D0554729

MICAH

VOLUME 24E

THE ANCHOR BIBLE is a fresh approach to the world's greatest classic. Its object is to make the Bible accessible to the modern reader; its method is to arrive at the meaning of biblical literature through exact translation and extended exposition, and to reconstruct the ancient setting of the biblical story, as well as the circumstances of its transcription and the characteristics of its transcribers.

THE ANCHOR BIBLE is a project of international and interfaith scope: Protestant, Catholic, and Jewish scholars from many countries contribute individual volumes. The project is not sponsored by any ecclesiastical organization and is not intended to reflect any particular theological doctrine. Prepared under our joint supervision, THE ANCHOR BIBLE is an effort to make available all the significant historical and linguistic knowledge which bears on the interpretation of the biblical record.

THE ANCHOR BIBLE is aimed at the general reader with no special formal training in biblical studies; yet it is written with the most exacting standards of scholarship, reflecting the highest technical accomplishment.

This project marks the beginning of a new era of cooperation among scholars in biblical research, thus forming a common body of knowledge to be shared by all.

William Foxwell Albright
David Noel Freedman
GENERAL EDITORS

THE ANCHOR BIBLE

MICAH

◆

A New Translation
with Introduction and Commentary

FRANCIS I. ANDERSEN
AND
DAVID NOEL FREEDMAN

THE ANCHOR BIBLE
Doubleday
New York   London   Toronto   Sydney   Auckland

THE ANCHOR BIBLE
PUBLISHED BY DOUBLEDAY
a division of Random House, Inc.
1540 Broadway, New York, New York 10036

THE ANCHOR BIBLE, DOUBLEDAY, and the portrayal of an
anchor with the letters A and B are trademarks of
Doubleday, a division of Random House, Inc.

Library of Congress Cataloging-in-Publication Data
Bible. O.T. Micah. English. Andersen-Freedman. 2000.
    Micah: a new translation with introduction and commentary/
  by Francis I. Andersen and David Noel Freedman. — 1st ed.
      p.   cm. — (The Anchor Bible; v. 24E)
  Includes bibliographical references and indexes.
        1. Bible. O.T. Micah Commentaries. I. Andersen, Francis I.,
    1925– . II. Freedman, David Noel, 1922– . III. Title. IV. Series: Bible.
    English. Anchor Bible. 1964; v. 24E.
  BS192.2.A1   1964.G3   vol. 24E
  [BS1613]
  220.7′7 s—dc21
  [224′.93077]   99-22814
                                                                CIP

    ISBN 0-385-08402-1

PREFACE

◆

Many persons and institutions have helped us in the making of this book. Andersen particularly wishes to thank his former colleagues and assistants in the Department of Studies in Religion, University of Queensland, and more recently New College for Advanced Christian Studies, Berkeley, for a grant of sabbatical leave that enabled the final revision to be completed. And we thank Dean and Ellen Forbes for much encouragement and many helps, including concordances of Micah and other computer products.

CONTENTS

◆

INDEXES

EVENTS REFLECTED IN
THE BOOK OF MICAH

Reigns of kings

Uzziah (783–742)
Jotham (750–735)
Jeho(ahaz) (735–715)
Hezekiah (715–687)

Date B.C.E. (some approximate) of events reflected in the book of Micah

742   Uzziah's death (Isa 6:1)
740   Menahem (Israel [2 Kgs 15:19]) and Ittobaal (Tyre) submit to Assyria
739   Pekahiah becomes king of Israel
738   Tiglath-Pileser defeats Azriyau of Yaudi
737   Pekah assassinates Pekahiah (2 Kgs 15:23–25)
735? Defeat of Ahaz by Rezin of Damascus (2 Chr 28:5)
735? Defeat of Ahaz by Pekah of Samaria (2 Chr 28:6–15; Micah 1?)
734   A coalition of Damascus, Samaria, Philistia, and Edom try to coerce Ahaz
      into an anti-Assyrian alliance (2 Kgs 16:5–6; 2 Chr 28:17–18; Isaiah 7–9)
733   Hoshea assassinates Pekah and becomes king of Israel
732   Aram, Gilead, Galilee conquered by Assyria (Isa 8:4)
722   Sargon (II) captures Samaria (2 Kings 17; Mic 1:4–7?)
715   Ahaz dies (Isa 14:28)
711   Sargon captures Ashdod (Isa 20:1)
705? Hezekiah's illness (Isaiah 38)
705? Merodach-Baladan visits Hezekiah (Isaiah 39)
701   Sennacherib (705–681) invades Judah (Isaiah 36–37)
687   Hezekiah dies
681   Sennacherib assassinated (Isa 37:38; 2 Kgs 19:37)
587   Fall of Jerusalem (Mic 3:12)
549   Cyrus founds the Persian empire
539   Persians capture Babylon
538   Cyrus's decree for the return of the Jews to Jerusalem; return of exiles
      (Mic 2:12–13)
520   Rebuilding of Temple resumed (Mic 4:1–5)

KINGS IN EIGHTH-CENTURY PROPHECIES

Amos	Hosea	Isaiah	Micah	Authors
Uzziah [Azariah]	Uzziah [Azariah]	Uzziah [Azariah]		
783–742	783–742	783–742		Albright
787–736	787–736	787–736		Begrich/Jepsen
785–733	785–733	785–733		Cogan/Tadmor
785–734	785–734	785–734		Hayes/Hooker
Jeroboam	Jeroboam			
786–746	786–746			Albright
789–748	789–748			Cogan/Tadmor
	Jotham	Jotham	Jotham	
	750–735	750–735	750–735	Albright
	756–741	756–741	756–741	Begrich/Jepsen
	758–743	758–743	758–743	Cogan/Tadmor
	759–744	759–744	759–744	Hayes/Hooker
	Ahaz	Ahaz	Ahaz	
	735–715	735–715	735–715	Albright
	741–725	741–725	741–725	Begrich/Jepsen
	743–727	743–727	743–727	Cogan/Tadmor
	743–728	743–728	743–728	Hayes/Hooker
	Hezekiah	Hezekiah	Hezekiah	
	715–687	715–687	715–687	Albright
	725–697	725–697	725–697	Begrich/Jepsen
	727–698	727–698	727–698	Cogan/Tadmor
	727–699	727–699	727–699	Hayes/Hooker

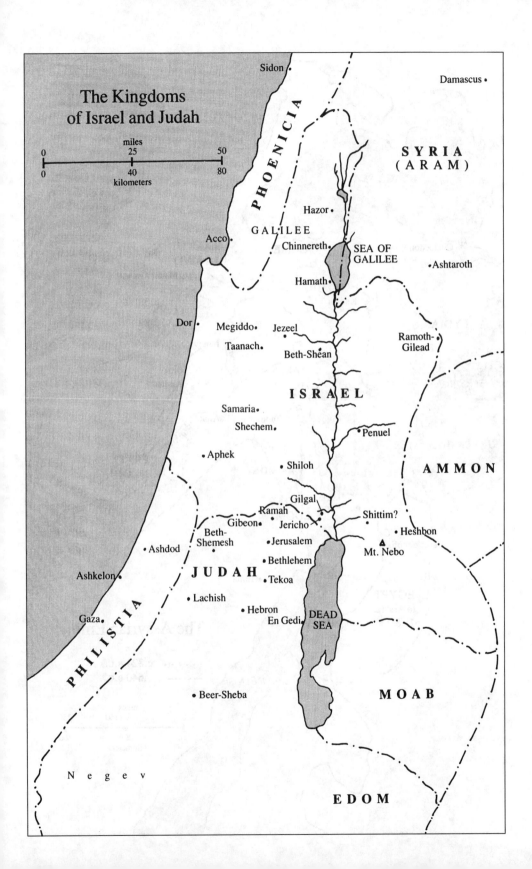

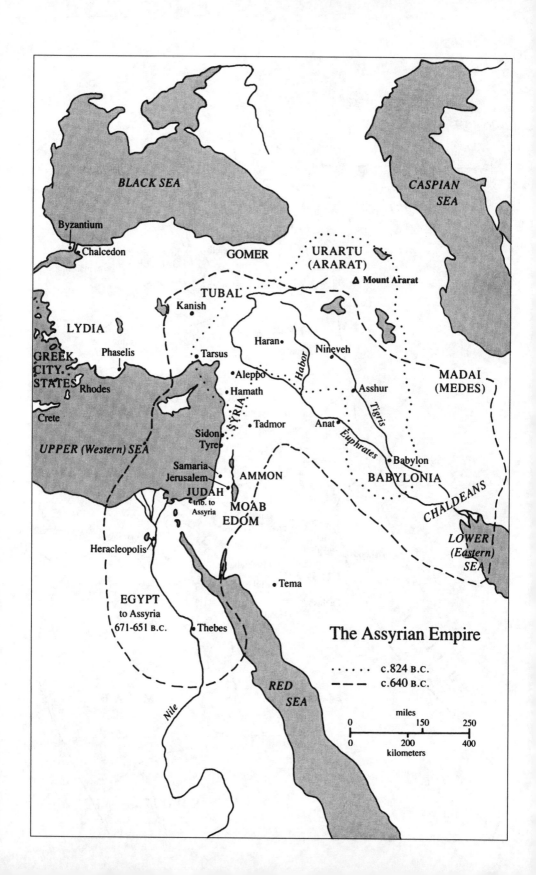

BLACK SEA

Byzantium
Chalcedon

GOMER

URARTU
(ARARAT)

△ Mount Ararat

CASPIAN
SEA

TUBAL

Kanish

LYDIA

Haran•

Nineveh•

Phaselis

•Tarsus

GREEK
CITY·
STATES

Rhodes

•Aleppo

Asshur

MADAI
(MEDES)

Crete

•Hamath

SYRIA

•Tadmor

Anat•

UPPER (Western) SEA

Sidon•
Tyre•

Samaria•
Jerusalem•

AMMON

JUDAH
trib. to
Assyria

MOAB
EDOM

Heracleopolis•

•Tema

EGYPT
to Assyria
671-651 B.C.

•Thebes

Nile

RED
SEA

Babylon•

BABYLONIA

CHALDEANS

LOWER
(Eastern)
SEA

The Assyrian Empire

•••••• c.824 B.C.
—— c.640 B.C.

miles

0   150   250

0   200   400

kilometers

PRINCIPAL ABBREVIATIONS

◆

Abbreviations not listed below are the same as those in *The Anchor Bible Dictionary*. The Dead Sea Scrolls and related manuscript sources are referred to using the now standard sigla as listed in Joseph A. Fitzmyer, *The Dead Sea Scrolls: Major Publications and Tools for Study*, rev. ed. Society of Biblical Literature Resources for Biblical Study 20 (Atlanta: Scholars Press, 1990).

A The Aleppo Codex
AB The Anchor Bible (Commentary)
ABD *Anchor Bible Dictionary*
AHI G. I. Davies, *Ancient Hebrew Inscriptions: Corpus and Concordance.* Cambridge: Cambridge University Press, 1992
AHw W. von Soden, *Akkadisches Handwörterbuch.* 3 vols. Wiesbaden: Harrassowitz, 1965–81
AI Arad Inscriptions
Akk Akkadian (a language of ancient Mesopotamia)
ANEP *The Ancient Near East in Pictures Relating to the Old Testament,* ed. J. B. Pritchard. 2d ed. with suppl. Princeton: Princeton University Press, 1954, 1969
ANET *Ancient Near Eastern Texts Relating to the Old Testament,* ed. J. B. Pritchard. 3d ed. with suppl. Princeton: Princeton University Press, 1955, 1969
AOAT Alter Orient und Altes Testament
Aram Aramaic language
ASV American Standard Version
BA *Biblical Archaeologist*
BAR *Biblical Archaeology Review*
BAT84 *Biblical Archaeology Today: Proceedings of the International Congress on Biblical Archaeology Jerusalem, April 1984.* Jerusalem: Israel Exploration Society
BAT90 *Biblical Archaeology Today, 1990: Proceedings of the Second International Congress on Biblical Archaeology Jerusalem, June–July 1990.* Jerusalem: Israel Exploration Society

BASOR	*Bulletin of the American Schools of Oriental Research*	DCH	*The Dictionary of Classical Hebrew*, ed. David J. A. Clines. Sheffield: Sheffield Academic Press, 1993–
B.C.E.	Before the Common Era		
BDB	F. Brown, S. R. Driver, and C. A. Briggs, *Hebrew and English Lexicon of the Old Testament*. Oxford: Oxford University Press, 1907, 1955	*DJD* 3	M. Baillet, J. T. Milik, and R. de Vaux, *Discoveries in the Judaean Desert of Jordan*. Oxford: Clarendon Press, 1962
BH³	Biblia Hebraica, 3d ed.	DN	Divine name
BHS	Biblia Hebraica Stuttgartensia	DNWSI	*Dictionary of the North-West Semitic Inscriptions*, ed. J. Hoftijzer and K. Jongeling. Leiden: Brill, 1995
Bib	*Biblica*		
BIOSCS	*Bulletin of the International Organization for Septuagint and Cognate Studies*	E	Elohist (author of a Pentateuchal source)
BJRL	*Bulletin of the John Rylands University Library of Manchester*	EAEHL	*Encyclopedia of Archaeological Excavations in the Holy Land*. 4 vols. Jerusalem: Massada Press, 1975–78
BZAW	Beihefte zur Zeitschrift für die alttestamentliche Wissenschaft	EI	*Eretz Israel*
		EncJud	*Encyclopedia Judaica* (1971)
C	Cairo Codex of the Prophets	ʾet	*Nota accusativi*, the sign of the definite object in Hebrew
CAD	*The Assyrian Dictionary of the University of Chicago*, ed. L. Oppenheim et al. Chicago: University of Chicago Press, 1956–	*ExpT*	*Expository Times*
		GKC	*Gesenius' Hebrew Grammar*, ed. E. Kautzsch, trans. A. E. Cowley. 2d ed. Oxford: Clarendon Press, 1910
CBQ	*Catholic Biblical Quarterly*		
C.E.	Common Era		
chap(s).	chapter(s)	H	Holiness Code (a source in the Book of Leviticus)
D	Deuteronomist (editor or "school" involved in editing the Primary History)		
		HAR	*Hebrew Annual Review*
D⁶²	The Karasu-Bazar Codex of the Latter Prophets in the Library of the Oriental Institute of the Academy of Sciences, Saint Petersburg	HAT	Handbuch zum Alten Testament
		HSS	Harvard Semitic Studies
		HTR	*Harvard Theological Review*
		HUCA	*Hebrew Union College Annual*
		IB	*Interpreter's Bible.*

	Nashville: Abingdon Press, 1951–57	KAT	*Kommentar zum alten Testament,* ed. E. Sellin, cont. J. Herrmann
IDB	*Interpreter's Dictionary of the Bible,* ed. G. A. Buttrick et al. Nashville: Abingdon Press, 1962	KB	L. Koehler and W. Baumgartner, *Lexicon in Veteris Testamenti Libros.* Leiden: Brill, 1958
IDBSup	*Interpreter's Dictionary of the Bible: Supplementary Volume.* Nashville: Abingdon Press, 1976	KB³	L. Koehler and W. Baumgartner, *Hebräische und aramäische Lexicon zum alten Testament.*
IEJ	*Israel Exploration Journal*		3d ed. Leiden: Brill, 1967–
IR	*Inscriptions Reveal: Documents from the Time of the Bible, the Mishna and the Talmud,* ed. R. Hestrin et al. Jerusalem: Israel Museum, 1973	KJV	*The Holy Bible Containing the Old and New Testaments* or Authorized Version (= King James Version)
J	Yahwist (author of a Pentateuchal source)	Krt	*Keret*
JAOS	*Journal of the American Oriental Society*	KS (Alt)	A. Alt, *Kleine Schriften zur Geschichte des Volkes Israel.* 3 vols. Munich: C. H. Beck
JB	Jerusalem Bible		
JBL	*Journal of Biblical Literature*	KS (Eissfeldt)	Otto Eissfeldt, *Klein Schriften.* 6 vols. Tübingen: Mohr, 1962–68
JNES	*Journal of Near Eastern Studies*		
JNSL	*Journal of Northwest Semitic Languages*	KTU	*Die keilalphabetischen Texte aus Ugarit,* ed. M. Dietrich, O. Loretz, and J. Sanmartin. AOAT. Neukirchen-Vluyn: Neukirchener Verlag, 1976
JPS	Jewish Publication Society		
JQR	*Jewish Quarterly Review*		
JSJ	*Journal for the Study of Judaism*		
JSOT	*Journal for the Study of the Old Testament*	L	*Codex Leningradensis*
JSS	*Journal of Semitic Studies*	LXX	Septuagint
		LXXᴸ	Lucianic recensions
JTS	*Journal of Theological Studies*	LXXᴮ	Vaticanus
		MQR	*Michigan Quarterly Review*
KAI	*Kanaanäische und aramäische Inschriften,* ed. H. Donner and W. Röllig. Wiesbaden: Otto Harrassowitz, 1962–64	MT	Masoretic Text
		n.a.	*Nota accusativi* ʾet
		NAB	New American Bible
		NASB	New American Standard Bible

NEB	New English Bible		Institute, 1972
NICOT	New International Commentary on the Old Testament	*RSP II*	*Ras Shamra Parallels.* Vol. II. Ed. Loren R. Fisher. Analecta
NIV	New International Version		Orientalia 50. Rome: Pontifical Biblical Institute, 1975
NJB	New Jerusalem Bible		
NJPS	The New Jewish Publication Society of America translations of the Holy Scriptures: *The Torah*, 2d ed., Philadelphia, 1967; *The Prophets: Nevi'im*, Philadelphia, 1978; *The Writings: Kethubim*, Philadelphia, 1978	*RSP III*	*Ras Shamra Parallels.* Vol. III. Ed. Stan Rummel. Analecta Orientalia 51. Rome: Pontifical Biblical Institute, 1981
		RSV	Revised Standard Version
		RTR	*Reformed Theological Review*
NRSV	New Revised Standard Version	RV	Revised Version
		SBL	Society of Biblical Literature
NT	New Testament	*StTh*	*Studies in Theology*
OT	Old Testament	*TA*	*Tel Aviv*
OTS	*Oudtestamentische Studiën*	TB	Babylonian Talmud
P	Codex Petropolitanus	TDOT	*Theological Dictionary of the Old Testament,* ed. G. J. Botterweck and H. Ringgren. Grand Rapids: Eerdmans, 1974–86
P	Priestly Source in the Pentateuch		
PEQ	*Palestine Exploration Quarterly*		
PJ	*Palästina-Jahrbuch*	TEV	Today's English Version
PRU	*Le Palais royal d'Ugarit*, ed. C. F. A. Schaeffer and J. Nougayrol. Paris, 1955–65	Tg	Targum
		TLOT	*Theological Lexicon of the Old Testament,* ed. Ernst Jenni and Claus Westermann. trans. Mark E. Biddle. 3 vols. Peabody, Mass.: Hendrickson, 1997
Q	Qumran		
REB	Revised English Bible		
RelSoc	*Religion and Society*		
RHPR	*Revue d'histoire et de philosophie réligieuses*	*TWAT*	*Theologisches Wörterbuch zum alten Testament,* ed. G. J. Botterweck, H. Ringgren, and H. J. Fabry. Stuttgart: Kohlhammer, 1970–88
RQ	*Revue de Qumrân*		
RS	Ras Shamra, field number of tablets		
RSP I	*Ras Shamra Parallels.* Vol. I. Ed. Loren R. Fisher. Analecta Orientalia 49. Rome: Pontifical Biblical	*TZ*	*Theologische Zeitschrift*
		UF	*Ugarit-Forschungen*
		UT	C. H. Gordon, *Ugaritic*

	Textbook. Rome, 1965; Supplement, 1967	ZAH	*Zeitschrift für Althebräistik*
V	Vulgate	ZAW	*Zeitschrift für die alttestamentliche Wissenschaft*
VT	*Vetus Testamentum*		
VTSup	Vetus Testamentum Supplements	ZDPV	*Zeitschrift des Palästina-Vereins*

INTRODUCTION

◆

TEXTS AND TRANSLATIONS OF
THE BOOK OF MICAH

Several ancient versions of the book of Micah claim attention. The nearer in time any version stands to the Hebrew original, the more seriously it needs to be studied. Translations into Greek (Septuagint = LXX), Aramaic (Targum), Syriac (Peshitta), and Latin (Vulgate) supply evidence of various kinds. These versions can be used as sources of information about the Hebrew text utilized by their translators only sparingly and always with caution; but at least they indicate how the Hebrew text was understood by the community in which the translation was prepared. Assuming that the translators were competent and honest, the Hebrew text that seems to lie behind these versions can be provisionally recovered by retroversion or back translation. Such a reconstructed *Vorlage* does not have the evidential value of an actual manuscript in Hebrew, and its use as a source of possible variant readings has to be monitored with the usual safeguards of disciplined text criticism (Tov 1981: 73–141). Tov concluded that "[t]here are hardly any criteria for distinguishing between retroverted variants existing in writing and similar variants existing only in the translator's mind" (1981: 140).

Keeping these cautions in mind, the Greek version has nonetheless a high claim as a form of the book of Micah, not only because it is the oldest translation, but also because of the prestige it enjoyed as the Christian Old Testament, influencing later Christian translations (Harl, Dorival, and Munnich 1988). The Book of the Twelve was translated from Hebrew into Greek in Alexandria in the first half of the second century B.C.E. (Harl, Dorival, and Munnich 1988: 97, 107). The evidence for this event is indirect. The strongest argument is the apparent use of a Greek text of the Minor Prophets by the translator of the *Wisdom of Jesus ben Sira*. Suggestions that selections from the prophets had been translated into Greek for liturgical purposes before whole books were translated are more speculative.

The earliest known manuscript of the Book of the Twelve in Greek is 8HevXIIgr (R943 in the Göttingen enumeration) from the cave at Naḥal Hever. Dated to the turn of the era, it represents a revision of the Old Greek, bringing it more in line with the Hebrew Text (Barthélemy 1963: 170–78; 1978: 38–50; Tov 1990). Because this and later versions and revisions for the most part adjusted the Greek text closer to the Hebrew, they offer confirmation of the Masoretic Text but, conversely, present fewer variant readings. The more an Old Greek text tradition deviates from the Masoretic Text, the more attention it deserves as a possible repository of variants with a prima facie claim to authenticity. Such variants could be the outcome of faithful translation of a variant Hebrew text not otherwise attested. Such a conclusion cannot be drawn with confidence, however. Other explanations are possible, and it is hard to exclude them. The difference between Greek and Hebrew could be due to slippage in translation, from whatever cause, and the causes could be many. A strange

LXX reading could be the outcome of an override of exact translation by a compelling interpretation that held sway in the mind of the translators, whether the result of their own scholarly work or supplied to them from a traditional understanding already established in their community. The degree to which this happened is much debated. The degree of literalness or otherwise paraphrase varies from book to book. To the extent that a translator handled the text with some freedom, the LXX is the oldest known commentary on the book of Micah (Harl, Dorival, and Munnich 1988: 216). If such is the case the Greek would not represent a reliable rendition of the Hebrew *Vorlage* from which the source Hebrew text might be recovered by retroversion. Alternatively (or in addition), the divergence could be due to transmission drift in the Greek version. As Harl, Dorival, and Munnich state, "Nous ne connaissons exactement ni l'état du texte hébraïque traduit par les LXX, ni l'état premier de la traduction grecque" (1988: 201).

A new mood comes to the fore in the second century C.E. The Greek translations become weapons in a war of words between Christians and Jews. Each side understandably accused the other of doctoring texts to suit their arguments. The motivations of partisan polemics have to be kept in mind when assessing conflicting readings. However, this consideration does not apply to the texts from earlier stages. The first translations of the Hebrew Bible into Greek were made by Jews for Jews. The Christians never made their own Greek Bible by translating from the Hebrew; they used the texts already in hand in the Jewish community. At first, of course, most Christians were converted Jews, and the Hellenophones among them simply brought their Bible with them into the new faith.

The whole story of the Greek versions of the Hebrew Bible has interest in its own right. The last two decades (since the foundation of the International Organization for Septuagint and Cognate Studies) have seen a revival of interest in LXX. The publications of Barthélemy (1963, 1978), Brooke and Lindars (1992), Fraenkel, Quast, and Wevers (1990), Gooding (1976), Harl, Dorival, and Munnich (1988), Jellicoe (1974, 1989), Katz (1956, 1957), Orlinsky (1959, 1961, 1974, 1989), Tov (1981, 1992), and Walters [= Peter Katz] (1973), and the work of Wevers and Ziegler for the Göttingen LXX have opened up new perspectives in Septuagint studies. In particular, the work of Gooding (1969) has drawn attention to the *interpretive* nature of the LXX translation, even to the point of regarding it as commentary or midrash (Olley 1975; de Waard 1984). Even if a substantial departure of LXX from MT does not feed back into the *textual* criticism of MT, i.e., does not contribute to the recovery of the best accessible Hebrew text of Micah, possibly better then MT, it could, all the same, give us insight into the competence or bias of the Greek translators. Study of LXX as evidence for the history of interpretation of the Hebrew Bible has been carried out for various books—Ezekiel (Lust 1986 [BIOSCS]) and notably Isaiah (Koenig 1982, 1988). We need to study LXX along similar lines if we are interested in the history of the interpretation of the book of Micah. Such work is now greatly facilitated by the publication of two new lexicons (Lust 1992; Muraoka 1993).

All too often LXX is consulted only when there is a hope that it might help solve a problem in the Masoretic Text; and only those variants that are found to be interesting from this perspective are likely to be reported in a textual apparatus, such as that in BHS, or in a critical commentary. When there is no perceived problem in the Masoretic Text, a variant reading in LXX is not likely to attract attention. However, the text of LXX is part of the larger story of the book of Micah.

Jewish translations into Aramaic (Targums) mainly reflect the mainstream Masoretic tradition, and in any case are usually so interpretive that their value for recovering variant Hebrew readings is slight. The Jewish scholarly tradition remains central for study of MT. For the relevance of Ibn Ezra's Biblical Hebrew lexicon for study of the Minor Prophets see Muraoka and Shavitsky (1990, 1991).

The present commentary is primarily interested in the Hebrew version of Micah, the complete text of which is available now only in the Masoretic recension. To assist that study, we supply a translation that is as literal as English can endure, sometimes painfully literal in the interests of exactitude. We reactivate obsolete *thou* because English *you* loses the distinction between singular and plural, which is often vital for interpretation. English makes no provision for distinctions in gender in second-person pronouns—often just as vital as grammatical number for distinguishing participants; so we attach [m.] or [f.]. Alongside this translation of MT we supply a translation of LXX in synoptic display. The translation of LXX is based on the Göttingen edition. The help of Gregory Fox with fine points of Greek is gratefully recognized. When LXX has a word with no evident match in MT, the translation is enclosed in ⟨. . .⟩. Such pluses could have been added by the translator, either because Greek idiom required them, or to secure some interpretive slant; but similar pressures could have brought about such additions in the transmission of the Greek text. It is also possible that such a detail, not now present in MT, was present in the copy of the Hebrew text used by the Greek translator. If that is the explanation of the variant Greek reading, the Hebrew recovered from it by retroversion could compete with the Masoretic reading as possibly "original," not in the sense of the wording of the text at its point of origination (that we can never hope to recover demonstrably), but only in the sense of being earlier and possibly better (nearer to the original) than what the Masoretic Text attests.

Words in the Hebrew text used by the Greek translators could also have been omitted (by them, or by later scribes) out of various considerations. However such differences came about, in each instance the possibility that features now in LXX were present in its *Vorlage* must be considered. Occasionally a Greek word of special interest will be transliterated in our display. A few explanatory glosses are supplied in [. . .]. Significant textual variants in Greek MSS are shown in {. . .}. Paraphrastic additions for the sake of English are in (. . .).

MICAH IN THE BOOK OF TWELVE
MINOR PROPHETS

The book of Micah is one of the twelve books of prophecy that are reckoned as the fourth scroll of the Latter Prophets in the Jewish tradition. In his praise of the "men of *hesed*" (Sir 44:1), Jesus ben Sira, writing in the first part of the second century B.C.E., began (44:16) and ended (49:14) with Enoch (Lee 1986; Mack 1985). Adam is mentioned last of all, even though he was "superior to every living thing in the creation." Ben Sira extolled the most noteworthy prophets, priests, and kings, but mainly prophets. Only the three kings who were not wicked—David, Hezekiah, Josiah (49:4)—are named. Toward the end of the review, after Jeremiah and Ezekiel, ben Sira refers to the "Twelve Prophets" (49:10) without giving their names. This seems to be the earliest evidence for the existence of the collection, along with the name of the scroll. With a prayer that their bones might sprout again from their place, he sums up the Twelve Prophets' ministry as "comforting Jacob"; and of twenty-six occurrences of the name Jacob in the Book of the Twelve, eleven are in Micah, more than in any other of the Minor Prophets.

The common designation "Minor Prophets" seems to be due to Augustine (*De civitate dei*, xviii.29). It refers to the small size of the books, not to the importance of their authors.

There is no reason to doubt that the same twelve books have always formed the collection. However, their sequence and the position of Micah in the set are different in the Hebrew and Greek versions of the Old Testament (Budde 1921). It is often said that the Hebrew arrangement—Hosea, Joel, Amos, Obadiah, Jonah, Micah—is based on chronological considerations, while that of the LXX—Hosea, Amos, Micah, Joel, Obadiah, Jonah—puts the books, at least the first five, in decreasing order of length (Eissfeldt 1965: 383). No explanation has been found for placing Jonah last in this set, considering that it is longer than Obadiah. There is no evidence that whoever made the decision to put Jonah last did so "because it is mainly a story about a prophet rather than a collection of prophetic oracles" (R. L. Smith 1984: xv). The LXX arrangement makes better historical sense than that of the MT. Ryle, quoted by Swete (1902: 227), suggested that the LXX order was the result of an attempt to improve the chronological arrangement, but this outcome is more evident in the earlier part of the listing, with the three eighth-century prophets appearing first. In the LXX sequence of Minor Prophets, twenty of the references to Jacob are in the first three books, and "Jacob" is a conspicuous word in Isaiah. This feature is even more striking when we remember that the sequence of prophetic writings attested by the Talmud (Beckwith 1985: 157, 450) puts Isaiah last of the big three (Jeremiah, Ezekiel, Isaiah), thus bringing the four (with Micah) eighth-century prophets together. (Note, however, that the Talmudic order matches diminishing length—Jeremiah [21,835 words], Ezekiel [18,730], Isaiah [16,933], Minor Prophets [14,355]). In some manuscripts and synodical lists of the books of the Greek Old Testament, Isaiah follows the Minor Prophets so that the four eighth-century prophets come in the sequence Hosea, Amos, Micah, . . . , Isaiah (Swete 1902: 201–14). We suspect that these details are the outcome of a grouping of these four books that could be the most ancient of all, reflecting the very first collection of prophetic writings. The headings of the four books disclose a common editorial policy (Freedman 1987a). The sequence Amos, Hosea, Isaiah, Micah (not attested) is required by the chronological information in the titles to the books, and the sequence in the Greek Old Testament comes close to it. Isaiah uses "Jacob" more than anyone (forty-one times in contrast to Ezekiel's four times). Taken together, these four prophetic books account for sixty-two of the ninety occurrences of the name "Jacob" in the Latter Prophets. This concentration could be the basis of ben Sira's observation about the ministry of the Twelve, which is even more pertinent when Isaiah is joined to the others.

It is plausible to connect the breaking up of this original set of four books with the reorganization of the book of Isaiah. This rearrangement of Isaiah was apparently a complex process that could have involved many stages that we do not need to trace here (Vermeylen 1978). Similar developments may be supposed so far as the Minor Prophets are concerned (Wolfe 1935). The first six books (considered to be from Assyrian period prophets, although Joel is questionable) were perhaps an early set, followed by three Babylonian and three Persian period prophets (Kuhl 1961: 202). Yet Obadiah hardly fits with the others, and Nahum would be better in the Assyrian era.

THE LITERARY UNITS OF THE BOOK OF MICAH

The book of Micah has been analyzed in various ways (see pp. 50–55). For convenience we recognize three sections, each with a distinctive mood and message. The sections are marked by well-formed beginnings, and each ends with a note of finality (3:12; 5:14; 7:20). These sections may be called:

I. The Book of Doom (1:2–3:12)
II. The Book of Visions (4:1–5:14)
III. The Book of Contention and Conciliation (6:1–7:20)

The general arrangement of the book of Amos is remarkably similar; it begins with judgment and ends on a positive note, with visions reported in between.

The Title (1:1)

The book of the prophet Micah opens with a conventional title (1:1). The title identifies the work as the word of Yahweh and names the receiver of that message as Micah the Morashtite. We are told as well the mode of that revelation: Micah had visions. There is also a date or rather a time period: the reigns of three successive kings of Judah, Jotham, Ahaz, and Hezekiah, who reigned from ca. 750 to 687 B.C.E. (on the dates, see the NOTE on 1:1). The subject matter is "Samaria and Jerusalem." Samaria and Jerusalem receive attention throughout the Book of Doom, chapters 1–3. Their sins are denounced and judgment is threatened against each city in turn—Samaria in 1:6–7, Jerusalem in 3:12.

I. THE BOOK OF DOOM (1:2–3:12)

I.1. The First Warning Oracle (1:2–7)

The message begins with a summons to disputation, suggesting that the prophecy will use the language and drama of litigation. The whole world is to observe this court hearing (1:2). Yahweh himself will come down *from his place*, and when he arrives the mountains and valleys will be convulsed (1:3–4). This drastic and destructive activity of God is his response to the *rebellion* and *sins* (sinful acts of sedition) of Jacob/Israel (1:5a). More precisely, this *rebellion* is located in the two capital cities, Samaria and Jerusalem (1:5b; cf. v 1), and the rebellion has been expressed in cultic activity disloyal to Yahweh. The threatened destruction of Samaria is described in 1:6–7, of Jerusalem in 3:12.

I.2. First Lamentation (Transitional) (1:8–9)

The prospect of such devastation causes the prophet (or perhaps God himself) to be deeply distressed, and the rest of the chapter is given over to lamentation. The catastrophe advances from Samaria (v 7) to Jerusalem (v 9).

I.3. Second Lamentation (1:10–16)

A group of regional cities is then addressed, with alarming remarks about various kinds of disasters that have befallen (or will befall) them. Finally a mother figure (Jerusalem?) is urged to go into deep mourning for her lost children (v 16).

I.4. Social Injustice Denounced (2:1–5)

The rest of the Book of Doom is taken up with additional accusations. Zion/Jerusalem is the only location explicitly identified. No names are mentioned, but the leaders—rulers (3:1, 9), priests, judges, prophets (3:11)—are held responsible. They are accused of greed and rapacity (2:1; cf. 2:8–10), notably in the illegal seizure of land (2:2–5). For this violation of the principles of the original settlement of Israel on the land that Yahweh gave them, the whole nation will be evicted from the sacred territory.

I.5. Attack on Prophets (2:6–11)

The prophets are the group that receives the most attention (2:6–7, 11; cf. 3:5–7). They are accused of supporting the wicked leaders, for a fee. Micah's own messages were directed against the leaders, as we can tell from the groups that he addresses by their titles (3:1, 9). The language in his attacks on the prophets gives the other side of this experience. It suggests that Micah's messages were rejected by the leadership, who found more acceptable the favorable oracles supplied by other prophets (2:6–11). In contrast to their reassuring messages, the mark of the authentic prophet—Micah himself—is fearless protest against national injustice (3:8). Micah insists that his words (God's genuine words) do good (2:7), and he exposes another case of callous oppression (2:8–10).

I.6. *Promise of Restoration (2:12–13)*

Everything that has happened, or will happen, to Israel is ascribed immediately to the personal activity of Yahweh. The language, however, suggests both a domestic breakdown of community values and devastation by a foreign invader, followed by exile of the population (1:16). That would seem to be final. Yet, in the midst of these threats, God makes a promise of restoration (2:12–13).

I.7. *Attack on Rulers (3:1–4)*

Returning to his accusations, the prophet describes in gruesome language the depredations of the rulers throughout the whole country (Jacob/Israel) (3:2–3).

I.8. *Condemnation of Prophets (3:5–8)*

The next section contains another oracle against false prophets, Micah's rivals (cf. 2:6–11). They will suffer an appropriate fate, the eclipse of their profession (3:6–7). Micah, in contrast, vows to be fearless in denouncing Jacob's *rebellion* and *sin* (v 8).

I.9. *Condemnation of Rulers (3:9–12)*

Turning to the rulers one more time, Micah exposes the collusion of the officers of court and cult and charisma, cloaked in the cant of conventional piety (v 11). They are chiefly to blame for the impending demolition of Jerusalem (v 12).

There are stories behind these oracles, yet no identifiable characters emerge; and the prophet himself is scarcely in view, except for a few autobiographical words in 3:1 and 3:8. His personal animus against the political and religious establishment, especially the rival prophets, is plain. Possibly his critique was compounded by the prejudice of a countryman against the big cities, their merchants (6:11), and bureaucrats. The humiliation of the proud (2:3) and the disgrace of the prophets (3:5–7) will be greeted with derision—they will be taunted by the singing of a dirge in mockery (2:4). Micah himself is not vindictive. He wails with grief at the calamity (1:8–16); he believes in the possibility of reformation (6:8), of forgiveness (7:18–20).

Except for 2:12–13, the note of judgment is struck continually in the Book of Doom. The justice is poetic. God schemes evil against the *mišpāḥâ*, "tribe" (2:3) because they schemed evil "upon their beds" (*miškĕbôtām*) (2:1). The gains from prostitution will be used for prostitution (1:7). Those who seized property (2:2) will forfeit property (2:5). Those who abused prophecy will be denied prophecy (3:5–6). Cities built on injustice (3:10) will be demolished (1:6; 3:12). The conjunction *therefore* spells out the logic of this justice.

Several kinds of discourse are used in this first prophecy (or collection of oracles). It begins with a call to attention (1:2), which is renewed in 3:1 and 3:9. The visionary aspect of Micah's experience comes out in the theophany of 1:3–4, and the prophet, using rhetorical questions (1:5b), explains that this is all because of the nation's sins (1:5a). The indictment at the beginning of chapter 2 is expressed as a woe oracle. Yahweh himself utters the threats of disaster (1:6–7; 2:3), the latter introduced by the messenger formula, which occurs again in 3:5. Chapter 2 ends with a promise to gather the scattered people under the combined leadership of the king and Yahweh (or under the sole leadership of Yahweh as king). This unit (2:12–13) is the hardest piece of all to fit in with the rest.

Condemnation gives thematic consistency to the Book of Doom (chapters 1–3). This feature was emphasized by Willis (1969b). The structural organization of the book in formal literary respects is harder to find. Hagstrom (1988) attempted to find features that pointed to the final integral form of the book. The announced topic is Samaria and Jerusalem (1:1). The sequence has surprised some readers, since Jerusalem was the more important city and receives most attention in the perspective of southern prophets. There is, however, a logic in the sequence not unlike that of the oracles against eight states in Amos 1–2. The sequence in the title supplies the structure of chapters 1–3 as a unit, Samaria first (1:5–7), Jerusalem second (1:8–3:12). It also reflects the actual historical developments. Samaria fell first and, in Micah's expectation, Jerusalem would have been next. Samaria is prominent to begin with, but Micah's main concern is clearly Jerusalem. The analysis shows how disproportionate is the attention given to the two cities. The oracles in chapters 1–3 are almost entirely lacking in historical specifics, so we should not assume that Samaria has dropped out of view just because it is not continually named (cf. Omri and Ahab in 6:16). There are geographical particulars in 1:10–15, but the event itself cannot be identified. There are plenty of details about the state of society in chapters 2–3, but none of the kings listed in 1:1 is ever mentioned again in the rest of the book, so we cannot readily recover the historical background of these injustices.

II. THE BOOK OF VISIONS (4:1–5:14)

The Book of Visions (chapters 4–5) consists of a series of eschatological oracles. These visions contrast the current status and state of Jerusalem (prominent in chapter 4) and Jacob (chapter 5) with their future prospects. The contrast is extreme. The conquered people will drive out Assyria and other nations. Peoples who gathered to gloat over Zion's humiliation will gather in humiliation to marvel at Zion's glory. In chapters 4–5 paragraphs or strophes beginning with *now* contrast with predictions beginning *in that day.* The whole is fantastic to the point of unreality, and there are no historical particulars that permit any of it to be dated to known events. Neither the current circumstances nor the future consequences attach to any known episode or era in Israel's history with the certainty we need for realistic interpretation. At the same time the references to both Assyria (5:4, 5a, 5b; 7:12) and Babylon (4:10) show that contemporary political realities are in mind. Micah clearly anticipated an invasion of Israel by Assyria (5:4, 5), and that was being realistic. In anticipating a successful counterattack by Israel into the territory of Assyria itself, he was too hopeful. Nothing like that happened. Incidentally, it is a tribute to the integrity of the scribes that they left that strange passage in the text, even after the complete disappearance of Assyria as a political entity made the prophecy irrelevant, unless the name "Assyria" has become a code word for the typical foreign aggressor.

The one firm peg seems to be 4:10, which predicts exile to Babylon and redemption from there. Yet the language is quite general, and none of the other things said in chapters 4–5 fit into what we know about the Babylonian Exile and its outcome. The reference to exile in 1:16 does not necessarily require the Babylonian Exile; our comment on that passage acknowledges other possibilities. While we concede, with the majority of scholars, that passages like 4:10 and others, such as 2:12–13, which anticipate exile to Babylon and subsequent return, might have made their way into the book during or after the Exile (sixth century B.C.E. or later), our minds are also open to the possibility that Babylon was part of the prophets' world map even in the eighth century (cf. Isaiah 39).

II.1. The End of the Days (4:1–5)

Chapter 4 begins with a glorious vision of *the end of days*, when Zion will be the center of the world (4:1–5). This most famous of all Micah's prophecies happens to be almost identical with Isaiah 2:2–5. The problems raised by this coincidence will be discussed in the introduction to the pericope. Here we note only that the universal scope and mythic imagery of 4:1–5 resembles that of 1:2–4. It sounds like the end of the story, the end of all stories; so its position here at the beginning of the Book of Visions is problematical.

II.2. Yahweh Rules the Remnant (4:6–8)

The scenario then seems to backtrack. The next verses (4:6–8) are similar to 2:12–13. God promises to assemble the exiles, and to rule over them in Zion. Here Yahweh is clearly the King.

II.3. The Anguish and Redemption of Zion (4:9–10)

Working backwards another stage, the next unit describes Zion in agony. Several time perspectives seem to be mixed together.

II.4. Zion Defeats the Nations (4:11–13)

In another rapid change of situation and mood, Zion—now a rampaging beast—will subdue and exploit *many peoples*. This political settlement bears a certain resemblance to the domination of the whole world by Jerusalem set forth in 4:1–5.

II.5. Zion(?) under Threat (4:14)

Changing tone again, the next verse describes the humiliation of Israel's ruler.

II.6. Advent of the Ruler (5:1–3)

Israel's ancient glory will be recovered under the leadership of a new ruler who is depicted as a second David, although that name is not mentioned (5:1–5).

II.7. Defeat of Assyria (5:4–5)

With the introduction of seven//eight other shepherds, to be "raised up" by an unidentified "we," the scenario becomes somewhat complicated. "He" (presumably the "ruler" from Bethlehem) will deliver "us" from Assyria. "They" will dominate the land of Nimrod.

II.8. The Remnant Benign (5:6)

The remnant of Jacob will bring both blessing and disaster to the other nations. The juxtaposition of scenes with utmost contrast continues in the next two units, comparing the *remnant of Jacob* with gentle, fruitful rain, then with the fiercest of beasts.

II.9. The Remnant Malign (5:7–8)

As in 4:13 and 5:6, Jacob is promised military victory over former enemies (5:8).

II.10. Israel Cleansed and Avenged (5:9–14)

In the end Yahweh will destroy all his enemies and eliminate all the means of war as well as false religions (5:9–14).

Chapters 4–5 contain no clear indication of the intended audience for the original spoken message or of the readership in mind for the final written form. The address to Zion, like those to Migdal-Eder (4:8) and to Bethlehem (5:1—masculine, in contrast to *Daughter Zion*), could be rhetorical. No specifics permit the identification of the communities represented by these personified cities. The masculine "thou" addressed in 5:9–14 seems to be Jacob, a name that evidently denotes the nation of Israel in general and as a whole. Some of the material is presented as direct speech of Yahweh (*I*) (4:6–7, 13; 5:10–15). Otherwise the actions of God are described using the third person (*he*).

III. THE BOOK OF CONTENTION AND CONCILIATION (6:1–7:20)

In some respects the third section of the book of Micah covers ground similar to that in the first two sections. There is a mix of condemnation, grief, and hope. It describes the breaking and mending of the covenant. Chapter 6 begins with judgment and justice; chapter 7 ends with mercy and forgiveness.

III.1. *Yahweh's Covenant Dispute (6:1–8)*

Like the Book of Doom, the Book of Contention opens with an arraignment. This is perhaps the best known of all the covenant disputes found in the Hebrew Bible. Although v 8 seems to round this unit off, the altercation continues with accusations (6:9–12)—none were found in the preceding dispute—and threats (6:13–16).

III.2. *More Accusations and Covenant Curses (6:9–16)*

Micah's vision extends deeply into future time. His references are gathered from the traditions of Israel's long past. The Book of Contention includes nine names of persons from bygone ages. The catastrophes now to overtake the nation are the evils threatened in the old covenant formulations as fitting punishment for a rebellious people.

III.3. *Lamentation (7:1–6)*

Prayers are more prominent in chapter 7, whether those of the responding people or of the prophet interceding on their behalf. An expression of anguish over prevalent iniquity (7:1–6) leads to a declaration of hope in God's salvation (7:7). (The boundary between this and the following unit is indeterminate; v 7 could be transitional—the end of vv 1–7, the beginning of vv 7–12.)

III.4. *Song of Confidence (7:7–12)*

The experience of humiliation at the hands of enemies can be perceived, experienced, and affirmed as God's just judgment and therefore as a token of future vindication (7:8–10).

III.5. *Vindication (7:13–17)*

Even if the whole world is reduced to primal chaos (7:13), creation can begin again (7:11–12), and Israel's early history of Exodus and Conquest can be recapitulated (7:14–17).

III.6. The Covenant Mended (7:18–20)

The prophecy ends with a powerful statement about the limitless scope of God's compassionate forgiving love (7:18–20). At this point the future prospect is anchored in the earliest memories of Israel's beginnings. The ancient promises to the founding ancestors will certainly be fulfilled, in spite of the consistent, even stubborn, refusal of Yahweh's covenant partner to abide by the stipulations of their relationship.

THE TRADITIONAL DIVISIONS OF THE BOOK OF MICAH

Long before the present system of chapters was imposed on the Hebrew Bible, the books had been broken up into portions. For purposes of synagogue readings, the text of the Pentateuch was divided into sections (*sedarim*). The system was extended to the rest of the Hebrew Bible. It was done differently in different parts of the Jewish community (Ginsburg 1897: 32–65; Yeivin 1980: 72–73). In the manuscripts, the onset of a new *seder* is marked by the letter *samek* in the margin. This is done three times in the book of Micah—at 1:1, 4:5, and 7:20. The first break makes sense, but the other two come just before the end of literary units. The boundaries do not occur at these places in all manuscripts. For example, the Yemenite manuscript Oriental 2211 in the British Museum begins the tenth *seder* of the Minor Prophets at Jon 4:11 instead of Mic 1:1, and the eleventh at Mic 4:7 instead of Mic 4:5 (Ginsburg 1897: 53). The beginning of a new *seder* with the last verse of Micah (7:20) is strange, but its position is certified by the use of the opening words of the verse as the catchword for this *seder* in the Masoretic lists. A division at this point shows that the breaks do not necessarily correspond to the boundaries of the literary units.

The text was divided further into paragraphs (*parashiyyoth*). The divisions between paragraphs were marked in two ways. A "closed" (*setumah*) division was marked by a space at the beginning or in the middle of a line. An "open" (*petuhah*) division was marked by a space at the end of a line or by a completely blank line. The antiquity of the system is attested by the occurrence of the divisions in ancient manuscripts, not only the Hebrew texts found at Qumran, but also the manuscripts of Greek translations found in nearby caves (DJD 2; Oesch 1979; Tov 1990). In modern printed editions, such as BHS, these divisions are marked by the letters *samek* (= S) and *peh* (= P), respectively, in open spaces in the printed text.

The open and closed divisions in the text of the Hebrew Bible are located in various positions in the manuscripts, and their identification as "open" or "closed" is not always the same. The differences between Qumran and medieval manuscripts are considerable (Tov 1992: 51, 211). Extensive differences between divisions in 4QJer^c (4Q72) and those in Masoretic manuscripts are reported by Tov (1991: 274–76). Often the divisions in **A** are closer to those in Qumran

Open and Closed Paragraphs in Prime Manuscripts of Micah

	Mur	8Hev	C	A	P	L
1:2	—	S	—	[.]	—	—
2:1	P	[.]	P	[.]	S	S
2:3	P	[.]	P	[.]	S	P
3:1	P	[.]	P	[.]	S	P
3:5	P	P	S	[.]	S	P
3:9	P	[.]	P	[.]	S	S
4:1	P	[.]	P	[.]	S	P
4:5	—	S	—	[.]	—	—
4:6	P	P	P	[.]	S	P
4:8	P	P	P	[.]	S	P
4:9	—	P	—	[.]	—	—
5:1	S	P	S	[.]	S	S
5:6	P	S	P	P	P	S
5:7	—	[.]	—	P	—	—
5:9	P	[.]	P	—	S	P
6:1	P	[.]	P	P	S	S
6:9	P	[.]	P	S	S	P
7:1	S	[.]	P	P	P	P
7:9	P	[.]	P	P	S	S
7:14	P	[.]	P	P	S	S

manuscripts than to those in **L**. The divisions of the book of Micah are fairly stable. We note only the prime witnesses: the Greek text of the Minor Prophets from Murabbaʿat Cave 5 (MurXII [Mur 88]), the Greek Minor Prophets scroll from Naḥal Ḥever (8ḤevXIIgr [Tov 1990]), **C** (Cairo Codex), **A** (Aleppo Codex), **P** (Petropolitanus), and **L** (Leningrad Codex). See Oesch (1979: T36*).

Very little use has been made of these data in modern study of the Hebrew Bible. De Moor (1993), in a study of the integrity of Isaiah 40, has demonstrated its usefulness and deplored its neglect (1993: 182). Oesch, while urging attention to the phenomenon of the paragraph breaks, nevertheless recommends caution. The *parashiyyoth* divisions usually come at obvious transition points in the text and merely confirm what we can discover without their aid. Sometimes the *parashah* break marks unequivocally the onset of a new literary unit. Sometimes the uncertainty of the manuscripts as to where the break comes is a warning signal that the matter is far from clear. This is often because there is continuity of theme across a formal break, and then the break should not be permitted to separate thematically related material. And not all the distinct literary units have their boundaries marked by this device. Every instance has to be assessed on its own merits, taking all factors into consideration. This commentary works with twenty-seven or so literary units, more than the eighteen or so *parashiyyoth* of the traditional text. When, however, thematic continuity is recognized and the unifying effect of larger literary structures is appreciated, the working units become larger and the number might be fewer than eighteen, as few as six or even five. For the most part we follow the Masoretic divisions. At some places the text presents problems in analysis that are not resolved by the locations of the *parashiyyoth*. Sometimes the *parashiyyoth* indicate the beginning of a new speech within a literary unit. The oracle that begins at 2:3 is clearly part of 2:1–5. We do not separate 2:3–5 away from 2:1–2; nor do we identify 2:3–11 as one literary unit on the basis of the *parashiyyoth* divisions. The literary unit of the "Song of Confidence" that we have identified in 7:7–12 is indicated by the first person speech throughout vv 7–10, and the feminine singular pronouns referring to "my enemy" carry the speech through v 11. The Masoretic division between vv 8 and 9 breaks this continuity.

The divisions at 2:3 and 7:9 break up coherent literary units. The opposite case is met when a *parashah* is not one coherent unit and further divisions have to be made. The *parashah* in 7:9–13 presents this problem. We have already observed that 7:9 is a continuation of 7:7–8 and that the speech goes at least through v 11. A new *parashah* begins with 7:14. It is not easy to work out whether vv 11–13 are a continuation of vv 7–10 or an introduction to vv 14–17. We have made the break at v 13.

Besides arguments based on internal coherence, literary units can sometimes be identified, or provisional identification can be confirmed, by arguments based on the analysis of larger literary structures. The structure of chapters 2–3 is partly indicated by the three *parashiyyoth* in chapter 3, and this evidence assists the analysis of chapter 2 as part of a larger whole. The result, however, requires that the traditional division at 2:3 not be used as part of the total structure. Similar considerations apply to chapters 4–5, in which all the portions fit into an overall literary structure. The portion in 4:6–8 is unified by the theme of Yahweh's kingship in Zion. The Masoretic tradition, confirmed by the two most ancient Greek manuscripts, MurXII [Mur 88] and 8ḤevXIIgr, has an open division between v 7 and v 8. Here, as at 2:3 and 7:9, the literary analysis and the traditional divisions pull in different directions. In the discussions that follow we shall pay attention to both of these factors.

THE ORGANIZATION OF THE BOOK OF MICAH

The outline of the prophecy of Micah used in this commentary takes it to be a collection of oracles that have been arranged in three "books." This approach, and the terms employed when we are talking about the "structure" of the book, are used for convenience. Numerous attempts have been made to identify literary units or pieces as constituents of the book and to work out the design, if any, in the arrangement of these materials as they are now presented in the edition that has come down through the scribal channels. Only one form of the book is now known. Where it came from and how it got to be that way are problems for which no solution is in sight. We shall confine our remarks to a few descriptive observations about the text we now have.

In the most recent attempts to establish the "structure" (Willis 1969b, 1969c), the "formation" (Renaud 1977), the "coherence" (Hagstrom 1988) of Micah, the authors have reviewed the work of dozens of previous scholars who have tried to resolve these kinds of questions. No consensus has emerged, but that does not mean that all the work has been futile. On the contrary, it rewards careful study. The outcomes of this research, conducted along so many different lines and from so many angles, are a treasury of valid and useful observations about the contents and connections of the book.

PREVIOUS RESEARCH

The older criticism mainly worked backwards from the final product in an attempt to track down sources and hopefully to sort out the original words of Micah himself from the accretions and additions of later editors and redactors and the glosses and glitches of even later scribes. The results of these investigations have ranged from emphasis on the diversity of the contents to recognition of the unification of the ingredients in the final edition. The variety of literary forms, the fluctuations of mood, and the contrasting theological points of view suggested to many scholars that there must have been a number of contributors over a long period of time. The analytical phase of research, which tried to track down all these components and to interpret them against their historical background, was inaugurated in 1867, when Ewald recognized that the book consisted of two distinct parts, chapters 1–5 and 6–7. That observation has been one of the most enduring outcomes of Micah research (S. R. Driver 1909: 326). Hagstrom (1988: 17) lists scholars who sustain this result. Jeppesen has reviewed nineteenth-century (1979) and recent (1978) research.

This, however, was only the first step. Ewald (1867–68, 1:525–37) concluded further that these portions were distinct books: the first (chapters 1–5) from Micah, the second a prophecy of an otherwise unknown prophet who lived in the time of Manasseh (687–642 B.C.E.). Burkitt (1926) identified Micah 6–7 as a northern prophecy. Van der Woude (1971a) concluded that the reference to Omri and Ahab in chapter 6 pointed to the same region.

Closer examination disclosed that the two portions identified by Ewald were not uniform or consistent within themselves, and each was divided further into smaller pieces. First the book was taken apart by finding the distinctive integral components and separating them from one another. This was done by combining three kinds of observation. Internally a self-standing item can be identified by a distinctive *theme* (or demonstrable historical background), consistently handled in a uniform *style*, especially when it takes the form of a familiar *genre*. Externally the boundaries of a constituent unit may be marked by well-defined onset and end, by clear transitions to something else, or even by deep breaks that isolate one unit from the next. The next major step was to split chapters 1–5 into chapters 1–3 and 4–5. Stade, in two influential papers (1881, 1883), identified chapters 4–5 as a distinct work, itself composite. At first it consisted of 4:1–4; 4:11–5:3; 5:6–14; later it was interpolated by 4:5–10 and 5:4–5. Many scholars reached similar conclusions (lists of names are given by Hagstrom [1988: 13, 15]). The splendid picture of Zion in the opening verses of chapter 4 contrasts with the desolate scene at the end of chapter 3, and many features found throughout chapters 4 and 5 are not found elsewhere in the book. The contrast between the threats in chapters 1–3 and the promises in chapters 4–5 was strongly emphasized by earlier commentators (G. A. Smith 1899; J. M. P. Smith 1914). There is a measure of consistency within chapters 1–3 and likewise within chapters 4–5 (but the unit in 2:12–13 stands apart from the rest and resembles chapters 4–5 in several particulars). The distinctiveness of chapters 4–5 is indicated by its contrasts with the rest of the book, especially in its eschatological vocabulary and imagery and in the way it lends itself to interpretation against the background of the Babylonian Exile as distinct from the earlier situation created by the relocation of populations by the Assyrians. The integrity of chapters 4–5 is shown by their inner consistency and by key words and structural arrangements that link these chapters together. The mood fluctuates between terror and grief, contrition and elation, but these contrasts are juxtaposed in a highly artistic way. This result of analysis, isolating chapters 4–5 from the rest, seems to have become the majority opinion, and we still find the arguments in its favor impressive.

The integrity of chapters 6–7 has been questioned along similar lines. Since Wellhausen ([Wellhausen-]Bleek 1893: 425; Wellhausen 1898: 149) there has been widespread agreement that 7:7(or 8)–20 is a distinct composition, exilic or even postexilic (Fohrer 1968).

The belief that the original Micah, like the other canonical eighth-century prophets, was a messenger of doom supplied a criterion relied on heavily by earlier researchers. All prophecies of hope, and especially those that seem to have a background in the Babylonian Exile or that are eschatological in thought and imagery, were identified as later additions. The simplest test of authenticity (a major concern of earlier critics) was that of consistency in the message, applied most readily to detach promises of redemption from proclamations of doom, only the latter coming from Micah himself. Fohrer (1968: 447) declared, "His only message, therefore, can be inescapable destruction." Otto (1991) highlights the formation history of the book of Micah as a refinement of the theological interpretation of the judgment and salvation experience of Israel in the light of later reflection on the major historical fulfillment of such prophecies in the events of the sixth century B.C.E. We shall have occasion to dispute the methodological cogency of the presuppositions on which this kind of conclusion is based. Some scholars, such as Procksch (1910), and more recently van der Woude (1969,

1973), accounted for the discrepancy between the judgment speeches in chapters 1–3 and the hope expressed in 2:12–13 by ascribing the latter to a false prophet of Micah's time (quoted to be rejected); see also Carroll (1992). But most scholars recognized the affinities of 2:12–13 with the message of Second Isaiah along with its similarities (in theme and diction) to the apparently exilic materials in chapters 4–5 and assigned these chapters to the sixth century B.C.E.

As a result of these successive separations, first of chapters 6–7 (dated to the seventh century) and then of chapters 4–5 (dated to the sixth century), only chapters 1–3 (and then not all of their contents) were dated to the eighth century. Here are two typical statements. Chapters 1–3 "derive almost in toto from Micah" (Fohrer 1968: 444). "Chapters 4–5 are composed almost entirely of oracles of salvation, and nearly all of these were produced after Micah's day" (McKeating 1971: 11). As a result of such argumentation, even the contents of chapters 1–3 came under suspicion, and the amount of text that remained as authentic original Micah prophecies was greatly diminished. This trend culminated in the radical results presented by Haupt (1910, 1911). He found genuine Micah oracles only in chapters 1–3, and then in only a small number of lines in those chapters.

The concerns of Lindblom (1929: especially 7–12, 134–62) were similar to those of Haupt. He was mainly interested in sifting out the authentic Micah materials in order to understand the prophet's experience of revelation. Since the work of Wolfe (1935), attention was focused more on the shape of the book in its successive editions, and the function of each such edition in the community that used it. Lescow (1972a) suggested that the edition at the end of the sixth century was used in rituals of lamentation over the destruction of the temple.

In the work of R. E. Wolfe (1935), very little, if any, of the present book of Micah comes from a prophet of that name who lived in the eighth century B.C.E. Wolfe used criteria of "differences in metrical structure, vocabulary, position, style, historical perspective, ideology, the forms of thought expression" (1935: 90) to distinguish thirteen "strata," of which seven involved pieces of the book of Micah. Lescow (1972a) still assigns most of 1:3–3:12 to Micah (with doubts about small portions, such as 1:13bc; 2:4; and parts of 2:6–11), while rejecting 1:2; 1:5b–7; 2:5; and 2:12–13. While there has been a consensus that most of chapters 4–7 (with the possible exception of some parts of chapter 6) are not from Micah, scholars who have worked on the problem independently have reached little agreement about when the various additions were made. Willi-Plein (1971), for instance, delays the addition of 4:1–8, 5:1, 5:3, and 7:1–4 until after the Babylonian Exile in the fifth century, with final additions, including 7:5–20, made about 350 B.C.E. Work along these lines attained its most elaborate expression in the studies of Renaud (1964, 1977).

Division of chapters 1–5 into 1–2 and 3–5 is another suggestion that has enjoyed a considerable vogue. Allen (1976), R. L. Smith (1984), and Hagstrom (1988: 19), following Willis (1969a), recognize the exhortations beginning with *šimʿû*, "Listen!" (1:2; 3:1; 6:1) as openers of major sections. They find a major break between chapter 2 and chapter 3 and continuity between chapter 3 and chapter 4. Cf. Shaw (1993). The word *šimʿû* occurs six times in the book (twice in chapter 6); it does not seem to be a very secure diagnostic for such a far-reaching conclusion.

So far as chapters 6–7 are concerned, it was an early conclusion, due mainly to Wellhausen (1898: 149), that 7:7(or 8)–20 was a distinct piece, a later addition. This, too, has stood the test of time. In similar fashion other passages, large or small, have been identified as later comments modifying, even contradicting, the original message of the prophet. Wolff (1990: 1), while recognizing that "many problems of dating the material remain unresolved," finds three main stages in the formation of the eventual book: from the neo-Assyrian era, original sayings from Micah himself; from the neo-Babylonian era, comments or adjustments providing "further orientation for Israel's continuing path in the midst of foreign nations"; from the Persian period, the response of the community "to hearing the liturgical readings of the old and new words of prophecy." We admit the cogency of the second point, which is analogous to the case of the book of Isaiah. We are doubtful about the continuation of revisions into the Persian period. In this regard the history of the book of Micah is part of the history of the Book of the Twelve, and its revision (we think its final revision) should be connected with the definitive assembly of that entire corpus of prophetic writings. With the complete lack of historical evidence for how and when this took place, we are left with inference and speculation. All we need say (all we can say) at this point is that we find no evidence within the book of Micah or within the Book of the Twelve as a whole that requires a date for its completion later than the fifth century B.C.E. We are prepared to recognize that final editorial work might well have taken place during the time of Ezra and under his patronage, since there is evidence for concern with sacred scriptures in that situation. Judgments about the dating of the possible additions to the original core will be discussed in the NOTES and COMMENTS on the individual pericopes and verses.

CHANGES IN METHODOLOGY

The more precise tools of form criticism and the more sensitive judgments of tradition-transmission studies have brought more subtlety to the enterprise of identifying the ingredients of the book of Micah and reconstructing the history of their assembly. Refined criteria have resulted in even more fragmentation, especially when form-critics worked with the assumption that prophetic oracles, in their first delivery, were short, pungent, poetic compositions, narrowly targeted to a concrete situation but very limited in their time perspective. This axiom is still maintained by Reventlow (1996: 376, n 6), who rejects the arguments of Andersen and Freedman (1989: 545–49) for the integrity of Amos's "woe" oracle (6:1–6) on the grounds that "this seems to overlook the shortness of most of Amos's utterances." But the assumption that prophetic oracles were short—it is only an assumption—has kept critics reading the text through narrow windows, so that they never see the final product as a large picture with extended structures and artistic designs that make for literary integrity. Scholars who are not imprisoned in the "short oracle" assumption are increasingly aware of the many different ways in which prophetic oracles might have been composed, of the different ways in which they might have been gathered, and of the innumerable things that might have happened to them as they were handed down from one generation to another. This more flexible approach has generated a wide range of solutions. But with so many possibilities, the chances of recovering what really happened between Amos's (or Micah's) street utterances and the "canonical" books that we now have become that much more uncertain. This indeterminacy has not, however, restrained some scholars from making confident pronouncements about the identity and history of various constituents of the book. Analysis was taken too far, in our opinion; constituent units, editorial additions, and redactional revisions were identified and dated with more precision and confidence than the method could sustain and seldom succeeded in winning wide acceptance. Renaud's (1977) detailed investigations are a rich source of material based on this approach. Vermeylen (1978: 519–601) has detected traces of a deuteronomic redaction of Amos and Micah. We shall not pursue all such suggestions at this point; that is best left to the introductions to the individual pericopes.

SYNTHETIC APPROACHES

In the last three decades there has been a new interest in the literary unity of the book of Micah as a whole. Attention has switched to the literary character of the final outcome of the possibly long and complex process of composition, transmission, adaptation, and editing that resulted in the book of Micah we now have. Earlier investigators into the origination, repetition, selection, revision, redaction, revision, editing, and copying of the material—with interpretation taking place all down the line—found it difficult to come out with results that succeeded in convincing the majority of scholars. It seems more manageable, if more modest, to take the surviving written form of the prophecy as the one thing that can be a given object of study, common to all of us. Wherever or whenever we search for the beginnings of the book of Micah, we have very little to go on apart from this final (canonical) text. When that was essentially finished is not known. The substantial contents might have been written down while the memory of what Micah said was still alive, perhaps already early in the seventh century B.C.E., in the last years of Hezekiah's reign. It could have been one or two hundred years after the time of Micah himself (late eighth century B.C.E.) before the book attained its present form, and who knows what might have happened over such a long period of time as the traditions were passed on (orally or in written form or both—again there is no evidence and no agreement among scholars as to how it happened) by tradents, through whose hands the material passed and in whose hands it might have undergone various changes. When it is claimed for such research that "the majority of scholars agree" on some result or other, the settling of issues by opinion poll might be reassuring to some, but the way the census was taken is seldom reported. And putting closure to research with such pronouncements does not advance knowledge. An open and on-going debate is much to be preferred, and in the instance of the book of Micah does not deserve Childs's comment: "In spite of many good insights and interesting observations of detail, the growing confusion over conflicting theories of composition [of the book of Micah] has increasingly buried the book in academic debris" (Childs 1979: 431).

There are several different approaches to this artifact. Redaction criticism focuses on the work of the major editor, assuming that one person was chiefly responsible for the overall design of the finished book. If the present form of the book is ancient and original, that person could be Micah himself, or at least a disciple close to him. If the originating selection, assembling, and integration of the available material associated with Micah as its central figure or even source was a major undertaking, done so successfully that from that point onwards the receivers of the book would be constrained to copy the text with care, but not to revise it, then the compiler or editor is to all intents the author, and we are correspondingly interested in what he did. That means studying the complete book as it eventually stabilized. It is impossible to ascertain why he (or they) did what he (or they) did, except by inference from the available text. We can find out what he did by literary analysis and description of the themes and their arrangement and of the rhetorical and artistic devices he used. To the extent that the book is a *composition*, insofar as we find evidence of deliberate organization, patterns, and structures, we gain a glimpse of the mind of this redactor-author.

The dissertation of Willis and his subsequent papers were a major contribution to this trend. The distinctiveness of the several portions of the book that had come to be recognized by most scholars was not denied; but now scholars paid more attention to the indications that somehow it all hangs together. The most influential change in method was the abandonment of uniformity and consistency as criteria for identifying materials that belonged together (same author or same date). This had been used extensively in the early stages of research, especially in the belief that oracles of judgment and oracles of salvation could not have been delivered by the same person. Now it was maintained that Micah could have uttered both kinds of prophecy (Luker 1987). The juxtaposition of oracles with one emphasis or the other was then seen to be part of a large artistic structure. Furthermore, each of these portions identified by Willis and others by the initial *šimʿû*, "Listen!" (1:2; 3:1; 6:1) begins with judgment and ends with hope. The distinctiveness of the note of promise at the end of the book permits the discovery of a four-part structure for the whole:

Chapters 1–3   Reproof and denunciation

Chapters 4–5   Promise of redemption

Chapters 6:1–7:6   Denunciation

Chapter 7:7–20   Promise of forgiveness

More detailed analyses by Nielsen (1954), Renaud (1977), and Willis (1969b) have disclosed concentric structures. Willis (1969b) highlighted an A-B-A pattern in both small and large units. At the same time he pointed out that relatively lengthy statements of doom or despair (such as 1:2–2:11 and 3:1–12) are followed by briefer statements of hope (such as 2:12–13 and 4:1–5). Renaud (1977: vii) finds an alternation of messages of judgment and salvation:

Judgment	Salvation
1:2b–2:11	2:12–13
3:1–12	4–5
6:1–7:6	7:7–20

Attempts to fit everything into such patterns are in danger of reaching a point where arguments have to be stretched and strained, and the results lose credibility. Allen (1976: 260) finds an opposite proportion of "short distress" and "long hope" in 4:11–13 and 5:1–6. There are limits to such quantification of the analysis; it can become artificial if pushed too far.

Recent research has returned to interest in the relationships within chapters 1–5 after the text had settled down to its final shape. After Lescow (1972) had studied the redaction history of these chapters, Mays (1976: 22f.) distinguished factors in the form of the book from those in its formation, highlighting once more the unity of chapters 1–5.

Even the long-standing separation of chapters 6–7 from the rest has been questioned. In particular Hagstrom (1988: 115–28) has found structural parallels, verbal links, common motifs, and other correspondences between these portions, showing how they seem to be related to each other as the two main constituents of the complete book. Even so, the break between them is recognized as a major cleavage, and no scholar working on the problem has proposed constituents that span that gap.

There is something to be said for all of these proposals insofar as they do no more than point out thematic and structural features actually present in the text. We cannot claim to have discovered the author's (or editor's) plan of composition. Nevertheless the numerous links among the various parts that have been brought to light by the observations of these scholars are evidence of the interconnectedness of the whole. At the very least they serve as aids to interpretation. Our critical method is not strong enough to decide whether such connections were worked out consciously by the editor(s) in order to achieve some overall unification of the material that came to his (their) hands, or whether they are just things that we are noticing. Either way, the facts and features are in the text, no matter how they got there. Furthermore, because these thematic connections and structural patterns are of various kinds (as we shall point out in detail as we go along), there is no need to struggle for the one and only valid (intended) outline or plan. Thus we prefer to divide chapters 1–5 into chapters 1–3 and 4–5. We think that each of these major units has an inner structure as well as clear onset and closeout. We arrive at this result because we attach more weight than some researchers do to the long-range inclusions that we find in each "book." Thus the Book of Doom has an oracle against Samaria near the beginning (1:6–7) and a similar oracle against Jerusalem at the end (3:12); the first and last oracles in the Book of Visions match in the theme of disarmament; and the conciliation that ends the third book (chapters 6–7) resolves the contention that opened it.

Both close-up and long-range perspectives are needed for analysis and interpretation. We are not prepared to side strongly with either Nielsen and Renaud or with Willis and Allen over the division of chapters 1–5. We maintain that the eschatological formula wĕhāyâ . . . unifies chapters 4–5 and separates them from the rest of the book, a structural feature to be added to the long-recognized distinctiveness of these chapters in mood, vocabulary, and apparent exilic background. Nevertheless we recognize, along with Willis and Allen, that 4:1–5 is a peculiar oracle of hope (unique in its connection with the almost identical piece in Isaiah) that suitably follows the doom of chapter 3. We point out firm verbal links between these two units. Both insights can be accepted. By beginning the Book of Visions (chapters 4–5) with an oracle of hope (4:1–5) the editor has achieved two effects at once. He has announced universal salvation to follow the judgments of the Book of Doom and he has set out the first block of a new (concentric) structure, the Book of Visions (chapters 4–5), that will be completed by the inclusion for 4:1–5 at 5:9–14.

RHETORICAL-HISTORICAL ANALYSIS

The work on this volume was completed before the publication of Charles S. Shaw's study The Speeches of Micah (1993) and of Brian Peckham's History and Prophecy (Anchor Bible Reference Library 1993). It was too late to incorporate many insights from these works into ours. Shaw's "rhetorical-historical analysis" applies classical rhetoric to the five speeches that he recognizes as constituting the book of Micah. He studies the art of persuasion in the presentation of a speech. His approach is quite different from the "rhetorical criticism" associated with the work of James Muilenburg. Muilenburg's method is literary and aesthetic, identifying and describing the formal and linguistic devices that achieve an artistic "composition." Shaw compares the biblical prophets with Greek orators, with emphasis on rhetoric as the art of persuasion.

Classical rhetoric studies the effective presentation of an argument. Shaw recognizes prophetic speech as "historical" because it is addressed to a "rhetorical situation"—"events, persons and objects firmly rooted in history" (Shaw 1993: 22). For each "speech" identified in the book of Micah, Shaw tries to reconstruct its "rhetorical situation," relying on evidence drawn from the speech itself.

When the historical situation at which the rhetoric of the speech is aimed has been reconstructed as far as indications from the text permit, the next move is to search in known history for something that matches the rhetorical situation thus recovered. The hazardous and largely speculative nature of these steps is manifest at every stage. And the two stages merge. From the outset one needs a hypothesis about some possible historical situation to guide numerous textual and exegetical decisions that have to be made in order to reconstruct the rhetorical situation.

Shaw's method can be illustrated by his handling of Mic 1:2–16 (Shaw 1987). He accepts this passage as a single rhetorical unit. Its unity arises from the supposed fact that it is a sustained argument addressed to the same situation throughout. Many decisions about the referential meaning of words (e.g., *ʿibrî* in v 11 means "Hebrew," *gālû, they have gone away,* in v 16 does not mean that "children" have gone into exile but that the cities listed have "defected from Jerusalem" [Shaw 1993: 44]), and not a few conjectural emendations (e.g., *bmwt* in v 5 refers to the death of Judah, not to its high places) are made so as to secure logical coherence and thematic consistency for the whole speech. Such moves might have a measure of plausibility if we already knew what the prophet was talking about. But Shaw gathers the pieces of the puzzle from the text by oblique or circular arguments, and the reconstructed rhetorical situation is largely imaginary. Attempted documentation from other texts, used as historical sources, is likewise tenuous and fragmentary.

Perhaps that is the best that we can ever hope to do with this kind of material. In spite of its fresh approach, Shaw's procedure is not different in principle from time-honored historical criticism that tries out some known historical circumstance as a possible occasion for a prophetic oracle and then uses knowledge of that supposed background to fill in the gaps, to settle the meaning of words, and even to suggest emendations. Shaw concludes that the best historical fit for the rhetorical situation that he has recovered from Mic 1:2–16 is "before" (1993: 61, 224) or "shortly after" (p. 65) the death of Jeroboam II (747 B.C.E.). To support his case, Shaw examines other theories about the date of the historical background of Mic 1:2–16 (allowing for the fact that many scholars who find more than one unit in this passage might have more than one date). The main suggestions have been: (1) the Syro-Ephraimite war (about 733); (2) the time just before or after the Assyrian capture of Samaria (about 722); (3) Sargon II's Philistia campaign of 712 B.C.E.; (4) Sennacherib's invasion of Judah in 701 B.C.E. By Shaw's showing, not one of these historical situations matches the rhetorical situation in 1:2–16 in sufficient detail to make the identification stick. The upshot of Shaw's work is that all attempts to date the background of Mic 1:2–16 have failed. But Shaw's new proposal is just as vulnerable as the others; it equally fails to meet the same kind of test, especially if we subtract the special readings and emendations that he has supplied from his hypothesis and planted in his exegesis.

The same can equally be said about his proposed dates for the other speeches: Mic 2:1–13 (he includes the widely disputed vv 12–13) in "the time of Menahem's coup"; Mic 3:1–4:8 in "the time of Pekah's takeover in Samaria"; Mic 4:9–5:14 "the Syro-Ephraimite siege of Jerusalem"; Mic 6:1–7:7 "shortly before the arrest of Hoshea in 725 B.C.E."; Mic 7:8–20 "sometime before the first capture of the city" (Samaria) (Shaw 1993: 224). In each instance the pointers from the text to the rhetorical situation are too sparse, too ambiguous, or too oblique to permit the reconstruction of a historical situation sufficiently concrete, sufficiently coherent, or sufficiently complete to disclose convincingly a unique historical situation, to secure a date for the prophetic speech, and so to license historical interpretation. Or, to put it another way, there are too many partly known historical situations that provide a partial match for the prophetic speech. Instead of forcing a fit, we should admit that our critical methods are not equal to the task. There is, however, some value in fruitless research. By demolishing the proposals of other scholars and by failing to prove his own theories, Shaw has mapped the limits of attainable knowledge in this field. For centuries biblical scholars have been trying to attach dates to these kinds of texts, to plug these texts into known history. It cannot be done.

For this reason, in the present study, we restrict our efforts almost entirely to purely literary analysis and interpretation. To that extent we are in sympathy with the strictly rhetorical features of Shaw's work. To treat the components of the book of Micah as only five long, intact, integral speeches is certainly a change from the usual practice that regards a prophetic book as a congeries of fragmentary oracles embedded in redactional material and overlaid by editorial comments. Shaw hesitates to resort to scribal glosses, editorial additions, or redactional revisions to solve textual and literary problems. In this respect his method is dramatically opposed to studies that attempt to reconstruct a long and complex transmission and development of the book. The work of Renaud (1964, 1977) is the most elaborate and competent in this mode. According to transmission-redaction studies, the final product is the outcome of layer upon layer of commentary and rewriting, beginning with a small nucleus of possibly authentic Micah sayings. Renaud recognizes three main phases—preexilic, exilic, postexilic—with many little touches added from time to time, some as late as the second century B.C.E. It is part of the aim of such work to date every stratum, and in some cases quite small phrases or even individual words are ascribed to individual contributors and given precise dates.

In the course of our studies we have compiled extensive tables of all the dates given by various scholars to all the parts—oracles, rewrites, glosses—of the book of Micah. The range of suggestions is very wide. We doubt if any good purpose would be served by publishing this information. Yet there may be some value in all these proposals. In other parts of the Hebrew Bible there are prophecies that do bear dates or do contain references to known historical events, and traditional historical-critical interpretation works well for them. But not in the book of Micah. Curiously, the only historical attachment of Micah's speeches is in Jeremiah 26, where Mic 3:12 is quoted (Jer 26:18) and dated in the reign of Hezekiah. Even if this tradition knows correctly that that oracle had an influence on Hezekiah, it does not follow that Micah first uttered that prophecy in the reign of Hezekiah, only that Hezekiah took the words to heart in his own time. It could be that specifics providing the kind of pointers to the historical situation that we need were lacking in Micah's speeches precisely because at the time of their delivery his audience did not need to be informed about the circumstances in which they all found themselves. The prophet could afford to use oblique or figurative language; they knew what he was talking about. We don't. The deliberate use of obscure or ambiguous language could also be part of the prophet's craft as an indirect communicator. Comparison with Greek political orators, with their lucidity and directness, could be pointing Hebrew rhetorical-historical criticism in the wrong direction.

MICAH AND JEREMIAH

The continuity of the preexilic prophetic tradition is evident in the indebtedness of Jeremiah to his predecessors, particularly Hosea (H. J. Hendriks 1975). The influence of Amos on later prophets in matters of social justice was enduring. The most conspicuous link between the book of Jeremiah and the book of Micah is the identified quotation in Jer 26:18. Cha (1996) has shown that four central themes of Micah reappear in Jeremiah: (1) predictions concerning Judah and Jerusalem (1996: 6–23); (2) polemics against other prophets (1996: 59–75); (3) criticism of social injustice (1996: 99–107); (4) confessions in the form of lamentation. While these are common *topoi* of biblical prophecy, Cha points out that Jeremiah's treatment of these themes often uses the distinctive vocabulary of Micah. He compares the following related passages: Mic 1:8 (Jer 4:8); 1:9, 14 (15:18); 1:10, 16 (6:26; 7:29); 2:4 (9:18); 2:11 (5:13a, 31); 3:1 (5:4f., 8:7); 3:5 (6:14 [= 8:11]; 23:13); 3:6f. (14:14f.; 23:16, 21, 31f.); 3:7 (6:15 [= 8:12]); 3:8 (6:11); 3:10 (22:13); 3:11f. (7:4, 9a, 10a, 11a, 12, 14a; 9:10; 26:6, 12); 4:9, 10a (4:31; 6:24; 22:23); 7:1f. (5:1; 7:28b); 7:5f. (9:3f.; 12:6).

Cha lists distinctive vocabulary items and idiomatic expressions common to these matching passages, twenty-three in all. It might be claiming too much to identify Micah as Jeremiah's *Vorgänger* (Cha 1996: 131); Jeremiah is in the succession, if not a direct successor. It will be noticed that most of the demonstrated linkages are with Mic 1–3, which are generally recognized as coming from the prophet. If Mic 4–5 contains exilic or postexilic additions, the linkage between Mic 4:9–10 and Jeremiah could have come from the latter. There are differences as well as similarities in usage, as Cha shows systematically. Cha is more inclined to explain the evidence in terms of oral tradition rather than written sources for Micah's message. In our discussion (111–16) we recognized the likely coexistence of written and oral transmission.

THE LITERARY INTEGRITY
OF THE BOOK OF MICAH

In spite of this diversity in theme and form, the book as a whole shows some signs of overall integration. It begins with a clear opening statement (1:1–4) and ends with a clear closing statement (7:18–20). The opening statement contains a number of key words that turn up again later in the book. The question *mî–'ēl kāmôkā* (7:18) is often taken as an inclusion for the name Micah (1:1). (We express reservations on this point in our NOTE on *Micah* at 1:1.) The announced theme of Samaria and Jerusalem is taken up immediately after the introduction (1:5) and gives a framework to the whole Book of Doom—Samaria (1:6) . . . Jerusalem (3:12). Most attention is given to Jerusalem, whose parallel Zion makes a chiasmus that embraces all the material from 1:9 and 12 to 3:12. The parallelism Zion // Jerusalem is used in 3:10, 12; 4:2, 8. This pattern locks the Book of Visions into the Book of Doom. "Zion" is the only name used in 4:10–13. The motif of mountains (heights) is introduced in 1:3, beginning a catena. Micah 3:12 is an inclusion for 1:3, with mountain // height in chiasmus. Mountain also serves as a domino link to 4:1, so that there is a series mountains (1:3), mountain (3:12), mountain, mountains (4:1). This word also marks the opening of the Book of Contention and Consolation (6:1–2). Here the invocation of Earth in parallel matches the invocation of Earth in 1:2. The opening invocation of peoples introduces another thread that runs through 4:1–3 to 5:14. God begins by treading on mountains (1:3); he ends by treading on iniquities (7:19—different verb). The first name in the oracles is Jacob (1:5), and this name occurs throughout the book and again at the end.

Besides these numerous links with the opening statement, the closing statement (7:18–20) picks up several motifs that were introduced as the prophecy unfolded. The questions about transgression // sin in 1:5 and 1:7 are answered in 7:18. The themes of the remnant (2:12; 4:7; 5:8, 9) and inheritance (2:2, 5) are tied together in 7:18. Most powerfully the virtue of ḥesed, required in man (6:8), is affirmed in God (7:18b; 20). Finally the last phrase, mîmê qedem, is a chiastic inclusion for miqqedem // mîmê ʿôlām in 5:1. The opening statements are programmatic; the closing statements are climactic. This architectonic structure of the whole book is reflected on a smaller scale in its three major sections. Jerusalem provides the inclusion for The Book of Doom (chapters 1–3). The End-time provides the inclusion for the Book of Visions (chapters 4–5). Sin and transgression are the inclusion for the Book of Contention and Consolation (chapters 6–7).

In spite of the diversity of theme and form and mood, there are four kinds of oracle that recur consistently throughout the entire book, with a general movement from doom through woe to salvation. The chart in Allen (1976: 260) shows that this movement occurs at least seven times. There are oracles of judgment spoken in anger, oracles of misery uttered in grief, oracles of promise uttered in hope, oracles of deliverance spoken in jubilation. The book begins with a powerful and terrifying revelation of God in angry judgment. It ends with an even more overwhelming disclosure of God in love and compassion. Both themes of judgment and redemption occur and recur from beginning to end—side by side in total contrast, and sometimes stated in extreme terms that do not seem to leave room for qualifications, let alone for opposite assertions to be reconciled. If all this material amounts to a total statement—if it all adds up to a valid revelation of the true character of God—then we have justice and mercy, anger and compassion, rejection and reconciliation, destruction and reconstruction.

The book begins with an outpouring of God's energies into the world. The destruction is global and total. But not final. God's mercy does not arrest his justice—it operates beyond judgment. His wrath does not quench his love; his compassion does not cancel his anger. But "he does not sustain his anger for ever" (7:18bA); mercy comes to expression once more after his anger is expended and relieved. His *ḥesed* is sustained for ever. Reconciliation is meaningful because the breach was real, serious, and apparently final, irreparable. It is possible to restore relationships because God himself takes up the task of salvation.

> It is God who promises to carry their sins away.
> He is the one who will trample them down.
> He himself will hurl all our sins into the depths of the abyss.

These are the final statements of the book, the ultimate message of the prophet. The way to this end is through the earthquake and fire of judgment. The city must become a heap of rubble before it can be splendidly rebuilt.

SCRIBAL TRANSMISSION

After the final redactor the text passed into the hands of scribes. The distinction between redactor and scribe is not absolute. It is rather a matter of degree. If we try to make the distinction at all, it would be in the attitude of a person making a copy of the text. If he felt he was still free to make changes, corrections, or clarifications, he was still an editor(-author). After the book had gained some kind of public acknowledgment in the Jewish community, resulting in its preservation and eventual veneration—however this might have taken place—the task of the copyist is to replicate the text without change. From now on any changes, or most of them, would be inadvertent and accidental. What happened to the book in its scribal transmission can be investigated using the evidence of manuscripts and versions (early translations into other languages—Greek, Aramaic, Syriac, Latin). Those matters are handled in the discipline of text-criticism.

In the long-prevailing wisdom of biblical criticism, the first task to be taken up was establishing a critical edition of the text (lower criticism). Then the work of literary criticism could follow. In this commentary we try to turn this process around. We believe that many decisions concerning the best textual readings, and judgments about the merits of proposed emendations to solve problems of various kinds, as well as identification of constituent units and speculation as to their date of composition and inclusion in the text, are best delayed until we have got our bearings on the whole text through compositional analysis. Management of the poetical patterns and rhetorical structures often places text-critical and form-critical issues in a very different light and can lead to solutions different from those enshrined in the older commentaries and text-critical apparatus.

BIBLIOGRAPHY

◆

BIBLIOGRAPHY

◆

This bibliography does not attempt a complete listing of the literature on the book of Micah. It provides references to sources used in the preparation of this commentary, many of which are referred to in the NOTES and COMMENTS. For a systematic bibliography see Adri van der Wal, *Micah: A Classified Bibliography* (Amsterdam: Free University Press, 1990). Abbreviations not listed in "Principal Abbreviations" (above) are the same as those in *The Anchor Bible Dictionary*.

Abraham, A. T.
    1975   Three Bible Studies on Struggle for Social Justice. *RelSoc* 22:3–10.
Abusch, T.
    1990   An Early Form of the Witchcraft Ritual *Maqlû* and the Origin of a Babylonian Magical Ceremony. In T. Abusch, J. Huehnergard, and P. Steinkeller, 1–57.
Abusch, T., J. Huehnergard, and P. Steinkeller
    1990   *Lingering over Words: Studies in Ancient Near Eastern Literature in Honor of William L. Moran.* HSS 37. Atlanta: Scholars Press.
Achtemeier, E. R.
    1963   How to Stay Alive (Exercising Love in Terms of Mi 6,8). *Theology and Life* 6:275–82.
Ackroyd, P. R., and B. Lindars, eds.
    1968   *Words and Meanings.* D. Winton Thomas Festschrift. Cambridge: Cambridge University Press.
Adas, M.
    1979   *Prophets of Rebellion.* Chapel Hill: University of North Carolina Press.
Aejmelaeus, A.
    1986   Function and Interpretation of *kî* in Biblical Hebrew. *JBL* 105:193–209.
Aharoni, Y.
    1968   Trial Excavation in the "Solar Shrine" at Lachish: Preliminary Report. *IEJ* 18:157–69.
    1976   The Solomonic Districts. *TA* 3:5–15.
    1980   *The Land of the Bible: A Historical Geography.* 2d ed. Trans. and ed. A. F. Rainey. Philadelphia: Westminster.
    1981   *Arad Inscriptions.* Jerusalem: Israel Exploration Society.
Aharoni, Y., and M. Avi-Yonah
    1968   *The Macmillan Bible Atlas.* New York: Macmillan.
Ahlström, G. W.
    1967   אֶדֶר. *VT* 17:1–7.
    1980   Is Tell Ed-Duweir Ancient Lachish? *PEQ* 112:7–9.
    1985   Lachish: Still a Problem. *PEQ* 117:97–99.

Albright, W. F.
1921   Contributions to the Historical Geography of Palestine. *AASOR* 2:1–46.
1923   The Sites of Ekron, Gath, and Libnah. *AASOR* 2–3:7–12.
1924a   The Assyrian March on Jerusalem, Isa X,28–32. *AASOR* 4:134–40.
1924b   Researches of the School in Western Judaea. *BASOR* 15:2–11.
1929   New Israelite and Pre-Israelite Sites: The Spring Trip of 1929. *BASOR*
            35:1–14.
1951   The Old Testament and the Archaeology of Palestine. In *The Old Testa-*
            ment and Modern Study, ed. H. H. Rowley, 1–26. Oxford: Clarendon Press.
1957a   *From the Stone Age to Christianity: Monotheism and the Historical Process.*
            2d ed. Garden City, N.Y.: Doubleday Anchor Books.
1957b   The High Place in Ancient Palestine. *VTSup* 4:242–58.
1958   An Ostracon from Calah and the North-Israelite Diaspora. *BASOR*
            149:33–36.
1961a   *Samuel and the Beginnings of the Prophetic Movement*. Goldenson Lec-
            ture for 1961. Cincinnati: Hebrew Union College Press.
1961b   The Archaeology of the Ancient Near East. In *Peake's Commentary on the*
            Bible, ed. M. Black and H. H. Rowley, 58–65. London: Thomas Nelson
            and Sons.
1964   *History, Archaeology, and Christian Humanism*. New York: McGraw-Hill.
1968   *Yahweh and the Gods of Canaan: A Historical Analysis of Two Contrasting*
            Faiths. Garden City, N.Y.: Doubleday.
Alexander, J. A.
1846–47   *Commentary on the Prophecies of Isaiah*. (Rev. J. Eadie [1875].) 8th print-
            ing (1977). Grand Rapids, Mich.: Zondervan.
Allegro, J. M.
1955   Uses of the Semitic Demonstrative Element Z in Hebrew. *VT* 5:309–12.
1968   *Qumran Cave 4*. DJD V. Oxford: Clarendon.
Alleman, H. C., and E. E. Flack, eds.
1948   *Old Testament Commentary*. Philadelphia: Muhlenberg.
Allen, L. C.
1973   More Cuckoos in the Textual Nest; at 2 Kings 23:5; Jeremiah 17:3–4;
            Micah 3:3; 6:16 (LXX); 2 Chronicles 20:25 (LXX)." *JTS* 24:69–73.
1976   *The Books of Joel, Obadiah, Jonah, and Micah*. NICOT. Grand Rapids,
            Mich.: Eerdmans.
Alonso-Schökel, L.
1975   Hermeneutical Problems of a Literary Study of the Bible. In *Congress Vol-*
            ume: Edinburgh 1974. VTSup 28:1–15. Leiden: Brill.
1988   *A Manual of Hebrew Poetics*. Trans. A. Graffy. Rome: Pontifical Biblical
            Institute.
Alt, A.
1930   Die territorialgeschichtliche Bedeutung von Sanheribs Eingriff in Paläs-
            tina. *PJ* 25:80–88. Reprint, Alt 1959, 2:242–49.
1949   Das Verbot des Diebstahls im Dekalog. In Alt 1959, 1:333–40.
1950   Jesaja 8,23–9,6. Befreiungsnacht und Krönungstag. In W. Baumgartner et
            al. 1950, 29–49. Reprint, Alt 1959, 2:206–25.
1951   Das Königtum in den Reichen Israel und Juda. *VT* 1:2–22 [= *KS* 2:116–34;
            English translation "The Monarchy in the Kingdoms of Israel and Judah,"
            in Alt 1968, 311–35].

1953   Jesaja 8,23–9,6. *Katolikus Szemle* 2:206–25.

1955   Micha 2,1–5 *ΓΗΣ ΑΝΑΔΑΣΜΟΣ* [Ges Anadasmos] in Juda. In *Interpretationes Ad Vetus Tetamentum Pertinentes Sigmundo Mowinckel Septuagenario Missae*, ed. N. A. Dahl and A. S. Kapelrud, 13–23. Oslo: Land og Kirche. Reprint, Alt 1959, 3:373–81.

1959   *Kleine Schriften zur Geschichte des Volkes Israel.* 3 vols. München: Beck'sche Verlagsbuchhandlung.

1966   *Essays on Old Testament History and Religion.* Garden City, N.Y.: Anchor.

Amiran, R., and A. Eitan

1965   A Canaanite-Hyksos City at Tell Nagila. *Arch* 18:113–23.

Anbar, M.

1994   Rosée et ondées ou lion et lionceau (Michée 5,6–7). *BN* 73:5–8.

Andersen, F. I.

1966a   Moabite Syntax. *Or* 35:81–120.

1966b   The Socio-Juridical Background of the Naboth Incident. *JBL* 85:46–57.

1969   Israelite Kinship Terminology and Social Structure. *BT* 20/1:29–39.

1974   *The Sentence in Biblical Hebrew.* Janua Linguarum, Series Practica 231. The Hague: Mouton.

1986   Yahweh, the Kind and Sensitive God. In *God Who Is Rich in Mercy: Essays Presented to Dr. D. B. Knox*, ed. P. T. O'Brien and D. G. Peterson, 41–88. Grand Rapids, Mich.: Baker Book House.

1994   The Poetic Properties of Prophetic Discourse in the Book of Micah. In *Biblical Hebrew and Discourse Linguistics*, ed. R. D. Bergen, 520–28. Dallas: SIL.

1995   Linguistic Coherence in Prophetic Discourse. In *Fortunate the Eyes That See* [David Noel Freedman Festschrift], ed. A. B. Beck et al., 137–56. Grand Rapids, Mich.: Eerdmans.

Andersen, F. I., and A. D. Forbes

1983   "Prose Particle" Counts of the Hebrew Bible. In C. L. Meyers and M. O'Connor, 165–83.

1986   *Spelling in the Hebrew Bible.* BibOr 41. Rome: Biblical Institute.

1989a   Methods and Tools for the Study of Old Testament Syntax. In *Les Actes de la 2ième conférence de l'AIBI Bible et Informatique: méthodes, outuils, résultats* (Jérusalem, 9–13 Juin 1988), 61–72. Genève: Slatkine.

1989b   *The Vocabulary of the Old Testament.* Rome: Biblical Institute Press.

Andersen, F. I., and D. N. Freedman

1980   *Hosea.* AB 24. Garden City, N.Y.: Doubleday.

1989   *Amos.* AB 24A. Garden City, N.Y.: Doubleday.

Anderson, B. W.

1978   *The Eighth-Century Prophets: Amos, Hosea, Isaiah, Micah.* Philadelphia: Fortress.

Anderson, B. W., and W. Harrelson, eds.

1962   *Israel's Prophetic Heritage.* New York: Harper.

Anderson, G. A.

1991   *A Time to Mourn, A Time to Dance: The Expression of Grief and Joy in Israelite Religion.* University Park: Pennsylvania State University Press.

Anderson, G. W.

1951   A Study of Micah 6:1–8. *SJT* 4:191–97.

Arbeitman, Y. L., ed.
  1988   *Fucus: A Semitic/Afrasian Gathering in Remembrance of Albert Ehrman.*
          Amsterdam Studies in the Theory and History of Linguistic Science 58.
          Amsterdam/Philadelphia: John Benjamins Publishing.

Auld, A. G., ed.
  1993   *Understanding Poets and Prophets. Essays in Honour of George Wishart
          Anderson.* JSOTSup 152. Sheffield: JSOT Press.

Avi-Yonah, M.
  1954   *The Madaba Mosaic Map.* Jerusalem: Israel Exploration Society.

Avi-Yonah, M., and A. Kloner
  1977   Maresha (Marisa). *EAEHL* 3:782–90.

Avigad, N.
  1976   *Bullae and Seals from a Post-Exilic Judean Archive.* Qedem Monographs
          of the Institute of Archaeology, The Hebrew University of Jerusalem 4.
  1979   Baruch the Scribe and Jerahmeel the King's Son. *BA* 42:114–21.
  1980   The Chief of the Corvée. *IEJ* 30:170–73.

Avigad, N., et al., eds.
  1971   *Hommages à André Dupont-Sommer.* Paris: Maisonneuve.

Avishur, Y.
  1971–72 Pairs of Synonymous Words in the Construct State (and in Apposition
           Hendiadys) in Biblical Hebrew. *Sem* 2:17–81.
  1975   Word-Pairs Common to Phoenician and Biblical Hebrew. *UF* 7:13–47.
  1981   Parallelism of Numbers in the Bible and in the Ancient Semitic Literature.
          Proceedings of the Seventh World Congress of Jewish Studies. Studies in the
          Bible and the Ancient Near East [Hebrew Section], 1–9.
  1984   *Stylistic Studies of Word-Pairs in Biblical and Ancient Semitic Literatures.*
          AOAT 210. Neukirchen-Vluyn: Neukirchener Verlag; Kevelaer: Verlag
          Butzon & Bercker.

Balentine, S. E., and J. Barton, eds.
  1994   *Language, Theology and the Bible: Essays in Honour of James Barr.* Oxford:
          Clarendon.

Balzer, H. R.
  1991   Eschatological Elements as Permanent Qualities in the Relationship
          between God and Nation in the Minor Prophets. *OTE* 4:408–14.

Banks, R.
  1987   "Walking" as a Metaphor of the Christian Life: The Origins of a Signifi-
          cant Pauline Usage. In E. W. Conrad and E. G. Newing 1987, 303–13.

Bardtke, H.
  1971   Die Latifundien in Juda während der zweiten Hälfte des achten Jahrhun-
          derts v. Chr. In *Hommages à André Dupont-Sommer,* ed. N. Avigad et al.,
          235–54. Paris: Maisonneuve.

Barr, J.
  1960   Theophany and Anthropomorphism in the Old Testament. *VTSup* 7:31–38.
  1968   *Comparative Philology and the Text of the Old Testament.* Oxford: Claren-
          don Press.
  1985   Why? in Biblical Hebrew. *JTS* n.s. 36:11–33.
  1989   *The Variable Spellings of the Hebrew Bible.* Schweich Lectures 1986. New
          York: Oxford University Press.

Barré, M. L.
1982   A Cuneiform Parallel to Ps 86:16–17 and Mic 7:16–17. *JBL* 101:272–75.
Barrick, W. B., and J. R. Spencer
1984   *In the Shelter of Elyon: Essays on Ancient Palestinian Life and Literature in Honor of G. W. Ahlström. JSOTSup 31.* Sheffield: University of Sheffield.
Barstad, H. M.
1984   *The Religious Polemics of Amos: Studies in the Preaching of Amos ii 7b–8, iv 1–13, v 1–27, vi 4–7, viii 14.* VTSup 34. Leiden: Brill.
1993   No Prophets? Recent Developments in Biblical Prophetic Research and Ancient Near Eastern Prophecy. *JSOT* 57:39–60.
Barthélemy, D.
1953   Redécouverte d'un chaînon manquant de l'histoire de la Septante. *RB* 60:18–29. Reprint, D. Barthélemy 1978, 38–50.
1963   *Les devanciers d'Aquila: Première publication intégrale du texte des fragments du Dodécaprophéton trouvés dans le Désert de Juda: Précédée d'une étude sur les traductions et récensions Greques de la Bible réalisées au premier siècle de notre ère sous l'influence du Rabbinat Palestinien.* VTSup 10. Leiden: Brill.
1978   *Études d'histoire du texte de l'Ancien Testament.* OBO 21. Göttingen: Vandenhoeck & Ruprecht.
1992a   *Critique textuelle de l'Ancien Testament: 3. Ézéchiel, Daniel et les 12 Prophètes.* OBO 50:3. Friburg, Suise: Editions Universitaires; Göttingen: Vandenhoeck & Ruprecht.
1992b   Les ruines de la tradition des Soferim dans le manuscrit d'Alep: La gageure de Sholomoh Ben Buyâ'â. *RB* 99:7–39.
Barthélemy, D., and J. T. Milik
1955   *Qumran Cave I.* DJD I. Oxford: Clarendon.
Bartlett, J. R.
1969   The Use of the Word ראש as a Title in the Old Testament. *VT* 19:1–10.
Baumgärtel, F.
1961   Die Formel נאם יהוה. *ZAW* 73:277–90.
Baumgartner, W., et al., eds.
1950   *Festschrift Alfred Bertholet zum 80. Geburtstag.* Tübingen: J. C. B. Mohr (Paul Siebeck).
Bazak, J.
1988   Numerical Devices in Biblical Poetry. *VT* 38:332–37.
Bea, A.
1937   Kinderopfer für Moloch oder für Jahwe? Exegetische Anmerkungen zu O. Eissfeldt, *Molk als Opferbegriff. Bib* 18:95–107.
Bechtel, L. M.
1991   Shame as a Sanction of Social Control in Biblical Israel: Judicial, Political, and Social Shaming. *JSOT* 49:47–76.
Beck, A. B., et al., eds.
1995   *Fortunate the Eyes That See: Essays in Honor of David Noel Freedman in Celebration of His Seventieth Birthday.* Grand Rapids, Mich.: Eerdmans.
Beck, E.
1972   *Gottes Traum: Eine menschliche Welt: Hosea, Amos, Micha.* Stuttgarter Kleiner Kommentar, Altes Testament, vol. 14. Stuttgart: Katholisches Bibelwerk.

Beck, J. T.
1898 *Erklärung der Propheten Micha und Joel: Nebst einer Einleitung in die Prophetie*: Herausgegeben von J. Lindenmeyer. Gütersloh: C. Bertelsmann.
Becker, J.
1980 *Messianic Expectation in the Old Testament*. Trans. D. E. Green. Edinburgh: T. & T. Clark.
Becking, B.
1992 *The Fall of Samaria: An Historical and Archaeological Study*. Studies in the History of the Ancient Near East, 2. Leiden: Brill.
Beckwith, R.
1985 *The Old Testament Canon of the New Testament Church and Its Background in Early Judaism*. London: SPCK.
Beek, M. A., et al., eds.
1973 *Symbolae Biblicae et Mesopotamicae F. M. Th. de Liagre-Böhl Dedicatae*. Leiden: Brill.
Begg, C.
1979 The Significance of the *Numeruswechsel* in Deuteronomy—the "Prehistory" of the Question. *ETL* 56:10–55.
1986 The Non-mention of Amos, Hosea and Micah in the Deuteronomistic History. *BN* 32:41–53.
Begrich, J.
1934 Das priesterliche Heilsorakel. *ZAW* 52:81–92.
1936 Die priesterliche Tora. *BZAW* 66:63–88. Reprint, Begrich 1964, 232–60.
1963 *Studien zu Deuterojesaja*. ThB 20.
1964 *Gesammelte Studien zum Alten Testament*. Ed. W. Zimmerli. Munich: Chr. Kaiser.
Benoit, F., J. T. Milik, and R. de Vaux
1961 *Les Grottes de Murabba'at*. DJD II. Oxford: Clarendon.
Bentjes, P. C.
1982 Inverted Quotations in the Bible: A Neglected Stylistic Pattern. *Bib* 63:506–23.
Bergant, D.
1982 Bethlehem-Ephrathah. *BToday* 20:26–27.
Bergen, R. D., ed.
1994 *Biblical Hebrew and Discourse Linguistics*. Dallas: SIL.
Bergmann, M. S.
1992 *In the Shadow of Moloch: The Sacrifice of Children and Its Impact on Western Religions*. New York: Columbia University.
Bergren, R. V.
1974 *The Prophets and the Law*. Monographs of the Hebrew Union College 4. New York: Hebrew Union College.
Beşer, Z.
1983–85 On the Penultimate Accent of *'ôyĕbôt/'ôyabtî*. *Leš* 48–49:5–8.
Best, T. F.
1984 *Hearing and Speaking the Word: Selections from the Works of James Muilenburg*. Chico, Calif.: Scholars Press.
Beuken, W. A. M., ed.
1994 *The Book of Job*. Leuven: University Press.

Bewer, J. A.
1949   *The Book of the Twelve Prophets.* Vol. I. *Amos, Hosea and Micah.* Harper's Annotated Bible. New York: Harper.
1950   Textkritische Bemerkungen zum Alten Testament. In *Festschrift Alfred Bertholet,* ed. W. Baumgartner et al., 65–76. Tübingen: Mohr.

Beyer, G.
1931   Beiträge zur Territorialgeschichte von Südwestpalästina im Altertum. ZDPV 54:113–70.

Beyer, K.
1984   *Die aramäischen Texte vom Toten Meer: samt den Inschriften aus Palästina, dem Testament Levis aus der Kairoer Genisa, der Fastenrolle und den alten talmudischen Zitaten.* Göttingen: Vandenhoeck & Ruprecht.

Beyerlin, W.
1959   *Die Kulttraditionen Israels in der Verkündigung des Propheten Micha.* FRLANT 72. Göttingen: Vandenhoeck & Ruprecht.
1960–61 Kultische Tradition in Michas Prophetie. *Vox Theologica* 31:2–12.

Biran, A., ed.
1981   *Temples and High Places in Biblical Times.* Jerusalem: The Nelson Glueck School of Biblical Archaeology of Hebrew Union College, Jewish Institute of Religion.

Black, M., and G. Fohrer, eds.
1968   *In Memoriam Paul Kahle.* BZAW 103. Berlin: Töpelmann.

Black, M., and H. H. Rowley, eds.
1962   *Peake's Commentary on the Bible.* London: Thomas Nelson and Sons.

Blank, S. H.
1969   *Understanding the Prophets.* New York: Union of American Hebrew Congregations.

Blau, J.
1976   *A Grammar of Biblical Hebrew.* Wiesbaden: Harrassowitz.
1977   *An Adverbial Construction in Hebrew and Arabic: Sentence Adverbials in Frontal Position Separated from the Rest of the Sentence.* Proceedings of the Israel Academy of Sciences and Humanities, VI/1. Jerusalem: Israel Academy of Sciences and Humanities.
1978   Hebrew and Northwest Semitic: Reflections on the Classification of the Semitic Languages. *HAR* 2:21–44.
1979   Non-Phonetic Conditioning of Sound Change and Biblical Hebrew. *HAR* 3:7–15.
1982   Remarks on the Development of Some Pronominal Suffixes in Hebrew. *HAR* 6:61–67.

Bleek, F.
1893   *Einleitung in das Alte Testament.* Sechste Auflage besorgt von J. Wellhausen. Berlin: Georg Reimer.

Bleeker, L. H. K., and G. Smit
1926–34 *De Kleine Propheten.* 3 vols. Tekst en Uitleg. Gronigen: J. B. Wolters.

Blenkinsopp, J.
1983   *A History of Prophecy in Israel from the Settlement in the Land to the Hellenistic Period.* Philadelphia: Westminster Press.

Blum, E., C. Macholz, and E. W. Stegemann, eds.
1990   Die Hebräische Bibel und ihre zweifache Nachgeschichte. Festschrift für Rolf
            Rendtorff zum 65. Geburtstag. Neukirchen-Vluyn: Neukirchener Verlag.
Bodi, D.
1990   The Book of Ezekiel and the Poem of Erra. OBO 104. Göttingen and
            Freiburg: Vandenhoeck & Ruprecht/Universitätsverlag.
Bodine, W. R., ed.
1992   Linguistics and Biblical Hebrew. Winona Lake, Ind.: Eisenbrauns.
Boecker, H. J.
1964   Redeformen des Rechtsleben in Alten Testament. WMANT 14. Neukirchen-
            Vluyn: Neukirchener Verlag.
de Boer, P. A. H.
1991   Selected Studies in Old Testament Exegesis. Ed. C. van Duin. OTS 27.
            Leiden: Brill.
Boling, R. G.
1960   "Synonymous" Parallelism in the Psalms. JSS 5:221–25.
1966   Some Conflate Readings in Joshua-Judges. VT 16:293–98.
1975   AB: Judges. Garden City, N.Y.: Doubleday.
Bomhard, A. R.
1988   The Reconstruction of the Proto-Semitic Consonant System. In Arbeitman,
            113–40.
Boogaart, T. A.
1981   Reflections on Restoration: A Study of Prophecies in Micah and Isaiah
            about the Restoration of Northern Israel. Ph.D. diss., Gröningen.
Bordreuil, P.
1971   Michée 4:10–13 et ses parallèles ougaritiques. Sem 21:21–28.
Bosshard, E.
1987   Beobachtungen zum Zwölfprophetenbuch. BN 40:30–62.
Bovati, P.
1994   Re-establishing Justice. JSOTSup 163. Sheffield: JSOT Press.
Boyd, B.
1976   Lachish. IDBSup. Nashville: Abingdon, 526.
Boyd, W. J. P.
1984   Galilaea: A Difference of Opinion between Augustine and Jerome's "On-
            omastica Sacra." StPatr 15:136–39.
Brandenburg, H.
1963   Die Kleinen Propheten. I–II. Das Lebendige Wort. Giessen:Basel: Brunnen
            Verlag.
Bravmann, M. M.
1977   Studies in Semitic Philology. Leiden: Brill.
Brekelmans, C.
1969   Some Considerations on the Translation of the Psalms by M. Dahood: The
            Preposition b = from in the Psalms according to M. Dahood. UF 1:5–14.
Brenner, M. L.
1991   The Song of the Sea: Ex 15:1–21. BZAW 195. Berlin/New York: de Gruyter.
Brettler, M. Z.
1989   God Is King: Understanding an Israelite Metaphor. JSOTSup 76. Sheffield:
            Sheffield Academic Press.

Briend, J.
1983   Bethlém-Ephrata. *MB* 30:29.
Brin, G.
1988   The Significance of the Form mah-ṭṭôb. *VT* 38:462–65.
1989   Micah 2,12–13. A Textual and Ideological Study. *ZAW* 101:118–24.
Brockelmann, C.
1956   *Hebräische Syntax*. Neukirchen Kreis Moers: Buchhandlung des Erziehungsvereins.
Brockington, L. H.
1973   *The Hebrew Text of the Old Testament: The Readings Adopted by the Translators of the New English Bible*. Oxford: Oxford University Press.
Brongers, H. A.
1965a   Bemerkungen zum Gebrauch der adverbialen wĕʿattâ im Alten Testament. *VT* 15:289–99.
1965b   Merismus, Synekdoche und Hendiadys in der Bibel-Hebräischen Sprache. *OTS* 14:100–14.
1981   Some Remarks on the Biblical Particle hǎlô'. *OTS* 21:177–89.
Bronznick, N. M.
1979   "Metathetic Parallelism": An Unrecognized Subtype of Synonymous Parallelism. *HAR* 3:25–39.
Brooke, G. J., and B. Lindars, eds.
1992   *Septuagint, Scrolls and Cognate Writings: Papers Presented to the International Symposium on the Septuagint and Its Relations to the Dead Sea Scrolls and Other Writings (Manchester 1990)*. SBLSCS 33. Atlanta: Scholars Press.
Broshi, M.
1974   The Expansion of Jerusalem in the Reigns of Hezekiah and Manasseh. *IEJ* 24:21–26.
Brown, M. L.
1987   "Is It Not?" or "Indeed!!!": *HL* in Northwest Semitic. *Maarav* 4:201–19.
Brown, S.
1991   *Late Carthaginian Child Sacrifice and Sacrificial Monuments in Their Mediterranean Context*. JSOTSup/ASOR Monograph Series, 3. Sheffield: JSOT Press.
Bruce, G. A.
1990   From Holy Mountains to the New Earth. *Theologica Evangelica* 23:27–34.
Brueggemann, W. A.
1981   "Vine and Fig Tree": A Case Study in Imagination and Criticism. *CBQ* 43:188–204.
1986   The Costly Loss of Lament. *JSOT* 36:57–71.
Brueggemann, W., S. Parks, and T. H. Groome
1986   *To Act Justly, Love Tenderly, Walk Humbly*. Mahwah, N.J.: Paulist Press.
Bruno, A.
1923   *Micha und der Herrscher aus der Vorzeit*. Leipzig-Erlangen, Uppsala, and Stockholm: A Deichertsche Verlagsbuchhandlung Dr. Werner Scholl/ Almqvist & Wiksell.
1957   *Das Buch der Zwölf: Eine rhythmische und textkritische Untersuchung*. Stockholm: Almqvist & Wiksell.
Bryant, D. J.
1978   Micah 4:14–5:14: An Exegesis. *ResQ* 21:210–30.

Buccellati, G.
1967   *Cities and Nations of Ancient Syria.* SS. Rome: University of Rome.
Buchanan, G. W.
1961   Eschatology and the "End of Days." *JNES* 20:188–93.
Büchler, A.
1910   אָדָר = Fell in LXX zu Micha 2,8. ZAW 30:64–65.
Büchner, D. L.
1993   Micah 7:6 in the Ancient Old Testament Versions. *JNSL* 19:159–68.
Budde, K.
1917–18   Das Rätsel von Micha 1. ZAW 37:77–108.
1919–20   Micha 2 und 3. ZAW 38:2–22.
1921   Eine folgenschwere Redaktion des Zwölfprophetenbuchs. ZAW 39:318–29.
1927   Verfasser und Stelle von Mi 4,1–4 (Jes 2,2–4). ZDMG 81 [N.F. 6]: 152–58.
Bullough, S.
1953   *Obadiah, Micah, Zephaniah, Haggai and Zechariah.* London: Saint Catherine Press.
Bülow, S., and R. A. Mitchell
1961   An Iron Age II Fortress on Tel Nagila. *IEJ* 11:101–10.
Burkitt, F. C.
1926   Micah 6 and 7: A Northern Prophecy. *JBL* 45:159–61.
Burnett, S. G.
1996   *From Christian Hebraism to Jewish Studies: Johannes Buxtorf (1564–1629) and Hebrew Learning in the Seventeenth Century.* Studies in the History of Christian Thought 68. Leiden: Brill.
Burns, R.
1987   *Has the Lord Indeed Spoken Only Through Moses: A Study of the Biblical Portrait of Miriam.* Atlanta: Scholars Press.
Buttenwieser, M.
1914   *The Prophets of Israel from the Eighth to the Fifth Century: Their Faith and Their Message.* New York: Macmillan.
Byington, S. T.
1949   Plow and Pick. *JBL* 68:49–54.
Cagni, L., ed.
1981   *La Lingua di Ebla: Atti del Convegno Internazionale (Napoli, 21–23 aprile 1980).* Seminario di Studi Asiatici: Series Minor XIV. Napoli: Instituto Universitario Orientale.
Calderone, P.
1961   The Rivers of "Masor." *Bib* 42:423–32.
Calkins, R.
1947   *The Modern Message of the Minor Prophets.* New York, London: Harper & Bros.
Calvin, J.
1846   *Commentaries on the Twelve Minor Prophets.* Vol. 3. *Jonah, Micah, Nahum.* Trans. J. Owen. Edinburgh: Calvin Translation Society.
1970   Calvin's Saturday Morning Sermon on Micah 6:6–8. Trans. A. D. Lewis. *SJT* 23:166–82.
1990   *Sermons on Micah by Jean Calvin.* Trans. B. Reynolds. Texts and Studies in Religion vol. 47. Lewiston/Queenston/Lampeter: Edwin Mellen Press.

Candelaria, M.
1983   Justice: Extrapolations from the Concept *mišpāṭ* in the Book of Micah. *Apuntes: Reflexiones Teológicas desde Margen Hispano* 3, no. 4:75–82.
Cannawurf, E.
1963   The Authenticity of Micah iv 1–4. *VT* 13:26–33.
Cannon, W.
1930   The Disarmament Passage in Isaiah II and Micah IV. *Theology* 24:2–8.
Caquot, A., and M. Delcor, eds.
1981   *Mélanges bibliques et orientaux en l'honneur de M. Henri Cazelles.* AOAT 212. Neukirchen-Vluyn: Neukirchener Verlag.
Caquot, A., S. Légasse, and M. Tardieu, eds.
1985   *Mélanges bibliques et orientaux en l'honneur de M. Mathias Delcor.* AOAT. Neukirchen-Vluyn: Neukirchener Verlag.
Carmignac, J.
1955   Précisions apportées au vocabulaire de l'hébreu biblique par la Guerre des Fils de Lumière Contre les Fils de Ténèbres. *VT* 5:345–65.
1961/62 Notes sur les peshârîm. *RevQ* 3:506–38.
1969–71 La notion d'eschatologie dans la Bible et à Qumran. *RevQ* 71:17–31.
1969–71 Le document de Qumran sur Melkisédeq. *RevQ* 71:343–78.
1986   L'Infinitif Absolu chez Ben Sira et à Qumrân. *RevQ* 12:251–61.
Carrez, M., J. Doré, and P. Grelot, eds.
1981   *De la Tôrah au Messie: Études d'exégèse et d'herméneutique bibliques offertes à Henri Cazelles pour ses 25 années d'enseignement à l'Institut Catholique de Paris, Octobre 1979.* Paris: Desclée.
Carroll, R. P.
1976   A Non-Cogent Argument in Jeremiah's Oracles Against the Prophets. *StTh* 30:43–51.
1979   *When Prophecy Failed: Cognitive Dissonance in the Prophetic Traditions of the Old Testament.* London: SCM.
1981   *From Chaos to Covenant: Uses of Prophecy in the Book of Jeremiah.* London: SCM.
1982   Eschatological Delay in the Prophetic Tradition? *ZAW* 94:47–58.
1990   Whose Prophet? Whose History? Whose Social Reality? Troubling the Interpretative Community Again: Notes towards a Response to T. W. Overholt's Critique. *JSOT* 48:33–49.
1992   Night without Vision: Micah and the Prophets. In *The Scriptures and the Scrolls: Studies in Honour of A. S. van der Woude on the Occasion of his 65th Birthday,* ed. F. García Martínez, A. Hilhorst, and C. J. Labuschagne, 74–84. VTSup 36. Leiden: Brill.
Casetti, P., O. Keel, and A. Schenker, eds.
1981   *Mélanges Dominique Barthélemy. Études bibliques offertes a l'occasion de son 60e anniversaire.* OBO 38. Göttingen: Vandenhoeck & Ruprecht.
Cassuto, U.
1975   Parallel Words in Hebrew and Ugaritic. In *Biblical and Oriental Studies II: Bible and Ancient Oriental Texts,* trans. I. Abrahams, 60–68. Jerusalem: Magnes Press.
Caspari, C. P.
1852   *Über Micah den Morasthiten und seine prophetische Schrift.* Christiana: Malling.

Cathcart, K. J.
  1968   Notes on Micah 5:4–5. *Bib* 49:511–14.
  1978   Micah 5,4–5 and Semitic Incantations. *Bib* 59:38–48.
Cathcart, K. J., and K. Jeppesen
  1987   More Suggestions on Mic 6:14. *SJOT* 1:110–15.
  1988   Micah 2:4 and Nahum 3:16–17 in the Light of Akkadian. In Y. L. Arbeitman, 191–200.
Causse, A.
  1938   Le mythe de la nouvelle Jérusalem. *RHPR* 18:377–414.
Cazelles, H.
  1947   Notes sur l'origine des temps convertis hébreux (d'après quelques textes Ugaritiques). *RB* 54:388–93.
  1967   Histoire et géographie en Michée IV 6–13. *Fourth World Congress of Jewish Studies: Papers,* 1:87–89. Jerusalem: World Union of Jewish Studies.
  1971   Micah. *EJ* 11:1480–83.
  1980   Qui aurant visé, a l'origine, Isaie II 2–5. *VT* 30:409–20.
  1981   Texte Massoretique et Septante en Is 2,1–5. In *Mélanges Dominique Barthélemy: Études bibliques offertes a l'occasion de son 60ᵉ anniversaire,* ed. P. Casetti, O. Keel, and A. Schenker, 51–59. OBO 38. Göttingen: Vandenhoeck & Ruprecht.
Cha, J.-H.
  1996   *Micha und Jeremia.* BBB 107. Weinheim: Beltz Athenäum.
Charles, R. H.
  1929   *A Critical and Exegetical Commentary on the Book of Daniel.* Oxford: Clarendon Press.
Charlesworth, J. H., ed.
  1983   *The Old Testament Pseudepigrapha.* Vol. 1. *Apocalyptic Literature and Testaments.* Garden City, N.Y.: Doubleday.
  1984   *The Old Testament Pseudepigrapha.* Vol. 2. *Expansions of the "Old Testament" and Legends, Wisdom and Philosophical.* Garden City, N.Y.: Doubleday.
  1990   From the Philopedia of Jesus to the Misopedia of the *Acts of Thomas.* In *By Study and Also by Faith: Essays in Honor of Hugh W. Nibley on the Occasion of His Eightieth Birthday 27 March 1990,* ed. J. M. Lundquist and S. D. Ricks, 1:46–66. Salt Lake City, Utah: Deseret Book Company.
Cheyne, T. K.
  1895a   *Micah, with Notes and Introduction.* CBSC. Cambridge: Cambridge University Press.
  1895b   *The Prophecies of Isaiah⁵.* New York: Thomas Whittaker.
Childs, B. S.
  1979   *Introduction to the Old Testament as Scripture.* Philadelphia: Fortress.
  1993   *Biblical Theology of the Old and New Testaments: Theological Reflections on the Christian Bible.* Minneapolis: Fortress.
Chisholm, R. B.
  1987   Wordplay in the Eighth-Century Prophets. *BS* 144:44–52.
  1990   *Interpreting the Minor Prophets.* Grand Rapids, Mich.: Zondervan.
Claassen, W., ed.
  1988   *Text and Context: Old Testament and Semitic Studies for F. C. Fensham.* JSOTSup 48. Sheffield: JSOT Press.

Clements, R. E.
1965   *Prophecy and Covenant*. SBT 43. London: SCM.
1982   The Form and Character of Prophetic Woe Oracles. *Semitics* 8:17–29.
Clifford, R. J.
1966   The Use of *hôy* in the Prophets. *CBQ* 28:458–64.
1972   *The Cosmic Mountain in Canaan and the Old Testament*. HSM 4. Cambridge, Mass.: Harvard University Press.
Clines, D. J. A.
1987   The Parallelism of Greater Precision: Notes from Isaiah 40 for a Theory of Hebrew Poetry. In E. Follis 1987a, 77–100.
Coates, J. R.
1934   Thou Shalt Not Covet [Ex. 20:17]. *ZAW* 52:238–39.
Coats, G. W.
1973   Balaam: Sinner or Saint? *BR* 18:21–29.
Coffin, E.
1987   The Binding of Isaac in Modern Israeli Literature. In *Backgrounds for the Bible*, ed. M. O'Connor and D. N. Freedman, 293–308. Winona Lake, Ind.: Eisenbrauns.
Cogan, M., and H. Tadmor
1988   *II Kings*. AB 11. Garden City, N.Y.: Doubleday.
Coggins, R. J., A. Phillip, and M. Knibb, eds.
1982   *Israel's Prophetic Tradition: Essays in Honor of Peter R. Ackroyd*. Cambridge: Cambridge University Press.
Cohen, A., ed.
1948   *The Twelve Prophets*. Bornemouth: Soncino.
Cohen, D., ed.
1970   *Mélanges Marcel Cohen: Études de linguistique, ethnographie et sciences connexes offertes par ses amis et ses élèves à l'occasion de son 80ème anniversaire*. The Hague: Mouton.
Collin, M.
1971   Recherches sur l'histoire textuelle du prophète Michée. *VT* 21:281–97.
Collins, J. J.
1977   Pseudonymity, Historical Reviews and the Genre of the Revelation of John. *CBQ* 39:329–43.
1977   *The Apocalyptic Vision of the Book of Daniel*. HSM 16. Missoula, Mont.: Scholars Press.
Collins, J. J., and J. H. Charlesworth
1991   *Mysteries and Revelations. Apocalyptic Studies since the Uppsala Colloquium*. JSPSup 9. Sheffield: Sheffield Academic Press.
Condamin, A.
1901   Les chants lyriques des prophètes. *RB* 10:352–76.
1902   Interpolations ou transpositions accidentelles? *RB* 11:379–97.
Conrad, E. W., and E. G. Newing, eds.
1987   *Perspectives on Language and Text: Essays and Poems in Honor of Francis I. Andersen's Sixtieth Birthday*. Winona Lake, Ind.: Eisenbrauns.
Coogan, M. D., J. C. Exum, and L. E. Stager, eds.
1994   *Scripture and Other Artifacts: Essays in Honor of Philip J. King*. Louisville: Westminster/John Knox Press.

Copass, B. A., and E. L. Carlson
1950   A *Study of the Prophet Micah*. Grand Rapids, Mich.: Baker Book House.
Coppens, J.
1950   *Les Douze Petits Prophètes*. Breviaire du Prophétisme. Bruges: Desclée de
          Brouwer.
1969   *Le messianisme royal: ses origines, son développement, son accomplisse-
          ment*. Paris: Éditions du Cerf.
1971   Le cadre littéraire de Michée V:1–5. In *Near Eastern Studies in Honor of
          William Foxwell Albright*, ed. H. Goedicke, 57–62. Baltimore and London:
          Johns Hopkins University Press.
Cornelius, I.
1988   Paradise Motifs in the "Eschatology" of the Minor Prophets and the Ico-
          nography of the Ancient Near East. The Concepts of Fertility, Water,
          Trees, and "Tierfrieden" and Gen 2–3. *JNSL* 14:41–83.
1989   The Lion in the Art of the Ancient Near East: A Study of Selected Motifs.
          JNSL 15:53–85.
Couroyer, B.
1977   Alternances de pronoms personnels en égyptien et en sémitique. *RB*
          84:365–74.
Cowley, A. E.
1923   *Aramaic Papyri of the Fifth Century* B.C. Oxford: Clarendon.
Craigie, P. C.
1977   The Problem of Parallel Word Pairs in Ugaritic and Hebrew Poetry.
          Semitics 5:48–58.
1985   *Twelve Prophets*. Vol. 2. The Daily Study Bible Series. Philadelphia:
          Westminster.
Cranfield, C. E. B.
1969   True Religion: A Sermon on Micah 6:8. *ComViat* 12, no. 4:191–95.
Crenshaw, J. L.
1971   *Prophetic Conflict: Its Effect upon Israelite Religion*. BZAW 124. Berlin:
          Walter de Gruyter.
1972   *Wedôrek ʿal-bamotê ʾareṣ*. CBQ 34:39–53.
1995   *Joel. A New Translation with Introduction and Commentary*. AB 24C. New
          York: Doubleday.
Crook, M. B.
1951   The Promise in Micah 5. *JBL* 70:313–20.
1954   Did Amos and Micah Know Isaiah 9:2–7 and 11:1–9? *JBL* 73:144–51.
Cross, F. M., Jr.
1953   The Council of Yahweh in Second Isaiah. *JNES* 12:274–77.
1962   Epigraphic Notes on Hebrew Documents of the Eighth–Sixth Centuries
          B.C.: II. The Murabbaʿât Papyrus and the Letter Found near Yabneh-Yam.
          BASOR 165:34–46.
1968   The Song of the Sea and Canaanite Myth. *Journal for Theology and the
          Church* 5:1–25.
1970   The Cave Inscriptions from Khirbet Beit Lei. In *Essays in Honor of Nelson
          Glueck: Near Eastern Archaeology in the Twentieth Century*, ed. J. A. San-
          ders, 299–306. Garden City, N.Y.: Doubleday.
1973   *Canaanite Myth and Hebrew Epic: Essays in the History of the Religion of
          Israel*. Cambridge, Mass.: Harvard University Press.

1994   A Phoenician Inscription from Idalion: Some Old and New Texts Relating to Child Sacrifice. In M. D. Coogan, J. C. Exum, and L. E. Stager, 93–105.

Cross, F. M., Jr., and D. N. Freedman
1952   *Early Hebrew Orthography: A Study of the Epigraphic Evidence.* AOS 36. New Haven, Conn.: American Oriental Society.

Crüsemann, F., C. Hardmeier, and R. Kessler, eds.
1992   *Was ist der Mensch . . . ? Beiträge zur Anthropologie des Alten Testaments. Hans Walter Wolff zum 80. Geburtstag.* Munich: Kaiser.

Cryer, F. H.
1994   *Divination in Ancient Israel and Its Near Eastern Environment. A Socio-Historical Investigation.* JSOTSup 142. Sheffield: JSOT Press.

Dahl, N. A.
1969   The Atonement—An Adequate Reward for the Akedah? (Ro 8:32). In *Neotestamentica et Semitica: Studies in Honour of Matthew Black,* ed. E. E. Ellis and M. Wilcox, 15–29. Edinburgh: T. & T. Clark.

Dahl, N. A., and A. S. Kapelrud, eds.
1955   *Interpretationes Ad VT Pertinentes Sigmundo Mowinckel Septuagenario Missae.* Oslo: Land og Kirche.

Dahood, M.
1958   Some Ambiguous Texts in Isaiah (30:15; 52:2; 33:2; 40:5; 45:1). *CBQ* 20:41–49.
1963   Hebrew—Ugaritic Lexicography I. *Bib* 44:289–303.
1965a   *Ugaritic—Hebrew Philology.* Rome: Pontifical Biblical Institute.
1965b, 1968, 1970
     Psalms I, II, III. AB 16, 17, 17A. Garden City, N.Y.: Doubleday.
1978   New Readings in Lamentations. *Bib* 59:174–97.
1980   Can One Plow without Oxen? (Amos 6:12). A Study of *BA-* and *'AL.* In G. Rendsburg et al., 13–23.
1983   The Minor Prophets and Ebla. In C. M. Meyers and M. O'Connor, 47–67.

Daly, R. J.
1977   The Soteriological Significance of the Sacrifice of Isaac. *CBQ* 39:45–75.

Daniels, D. R.
1987   Is There a "Prophetic Lawsuit" Genre? *ZAW* 99:339–60.

Davies, E. W.
1981   *Prophecy and Ethics. Isaiah and the Ethical Tradition of Israel.* JSOTSup 16. Sheffield: JSOT Press.

Davies, G. I.
1985   Tell Ed-Duweir: Not Libnah but Lachish. *PEQ* 117:92–96.
1991   The Use and Non-Use of the Particle *'et* in Hebrew Inscriptions. In K. Jongeling, H. L. Murre-van den Berg, and L. van Rompay, 14–26.
1992   *Ancient Hebrew Inscriptions: Corpus and Concordance.* Cambridge: Cambridge University Press.

Davies, P. R., and B. D. Chilton
1978   The Aqedah: A Revised Tradition History. *CBQ* 40:514–46.

Davies, P. R., and D. J. A. Clines, eds.
1993   *Among the Prophets: Language, Image and Structure in the Prophetic Writings.* JSOTSup 144. Sheffield: JSOT Press.

Davies, T. W.
1898   *Magic, Divination, and Demonology.* Reprint, New York: KTAV, 1969.
Dawes, S. B.
1988   Walking Humbly: Micah 6.8 Revisited. *SJT* 41:331–39.
Day, J.
1989   *Molech: A God of Human Sacrifice in the Old Testament.* University of
         Cambridge Oriental Publications 41. Cambridge: Cambridge University
         Press.
De Vries, S. J.
1976   *Yesterday, Today and Tomorrow: Time and History in the Old Testament.*
         London: SPCK.
1978   *Prophet Against Prophet. The Role of the Micaiah Narrative (I Kings 22) in the
         Development of Early Prophetic Tradition.* Grand Rapids, Mich.: Eerdmans.
Dearman, A.
1988   *Property Rights in the Eighth-Century Prophets. The Conflict and Its Back-
         ground.* Atlanta: Scholars Press.
1989   *Studies in the Mesha Inscription and Moab.* Archaeology and Biblical
         Studies 2. Atlanta: Scholars Press.
Deden, D.
1953–56 *De kleine Profeten uit de grondtekst vertaald en uitgelegd.* De Boeken van
         het Oude Testament 12. Adrianus ven den Born, ed. Roermond: Romen.
DeGuglielmo, A.
1955   Sacrifice in the Ugaritic Texts. *CBQ* 17:76–96.
Deissler, A.
1959   Micha vi,1–8: Der Rechtsstreit Jahwes mit Israel um der rechte Bundes-
         verhältnis. *TTZ* 68:229–34.
1984   *Zwölf Propheten II. Obadja, Jona, Micha, Nahum, Habakuk.* Die Neue
         Echter Bibel. Würzburg: Echter Verlag.
Deissler, A., and M. Delcor
1964   *Les petits prophèts. 2: Michée–Malachie.* La Sainte Bible 8:1. Paris: Letouzey
         et Ané.
Delavault, B., and A. Lemaire
1976   Une stèle "Molk" de Palestine: Dédié à Eshmoun? RÉS 367 reconsidéré.
         RB 83:569–83.
Delcor, M.
1966   Les attaches littéraires, l'origine et la signification de l'expression bib-
         lique, "prendre à témoin le ciel et la terre." *VT* 16:8–25. Reprint, Delcor
         1976, 49–66.
1967   Two Special Meanings of the Word *yd* in Biblical Hebrew. *JSS* 12:230–40.
         Reprint, Delcor 1976, 139–49.
1969   Sion, centre universel Is 2:1–5. *Assemblées du Seigneur* 2/5:6–11. Reprint,
         Delcor 1976, 92–97.
1976   *Religion d'Israël et Proche Orient ancien: Des Phéniciens aux Esséniens.*
         Leiden: Brill.
Delekat, L.
1964   Zum hebräischen Wörterbuch. *VT* 14:7–66.
Delitzsch, F.
1897   *Biblischer Commentar über den Propheten Jesaia.* 3d ed. Leipzig: Dörffling
         und Franke.

Demsky, A.
1966   The Houses of Achzib: A Critical Note on Mi 1,14b. *IEJ* 16:211–15.
Demsky, A., and M. Bar-Ilan
1988   Writing in Ancient Israel and Early Judaism. In M. J. Mulder, 1988, 1–38.
Derchain, P.
1970   Les plus anciens témoignages de sacrifices d'enfants chex les Sémites occidentaux. *VT* 20:331–55.
Deurloo, K. A.
1994   Because You Have Hearkened to My Voice (Genesis 22). In M. Kessler, 113–30.
Dever, W. G.
1969–70 Iron Age Epigraphic Material from the Area of Khirbet El-Kom. *HUCA* 40–41:139–204.
Dhorme, É.
1984   *A Commentary on the Book of Job.* Trans. H. Knight. Nashville: Thomas Nelson.
Dietrich, M., and O. Loretz
1977   *Anš(t) und (m)inš(t) im Ugaritischen. UF* 9:47–50.
1993   *Mesopotamica, Ugaritica, Biblica: Festschrift für Kurt Bergerhof zur Vollendung seines 70. Lebensjahres am 7. Mai 1992.* AOAT 232. Kevalaer: Verlag Butzon & Bercker/Neukirchen-Vluyn: Neukirchener Verlag.
Dijkstra, M.
1995   Is Balaam Also among the Prophets? *JBL* 114:43–64.
Dillmann, A.
1899   *Grammatik der Äthiopischen Sprache.* Reprint, Graz: Akademische Druck, 1959.
Dirksen, P. B., and M. J. Mulder
1988   *The Peshitta: Its Early Text and History.* Monographs of the Peshitta Institute Leiden IV. Leiden: Brill.
Dobbs-Allsopp, F. W.
1993   *Weep, O Daughter Zion: A Study of the City-Lament Genre in the Hebrew Bible.* BibOr 44. Rome: Biblical Institute.
Donat, H.
1911   Micha 2,6–9. *BZ* 9:351–66.
Donne, J.
1953–62 *The Sermons of John Donne.* Ed. G. R. Porter and E. M. Simpson. Berkeley and Los Angeles: University of California Press.
Donner, H.
1963   Die soziale Botschaft der Propheten im Lichte der Gesellschaftsordnung in Israel. *OrAnt* 2:229–45.
1964   *Israel unter den Völkern: Die Stellung der 8. Jahrhunderts v. Chr. zur Aussenpolitik der Könige von Israel und Juda.* VTSup 11. Leiden: Brill.
1994   *Mosaic Map of Madaba: An Introductory Guide.* Palaestina antiqua 7. Grand Rapids, Mich.: Eerdmans.
Donner, H., and W. Röllig
1962–64 *Kanaanäische und aramäische Inschriften.* Wiesbaden: Harrassowitz.
Donner, H., R. Hanhart, and R. Smend, eds.
1977   *Beiträge zur alttestamentliche Theologie: Festschrift für Walther Zimmerli zum 70. Geburtstag.* Göttingen: Vandenhoeck & Ruprecht.

Draisma, S., ed.
1989   *Intertextuality in Biblical Writings. Essays in Honour of Bas ven Iersel.*
          Kampen: Uitgeversmaatschappij J. H. Kok.
Dreytza, M.
1990   *Der theologische Gebrauch von RUAH im Alten Testament. Ein wort—und*
          satzsemantische Studie. Giessen/Basel: Brunnen.
Drijvers, P.
1971   Wo steht Micha? *Schrift* 17:163–68.
Driver, G. R.
1936   *A Treatise on the Use of the Tenses in Hebrew.* Edinburgh: T. & T. Clark.
1938a   Linguistic and Textual Problems: Minor Prophets II. *JTS* 39:260–73.
1938b   Linguistic and Textual Problems: Minor Prophets III. *JTS* 39:393–405.
1940   Hebrew Notes on Prophets and Proverbs. *JTS* 41:162–75.
1954   Reflections on Recent Articles. *JBL* 73:125–36.
1956   *Canaanite Myths and Legends.* Edinburgh: T. & T. Clark.
1957   On עלה "went up country" and ירד "went down country." ZAW 69:74–77.
1960   Abbreviations in the Massoretic Text. *Textus* 1:112–31.
1970   Colloquialisms in the Old Testament. In D. Cohen, 233–39.
Driver, S. R.
1874   *A Treatise on the Use of the Tenses in Hebrew.* Oxford: Clarendon Press.
1909   *An Introduction to the Literature of the Old Testament*[8]. Edinburgh: T. & T.
          Clark.
Dronkert, K.
1953   *De Molochdienst in het Oude Testament.* Leiden: Brill.
Duhm, B.
1911   Anmerkungen zu den Zwölf Propheten: III Buch Micha. ZAW 31:81–93.
1912   *The Twelve Prophets: A Version in the Various Poetical Measures of the*
          Original Writings. Trans. A. Duff. London: A. & C. Black.
1968   *Das Buch Jesaja.* HAT III. 5th ed. Göttingen: Vandenhoeck & Ruprecht.
          [1st ed. 1892]
Durand, J. M.
1982   In vino veritas. *RA* 76:43–50.
Dus, J.
1965   Weiteres zum nordisraelitischen Psalm, Micha 7,7–20. ZDMG 115:14–22.
Edelkoort, A. H.
1948   Prophet and Prophet. *OTS* 5:179–89.
Edelman, D.
1987   Biblical Molek Reassessed. *JAOS* 107:727–31.
Edgar, S. L.
1962   *The Minor Prophets.* Epworth Preacher's Commentaries. London: Epworth.
Ehrlich, A. B.
1912   *Randglossen zur hebräischen Bibel.* Leipzig: Hinrichs.
Ehrman, A.
1959   A Note on Yešah in Mic. 6:14. *JNES* 18:156.
1970   A Note on Micah II 7. *VT* 20:86–87.
1973   A Note on Micah VI 14. *VT* 23:103–5.
Eichholz, G., ed.
1961   *Herr, tue meine Lippen auf.* Wuppertal-Barmen: Emil Müller.

Eissfeldt, O.
1935   *Molk als Opferbegriff im Punischen und Hebräischen und das Ende des Gottes Moloch.* Halle: Saale.
1962   Ein Psalm aus Nord-Israel, Micha vii,7–20. ZDMG 112:259–68. Reprint, KS 4:63–72.
1962–79   *Kleine Schriften* [KS]. Ed. R. Sellheim and F. Maass. 6 vols. Tübingen: Mohr.
1965   *The Old Testament: An Introduction, Including the Apocrypha and Pseudepigrapha and Also the Works of Similar Type from Qumran. The History of the Formation of the Old Testament.* Trans. P. R. Ackroyd. Oxford: Blackwell.
1968   Gottesnamen in Personennamen als Symbole menschlicher Qualitäten. In *Kleine Schriften* 4, ed. R. Sellheim and F. Maas, 276–84. Tübingen: Mohr. (Original publication: Festschrift Walter Batke dargebracht zu seinem 80 Geburtstag. Ed. K. Rudolph. Weimar: Herman Bohlaus.)
1977   *ʾādhôn.* TDOT 1:59–72.
Elliger, K.
1934   Die Heimat des Propheten Micha. ZDPV 57:81–152.
1964   *Das Buch der Zwölf kleinen Propheten II.* ATD 25/II. Göttingen: Neues Göttinger Bibelwerk.
Ellul, D.
1981   Michée 1–3 Knappe Analyse. *ÉTR* 56:135–47.
Elwolde, J.
1990   Non-biblical Supplements to Classical Hebrew *ʾim.* VT 60:221–23.
Emerton, J. A.
1982   New Light on Israelite Religion. ZAW 94:2–20.
Engnell, I.
1970   *Critical Essays on the Old Testament.* Trans. J. T. Willis. London: SPCK.
Ernst, A.
1990   "Wer Menschenblut vergiesset . . . " Zur bersetzung von *bʾdm* in Gen 9,6. ZAW 102:252–53.
Eslinger, L., and G. Taylor, eds.
1988   *Ascribe to the Lord. Biblical and Other Studies in Memory of Peter C. Craigie.* JSOTSup 67. Sheffield: University of Sheffield Press.
Evans, C. A.
1984   On the Vineyard Parables of Isaiah 5 and Mark 12. BZ 28:82–84.
Ewald, G. H. A. von
1867–68   *Die Propheten des alten Bundes.* 3 vols. Göttingen: Vandenhoeck & Ruprecht.
1875–81   *Commentary on the Prophets of the Old Testament.* Trans. J. F. Smith. London and Edinburgh: Williams and Norgate.
Exum, J. C.
1981   Asseverative *ʾal* in Canticles 1,6? *Bib* 62:416–19.
Eybers, I. H.
1968   Micah, the Morashthite: The Man and His Message. *Die Ou Testamentiese Werkgemeenskap in Suid-Afrika* 11:9–24.
Fensham, F. C.
1967   Righteousness in the Book of Micah and Parallels from the Ancient Near East. *Tydskrif vir Geesteswetenshappe* 7:416–25.

1973   The Divine Subject of the Verb in the Book of Micah. *Die Ou Testamen-
            tiese Werkgemeenskap in Suid-Afrika* 16:25–34.
1978   The Use of the Suffix Conjugation and the Prefix Conjugation in a Few
            Old Hebrew Poems. *JNSL* 6:9–18.
Fernández Tejero, E.
1986   Corregido y correcto: La segunda mano del Códice de Profetas de El
            Cairo en el libro de *Profetas Menores. Sef* 46:191–96.
Fichtner, J.
1957   *Obadja, Jona, Micha.* Stuttgarter Biblehefte. Stuttgart: Quell.
Fields, W. W.
1992   The Motif "Night as Danger" Associated with Three Biblical Destruction
            Narratives. In M. A. Fishbane, E. Tov, and W. W. Fields, 17–32.
Fisch, H.
1988   *Poetry with a Purpose. Biblical Poetics and Interpretation.* Indiana Studies
            in Biblical Literature. Bloomington: University of Indiana Press.
Fishbane, M. A.
1971   Studies in Biblical Magic: Origins, Uses and Transformations of Termi-
            nology and Literary Forms. Ph.D. diss., Brandeis University.
1985   *Biblical Interpretation in Ancient Israel.* Oxford: Clarendon Press.
Fishbane, M. A., E. Tov, and W. W. Fields, eds.
1992   *Shaʿarei Talmon.* In *Studies in the Bible, Qumran, and the Ancient Near
            East Presented to Shemaryahu Talmon.* Winona Lake, Ind.: Eisenbrauns.
Fisher, L. R.
1970   A New Ritual Calendar from Ugarit. *HTR* 63:485–501.
Fisher, M. C.
1974   Some Contributions of Ethiopic Studies to the Understanding of the Old
            Testament. In *The Law and the Prophets: Old Testament Studies Prepared
            in Honor of Oswald Thompson Allis,* ed. J. H. Skilton, M. C. Fisches, and
            L. W. Sloat. Nutley, N.J.: Presbyterian and Reformed.
Fitzgerald, A.
1975   *BTWLT* and *BT* as Titles for Capital Cities. *CBQ* 37:167–83.
Fitzmyer, J. A.
1956   *lĕ* as a Preposition and a Particle in Micah 5,1 (5,2). *CBQ* 18:10–13.
1957   The Syntax of *kl, klʾ,* "All," in Aramaic Texts from Egypt and in Biblical
            Aramaic. *Bib* 38:170–84. Reprint, Fitzmyer 1979, 205–17.
1969   A Further Note on the Aramaic Inscription Sefire III. 22. *JSS* 14:197–200.
1979   A *Wandering Aramean: Collected Aramaic Essays.* SBLMS 25. Chico,
            Calif.: Scholars Press.
Fitzmyer, J. A., and D. J. Harrington
1978   A *Manual of Palestinian Aramaic Texts.* BibOr 34. Rome: Biblical Institute
            Press.
Fohrer, G.
1951   Neuere Literatur zur alttestamentlichen Prophetie. *Theologische Rund-
            schau* N.F. 19:277–346.
1952   Neuere Literatur zur alttestamentlichen Prophetie (Fortsetzung). *Theolo-
            gische Rundschau* N.F. 20:192–271; 295–361.
1954   Über den Kurzvers. *ZAW* 66:199–236.
1955   Umkehr und Erlösung beim Propheten Hosea. *TZ* 11:161–85.
1961   Remarks on Modern Interpretations of the Prophets. *JBL* 80:309–19.

1962   Zehn Jahre Literatur zur alttestamentlichen Prophetie (1951–1960). *Theologische Rundschau* 27:1–75; 235–97; 301–74.

1967   Micha 1. In *Das ferne und nahe Wort: Festschrift Rost*, ed. F. Maass. BZAW 105:65–80.

1968   *Introduction to the Old Testament.* Trans. D. E. Green. Nashville: Abingdon.

1969   *Studien zur alttestamentlichen Theologie und Geschichte (1949–1966).* BZAW 115.

1974   *Die Propheten des Alten Testaments.* Gütersloher: Gütersloher Verlaghaus.

1975   Neue Literatur zur alttestamentlichen Prophetie (1961–1970). *Theologische Rundschau* 40:193–209; 337–77.

1976   Neue Literatur zur alttestamentlichen Prophetie (1961–1970). *Theologische Rundschau* 41:1–12.

1980   Neue Literatur zur alttestamentlichen Prophetie 6. Micha. *Theologische Rundschau* 45:212–16.

1981   Micha 1. BZAW 155:53–68.

1982   Der Tag Jhwhs. *EI* 16:43–50.

Fokkelman, J. P.
1991   Iterative Forms of the Classical Hebrew Verb: Exploring the Triangle of Style, Syntax, and Text Grammar. In K. Jongeling, H. L. Murre-van den Berg, and L. van Rompay, 38–55.

Follis, E. R.
1987a   *Directions in Biblical Hebrew Poetry.* JSOTSup 40. Sheffield: University of Sheffield.
1987b   The Holy City as Daughter. In Follis 1987a, 173–84.

Forshey, H. O.
1975   The Construct Chain *naḥ^alat YHWH/ʾĕlōhîm.* BASOR 220:51–53.

Foster, B. R.
1977   Ea and Saltu. In *Essays on the Ancient Near East in Memory of Jacob Joel Finkelstein*, ed. M. de Jong Ellis, 79–84. Memoirs of the Connecticut Academy of Arts and Sciences 19. Hamden, Conn.: Archon Books.

Fowler, J. D.
1988   *Theophoric Personal Names in Ancient Hebrew. A Comparative Study.* JSOTSup 49. Sheffield: JSOT Press.

Fox, M. V.
1980   The Identification of Quotations in Biblical Literature. ZAW 92:416–31.

Fox, M. V., et al., eds.
1996   *Texts, Temples, and Traditions. A Tribute to Menahem Haran.* Winona Lake, Ind.: Eisenbrauns.

Fraenkel, D., U. Quast, and J. W. Wevers, eds.
1990   *Studien zur Septuaginta: Robert Hanhart zu Ehren; aus Anlass seines 65. Geburtstages.* Abhandlungen der Akademie der Wissenschaften in Göttingen; Philologische-historische Klasse, dritte Folge 190. Göttingen: Vandenhoeck & Ruprecht.

de Fraine, J.
1954   *L'Aspect religieux de la royauté israélite: l'Institution monarchique dans l'Ancien Testament et dans les textes mésopotamiens.* Rome: Pontifical Biblical Institute.

Freedman, D. N.
1953   Notes on Genesis. ZAW 64:190–94.
1960   Archaic Forms in Early Hebrew Poetry. ZAW 72:101–7.
1961   The Chronicler's Purpose. CBQ 23:436–42.
1969   The Orthography of the Arad Ostraca. IEJ 19:52–56.
1972   Prolegomenon to G. B. Gray, The Forms of Hebrew Poetry, reprinted, New York: KTAV, 1972.
1980   Pottery, Poetry, and Prophecy: Studies in Early Hebrew Poetry. Winona Lake, Ind.: Eisenbrauns.
1981   Temples without Hands. In Temples and High Places in Biblical Times, ed. A. Biran, 21–30. Jerusalem: The Nelson Glueck School of Biblical Archaeology of Hebrew Union College.
1982   Discourse on Prophetic Discourse. In The Quest for the Kingdom of God: Studies in Honor of George E. Mendenhall, ed. H. B. Huffmon, F. A. Spina, and A. R. W. Green, 141–58. Winona Lake, Ind.: Eisenbrauns.
1986a   Acrostic Poems in the Hebrew Bible: Alphabetic and Otherwise. CBQ 48:408–31.
1986b   Deliberate Deviation from an Established Pattern of Repetition in Hebrew Poetry as a Rhetorical Device. In Proceedings of the Ninth World Congress of Jewish Studies: Jerusalem, August 4–12, 1985. Division A: The Period of the Bible, 45–52. Jerusalem: World Union of Jewish Studies.
1987a   Headings in the Book of the Eighth-Century Prophets. AUSS 25:9–26.
1987b   Another Look at Biblical Hebrew Poetry. In E. R. Follis 1987a, 11–28.
1987c   Yahweh of Samaria and His Asherah. BA 50:241–50.
1989   The Nine Commandments. The Secret Progress of Israel's Sins. BRev 5/6:28–37, 42.
1990   Confrontations in the Book of Amos. PSB 11:240–52.
1991   The Unity of the Hebrew Bible. Ann Arbor: University of Michigan Press.
1994   The Structure of Psalm 119: Part II. HAR 14:55–87.
1995   The Structure of Psalm 119: Part I. In D. P. Wright, D. N. Freedman, and A. Hurvitz, 725–56.
Freedman, D. N., A. D. Forbes, and F. I. Andersen
1993   Studies in Hebrew and Aramaic Orthography. Biblical and Judaic Studies from the University of California, San Diego. Vol. 2. Ed. W. H. Propp. Winona Lake, Ind.: Eisenbrauns.
Freehof, S. B.
1941–42 Some Text Rearrangements in the Minor Prophets. JQR 32:303–8.
Fretheim, T. E.
1984   The Suffering of God: An Old Testament Perspective. Philadelphia: Fortress.
1988   The Repentance of God: A Key to Evaluating Old Testament God-Talk. HBT 10:47–70.
1989   Suffering God and Sovereign God in Exodus: A Collision of Images. HBT 11:31–56.
Freund, Y.
1986–87 And Nations Shall Flow to It. Beth Mikra 32:154–61 (Hebrew).
Frezza, F.
1977   Il libro di Michaea: Ascendenze filogico-letterarie semiticonordoccidentali. Rome: Pontifical Biblical Institute.

Frick, F. S.
1977   *The City in Ancient Israel.* SBLDS 36. Missoula, Mont.: Scholars Press.
Fritz, V.
1974   Das Wort gegen Samaria Mi 1,2–7. ZAW 86:316–31.
Fritz, V., K.-F. Pohlmann, and H.-C. Schmitt, eds.
1989   *Prophet und Prophetenbuch: Festschrift für Otto Kaiser zum 65. Geburts-*
          tag. BZAW 185. Berlin: Walter de Gruyter.
Fuerst, W. J.
1982   A Study of Prophetic Disagreement. *BToday* 20:20–25.
Fuhs, H. F.
1968   *Die äthiopische Übersetzung des Propheten Micha. Edition und textkriti-*
          scher Kommentar nach den Handschriften in Oxford, London, Paris, Cam-
          bridge, Wien und Frankfurt am Main. Bonner biblische Beiträge. Bd. 28.
          Bonn: P. Hanstein.
1978   *Sehen und Schauen, Die Wurzel ḥzh im Alten Orient und im alten Testa-*
          ment. FB 32. Würzburg: Echter Verlag.
Fuller, R.
1993   4QMicah: A Small Fragment of a Manuscript of the Minor Prophets from
          Qumran, Cave IV. *RevQ* 16:193–202.
Fullerton, K.
1916   Studies in Isaiah I: On Is 2,5 and Mi 4,5. *JBL* 28:134–40.
Gailey, J. H.
1962   *Micah, Nahum, Habakkuk, Zephaniah, Haggai, Zechariah, Malachi.* The
          Layman's Bible Commentary 15. KellRichmond: John Knox.
Gammie, J. G., and L. G. Perdue, eds.
1990   *The Sage in Israel and the Ancient Near East.* Winona Lake, Ind.: Eisen-
          brauns.
Gammie, J. G., et al., eds.
1978   *Israelite Wisdom: Theological and Literary Essays in Honor of Samuel*
          Terrien. New York: Union Theological Seminary, Scholars Press.
Garcia de la Fuente, O.
1967   Notas al texto de Miqueas. *Aug* 7:145–54.
Gaster, T. H.
1937   Notes on the Minor Prophets. *JTS* 38:163–65.
Gelston, A.
1987   *The Peshitta of the Twelve Prophets.* Oxford: Clarendon.
1988   Some Readings in the Peshitta of the Dodekapropheton. In P. B. Dirksen
          and M. J. Mulder, 81–98.
Gemser, B.
1955   The *Rîb*- or Controversy-Pattern in Hebrew Mentality. In *Wisdom in Israel*
          and in the Ancient Near East: Presented to Professor Harold Henry Rowley
          by the Society for Old Testament Study in Association with the Editorial
          Board of VT in Celebration of His Sixty-fifth Birthday, 24 March, 1955.
          VTSup 3:120–37. Leiden: Brill.
George, A.
1952   *Michée, Sophonie, Nahum.* La Sainte Bible Vol. 27. Paris: Cerf.
1955   Michée (Le livre de). *DBSup* 5:1252–63. Paris: Letouzey et Ané.
1958   *Michée, Sophonie, Nahum.* 2d ed. La Bible de Jerusalem. Paris: Cerf.

Gerleman, G.
1973　　　Die lärmende Menge: Der Sinn des hebräischen Wortes *hamon.* AOAT
　　　　　18:71–75.
Gerstenberger, E.
1962　　　The Woe-Oracles of the Prophets. *JBL* 81:249–63.
Gese, H.
1957　　　Die hebräischen Bibelhandschriften zum Dodekapropheton nach der
　　　　　Variantensammlung des Kennicott. *ZAW* 69:55–69.
1964　　　Der Davidsbund und die Zionserwählung. *ZThK* 61:10–26.
Gesenius, W.
1910　　　*Gesenius' Hebrew Grammar.* 2d rev. ed. Ed. and enlarged by E. Kautzsch,
　　　　　trans. and rev. A. E. Cowley. Oxford: Clarendon Press.
Gevirtz, S.
1963　　　*Patterns in the Early Poetry of Israel.* SAOC 32. Chicago: University of
　　　　　Chicago Press.
Gianto, A.
1987　　　Some Notes on the Mulk Inscription from Nebi Yunis (RES 367). *Bib*
　　　　　68:397–401.
Gibson, J. C. L.
1971　　　*Textbook of Syrian Semitic Inscriptions.* Vol. I. *Hebrew and Moabite In-*
　　　　　scriptions. Oxford: Clarendon Press.
1978　　　*Canaanite Myths and Legends.* Edinburgh: T. & T. Clark.
1993　　　The Anatomy of Hebrew Narrative Poetry. In A. G. Auld, 141–48.
Gilʿadi, A.
1989　　　Ṣabr (Steadfastness) of Bereaved Parents: A Motif in Medieval Muslim
　　　　　Consolation Treatises and Some Parallels in Jewish Writings. *JQR* 80:35–48.
Gilula, M.
1974　　　*bî* in Isaiah 28,1—A Head Ornament. *TA* 1:128.
Ginsberg, H. L.
1967　　　Lexicographical Notes. *Hebräische Wortforschung.* VTSup 16:71–82.
Ginsburg, C. D.
1867　　　*The Massoreth Ha-Massoreth of Elias Levita, Being an Exposituin of the*
　　　　　Massoretic Notes on the Hebrew Bible. Reprint, New York: KTAV, 1968.
1897　　　*Introduction to the Massoretico-Critical Edition of the Hebrew Bible.* Lon-
　　　　　don, Trinitarian Bible Society. Reprint, with a prolegomenon by Harry M.
　　　　　Orlinsky: *The Masoretic Text; A Critical Evaluation.* New York: KTAV,
　　　　　1966.
Glueck, N.
1936　　　The Theophany of the God of Sinai. *JAOS* 56:462–71.
1967　　　Ḥesed *in the Bible.* Trans. A. Gottschalk. Intro. G. L. Larue. Cincinnati:
　　　　　Hebrew Union College.
Goedicke, H., ed.
1971　　　*Near Eastern Studies in Honor of William Foxwell Albright.* Baltimore and
　　　　　London: Johns Hopkins University Press.
Goldenberg, G.
1991　　　On Direct Speech and the Hebrew Bible. In K. Jongeling, H. L. Murre-
　　　　　van den Berg, and L. van Rompay, 79–96.

Gonçales, F. J.
1986   *L'expédition de Sennachérib en Palestine dans la littérature hébraïque an-cienne.* ÉBib nouvelle série 7. Paris: J. Gabalda.

Good, G.
1983   *The Sheep of His Pasture: A Study of the Hebrew Noun ʿM(M) and Its Semitic Cognates.* HSM 29. Chico, Calif.: Scholars Press.

Gooding, D. W.
1969   Problems of Text and Midrash in the Third Book of Reigns. *Textus* 7:1–29.
1976a   An Appeal for a Stricter Terminology in the Textual Criticism of the Old Testament. *JSS* 21:15–25.
1976b   *Relics of Ancient Exegesis. A Study of the Miscellanies in 3 Reigns 2.* SOTSMS 4. Cambridge: Cambridge University Press.

Gordis, R.
1934   A Note on *ṭôb*. *JTS* 35:186–88. Reprint, Gordis 1976, 313–14.
1937   *The Biblical Text in the Making: A Study of the Kethib-Qere.* Philadelphia: Dropsie College for Hebrew and Cognate Learning. Reprint, with new prolegomenon, New York: KTAV 1971.
1950   Micah's Vision of the End Time. In R. M. MacIver, 1–8. Reprint, Gordis 1971a, 268–79.
1959   Primitive Democracy in Ancient Israel. In *Alexander Marx Jubilee Vol-umes,* ed. S. Lieberman, 369–88. New York: Jewish Theological Seminary of America. Reprint, Gordis 1971a, 45–60.
1971a   *Poets, Prophets, and Sages: Essays in Biblical Interpretation.* Bloomington: Indiana University Press.
1971b   The Origins of the Masorah in the Light of the Qumran Scrolls and Rab-binic Literature. Prolegomenon to reprint of Gordis 1937. New York: KTAV. Reprint, Gordis 1976a: 29–74.
1976a   *The Word and the Book: Studies in Biblical Language and Literature.* New York: KTAV.
1976b   The Faith of Abraham: A Note on Kierkegaard's "Teleological Suspension of the Ethical." *Judaism* 25:415–20.
1978   *The Book of Job: Commentary, New Translation, and Special Studies.* New York: Jewish Theological Seminary of America.

Gordon, C. H.
1949   *Ugaritic Literature.* Rome: Pontifical Biblical Institute.
1955   North Israelite Influence on Post-Exilic Hebrew. *IEJ* 5:85–88.
1965   *Ugaritic Textbook.* Rome: Pontifical Biblical Institute. [= *UT*]

Gordon, C. H., and G. A. Rendsburg, eds.
1990   *Eblaitica: Essays on the Ebla Archives and Eblaite Language.* Vol. 2. Wi-nona Lake, Ind.: Eisenbrauns.

Gordon, C. H., G. A. Rendsburg, and N. H. Winter, eds.
1987   *Eblaitica: Essays on the Ebla Archives and Eblaite Language.* Vol. 1. Wi-nona Lake, Ind.: Eisenbrauns.

Gordon, R. P.
1978   Micah VII 19 and Akkadian *kabâsu.* VT 28:355.

Gordon, R. P., ed.
1995   *The Place is Too Small for Us: The Israelite Prophets in Recent Scholarship.* Winona Lake, Ind.: Eisenbrauns.

Gorgulho, F. L. B.
1963　　　　Notas sôbre Betlem-Efratá en Miq 5,1–5. *RCT* 3:20–38.
Gossai, H.
1988　　　　*Ṣaddîq* in Theological, Forensic and Economic Perspectives. *SEÅ* 53:7–13.
Gottlieb, H.
1963　　　　Den taerskende kvie Mi IV 11–13. *DTT* 26:167–71.
1967　　　　Die Tradition von David als Hirten. *VT* 17:190–200.
Gottwald, N. K.
1964　　　　*All the Kingdoms of the Earth. Israelite Prophecy and International Rela-*
　　　　　　tions in the Ancient Near East. New York: Harper & Row.
1979　　　　*The Tribes of Yahweh: A Sociology of the Religion of Liberated Israel, 1250–*
　　　　　　1050 B.C.E. Maryknoll, N.Y.: Orbis.
1993　　　　Social Class as an Analytic and Hermeneutical Category in Biblical Studies.
　　　　　　JBL 112:3–22.
Graetz, H.
1895　　　　*Emendationes in plerosque Sacrae Scripturae Veteris Testaenti Libri²*. Ed.
　　　　　　W. Bacher. Breslau: Schelsische Buchdruckerei.
Graffy, A.
1979　　　　The Literary Genre of Isaiah 5,1–7. *Bib* 60:400–9.
1984　　　　*A Prophet Confronts His People. The Disputation Speech in the Prophets.*
　　　　　　AnBib 104. Rome: Pontifical Biblical Institute Press.
Graham, W. C.
1930–31　　Some Suggestions toward the Interpretation of Micah 1:10–16. *AJSL*
　　　　　　27:237–58.
Gray, G. B.
1896　　　　*Studies in Hebrew Proper Names.* London: A. & C. Black.
1915　　　　*The Forms of Hebrew Poetry: Considered with Special Reference to the Criti-*
　　　　　　cism and Interpretation of the Old Testament. London: Hodder and Stough-
　　　　　　ton. Reprint, with prolegomenon by D. N. Freedman, New York: KTAV,
　　　　　　1972.
Green, A. R. W.
1975　　　　*The Role of Human Sacrifice in the Ancient Near East.* Missoula, Mont.:
　　　　　　Scholars Press.
Greene, J. T.
1992　　　　*Balaam and His Interpreters: A Hermeneutical History of the Balaam*
　　　　　　Traditions. BJS 244. Atlanta: Scholars Press.
Greenfield, J. C., and J. Naveh
1984　　　　Hebrew and Aramaic in the Persian Period. Chapter 6 in *CHJ: Volume*
　　　　　　One. Introduction; The Persian Period, 115–29. Cambridge: Cambridge
　　　　　　University Press.
Greengus, S.
1969　　　　The Old Babylonian Marriage Contract. *JAOS* 89:505–32.
Grelot, P.
1986　　　　Michée 7,6 dans les evangiles et dans la litterature rabbinique. *Bib*
　　　　　　67:363–77.
Grol, H. W. M. van
1983　　　　Paired Tricola in the Psalms, Isaiah and Jeremiah. *JSOT* 25:55–73.
1986　　　　*De Versbouw in het klassieke Hebreeuws. Fundamenteele verkenningen.*
　　　　　　Deel een: metriek. Amsterdam: Katholieke Theologische Hogeschool.

Grollenberg, L.
1971   Micha 7: Eine Buss-Liturgie? *Schrift* 17:188–91.

Gröndahl, F.
1967   *Die Personennamen der Texte aus Ugarit.* Studia Pohl 1. Rome: Pontifical Biblical Institute.

Gross, W.
1976   *Verbform und Funktion, wayyiqtol für Gegenwart. Ein Beitrag zur Syntax poetischer althebräischer Texte.* Ed. W. Richter. ATSAT 1. St. Ottilien: EOS Verlag.

1987a   *Die Pendenskonstruktion im Biblischen Hebräisch: Studien zum althebräischen Satz I.* Ed. W. Richter. ATSAT 27. St. Otillien: EOS Verlag.

1987b   Zur Syntagmen-Folge im Hebräischen Verbalsatz die Stellung des Subjekts in Dtn 1–15. *BN* 40:63–96.

1988   Satzgrenzen bei Pendenskonstruktionen: Der Pendenssatz. In W. Claassen, 249–58.

Guillaume, A.
1938   *Prophecy and Divination among the Hebrews and Other Semites.* London: Harper.

Gunkel, H.
1924   Der Micha-Schluss: Zur Einführung in die literaturgeschichtliche Arbeit am Alten Testament. *Zeitschrift für Semitistik und verwandte Gebiete* 2:145–78.

1928   The Close of Micah: A Prophetical Liturgy. In *What Remains of the Old Testament and Other Essays.* Trans. A. K. Dallas of Gunkel 1924, 115–49. London: George Allen and Unwin.

1933   *Einleitung in die Psalmen.* [Completed by J. Begrich.] Göttingen: Vandenhoeck & Ruprecht.

Gunnel, A.
1982   Ecstatic Prophecy in the Old Testament. In N. G. Holm, 187–200.

Guthe, H.
1923   Der Prophet Micha. In *HSAT*[4]. Vol. 2. Ed. D. Bertholet, 53–66. Tübingen: Mohr.

Haak, R. D.
1982   A Study and New Interpretation of *qṣr npš. JBL* 101:161–67.

Hackett, J. A.
1984   *The Balaam Text from Deir ʿAllā.* HSM 31. Chico, Calif.: Scholars Press.

1987   Religious Traditions in Israelite Transjordan. In P. D. Miller, P. D. Hanson, and S. D. McBride, 125–36.

Hagstrom, D. G.
1988   *The Coherence of the Book of Micah: A Literary Analysis.* SBLDS 89. Atlanta: Scholars Press.

Hailey, M.
1972   *A Commentary on the Minor Prophets.* Grand Rapids, Mich.: Baker.

Halévy, J.
1904   Le Livre de Michée. *Revue Sémitique d'Épigraphie et d'Histoire Ancienne* 12:97–117, 193–216, 289–312.

1905   Le Livre de Michée. *Revue Sémitique d'Épigraphie et d'Histoire Ancienne* 13:1–22.

Hallo, W. W., ed.
1997   *The Context of Scripture. Canonical Compositions, Monumental Inscrip-
         tions, and Archival Documents from the Biblical World.* Vol. I. *Canonical
         Compositions from the Biblical World.* Leiden/New York/Köln: Brill.
Hallo, W. W., J. C. Moyer, and L. G. Perdue, eds.
1983   *Scripture in Context II: More Essays on the Comparative Method.* Winona
         Lake, Ind.: Eisenbrauns.
Halpern, B.
1993   The Baal (and the Asherah) in Seventh-Century Judah: Yhwh's Retainers
         Retired. In *Konsequente Traditionsgeschichte: Festschruift für Klaus Baltzer
         zum 65. Geburtstag,* ed. R. Bartelmus, T. Krüger, and H. Utzschneider,
         115–54. Orbis Biblicus et Orientalis 126. Freiburg, Schweiz: Universitäts-
         verlag; Göttingen: Vandenhoeck & Ruprecht.
Hammershaimb, E.
1961   Einige Hauptgedanken in der Schrift des Propheten Micha. *Studia Theo-
         logica* 15:11–34.

1966   Some Leading Ideas in the Book of Micah. In *Some Aspects of Old Testament
         Prophecy from Isaiah to Malachi,* 29–50. Teologiske Skrifter 4. Kopenhavn:
         Rosenkelde og Bagger.
Handy, L. K.
1988   Hezekiah's Unlikely Reform. ZAW 100:111–15.
Hanson, P. D.
1975   *The Dawn of Apocalyptic.* Philadelphia: Fortress.
Haran, M.
1972   Graded Numerical Sequence and the Phenomenon of "Automatism" in
         Biblical Poetry. VTSup 22:238–67.
1977   From Early to Classical Prophecy: Continuity and Change. *VT* 27:385–97.
Hardmeier, C.
1978   Texttheorie und Biblische Exegese: Zur Rhetorische Funktion der
         Trauermetaphorik in der Prophetie. BEvT 79. Munich: Kaiser.
1991   Die Propheten Micha und Jesaja im Spiegel von Jeremia XXVI und 2
         Regum XVIII–XX. Zur Prophetie-Rezeption in der nachjoschijanischen
         Zeit. In *Congress Volume: Leuven 1989,* 172–89. VTSup 43. Leiden: Brill.
Harl, M., G. Dorival, and O. Munnich, eds.
1988   *La Bible Grecque des Septante*: Du Judäism hellénistique au Christian-
         isme ancien. «Initiations au christianisme ancien.» Paris: Cerf/C.N.R.S.
Harper, R. F., F. Brown, and G. F. Moore, eds.
1908   *Old Testament and Semitic Studies in Memory of W. R. Harper.* 8th ed. 2 vols.
         Chicago: University of Chicago Press.
Harrelson, W.
1962   Nonroyal Motifs in the Royal Eschatology. In B. W. Anderson and W. Har-
         relson, 147–65.
1994   Isaiah 35 in Recent Research. In S. E. Balentine and J. Barton, 247–60.
Harvey, J.
1962   Le "Rîb-Pattern," réquisitoire prophétique sur la rupture de l'alliance. *Bib*
         43:172–96.
1967   *Le plaidoyer prophétique contre Israël après la rupture de l'alliance: Étude
         d'une formule littéraire de l'Ancien Testament.* Studia 22. Bruges: Desclée
         de Brouwer.

Hasel, G. F.
1972   *The Remnant: The History and Theology of the Remnant Idea from Genesis to Isaiah.* Andrews University Monographs: Studies in Religion 5. Berrien Springs: Andrews University Press.
1976   Remnant. *IDB*Sup, 735–36.
1988   Old Testament Theology from 1978–1987. *Andrews University Seminary Studies* 26:133–57.

Haupt, P.
1910a   Micah's Capucinade. *JBL* 29:85–112.
1910b   Critical Notes on Micah. *AJSL* 26:201–52.
1911   The Book of Micah. *AJSL* 27:1–63.
1919   *The Book of Micah.* Reprinted from *AJSL* 26 (1910): 201–52, and 27 (1911): 1–63. Chicago: University of Chicago Press.

Hayes, J. H., ed.
1974   *Old Testament Form Criticism.* San Antonio: Trinity University Press.

Hayes, J. H., and J. K. Kuan
1991   The Final Years of Samaria (730–720). *Bib* 72:153–81.

Heer, J.
1970   Der Bethlehemspruch Michas und die Geburt Jesu (Micah 5:1–3). *BK* 25:106–9.

Heider, G. C.
1985   *The Cult of Molek. A Reassessment.* *JSOT*Sup 43. Sheffield: JSOT.

Hemmerle, K.
1989   Wandern mit deinem Gottreligionsphilosophische Kontexte zu Mi 6,8. In R. Mosis and L. Ruppert, 234–50.

Hendricks, H. J.
n.d.   Juridical Aspects of the Marriage Metaphor in Hosea and Jeremiah. Ph.D. diss., University of Stellenbosch.

Hennesy, J. B.
1985   Thirteenth-Century b.c. Temple of Human Sacrifice at Amman. *Studia Phoenicia* 3:85–104.

Henry, M.
1827   *An Exposition of the Old and New Testament.* Vol. 3. The Prophetical Books. New York: Robert Carver.

Henten, J. W. van, et al., eds.
1986   *Tradition and Re-interpretation in Jewish and Early Christian Literature: Essays in Honour of Jürgen C. H. Lebram.* Leiden: Brill.

Hentschke, R.
1957   Die Stellung der vorexilischen Schriftpropheten zum Kultus. BZAW 75:104–7.

Herder, J. G.
1782–83 *The Spirit of Hebrew Poetry.* Trans J. March of *Vom Geiste der Ebraeischen Poesie.* Burlington: Edward Smith, 1833. Reprint, Naperville: Aleph, 1971.

Herman, W. R.
1988   The Kingship of Yahweh in the Hymnic Theophanies of the Old Testament. *Studia Biblica et Theologica* 16:169–211.

Herrmann, J.
1927   Das zehnte Gebot. In *Sellin-Festschrift: Beiträge zur Religionsgeschichte und Archäologie Palästinas*, ed. W. F. Albright et al., 69–82. Leipzig: Deichertsche Verlagsbuchhandlung.

Herrmann, S.
1976   *Ursprung und Funktion der Prophetie im alten Israel*. Rheinisch-Westfälische Akademie der Wissenschaften G 208. Opladen: Westdeutscher Verlag.
1989   The So-called "Fortress System of Rehoboam," 2 Chron 11:5–12: Theoretical Considerations. *EI* 20 [Yigael Yadin Memorial Volume]: 72–78.

Hertz, J. H.
1934–35 Micah vi.8. *ExpT* 46:188.

Heschel, A.
1962   *The Prophets*. 2 vols. New York: Harper & Row.

Hetzron, R.
1969   The Evidence for Perfect **yáqtul* and Jussive **yaqtúl* in Proto-Semitic. *JSS* 14:1–21.

Hillers, D. R.
1964   *Treaty-Curses and the Old Testament Prophets*. BibOr 16. Rome: Pontifical Biblical Institute.
1965   A Convention in Hebrew Literature: The Reaction to Bad News. *ZAW* 77:86–90.
1983a   Imperial Dreams: Text and Sense of Mic 5:4b–5. In H. B. Huffmon, F. A. Spina, and A. R. W. Green, 137–39.
1983b   Hôy and Hôy Oracles: A Neglected Syntactic Aspect. In *The Word of the Lord Shall Go Forth: Essays in Honor of David Noel Freedman in Celebration of His Sixtieth Birthday*, ed. C. L. Meyers and M. O'Connor, 185–88. ASOR 1. Winona Lake, Ind.: Eisenbrauns.
1984   *Micah: A Commentary on the Book of the Prophet Micah*. Hermeneia. Philadelphia: Fortress.

Hitzig, F.
1881   *Die zwölf kleinen Propheten*. 4th ed. KEHAT. Heinrich Steiner, ed. Leipzig: S. Hirzel.

Hoffmann, E.
1987   Das Hirtenbild im Alten Testament. *Fundamentum* 4:33–50.

Hoftijzer, J.
1985   *The Function and Use of the Imperfect Forms with* nun paragogicum *in Classical Hebrew*. SSN 21. Assen/Maastricht: Van Gorcum.

Hoftijzer, J., and G. van der Kooij, eds.
1991   *The Balaam Texts from Deir 'Alla Re-evaluated: Proceedings of the International Symposium Held at Leiden 21–24 August 1989*. Leiden: Brill.

Holladay, J. S.
1970   Assyrian Statecraft and the Prophets of Israel. *HTR* 63:29–51.

Holladay, W. L.
1960   Prototype and Copies: A New Approach to the Poetry-Prose Problem in the Book of Jeremiah. *JBL* 79:351–67.

Holm, N. G., ed.
1982   *Religious Ecstasy*. Symposium held in August 1981 at Åbo, Finland. SIDÅ XI. Stockholm: Almquist & Wiksell International.

Holt, E. K.
1987   *dʿtʾlhym* und *ḥsd* im Buche Hosea. *SJOT* 1:87–103.
Hoonacker, A. van
1908   *Les douze petits prophètes, traduits et commentés.* ÉBib. Paris: Gabalda.
Horine, S.
1989   A Study of the Literary Genre of the Woe Oracle. *Calvary Baptist Theological Journal* 5:74–97.
Hospers, J. H.
1991   Some Remarks about the So-called Imperative Use of the Infinitive Absolute (Infinitivus pro Imperativo) in Classical Hebrew. In K. Jongeling, H. L. Murre-van den Berg, and L. van Rompay, 97–102.
Hossfeld, F. L., and I. Meyer
1973   *Prophet gegen Prophet. Eine Analyse der alttestamentlichen Texte zum Thema: Wahre und falsche Propheten.* Biblische Beiträge 9. Fribourg: Schweizerisches Katholisches Bibelwerk.
1974   Der Prophet vor dem Tribunal: Neuer Auslegungsversuch von Jer 26. ZAW 86:30–50.
House, P. R.
1990   *The Unity of the Twelve.* JSOTSup 97. Bible and Literature Series 27. Sheffield: Almond.
————, ed.
1992   *Beyond Form Criticism: Essays in Old Testament Literary Criticism.* Sources for Biblical and Theological Studies 2. D. W. Baker, ed. Winona Lake, Ind.: Eisenbrauns.
Housman, A. E.
1933   *The Name and Nature of Poetry.* Cambridge: Cambridge University Press.
Huehnergard, J.
1988   The Early Hebrew Prefix-Conjugation. *HS* 29:19–23.
Huesman, J.
1956   The Infinitive Absolute and the *waw* + Perfect Problem. *Bib* 37:410–34.
Huffmon, H. B.
1959   The Covenant Lawsuit in the Prophets. *JBL* 78:285–95.
1965   *Amorite Personal Names in the Mari Texts: A Structural and Lexical Study.* Baltimore: Johns Hopkins University Press.
1966   The Treaty Background of Hebrew Yadaʿ. BASOR 181:31–37.
Huffmon, H. B., F. A. Spina, and A. R. W. Green, eds.
1983   *The Quest for the Kingdom of God: Studies in Honor of George E. Mendenhall.* Winona Lake, Ind.: Eisenbrauns.
Hummel, H. D.
1957   Enclitic *mem* in Early Northwest Semitic, Especially Hebrew. *JBL* 76:85–107.
Hunter, J. H.
1989   The Literary Composition of Theophany Passages in the Hebrew Psalms. *JNSL* 15:97–107.
Hutton, R. R.
1987   Eating the Flesh of My People: The Redaction History of Micah 3:1–4. *PEGLAMBS* 7:131–42.
Hyatt, J. P.
1952   On the Meaning and Origin of Micah 6:8. *ATR* 34:232–39.

1965   *The Bible in Modern Scholarship.* Nashville: Abingdon Press; London: Carey Kingsgate, 1966.

Ilan, Z.
1975   Gedud and Lehi in the Book of Micah. *Beth Mikra* 61:209–18.

Imschoot, P. van
1930   Le prophète Michée et son temps. *Collationes Gandavenses* 17:176–81.

Innes, D. K.
1967   Some Notes on Micah, Chapter I. *EvQ* 39:225–27.
1969   Some Notes on Micah, Chapter II. *EvQ* 41:10–13, 109–12, 169–71, 216–20.

Irvine, S.
1991   *Isaiah, Ahaz, and the Syro-Ephraimitic Crisis.* Atlanta: Scholars Press.

Isaksson, B.
1987   *Studies in the Language of Qoheleth: With Special Emphasis on the Verbal System.* Acta Universitatis Upsaliensis: Studia Semitica Upsaliensia 10. Uppsala: Almqvist & Wiksell.

Jackson, B.
1975   Liability for Intention in Early Jewish Law. In *Essays in Jewish and Comparative Legal History*, 202–34. SJLA 10. Leiden: Brill.

Jacob, E.
1957   Quelques remarques sur les faux prophètes. *Theologie en Zielzorg* 13:479–86.

Jacobs, L.
1981   The Problem of the *Akedah* in Jewish Thought. In *Kierkegaard's* Fear and Trembling: *Critical Appraisals*, ed. R. L. Perkins, 1–9. [Tuscaloosa]: University of Alabama Press.

Janzen, W.
1972   *Mourning Cry and Woe Oracle.* BZAW 125. Berlin: Walter de Gruyter.
1975   God as Warrior and Lord. A Conversation with G. E. Wright. *BASOR* 220:73–75.

Jellicoe, S.
1974   *Studies in the Septuagint: Origins, Recensions, and Interpretations.* Ed. H. M. Orlinsky. LBS. New York: KTAV.
1989   *The Septuagint and Modern Study.* Winona Lake, Ind.: Eisenbrauns.

Jemielity, T.
1992   *Satire and the Hebrew Prophets.* Literary Currents in Biblical Interpretation. Louisville, Ky.: Westminster/John Knox Press.

Jenni, E.
1968   *Das hebräische Pi'el: Syntaktisch-semasiologiche Untersuchung einer Verbalform im Alten Testament.* Zürich: EVZ-Verlag.
1977   ZAQEN. Bemerkungen zum Unterschied von Nominalsatz und Verbalsatz. In H. Donner, R. Hanhart, and R. Smend, 185–95.

Jeppesen, K.
1977   Fire nye Mikakommentarer: et forsoeg pa en Forkningsstatus. *DTT* 40:243–62.
1978   New Aspects of Micah Research. *JSOT* 8:3–32.
1979   How the Book of Micah Lost Its Integrity: Outline of the History of the Criticism of the Book of Micah with Emphasis on the 19th Century. *ST* 33:101–31.
1984a   The Verb *ya'ad* in Nahum 1:10 and Micah 6:9? *Bib* 65:571–74.

1984b   Micah 5:13 in the Light of a Recent Archaeological Discovery. *VT* 34:462–66.

Jepsen, A.
1967   Warum? Eine lexicalische und theologische Studie. In F. Maass, 106–13.

Jepsen, A.
1934   *Nabi. Soziologische Studien zur alttestamentlichen Literatur und Religions-geschichte.* Munich: C. H. Beck.
1937   *Das Zwölfprophetenbuch: Bibelhilfe für die Gemeinde.* Leipzig und Hamburg: Gustav Schloessmanns Verlags.
1938   Kleine Beiträge zum Zwölfprophetenbuch. 2. Micha. *ZAW* 56:85–100.

Jeremias, J.
1933   Moreseth-Gath, die Heimat des Propheten Micha. *PJ* 29:42–53.

Jeremias, J.
1965   *Theophanie: Die Geschichte einer alttestamentlichen Gattung.* WMANT Vol. 10. Neukirchen-Vluyn: Neukirchener.
1970   *Kultprophetie und Gerichtsverkündigen in der späteren Königszeit Israels.* WMANT 35. Neukirchen-Vluyn: Neukirchener.
1971a   Lade und Zion: Zur Entstehung der Zionstradition. In *Probleme biblischer Theologie: Gerhard von Rad zum 70. Geburtstag,* ed. H. W. Wolff, 183–98. Munich: Kaiser Verlag.
1971b   Die Deutung der Gerichtsworte Michas in der Exilzeit. *ZAW* 83:330–54.
1992   Tau und Löwe (Mi 5,6f). In F. Crüsemann, 221–27.

Jerome
1969   *S. Hieronymi Presbyteri Opera. Pars I: Opera Exegetica, Vol. 6, Commentarii in Prophetes Minores.* Corpus Christianorum, Series Latina, Vol. 76. Turnhout: Brepols.

Jobling, D., P. L. Day, and G. T. Sheppard, eds.
1991   *The Bible and the Politics of Exegesis. Essays in Honor of Norman K. Gottwald on His Sixty-fifth Birthday.* Cleveland: Pilgrim.

Johnson, A. R.
1944   *The Cultic Prophet in Ancient Israel.* Cardiff: University of Wales.

Johnson, J. F.
1983   The Nativity of Our Lord, Christmas Day. *Concordia* 9:238–39.

Jones, B. W.
1972   *Ideas of History in the Book of Daniel.* Ph.D. diss., Graduate Theological Union, Berkeley, Calif.

Jongeling, B.
1971   Pseudo-Propheten Entlarvet. *Schrift* 17:169–75.

Jongeling, K., H. L. Murre-van den Berg, and L. van Rompay, eds.
1991   *Studies in Hebrew and Aramaic Syntax Presented to Professor J. Hoftijzer on the Occasion of His Sixty-fifth Birthday.* Studies in Semitic Languages and Linguistics 17. Leiden: Brill.

Joüon, P.
1947   *Grammaire de l'Hébreu biblique.* 2d ed. Rome: Pontifical Biblical Institute.
1991   *A Grammar of Biblical Hebrew.* Trans. and rev. of Joüon 1923 by T. Muraoka. Subsidia Biblica 14/I, II. Rome: Pontifical Biblical Institute.

Junker, H.
1959   Die literarische Art von Is. 5:1–7. *Bib* 40:259–66.

Kaiser, O.
1974   *Isaiah 13–39. A Commentary.* Trans. of 2d German ed. R. A. Wilson. OTL. London: SCM; Philadelphia: Westminster Press.
1983   *Isaiah 1–12. A Commentary.* OTL. 2d ed. Westminster: John Knox.
Kallikuzhuppil, J.
1985   Liberation in Amos and Micah. *Bible Bhashyam* 11:215–23.
Kapelrud, A. S.
1961   Eschatology in the Book of Micah. *VT* 11:392–405.
1981   Eschatology in Micah and Zephaniah. In M. Carrez, J. Doré, and P. Grelot, 255–62.
1988   Sigmund Mowinckel's Study of the Prophets. *SJOT* 2:72–82.
Kassis, H. E.
1965   Gath and the Structure of the "Philistine" Society. *JBL* 84:259–71.
Katz, E.
1970   *A Classified Concordance to the Late Prophets in Their Various Subjects.* Jerusalem: Central Press.
Katz, P.
1956   Septuagintal Studies in Mid-Century. Their Links with the Past and Their Present Tendencies. In *The Background of the New Testament and Its Eschatology* [C. H. Dodd *Festschrift*], ed. W. D. Davies and D. Daube, 176–208. Cambridge: Cambridge University Press.
1957   Justin's Old Testament Quotations and the Greek Dodekapropheten Scroll. *StPatr* 1:343–53. Texte und Untersuchungen zur Geschichte der altchristlichen Literatur 63. V Reihe, Band 8.
Kaufman, Y.
1960   *The Religion of Israel.* Abr. and trans. M. Greenberg. Chicago: University of Chicago Press.
Kaufmann, S. A.
1982   Reflections on the Assyrian-Aramaic Bilingual from Tell Fakhariyeh. *Maarav* 3, no. 2:137–75.
Keel, O., ed.
1980   *Monotheismus im alten Israel und seiner Umwelt.* Biblische Beiträge 14. Fribourg: Verlag Schweizerisches Katholisches Bibelwerk.
Keil, C. F.
1866   *Biblischer Commentar über die Zwölf kleinen Propheten.* Biblischer Commentar III/4. Leipzig: Dorffling und Franke.
Kellerman, D.
1978   Überlieferungsprobleme alttestamentlicher Ortsnamen. *VT* 28:423–32.
Kennett, R. H.
1905   The Origin of the Aaronite Priesthood. *JTS* 6:161–86.
Kessler, M., ed.
1994   *Voices from Amsterdam: A Modern Tradition of Reading Biblical Narrative.* Society of Biblical Literature Semeia Studies. Atlanta: Scholars Press.
Kesterson, J. C.
1986   Cohortative and Short Imperfect Forms in Serakim and Dam. Doc. *RevQ* 12:369–82.
Khan, G.
1984   Object Markers and Agreement Pronouns in Semitic Languages. *BSOAS* 47/3:468–500.

1987 Vowel Length and Syllable Structure in the Tiberian Tradition of Biblical Hebrew. *JSS* 32:23–82.
1988 *Studies in Semitic Syntax.* London Oriental Series Vol. 38. Oxford: Oxford University Press.

Kilian, R.
1970 *Isaaks Opferung.* Stuttgarter Bibel-Studien 44. Stuttgart: Verlag Katholisches Bibelwerk.

King, P. J.
1968 Micah. In *The Jerome Biblical Commentary,* ed. R. E. Brown, J. A. Fitzmyer, and R. E. Murphy, 283–89. Englewood Cliffs, N.J.: Prentice-Hall.
1988 *Amos, Hosea, Micah: An Archaeological Commentary.* Philadelphia: Westminster.
1989 The Great Eighth Century. *BRev* 5, no. 4:22–33, 44.

Kingsbury, E. C.
1964 The Prophets and the Council of Yahweh. *JBL* 83:279–86.

Kleinert, P.
1893 *Obadja, Jona, Micha, Nahum, Habakkuk, Zephanja.* Theologisches-homiletisches Bibelwerk. 2d ed. Ed. J. P. Lange. Bielefeld & Leipzig: Velhagen und Klasing.

Knabenbauer, J.
1924 *Commentarius in prophetas minores.* 2d ed. Ed. M. Hagen. Cursus Scripture Sacrae 2d section, 24. Paris: Lethielleux.

Köbert, G.
1958 *Môrad* (Mi 1,4) Tränke. *Bib* 39:82–83.

Koch, K.
1961 Tempeleinlassliturgien und Dekaloge. In R. Rendtorff and K. Koch, 45–60.
1969 *The Growth of the Biblical Tradition: The Form-Critical Method.* Trans. S. M. Cupitt. New York: Charles Scribner's Sons.
1971 Die Entstehung der sozialen Kritik bei den Propheten. Pp. 235–57 in H. W. Wolff.
1982 *The Prophets: The Assyrian Period.* Trans. M. Kohl. Philadelphia: Fortress.
1988 Aschera als Himmelskönigin in Jerusalem. *UF* 20:97–120.

Koenig, J.
1982 *L'hermeneutique analogique du Judaisme antique d'apres les temoins textuels d'Isaïe.* VTSup 33. Leiden: Brill.
1988 *Oracles et liturgies de l'exile babylonien.* Paris: Presses Universitaires de France.

Koepke, W., ed.
1982 *Johann Gottfried Herder: Innovator Through the Ages.* Bonn: Bouvier Verlag Herbert Grundmann.

Kogut, S.
1987/88 The Biblical Expression *yēš/ʾên lěʾēl yad*: The Interpretation and Development of a Mistake. *Tarbiz* 57:435–44.

Koopmans, W. T.
1990 *Joshua 24 as Poetic Narrative.* JSOTSup 93. Sheffield: JSOT Press.

Korpel, M. C. A.
1988 The Literary Genre of the Song of the Vineyard (Isa 5:1–7). In W. van der Meer and J. C. de Moor, 119–55.

1989   The Poetic Structure of the Priestly Blessing. *JSOT* 45:3–13.

Korpel, M. C. A., and J. C. de Moor
1986   Fundamentals of Ugaritic and Hebrew Poetry. *UF* 18:173–212. Reprint, van der Meer and de Moor 1988, 1–61.

Kosmala, H.
1963   At the End of the Days. *ASTI* 2:27–37. [= Kosmala 1978, I:73–83]
1964   Form and Structure in Ancient Hebrew Poetry. *VT* 14:423–45.
1966   Form and Structure in Ancient Hebrew Poetry. *VT* 16:152–80.
1978   *Studies, Essays and Reviews.* 3 vols. Leiden: Brill.

Kottsieper, I.
1984   KTU 1.100—Versuch einer Deutung. *UF* 16:97–110.

Kraeling, C. H., and R. M. Adams, eds.
1958   *City Invincible. A Symposium on Urbanization and Cultural Development in the Ancient Near East.* Chicago: Oriental Institute.

Krašovec, J.
1977   *Der Merismus im biblisch-hebräischen und nordwestsemitischen.* BibOr 33. Rome: Biblical Institute Press.
1984   *Antithetical Structure in Biblical Hebrew Poetry.* VTSup 35. Leiden: Brill.

Kraus, H.-J.
1973   *hôj* als prophetische Leichenklage über das eigene Volk im 8. Jahrhundert. *ZAW* 85:15–46.

Kreuzer, S.
1986   Das Opfer des Vaters—die Gefährdung des Sohnes. Genesis 22. *Amt und Gemeinde* 37, no. 7/8:62–70. [= *Schaut Abraham an, euren Vater! Festschrift für Professor Dr. Georg Sauer zum 60. Geburtstag.*]

Krinetzki, L.
1970   Die Gerichts—und die Heilbotschaft des Propheten. BK 25:104–6.

Kselman, J. S.
1975   A Note on Isaiah II 2. *VT* 25:225–27.

Kugel, J. L.
1981   *The Idea of Biblical Poetry: Parallelism and Its history.* New Haven: Yale University Press.
1991   *Poetry and Prophecy: The Beginning of a Literary Tradition.* Ithaca and London: Cornell University Press.

Kuhl, C.
1961   *The Old Testament: Its Origins and Composition.* Trans. C. T. M. Herriott. Richmond: John Knox Press.

Kurylowicz, J.
1972   *Studies in Semitic Grammar and Metrics.* Prace Jezykoznawze 67. Wroclaw: Polska Akademia Nauk.

Kuschke, A., ed.
1961   *Verbannung und Heimkehr: Wilhelm Rudolph zum 70. Geburtstage.* Tübingen: J. C. B. Mohr.

Kutscher, E. Y.
1957   The Language of the Genesis Apocryphon. *ScrHier* 4:1–35.
1970   The Genesis Apocryphon of Qumran Cave I. *Or* 39:178–83.
1982   *A History of the Hebrew Language.* Ed. R. Kutscher. Jerusalem and Leiden: Magnes Press and E. J. Brill.

Labuschagne, C. J.
1966   *The Incomparability of Yahweh in the Old Testament.* Pretoria Oriental
          Studies 5. Leiden: Brill.
Labuschagne, C. J., et al.
1973   *Syntax and Meaning: Studies in Hebrew Syntax and Biblical Exegesis.*
          OTS 18. Leiden: Brill.
Ladame, F.
1902   Les chapitres IV et V du livre de Michée. *RTP* 35:446–61.
Laetsch, T.
1956   *Bible Commentary: The Minor Prophets.* St. Louis: Concordia.
Lambdin, T. O.
1971   *Introduction to Biblical Hebrew.* New York: Scribner's.
1978   *Introduction to Classical Ethiopic* (Geʿez). HSS 24. Missoula, Mont.:
          Scholars Press.
Lambert, W. G.
1988   Old Testament Mythology and Its Ancient Near Eastern Context. In *Con-
          gress Volume (Jerusalem 1986)*, ed. J. A. Emerton, VTSup 40. Leiden:
          Brill.
Lambert, W. G., and A. R. Millard
1969   *Atra-Ḥāsîs: The Babylonian Story of the Flood.* Oxford: Clarendon.
Landy, F.
1984   Poetics and Parallelism: Some Comments on Kugel's *The Idea of Biblical
          Poetry. JSOT* 28:61–87.
Lang, B.
1981   Die Jahwe-allein Bewegung. In *Der einzige Gott: Die Geburt des bibli-
          schen Monotheismus*, ed. B. Lang, 47–83. München: Kösel-Verlag.
1982   The Social Organization of Peasant Poverty in Biblical Israel. *JSOT*
          24:47–63.
LaRocca, E. C.
1989   Archaeology and the "Asherah." *BToday* 27:288–92.
Laurentin, A.
1964   Weʿattâh—*kai nun*: Formule caractéristique des textes juridiques et
          liturgiques (à propos de Jean 17,5). *Bib* 45:168–97, 413–32.
Lawton, R.
1984   Israelite Personal Names on Pre-Exilic Hebrew Inscriptions. *Bib* 65:33–46.
Layton, S. C.
1990   *Archaic Features of Canaanite Personal Names in the Hebrew Bible.* HSM 47.
          Atlanta: Scholars Press.
1992   Whence Comes Balaam? Num 22.5 Revisited. *Bib* 73:32–61.
Lee, T. R.
1986   *Studies in the Form of Sirach 44–50.* SBLDS 75. Atlanta: Scholars Press.
Leeuwen, R. C. Van
1990   The Sage in the Prophetic Literature. In Gammie and Perdue, 295–306.
Lefèvre, A.
1957   L'expression "En ce jour-là" dans le Livre d'Isaïe. In *Mélanges bibliques ré-
          digés en l'honneur d'André Robert*, 174–79. Travaux de l'Institut Catholique
          de Paris, 4. Paris: Bloud [et] Gay.
Lemaire, A.
1977   L'Ashérah de Yahweh. *RB* 84:603–6.

Lescow, T.
1966   Micha 6,6–8: Studien zu Sprache, Form und Auslegung. Arbeiten zur The-
          ologie, I Reihe, Heft 29. Stuttgart: Calwer.
1967   Das Geburtsmotiv in den messianischen Weissagungen bei Jesaja und
          Micha. ZAW 79:172–207.
1972a   Redaktionsgeschichtliche Analyse von Micha 1–5. ZAW 84:46–85.
1972b   Redaktionsgeschichtliche Analyse von Micha 6–7. ZAW 84:182–212.
Leslie, E. A.
1962   Micah the Prophet. IDB 3:369–72.
Levenson, J. D.
1993   The Death and Resurrection of the Beloved Son: The Transformation of
          Child Sacrifice in Judaism and Christianity. New Haven: Yale University
          Press.
Levine, B. A.
1993   Numbers 1–20. AB 4. New York: Doubleday.
Lewis, R. L.
1959   The Persuasive Style and Appeals of the Minor Prophets Amos, Hosea and
          Micah. Ph.D. diss., University of Michigan.
Lieb, M.
1991   The Visionary Mode: Biblical Prophecy, Hermeneutics, and Cultural
          Change. Ithaca and London: Cornell University Press.
Limburg, J.
1969   The Root ryb and the Prophetic Lawsuit Speeches. JBL 88:291–304.
Lindblom, J.
1929   Micha literarisch untersucht. Acta Academiae Åboensis, Humaniora VI 2.
          Helsingfors: Åbo Akademi.
1962   Prophecy in Ancient Israel. Philadelphia: Fortress.
Lipiński, E.
1970   B'ḥryt hymym dans les textes préexiliques. VT 20:445–50.
1975   Studies in Aramaic Inscriptions and Onomastics I. OLA 1. Leuven: Leuven
          University Press.
Lippl, J., J. Theis, and H. Junker
1937   Die Zwölf Kleinen Propheten übersetzt und erklärt 1. HSAT 8/3. 1 Halfte.
          Bonn: P. Hanstein.
Lohfink, G.
1986   "Schwerter zu Pflugscharen." Die Rezeption von Jes 2,1–5 par Mi 4,1–5
          in der Alten Kirche und in Neuen Testament. Theologische Quartalschrift
          166:184–209.
Lohfink, N.
1983   Die Bedeutung von hebr. jrš qal und hif. BZ 27:14–33.
Long, B. O., and G. W. Coats, eds.
1977   Canon and Authority: Essays in Old Testament Religion and Theology.
          Philadelphia: Fortress.
Loretz, O.
1971   Studien zur althebräischen Poesie 1. Das althebräische Liebeslied. Unter-
          suchungen zur Stichometrie und Redaktionsgeschichte des Hohenliedes und
          des 45. Psalms. AOAT 14/1. Kevelaer: Butzon & Bercker.
1975   Weinberglied und prophetische Deutung im Protest-Song Jes. 5:1–7. UF
          7:573–76.

1977a   Hebräische *TJRWŠ* und *JRŠ* in Mc 6,15 und Hi 20,15. *UF* 9:353–54.
1977b   Fehlanzeige von Ugaritismen in Micha 5,1–3. *UF* 9:358–60.
1986   Kolometrie ugar. und hebr. Poesie: Grundlagen, informationstheoretische und literaturwissenschaftliche Aspekte. *ZAW* 98:249–66.
1989   Hexakola im Ugaritischen und Hebräischen, Zu KTU 1.3 IV 50–53 *et par. UF* 21:237–40.

Lowth, R.
1778   *Isaiah: A New Translation; with a Preliminary Dissertation and Notes, Critical, Philological, and Explanatory.* Reprint, London: William Tegg, 1868.
1787   *Lectures on the Sacred Poetry of the Hebrews.* Trans. G. Gregory. London: J. Johnson. This translation from the Latin of *De Sacra Poesi Hebraeorum* (1st ed. 1753, 2d ed. 1763) adds a selection of the notes by John David Michaelis (added to the Göttingen edition), the translator, and others from lectures given in 1741; the U.S. edition of 1829 adds further notes by Calvin Stowe. Reprint, New York: Garland, 1971.

Luker, L. M.
1987   Beyond Form Criticism: The Relation of Doom and Hope Oracles in Micah 2–6. *HAR* 11:285–301.

Luria, B. Z.
1977   The Political Background for Micah: Ch. 1. *Beth Mikra* 71:403–12 [Eng. 532].
1980   In the Days of Hezekiah, King of Judah. *Beth Mikra* 82:195–98.
1982   Judea in the Time of the Prophet Micah and the King Hezekiah. *Beth Mikra* 92:6–13 [Eng. 100].
1989–90 For the Statutes of Omri Are Kept . . . (Micah 6:16). *DD* 18:69–73.

Lust, J.
1971   Dat ik toch vroom mag blijven: Prophet en Kultus. *Schrift* 17:184–87.
1986   Exegesis and Theology in the LXX of Ezekiel. *VI Congress of the International Organization of the LXX and Cognate Studies*, Jerusalem 1986. Septuagint and Cognate Studies 23. Atlanta: Scholars Press.
1991   "For Man Shall His Blood be Shed": Gen 9:6 in Hebrew and in Greek. In G. J. Norton and S. Pisano, 91–102.

Lust, J., E. Eynikel, and K. Hauspie, eds.
1992   A *Greek-English Lexicon of the Septuagint.* Stuttgart: Deutsche Bibelgesellschaft.

Luther, M.
1975   *Luther's Works, Vol. 18: Lectures on the Minor Prophets, I.* [Lectures on Micah delivered 1524–1526.] Ed. H. C. Oswald. St. Louis: Concordia.

Lutz, H. M.
1968   Jahwe, Jerusalem und die Völker. In *Studien zur israelitischen Spruchweisheit*, ed. H-J. Hermisson. WMANT 28. Neukirchen-Vluyn: Neukirchener Verlag.

Lux, R. C.
1976   An Exegetical Study of Micah 1,8–16. Ph.D. diss., Notre Dame University.

Lys, D.
1962   Rûach: *Le souffle dans l'Ancien Testament.* Études d'histoire et de philosophie religieuses 56. Paris: Presses universitaires de France.
1974   La vigne et la double je. Exercise de style sur Esaia 5:1–7. In *Studies on Prophecy*, 1–16. VTSup 26. Leiden: Brill.

Maass, F., ed.
1967   *Das ferne und nahe Wort. Festschrift Leonhard Rost zur Vollendung seines 70. Lebensjahres am 30.XI. 1966.* BZAW 105. Berlin: A. Töpelmann.

Maccoby, H.
1983   *The Sacred Executioner: Human Sacrifice and the Legacy of Guilt.* London: Thames and Hudson.

MacIver, R. M., ed.
1950   *Great Expressions of Human Rights.* New York: Harper & Row.

Mack, B. L.
1985   *Wisdom and the Hebrew Epic: Ben Sira's Hymn in Praise of the Fathers.* Chicago Studies in the History of Judaism. Chicago: University of Chicago Press.

Maier, J., and V. Tollers, eds.
1979   *The Bible in Its Literary Milieu: Contemporary Essays.* Grand Rapids, Mich.: Eerdmans.

Maillot, A., and A. Lelievre
1976   *Actualité de Michée. Un grand "petit prophète."* Geneva: Éditions Labor et Fides.

Malchow, B. V.
1980   The Rural Prophet: Micah. *Currents in Theology and Mission* 7:48–52.

Malone, J. L.
1983   Generative Phonology and the Metrical Behavior of *u-* "and" in the Hebrew Poetry of Medieval Spain. *JAOS* 103:369–81.
1990   Pretonic Lengthening: An Early Hebrew Sound Change. *JAOS* 110:460–71.
1993a   Generative Phonology and Analogical Change: The Case of the Hebrew Suffix "you(r)." *JAOS* 113:25–34.
1993b   *Tiberian Hebrew Phonology.* Winona Lake, Ind.: Eisenbrauns.

Manahan, R. E.
1980   A Theology of Pseudoprophets: A Study in Jeremiah. *GTJ* 1:77–96.

Margalit, B.
1986   Why King Mesha of Moab Sacrificed His Oldest Son. *BARev* 12/6:62–63, 76.
1989   Some Observations on the Inscription and Drawing from Khirbet El-Qôm. *VT* 39:371–78.
1990   The Meaning and Significance of Asherah. *VT* 60:264–97.

Margolis, M. L.
1908   *Micah.* Philadelphia: Jewish Publication Society of America.

Marsh, J.
1959   *Amos and Micah. Introduction and Commentary.* TBC. London: SCM.

Marti, K.
1904   *Das Dodekapropheton.* Kurzer Hand-Commentar zum Alten Testament 13. Tübingen: J. C. B. Mohr.

Marty, J.
1947   Michée. In *Bible du Centenaire.* Vol. 2, *Les Prophètes,* xxxiii–xxxiv, 768–83. Paris: Société Biblique de Paris.

Matthiae, P.
1981   *Ebla: An Empire Rediscovered.* Trans. Christopher Holme. Garden City, N.Y.: Doubleday.

Mauchline, J.
1970   Implicit Signs of a Persistent Belief in the Davidic Empire. *VT* 20:287–303.

Mayerson, P.
 1959 Ancient Agricultural Remains in the Central Negeb: The Teleilat El-ʿAnab. *BASOR* 153:19–31.
Mayes, A. D. H.
 1974 *Israel in the Period of the Judges.* Naperville, Ill.: Allenson.
Mays, J. L.
 1976 *Micah: A Commentary.* OTL. London: SCM.
 1977 The Theological Purpose of the Book of Micah. In H. Donner, R. Hanhart, and R. Smend, 276–87.
Mays, J. L., and P. J. Achtemeier, eds.
 1987 *Interpreting the Prophets.* Philadelphia: Fortress.
Mazar, A.
 1990 *Archaeology of the Land of the Bible, 10,000–586 B.C.E.* New York: Doubleday.
Mazar, B.
 1954 Gath and Gittaim. *IEJ* 4:227–35.
 1956 Tell Gath. *IEJ* 6:258–59.
McCarter, P. K.
 1976 Obadiah 7 and the Fall of Edom. *BASOR* 221:87–91.
 1980 *I Samuel.* AB 8. New York: Doubleday.
 1984 *II Samuel.* AB 9. New York: Doubleday.
McCarthy, D. J.
 1971 Some Holy War Vocabulary in Joshua 2. *CBQ* 33:228–30.
McCarthy, J. J.
 1985 *Formal Problems in Semitic Phonology and Morphology.* Outstanding Dissertations in Linguistics. General editor J. Hankamer. New York: Garland.
McComiskey, T. E.
 1981 Micah 7. *TJ* 2:62–68.
McFadden, W. R.
 1983 Micah and the Problem of Continuities and Discontinuities in Prophecy. In W. W. Hallo, J. C. Moyer, and L. G. Perdue, 127–46.
McFall, L.
 1982 *The Enigma of the Hebrew Verbal System.* Sheffield: Almond Press.
McKane, W.
 1979 Prophecy and the Prophetic Literature. In *Tradition and Interpretation: Essays by Members of the Society for Old Testament Study,* ed. G. W. Anderson, 163–88. Oxford: Clarendon Press.
 1995 Micah 1,2–7. *ZAW* 107:420–34.
McKeating, H.
 1971 *The Books of Amos, Hosea and Micah.* Cambridge Bible Commentary. Cambridge: Cambridge University Press.
McKenzie, J. L.
 1959 The Elders in the Old Testament. *Bib* 40:522–40.
Meek, T. J.
 1929a Some Emendations in the Old Testament (1 Mi 4,4–Isa 2,2). *JBL* 48:162–68.
 1929b The Co-ordinate Adverbial Clause in Hebrew. *JAOS* 49:156–59.
 1930–31 The Co-ordinate Adverbial Clause in Hebrew. *AJSL* 47:51–52.
 1945 The Syntax of the Sentence in Biblical Hebrew. *JBL* 64:1–13.

1955–56   Result and Purpose Clauses in Hebrew. *JQR* 46:40–43.

Meer, W. van der, and J. C. de Moor, eds.
1988   *The Structural Analysis of Biblical and Canaanite Poetry.* JSOTSup 74. Sheffield: University of Sheffield Press.

Meier, S. A.
1992   *Speaking of Speaking: Marking Direct Discourse in the Hebrew Bible.* VTSup 46. Leiden: Brill.

Melamed, E. Z.
1961   Break Up of Stereotype Phrases as an Artistic Device in Biblical Poetry. In C. Rabin, 115–53.

Mendecki, N.
1981   Die Sammlung und der neue Exodus in Micha 2:12–13. *Kairos: Zeitschrift für Religionswissenschaft und Theologie* 23:96–99.
1982   Autentycznosc Mi 4:6–7. *ColT* 52:85–88.
1983   Die Sammlung der Zerstreuten in Mi 4,6–7. *BZ* 27:218–21.

Mendenhall, G. E.
1955   *Law and Covenant in Israel and the Ancient Near East.* Pittsburgh: Biblical Colloquium.
1958   The Census Lists of Numbers 1 and 26. *JBL* 77:52–66.
1973   *The Tenth Generation.* Baltimore: Johns Hopkins University Press.

Merwe, B. J. van der
1973   Micah 1:12 and Its Possible Parallels in Pre-Exilic Prophetism. *Die Ou Testamentiese Werkgemeenskap in Suid-Afrika* 16:45–53.

Meyer, I.
1977   *Jeremia und die falschen Propheten.* OBO 13. Freiburg Schweiz: Universitätsverlag. Göttingen: Vandenhoeck & Ruprecht.

Meyer, R.
1960   Michabuch. *RGG*³ 4:929–31.

Meyers, C. L.
1991   Of Drums and Damsels: Women's Performance in Ancient Israel. *BA* 54:16–27.

Meyers, C. L., and M. O'Connor, eds.
1983   *The Word of the Lord Shall Go Forth: Essays in Honor of David Noel Freedman in Celebration of His Sixtieth Birthday.* Winona Lake, Ind.: Eisenbrauns.

Meyers, C. L., and E. M. Meyers
1987   *Haggai, Zechariah 1–8.* AB 25B. Garden City, N.Y.: Doubleday.
1993   *Zechariah 9–14.* AB 25C. Garden City, N.Y.: Doubleday.

Michaelson, P.
1989   Ecstasy and Possession in Ancient Israel. A Review of Some Recent Contributions. *SJOT* 2:28–54.

Milgrom, J.
1991   *Leviticus 1–16.* AB 3. Garden City, N.Y.: Doubleday.

Milgrom, J.
1988   *The Binding of Isaac: The Akedah—A Primary Symbol in Jewish Thought and Art.* Berkeley, Calif.: Bibal Press.

Milik, J. T.
1952   Fragments d'un midrash de Michée dans les manuscrits de Qumran. *RB* 59:412–18.

Millard, A. R.
1980   YW and *YHW* Names. *VT* 30:208–12.

Miller, C. H.
1982   Micah: A Word of Our Time. *BToday* 20:13–17.

Miller, C. L.
1994   Introducing Direct Discourse in Biblical Hebrew Narrative. In R. D. Bergen, 199–241.
1995   Discourse Functions of Quotative Frames in Biblical Hebrew Narrative. In W. R. Bodine, 155–82.
1996   *The Representation of Speech in Biblical Hebrew Narrative: A Linguistic Analysis.* HSM 55. Atlanta: Scholars Press.

Miller, P. D.
1980   Synonymous Sequential Parallelism in the Psalms. *Bib* 61:256–60.
1982   *Sin and Judgment in the Prophets: A Stylistic and Theological Analysis.* SBLMS 27. Chico, Calif.: Scholars Press.

Miller, P. D., P. D. Hanson, and S. D. McBride, eds.
1987   *Ancient Israelite Religion: Essays in Honor of Fran Moore Cross.* Philadelphia: Fortress.

Moberly, R. W. L.
1988   The Earliest Commentary on the Akedah. *VT* 38:302–23.

Moffitt, J.
1982   Difficult Texts from Micah, Nahum, Habakkuk, Zephaniah and Haggai. In *Difficult Texts of the Old Testament Explained: Fifth Annual Fort Worth Lectures 1981,* ed. W. Winkler, 415–25. Hurst, Tex.: Winkler.

Moor, J. C. de
1986   The Poetry of the Book of Ruth (Part II). *Or* 55:16–46.
1988   Micah 1: A Structural Approach. In W. van der Meer and J. C. de Moor, 172–85.
1993   The Integrity of Isaiah 40. In *Mesopotamica, Ugaritica, Biblica: Festschrift für Kurt Bergerhof zur Vollendung seines 70. Lebensjahres am 7. Mai 1992,* ed. M. Dietrich and O. Loretz, 181–216. AOAT 232. Kevelaer: Verlag Butzon & Bercker/Neukirchen-Vluyn: Neukirchener Verlag.

Moor, J. C. de., and W. G. E. Watson, eds.
1993   *Verse in Ancient Near Eastern Prose.* AOAT 42. Neukirchen-Vluyn: Neukirchener Verlag.

Moore, M. S.
1990a   *The Balaam Traditions: Their Character and Development.* Atlanta: Scholars Press.
1990b   Another Look at Balaam. *RB* 97:359–78.

Morag, S.
1962   *The Vocalization Systems of Arabic, Hebrew and Aramaic: Their Phonetic and Phonemic Principles.* Janua Linguarum 13. 'S-Gravenhage: Mouton.
1974   On the Historical Validity of the Vocalization of the Hebrew Bible. *JAOS* 94:307–15.
1988   Qumran Hebrew: Some Typological Observations. *VT* 38:148–64.

Moran, W. L.
1950   The Putative Root ʿtm in Is 9:18. *CBQ* 12:153–54.

1961   The Hebrew Language in Its Northwest Semitic Background. In *The Bible and the Ancient Near East: Essays in Honor of William Foxwell Albright*, ed. G. E. Wright, 59–84. Garden City, N.Y.: Doubleday.

1963   The Ancient Near Eastern Background of the Love of God in Deuteronomy. CBQ 25:77–87.

1967   The Conclusion of the Decalogue (Ex. 20,17 = Dt. 5,21). CBQ 29:543–54.

Moreschet, M.

1966–67   Whr hbyt lbmwt yʿr. Beth Mikra 12:123–26.

Morgenstern, J.

1911   Biblical Theophanies. ZA 25:139–93.

1914   Biblical Theophanies. ZA 28:15–60.

Mosis, R., and L. Ruppert, eds.

1989   *Der Weg zum Menschen. Für A. Deissler.* Freiburg: Herder.

Mowinckel, S.

1921–24   *Psalmenstudien* I–VI. Videnskapsselskapets Skrifter. II Hist. Filos. Klasse. Kristiania. Reprint, in two volumes, Amsterdam: P. Schippers, 1961.

1925   Zwei Beobachtungen zur Deutung der פֹּעֲלֵי אָוֶן. ZAW 43:260–62.

1928   Mikaboken. NTT 29:3–42.

1934–35   Ecstatic Experience and Rational Elaboration in Old Testament Prophecy. AcOr 13:264–91.

1947   *Prophecy and Tradition: The Prophetical Books in the Light of the Study of the Growth and History of the Tradition.* Oslo: Dybwad.

1957   *Real and Apparent Tricola in Hebrew Psalm Poetry.* Avhandlinger utgitt av Det Norske Videnskaps-Akademi i Oslo. II Hist. Filos. Klass. No. 2. Oslo: I Kommisjon Hos H. Aschehoug (W. Nygaard).

1961   "Ich" und "Er" in der Ezrageschichte. In A. Kuschke, 211–33.

Muilenburg, J.

1940   The Literary Character of Isaiah 34. JBL 59:339–65. Reprint, Muilenburg 1984, 59–85.

1953   A Study of Hebrew Rhetoric: Repetition and Style. VTSup 1:97–111.

1961   The Linguistic and Rhetorical Usages of the Particle *kî* in the Old Testament. HUCA 32:135–60. Reprint, Muilenburg 1984, 208–33.

1965   The Office of Prophet in Ancient Israel. In J. P. Hyatt, 74–97. Reprint, Muilenburg 1984, 127–50.

1968   The Intercession of the Covenant Mediator: Ex 33:1a, 12–17. In P. R. Ackroyd and B. Lindars, 159–81. Reprint, Muilenburg 1984, 170–92.

1969   Form Criticism and Beyond. JBL 88:1–18.

1984   *Hearing and Speaking the Word: Selections from the Works of James Muilenburg.* Ed. T. F. Best. Homage Series. Chico, Calif.: Scholars Press.

Mulder, M. J.

1988   *Mikra: Text, Translation, Reading and Interpretation of the Hebrew Bible in Ancient Judaism and Early Christianity.* CRINT. Assen/Maastricht: VanGorcum; Philadelphia: Fortress.

1991   Die Partikel אִם als Konjunktion und Interjektion im biblischen Hebräisch. In K. Jongeling, H. L. Murre-van den Berg, and L. van Rompay, 132–42.

Müller, H. P.

1984   Ebla und das althebräische Verbalsystem. Bib 65:145–67.

Muller, R. A.
1980   The Debate over the Vowel Points and the Crisis in Orthodox Herme-
        neutics. *Journal of Medieval and Renaissance Studies* 10:53–72.
Muraoka, T.
1972   Notes on the Aramaic of the Genesis Apocryphon. *RevQ* 8/29:7–51.
1975   The *Nun energicum* and the prefix conjugation in Biblical Hebrew. *AJBI*
        1:63–71.
1976   Segolate Nouns in Biblical and Other Aramaic Dialects. *JAOS* 96:226–35.
1985   *Emphatic Words and Structures in Biblical Hebrew.* Leiden: Brill.
1989   Review of *Sintassi del verbo ebraico nella prosa biblica classica,* by A. Nic-
        cacci. *AbrN* 27:187–93.
1991a   A *Grammar of Biblical Hebrew.* Trans. and rev. of Joüon 1923. Subsidia
        Biblica 14/I, II. Rome: Pontifical Biblical Institute.
1991b   The Biblical Hebrew Nominal Clause with a Prepositional Phrase. In
        K. Jongeling, H. L. Murre-van den Berg, and L. van Rompay, 143–51.
1993   A *Greek-English Lexicon of the Septuagint. Twelve Prophets.* Louvain:
        Peeters.
Muraoka, T., and Z. Shavitsky
1990   Abraham Ibn Ezra's Biblical Hebrew Lexicon: The Minor Prophets I.
        AbrN 28:53–75.
1991   Abraham Ibn Ezra's Biblical Hebrew Lexicon: The Minor Prophets II.
        AbrN 29:106–28.
Murray, D. F.
1987   The Rhetoric of Disputation: Re-examination of a Prophetic Genre. *JSOT*
        38:95–121.
Murtonen, A.
1953   On the Interpretation of the *Matres Lectionis* in Biblical Hebrew. *ABR*
        14:66–121.
Myers, J. M.
1959   *The Books of Hosea, Joel, Amos, Obadiah and Jonah.* The Laymen's Bible
        Commentary 14. Atlanta: John Knox.
Na'aman, N.
1974   Sennacherib's "Letter to God" on His Campaign to Judah. *BASOR*
        214:25–39.
1979   Sennacherib's Campaign to Judah and the Date of the *LMLK* Stamps. *VT*
        29:61–86.
1986   Hezekiah's Fortified Cities and the *LMLK* Stamps. *BASOR* 261:5–21.
1990   The Historical Background to the Conquest of Samaria (720 B.C.). *Bib*
        71:206–25.
1995   "The house-of-no-shade shall take away its tax from you" (Micah i 11). *VT*
        45:516–27.
Neary, M.
1986   The Importance of Lament in the God/Man Relationship in Ancient Israel.
        ITQ 52:180–92.
Neiderhiser, E. A.
1981   Micah 2:6–11: Considerations on the Nature of the Discourse. *BTB*
        11:104–7.
Nestle, E.
1909   Miszellen. Micha 4,3. ZAW 29:234.

Neumann, P. K. D.
  1973   Das Wort, das geschehen ist . . . *VT* 23:171–217.
Newman, L.
  1918   *Studies in Biblical Parallelism.* Berkeley: University of California Press.
Newsom, C. A., and S. H. Ringe, eds.
  1992   *The Women's Bible Commentary.* London: SPCK; Louisville, Ky.: West-
               minster/John Knox Press.
Newsome, J. D.
  1986   *The Hebrew Prophets.* Louisville, Ky.: Westminster/John Knox Press.
Newton, T.
  1826   *Dissertations on the Prophecies Which Have Remarkably Been Fulfilled,*
               and at This Time Are Fulfilling in the World. London: Thomas Tegg.
Niccacci, A.
  1987   A Neglected Point of Hebrew Syntax: *Yiqtol* and Position in the Sentence.
               Liber Annuus 37:7–19.
  1988   Basic Principles of the Biblical Hebrew Verbal System in Prose. *Liber*
               Annuus 38:7–16.
  1989   *Un profeta tra oppressori e oppressi. Analisi esegetica del capitola 2 di*
               Michea nel piano generale del libro. Studium Biblicum Franciscanum
               Analecta 27. Jerusalem: Franciscan Printing Press.
  1990   *The Syntax of the Verb in Classical Hebrew Prose.* Trans. W. G. E. Watson.
               JSOTSup 86. Sheffield: Sheffield Academic Press.
Nicholson, E. W.
  1970   *Preaching to the Exiles.* New York: Schocken.
  1986   *God and His People: Covenant and Theology in the Old Testament.* Oxford:
               Clarendon Press.
Nielsen, E.
  1954   *Oral Tradition: A Modern Problem in Old Testament Introduction.* SBT 11.
               London: SCM.
Nielsen, K.
  1978   *Yahweh as Prosecutor and Judge: An Investigation of the Prophetic Lawsuit*
               (Rîb-*Pattern*). JSOTSup 9. Sheffield: University of Sheffield.
Norin, S.
  1979   JÔ Namen und J^eHÔ Namen. *VT* 29:87–97.
  1980   YW-Names and YHW-Names: A Reply to A. R. Millard. *VT* 30:239–40.
  1986   *Sein Name allein ist hoch*: Das Jhw-haltige Suffix althebräischer Personen-
               namen untersucht mit besonderer Berücksichtigung der alttestament-
               lischen Redaktionsgeschichte. CBOTS 24. Lund: Gleerup.
  1988   Die Wiedergabe JHWH-haltiger Personennamen in der Septuaginta.
               SJOT 1:76–95.
Norton, D.
  1993   *A History of the Bible as Literature.* Cambridge: Cambridge University
               Press.
Norton, G. J., and S. Pisano, eds.
  1991   *Tradition of the Text: Studies Offered to Dominique Barthélemy in Celebra-*
               tion of His 70th Birthday. OBO 109. Freiburg/Göttingen: Vandenhoeck &
               Ruprecht.

Noth, M.
1928   *Die israelitischen Personennamen im Rahmen der gemeinsemitischen Na-mengebung.* BWANT III, 10. Stuttgart: Kohlhammer. Reprint, Hildesheim: Olms, 1966.
1948   *Überlieferungsgeschichte des Pentateuch.* Stuttgart: Kohlhammer.

Nötscher, F.
1949   *Zwölfprophetenbuch oder kleine Propheten.* Echter-Bibel. Würzburg: Echter.

Nowack, W.
1884   Bemerkungen über das Buch Micha. ZAW 4:277–91.
1922   *Die kleinen Propheten.* 3d ed. HAT III Abteilung, 4 Band. Göttingen: Vandenhoeck & Ruprecht.

Nunes Carriera, J.
1981   Micha—ein Ältester von Moreshet? TTZ 90:19–28.
1982   Kuntsprache und Weisheit bei Micha. BZ 26:50–74.

O'Connor, M. P.
1980   *Hebrew Verse Structure.* Winona Lake, Ind.: Eisenbrauns.
1987a   The Pseudosorites in Hebrew Verse. In E. W. Conrad and E. G. Newing, 239–53.
1987b   The Pseudosorites: A Type of Paradox in Hebrew Verse. In E. R. Follis, 161–72.
1987c   Irish Bull and Pseudosorites: Two Types of Paradox in English. *Ars Semeiotica* 10:271–85.
1988   Yahweh the Donor. *AulaOr* 6:47–60.

Oberholzer, J. P.
1972   Micah 1:10–16 and the Septuagint. *Hervormde Teologiese Studies* 28:74–85.

Oded, B.
1979   *Mass Deportations and Deportees in the Neo-Assyrian Empire.* Wiesbaden: Reichert.

Oeming, M.
1989   "Ich habe einen Greis gegessen." Kannibalismus und Autophagie als Topos der Kriegsnotschilderung in der Kilamuwa-Inschrift, Zeile 5–8, im Alten Orient und im Alten Testament. *BN* 47:90–106.

Oesch, J. M.
1979   *Petucha und Setuma: Untersuchungen zu einer überlieferten Gliederung im hebräischen Text des Alten Testaments.* OBO 27. Göttingen: Vandenhoeck & Ruprecht.

Ollenburger, B. C.
1987   *Zion, the City of the Great King.* JSOTSup 41. Sheffield: JSOT Press.

Olley, J. W.
1975   Biblical Exegesis in a Cross-Cultural Context: The Study of the Septuagint. *SEAJT* 16/1:1–12.

Olyan, S. M.
1987   Some Observations Concerning the Identity of the Queen of Heaven. *UF* 19:161–74.
1988   *Asherah and the Cult of Yahweh in Israel.* SBLMS 34. Atlanta: Scholars Press.

Orelli, C. von
  1908   *Die zwölf kleinen Propheten.* 3d ed. Kurgefasster Kommentar zu den Heili-
            gen Schriften Alten und Neuen Testaments. Munich: Becksche.
Orlinsky, H. M.
  1956   Notes on the Present State of the Textual Criticism of the Judean Biblical
            Cave Scrolls. In A *Stubborn Faith, Papers on Old Testament and Related
            Subjects Presented to Honor William Andrew Irwin,* ed. E. C. Hobbs, 117–
            31. Dallas: Southern Methodist University Press.
  1959   Qumran and the Present State of Old Testament Text Studies: The Septu-
            agint Text. *JBL* 78:26–33.
  1961   The Textual Criticism of the Old Testament. In *BANE* (Wright 1961),
            113–32.
  1965   The Seer in Ancient Israel. *Oriens Antiquus* 4:153–74. [Parts of this paper
            were used in *The World History of the Jewish People,* ed. B. Mazar. Vol. 3,
            chap. 12.] Reprinted as "The Seer-Priest and the Prophet in Ancient Israel"
            in Orlinsky 1974, 39–63.
  1974   *Essays in Biblical Culture and Bible Translation.* New York: KTAV.
  1989   The Septuagint. In *CHJ, vol.* 2, ed. W. D. Davies and L. Finkelstein, 534–
            62. Cambridge: Cambridge University Press.
Osborn, A. R.
  1932   The Nature of True Religion: Micah 6:1–8. *BRev* 17:232–39.
Osswald, E.
  1962   *Falsche Prophetie im Alten Testament.* Tübingen: Mohr.
Otto, E.
  1991   Techniken der Rechtssatzredaktion israelitischer Rechtsbücher in der
            Redaktion des Prophetenbuches Micha. *SJOT* 2:119–50.
  1992   Micha/Michabuch. *TRE* 22, no. 4/5:695–704.
Otzen, B.
  1984   Heavenly Visions in Early Judaism: Origin and Function. In W. B. Barrick
            and J. R. Spencer, 199–215.
  1989   Indskrifterne fra Kuntillet Ajrud. Tekst-Form-Function. *SEÅ* 54:151–64.
Overholt, T. W.
  1970   *The Threat of Falsehood: A Study in the Theology of the Book of Jeremiah.*
            SBT 16. London: SCM.
  1989   *Channels of Prophecy: The Social Dynamics of Prophetic Activity.* Minne-
            apolis: Fortress.
  1990   Prophecy in History: the Social Reality of Intermediation. *JSOT* 48:3–29.
Pannell, R. J.
  1988   The Politics of the Messiah: A New Reading of Micah 4:4–5:5. *PRS*
            15:131–43.
Pardee, D.
  1978   A Philological and Prosodic Analysis of the Ugaritic Serpent Incantation
            UT 607. *JANES* 10:73–108.
  1982   *Handbook of Ancient Hebrew Letters.* SBLSBS 15. Chico, Calif.: Scholars
            Press.
  1988   *Ugaritic and Hebrew Poetic Parallelism: A Trial Cut (ʿnt I and Proverbs 2).*
            VTSup 39. Leiden: Brill.
Parker, S. B.
  1978   Possession Trance and Prophecy in Pre-Exilic Israel. *VT* 28:271–85.

1993 Official Attitudes toward Prophecy at Mari and in Israel. *VT* 43:50–68.

1994 The Lachish Letters and Official Reactions to Prophecies. In *Uncovering Ancient Stones: Essays in Memory of H. Neil Richardson*, ed. L. M. Hopfe, 65–78. Winona Lake, Ind.: Eisenbrauns.

Paul, S. M., and W. G. Dever
1973 *Biblical Archaeology.* Jerusalem: Keter.

Peckham, B.
1993 *History and Prophecy. The Development of Late Judean Literary Traditions.* The Anchor Bible Reference Library. New York: Doubleday.

Pelser, H. S.
1973 Some Remarks Regarding the Contrast in Micah 5:1 and 2. *Die Ou Testamentiese Werkgemeenskap in Suid-Afrika* 16:35–44.

Petersen, D. L.
1977 *Late Israelite Prophecy. Studies in Deuteroprophetic Literature and in Chronicles.* SBLMS 23. Missoula, Mont.: Scholars Press.

1981 *The Roles of Israel's Prophets.* JSOTSup 17. Sheffield: University of Sheffield Press.

1987 *Prophecy in Israel.* IRT 10. London: SPCK.

Petersen, D. L., and K. H. Richards
1992 *Interpreting Hebrew Poetry.* Minneapolis: Fortress.

Petrotta, A. J.
1991 *Lexis Ludens: Wordplay and the Book of Micah.* American University Studies; Series VII, Theology and Religion 105. New York/San Francisco/ Bern: Lang.

Pettinato, G.
1975 Testi cuneiformi del 3. millennio in paleo-cananeo rinvenuti nella campagna 1974 a Tell Mardikh = Ebla. *Or* 44:361–74.

1976 The Royal Archives of Tell-Mardikh-Ebla. *BA* 39:44–52.

1980 Polytheismus und Henotheismus in der Religion von Ebla. In O. Keel, 31–48.

Pfeiffer, R. H.
1952 *Introduction to the Old Testament.* London: Adam and Charles Black.

Pixley, G. V.
1991 Micah—A Revolutionary. In D. Jobling, P. L. Day, and G. T. Sheppard, 53–60.

Ploeg, J. P. M. van der
1972 Eschatology in the Old Testament. *OTS* 17:89–99.

Polzin, R.
1976 *Late Biblical Hebrew: Toward an Historical Typology of Biblical Hebrew Prose.* HSM 12. Missoula, Mont.: Scholars Press.

Pope, M. H.
1973 *Job.* AB 15. Garden City, N.Y.: Doubleday.

Popper, W.
1918–23 *Studies in Biblical Parallelism.* Berkeley: University of California Press.

1931 *The Prophetic Poetry of Isaiah Chapters 1–37.* Berkeley: University of California Press.

Posner, A.
1924 *Das Buch des Propheten Micha.* Frankfurt am Main: Kauffmann.

Posner, R.
1982   *Rational Discourse and Poetic Communication: Methods of Linguistic, Literary, and Philosophical Analysis.* Janua Linguarum, Series Maior 103. The Hague: Mouton.
Poulter, A. J., and G. I. Davies
1990   The Samaria Ostraca: Two Onomastic Notes. *VT* 60:237–40.
Praetorius, Fr.
1924   Zum Micha-Schluss. *Zeitschrift für Semitistik* 3:72–73.
Premnath, D. N.
1988   Latifundialization and Isaiah 5:8–10. *JSOT* 40:49–60.
Price, J. D.
1990   *The Syntax of Masoretic Accents in the Hebrew Bible. Studies in the Bible and Early Christianity* 27. Lewiston, N.Y.: Edwin Mellen Press.
Proksch, O.
1910   *Die kleinen prophetischen Schriften vor dem Exil.* Erläuterung zum Alten Testament, 3 Teil. Calwer & Stuttgart: Vereinsbuchhandlung.
Puech, É.
1974   L'inscription du tunnel de Siloé. *RB* 81:196–214.
Pusey, E. B.
1866   *The Minor Prophets.* Oxford: Parker.
Qimron, E.
1986–87   Consecutive and Conjunctive Imperfect: The Form of the Imperfect with WAW in Biblical Hebrew. *JQR* 77:149–61.
1986   *The Hebrew of the Dead Sea Scrolls.* Atlanta: Scholars Press.
Rabin, C., ed.
1961   *Studies in the Bible.* ScrHier 8. Jerusalem: Magnes Press, the Hebrew University.
Rabinowitz, I.
1984   *'āz* Followed by Imperfect Verb-Form in Preterite Contexts: A Redactional Device in Biblical Hebrew. *VT* 34:53–62.
Radday, Y. T.
1986   "Wie ist sein Name?" (Ex 3:13). *LB* 58:87–104.
Radday, Y. T., and H. Shore
1976   The Definite Article: A Type- and/or Author-Specifying Discriminant in the Hebrew Bible. *Association for Literary and Linguistic Computing Bulletin* 4:23–31.
Rainey, A. F.
1974   Dust and Ashes. *TA* 1/2:77–83.
1975   The Identification of Philistine Gath. *EI* 12:63–76*.
1978   The Toponymics of Eretz-Israel. *BASOR* 231:1–17.
1983   The Biblical Shephelah of Judah. *BASOR* 251:1–22.
1986   The Ancient Hebrew Prefix Conjugation in the Light of Amarnah Canaanite. *HS* 27:4–19.
1988   Further Remarks on the Hebrew Verbal System. *HS* 28:35–42.
Ramsey, G. W.
1977   Speech-Forms in Hebrew Law and Prophetic Oracles. *JBL* 96:45–58.
Ratner, R.
1987   *Derek*: Morpho-Syntactical Considerations. *JAOS* 107:471–73.

1988   Does a *ṭ*-Preformative Third Person Masculine Plural Verbal Form Exist in Biblical Hebrew? *VT* 38:80–88.

Rebera, B.

1981   The Book of Ruth: Dialogue and Narrative. Ph.D. diss., Macquarie University.

1987   Lexical Cohesion in Ruth: A Sample. In E. W. Conrad and E. G. Newing, 123–49.

Reicke, B.

1947   Mik. 7 såsom "messiansk" text med sörskild hänsyn till Matt. 10,35f. och Luk. 12,53. *SEÅ* 12:279–302.

1967   Liturgical Traditions in Micah 7. *HTR* 60:349–67.

Reider, J.

1930   The Present State of Textual Criticism of the Old Testament. *HUCA* 7:285–315.

1954   Etymological Studies in Biblical Hebrew. *VT* 4:276–95.

Reiling, J.

1971   The Use of *ΨΕΥΔΟΠΡΟΦΗΤΗΣ* in the Septuagint, Philo, and Josephus. *NovT* 13:147–56.

1973   *Hermas and Christian Prophecy: A Study of the Eleventh Mandate.* NovTSup 37. Leiden: E. J. Brill.

Reiner, E.

1958   *Šurpu: A Collection of Sumerian and Akkadian Incantations.* Archiv für Orientforschung. Beiheft 11. Graz: Im Selbstverlage des Herausgebers.

Reinke, L.

1974   *Der Prophet Micha.* Geissen: Emil Roth.

Renaud, B.

1961   La prophétie de Michée. *BTS* 42:4–5.

1964   *Structure et attachés littéraires de Michée IV–V.* CahRB 2. Paris: Gabalda.

1977   *La formation du livre de Michée. Traditions et actualisation.* ÉBib. Paris: Gabalda.

1983   Et toi, Bethléem, petite parmi les clans de Juda. *MB* 30:31–32.

Rendsburg, G. A.

1980a   Evidence for Spoken Hebrew in Biblical Times. Ph.D. diss., New York University.

1980b   Late Biblical Hebrew and the Date of "P." *JANES* 12:65–80.

1982   Dual Personal Pronouns and Dual Verbs in Hebrew. *JQR* 73:38–58.

Rendsburg, G., et al., eds.

1980   *The Bible World: Essays in Honor of Cyrus H. Gordon.* New York: KTAV and The Institute of Hebrew Culture and Education of New York University.

Rendtorff, R., and K. Koch, eds.

1961   *Studien zur Theologie der alttestamentlichen Überlieferungen.* Neukirchen: Neukirchener Verlag.

Renz, J., and W. Röllig

1995   *Handbuch der althebräischen Epigraphik.* Darmstadt: Wissenschaftliche Buchgesellschaft.

Revell, E. J.

1970   Studies in the Palestinian Vocalization of Hebrew. In J. W. Wevers and D. B. Redford, 51–100.

| 1979 | The Conditioning of Stress Position in WAW Consecutive Perfect Forms in Biblical Hebrew. *HAR* 3:277–300. |

1979   The Conditioning of Stress Position in WAW Consecutive Perfect Forms in Biblical Hebrew. *HAR* 3:277–300.

1984   Stress and the *Waw* "Consecutive" in Biblical Hebrew. *JAOS* 104:437–44.

1987   Stress Position in Hebrew Verb Forms with Vocalic Affix. *JSS* 32:249–71.

1988   First Person Imperfect Forms with *waw* Consecutive. *VT* 38:419–26.

1989   The System of the Verb in Standard Biblical Prose. *HUCA* 60:1–37.

1990   *VIII International Congress of the International Organization for Masoretic Studies, Chicago 1988.* Atlanta: Scholars Press.

Reventlow, H. G.

1968   *Opfere deinen Sohn.* Biblische Studien 53. Neukirchen-Vluyn: Neukirchener Verlag.

1996   Participial Formulations: Lawsuit not Wisdom—A Study in Prophetic Language. In M. V. Fox et al., 375–82.

Reviv, H.

1977   "Elders" and Saviors." *OrAnt* 16, no. 3:201–4.

1989   *The Elders in Ancient Israel. A Study of a Biblical Institution.* Jerusalem: Magnes.

Richter, G.

1914   Erläterungen zu dunkeln Stellen in den kleinen Propheten. BFCT 18, 3/4 Heft: 275–473.

Richter, W.

1987   Lakiš 3—Vorschlag zur Konstitutionen eines Textes. *BN* 37:73–103.

Reiszler, P.

1911   *Die Kleinen Propheten oder das Zwölfprophetenbuch.* Rottenburg: Bader.

Rin, S.

1963   Ugaritic–Old Testament Affinities. *BZ* 7:22–33.

Rinaldi, G.

1969   *I Profeti Minori, Fascicolo III: Michea Nahum Abacuc Sofonia Aggeo Zaccaria Malachia.* Turin: Marietti.

Roberts, J. J. M.

1973   The Davidic Origin of the Zion Tradition. *JBL* 92:329–44.

1985   Isaiah 2 and the Prophet's Message to the North. *JQR* 75:290–308.

Robertson, D. A.

1972   *Linguistic Evidence in Dating Early Hebrew Poetry.* SBLDS 3. Missoula, Mont.: Scholars Press.

Robinson, T. H.

1921   The Ecstatic Element in Old Testament Prophecy. *The Expositor* (8th ser.) 21:217–38.

1938   *Die zwölf kleinen Propheten.* HAT 14. Tübingen: Mohr.

1947   *The Poetry of the Old Testament.* London: Gerald Duckworth.

1953a   *Prophecy and the Prophets in Ancient Israel².* London: Gerald Duckworth.

1953b   Hebrew Poetic Form. In *Congress Volume: Copenhagen 1953.* VTSup 1:128–49. Leiden: Brill.

Robinson, T. H., and F. Horst

1964   *Die zwölf kleinen Propheten.* 3d ed. HAT 1/14. Tübingen: Mohr.

de Roche, M.

1983   Yahweh's *rîb* against Israel: A Reassessment of the So-called Prophetic Lawsuit in the Preexilic Prophets. *JBL* 102:563–74.

Rodd, C. S.
1986   Talking Points from Books: L. Epsztein, *Justice in the Ancient Near East* and the *People of the Bible*. *ExpT* 97:354–55.
1986   Talking Points from Books: Oracles of God. *ExpT* 98:66–68.
Romerowski, R.
1990   Que signifie le mot ḥesed? *VT* 40:89–103.
Roorda, T.
1869   *Commentarius in Vaticinium Michae*. Leipzig: Weigel.
Rosen, A. M.
1986   Environmental Change and Settlement at Tel Lachish. *BASOR* 263:55–60.
Rosenbaum, J.
1979   Hezekiah's Reform and the Deuteronomistic Tradition. *HTR* 72:23–43.
Rosenberg, J.
1986   *King and Kin: Political Allegory in the Hebrew Bible*. Indiana Studies in Biblical Literature. Bloomington: Indiana University Press.
Rosenberg, R. A.
1965   Jesus, Isaac, and the "Suffering Servant." *JBL* 84:381–88.
Roth, W. M. W.
1962   The Numerical Sequence x/x+1 in the OT. *VT* 12:300–11.
1965   *Numerical Sayings in the OT. A Form-Critical Study*. VTSup 13. Leiden: Brill.
Rottenberg, M.
1979   *šimʿû ʿammîm kullām*. Beth mikra 24:266–68.
Rowley, H. H.
1945   The Nature of Old Testament Prophecy in the Light of Recent Study. *HTR* 38:1–38.
1963   Hezekiah's Reform and Rebellion. In *Men of God*, 98–132. London: Nelson.
Rowley, H. H., ed.
1950   *Studies in Old Testament Prophecy*. Presented to Professor Theodore H. Robinson. Edinburgh: T. & T. Clark.
Rudolph, W.
1972   Zu Micha 1,10–16. In J. Schreiner, 233–38.
1975   *Micha-Nahum-Habakkuk-Zephanja*. KAT Bd. 13/3. Gütersloh: Gütersloher Verlaghaus Gerd Mohn.
Ryder, E. T.
1962   The Languages of the Old Testament. In M. Black and H. H. Rowley, 66–69.
Ryssel, V.
1885   Die arabische Übersetzung des Micha in der Pariser und Londoner Polyglotte. *ZAW* 5:102–38.
1887   *Untersuchungen über die Textgestalt und die Echtheit des Buches Micha. Ein kritischer Commentar zu Micha*. Leipzig: S. Hirzel.
Sachsse, E.
1925   Untersuchungen zur hebräischen Metrik: Jes 2,2–4; Mi 4,1–3. *ZAW* 43:173–92.
Safren, J. D.
1988   Balaam and Abraham. *VT* 38:105–13.
Sakenfeld, K. D.
1978   *The Meaning of Ḥesed in the Hebrew Bible: A New Inquiry*. HSM 17. Missoula, Mont.: Scholars Press.

Sanders, J. A.
1977   Hermeneutics in True and False Prophecy. In *Canon and Authority: Essays in Old Testament Religion and Theology*, ed. B. O. Long and G. W. Coats, 21–41. Philadelphia: Fortress.
Sanderson, J. E.
1992   Micah. In C. A. Newsom and S. H. Ringe, 215–16.
Saracino, F.
1983   A State of Siege; Mi 5:4–5 and an Ugaritic Prayer. *ZAW* 95:263–69.
Sarfatti, G. B.
1990   Gleanings from Hebrew Epigraphy. *Leš* 55:43–53.
Sasson, V.
1986   The Book of Oracular Visions of Balaam from Deir ʿAlla. *UF* 17:283–309.
Saydon, P. P.
1955   Assonance in Hebrew as a Means of Expressing Emphasis. *Bib* 36:36–50, 287–304.
1959   The Use of Tenses in Deutero-Isaiah. *Bib* 40:290–301.
Scagliarini, F.
1990   Precisazioni sull'uso delle *matres lectionis* nelle iscrizioni ebraiche antiche. *Hen* 12:131–46.
Scheffler, E. H.
1985   Micah 4:1–5: An Impasse in Exegesis? *OTE* 3:46–61.
Schenker, A.
1988   L'origine de l'idée d'une alliance entre Dieu et Israël dans l'Ancien Testament. *RB* 95:184–94.
Schmidt, H.
1923   "Micha." *Die grossen Propheten*. SAT Abteilung 2, Band 2. Göttingen: Vandenhoeck & Ruprecht.
Schmitt, G.
1990   Moreschet Gat und Libna mit einem Anhang: zu Micha 1:10–16. *JNSL* 16:153–72.
Schneider, D. A.
1979   The Unity of the Book of the Twelve. Ph.D. diss., Yale University.
Schnutenhaus, F.
1964   Das Kommen und Erscheinen Gottes im Alten Testament. *ZAW* 76:1–21.
Schottroff, W.
1970   Das Weinberglied Jesajas, Jes. 5:1–7; Ein Beitrag zur Geschichte der Parabel. *ZAW* 82:68–91.
Schramm, G.
1964   *The Graphemes of Tiberian Hebrew*. University of California Publications: Near Eastern Studies 2. Los Angeles and Berkeley: University of California.
Schreiner, J., ed.
1972   *Wort, Lied und Gottesspruch: Beiträge zur Septuaginta: Festschrift für Joseph Ziegler*. FB. Würzburg: Echter Verlag.
Schumpp, M.
1950   *Das Buch der zwölf Propheten*. Herders Bibelkommentar 10/2. Freiburg i. B.: Herder.
Schwantes, S. J.
1962   A Critical Study of the Text of Micah. Ph.D. diss., Johns Hopkins University.

1963 A Note on Micah 5:1 (Hebrews 4:14). *AUSS* 1:105–7.
1964 Critical Notes on Micah 1:10–16. *VT* 14:454–61.

Scoggin, B. E.
1985 An Expository Exegesis: Micah 6:6–8. *Faith and Mission* 2:50–58.

Sebök, M.
1887 *Die syrische Uebersetzung der zwölf kleinen Propheten.* Breslau: Preuss und Jünger.

Seebass, H.
1974 אחרית *'achᵃrîth.* TWAT 1:207–12.

Segert, S.
1983 Ethiopic and Hebrew Prosody: Some Preliminary Observations. In *Ethiopic Studies Dedicated to Wolf Leslau*, ed. S. Segert and A. J. E. Bodrogligeti, 337–50. Wiesbaden: Otto Harrassowitz.
1984 *A Basic Grammar of the Ugaritic Language with Selected Texts and Glossary.* Berkeley: University of California Press.
1986 Symmetric and Asymmetric Verses in Hebrew Biblical Poetry. In *Proceedings of the Ninth World Congress of Jewish Studies: Jerusalem, August 4–12, 1985*, 33–37. Division A: The Period of the Bible. Jerusalem: World Union of Jewish Studies.

Sellin, E.
1925 Wann wurde das Moselied Dtn 32 gedichtet? ZAW 43:161–73.
1930 *Das Zwölfprophetenbuch übersetzt und erklärt.* 3d ed. KAT 12/1. Leipzig: A. Dichtersche Verlagsbuchhandlung D. Werner Scholl.

Shaw, C. S.
1987 Micah 1:10–16 Reconsidered. *JBL* 106:223–29.
1993 *The Speeches of Micah: A Rhetorical-Historical Analysis.* JSOTSup 145. Sheffield: JSOT.

Shea, W. H.
1988 Sennacherib's Description of Lachish and of Its Conquest. *AUSS* 26:171–80.
1990 The Khirbet el-Qom Tomb Inscription Again. *VT* 60:110–16.

Sheppard, G. T.
1982 More on Isaiah 5:1–7 as a Juridical Parable. *CBQ* 44:45–47.
1988 True and False Prophecy within Scripture. In G. M. Tucker, D. L. Petersen, and R. R. Wilson, 262–82.

Shoot, F. van B.
1951 The Fertility Religions in the Thought of Amos and Micah. Ph.D. diss., University of Southern California.

Sievers, E.
1907 Alttestamentliche Miscellen. *Berichte über die Verhandlungen der königlichen sächsischen Gesellschaft zu Wissenschaften* 59:76–109.

Sievi, J.
1970 Wie es zur Zeit des Propheten Micha in Juda aussah. Situation und geistiger Hintergrund des Auftretens des Propheten. *BK* 25:102–3.

Sinclair, L. A.
1983 Hebrew Text of the Qumran Micah Pesher and Textual Traditions of the Minor Prophets. *RevQ* 11:253–63.

Sirat, R. S.
1971 Est-ce que *yam*, en hébreu biblique, désigne toujours la direction de l'occident? In Avigad et al., 209–20.

Ska, J. L.
   1988   Gn 22,1–19. Essai sur les niveaux de lecture. *Bib* 69:324–39.
Skipwith, G. H.
   1894   On the Structure of the Book of Micah and on Isaiah ii.2–5. *JQR* 6:583–86.
Smith, G. A.
   1899   *The Book of the Twelve Prophets Commonly Called the Minor*. 6th ed. Vol. 1.
                Amos, Hosea and Micah. ExB. London: Hodder and Stoughton.
   1931   *The Historical Geography of the Holy Land*. 25th ed. Reprint, New York
                and Evanston: Harper & Row, 1966.
Smith, J. M. P.
   1908   The Strophic Structure of the Book of Micah. In R. F. Harper, F. Brown,
                and G. F. Moore, 415–38.
   1914   *A Commentary on the Books of Amos, Hosea and Micah. The Bible for
                Home and School*. New York: Macmillan.
Smith, J. M. P., W. H. Ward, and J. Bewer
   1911   *A Critical and Exegetical Commentary on Micah, Zephaniah, Nahum,
                Habakkuk, Obadiah and Joel*. ICC. Edinburgh: T. & T. Clark.
Smith, L. P.
   1952   The Book of Micah. *Int* 6:210–27.
Smith, M.
   1975   A Note on Burning Babies. *JAOS* 95:477–79.
Smith, R. L.
   1984   *Micah–Malachi*. Word Biblical Commentary. Vol. 32. Waco, Tex.: Word
                Books.
Smith, W. R.
   1895   *The Prophets of Israel and Their Place in History*. Ed. T. K. Cheyne. London:
                Adam and Charles Black.
Snaith, N. H.
   1956   *Amos, Hosea, and Micah*. Preacher's Commentaries. London: Epworth.
Soden, W. von
   1988   Hurritisch *uatnannu* > Mittelassyrisch *utnannu* und > Ugaritisch *itnn* >
                Hebräisch *'ätnan* "ein Geschenk, Direnlohn." *UF* 20:309–11.
   1990a   Rhythmische Gestaltung und intendierte Aussage im Alten Testament
                und in babylonischen Dichtungen. *ZAH* 3:179–206.
   1990b   Zu einigen Ortsbenennungen bei Amos und Micha. *ZAH* 3:214–20.
Speiser, E. A.
   1958   In Search of Nimrod. *Eretz-Israel* 5:32*–36*. Reprint, Speiser 1967, 41–
                52.
   1960   "People" and "Nation" of Israel. *JBL* 79:157–63. Reprint, Speiser 1967,
                160–70.
   1964   *Genesis*: Anchor Bible I. Garden City, N.Y.: Doubleday.
   1967   *Oriental and Biblical Studies: Collected Writings of E. A. Speiser*. Ed. J. J.
                Finkelstein and M. Greenberg. Philadelphia: University of Pennsylvania
                Press.
Sperber, A.
   1962   *The Bible in Aramaic*. Vol. 3. Leiden: Brill.
   1966   *A Historical Grammar of Biblical Hebrew: A Presentation of Problems with
                Suggestions to Their Solutions*. Leiden: Brill.

Spiegel, S.
1967   *The Last Trial: On the Legends and Lore of the Command to Abraham to Of-fer Isaac as a Sacrifice: The Akedah.* Trans. J. Goldin. New York: Pantheon.

Stacey, W. D.
1982   A Pre-Battle Rite in Ancient Israel? *Studia Evangelica* 7:471–73.

Stade, B.
1881   Bemerkungen über das Buch Micha. ZAW 1:161–72.
1883   Weitere Bemerkungen zu Micha 4.5. ZAW 3:1–16.
1884   Bemerkungen zu Nowack über das Buch Micha. ZAW 4:277–91.
1886a   Miscellen 12. Mic. 2,4. ZAW 6:122–23.
1886b   Miscellen 15. »Auf Jemandes Knieen gebären« Gen. 30,3; 50:23; Hiob 3:12 und אֲבָנִים Exod. 1,16. ZAW 6:143–56.
1903   Micha 1,2–4 und 7,7–20 ein Psalm. ZAW 23:163–77.
1904   Streiflichter auf die Entstehung der jetzigen Gestalt der alttestamentlichen Prophetenschriften. ZAW 23:153–71.

Staerk, W.
1891   Der Gebrauch der Wendung *bĕ'aḥărît hayyāmîm* im alttestamentlichen Kanon. ZAW 11:247–53.

Stager, L. E.
1980   The Rite of Child Sacrifice at Carthage. In *New Light on Ancient Carthage*, ed. J. G. Pedley, 1–11. Ann Arbor: University of Michigan Press.

Stager, L. E., and S. R. Wolff
1984   Child Sacrifice at Carthage: Religious Rite or Population Control? BAR 10:30–51.

Stamm, J. J.
1980   *Beiträge zur hebräischen und altorientalischen Namenkunde: Zu seinem 70. Geburtstag herausgegeben von Ernst Jenni und Martin A. Klopfenstein.* OBO 30. Friburg, Suise: Editions Universitaires; Göttingen: Vandenhoeck & Ruprecht.

Stansell, G.
1988   *Micah and Isaiah: A Form and Tradition Historical Comparison.* SBLDS 85. Atlanta: Scholars Press.

Stec, D. M.
1987   The Use of *hen* in Conditional Sentences. *VT* 37:478–86.

Steiner, R. C.
1979   From Proto-Hebrew to Mishnaic Hebrew: The History of ךָ and הָ. HAR 3:157–74.
1987   *Lulav* versus **lu/law*: A Note on the Conditioning of **aw > u* in Hebrew and Aramaic. *JAOS* 107:121–22.

Sternberg, M.
1987   *The Poetics of Biblical Narrative: Ideological Literature and the Drama of Reading.* Indiana Studies in Biblical Literature. Bloomington: Indiana University Press.

Stoebe, H. J.
1959   Und demütig sein vor deinem Gott. Micha 6,8. WD 6:180–94.

Stohlmann, S.
1983   The Judean Exile after 701 B.C.E. In W. W. Hallo, J. C. Moyer, and L. G. Perdue, 147–75.

Strugnell, J.
1970   Notes en marge du volume V des "Discoveries in the Judaean Desert of
            Jordan." *RevQ* 26:163–276.
Strus, A.
1985   Interprétations des noms propres dans les oracles contre les nations. In
            Congress Volume: Salamanca, 1983, ed. J. A. Emerton, 272–85. VTSup 36.
            Leiden: Brill.
Strydom, J. G.
1986   A Critical Evaluation into A. S. van der Woude's Analysis of Micah with
            Special Reference to Micah 2:6–11b. *OTE* 4:197–215.
Stuart, D. K.
1976   *Studies in Early Hebrew Meter*. HSM 13. Missoula, Mont.: Scholars Press.
Suder, R. W.
1984   *Hebrew Inscriptions: A Classified Bibliography*. Selinsgrove, Pa.: Susque-
            hanna University Press.
Sweeney, M. A.
1987   Structure and Redaction in Isaiah 2–4. *HAR* 11:407–22.
1988   *Isaiah 1–4 and the Post-Exilic Understanding of the Isianic Tradition*.
            BZAW 171. Berlin: de Gruyter.
Swete, H. B.
1902   *An Introduction to the Old Testament in Greek*. Cambridge: Cambridge
            University Press. Reprint, New York: KTAV, 1968.
Swiggers, P.
1991   Nominal Sentence Negation in Biblical Hebrew: The Grammatical Sta-
            tus of אִין. In K. Jongeling, H. L. Murre-van den Berg, and L. van Rompay,
            173–79.
Tadmor, H., and M. Cogan.
1979   Ahaz and Tiglath-Pileser in the Book of Kings: Historiographic Consider-
            ations. *Bib* 60:491–508.
1988   *II Kings*. AB 11. New York: Doubleday.
Talmon, S.
1953   The Qumran *yḥd*—A Biblical Noun. *VT* 3:133–40. Reprint, Talmon 1989,
            53–60.
1978   The Presentation of Synchroneity and Simultaneity in Biblical Narrative.
            In *Studies in Hebrew Narrative Art throughout the Ages*, ed. J. Heinemann
            and S. Werses. *ScrHier* 27:9–26.
1989   *The World of Qumran from Within*. Collected Studies. Jerusalem: Magnes
            Press; Leiden: Brill.
Talstra, E.
1991   Biblical Clause Types and Clause Hierarchy. In K. Jongeling, H. L.
            Murre-van den Berg, and L. van Rompay, 180–93.
1994   Dialogue in Job 21. "Virtual Quotations" or Text Grammatical Markers?
            In W. A. M. Beuken, 329–48.
Tångberg, K. A.
1987   Eblaite. An Introduction to the State of Research on the Cuneiform Tablets.
            SJOT 2:111–20.
Taylor, J.
1890   *The Massoretic Text and the Ancient Versions of the Book of Micah*. London:
            Williams and Norgate.

Théodoridès, A., P. Naster, and J. Reis, eds.
1980   *L'enfant dans les civilisations orientales: Het kind in de oosterse beschavin-gen.* Acta Orientalia Belgica 2. Leuven: Éditions Peeters.

Theodore of Mopsuestia
1864   *Commentarius in XII Prophetas Minoras.* PG Tomus LXVI. Paris: J. P. Migne.

Thiele, E. R.
1965   *The Mysterious Numbers of the Hebrew Kings.* Grand Rapids, Mich.: Eerdmans.

Thompson, M. E. W.
1982   *Situation and Theology: Old Testament Interpretations of the Syro-Ephraimite War.* Prophets and Historians Series, 1. Sheffield: Almond Press.

Tidwell, N. L. A.
1975   *Wā'āmar* (Zech. 3:5) and the Genre of Zechariah's Fourth Vision. *JBL* 94:343–55.

Tobin, Y.
1991   Process and Result and the Hebrew Infinitive: A Study in Linguistic Iso-morphism. In K. Jongeling, H. L. Murre-van den Berg, and L. van Rompay, 194–209.

Torrance, T.
1952   The Prophet Micah and His Famous Saying. *EvQ* 24:206–14.

Tournay, R.
1964   Quelques sélectures bibliques antisamaritaines. *RB* 71:504–36.

Tov, E.
1981   *The Text-Critical Use of the Septuagint in Biblical Research.* Jerusalem: Simor.
1990   *The Greek Minor Prophets Scroll from Nahal Ḥever (8ḤevXIIgr) (The Seiyâl Collection I).* DJD VIII. Oxford: Clarendon Press.
1991   4QJer^c (4Q72). In G. J. Norton and S. Pisano, 249–76.
1992   *Textual Criticism of the Hebrew Bible.* Minneapolis: Fortress; Assen/Maa-stricht: Van Gorcum.
1994   Glosses, Interpolations, and Other Types of Scribal Additions in the Text of the Hebrew Bible. In S. E. Balentine and J. Barton, 40–66.

Treves, M.
1969   The Reign of God in the Old Testament. *VT* 19:230–43.

Trible, P.
1989   Bringing Miriam out of the Shadows. *BRev* 5:14–25, 34.

Tsumura, D. T.
1986   Literary Insertion, AXB Pattern, in Hebrew and Ugaritic. *UF* 18:351–61.
1988   "Inserted Bicolon," the AXYB Pattern, in Amos i 5 and Psalm ix 7. *VT* 38:234–36.

Tucker, G. M., D. L. Petersen, and R. R. Wilson, eds.
1988   *Canon, Theology, and Old Testament Interpretation: Essays in Honor of B. S. Childs.* Philadelphia: Fortress.

Ungern-Sternberg, R. F. von
1958   *Der Rechtsstreit Gottes mit seiner Gemeinde. Der Prophet Micha.* BAT Bd. 23.3. Stuttgart: Calwer Verlag.

Ussishkin, D.
1978   Excavations at Tel Lachish 1973–1977, Preliminary Report. *TA* 5, nos. 2–
            3:1–97.
1980   The Battle at Lachish, Israel. *Arch* 33, no. 1:56–59.
1982   *The Conquest of Lachish by Sennacherib*. Tel Aviv University Publications
            of the Institute of Archaeology 6. Tel Aviv: Tel Aviv University.
1983   Excavations at Tel Lachish 1978–1983, Second Preliminary Report. *TA*
            10:97–175.
1990   The Assyrian Attack on Lachish: The Archaeological Evidence from the
            Southwest Corner of the Site. *TA* 17:53–86.

van Rooden, P. T.
1989   *Theology, Biblical Scholarship and Rabbinical Studies in the Seventeenth
            Century: Constantijn L'Empereur (1591–1648) Professor of Hebrew and
            Theology at Leiden.* Studies in the History of Leiden University 6. Leiden:
            Brill.

Vanstiphout, H. L. J., et al., eds.
1986   *Scripta Signa Vocis: Studies about Scripts, Scripture, Scribes and Lan-
            guages in the Near East Presented to J. H. Hospers by his Pupils, Colleagues,
            and Friends.* Groningen: Egbert Forsten.

Vaughan, P. H.
1974   *The Meaning of "bâmâ" in the Old Testament.* SOTSMS 3. New York:
            Cambridge University Press.

Vawter, B.
1981   *Amos, Hosea, Micah with an Introduction to Classical Prophecy.* Old Testa-
            ment Message 7. Wilmington, Del.: Glazier.
1986   Yahweh: Lord of the Heavens and the Earth. *CBQ* 48:461–67.

Vegas Montaner, L.
1980   *Biblia del Mar Muerto, Profetas Menores, edición critica según manuscritos
            hebreos procedentes del Mar Muerto.* Textos y Estudios "Cardenal Cisneros,"
            29. Madrid: Instituto "Arias Montano."

Veijola, T.
1988   Das Opfer des Abraham—Paradigma des Glaubens aus dem nachexili-
            schen Zeitalter. *ZTK* 85:129–64.

Vergone, S.
1976   Micah 4, 14. *Beth Mikra* 66:392–401.
1981   Two Dirges Concerning Cities in Judah: A Literary-Historical Analysis of
            Mic. 1,10–16. In *Sefer Dr. Barukh Ben-Yehudah: mehkarim ba-Mikra uve-
            mahshevet Yîsra'el [Jubilee Volume Baruch Ben-Yehudah]*, ed. B. T. Lurya and
            M. Goldstein, 259–80. Tel-Aviv: ha-Hevrah le-heker ha-Mikra be-Yîsra'el
            be-shituf ha-Gimnasyah "Hertseliyah" u-"Vet ha-Tanakh" be-Tel-Aviv.

Vermeylen, J.
1977–78   *Du prophète Isaïe à l'apocalyptique: Isaïe, I–XXXV, miroir d'un demi-
            millenaire d'experience religieuse en Israel.* Etudes bibliques 47. Paris:
            J. Gabalda.

Vernant, J. P., et al.
1974   *Divination et rationalité.* Paris: Éditions du Seuil.

Victor, P.
1966   A note on *ḥoq* in the Old Testament. *VT* 16:358–61.

Vilnay, Z.
1939   The Topography of Israel in the Book of the Prophet Micah. *BJPES* 1:1–19.
Vincent, J. M.
1986   Michas Gerichtswort gegen Zion (3,12) in seinen Kontext. *ZTK* 83:167–87.
Vogt, E.
1953   Fragmenta Prophetarum Minorum Deserti Juda. *Bib* 34:219–72.
Vollers, K.
1883   Das Dodekapropheton der Alexandriner. *ZAW* 3:219–72.
1884   Das Dodekapropheton der Alexandriner (Schluss). *ZAW* 4:1–20.
von Rad, G.
1966   The City on the Hill. In *The Problem of the Hexateuch and Other Essays*, 232–42. New York: McGraw-Hill.
Vriezen, T. C.
1958   Einige Notizen zur Übersetzung des Bindewortes *kî*. In *Von Ugarit nach Qumran: Beiträge zur alttestamentlichen und altorientalischen Forschung. Otto Eissfeldt zum 1. September 1957 dargebracht von Freunden und Schülern*, ed. J. Hempel and L. Rost, 266–75. BZAW 77. Berlin: A. Töpelmann.
Vuilleumier, R., and C. A. Keller
1971   *Michée Nahoum Habacuc Sophonie*. Commentaire de l'Ancien Testament Xlb. Neuchâtel: Delachaux et Niestlé. 2d ed., 1990.
de Waard, J.
1979   Vers une identification des participants dans le livre Michée. *RHPR* 59:509–16.
1984   La Septante: Un traduction. In *Études sur la judäisme hellénistique*, 133–95. LD 119. Paris: Cerf.
Wade, G. W.
1925   *The Books of the Prophets Micah, Obadiah, Joel and Jonah*. Westminster Commentaries. London: Methuen.
Wagner, M.
1966   *Die lexikalischen und grammatikalischen Aramaismen im alttestamentlichen Hebräisch*. BZAW 96. Berlin: de Gruyter.
Waldman, N. M.
1989   *The Recent Study of Hebrew: A Survey of the Literature with Selected Bibliography*. Winona Lake, Ind.: Eisenbrauns.
Walters, P.
1973   *The Text of the Septuagint, Its Corruptions and Their Emendation*. Cambridge: Cambridge University Press.
Waltke, B. K., and M. O'Connor
1990   *An Introduction to Biblical Hebrew Syntax*. Winona Lake, Ind.: Eisenbrauns.
Ward, J. M.
1976   Micah the Prophet. In *IDBSup*, 592–93.
Warmuth, G.
1976   *Das Mahnwort: Seine Bedeutung für die Verkündigung der vorexilischen Propheten Amos, Hosea, Micha, Jesaja und Jeremia*. BBET 1. Frankfurt am Main: Peter Lang.
Watson, P.
1963   Form Criticism and an Exegesis of Micah 6:1–8. *ResQ* 7:62–72.

Watson, W. G. E.
1977   Reclustering Hebrew *'l yd-*. *Bib* 58:213–15.
1983   Further Examples of Semantic-Sonant Chiasmus. *CBQ* 45:31–34.
1984a   *Classical Hebrew Poetry: A Guide to Its Techniques*. JSOTSup 26. Sheffield: JSOT Press.
1984b   Allusion, Irony and Wordplay in Micah 1:7. *Bib* 65:103–5.
1984c   The Hebrew Word-Pair *'sp // qbṣ*. ZAW 96:426–34.
1988a   More on Metathetic Parallelism. WO 19:40–44.
1988b   Some Additional Wordpairs. In L. Eslinger and G. Taylor, 179–201.
1989   Internal or Half-Line Parallelism in Classical Hebrew Again. *VT* 39:44–66.
1993   Problems and Solutions in Hebrew Verse: A Survey of Recent Work. *VT* 43:372–84.

Watters, W. R.
1976   *Formula Criticism and the Poetry of the Old Testament*. BZAW 138. Berlin: de Gruyter.

Weil, G. E.
1971   *Massorah Gedolah iuxta codicem Leningradensem B 19a. Vol. I Catalogi*. Rome: Pontifical Biblical Institute.
1981   Les décomptes de versets, mots et lettres du Pentateuque selon le manuscrit B 19a de Leningrad. In *Mélanges Dominique Bartélemy. Études bibliques offertes a l'occasion de son 60e anniversaire*, ed. P. Casetti, O. Keel, and A. Schenker, 651–703. OBO 38. Göttingen: Vandenhoeck & Ruprecht.

Weil, H. M.
1940   Le Chapitre 2 de Michée expliqué par le Premier Livre de Rois, Chapitre 20–22. *RHR* 121:146–61.

Weinfeld, M.
1972   The Worship of Molech and of the Queen of Heaven and Its Background. *UF* 4:133–54.
1977   Ancient Near Eastern Patterns in Prophetic Literature. *VT* 27:178–95.
1978   Burning Babies in Ancient Israel. *UF* 10:411–13.
1981   Sabbath, Temple and the Enthronement of the Lord—The Problem of the Sitz im Leben of Genesis 1:1–2:3. In *Festschrift H. Cazelles*, 501–12. AOAT 212. Neukirchen-Vluyn: Neukirchener Verlag.
1984   Kuntillet Ajrud Inscriptions and Their Significance. *Studi epigrafici e linguistici* 1:121–30.
1991   *Deuteronomy 1–11*. AB 5. New York: Doubleday.

Weiser, A.
1956   *Das Buch der zwölf kleinen Propheten I: Die Propheten Hosea, Joel, Amos, Obadja, Jona, Micha*. ATD Teilbd. 24. Göttingen: Vandenhoeck & Ruprecht.

Welch, A. C.
1902   Micah V.1–3 (Eng. 2–4). *ExpT* 13:234–36.

Welch, J. W.
1981   *Chiasmus in Antiquity: Structures, Analyses Exegesis*. Hildesheim: Gerstenberg Verlag.

Wellhausen, J.
1892   *Die kleinen Propheten übersetzt und erklärt, mit Noten: Skizzen und Vorarbeiten 5*. Berlin: Reimer. (2d ed., 1893; 3d ed., 1898.) 4th ed. (unaltered reprint of the 3d ed.), Berlin: Walter de Gruyter, 1963.

Wendlund, E. R.
1995   *The Discourse Analysis of Hebrew Prophetic Literature. Determining the Larger Textual Units of Hosea and Joel.* Mellen Biblical Press Series 40. Lewiston/Queenston/Lampeter: Mellen Biblical Press.

Wénin, A.
1989   Abraham à la rencontre de YHWH. Une lecture de Gn 22. *RTL* 20:162–77.

Werbeck, W.
1960   Michabuch. *Die Religion in Geschichte und Gegenwart*[3] 4:929–31. Tübingen: Mohr.
1969–70   Zwölfprophetenbuch. *RGG*[3] 6. Tübingen: Mohr.

Werblowsky, R. J. Z.
1956   Stealing the Word. *VT* 6:105–6.

Wernberg-Møller, P. C. H.
1959   Observations on the Hebrew Participle. *ZAW* 71:54–67.

Werner, W.
1981   Israel in der Entscheidung Überlegungen zur Datierung und zur theologischen Aussage von Jes 1,4–9. In *Eschatologie: Bibeltheologische und philosophische Studien zum Verhältnis von Erlösungswelt und Wirklichkeitsbewältigung. Festschrift für Engelbert Neuhausler zur Emertierung gewidmet von Kollegen, Freunden und Schülern,* ed. R. Kilian, K. Funk, and P. Fasl, 59–72. St. Otillien: EOS Verlag.
1982   *Eschatologische Texte in Jesaja 1–39; Messias, Heilige Rest, Völker.* FB 46. Würzburg: Echter Verlag.
1988   Micha 6,8—eine alttestamentliche Kurzformel des Glaubens? Zum theologischen Verständnis von Mi 6,8. *BZ* 32:232–48.

Westermann, C.
1961   Predigtmeditation zu Micha 5,1–3. In G. Eichholz, 5:54–59.
1967   *Basic Forms of Prophetic Speech.* Trans. H. C. White. Philadelphia: Westminster.
1986   Zur Erforschung und zum Vertändnis der prophetischen Heilsworte. *ZAW* 98:1–13.
1989   Bedeutung und Funktion des Imperativ in den Geschichtsbüchern des Alten Testaments. In R. Mosis and L. Ruppert, 13–27.
1991   *Prophetic Oracles of Salvation in the Old Testament.* Trans. K. Crim. Louisville, Ky.: Westminster/John Knox Press.

Westhuizen, J. P. van der
1973   The Term ʾetnān in Micah. *Die Ou Testamentiese Werkgemeenskap in Suid-Afrika* 16:54–61.

Wevers, J. W., and D. B. Redford
1970   *Essays on the Ancient Semitic World.* Toronto Semitic Texts and Studies. Toronto: University of Toronto Press.

Whedbee, J. W.
1971   *Isaiah and Wisdom.* Nashville: Abingdon Press.

Whitelam, K. W.
1979   *The Just King: Monarchical Judicial Authority in Ancient Israel:* JSOTSup 12. Sheffield: JSOT Press.

Whitney, J. T.
1979   "Bamoth" in the Old Testament. *TB* 30:125–47.

Wickes, W.
1970   *Two Treatises on the Accentuation of the Old Testament*, ed. H. M. Orlinsky. LBS. New York: KTAV.

Widengren, G., et al.
1959   *The Sacral Kingship*. Contributions to the Central Theme of the VIIIth International Congress for the History of Religions (Rome, April 1955). Studies in the History of Religions (Supplements to *NVMEN*) IV. Leiden: Brill.

1984   Yahweh's Gathering of the Dispersed. In W. B. Barrick and J. R. Spencer, 227–45.

Wiklander, B.
1984   *Prophecy as Literature: A Text-Linguistic and Rhetorical Approach to Isaiah 2–4*. Coniectanea Biblica: Old Testament Series 22. Stockholm: CWK Gleerup.

Wildberger, H.
1957   Die Völkerwallfahrt zum Zion, Jes. II 1–5. *VT* 7:62–81.

1972   *Jesaja 1–12*. BKAT X/1. Neukirchen-Vluyn: Neukirchener Verlag.

1991   *Isaiah 1–12: A Commentary*. Trans. T. H. Trapp. Minneapolis: Fortress.

Wilken, R. L.
1976   Melito, the Jewish Community at Sardis, and the Sacrifice of Isaac. *TS* 37:53–69.

Willi-Plein, I.
1971   *Vorformen der Schriftexegese innerhalb des A.T. Untersuchungen zum literarischen Werden der auf Amos, Hosea und Micha zurückgehenden Bücher im hebräischen Zwölfprophetenbuch*. BZAW 123. Berlin: Walter de Gruyter.

Williams, J. G.
1967   The Alas-Oracles of the Eighth Century Prophets. *HUCA* 38:75–91.

Williams, R. J.
1976   *Hebrew Syntax: An Outline*[2]. Toronto: University of Toronto Press.

Willis, J. T.
1966   *The Structure, Setting and Interrelationships of the Pericopes in the Book of Micah*. Ph.D. diss., Vanderbilt Divinity School.

1967   On the Text of Micah 2,1aα–β. *Bib* 48:534–41.

1967–68   *Mimměkā lî yēṣē᾽* in Micah 5:1. *JQR* 58:317–22.

1968a   Micah 4:14–5:5, a Unit. *VT* 18:529–47.

1968b   A Note on *wa᾽omar* in Micah 3:1. *ZAW* 80:50–54.

1968c   Review of Theodor Lescow, Micah 6,6–8. *Studien zu Sprache, Form und Auslegung*. *VT* 18:273–78.

1968d   Some Suggestions on the Interpretation of Micah 1:2. *VT* 18:372–79.

1969a   The Structure of Micah 3–5 and the Function of Micah 5:9–14 in the Book. *ZAW* 81:191–214.

1969b   The Structure of the Book of Micah. *SEÅ* 34:5–42.

1969c   The Authenticity and Meaning of Micah 5:9–14. *ZAW* 81:353–68.

1970a   Fundamental Issues in Contemporary Micah Studies. *ResQ* 13:77–90.

1970b   Micah 2:6–8 and the "People of God" in Micah. *BZ* 14:72–87.

1974   A Reapplied Prophetic Hope Oracle. Studies in Prophecy. *VTSup* 26:64–76.

1977   The Genre of Isaiah 5:1–7. *JBL* 96:337–62.

1978   Thoughts on a Redactional Analysis of the Book of Micah. *SBLSP* 13:87–107.

1979   The Expression *be'acharith hayyamim* in the Old Testament. *ResQ* 22:60–71.

1987   Alternating (ABA'B') Parallelism in the Old Testament Psalms and Prophetic Literature. In E. R. Follis, 49–76.

Wilson, R.

1979   Prophecy and Ecstasy: A Reexamination. *JBL* 98:321–37.

1980   *Prophecy and Society in Ancient Israel.* Philadelphia: Fortress.

Van Winkle, D. W.

1989   1 Kings XIII: True and False Prophecy. *VT* 29:31–43.

Winton Thomas, D.

1948–49   The Root צנע in Hebrew and the Meaning of קדרנית in Malachi III,14. *JJS* 1:182–88.

1962   Micah. In M. Black and H. H. Rowley, 630–34.

1967   *Archaeology and Old Testament Study.* Oxford: Clarendon Press.

Wolfe, R. E.

1935   The Editing of the Book of the Twelve. *ZAW* 53:90–129.

1956   The Book of Micah. *IB* 6:897–949. Nashville: Abingdon.

Wolff, H. W.

1977   Wider die Propheten, die mein Volk verführen. *Widerstand und Anpassung beim Propheten Micha und Heute:* TBei 8:97–108.

1978a   *Mit Micha reden: Prophetie einst und jetzt.* Munich: Kaiser Verlag.

1978b   Wie verstand Micha von Moreschet sein prophetisches Amt? VTSup 29:403–17.

1978c   Micah the Moreshite—the Prophet and His Background. In J. G. Gammie et al., 77–84.

1980   *Dodekapropheton 4. Micha.* BKAT XIV/12. Neukirchen-Vluyn: Neukirchener.

1981a   *Dodekapropheton 4. Micha.* BKAT XIV/13. Neukirchen-Vluyn: Neukirchen Verlag.

1981b   *Micah the Prophet.* Trans. R. D. Gehrke. Philadelphia: Fortress.

1982   *Dodekapropheten 4. Micha.* BKAT XIV/14. Neukirchen-Vluyn: Neukirchener Verlag.

1985   Swords into Plowshares: Misuse of a Word of Prophecy. *Currents in Theology in Mission* 12:133–47.

1987   Use of the Bible in Theology: A Case Study. *ERT* 11:37–52.

1990   *Micah: A Commentary.* Trans. G. Stansell. Minneapolis: Augsburg Fortress Press.

Wolff, H. W., ed.

1971   *Probleme biblischer Theologie; Gerhard von Rad zum 70. Geburtstag.* Munich: Kaiser Verlag.

Woude, A. S. van der

1968   Micha 2:7a und der Bund Jahwes mit Israel. *VT* 18:388–91.

1969   Micah in Dispute with the Pseudo-Prophets. *VT* 19:244–60.

1970   Waarheid als Leugen (Micha 2,6–11). *Vox Theologica* 42:65–70.

1971a   Deutero-Micha: Ein Prophet aus Nord-Israel? *NedTTs* 25:365–78.

1971b   Micah I 10–16. In *Hommages à André Dupont-Sommer,* ed. N. Avigad et al., 347–53. Paris: Adrien-Maisonneuve.

1973   Micah iv 1–5: An Instance of the Pseudo-Prophets Quoting Isaiah. In M. A. Beek et al., 396–402.

1976   *Micah. De Prediking van het Oude Testament.* Nijkerk: Callenbach.
1981   Bemerkungen zu einigen umstrittenen Stellen im Zwölfprophetenbuch.
          In A. Caquot and M. Delcor, 483–99.
1982   Three Classical Prophets: Amos, Hosea, and Micah. In R. J. Coggins,
          A. Phillip, and M. Knibb, 32–57.
1989   Zur Geschichte der Grenze zwischen Juda und Israel. *OTS* 25:38–48.

Wright, D. P., D. N. Freedman, and A. Hurvitz, eds.
1995   *Pomegranates and Golden Bells.* Studies in Biblical, Jewish, and Near
          Eastern Ritual, Law, and Literature in Honor of Jacob Milgrom. Winona
          Lake, Ind.: Eisenbrauns.

Wright, G. E.
1962   The Lawsuit of God: A Form-Critical Study of Deuteronomy 32. In
          Israel's Prophetic Heritage: Essays in Honour of James Muilenburg, eds.
          B. W. Anderson and W. Harrelson, 26–67. New York: Harper and Brothers.
1966   Fresh Evidence for the Philistine Story. *BA* 29:70–86.
1971   Problems of Ancient Topography, Lachish and Eglon. *BA* 34:76–86.

Wright, W.
1896–98   A *Grammar of the Arabic Language.* 3d ed. 2 vols. Cambridge: Cambridge
          University Press.

Würthwein, E.
1952   Der Ursprung der prophetischen Gerichtsrede. *ZTK* 49:1–16.

Xella, P.
1976a   A proposito del sacrificio umano nel mondo mesopotamico. *Or* 45:185–96.
1976b   Sacrifici umani ad Ugarit? Il problema di *NPŠ. Religioni e Civilita* N.S.
          2:355–85.

Yadin, Y.
1957   *The Scroll of the War of the Sons of Light against the Sons of Darkness.*
          Jerusalem: Bialik Institute.

Yee, G. A.
1981   The Form Critical Study of Isaiah 5:1–7 as a Song and as a Juridical Para-
          ble. *CBQ* 43:30–40.

Yeivin, I.
1980   *Introduction to the Tiberian Masorah.* Trans. E. J. Revell. SBLMasS 5.
          Chico, Calif.: Scholars Press.

Young, E. J.
1952   *My Servants the Prophets.* Grand Rapids, Mich.: Eerdmans.
1965–72   *The Book of Isaiah.* NICOT. Grand Rapids, Mich.: Eerdmans.

Young, I.
1993   *Diversity in Pre-Exilic Hebrew.* Forschungen zum Alten Testament 5.
          Tübingen: Mohr.

Zadok, R.
1988   *The Pre-Hellenistic Israelite Anthroponymy and Prosopography.* Orientalia
          Lovaniensia Analecta 28. Leuven: Peeters.

Zeidel, M.
1945   Micha Chap. VI (Its Parallels and a Commentary). *Tarbiz* 17:12–20.

Zerfass, R.
1970   "Es ist dir gesagt, Mensch, was du tun sollst" (Mi 6,8). *BK* 25:109–10.

Zevit, Z., S. Gitin, and M. Sokoloff, eds.

1995   *Solving Riddles and Untying Knots.* Biblical, Epigraphic, and Semitic Studies in Honor of Jonas C. Greenfield. Winona Lake, Ind.: Eisenbrauns.

Ziegler, J.

1934–35   Die Einheit der Septuaginta zum Zwölfprophetenbuch. *Beilage zum Vorlesungsverzeichnis der Staatl. Akademie zu Braunsberg/Ostpr*, 1–16.

1943   Beiträge zum griechischen Dodekapropheton. In *Nachrichten von der Akademie der Wissenschaften in Göttingen: Philolog-Hist. Klasse*, 345–412. Göttingen: Vandenhoeck & Ruprecht.

1944a   Der griechische Dodekapropheton-Text der Complutenser Polyglotte. *Bib* 25:97–310.

1944b   Studien zur Verwertung der Septuaginta im Zwölfprophetenbuch. *ZAW* 60:107–31.

1945   Der Text der Aldina im Dodekapropheton. *Bib* 26:37–51. Reprint, Zeigler 1971, 306–20.

1971   *Sylloge.* Gesammelte Aufsätze zur Septuaginta. Mitteilungen des Septuaginta-Unternehmens der Akademie der Wissenschaft in Göttingen X. Göttingen: Vandenhoeck & Ruprecht.

1988   Die Wiedergabe der nota accusativi ’*et*, ’*æt*- mit *syn*. *ZAW* 100:222–33.

Zijl, A. H. van

1973   Messianic Scope in the Book of Micah. *Die Ou Testamentiese Werkgemeenskap in Suid-Afrika* 16:62–72.

Zijl, P. J. van

1973   A Possible Explanation of Micah 5,13 in Light of Comparative Semitic Languages. *Die Ou Testamentiese Werkgemeenskap in Suid-Afrika* 16:73–76.

Zimmerli, W.

1969   *Ezechiel.* I Teilband, BK, XIII/I. Neukirchen-Vluyn: Neukirchener.

TRANSLATION,
NOTES, AND
COMMENTS

◆

THE TITLE (1:1)

TRANSLATION

MT

děbar-yhwh	The word of Yahweh,
ʾăšer hăyâ ʾel-mîkâ hammōraštî	that came to Micah the Morashtite
bîmê yôtām ʾāḥāz yěḥizqiyyâ	in the days of Jotham, Ahaz, Hezekiah,
malkê yěhûdâ	the kings of Judah,
ʾăšer-ḥāzâ	which he saw in (or, who had) a vision
ʿal-šōměrôn wîrûšālēm	concerning Samaria and Jerusalem.

LXX The Title (1:1)

⟨And⟩ the word of Kyrios came to Mikhaias the one of [= son of] Morasthi in the days of Ioatham ⟨and⟩ Akhaz ⟨and⟩ Ezekias, kings of Judah, because (of the things) which he saw concerning Samaria and ⟨concerning⟩ Jerusalem.

INTRODUCTION TO THE TITLE

By editorial convention, certain information is given at the outset of most prophetic books; but each book has its own peculiarities. A full discussion of these titles is given in the NOTES on Hosea 1:1 in Andersen and Freedman (1980). The heading for Micah contains five points: (1) the oracular character of the book; (2) the identity of the prophet; (3) the date of his activity; (4) the mode of divine revelation; and (5) its subject matter. Similar ingredients are found in the titles of other prophetic books. There is enough resemblance among them to suggest that a template was in use for a long period or that all the books of prophecy were finished by later editors who followed a common policy.

No two titles are exactly the same. The components of the full formula used in Mic 1:1 are found in other books. The title děbar-yhwh stands in the same lead position in Hos 1:1; Joel 1:1; Zeph 1:1; the phrase appears at a later point in Jer 1:2; Ezek 1:3; Hag 1:1; Zech 1:1; Mal 1:1. An alternative style names the book for the prophet himself—his "vision" (Isa 1:1; Obad 1), "burden" (Nah 1:1; Mal 1:1; cf. Hab 1:1), or "words" (Jer 1:1; Amos 1:1). Micah, Hosea, Joel, and Zephaniah all modify the prime title with a relative clause that begins with ʾăšer hăyâ ʾel-. In some books this event ("And the word of Yahweh was unto so-and-so") starts the prophecy as narrative without a real title (Jon 1:1). When the prophet's name is given first, his status can be immediately defined by a relative clause of the shape ʾăšer hăyâ děbar-yhwh ʾel- . . . (Jer 1:2), but more often by a relative clause similar to the one in Mic 1:1b—ʾăšer-ḥāzâ . . . , "who had visions . . ." (Isa 1:1; Amos 1:1; Hab 1:1 [Nahum is called "The Vision-Book of Nahum the Elqoshite"]). The limited use of this highly technical verb as part of the titles of prophetic books could tell us something about the history of the phenomenon of Israelite prophecy or about how it was perceived in later literary reflexes. This point will be taken up in the NOTE on *vision* below.

The form of the prophet's name varies from book to book, as does the provision of further identifying details, such as place of origin (or residence) and family connection. They are at once specific and meager. The significance of this feature for editorial practice will be discussed in more detail in the NOTE on *Micah the Morashtite*. The content of the visions and the resulting subject matter of the prophecies can be carried by the preposition *'al*, "concerning" (perhaps "against"), naming a country ("Israel" in Amos 1:1) or cities ("Samaria and Jerusalem" in Mic 1:1) or both ("Judah and Jerusalem" in Isa 1:1). The last combination raises the question of how precisely Micah's messages are targeted against the cities, whether as capitals representing the whole land or whether as centers of wickedness in contrast to the rest of the country. Finally the chronological information given in the title, when any is present, varies in its form from book to book. The unique way in which the title of each prophetic book has been composed suggests that the editor had specific, but sometimes limited, knowledge of each case. It is less likely that the variety is due to guesswork or to a careless use of a stereotypical formula.

The titles of prophetic books are clearly editorial, and for that reason have been regarded as of doubtful historical value. McKeating (1971: 3 [Hosea], 4 [Micah]) simply says that they are not to be trusted, without showing where or why they are untrustworthy. By taking the information in the titles seriously, Freedman (1987a) has shown that they provide helpful guidance for the student. The similarities among them all show a conscientious editorial policy and a concern to locate each prophet in his times with some precision. The differences among them, if they are not to be set aside as merely fanciful, purport to claim distinct knowledge about the personal background and time of the activity of each prophet.

The title of the book of Micah presents some linguistic peculiarities. The use of the preposition *'al* only once with the phrase "Samaria and Jerusalem" is less usual than the repetition of the preposition with each noun. O'Connor (1980: 310–11) calls this rarer construction "preposition override." Its use suggests that there is a common message for both cities. The suggestion that "and Jerusalem" was added later, along with references to Judah (as also in 1:5) is a speculation that can be neither proved nor falsified. Another oddity is the coordination of the names of three kings without the use of "and" and the government of this phrase by the single use of the construct noun "the days of." The effect is to present the three successive reigns as a single period, not only for the career of the prophet, but also for the destiny of the nation. Finally we note the awkwardness of having two relative clauses in succession. This pattern makes the antecedent of the second relative clause indeterminate (whether "the word of Yahweh" or "Micah"). The resulting title is more elaborate than that of most other prophecies, and the suspicion has been continually voiced that v 1a is the original title and that v 1b was added later, imitating Amos 1:1 and Isa 1:1 (Lescow 1972a; Lindblom 1929; Mays 1976: 37; Renaud 1977: 1–7; Rudolph 1975: 31; J. M. P. Smith 1911; Wellhausen 1898: 134 [*zu vage*]; Willi-Plein 1971). But the affinity of Mic 1:1 with Amos 1:1 and Isa 1:1 in this detail has suggested to other scholars that the pattern in Amos 1:1 and Isa 1:1 is more likely to be the original one and that it was the first relative clause that was added later, imitating Hos 1:1 (Duhm 1911: 81; George 1958; Wolff 1990: 33; van der Woude 1976). This last consideration, however, has the same weight as the affinity of Mic 1:1 with Amos 1:1 as an argument for the originality of the first relative clause. If, as we suggest, all four eighth-century prophets were edited in conjunction or succession by the early seventh century to constitute a kind of proto-corpus of prophetic writings, then it is entirely possible—indeed, we think it is more likely—that the original collection had four books, one for each of the four generations of eighth-century prophets in chronological order—Amos, Hosea, Isaiah, Micah. The editor of Micah combined the formulas already in place in previously existing editions of the books of Amos and Hosea.

NOTES AND COMMENTS

Notes on Micah 1:1

The word of Yahweh. This term is used abundantly in the Hebrew Bible to denote the personal utterance of the deity, conveyed to the public by a prophet. As such, it can describe any specific message from God, such as an individual oracle delivered on a particular occasion. By extension, it can cover a collection of such speeches; the plural, "words of Yahweh," is rarely used. By further extension, the expression can serve as the name of a book containing such revelations (eventually for the whole Bible), even when it includes other things as well, such as biographical information about the prophet himself, or pieces on the history of the times. Such supplementary narratives are found in other prophetic collections, notably in Amos, Hosea, Isaiah, Jeremiah, and Ezekiel, but not in Micah. All the book is "the word of Yahweh," that is, prophetic declaration. The lack of notes about the historical circumstances of these proclamations makes their interpretation more difficult for us. The audiences of the original proclamations did not need to be told about the situations they were in, such as the story behind the injustices denounced in 2:1–2 and 3:9–11 or the atrocities condemned in 2:8–10 and 3:1–3. They knew all that, only too well. Even after such oracles had been written down, the background needed for their interpretation would be common knowledge.

For the next generation, however, someone would have to tell the story in order to make sense of the written sayings. The situation and the oracle were each needed to understand the other. If both story and saying were handed down together in oral tradition for any length of time, then they would have become inseparable, and both would have been recorded together in due time.

At first people knew the story and only needed to be told the prophecy. By the time knowledge of the circumstances had faded, the written form had been fixed with an identity of its own, not receptive of a rewrite that belatedly incorporated the narrative materials that were really integral to the total message. That is now our loss. One can suppose, however, that this loss was not felt very strongly in the early stages of formation of the prophetic corpus; otherwise the situation stories could have been salvaged before the oral tradition lost them entirely. This could be the case with the unique story in the book of Amos, his encounter with the priest Amaziah (Amos 7:10–17), which has been sandwiched (perhaps "woven" is a better word) into the autobiographical report of Amos's visions (Freedman 1990). Or, if speculation was now the only means of supplying the needed background, midrashic tales could have been invented and attached to the oracles. We can see this process in the apocryphal *Lives of the Prophets* and already perhaps in the book of Jonah. The opening narrative chapters of the book of Hosea have a midrashic feel to them. They have a different literary quality from the oracles in chapters 4–14. And, while they supply general background for the prophet's career of a biographical kind, they are essentially private and do not give any specific clues for the particular oracles that make up the body of the book. When it comes to the historical background of Hosea's oracles, we remain largely in the dark.

All four books of eighth-century prophecy present this tantalizing feature: oracles without stories about their circumstances. This lack (as felt by us) could be the result of the written records' having acquired some kind of canonical status that limited or blocked further literary development, specifically the addition of narrative material. In saying this we are well aware that many scholars suppose that the prophetic writings were continually revamped for centuries. But it is strange to us that, with all the liberty these postulated successive editors are supposed to have exercised, they did not feel free to supply stories about Micah to give flesh to the bones of his oracles. We suggest that one of the reasons for this restraint, apart from veneration for the authentic words of the prophets now preserved in written form, was the availability of the needed background material in the form of the Primary History (Genesis–Kings). Especially in the so-called Deuteronomistic editorial comments on the disasters that overwhelmed the two kingdoms, the point is continually made that they did not heed the voices of the prophets whom Yahweh had sent to them through all those years (2 Kgs 17:23). Freedman (1991: 41–73) has developed the thesis that the two kinds of writing, history and prophecy, were complementary and mutually interpreting. The opposite view has been expressed, namely that the Deuteronomic editors of the Primary History made no reference to the writing prophets, except for Isaiah, because the theology of those prophets did not fit that of the Deuteronomic movement. In particular it has been asserted (Begg 1986) that Amos, Hosea, and Micah were messengers of irrevocable doom, while the Deuteronomists left room for repentance. What prophets, then, did the Deuteronomistic editors of the Primary History have in mind when they made their repeated references to unheeded prophets? This alleged theological disagreement is the result of circular argumentation, for the passages in their books that show that Amos, Hosea, and Micah *were* preachers of repentance have been labeled as inauthentic, as, in fact, the outcome of Deuteronomistic revisions of those books! In spite of the absence of the names of most of the writing prophets from the historical books (Begg 1986), the titles of the four eighth-century prophecy books, with their precise specification of the kings in whose reigns the prophets delivered their messages, facilitate these cross-linkages. In fact we think that the titles were likely designed to secure this attachment of the prophecy books to the history books.

The title of the book of Micah gives only the general time setting of his oracles. The collection attributed to Micah is not uniform. Each "word of Yahweh" reported is not a formal pronouncement by the sovereign Lord in some governing capacity, such as king or judge. Included as well are compositions of many kinds, among them poems of misery ("lamentations"). These most obviously express the prophet's personal grief over the disasters that have come (or might come) on his people; but it is possible that these, too, reflect the sorrows of Yahweh, whose pain is expressed in the questions of 6:3–4.

Even on the more natural view, the prophet is no mere channel for a divine word that comes from a distance and remains transcendent. The word becomes incarnate in Micah's own thoughts and feelings. Their intense sincerity sometimes approaches hysteria, reflected in the turbulence, even incoherence, of their literary realization—another problem for the interpreter (Andersen 1995). Their individual, occasional character is the very opposite of the propositional expression of timeless truths (sometimes asserted as the appropriate medium for a message from God), and without knowledge of the original setting many of the references elude us. The hermeneutical task of extracting relevant principles from such texts and applying them to moral and theological issues of other times and places is even more hazardous. In biblical texts the word of God is brought right into the contingencies of history, into the relativities of one man's mind. In such a form, the word of Yahweh is quite at risk. It has no coercive power. As Diognetus's nameless correspondent said: βία γὰρ οὐ πρόσεστι τῷ Θεῷ — "coercion is not part of God's character" (*Ep. Diog.* 7:4). To discern and to receive that word, faith is always needed and never compelled. In Micah's mouth the word is weak, with no legitimation apart from its intrinsic authenticity perceived perhaps by the listener as the very presence of the sovereign Lord accompanying the testimony of his servant. In biblical prophecy the word of God comes in this roundabout way, almost in disguise; the prophet's own involvement in the events of his time is as the instrument of insight into the divine mind, at once a human achievement bearing all the marks of his own individuality and also a gift by inspiration from on high. The validity of the prophet's perception cannot be demonstrated by positivistic investigation and so falls outside the scope of this philological note; but at least it can be said that, for the prophet himself and also, we must suppose, for some of his listeners, the event of speaking and hearing the word of Yahweh had the awesome finality of a personal encounter with the living God.

came. Literally "was," the usual idiom; "became" or "happened" is closer to the meaning of *hyh*. The idea of movement through space is not present in the verb, but in the preposition "unto." The mode of impartation is indicated cryptically in the word *ḥāzâ* (see the later NOTE on this word), and this equally implies that the visionary experience is granted to the prophet, not acquired by any kind of theurgy. The word comes to the prophet; he does not go after it. The idiom *hāyâ ʾel-* is thus quite different from *hāyâ l-*. The latter implies acquisition, possession, control; in the former the verb remains dynamic, and the word comes into existence "unto" the prophet. This peculiar use of the simple words *hāyâ* rather than, say, *bāʾ*, "came," and *ʾel-*, "unto," rather than *l-*, "to," thus secures a clear distinction between prophecy and divination. The diviner is the master of certain arts and has real powers at his disposal. The word is never at the disposal of the prophet. It cannot be requisitioned at will, yet it is committed to the prophet and becomes a real presence in him. He bears it (the "message" is often called a "burden," *maśśāʾ*); and the word in his mouth (Jer 1:9) makes the prophet a truly formidable person.

Micah the Morashtite

The name Micah exists in several forms and was borne by more than a dozen different persons mentioned in the Bible (Norin 1986: 66–68). The six different Hebrew names that begin with *mîkā-* present a complex picture. The shortest form, *mîkâ* (1:1), is attested thirty-three times in the MT. More than half of these occur as the name of the Ephraimite of Judges 17, 18, who is also twice called *mîkāyĕhû* (Judg 17:1, 4). Besides the Ephraimite of the book of Judges, *mîkāyĕhû* is the name of two other persons—a contemporary of Jeremiah (Jer 36:11, 13)—and Micaiah ben Imlah (1 Kings 22; 2 Chronicles 18)—eighteen occurrences. The genuinely Yahwistic name, *mîkāyāhû*, occurs only twice in the Hebrew Bible (2 Chr 13:2 [the mother of Abiyyâ, who is elsewhere called Maʿakah (Stamm 1980: 110, 133)]; 17:7 [an official of Jehoshaphat]). The matching *mîkayaw* (spelled ᶦmì-ka-ya-a-ma) is attested once in the Murašû archives (Coogan 1976: 28).

The name *mîkāʾēl* is borne by ten men and one angel in the Hebrew Bible (Fowler 1988: 349). The most famous bearer of this name is the archangel Michael. To judge from the names of his companions, Gabriel and Raphael, this trio (the most stable core of numerous listings of superangels in later tradition) could be a reification of ancient associates or manifestations of El, superseded in Mosaic monotheism by Yahweh(-El). This suggests that the origin of the series *gbr*, *rpʾ*, *m(y)k*, *yhw*, and something common among them all, should be sought in North-West Semitic, even though we cannot nominate more precisely Canaanite, Amorite, or some even less well attested ancestral Hebrew as the most likely source.

In the shortest form, *mîkâ*, it is possible that the abbreviated forms of *mîkāʾēl* and *mîkāyāhû* coincide. It is also possible that *mîkâ* was the only name the prophet ever had. This would account for a glaring inconsistency in v 1 where *mîkâ* is used side by side with the partly shortened form of the name of Hezekiah, in contrast, for instance, to the occurrence of three names with the fullest *-yāhû* form in Isa 1:1 (MT). The same dissonance is met in the name *mattanyâ ben-mîkâ* (Neh 11:17); why not level them to **mattanyâ ben-mîkāyâ*?

Morashtite. Jeremiah 26:18 similarly designates Micah as "the Morashtite." The significance of the title is discussed by Jeremias (1933), Elliger (1934), and Neumann (1973). Some of Micah's messages are addressed directly to the authorities in Jerusalem (3:9–10), so we must suppose that he traveled the thirty-five kilometers to the capital to deliver them, if not to reside permanently. Micah is more likely to have been called "the Morashtite" in Jerusalem than in his home-town, where the normal custom would be to use a patronym in the full name, since his father would have been known there. His own identity in the community would derive from his family. In the village, "the Morashtite" would have been redundant and ambiguous as well, since it would not have distinguished him from any other Micah in that town.

We do not know what prejudice might have prevailed in Israel between tribe and tribe and between city and village. Human nature being what it is, it is not likely that ancient Israelites were any different from anyone else in this respect. The expulsion of Amos (Amos 7:12) can be explained sufficiently by his unwelcome message, but the opprobrious manner of his expulsion suggests contempt in the royal city for the rustic from the south. Yet such obloquy can be turned to honor, and at least among Micah's disciples or later admirers the designation could not have been derogatory, since it survived with his prophecies as his only title. Compare Elijah the Tishbite.

Jeremiah (26:18) says that Micah "prophesied" in the days of Hezekiah. LXX (at 33:18) lacks this verb, saying simply that "Mikhaias the Morathites was in the days of Hezekiah." There is no indication that he was given the title "prophet" in his lifetime. Perhaps, like Amos, he would have been called *hōzeh,* "visionary;" but, in light of his derogatory words in 3:6–7, it is open to doubt whether he would have accepted the title, let alone used it of himself. His place in society remains unknown. A somewhat romantic approach cast Micah, like Amos, as the voice of rural protest, raised in the city—"a small-town artisan, . . . more at home in a labor hall than in a cathedral" (*IB* 6:898). In several places Wolff (1978a; 1978b; 1978c; 1981b: 17–25; 1990: 6–7) has canvased the idea that Micah was an elder in his hometown, and in that capacity joined the assembly of elders in Jerusalem, speaking there as an official delegate to consultations at the national level. He was not a proletarian attacking the upper class. He was a fellow magistrate remonstrating with his peers over their abuse of power. At the same time Wolff saw Micah's eldership as involving more than a responsibility for "justice." He was also the custodian of rural wisdom and piety (1978c). It was because the elders esteemed him and treasured his words that "the elders of the land" were later able to quote his prophecy, now in Mic 3:12, during public hearings on Jeremiah's behavior (Jer 26:17–19). Part of Wolff's argument is that Micah saw himself as a bearer of "justice" (*mišpāṭ*) (3:8), which was supposed to be the responsibility of the "heads" and "rulers" (3:1), but which those of his time abhorred (3:9). This language can be explained equally well by the prophet's role as a messenger delivering the judgment speeches of Yahweh. Micah's passion for justice does not imply that he was himself a community magistrate or elder. His words to the leaders in Jerusalem sound more like those of a hostile outsider than a colleague. Blenkinsopp (1983: 124), with reservations, agrees with Wolff's identification of Micah as "an elder in Moresheth." McFadden (1983: 145) accepts Wolff's position, and even asserts that Micah's support group may be seen to be "the elders of the land" (1983: 137). Presumably this would give Micah a recognized and respectable social function. Yet McFadden accepts Wilson's identification of Micah as a "peripheral" intermediary, on "the fringes of the centers of power" (1983: 136). We find no evidence in the book of Micah to support these claims. See Nunes Carreira (1981) for more dissenting arguments. Behind Wolff's sustained use of the term *Amt* is the notion that Micah held some "office" whose identification will help us to understand him. Petersen (1981: 9–15) has shown that the presuppositions of this line of inquiry are mistaken. On the institution of elders see Reviv (1977; 1989).

Micah includes his home in the list of towns in his second oracle (1:14), but no more is made of it than of any of the others. This reference supplies the additional information that its full name was Moresheth-Gath. This detail does not necessarily connect it with the well-known Philistine city of Gath. Many cities of Israel were compounded with Gath ("winepress"). Because of the reference to Philistine Gath in 1:10, McKeating suggests that Micah's own village "was close enough to *Philistine* Gath to be regarded as a satellite of that city" (1971: 160). But the best guess about the location of Moresheth-Gath places it on the road linking Azekah and Lachish (Aharoni and Avi-Yonah 1968: Map 119), well out of range of Philistine Gath. The site of this Moresheth is generally identified with Tell-ej-Judeideh, which is about two kilometers north of Eleutheropolis and ten kilometers from Lachish. If this is correct, the town is strategically located on the vital north-south route that skirts the mountain country of Samaria and Judah through the Shephelah, linking the valley of Aijalon with Lachish. This road ran through such important places as Sochoh and Azekah. Aijalon, Sochoh, and Lachish were the most strategic, since they were at crossroads of routes giving access by convenient valleys to the mountains further east. This network of communications received special attention in the reconstruction undertaken by Rehoboam (2 Chr 11:5–12). The present position of this notice gives the impression that these measures were taken in the wake of Jeroboam's rebellion; even though no extensive fighting between Israel and Judah in this region is reported. Shishak's successful siege of Jerusalem, although not recorded until 2 Chronicles 12, must have required some action against Judah's ring of defensive fortresses in the lowland approaches. So it is probable that 2 Chr 11:5–12 records Rehoboam's rebuilding after Shishak's invasion. Micah's inventory in 1:10–16, especially the cluster of names in vv 13–15, is worth comparing with Rehoboam's list in 2 Chr 11:6–9. Neither traces a line of march, so dubious identifications cannot be settled by extrapolation. (The organization of the list in 2 Chronicles 11 is discussed by Beyer [1931] and by Alt [1959, 2:306–15]). There is a Gath in both sources, but identification of one with the other is not demonstrable, nor of either with the more famous Philistine Gath. If Philistine Gath is correctly located somewhere on the route between Azekah and Ashdod (Aharoni 1980: 250–51) then it is too far west to be part of Rehoboam's frontier complex. And in any case it was still in Philistine hands in his reign (1 Kgs 2:39), because Amos later (6:2) refers to its destruction. So it is not likely that the Gath of 2 Chr 11:8 is Philistine Gath. It is almost certainly Moresheth-Gath, since Moresheth as such is not found in Rehoboam's list (Aharoni 1980: 291–92 suggests that the word might have fallen out). In any case, the affinities of Mic 1:13–16 with Rehoboam's list are close; and this has a bearing on the interpretation of Micah's oracle. If Moresheth is an old Judaean fortress town, it ought not to be spoken of as a mere country village.

The town remained significant into Christian times. It figures on the Madeba map (Avi-Yonah 1954). A summary of Christian traditions of its connections with Micah is given by Gold (*ISB* [1962] *ad loc.*). The identification of Tell-ej-Judeideh as Moresheth(-Gath) is not firm, however. Vargon (1992) has argued cogently that Tell-ej-Judeideh is the city Gedud of Mic 4:14, rejecting Bath-Gedud as a poetical name for Jerusalem. See the NOTE on Mic 4:14. Micah 1:1 presents the *defective* spelling of the gentilic, whereas in Jer 26:18 it is *plene*; but the town name is *plene* in v 14 (contrast *mārēšâ* in v 15). The form resembles that of other names on Micah's list, such as *yôšebet šāpîr* "Occupant of Shapir." The participle *môrešet* (an actual name) was apparently imitated in the similar phrases with *yôšebet*, which does not have much semantic content, like *bat-ṣiyyôn*, which is not "daughter of Zion" but Daughter-Zion, i.e., Zion presented as a girl.

days. The epoch marked by their combined reigns. LXX translated *ymy* as *basileian* in Isa 1:1, but is literal (*hēmerais*) in Hos 1:1; Amos 1:1; Mic 1:1. Comparison with the titles of Hosea and Isaiah discloses a similar editorial practice. The listings of the Judaean kings, in particular, have several peculiar features in common: the use of the construct noun "days" only once with a phrase made up of all the names, rather than listing each reign separately; the listing of the names without the usual "and"; and the blanket designation of them all as "kings of Judah" rather than giving the title "king of Judah" individually to each, as one would expect in normal or formal composition. All these details suggest that the period covered by the combined reigns of these three kings is viewed as a single epoch, during which, or at least concerning which, the word of Yahweh came to Micah.

This fact is of considerable value in settling the background for the interpretation of the book as a whole. Furthermore, the absence of Uzziah's name (Isa 1:1; Hos 1:1; Amos 1:1) shows that a general formula has not been used thoughtlessly. The author of the verse did not consider that Micah prophesied in or concerning Uzziah's reign; and he probably wrote in possession of sound knowledge of the circumstances. In his famous paper on "The Riddle of Micha 1," Karl Budde (1917–18) set Jer 26:18 against Mic 1:1 (p. 78), concluding that the whole chapter must have been written after the destruction of Jerusalem (p. 108). But the book of Micah itself betrays no awareness of this development, not even of the dramatic events of 701 B.C.E., which would have placed Micah's prophecies in a different light. Hezekiah's response to Micah's prophesying, as known in the time of Jeremiah, but not reported anywhere else, could be no more than an inference made in retrospect. We think, on the contrary, that it is more likely to be a genuine memory of one of the reasons for Hezekiah's reforms. The reference by the elders of Jeremiah's time to the oracle of Micah also expresses the view that kings should take notice of prophets. In taking the story in Jeremiah 26 at face value, we are not overlooking the opinion of scholars who find in this chapter marks of a Deuteronomistic editor who brought in Mic 3:12 to support his belief that the destruction of Jerusalem was a fulfillment of old prophecies (Nicholson 1970: 52–55; Hossfeld and Meyer 1974: 30–50; Carroll 1981: 91–95). But the point being made in Jeremiah 26 is quite different: the nonfulfillment of Micah's prophecy showed that the fall of the city was not inevitable.

The tradition behind Jer 26:18 does not require that Micah's activity continued long into Hezekiah's reign (Hardmeier 1991). The reign of Ahaz provides the most tangible background for the contents of the book of Micah. And it is possible, in spite of the widespread acceptance of the Thiele-Albright date for Hezekiah's accession (715 B.C.E.), that Hezekiah's reign (and Micah's activity during his reign) comes before that date. Cogan and Tadmor (1988: 15) give Hezekiah's dates as 727–698 B.C.E. The precision of the notice in Mic 1:1 places Micah's work as beginning later than that of the other three eighth-century prophets, although not necessarily continuing later than that of Isaiah, whose activity went on at least to the end of the century.

There is also in Mic 1:1 an awareness, in the very act of preserving and publishing the writings of four prophets as a single corpus, that with (the end of) the reign of Hezekiah, Israel had come to the end of an age. The two most conspicuous events of the period were the disappearance of the northern kingdom and the survival of the southern kingdom. The difference in the fates of the two kingdoms is explained by the biblical historians as due to Hezekiah's reforms (Handy 1988). These developments enhanced and established the bona fides of those prophets who took the line we now regard as classical (canonical); but at the time the ordinary person must have found it hard to decide between them and their rivals, prophets whom all four prophets regarded as false (they promised safety, contradicting the warnings of disaster given by Amos, Hosea, Micah, Isaiah), and against whom they have occasion to inveigh. We have no way of knowing how widespread or public was the vindication of these four, as represented by the preservation of their oracles and their possible circulation during the dark reaction that followed Hezekiah's death. It would seem from the existence of similar and conflicting points of view during the reign of Josiah and his successors that public opinion remained divided over these vital issues, and "false" prophets still succeeded in gaining a following and even a hold on national policy.

From the editorial headings of the four eighth-century prophecies we seem to have a *terminus ad quem* in the reign of Hezekiah (to 687 [Albright] or 698

[Tadmor]), which might indicate that the books were assembled first in the latter years of the reign of Hezekiah. Beyond these general conclusions the title of Micah does not help to date individual oracles in the book. None of the individual oracles in the book is dated, directly or indirectly. There is no biographical material about Micah himself. When such narratives are present, as in Amos and Isaiah, the names of other persons are usually found as well. In this way we can date several chapters in Isaiah to the reigns of Ahaz or Hezekiah. In Jeremiah and Ezekiel such documentation is abundant. For Micah, however, we are in the dark. There are no dates, no references to identifiable contemporary events, no mention of any of the reigning kings in specific oracles. The only historical persons Micah mentions belong to earlier ages.

Jeremiah 26:18–19 shows that a tradition about Micah survived as a narrative of events. It notes that Mic 3:12 was delivered during Hezekiah's reign. The phrase "the days of Hezekiah, king of Judah" (Jer 26:18) resembles the language of the titles of the books of prophecy. This does not necessarily date the composition of Mic 3:12 to Hezekiah's reign (*pace* Budde 1917–18), let alone that all his activity took place in Hezekiah's reign. If, as we shall show below, chapters 1–3 are a literary unit, then it is possible that all of it was composed while Samaria was still standing; that is, in Ahaz's reign or even in the first years of Hezekiah's reign, accepting the Cogan-Tadmor chronology. Jeremiah's practice (chapter 36) shows that such messages could be declared again and again and republished in the reign of a later king. The fulfillment of half of Micah's prophecy, through the fall of Samaria, would have given fresh seriousness to the section on Jerusalem, with irresistible appeal to a person like Hezekiah. Jeremiah's supporters have knowledge of Hezekiah's personal reaction to the prophecy, a fact not preserved anywhere else. Micah 3:12 is integral to 3:9–12; but even if Jer 26:18–19 is accepted as settling its date, this cannot be extended with confidence to other passages in the Book of Doom. Insofar as chapters 1–3 are a large unit, the whole (its editing, if not the original production of its parts) might well belong in Hezekiah's reign. Hezekiah's reign was a long one, and it is fairly well documented in Isaiah, Kings, and Chronicles; or, to put the matter more cautiously, it has left more records than the decades before Hezekiah's accession. One consequence of this uneven reporting is that events in Hezekiah's reign are more easily used as settings for Micah's oracles, simply because we know about them, so other possibilities are given less consideration. The dating of Mic 1:10–16 is a good example of this practice. It is usually placed against Sennacherib's invasion, because that event is so well known. However, as we shall argue in the commentary on that passage, there is no detail within Mic 1:10–16 that identifies the Assyrian as the aggressor, and some internal details do not fit 701 B.C.E. at all. In fact, the indications that Samaria and Jerusalem are under similar threats point to an earlier period and the references to Jotham and Ahaz in verse 1 make it possible, if not certain, that some of Micah's prophecies were delivered in their reigns.

The quotation in Jeremiah is important for the light it throws on the later history of Micah's prophecies. It shows that information about his activity, including quite concrete particulars, survived for more than a hundred years as common knowledge. The facts produced as evidence in Jeremiah's trial were not disputed and they were known to "the elders of the land," not the cult officers. In fact, the lay leaders quote this precedent in opposition to the arguments of the priests and prophets. The disagreement between "the princes of Judah" (not the lay leaders of Jerusalem necessarily) and the cult officials of the city could be another instance of differences of attitude found earlier in the clash between Micah and the prophets and priests of his day, who are explicitly blamed (Mic 3:11) for the perils confronting Jerusalem. The Jerusalem hierarchy would never have treasured up Micah's words; but Jeremiah's later messages are essentially the same as Micah's, his relationship to elements in society similar to Micah's. Hence the pertinence of the comparison made by Jeremiah's supporters.

The tactics of Jeremiah's supporters reveal another factor too. They bring the king into the matter. It was always up to the king to decide what to do about a prophecy, because such a decision could not be made by a lower court. This was an old pattern, already present with the prophets of Mari. From Nathan onwards (2 Samuel 12), through Ahijah, Elijah, Micaiah, Oded, and Isaiah, prophets dealt mainly, and immediately, with kings; and kings were expected to take the initiative in responding to the word brought to them by a prophet, an arrangement as old as the career of Samuel, whose successors continued to claim the ancient right of telling kings what to do. The attacks of Amos and of Micah are restricted to the bureaucracy—priests, prophets, magistrates, military, merchants—but in the one glimpse we have of Amos in confrontation with this establishment, he is reported to the king as seditious (Amos 7:10–17; Freedman 1990). Micah is similarly oblique; he does not address or name any king. Yet the king is the most likely official to be held responsible for following the statutes of earlier kings (6:16): it was bad enough for the kings in Samaria to do that, but when those in Jerusalem did likewise, the treachery of Judah was worse than the backsliding of Israel (Jer 3:11).

Three additional details are worth remarking. First, the example set by Hezekiah's recognition of Micah was not decisive for settling the fate of Jeremiah. The validity of Jeremiah's work and words, his entitlement to immunity, are not settled by comparison with his predecessor. In the end his deliverance was not due to a clear decision of the court, but to the personal intervention of an influential leader.

Second, although the words in Jer 26:18 correspond to Mic 3:12, they are not produced as a quotation from a book, rather they are quoted as if they existed as oral tradition. Mowinckel (1947) maintained the coexistence and concomitant transmission of oral traditions and written records concerning the prophets; see also Kapelrud (1988). The fact that no book is mentioned in Jeremiah 26 does not prove that a book of Micah did not exist at that time. On the contrary, the wording of Jer 26:18 is close to that of Mic 3:12, suggesting that the control arose from a written authority. But what is quoted as a complete oracle in Jer 26:18, with a normal introductory formula, is only part (the concluding part) of a much longer message in Mic 3:9–12. Jeremiah's supporters may simply have given the climax of the message as a way of referring to the longer unit preserved in Micah, i.e., we may have the result of the quotation technique of the author of Jeremiah, not the mode in which the evidence was presented to the court by the elders. The significance of this circumstance will be looked at more closely below. Here we simply note that in Jer 26:18 the words are not identified as a quotation from a book, and are accompanied by information not found in the present book. The written forms of old prophecy did not, at that stage, have a canonical authority that excelled that of oral tradition.

Third, the book of Micah that we now have contains no information of the kind that the elders of Jeremiah's day still possessed. It is possible that this narrative material was never written down and consequently perished readily in the great losses when Judah was destroyed not long after the incident reported in Jeremiah. The book of Micah itself does not represent the salvaging of memories of the prophet by writing his oracles down from the oral tradition at that late crisis stage; rather the existence of the book of Micah suggests that it comes from written records.

This analysis of the connections between Jeremiah 26 and the book of Micah points to a distinction that can be made between the oracular utterances of a prophet and the stories about him, including the narrative setting of the utterances themselves. The former would be preserved in fixed form (subject to the inevitable minor variations and accidents of transmission). Stabilization of the prophecy in written form is to be expected, considering both the intrinsic authority of the prophet's utterances as messages from God himself, and also the formal aspects of their literary composition, even when the poetry is not regular. The stories that went with these oracles were not under the same constraints. They were only human narratives, not speeches of God; and their content was not vital, their form open to more variation. This vulnerability to change or loss would have been diminished if such traditions had been written along with the oracles for which they provided or could have supplied a framework. The existence of some such distinction between oracle and story explains the extraordinary (and for us annoying) fact that a book like Micah is all oracle and no story. It is because we don't have the stories that we don't understand the oracles. To judge from Jer 26:18, the ancients did not suffer from this disadvantage insofar as they still had some stories available in the oral tradition. Unfortunately again for us, their better understanding of the oracles with the aid of such stories has not been preserved.

The relationship between oral and written tradition can now be stated more precisely. The connection is not stadial—as if all the material concerning a prophet had been handed down orally at first, and then later some of it was written. It seems as if the traditions existed in both oral and written forms, both running side by side, until only the written record survived. The two were complementary. What was written was mainly oracles, with fixed form suited to their authority and literary character. These documents were normally accompanied by oral stories of their original delivery, without which they would be less intelligible. The existence of written oracles would also perpetuate the sto-ries in which they functioned. For some prophets, such as Micah, such narra-tive has entirely disappeared (except for the fragment in Jer 26:18). None of it found its way into the book we now have; perhaps none of it was ever written. This is the case also with prophecies like Habakkuk and Zephaniah. In the other eighth-century prophets small amounts of such narrative have been sal-vaged; either by integrating the oracles with it (examples: Isaiah 7, Amos 7), or as a narrative supplement (Hosea 1–3). Otherwise there are great chunks of oracular material (Amos 4–6; Isaiah 1–3; Hosea 4–14) that resemble the oracles in the book of Micah in having no specific references to persons, places, events, or dates. This is partly true of the books of Jeremiah and Ezekiel too, but the introductory and supplementary matter that accompanies many of their oracles makes a great difference in our ability to understand them.

The mention of Samaria side by side with Jerusalem in v 1b suggests that some of Micah's work was done in the last days of the northern kingdom, even though no kings of Israel are mentioned. The silence of eighth-century proph-ets about Israelite kings after Jeroboam II, even though they recognize the later kings of Judah, requires explanation. Samaria and Jerusalem are both objects of prophecy but only kings of the latter are named. Isaiah's opening lines sim-ilarly name only kings of Judah (beginning with Uzziah), even though he also has much to say about Samaria, and actually names Pekah ben-Remalyahu, king of Israel (Isa 7:1). Amos and Hosea put in the name of Jeroboam as well as kings of Judah, but no other kings of Israel are mentioned, even though several succeeded Jeroboam and were contemporaries of Uzziah's successors in Judah. The listings could be precise indications of the times when these four prophets mainly functioned.

State	Amos	Hosea	Isaiah	Micah
Israel (Samaria)	Jeroboam	Jeroboam	———	———
Judah (Jerusalem)	Uzziah	Uzziah	Uzziah	———
	———	Jotham	Jotham	Jotham
	———	Ahaz	Ahaz	Ahaz
	———	Hezekiah	Hezekiah	Hezekiah

The names of the kings tell us when, and the locations tell us where the proph-ets delivered their messages. Isaiah and Micah were southerners and they were active in the south during the reigns of the kings mentioned. Amos and Hosea were from the south and north respectively, but according to the headings, they prophesied in both kingdoms at different times. The information pro-vided says that Amos prophesied in the north during the reign of Jeroboam and in the south during the reign of Uzziah. The title to the Book of Amos men-tions no successors to those two kings, because he did not prophesy during the reigns of these later kings. Hosea prophesied in the north only in the reign of Jeroboam, not later. Just as Amos became *persona non grata* in the north, and either left under his own power or was put to death, so Hosea probably was expelled from the northern kingdom and sought refuge in Judah, where he continued to talk about Samaria, including developments after the death of Jeroboam, which seem to be reflected in some passages. Like Isaiah, Hosea prophesied in the south during the reigns of four successive kings. Hosea's references to Judah and David (he does not mention Jerusalem or Zion) come from this background.

We have already argued that the common features suggest similar editorial policy (if not an identical editorial hand) in the gathering of these writings, perhaps into a single corpus, and possibly already during the reign of Hezekiah, since the books disclose no knowledge of developments during Manasseh's reign. This puts Hezekiah into prominence. He saved the southern kingdom from a fate matching the destruction of the northern kingdom, because he repented at the preaching of the prophets. His relationship to Isaiah (chapters 36–39) agrees with what Jer 26:18 says about his response to Micah and contrasts with the behavior of Jotham and Ahaz, to say nothing of the eighth-century kings of Israel, who in general are reported as hostile to the prophets of Yahweh (1 Kings 22; 2 Kings 3, especially v 14; but note the opposite case of Jeroboam II and Jonah [2 Kgs 14:25]). There is a tradition that Hezekiah was a patron of literature (Prov 25:1). His respectful attitude toward Isaiah and the report in Jeremiah (26:18) that he heeded Micah make it plausible to suggest that he might have had something to do with the collection and publication of the first corpus of prophetic writings.

There is no way of deducing the actual length of Micah's public activity from the data in v 1. At face value it would require at least the length of Ahaz's reign (731–715 B.C.E. [Thiele-Albright], 743–727 [Cogan-Tadmor]). Calvin made a guess of half the reign-spans of the preceding and following kings to arrive at thirty-eight years (1990: 2). If there were coregencies (Ahaz for Jotham, Hezekiah for Ahaz), then it could all be confined to Ahaz's actual reign. Jeremiah 26:18 takes it into Hezekiah's actual reign only if it means when Hezekiah was full king after Ahaz's death. The difficulty with extending Micah's activity too far into Hezekiah's time is that the book shows no awareness of the fall of Samaria, unlike Isaiah.

which he saw. Verse 1 has two relative clauses in immediate succession. There are three ways in which this can happen:

(1) The two relative clauses have the same antecedent. They are really coordinated, and in a well-formed construction the successive relative clause(s) will be linked together by "and": "Yahweh the God of heaven, *who* took me. . . . , *and who* spoke to me, *and who* swore to me . . ." (Gen 24:7).

(2) The "and" can be omitted, however, as in Amos 1:1, where "Amos" is clearly the antecedent of both relative clauses: "The words of Amos, who was one of the sheep-raisers from Tekoa, [and] who had vision(s) . . ." The antecedent of the first relative clause in Mic 1:1 is clearly *the word of Yahweh*; and, if both relative clauses have the same antecedent, as they do in Amos

1:1, then the second relative clause refers back to *the word of Yahweh*, which he [Micah] saw in a vision. The antecedent *word* is the implied object of the verb. Such is the grammar of Isa 2:1: "The word which Isaiah saw in a vision." This latter idiom shows that "word" can be the virtual object of *ḥāzâ*. The general similarity between Isa 2:1 and Mic 1:1 makes a strong case for finding the same grammar in both places.

(3) Amos 1:1 and Isa 2:1 are different, however; each has a different antecedent for the relative clauses—the name of the prophet in Amos 1:1 (the phrase *the word of Yahweh* does not occur in the title), while Isa 2:1 is titled *haddā-bār*. Both kinds of antecedent are available in Mic 1:1. If each relative clause has a different antecedent, then *the word of Yahweh* is the antecedent of the first relative, and *Micah* is the antecedent of the second: *Micah . . . who had visions*. The internal grammar of each relative clause is then different; when *Micah* is the antecedent, the relative is the virtual subject, and the verb is apparently intransitive. This absolute usage implies an inner object or elliptical cognate object, and this construction does occur (Isa 30:10; Job 27:12, 34:32; Prov 24:32). The rather free paraphrase of LXX could be a response to the difficulty found in the double relative clause. It begins as if they had read *wayĕhî dĕbar Yhwh 'el M.*, eliminating the first relative clause. The second appears as *hyper hōn*, showing that they did not consider "Micah" to be the antecedent of the second relative clause. Translators and commentators are pretty well unanimous that *the word of Yahweh* not *Micah* is the antecedent of the second relative clause: "which he saw" (KJV, RV, ASV, RSV, NRSV, NASB; cf. R. L. Smith), "the vision he saw" (NIV), "that is, the vision he received" (NACE, NAB), "which he received in visions" (NEB), "he received it in visions" (REB), "His visions about . . ." (NJB—making it a subtitle), "the message . . . received by revelation" (Allen 1976: 264—a paraphrase). Hillers (1984: 13) has "which he prophesied," with arguments that the verb *ḥāzâ* can be used generically. NJPSV alone among current translations has "who prophesied," which we think is correct.

These available renditions range in focus from the perception of a vision or visions through the reception of a revelation (the emphasis is on the word heard, not the sight seen) to the proclamation. Although we prefer *Micah* as the antecedent of the second relative clause (*who had a vision [or visions] . . .*), we record the alternative out of regard for the consensus that prefers the other reading.

The point is finely balanced, and the outcome is not very different. The value of conducting the exercise is to show that the heading to the book of Micah, though somewhat cumbersome, is not necessarily composite (i.e., a mix of ill-fitting editorial accretions). Lined up with the titles of the other books, Micah's title agrees with them that all three prophets had visions. If *dbr* is the antecedent of both relative clauses, then, as with Isa 2:1, the focus is on the fact that what emerges in public as a proclamation of *the word of Yahweh* originates in vision. If *Micah* is the antecedent of the second relative clause, then the focus is on the prophet himself as the recipient of the word through vision. We prefer the second alternative, and we suspect that scholars have shied away from it partly through neglect of strictly grammatical considerations, partly out of ideological discomfort with the thought that biblical prophets might have been tainted with ecstasy. For the history of this prejudice, see Andersen (1995) and Norton (1993). For a review of recent studies, see Michaelson (1989).

vision. See Fuhs (1978). Micah does not describe his visions the way Amos does. The similar language in the titles of each book points to experiences that are essentially the same. The testimony of Amos is invaluable in that he reports a series of visions (at least five). So the verb *ḥāzâ* covers more than an initial vision. We translate *who had a vision*, because the placement of that language in the title makes *ḥāzâ* a generic term covering the whole outcome of his call and career. "Who saw visions" would have done just as well, except for suggesting that he had a multiplicity or variety of separate visionary experiences. Maybe he did, but the book of Micah does not report them the way the book of Amos does. Even so, the affinities of Micah with Amos implied by the use of this common terminology encourage us to be more alert to visionary elements in his reported oracles. There is much visual imagery here; and while it could have arisen from the poetic imagination, the stimuli might well have been renewed encounters with Yahweh in which "vision" was the originating and driving impulse, even though Micah, unlike Amos, chose not to include such autobiographical details in his reports. We get a glimpse of prophetic "inspiration" in the one autobiographical passage Micah does supply (3:8).

The title of the book recognizes "vision" as the occasion and medium of *the word of Yahweh*. There is no English verb equivalent to *ḥāzâ*. The verb describes extraordinary kinds of seeing and particularly those connected with the reception of messages from a deity. None of the contents of the book bears the explicit title "vision," *ḥāzôn*, not even the "vision" reported in 4:1–5, which does have that title in Isa 2:1. In fact the book of Isaiah is titled *ḥāzôn*, and the titles to Amos and Habakkuk each have a relative clause similar to the one in Micah 1:1. In all these books there seems to be a difference in the respectability of these terms, the verb *ḥāzâ*, the participle *ḥōzeh*, the noun *ḥāzôn*, when used by the editor, and their equivocal connotations when used in the body of the book. Amaziah calls Amos *ḥōzeh* (Amos 7:12), with disapproval, if not contempt. Amos was not even happy with the title *nābî'*. Because the book of Micah gives no personal information about the "prophet," we have no idea what he conceived himself to be or what title he would have accepted. In the book the terms "seer" and "prophet" are used only in condemnation (2:6–11; 3:5–8). Micah describes his own activity as "declaration," *hgyd* (3:8). Micah does not describe his experiences, nor do his oracles have the visual component so prominent in Amos, for instance, backed up in the case of Amos with personal memoirs of his visions (chapters 7–9). In fact the entire career of Amos was driven by visions. The report of his visions was part of the substance of his proclamation: "Thus Yahweh showed me" (Amos 7:1, 4, 7; 8:1) as a formula is equivalent to the more abundant "Thus said Yahweh." In this tradition we would expect that the verb *ḥāzâ* in the title of Micah documents something similar. In the context of the title the perfect verb *ḥāzâ* does not refer to just one experience but means that he functioned as a visionary prophet over the stated period. It is equivalent to the statement in Jer 1:2 that "the word of Yahweh came to him."

Verse 1b has been studied mainly with a view to settling its place in the editorial history of the book (Renaud 1977: 1–7). Either it was part of an early, even original title; or it was added at a later stage in imitation of other books that had a similar formula in their titles. The appropriateness of the language used, especially the verb *ḥāzâ*, at this position in the book has received less attention, except perhaps to set it aside as merely editorial. Modern scholars have not been comfortable with the biblical statements about prophets, such as Isaiah and Micah, having perceived and received the word of Yahweh in (as) "vision." Biblical prophets have been given respectability in the esteem of modern culture by distancing them from soothsayers and prognosticators. Because ecstasy was considered unwholesome, and trance states were psychopathological, real prophets were said to be free from them (Buttenwieser 1914; Orlinsky 1965). Additional arguments against the notion that biblical prophets were ecstatics were drawn by Wolff from the indications that Mari prophets were not ecstatics and on the general grounds that ecstasy is incompatible with the prophet's function as messenger (Westermann 1967: 63). The prophets were proponents of "ethical monotheism" (the great breakthrough), as innocuous (and they would have been just as ineffectual) as rationalistic moralists, as pallid as liberal educationalists. This dismal laundering reached a limit of vacuity when R. H. Charles declared that biblical prophecy was concerned "only with the development of character and its issues" (1929: xxvii).

Modern study contrasts the experience and mentality of the classical prophets of Israel with that of the seers who came before them (Rowley 1945) and the apocalyptic visionaries who came after them. The *modus operandi* of canonical prophets is alleged to be distinctive, rational, superior, unique to Israel (Orlinsky 1965). Yet, in the early days, even Israelite prophets resembled the diviners of surrounding cultures. Robinson (1921) acknowledged the persistence of ecstasy, but continued to struggle with the "shock on realising that men like Amos and Jeremiah were not readily distinguishable by their contemporaries from the Ecstatics whose symptoms resembled those of the epileptic or even the insane" (1953a: 36). Guillaume's study (1938), while overstating the similarities of Israelite prophetic procedures to certain divinatory practices among Arabs, showed how misleading it was to domesticate Israel's prophets to Western intellectualism. More recent study, rectifying that treatment, has drawn (perhaps overdrawn) comparisons with the social roles of shamans in various cultures (Wilson 1980), including the experience of ecstasy (Wilson 1979; Holm 1982).

After the decline of prophecy in Israel, the apocalyptical medium has struck modern readers as a poor substitute. This judgment again was biased by the marginalization of apocalyptic modes of thought from our contemporary world-views and from our decorous religious communities. Modern readers of the Bible have managed to retain the prophets as acceptable guides, even as heroes, by redefining them as the champions of this cause or that in civilized political life — now meliorist social progressivism, now liberation theology.

By the end of the nineteenth century, prophetic religion was seen as the high point in the evolution of Israel's understanding of God. Between the primitive beginnings when a prophet like Samuel was indistinguishable from a divining seer, and the later decline when apocalyptic dreamers were more interested in the end of this world than fighting for social justice here and now, was the great age (eighth through sixth centuries B.C.E.) when most of the prophetic writings were produced, at least in first editions. Modern scholars isolated the religiously correct Old Testament prophets from practitioners of the mantic arts who have always been in operation, even in Israel at the same time as the mainline prophets, and from the astrologers and forecasters who flourished from Hellenistic times, whether within Judaism or in surrounding communities.

Such strictly categorical distinctions are too simplistic to do justice to such a complex phenomenon as Israelite prophetism. First, dividing the history of Israelite prophecy into three successive periods — seer, prophet, and apocalypticist — is schematic and artificial. A transitional phase can be recognized in the tenth–ninth century in which bands or guilds of prophets exercised charismatic gifts (Albright 1961); and there was a long transition from late prophecy to full-blown apocalypticism (Hanson 1975). Second, and more serious, the differences between classical prophecy and its forebears and heirs were exaggerated to make the data fit the scheme; evidence that the canonical prophets were still visionaries and already apocalypticists was played down or even deleted from the biblical texts. It was especially the case that any passages that smacked of apocalyptic were explained as later additions, to be ignored when we wish to study Micah himself.

Micah is no different from the other biblical prophets in these matters. The title says that he had a vision (or visions), and there are several "apocalyptic" passages in the book. He has been simplified into a textbook prophet by denying the visionary ingredient in his experience and in its literary expression and by cutting away the "apocalyptic" passages from the authentic, original oracles.

To arrive at their oversimplified reconstruction of the history of Israelite prophecy, scholars made too much of a few pieces of evidence: first, the sinister figure of Balaam ben-Beor. Orlinsky (1965: 174) set him aside as a "non-Israelite" diviner, asserting that "divination nowhere developed into prophecy" (170). Lindblom (1962: 90–95), finding Balaam close to the *kahin* of Arabic religious culture, accepts the complex biblical portrait and finds in him a typical combination of seer and prophet (cf. Coats 1973). Balaam's experience — *maḥăzēh šadday yeḥĕzeh*, "he received a vision from Shadday" (Num 24:4, 16) — and the strange behavior that went with it are reported as if they were valid; and his prophecies were true! The verb *ḥzh* is used only two more times in the Primary History

(Exod 18:21 [meaning unclear]; 24:11 [the elders had a vision of God; they "saw" him {v 10}]); the participle twice (2 Sam 24:11 [Gad]; 2 Kgs 17:13 [there are textual problems]). The noun *ḥāzôn* occurs only once in the Primary History (Genesis–Kings), in 1 Sam 3:1, describing the deplorable state of affairs when the word of Yahweh was rare (precious) because "visions were restricted in number and infrequent at the time with which the story is concerned" (McCarter 1980: 97). More often than *ḥāzôn* the equivalents *maḥăzeh* and *mar'eh* are used. The latter refers to Jacob's (Gen 46:2) and Samuel's (1 Sam 3:15) nocturnal apparitions (associated with dreams in Num 12:6); and later Ezekiel and Daniel received revelations in "visions of God." The language used to describe Balaam's experiences can be used of quite respectable persons, neither exotic nor pagan. Abram had such a vision (Gen 15). Since the statement is quite clear that Samuel had a *mar'eh*, it is strange that Jepsen (*TDOT* IV: 290) insists that all that happened was "nocturnal perception of a divine voice during deep sleep" and McCarter states that "Yahweh addresses Samuel from the ark" (1980: 98). But the text says that "the Lord came and stood," and the language is the same as that of Gen 28:13 (as most translations now recognize). Jacob and Samuel saw the Lord standing beside them (his feet near their head as they lay there). The same language occurs in Amos 9:1, and nothing could be plainer: Amos saw Yahweh.

Second, in 1 Samuel 9, Samuel is called *hārō'eh*, "the seer," by the people in the story—by Saul and his assistant (1 Sam 9:11, 18) and by Samuel himself (1 Sam 9:19). The narrator (or a glossator) supplies an antiquarian note, explaining that formerly in Israel a person who went to get information from God said, "Let's go to *hārō'eh*" (because the *nābî'* of today was formerly called the *rō'eh* [1 Sam 9:9]). The narrator himself calls Samuel *'îš 'ĕlōhîm*. The note simply records a change in terminology, not a shift in the mode or value of prophecy. The use of *rō'eh* in Chronicles, not only for Samuel (1 Chr 9:22; 26:28; 29:29) but for Hanani (2 Chr 16:7, 10), makes one wonder why someone thought that the gloss in 1 Sam 9:9 was needed. The two terms continued to be used in parallel (Isa 30:10). Chronicles also perpetuates the use of *ḥōzeh* as well as *rō'eh* (Iddo [2 Chr 9:29; 12:15], Jehu [2 Chr 19:2], Asaph [2 Chr 29:30]), with various persons being named "the king's *ḥōzeh* (1 Chr 21:9; 25:5; 2 Chr 29:25; 35:15; cf. 2 Sam 24:11). This usage raises the question of whether distinctions in function or status are secured by the use of the different terms, especially when all three are used in the same list—Samuel the *rō'eh*, Nathan the *nābî'*, Gad the *ḥōzeh* (1 Chr 29:29).

Many scholars recognized that Israelite prophecy had ancient roots; just how ancient and enduring can be appreciated if prophecy at Mari already functioned along similar lines. Within Israel, the prophets as individual charismatics operating in society with considerable success and without the benefit of an institutional base had affinities with the "judges" of old, at least in the case of Deborah. Neither judge nor prophet was appointed to an office. A completely opposite interpretation saw prophets as officials in the cultus (Johnson 1944). If the note in 1 Sam 9:9 is essentially correct in stating that "prophet" and "seer" are the same, it weakens the claim of Robinson (1953a: 28) that in early Israel there were two "classes of religious persons, . . . originally largely independent"—the seer (*ḥōzeh* or *rō'eh* [Samuel is typical]) and the ecstatic (*nābî'*). While acknowledging the roots of Israelite prophetism in the bands of prophets that existed from Samuel through Elisha (their disappearance has never been explained), older criticism postulated a radical shift to the individualistic prophets of the eighth century B.C.E., who were neither seers nor ecstatics. They are made out to be more intellectual, preachers of doctrines, men with a "ministry." Engnell speaks of "reaction prophetism" (1970: 131). Mowinckel (1934–35) makes some strong statements about the use of rational tests by the prophets to discern the authentic word of the Lord: "he knows this from the *clear, intelligible moral and religious content of the word*" (287; italics his); "the prophets are religious and moral *personalities who weigh and judge rationally*" (289; italics his). Applied to a person like Micah, these definitive characteristics empty the word *ḥōzeh* of its specific denotative reference, retaining only some of its connotation.

Discussions of the meaning of *ḥōzeh* and its cognates have been distracted by an ongoing debate over the origin of the word. The influential arguments of Wagner (1966, nos. 93–98:53–54) that *ḥzh* is a loan from Aramaic depend mainly on the point that *ḥzh* is the general verb for "see" in Aramaic, covering the same ground as *r'h* in Hebrew; it was not needed in Hebrew. An additional argument is that *ḥzh*, "see," is not clearly attested in other Semitic languages; it is not Common Semitic. The evidence for this last point is less clear. However, the etymological puzzle has little to do with the meaning that *ḥzh* has in Biblical Hebrew. If it was borrowed, it was domesticated. Besides the verb there are five or six nouns, and the derivatives are found in more than a hundred passages all over the Hebrew Bible, mainly connected with prophecy. The verb is used in a technical sense in a way that *r'h* rarely is; it mostly has a positive connotation; and it supplied language for the phenomena of prophecy not provided by other roots.

The word-field for the phenomena of prophecy drew on a number of roots. The four main labels (*rō'eh*, *'îš* [*hā*]*'ĕlōhîm*, *ḥōzeh*, *nābî'*) have been studied by Petersen (1981) with the help of role theory. He arrived at the following distinctions: the *rō'eh* was "a resident, urban figure who functioned in the public sacrificial cultus and who could act as a consultant on a fee basis" (p. 98). This result is obtained by generalizing from just one specimen, the unnamed personage in the folktale in 1 Samuel 9 to whom the name of Samuel was later attached (pp. 38–39). The *'îš* (*hā*)*'ĕlōhîm* was "an itinerant holy man who was related to urban support groups," "the sons of the prophets," Elisha being taken as typical (p. 98). "The role labels *ḥōzeh* and *nābî'* do not refer to two different roles. Rather, they comprise two sociopolitically oriented role labels used to refer to individuals who performed one basic role" (p. 99). Petersen applies the social anthropology term of Lewis—"central morality prophet."

Petersen's study does not directly address the question, so very important for the prophets themselves, of legitimation. His result fits the curious fact that these two role-equivalent terms are neutral in that respect. There were no special role labels for false seer or false prophet. That distinction was secured by referring to the message. From the phenomenological point of view, the behaviors of true and false prophets in Israel were indistinguishable. The same word *nābî'* described them all. Both claimed to have "visions" from which issued the word of Yahweh. The deciding factor for discriminating between the authentic and the bogus—did Yahweh give the word or not?—was not accessible for testing. The use of *ḥāzôn* in connection with divination (Mic 3:6) or referring to fake prophecy (then it has a qualifier [Jer 14:14; 23:16; Ezek 12:24; 13:7]) does not disqualify the term as such.

In spite of the popular notion that biblical prophets were proclaimers, there is no indication that either of these terms meant spokesperson or herald. The noun *nābî'* is the standard term for "prophet." The denominative *nip'al* and *hip'il*, derived from the noun, described the activity of prophesying—delivering the message—but not the experience of receiving it; nor did this root supply a term for the message as such. For a divine oracle, delivered by the prophet, *dbr yhwh* or *n'm yhwh* were used. The cognate noun *nĕbû'â*, "prophecy," is rare and late (2 Chr 15:8 [authentic]; Neh 6:12 [bogus]; 2 Chr 9:29 [written]). A longstanding term was *maśśā'*, the "burden," that is, of the prophet.

Petersen's conclusions about the indistinguishability of *ḥōzeh* and *nābî'*, with reference to role, leave unresolved the question of why *ḥōzeh* and *ḥāzôn* were preferred, in spite of their ambivalence, in referring to the experience of the prophet at the point of reception of his message (Ezek 12:27) and also to what the people got at the point of delivery (Ezek 7:26; Hos 12:11), even a book (Isa 1:1; 2 Chr 32:32; cf. Obad 1; Nah 1:1; Hab 2:2)—the more so if the root was exotic. Like *mar'eh*, *ḥāzôn* is associated with dreams (Isa 29:7; Joel 3:1; Job 4:13; 7:14; 20:8; 33:15).

Scholars continue to be unfriendly to interpretations that give the word *ḥzh* its simple meaning. Micah had visions; so did the other prophets. The term *ḥōzeh* has content, yet Jepsen (*TDOT* IV: 283) is categorical. When the root *ḥzh* is used what is received is "not a visual image but a word from God." Even when it is acknowledged that the experience often came at night, Jepsen insists that "the essential element is . . . a nocturnal audition" (p. 283). Jepsen even finds no visual component in Balaam's experience, even though Balaam says, "I see him, . . . I behold him" (Num 24:17). Hearing God speak was accompanied by apparitions throughout the entire period. "God spoke in a *ḥāzôn*" (Ps 89:20). True, the important outcome was a message to deliver, and often little or nothing is said about the visual component; but that does not mean that it was all hearing and no seeing. The vision is the occasion and medium of receiving the word, not the substance of prophecy as a spoken message. In the first place it is the vision of God, as in Isaiah 6, but it could also be a vision of the future, impending as in Amos's visions, or more distant as in the later apocalypses. It is an entirely modern conception to equate this "seeing" with the reflective perception of divine reality ("insight"), for which Israel's prophets possessed a special capacity, not unique but the highest expression of a nation with a genius for religion. Nor should the extraordinary features be identified with the ecstasy of the mystic or the hallucinations of the psychopath. Prophetic visions were always occasional and particular, considered by their recipients to come from God, not from their own minds, and their characteristic outcome was a spoken oracle.

Renaud (1977: 6) infers from the general use of *ḥzh* or *ḥzwn* in the headings of prophetic collections or books that the root had lost its original denotative technical reference to seeing and had moved its reference not just to a generic sense (prophecy in general) but to its original connotation ("receive a revelation in words [by hearing]"). This semantic shift was postexilic. The implication is that classical Israelite prophecy never included a significant, let alone definitive, visionary component. Renaud's argument depends in part on the use of *ḥzwn* in Isa 2:1 as a title for a prophecy that he takes to be "undoubtedly postexilic" (1977: 6). He goes further, and concludes that the same editorial hand placed the doublet Isa 2:2–4 and Mic 4:1–4 in these books and also supplied the headings with their similar use of the root *ḥzh*. We suggest, on the contrary, that the plain meaning of these terms facilitates appreciation of the highly visual nature of the poetic imagery that suffuses the messages of the eighth-century prophets, including Micah.

concerning. The preposition *ʿal* can mean "against." LXX translated it *kata* ("against") in Isa 1:1, but here *peri* ("concerning"). The preposition can govern a noun (Isa 1:1; 2:1) or pronoun (1 Kgs 22:8) that refers to the subject matter of a prophecy. But, since *l-* is commonly used to refer to the content of a speech (Jer 23:9, in contrast to *ʿal* in v 15), here the meaning "against" might apply.

Samaria and Jerusalem. The focus is on the cities, but attention is not confined to them. It extends to both countries named by their capitals, that is, to Israel as a whole. But Samaria is discussed explicitly only in the first oracle (1:5–6), where it is parallel to Jerusalem. There is an unnamed city in 6:9 which could be the northern capital although most commentators think it is Jerusalem. See the NOTE there. Thus this detail of the title applies better to the first oracle (1:2–9) than to the rest of the book. This could account for the rather cumbersome structure of v 1, and in particular for the presence of a second relative clause, which does not attach smoothly to the antecedent. The titles to Amos and to Jeremiah also have two relative clauses, but they are more in keeping with the norms of Hebrew prose—especially in dealing with subordinate clauses. Comparison with them and with Hab 1:1 suggests that Mic 1:1b could be a fragment of a distinct title to the first oracle, conflated with the more comprehensive heading when the whole book was assembled. If this is so, the book as a whole contains oracles given during the reigns of three kings; but visions about Samaria are not to be sought in all chapters.

Lescow (1972: 61) argued that "Samaria and Jerusalem" is not original to the heading; it was added later to the original title in which Mic 1:1 resembled Hos 1:1. He maintained that, if authentic, the prophecy against Samaria should have been associated with a reference to the king in Samaria during whose reign it was delivered. Certainly the silence of Micah on this point contrasts with Hosea's inclusion of rulers' names from both kingdoms. Viewing the matter differently, Renaud (1977: 2) argued that Mic 1:1b is the original title of the core oracle of Micah against Samaria and Jerusalem that follows immediately. In a later redaction, v 1a was added as the title of the whole book.

A grammatical peculiarity of verse 1b was noted above. It is usual in Hebrew, when two phrases are coordinated, to repeat the preposition. Grammar books usually state this rule for *bên*, "between," because its repetition is not acceptable in English syntax. But the rule is general, and if it had been followed here, the result would have been "concerning Samaria and [concerning] Jerusalem." Thus LXX. Because the use of one preposition to govern a phrase consisting of two coordinated nouns is acceptable in Greek, we must suppose that LXX had a *Vorlage* that followed the rule for Hebrew. It is worth noting, on the one hand, that postexilic or Late Biblical Hebrew drifted from the classical standard in this matter; Chronicles often has a preposition and even a construct noun governing a coordination phrase. The present reading of Mic 1:1b could then be due to the same drift, and the *Vorlage* of LXX could be more original.

On the other hand, the transmitted text has a nuance that could have been intentionally secured by deviation from the classical norm. This would have used the preposition twice, even if the two nouns were closely linked. Without the repeated preposition, the coordination of "Samaria and Jerusalem" is even more striking. It is as if they are regarded as a single entity, the nearest possible way of emphasizing the unity of the nation. Compare "Judah and Jerusalem" in Isa 1:1. This linking of the two cities reflects theological not political reality. In view of Micah's interest in Jerusalem, his coupling of the original capital with the capital of the breakaway kingdom is all the more remarkable. It is true that in the oracle that follows he turns the connection against Jerusalem, by arguing that it is just as bad as Samaria. (Compare Amos's similar progression in chapters 1–2.) Even so, the identity of Israel (of Jacob) as the whole people of God is the basis of the joint address. That the conjunction of "Samaria and Jerusalem" in verse 1 is not merely editorial is shown by their equal treatment in the first oracle. They are on the same footing in v 5b, and the ruin of both cities is predicted in similar terms in vv 6–9, beginning with Samaria (v 6a) and ending with Jerusalem (v 9b). Neither has preferential treatment, lenient or severe, in the divine economy. This equal treatment shows a certain detachment on Micah's part.

The terminology—naming the kingdoms after their capital cities—was not traditional practice in Israel. It reflects, however, contemporary usage. It is not just editorial, for this is how other states of the period were named, especially on the international scene. This usage was paramount for the city-based empires of the ancient Near East and reflects their political growth. Akkad, Babylon, Asshur, and the rest expanded from the city as the temple estate (Kraeling and Adams 1958) to hegemony and to territorial empire, retaining the name of the base, just as Rome did later. In Israel these administrative centers were secondary to the tribal league, and in the minds of those who preferred the premonarchical order, artifacts modeled on hated foreign practice, which never became an organic part of Israel's national ideology. The persistent terminology "Judah and Jerusalem" shows a development the reverse of the usual city-state. It reflects the origins of Jerusalem as an extratribal personal acquisition of the king (Zion remained "David's city" to the end). The capital was almost a separate realm. Samaria, acquired by Omri, enjoyed a similar status in the north.

The ambivalent attitude toward Jerusalem could polarize to extremes. There was hostility and detestation for centralized government, and there was a Zion theology, prominent in Isaiah and in some psalms, present also in Micah, persisting in Zechariah, which viewed the temple-palace complex in Jerusalem as a primeval creation of Yahweh himself and the chief locus or focus of his activity in the world. The first point of view is found in the Book of Doom (chapters 1–3), the second in the Book of Visions (chapters 4–5). Compare Mic 4:2b with Mic 3:10; and compare Mic 4:13 with Mic 4:10. According to Mic 1:5b, the sins of the two kingdoms, Jacob and Judah, are concentrated in the capitals, and Mic 1:7 gives the impression that this is mainly because of the idolatrous cults found there. Even if Mic 1:7 refers to Samaria in the first place, there are no indications that Jerusalem was thought to be any better. Yahweh said through Jeremiah: "This city has aroused my anger and wrath from the day it was built to this day" (Jer 32:31). Micah's evenhandedness in his opening condemnation of both capital cities makes it difficult to decide whether the unnamed city in Mic 6:9 is Samaria or Jerusalem (the latter is the opinion of most commentators, in spite of the reference to northern kings later in that chapter), and the "cities" of Mic 5:10–15 are best referred to the two capitals, although provincial towns might be included as well.

Micah's evenhandedness also makes it difficult to decide whether reference to Samaria continues after 1:7. If there is any kind of continuity into v 8, its opening phrase, *on account of this*, refers immediately to the destruction of Samaria, which causes the prophet grief. The referent of *her*, in *her wounds* in v 9aA, could also be Samaria. By the time we reach the end of that verse, Jerusalem is named and remains the center of attention until the end of chapter 3. It is therefore possible that Mic 1:8 begins a completely new series of oracles, devoted exclusively to Jerusalem; *this* in v 8aA refers forward, not backwards. If that is so, Samaria receives no certain attention after Mic 1:7. After we have analyzed v 8 more carefully, we will set this result aside. The main reference of *this* in v 8 is backwards. Samaria is not dealt with in vv 5–7 and then left behind. The whole book is about both cities, as the title says. A further indication of this sustained interest is the reference to Omri and Ahab in Mic 6:16. The destruction of both cities under similar circumstances is clearly anticipated. Similar mood and language put Mic 3:12 (Jerusalem) into an inclusion with Mic 1:6 (Samaria). We therefore think it is more likely that Micah would be equally distressed over both cities, retaining the perspective of 1:5 throughout.

By the end of the eighth century the situation had completely changed. Samaria had been taken by the Assyrians, even though it was not destroyed as predicted by Micah. The Assyrians brought in new settlers (2 Kgs 17:24–41). The situation in Jerusalem had been transformed as a result of Hezekiah's reforms and had survived, contrary to Micah's similar prediction for that city. There are no indications that Micah's prophecies were revised to match these historical sequelae, which showed that his forecast for Samaria was (partly) correct, his forecast for Jerusalem (entirely) wrong. It is only in Jeremiah that we find out how the prediction of Mic 3:12 failed. It was not discredited in any way by this different turn of events. On the contrary, it was made even more memorable by the fact that Hezekiah defused it by his reforms. It was fulfilled in the sense that Hezekiah listened to it and did something about it. Ezekiel discusses this matter at length in chapter 33 about the role of the prophet as watchman. He discharges his duty when he gives warning, which is how Mic 3:12 is to be understood. The outcome will depend upon the response; but whatever happens, and however people respond, the prophet's role will be vindicated and his word fulfilled: either through the repentance of king and people in the renewal and survival of the city or in their rejection of the word and the fulfillment of the threat in the destruction of the city. The word can be fulfilled in two ways: in the response of the audience or, failing that, in the realization of the words in the life (and death) of the city. This shows, furthermore, that such prophecies, even when made without qualification, were implicitly conditional. Repentance was always possible, and this was the abiding lesson of the opposite fates of the two cities.

Comment on Micah 1:1

The title (1:1) is appropriate. It lines up with the titles of the other three eighth-century prophetic books and suggests a common editorial policy, even the same editorial pen. The names of kings give historical sequence to the four books of the corpus as well as suggesting a theological focus for each book. We have not found any of the numerous proposals for tracing stages in the redaction of the title convincing.

Renaud (1977: 3–4) has shown that there are three kinds of formulas used in the headings for prophetic oracles, whether collections or whole books. He associates the usages with two editorial traditions. One practice, featuring *hyh dbr yhwh 'l* in various modulations, is characteristic of Jeremiah and Ezekiel and is found also in Hosea, Joel, Jonah, Zephaniah, Haggai, and Zechariah 1–8. The other practice features the root *hzh* in various combinations and the term *mś'* attached to individual oracles. The first formula is Deuteronomistic; the other formulas are later. Renaud then points out that Mic 1:1 "represents the only instance where the diversified formulas of these two ensembles are found together." He interprets this fact as evidence that the book of Micah has passed through a complex process of formation. Attempts by various scholars to assign the several components of the title to the book of Micah to distinct and even datable stages in the redaction of the whole book have yielded no consensus.

Wolfe (1935) concluded that v 1 was added in the twelfth stage (third century B.C.E.), no longer editorial or redactional but scribal.

In view of the indecisive outcome of so much research, one might wish to set the whole problem aside as insoluble; however, it is not inconsequential. It makes a big difference to the interpretation of many parts of the book, especially if one tries to attach them to possible historical situations, if the data supplied by the title (1:1) are to be accepted as a control. If the Samaria of the title and elsewhere is the capital of (northern) Israel in the eighth century, there will be one reading. If the references to Samaria arise from the polemics of the later Jewish-Samaritan schism (Tournay 1964), there will be another reading. It might not be necessary, however, to make a choice between these two readings. As we will see with our study of the use of Babel as a prototypical city in the book of Micah (as in many other places in the Hebrew Bible), language that takes its rise in prophetic comment on a specific historical event remains available for application to similar events at a later time. If Micah made remarks about the Samaria of his day, they would doubtless be seized upon by readers of a later time and applied to the Samaria they knew. It was not even necessary to have the same name. As we see in the Qumran Habakkuk *pesher*, a hermeneutic was constructed that could exploit an old text as if it were exclusively a prophecy of contemporary events. The Qumran people did not have to write the texts they needed into the book of Habakkuk. The old prophecies lent themselves to continual application to similar situations in later times. Critics of Samaria in Hellenistic times could find Micah's critique of Omri and Ahab germane to their situation. Such relevance does not mean that that is when the book was written or edited. Micah had already used the names of these kings from a much earlier time as code for the Samarian kings of his day. His use of the name *Nimrod* is similar exploitation of a legendary and prototypical figure to refer to some Assyrian king of his own day.

I: THE BOOK OF DOOM (1:2–3:12)

◆

The first three chapters of the book of Micah exhibit a coherence of theme and a structural organization that warrant the identification of a distinct literary composition that may be called a "book." Many scholars have come to the conclusion that this section represents the original work, possibly the only part that comes (mainly or entirely) from the prophet himself. The dominant note is one of impending disaster, a destiny determined on Israel by the supreme Judge. So we call it "The Book of Doom."

Judgment is first pronounced against both Samaria and Jerusalem (1:5). In 2:1–5 an unidentified group of schemers and evil doers are condemned for illegal seizure of others' property. The obscure oracle(s) in 2:6–11 denounce the oppression of women and children and rebuke also those who wish to silence the voice of truthful prophecy (2:6, 7, 11). In chapter 3 the leaders of Israel are addressed, the rulers in 3:1–4 and 3:9–12, the prophets in 3:5–8. They are accused of terrible atrocities and abuses. The outcome will be the total demolition of Jerusalem (3:12), an event described in language similar to that used for Samaria in 1:6.

The match between 1:6 and 3:12 constitutes an overarching inclusion so that 3:12 ends and unifies the Book of Doom. The similar fate of the two cities shows the aptness of the statement in the title (1:1) that Micah had visions concerning Samaria and Jerusalem.

The Book of Doom is not all condemnation and threatened punishment. The tragic situation evokes profound feelings of grief, expressed in the lamentations of 1:8–16. Whether these poems express the agonies of God himself, or only the horrified response of the prophet, they give the lie to the popular opinions (a Christian heresy that goes back to Marcion) that the deity of the Old Testament is an implacable god of wrath and that his prophets are vindictive and uncompassionate.

Nor is the message of condemnation final. In 6:8 God defines his requirements, namely "to do justice, to love ḥesed, and to walk humbly with (thy) God." In 2:7b he asks, "Do not my words achieve good to him who walks with the upright?" The similar language of these two passages suggests that God himself is the "upright one" with whom they are to walk. Walking with God is a common image in the Bible for life as a journey, a pilgrimage—the good life ("what is good?" [6:8]), doing good and receiving good. That is clearly the unchanged intention of the Creator; judgment is needed only for those who have lost this way. And judgment is intended to bring them back to the right path, to resume the journey in which the Lord himself is their leader (2:13). The Book of Doom has as its centerpiece a clear expression of this ultimate hope (2:12–13).

The first section of the Book of Doom (1:2–16) is a unit. Masoretic manuscripts have an "open" division between chapter 2 and chapter 3. There are no traditional divisions in chapter 1. For criticism of the chapter see Budde (1917–18), Fohrer (1981: 53–68), Fritz (1974), Innes (1967), Shaw (1993).

Quantitatively, the opening theophany and judgment oracle (vv 2–7 — 206 syllables) is the same length as the lamentation (vv 9–16 — 207 syllables), with v 8 (31 syllables) in the middle as the pivot of the whole construction. Inasmuch as v 8 links both backwards to vv 2–7, completing the development of the first warning oracle, and forward to vv 9–16, initiating the lamentation, it gives the whole unit the tone of a lament. The preceding verses spell out the cause, the occasion, and the threatened action, while the following verses evoke and depict the disaster itself as it approaches and reaches Jerusalem.

Both these portions are composite. The first speech opens with a call to attention (v 2) followed by a report of a theophany (vv 3–4), explained as a response to the wickedness of Samaria and Jerusalem (v 5). Judgment is pronounced against Samaria (vv 6–7). No hope of salvation is expressed, either in the avoidance of the disaster by successful appeal to divine clemency or by restoration after divine justice has been implemented. Nor is satisfaction expressed, whether in praise of divine justice or in vindictiveness against the wicked. The only response to Micah's terrible prospect of a similar fate for Samaria and Jerusalem is grief. The oracle of doom is followed by lamentation (vv 8–16).

A considerable body of scholarly opinion recognizes the unity of vv 2–16. Donner (1964) and Fohrer (1967) review the earlier discussion. Wolff (1990) argues for the integrity of the whole chapter, interpreting the lamentation as an indirect judgment oracle anticipating the disaster that will overtake all the cities that are named. The question of the thematic unity of the whole piece, as finally redacted, is distinct from the question of the origins of the material. Shaw (1993) presents the strongest case for the "rhetorical" unity of vv 2–16, grounded in a single historical setting, expressed in a unified composition by Micah himself. Other scholars have found more difficulty in connecting the opening theophany and the concluding lamentation. Decisions about dating have influenced literary judgments. A common approach suggests that vv 2–7 (or at least its original nucleus, which some scholars find to be quite small) was an oracle of judgment against Samaria delivered before the city was captured by the Assyrians (before 722 B.C.E.), while the following lamentation reflects an actual disaster in Judah, either in 711 B.C.E. or more likely in 701.

When two distinct pieces are recognized, several suggestions have been made about their boundaries. Attention fastens on how vv 8–9 relate to the rest. There are several ways of looking at this material, depending mainly on whether it is viewed as dealing with Samaria and Jerusalem separately or together: (1) This unit (vv 8–9) concludes the first oracle, but has no connection with the following lamentation (vv 10–16). (2) Wolfe (1935) accepted vv 8–16 as a unity, original with Micah, but attributed little, if any (perhaps v 5c), of vv 2–7 to the prophet. (3) Sellin (1930: 309–17) found a break between v 8 and v 9; however, this proposal did not attract support from other scholars. We try to extract the merit from all these proposals, recognizing both the breaks and the continuities. We reinstate the observation made by Sellin, finding a change of focus from Samaria to Jerusalem within vv 8–9 as a transitional unit.

I.1. THE FIRST WARNING ORACLE (1:2–7)

TRANSLATION

MT

2aA	*šimʿû ʿammîm kullām*	Listen, peoples, all of them!
2aB	*haqšîbî ʾereṣ ûmělōʾāh*	Pay attention, Earth and her fullness!
2bA	*wîhî ʾădōnāy yhwh bākem lěʿēd*	And let my lord Yahweh be against you as a witness,
2bB	*ʾădōnāy mēhêkal qodšô*	my lord from his holy temple.
3a	*kî-hinnēh yhwh yōṣēʾ mimměqômô*	For behold, Yahweh is setting out from his place,
3b	*wěyārad*	and he will descend
	wědārak ʿal-bāmôtê-ʾāreṣ	and he will trample upon the *bāmôt* of Earth;
4aA	*wěnāmassû hehārîm taḥtāyw*	and the mountains will melt beneath him,
4aB	*wěhāʿămāqîm yitbaqqāʿû*	and the valleys will split open
4bA	*kaddônag mippěnê hāʾēš*	like the wax in the presence of the fire,
4bB	*kěmayim muggārîm běmôrād*	like water cascading down a sluice.
5aA	*běpešaʿ yaʿăqōb kol-zōʾt*	Because of Jacob's rebellion is all this,
5aB	*ûběḥaṭṭōʾwt bêt yiśrāʾēl*	and because of the sins of the House of Israel.
5bAα	*mî-pešaʿ yaʿăqōb*	Who—Jacob's rebellion?
5bAβ	*hălôʾ šōměrôn*	Is it not Samaria?
5bB	*ûmî bāmôt yěhûdâ*	And who—the *bāmôt* of Judah?
5bC	*hălôʾ yěrûšālēm*	Is it not Jerusalem?
6aA	*wěśamtî šōměrôn lěʿî haśśādeh*	And I will make Samaria into a stone heap of the field
6aB	*lěmaṭṭāʾê kārem*	into planting places of a vineyard.
6bA	*wěhiggartî laggay ʾăbāneyhā*	And I will pour into the valley her stones;
6bB	*wîsōdeyhā ʾăgalleh*	and her foundations I will lay bare.
7aA	*wěkol-pěsîleyhā yukkattû*	And all her carved images will be shattered,
7aB	*wěkol-ʾetnanneyhā yiśśārěpû bāʾēš*	and all her earnings of prostitution will be burned in the fire,
7aC	*wěkol-ʾăṣabbeyhā ʾāśîm šěmāmâ*	and all her idols I will make a desolation
7bA	*kî mēʾetnan zônâ qibbāṣâ*	For from the fee of a prostitute she gathered [them];
7bB	*wěʿad-ʾetnan zônâ yāšûbû*	and for the fee of a prostitute they will go back.

LXX I.1. The First Warning Oracle (1:2–7)

2aA	Hear, peoples, words;
2aB	⟨And⟩ let the earth and ⟨all⟩ that are in it give heed!
2bA	And Kyrios {Kyrios} will be among you as a testimony,
2bB	Kyrios from his holy house.
3a	For behold, Kyrios is going out from his place,
3b	and he will descend
	and he will tread upon the heights of the earth;
4aA	and the mountains will be shaken beneath him,
4aB	and the gorges will melt
4bA	like wax in the presence of fire,
4bB	⟨and⟩ like water cascading down a declivity.
5aA	On account of Jacob's ungodliness are all these things,
5aB	and on account of the sin of the house of Israel.
5bAα	Who is Jacob's ungodliness?
5bAβ	Is it not Samaria?
5bB	And who is the sin of ⟨the house of⟩ Judah?
5bC	Is it not Jerusalem?
6aA	And I will make Samaria into a fruit shed of the field
6aB	⟨and⟩ into a plantation of a vineyard.
6bA	And I will drag down into chaos her stones;
6bB	and her foundations I will reveal.
7aA	And all her carved images they will cut to pieces,
7aB	and all her hired things they will burn with fire,
7aC	and all her idols I will put to destruction.
7bA	For from fees of prostitution she gathered (them);
7bB	and from fees of prostitution she collected (them).

INTRODUCTION TO MICAH 1:2–7

The Poetry of Micah 1:2–7

There are twenty-five colons in this unit. The individual colons are quite diverse and range in length from four syllables to twelve. A more familiar procedure for finding regularity in Hebrew poetry is to count the stresses as if they were beats. In Mic 1:2–7 the colons range in length from two beats to five, according to the Masoretic cantillations. If the text as we now have it still represents the original composition (even allowing for minor changes in transmission, from whatever causes), this range (whether measured by syllables or beats) shows that Hebrew prophetic poetry was not made with colons that were even approximately constant in length. Scholars who expect Hebrew poetry to be more regular than what we find in the book of Micah have a number of remedies. Some use a very flexible system of counting beats. A colon that does not seem to have enough words to supply the expected number of beats can be given more beats than were assigned by the Masoretes. A proclitic word, unstressed by the Masoretes, can be given a beat, or a long word can be given an additional secondary accent. When there seem to be too many words, some can be left unstressed, even if it means revising the Masoretic accentuation. The net result of admitting such license into the scansion of Hebrew poetry is often the pronouncing of the same word quite differently in different parts of the same poem. This arbitrary procedure is defended by Gordis (1978: 501–18) and practiced on Micah by Allen (1976), R. L. Smith (1984), and others. The disagreements among Allen, Smith, and others in the scansion of the same passages in Micah make it clear that their decisions arise from what they think the beat count should be. Theory founders in circular reasoning.

A third strategy for knocking the text into a more regular scheme is to suppose that a short colon has lost a word in transmission and to supply the missing word by conjectural emendation. Alternatively an overly long colon might have acquired an extra word in transmission, and this intruder can now be deleted. There are plenty of examples of such adjustments in the literature, and we shall discuss some of the proposals as we go along. See the NOTE on v 2bA, a colon of twelve syllables that many wish to shorten. At this point we simply indicate that all such practices, while not illicit in themselves—anything is possible both in the original composition of poetry and in the scribal transmission of poetic texts—should be invoked only as a last resort, and then with diffidence. It is easy enough to trim some of the longer colons to a more average size, even though this begs the whole question of uniformity in colon length, yet some colons resist such mutilation. Thus it is commonplace to remove the first ʾădōnāy from v 2b, and to excise one of the verbs from v 3b. Both colons in v 3b, having eleven syllables or four beats, are considered too long, because of common belief that the whole is written in trimeters. Verse 3a (also eleven syllables and four beats) is not so easy to change. Once more we do not intend to refute every such proposal. It lies in the elusive nature of the subject that no one can claim much certainty; but a dogmatic approach that derives a doctrine of "three beats per colon" from theory rather than from the poem itself is deplorable.

Verses 2–7 display all the usual features of classical Hebrew poetry, notably parallelism between adjacent pairs of colons. But once more the whole cannot be forced into bicolons of Lowthian type, although these are certainly the most conspicuous. Powis Smith (1911: 32) succeeded in displaying the whole of vv 2–9 as six strophes of four colons each, but only by removing v 4b and v 7 altogether, and by reading v 5b as two long colons rather than as four short ones. There is no need to quarrel over this last point, for the text is the same no matter how it is printed; but the removal of seven whole colons is another matter.

Form Criticism of Micah 1:2–7

There are at least two speakers in vv 2–7. At first the prophet, announcing Yahweh's impending epiphany (v 3), calls all the peoples of the world to observe the proceedings (v 2). The effect of Yahweh's impact when he comes down to the earth (v 4; Cf. Exodus 19) is described in vivid language. In these verses Yahweh is referred to in the third person. Verses 6–7 are a judgment speech, in which the "I" is Yahweh. A transitional passage (v 5) analyzes the reason for this visitation, the sinful rebellion of "the house of Israel," concentrated in the religious practices of the two main cities, Samaria and Jerusalem. Either the prophet or the LORD could be the speaker.

The variety of literary genres employed in this oracle makes it difficult to assign conventional roles to the participants. The immediate audience is the peoples of the world. The real audience, Israel, does not take part and is not even addressed, unless *bākem*, "in [against or among?] you" (v 2bA), marks a focusing of the address on the accused. Yahweh has come to investigate and expose and eradicate the evil practices of his people, and some of the language of covenant disputation is used, notably *'ēd*, "witness" (v 2bA). But the procedures are not dramatized as a formal court hearing or trial. Form-criticism takes us only part way into the literary character of this material.

The Composition of Micah 1:2–7

Tradition-transmission criticism and redactional analysis have come up with some very complicated explanations of the compositional features of this unit. The history of scholarship in this regard was reviewed up to the time of publication by Renaud (1977). The methods seem to have exhausted themselves. The most fragmented approach seems to have been that of Wolfe (1935); he found a possible Micah source only in v 5bB (Micah being interested in Judah, but not in Samaria). Verses 2–4 were added after the Exile (it was thought that apocalyptic materials could not be pre-Exilic). The material aimed at Samaria (the rest of v 5 and vv 6–7) was added in the third century B.C.E. as polemic against the Samaria of that time. There is no need to report any more examples of this kind of work. Its day has passed and research is now more interested in addressing questions of the final outcome, the stabilized "canonical" text, no matter how it came to be that way.

Various artistic defects have been found in vv 2–7, such as irregularities in meter or undisciplined use of formal literary genres. If such features are deemed to be aesthetic blemishes, they are more than remedied by the intricate word patterns that link the whole together into a tapestry of ideas. Not only that; as the opening oracle, this piece already states themes and introduces language that will be used throughout the book, unifying the whole. It is precisely our new sensitivity to such compositional features that permits us to claim that artistry of this quality is more likely to come from one capable author than from several successive editors.

Symmetrical Structure in Micah 1:2–4

2aA		⌐ *šimᶜû ᶜammîm kullām* ⌐	
2aB		*haqšîbî ʾereṣ ûmĕlōʾāh*	
2bA	34 syl.	*wîhî ʾădōnāy yhwh bākem lĕᶜēd*	45 syl.
2bB		⌐ *ʾădōnāy mēhêkal qodšô* ⌐	
3a	22 syl.	⌐ *kî-hinnēh yhwh yōṣēʾ mimmĕqômô* ⌐	
3b		⌐ *wĕyārad wĕdārak ᶜal-bāmôtê-ʾāreṣ* ⌐	
4aA		⌐ *wĕnāmassû hehārîm taḥtāyw* ⌐	
4aB		*wĕhāᶜămāqîm yitbaqqāᶜû*	
4bA	34 syl.	*kaddônag mipĕnê hāʾēš*	45 syl.
4bB		⌐ *kĕmayim muggārîm bĕmôrād* ⌐	

The ten colons (90 syllables) in vv 2–4 can be construed as two quatrains (vv 2, 4), each thirty-four syllables long, arranged symmetrically around a bicolon (v 3). In another view, the opening call, a bicolon (v 2a), is followed by four colons that announce and describe the descent of Yahweh (vv 2b–3) and four colons that describe the outcome (v 4). In another view again, the poem divides into two pentacolons, each forty-five syllables long. The first half (vv 2–3a) calls the world to attend the disputation, with v 3a a subordinate clause attached to v 2 giving the reason for the call—*for Yahweh is setting out from his place*. In the second half, v 4 is the result of the movement described in v 3b. There are thus three superimposed structures in vv 2–4. The perfect symmetry of the pattern of colons in the text exactly as it now is would be marred if some of the seemingly superfluous words were deleted, as is commonly done.

The Structure of Micah 1:2–4

Verse	Syllables	Scheme I	Scheme II	Scheme III
2aA	6		Call	
2aB	8	34 syllables		45 syllables
2bA	12		Descent	
2bB	8			
3a	11	22 syllables		
3b	11			
4aA	9			
4aB	9	34 syllables	Outcome	45 syllables
4bA	8			
4bB	8			

Having said that, we must add that the three superimposed structures described in the preceding paragraph secure continuity in the dramatic development. The verbs in v 3 —*sally forth, descend, march*—refer to the stages in a military expedition. In fact, all the material in vv 2–4 is interconnected; but the unfolding of the themes is not so simple. The vocabulary evokes a profusion of mythic imagery and sets the cosmic stage for the whole book as befits the visionary experience of the prophet (v 1). The forensic language of the opening words sets the stage, or rather the court, for covenant disputation; but Yahweh's role, as litigant or magistrate, is not yet defined. Only part of the traditional invocation of "heaven and earth" is used, with "all the peoples [of the earth]" substituted for "heaven." This combination brings history into the myth, realism into the fantasy. The expected formalities of a *rîb* do not follow. Instead of conducting the investigation like a king in his palace, Yahweh comes out as a warrior; and the combat is a reenactment of the old cosmic battle with the primal elements, here represented by "mountains."

The movement into contemporary actuality is completed in v 5, barely intimated in vv 2–4. The twice-mentioned "Earth" (vv 2, 3) retains its mythic connotations and the "mountains" and "valleys" likewise belong more in primal creation stories than in contemporary geography. In making this distinction we do not intend to suggest that the prophet distinguished and separated the cosmic-mythic and the historical-actual realms. This distinction, as we now perceive it, is for us a literary one; and we do not pretend to have captured the prophet's conceptualizations. We think that there is only one worldview here, a perception of the real world with the benefit of prophetic vision, inspired into poetry with imagery drawn from the old myths. So we do not have to ask if "his holy temple" (v 2bB) is the building on Mount Zion, the original model displayed to Moses on Mount Sinai, or a residence located in the sky somehow (Freedman 1981). The phrase evokes all three associations. In similar fashion the "mountain-house" of 3:12–4:1 is both the temple mount of Jerusalem and the cosmic mountain of myth. The collapse of the fabric of the world (v 4) passes into the devastation of Samaria (vv 6–7) and of Zion (3:12). The cosmic setting of the opening theophany returns in 6:1–2, notably in the association "mountains" // "foundations of earth." Here at last the role of Yahweh as "accuser" (*ʿēd*), announced at the very beginning of the book, comes to dramatic expression. The cosmic court is the setting for the covenant dispute that touches real history in Israel (6:2b). Verses 2–4 thus put into place the themes of the entire book.

The first word of command, *šimʿû*, "Hear!" is used five more times in the book. There is one set of three occurrences in the Book of Doom and one set of three in the Book of Contention. It is the first word in each of these books. After the initial call to the "peoples" in 1:2, there is a double summons to the leaders of Israel (3:1, 9). In the second set the audience of the first call (6:1) is not identified (all the other five have a vocative noun); but it links up with the pair in chapter 3 in having *nāʾ*. When no new addressee is identified, the inference would be that the audience has not changed; chapter 6 continues the indictment of the leaders of Israel. The call in 6:2 is to the mountains. Its cosmic scope matches the global scope of 1:2. The final call (6:9) is to *maṭṭeh*, "tribe." Just who is being addressed in this way is not clear; this is the only occurrence of that word in Micah. The preliminaries in 6:9 say that "the voice of Yahweh is calling to the city," evidently Jerusalem, because the accusations in vv 9–12 continue on the lines of chapter 3, concentrating this time on the city merchants. But Samaria is also a possibility in view of the reference to Omri and Ahab in 6:16. All six occurrences of *šimʿû* are thus part of the same operation, or of two similar operations in which the leaders of Israel are accused and condemned in the presence of global or cosmic observers and adjudicators.

The next word, *ʿammîm*, "peoples," introduces a prime participant in the drama. Yahweh's dealings with Israel are continually placed in a global setting. The whole world has an interest in the matter. The word *ʿammîm* occurs seven times, six in the Book of Visions, so the other occurrence in 1:2 provides a link that ties the Book of Doom into the Book of Visions. Four times this word occurs in the phrase *ʿammîm rabbîm*, "many peoples," and the equivalent expressions *ʿammîm kullām* and *kol-hāʿammîm* show that the entire population of the world is embraced. The synonymous *gôyim* is used six times, five in the Book of Visions. The sixth occurrence (7:16) ties the Book of Contention back into the Book of Visions. The equivalence of "peoples" and "nations" is shown by their use as poetic parallels (4:2, 3) and by giving them the same attribute "many." Israel is called a *gôy* only in 4:7, otherwise *ʿam* (twelve occurrences, in all parts of the book; nine times *ʿammî*, "my people" [God speaking]).

"Earth" is invoked in v 2aB. The word *ʾereṣ* is used fifteen times. A clear grammatical distinction is maintained between the cosmic reference (the definite article is not used, even though the noun is definite [1:2, 3; 5:3; 6:2; 7:17], except in 4:13) and specific references to "the land of Egypt" (6:4; 7:15), "the land of Assyria (Nimrod)" (5:5), and the land of Israel (with pronoun suffix [5:4, 5, 10], or the definite article [7:2, 13]).

The title *ʾădōnāy* is a particular favorite with the prophets. In Micah it occurs twice in v 2 and is used once more in the longer "Lord of the whole earth" in 4:13, there in parallel with "Yahweh." In contrast to the use of "Yahweh" (forty times), Micah uses "God" only eleven times (never in the Book of Doom and only once as a proper noun [3:7, where it might not even refer to Yahweh]).

The first two colons have built up the impression that we are going to have some classical Hebrew composition. The resultant bicolon is well formed; the parallelism is complete; the rhythm, whether measured by syllables (14) or beats (3:3), is excellent. This expectation is not met; the next colon (v 2bA) is overly long, and it has already made a twist. If the discourse is coherent, the available referents for *bākem*, "against you," are the parties addressed in v 2a, all the peoples of the earth. When used with either the noun *ʿēd* or the denominate *hipʿil* verbs derived from it, the preposition *b-* means "against" (the noun in Num 5:13; Josh 24:22; 1 Sam 12:5; Jer 42:5; and others; the verb in Deut 8:19). Furthermore, the cosmic powers of heaven and earth were invoked as witnesses of the original covenant agreements and remain as observers and custodians of the performance of the contracting parties. God said: *haʿîdōtî bākem hayyôm'ēt haššāmayim wĕ'ēt hā'āreṣ,* "I have appointed to be witnesses *against you* today the heavens and the earth" (Deut 30:19). Here *you* refers to Israel, the audience at that time. There is something strange about the picture in Mic 1:2: The accuser (Yahweh) and the audience ("peoples") have assembled; but the accused is not present, or at least not yet identified. If the third party is absent, v 2bA could mean "and let my Lord Yahweh give testimony *to* you [the peoples]," but that would be straining the idiom. The discourse that follows in Micah does not indicate that Yahweh is about to testify against the peoples. The picture is incomplete. The accuser (Yahweh) and the panel of adjudicators (the peoples) have assembled. The *you* in v 2bA (against whom Yahweh is about to testify) can only be Israel, the usual target of Yahweh's covenant dispute and the object of the complaints that follow in v 5.

If vv 2–7 are an oracle proclaimed by a prophet in some public place, then the accused, Israel, is represented by his audience. What has happened is that the prophet, who is addressing an actual audience of Israelites, having rhetorically invoked the peoples of the world (who are not present), says directly to his audience that Yahweh will testify *against you*. When Jesus switches audiences in mid-speech in Mark 2:10–11, the evangelist helpfully marks the transition with an aside ("—he turned to the paralyzed man—"). A similar switch takes place in Ruth 4:4. In the middle of a speech to the *gō'ēl,* who is at first addressed directly ("If you will redeem, . . . "), Boaz turns to the panel of elders and refers to the *gō'ēl* in the third person ("and if he will not redeem, . . . "). There is no need to level the text of Ruth 4:4 to a uniform second person, as is widely done by text critics and commentators. In a similar way, Micah has pounced on his audience abruptly. The effect is dramatic. We suspect that this partial development of a picture and the sudden transition to a new line of thought are marks of the subliminal state in which the prophet had his vision. The prophet delivered his message while actually in that state, not as a later report on a visionary experience.

There is continuity in the transition from v 2bA to v 2bB in the repetition of *'ădōnāy,* another good reason for retaining that word in v 2bA. There is also a fissure between v 2bA and v 2bB. There is nothing in the preceding text for *mēhêkal qodšô, from his holy temple,* to modify. *His holy temple* is not the site of the assize into which all the peoples of the world have somehow congregated. It is true that Yahweh speaks *in* this audience chamber, and his word issues *from* it (Mic 4:2; Amos 1:2; and others). But there are no indications that Micah was a cult official of the Jerusalem temple and in that capacity issues decrees in the name of Yahweh. It is more likely that the holy temple of v 2 is the heavenly residence of Yahweh. A common, almost standard experience of a visionary prophet was to be admitted to the consultations that took place there in the company of the heavenly beings (1 Kgs 22:19; Isa 6:1; Amos 3:7). Here, too, he learns about the planned excursion of Yahweh down into his earthly domain to deal with the situation there. This kind of mythic talk is the very stuff of prophetic visions. The phrase *mēhêkal qodšô* is in parallel with *mimmĕqômô* (v 3a), and anticipates the descent described in v 3.

Parallelism, or even the repetition of a key word, does not necessarily supply a close linkage. The title "My Lord Yahweh" occurs in v 2bA, and its parts follow in the next two colons. This secures continuity between v 2 and v 3. There is also the parallelism of "his holy temple" and "his place," which makes it clear that the expedition sets out from the heavenly headquarters. A connection between v 2bB and v 3a also relieves the strain on the phrase "from his holy temple," which modifies *is setting out* but does not fit so well into v 2bA. In fact v 2bA is the end of the process that begins with vv 2bA–3a and that runs through v 4. Yahweh will appear as a witness at the assize, but he will start out from his heavenly temple and march through the earth to get there. At the same time there is a break between v 2 and v 3. Verse 2 is the introduction, while v 3 begins the body of the oracle. *For behold* makes a fresh start. The direct address that begins with *against you* in v 2bA does not continue.

The language of v 2, with its echoes of covenant formulation and its use of forensic terms creates the expectation that a full-blown law suit is about to take place. Yahweh will appear as litigant, plantiff, with Israel as the defendant. This expectation is not fulfilled; the discourse takes another turn, casting Yahweh in a more soldierly role. The participle *yōṣē'* has connotations of sallying forth on a military campaign. The language of v 3 evokes memories of old theophanies, and the archaic expression *bāmôtê-'āreṣ* makes it sound like an episode from an old myth (Hunter 1989). The effect of Yahweh's impact on the world is to convulse the fabric of mountains and valleys, the kind of lurid scene that is likely to be found in a later apocalypse. Zechariah 14:3–4 has the same scenario.

And Yahweh will sally forth (*yṣ'*), and his feet will stand . . . upon the Mount of Olives; and the Mount of Olives will be split asunder (*nibqa'*).

The two verbs at the beginning of v 3b have attracted the suspicion of textual scholars and literary critics, who propose to delete one so as to shorten and simplify the colon. There is meager textual support for the emendation, and the literary arguments are weak. The two colons in v 3 are exactly the same length (eleven syllables each), and, after the long colon in v 3a, the sudden succession of verbs speeds up the pace and moves into the violence that continues into v 4.

Because of the parallelism of "mountains" // "valleys" and of "wax" // "water," two bicolons can be recognized in v 4. The first (v 4a) has the verbs in chiasmus. The images of melting and flowing in v 4b are congruent, but Yahweh's impact on the world has two quite different effects. The verb *drk* is slightly ambiguous. It could describe the warrior's progress along the tops of the mountains; or it could indicate seismic effects as he tramples rocks and shatters the earth. Added to this scene is a picture of Yahweh as fire, melting the mountains like wax so that they flow like water. The double simile of v 4b elaborates on v 4aA, while the picture of the valleys splitting apart is not developed any further. (The Greek translator evidently felt the incongruity and switched the imagery to something more conventional so that v 4aA followed logically on v 3 ["the mountains will be shaken"], and v 4aB fitted in with v 4b.)

Verse 5 has two parts. Verse 5a gives the explanation for all that has been declared in vv 2–4. "All this is for Jacob's rebellion and for the sins of the house of Israel." Verse 5b then proceeds to identify this rebellion more exactly. The fault is located in the two main cities, Samaria and Jerusalem; and it is connected with the *high places.* Whereas v 5a is a categorical statement, v 5b has the form of parallel rhetorical questions and answers. A different poetic pattern is used in each half-verse.

Verse 5a is a bicolon of classical quality. It is just one clause: the subject (*all this*) carries a two-part predicate. The parallel to *peša'* is a longer word (*ḥaṭṭō'wt*), and *Jacob* is matched by a two-word phrase *House of Israel.* Even though v 5aB lacks a parallel to *all this*, it is longer than v 5aA. The single subject *all this* shows that vv 2–4 are a single action against all Israel as a unit. Both names, *Jacob* and *House of Israel*, refer to the whole nation. Verse 5b can be construed as two long colons, each with a question and answer, or as four colons, as shown above. Verse 5b grows out of v 5a, and the repetition of *Jacob's rebellion* creates the expectation that its parallel (*the sins of the House of Israel*) will also be used again. This expectation is not fulfilled. Micah keeps on doing this kind of thing, twisting away from an expected line of thought, not completing an expected poetic pattern. Instead of the expected *the sins of the House of Israel*, there is *the high places of Judah.* The early versions have already leveled v 5b to v 5a, and their evidence has been used by textual scholars to emend MT. See the NOTE.

The oracle in vv 2–7 is completed by the threat of punishment uttered against one of the cities in vv 6–7. In this subunit there are nine colons, seventy-nine syllables (mean 8.8 syllables per colon). The subunit is unified by its theme and also by numerous compositional devices. All the colons except for v 6aB have a verb; that is, each colon is a distinct clause. The first seven colons are marked by verbs in the first person and by the itemization of the objects of destruction. The seven colons are embraced by an inclusion:

wĕśamtî šōmĕrôn . . . 'āśîm šĕmāmâ

The last word is a cruel sound play on "Samaria," using double alliteration plus consonantal assonance. Verse 6a is an opening bicolon, the only one with a double-duty verb. It names Samaria. The next five colons list the things in the city that will be destroyed. They fall into two sets: first stones and foundations (or foundation stones), then sculptures and idols (or carved images). The latter pair occur in a tricolon whose middle colon apparently does not list a third item but identifies the images as *earnings of prostitution.* The final bicolon (v 7b) is governed by the subordinating conjunction *because.* It explains the logic of the judgment.

Besides the familiar patterns of parallelism between contiguous colons, there are larger patterns in the matching of the running series of verbs and nouns.

6aA	wĕśamtî		And I will make	
6bA	wĕhiggartî		And I will slide	
6bB		ʾăgalleh		I will lay bare
7aA	yukkattû		they will be shattered	
7aB	yiśśārĕpû		they will be burned	
7aC		ʾāśîm		I will make
7bA	qibbāṣâ		she gathered	
7bB	yāšûbû		they will go back	

In vv 5–7 the use of proper nouns unfolds the theme announced in v 1, and this continues into the transitional vv 8–9.

5aA	Jacob				
5aB			Israel		
5bAα	Jacob				
5bAβ				Samaria	
5bB					Judah
5bC						Jerusalem
6aA				Samaria	
9a					Judah

The whole of vv 2–7 can be arranged in sets of two, three, or four colons that exhibit all the usual features of poetic parallelism. There are two bicolons that have complete synonymous parallelism, vv 2a, 7b. Verse 4b has two similes in parallel, but the inner designs of the two colons do not match. Incomplete synonymous parallelism is more common. Verse 3 is the only exception. It has no parallelism, unless we accept "synthetic" parallelism; it reads more like prose, except for the archaic last phrase. In v 3, the detailed narrative development and the progression of verbs (*goes out, goes down, tramples*) does not use conventional parallelism that would slow down the pace. This verse is thus at the end of the range from complete parallelism to no parallelism (Freedman 1972: XXV–XXVI); and since v 3 fits snugly into the surrounding material, there is no need to call it prose in contrast to the poetry of the rest, even though we did this provisionally above. All other colons have parallelism, even when they are quite uneven in length, and v 3 is integral to the development. The patterns of matching pairs in parallel are quite diverse. None can be considered as characteristic of the piece as a whole, and this chimes in with the diversity of genres and the alternation of speakers.

The parallelism develops triads as well as pairs. This is obvious in v 7a, with the triple *wĕkol- . . . -hā*, and this trio matches the three objects of destruction in v 6, *Samaria . . . her stones . . . her foundations*. And there are three results, indicated by *l-*, but they do not correspond simply to the three objects of destruction. The relationships among the items are intricate, as we have seen also in v 4, where v 4b as a whole matches v 4a as a whole. Thus in v 6 two results are associated with Samaria, none with her foundations. Verse 6b as a whole matches v 6a, the building stones become field stones, the foundations become the lines laying out a plantation. Armed with these insights, we can add v 7b to the rest, so that *'etnan* comes three times in the unit.

Imposed on all that, there is an extended design in the syntactic sequence patterns of matching colons that are not contiguous. The possibility that some pairs of nouns are a kind of hendiadys has been hinted at above. The stone heaps will serve as planting places for vines. The foundations will be exposed by sliding the stones down into the valley. The idols will be smashed and burned.

A moral of these little exercises in poetic analysis is that neither the colon, nor the bicolon, is the working unit of composition in the original craftsmanship of the author. So neither the colon, nor the bicolon, should be the working unit of interpretation for the subsequent reader. In order to explore the rhetorical connections of any one of the colons in the unit, we have to read v 4 as a unit of four colons, v 5 as a unit of six colons, vv 6–7 as a unit of nine colons.

The syntax of vv 2–7 is that of poetry, not prose. This was shown in the introductory section on the use and nonuse of the prose particles. A definite article which is only there by courtesy of an inseparable preposition, such as in *kaddônag* (v 4b, parallel to *kĕmayim*!) does not count. The definite article with *lĕʿî haśśādeh* (v 6) is rendered suspect by its absence from the following parallel *lĕmaṭṭāʾê kārem*. Even so, the instinct of the Masoretes was sound, for the nouns in question are definite in meaning (gnomic generic); that is, there is a real absence of the definite article, it is not lacking because the nouns could be indefinite. The lack of the definite article with *Earth* (vv 2, 3) is striking and seems archaic. This contrasts with the use of the definite article with *mountains* and *valleys* (v 4a). In this matter Micah's usage is mixed, but the cosmic Earth more often lacks the definite article (1:2, 3 [1QpMic {*DJD* I PL. XV} reads the definite article at this point, and LXX has *tēs gēs*]; 5:3; 6:2; 7:17 — exceptions 4:13; 7:2, 13). In view of this poetic avoidance of prose particles one must ask if *zônâ* too (v 7b) should be considered definite in reference, [the] Prostitute (i.e., the goddess [Olyan 1988]).

Conspicuous is the nonuse of *nota accusativi*, although grammar would require it for the objects in vv 6 and 7. Not to use it when the object is a proper noun, *Samaria* in v 6, would never be tolerated in prose. There is no place where the relative pronoun should have been used but was not; its absence shows that complex sentences (so common in the oratory of Deuteronomy, for instance) have been avoided. Word sequences also depart from the norms of prose and can be explained as a deliberate attempt to secure a poetic effect, particularly chiasmus (v 6bB). Note the unusual placement of the object in v 6bB (which achieves chiasmus with v 6aA) and the position of the subject in v 5a. "A witness against you" (v 2bA) would normally be *lĕʿēd bākem* as in 1 Sam 12:5; Josh 24:22; Num 5:13; compare Gen 31:44, 48, 50; and see the NOTE on v 2.

As against these indications of the use of the language of poetry rather than that of prose, it should also be remarked that the *waw*-consecutive verb construction is more at home in Hebrew prose than in poetry. Yet it is used here several times (vv 3b [twice], 4aA, 6aA, 6bA), but only for future sequences.

One of the valid features of the method of scansion of a colon by beats is the recognition that most colons have only two or three "ideas," such as verb, object, adverb, and the like. So most clauses are minimal, yet complete, and nothing remains to be added in the next colon, which merely echoes what has already been said (synonymous parallelism). But when more than three items of information are needed, new material may be introduced in the second colon, and there is less repetition or none at all. Thus v 2b says: "And let my Lord Yahweh be a witness against you from his holy temple." The repetition of "my Lord" before "from his holy temple" changes this statement from prose to poetry. Yet if the author had followed conventional practice, he would have broken up the phrase "my Lord Yahweh" and spread it over the two colons. One can appreciate the impulse to tidy it up by deleting "my Lord" from v 2bA.

Another development in vv 2–7 achieves an almost imperceptible shift from the apocalyptic to the historical. The theophany of vv 3–4 is only a fragment, but it is enough to evoke memories of ancient poems dealing with the same themes, the cosmic convulsions caused by the angry advent of Yahweh. The events described in vv 6–7 continue the imagery, with ruins tumbling down into the valley and everything in flames (*fire* is repeated [vv 4, 7]). The second picture is more realistic and shows that the language of vv 3–4 is an extravagant way of talking about the transcendent component in historical actuality. The military connotations of the old theophanies, still present in such verbs as *yōṣēʾ* ("sally forth") and *dārak* ("trample" or "march"), suggest that vv 6, 7, 9 describe the devastations of Yahweh acting as warrior.

The use of all the "tense" forms of the Hebrew verbal system in vv 2–7 makes it difficult to determine the time perspective. The jussive of v 2b does not seem to be as suitable as a future indicative found in 1QpMic and reflected in LXX *estai*. The construction in v 3a (*hinnēh* + subject + participle) usually predicts imminent action, and all the following verbs are future, whether imperfect (vv 4aB, 6bB, 7aA, 7aB, 7bB) or consecutive perfect (3b [twice], 4aA, 6aA, 6bA). This is classical narrative style.

Quite apart from the several genres that have been mixed into the whole, there is no lyrical unity—no sustained expression of one dominant emotion by a single speaker. There are at least two speakers, Yahweh and the prophet, but the audience is not demonstrably the same throughout. As an oracle of judgment to be pronounced against the guilty cities, it simply does not have the required form of direct address in accusation and sentence. Instead, the cities are viewed as it were from a distance and described in the third person.

In more detail the most likely assignments are:

v 2a   Summons (by the prophet?) to the whole world (to adjudicate the dispute between Yahweh and Jacob?).

v 2b   Warning (by the prophet?) to Israel (?) that Yahweh will lay charges.

vv 3, 4   The prophet (?) as herald announces to an unidentified audience (the
same as those spoken to in v 2?) the impending arrival of Yahweh (for
the assize?). But this could be Yahweh announcing his own epiphany, referring to himself in the third person, as often occurs in such
self-declarations.

vv 6, 7   A single speech, spoken by Yahweh, stating his intended action against
Samaria; but not addressed directly to that city. There is no indication
of who the audience of this speech is, unless it is the nations of v 2.

This analysis leaves v 5 unassigned. The interrogation in v 5b, which is entirely
rhetorical, could be an accusation made by God (in a speech to the court?) or
a denunciation made by the prophet. The former suits the general dramatic
setting and the role of God as accuser of his people. The fact that Jacob and
Judah are not directly charged, but spoken *about* in the third person, is accounted for if the whole is addressed to the "nations" as a panel of judges, in
continuation of the mode of discourse in v 2b, which we have (cautiously) assigned to the prophet. The argumentative tone of v 5b suits the idea that the
one who utters v 5 is the prophet in his own person, not as mouthpiece of God.
The similar use of *this* in vv 5 and 8 is another pointer to this result (assuming
that vv 8–9 are spoken by the prophet). *All this*, which causes the prophet such
grief (v 8), is the manifestation of divine power (vv 3, 4) in the destruction of
Samaria (vv 6 and 7) and Jerusalem (v 9). This is due to the sins of the two kingdoms, concentrated in the capitals (v 5b), the theme of *the word of Yahweh*
according to the Title (1:1).

NOTES AND COMMENTS

Notes on Micah 1:2

The incongruent images and the lack of logical connections within vv 2–7 have
suggested to many scholars that v 2 is the end result of successive revisions of
the text—attempts to make it better that only made it worse. In this opening position, v 2 creates the expectation that the oracle will be some kind of disputation or *rîb*. But v 3 announces a theophany, and many readers have been
unable to discover any organic connection between these two genres. Budde
(1917–18: 83) considered that v 3 was a better starting point beginning with *hinnēh*, omitting *kî*, since logically God would manifest himself first in the theophany (vv 3–4) before beginning the controversy (v 2) with a speech that comes in
v 5. Hence Budde read vv 1, 3–4, 2, 5. Suspecting that editorial work had been
done on both opening verses, Stade (1903: 163) rejected all of v 2. Verse 2a was
retained by Lindblom (1929: 18) and Sellin (1930 *ad loc.*). Jeremias (1965: 11,
n. 2) at first agreed that the theophany proper was a better way to begin an oracle.

In a later article, however (1971b), he reinstated "the peoples" as observers by accepting v 2a as original. See also Willis (1968d). Lescow (1972a: 58) identi-fied v 2, along with 5:14, as the very last redactional touchup. On the basis of an analysis of other passages that begin with an "alarm-call" (*Weckruf*), Lescow concluded that v 2 binds the following material into a "prophetic judgment liturgy" that embraces chapters 1–5 (1972a: 58). Renaud likewise attributed v 2 to the final editor. It gives the final edition "a universalistic and probably escha-tological" perspective that was quite lacking in the book until the very last mo-ment of its evolution (1977: 58). Such reconstructions of the redactional process, having severed v 2 from v 3, are obliged to recognize the logical con-nection secured by *kî*, "because," the first word in v 3, as a "redactional suture" (Renaud 1977: 58).

The integrity of this opening bicolon (v 2) has thus not been universally ac-cepted. Internal dissonance has been found. First, the two colons are not well matched; second, v 2aA is suspected of being an editorial or scribal intrusion from 1 Kgs 22:28; third, the expectation that the *"peoples"* addressed will have some judicial role in what follows is not fulfilled.

So far as the poetic composition of v 2a is concerned, there is grammatical parallelism in the sequence in each colon of Verb + Noun (the lack of definite article with each noun is distinctly poetic) + Suffixed Noun. In a general way *peoples* matches *Earth*, and *all of them* matches *its fullness*. But they are not lexemic synonyms. The phrase (*kol*)-ʿammê hāʾāreṣ occurs throughout the He-brew Bible (Deut 28:10; Josh 4:24; 1 Kgs 8:43, 53, 60; Ezek 31:12; Zeph 3:20; Esth 8:17; Ezra 10:2, 11; Neh 10:31, 32; 1 Chr 5:25; 2 Chr 6:33; 32:19). In post-exilic writings an equivalent is ʿammê hāʾărāṣôt (Ezra 3:3; 9:1, 2, 11; Neh 9:30; 10:29; 2 Chr 13:9; 32:13). Micah's arrangement can be recognized as a breakup of a "stereotype phrase" (Melamed). Another stereotype phrase is ʾereṣ ûmĕlōʾāh (Deut 33:16; Isa 34:1; Jer 8:16; 47:2; Ezek 12:19; 19:7; 30:12; 32:15; Ps 24:1). The ingredients of the phrase mĕlōʾ kol-hāʾāreṣ (Isa 6:3) are present in Mic 1:2a. The language is prophetic, poetic, and cosmic.

The second difficulty—possible contamination from 1 Kgs 22:28 (= 2 Chr 18:27)—is harder to get a handle on. The clause is problematic in both places. Micaiah's call seems to be addressed to the two Israelite nations, at least to their assembled armies. The language of Mic 1:2a suggests that Micah is calling on the world community. The similarity of the names of the two prophets could have prompted the borrowing. In Micaiah's case the words conclude his speeches. In the context the audience is the armies of Israel and Judah. One wonders if it is a set phrase that could have been quite commonly used, but which happens to have survived in just these two places. That does not mean that it has been quoted from one place to the other, or that the similarity goes beyond the fact that the words were spoken by prophets. But the borrowing could have gone in the other direction, from Micah to 1 Kings (De Vries 1978: 16). The statement is rather pointless in the latter location, coming as it does at the end of Micaiah's speeches, almost as an afterthought. So we cannot take its apparent local meaning there as the meaning in Micah. Micah's original global reference does not suit the situation of his namesake. Doubt concerning the authenticity of the words in 1 Kgs 22:28 is supported by their absence from LXX. There is no reason why the Greek translator should have deleted them, and LXX is generally reliable in its treatment of the Primary History. The LXX evidence is firm. The Cambridge LXX certifies the gloss only in Armenian and Syriac versions. When it does turn up in late Greek texts, this is probably from the MT via Hexapla. See Lagarde's 𝕲^L in BH^3.

As for the third problem—the puzzling involvement of "all the peoples"— we shall pick up this language later in the book. "Many peoples" are involved, especially in the Book of Visions. A connection between Mic 1:2 and chapters 4–5 can be taken seriously if the book is read as a whole.

Listen. The imperative verb *šimʿû* is the call of the herald. Its six occurrences in Micah (1:2; 3:1, 9; 6:1, 2, 9) head major sections. They are a link between the Book of Doom and the Book of Contention. The verb may have an object: "this" (3:9), "this word," "the word of the LORD," or the like (cf. 6:1); it may be followed by a vocative, as here and in 3:1, 9; 6:2, and possibly 6:9b; or by the reason for the call to listen, using *kî,* "because," as in 1:3; 6:2bA. Rottenberg (1979) revocalizes to *piʿel* and paraphrases, "Gather people and proclaim to all of them." The juridical intention of the summons shows that the nations are not just an audience. The verb does not decide the role of the *peoples*; it can be used either way to call litigants or witnesses. Both ways are found in Mic 6:1–3, where Yahweh addresses first the mountains (the witnesses) and then his people (the accused).

peoples. In Standard Biblical Hebrew a noun that has a vocative function in an utterance is usually marked with the definite article. Waltke and O'Connor (1990: 247), citing Mic 1:2 and quoting Prov 6:6 and Qoh 11:9, state that the definite article is not used "when the reference is to persons not present or who are more or less imaginary" (cf. "when reference is made to persons who are not present or who are more or less imaginary" [Joüon {Muraoka} 1991: 508]). At another place, Waltke and O'Connor state that the definite article is used to mark *"nouns definite in the imagination"* (1990: 243, italics theirs). These observations are not valid. When parents call children (who are present and not imaginary) to receive instruction, they say *bānîm,* "(my) children!" (Isa 30:1; Jer 3:14, 22; Ps 34:12; Prov 4:1; 5:7; 7:24; 8:32). When the expected definite article is lacking, as here (cf. Isa 1:2), the diction is poetic. All the examples quoted by Waltke and O'Connor and by Muraoka are from poetical texts. No difference in reference or function is implied.

Who are the *ʿammîm kullām* addressed here? Foreign nations could be identified more unambiguously as *gôyîm* or as (*kol*)-*ʿammê hāʾāreṣ* (occurrences listed above). The latter phrase could here be split up over the bicolon. The whole of the parallel phrase *ʾereṣ* (or *tēbēl*) *ûmēlōʾāh* seems universal in reference, to judge from its setting in Deut 33:16 and Pss 24:1; 50:12; 89:12. But in Jer 8:6; 47:2; Ezek 19:7; 30:12; 32:15 the reference is local. At this point, at the very beginning of the book, and comparing Isa 1:2, a call to listen could be a summons to the cosmic powers, the witnesses of the covenant. The word *Earth* in v 2aB supports this. They are to listen to Yahweh's dispute (Mic 6:1). Here it is "peoples all of them" who are told to listen, but they are not told what else they might be expected to do. If the ancient mythological background of this kind of language has been preserved, the cosmic powers (gods of sky, earth, mountains, etc.) are supervisors of the behavior of contracting parties. In such a role they might now be expected to observe the dispute between Yahweh and Israel. If Israelite monotheism retained such language as mere literary decoration, it was so completely demythologized that the powers were retired from any possible role as judges. Casting Yahweh in the dramatic presentation as the only one qualified to arbitrate gives him a dual role as both prosecutor and judge, a complication confirmed by and complained about vociferously by Job. It could be that the selection of *peoples* rather than cosmic powers to listen to the proceedings is a compromise or rather a way of avoiding compromise with polytheism. Consider the invitation to Ashdod and Egypt to gather on the mountains of Samaria in order to observe the tumults and oppressions in that region (Amos 3:9). The peoples, however, take no further part in the proceedings; thus we suggest that too much has been made of the use of forensic language in the presentation of a prophetic message as a "covenant dispute," as implying adherence to due process in a formal court of law. The same problem has to be addressed in chapter 6. There, as here, once the dispute has been initiated by a call to observers, the confrontation takes place entirely between the two parties, Yahweh and Israel, and the argument is conducted in an informal and even conciliatory manner that suggests a preference on God's side to have the matter settled out of court.

The obvious meaning of the plural *peoples* is "nations," as it clearly is in the rest of the book. Even clearer are "all (the) peoples" (Deuteronomic) or "all the peoples of the earth." But it cannot be assumed that *ʿammîm kullām* is just a variant of those expressions.

The Masoretic Text presents several difficulties. One problem is the identity of the audience; if Israel, why are they called *peoples*? The same problem is met in 1 Kgs 22:28, where the call is to Israel. Another problem is the need for an object of the verb; but an object is often lacking in such an initial invocation (cf. 3:1; but the verb does have an object in 3:9; 6:1, 2 [in 6:9 it is not clear whether *maṭṭeh* is subject or object—see the NOTE]). Emendations try to come up with a better subject or a suitable object. LXX reflects the difficulty, for it reads "hear words." Because it does not add "these" or "my," Ryssel (1887: 13) suggested *logous pantas* as an intermediate reading. This is plausible, because of *klm*, "all of them"; but it does not warrant emending *ʿammîm*, "peoples," to *dbrym*, "words." An alternative to the latter is to read *mlm* (*millîm* [archaic defective spelling]), "words," or to find in *klm* a cognate of Arabic *kalām*, "speech" (Rudolph 1975: 32). The problematical *klm* has been targeted as a mistake for the original object "words" (*mlym* [later standard *plene* spelling]), proposed by Roorda (1869) and discussed by Schwantes (1962). Schwantes suggests (p. 20), the other way around, that *mlm* as possible source of LXX could have been a misreading of *klm*, *k* and *m* being similar in the Paleo-Hebrew script. Either way, retrojection of LXX to *mlm* does confirm that the Hebrew word ended in -*lm*, and not -*lkm* as the emendation to "all of you" (**klkm*) would require. The emended reading cuts across the Hebrew usage in which this verb is usually followed by a vocative. In this respect Sellin's emendation to *šmym* (changing only one letter) provides a vocative and a more conventional parallel to *Earth*, in line with Isa 1:2. The Greek evidence is not unanimous; some manuscripts and patristic quotations agree with MT (in matters of this kind we assume that the interested student will consult the Göttingen edition [Ziegler 1967]). The other ancient versions support MT, and in particular the problematical *klm*— Targ. *kwlhwn*, Pesh. *klkwn* (making it 2d person), V *omnes*. The change to 2d person is harmonizing; but Duhm (1911: 82), followed by Robinson (1964: 130), preferred it to MT as a more original reading. Emendation to *klkm* draws support from Mic 2:12—"Jacob, all of you" (compare LXX *syn pasin*), where emendation the other way, to *kullô*, has been advised! We disagree with these judgments. Whatever the connection between v 2 and 1 Kgs 22:28 might be, the identity of the two texts in this detail suggests that it passed muster with ancient Hebrew speakers. We shall shortly look at other instances of a similar switch of grammatical person in midclause.

The *peoples* are not identified and they have no identifiable role in what immediately follows. The phrase *against you* (v 2bA) suggests that *they* are the ones to be indicted. There is no other direct address in the opening oracle; Israel is not addressed by name. We wonder if this might be deliberate mystification, as often practiced by prophets, vague hints that leave the actual audience in suspense. In no other passage do the nations serve as witnesses of Yahweh's dispute with his people unless perhaps Amos 3:9. The summons to the nations in Second Isaiah is so that they may be judged. Micah does not have the idea, found in the prophecies of his contemporary Isaiah, that Yahweh sends the invader as his executioner. Micah does not go as far as Isaiah in saying that Yahweh will bring the Assyrian to the land, even when he discusses this possibility in chapter 5. In what follows Yahweh acts directly, and there are no foreign armies in the disasters he brings, although the anonymous agent of the invasion that causes the grief in vv 10–16 could be a foreign army.

Another possibility for v 2a is that the warning, at least in v 2bA, is addressed to Israel as the defendant in a dispute with Yahweh. Compare the indictments in Hos 4:1; 5:1; Amos 3:1, 13; 4:1; 5:1; 8:4; Mic 3:1, 9, and others. Israel alone is usually a people, rarely "peoples." Yet a few instances show that the term can have this limited reference. Twice Jacob is the ancestor of "an assembly of peoples" (Gen 28:3; 48:4), as if each tribe is an *ʿam*, a "people," "tribe," in the ethnic sense, while *gôy* more often is a political entity. When used in parallel with *gôyim*, as in Mic 4:1–3, *ʿammîm* brings out the ethnic diversity of nations, but in other contexts it can mean "kin," closer to the original etymology. This is most evident in the idiom "he was gathered to his kinsfolk" (he died). The singular can do equally well (Gen 49:29). In this context *ʿammîm* is almost individualizing—"relatives." Compare Deut 33:3; Isa 3:13, where the versions show that the text was considered to be difficult:

Yahweh stands to dispute,
standing to judge peoples.

Again there is no need to follow the versions and change to "his people" (NEB). 1QIsa^a confirms MT. Isa 3:13 is contemporary with Micah, and its meaning is clinched by the parallel "the elders and princes of his people." Micah 1:2 and Isa 3:13 thus support each other in the authenticity of the difficult plural. Furthermore it is clear in Isa 3:13–15 that the "peoples" (Judah) are to listen to their own indictment; and "against you" in Mic 1:2b suggests something similar here. So v 2 is not an unequivocal call to the (other) nations of the world to listen or adjudicate. The plural thus matches *Samaria and Jerusalem* in the title. Both cities come under attack in what follows, but no further word is addressed to the international community. The tantalizing ambiguity in the language of v 2 is not resolved until v 5.

This last point is not decisive, however. There are other disputations that begin with an invocation of cosmic powers, who immediately disappear from view. Micah 6 is an example. The position of *all* after *peoples* tips the balance to a global perspective. Unless it is a mere borrowing, the occurrence of the identical expression in 1 Kgs 22:28 (= 2 Chr 18:27) confirms the construction. The phrase occurs again in Zeph 3:9 (discontinuously).

all. There is a lack of grammatical agreement between the pronouns. The third-person suffix *-ām* clashes not only with the second person verbs, but also with *-kem* in v 2b. If *peoples* is vocative after the imperative verb (2d m. pl. "you"), then it too is second person ("you peoples"). "All of them," rather than "all of you" in apposition presents a problem. The construction is used not infrequently in various Semitic languages (Arabic [Wright 1896–98: 2:278], Aramaic [Fitzmyer 1957]) in lieu of the more usual "all the nations," with *all* in construct. It is possible that here we have, not pronominal *-m*, but enclitic. But it is more likely that "nations—all of them" has been frozen and is used in spite of the clash of person. A similar sequence is met in Isa 64:8.

The simplest explanation of the construction is that *'ammîm kullām* is an oratorical equivalent of *kol-hā'ammîm*. Failing that, the suffix could be explained (away) in various ways. Resorting to enclitic *mem* would resolve the morphological discord, for it is a lexical cipher. But the syntactic problem would remain. An adverb ("completely") might be the explanation—"all together" (NEB). Compare the apparently redundant *kullām* in Num 16:3; Isa 14:18 (pleonastic subject or adverb?); 44:9; or better, the appositive use as in Ps 8:8a and in Ezekiel 23 (six times) and the incantational repetition in Ezek 32:22–26. There seems to be something special about the use of *kl* in this way. It is like *k^welu* in Ethiopic, which occurs with third person suffixes, even when they are not functional (Dillmann 1959: 321; Lambdin 1978: 45–46). The construction is rare in Aramaic. Its occurrence in the Tell Fekheryeh Inscription has been attributed to Akkadian influence (Kaufman 1982: 152; cf. Fitzmyer 1979: 205–17), but its occurrence in Hebrew (e.g., Isa 14:18) and in Qumran Aramaic (1QapGen 10:1; 12:10, 13) suggests a touch of style. Such a switch in the person of the pronoun is not unlike the use of third person in relative clauses modifying second person antecedents (Isa 48:1; Amos 6:1). The same thing happens in Mal 3:9 — "it is I you are robbing, the nation, his all." So no change is needed. The use of *kullām* by all the eighth-century prophets deserves study. Its position in Mic 3:7 is strange, if it is the subject (see the NOTE), but suited for an adverbial function.

The wide attestation of this kind of construction and the impression given by its fixed form that has frozen the suffix even when we would expect second person makes it impossible to give a date for its first use in Hebrew. These circumstances weaken the argument of Renaud (1977: 32) that, because the phrase occurs in Lam 1:18 and Ps 67:4, 6, its inclusion in the book of Micah must be postexilic.

In discussing this problem, an important piece of evidence is usually overlooked. The same kind of discord occurs in v 2aB, where *Earth* is vocative (second person), but the referential pronoun is *her*, which is parallel to *their*, just as *fullness* is parallel to *all*. The authenticity of the switch from second to third person in the same colon is supported by the poetic pattern, for it is the same in each colon:

Listen (you) peoples—all of *them*!
Pay attention (you) earth—and *her* fullness!

The sequence in the second colon is required by the final phrase. The second colon could account for the inverted construction preferred in the first colon, which brings the two third-person pronoun suffixes into line. When the bicolon is all put together, the call is addressed to all the peoples of the whole earth.

A related problem is the discord in definiteness. One would expect both items in apposition to be definite—"*the* nations, all of them." Moreover, a vocative marker, identical in form with the definite article, is expected with a noun used vocatively. On both counts the lack of the definite article is a sure sign of poetic usage. The lack of the definite article with "Earth" (vv 2, 3) is archaic and poetic. This lack contrasts with the use of the definite article with *mountains* and *valleys* (v 4a). In this matter Micah's usage is mixed, but the cosmic *Earth* more often lacks the definite article (1:2, 3 [1QpMic (*DJD* I PL. XV) reads the definite article at this point, and LXX has *hē gē, tēs gēs*]; 5:3; 6:2; 7:17—exceptions 4:13; 7:2, 13).

Pay attention. Hip'il *haqšîbî*. The verb occurs forty-five times in the Hebrew Bible, exclusively in prophetic discourse and other poetry. Its sole occurrence in the Primary History is in Samuel's famous oracle: "Behold to listen (*šm'*) is better than sacrifice; and to heed (*hqšyb*) than the fat of rams" (1 Sam 15:22). The following words show that the implicit object of these verbs is the word of Yahweh (cf. Isa 48:18; Neh 9:34). The verb can be used on its own (fourteen times: Isa 10:30; 21:7; 48:18; Jer 6:17, 17, 19; 18:18; Ps 142:7; Prov 1:24; 2:2; 29:12; Neh 9:34; 2 Chr 20:15; 33:10), but mostly in association with some almost synonymous expression. The commonest pattern is in a matched pair of verbs *šm'* // *hqšyb*, (fourteen times: 1 Sam 15:22; Isa 34:1; 49:1; Jer 6:10; Mic 1:2;

Zech 1:4; Pss 10:17; 17:1; 61:2; 66:19; Job 13:6; Prov 4:1; 7:24; Dan 9:19). Micah's usage is thus conventional. But the inverted sequence is not uncommon (Jer 8:6; 18:19; 23:18; Zech 7:11; Mal 3:16; Job 33:31; Cant 8:13. Another match is h'zyn, with hqšyb before (Isa 51:4; Prov 17:4) or after (Pss 5:2–3; 55:2–3; 86:6). Sometimes all three can be used in varying sequences (Isa 28:23; 42:23; Hos 5:1). Compare Prov 5:1. The language of Mic 1:2 is found again in Isa 34:1, with a reprise in Isa 49:1. The resemblance is the more striking when we note that Isa 34:1 is the real beginning of Second Isaiah.

> Draw near, ye nations, to hear,
> And ye peoples, pay attention!
> Let the earth and her fullness hear,
> The world and all that comes from her!

First Isaiah begins with an invocation of heaven and Earth (Isa 1:2); Second Isaiah invokes the nations. It could be that Mic 1:2 aims between the mythological invocation of the cosmic powers, as in the primal covenant formulations (Deut 32:1 [which has the same mixture of second- and third-person verbs], and also in Mic 6:1), and the historical address to the peoples of the world. "The Earth and her fullness" has an echo of creation, but its global scope, and the addition of klm to peoples in v 2aA keeps it a somewhat unrealistic apostrophe.

Earth. This word is a familiar parallel for "heaven." The parallel of peoples // Earth is found, not only in Hebrew (Isa 34:1), but also in Ugaritic (RSP 1975: 411–14). Instead of recognizing the ancient mythic roots of this language, Lescow (1972) argues that, since Isa 34 is postexilic, Mic 1:2 must come from a similarly late period.

fullness. Population. mĕlō'āh means "that which fills her." The original command to "fill the Earth" (Gen 1:28) shows that the earth's "fullness" is its population, all living creatures, not just humans. Losing the word ml', LXX makes the appeal more personal, "all who are in it," suggesting human inhabitants. Compare ṣ'ṣ'yh in Isa 34:1, in parallel with "fullness." In other places the equivalent is (kol-)yôšĕbê bāh (compare Hos 4:3), and sometimes the two are parallel (Jer 8:6; 47:2; Ezek 12:19). We have already shown that in this global setting, the "peoples" replace the cosmic powers as the observers of the covenant dispute. Amos 3:9–11 shows that (foreign) peoples can be summoned as witnesses to see, hear, and testify—or at least confirm testimony. They are not asked to judge, rather to endorse the rightness of Yahweh's judgment. It is going too far to assert that "the prophet sets his pronouncement against a vast backcloth of world judgment" (Allen 1976: 269). The nations are not indicted here (we do not think that bākem in v 2bA is addressed to them). Only Samaria and Jerusalem are in view at first. But v 2 could anticipate the global scope of the Book of Visions, where the "nations" are universal. The cosmic perspective of the theophany in vv 3 and 4 does not settle the point either, for that is traditional, and it can be used as a literary setting for an account of a quite localized event, such as the battle of Kishon, as Judges 5 shows. This problem has been thoroughly studied by Willis (1968a). In conclusion we confess that the arguments are so delicately balanced—both options for interpreting "peoples" are attested elsewhere, and both make sense in this context—that the problem must be left unsolved. Whatever the nuance of the global scope of the opening call, the position of such words at the very beginning of the book indicates that the book was intended for a readership wider than the people of Israel.

And let . . . be. The summons to *listen* (v 2a), in this book and elsewhere, is often followed by accusation, by interrogation, or by the reason for the call to disputation (using *kî*, "because," as in v 3). Here precative speech continues into v 2b. The jussive continues the precative mood of the two preceding colons. It is awkward, all the same. The nations are to assemble because Yahweh is about to appear (v 3).

1QpMic (*DJD* I, PL. XV) has *y]hiwh* [*'dny yhy]h bkm l'd*, indicative "he will be." The lacunae leave it in doubt whether the quotation began with "and" but the reading of the tetragrammaton is certain, since the paleo-Hebrew script is used. LXX *estai* either used a similar *Vorlage* or made the same adjustment. The versions are divided: Vulgate *sit* confirms MT jussive. The preference for the indicative rather than the jussive is characteristic of Qumran, so the variant is probably secondary. If the more unusual jussive of MT is retained, rather than the indicative of 1QpMic, it continues the imperatives of v 2, making a double summons, calling the nations to listen, Israel to be judged.

my lord. This title occurs in Micah only here. 1QpMic has both names, but inverted. The Qumran reading with the sequence *yhwh 'dny* has some biblical support (Hab 3:19; Pss 68:21; 109:21; 140:8; 141:8; also Amos 5:16, where the phrase is distributed over the two lines of a bicolon, as would be the pattern in verse 2b, if the first *'dny* were removed). The sequence in 1QpMic also secures chiasmus with the sequence *yhwh 'dny . . . 'dny yhwh.* The double name is supported by Targum, Peshitta, and Vulgate. It is plausibly restored in the Qumran Micah *pesher* by Milik. The deletion of *'ădōnāy* from v 2 has been recommended (BH³, BHS) on several grounds and is widely accepted (Duhm, George, Schwantes, Powis Smith, Robinson). First, it is lacking in two Hebrew manuscripts, numbers 2 and 150 in Kennicott; but this evidence needs closer scrutiny before it is given weight. In Kennicott 2 the tetragrammaton is at the beginning of a line, in Kennicott 150 at the end. These positions would be more vulnerable to pseudo-haplography than positions within a line. The omission is obviously due to scribal inadvertence. Moreover, the missing *my lord* has been restored by a second hand. Second, it is lacking in some Greek manuscripts, particularly the "Old Greek," with quotations in Origen and Eusebius. Leveling divine names to *Kyrios* is fairly common in this tradition. The later movement of Greek translations or revisions closer to MT is seen in the mixed evidence. 𝕲ᴮ reads *Kyrios Kyrios*, confirming MT. But 𝕲ᴬ and 𝕲ᵠ read *Kyrios* once, although 𝕲ᵠ has *Kyrios ho theos* in the margin, a link with 1QpMic. The Greek evidence does not have much weight. Third, "It is superfluous to the metre" (Powis Smith 1911: 34); but, since the poem does not have regular meter, and this colon is no longer than some others, this consideration would weigh only if there was good textual support in the first place. The title "My Lord Yahweh" is unobjectionable in itself; it is used nearly three hundred times in the Hebrew Bible, particularly by Micah's earlier contemporary, Amos. So it could have attracted *'dny* from the next colon as a gloss on *yhwh*, the usual modern explanation. The size of the lacuna in 1QpMic requires the restoration of *'dny*, an important fact to set against the arguments for its deletion reviewed above. Allowing for the mix-up of *wyhy* → *yhwh* and *yhwh* → *yhyh*, 1QpMic supports MT in this detail too. It is not a very strong defense of the MT to argue that "repetition is a feature of Micah's poetry" (Allen 1976: 266 n. 7). Allen does not have many examples of this kind of repetition. If we had only v 2b, the parallelism *'dny yhwh // 'dny* would not be as good as *'dny // yhwh*. But the organic links between vv 2 and 3 are served by the device of splitting up the phrase *'dny yhwh* and using the two parts in succession.

When referring to God the term is apparently singular, although literally plural "my lords." As such it resembles other plural honorifics or "plurals of majesty," not only the familiar *'ĕlōhîm*, "God," but *qĕdōšîm*, "Holy [One]," and the like. This kind of plural designation of the one God, Yahweh, seems to be used only when there is a pronoun suffix—"my Lord{s}"; otherwise the singular is used— "Lord of all the earth" (4:13). It is possible, however, that the *-āy* ending is an archaic intensifying suffix (Eissfeldt 1977). We now have no way of knowing if these origins were remembered by later Hebrew speakers, so we do not know what was in the mind of a prophet when he called God, or referred to him as *'ădōnāy*.

against you. Duhm (1911: 82) omitted *bākem* to improve the meter. For *b-* with the meaning of *against* see Gen 16:12; 2 Sam 24:17. "Peoples" and "Earth" are invoked in v 2a, but the target is Israel, not identified until v 5. The universal language of v 2a, or even just the plural "peoples," suggests that the call is to all the peoples of the world, referred to by the fixed phrase that is broken up and distributed between the two parallel colons in v 2a. Yet these are to be witnesses to the arraignment of Israel. In spite of the strain on usage, the pragmatics of the speech indicate that the pronoun *you* in v 2bA is not anaphoric to the nouns in v 2a, even though that would be the natural reading and for the time being the salient reading. It is only when v 5 identifies the accused as Jacob // Judah that this initial reading can be revised and the pronoun understood to be kataphoric. Clines (1987: 94–96) has a good discussion of this kind of "unpredictability" in Hebrew poetry. The identical idiom in Josh 24:27 confirms the fact that Mic 1:2 begins a dispute between Yahweh and Israel over the central issue of apostasy. The tribal settlement documented in Joshua 24 is not just the constitution of the old league, not even ostensibly that, although modern scholarship has tended to assume that this was its purpose. The ceremony is represented as a renewal of an existing covenant whose main concern was agreement among the tribes in common worship of the same God. The ritual highlighted the incorporation of converted pagans. The "us" and "you" of Josh 24:27 matches similar phrases in Genesis 34 (also at Shechem). Hence the twofold assertion:

"us"   *tihyeh . . . bānû lĕʿēd*
"you"   *wĕhāyĕtâ bākem ʿēdâ*

It is a mutual agreement among the peoples to serve the same God. This could be the tradition behind Mic 1:2. The accused are Israel and Judah, both indicted in v 5. The Lord is not going to be a witness against the outside nations. He will be a witness against Israel. There is thus a change in the direction of the address between v 2a and v 2b. In v 2a the prophet summons all the nations of the world; in v 2b he turns to Samaria and Jerusalem. In spite of its proximity, "peoples" in v 2a is not the antecedent of "you" in v 2b. The use of *bākem* in Deut 30:19 suggests that v 2b is addressed to the culprits (Israel and Judah) by the prophet as a kind of bailiff.

   witness. LXX *martyrion*, "testimony," interprets *ʿēd* as an activity; but other versions agree that *ʿēd* is the person who testifies. This important term designates the role of God in the altercation, but its range of reference is wide, so that even Yahweh as the accused can be called *ʿēd* (Mal 3:5). This late usage provided Lescow with an additional argument that v 2 is postexilic (1972: 59). It should not be permitted to attract its modern juridical connotations—a person who supplies evidence. In biblical usage *ʿēd* is a person or object that cements a bond of agreement between two parties. He will maintain the bond and adjudicate when there is a dispute. If he testifies, it will be by reaffirming the terms of the agreement. Thus the elders and people of Bethlehem serve as "witnesses" of the transaction between Boaz and Naomi (Ruth 4, compare Jer 32; Josh 24:22; Isa 8:2), confirming its validity and engaging to vindicate it against possible future challenges. In other words, the "witnesses" constitute the court. Such a "witness" is distinguished from an "eyewitness" in Lev 5:1; but in Num 5:13 and Jer 29:23 *ʿēd* is eyewitness, and in Exod 22:12 it is material evidence. In a murder trial, a panel of at least three such "witnesses" is required, this being the minimum number that permits a majority decision (Num 35:30; Deut 17:6— note that this court also has the prime responsibility for carrying out the sentence; Deut 19:15–16). Agreement of two is necessary, and sufficient. A person who upholds such a charge is a faithful witness (Jer 42:5). The system would only work if witnesses could be trusted, Yahweh being the model. The testimony this witness brings to the dispute is confirmation of the terms of the original agreement, not necessarily evidence of its violation. Both are needed to establish guilt; and it is possible that the same person, such as God himself, would make both contributions serving as both accuser and quoter of the terms of the contract breached. A person who reneges on this duty (Lev 5:1) is a "false witness." Hebrew has quite a repertoire of attributes for such false witnesses.

ʿēd šāwʾ   Deut 5:20
ʿēd šeqer   Exod 20:16; Deut 19:18; Ps 27:12; Prov 6:19; 12:17; 14:5; 19:5, 9;
                 25:18
ʿēd ḥāmās   Exod 23:1; Deut 19:16; Ps 35:11
ʿēd ḥinnām   Prov 24:28

ʿēd bĕliyyaʿal Prov 19:28
ʿēd kĕzābîm   Prov 21:28

This role of "witness" was the same in Old Babylonian jurisprudence. A typical document, such as a bill of sale or marriage agreement, has names of witnesses. The contract itself consists of the promises spoken by the contracting parties in the presence of these witnesses. The record of these statements (the tablet itself) is not the contract (Greengus, 1969); it is a memorandum that enables the original witnesses to be reassembled to confirm what is recorded on the tablet. Procedures changed with time. It was easy to accept the tablet itself as sufficient evidence. At Ugarit the regular formula is that the tablet will settle future disputes, especially one issued by the royal court with the king as sole judge. A common formula at the end of the document states that, in case of any future dispute, the tablet "will prevail" over the person who questions the agreement. So, in the Bible some physical object that memorializes an agreement remains its abiding "witness"—preeminently the book of the Torah (Deut 31:26), including the Song of Moses (Deut 31:19, 21).

Important in the context of Micah, especially Mic 2:1–4 along with Hosea 5:8–12, is the designation of a boundary marker as "witness" in the settlement of an intertribal territorial dispute: the cairn at Gilead (Gen 31:44–52), the altar in Transjordan (Josh 22:10–29), the pillar at the frontier of Egypt (Isa 19:20). Compare Gen 21:30. The big stone erected by Joshua under the oak tree in the sacred precinct of Yahweh at Shechem is a "witness" whose function is clearly defined—"it has heard all the words of Yahweh that he spoke to us" (Josh 24:27), just like the "witnesses" in human courts of law. On a supreme level God is the custodian of agreements, the "witness" (Gen 31:50; 1 Sam 12:5; Jer 42:5; Mal 3:5), and the court for disputes about those agreements; hence appeal to this "witness" as vindicator (Job 16:19). This is God's role also in Ps 89:38, where a misreading of the poetic structure has led to a wrong identification of the moon as the witness. After a preamble of repeated asseverations (vv 34–35), Yahweh's oath to David in vv 36–38 is:

> Once I swore by my holiness,
>   I will not lie to David.
>   His seed will be forever,
>   and his throne like the sun
>   like (the) moon it will be established (for)ever
>   and a faithful witness in the skies

"David" in v 36b is matched by "his seed" in v 37a; "moon" in v 38a is matched by "sun" in v 37b, giving two firm bicolons. The traditional verse divisions and conventional versions do not reflect the poetic structure. The parallelism of the outlying colons, v 36a and v 38b, indicates a split bicolon serving as inclusion around the unit and shows that God, as a faithful witness, has sworn by his holiness in the skies. Neʾĕmān is an attribute of God as "witness" (Jer 42:5), the complete opposite of the list of "false" witnesses given above; and Job says that his "witness" is in heaven (Job 16:19), the location of the holy palace in Mic 1:2. The association of the Messiah with Yahweh as witness in 1 Sam 12:5 (so as to have the needed minimum of two?) helps to explain the role of David as "witness" in Isa 55:4. By a dependable covenant, as in Psalms 2 and 89, David has a position of authority as "leader and commander" over "peoples."

   temple. Or palace, corresponding to *mě'ôn qodšô* in Ps 68:6. Since the preposition *m-* here matches *b-* there, this supports Dahood's translation of the latter as "from" (1968: 136–37). The earthly shrine was but an outpost, a replica of the real headquarters in heaven (Freedman 1981). Because the design and function of the two palaces were the same, and because there was a nexus between them, it is not always possible to say where the main focus is in any specific case. Here, however, the movement of coming down points to the heavenly sanctuary as the starting point for the expedition.

Comment on Micah 1:2

The older critical methods denied much of vv 2–7 to Micah on the grounds that his original message could not have had such wide geographical scope, including Samaria as well as Jerusalem, Israel as well as Judah, not to mention nations outside Israel. Renaud (1977: 31) found the "universal dimension" of v 2 incompatible with the regional limitations of what follows. The apocalyptic perception that often goes with this kind of universalism is another reason for giving v 2 a postexilic date. When, however, v 2 is left in place and is permitted to open out into vv 3–4, the vision has more affinities with ancient theophanies than with later apocalypses. It is precisely as creator and ruler of the whole world—all the nations—that Yahweh reveals himself in concern for his covenant people. Ps 97:2–6 is one of many compositions with the same mix. In Nah 1:5, "the world and all who live in it" are affected by the theophany. Instead of accepting the occurrence of the plural *'ammîm* elsewhere in Micah as an indication that *'ammîm kullām* could have been part of his vocabulary, the conclusion already reached about *'ammîm kullām* as a postexilic addition is used to deny that he used *'ammîm* anywhere. In this way, all references to a larger geographical setting for the oracles of Micah are washed out of the text, and his original message becomes parochial. With nothing except the final text to go on, it is now impossible to *prove* that there is anything in that text that Micah himself could not have said. Willis's comparison of Mic 1:2 with the scope of Amos's opening oracles (1968d) is cogent.

   The retention of "all the nations" as called upon to listen at the very outset of the prophecy has been made unnecessarily difficult by an overdrawn appeal to tradition as a source of their role in the proceedings that follow, taken to be a covenant dispute. When cosmic powers—heaven, earth, mountains, etc.—are invoked, it is easier to postulate ancient ceremonies of covenant making as the source of the imagery. In international treaties the negotiating parties invoked their gods; in private property transactions, the titular god(s) of the city along with the king. While there is some similarity between ancient treaties and Yahweh's covenant with Israel, the differences are substantial, not least in the detail that the forms have been radically demythologized. A shadow of the gods of sky, earth, mountains, streams remains in the invocation of these cosmic entities. They have become quite inactive, and if sometimes the heavens declare God's glory or righteousness, it is as creatures, not as ranking deities. Any original involvement of gods has now been downshifted to human inhabitants of the world, but they do and say nothing. While heaven and earth would long be apostrophized as silent and inactive observers (1 Macc 2:37), any and all active roles of supernatural beings in covenant surveillance have now been taken over completely by Yahweh.

Notes on Micah 1:3–4

Verses 3–4 describe a theophany. R. E. Wolfe (1935) dated the addition of these verses to the book of Micah to his third stage (early postexilic) on the grounds that such apocalyptic material was not known before that time. Lescow (1972a) accepted vv 3–5a as preserving Micah's own words. The long history of descriptions in the Hebrew Bible of such self-disclosures of God has been written by Jeremias (1965). The two traditional components are the travel of God from his (celestial) abode and the convulsions of nature that result from his arrival on the earth (Jeremias 1965: 11–15). Chaos in the world caused by the presence of God is a standard topos in biblical theophanies (Morgenstern 1911, 1914; Hunter 1989). This use of conventional language and established imagery enables the author to assume a backdrop of familiar compositions and to evoke their more elaborate accounts by association. Beyerlin (1959: 29–42) has shown that the theophanic motifs in the book of Micah, and especially in 1:3, are grounded in the traditions of the Sinai theophany. The form of Yahweh in biblical theophanies has been investigated by Barr (1960). Like his near contemporary Amos, Micah makes no attempt to describe what Yahweh himself looks like. Nor does he hint that Yahweh is accompanied by a retinue. Micah's interest lies exclusively in what Yahweh will do.

Yahweh's interaction with the world is restricted to two elements only, mountains and valleys (v 4); these by merismus represent the entire surface of the earth. A longer inventory of cosmic elements, from highest heaven to lowest abyss, so often present in compositions of this kind (Judg 5:4–5), is lacking. Lacking also is any description of the effect of this unleashing of destructive power on the human inhabitants of the world, whether in large-scale slaughter (as in Isa 34) or in terrified panic. (The prophet's own response could be what comes in v 8; compare Hab 3:16 and Hillers 1965).

The description of the event is so spare that the instrumental causes of the ruin of the earth's surface are not identified. The verb yṣ' often describes a warrior or an army setting out (Schnutenhaus 1964: 2–3), but the portrait of the divine warrior, with his heavenly cohorts and full armament, is undeveloped (contrast Hab 3; 2 Sam 22 = Ps 18; Judg 5; Exod 15). Knowledge of all these great ancient poems can be assumed on the part of the Israelite listener. This picture of the descent of Yahweh provides the background for prayers for divine intervention: "Oh that thou wouldst rend the heavens and come down!" (Isa 64:1; compare Ps 144:5–7). The conventions are revitalized in later apocalypses, whose authors show none of the restraint of the early writing prophets. The opening scenes of 1 Enoch are typical of the full-blown form.

> The Holy and Great One will come out from his dwelling,
> and the Eternal God will tread from there upon Mount Sinai;
> and he will appear with his host,
> and he will appear in the strength of his power from heaven. . .
> And the high mountains will be shaken,
> and the high hills will be made low,
> and will melt like wax before the flame;
> and the earth will sink down. (1 En 1:3b–4; 6–7a)

After the first action, *setting out from his place* (v 3a), Micah describes two activities of Yahweh—he comes down, he tramples (v 3b); two objects of his fury—mountains and valleys (parallel in v 4a); two effects on them—the mountains melt, the valleys split (parallel in v 4a); and uses two similes to enrich the picture (the similes are parallel in v 4b). The incongruity in the last bicolon has led some scholars to discard the similes as a later and unsuitable embellishment (Powis Smith 1911: 36). Certainly v 4bA goes well with v 4aA; in fact the construction is a cliché (Pss 68:3; 97:5). However, to say that the valleys are split apart . . . like water cascading down a sluice does not make sense, unless the picture is considered to be quite vague, describing a universal convulsion in rather general terms. The similarity of melted wax and water as liquids enables both colons in v 4b to be seen as a double simile that goes with v 4aA, but not at all with v 4aB. That is, mountains can flow like melted wax (compare Nah 1:5), but valleys are not "like water," unless the splitting open of the valleys is to be compared with the gullies made by a torrent in a hillside. The lack of "and" at the beginning of v 4bB tells against interpretations that coordinate the two similes. (LXX has done just that by supplying *kai*.)

The poem then pictures the melted mountains flowing down into the valleys (just as all the buildings of Samaria will slide down the hillside [v 6]). But in that case the valleys will be filled in, not split asunder. The latter is clearly seismic and matches passages in other poems where the earth is shaken to pieces as it rocks under the impact of Yahweh's trampling feet (Isa 24:19–20; Judg 5:4; 2 Sam 22:8; Hab 3:6). One could always try to be realistic, arguing that an earthquake could split open a crevice in the earth down which water would cascade. But all that is needed is to keep the similes close to, but not necessarily identical with, the phenomena. So it is best to see a composite of images that are not altogether consonant. They derive from the three major comparisons that are used to emphasize the titanic forces that are virtually identified with the presence of God himself. These are itemized in 1 Kgs 19:11–12 — earthquake, wind (that is, hurricane with torrential rain) and fire (lightning). This, in turn, goes back to Moses's original experience. "The description is embellished from that tremendous scene that was exhibited upon Mount Sinai" (Lowth 1829, I: 197). The theophany is a manifestation of Yahweh the storm god, and the iconography of Enlil, Hadad, Teshub, and Baal supplies the general background (Jeremias 1965: 73–90). While the thunder can be explained as the rumble of the chariot wheels as the warrior drives along the mountain tops (Habakkuk 3), the landslides are due to the trampling of his feet.

Several motifs of this theophany are elaborated in the apocalypse in Zechariah 14. The military connotations of some of the language are made more explicit there than in Mic 1:3; there is a larger cosmic backdrop: *wĕyāṣā' yhwh wĕnilḥam baggôyim hāhēm*, "and Yahweh will go out and make war on those nations" (that is, "all the nations") (Zech 14:3). At the same time Zechariah's scenario is closer to Micah's than to that quoted above from 1 Enoch in preserving the archaic feature of Yahweh as a solitary warrior. No hosts accompany or assist him. "And his feet will stand . . . upon the Mount of Olives" (the geographical location is very precise), and the Mount of Olives will split (making a great east-west cleavage, with half the mountain moving northward, half southward—again precise details). Zechariah goes on to describe the reaction. "You will flee . . . as you fled before the earthquake in the days of Uzziah, the king of Judah" (v 5). Thus Mic 1:3b combined with v 4aB describes an earthquake. We remember the imagery of Micah's predecessor, Amos, who likewise saw visions of seismic upheavals as well as large-scale destruction by cosmic fire. Verses 4aA and 4bA highlight fire, which is explicit in the simile. The verb *yrd*, "descend," refers to fire in several theophany passages (Isa 63:19; Pss 18:10; 144:5; Schnutenhaus [1964: 5–6]), and the remaining expressions "he will descend . . . like waters cascading down a sluice" are drawn from the rainstorm. Yahweh will come down like a cloudburst.

It is inviting to link together *wĕyārad* and *bĕmôrād*, which have the same root and which constitute an inclusion. The six grammatical units in vv 3b–4 thus consist of three pairs of related statements, but no pair is contiguous; rather there is an interdigitated structure surrounded by an envelope construction.

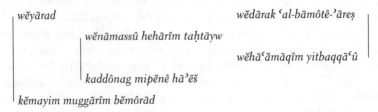

The envelope describes meteorological phenomena; the bicolon constituted by the second and fourth colons is seismic; the third and fifth are volcanic. Renaud (1977: 13) compares the sequence of colons in v 4 as alternation rather then juxtaposition of pieces with the same reference, with the alternation in Ps 113:5–6 with its elative *hip'ils*:

> Who is like Yahweh our God—
>> the one who goes up as high as possible to sit . . . ①
>> the one who goes down as low as possible to see . . . ②
>>> ①   in the heavens
>>> and ②   in the earth?

NEB connected the two prepositional phrases in Ps 113:6b to the opening question of v 5a and relocated them accordingly. Leaving the text as it is, it is possible to read vv 5a and 6b as an envelope construction. Recognizing the connection is not a warrant for dismantling the poetry. It is better, however, to attach the prepositional phrases in alternation to the preceding participles, a ① . . . ② . . . ①② construction similar to that in Mic 1:3–4.

The root *yrd* begins and ends the unit. These considerations render null the decision of NEB to shuffle the colons of v 4 (as it did with Ps 113:5–6) so that each simile follows its supposed reference. If the scheme in NEB implies a restoration of a dislocated text, it is gratuitous. If it is simply a translator's decision, it loses the poetry. What difference does it make? If the only objective were to unravel the intricacies, it would not matter whether the text is shuffled around or not. We are all observing the same relationships. Yet the point is not trivial. We think that the sounder method is to give the text we now have the benefit of the doubt, since it is quite intelligible. Accepting it leaves our minds open to perceive similar poetic devices in other places. (We shall meet the same problem, but on a more horrendous scale, when we come to vv 10–16 below.)

There is more than logic involved in the analysis of vv 3–4. Interlocking structures and long-distance connections are encountered all the time in prophetic discourse, and as soon as one escapes from the myopic vision that reads only two contiguous colons at a time, such compositions are found to be not only intelligible, but much more interesting and more satisfying artistically than the simplified and pedestrian rearrangements of the kind advanced by NEB. It remains to point out that the full detail and balance of the scheme displayed above is spoiled if one of the verbs in v 3b is excised, as is often done. Both verbs are needed. We cannot delete *wĕyārad* without losing the inclusion; *wĕdārak* is idiomatic with the following phrase (see below); and the omission of either would spoil the balance in length between the opening and closing colons. It is no objection that the unit of analysis has five colons. Two contiguous pairs do make formal bicolons. The second and third colons have mountains and valleys in parallel; and the fourth and fifth are both similes. The two interwoven images of thunderstorm and earthquake are the results of the concomitant actions described by the verbs *yrd* and *drk*.

3. *For behold.* Even if *kî* is editorial (Budde and others), it should be retained, for we are studying the edited text. The conjunction provides continuity with v 2, and *hinnēh* marks the onset of predictive narrative. The participial construction

is continued by consecutive perfect verbs marking four successive moments in the event—*set out, descend, trample, melt*. The imperfect verb in v 4aB is simultaneous with its parallel in v 4aA. An identical statement is found in Isa 26:21. Emendation to *hinnēhû* (*metri causa*) (BH³, BHS) proposed by Procksch, endorsed by Schwantes (1962: 22), is gratuitous. It has no textual support. The adjustment goes with the deletion of a verb from v 3b to secure 3 :: 3 meter. Other scholars, such as Budde, find the 4 :: 4 meter of MT acceptable.

Although it is a new beginning, v 3a also grows out of v 2. Verse 3 echoes and complements elements in v 2. The sequence *'dny yhwh . . . 'dny . . . yhwh* provides one connection; and v 2 identifies *his place* as *his holy palace*. With this equation, the verb *descend* shows that the *place* or *temple* is celestial. This reference in turn gives to *Earth, mountains*, and *valleys* a cosmic connotation, pointing to a universal setting for the judgment, not just a local disturbance. And the cosmic backdrop supports the conclusion that the peoples of v 2a are all the nations of the world. We vacillated on this point above and admit that a localized use of cosmic imagery is possible. We need, in any case, to recognize the continuity in theme and vocabulary within vv 2–4 while at the same time acknowledging the variety in genre as well as the clear grammatical transition between v 2 and v 3.

setting out. The connotations are military, but none of the accoutrements of the divine warrior are present in what follows, except perhaps in v 13. The same words *yṣ' mimmĕqômô* describe the lion's egress in Jer 3:7 (compare Hos 5:15 [Yahweh goes back home]).

his place. Short for "his place of residence," *mĕqôm šibtĕkā* (1 Kgs 8:30 = 2 Chr 6:21) or "lair," the dual meaning of the parallels *mā'ôn* and *mĕ'ônâ*. Meyers and Meyers (1987: 55) have shown that *māqôm* can mean "shrine."

descend. Psalm 18:10. The deletion of this verb is not warranted. Even less the deletion of *trample*, widely favored by critics (Nowack, Sievers, H. P. Smith, Procksch) and advised by BH³, BHS. The reasoning was that the long colon upsets the meter, and the second verb could have been a gloss on the first, or the present text is a conflate reading of texts that had these verbs as variant readings. Some manuscripts of Greek versions contain a simpler text with only one verb, but the facts are not always correctly reported. Crenshaw's statement (1972) that *drk* is missing from LXX is incomplete. Three readings are well represented.

kai	*katabēsetai kai epibēsetai epi*	*ta*	*hypsē* . . .	(W' Bᶜ O L'–613, etc.)
kai	*katabēsetai*	*epi*	*ta*	*hypsē* . . .	(B*-V–456 *III*, etc.)
kai	*epibēsetai epi*	*ta*	*hypsē* . . .	(A″, etc.)

Alexandrian manuscripts prefer "march," lacking a verb that matches MT *yrd*; Lucianic manuscripts prefer "descend," lacking a verb that matches MT *drk*.

The removal of one verb from the text seemed to find confirmation from the Micah text found at Qumran, in the absence of *wdrk* from the Micah *pesher* (Milik 1952). There are two questions here that should not be confounded.

Qumran proves that the reading already known from some versions also existed in a Hebrew text tradition. It does not follow that this evidence becomes a casting vote against MT. The rival claims still have to be debated using the proper method. First, one distinct problem is the intrinsic acceptability of MT, whether (the poetical question) the long colon that results from the "extra" verb is too long, or whether (the grammatical question) the coordinate construction is inferior, pointing to one or other of the verbs as a gloss.

Orlinsky turned to this problem more than once (1956; 1959 [the latter reproduced in *BANE*]). His main target was the misrepresentation of the evidence of the versions in the apparatus of BH³. The Hebrew texts are firm; the versions are another matter. While the full reading is widely attested in versions that have two verbs, one or other of the verbs is lacking in certain traditions. The fact that some Greek manuscripts lack the first verb while others lack the second suggests that each of these groups is secondary to a tradition that has both verbs. The verbs are similar in Greek (*kai katabēsetai kai epibēsetai*), so loss of either by haplography could easily have happened within Greek. Or an ancient scribe, suspecting dittography or gloss just as his modern cousins have done might have already thought of their solution. These variants are thus more likely to have arisen through inner-Greek simplifications than from exact translation of Hebrew originals; together the three Greek traditions preserve both verbs and verify the originality of MT as the source of all recensions. Such variation within the Greek transmission is a more likely explanation than that each of the Greek readings reflects accurate translation from a Hebrew *Vorlage*. It is "an inner-Greek problem" (Orlinsky 1961: 119). The alternative to recognizing streamlining of the Greek text would be to postulate that each of the shorter Greek readings accurately reproduces a distinct Hebrew original, and then that these shorter readings produced longer conflate readings in MT (dominating the tradition) and LXX (well attested). While anything can happen theoretically, such a complicated scenario, and such a coincidence in the outcome in two distinct bodies of text, put too much strain on credulity.

The pressure of idiom is a second consideration. Given that the variant in the Qumran fragment is original, knowledge of this idiom would be pressure to bring the text of Micah into line by adding *wdrk*. Orlinsky points out that comparison of the idiom where *drk* is used with *ʿal-bāmôtê-* plus various nouns (discussed in detail in the following NOTE) tips the balance in favour of MT. This is the standard idiom (Deut 33:29; Amos 4:13; Hab 3:19; Job 9:8), and Micah could have used it from the outset. Even so, the textual judgment is finely balanced. The fact that "trample upon the high places of the earth" is a stock phrase could validate Micah's original choice or it could explain why a scribe put it in later.

bāmôt. 1QpMic reads *]ty h'r[*. The definite article here is clearly secondary. Orlinsky (1961: 119) disposes of the argument from the presence of the definite article in LXX. Given Orlinsky's sustained animus against the Qumran texts, this variant should not be brushed aside so abruptly. The argument that the definite article was supplied in LXX by the requirements of Greek idiom has

truth in it. It recognizes that the word is intrinsically definite. By the same token, the definite article could have been added by a Hebrew scribe, as seems to
have happened with *hrym* in Isa 2:2. LXX could have had a *Vorlage* like that
now attested at Qumran. The definite article in LXX could be the result of
faithful translation of such a source reading, not just a move to Greek idiom.
That, however, does not give the Qumran reading any advantage over MT.

The phrase *bāmôtê-'āreṣ* is an ancient expression describing the rumpled surface of the earth consisting of both hills and valleys (v 4a). The "high places,"
bāmôt, locations of legitimate Yahweh worship in early monarchical times but
proscribed as centers of illicit paganism in later times, are a mundane adaptation of the word (Albright 1957b; Whitney 1979). At the same time its use to
describe cult places carries with it a memory of the mythological function of
such places as an interface between heaven and earth. The equivocal spelling
and vocalization of the word *bm(w)ty* in its ten occurrences points to **bāmôtê-*
as an alternative to the Masoretic *bomŏtê-*. It is a tenacious mythological term
that survives in association with various nouns and verbs.

Isa 14:14	*'e'ĕleh 'al-bmty-'āb*
Job 9:8	*wĕdôrēk 'al-bmty-yām*
Amos 4:13	*wĕdôrēk 'al-bmty-'āreṣ*
Mic 1:3	*wĕdārak 'al-bāmôtê-'āreṣ*
Deut 33:29	*wĕ'attâ 'al-bmwtymw tidrōk*
Hab 3:19	*wĕ'al-bāmôtay yadrikēnî*
Ps 18:34 = 2 Sam 22:34	*wĕ'al-bmty ya'ămîdēnî*
Deut 32:13	*yarkibēhû 'al-bāmôtê-'āreṣ*
Isa 58:14	*wĕhirkabtîkā 'al-bāmôtê-'āreṣ*

Etymologically, *bmwt* derives from *bhmt*, referring originally to the humps of
the primal monster. Traces of these cosmic entities remain in the phrases *bmty
'āb* ("cloud," associated with God's true domain [Isa 14:14]), *bmty-yām* ("sea,"
that is, the god [Pope 1973: 70], [Job 9:8]), *bmty-'āreṣ* ("earth," demythologized
from the god of the underrealm whose subjugation is celebrated in the appellative in Amos 4:13 [Deut 32:13; Isa 58:14; Amos 4:13; Mic 1:3]). Something of
the original denotation remains in Deut 33:29, the backs of the enemies on
which the victor treads. Equally old, and perhaps retaining the same connotation, is 2 Sam 22:34 (= Ps 18:34); here the victor is the king, but what the
psalmist means by "my high places" is not clear. Likewise Hab 3:19. The connection seems to be that these heights are the ones that God has placed under
his feet, and his followers are brought to the same position. This tradition gives
Mic 1:3b a military connotation, an association not incompatible with the nat-
uralistic phenomena (storm, earthquake, volcano) identified as theophanic.
Such convulsions take place in the battle with the monstrous forces. The
meaning of *bāmâ* thus shifts around from "back" to "ridge" to "high place." See
Crenshaw (1972).

The verb *drk*, "trample," describes assault (Deut 33:29; Amos 4:13; Mic 1:3; Hab 3:19), but it might also describe the stance of the victorious warrior with his foot on the back of the neck of a defeated foe (Deut 33:29). Hence the verb "stand" (2 Sam 22:34; Ps 18:34). The other verb "ride" (Deut 32:13; Isa 58:14) need not imply the use of a chariot but the use of the subjugated creature as a mount. Like Ba'al, Yahweh is the Cloud-Rider (Ps 68:5); and a comparison of Isa 19:1 ("Behold, Yahweh is riding on a fast cloud") with Isa 14:14 shows that the impudence of Helel ben-Shahar was that he tried to usurp the exclusive prerogatives of Elyon, not by ascending "above the heights of the clouds" (RSV), but by riding up to heaven on the back of a cloud:

> (To) heaven I shall ascend [13a]
>
> . . .
>
> I shall ascend upon the back(s) of a cloud [14a]

Verses 13a and 14a of Isaiah 14 are a discontinuous bicolon that encompass a tetracolon. The prophetic use of the familiar motif reifies the mythological incident to describe a historical disaster, both acts of the same God. For possible Mesopotamian background of the imagery see Gallagher (1994).

Earth. The noun without the definite article is poetic, archaic, mythic. We try to retain this nuance by rendering "Earth" rather than "the earth."

4. *mountains . . . valleys.* The plurals suggest a global scale, as befits the immensity of God. The effect is enhanced by the use of the definite article, although this diminishes the poetry, which usually lacks the article (Ps 97:5). The formal similarity between the colons in v 4a does not mean that they are parallel descriptions of the same event. Our structural analysis has separated them. "Mountains" are a closer parallel to *bāmôt* ("ridges") in v 3. And the two similes in v 4b, although their construction is formally the same, have different connections, as we have already explained above.

melt. The verb *ms(s)* is routinely translated *tēkō* in the Greek versions, and here too by Aquila and Theodotion. But the Old Greek has *seleuthēsetai*, and *seleuō* corresponds to *r'š*. LXX has transferred "melt" to the next colon, to obtain a more conventional picture. It also brings *melt* nearer to its stock simile *like wax*. We have already argued that it is precisely this collocation of *ms(s)* with *kdnwg* that points to a structural analysis that links v 4aA with v 4bA. There is no need to move them into contiguity. On *mwg* in holy-war vocabulary, see McCarthy (1971: 230).

split open. We see no need to even up the lengths of vv 4aA and 4aB by adding *thtyw*, "beneath him" (Schwantes 1962: 23). The verb secures assonance with the subject ('*mq bq'*) but the cognate *biq'â*, "valley," could have been used. The picture does not fit either the melting of the hills (v 4aA) or the similes that follow. The verb does not describe the cleavage of valleys to make deep fissures; rather it connotes the bursting out of liquids — water from a cloud (Job 26:8), wine from a leather bottle (Josh 9:13; Job 32:19). This theophany is close to mythology, and in archaic texts *bq'* describes the uprush of waters from the great abyss to match the downrush of waters from the celestial Tehom (Gen 7:11; Prov 3:20), for which the last simile (v 4bB) is more suitable. Thus v 4aB describes the release of the underground waters, as during the Flood. In creation this element was brought under control (Job 38:8–11); in the theophany this control is relaxed, a taste of the complete dissolution of the universe that will occur at the eschaton. Similarly, the shaping of mountains was one of God's primal achievements (Amos 4:13; Ps 90:2; Prov 8:25; Isa 40:12), and now they are melted down.

like . . . wax. The noun is met in the Hebrew Bible only in a simile. The simile is used again in 2 Esd 13:4. The verb is always *mss*. It describes diverse events — the melting of the heart (Ps 22:15, where the image is not completed by the explanation "before the fire"), the wicked (Ps 68:3), as well as the mountains (Ps 97:5, where fire marches in front of Yahweh). The imagery of lava is present. The mountains literally flow down into the valleys.

cascading. The form is passive, an irregular *hop'al* formation of *ngr*. It gives the impression that this development is not the result of natural flow, but of applied force. The identity of the agent is eventually disclosed in the *hip'ils* of v 6. Verse 4bB could be a second simile for the flow of molten mountains in the fiery theophany, leaving verse 4aB without a comparison. Yet the two are not congruent. The mountains melt like wax; they do not melt like water pouring down a slope. It requires considerable paraphrase to connect the pictures — the mountains melt like wax (and then flow down into the valleys [this will not split the valleys open] like water poured down a slope). The violent torrent causes the destruction; this is why we connect the simile with Yahweh's descent. Note the assonance of *m* and *r* in v 4bB: *kĕmayim muggārîm bĕmôrād*.

sluice. The exact denotation of *môrād* is not known. It could be part of the topographical imagery, the "slope" (of a mountain side). Köbert (1958) compared the structure of v 4 with Ps 113:5–6 and correctly observed the alternation in the linkage of the colons. He equated *môrād* with Arabic *maurid* to obtain the meaning "drinking channel." But it is going too far to make the verb in v 4aB "gush," with "valleys" as its subject.

The same double simile occurs in 1QH 4:33–34 and 8:32–33: "My heart melted like wax from before fire" [no definite article!], *kmym mwgrym bmwrd*.

Notes on Micah 1:5

Verse 5 is in two parts. Verse 5a is a well-formed bicolon. It is a comment (of the prophet?), explaining the reason for the theophany. The two-part predicate has parallelism of a traditional kind:

bĕpešaʿ yaʿăqōb // ûbĕḥaṭṭōʾwt bêt yiśrāʾēl

Yet it seems as if the prophet has followed the conventions loosely, with a feminine plural noun following a masculine singular noun. (In 3:8 he has simply "Jacob" // "Israel" and "rebellion" // "sin".) The language of v 5a sets things up for v 5b. Verse 5b becomes more rhetorical. It consists of two questions and two answers—four clauses—which can be displayed as four (short) colons that match alternatively; but each question and its answer could be one (long) colon (9 and 13 syllables, respectively). Verse 5b begins with the phrase "Jacob's rebellion" from v 5a, creating an expectation of a parallel question about "the sins of the house of Israel." This expectation is not satisfied in MT. In LXX there is more correspondence between v 5a and v 5b. In the Hebrew text the details become more specific, even though the phrase "the high places of Judah" does not provide a comfortable parallel for "the rebellion of Jacob." This is an example of what Clines (1987) calls "parallelism of greater precision."

Verse 5b purports to explain the term *rebellion* just used in v 5a. It apparently identifies the sins of the two countries with their capital cities. The balance of "Jacob" : "Samaria" :: "Judah" : "Jerusalem" is excellent. The match of "Judah" with "Jacob" feeds back into v 5a with the implication that "Jacob" here refers to the northern kingdom and even that "house of Israel" refers to Judah. Such an identification of referents could be pressing on the terminology more precision than the poet intended; perhaps v 5a refers to the whole nation (both kingdoms together), and then v 5b distinguishes the two kingdoms. In any case a holistic reading of the verse requires that matching terms be applied to both kingdoms. Their "rebellion" (// "sins") is epitomized in the "high places" of both Samaria and Jerusalem.

The language of v 5b poses a problem, for how can a city be a *rebellion*? The terminology of the two parts of v 5 is not identical (another surprise turn by the prophet), and this internal skewing has been rectified in various ways. Verse 5a speaks only about *Jacob* and *the House of Israel*, and v 5bA identifies Jacob with the main city of the northern kingdom. Verse 5b asks two questions in identical form about the two kingdoms, *Jacob* and *Judah*. The symmetry of v 5a and v 5b can be improved by replacing *House of Israel* by "Judah" in v 5aB; or the verse can be made more uniform by deleting v 5bB, eliminating all reference to Judah at this point. "In verse 5b the reference to Judah and Jerusalem was no doubt inserted later and harmonized with the title" (Weiser 1961: 253). There is no textual evidence that the colon is a gloss, but some general arguments suggest that it is. In v 5a *sin(s)* is a good parallel for *rebellion*; in v 5b *high places* is a less suitable parallel. The threat that follows (vv 6–7) is aimed exclusively at Samaria.

Intense research has not been able to produce an account of the redactional history of v 5 that receives general acceptance. In the title (v 1) Samaria and Jerusalem are named together (one preposition—see the NOTE). There is a proper noun in each colon of v 5, five different names in all: Jacob, Israel, Judah, Samaria, Jerusalem. On the grounds that an original oracle would have been spoken specifically and realistically to just one object of divine judgment, opposing conclusions have been reached as to just which city it was. Elimination of the references to Judah and Jerusalem in v 5 makes it possible for scholars to claim that there was at first no connection between vv 3–7 and vv 8–16. The former, in its first form, was focused exclusively on the northern kingdom

and must be dated before the fall of Samaria (Renaud 1977: 58). It is not a *vaticinium ex eventu*, for the demolition it predicts does not match what actually
happened. Verses 5–7 cannot therefore go with vv 10–16, which are focused on
the southern kingdom and are to be dated to 701 B.C.E. While details vary from
scholar to scholar, there are several researchers (Donner 1964; Jeremias 1971b;
Lescow 1972a) who account for the bicolon in vv 5bB–C as added during the
exile, after Jerusalem had met the same fate as Samaria.

This line of argumentation can, however, be turned on its head. Jepsen (1938:
96–99) argued against the originality of vv 6–7 that the language is not that of
Micah and that nothing is said about Samaria anywhere else in the book. The
original oracles in chapter 1 (vv 2–5 and 8–16) were concerned with Jerusalem
only. Jepsen's appeal to vocabulary statistics has been refuted by Renaud, who
points as well to the verbal links between vv 6–7 and 3:12. The authenticity of
the latter is not in doubt. Although Jepsen found the vocabulary of vv 6–7 to be
in affinity with Hosea, Lescow (1972a: 82) concluded that the common language of polemic against the cult was all postexilic. Given that Micah originally said nothing about Samaria, it has been inferred that the addition of
Samaria to the text was the very last scribal change or gloss motivated by anti-
Samaritan feelings in Hellenistic times (Renaud 1977: xvii, 43, 54, 59).

As against all this kind of work, the study by Shaw (1993) has found numerous rhetorical indicators of compositional unity within the whole chapter and
has also shown the weakness of the arguments dating vv 10–16 to 701 B.C.E., a
point on which many other critical decisions have been based. According to
Shaw, the whole of vv 2–16 comes from a time when the two cities were on the
same footing and could be addressed in similar terms.

The suggestion that v 5bB should be deleted as a later scribal addition intended to include Judah in the picture would hardly have been taken seriously
were it not for a general belief that the eighth-century prophecies, whether in
oral or written form, remained open to such changes for a long time after their
original composition. Some critics have removed nearly all references to Judah
from Hosea. Did these prophets address only the community to which they belonged? Micah is a southern prophet, and the title of the book makes it clear
that he has both halves of the nation in his sights. We do not believe that such
drastic emendation is needed in either book, since good internal arguments
show that both nations were continually placed on the same footing by the
prophets, whether the prophet came from north (Hosea) or south (Amos,
Micah, Isaiah), or spoke in the north (Amos) or south (all of them!). All the
prophets regarded themselves as prophets to all Israel.

The decision about the authenticity of colons like verse 5bB depends also on
beliefs about the size and scope of typical prophetic messages. If each complete oracle was short and dealt simply and directly with but one point, then
the rebellion of Samaria would be enough for one such declaration. However,
the prophecies in the book of Micah can be viewed as sustained compositions
of wide scope, so that an analysis embracing both states was achieved in his
thought and expressed in his message. The prophets did not speak only *about*

the people they were speaking *to*. We have already drawn attention to the peculiar phrase *concerning Samaria and Jerusalem* (one preposition). (See the
NOTE on v 1.) Both cities are dealt with on the same basis. Both are summoned
to the bar in the presence of all the nations in v 2 (v 2a is addressed to the
nations, v 2b to all Israel, including Judah). The devastations of Samaria (1:6–7)
and of Jerusalem (3:9–12) are described in similar terms (the language of 3:12
has much in common with 1:7, even though the imagery of 3:12 is a little more
mythic than the language of 1:7). If the whole of chapters 1–3 is viewed as a
single discourse *concerning Samaria and Jerusalem*, then the remarks about
the two cities expand stage by stage. In fact, Jerusalem receives more attention
than Samaria. Even though both are indicted side by side in v 5b, the fate of
each is forecast separately. And we can draw another deduction from such features. Micah's wide-ranging vision would mean that no one small local audience would include all the people for whom his message was intended, except
that any group would be addressed as representatives of the nation as a whole.

The name *Jacob* has the advantage of avoiding the confusion of *Israel*, the
ancestor, with the later northern kingdom. When it is in contrastive parallelism
with *Judah*, as in v 5b, *Jacob* means (northern) Israel, as the link with Samaria
places beyond doubt. Otherwise *Israel* in parallel with *Jacob* could be synonymous, but less clearly defined. *House of Israel* (v 5a) could be deliberately chosen to describe the whole nation. So it is the word *Jacob* that changes its
meaning between v 5a and v 5b. In Mic 3:9 *House of Jacob* is paralleled by *House
of Israel*, and this verse introduces an oracle against Jerusalem. So one should not
be overly precise in pinpointing the meaning of *Jacob* or *Israel*. In fact, since
Judah was also (part of) Israel, the name "Israel" continued to be used in referring to the people after (northern) "Israel" had ceased to be a political entity.

Verse 5b gathers in words from the beginning of the unit—"Samaria and Jerusalem" from v 1, *bmwt*, "high places," from v 3. In v 3 *bmwty* has cosmic-mythic
connotations, while in v 5b the *bmwt* are historical and real. Instead of arguing
that the difference in reference shows that the two verses cannot be part of the
same composition, we recognize (on the contrary) that Micah has achieved
several artistic effects at once. Instead of the expected "sins" his surprise *bmwt*
becomes suddenly very specific and at the same time picks up a word already
used to make a kind of inclusion. This pattern links the two occurrences of
bmwt so that each colors the other. The mythic world ridges that Yahweh tramples turn out to be precisely the familiar "high places" of the people of Israel.
The same blend of mythic and actual is achieved also in the two occurrences
of fire (v 4 [mythic]; v 7 [real]).

There is no need to keep on saying that certainty about the original text cannot be attained at our late date. In the absence of any compelling reason to
change it, the text of v 5 may be left as it is. The changes that take place between
v 5a and v 5b, however—the change in the mode of speech and the change in
the meaning of *Jacob*—could indicate that v 5a is a concluding comment on
the theophany and v 5b begins to develop a new line of thought, without, however, being a distinct literary unit.

all this. In contrast to *this* in the opening of a speech, which refers forward (as in 3:9), *all this* always refers back to earlier material (Gen 41:39; Deut 32:27; Judg 6:13; 2 Sam 14:19; Jer 3:10; Hos 7:10; Pss 44:18; 78:32; Job 1:22; 2:10; Neh 10:1; 2 Chr 21:18; 31:1; 35:20). Thus the phrase as used here refers in the first place to the theophany just described in vv 3–4; but, insofar as the destruction predicted in vv 6–7 can be understood as the outcome of the activities described in v 4, v 5 interrupts the development of that theme and anticipates also the destruction of both cities to be described shortly. Note the further link with *this* in v 8. *All* has been found problematical. Wellhausen (1898: 135) questioned it. There are two problems. One is why *all* has to be added to *this* in order to refer back to v 4. Hence the proposal to read a noun *kālâ*, "destruction" (Schwantes 1962: 24). The other problem is grammatical; hence the proposal to read a verb *killêtî* (Budde 1917–18: 26). There is no need for such changes.

Not much attention has been given to the sequence Predicate (P) + Subject (S) in this verbless (or "nominal") clause. Muraoka (1991) has shown that there is a trend from S + P in biblical prose (his data [p. 145] are from Genesis and Judges) to P + S in Late Biblical Hebrew; but both sequences are well represented in both corpora. Conditioning variables, such as the presence of a conjunction in the clause (many are "circumstantial") and other discourse-grammar factors need to be allowed for. Muraoka recognizes that the under-preferred sequence P + S is met when the subject is a personal pronoun, so one must ask if a demonstrative pronoun has a similar effect. The less common sequence brings the predicate into "prominence." The clause in v 5aA is the only instance in the Hebrew Bible of a verbless clause with *kol-zō't* as S and a prepositional phrase as P. In other kinds of clauses a demonstrative pronoun referring back anaphorically to the preceding text usually comes first (cf. v 8). We conclude that the sequence highlights the prepositional phrase and that the deviant syntax is poetic.

because. This word translates, not one of the usual prepositions meaning "on account of," such as *'al* (v 8); but *b-*, which often indicates the reason for condign punishment. Thus Joab summarily executed Abner "for" (*b-*) the murder of Asahel (2 Sam 3:27); compare Gen 9:6 ("for that man"; NEB, not "by man"—Lust [1991]); 2 Sam 14:7; Deut 24:16; and others.

rebellion. The word *peša'* is often translated "transgression." In a political setting it means "treason," in religion "apostasy." Both ideas merge in idolatry as Israel's worst violation of covenant obligations to Yahweh. Although "high places" are mentioned in v 5b, the crimes attacked in what follows are social and political, not religious, at least in the superficial sense of cultic or ecclesiastical. They are religious in the most profound sense, because the covenant was with Yahweh. Violations of the moral stipulations of the covenant were infringements of the sovereign rule of God that made Israel his people. Any violation of covenant stipulations was *peša'*, "rebellion." As such, the singular *peša'* does not refer to any specific act of Jacob, but collectively to all that contravened Yahweh's requirements.

Jacob. The name "Jacob" occurs eleven times in Micah, in all of the chapters but one (chapter 6). The name "Israel" is used twelve times. Both names have a range of connotations. Sometimes they are specified more precisely by means of a preceding construct noun, but this does not always secure a more certain identification.

1) Jacob (1:5a) // House of Israel
2) Jacob (1:5b) ~ Samaria
3) Judah (1:5b) ~ Jerusalem

The symmetry in v 5b points to *Jacob* as a name for the northern kingdom. Feeding this result back into v 5a, the parallel *House of Israel* can be taken as synonymous, another name for the northern kingdom, as in Amos. In this analysis v 5a and v 5bA both refer to the north, only one colon (v 5bB) to the south. But, if the two bicolons match, *House of Israel* (v 5aB) = Judah (v 5bB). We think that this alternative interpretation is quite improbable.

4. Judah // Jerusalem (1:9)
5. *kings of Israel* (1:14)—unidentified, but see the NOTE
6. *the glory of Israel* (1:15)—unidentified, but our NOTE on that verse points to the north
7. *House of Jacob* (2:7)—unidentified
8. *Jacob // remnant of Israel* (2:12)—unidentified; cf. nos. 16, 17
9. *heads of Jacob // rulers of the House of Israel* (3:1); cf. no. 1

To judge from chapter 1, the main associations of "Jacob" are with the north; and, in the absence of evidence to the contrary, this could be the continued connotation here. The accompanying references to *my people*, however (3:2, 3, 5), apply best to the nation as a whole. In 3:9 (no. 11) the same terms are associated with Zion.

10. *Jacob // Israel* (3:8); same parallelism of *pešaʿ* and *ḥṭʾ* as 1:5
11. *heads of the House of Jacob // rulers of the House of Israel* (3:9; cf. no. 9, associated with Zion in vv 11–12)
12. *Yahweh // God of Jacob* (4:2); associated with Zion // Jerusalem
13. *judge of Israel* (4:14)—unidentified
14. From Bethlehem in Judah will come a ruler over *Israel* (5:1)—a David figure, so here Israel is the whole nation.
15. *sons of Israel* (5:2)—the whole covenant people(?)
16. *remnant of Jacob* (5:6)—gentle
17. *remnant of Jacob* (5:7)—rampant
18. *his people // Israel* (6:2)—the whole nation, as the historical recital in vv 3–5 shows
19. *Jacob // Abraham* (7:20)—the patriarchs

The references to the cities can be taken at face value. References to Judah (1:1, 5, 9; 5:1) are unequivocal. Leaving aside the one clear reference to Jacob the patriarch (7:20), "Jacob" is used twice in "House of Jacob" (2:7; 3:9), eight times alone. "Israel" is used alone eight times, three times with "house," once with "sons" (5:2). It is only when "Jacob" or "Israel" contrasts with "Judah" or is linked exclusively with Samaria that either can be taken as a name for the northern kingdom as such. By the same argument they are names for the southern kingdom in chapter 3, because of associations with Jerusalem. It is facile to assign each major nuance (all, north, south) to a different source. As soon as we begin to appeal to vocabulary, such arguments work both ways. Micah 3:8b is very close to 1:5a. But the former leads to Jerusalem, the latter to Samaria. The usage seems to be fluid, and even when one of the kingdoms is in focus, the other is not out of the picture.

The political terminology used in Amos has been fully investigated by Andersen and Freedman (1989: 98–139). It would be no surprise if Micah stood in the same tradition, but it would be unwise to assume too much similarity. We note, on the one hand, that Micah does not refer to "Joseph." On the other hand, we have become so used to the critical literature on Micah that we assume that the references to a remnant that will be reassembled have the sixth-century Exile as their historical background, so that *the remnant of Israel* (2:12) and *the remnant of Jacob* (5:6, 7) are the same and are actually the remnant of Judah! We suggest rather that here, as generally in Micah, the name "Jacob" can refer to either kingdom (Samaria [no. 2], Jerusalem [no. 12]) or to both. Micah is prophesying at a time when no distinction can be made in the destiny of the two states. In his vision both cities are doomed, and the remnant will consist of the survivors from both realms, called either "Jacob" or "Israel." Micah's political terminology is thus not as precise or consistent as Amos's usage.

sins. LXX has singular, harmonizing with *pešaʿ*.

Israel. The versions confirm *Israel* as the parallel to *Jacob*. The proposal to replace *the House of Israel* with "(house of) Judah" (BHS) goes back through Wellhausen (1898: 135) to Sebök, endorsed by H. P. Smith. It is intended to achieve congruity with v 5b. It is vacuous to suggest that the mistake arose from misreading of the letter *yod*, supposedly used as an abbreviation (Schwantes 1962: 24). The value of such a hypothesis is dubious to begin with (Driver's [1960] proposals have not established themselves in the discipline); and in any case the very ambiguity of *yod* would make it useless as an abbreviation for both "Judah" and "Israel." Furthermore, the bent of LXX is to leveling (previous NOTE).

Who . . . ? The use of the personal interrogative pronoun *mî* rather than "what?" is problematic. Wellhausen (1898: 135) preferred *mh*, "What . . . ?" Peshitta has *mh*. LXX *tis* cannot be retrojected to *mh*, because it is required for grammatical concord of gender. It is not surprising that some manuscripts, and 1QpMic from Qumran, read *wmh*. This is the easier reading. Yet it is hard to believe that the Masoretic Text could be wrong in such an elementary matter. Perhaps the difference between *mî* and *mâ* is not as simple as we think. A solution should do justice to the animate reference of *mî*. Reading superficially, since the predicate is "rebellion," Budde concluded that this word is personified. Since the answer is "Samaria," the city could be personified, a common

figure. Compare the blaming of Lachish in v 13. But real people are usually responsible for sin; so naming the city blames the people in charge (cf. 3:1, 9).
There are other cases of the use of *mî* referring to things (GKC §37a). The several places where *mî* has atypical impersonal reference, and several where *mâ*
has personal reference are listed by Radday (1986). Texts in which it is alleged
that *mî* means "what?" are usually connected with a person's identity (2 Sam
7:18), expressed in their name (Judg 13:17). In Gen 33:5 *mî* refers formally to
Jacob's family, in v 8 to his animals. A similar interpretation is called for in Mic
1:5. What is in common is the animate referents. This is lost in translations
such as NIV: "What do you mean . . . ?" The question "What's your name?"
can be asked with either *mî* or *mâ* (Judg 13:17), as if *mî 'attâ* and *mâ šĕmekā*
are mixed. Clearly *mî* can be used with a nonpersonal noun only when that
noun stands for a person, even if in somewhat roundabout fashion. For this
reason we sustain a literal translation, but suggest the ellipsis. Giving *mî* its
regular value then, the question concerns some person. But a person cannot
be a sin; nor can a city. Hence we suspect a highly compact idiom — "Who (is
responsible for) Jacob's rebellion?" If Samaria (personified) is the sin of Jacob,
then the language is colorful indeed. In modern practice we say "Washington,
D.C." or "London" or "Moscow," meaning the federal government or Congress,
or some equivalent agency. The capital city identifies the people in their political and responsible capacity. Personification may be present, as in speeches
against other cities, like those in Amos 1–2. The rulers are really meant, and
the same is true of many references to Babylon or Egypt (Pharaoh). Samaria is
the target for punishment, but it represents the whole state or rather locates the
leadership, openly accused in the parallel case of Jerusalem (3:1–9).

bāmôt. "High places," "cult shrines." This word does not seem to match *pešaʿ*
the way *ḥṭʾwt*, "sin(s)," does in v 5a. There are two favored ways of securing
more symmetry. MT *bmwt* has been widely discarded in favor of *ḥṭʾwt*, "sin(s),"
bringing v 5b into line with v 5a; or *byt* is read for *bmwt* and "sin" is supplied,
following some versional evidence (LXX [*hē hamartia*], Targum). Peshitta reads
"sin," but not "house." The versions are not unanimous. Vulgate and Sym. (*ta
hypsēla*) support MT, as does 1QpMic, an important witness. The supporting
argument from context, that "sin" fits better than *bmwt*, could explain equally
well the ancient substitution of the easier reading. An ideal solution explains
all the evidence, but that is difficult to achieve when so many factors are at
work. The best solution would be one that accounts for most of the evidence,
and here the main difficulty is to explain how *bmwt* could have come into the
text. Cheyne (1895b: 20) accounted for the intrusion of *bmwt* as a gloss from
Hos 10:8. But the recurrence of this word in 3:12, where it makes an inclusion,
speaks for its authenticity in both places.

In v 5a *bĕpešaʿ* and *ûbĕḥaṭṭōʾwt* are suitable parallels, despite the difference in
number (Gen 31:36). When *pešaʿ* is repeated in v 5b, one expects the same
parallel to follow. Instead *bmwt* is used, and the statement that the high places
of Judah *are* Jerusalem seems tame compared with v 5bA — Samaria is Jacob's
rebellion. It is implied, of course, that the *bmwt* are locations of sin, and this

could be taken as pinpointing the sin quite specifically. The word *bmwt* is usually rendered "high places" (Albright 1957b). Since this is not a good parallel to "rebellion," it is not surprising that LXX and other versions read "sin." RSV conflates: "the sin of the house of Judah." By using *bmwt* rather than some conventional parallel for "rebellion," Micah has done two things. First, he has once more startled his hearers (now us, his readers) by twisting away the discourse from its expected path. Second, he has set things up for the long-range inclusion secured by the use of *bmwt* in Mic 3:12, the one statement of Micah whose authenticity few would deny. Micah 3:12 completes what begins in Mic 1:5. Because Jerusalem fostered *bmwt* it will revert to *bmwt*, just as Samaria's harlot earnings will revert to the same use (v 7). Besides this link to 3:12, *bmwt* is an echo of *bmty* in v 3. The LXX reading, even if it does go back to a variant already within Hebrew texts, as the Targum suggests, is even so an obvious leveling to v 5a. The word *bmwt* defines the rebellion, not as a parallel, but as a discontinuous *nomen rectum*, or at least as a qualifying complement. And both cities are equally guilty of the "rebellion of high places."

Is it not . . . ? 1QpMic preserves the *defective hlʾ*. The rhetorical question implies an obvious answer. Yet in answer to the question "who?" one would have expected something like "the king of/in Samaria," which could be implied. The connection between country, capital and king is made plain in Isa 7:8:

> The head of Aram is Damascus,
> and the head (compare Mic 3:1, 9) of Damascus is Rezin.

Isaiah 7:9 has a similar statement about Samaria. The kings were certainly responsible for the *bmwt* in both Judah and Israel, and the final corruption was their installation in the capitals.

In placing such a charge against Samaria, Micah condemns the religion of the northern kingdom differently from Amos and Hosea. They have animus against Bethel, although Amos exposes the pagan(izing) cult of Samaria as well (Amos 8:14). There seems to have been a goddess involved, and this is reflected in the harlot figure (Barstad 1984; Emerton 1982; Freedman 1987c; Halpern 1993; Koch 1988; LaRocca 1989; Lemaire 1977; Margalit 1989; Olyan 1987, 1989; Otzen 1989; Weinfeld 1984). The lack of symmetry in the attention given to the religion practiced in the two capitals in v 5 probably reflects the real differences between them at the time. Jerusalem had *high places*, but Samaria had *carved images* (v 7).

There is another reason for believing that v 5 is as Micah composed it. Micah is a Judaean. He would be expected to criticize Samaria as apostate. To turn the same charge back even more explicitly on Jerusalem might be unexpected and unacceptable in southern circles, but its shock value would be great, and Micah's contemporaries used it effectively. The best known case is Amos 1–2. Amos begins abroad and ends at home. All nations are placed on the same footing. Isaiah, using the same terminology as Micah (Isa 1:10) brands Jerusalem with the name of the worst cities ever known (Sodom and Gomorrah) and ends by calling it a harlot (Isa 1:21), which is what Micah calls Samaria in v 6. The use of suspense and surprise makes the charge unanswerable. If the Judaean listeners consented readily that the sentence on Samaria in vv 6–7 was just, then the evidence proving that Jerusalem was no different makes a similar fate for the southern capital (3:9–12) inevitable.

Judaeans were used to congratulating themselves that they were not as bad as their northern cousins, at least in the capital matter of idolatry, particularly the pagan (or paganized Yahwistic) district shrines on the "high places." In the north the officially sponsored worship of Yahweh at Dan and Bethel was conducted in ways that the self-righteous south viewed with abhorrence. Thus the "sin of Jeroboam the son of Nebat with which he made Israel to sin" was the use of animal images (the bull calf). So to speak of "high places" in Judah, but not in Israel, lays the crime against the usual accuser. Intentionally so. Judaeans did not need to be convinced about the guilt of northern Israel; they had to be made aware of their own. Although there is some allocation of distinct and characteristic sins to each kingdom, both are equally guilty of all sins. That Israel was guilty of "high places" went without saying (Amos 7:9). A psalmist saw this ancient national sin as the reason for the destruction of Shiloh (Ps 78:58). Even the great Solomon had built a high place (1 Kgs 11:7). In spite of the historian's desire to show Uzziah and Jotham in the best light, the historian is forced to concede that in their reigns the high places were not taken away (2 Kgs 15:4, 35). Ahaz is reported in the same terms as Jeroboam I, taking all idolatrous practices to the limit (2 Kgs 16:1–4). It was believed in Jeremiah's time that some of Hezekiah's reforms were provoked by Micah's words, and the historian puts the removal of high places at the forefront of Hezekiah's cleanup (2 Kgs 18:4). If Micah's denunciation of high places in Jerusalem itself is to be taken as plain fact, then the reign of Ahaz or earlier is the obvious time for it.

Notes on Micah 1:6

Verses 6–9 are characterized by first-person verbs, not used so far. The speaker is obviously Yahweh, at least through v 7. The *waw*-consecutive constitutes an abrupt beginning for a speech. The normal transition from an accusation (v 5) to the sentence (v 6) is "therefore." The use of the consecutive construction *wĕśamtî* suggests the continuation of some action already begun. This earlier stage is probably represented by vv 3–4, in spite of the switch from third to first person. In fact, it is precisely the continuity secured by the salient use of the consecutive verb construction that points to the cohesion of vv 6–7 with 3–4. Verse 5 is then a parenthetical explanation for the full program set out in vv 3–4, 6–7. Both phases are equally called *this* (vv 5aA, 8a). The activity of v 4 passes into that of v 6.

The syntax of vv 6–7 is consistent. Clause-initial verbs are consecutive perfects (6aA, 6bA), and imperfect verbs come later in their clauses (6bB, 7). In v 7a a bicolon with two passive verbs is inserted in a passage dominated by active verbs. There can be no doubt, however, that all equally are acts of God. Jepsen

(1938) doubted the authenticity of vv 6–7 and was suspicious of v 5b as well. The question can be turned around to ask if Yahweh has been the speaker from the beginning, even though he speaks about himself in the third person (Renaud 1977: xviii). Once we realize that there is nothing incongruous about this, in fact it can be identified as *Hofstil*, we can be on the lookout for more divine speech in this indirect mode in the rest of the prophecy.

Although most scholars retain vv 6–7 as the threat that naturally follows the accusation in v 5, some, notably Jepsen (1938) and Lescow (1972a), identified vv 6–7 as a later (even the last) addition to the book. Those who recognize that a word of reprimand (v 5) should be followed by a word of menace do not necessarily accept vv 6–7 as that *Drohwort*, at least in its original form. Elliger (1934: 138 n. 4), followed by Jeremias (1971b: 335–37), considered that the Hosean-Deuteronomic language of v 7a shows that it is a gloss on v 7b. To illustrate: the expression "burn [idols] in the fire" occurs (elsewhere) only in Deuteronom[ist]ic texts; the idiom "put to desolation" (*śym šmmh*) is characteristic of Jeremiah (but compare Josh 8:28). The inference is not self-evident, and it has not been irrefutably proved that all Deuteronomistic traditions are later than the eighth century.

make. The ruin of Samaria has two aspects: the buildings will be demolished and the idols destroyed. If the oracle has a single target, the stones that are hurled into the valley could be those of the Temple. This seems to be the case in the parallel instance of Jerusalem (Mic 3:12); but the stone superstructure is probably that of the walls, a magnificent feature of the city that Isaiah described as "the proud crown . . . on the head of the rich valley" (Isa 28:1; Gilula [1974]). Furthermore Isaiah describes the devastation of the city by means of a violent storm (Isa 28:2) in language that has affinities with Mic 1:4. In Isa 28:2 "My Lord" has (or is) a violent destroyer who comes down with hurricane force as driving rain and pelting hail. He is also described as trampling Samaria with his feet (Isa 28:3; cf. Mic 1:3b).

Like a storm of hail,
a tempest of destruction,
like a storm of waters
mighty, overflowing,
he will hurl to the earth with his hand,
with his feet he will trample
the crown of pride of the drunkards of Ephraim.

into. The preposition *l-* marks the object complement; it does not make a simile ("as . . . as . . . " in RV).

stone heap. The word *ʿî* has attracted suspicion. Now that the reading is confirmed by 1QpMic this suspicion has diminished somewhat. Numerous proposals to read it differently were reviewed by Schwantes (1962: 25). Some follow LXX to read "and plantings of a vineyard." Lindblom (Schwantes 1962: 27) recovers a 3 :: 3 bicolon with better parallelism:

And I shall put Samaria to ruins,
and her fields to vineyard plantings.

Schwantes (1962: 26) takes two more steps beyond this. First, he discards *maṭṭā'ê* to achieve 3 :: 2 meter (he has to change *hśdh* to *wśdyh*); second, he accepts a proposal of Weidner to equate *krm* with Assyrian *karmu*, "ruin," improving the parallelism. The analogy with the Assyrian cliché is impressive, but would Micah have known such texts? The proposal loses credibility when three words have to be adjusted to make it work, one by rewriting, one by deletion, and one by replacing the meaning of a familiar Hebrew word with a foreign borrowing. We do not consider either the grammatical incompleteness or the metrical imbalance of v 6bA to be a blemish. The aggregate of sixteen syllables for a bicolon is standard.

At first sight the imagery in v 6a is an incongruous mixture. Two ideas are suggested: first, that the city site will become a useless ruin; second, that it will revert to agriculture. The associations of (grain)field and vineyard are positive and could represent the countryman's prejudice against urban development. Such a future for Samaria moderates the severity of the judgment, for then the land can be put to the use intended by God himself. "Again you shall plant vineyards on the mountains of Samaria; the planters shall plant and shall enjoy the fruit" (Jer 31:5). On the use of hillsides for viticulture, see Mayerson (1959). In more extreme cases a site can revert to wilderness or desert (Isa 7:23–25, 34). The perceived discord between v 6aA and v 6aB arises from the traditional gloss of *'î* as "ruin" (cf. *'ay*). The related words *'î* (Job 30:24), plural Mic 3:12 (= Jer 26:18, but with a different ending); Ps 79:1, *mĕ'î* (Isa 17:1), or *'awwâ* (Ezek 21:32), generally describe the heaps of rubble in a demolished city. The city of Ai has a name that can be construed as "ruin," whether that was its original meaning or not. Biblical usage implies destruction in war, which turns a town back to country terrain. Micah's qualification—"a heap of stones in a field"—and the parallelism of the vineyard suggest that it is not wasteland. There is an implied comparison between the piles of stones such as one finds in the field, gathered out and heaped up by the farmer—a constructive act—and the ruined city. The site of Samaria was originally a private estate (1 Kgs 16:24) devoted to agriculture and, to judge from present-day practice, to the vine and the olive. What Yahweh will do, when he takes the stones erected by Omri and his successors and hurls them violently into the valley below, will be the work of a good farmer. Yahweh is described in exactly those terms in Isa 5:1–3. In this way Samaria will become a well-planned vineyard, as Yahweh always intended for his land (Isa 5:7; Ezek 31:4), so that like Jerusalem it might be called Yahweh's "plantation" (Isa 61:3). Such a pleasing prospect, however, is hardly glimpsed; and it would not have been pleasing to the Samarians. The emphasis is on the destruction of buildings and on depopulation. There is also an irony like that of v 7b. There will be reversion, some good, some bad.

pour. The same root as in v 4bB. The root *ngr* is an important verbal link between the theophany and the judgment speech. The basic idea is to pour something out: water (2 Sam 14:14), wine (Ps 75:9), tears (Lam 3:49), blood (implied, because the sword is used: Jer 18:21; Ezek 35:5; Ps 63:11). Micah 1 is the only text in which solids are "poured"—the mountains in v 4, the stones of Samaria in v 6. The two pictures are similar and complement each other. In each case rocks pour down a slope into a valley. The repetition of the verbal root points to the same agency both times, or even to the same event. The visionary aspect of the theophany continues into the judgment speech. Samaria will be destroyed by the advent of Yahweh.

valley. Spelled either *gy* or *gy'*. It is possible that here *alef* was lost by haplography; but this does not explain the other occurrences of *gy*.

stones. The building projects of Omri and Ahab (the contributions of each king cannot be distinguished, any more than those of David and Solomon can) represented a significant advance in Israelite architecture, especially the masonry. See Paul and Dever (1973), especially chapter 3, and Mazar (1990: 406–10). Doubtless there was pride in its durability. The "stones," stone buildings of Samaria, were palaces and defense walls. The pictorial language suggests the collapse of the latter, as described with equal vividness by Isaiah (28:2). Isaiah compares the imposing ramparts of Samaria (featured like the walls of Uruk in Gilgamesh or the walls of Zion in the Psalms) to a beautiful crown encircling the brow of the hill. Isaiah's language suggests that this structure was undermined and tumbled into the valley below by a torrential downpour just like the rushing waters of Mic 1:4bB. See the passage quoted above.

lay bare. The verb *'ăgalleh* means "reveal" or "expose." The buildings are demolished, but not razed (Meyers and Meyers 1987: 63f.) The foundations are laid bare, but not removed. This pictorial detail is quite realistic. A common feature of a tell in the Near East is the presence in its sloping sides of visible lines of foundation stones (or lower courses) of ancient walls. Exposure of the foundations (Ps 137:7) means deliberate systematic destruction. The actions in vv 6bA and 6bB are correlative.

The verb is only a hint at this point in the oracle. The verb "I will strip bare" has a further connotation, since Samaria will shortly be called a prostitute. The word *earnings* links v 7b to v 7aB, and makes more explicit the branding of Samaria as a prostitute, which is already implied by calling her images and idols her harlot earnings. Samaria . . . her . . . her . . . her . . . her . . . her . . . harlot . . . harlot make a single thread through vv 6–7. And this continuity gives a nuance to *lay bare* in v 6bB. Stripping and exposure to public disgrace were fitting punishment for a wife whose infidelity took this form (Hos 2:12—same word; see the full discussion in Andersen and Freedman 1980: 246). Compare Isaiah's similar threat against the wanton women (Isa 3:18–24) in harlot Jerusalem (Isa 1:21).

Notes on Micah 1:7

Because it condemns the cultus, the originality of v 7 was questioned by Bruno (1923: 20). The word *bmwt* in v 5 is eliminated for the same reason. Most scholars retain v 7, but parts of it attract suspicion. Scholars who work with the doctrine that Hebrew poets worked exclusively (or mainly) with bicolons suspect the tricolon in v 7a. Scholars who work with the doctrine that Hebrew poets strove to achieve synonymous parallelism in each bicolon are troubled by the fact that not one of the three colons in v 7a is a perfect match for any of the others by this criterion. The closest synonyms are *pĕsîleyhā* and *ʿăṣabbeyhā*, but the verbs in their colons are different in reference, person, and voice. The verbs in vv 7aA and 7aB have the same voice, and this fact, together with contiguity, encourages acceptance of this unit as a bicolon. The noun *ʾetnanneyhā* (*earnings*), however, is not a synonym for *pĕsîleyhā* (*carved images*). Wellhausen (1898: 135) changed *ʾetnanneyhā* to *ʾăšēreyhā* ("her *asherahs*"), and this has been the most popular emendation. Part of the argument is that *asherim*, "wooden poles," could be *burned*. Powis Smith (1911: 35) objected, stating that *ʾăšēreyhā* would require a feminine verb. Hillers (1984: 18) and R. L. Smith (1984: 16) accepted this point and rejected Wellhausen's emendation. The argument based on gender is not itself very strong; an adjustment in the gender can be made easily. Even so, the more changes needed for an emendation, the less convincing it is. Willi-Plein (1971: 71) and Vuilleumer (1971: 17 n. 7) sustain Wellhausen's emendation. Mays (1976: 46) argued that the original *ʾăšēreyhā* might have been damaged, and wrongly repaired by bringing in *ʾetnanneyhā* from v 7b. As Renaud (1977: 15) points out, there is no textual support for this proposal.

A more drastic solution (BHS) is to delete v 7aB altogether (Rudolph 1975: 33). The present state of v 7aB is further suspect because of its length (four words, eleven [or twelve] syllables). None of these arguments against the originality of v 7aB has weight. Verse 7aC is almost as long. Hebrew prophet-poets worked with units of any number of colons and with colons of varying lengths. Our overall analysis of the nine-colon unit in vv 6–7 has shown that the colons line up in all kinds of combinations and patterns, including many trios. Matched items between colons are not necessarily synonyms; nor are all matched pairs in contiguous colons. In particular, the intrusion of *earnings* into v 7a constitutes an interdigitated link with v 7b; the passive verb makes a match with v 7aA; and *fire* makes a longer linkage with v 4.

images. The three colons are linked by the repetition of "all." The parallelism shows that both *images* and *idols* are related somehow to her prostitute *earnings*, the middle term. The technology of the manufacture of figurines of divine beings, as described in various polemical passages, such as Isa 40:19–20; 41:6–7, indicates wood carving, gilded or otherwise adorned with precious metal. Such objects can be cut up (*krt* [Mic 5:12] or *gdʿ* [Deut 12:3]; here in v 7aA *ktt* means to smash by hammer blows) and burnt (Deut 7:5, 25). The gold bull was "burned in fire" (Exod 32:20), "crushed" and "ground" (Deut 9:21). A sculpture or a casting could also be called a *pesel*, so the term is quite general.

The parallelism of *pĕsîleyhā* and *ʿăṣabbeyhā* is quite significant, because the latter had its main currency in the eighth-century prophets, Isaiah, Micah, and especially Hosea, who uses the plural as a proper noun, the name of Baal. In Isa 10:10–11 a speech placed in the mouth of the Assyrian official refers to both

Samaria and Jerusalem (Micah's terminology) as "kingdoms of the idol (*'ĕlîl*)." Their idols (*'ĕlîlîm*) are both *pĕsîlîm* and *'ăṣabbîm* (Micah's sequence). Hosea does not use *'ăṣabbîm* as a common noun (Andersen and Freedman 1980: 649), whereas Micah's modifiers, both *kol* and the pronoun suffix, emphasize the multiplicity of the idols rather than the identity of the false god. Their presence in Samaria shows what is meant by "the rebellion . . . of *bmwt*" in v 5.

shattered . . . burned. This is what the Israelites should have done under the covenant that prohibited the manufacture and banned the use of idols—Deut 7:5, and others. This is what good King Josiah did (2 Chr 34:3–7). The verb *shatter* shows that stone *pĕsîlîm* were destroyed like the *maṣṣēbôt* ("standing stones") mentioned in Deut 7:5. God entrusted to his people the rectification of the faults in his world, in this instance the eradication of idols. When they failed, he would do it himself. This would happen, according to Micah, because the Israelites not only failed to eradicate the idols themselves, but even added to the number and became practitioners of the idolatry they were ordered to remove.

The use of passive verb forms in this bicolon contrasts with the other active verb forms and has attracted the suspicion that these statements are secondary. Embedded in four clauses (three in v 6, one in v 7aC) that identify Yahweh as agent, there is no need to complicate the story by arguing that the destruction in v 7a will be carried out by another agent. Even if such things are done by a human agent (an invader—Assyria[?]), in prophetic perception any such events are as much acts of God as acts of humans. There are other oracles in which an initial threat of punishment uttered by God using first-person speech is followed by a more impersonal statement, sometimes with a passive verb.

I shall eat them there like a lion,
　　a wild beast will tear them apart. (Hos 13:8b)
Behold I am doing a wonder with this people . . .
　　and the wisdom of the wise will perish. (Isa 29:14)
Behold days are coming,
　　and I will cut off thine arm . . .
　　and thou shalt see . . . (1 Sam 2:31—MT is in disorder)
Behold I am expelling you from upon the face of the ground;
　　this year you are going to die. (Jer 28:16)

earnings. There is no serious reason for doubting that the word *'etnannîm* is original in all three occurrences and has the same meaning ("harlot's pay") each time. Derivation from the root *ntn*, "give," "pay," is doubtful. The pattern does not fit any other Hebrew noun type. It is almost certainly identical with Ugaritic *itnn*, "marriage gift" (Kottsieper 1984: 108), but a close connection in meaning is unlikely (Pardee 1978). The derivation in Ugaritic is just as problematic as it is in Hebrew (von Soden [1988] suggests a Hurrian etymology). The word seems to have acquired a specialized use in Hebrew; its meanings in other languages do not contribute to the understanding of Mic 1:7.

The best object for the verb *burn* would be something made out of wood; hence Wellhausen's changed *'etnanneyhā* to *'ăšēreyhā* because the former "does not fit the sentence in which it stands or echo 'images // idols'" (Mays 1976: 46). Driver (1954: 242) had a more ingenious solution that had it both ways, retaining the word but giving it a meaning closer to its parallels. He suggested "effigy" on the basis of a supposed Arabic cognate. This is presumably the basis for "images" in NEB and REB. Watson's note on v 7 illustrates the methodological predicament. He writes (1984a, 104):

> The Hebrew word *'tnn* occurs three times in our Micah passage. In the final couplet it undeniably means "(prostitute's) price" as elsewhere in Hebrew. In the preceding tricolon, however, as already noted, *it cannot possibly have the same meaning* [our italics], parallel, as it is to the two words *psl* and *'ṣb*.

Under the spell of synonymous parallelism, Watson argues that *'tnn* in v 7aB must refer to an object of worship and explains the form as *tannîn* ("sea-monster") plus prosthetic *aleph*. This is ingenious, but a solution that requires the postulation of an otherwise unattested Hebrew word is too far-fetched, and should be tried out (and then cautiously) only when the text is utterly intractable. Once the dogma of synonymous parallelism is set aside, we can accept the common meaning of *'tnn* in all three occurrences, and we can appreciate the way its placement in the colons that refer to objects of worship ties together the related ideas of idolatry and prostitution.

Micah's arrangement associates the idols with prostitute earnings in preparation for v 7b. The combination of nouns also suggests that carved images donated to the prostitute or purchased with her earnings will be smashed and burned in the fire. In spite of the threefold *all*, and the different verbs that describe their destruction, we do not think that three distinct kinds of objects are being itemized. All the verbs apply to all, with the last (v 7aC) being general and comprehensive. At the same time each noun suits the verb in each colon. The noun *earnings* fits *burn* by a kind of transference because the verb "burn" is associated with the penalty for prostitution, especially in a priestly family (Gen 38:24; Lev 21:9).

It is not clear in what sense the idols of Samaria could be labeled as prostitute earnings. The objects themselves as votive oblations could be impugned in such language, even though such gifts would have been legitimate in the minds of the donors. Or the idols could have been obtained by using the proceeds of activities that, in the view of the prophet, constituted prostitution. However, there is no direct evidence, except in the language of hostile critics like Micah (who could be speaking figuratively), that ritual prostitution was exploited for monetary profit in Israelite sanctuaries. If the *earnings* are distinct from the *images*, they could refer to (state?) treasures deposited in shrines for safekeeping. Furthermore, these might not be any different from the valuable equipment of the cultus (dishes and chalices) or the jewels adorning the statues of gods.

desolation. Samaria the prostitute will be exposed (v 6bB) and burned; the verbs have more than one level of meaning. The picture is fluid. Samaria and her idols are sometimes identified, sometimes distinguished in vv 6–7a. This fluidity permits *šĕmāmâ* to be used in v 7aC. The nouns *šĕmāmâ* and *šammâ* are applied to a land or a city, never to an object. So the reference changes perceptibly in the middle of v 7aC. The word *šĕmāmâ* makes this transition because it describes more appropriately the demolition of a city (v 6) than the smashing and burning of idols (v 7a). The verb *śym* is repeated for an inclusion from v 6aA, and its idiom puts *desolation* in parallel with *stone heap*; the preposition *l-* is not repeated, it does long-distance double duty. The assonance in *šĕmāmâ* makes an inclusion with *Samaria* in v 6aA. By means of this device the thought returns to the city at the end of v 7a, and Samaria is the topic (*she*) in v 7b.

prostitute. There are three candidates: (1) the city as such, personified (cf. Jerusalem in Isa 1:21, Nineveh in Nahum); (2) some woman, who would have to be a public or representative figure, such as a queen like Jezebel (the language of 2 Kings 9), or a member of the priestly caste; (3) some goddess worshiped in Samaria, perhaps Ashimah (Amos 8:14). The first is the best solution because the pronouns in v 6b seem to refer to Samaria as such, and those in v 7 seem to sustain that reference. But v 7 presents a difficulty if Samaria gathered the idols *from* her own earnings as a prostitute. *From* suggests that she (Samaria) obtained them from a source distinct from herself. If she were the prostitute, she would have obtained them from her clients.

fee. It is usual to supply an object "them," but the result is nonsensical. They (the idols) *are* the earnings. Samaria is the *zônâ* and her idols are her professional fees, according to the equations in v 7a; or at least, if the parallelism does not require identification, it requires that the wages and the idols be put all together. But it is empty to say that she gathered her prostitute's fees from a prostitute's fee. So the point remains obscure. The strains in the text have been eased in various ways. "She collected them *as* the fee of a harlot" (Mays 1976: 46); but *min-* is never used to mark a complement in this way, and the idiom *min-* . . . *wĕʿad-* must be respected. "They have been collected with prostitutes' earnings" (JB) weakens the identity in v 7a by regarding the idols as things acquired from income gained as a prostitute. Again *min-* does not have this instrumental meaning. Thus it is best to regard the idolatrous cult itself as whoredom, as Hosea certainly does. The strain is eased, as in NEB and REB, by replacing *her earnings* by "images" and reading v 7bB "she amassed them out of fees for harlotry," presumably fees paid to herself. This feature is unfortunately obscured in translations that take *zônâ* as generic and render it as plural (JB, NIV), which would imply that harlotry was a source of city income, not that Samaria was the harlot. NIV further obscures the fact that the same word for earning(s) is used three times (vv 7aB, bA, bB), translating the first occurrence "temple gifts" (already in the Geneva Bible), the others as "wages." Translations like "earnings" (NASB; JB) or "wages" (NIV) obscure the difference between plural (v 7a) and singular (v 7b). "Fee" (Mays) or "hire" (KJV; RSV) can serve, but NEB translates "fees" // "fee" in v 7b, which is irresponsible.

The use of the suffix *-hā* (*her*) five times in vv 6–7a shows that these "fees" are part and parcel of the Samaria complex—walls, foundations, images, idols. The connections would be even closer if the building in mind was the temple. But, apart from that, if v 7b refers back to all that has been mentioned, then all Samaria's wealth, whether devoted to the cult or used in civil buildings, came from harlotry. Taking seriously the overlap in terminology between Hosea and Micah, we can see their common use of the term *harlot(ry)* as covering both religious engagement with the goddess and political treaties with idolatrous nations.

she gathered. The interpretation of the last line (v 7bB) is even more difficult. The difficulty in the syntax of the active verb of MT (confirmed by LXX, which like MT has no object, unless it be the *min-* [= *ek*] construction taken as partitive) has been resolved by versions that make the verb passive. Some Hebrew manuscripts read a passive verb (Hillers 1984: 18 n. *u*). A full discussion of the agelong debate is to be found in Barthélemy (1992a: 713–16). The use of the verb *gathered* for the collection of a professional fee is another problem in itself. The *Qal* would serve for the gathering of revenue (2 Chr 24:5—with *min-* marking the source—; Prov 13:11). The *pi'el* always describes the gathering together of animals or humans previously dispersed. In the present context this choice of the verb could hint at the far-flung sources of Samaria's revenues, and at the diversity of the objects collected. It suggests, in fact, that her business was international in scope. The idols came from outside and they will go back where they came from.

they will go back. LXX has lost this. It brought v 7bB into line with 7bA, repeating it almost word for word. The subject of *yāšûbû* is unidentified, and the previous verb has no object. They are usually assumed to be the same, and they are assumed to be the idols of v 7a; but v 7a has predicted their utter destruction, and this can hardly be the same as using them once more to pay a prostitute. The representation of a country or, more precisely, a city as a prostitute is a figure of speech used so often in the Bible as to become a convention whose details may be taken as understood without much explication. Tyre (Isaiah 23), Nineveh (Nahum 3), Jerusalem (Isa 1:21), Babylon (Revelation 17) are the harlots of history. Hosea's focus was more on the nation; Micah's interest is in the two cities; the two merge in Ezekiel's restatements (chapters 16, 23). The extended metaphor can be developed along two main lines, which often blend. Marital infidelity and the sale of oneself can be apostasy in religion, and it can be treachery in politics. The gaining of wealth involves the commercialization of both religion and diplomacy, and any or all of these ingredients may be present in the harlot's behavior. So Babylon of the Apocalypse:

All nations have drunk the wine of her impure passion, and the kings of the earth have committed fornication with her, and the merchants of the earth have grown rich with the wealth of her wantonness. (Rev 18:3)

Another association of *'etnan zônâ* could be present (van der Westhuizen 1973). The association of Samaria's harlot's fees with images and idols in v 7a suggests either that the earnings were donated to the temple as votive offerings or that the materials gained in this way were actually used to make the graven gods. In either case this was illegal. In fact Deut 23:19 bans this practice with abhorrence.

In a comprehensive sense, all the treasures accumulated by Samaria, national wealth usually stored in the temple treasury for safekeeping under divine protection, were gained either through forbidden trade pacts with foreign powers or by commercialized prostitution under a guise of religion within Israel itself. The international trade of Tyre is called prostitution (Isa 23:17). The same term *'etnan* is used for commercial gain (Isa 23:17, 18), but it is more likely that this is a figurative use of a term that precisely refers to a harlot's fee than that the latter is only one part of its general commercial meaning. The seductions of Nineveh are associated more with magic (Nah 3:14). The religious component in such relationships arose from political treaties or trade agreements that required acknowledgment of foreign gods or even the installation of their images as concessions to merchant colonies or through cosmopolitan syncretism. If some of the idols were exotic, gathered in as the harlot's fees, or purchased with such fees, then "they will go back" to where they belong. Alternatively, the removal of Samaria's gods to foreign countries as spoils of war is another possibility common enough in ancient times. This outcome conflicts with the expectation of their physical destruction (v 7a), but both things would happen commonly in war when cities were sacked and plundered. Behind it all is the general maxim that ill-gotten gain will not be retained as well as poetic justice that makes end match origin.

In Ezekiel 16 the *'etnan zônâ* is put to another use. In a passage of unmatched vileness, Jerusalem is shown to be even more depraved than Sodom or Samaria, so that these two cities, bywords for turpitude, seem righteous by contrast (v 52). The difference lay in the fact that Jerusalem scorned the fee (v 31) *lĕqallēs 'etnan* (which should not be changed to *qbṣ*, as often proposed in spite of versional support). Instead, "you paid the fee." It is doubtful if this extreme idea is present in Mic 1:7b; but if it is, it means that what came in as a fee will go out as a fee. This is the usual interpretation, although the picture remains vague. It fails to convince because the idiom "return unto" is spatial (our translation of *'ad-* as *for* is not satisfactory), and does not mean to revert to a previous condition or status. It can mean "repent" (Isa 19:22 and Amos 4 *seriatim*), but this is not apposite here.

The idiom *šwb 'el* can mean to return to origins, as in Gen 3:19; by extension *šwb* can mean "to go off." Thus Job expects to go off into death naked, not to return to his mother's womb (Job 1:21). If *yāšûbû* has this more neutral meaning in v 7b, then it could be similar to *qibbāṣâ* not in contrast. Here the reading of the Aramaic versions "they were gathered," is of interest, for its Hebrew counterpart, the passive *qubbāṣâ*, requires only a minimum emendation in the vocalization. It depends on the perspective and whether *kî* is a conjunction, giving the reason for the destruction of the idols in v 7a, namely, "*because* she gathered (them) from a prostitute's fee." But the logical connection has also been found within v 7b, taken as a separate sentence. They will be used once more as a prostitute's fee *because* that is how she acquired them in the first place. But the utter destruction of the images (v 7a) and their recycling to pay (another?) prostitute are two quite different things. Is Micah proposing two quite different fates for the idols of Samaria, each appropriate in its own way? It is more likely that the wooden statues would be chopped up and burned, the stone ones knocked to bits and strewn around, by a reformer like Hezekiah rather than by a conqueror like Sargon (Becking 1992). It was a big thing for Mesopotamian conquerors to carry off the gods of their victims, not just as loot but as talismans that might bring blessings if treated with honor. And as symbols of authority over the conquered land. In the case of Jerusalem the temple vessels were taken off in this way and eventually returned under the decree of Cyrus, according to biblical tradition. The history of the god Marduk, normally residing in Babylon, is interesting in this respect. Captured and carried away to Assyria, the god was installed in a temple there, and the theological legitimation was worked out. Marduk had decided to live there for a while, but later he decided to come back (*ANET* 309).

On the level of practical politics, such treasures were useful for bargaining. In his campaigns against the Arabs, Sennacherib had captured images of their gods as well as their queen. In the reign of Esarhaddon, Hazail, king of the Arabs, was able to recover his gods by payment of a ransom (*ANET* 291). Hosea predicted (10:5–6) that the calf-idol (he calls it "Israel's sin" — Micah's term) of Beth-El (he calls it, not only *Beth-Awen* [10:5] but even *Bamoth-Awen* [10:8; compare Mic 1:5]) would be carried off to Assyria in the same way as a "present" for the Great King. Such a fate for the idol could be interpreted as a harlot fee paid to Ishtar in Nineveh (Nah 3:4).

Comment on Micah 1:2–7

The "Samaria" referred to in these verses has been variously identified. It is generally held that the oracle, or at the least its original core, was delivered as a prophecy of judgment against the capital of the northern kingdom of Israel. It must have been delivered before the Assyrian capture of that city in 722/1 B.C.E. It is a threat. The book of Micah betrays no knowledge of its fulfillment let alone awareness that vv 6–7 do not describe what the Assyrians actually did to the city.

Lescow finds the entire polemic against idolatry to be postexilic. Verses 6–7 are a criticism of the breakaway Samaritans. Each of these interpretations is concerned to attach the oracle as realistically as possible to a concrete *historical* situation.

Fritz (1974) finds an essentially *theological* motivation for the composition. It is the outcome of a major editorial effort after the Exile. Fritz accepts the authenticity of Mic 3:12, but suggests that vv 6–7 were composed in imitation of 3:12. Renaud (1977: 59 n. 143) labels this an evasion (*échappatoire*). Renaud points out that the theological interpretation of the similar fates of Samaria and Jerusalem now embodied in the wording of Mic 1:1 and found in the overall organization of chapters 1–3, held together firmly by the similarity between 1:6–7 and 3:12, is characteristic of the exilic period. This perspective is strongly present in Jeremiah and Ezekiel and prominent in the Deuteronomistic editorial arrangement of the book of Kings, which is organized throughout as a parallel history of the two kingdoms. After the Exile, interest narrowed to the plight of Jerusalem and hopes for its renewal. Second Isaiah is not interested in Samaria. The Second History (Chronicles-Ezra-Nehemiah) leaves out nearly all the material on the northern kingdom. From this point of view we think that Renaud has made a better case for the authenticity of vv 5–7 (most of it anyway) as originating before 722 B.C.E.

I.2. FIRST LAMENTATION (TRANSITIONAL) (1:8–9)

TRANSLATION

MT

8aA	ʿal-zōʾt ʾespĕdâ wĕʾêlîlâ	On account of this I shall weep and wail,
8aB	ʾêlĕkâ šîlāl wĕʿārôm	I shall walk around stripped and naked,
8bA	ʾeʿĕśeh mispēd kattannîm	I shall make a mourning cry like the jackals,
8bB	wĕʾēbel kibĕnôt yaʿănâ	and a lamentation like ostriches:
9a	kî ʾănûšâ makkôteyhā	For she is incurable—her wounds,
9bA	kî-bāʾâ ʿad-yĕhûdâ	for she came unto Judah;
9bBα	nāgaʿ ʿad-šaʿar ʿammî	he reached unto the gate of my people,
9bBβ	ʿad-yĕrûšālēm	unto Jerusalem.

LXX I.2. First Lamentation (Transitional) (1:8–9)

8aA	On account of this she will beat (the breast) and wail,
8aB	She will go barefoot and naked,
8bA	She will make a wailing like dragons,
8bB	and a lamentation like daughters of sirens.
9a	For her plague has gained the mastery
9bA	for it came unto Judah;
9bBα	and reached unto the gate of my people,
9bBβ	unto Jerusalem.

INTRODUCTION TO MICAH 1:8–9

The Literary Constituents of Micah 1

The oracle of doom (1:2–7) is followed by lamentation (1:8–16). The lamentation comes in two instalments, each of which speaks of a disaster that reaches Jerusalem (vv 9, 12). The phrase "gate of Jerusalem" (v 12) is split up in v 9. This language shows that there is a connection between the two pieces, but the question is whether vv 8–9 are the introduction to vv 10–16, whether there are two distinct dirges on the same or similar and related events, or whether vv 8–9 and vv 10–16 were connected only by an editorial decision based on their similar genre and language. Micah studies have generally accepted vv 8–16, not only as a unit, but also as containing (mostly) authentic Micah materials. Some modern editions (NIV, NJB, JB) and commentaries (Mays) identify vv 8–16 as one composition. Others (RSV) make a break between v 9 and v 10. Elliger (1934: 137–39) found a major break between v 10 and v 11. He insisted (p. 138) that vv 8–10 have nothing to do with the preceding material; and he was equally emphatic that vv 8–10 are "a complete self-standing unity." His argument (p. 138) rested on the change of genre at v 8 (not in dispute), on the change in meter (not very marked), and on the belief that the reference of ʿal-zōʾt is forward (not self-evident). Most of all, Elliger's conclusion about the break between v 10 and v 11 derived from his dating of vv 11–16 to 701 B.C.E.; vv 8–10 did not fit that background. The dating of individual oracles in the book of Micah is so precarious, in our judgment, that this task is better left until the work of literary analysis can assist historical decisions. Secure literary conclusions cannot result from uncertain historical criticism.

The continuity of v 8 with vv 2–7 is secured by the logic of the movement through theophany (vv 3–4), through indictment (v 5), through punishment (vv 6–7) to lamentation (vv 8–16). This scenario unifies the whole chapter. Within that thematic structure there are features in v 8, notably the bird simile, that make an inclusion with v 16; and there are features in v 9 that continue some of the motifs of the theophany, making an inclusion from v 3 to v 9. See the NOTES on v 9. Together these two inclusions make a formal interlocking structure. The use of ʿal-zōʾt to make the abrupt transition from the judgment theophany in vv 2–7 to the lamentations in vv 8–16 creates both a break and a linkage.

Whether or not vv 8–9 have been identified as a distinct lament (perhaps the outcome of the judgment oracle in vv 2–7) or as the beginning of a single lament (vv 8–16) over the fate of the cities of Judah, there has been widespread agreement that vv 8–9 are a literary unit: v 8 describes the mourning, v 9 gives the reasons for it. Some awkwardness has been felt with the double *kî* pattern in v 9. Naʾaman (1995: 517) observed the same pattern in v 12 and inferred from this that the unit is vv 9–16, with each pair of *kî* clauses opening a strophe consisting of eight bicolons. He then explains the similarity between v 8 and

v 16 as "a two-line dirge" in v 8 matching the "two-line summons to lament disaster" in v 16. In other words, the two main units in the chapter (vv 2–8 and vv 9–
16) end in a similar way. We have concluded that v 8 and v 16 are an inclusion
that embraces vv 8–16 as a unit, but we recognize that this is a difficult call and
that other structural features have to be factored into the decisions. Naʾaman
has made a number of acute observations about Mic 1:8–16, and we shall discuss some of them in the NOTES. The main methodological difference between
our approaches is that Naʾaman uses the structure he has found in vv 9–15 as an
aid to text-critical decisions. We have no disagreement with that strategy in
principle. There is a lot to be gained by doing "higher" criticism before "lower"
criticism, reversing the classical sequence. It is even better to allow interplay
between the "bottom-up" approach through text-criticism and the "top-down"
approach through literary analysis, so that each approach helps to fine-tune the
other by successive approximations. We have been greatly encouraged by
Naʾaman's positive conclusion (so different from the opinion in the apparatus of
BHS—*omnia mutilata sunt!*) that "Micah's words in *vv.* 9–16 have a well-
planned literary structure and reflect the work of an author who has transformed the oral prophecy into a literary work" (1995: 517). However, as more
and more emendations are invoked to secure a suspected structure or inferred
from it, the demonstration becomes less convincing.

Verses 8–9 as Transitional

What we have then in vv 8–9 is an elegant specimen of composition in which
formal structures and thematic development do not coincide. There is inner
structural cohesion in vv 8–9. There is continuity in theme from vv 6–7 to v 8,
given the anaphoric function of ʿal-zōʾt (see below) and the salient reading of
the feminine singular pronouns in v 8 and v 9a as referring to Samaria. The
change of theme from Samaria to Judah takes place between v 9a and v 9b, in
the middle of a well-made poetic unit.

The strongest arguments for identifying v 8 as the introduction to the following lament (vv 8–16) are those of Lindblom (1929: 92). He considers ʿal-zōʾt to
be equivalent to ʿal-kēn at the onset of a new oracle, as in Jos 14:14; 2 Sam 7:22;
Isa 9:16; 16:9; 22:4; 25:3; Jer 5:6; 48:36. Transition to a lament is marked by
ʿal-kēn in Hos 4:3. Both pronouns are deictic, and their salient reference is
anaphoric, referring backwards to preceding material, in this case the judgment speech in vv 6–7 or (as we prefer) to the whole of vv 2–7. We could translate "Because of *that* . . . " Elliger (1934: 139), however, argued that ʿal-zōʾt is
often cataphoric, pointing to the material in the following verses. He referred
to Hos 5:1; Amos 8:4; Joel 1:2; Mic 3:9. But these verses have šmʿ zʾt, not ʿl-zʾt.
Renaud (1977: 38–41) examined every occurrence of ʿal-zōʾt in the Hebrew
Bible and came to the following conclusions: (1) "The expression always resumes what precedes and draws out the consequences of a situation or of a
specified (*précis*) event"; there are no exceptions, and Renaud expressed aston-
ishment that the contrary had been so often asserted. (2) It sometimes marks a

turning point in the development of a thought, so much so that it can introduce (just as in Mic 1:8) a new literary form. (3) Very often, especially in poetry, it comes at the head of a phrase or verse. (4) It is never found, however, at an absolute beginning; it always comes within a development of which it introduces a fresh stage. We think that Renaud's conclusions are sound.

The opening phrase of v 8 (*On account of this*) seems to be an echo of *all this* in v 5. Verse 5 relates the arrival of Yahweh in judgment upon the rebellion of both Samaria and Jerusalem, in keeping with the mention of those cities in v 1. Verses 6–7 describe the impending devastation of Samaria and provide v 8 with its nearest reference. It is simpler, then, to take v 8 as the prophet's (or Yahweh's) grief over Samaria. Verse 9a is linked to v 8 by the conjunction *kî, for,* and *her wounds* in v 9a could be the blows described in vv 6–7. If, however, v 9 is considered to be an independent unit (because the verbs in it switch from non-perfective to perfective), the pronoun *her* in v 9a must refer cataphorically to Jerusalem, which is a little awkward although not impossible. But, if v 9a refers to Samaria, the repetition of *kî* at the beginning of v 9b can then be explained as another distinct reason for grief, this time over Jerusalem. Verses 6–9 are then included in the larger unit of vv 1–9 by this third occurrence of *Samaria . . . Jerusalem.*

Continuity from v 8 to v 9 is also recognized; the lamentation of v 8 could be (we think it is, at least in part) a response to the calamity described in v 9. That connection is sufficiently secured by the conjunction *kî*. If *'al-zō't* anticipates v 9, then *kî* will have to be construed as resumptive of preposed *'al-zō't*. We consider this strained; but it does not exclude a backward reference to vv 3–7 as well. In other words, v 8 bewails the double calamity on Samaria (vv 6–7) and Jerusalem (v 9). Its position inside the two-part description of the judgment on the two cities is then structurally similar to the placement of the indictment (v 5) between the theophany (vv 3–4) and the judgment (vv 6–7).

The Poetry of Micah 1:8

The poetry of v 8 is well formed. Each colon has three beats. The quatrain has thirty-one syllables (thirty-two standard). The grammatical and the poetic structure do not coincide so that each colon is one clause and vice versa. Verse 8b is a perfectly classical bicolon with incomplete synonymous parallelism and rhythmic compensation. Micah knows how to do it. But v 8a is skewed, with two parallel verbs in the first colon, and two parallel complements (*stripped and naked*) in the second. The verb *spd* in the first colon is picked up by the cognate noun in the third. The noun *mispēd* has its conventional parallel in the following colon (Amos 5:16). The use of three cohortative verbs in succession in v 8a is striking, and the fourth (*I shall make*) in v 8bA must be the same mood. Although the morphology does not necessarily show it, the cohesion of the unit requires continuity in mood. This series achieves rhyme, and the assonance is enhanced by the abundance of the consonant *l*. In v 8 the animal and bird comparisons are close parallels; but the repetition of *spd* shows that the third colon goes also with the first. This suggests that the fourth might go with the second, that is, his frenzied ambulation, not his wailing, resembles the conduct of an agitated ostrich.

The Verbs of Micah 1:8

A difficulty in settling the overall perspective and the chronological and logical connections among the various pieces in chapter 1 arises from the use of verb forms. Most of the statements in vv 3–7 seem to be predictive, whereas those in vv 9–15 seem to describe events that have already happened. The verbs in v 8 are cohortative (the fourth one by implication, since it cannot receive the morphological distinction of terminal long -â). Before attaching v 8 to the preceding or following block, we need to ask whether the prophet's behavior is grief when the disaster has occurred or a penitential ritual that might perhaps avert it before it occurred. The verbs are variously translated present (NAB) as if the prophet is actually doing what he describes, or future (RSV, NIV), as if he is predicting what he will do when the time comes. NEB "I must mourn" expresses resolution, if not compulsion. This problem remains unsolved.

The Speaker of Micah 1:8–9

Because vv 8–9 have links in both directions, we regard this unit as a transition piece between the judgment oracle in vv 2–7 and the lamentation in vv 10–16. In any case it is important to note the integral connections between condemnation and compassion, in both Yahweh and his prophet. The blows of the just Yahweh are reluctant, not vindictive. We are not sure whether the lamentation in vv 8–9 is oracular (divine utterance) or prophetic commentary. The latter is the usual understanding. The abrupt switch to expressions of grief suggests that this is the prophet's more personal response to the appalling prospect of the destruction just announced. We can dismiss as prejudiced the notion that Micah was a chauvinist who would have wept over Jerusalem (v 9) but would have gloated over Samaria (vv 6–7) (Rudolph 1975: 43).

Micah's reaction resembles the characteristic response of dismay in the presence of a theophany and of horror at the prospect of judgment found in many stories (Isa 6:5 and Amos's spontaneous response to his first two visions). Weeping as a conventional response to a vision of catastrophe is attested in the Deir 'Allā inscription; Balaam arose the next morning and wept. That may be all there is, but we think that this traditional interpretation should be questioned. The break between vv 6–7 and v 8 is diminished if the speaker ("I") is the same throughout. The speaker in v 6 is certainly Yahweh. Could he be the mourner in v 8? Renaud (1977: 26) conceded that passage from the "I" of the prophet to the "I" of Yahweh is plausible in an oracle of judgment, but not in a lamentation. Why not? In v 15 the "I" is clearly Yahweh ("Again the dispossessor I shall bring to thee") and LXX *agagō* confirms first person. But *'by(')* is commonly amended to *ybw'*, "he will come," something that the prophet could say. The thought that God feels and expresses grief at the prospect of the disasters he has just announced does not come easily to modern readers. We have been brought up on the largely Aristotelian metaphysical doctrine of the impassibility of God, and the terms "anthropomorphic" and "anthropopathic" have been used to empty the language of the Bible of truthfulness when it talks about God in such ways, explaining them (away) as merely figurative, analogical, or just mythological. Our difficulties in conceptualizing the emotions of God as, in fact, similar to our own are likewise great when we are under the spell of largely Stoic ethics that disapproves of emotion and finds admirable human character, and even holiness, in the calm triumph of reason over passion. We think of God as tranquil, not turbulent, especially when that grief of God is expressed in such a wild and uncontrolled fashion as vv 8–9 reveal. Quite apart from the question of divine dignity and decorum, Yahweh has a reputation, at least among superficial and conventional readers of the Bible, for wrath, but not for tender feelings. He is so often presented as a vengeful, or even cruel deity, that the idea that he feels the misery and tragedy of the human situation, identifies with his people as the painful consequences of their evildoing overtake them—this does not even occur to us. Why not? Once it is recognized that in a lamentation, as in a judgment oracle, the prophet can identify with the feelings of God, the whole of vv 2–16 can be recognized as an oracle, "proclaiming disaster" (Wolff 1990: 3), but in sorrow, not anger. There is no indication in the text itself that there has been a change of speaker at v 8. In vv 6–7 Yahweh says what he will do. In v 8 he says how he will feel. It may seem bizarre to suggest that Yahweh is the speaker of vv 8–9, but he is equally emotional over the same matter in Hos 11:8–9, and equally daring imagery is found in other divine utterances. "My people" (v 9) is the way Yahweh, not a prophet, usually refers to Israel. God is profoundly upset by this end to his hopes for his people. (In our "Excursus: When God Repents" [Andersen and Freedman 1989: 638–79] we concentrated on the cognitive and moral aspects in God's change of mind; Fretheim [1984, 1988, 1989] has emphasized the affective side.) If we accept the conventional view, the prophet's response to the terrifying revelation of vv 2–7 is not to praise God for his justice, but to bewail the calamity.

NOTES AND COMMENTS

Notes on Micah 1:8

On account of this. The phrase introduces predictions about mourning in Jer 4:28; Amos 8:8. The direction of the linkage is both backward and forward, as discussed above. When vv 8–16 are taken together as a new unit, this implies that *'al-zō't* in v 8 refers forward to the disasters of vv 9, 11–15 as the reason for the mourning enjoined in vv 8, 10, 16. But in the examples cited above and others, *zō't* refers backward to a disaster just described or predicted. This does not mean that the backward reference is immediate and close, that the mourning is only for the destruction of Samaria described in vv 6 and 7. The *this* at the beginning of v 8 picks up "all this" from v 5, going right back to the theophany.

I shall weep and wail. The cohortative mood expresses an intention to mourn in anticipation of impending catastrophe. Mourning behavior as a symbolic act can be a prophetic proclamation of disaster (Wolff 1990: 3). On the social conventions for such behavior, see Hillers (1965). The problem of the identity of the mourner could be the explanation of the movement of the verbs to third person in LXX (sg.) and Targum (pl.). Peshitta confirms MT. Hebrew has a rich vocabulary to describe the behavior of mourners and penitents, and most of it has both associations (G. A. Anderson 1991). Mourning was a ritual, carried out vicariously by professionals (Jer 9:17), or a ceremony in the temple, performed representatively by the priests (Joel 1:9). A prophet could mourn on behalf of the nation, Jeremiah preeminently (Jer 8:23 [Eng. 9:1]; 17:12–15), and not less painfully and sincerely for its being a social duty. Such conduct could itself be prophetic, a dramatic anticipation of what others would not be able to avoid when the time came. So Isaiah (20:3) walked around "naked and barefoot" (the same idiom as in Mic 1:8aB) "as a sign and a portent against Egypt and Ethiopia," predicting that the Assyrians would lead them away captive in the same condition. A song of grief also could be sung as a taunt, reminding the smug that their complacent joy would turn to misery. It was better to mourn in penitence than in bereavement. We cannot tell at what point in this process Mic 1:8 stands.

No one account of mourning behavior includes all the details that might be found, so we do not know how much was required, what was optional, or what details changed with times and circumstances. This limits our interpretation of Mic 1:8. The mourner put on a distinct appearance. Clothes were ripped or exchanged for sackcloth. Shoes could be discarded (2 Sam 15:30; Ezek 24:17), but the nakedness of Micah and Isaiah seems rather to have been a prophetic mime of prisoners of war since public nakedness was taboo in Israel. The pagan custom of slashing one's body was banned in Israel (Lev 19:28; Deut 14:1; Jer 16:6), but the associated practice of shaving some or all of the head hair was sometimes enjoined, as in Mic 1:16 (compare the use of the verb *qrḥ* in Ezek 27:31 and of *gzz* in Jer 7:29, where it is accompanied by a dirge). Expected behavior was to sit in dirt and ashes, or to throw dirt over one's head, even to roll around in the dust (v 10); to beat upon the breast; to wail aloud or utter choking sobs, or to be completely silent.

Ezekiel 27:30–32a contains one of the richest concentrations of the Hebrew vocabulary of mourning:

And they will cause their voices to be heard for you,
and they will cry out bitterly,
and they will throw dust over their heads,
in ashes they will wallow (cf. Mic 1:10b)
and they will make their baldness bald for you (cf. Mic 1:16),

and they will wrap sackcloth around themselves.
And they will weep for you with a bitter soul (cf. Mic 1:10a),
bitter mourning (cf. Mic 1:8).
And they will raise (their voices) for you a dirge in their wailing,
and they will lament for you.

Similar vocabulary is found in Jer 6:26 and 25:34–36. The verses in Micah 1 where the same vocabulary is found are shown in parentheses. While there is considerable overlap, some common terms found in Ezekiel 27 (such as "sackcloth," "bitterness," and "dirge") are not used by Micah, and two quite common terms used by Micah (*yll* and *'bl*) are not found in Ezekiel 27, although Jeremiah (6:26; 25:34–36) uses both in association with rolling in the dust. In sum, Micah 1 contains eight of the prime words in the Hebrew vocabulary of mourning, distributed without repetition over three separated verses. Even though this mourning is ascribed to possibly three different subjects (and at least two: first singular in v 8; second singular feminine in vv 10b and 16; second plural masculine in v 10a). These subjects reflect three facets of mourning that would normally be found all together in any real situation. Both gestures and cries would always be involved, so the pieces scattered over Micah 1 are all needed for a complete picture. This suggests that vv 8–16, if not the entire chapter, could be viewed as a unit. (Methodologically we do not accept the argument that different vocabulary requires a different author.) Besides this evidence from vocabulary, the use of three animal and bird similes in vv 8 and 16 achieves additional unity in the composition.

walk. The spelling of *'ēlĕkâ* [*'ylkh*], *I shall walk*, is unique. It could have arisen from imitating the preceding word. The manuscripts that read *'lkh* are obvious corrections. **L** protects the peculiarity with a Masora, but **P** and many manuscripts have the usual *'lkh*. **P** reads *'lylh* as well. A *pi'el* or even *hip'il* based on the secondary root *ylk*, a back formation attested in Ugaritic and in derived stems in Aramaic, is possible. This would secure an important distinction; instead of "I shall walk off" (*qal*), as accepted by the Masoretes, the reconstructed intensive *pi'el* or iterative *hip'il* could mean "I shall (continually) walk around." This is the verb form that describes the activities of miserable persons who walk around naked (Job 24:10). Job 30:28 proves that the *pi'el* is required. It occurs in a passage full of the language of grief, and Job says, just as in Mic 1:8,

I have become a brother of jackals,
and an acquaintance of ostriches.

stripped. Alternative readings are available: *ketib šyll* and *qere šwll* (in some manuscripts these are reversed). It is impossible to choose between them. The reading in 1QpMic is unclear: *šll* is possible (*DJD* 1:78). Gordis (1937: 183, n. 273) explains *šyll* as a *šap'el* formation from *yll*, meaning "wailing." This preserves parallelism with *yll* in the first colon and, besides, a different word for mourning in each colon. The preferred reading of the verb 'ylkh also combines to make "walking around mourning" better than "walking (away) stripped," but the rarity of šap'el in Hebrew weakens his point somewhat. The alternatives could be simply a misspelling due to the common confusion of yod and waw. On the one hand, the rare and original form of šyll could equally mean "stripped." On the other hand šwll, if it means "stripped," introduces the ancillary image of the war captive, a link with v 16. The passage can be compared with Isa 20:3, "walk naked and barefoot," with "barefoot" instead of šy/wll. (David walked "barefoot" in mourning [2 Sam 15:30].) If the šap'el is excluded, neither the etymology nor the morphology of šy/wll is evident. It evokes the word šālāl, "spoil," and assonance with 'ylylh, not repetition of the root, could be intended. Nakedness suits a captive better than a mourner. So the balance is even. In v 16 a mother mourns her captured children; in v 8 the prophet mimes both captives and their mourners in one acted prophecy.

Job 12:17, 19 says that God "leads away (mwlyk) counselors // priests šwll." The meaning of the term is unclear, but it surely has the same meaning as in Mic 1:8. As a complement, one might have expected a plural. But the singular may stand in Job as distributive: each one is šwll. As an example to be added to the qere of Mic 1:8, it is not as weak as Gordis supposes; its acceptance is almost universal. But again it is possible that the word whose existence is attested by Job 12:17, 19 is responsible for the qere of Mic 1:8. If šwll does mean "stripped," this meaning could have been laid on top of šyll ([de]spoiled) with a change of spelling, under the influence of 'ārôm found in both passages.

naked. If the associations of šy/wll are with war captives, Micah is miming that outcome. The associations of 'ārôm lean to a mourning ritual. A mourning woman is described as "naked" ('rym) in Krt 1.16:II.30. The scope of a mourner's nakedness is unclear. In view of Israel's taboo against nudity, it was doubtless symbolic. David covered his head and went barefoot (2 Sam 15:30). When told not to mourn, Ezekiel was to keep his shoes on (Ezek 24:17).

make. The verb 'śh implies the performance of customary mourning rituals.

jackal. The reading in LXX of "dragons" (cf. Vulgate) has confused the plural of tan, "jackal," with tannîm a variant of tannîn. We cannot account for the "sirens" and "lions" of the other Greek versions. The jackal and ostrich are associated in Job 30:29; Lam 4:3; Isa 13:21–22, all in quite different connections. The wailing of the grief-stricken might sound like the howl of that wild animal. The bird is not to be identified with certainty as the ostrich; it could be some kind of owl (NEB, adopting a proposal of G. R. Driver in PEQ 87 [1955]: 12f.). In any case, its strange cry was compared with some sob or scream of a mourner.

Introduction to Micah 1:9

The poetry limps. It should not be assumed without testing that the four colons in this verse constitute a unit. The threefold 'ad- links the last three colons, all carried by the one kî and "Judah," "the gate of my people," and "Jerusalem" constitute a good series. They show that the assault on Jerusalem is a second stage in the movement that began in v 3 (Wolff 1990: 34). The repetition of the verb *yrd* in v 12b shows that the consternation registered in vv 10–15 is a further outcome of the same movement. The repetition of *kî* suggests that there is a break in the discourse between v 9a and v 9b. Verse 9a has one focus, v 9b another. The whole verse has military connotations; it seems to describe an invasion. The referents for *-hā* in "her wounds" and for the subject of *bā'â*, "she came," are not evident and can hardly be the same, unless the first means "the wounds (inflicted by) her," subjective genitive. Verse 9a describes a victim; the subject of v 9bA must be the aggressor. So far the only candidate for this role is Yahweh (v 3). If the whole verse is about Jerusalem, then she is the one wounded, and she cannot be the one who came to Judah. In addition, there is a disconcerting change of gender between *bā'â* and *nāga'*; and this, together with the lack of "and" before the latter, suggests that vv 9a–9bA and v 9bB might be distinct, that is, there is another break in theme between v 9bA and v 9bB. If the feminine singular referents for vv 9a and 9bA are the same, then the most eligible candidate is Samaria, crippled by the blows described in vv 6 and 7 (which are threats of something still future), who nevertheless assaults Judah (but the verbs in v 9 are past tense). This has become a complicated scenario, and we would not consider it were it not for the details coming up in vv 10–15 in which "kings of Israel" seem to be ravaging cities in Judah, including Jerusalem. It is therefore possible that the repeated *kîs* of v 9 subordinate their clauses to different principal clauses, v 9a linking backwards (cf. Masoretic *'athnaḥ*).

The mourning in v 8 is for Samaria whose blows (as in vv 6–7) are (or will be—there is no verb in v 9a) so injurious. This leaves v 9b to be connected with similar injuries sustained by Judah and Jerusalem, for which the prophet will mourn, joined by others (v 16). While the subject of *she came* remains to be identified, the subject of *nāga'* could be "evil," since v 12b echoes v 9b by saying that evil has come down from Yahweh to the gate of Jerusalem. The phrase *gate of Jerusalem* is split up over the two colons in v 9b, and it is best to link both references to the same occasion and to identify *nāga'* and *yārad* (v 12) with the same subjects, namely *rā'*. Since Mic 3:11 reports people as saying, "Evil will not come (*tābô'*) to us," *rā'â* could be the subject of *bā'â* in v 9, *rā'* could be the subject of *yārad* in v 12. The common subject achieves a closer link between the verbs. It remains, however, to ascertain whether the fluctuation between masculine and feminine *evil* is purely stylistic or whether gender distinguishes two different agents. We conclude that vv 8–9a look back to vv 6–7, while v 9b looks forward to vv 10–16. All of vv 8–9a are about Samaria, and the repeated *for* in v 9bA is resumptive—attention switches to Jerusalem. Verses 8–9 are thus a transition and a bond between vv 2–7 and vv 10–16.

Notes on Micah 1:9

incurable. The word *'ănûsâ* caused the ancient versions much difficulty (assuming that it was in their *Vorlage*). They agree that it is singular, and they conform the subject to it. LXX reads "she has gained the mastery." No convincing Hebrew alternative reading has been recovered by retrojection of the versions. The use of the cognate verb in 2 Sam 12:15 indicates that a sickness inflicted by God as punishment for sin cannot be cured by anyone but God himself. It shows too that the subject of *'nš* can be a person as well as an ailment. Once more we have a word with multiple connotations. The theophany in vv 3–4 emphasizes "natural" acts of God, with only slight hints of military assault. The destructions described in vv 6–7 could be the result of war, and *makkôt* could be combat injuries. The military imagery continues through v 9. The personification of the cities (cf. "harlot" in v 7) secures the picture (or simile) of a sick person as well.

her wounds. Two identifications are possible, since there are two cities, Samaria and Jerusalem, in Micah's sights. *Her* could refer to either city. If *her* refers to Samaria, the wounds are the punishments described in vv 6–7. Then the referent of the pronoun modifier *her* is objective (the wounds she has sustained, not inflicted). Or the victim is Jerusalem, the aggressor possibly Samaria. The modifier is subjective—Samaria inflicted *her* wounds on Jerusalem when *she came unto Judah.* We think that the former is more likely, in the light of general usage. The term *makkâ* describes an injury inflicted by a blow with fist, stick, scourge, or weapon. The cursing texts threatened seven blows (different, or sevenfold?) in punishment for covenant contrariety (Lev 26:2), and the plural here might reflect such diverse calamities, since one crushing plague or military defeat (even multiple defeats) was usually called *makkâ rabbâ* (Num 11:33) or *makkâ gĕdôlâ* (Josh 10:10). The combination of war, famine, and disease is described as a very grievous *makkâ* in Jer 14:17. Second Chronicles 28:5 says that Pekah of Israel defeated Ahaz of Judah with *makkâ gĕdôlâ*. The plural is less common and usually refers to the chastisements of a covenant violator (Deut 28:59; 29:21) or the multiple injuries of an individual who has been repeatedly attacked. The latter is in keeping with the personification of Samaria (or Jerusalem); compare Jer 19:8. Micah lines up with Deuteronomy and Jeremiah in this usage; but the clinical term *'ănûšâ* keeps the figure closer to "injury" than "defeat," resembling the picture in Isa 1:5–8. The devastation described by Isaiah is generally connected with Sennacherib's invasion of Judah in 701 B.C.E., but 2 Chr 28:18 provides another (and in our opinion better) occasion as a possible background for both Micah 1 and Isaiah 1.

There is grammatical discord between the plural subject ("wounds") and the singular predicate ("incurable"). We can think of no explanation for this discord. The versions, ancient and modern, make the subject singular, and some scholars (Hillers, R. L. Smith), following Wellhausen, wish to emend MT accordingly. This proposal continues to enjoy favor (NEB, JPS). REB paraphrases "Israel has suffered a deadly blow." It is unconscionable to add the word "Israel" without informing readers that there is no textual basis whatsoever for this addition. It is going too far to explain the ending -*yh* as the divine name—"Yahweh's stroke." This proposal (Duhm [1911], accepted by Budde [1917–18], Elliger [1934],

Renaud [1977: 21], and Wolff [1990: 40]) is ingenious (it requires only one change in the consonants); it was widely accepted by text critics of that generation and is still ventilated by BHS. NJB reads "the wounds that Yahweh inflicts." The supporting arguments become very convoluted: the noun was originally singular (*mkt*), reflected in various translations. Misreading the name *yh* as a suffix created a spurious plural, fixed by adding -*w*-. The expression is not attested. The Masoretic orthography *mkwtyh* does not permit singular to be read without emendation. Jeremiah has all possible spellings *mkwtyh* (50:13), *mkwth* (49:17), *mkth* (19:8). Only the latter might be singular, and at first Mic 1:9 could have been written in this doubly defective way. Such a text could be behind the unanimous attestation of singular in the ancient versions, e.g., *hē plēgē autēs* (LXX); *plaga eius* (Vulgate); Targum, Peshitta. The ambiguous **mkth*, if original, could have been taken as singular because it is more common than plural. But how, then, is the plural—the rarer and more difficult reading—to be explained? Allen (1976: 267 n. 17) suggested that the plural nouns in v 7 could have spread to the Masoretic plural in v 9a, but there is no real analogy. Renaud (1977: 21), beginning with *mktyh*, *le coup de Y*HWH, argued that misreading the final -*h* as "her" left the stem *mkty*, which could only be plural. The vowel letter *w* was then added. The singular, however, can be explained as easing the clash in number between MT "blows" and "sick." The predicate of the verbless clause corresponds to the attributive adjective. Jeremiah complains: "My *makkâ* is *'ănûšâ*, it has refused to be healed" (15:18); *'ănûš* is an attribute of synonyms of *makkâ*, *šeber*, "fracture," in Jer 30:12, 15; *kĕ'ēb*, "pain," in Isa 17:11. The MT can be retained once it is recognized that Samaria is the referent for "her" and "sick," while "blows" is a causal complement: "She is incurably ill [because of] her wounds." This is another instance of the lean language of poetry omitting a preposition.

for. The second *kî* (v 9bA) is confirmed by LXX and Vulgate. The two subordinated clauses in sequence have aroused the doubts of modern scholars. If not simply deleted, *kî* can be read as resumptive ("Surely" [Wolff 1990: 40]); or the first *kî* can be replaced by *'yk* (Schwantes 1962: 31).

came. The contrast between future reference of the verbs in vv 6–8 and the past reference of the verbs in v 9 can be retained (RSV, NEB, NIV), or evaded by making the latter present (JB), or resolved by invoking the prophetic perfect in vv 8–9. If all of vv 2–9 are speaking about the future, then v 9 is part of the prediction, or, if the actions of v 8 were actually performed as part of the proclamation, it is a proleptic mime. In view of the connection between v 9b and v 12b, it is best to regard the former as a preliminary statement that is amplified in vv 10–16. This has the vividness of something experienced in actuality, not just anticipated in the imagination. But what is the implied *feminine* subject of *bā'â*? It cannot be Jerusalem. The only other singular feminine noun used so far is Samaria, and that does not fit very well, although we are prepared to recognize an invasion of Judah from the north as the cause of Jerusalem's sickness. Hebrew often uses feminine where other languages use neuter for impersonal "it" or "this" of vv 5 and 8. Otherwise some feminine noun meaning "disaster" must be understood, perhaps *makkâ* if that can be read in v 9a, a further argument for the ancient and modern alternative singular reading. Since v 12 says that *rāʿ* came down from Yahweh, perhaps *rāʿâ* is meant in v 9bA (cf. Judg 20:34, 41), hence the irony of Mic 3:11.

reached. The verb is masculine, but many scholars (from Wellhausen through Schwantes) wish to read feminine, as already in the Aramaic versions. The verb has no subject in its clause. The cognate *negaʿ*, understood, is the best candidate, but *rāʿ* is possible; see Job 5:19. The same verbs (with no subjects and apparently impersonal) are used in the same sequence in Job 4:5.

It *comes* to you,	and you are incapacitated;
it *strikes* you (*tiggaʿ ʿădeykā*)	and you are aghast.

In Job 1:19 the subject is feminine, the verb sequence is the same as in Mic 1:9—same verbs, same sequence, same change in gender! The language shows that *negaʿ* describes a heavy blow, not just contact ("touch"). The noun *negaʿ* is a synonym of *makkâ* and often describes a divinely inflicted plague. See the parallelism of these roots in Isa 53:4, while Isa 53:8 says that the Servant received the *negaʿ* as punishment for the "rebellion" of the people. Amos 9:5 provides a link with v 3. Yahweh "touches [*ngʿ*] the earth and it melts." Compare Pss 104:32; 144:5.

gate. Targum has the more familiar "gates," but the other ancient versions support the singular of MT. If the intention was to report the investiture of Jerusalem in siege one might have expected "city gate" (2 Kgs 23:8); compare Isa 14:31, where the construct phrase "the gate of . . . the city" is broken and distributed over two colons of poetry. It is more likely, in the larger context of the chapter (especially if we read vv 2–9 as a unit) that the goal of the theophany announced in v 3 is "Yahweh's triumphal entry into the temple precincts of the holy city Jerusalem" (Hanson 1975: 375).

my people. It is more appropriate for God to refer to Israel as "my people" than for the prophet. But the latter usage is not impossible as Ruth 3:11 shows (compare Deut 21:19; Ruth 4:10). Wolff (1990: 7), assuming that the speaker is Micah, uses this detail to support his theory about Micah's standing in the community as an "elder." He finds in the usage the vocabulary of clan wisdom. Here it refers to "that particular group of people entrusted to Micah's care as an elder." The use of "people" adds poignancy, whether it is Micah who is mourning or Yahweh.

There does not seem to be any technical "wisdom" vocabulary in the book of Micah. In disagreement with scholars who find such a background in the role of Micah, R. C. Van Leeuwen concludes that "none of the writing prophets can be proven to be sages in a technical sense, nor were they sages prior to their prophetic activity" (in Gammie and Perdue 1990: 298; note 15 supplies documentation of the discussion).

Jerusalem. The single stress of the final colon completes the woeful oracle like a solitary drumbeat. It matches the end of v 5, the halfway mark of vv 2–9. The authenticity of this final phrase is attested by all the versions. Its brevity has raised doubt in the minds of modern scholars, who either discard it as a gloss (Wellhausen, who argued that it had come from Obad 11, 13 [1898: 136]) or else emend it to make it longer, and so improve the meter.

Comment on Micah 1:9

The past-tense verbs in v 9 suggest that the distressing events have already come to pass, so that the prophet's mourning is actual ("because" is used twice in v 9); but the future-tense verbs in vv 6 and 7 suggest that it is the prediction that causes the lamentation (*'al-zō't* refers back to vv 6 and 7). Verse 8 thus has logical connections with what precedes and with what follows, bringing vv 6–7 and v 9 together as dual causes of anguish. This fits in with the association of Samaria and Jerusalem in vv 1 and 5b. The clash of tenses between vv 6–7 (future) and v 9 (past) is thus inexplicable, and there is no historical explanation, unless Samaria is condemned for an attack on Jerusalem. There was a time when Samaria was destroyed and Jerusalem was threatened, but never the reverse situation. Aside from this problem, the rest of the oracle in vv 2–7 makes sense in terms of the assignments we have proposed. At the same time the distinction between the prophet and Yahweh should not be pressed, for Yahweh speaks only through the prophet, and the prophet speaks only Yahweh's word. An opening call by the prophet (vv 1–4) is followed by the oracle proper (vv 5–7), but without the usual "Thus says Yahweh" or the like (TEV supplies such words at this point!). Finally the prophet responds more personally (vv 8–9) (TEV adds "And Micah said"). The differences between the accounts of the destruction of the two cities, Samaria in vv 6–7, Jerusalem in v 9, arise from the fact that the first is a prediction made by God, whereas the second is a fact described by the prophet. If this is a fact in anticipation, the verbs in v 9 are examples of the prophetic perfect. The two cities occupy a different perspective in the prophet's view. His southern location makes Samaria seem a little more remote. The impression is given that destruction will begin with Samaria but will eventually reach Jerusalem. But every effort should be made to give the verb forms their salient meanings and to pay close attention to the use of pronouns. In vv 6–7 "she" is Samaria; and this city is the best candidate as subject of v 9bA "*she* came unto Judah." So in v 9a, *her wounds* are the wounds of Samaria, that is, inflicted by Samaria. Samaria came into Judah, right up to the gate of Jerusalem, and inflicted incurable wounds. As we shall see below, this hypothesis fits into 1:10–16 and 2:1–2 as well. Anticipating the discussion, we mention here only the impact of this conclusion on the common hypothesis that the background of vv 10–16 is to be sought in Sennacherib's invasion of Judah in 701 B.C.E.

I.3. SECOND LAMENTATION (1:10–16)

TRANSLATION

MT

10aA	*bĕgat ʾal-taggîdû*	In Gath don't report [2d m. pl.] [it]!
10aB	*bākô ʾal-tibkû*	Don't weep [2d m. pl.] at all!
10bA	*bĕbêt lĕʿaprâ*	In Beth-le-Aphrah
10bB	*ʿāpār hitpallāštî*	roll thyself [f.] in the dust!
11aAα	*ʿibrî lākem*	Pass on [f. sg.], for you [2d m. pl.]!
11aAβ	*yôšebet šāpîr*	The inhabitant [f. sg.] of Shaphir,
11aB	*ʿeryâ-bōšet*	[is] [in] nakedness [and] shame.
11bAα	*lōʾ yāṣĕʾâ*	She did not go forth [3d f. sg.]—
11bAβ	*yôšebet ṣaʾănān*	the inhabitant [f. sg.] of Zaʾanan
11bB	*mispad bêt hāʾēṣel*	The wailing of Beth-haʾezel,
11bC	*yiqqaḥ mikkem ʿemdātô*	he will take away from you [2d m. pl.] his standing place.
12aA	*kî-ḥālâ lĕṭôb*	For waited anxiously for Good;
12aB	*yôšebet mārôt*	the inhabitant [f. sg.] of Maroth
12bA	*kî-yārad rāʿ mēʾēt yhwh*	but Evil came down from Yahweh
12bB	*lĕšaʿar yĕrûšālēm*	to the gate of Jerusalem.
13aA	*rĕtōm hammerkābâ lārekeš*	Harness [2d m. sg.] the chariot to the steed,
13aB	*yôšebet lākîš*	inhabitant [f. sg.] of Lachish!
13bA	*rēʾšît ḥaṭṭāʾt hîʾ lĕbat-ṣiyyôn*	She is first(fruit) of sin to Daughter-Zion,
13bB	*kî-bāk nimṣĕʾû pišʿê yiśrāʾēl*	for in thee [f.] were found the rebellions of Israel.
14aA	*lākēn tittĕnî šillûḥîm*	Therefore thou [f.] shalt give parting gifts
14aB	*ʿal môrešet gat*	on account of Moresheth-Gath;
14bA	*bāttê ʾakzîb lĕʾakzāb*	houses of Akzib to [the] deceiver (ʾakzāb),
14bB	*lĕmalkê yiśrāʾēl*	to the kings of Israel.
15aA	*ʿōd hayyōrēš ʾābî lāk*	Again the dispossessor I will bring to thee [f.],
15aB	*yôšebet mārēšâ*	inhabitant [f. sg.] of Mareshah;
15bA	*ʿad-ʿădullām yābôʾ*	To Adullam will come
15bB	*kĕbôd yiśrāʾēl*	the glory of Israel.
16aA	*qorḥî wāgōzzî*	Make thyself [2d f. sg.] bald and cut off thy [2d f. sg.] hair,
16aB	*ʿal-bĕnê taʿănûgāyik*	for the children of thy [2d f. sg.] delight!
16bA	*harḥibî qorḥātēk kannešer*	Make thyself [2d f. sg.] as bald as the eagle,
16bB	*kî gālû mimmēk*	for they have gone from thee [2d f. sg.] into exile.

LXX I.3. Second Lamentation (1:10–16)

10aA	You in Geth don't exult!
10aB	And you in Akim, don't rebuild from a house with derisions!
10bA	Sprinkle earth with your derisions!

11aA	Living well in her cities,
11aB	
11bAα	did not go out
11bAβ	the inhabitant [f. sg.] of Sennaan
11bB	to lament over the house next to her.
11bC	She will receive from you a grievous wound.
12aA	Who has begun for good
12aB	to her who dwells in grief?
12bA	For evils came down from Kyrios
12bB	upon the gates of Jerusalem.
13aA	The sound of chariots and horsemen.
13aB	Inhabitant [f. sg.] of Lachis—
13bA	Leader of sin is she to the daughter of Zion,
13bB	for in thee were found impieties of Israel.
14aA	Therefore thou shalt give ambassadors
14aB	as far as the inheritance of Geth;
14bA	vain houses,
14bB	it {they [**B**]} became vain for the kings of Israel.
15aA	Until I will bring the heirs to thee,
15aB	inhabitant [f.] of Lachis—inheritance;
15bA	Unto Odollam will come
15bB	the glory of ⟨the daughter of⟩ Israel.
16aA	Shave thyself and shear thyself,
16aB	for thy delicate children;
16bA	Extend thy widowhood as the eagle,
16bB	for they have been taken from thee into captivity.

INTRODUCTION TO MICAH 1:10–16

The main tone of this unit is panic. It is full of consternation, indeed hysteria, brought about by anticipation of what will happen in the world when Yahweh comes down from his place and marches across the countryside (v 3). The colons that frame the unit (vv 8–10 and v 16) are rich with the language of lamentation over a catastrophe and of grief for lost children. The city of Jerusalem is at the center of these events (v 12), and Zion is urged to mourn (v 16).

Connecting this unit with the opening theophany (vv 3–4), the whole can be understood as the report of a terrifying vision (v 1) received by Micah. As he views the threatened outcome of Yahweh's relentless destruction of city after city, the prophet is overcome by grief and driven to frenzy. The disordered speech, like broken sobs, expresses Micah's (perhaps even Yahweh's) turbulent state of mind (Andersen 1995).

Most scholars have accepted vv 10–16, or even vv 8–16, as an authentic composition of Micah. At the same time the apparently mutilated condition of the text prevents it from being received as something still close to the original. The task of criticism has been to explain how the text got into its present corrupt state and to recover, if possible or as near as possible, its original form. Studies in minute detail have identified places where the text seems to have lost something and other places where a word or phrase might have been added. We shall discuss these specifics in the NOTES.

There have been many valiant attempts to unravel the riddle of Mic 1:10–16. Notable are Haupt's defiant study of Micah's "Capucinade" (1910a) followed by Budde (1917–18), Graham (1930–31), Elliger (1934), Schwantes (1964), Fohrer (1967), van der Woude (1971b), Rudolph (1972), Naʾaman (1979, 1995), and Shaw (1993).

There are several indications of the internal structural arrangement of the material. The opening colon (v 10a) prohibits mourning and the closing quatrain (v 16) urges it. The middle section (vv 10b–15) is taken up with comments on a number of cities (the exact number is not clear). The conjunction lākēn, "therefore," marks the beginning of a new portion, and the use of the conjunction kî separates vv 12–13 from the rest. The repetition of the verb yrd in vv 3 and 12 is a unifying link between the theophany and the calamity; Yahweh came down as something harmful (rāʿ). The movement began with Samaria and ended at Jerusalem. The mention of Yahweh and of Jerusalem // Zion in the middle section of the book of Micah (book II, chapters 4–5) suggests that the rest of the composition has been built around these explanatory statements. There is thus some rough symmetry, but it is not quantitative. The opening (v 10a) and closing (v 16) match (inclusion, with theme of weeping), and the three parts between them (vv 10b–11, 12–13, 14–15) have a measure of symmetry around the middle. Although the locations of the various cities named have not all been determined, it is possible that Lachish, in Part II, marks the midpoint of the expedition, dividing the cities into two groups, one in Part I, the other in Part III. Significantly Jerusalem, which logistically would represent the end of the excursion and the end of the story, in terms of composition is structurally in the centerpiece.

Van der Woude (1971b) seems to be the only scholar with doubts about the unity of vv 10–16. He finds differences in meter between vv 10–12 (2 + 2) and vv 13–15 (3 + 2); he argues that the cities fall into two unrelated groups. The tone of finality in v 12b marks the end of the first unit. He recognizes vv 10–12 as a lamentation, but concludes that vv 13–15 are a judgment oracle. These arguments are not very strong. It is not self-evident that any one poem must have the same meter throughout. The meter is not as regular as he claims. The Masoretic accentuation indicates colons with 1, 2, 3, 4, and 5 beats. The dominant 3 + 3, 3 + 2, 2 + 2 bicolons are distributed throughout. Moreover, the part that van der Woude identifies as a judgment oracle is the part in which he finds qînâ meter! Arguments based on a suspected grouping of the towns are weak; in fact some identifications have been made on the assumption that there is some grouping in the presentation. Far from the climactic v 12b marking the end of a unit, we shall argue that it occupies a position in the center of a symmetrical structure.

As for the genre—lamentation or judgment speech—the unit (at least vv 10–15) as a whole has been identified as one or other by various scholars. Elliger (1934), among others, explained the unit as a lament over a calamity that has already taken place. This seems to be the majority opinion, with the event identified as Sennacherib's invasion of Judaea in 701 B.C.E. (Gonçales 1986). Fohrer (1967: 78) identified vv 10–16 as a judgment oracle. Like Isa 10:17–32, which it resembles in a number of ways (notably in the play on paronyms [Strus 1985]), Mic 1:10–16 bewails the disaster in anticipation. It has the *form* of a lament; it *functions* as a warning (Renaud 1977: 37). This explanation of the mixed nature of the genre is made certain, in our opinion, when the whole lament (vv 8–16) is seen as the sequel to vv 2–7. Renaud (1977: 35) also points out that vv 10–15 are unified by the clear allusions to royal history in vv 10a, 14b, and 15b. Renaud sees in these allusions an indirect threat to the monarchy of Micah's day, even though he is not able to explain why that threat is so oblique (1977: 36).

The whole of chapter 1 can thus be understood—and is best understood—as a single unit of prophetic composition with thematic, dramatic, and rhetorical integrity on the literary level (Wolff 1990; Shaw 1993). It derives this unity from the actuality of the vision that created the report of the theophany (vv 3–4), the threat (vv 5–7), and the agonized response (vv 8–16).

The language of vv 10–16 seems so incoherent on first (and subsequent!) readings that one might suppose either that the text has sustained massive injuries in transmission or that it was deliberately intended to create an effect of extreme emotional turbulence. The quest for poetic regularity has yielded a cleaner text, but only through heroic emendation, and the results express the individual scholar's expectations. How differently the data can be approached and the original text reconstructed can be illustrated by the divergent reconstructions of Haupt and Elliger.

Haupt, looking for the 3 : 2 *qînâ* meter, explained the presence of many "lines" of four or more beats as the outcome of extensive glossing. By removing many words, he was able to "restore" an original version much shorter than that in the Masoretic Text.

Elliger (1934), believing that the most appropriate poetic form for a lament was a *qînâ* with 3 : 2 meter, explained the abundant 2 : 2 meter by a theory that a strip was torn from one edge of the sheet bearing the text. This entitled him to restore the missing words to the best of his ability. In addition he expected all the colons to fit into tetracolons, and hence inferred that two colons had been lost from v 11, two from 13. These he did not venture to restore.

To be realistic, it is hard to imagine such an accident, which must have happened to the only available copy, being left without rectification. How many times in the history of its transmission did the preservation of this text depend on one single manuscript and that unsupported by any knowledge of the true text in anybody's head? Most scholars who have struggled with the text have encountered problems everywhere, not just at the onset of colons.

Fohrer (1967) accepts the dominance of 2 : 2 meter in what survives, and manages to bring the whole piece into this pattern, although this still requires extensive emendation. Allen (1976) has more regard for the text and so is forced to recognize a mixture of meters. He accepts some of Elliger's emendations, now available in the apparatus of BHS. Allen finds eight bicolons of 2 : 2, five of 3 : 2, one of 3 : 3, and two tricolons of 2 : 2 : 2. Even so, it would be even less regular had not Allen balked at a one-beat colon by giving the preposition *mē'ēt* a beat in v 12, while reducing the four-beat colon in v 15 to three beats.

The search for prosodic units that begins with syntactic units in the expectation that most colons will consist of discrete clauses is hampered by the atrocious grammar in vv 10–15 that leaves many clause boundaries indeterminate. Most of it is fragmentary, but there are some long clauses, notably vv 12b, 13b, both with benefit of conjunctions that show where the clause begins. These are about the only two intelligible statements in the entire composition; but to scan them as poetry when there is no parallelism at all requires caesuras at arbitrary points.

The hallmark of Hebrew verse—parallelism between adjacent colons—does not offer much help. There is not one classical bicolon in the whole piece, unless in v 10a; but there the expectation of parallelism might go too far when it finds in *bkw* an item to match *bgt*. In v 16 we do find some parallelism between v 16aA and v 16bA; but verse 16 is the only coherent four-colon unit that can be recognized.

The brevity of most of the clauses in vv 10–16 is partly due to the limited use of grammatical particles. Without them it is hard to explore the linguistic structure or to work out the connections between the nouns and verbs. A major cause of difficulty is the almost total lack of conjunctions. "And" is used only once (v 16aA)—surely a record for the Hebrew Bible. There it coordinates two synonymous verbs within a colon. In its four occurrences, *kî* offers a welcome toehold in otherwise slippery terrain, for one expects a subordinate clause to begin with this conjunction. Even so the help is minimal. Except for v 16, where *kî* clearly means "because," we cannot be sure that it is a subordinating conjunction. It could be asseverative, for instance. Assuming that *kî* in v 13b means "for" and that v 13a is the principal clause, then that requires the revision of v 13a to relieve the clash between *thou* (m. sg.) *harness . . . she . . . in thee* (f. sg.). The use of *kî* twice in v 12 compounds the problem. There is some play on the contrast between "good" and "evil"; but the logical connection between v 12a and v 12b cannot be that Maroth expected good *because* evil came down to Jerusalem. It could be adversative: "she expected good . . . *but* evil came." But what, then, is the nexus between Maroth and Jerusalem?

The composition does not altogether lack indications of linguistic coherence. The long inventory of place-names, with similar titles (*bat-* and *yôšebet*), and the puns on these names point to planned, sustained literary work. This is the one feature of vv 10–16 that all students are agreed on, and this starting point invites the search for an overall structure in the arrangement, for some sustained message in this theme. This clue does not get us very far. All these names do not serve the same grammatical functions, to judge from the interpretations that are actually present in the text. With so many imperative verbs one might expect a number of vocative names. But there are indicative verbs as well, and it is often unclear what the grammatical connections are between a verb and a nearby noun. In poetry, which does not follow strict word order, the subject could come anywhere. Without the use of *nota accusativi*, an object may be hard to detect. Prepositions often help to realize familiar idioms; but *b-* is lacking from "dust" in v 10 (contrast Jer 6:26; Ezek 27:30), and *nota accusativi* is never used, although opportunities are present in vv 11bC, 13aA, 16bA. Such indications of the use of poetic language, along with terseness and turbulence, offer little hope that normal syntax sequences will be found. If most of the staccato clauses contain only two or three words at the most, they must be laconic to the point of complete opaqueness. There are enough run-on colons to leave the question of clause boundaries well open. In what follows we shall check out the clause assignments implied by the Masoretic punctuation and traditional translations, and test some alternate possibilities.

Purely formal considerations, involving both grammatical and prosodic phenomena, are not the most formidable barriers to our understanding of Mic 1:10–16. And it is not just our understanding that needs help; the state of the text creates grave misgivings about any efforts to make sense of it; for, to put the matter bluntly, vv 10–16 are all but incomprehensible as they now stand. It is true that the composition contains a number of names of real places. It is a response to a calamity that affected them all. Some kind of military disaster had evidently overtaken them (or is predicted for them). That much is clear. It is also apparent that the prophet is playing on the (sounds of the) names of these towns; but the significance of this paronomasia is clear in hardly any instance. These features have created quite different impressions on different people. Duhm, for example, admitted candidly that he could make no sense of the content of the oracle (or whatever it is). Others strive to obtain as much realistic information as possible from the reference to geographical places, linking them with some real political events actually experienced by Micah (most commonly the Assyrian invasion of 701 B.C.E.). All the towns, at least those that can be identified with reasonable certainty, lie within a radius of Micah's hometown. Different again is Graham's attempt (1930–31) to explain the text as having a cultic function.

Each individual problem will be studied closely in the NOTES on the geographical names. The results are admittedly lean and merely go to prove in other ways that the text we have is incoherent. Honest readers find themselves in a distressing predicament. Here we have one of the great partings of ways in biblical criticism. For most readers of the Bible as a sacred text, inspired indeed by God himself, it is shocking and unthinkable that a prophet should produce such poor composition. Even without such a theological prejudice, scholars have looked upon the prophets of Israel as clear thinkers and skilled verbal craftsmen. Micah himself could not have composed such a piece. It must originally have expressed clear ideas, in grammatical Hebrew, in regular verse. Scholars who take this position blame the present state of the text on later scribes or copyists, who, by accident or carelessness, have lost the original text. It is then the task of modern scholars to do their best to recover that lost text. To be acceptable, any text they recover by means of critical method must be clear, grammatical, and regular.

The state of the text is not a problem for modern readers only. And this is not the only place in the Hebrew Bible where problems of this kind present themselves. There is much in the Bible that is obscure and untidy, an offense to neat thinkers and a nuisance for all readers. And it was already noticed by the earliest commentators. Furthermore scholars in antiquity were aware of the phenomena of ecstatic utterance, which received quite ambivalent evaluations. On the one hand, abnormal behavior could be rejected with abhorrence as the very opposite of rational conduct, either sheer madness or else a fraudulent affectation. On the other hand, some people felt that such paranormal behavior, especially when the performer was evidently "possessed" by some spirit power, should be accepted as "enthusiasm" in the proper meaning of that term. The person had been filled by a god. A divine being had come to that person; he or she was a medium for inspired utterance arising from a god or demon that had taken up residence in and was in control of that person.

From the strictly phenomenological point of view, such experiences are attested as clearly within the Bible as outside it. For any stable and organized religious community, such eruptions of spirit would be threatening and unacceptable. There are plenty of indications that in Israel too the establishment viewed the recipients of such experiences with alarm and disapproval. Even the prophets whom time vindicated, so that they became "canonical," were often and at first considered to be crazy. Albright (1961) pointed out the creative and constructive role that such movements have played in the long history of biblical religion.

The prophets were often very emotional, and—this is even more important, because it is more embarrassing to the philosophically minded readers of Scripture—Yahweh is revealed as a passionate deity. His emotions, tender as well as violent, are often expressed in turbulent language, turbulent sometimes even to the point of incoherence. Even if we restrict ourselves to Micah as the speaker of these words, we can accept them as an authentic expression of a profound and genuine emotional disturbance. As such, they can be taken in either of two ways. Either they are an accurate transcript of a spontaneous outburst; in broken sobs the prophet allows the names of the various towns to trigger associated words and ideas. As such, they still make a lot of sense; indeed they have great power. They catch the mood of terror, outrage, helplessness, tragedy. Or, alternatively, they are a more artistic composition such as would be made by a dramatist, capturing the feelings of desolation and grief that must be felt by any participant in events so catastrophic. In the final result, and so far as later readers are concerned, there is not much difference between these two readings. In either case the text can be accepted as it stands. That is what the prophet uttered (or wrote); it is the way he wanted it; the effects we still feel (with a high emotional content bordering on hysteria) are what he intended. And, in terms of revelation or theology, such a composition is not at all out of place in the repertoire of the words of the living God, who "was afflicted in all their afflictions" (Isa 63:9).

On the phenomenology of ecstatic utterance see Andersen (1995). If this is a more perceptive reading of Mic 1:10–16, its "message" lies more in its emotional impact than in its conceptual content. If we can take the formal incoherence as part of its message, we can mitigate a nagging problem in the textual criticism of the passage (Freedman 1982.)

THE PLACES IN MICAH 1:10–16

Identification of the Places in Micah 1:10–16

It is clear that vv 10–15 contain the names of several identifiable, even well-known cities. By analogy it is inferred that other cities might be mentioned whose names are not otherwise attested. And it is suspected that other places were originally listed but the names have been lost, the obscurity of the reference making the word vulnerable to scribal error.

In several instances LXX preserves the name of a town by transliteration; in other instances it translates the Hebrew word(s) (Oberholzer 1972):

> *bêt lĕʿaprâ,* "house of derision"
>
> *šāpîr,* "beautifully"
>
> *bêt hāʾēṣel,* "house of the neighbor"
>
> *mārôt,* "sorrow"
>
> *môrešet-gat,* "heritage of Gath"
>
> *bāttê-ʾakzîb,* "houses of vanity"

The place-names of MT are manifestly the source of the LXX renderings (Oberholzer 1972), not the reverse. Renaud cogently argues that "the Greek translation is incontestably interpretive and intended to make things easier *(facilitante)*" (1977: 20). This feature weakens the case of Collin (1971) that LXX reflects a Hebrew text that focused on cities in the vicinity of Samaria rather than in Judaea.

The Towns Named in Micah 1:10–16

1. Gath

There are plenty of candidates, beginning with the most famous Gath of all—Philistine Gath. Its nomination is strongly supported by the fact that it is certainly the Gath in 2 Sam 1:20, the source of the quotation that begins the whole recital; and it is simplest to assume that the reference remains the same. Unfortunately the location of this Gath remains unknown, although there have been several suggestions. Albright (1923; also Kassis 1965) favored Tell ʿErani (Tell Sheikh Ahmed el-ʿAreini). Wright (1966, 1971) proposed Tell ʾeš-Šariʿah. Tell ʾeṣ-Ṣafi, twelve miles east of Ashdod (Aharoni), is possibly to be identified as Libnah. Tell Nagila (Bülow and Mitchell 1961) is impossible (Amiran and Eitan 1965). For a full discussion, see Rainey (1974). A location southeast of Ekron now enjoys considerable favor as the site of this Gath (*ABD* 2: 909).

The versions confirm the name. Even so, its presence in the poem has attracted much suspicion from modern scholars. All the other places that can be identified lie in the vicinity of Micah's hometown, so a reference to Philistine Gath is deemed unlikely, and a nearby Judaean Gath has been sought. An additional argument against Philistine Gath is based on dating Mic 1:10–16 to 701 B.C.E., by which time Gath had been in Assyrian hands for ten years. It was captured by Sargon in 711 B.C.E. (*ANET* 286; Becking 1992). Scholars such as Lindblom (1929: 43), who retain Gath in the list, infer a campaign in which Philistine and Judaean cities suffered a common fate, defeat by Sargon in 711 B.C.E.

Gath is first on the list and not necessarily linked with the others. The political status of Gath changed with the rise and fall of Judaean control of the disputed territory between themselves and the Philistines. It was evidently part of David's (1 Chr 18: 1) and Solomon's realm, with Achish as Solomon's vassal(?) (1 Kgs 2:39–41). It was lost and regained by Rehoboam (2 Chr 11:8–10), captured by Hazael, the Aramaean usurper, sometime before 800 B.C.E. on his way to Jerusalem (2 Kgs 12:17), regained by Joash, and subsequently by the Philistines, since Uzziah expelled them (2 Chr 26:6). But it was Philistine once more when Sargon II destroyed it in his campaign of 711 B.C.E. This is the last mention of Gath in ancient sources, unless Mic 1:10 be dated to 701 B.C.E.

Bākô

On the basis of poetic parallelism, the first word in v 10aB has been suspected to be a place-name to match Gath in v 10aA. It is further surmised, not only that each place-name will evoke wordplay on its sound, but that any word should have a matching place-name. As the infinitive absolute *bākô* makes good grammar and good sense. No satisfactory proposal has been advanced, whether to infer that *bākô* must be a place, or to suggest some sound-alike, such as *Kabbon* (Strus 1985: 277). Other suggestions are Akko (LXX Akim) or Sokoh. Renaud (1977: 20) argues that emendation or reinterpretation of *bkw* to recover the name of a city is not plausible if the general rule is that each bicolon deals with only one city.

2. Bêt lě'aprâ

This city is attested only here. We assume that all twelve places mentioned by Micah have something in common and at least that they are near enough to one another to constitute a group. We assume that they all share in a common historical fate, whether Micah is predicting this or bemoaning its accomplishment. Taking a lead from the places that we can identify, it is best to suppose that they are all in Judah and all in or near the Shephelah. On this basis, connection with Ophrah in Benjamin (Josh 18:23; 1 Sam 13:17–18) seems most unlikely, with the Ophrah of Abiezer (Judg 6:11, 24; 8:32) quite out of the question.

It has been suggested by von Soden (1990b: 694) that some of the names on Micah's list might have been deliberately deformed to assist the wordplay. *Bêt lě'aprâ* could be a reference to Beth-lehem Ephratha (5:1). Na'aman emended the puzzling preposition *l-* to *l'* "in the house-of-no-dust," an "ironic twist" on the real name "of the place where the rite of mourning by rolling in the dust would take place" (1995: 519).

3. *Shaphir*

Unknown, except for this mention. Eusebius mentions a *Shafeir* near Ashkelon (*Onom.* 156); but this seems to be too far away from Judah to be eligible. Gold (*IBD* 4: 308) cautiously suggested a site west of Hebron near Wadi es-Saffar, assuming a link of the latter with *šāpîr*. But this takes us out of the Shephelah in the other direction. Dever (*EAEHL* 4:976–77) presents a strong case for Khirbet el-Kôm, west of Hebron.

4. *Ṣaʾănān*

Unknown. Possibly the same as *ṣĕnān* (Josh 15:37), which at least is in the right general area, the Shephelah of Lachish; but even so, the location of this place is not known. Accepting *ṣĕnān* as the place Micah had in mind, von Soden (1990b) thinks that Micah twisted the name to *ṣaʾănān* to make it sound more like *šaʾănān*, "careless." Naʾaman repeats this suggestion (1995: 519). This reading has meager attestation in manuscripts and could be behind Symmachus's translation "flourishing." Luker (*ABD* VI 1029) suggests that Micah added *alef* "to make clear his wordplay on *yāṣĕʾâ*."

5. *Bêth-hāʾēṣel*

Known only from this reference, it has been provisionally identified with Deir el-ʿAsal, two miles east of Tell Beit Mirsim. However, this is south of Hebron, almost in the Negev, and too far away to satisfy our expectation; and it would complicate even more any reconstruction of the developments, assuming that the sequence of towns reflects some kind of actual event, such as an army's line of march. Aharoni and Avi-Yonah (1968, Map 154) connect Mic 1:8–16 with Sennacherib's 701 B.C.E. campaign by reconstructing a main thrust from the coastal plain to capture Lachish, followed by forays to the north and east to secure some of the towns mentioned by Micah. Naʾaman, however, argues that "the names of towns have been selected mainly on the basis of their suitability for the play on words sought by the prophet. Therefore I very much doubt all efforts to find a strategic layout or line of march in the list of towns mentioned in the prophecy" (1986: 523). Naʾaman does not think that *bêt hāʾēṣel* is a Judaean place-name at all. He accepts von Soden's reading *bêt-hāʾî-ṣel*, "house-of-no-shade" as a "mocking designation for the ruling house of Assyria (1995: 520).

6. *Maroth*

Unknown, apart from this text, its suggested identification with Maʿărat (Josh 15:59) (Gold in *IDB* 3: 196, 278) seems most unlikely: first, because of *ʿayin*; second, because Maʿărat is in the hill country of Judah, too far south.

So far we have been unable to get our bearings. Not one of the six cities mentioned in vv 10–12a can be located on the map. Indeed five of them are completely unheard of outside Micah's lament. The first, Gath, does not give us a point from which to commence our journey in Micah's footsteps (or in his imagination). In this case the name is too common. We are not certain if the connection with 2 Sam 1:20 points to Philistine Gath, although we think that this is the simplest and best assumption. Even if we could settle that point, we would still be no better off, for the site of that city remains undiscovered by modern archaeology. All that can be conjectured about it is that, because of its prominence in relations between Philistines and Judaeans, it was probably the most inland of the major cities of Philistia. And often passing into Judaean hands, it could be reckoned as one of the frontier posts of the southern kingdom. As such, it could have been the first to bear the brunt of an attack from the west. If, however, it is one of the Gath's of Israel (usually "Gath" is part of a compound name, either first or last part), it could be anywhere.

7. Jerusalem
One of two indisputable places on the list! The other is Lachish. Fohrer (1967: 79) adopts the view that Micah is looking around at the towns that surround Moresheth-Gath, principally from east to west (not from north to south, which is the expectation of readers who think that the main line of march is from Samaria to Jerusalem). Jerusalem is not in Micah's view. The reference in v 12 is a corruption of an original *lĕša'ărayim*. The parallel reference to "Daughter-Zion" in v 13 is a later addition generated by the corrupted text. We are wary of the kind of hypothesis that goes on to change the text in order to obtain supporting arguments.

8. Lachish
At last we have a place we know a good deal about. It was an old Canaanite city-state, prominent in Joshua's conquest (Josh 10:31). It became a major fortress of Israel, or rather Judah, a chariot city from the time of Solomon onward. It was the key to Sennacherib's assault on Jerusalem in 701 B.C.E. (2 Kgs 18:14, 17; Isa 36:2; 2 Kgs 19:8; Isa 37:8). It has been well excavated, and its stratigraphic history is reasonably well known (Ussishkin 1982; A. M. Rosen 1986; Shea 1988; Mazar 1990: 427–35). The famous Lachish Letters reveal its significance for the later Babylonian invasion. The stratigraphy of eighth-century Lachish suggests that Lachish III was the city captured by Sennacherib in 701 B.C.E., but the details remain debatable (Ussishkin 1978a, 1978b, 1980, 1982). Micah associates Lachish with Jerusalem; in fact, he sandwiches it between the parallels "Jerusalem" // "Daughter-Zion." This arrangement makes it impossible to interpret the lament as a blow-by-blow account of an actual campaign, reported in any kind of chronological order, reflecting actual events.

9. Daughter-Zion
Compare Jerusalem. See the parallelism in Mic 4:8 and cf. Fitzgerald (1975) and Follis (1987b).

10. Moresheth-Gath
Probably, but not certainly, Micah's hometown. Commonly identified with Tell ej-Judeideh. This is supported by early Christian tradition about the tomb of Micah. But the latter attestation cannot bear much weight, and doubt remains

over both equations—the equation of Moresheth-Gath (1:14) and Moresheth (1:1) and the equation of either or both with Tell ej-Judeideh.

11. *Achzib*

There are two known places with this name (Josh 19:29; Judg 1:31). Joshua 15:44 locates Achzib near Mareshah on the border of the Shephelah of Judah. Eusebius (*Onom.* 172) has Χασβι near Adullam. So the last three names on Micah's list make a cluster. Achzib is plausibly identified with Tell el-Beida. The better-known Achzib in Asher (West Galilean hills) is not a candidate.

12. *Mareshah*

Located at Tell Sandaḥanna (Hermann 1989: 73), it is sufficiently attested in ancient sources to permit identification with Marisa (1 Macc 5:66; 2 Macc 12:35). It belonged to the tribe of Judah (Josh 15:44) and was settled by Calebites (1 Chr 2:42). Rehoboam fortified it, according to 2 Chr 11:5–10. The discovery of seventeen *lmlk* seals from the Iron Age 2C stratum of Israelite occupation confirmed the importance of the city as part of the south-west defense system of the kingdom of Judah (Na'aman 1986). The most extensive remains belong to the Hellenistic city.

13. *Adullam*

Khirbet esh-Sheikh Madkur (Albright 1924b: 3–4). The history of this settlement is well documented. Like Lachish it was a fortress town (2 Chr 11:7). The cave of that name, apparently nearby, has romantic associations with David. So the places that begin and end the piece (Gath and Adullam) have ancient memories. It was the hometown of Judah's friend Hirah (Genesis 38:12). It was David's hideout (1 Samuel 22:1). We cannot tell, however, whether these traditions were in Micah's mind or whether Gath and Adullam had more recent significance. Adullam is named as a town fortified by Rehoboam (2 Chr 11:7 [Herrmann 1989]), perhaps by Hezekiah (Na'aman 1986).

The locations of the first six towns are quite unknown. We know where the other six were, except for some residual doubt about the identity of Moresheth-Gath. The last four (Moresheth-Gath, Achzib, Mareshah, Adullam) are located in the foothills of Judah, southwest of Jerusalem. They lie between Lachish and Jerusalem, but not on a line of march in the order named. An invader would have to backtrack from Achzib to Mareshah before going on to Adullam.

There can be no doubt that Jerusalem is the ultimate goal of the oracle, although it has to be admitted that there is very little language that suggests military activity. In this respect Mic 1:10–16 differs from Isa 10:27b–30, which Fohrer (1967) thinks has influenced the composition of Mic 1:10–16. There the military scenario is evident, and the field movements can be reconstructed, at least in part. The realism of Isaiah's attachment of his oracle to geographical places in 10:27b–30 and the credibility of its scenario do not mean, however, that the text documents actual events; certainly no identification of such a campaign with any of the known movements of the Assyrian army has ever been achieved. There, too, Jerusalem is the final goal. Jerusalem is the only place mentioned twice by Micah (v 12). It is mentioned in the center of the lament, and v 12 says clearly that the evil has reached the gate of the capital. The close association of Lachish with Jerusalem, even though geographically it is the most distant from Jerusalem of all the towns in Micah's inventory whose locations we know, might have been intended to place it in a position of comparable importance to the capital for any conquest of the whole country. But there does not seem to be any basis for finding logistical or strategic considerations in either the list of towns themselves or the sequence in which they are listed.

The recital ends with Adullam. But it does not say that the invader has reached Adullam, thus posing a threat to Jerusalem (Adullam is nearest to Jerusalem of all the towns whose locations we know). Verse 15b says that the glory of Israel will come to Adullam, a statement whose total meaning is as obscure as its individual words are lucid. In any case v 12 has already said that the disaster has reached the gate of Jerusalem, and we would think that that would be the end of the story, if there is one behind the lamentations. Even if v 15 does report Adullam as the last place reached before the final assault on the capital city, there does not seem to be any geographical basis for tracing the lead-up battles through the other cities in the order named. There is no reason to believe that Micah began with Gath "because the Assyrian invasion was to begin at Gath" (Smith 1984: 21). We know in fact from Sennacherib's own account that his southern campaign began with Ashkelon and Ekron, followed by an engagement with the Egyptian army at Eltekeh. He does not mention Gath. Micah's account could be just as imaginary as Isaiah's.

As already pointed out, we don't know where any of the towns mentioned in vv 10–12a actually were. We have not succeeded in making sense out of the order of the six places whose locations we do know (vv 12b–15). In this, as in so many other respects, Mic 1:10–16 remains a complete enigma.

The Wordplay in Micah 1:10–16

Everyone agrees that vv 10–16 contain wordplay. Petrotta (1991) has pointed out that a play on words is found throughout the book of Micah, not just in 1:10–15. There is a play on the sound of the name of the city Samaria in the word *devastation* (*šĕmāmâ*) in v 7. There is a similar play on a city name in 4:14 (cf. Petrotta 1991). This feature provides more than literary decoration. It is a pervasive and unifying literary device; each instance reinforces the rest. But the composition is not consistently and systematically built on puns. In 1:10–15 the puns are most conspicuous with Beth-le-Aphrah, Lachish, and Achzib; and this has encouraged scholars to look for similar wordplay in the other names or even to use the expectation of a pun as an aid in textual emendation. When no known town can be identified with a name on the list, it has been suggested that the "name" is a perversion of the real name (von Soden 1990b; Na'aman 1995).

1. Gath—no pun, unless we are impressed with the chiastic assonance (*g t–t d*).
2. Beth-le-Aphrah—ʿ*āpār*, "dust."
3. Shaphir—no pun; *šôpār*, "horn," has been smuggled into the text (JB: "sound the horn"); see NOTE. There is sound play, however; all the consonants in *yšbt špr* except *p* are in ʿ*ry bšt*.
4. Zaanan—the verb *yāṣěʾâ* has two consonants in common.
5. Beth-haʾezel—no wordplay has been discovered (but see von Soden's suggestion above). The Hebrew word ʾ*ēṣel* is a noun used mainly as a preposition meaning "beside" (van Hoonacker 1908: 360). There is a verb root ʾ*ṣl*, "withhold." Attempts to find in the name implied wordplay with either of these vocabulary items are reported by Luker (*ABD* I: 686), who suggests that the name is connected somehow with the following statement about taking away his standing place. Strus (1985: 277) found one of his *jeux sonores* between *mispad* and the place-name; but there is really no similarity.
6. Maroth—if it means "bitter (ones)" (compare LXX "sorrows"), a contrast has been found by giving *ṭôb* the meaning "sweetness"; otherwise the town is accused, by implication found in the name, of "rebellions." We are supposed to be able to guess that a pun on some word with root *mr* is intended. Strus finds the sound play in the consonants *r* and *t* in v 12bA.
7. Jerusalem—no pun.
8. Lachish—*rekeš*, two consonants in common, and the third pair (*l* and *r*) are liquids.
9. Daughter-Zion—no pun.
10. Moresheth-Gath—attempts have been made to link *šillûḥîm*, "dowry," with *měʾôrešet*, "betrothed," because the latter sounds like *môrešet*. This is rather tenuous.
11. Achzib—a pun is clearly intended with ʾ*akzāb*, but the meaning of the latter is disputed. See the NOTE.
12. Mareshah—*yōrēš*, "(dis-)inheriting" ("plunderer" [NJB]) is a pun on the name.
13. Adullam—no wordplay, apparently, unless in the preposition ʿ*ad*. There is some assonance of vowels and consonants.

So, of the thirteen names, at least five are associated with words of similar sounds:

ʿ*aprâ*	ʿ*āpār*
ṣaʾănān	*yāṣěʾâ*
lkyš	*rkš*
ʾ*kzyb*	ʾ*kzb*
mršh	*yrš*

Most, if not all of the words that are placed alongside the names of the towns are negative in their suggested ideas. They are not the natural meanings of the names. Negative statements are also made without resorting to wordplay, notably in the case of Jerusalem. All the remarks are somewhat disjointed, as if thrown off on the run. They seem to be improvised, as if by free association. They are not systematic; there is no logical argumentation. The author did not succeed in carrying through a common pattern for them all. Given time and ingenuity, doubtless he could have done this, assuming that wordplay was the main intention of the exercise. The fact that it was not even half-done confirms our impressions, gained already on the basis of grammar and poetic structure, that there is a spontaneous, disorderly, makeshift character to the outburst. It also indicates that the names were not selected so that they could be exploited in this way. Nor does the use of five puns supply a warrant for searching for puns on all the names, or for using the expectation of such wordplay as an aid to the solution of textual problems. Various attempts have been made by text critics to enhance the wordplay on the names for which the present text has no such material. It seems to us that this is going too far, and the results of such endeavors have gained little hold on modern students of the problem.

We have been unable to hit on any explanation for the choice of these twelve cities (thirteen names) or for the sequence in which they are listed. They don't correspond to any military campaign that can be realistically constructed, except in a vague and general way. They are all (apparently, so far as we can tell) cities of Judah that would be likely to be involved in any attack on Jerusalem from the southwest. We cannot even tell whether they record or predict. We cannot determine whether the recital is a lament in mourning or a taunt in warning. Either way the effect of chaos and confusion is brilliantly achieved. But this effect is diminished the more we look for logic or logistics in the presentation.

NOTES AND COMMENTS

Notes on Micah 1:10

Each colon in v 10 has two beats, and each bicolon has eleven syllables. They are a bit short compared with classical verse, but close to poems in 2:2 meter. The entire piece is consistent in this feature, and we accept it as what we have to work with.

In Gath don't report [it]. No reasonable doubt can be entertained about the integrity of this clause. It is supported by its resemblance to the famous opening line of David's lament (2 Sam 1:20), from which it is a quotation. The only difference is that the sequence is inverted in Micah. In both places the verb lacks an implicit object—an unusual feature. Presumably the implied object is the same in both places, that is, they are not to report a monumental disaster suffered by Israel in which the Philistines would rejoice. MT is confirmed by Targum *thwwn*, by the Vulgate, and some Greek manuscripts.

In spite of this seemingly firm ground, the wording has attracted wide suspicion, and several emendations have been proposed. It is surprising that some ancient versions do not agree with the MT. But LXX *megalynesthe* retrojects to *tgdylw*, "boast" (preferred by Wolff and others); and Peshitta *tḥdwn* can be retrojected to *tgylw*, "rejoice" (accepted by many commentators, notably Elliger and hence BHS). Carmignac (1961/62: 517) recovered *bgwdly* from a Qumran fragment 1QpMi (*DJD* I 78, Plate XV), and conjectured that this reading could have derived from *tgdylw* retrojected from LXX. Collin (1971: 289) accepted this connection; but Barthélemy (*CT* 719) has pointed out that the word in the fragment of 1QpMi is not in v 10. Ehrlich proposed *tānûdû*. Driver (1938: 265) on the basis of an Arabic cognate, recommended *tāgîdû*, which is the basis of NEB "Will you not weep your fill, weep your eyes out in Gath?"

The present MT reading is then explained as a false adjustment to 2 Sam 1:20. The argument is (1) that v 10 originally had nothing to do with 2 Sam 1:20; (2) that originally, if Gath was even mentioned, which some doubt (see the emendation *gnt*, "gardens," below), it was not Philistine Gath. The geographical problem of Philistine Gath being the odd city out excludes it from the scene. The expectation of a pun on the city name leads further to the proposal to replace Gath by Giloh (proposed by Cheyne, still in BHS) or Gilgal (Budde 1917–18: 95; cf. BH³). Even so, neither of these cities is suitably situated to make a set with the others. Nor do the shock waves of emendation stop there. The assonance of *gt* and *tgydw* in MT is satisfactory, but the change to *tgylw* loses it. The new reading requires a better pun; hence Elliger proposed *bgnt*, "in the gardens of." Part of Elliger's strategy is to recover a three-beat colon. The original Hebrew text has completely disappeared! The only word in the colon that survives is "not"! In the end Schwantes (1962: 36) settles for Elliger's (1934: 85) solution: *běgannōt gilōh 'al-tāgîlû*, "In the gardens of Giloh don't rejoice!" Cf. Lindblom 1929. Nor did it stop there. "Gardens" required a parallel, so Elliger changed v 10bA to *bkrmy*, "in the vineyards of Beth-le-Aphrah," again securing three beats; and this duly appeared in BHS, despite the total lack of textual support. We notice once more the influence of the doctrine of synonymous parallelism on textual judgments. An emendation that requires another emendation to support it immediately loses credibility.

Gath. It is theoretically possible that Gath is not the same in the two poems, the original in 2 Samuel and Micah's quotation. The Gath of 2 Sam 1:20 is Philistine Gath, but when Micah quoted it he was perhaps bitterly transferring the reference to some Judaean Gath. There were several places called "Gath" in Israel and Philistia (Rainey 1974). The connections between Mic 1:10 and 2 Sam 1:20 are important for the criticism of both compositions. Micah 1:10 is a commentary as well as a quotation. It shows that vv 10–16 are intended to be a real lament in the same vein, grieving over a disaster that has happened. How much similarity are we warranted to find between the two occasions? The name "Gath" is the firmest link, and this suggests that it is the same place. This does not mean, however, that the concern to suppress the news so as to prevent the jubilation of the Philistines supplied the same motivation now as then. We suspect, rather, that the phrase has become a byword (it is still used like that, even in these days of biblical illiteracy). The Philistines have become symbolic of any enemy who might rejoice over one's downfall.

Renaud takes the point further. The quotation from 2 Sam 1:20 in Mic 1:10 evokes (and was intended to evoke) memories of one of the worst disasters to befall the monarchical institution of Israel, nothing less than the termination of a dynasty. Renaud finds similar allusions in other places, notably in vv 14b and 15b. In other words, vv 10–16 are about kings as well as cities (1977: 20, 22).

Given the similarity to 2 Sam 1:20, the word order in Mic 1:10aA calls for an explanation. This is abnormal order, because imperatives (here negative plus jussive) usually come first in a clause. This rearrangement could have been intended to secure the series (with assonance) *bgt . . . bkw . . . bbyt*. But, if so, why not complete the series in the fourth colon with *b-ʿpr* the usual idiom, from which *b-* must have been deliberately suppressed?

2 Samuel 1:20 required that news of the death of Saul and Jonathan be withheld from the Philistines so that their womenfolk would not celebrate their victory in the customary manner (Exod 15:20; 1 Sam 18:6–7). The remark was rhetorical; the Philistines knew, and nothing could stop their jubilation. David's original remark was itself an expression of grief, a futile wish that the Philistines would not take their good news back home, as the parallelism shows: "Publish it not in the streets of Askelon." And in 2 Sam 1:24 the Israelite people are told to weep for Saul and Jonathan. In Mic 1:10 the prohibition of publicity is fortified by a ban on weeping (Ezek 24:15–17). This second prohibition (v 10aB) parallels the first one in v 10, but it contradicts the resolutions of v 9 and the commands of vv 10b and 16. While the latter could imply silent grieving, the former implies wailing. Contradictory behavior is only to be expected in a grief-crazed person and fits in with other indications of hysteria in vv 11–15. There is a similar contrast between positive *ʿibrî* and negative *lōʾ yāṣěʾâ*. The two prohibitions of v 10 could be addressed to two distinct groups of persons, and so cover both extremes of possible and even conventional responses to calamity.

Micah 1:8–16 is not the only place in the Hebrew Bible where both wailing and silence are encouraged as expressions of grief. In Isa 23:2 *dōmmû*, "Be silent!" follows *hêlîlû*, "Wail!" BDB, following Delitzsch, invokes a second root word *dmm*, "wail," to secure synonymous parallelism. This *hapax legomenon* has not established itself in the Hebrew lexicon.

For some the news is good, and they would announce it with jubilation. This is prohibited (v 10aA). For others, the news is bad, and they weep. But this also is banned (v 10aB). Ezekiel, a special case, was forbidden to mourn for Jerusalem or his wife, but others were expected to do so. As in the case of David's strange reaction to the death of his child by Bathsheba, only a person directly involved is likely to be excused for eccentric behavior. Mourning could be prohibited when the dead person had come to a deserved end (Jer 22:18). There is one circumstance under which the conventions would be suspended— when there were no survivors! But usually it was expected that someone would live to tell the tale, to rejoice or to grieve. Perhaps here we have an extreme situation in which specific instructions override custom. The Philistines are not to rejoice. But then the command not to weep must be addressed to someone else. In any case, even as the text stands, it is clear from the changes in number and gender that the audience changes. The unit begins with second-person masculine plural, then changes to second-person feminine singular for the rest of the poem. The former are messengers; the latter are (the inhabitants of) the various cities.

don't weep at all. This is enough for a two-beat colon. It has good parallelism with v 10aA, especially if *bkw* is read, not as an infinitive absolute (MT), but as some kind of locative to match *bgt*. The LXX reading of the first word—"those in (or, you in) Akim"—could come from Hebrew *b(w)kym*, "weepers." The pun on *bkym* is already met in Judges 2. This is better than supposing that *m* is secondary in LXX, picked up by dittography from the following *mē* (Powis Smith 1910: 42). But the location of Bokim, near Gilgal, is quite unsuitable. And it is gratuitous to replace Gath by Gilgal in the preceding colon to secure this parallelism.

at all. Rendition of infinitive absolute. For the idiom compare *bākô lō'-tibkeh*, "you will never weep again" (Isa 30:19). The pattern in other parts of the poem, and especially in the colons immediately preceding and following, suggests a place-name on which the verb is a pun. Hence the various suggestions to read Bako, or something like it, as such a place-name. So LXX, which could reflect Acco. An extraordinary number of candidates have been nominated besides Acco—Bokim, Eshkol, Kabbon, Bakah, Ekron (Elliger 1934: 87 n. 7, for their proposers). Bakah would be easiest, since it would require no change in the Hebrew consonants. If 2 Sam 1:20 is in mind, Ashkelon would be the parallel of Gath. This is so conventional that we should regard the departure of the quotation from its original as deliberate. To mention Ashkelon would have made it certain that the Gath is Philistine Gath. Without Ashkelon as a parallel, the point remains moot. But the nonuse of Ashkelon here could indicate that now in Micah's day the political situation is different from what it was in David's time. Assuming that the original circumstances of 2 Sam 1:20 do not apply at all—the enemy was not the Philistines, and Gath is not a Philistine city, since all the others are Judaean—this would still not explain why the news is not to be reported in Gath. The point is the same whether this Gath is the original one of 2 Sam 1:20 or not. *Who* are told not to report *what* in Gath? If Jerusalem has been attacked, or if an enemy is coming, why should such a fact be concealed from the country towns. The usual procedure would be to sound the alarm. Perhaps the cliché has become a conventional response to bad news, not to be taken literally.

For the main verb *weep*, LXX *anoikodomeite*, "build," points back to *tbnw*, a misreading rather than an alternative reading.

The difficulty in accepting a ban on mourning when this is obviously required and when apathy would not be accepted by the community, has been resolved by inverting the meaning of the verb! If one accepts this solution, the contrast between v 10a ("Don't rejoice!") and v 10b ("Don't weep!") still remains as a problem. This problem has been solved either by omitting the second *'al* (Budde) or replacing it with *'ap* (Elliger). Renaud's one adjustment in v 10 is to resolve the contradiction usually found within v 10aB, which forbids weeping in a lament! He reads *'p* for *'l—Oui pleurez!* (1977: 22). Schwantes (1962: 37) comments: "All agree that *'l* as a negative is out of place here." This judgment arises from a too stringent expectation that two parallel colons will have similar meanings. Schwantes retains *'l* in part by proposing emphatic *l-*. None of these changes is needed to make v 10aB a positive assertion. One simply postulates asseverative or emphatic *'al*. This is what Gibson did (*Canaanite Myths and Legends*, glossary, under *'al*). Other passages in which *'al* asseverative has been proposed include 1 Sam 27:10 (Rin 1963); 2 Kgs 6:27 (the prohibitive *'al* makes no sense; either it is detached to make a clause of its own— "Don't [ask me]" [NJPS]; "No!" [NAB, NRSV], which would require different punctuation [cf. 2 Kgs 3:13b]—or read as conditional—"If Yahweh doesn't save you, where could I find help" [RSV, REB, NJB], which is so forced as to prompt emendation to *'im lō'*); Jer 5:10; Jer 18:18b (where LXX lacks the negative [Dahood 1965a §9.19]); Ps 59:12 (*'al tahargēm*, "Don't [or *do*] slay them!" [Dahood 1963: 294; 1968, *ad loc.*, however, he read "O El!"]); SS 1:6 (Exum 1981); cf. Muraoka (1985: 124). The difficulty with a particle that can have a positive or a negative meaning is that each reading makes sense, and appeals to context may not be enough to decide the balance. The judgment on this particle depends also on how much affinity is recognized between Hebrew and Ugaritic. The recognition of asseverative *'al* has merit in several of the texts referred to above, but we do not recommend it in Mic 1:10. We suggest that the exercise has been misguided by an irrelevant quest for consistency between the two colons.

Beth-le-Aphrah. The preposition *l-* attracts suspicion because none of the many place-names compounded with *Beth-* has such a grammatical structure. It is easy enough to excise the *l-*, following the lead of the Aramaic versions, or to transfer it to *'āpār* in v 10bB (Lindblom). Modern solutions have restored a more ample text, such as *(m-)byt-['l] [']l-'prh* (Budde 1917–18: 77). Compare the proposals of von Soden and Na'aman discussed above. Budde's adjustment replaces the 2 :: 2 scansion with 3 :: 2 (*qinah*) meter. Any extra word supplied at the beginning of the colon will do that: *bkrmy* (Elliger) or *bḥwṣwt* (Schwantes).

roll. The *qere* is imperative, in line with *'ibrî* in v 11aA. Mur 88 reads *htplšy*. The *ketib* is perfect, not first person, but archaic second feminine, possibly precative. Emendation to *hitpallāšû* follows LXX and is widely adopted (Na'aman 1995: 519); but that is just another case of harmonizing leveling to nearby plurals (Powis Smith in *ICC*). And the case for this emendation is weakened when *'ibrî* in v 11aA is adjusted to *'ibrû*. The traditional meaning "roll around" is not certain; and it is not suitable. The etymology of the root is uncertain or, at least, misleading. In Hebrew it always occurs as *hitpa'el* and in a similar idiom. It describes an act of mourning done to oneself with dust, *'āpār*, or ash, *'ēper*.

Neither noun is explicit in Jer 25:34, but one or the other must be implied and is normally supplied in translation. The other occurrences are: Jer 6:26—*hit-pallĕšî bā'ēper*; Ezek 27:30—*bā'ēper yitpallāšû*.

dirt. '*āpār* in this context refers to the dusty surface of the ground. Although the evidence is meager, two inferences might be ventured. First the preposition *b-* may be understood in Mic 1:10 also, omitted as in poetry, or double duty from v 10aA. There is no need to make a distinction between "complement" and "adverbial accusative" (Rainey 1974: 78). Second, the interchangeability of "dust" and "ash" does not mean that they are synonyms, as commonly argued. These words are not interchangeable in all contexts. On the contrary, either serves as a short equivalent of the complete phrase "dust and ashes" (Gen 18:27; Job 30:19; 42:6). The posture of a mourner or penitent was to sit "upon (the) dust and ashes" or, simply, "on the ground" (Job 2:13; Lam 2:10). In spite of LXX Job 2:8, which adds the words *eksō tēs poleōs,* "outside the city," there is no evidence that such a person was expected to sit "on the dung heap." The street, or the public square ("gate") within the city would do. Furthermore several passages indicate that "dust" or "ashes" might be put on the head as a further pathetic token of humiliation, and some even speak of "eating" these substances; the latter perhaps metaphorical (references in Rainey 1974). Archaeological evidence converges on these circumstances to show that the phrase "dust and ashes" describes a mixture that was used for surfacing the streets and squares of ancient cities (Rainey 1974: 81). That "dust and // or ashes" is something you walk on is shown by the cliché, *epru* (= '*āpār*) *ša šepêšu,* "the dust of [or beneath] his feet" and similar phrases (evidence in Rainey 1974: 79); while Mal 3:21 speaks of "ash beneath the soles of your feet."

There is no evidence that a person was expected to roll in the dirt, although by a stretch of the word a person sitting on the ground and sprinkling the loose dirt on his head might be said to "wallow." At least *hitpallēš* connotes "strew" as the LXX translations of Jer 6:26; Ezek 27:30; and Mic 1:10 show. Supportive evidence comes from Ugaritic, where GUT 67 (= CTA5): VI 14–16 describes such an activity, including the phrase '*pr pltt,* "the dust of mourning." Cassuto pointed out the resemblance to Mic 1:10 already in 1940–41.

In analyzing the double prohibition in v 10, we have already concluded, if somewhat tentatively, that there is a break between v 10a and v 10b. There are two different recipients of the prophet's messages, with two different assignments. Mourning is banned in v 10a, encouraged in v 10b. From the grammatical point of view there is no reason why the complete clause that begins in v 10a should not include "in Beth-le-Aphrah" as its locative adverb, a chiastic inclusion for *bgt.* The lament then begins with a tricolon (vv 10a–10bA) followed by a bicolon (vv 10bB–11aAα). Conventional wisdom about Hebrew poetry is against such a reading: (1) Two-colon units are preferred, and there is enough parallelism between 10aA // 10aB and 10bA // 10bB to satisfy most people that v 10 consists of two bicolons. (2) A run-on colon is not favored. (3) Expectation of a pun on '*pr* dictates that 10bA be linked to 10bB. (4) There is a change from plural to singular between 10a and 10b. These are powerful arguments, but they are not wholly compelling. The switch from plural to singular is not manifest until v 10bB, and v 11aA is likewise second-person feminine singular, so that 10bB // 11aA is a bicolon. And there could be a pun between *ʿpr* and *ʿbr*. Accepting in v 10aB the cognate infinitive absolute of MT, 10aA // 10aB // 10bA make a good tricolon. The two ingredients of 10aA—locative and verb phrase—are paralleled chiastically by the two colons of 10aB (the verb phrase) and 10bA (the location). If 10aB + 10bA are one clause with the same grammar as 10aA (infinitive absolute + negative + verb + locative), the grammar is impeccable, and it is purely an academic question whether it should be printed as one colon or two. If Gath and Beth-le-Aphrah constitute an inclusion in the opening colons of the poem, then they could mark the extreme limits of the range of territory in which all the other towns lie.

If the parallelism between *hitpallāštî* and *ʿibrî* warrants recognition of 10bB // 11aAα as a bicolon, then an opening five-colon unit with good structure can be recognized. In the first bicolon two negated second-person masculine plural verbs are in parallel; in the last bicolon two second-person feminine singular verbs are in parallel (and in chiasmus, to match the chiasmus of locatives and verbs in the first three colons). Furthermore, v 10bA can be explained as a two-way middle colon. As a locative it matches the opening *bgt*; and *ʿprh* is a domino (in chiasmus if you like) with *ʿpr*, so the pun is not denied. Finally *lākem* returns to the masculine plurals of the opening verbs—a long-range ethical dative that otherwise has no grammatical connection with the immediately adjacent words. If, looking at it another way, *yôšebet šāpîr* is the subject of *ʿibrî*, the intervention of *lākem* is very difficult to accept. Most critics discard it or rewrite it.

Introduction to Micah 1:11

The play on *ʿāpār* in vv 10bA // 10bB is a link strong enough to show that v 10b is a bicolon. At the same time it is valid to look for additional links between v 10bB and v 11aA through the play on *ʿāpār* // *ʿibrî* and the congruent imperative verbs. The sudden switch from singular *ʿibrî* to plural *lākem* at the beginning of v 11 detaches the latter so that it matches the plural *mikkem* at the end of v 11, and we do not have to explain *lākem* (away) by reference to the preceding material. Verse 11 then stands as a distinct, if complex, unit of seven colons. The short, jerky colons (two or three beats, three through seven syllables) show little or no connection with one another. The lack of conjunctions leaves it all open.

Verse 11aA has the last of the initial imperative verbs; it completes the opening exhortation. The following verbs are indicative; *yôšebet šāpîr* begins the middle section. That is, the command "Pass over!" is not addressed to "Inhabitant (of) Shaphir." Instead, the rest of v 11 can be seen as two tricolons, one dealing with Shaphir, one with Zaʾanan. Alternatively, v 11 could be three bicolons, the third one for Beth-haʾezel. Neither analysis makes the accompanying words any more intelligible.

11aAβ   *yôšebet šāpîr*
11aB   *nakedness shame*
11bAα   *she did not go forth*
11bAβ   *yôšebet ṣa'ănān*
11bB   *wailing of beth-ha'ezel*
11bC   *he will take away from you his standing place*

Notes on Micah 1:11

Pass. It is not easy to draw a line between assonance and paronomasia. There is considerable assonance between *'ibrî* and *šāpîr*; in addition, *'ibrî* has much in common with *'āpār*. Thus, if there is sound play here, it sets up a chain between v 10bB and v 11aAα and between v 11aAα and v 11aAβ. And there is another connection forward for *'ibrî*; this verb of movement lines up with *she went out* in v 11bAα. Both are so general in meaning that it is hard to determine what is being described here. The act of passing by or through is usually a normal and peaceful transit (compare the trusting travelers of Mic 2:8). It does not have the urgency of refugees fleeing from defeat. If the words "nakedness" and "shame" describe the condition in which the inhabitants of Shaphir pass along, then these could be prisoners from the town. But why should the prophet command them to pass along? And why is the verb singular? Is he imitating the commands of their captors, taunting them? But such vindictiveness seems incompatible with the grief that we find in this entire composition.

you. Perhaps the most troublesome single word in this unit is *lākem*. Few critical scholars have been able to accept it. Emendation to *lāk* is simple (BHS). Most recently Na'aman proposed *lāken* (1995: 517, 519), improving the symmetry between v 11 and v 14. However, a conjunction after an imperative makes the text difficult in another way. We retain *lākem* for three reasons: first, LXX, Targum, and Vulgate confirm the plural, but normalize the preceding verb to plural. Peshitta has singular. In other words, the versions have leveled in one direction or the other a source that had singular and plural in discord. Second, similar inconcinnities are found in other places, as pointed out above. Third, we think that there is a long-range rhetorical link with *mikkem* in v 11bC. The clash of singular and plural *lākem*—between the verb and its supposed subject, assuming ethical dative!—is thus alleviated. The delicate shift from plural to distributive singular ("each") usually moves from plural verb to singular subject (*'îš*); here it is reversed. A further difficulty is the switch in gender. In the COMMENT below we suggest an interpretation that accepts the different pronouns as pointing to two distinct but interrelated groups.

Renaud (1977: 24) emended *lkm* to *lkh*, "go!" the masculine form being an interjection that can be used when addressing a female. When used in this way, however, this kind of interjection comes before, not after, the main imperative verb.

inhabitant. Graham (1930–31) interpreted this word as the title of a resident female deity. The proposal as such is not implausible, the more so now that we have so much evidence, not available to Graham, that the cult of a goddess was more common in Israel during this period than even the biblical record suggests. There is no confirmation in the rest of the book that Micah was concerned about such a cult in these country towns. And the whole tone of Micah's lament is compassionate, not derisive or condemnatory. Graham's work is self-refuting when he has to find ceremonial processions and dances in the vocabulary and to delete about one-third of the text that does not fit his theory. Elliger's refutation (1934: 147 n. 2) is sufficient.

nakedness. The idea suggests shame, but the phrase "nakedness" (absolute, unaccented, and with *maqqeph*) "shame" is not satisfactory from the grammatical point of view. A construct would be better. The expected phrase is "the shame of nakedness" just as in 1 Sam 20:30; it is as if Micah has reversed the normal sequence of the construct phrase. The Aramaic versions confirm "nakedness." The much more common *ʿerwâ* emphasizes nudity that exposes the genitalia. Perhaps some nuance attaches to the rarer form *ʿeryâ* used here. In Hab 3:9 *ʿeryâ* is obscure; otherwise it occurs only in the fixed phrase *ʿērōm* (or *ʿêrōm*) *wĕʿeryâ* (Ezek 16:7, 22, 39; 23:29), which describes both the innocent nakedness of an infant or pubescent girl as well as the infamy of an exposed adulteress. The stock phrase attested by Ezekiel is found split up in Micah—*ʿārôm* in v 8, *ʿeryâ* here—so there could be a connection. The difference in spelling and vocalization does not seem to carry any difference in meaning. Micah, like Isaiah, goes naked in sympathy for the humiliation of the prisoners.

shame. The grammar of *bšt* remains a problem. Because LXX lacks any corresponding word, *bšt* has been deleted as a gloss on *ʿeryâ*. Vulgate confirms "shame." BHS lists *tēšēb* as a possible emendation (proposed by Duhm, favored by Sellin and G. R. Driver). A problem for some modern students of the passage is the apparent lack of a pun on the word *šāpîr*. This problem was solved by Duhm (1911: 83), who supplied *šôpār yaʿăbîrû*, following Lev 25:9. This was rejected by Budde (1917–18: 96), rehabilitated by Elliger (1934: 85), touched up by Driver (1968: 264), accepted by Schwantes (1964: 457), and is still recommended in BHS. With even more subtlety, van der Woude (1971b: 349) read *tʿbyr* (gathering *t* from the preceding word) without *šôpār*. He argued (n. 5) that the complete idiom, which is attested only in Lev 25:9, is only suggested, the pun being discovered in the listeners' recollection (from Lev 25:9) that the word *šôpār* was to be "understood."

Even more tortuous are Naʾaman's suggestions that ʿEriah is a place, with *bšt* added to distort the meaning to "nakedness," or that the toponym was Baʿal, read as *bšt*. While we give the verb *yāṣĕʾâ* its common military connotations, Naʾaman sees someone "naked" remaining indoors to avoid "shame."

The more conventional text-critical reasoning is that *bšt* was abandoned as a gloss on *ʿeryâ*, and the latter was then rewritten as *ʿîrâ* and touched up further either to *ʿîrâ tēšēb lōʾ yāṣĕʾâ* (Budde) or *mēʿîrālōʾ yāṣĕʾâ* (Elliger). It is only the status accorded to these readings—they are not emendations, they are new texts—in BHS that obliges us to notice them and to set them aside as far too elaborate to have any place in serious text criticism. We conclude, with all due diffidence, that *'eryâ-bōšet* is either the complement of *'ibrî*—"Pass by (in) shameful nakedness"—or the predicate of "the inhabitant of Shaphir," as in the translation at the head of this section.

go forth. The pun on the consonants *ṣ'* secures the integrity of the clause "(The) inhabitant (of) Za'anan did not go out." It is less clear whether the following six words in v 11bB continue this clause. The propensity of the author for short statements suggests otherwise. His style leaves the statement quite cryptic. Most researchers have given up the attempt to find (or to restore) a pun in this bicolon (v 11bB–C). Some have tried to improve the parallelism by means of various emendations (details in Schwantes [1962: 42]). Cautious for once, Elliger found only fragments of two mutilated lines (1934: 85), but did not attempt to restore the lost front ends. Schwantes himself (1962: 19) restored *'ăśēh* in his revised text, referring to the idiom in v 8.

The chaos in the text expresses the turbulence in the poet's mind, which reflects the confusion in the towns of Judah. It all adds up to a full picture, a whole catalog of activities (and their opposites) as elements in the experience of assault, siege, defeat, capture, death, mourning. Some would die, some would survive; some would stay, others would go. The ones remaining could sit in stunned silence or run about in frenzied grief. Some would rush off to escape, some would be dragged off as prisoners. Verses 10–16 give numerous fleeting fragmentary glimpses of this kaleidoscope. Does the case of Za'anan contrast with that of Shaphir? The residents of Shaphir went off as prisoners, those of Za'anan did not go out. In v 3 we associated *yṣ'* with a military expedition. In a siege, a city garrison could "go out" in a sally. Does v 11bA record a failure of Za'anan to do that? Or does it describe seclusion in mourning (compare Deut 21:10–14). Gordis (1978: 24–25) asserts that mourners were not supposed to go out-of-doors. If the latter, the following reference to mourning could be a continuation of the account. If this perfect verb also is precative, then it could be an exhortation to Za'anan to remain in seclusion, like a woman in mourning, hiding the disgrace of her nakedness.

wailing. The grammatical awkwardness of *mspd* has made it the target for correction; but no proposed solution has won general acceptance. Hillers does not defend his translation "Mourn greatly" (1984: 24). He seems to have accepted Schwantes's "restoration" of the verb "make!" We feel that if any word in the text is genuine, it is "mourning"; and the disjointed language is characteristic of the whole piece.

The arrangement of the names in vv 10 and 11 is chiastic:

    bĕbêt lĕ'aprâ

        yôšebet šāpîr

        yôšebet ṣa'ănān

    bêt hā'ēṣel

So it is possible that the mourning ritual enjoined for *bĕbêt lĕʿaprâ* is matched by wailing for *bêt hāʾēṣel*. The construct *mspd* is used only here and in Jer 6:26 and Zech 12:11, which show that it means mourning for, not by, *bêt hāʾēṣel*.

take. The imperfect verb could be future or jussive. We cannot be sure that the verb is future in reference. The end of the story is probably when evil reaches the very gate of Jerusalem (v 12), and this has happened, to judge from the form of the verb *yārad*, "it came down." Compare the perfect verbs in v 9. The profusion of verb forms is certainly bewildering. It is desirable to bring everything into line as either past or future, rather than to suppose a time perspective that continually changes. And it is easier to bring imperfect forms into line with perfects as past, than to strain verbs like *ḥālâ*, *yārad*, and *gālâ* into future. It is all retrospective, after the worst is over; but it is described using verbs of all aspects because the prophet is speaking in a multitude of discrete elements that rush into his mind in jumbled sequence, creating a nightmare effect. Hence v 11b is bewailing the calamity in which Yahweh took away "his standing place" from the cities just mentioned or from the people of Beth-haʾezel.

from you. It seems as if LXX read some form of *makkâ*, "blow," but attempts from Wellhausen on to recover a better Hebrew text from this clue have not secured a consensus. The sudden introduction of the plural *mikkem*, although it is masculine, not the expected feminine in reference to two or more cities (but "house" is masculine), could be the result of the inclusion of both in mourning. We have already mentioned the match with the equally problematic *lākem* in v 11aA; we think that together they constitute some kind of inclusion. If there were only one such plural, we would feel more at liberty to question it and emend it; but with two it becomes harder to do that. But who can Micah's audience be, apart from the individual cities apostrophized in the singular? Where did he say this? In public? If so, the "you" addressed twice in v 11 could be that immediate human audience, some group most likely in Jerusalem itself. In the COMMENT below we look further afield for an antecedent for these plural *you*'s.

standing place. Nobody knows what v 11bC means. Hillers (1984: 26) declares it to be "nonsense." It is one thing to admit that we don't know what it means; it is another thing to claim that we know that it's nonsense. There is no hint of wordplay on the name Beth-haʾezel and the word *ʿemdâ*. The noun occurs only here in the Hebrew Bible. It could be a feminine variant of *ʿōmed* (postexilic) or *moʿŏmād* (Ps 69:3). The most likely meaning is a secure place to stand, or a post to which one is assigned. Wordplay has been suspected between the verb *yiqqaḥ* and the verb *ʾāṣal* (same root as *ʾēṣel*), which means "withhold." The one who performs this act (masculine singular) is unidentified. Other masculine singular agents in the passage are "evil" (12bA), "the dispossessor," and "the glory of Israel." Since taking something away sounds like a hostile act, by the rule of parsimony it is simplest to suppose that one enemy did all these things to the several cities. Furthermore, v 12 makes it clear that "evil" comes from Yahweh, and Yahweh is probably the speaker in v 15, who brings the dispossessor to Mareshah again. So Yahweh is the best candidate to be the subject of *yiqqaḥ* in v 11. If not he, then some agent of his, the active referent of the subject of the third-person masculine singular forms. Whose *ʿemdâ* does he take away? That of some otherwise unidentified person, removed from his post? His own? The most dismaying of all tokens of divine displeasure is when God destroys his own familiar haunts. It was unthinkable; yet it happened. The eventual demolition of Solomon's Temple was the supreme instance. And the best kind of faith saw this as God's strong action, not as proof of his impotence to guard his own shrine. We shall return to this problem in the concluding COMMENT.

Introduction to Micah 1:12

Verse 12 contains the most (almost the only) intelligible sentence in the entire piece: *but* (or *for*) *Evil came down from Yahweh to the gate of Jerusalem.* Hardly lyrical poetry! There is no parallelism. If it is a bicolon, it is the longest in the unit (fourteen syllables). The bicolon in v 12a has only nine syllables. In spite of its great length, v 12b may be accepted as part of the composition, and not rejected as a scribal gloss. The position of Jerusalem in the middle of the series befits its central importance, but shows that the march of an army to its final goal is not being chronicled in a documentary fashion. The links between v 12b and vv 3 and 9 suggest that the same development has been traced to its climax—*yārad* (v 3) . . . *šaʿar* . . . *Jerusalem* (v 9). Verse 9 and v 12 report the same situation. Note the occurrence of *kî* twice in both verses, with parallelism of the verbs.

kî ʾănûšâ	*kî-ḥālâ*
kî bāʾâ	*kî-yārad*

If the disasters that overtook all the towns represent evil that came down from Yahweh, then this is a theological interpretation placed on a combination of natural disasters (prominent in the ruin of Samaria) and military defeats (prominent in the ruin of Jerusalem and her cities).

Notes on Micah 1:12

Good. Gordis (1934: 187 [= 1976: 314]) suggested an adverbial meaning "greatly" for this expression. Driver translated "she is in very great anguish" (1938: 265). In view of the following *Evil* it is best to retain the salient meaning "good." Hillers (1984: 24) has "sweetness" (adducing this meaning for the Ugaritic and Akkadian root) to secure an antithesis to the idea of "bitterness" in Maroth. The juxtaposition of *Good* and *Evil* in this verse encourages belief that there is an inner connection between them. But there are no specifics. We have capitalized the words to suggest possible reference to an agent rather than an abstract notion, Yahweh being "(the) Good (one)." There seems to be a causal or logical connection between the event at Jerusalem (v 12b) and the reaction of the people of Maroth (v 12a). The fact that both halves of the verse begin with *kî* makes this more difficult to work out; and many translators suppress or change either or both of these conjunctions. The same problem was met in v 9. LXX *tis ērksato* implies *mî*, "who," for *kî*. This has been widely adopted in modern translations.

   waited anxiously. The LXX verb points to *yiḥălâ* or the like. This could be read in any case, since the additional *yod* is available in *ky*. The *pi'el* is an attractive reading, since it is used in Mic 5:6. It has enjoyed much favor since Wellhausen (1898: 136). Verbs containing *ḥ* and *l* are notoriously difficult, because there are nearly a dozen eligible roots to choose from. MT *ḥālâ* could be a third-person masculine singular *qal* of *ḥly*, "he was sick" (usually a terminal illness), or third-person feminine singular *qal* of *ḥw/yl*, "she writhed in pain." But the meaning "wait" could be present without restoring **yḥlh*, since *ḥl* could be a byform of *yḥl* (Andersen 1970). A feminine verb is certainly better if "Inhabitant Maroth" is the subject, and BDB (297a), comparing it with Judg 3:25, interprets it as "longing anxiously." We have used this in the translation, but without conviction. Such a nuance is not otherwise attested. In the context of pain and misery in Mic 1:10–16 *ḥālâ* might have its ordinary meaning, since the language of Mic 4:10 is very close, and the circumstances are very similar. Collocation with *Good* suggests a more positive verb. The root *yḥl*, common parallel of *qwy*, expresses hopeful expectation. Powis Smith (ICC) preferred the latter option, using LXX to recover *myḥlh* (**miyyiḥălâ*), "How it has hoped?" The consonants of this restoration became the starting point for several similar proposals. The meaning "How?" for *my* was brought in from Amos 7:2, 5. A better basis for this meaning was then found in *'êk* ("attractive" [Hillers 1984: 26 n. i]). This seems to be building conjecture on conjecture.

   Evil. See the NOTE on *Good* above.

   came down. The idiom *yrd l-* is unusual. LXX has *epi* (= *'al*) but the occurrence of the idiom in Judg 5:11 confirms its authenticity. The pictures could be the same—"Then the (heavenly?) army of Yahweh descended to the gates."

   gate. LXX and the Aramaic versions have "gates," the commoner expression. If correct, then either the original had a double reading of one *yod*, or *yod* was lost by haplography. Or the plural was leveled to the singular in v 8. But again the singular of v 8 could validate that of v 12.

Introduction to Micah 1:13

It is ironic that one of the few places in Mic 1:10–16 that can be read with reasonable clarity (v 13b) is, perhaps for that very reason, considered by many critics to be redactional. As is often the way, the Exile is nominated as the time when this kind of interpretation was added to older texts (Jeremias 1971b; Lescow 1972a; Renaud 1977: 11, 55). Like the similar suspected additions in v 5, the comment highlights the responsibility of the capital cities for national disasters, and Judah is blamed for imitating the northern kingdom. Calling Jerusalem "Daughter-Zion" (v 13bA) is said to be secondary. Part of the argument against the authenticity of parts of v 13 is the disorder in the grammatical persons (Renaud 1977: 25). But, while allowing that the change in gender introduces further complications, v 13a and v 13bB make a second-person envelope around a third-person statement (v 13bA). Thus attention fastens on the seemingly aberrant "she" of v 13bA. The manuscripts (including Mur) and versions are unanimous that this is the correct reading. Even so, harmonizing translations from Luther onward, too numerous to list (KJV, ASV are exceptions), have replaced it with "thou," usually without note. Slender textual arguments for 't as the original pronoun are sometimes given (the two words have one letter in common), but such a disturbance of the coherence of the verse would surely have been corrected in a hurry. The clash of gender can be softened a little if the feminine is taken to be virtual neuter ("it" [NRSV]); but the price paid is that, whereas "she" has an available referent in "Lachish," with a plausible exegesis, without a referent for "it" we do not know what the author (or redactor) was talking about. Discourse linguistics recognizes other ways in which this text might be received as coherent. The switch to third-person discourse in the middle of a second-person speech could indicate embedding (subordination), or that the remark is parenthetical (an aside, but still part of the exposition). There is not much difference linguistically between these two explanations, and there is no way of telling the difference between a parenthetical remark made by the original author and an interpretive comment inserted by a later scribe.

Notes on Micah 1:13

Harness. Hapax legomenon. The Aramaic versions confirm MT. The other versions seem to be floundering. This word has suffered much at the hands of text critics. The root is one problem. The number and gender are another (it is the only 2d. m. sg. verb in the unit). We see no merit in the gratuitous substitution of a more familiar root—*mhr* (Budde), *'rk* (Elliger), *'sr* (Schwantes). A simpler way to get rid of the lone masculine form would be to read *rātôm*, infinitive absolute, used as a generic imperative, so that the command could be addressed to Lachish. Perhaps it is masculine because that command is always addressed to a groom. The context suggests some activity having to do with chariotry.

the chariot. This word is not in doubt. It presents four anomalies. First, the use of the definite article, the only case in vv 10–16, raises the question of its function in making the noun definite. Why use the definite article? (Duhm transferred the *h-* to the preceding verb.) Which chariot? We suggest that it implies possession, *the* chariot of the person spoken to. Hence the masculine gender of the verb, since the operator would be male. Second, since Lachish is likely to have more than one chariot, why use *merkābâ*, if the whole chariot force is to be readied for war? The collective noun *rekeb* is usual for that or else the individualizing feminine *merkābâ* can be pluralized. The singular is distributive—"Each of you harness his chariot." Finally we note that *nota accusativi* is not used to mark the definite object.

Megiddo and Hazor were Solomon's chariot cities. When these were lost to Judah with the secession of the northern tribes, it is likely that Lachish, which was the largest city in Judah next to Jerusalem, would be strengthened as a military fortress. It occupied a strategic position and is frequently mentioned in wars, most notably in Sennacherib's invasion, when its capture was assumed by the Assyrian to seal the doom of Jerusalem. See Tufnell in D. Winton Thomas (1967) and the reports of Ussishkin. Micah's remark here suggests that it was a chariot city; but the fact is that Judah never went in for chariots after the heyday of Solomon, at least there is no documentation of this service in the armies of Judah. In this connection the silence of 2 Chr 11:5-12 may be significant. It reports how Rehoboam built numerous cities, including four in Micah's inventory (Adullam, Gath, Mareshah, Lachish). These were fortified as strongholds, with garrisons and supplies. But the only weapons mentioned are shields and spears. And the Assyrian taunted Hezekiah on his lack of chariotry at the very time when Lachish was under siege, since Hezekiah had to rely on Egypt for such military aid (Isa 36:9).

steed. The noun *rekeš* is also a rare word. It could have been chosen to secure assonance. Micah's statement presents several difficulties. The noun *rekeš* refers to some kind of steed that may be ridden (Esth 8:10, 14), but 1 Kgs 5:8 distinguishes *rekeš* from horses. LXX had difficulty with this word in Esther, but the situation there suggests speedy animals used by couriers to carry urgent messages. The traditional interpretation—"hitch the horses to the chariots"— encounters numerous grammatical difficulties on top of the problem of the meaning of two of the three words. The usual idiom is "Harness the horse to the chariot," not "Harness the chariot to the horse." The verb *'sr* (which Schwantes wishes to restore out of *rtm*) has "chariot" as its object (*merkābâ* [Gen 46:29], *rekeb* [Exod 14:6; 2 Kgs 9:21]), or "horses" (Jer 46:4). The full idiom is found in 1 Sam 6:7—*wa'ăsartem 'et-happārôt bā'ăgālâ.* Elliger prefers *'irkî,* but this verb describes the setting of things in array, including the battle line. Here it would mean arranging the chariot(s) against the *rekeš* (cavalry?). Renaud argues that the anomalous idiom as well as the rare word facilitates the wordplay on Lachish (1977: 25).

She is first of sin. The third person *hî'* contrasts with the second person before (presumably, if *yôšebet lākîš* is vocative) and after. The whole clause could be a later interpretive comment (Elliger). This kind of "solution" appealed to a previous generation of scholars who were still trying to sift out the original words of Micah from later accretions. Now that so many scholars are convinced that much of the book is the result of successive editions and rewrites, such glosses and comments (if that is what they are) are taken more seriously as part of the tradition of interpretation, indeed as part of the text of the book of Micah we now have.

One would expect an explanatory comment to make the text better, not worse, clearer, not more obscure. What does it mean to say that *she* (presumably Lachish) is *the first of sin to* (or *for*) *Daughter-Zion*? If the next clause, beginning with *kî,* gives the reason (*because*), what exactly are *the rebellions of*

Israel that were found there? And why does the speech switch from *she* to *thee*? Can these two pronouns have the same referent? Is Micah talking *to* some male personage in v 13aA, *about* Lachish in v 13bA, and *to* Lachish (f.) in a subordinate clause in v 13bB?

"She" can be changed to "you" (NEB). Or "in you" can be changed to "in her" (Duhm). If v 13bB is talking *to* Lachish (Daughter-Zion seems to be third person in v 13bA), then the charge is that the crimes of Israel were found in Lachish. If, however, Micah is in Jerusalem, talking about the surrounding towns, addressing those towns rhetorically, but also talking *about* them, then just as vv 3, 9, 12 trace the progress of Yahweh (or "Evil") right up to Jerusalem, so v 13 shows how the two main cities share in the common guilt of Jacob's *rebellion* (*pešaʿ*), "the sin (*ḥaṭṭāʾâ*) with which Jeroboam I made Israel to sin." After naming Zion in v 13bA, the prophet addresses that city directly in v 13bB, saying to her that those same rebellions *were found in thee*. The use of the same vocabulary in vv 5 and 13 invites the use of one to clarify the other. There is a complex chiastic pattern in the sequence:

v 5	*pešaʿ*	singular	*ḥaṭṭōʾwt* plural
v 13	*ḥaṭṭāʾt*	singular	*pišʿê* plural

These nouns are in construct with four different nouns, Jacob : House of Israel :: Daughter-Zion : Israel. Symmetry, chiastic or otherwise, is hard to find in this set of names; but we think that it is more likely to involve parallelism of north and south rather than synonymous parallelism, that is, "Israel" following "Daughter-Zion" is more likely to point to the north than to the south. The characteristic sin of Israel (the northern kingdom, as again in v 14) spread to Jerusalem, with Lachish as the intermediate first stop in Judah. *The beginning of sin* in v 13bA suggests some inauguration of a standing offense. What then is the logical connection between v 13a and v 13b?

The discovery of Israel's sins in Lachish does not seem to be a cogent reason for harnessing the chariot. The command to prepare the war chariot is in line with the urgent response to a military threat, reflected in some other language of field combat found in the unit. If Lachish is addressed, vocative, in v 13a and is also "thee" in v 13bB, then "she" of v 13bA cannot be Lachish (unless the remark is an aside). It refers to someone (or something) who was "first of sin" in relation to Jerusalem. The word "first" is also unclear; is it first in rank or in time? It is more likely that this means the source of sin rather than the leader in sin or worst sin and that this sin seems to be the same as "the crimes of Israel" (v 13bB). The *pešaʿ* (sg.) of Jacob in v 5 is paralleled by "sins," and Samaria and Jerusalem are evidently guilty of the same things. Moreover the word *bāmôt*, which many have found puzzling, is a firm indication that the covenant rebellion condemned in v 5 is located in or represented by the cult. Amos likewise (2:4–8) connects the rebellion of both Israel and Judah with the paganizing of the Yahweh cultus, and specifically with a goddess, given that The Girl of Amos 2:7 is the same as Ashmat of Samaria (Amos 8:14). Amos's references to various shrines suggest that this defection had spread all over the country. He uses the verb *pšʿ* to describe what is going on in the shrines (Amos 4:4). Now Micah 1:13 links firmly to 1:5 by the chiasmus pointed out above. All this suggests, or at least permits, the idea that "She" is the goddess whose image and cult were exported from Samaria to various other places and that the capital sin of the north (idolatry) reached Jerusalem via Lachish. The sin was setting up idols (and precisely idols of that goddess) in the high places of Judah (v 5).

A few other considerations support this proposal. There are two prongs in the development of the dual prophecy against Samaria and Jerusalem (v 1). Both are summoned in v 2. In vv 3–9 Samaria is prominent, Jerusalem secondary. In vv 10–16 the focus is on Jerusalem, with Samaria in the background. But Israel is part of the picture, being mentioned three times in vv 10–16. In the middle of vv 3–9 (in v 5), the two cities are looked at together. Jerusalem and Judah in v 9 are transitional. It would therefore complete the development if in the middle of vv 10–16 (in v 13) the similarity of the two capitals in the matter of their common sin were stated again.

If we are correct in seeing the connection between v 5 and v 13 as the trail of the spread of the cult of the goddess from Samaria to Jerusalem via Lachish, then a combination of what Jeremiah says about a goddess cult in Jerusalem with the account of Hezekiah's reforms in the book of Chronicles gives mutual support among these very incomplete reports. There is no indication that any of these texts was composed with knowledge of the others. The book of Micah gives no hint that the prophet's message influenced Hezekiah, as reported in Jer 26:18. Jeremiah does not say *what* Hezekiah did in response to Micah's oracle. The Chronicler (2 Chronicles 29) does not attribute Hezekiah's policies to Micah's preaching, and his language is rather general. The reference to Ahaz's transgression in 2 Chr 29:19, however, points to the time when we think it is most likely that Micah was mainly active. Among Ahaz's many sins the Chronicler lists making and using images of many foreign gods and sacrificing his children. From Micah 1 we might infer that among those gods was the goddess from Samaria. Handy (1988: 115) has asserted that "it is quite unlikely that Hezekiah made a sweeping reform of the religion of Israel." His arguments are *a priori*, based on what the king "would have done." On the contrary, we find the convergence of these three independent sources impressive, especially as there is no reason to doubt the authenticity of Mic 1:13; and the best sense we can make out of that verse is that it documents the spread of a serious sin from Samaria to Jerusalem.

were found. The passive verb "they were found" means that God found them. And this is what Assyria says in Isa 10:10–11, which analyzes the same historical situation in the same way as Micah, using the language of Mic 1:7 and comparing both countries with "kingdoms of the idol." He threatens:

As I did to Samaria and to her images,
So I shall do to Jerusalem and to her idols.

Introduction to Micah 1:14

To explore the relations between linguistic structure and poetic structure we have used a rule of thumb that tries as much as possible to identify a complete grammatical unit, preferably a clause, as a poetic unit, sometimes a bicolon, often a colon. When the two kinds of unit do not obviously coincide, one might help to find the other, working in either direction. In v 14 neither consideration gets us very far, and we have accepted the Masoretic punctuation. The syntax is not clear. There is only one verb and there are actually five noun phrases available to be connected grammatically to that verb. If the prepositions are taken seriously *l-* should mark the indirect object of *give*. There are two such phrases. The noun phrases without prepositions (*parting gifts* [v 14aA] and *houses of Akzib* [v 14bA]) could be direct objects of "give," and it is easiest to regard them as standing in apposition. Their similar functions and parallelism suggest that they might refer to the same things; that is, the houses of Akzib are characterized as "parting gifts." This leaves the fifth phrase—*'al môrešet gat.* The preposition compounds the difficulties. There is no idiom that would draw *'al* into the sentence (Mays). Nor can it mark Moresheth-Gath as the indirect object (KJV; R. L. Smith). With *ntn*, *'al* means "concerning" or "on account of."

Conjunction	Verb	Object	Reference	Indirect Object
Therefore	*you will give*	*gifts*	*on account of*	*to Akzab*
		houses of Akzib	*Moreshet Gat*	*to kings of Israel*

Once more the logical connection from verse to verse is quite unclear. We were unable to decide whether the last protagonist addressed in v 13 (the *thee* [f.] in v 13bB) was Lachish or Jerusalem. If v 14 is a single detached statement, we are still obliged to work out to whom the prophet is talking, who he says will give these gifts to the kings of Israel. The best place to look is in the preceding text. If the same person (city) is still being addressed in v 14, then the logical force of the connective *lākēn, therefore,* is that she will give parting gifts because the sins of Israel were found in her. But v 14aB suggests that the *parting gifts* will be given *on account of Moresheth-Gath.* In spite of the difficulty of working out the logical continuity between vv 13 and 14, there seems to be some thematic continuity in the way the phrases *pišʿê yiśrāʾēl* and *malkê yiśrāʾēl* balance each other at the ends of these verses.

Notes on Micah 1:14

Therefore. The opening conjunction *lākēn* has been identified as an exilic addition required by the redactional changes made in v 13 (Renaud 1977: 11, 25). We accept it as marking a transition from the largely descriptive mode of vv 11–13 (three perfect verbs, one imperfect) to the predictive mode of vv 14–15 (three imperfect verbs). Because of the difficulties in finding the logical connection between v 13 and v 14 secured by this conjunction, the first two words have often been emended. An indirect object has been recovered from the opening conjunction by rereading *lkn ttny* as *lk ntnw* (BHS—accepted by Mays, Allen, and others). *Ntnw* can be vocalized as either active or passive. Hillers sees no need for this emendation, and we agree. The emendation is drastic; it involves moving one letter, deleting one letter, changing one letter. And it requires also the removal of the preposition *ʿal*. We do not rehearse here the more adventurous proposals of earlier scholars who have come up with at least four different verbs to replace *ttny* (details in Schwantes 1962: 48).

shalt give. Or "hast given." For the tense, see the NOTE on *take away* in v 11 above. The feminine subject of MT *ttny* could be a difficulty if the statement describes the bestowal of a dowry, usually the responsibility of the father of the bride. But this meaning for *šillûḥîm* is not certain. Since *lqḥ* and *ntn* are correlate in Hebrew, and both occur here, the two should be kept in line if possible. The verb *ntn* can mean "pay." So the first verb could refer to seizure of an asset (v 11bC), the second to payment or compensation (v 14).

parting gifts. The questions to be answered are (1) Who makes the gift? (2) What are the *šillûḥîm*? (3) To whom are they given? (4) Why? The noun *šillûḥîm* is a technical term that occurs three times in the Hebrew Bible. In this context, a departure payment to the kings of Israel might seem to be dane-geld, a bribe to an invader to go away. Since the passage speaks of dispossession (v 15), refugees (v 11), and prisoners of war (v 16), gifts could be for saying goodbye to departing residents of Moresheth-Gath (Mays). But this seems to be too peaceful to fit the terror of the rest of the lament. The contexts of the other two occurrences of the word identify *šillûḥîm* as dowry given to a bride by her father when she leaves her home. For the practice, see van der Woude, (1964: 188–91). Haupt (1910a: 105) compares Caleb's gift to Achsah. A basis for its use here could be a pun on the word *môrešet*, which sounds like *mĕʾōrāśâ*, "affianced." In fact Haupt (1910a: 92) translated the phrase "Gath, the bride." But the feminine verb *tittĕnî* shows that it is a female (the bride?) not a male (her father) who gives the gifts. It is no solution to this to change the verb to *yittĕnû*, "they will give" (T. H. Robinson 1954: 132; recommended by BHS), or *yuttĕnû*, (suggested by Lindblom and preferred by Allen), or *yinnātĕnû* (Elliger). LXX *dōsei* attests the difficulty, but does not solve the problem.

The second problem is the meaning of *šillûḥîm*. There is nothing in the meaning of the root *šlḥ* that connects it necessarily with the technicalities of marriage. It means simply "send (away)" and it is quite general—anyone can send anyone or anything for any reason or purpose. So it would be better not to try to nail this word down first and then to use its meaning to control the interpretation of all the other words in v 14. A literal translation of the unchanged text points to the answers. Question 4: They are given "on account of Moresheth-Gath." Question 3: They are given to the kings of Israel, also called "deceiver," if the two indirect objects are parallel. Question 2: The gifts consist of "houses of Akzib." Question 1: In the absence of a clear candidate to be subject of the verb, Jerusalem is the probable giver. If marriage customs are implied, they are present only as a faint metaphor.

Exodus 18:1–12 recounts the reunion of Moses' family at Horeb. His wife and children are repeatedly mentioned. Verse 2 ends with the phrase "after her *šillûḥîm.*" This is obscure; the gifts are not identified, but they clearly belong to Zipporah. If *'aḥar* meant "together with" then it would make sense, and indicate that the dowry was movables. First Kings 9:16 reports that Pharaoh captured Gezer from the Canaanites, "and he gave it as parting gifts (*šillûḥîm*) to his daughter, Solomon's wife." So Gezer became the queen's city. Such a practice is commonly attested in the political and economic documents from Alalakh and Ugarit. The dowry was real estate. But the exchange of villages could be part of international treaty making without necessarily involving a dynastic marriage; at least no intermarriage is mentioned in the well-known case of Hiram and Solomon. Pointing out 1 Kgs 20:34, van der Woude (1964) concluded that Mic 1:14 is talking about a similar action; the gifts are to formalize a treaty.

The *šillûḥîm* of Mic 1:14 might have had political significance without necessarily including any marriage or betrothal gifts. As we shall show in the comment on chapter 2, the word "house(s)" in vv 2 and 9 refers to estates—land as well as houses, and the "houses of Akzib" mentioned here could have a similar meaning. In 1 Kgs 9:16 *šillûḥîm* is the complement—"he gave her Gezer (as) (her) *šillûḥîm*"; the modifier used in Exod 18:2 is understood. So here the unmodified noun is similar, implying "You gave away (your) *šillûḥîm* [that is, the houses of Akzib]." If Jerusalem is the subject, then, as Daughter-Zion she received these country properties as part of a marriage settlement. (There is no need to work the figure up into a complete allegory by trying to identify the husband.) The point is that Jerusalem has given away her endowment by ceding territory to Israel in settlement at the end of a losing war. The notion of endowment might be marginal to the political figure of speech. If the lost territories were in some sense an endowment, the thought behind that might be the gift of land by Yahweh to Israel as his partner. Whatever the deal was, it involved deceit. We strongly suggest that Mic 2:1–5 is talking about the same incident, or at least the same kind of thing, the relinquishment of territory under the figure of giving away an endowment.

on account of. If Moresheth-Gath receives the dowry, the idiom "give . . . upon" (Allen) is uncorroborated. It requires extensive emendation to recover an indirect object **'ēlayik* (BHS) via **'ālayik* (Elliger). Or Moresheth-Gath can be made vocative by dropping *'al* altogether (Mays). A solution that retains the preposition and gives it its usual meaning is preferable.

Moresheth. The versions took this word as a common noun, *inheritance* (LXX). Haupt's emendation to "affianced" has been discussed above.

houses. Targum and LXX confirm the plural; other versions have singular. Elliger changes *bty* to *yôšebet*; others prefer *bat* or singular *bêt*. The very analogy used by Elliger to "restore" *yôšebet* to line up with the titles of other cities is the one that Haupt argued had already misled ancient scribes into using *yôšebet* for too many cities. So Haupt (1910a: 101) deleted *yôšebet* in v 11 and changed it to *bat* in v 15! For such drastic emendations we should expect some kind of support from ancient versions, or at least compelling internal arguments, in three distinct parts: (1) Proof that *bty* is impossible (but the phrase is unobjectionable; it can be given a distinctive meaning in this context; and the plural with the same reference turns up immediately in 2:2); (2) proof that *bt* or some other alternative is better, if not absolutely required (this has not been done; cannot be done); (3) explanation of the reading we have—how it arose, why it survived (as *lectio difficilior*, it has the better claim). We argue that our acceptance of the text as it is leads to a reasonable result and fits in, not only with vv 10–16 as a whole, but with other background in chapters 1–3.

We have interpreted the term *houses* as political-territorial, trying to make sense of v 14 as one unit by identifying "houses of Akzib" as something given to the kings of Israel by way of *šillûḥîm* (the plural agrees with "houses") on account of Moresheth-Gath. Renaud (1977: 26) interprets "houses" as "workshops," which he identifies with those of the potters of Kozeba (1 Chr 4:23), an industry owned by the king and producing vessels with *lmlk* seals. The weak point in his argument is that he must identify the "kings of Israel" as kings of Judah. Na'aman reviews the debate on the identity of these "houses," rejecting the suggestion of Mittmann that *bat* is the measure. He also draws attention to the fact "that *byt* has a different meaning each time it appears: 'within' (*v.* 10), 'ruling house' (*v.* 11b), and 'house/workshop' (*v.* 14)" (1995: 523). The observation is methodologically important. If Micah is playing on the several meanings of a word, we cannot appeal to consistency in reference when deciding difficult instances.

deceiver. We have been quite unable to identify or date the military activity that evokes the lamentations of vv 8–16; but v 14 seems to have something quite concrete and specific in mind, something known to Micah and his audience, and so not needing any further explanation or identification. Unfortunately we are completely in the dark. Presumably the transaction was a matter of indemnity or tribute or payment of blackmail. The word *'akzāb* is a pair of homonyms, one meaning "cruel" the other "deceptive." Either would fit here; but "deceiver" is more suitable to describe Israel's conduct in a war between the states. It is well known that dane-geld brought even more Scandinavians to Britain, and Israel's treachery could lie in the fact that they invaded again after a settlement and treaty. See Demsky (1966).

kings. Once again the more difficult plural reading should be retained, along with "Israel." The support of the versions is unanimous. Wellhausen (1898: 137) accepted the reading, but not the plural meaning. Most text critics delete the final *yod* as dittography from the first letter of the next word. Assuming that the date is 701 B.C.E., Allen (1976: 242) infers that "Israel" means the southern kingdom. We think that that terminology is most unlikely at that time, and the difficulty of making "Israel" mean "Judah" is one of many reasons why we cannot accept the 701 B.C.E. date. Haupt (1910a: nn. 27, 85, 93) changed all three occurrences of "Israel" to "Judah." We consider this altogether too drastic, for methodological reasons set out in the INTRODUCTION above. We are looking for a situation in which "kings of Israel" were involved in the cities of the Judaean Shephelah and received territory of Akzib as some kind of payoff. Either it means more than one such act to successive kings of Israel; or it refers to a time when the northern kingdom was divided or had more than one claimant, or when there was a coregency (Thiele 1965: 205).

The reign of Ahaz is the most likely time for such a circumstance (Irvine 1991: 191). Although the records are fragmentary and scattered, they make it clear that Ahaz was invaded from all sides—by Edom (2 Kgs 16:6), by the Philistines who raided the cities of the Shephelah (2 Chr 28:17–18), and by Rezin of Aram and Pekah of Israel, acting either in coalition (2 Kgs 16:5; Isaiah 7) or separately (the impression given by 2 Chr 28:5–8). Isaiah 7 makes it clear that Jerusalem was besieged in one such invasion (compare Mic 1:9, 12). The enemy forces could hardly have bypassed all outlying defense posts to get there. The state of panic in Jerusalem (Isa 7:2) suggests demoralization at the news of defeats like those described in 2 Chronicles 28 and also Micah 1. The biblical historians blame these disasters on Ahaz's imitation of the ways of *the kings of Israel* (2 Kgs 16:2–4; 2 Chr 28:1–4; compare Mic 1:13), and they say specifically that in every individual city (*'îr wā'îr*) of Judah Ahaz made *bāmôt* (2 Chr 28:25; cf. Mic 1:5). All the horrors of those wars—loss of territory, enormous casualties, numerous captives and vast booty (reported in Kings and Chronicles, especially the latter)—provide a background into which the whole of Micah 1–3 (and possibly Isaiah 1 also) fits better, we suggest, than any other time. For the theology of that situation see M. E. W. Thompson (1982).

Notes on Micah 1:15

Again. MT *'ōd* is placed in doubt by the *defective* spelling and by the presence of *'ad* in v 15b. The vocalization is safeguarded by a Masora. LXX and Vulgate point back to *'ad*. Elliger (1934: 85, 96) adds *hă-* to make it a question. Schwantes (1962: 51; 1964: 459) canceled it by negation. There is sound play on *'ad 'adul-lām*, and this is lost when the word Adullam is emended to *'wlm* (Elliger 1934: 97). That a reference to Adullam is original and intended to arouse memories of David's adventures seems to be certain.

dispossessor. The noun (participle) *yôrēš* sometimes means "heir" (2 Sam 14:7; Jer 49:1). There is no clue as to the identity of this "dispossessor." Compare *haš-šōdēd* in Jer 6:26. The play on the name *mārēšâ* is transparent. The root *yrš* is commonly associated with Israel's conquest of Canaan, particularly in the Deuteronomic tradition. See Deuteronomy 7–8. There is an ironical reminder that those who dispossessed the Canaanites will be dealt with in the same way when they revert to the same kind of religious culture.

I will bring. Duhm (1911: 84) made the brilliant suggestion to read the rare exclamation *'ābî*, an expression of dismay. This would eliminate the vexing need to identify the speaker implied by the use of the first-person verb, the only one in the unit. But LXX *agagō* and other versions fully support MT. The defective reading *'ābî* for *'ābî'* does not have the expected *qere* although there are six instances in which the missing *alef* is supplied in *qere*, four involving this verb (2 Sam 5:2; 1 Kgs 21:21; Jer 19:15; 39:16). The other two are 2 Kgs 13:6;

Jer 32:35. In all these cases the first letter of the following word is *alef*, which thus does double duty, as if *scripta continua* had been used. Compare the redundant *alef* in Josh 10:24. There is no reason to doubt the genuineness of the text of v 15aA, no need to accept BHS's proposal to change it to *yābô'*, which occurs in the next colon, even though this emendation commands a near consensus among textual scholars. Here, at last, the divine mover of history discloses himself. There should be no doubt that Yahweh is the speaker; and this carries weight in our suggestion (which we made with caution because most people would consider it outrageous) that Yahweh is the one grieving in this chapter (see the COMMENT on vv 8–9). The verb could refer to past time, given a preterite prefixed verb; but its threatening tone agrees with that of v 12b.

An ingenious emendation, perhaps too ingenious, proposed by Renaud (1977: 27) requires fewer consonantal changes: *y'bylk*, with the *hip'il* meaning "the conqueror will give you occasion to practice mourning rites" (cf. Ezek 31:16; Lam 2:8).

to thee. The words *lāk* here and *bāk* in v 13 match *lākem* and *mikkem* in v 11.

Mareshah. The town Mareshah is well known and not to be confused with Moreshet(-Gath), Micah's hometown. It is easy to make the mistake of identifying them. This already happened in the ancient Aramaic versions and received modern advocacy from George Adam Smith, followed by Haupt, Budde, Marsh, Wolfe. But Jerusalem is the only place mentioned twice in Mic 1:10–16, and there should be no doubt that Mareshah and Moreshet are two different places. There is no warrant for revising it to "Moreshah" (R. L. Smith 1984: 19).

the glory of Israel. Nothing could be clearer than v 15b. The words are familiar and the grammar is flawless. Yet we don't know what Micah is talking about. If v 15b flows on from v 15a, then the use of the cognate verb makes it possible that the object of *bring* is the subject of *come*. So it is not certain that "glory of Israel" is the subject of the verb "come." Micah's contemporary, Isaiah, speaks of the fate of the glory of Israel as the same as that of the remnant of Aram, and the fate of the glory of Jacob (Isa 17:3–4) will be the same. These and similar expressions in Isa 16:14; 21:16 suggest the decimation of military forces. So v 15b could record the arrival of the Israelite army at Adullam. If in defeat, the splendid language is used in sarcasm or contempt. Adullam evokes memories of David's career, "glory" is also an attribute of Yahweh, or even his proper name (Psalm 29). He is "Israel's glory" (compare "The Holy One of Israel"). This phrase could be the delayed subject of "bring" — "I, Israel's glory, will once more bring the dispossessor to you, inhabitant of Mareshah; he will come as far as Adullam."

come. The versions support MT. The substitution of *'ābad* or *yō'bad* is motivated by the need for something more dramatic and drastic at the climax. It has no textual basis.

To Adullam. The alliteration *'d 'dlm* is good. Changes have been proposed: *'ad 'ôlām* (*w* instead of *d*, supported by Syriac); or *lō' 'ôd* (Schwantes, accepted by Mays) to reverse the meaning. Since Adullam is to the south, perhaps *'ad* in v 15b completes the series begun in v 9.

Introduction to Micah 1:16

There is a common opinion that v 16 is not part of the original composition. This status is so obvious to some scholars that they seem to feel no need to argue the point. Thus Fohrer (1967: 76) pronounced v 16 a gloss supplying the reason that the preceding text is an oracle of doom (in strict 2 : 2 meter), not a lament (which requires 3 : 2 meter). There is a similar pronouncement in Fohrer (1968: 445). From Fohrer's general stance on Micah 1, one can infer that his arguments are along the same lines. First, Fohrer considers vv 10–15 to be, not a dirge, but a threat. (On vv 10–16 as a dirge see Vergone [1981].) Second, the talk about exile in v 16 is enough to convince many scholars that the verse must have been added after the fall of Jerusalem to the Babylonians (Mays 1976: 60). But populations were deported in the eighth century too (Oded 1979). It is often observed that v 16 is the only verse in vv 8–16 that (apparently) has no place-name. This lack has been remedied by supplying "Daughter-Zion" or some such expression (see BHS). Some basis for this emendation has been found in LXX, which reads "the glory of the *daughter* of Israel" at the end of v 15. Wolff (1990: 50) finds these arguments weak and concludes that v 16 is authentic. The verse contains some features characteristic of Micah. So far as the poetry is concerned, it is like much in the rest of the book and can be accepted as it is so long as we do not insist that it should be in strict *qinah* meter. We recognize that in such a small book it is hardly possible to arrive inductively at any features that are "characteristic"; but we note the peculiar use of the noun *ta'ănûgāyik* (2:9) and the use of two verbs in one colon (v 16aA). Renaud (1977: 37, 57) has observed that v 16 makes an inclusion with v 8. We have already pointed out that v 16 makes an inclusion with v 10.

The four colons in v 16 do not show enough parallelism to permit bicolons to be charted. They are all interconnected in a variety of ways. Verse 16a is one clause in which the prepositional phrase that constitutes v 16aB gives the reason for the action described by the double verb in v 16aB. A similar action is enjoined in v 16bA, using a noun cognate with the first verb in v 16aA, so vv 16aA and 16bA can be taken as a split bicolon. By the same token v 16aB gives the reason for all three actions commanded by the verbs; it belongs equally with the preceding and following colons. The noun in v 16aB is the subject of the verb in v 16bB, another split bicolon. The final colon (v 16bB) is a subordinate clause (no parallel) that modifies the rest of the verse as a single construction.

Notes on Micah 1:16

bald. There are three verbs, all imperative (2d f. sg.). The repetition increases the intensity of the command. The second verb *gzz* indicates the technique— shearing. The first imperative, *qorḥî*, describes the result of shaving, "baldness," so the sequence is not chronological; the result is mentioned before the process. Both verbs are transitive, yet neither has an object. In such cases one would expect a reflexive—"shave yourself!" The first imperative, *qorḥî*, usually has the cognate object *yiqrĕḥû qorḥâ* (Lev 21:5—forbidding such an action in the case of priests; cf. Deut 14:1). The missing object turns up with the third verb, which is *hipʿil* and elative—"expand your baldness to the limit!" Shaving is part of the mourning rites of Moab in Isa 15:2, omitted for the wicked (Jer 16:6). Here as in Amos 8:10 and Mic 1:16 the action is associated with the most extreme loss—darling children (Mic 1:16), an only son (Amos 8:10).

children. Literally "sons." Since the cities of Judah are Jerusalem's "daughters," a distinction is being made here between captured towns and exiled citizens.

delight. The phrase supports reading *bat-taʿănûgîm, "daughter of delights" at Cant 7:7, as in Syriac and Aquila. It suggests further that we might read *mib-bat-taʿănûgeyhā at Mic 2:9, which makes a better parallel to ʿôlāleyhā. See the NOTE there.

eagle. The noun *nešer* is a generic term for eagles or vultures. The so-called "bald" eagle (actually the griffon-vulture of Syria-Palestine) is not actually bald; the white down on its head only looks like baldness. It is a strange simile and does not seem to extend to any other aspects of this bird that might be applied also to a mourning mother.

have gone. Many commentators wish to interpret the perfect verb form as prophetic so that the mourning is in anticipation. It is more likely, in our opinion, that the several perfect verbs in Mic 1:2–16 describe the events seen in Micah's vision. At the same time, there is no need to exclude historical realism. Massive relocation of population after conquest was already common policy in the eighth century B.C.E. All references to "exile" do not have to be attached to the Babylonian Exile of the sixth century, just because it has been given so much space in the Hebrew Bible. If 2 Chronicles 28 provides the background for Micah 1 we are at a moment where captives have been taken, but not yet returned.

Comment on Micah 1:10–16

In this lamentation, the prophet runs down a list of towns and villages guarding the southern and southwestern approaches to Jerusalem, the classic route of invading armies, to be followed by the infamous Sennacherib within a generation. Micah binds all together in a litany of disaster giving a kaleidoscopic view of various scenes of frantic defense and panicky response, impending and occurring ruin, the folly of resistance, and the fate of the defeated—an unrelenting and unremitting tragedy that ends in the conquest of the land and the death and exile of its citizens. At the center is Jerusalem, Daughter-Zion, a bereaved mother wailing for children lost in war, banished to captivity (Dobbs-Alsop 1993). The passage draws out the previously mentioned grief and hysteria of the prophet, if he is the speaker in vv 8–9. We have also ventured the opinion that the piece could be oracular; the speech is actually the deity's.

Immediately noted features of the passage include the extensive use of paronomasia and the profusion of the different pronominal elements, creating both intensification and confusion, if not incoherence. Verses 10–16 are built around a series of place-names, cities and villages that belong to the region of Jerusalem. There may be as many as fourteen such names including the central city—Jerusalem = Daughter-Zion. Under the threat and reality of military invasion, the cities symbolic of their populations are described in various postures of despair and grief, while being encouraged to wail and lament their fate. Aside from the elaborate paronomasia and the introduction of unusual or unique terms, the general idea can be captured, and the meaning seems to be consistent with the use of wordplay. There are, however, other threads running through the material. These elements complicate the picture. They are not readily classified, and they put intolerable strains on ordinary, or even poetic grammar and syntax.

Following the basic principle of parsimony, we shall try to keep the participants to a minimum. The first step is to group grammatically congruent components. The opening colon has verbal forms in the second-person masculine plural: "Do not announce . . . do not weep." The people to whom these masculine plural verbs refer are not identified in the section, but their presence may be noted, not only in v 10, but also in v 11, twice in prepositional constructions. Who they are may remain a mystery, but we are obliged to look for an appropriate referent for the pronouns, preferably an antecedent. The only one that commends itself is the subject of the initial summons and command in 1:2: "Hear O peoples (all of them), pay heed O earth (and its fullness)." (For the intrinsic difficulties in the collocation of second- and third-person forms, see the NOTES on that verse.) Whether or not this is the correct connection, there can be no doubt about the grammar: two masculine-plural persons are addressed twice in v 10a, whereas v 10b shifts abruptly to two second-person feminine singulars, with an unusual and archaic verb form. Here the subject is apparently the personified city, as represented throughout the piece by several or many of the names preceded by the terms *inhabitant* or *daughter* to justify and explain the feminine singular forms of verbs and pronouns. (The dramatic shift from two masculine plurals to two feminine singulars is obscured in English, where we use the same word "you" for all four forms, masculine and feminine, singular and plural.) The verse can be rendered:

> In Gath do not *you* tell (it)
> In Bako(?) do not *you* weep (or Do not weep at all).
> In Beth-le-Aphrah roll *thyself* in the dust,
> *Thou* pass by for *you*, O inhabitant of Shaphir
> (with) the shame of (thy) nakedness.

In v 11 we have the curious phenomenon of double direct address. This can hardly be expressed intelligibly in English, or in Hebrew, for that matter. Put literally, we have "Thou pass by [imperative 2d f. sg.] for you [2d m. pl.]." The latter must be the same people addressed in the opening colon but different from the participant addressed by the second-person feminine singular verb (against RSV and other translations, which equate them, erasing the distinction in the Hebrew), while the former is identified as the city of Shaphir, presented as a woman. Behind all the towns is the central city of Jerusalem, Daughter-Zion, which is never out of sight.

The notion of simultaneous direct address to different parties is difficult to accommodate, either grammatically or conceptually. Yet an effort has to be made to enter into the prophet's strange thinking, unless we either identify the groups under different figures or else eliminate one of them as an error introduced into the text by some mishap in transmission. Actually the messages are in conflict if not in contradiction, since the instruction to the second-person masculine plural group is not to proclaim, not to weep, whereas the mandate for the city is to roll in the dust, a vivid image of public mourning and self-abasement in the face of tragedy. In short, outsiders are not to be told; it is not fitting to seek their sympathy, because the judgment is completely justified and the punishment is thoroughly deserved. Micah has thus given a cruel twist to the words he quotes from 2 Sam 1:20. There the instruction was given so as to preclude or postpone the inevitable rejoicing of the Philistine women over the defeat of the Israelites. The subjects of the opening prohibitions are no more identified in 2 Sam 1:20 than in Mic 1:10. They are hardly fellow Israelites. Why should they tell it in Gath? Not Philistines; it would be pointless to prohibit *them*. It could be indefinite (any group of onlookers or bystanders), almost impersonal—"let it not be declared." Otherwise we have to fall back on the more remote referent "peoples" of v 2. The circumstances of David's lamentation are perfectly clear; in the passage in Micah the circumstances may be only partly similar (disaster on a national scale due to military defeats, but not, apparently, the death of the king and his heir), and the reason correspondingly more obscure. We are not even sure whether Gath in Mic 1:10 is to be taken as a real city, the same city as in 2 Sam 1:20. If so, Gath represents the enemy, the victor; and they know that they have won. But if Gath here is the first of the series, and all of them are Judaean cities (it is possible that Philistine Gath was under Judaean hegemony at this time), then the brevity of Micah's quotation could be intended to leave out the original motivation (so the enemy won't rejoice) and to leave room for a different motivation (a different kind of mourning by the defeated). The inhabitants, the participating group—the ones addressed by the prophet—must give full expression to grief or self-laceration in a mode quite different from David's original threnody but for the same reason that outsiders are to be excluded. Only by a show of remorse and repentance (in the mood and consciousness expressed in chapter 7) can the guilty victims make a proper response to the judgment of their angry God.

The second-person masculine plural forms occur through v 11 and then cease. We have identified these people as outsiders, spectators of the scene of devastation and catastrophe, who are admonished not to spread the news or weep in mourning. We can reach back to v 2 for an appropriate antecedent: "the peoples of the Earth." (We need to bear in mind at the same time that the identity of that group was not completely clear in the opening invocation.) The meaning of the prepositional phrases in v 11 is less clear: *for you* and *from you*. In neither case does the immediate context offer much help, although the entanglement in the action of the second-person feminine singular forms indicates that both of Micah's addressees are at the same scene. (We do not assume that this is a real situation; it could be in the prophet's imagination. But he speaks as if both the masculine group and the feminine individual are within earshot.) *For you* may be ethical (reinforcing—a kind of reflexive: "do not weep for yourselves") or benefactive ("for your benefit or advantage"). The former would be more appropriate if the second-person masculine plural group were among the sufferers; the latter if they are a little removed from the experience, albeit having an interest in it that would normally lead to grief if that were not specifically and unexpectedly forbidden. The second phrase (*from you*) may be linked more closely to its context. Tentatively we may translate: "He will take from you mourning appropriate to his station." Now we have third-person masculine singular verb and pronoun, which must refer to someone different again: perhaps the subject is God or an agent of God; or the construction may be impersonal, while the suffixed pronoun may refer to the person for whom mourning normally would be appropriate, i.e., the king. In Jer 22:10–19 there is an interdict against mourning for a dead king. If the "wailing of Beth ha-ʾezel" is "taken away," then a ban on mourning for that city would fit with the opening prohibition against audible wailing.

Now we must grapple with the second-person feminine singular forms. These dominate the unit. The central figure or person clearly is Jerusalem // Daughter-Zion (vv 12–13). This kind of personification is frequent in the prophets, especially those of the eighth century B.C.E.: Jerusalem // Zion is portrayed as a woman or girl (but in a variety of life's stages, ranging from nubile girl to bride to mother or widow or even adulteress and/or prostitute). This last possibility was already considered in the case of Samaria (v 7). The female represents the city as a whole, its population, or various groups. Along with Jerusalem // Zion, Micah mentions about a dozen cities or villages in the surrounding area, mainly in the southwest environs along a major military route. The most common designation of these "inhabitant(s)" is *yôšebet* + the name of a city, with collective force similar to the phrase *bat-ṣiyyôn*. In each construct phrase the two nouns are in apposition—"Daughter-Zion," "Resident-Shaphir," and so on. The expression *yôšebet* + the name of a city occurs five times in the passage:

v 11	*yôšebet šāpîr*	Resident-Shapir
v 11	*yôšebet ṣaʾănān*	Resident-Zaanan
v 12	*yôšebet mārôt*	Resident-Maroth
v 13	*yôšebet lākîš*	Resident-Lachish
v 15	*yôšebet mārēšâ*	Resident-Mareshah

The apparent gap between the last two members of the list is actually filled by a similar-sounding but different expression, *môrešet* ("possessor" perhaps, or "possession," "territory"), which is joined to the city name Gath to produce

Moresheth-Gath. It is a common practice of the poets and prophets of Israel/ Judah to vary a sequence of repetitions by a single change in a long list. At first glance this may seem anomalous; but the practice of varying from a norm, or avoiding monotony, is well known, and in the case of biblical poetry this variation itself has become a principle (Freedman 1986b). Here are a few illustrative examples that only need be listed without additional comment:

Amos 1-2: *wěšillaḥtî ʾēš* (1:4, 7, 10, 12; 2:2, 5), varied by *wěhiṣṣattî ʾēš* (1:14).

Jer 51:20-23: *wěnippaṣtî běkā* (51:20, 21[2], 22[3], 23[3]) varied by *wěhišḥattî běkā* (51:20).

Gen 49:25-26: *birkôt* (49:25[3], 26[2]), varied by *taʾwat* (26).

The parallel passage in Deut 33:13-16 has the same feature: *mimmeged* (33:13, 14[2], 15, 16) varied by *mērōʾš* (15).

The book of Micah contains another example in 5:9-13, only there the pattern itself is more complex and elaborate. Thus each of the repeated words is balanced by a parallel expression or paraphrase; in the last case the initial term of the pair is also changed:

5:9	*wěhikrattî sûseykā miqqirbekā*	*wāhaʾăbadtî markěbōteykā*
5:10	*wěhikrattî ʿārê ʾarṣekā*	*wěhārastî kol-mibṣāreykā*
5:11	*wěhikrattî kěšāpîm miyyādekā*	*ûměʿôněnîm lōʾ yihyû-lāk*
5:12	*wěhikrattî pěsîleykā . . . miqqirbekā*	*wělōʾ-tištaḥăweh ʿôd lěmaʿăśēh yādeykā*
5:13	*wěnātaštî ʾăšêreykā miqqirbekā*	*wěhišmadtî ʿāreykā*

Returning to Mic 1:10-16, we can count probably twelve different city names, not including the pair Jerusalem // Daughter-Zion. This is obviously the center of attention. The other twelve serve as attendants or subordinate associates: suburbs and exurbs of the capital. The whole passage is organized around the names of the cities: the occurrences of the repeated expression *yôšebet* (and its substitute *môrešet*) form a framework around which the other names are inserted.

The conclusion, perhaps drastic, is that all the cities together represent the single entity Judah. Or, a little more precisely, we remember that the full name for the southern state was "Jerusalem and Judah" or sometimes "Jerusalem" // "Cities of Judah," as in Isaiah 40. But more is involved here than complete, if only representative, coverage of the realm. Jerusalem is special; it can stand for the whole country and is so used in v 1, while all these cities are important because they help to guard Jerusalem. What is said about one could be applied in some measure to them all. The activities ascribed to the separate localities together add up to the frenzied and hysterical behavior of the inhabitants of the invaded country and besieged city in the last throes of desperate struggle before the final collapse of resistance, followed by destruction, desolation, captivity, and mourning. These activities are glimpsed haphazardly as the eye of the prophet wanders over the scene of anguish and devastation, picking out individual figures and settings at different stages of the disaster. The lack of overall clarity reflects the confusion of battle and defeat, but of the overarching tragedy there can be no doubt.

Three prepositional phrases, each with the second-person feminine singular suffix, provide a key to understanding the sweep of the prophet's vision:

(1) v 13: For in thee (*bāk*) are found the transgressions of Israel.
(2) v 15: Yet again I will bring the dispossessor to thee (*lāk*).
(3) v 16: Strip and shave thyself over thy delightful sons!
  Make extensive thy baldness like the vulture,
  For they have gone into captivity from thee (*mimmēk*).

In sequence, the three clauses give the rationale and the reality of divine punishment. Judgment has come upon Judah because the sins characteristic of the northern kingdom (spelled out at length elsewhere) have been imported into and adopted in Judah, so that the latter will share in the destiny of the former. As a consequence, God (speaking through the prophet in the first person) has brought, is bringing, or will bring the conqueror to the land. In the third sentence the end of the drama is portrayed: "they (thy children) have gone away into exile." The immediate associations with individual locales are subordinated to the overall picture with its focus on the central city and on the consequences spread out through the vicinity.

While we acknowledge that we have not succeeded much better than previous researchers in making coherent sense out of the passage as it stands, the preceding discussion shows that it is possible to isolate the central theme and to group elements that seem to belong together. Thus we can follow the prophet's message through its various embodiments and representations to some kind of conclusion. We wish to emphasize that we have done this without changing a single letter of the MT; in fact, it has often been the trouble spots in the text, notably the bewildering fluctuations in person, number, and gender of verbs and pronouns that have given us a promising lead. These apparent inconcinnities in grammar have been for other readers the main triggers for emendations, beginning with ancient copyists and translators.

We have found several structures that point to vv 12–13 as the centerpiece of the complete unit. These verses happen also to be the physical center, and they talk about the political center. So we look to vv 12–13 for the major theme, and the theme to which all the subthemes should be related. In v 12b we read: "For evil (harm) has come down from Yahweh to the gate of Jerusalem." Nothing could be clearer. This theme has already been expressed in Mic 1:9: "For it has come as far as Judah; he has struck at the gate of my people, as far as Jerusalem." Parallel to v 12b is v 13b (the interlocking structure has already been described), which we try to render literally: "The first (or chief) of sin (was) she for Daughter-Zion, because in thee were found the transgressions of Israel." The opening and closing colons of this central group express clearly the intention of the prophet: judgment in the form of military disaster has been decreed by Yahweh; the underlying reason is the transgressions of Judah, who has imitated Israel in this respect. The background and connections are explained earlier by the prophet himself (1:2–7) and confirmed elaborately by the Deuteronomic editor of 2 Kings 16–18. The middle clause is different, but the "she" who constitutes the chief sin is not identified with Daughter-Zion // Jerusalem, but as someone or something in the city. The feminine singular pronoun ("she") here suggests that the figure is an image of the chief goddess of Canaan, Asherah, whose worship in Israel is mentioned often in historical and prophetic books, or perhaps the Queen of Heaven, an epithet of Astarte, as reported in Jeremiah. There are specific references to this figure in Israel, and the implication here is that the same goddess is now being worshiped in Judah, and especially in Jerusalem. (If this conclusion is close to the truth, we have another reason for dating the background of Micah 1 away from the reign of Hezekiah and for looking for circumstances in the reign of one of his predecessors, probably Ahaz.) The parallelism between Samaria and Jerusalem, precisely in the matter of a forbidden cult, is affirmed in Mic 1:5, so we cannot be far off the track. There is another intriguing feature of the two passages: In 1:5 we have *pešaʿ* (sg.), "transgression," matched with *ḥaṭṭōʾwt* (pl.), "sins," whereas in 1:13 the reverse is the case: *ḥaṭṭāʾt* (sg.) is paralleled with *pišʿê* (pl.). The meaning is hardly affected, but the forms are carefully arranged in chiastic and interlocking fashion.

We may now turn to the list of activities linked with the inhabitants of the various cities and gather from them glimpses of the frenzied hysteria that gripped the country in its time of peril. On other, historical grounds, we believe that the Micah oracle reflects the period when Judah was invaded by Israel and Aram around 735 B.C.E., and when, according to the accounts in Kings and Chronicles, much of Judah was overrun, its armies routed, and many of its citizens taken captive by the victorious Israelites and Arameans. The armies of the latter invested Jerusalem and laid siege to that city, which with its suburbs was apparently the only surviving territory of Judah. In this emergency, Ahaz the king of Judah appealed to Tiglath-Pileser III, the king of Assyria, for help. The crisis is depicted by the prophet Isaiah in a notable passage (chapter 7). While Isaiah adamantly urged calm reliance on Yahweh for succor, the king understandably turned to a somewhat more visible source of aid. In any event the prophet, with his omnitemporal eye, fusing past, present, and future into a single picture of disaster, speaks of the crisis and impending doom. See van der Woude (1989).

The ensemble of oracles in Micah 1 begins with a call or warning to the peoples of the world (1:2). Given the literary unity of chapter 1, and assuming some continuity of theme (Shaw 1993), the plural verbs in v 10 suggest that this same group is urged in v 10 not to waste tears or sympathy on the cities listed. The analysis in v 5 shows that appropriate divine justice is being administered to the two sinful nations that constitute Israel. The oracle predicts the destruction of Samaria, then the cities of Judah, with Jerusalem (vv 5bB, 9bB, 12b) as the main targeted victim. She is not only permitted to mourn, but commanded to do so. "Roll in the dust" is a typical if exaggerated expression of grief. The next element is exposure (v 11), nakedness coupled with shame. This is a common consequence of defeat that especially symbolizes the humiliation and degradation of women. "Pass by in shameful nakedness" is a reflex, perhaps, of captives going into exile; cf. Amos 4:1–3. The next colon (v 11b) speaks of the seclusion associated with mourning, but neither expression is clear. The presence of this kind of language shows that the judgment is not to be celebrated. It is a tragedy, and, if our reading of vv 8–9 is valid (the mourner is Yahweh!), the divine compassion tempers the severity of the judgment. Even if the mourner in vv 8–9 is the prophet, the effect is similar.

Verse 12a is obscure, but perhaps the expectation of or waiting for the "Good" is antithetical to "Evil" that Yahweh has decreed and sent down from Heaven (v 12b). Coupled with the vain waiting for the "Good" is the presumably ironic instruction (v 13) to harness the chariots to the horses (or vice versa), perhaps for battle, perhaps for flight, either of which would be futile.

Beginning with v 14 matters become somewhat more confusing, but a structural analysis may help to untangle themes and threads that can be made to yield meaning. In v 14 we recognize an envelope construction linking v 14aA and v 14bB: "Therefore you shall pay tribute (*parting gifts*, i.e., to buy off the invader) . . . to the kings of Israel"; perhaps then as part of the same structure payment is to be made from the storehouses of Akzib, used here symbolically as a link to the next word, which means "to the false or deceptive one." This last word may well be another designation of the "dispossessor," namely the "glorious one," the king(s) of Israel. (We are not sure which of the nouns in this section might go together; there is so much irony in the entire piece that we cannot rely on the plain meanings of the words to make the connections.) The plural "kings" is a special problem. It is strange since the other three forms are all singular. We must hesitate before emending the text, even so mildly as to remove only one letter, *yod*, which moreover can be easily and legitimately justified as a case of dittography, since the next word, Israel, begins with *yod*. This emendation is an attractive option and has been widely adopted by translators as well as commentators. Perhaps the plural here refers to a group of Israelite kings in the period, or, as seems more likely, to a dual monarchy or coregency arrangement, the existence of which at that time is confirmed more than once in the history of this kingdom; cf. Hos 8:4. There seems also to be a play on *'akzāb*, "false," and *kābôd*, "glory" (in contrast), since they share two of the same consonants. If the result is hendiadys, the fused meaning is "the false or deceptive glory."

Verse 15 offers a fairly clear frame of reference:

Again will I bring to thee a dispossessor—
the glory (glorious one) of Israel will come.

It is clear that the conqueror is the glorious one of Israel, presumably the king of that country currently leading the invasion of Judah.

The conclusion (v 16) brings us back to the central theme in terms of its ultimate consequences: unceasing grief for the loss of the population of the country. The survivors are taken away in exile as the passage ends: "They have gone from thee into exile."

What is still needed is some explanation of the radical confusion and disorientation of the text. The lack of agreement among verbs, nouns, and pronouns, the apparently indiscriminate use of all the available Hebrew verb forms (tense/aspect), the leaping about from subject to subject, and the incoherent variety of circumstances, all these features go far beyond the normal range of scribal (i.e., inadvertent) error. We make an important distinction here between an unwitting slip and a deliberate change; both have doubtless occurred, but the latter would be a conscious "correction," whether warranted or not, and would make the text easier to read, and by that token would also be hard if not impossible for us to detect as an ancient emendation. We seldom stop to suspect that a text that gives us no trouble has been tampered with, so that we reverse it into something problematical! In other words, no scribe would knowingly rewrite a text into the form we now have. But the question is, would anyone ever compose such a text? Patching up the piece to make it read like ordinary poetry or prose would require extensive rewriting, and this has actually been done several times (Allen 1976, Budde 1917–18, Elliger 1934, Graham 1930–31, Haupt 1910a, Schwantes 1964, van der Woude 1971b). But it does not make the real text any more intelligible. Is it possible to account for the product without either appealing to the emendatory recourse or consigning the passage to oblivion because it is simply impossible to accept as a piece of genuine Hebrew prophecy, or even as a specimen of the Hebrew language? Perhaps a look at the prophetic experience will help. (The discussion here is drawn in part from Freedman [1982].)

In studying the biblical material about the prophets and the material from the prophets, we find in effect two traditions. One is commonly recognized and used as a basis for interpreting oracular compositions: prophets are poets or very close to them. Their utterances (or writings) fall into well-known patterns; and given the general difficulties of dealing with poetry in any language or period, we can make reasonable headway and come out with satisfactory results. In this approach we assume conscious (creative yet disciplined) composition by the prophet with a certain amount of arranging and editing by disciples and later editors. Most of the book of Micah can be handled reasonably well on this basis. But with 1:10–16 such an approach won't work, so we must look again at the tradition. Some, perhaps most, prophets were visionaries; many, perhaps most, were ecstatics, and presumably gave utterance under the power of the spirit of Yahweh. Now religious ecstasy and "enthusiasm" (infusion of divine presence and power with dramatic or sensational deviations from normal behavior) are widespread phenomena of extraordinary complexity and variety (Holm 1982). The specifics of biblical "inspiration" can be ascertained, not by projections and extrapolations from general theories, but by the testimony of the experiencers themselves, by descriptions of their behavior supplied by the Bible, and by the rational (or it could be irrational) and literary properties of their utterances. In the case of Micah we have several such clues. He affirms explicitly in 3:8, "But as for me, I am full of the mighty spirit of Yahweh, with power and judgment." As for his behavior, he says (1:8), "On account of this I am grief-stricken and wail inconsolably. I howl like the jackals and scream like young female ostriches." The prophet is not composed, and we can hardly expect his utterances while in that state to be composed. So we may suggest that the oracle of lamentation in vv 10–16 was uttered during an ecstatic transformation (or is based on his utterances during such an episode), occasioned by his almost hysterical grief at what he foresaw to be the fate of his beloved country and people. In a paroxysm of anguish, sharpened by a panoramic vision of desolation and ruin, the prophet pours out his woe in fits and starts, in bits and pieces. See Andersen (1995).

Of this general result we are fairly confident. But there are several other considerations. First, we do not wish to infer that the prophet was out of his mind, or that he had no self-control. Verses 10–16 are not the ravings of a lunatic. They make a lot of sense, or we think we can make quite a bit of sense out of them, and we think that this is what the prophet intended. Ecstatic utterance has enormous emotional power, and here we have as well a considerable amount of system and structure.

Our second point is that we cannot tell (and it does not matter) whether the words that came pouring out were recorded by a scribe who simply set down what he heard or what he could make out in words and sentences of what was uttered; or whether Micah himself, in retrospect and recollection, made up this lament out of what he had said under the impact of historical events and the impulse of the irresistible spirit (3:8). Either way, apparently little or no effort was made to reconstruct a sensible or intelligible speech. What was preserved and transmitted were the key words, mainly the city names and the remarks they triggered, the basic clues to the inmost feelings and uppermost thoughts of the overwrought prophet. If it is possible to probe into the psyche of this prophet, without making it easy for ourselves by some kind of reductionist methodology, then here are the essential data, raw and sincere, requiring not reconstruction or rewriting, but rather analysis and appreciation and response.

Third, in terms of the biblical understanding of a prophet such as Micah, in and behind his mind there lies an encounter and dialogue with Yahweh himself, a vision and communication to which the prophet consents. To put it negatively, the prophet would not say, when he comes to the end of his speech, "That's only the way I feel, the word of Yahweh is something else." The lament in vv 10–16 is meant to be a message, a revelation, an analysis and interpretation with exhortations that are certainly not just a private religious experience of the prophet. The composition was preserved and presented as part of a book that in its completeness is titled "The word of Yahweh" (1:1). One of the most mysterious features of biblical prophecy is this linkage of the mind of a man with the mind of God. It is a very dynamic connection; the language of mystical union is never used. The human remains vividly aware of his or her own identity and of the tremendous difference between creature and Creator. Yet the prophet speaks for God, as if repeating God's very words (note the first-person "I" in v 15). We therefore suggest that vv 10–16 uncover the feelings of God himself about these terrible developments, however startling it might be to project that kind of turbulence into the being of God.

On another occasion, the prophet, in a calmer frame of mind, reflecting on the same situation, might well have organized his thoughts along normal lines of poetic expression, as found in the rest of his book and generally in the pro- phetic literature. Here in 1:10–16 we seem to have the raw product, straight from the soul of the prophet, who could not restrain the torrent of words (or sounds)—an almost incoherent speech forced from his lips by the spirit of God. This could be a rare specimen and striking example of things said in the height of ecstatic inspiration, about which we read in various parts of the Bible (cf. Jer 20:7–9; 1 Corinthians 12–14). If Mic 1:10–16 belongs to the category of ecstatic utterances characteristic of certain classes of prophets, then we note that it is in Hebrew; it is neither an alien tongue (whether of men or of angels) nor the babble without discernible linguistic structure that is generally found in "speaking in tongues." There is something eerie about it, as if coming from a subliminal level of consciousness; and its most effective reception also lies on the subliminal level. It is certainly emotional; but it is not irrational.

This last point leads to a final word of caution. Our investigation has shown that the passage cannot be analyzed or parsed according to the common rules of Hebrew syntax. Nor does it conform to the rules of Hebrew prosody, so far as we might think that we know them. At the same time, the more carefully we ex- amine the components the more connections and structural patterns emerge. It is important to emphasize that these patterns and connections pervade and embrace the whole composition and are quite different from the short-range connections we look for in single colons and clauses. It is thus a paradox that the composition seems to be better planned and more controlled on those higher levels of discourse than in the lower levels of phrase structure, clause structure, and colon design. It is possible that such features are an aspect of the prophet's subconscious, expressed in the involuntary speech of ecstatic experi- ence. It is also possible that these organizational features, as distinct from the ragged little jerky bits, are the result of a carefully planned presentation, which resembles ecstatic utterance but was deliberately designed that way. If so, we may ascribe its success in achieving the desired and designed effects to genius. In part our abiding sense of its incoherence may be a reflection of our own ig- norance, not only of some of the more marginal usages of the Hebrew lan- guage, but also of the tricks that can be played with language, especially when there is deliberate wordplay, as is certain in this instance. Or our remaining dif- ficulties may be due to a failure to recognize more intricate patterns and ar- rangements, which differ from normal composition, but have a subtle system of their own. Perhaps we will finally discover that the interaction of ecstatic ex- perience and intellectual planning is adequate to explain the whole range of prophetic poetic utterance. We certainly have a more open mind on this question than when we began our study of Micah, and we are encouraged to think that we might have made some progress. We need a much larger base; and we are hopeful that investigation of some of the notoriously difficult passages in other prophets, especially Micah's contemporaries and most of all Isaiah, will uncover more of their secrets.

At present and perhaps for the foreseeable future, we will not be able to answer the questions we have tried to raise about prophetic composition generally and this oracle in particular. If we cannot now discern motivation and intention, we nevertheless have the inescapable obligation to deal with the finished product and to analyze and interpret the text that has come down to us.

COMMENT ON MICAH 1

We recognize that the problems of Micah 1 are many, and many of them are intractable. We cannot hope to make much progress with their resolution. The modern practice of rewriting the text extensively we do not regard as a solution at all. Some results, particularly those of Elliger, have gained a certain vogue, as seen for instance in the publicity given to his emendations in BHS, which he edited. But the very different treatments of Haupt and Budde (before Elliger) and Fohrer and Lescow (after him), to mention only a few who have tried their hands on it, cancel one another out to a large extent. The more cautious approach of recent studies is to be welcomed, but theories about sources and their dates, about poetry, about "forms," and about Hebrew syntax, are one thing when applied to a reasonably sound text, another when they become the instruments of text restoration.

Taking the text as we find it is not blind conservatism. For all we know, the text might be more corrupt than anyone has yet said. But that conviction should be reached at the end of patient work, and then the scholar should quit. The conclusion that the text is badly damaged—in every line, almost—means that the original is lost forever.

There are several good reasons for assuming that the text is not as bad as commonly supposed. First is the fact that other places in Micah can be managed reasonably well; so how did one block, notably 1:10–16, deteriorate out of line with the rest? Second, and more significant, is the fact that almost every individual word is recognizable Hebrew, most of it familiar. Third, most of the alternate readings proffered by the ancient versions are evidence that ancient scholars already faced the difficulties we still have in the traditional Hebrew text in its pre-Masoretic stage. More often their combined evidence confirms the text we now have; individual readings in this version or that are of limited strength as pointers to better original Hebrew readings.

In spite of the peculiarities that distinguish the lament in vv 8–16, and especially the difficulties that characterize vv 10–15, we recognize an overarching unity in vv 2–16. This is not evident on first reading, and many readers do not perceive it at all. There are at least five distinct genres, at least two voices, and many implied audiences. How can such diversity converge into literary unity?

There is a logical, dramatic progression from invocation (v 2) through theophany (vv 3–4), accusation (v 5), judgment (vv 6–7), to lamentation (vv 8–16). This is the broad sweep of the chapter. Some of these constituents might be analyzed further; we recognize two parts in the lamentation. Some might be joined; a threat frequently follows an accusation (they are "inseparable" in a judgment oracle, according to Westermann [1967: 30]), and a theophany is a suitable lead-in to such a two-part prophetic message. For the affinities among the pieces of differing genres see Fohrer (1967: 72).

Although many scholars have detected sutures in vv 2–16, we are persuaded that they could have been part of the original composition. More important, most of the integrating devices are not at the interfaces of the constituents, but within the body of their texts. These include:

(a) The names of God linking v 2 and v 3.

(b) The two stages of the theophany linking v 3 and v 4.

(c) The words *bmwt* linking v 3 and v 5, and *yrd* linking v 3 and v 12.

(d) The anaphoric *kol-zō't* (v 5) linking the accusation with the theophany.

(e) The names Samaria and Jerusalem, introduced in the title (1:1), declared in v 5, and making an inclusion for vv 6–9. These names are the central themes embedded in the texts. They are not editorial (unless under the most violent reconstruction). Even if the linkage is called "domino," that sequence pattern does not make it redactional. The references are the same, the fabric of vv 6–9 grows out of v 5.

(f) The threat (vv 6–7) is a highly unified composition, as shown above.

(g) In v 8aA *'al-zō't* links the first lamentation (vv 8–9) or vv 8–16 in their entirety to the preceding judgment oracle. "This" refers to everything that has been announced in vv 2–7, not to any one detail, as the qualifier "all" indicates.

(h) The structural unity of vv 8–16 (as in Renaud's scheme) and the spread of repeated themes and motifs all over is compositional rather than redactional.

We agree in general with the conclusion of Renaud (1977: 38) that, apart from a little touching up, "the chapter as a whole, *in its actual state* [Renaud's italics] was composed on the occasion of a definite event or historical situation, but that the prophet has reused materials of an earlier date." His final qualification is not altogether clear, especially when he says later that the unity of Micah 1 "seems more redactional than original" (1977: 47), and we see no need for it. The whole thing could have come out of Micah's vision, which supplied the visual components and created the pervasive emotional tone.

Given the thematic continuity in vv 2–7 and the structural unity of vv 8–16, it remains to ask if these two compositions make up a larger whole. In our work we have recognized vv 8–9 as a distinct unit. We accept fully that vv 8–16 can be read as a single lament. At the same time there are clear signals that vv 8–9 are a continuation of vv 3–7. Nothing could be stronger than *'al-zō't*, "on ac-count of this," as a link between the judgment speech in vv 5–7 and the lamenta-tion that begins in v 8. The prophet's grief is caused by his vision of the calamity he has just announced; public display of alarm in the form of dramatic mourn-ing ritual behavior would drive home the seriousness of the threat. The warn-ing portion of the judgment speech (vv 6–7) and the first part of the full lament (vv 8–9) are bound together by the placement of Samaria (v 6aA) and Jeru-salem (v 9bB) in envelope parallelism around the whole. And this pair makes an inclusion for the phrase "Samaria and Jerusalem" in v 1. So vv 8–9 have solid connections with what precedes (vv 1–7), as we have just shown, and with what follows (vv 10–16), as Renaud's analysis (1977: 39) shows, integrating the whole.

Other marks of integrity for the whole of chapter 1 can be found in a number of connections to be observed among the several parts. In spite of their seem-ingly different genres, the summons, theophany, indictment, sentence, lament, and whatever vv 10–16 might be (a mix of judgment and lament), they are clearly dealing with Israel and Judah, Samaria and Jerusalem. A hypothesis that puts everything into the same historical situation is to be welcomed.

A major clue to the organization of the whole chapter is supplied by the first verse, which should not be set aside from the main body just because it is "ed-itorial." The two cities that are there declared to be the subject matter of Micah's vision are condemned in similar terms in v 5, but their punishment is stated dif-ferently, as if actual historical events are in mind. Verses 9–16 report disasters, apparently military, spread widely over Judah. And Israel seems to be the dou-ble source. From Israel came the cause, idolatry (v 13b); from Israel came the punishment, an invading army (vv 14–16) that destroyed cities and collected booty (v 14) and captives (v 16). Unlike Isaiah 7, which has Rezin and Pekah as allies in a joint expedition, 2 Chronicles 28 gives the impression of separate in-vasions. But large-scale operations of Aram in Judah would hardly have been possible without the collaboration of the king of Israel.

> The LORD his God delivered him [Ahaz] over to the king of Aram, who de-feated him and took many of his men captive, and brought them to Dam-ascus. He was also delivered over to the king of Israel, who inflicted a great defeat on him. Pekah son of Remaliah killed 120,000 in Judah—all brave men—in one day, because they had forsaken the LORD God of their fathers. Zichri, the champion of Ephraim, killed Maaseiah the king's son, and Azrikam chief of the palace, and Elkanah, the second to the king. The Isra-elites captured 200,000 of their kinsmen, women, boys, and girls; they also took a large amount of booty from them and brought the booty to Samaria. (2 Chr 28:5–8 [NJPS])

If this is the background of vv 10–16, it has already happened and is the cause of lamentation all round. The fate of Samaria is described differently (vv 6–7), and seems to be still in the future. Her country towns are not involved, and the causes seem to be more supernatural (v 3–4). Samaria is doubly guilty if, on top of her own idolatry, she has corrupted Judah and also savaged Judah "with a rage that has reached up to heaven" (2 Chr 28:9), planning to subjugate all Judaeans as slaves—as if Samaria did not already have enough sins of her own (2 Chr 28:10). The analysis of the prophet Oded in 2 Chronicles 28, even if somewhat midrashic, whether historical or not, would fit Micah 1 very well; and Micah 1 gives the Judaean perspective on events that the Chronicler, for once, describes from the northern point of view. The conclusions in this paragraph, admittedly tentative, were reached before we were able to study the monograph of Shaw (1993), who was able to make most sense out of Mic 1:2–16 as a whole against the historical situation near the end of Jeroboam II's reign (1993: 61, 65, 224). We remain cautious, however, about our ability to attach all the details of Mic 1:2–16 to a specific date in "real" history. If the reference to "kings of Israel" is to be retained, it could refer, not to a time when the northern kingdom was divided, or had a coregency, but to a conspectus of events that occurred in several different reigns. After all, it is a vision. Our main concern is to grasp the whole chapter as a unified *literary* product of Micah's vision.

Recognition of the literary integrity of Mic 1:2–16 and acceptance of it as close to the prophet's original message are enhanced when its correspondence to actual historical events is not overpressed. It is a vision, not a prediction. In its view, the destruction of Samaria, the devastation of Judah, and the threat to Jerusalem are parts of a single scenario, the outcome of the arrival of Yahweh in judgment announced in vv 3–4. Expanding the vision to include Mic 3:12 suggests that the fate of the two cities would be practically identical. History turned out otherwise. Each city suffered its own fate, and neither exactly matched what Micah saw. It is only in hindsight that scholars have separated the judgment against Samaria (vv 6–7) from the materials dealing with Jerusalem. This move is familiar in the separation of vv 10–16 from the rest and giving them a different date. But the two cities are on the same footing throughout the Book of Doom.

Paul Haupt's Reconstruction of Micah 1:10–16 (1910)

11aAα	'Ivrû lakhém miš-Šāpîr,	Pass ye away from Saphir;
11bC	iqqaḥ 'emdathô;	this post will be taken!
13aA	Rathôm ham-märkavâh la-rákhš	Pack off with bag and baggage,
13aB	yôšévth Lakhîš!	Ye dwellers of Lachish!
14aA	La-khén tittĕnî šilluḥîm	So give now parting gifts
14aB	lĕ-môréšĕth Gáth	to Gath, the bride.
14bA	Báth Akhziv lĕ-akhzáv	Nevermore will Akhzib accede
14bB	lĕ-malkhê Yĕhadhâh	to Judah's wooing.
15aA	Hai-yôréš yabô eláikh	A new lord will be marshaled
15aB	báth Marešâh;	into Mareshah's borough.
15bA	'Adhê-'ôlám yôvédh	For ever and aye will perish
15bB	kĕvôdh Yĕhudhâh	the glory of Judah.

Karl Elliger's Reconstruction of Micah 1:10–16 (1934)

(NOTE: In the transliteration below, Elliger's reconstruction is underlined and in italics, while the Masoretic Text is in bold and italics.)

10aA	*bĕgannôt gīlōh]* **'al-tāgîlû**	In the gardens of Gilo don't rejoice,
10aB	**bĕkû 'ap-tibkû**	mourn, only mourn!
10bA	*bĕkarmê]* **bêt 'aprâ**	In the vineyards of Beth-Aphrah
10bB	**'āpār hitpallĕšû**	roll in the dust!
11aAα	*šôpār ya]***'ăbîrû lāk**	Let them blow the shophar for thee
11aAβ	**yôšebet šāpîr**	community of Shaphir!
11bA	*mē]***'îrāh lō' yāṣĕ'â**	From her city did not go forth
11bAβ	**yôšebet ṣa'ănān**	the community of Za'anan!
11bB	. . . .]	On all sides one hears
11bB	**mispad bêt hā'ēṣel**	the wailing of Beth-ha'ezel!
11bC	. . . .]	Inhabitant of the fortress Eshan {אֶשְׁעָן}
11bC	**yiqĕḥû mikkem 'emdāh**	one takes from you support!
12aA	*mî yi]***ḥălâ lĕṭôb**	Who can hope for good
12aB	**yôšebet mārôt**	community of Maroth,
12bA	**kî-yārad rā' mē'ēt yhwh**	when evil has come down from Yahweh
12bB	**lĕša'ărê yĕrûšālēm**	to the gates of Jerusalem?
13aA	*'irkî]* **hammerkābâ lārekeš**	Prepare the chariot for the steed,
13aB	**yôšebet lākîš**	community of Lachish!
13bA	. . . .	
13bB	. . . .	
14aA	*yinnā]***tĕnû šillûḥîm 'ālayik**	Parting gifts will be given to thee,
14aB	**môrešet gat**	Moresheth-Gath!
14bA	*yôše]***bet 'akzîb lĕ'akzāb**	The community of Akzib is a deceiver
14bB	**lĕmelek yiśrā'ēl**	for the king of Israel!
15aA	*ha]***'ōd hayyōrēš 'ābî lāk**	Will an [ein (sic)] heir yet come to thee,
15aB	**yôšebet mārēšâ**	community of Mareshah?
15bA	**'ākēn]** **'ad-'ôlām 'ābad**	Surely, unto eternity is destroyed
15bB	**kĕbôd yiśrā'ēl**	the glory of Israel!
16aA	*bat ṣiyyôn]* **qorḥî wāgōzzî**	Daughter-Zion, make thyself bald and cut off thy hair,
16aB	**'al-bĕnê ta'ănûgāyik**	for the children of thy delight!
16bA	**harḥibî qorḥātēk kanneš er**	Make thy baldness wide like the eagle,
16bB	**kî gālû mimmēk**	for they have gone from thee into exile!

INTRODUCTION TO MICAH 2

The rest of the Book of Doom (chapters 2 and 3) continues the mood of chapter 1 and elaborates on its themes. Chapter 2 begins with a woe oracle (vv 1–5) that denounces the social injustice of the forcible and illegal seizure of land. It is followed by an attack on prophets (2:6–11) that has a companion piece in 3:5–8. The latter is embedded in a twofold address to the "heads" and "rulers" of Jacob-Israel (3:1–4, 9–12). Responsibility for the wrongs exposed in 2:1–5 is thus traced to two groups of community leaders, prophets and rulers, each group being addressed twice in alternation. Embedded in these judgment speeches (between the second and third) is an oracle of hope (2:12–13). It promises to reassemble the remnant of Israel. This message does not contradict the others; it does not mitigate them. On the contrary, it assumes that the punishments threatened—expulsion from the community (2:5), withdrawal of the presence of Yahweh (3:4), extinction of prophetic vision (3:6), demolition of Zion (3:12)— will be fully administered. The nation will be destroyed and dispersed. Only then will the ruined and scattered people be gathered once more. That is a hope for the future; but no joy for Micah's present audience.

The basis of these messages is the age-old relationship between Yahweh and Israel. There is an explicit reminder of this at the very end of the book, with its listing of the patriarchs (7:20). At other points, as well, there are recollections of God's past dealings with this people, right back to the olden days (5:1), in the names Nimrod (5:5), Balaam (6:5), Moses, Aaron, and Miriam (6:4), even possibly Adam (6:8). Add to these names the numerous evocations of great occasions in the past enshrined in ancient poems whose echoes are heard in 1:2, 3, 10; 4:1, 4; 6:1; 7:14, 18. And who knows how many other traditions we do not recognize because their sources have not survived.

From all these past dealings of Yahweh with Israel came a conscious national identity as "the people of Yahweh." The arrangements of the covenant gave the people a sense of security. The institutions, set up by God himself, as they believed, were available and dependable. Ceremonies, supervised by cult professionals, dealt with the seasonal round of agricultural life and the rites of passage. In the liturgy the people were active and God presumably receptive. Ceremonial audience with the fearsome presence of the deity was restricted to authorized personnel; it was conducted at sacred places (temples) in traditional prescribed rituals. Such amenities were a standing token of the engagement of Yahweh to be "with" his people, "in their midst." Memories of the terrible deeds performed by this mighty spirit on their behalf could be reassuring. Faith that Yahweh actually resided among his favored people encouraged them to think that they were the darlings of the deity, and that under his shelter they would be safe from harm: they could cry out to him, and he would answer them (3:4a). Their slogans expressed the comfort, security, and complacency of those who felt that God was and would be there when they needed him:

Is not Yahweh in our midst?
Evil will not come against us. (3:11)

The other outlet for divine dealings with the situations that arose from time to time worked outside these established arrangements. The human agent was a prophet. The prophet was an immediate agent of the deity. He operated without the benefit of an institutional function or a social base. Like the God he represented, the prophet was unpredictable and uncontrollable. His unwelcome task was to speak the truth from God's point of view, not to supply the consolations of religion, the promise of "Peace!" (3:5) that the people wished to hear. Part of the prophet Micah's assignment was to denounce the popular belief that with such a powerful patron god as Yahweh, their partner and protector, no "evil" (*rā'â*) would befall them, only "good" (*ṭôb*). His was not the only voice speaking on this subject. Micah was not the only prophet. There were plenty of others claiming to bring messages from the deity, the opposite messages of benediction and well-being. To them, and to their willing hearers, the warning that Yahweh was going to send evil, not good, must have sounded like blasphemy. These words *rā'* and *ṭôb* weave themselves through the entire book. They come to a climax with the question "What is good?" (6:8) which is answered by the classic definition of true religion:

What is Yahweh seeking from thee?
Only to do justice,
to love *ḥesed*,
and to walk humbly with thy God. (6:8)

Why, then, when they hoped for "good," did "evil" come down from Yahweh (1:12)? According to Micah, it was an accumulation of covenant violations (*pĕšā'îm*), including the paganizing of the cultus in the "high places" (1:5), the building of the economy on exploitation and violence (3:10; 6:12), the oppression of men (2:2), women, and children (2:9), and worst of all the corruption of the leadership—heads, princes, judges, priests, prophets (3:1, 5, 9, 11). Here was a power complex at the top of the nation's life and institutions—business persons and bureaucrats, military and magistrates, prophets and priests—all together in collusion and collaboration. These are the people addressed by God through his spokesman, the prophet. These are the power brokers and power wielders blamed and warned by Micah.

Among that coalition of corruption the prophets are the most responsible. Micah has more to say against them than against any of the others. The five distinct addresses in chapters 2–3 begin with a general indictment directed, not at a named category of officials, but generally at "planners of iniquity" and "doers of evil" (2:1–5). This is followed by more specific condemnations of two special-interest groups. Each group is dealt with twice, in alternation—the prophets in 2:6–11 and 3:5–8; the administrative leadership in 3:1–4, 9–12. Another pair of similar speeches against the wealthy comes in the Book of Contention—the dishonest city merchants (6:9–12) and the farmers (6:13–15). The general collapse of the values of the covenant is shown in the breakdown of law and order, the scale of unchecked crime against property (2:1–5), the appalling cruelty of the leaders (3:2–3; 7:2–3), the fragmentation of society, even the family (7:5–6). The prophets are more to blame for this than anyone else, for they have failed in their duty as watchmen of the covenant. Instead of exposing and condemning violations of the rules and principles of the covenant, they have condoned the status quo and comforted the privileged. In 2:6–11 and 3:5–8 Micah assails these prophets with a word from God contrary to their own favorable oracles. These two complementary oracles are the twin pillars of the Book of Doom (chapters 1–3).

Micah 2 contains a condemnation of various sins—rapacity (vv 1–2, 8–10) and false prophecy (vv 6, 11)—woes (vv 1, 4) and threats (vv 3–5) against evildoers. But after all these threats have been fulfilled in judgment there will be a marvelous recovery (vv 12–13), vindicating the goodness of Yahweh's spirit (v 7). The ideas in chapter 2 are not developed logically or arranged in a simple pattern.

The unity of the chapter, whether from author or editor, is far from assured. In fact, most commentators expound it as three or more units. Verses 12–13 attract suspicion as probably postexilic, and even when vv 6–11 are seen to be unified by the opening and closing references to pseudo-prophets, the composite material in vv 7–10 suggests a complex development—from original oracle through oral transmission and literary redaction.

Compared with chapter 1 the composition is good and clear. More shapes of classical prosodies and speech forms can be delineated; it is poetry, but it is not the same as the lyrical and cultic poetry of Psalms and Wisdom and victory odes from which scholars have worked out the rules of Hebrew versification. Not much is achieved by trying to scan it by beats, the way Allen, Robinson, R. L. Smith, and others do; and it is an atrocity to knock it into better shape by making the colons more regular, as with Stade's trimming it all into *qinah* meter. It is prophetic oratory in which the occasional development of parallelism generates enough bicolons to show that it is poetic. These passages are organic with statements that are more like prose. Micah 2:5 is a good illustration. If a clause like this turned up in narrative it would be considered prose. It is just one long clause. In the context of so much poetry it is part of the whole poem.

The Five Judgment Oracles in Micah 2–3

Social Injustice Denounced 2:1–5	
	Attack on Prophets 2:6–11
Attack on Rulers 3:1–4	
	Condemnation of Prophets 3:5–8
Condemnation of Rulers 3:9–12	

I.4. SOCIAL INJUSTICE DENOUNCED (2:1–5)

TRANSLATION

MT

1aA	*hôy ḥōšĕbê-ʾāwen*	Hôy—planners of iniquity,
1aB	*ûpōʿălê rāʿ ʿal-miškĕbôtām*	and doers of evil on their beds!
1bA	*bĕʾôr habbōqer yaʿăśûhā*	In the light of the morning they did it,
1bB	*kî yeš-lĕʾēl yādām*	for their hand belongs to El (God).
2aA	*wĕḥāmĕdû śādôt wĕgāzālû*	And they coveted fields and seized [them],
2aB	*ûbāttîm wĕnāśāʾû*	and houses and stole [them];
2bA	*wĕʿāšĕqû geber ûbêtô*	and they defrauded a man and his house,
2bB	*wĕʾîš wĕnaḥălātô*	and a man and his estate.
3aA	*lākēn kōh ʾāmar yhwh*	Therefore thus has said Yahweh:
3aB	*hinĕnî ḥōšēb ʿal-hammišpāḥâ hazzōʾt rāʿâ*	Behold, I am planning against this tribe evil,
3bAα	*ʾăšer lōʾ-tāmîšû miššām ṣawwĕʾrōtêkem*	from which you will not be able to withdraw your necks.
3bAβ	*wĕlōʾ tēlĕkû rômâ*	And you will not walk upright,
3bB	*kî ʿēt rāʿâ hîʾ*	for it is a time of evil!
4aAα	*bayyôm hahûʾ yiśśāʾ ʿălêkem māšāl*	On that day he will raise against you a proverb
4aAβ	*wĕnāhâ nĕhî nihyâ*	and mourn (with) a mournful lamentation.
4aAγ	*ʾāmar šādôd nĕšaddūnû*	He said: We have been utterly devastated,
4aB	*ḥēleq ʿammî yāmîr*	He has exchanged my people's portion.
4bA	*ʾêk yāmîš lî*	How he has removed (what is) mine!
4bB	*lĕšôbēb śādênû yĕḥallēq*	To the apostate he apportioned our fields.
5aA	*lākēn lōʾ-yihyeh lĕkā*	Therefore thou [m.] wilt not have anyone
5aB	*mašlîk ḥebel bĕgôrāl*	working out the boundaries by lot
5b	*biqĕhal yhwh*	in the assembly of Yahweh.

LXX I.4. Social Injustice Denounced (2:1–5)

1aA	There came planners of troubles
1aB	and workers of evils in their beds!
1bA	And immediately it is day, they carry them out,
1bB	because they did not lift up their hands to God.
2aA	And they were coveting fields and they were plundering orphans,
2aB	and houses they were oppressing;
2bA	and they plundered a man (*aner*) and his house,
2bB	and a man (*aner*) and his inheritance.
3aA	Therefore thus says Kyrios:
3aB	Behold, I am planning against this tribe evils
3bAα	from which you will not be able to lift your necks.
3bAβ	And you will not walk upright immediately,
3bB	for it is a time of evil!
4aAα	On that day will be raised against you a parable
4aAβ	and will be mourned a mournful lamentation.
4aAγ	Saying: We have become miserable in our misery.

4aB   The portion of my people has been measured out with a cord
4bA   and there was nobody to prevent him, to turn (him) away.
4bB   Our fields have been divided up.
5   Therefore there shall not be for thee one who casts a cord in the lot in the *ekklesia*
      of Kyrios.

INTRODUCTION TO MICAH 2:1–5

This unit is a judgment oracle against those who greedily, unjustly, and violently seize others' property. Bardtke (1971: 235) points out its similarity to Isa 5:8–10. The unity of its theme could reflect a concrete historical situation (Shaw 1993), but its literary expression uses at least three genres — woe, lament, verdict. Dearman (1988: 45) finds only two components in this "woe speech" which he calls also a "judgment speech": "the reasons for the woe (vv 1–2) followed by an announcement of future judgment."

Verses 1–5 as a whole are characterized by a wide range of colon lengths and by a variety of parallelism patterns. Hebrew oracular poetry is not as regular and uniform as cultic compositions. So the less poetic parts, the judgment pronouncements (vv 3 and 5), can also be accepted as parts of the oracle.

From the thematic point of view the oracle in 2:1–5 has four parts, in which some scholars have identified distinct genres and sources to match the different themes. Lescow (1972a), for instance, assigns vv 1–3 to Micah, but not the verses that follow them.

1. A declaration of woe against the miscreants (vv 1–2). Here is a fine poetic unit, eight colons, four bicolons, two quatrains. It is followed logically by:

2. A threat of punishment (v 3). This unit is introduced by the messenger formula (v 3aA). From the grammatical point of view it is one long clause, including a very elaborate relative clause (v 3b). The use of the relative pronoun and the definite article shows that the language is that of prose. But the use of prose diction or syntax at this point does not mean that v 3 cannot be part of the larger poem. Quite apart from the dramatic and thematic necessity of moving from accusation to denunciation in the woe passage (vv 1–2) to the pronouncement of doom in v 3, the judgment speech uses vocabulary that ties it right in to the woe speech. There is a correspondence between what they have done to their victims and what Yahweh is going to do to them. They are *planning . . . evil upon their beds* (ʿal-miškĕbôtām); he is *planning evil against this tribe* (ʿal-hammišpāḥâ hazzōʾt). The match of *miškĕbôtām* and *hammišpāḥâ* is hardly a pun, but there need be no doubt about the play on the similarity of the sounds in conjunction with the repetition of the same verb. We note as well that the subordinated clause in v 3bB is an echo of the clause in v 1bB.

3. The condemnation and threat are followed logically by lamentation (v 4). Exactly the same development took place in 1:2–16. There is no question about the poetic character of the three bicolons in v 4. Their outstanding feature is the repeated play on the similar sounds of words, a feature already present in vv 1–3. The genre of v 4 is more problematic, especially when the entire verse is

identified as the *proverb*. We shall argue shortly that vv 4aAγ–4b are not to be identified as the text of the *proverb*. In v 4aAβ the *proverb* is identified as *a mournful lamentation*, that is, the lamentation is to be used as a proverb *against you* on the day of reckoning. How does it work? The proper use of a lament is as an expression of one's own misery, and this is the case with vv 4aAγ–4b, as it is with 7:1–6. As such it can also be a protest, an appeal to divine justice or pity, an indirect accusation of the one who caused the misery, a prayer. Lament can be used in sincere commiseration; we think that this applies to the laments in chapter 1. As a *proverb* a lament is used improperly, and prophets frequently use it to warn a wrongdoer of coming disaster, or to taunt him when his misery is seen as vindication of divine justice. The latter application is implied by the phrase *against you* in v 4aA.

4. Finally there is a concluding judgment speech (v 5). Thematically it belongs with the rest. The whole unit is dealing with the right to enjoy the allotments of land that had been apportioned to the people as members of Yahweh's community (*qhl*). The oppressors of v 1 had violated these sacred arrangements. The crime against people was a sin against Yahweh. The appropriate punishment was to evict these culprits from the privileges that they had denied to others (Premnath 1988). That much is clear, and the conclusion of the whole oracle is fitting. This thematic cohesion overrides any misgivings one might have about the integral connection of v 5 with the rest on the grounds of its limited poetic development. Rhythmically it can be read as a tricolon with one prepositional phrase in each colon.

There is more work to be done on the dramatic side of this oracle. That will be taken up in the COMMENT that follows the NOTES. Micah is making a proclamation on behalf of God, but only some of the words (notably vv 3aB–3b) are labeled as a divine utterance by the messenger formula used in v 3aA. This conventional protocol formula (spoken by the prophet) initiates the quotation of what is in the strictest sense the word of Yahweh, who is the "I" of v 3aB. The individual in v 4 is not protesting against the violation of his private property rights; he is speaking in solidarity with the whole people (the *qhl* of Yahweh [v 5]) who received allotments of land as part of the covenant settlement. Beyond this there are not enough data in the text to reconstruct the scenario. The words are reported, but the story is not told.

The divine response to this injustice is caught in a paradox. For the victims, it is not enough to evict the illegal occupants; the innocent must be restored (vv 12–13). The violated covenant entitlements must be maintained for the remnant. For the guilty, it is not enough to evict them from land they are not entitled to. They have forfeited their covenant entitlements; and they must never get them back (v 5). It is only because readers have not sorted out the participants, but have supposed that prophecies were addressed to "Israel" in general, that they find a contradiction between the threat of permanent exclusion in v 5 and the promise of restoration in vv 12–13. It is because they have not appreciated the solidarity of individual and national identity within Israel as "people" of Yahweh, the community of the covenant, that they have attributed the protest about the violation of individual landownership rights to Micah and the eighth century, but found the language of the whole community (*people* [v 4], *assembly* [v 5]) to be appropriate only after the nation had experienced eviction from the land during the Exile. We see no need for Mays's conclusion that these more nationalistic features "belong to interpretation of Micah's prophecy as one which was fulfilled about a century later in conquest of Judah by Babylonians" (1976: 62). That the text can bear such an interpretation is recognized; and that such an interpretation was made we do not doubt. But the language itself, especially that of v 5 (which is especially suspected of being an exilic addition, partly because it is less poetic than the rest of the oracle) is still talking about the apportionment of land within the assembly, not just the resettlement of the whole people on Yahweh's estate, viewed as one holding. Verse 5 in its literal meaning is a suitable ending for the oracle; in its metaphorical meaning it became a prophecy for the nation.

NOTES AND COMMENTS

Introduction to Micah 2:1

The oracle in vv 1–5 is remarkable for the integration of diverse genres into a single literary composition. Each verse belongs to a distinct genre. Verse 1 pronounces "Woe!" against those who scheme evil; v 2 describes the execution of their plan; v 3 is a judgment speech; v 4 refers to a *proverb*, apparently a *mournful lamentation* used as a taunt, mocking derision of the wrongdoers when they suffer a fate like that of their victims. The latter part of v 4 seems to be a "woe" that gives the victim's side of the crimes described in v 2. Verses 3 and 5 both begin with "therefore" and together state the punishment for the crimes of vv 1–2, as the repetition of the ideas and even the vocabulary show.

The whole of vv 1–2 traces a single narrative development, from scheming while in bed (v 1) to carrying through the scheme (v 2). The successive stages in the action are reported by different kinds of verbs, first two participles (v 1a), then a prefix verb (v 1bA), then four suffix verbs each with a preceding *and*. In a later age, Western moral philosophy would locate the merit or demerit of human behavior in intention; the Bible emphasizes wrong actions as constituting crimes of disobedience to the statutes laid down by the divine ruler of the people of Israel, while at the same time tracing sin as rebellion to underlying attitudes toward the deity. The outcomes are interpreted as blessing (by God) or cursing (by God). The scenario in vv 1–2 traces the injustice of violent seizure of another's land back to covetousness, the only commandment of the ten that concentrates on a wrong attitude of mind or desire. The subsequent words of judgment in vv 3–5 show that they not only planned iniquity, they did evil. Verses 1 and 2 go together, and the initial *hôy* covers all eight colons.

Verse 1 declares Woe against *planners of iniquity* and *doers of evil*. Who are these doers of evil, and what are they up to? It is usually supposed that Micah is documenting the familiar economic development in which inequalities of wealth place the poor more and more at the mercy of the rich, who grab the little farms and make vast estates for themselves. A similar state of affairs lies behind Isa 5:8–10, which Fohrer (1968: 444) thinks has influenced Mic 2:1–3. On the socioeconomic background of these developments in the distribution of landholdings in ancient Israel, Bardtke (1971: 235) links Mic 2:1–5 with Isa 5:8–10. Good sense can be made of the passage along these lines. But there are many details that do not entirely fit. The perspective of v 2, with its focus on the oppression of individual landowners, is complemented by language later on in the oracle that looks at the problem in terms of the whole community. Important in this connection is the identification of the evildoers as "this tribe" (or "family") (v 3aB—see the NOTE).

Much of the interest of Micah's poetry is created by his use of pairs of related words that are not necessarily the stock pairs generally preferred by Hebrew poets. Thus the preferred idiom for "plan evil" is *ḥšb rāʿ* (Gen 50:20; Hos 7:15; Mic 2:3; Pss 35:4; 41:8; 140:3), and "doers of iniquity" (*pōʿălê-ʾāwen*) is a cliché. Micah has switched the nouns, and the expressions he uses in v la (*ḥōšĕbê-ʾāwen* and *ûpōʿălê rāʿ*) occur only here in the Hebrew Bible. The matching of synonyms of these words is discussed by Avishur (1984: 283). Melamed (1961: 134) identified the "break-up of a stereotype phrase" in Micah's arrangement. Bronznick (1979: 32) explained it as "metathetic parallelism." Instead of the usual *ḥlq wnḥlh* we have *byt . . . nḥlh* in v 2b. The noun *bqr*, "morning," is usually paired with *ʿrb*, "evening"; here it matches "upon their beds."

Micah uses seven verbal roots in vv 1–2 to describe the activities of those against whom he pronounces woe. The lack of "and" at the beginning of v 1b and the use of "and" at the beginning of v 2 shows that v 1a is the more general opening statement (using participles) followed by six colons that spell out the specifics using finite verbs. There is a prefix verb in v 1b and four suffix verbs with "and" in v 2. In prose the latter construction (*waw*-consecutive) would predict a series of successive future actions, especially when the *waw*-consecutive constructions follow an opening clause that uses a prefix verb, here *yaʿăśûhā*. The usual future time reference of this string of verb forms cannot be sustained. Micah is not describing things that might happen or will happen; he is reacting to what has already been done, the sins in Israel that have already provoked Yahweh. In Hebrew, participles are often used as labels or titles of persons who have done specific things. Translation of all the verbs by neutral present tense makes the woe oracle into a bland generalization, not targeted at anyone in particular, mere moralism. The oracle has prophetic power if it is addressed directly to persons who have actually done these things. If the verb usage is not that of classical prose but of archaic poetry, then they can all be past tense.

In view of this rich concentration of poetic artistry in vv 1–2, it does not matter that the colons vary widely in length (the shortest is five, the longest ten syllables), or that v 1b does not read as a bicolon with parallelism. It is precisely this lack of parallelism between v 1bA and v 1bB that alerts us to the connection between v 1aB and v 1bA (*ûpōʿălê rāʿ* // *yaʿăśûhā*—the verbs are parallel, but the objects have different gender).

Notes on Micah 2:1

Hôy. Woe. The ascription or assignment or imprecation of misfortune or misery to certain miscreants in a "woe" oracle is characteristic of Israelite prophecy from its inception. Amos has a series or schedule of such woes (Andersen
and Freedman 1989: 462–64). Amos uses participial constructions to identify
those deserving disaster. Isaiah has a series of "woe" oracles in chapters 5 and 10.
On the form-critical features and situational use of "woe" compositions in prophetic oracles, see Gerstenberger (1962), Clifford (1966), Williams (1967), Janzen (1972), Clements (1982), Hillers (1983).

The background and origin of this mode of discourse have been found in
four different situations in ancient Israelite culture. Mowinckel (1924: V 120)
recognized the formal similarity between "Woe" uttered in the cult and the
cursing formulae of the commination rituals (Deut 27:15–26); hôy corresponds
to 'ārûr. There is a similar correspondence between beatitude ('ašrê) and blessing
(bārûk) (Mowinckel 1924: V 2). Given the background of covenant stipulations
as providing the standard of right conduct, it is notable that the deeds that attract woe are often described in terms of disobedience to these requirements
(cf. "covet" in v 2). Even if this connotation explains the common judgmental
tone of curses and woes, the former were minatory rather than condemnatory. It
was too late for the prophets simply to repeat such admonitions in a different
form. Prophetic woes are concrete and specific; the participles are mainly plural (cursing and blessing formulas are singular); the implied charge of actual
wrongdoing is often elaborated from the participle into narrative by the use of
finite verbs (as in Mic 1:2–5). Westermann (1967: 193) considered the prophetic
"woes" more original. In an influential study, Gerstenberger (1962) found the
background of prophetic "woe" oracles in the admonitions of wisdom teachers,
a linkage that Wolff (1964) emphasized in his study of Amos. Another possibility
is that "woe" messages are imitations of funeral chants (Clifford 1966; Janzen
1972). While to some degree there seems to be an overlap in usage between hôy
and 'ôy, the former is preferred in mourning for another, while the latter characteristically expresses anguish felt by the speaker (cf. 'alĕlay lî in Mic 7:1).

The trend in recent scholarship has favored the affinity between "woe" and
"mourning cry." The language of Mic 2:4 supports this. In Amos 5:16–17 lamentation is linked with woe oracles, resembling the connection between Mic 2:1
and Mic 2:4. What is less clear is the extent to which prophetic usage is metaphorical. The use of the label māšāl takes us back to "wisdom" talk and points
to figurative language, suggesting that the mourning cry (nĕhî) is not literal,
but indicates the prophetic use of traditional language as a taunt or as a threat.
If the translation "Alas!" is accepted, this does not take us very far. It all depends
on the prophet's tone of voice, and at this we can only guess. If the word is sincere, it could express the prophet's own personal dismay and grief, not only
over the sufferings of the victims, so that his commiseration could function as
an appeal to the divine pity, but even over the fate of their oppressors, however

justly deserved. It is perhaps going too far to say that the prophet is mourning over the evildoers in anticipation of their punishment. If, however, the prophet sings a dirge in mockery, then the language is sarcastic. Wildberger says of the woe oracles in Isaiah, "The woe-oracle is not far away from the curse: it bewails [Trapp's translation of *beklagt* (Wildberger 1980: 182) as 'complains' (1991: 196) could give the wrong impression that the prophet is protesting] those who are already to be found in the realm of death." This is somewhat forced. If it has any validity, it places the woe oracle close to a dirge. As Wildberger had said immediately before the words just quoted, "If the prophets take over this *hôy* from the lament for the dead as the introduction for their reproach (*Scheltwort*), it is because they wanted to proclaim that the germ of death dwelt within the observed crime" (Wildberger 1991: 182). This is overdoing it. Even so, the intention of a prophetic "woe" seems to have been denunciation, perhaps derision, rather than warning or commiseration.

In spite of the conventional and familiar use of *hôy*, *woe*, to begin this oracle, the versions part company. LXX *egenonto* suggests a source reading **hāyû*, "they were," while Targum suggests *'ayyēh*, "where?" It is hardly likely that the sources used for these translations contained such variants, which do not represent improvements over MT. But, if their sources read *hôy*, it is hard to see the motivation for the changes. What lies behind this uncertainty is a recognition that a "woe" pronounced against a wrongdoer does not express commiseration but denunciation. The accusatory tone of this oracle brings it close to the prophetic *rîb* (Horine 1989).

planners of iniquity. The usual expression is *pôʿălê-ʾāwen*, "evildoers," while *rāʿ* is often the object of *ḥšb* (Pss 35:4; 41:8; Jer 26:3; 36:3; Nah 1:11; compare Jer 29:11). Micah has switched the idioms, deliberately, we think. It is also part of his unconventional use of conventional formulas that he has delayed the modifier *upon their beds*, which goes better with *planners*, and placed it with *doers*, an incongruity that has troubled some modern readers. The effect of the delayed modifier is to clamp together the two participial expressions: "on their beds they plan to do evil."

The versions fully support MT and indeed read participles. There can be no doubt that what we now have in MT was the settled text. Yet, in spite of this united front, the text has been doubted on *a priori* and on internal grounds. There are problems of logic, of poetry, and of grammar. First, it is not logical to say that planners of iniquity do evil on their beds. There is a further contradiction with v 1b, which says that they do it when morning dawns. Second, the scansion of v 1a in which the second colon is longer than the first does not match the expected *qinah* meter (3 : 2). The third problem is the clash of gender if *rāʿ* (m.) is the antecedent of the pronoun suffix object *-hā* (f.), *they did it*.

The text has been heavily rewritten in several ways since Wellhausen (1898). The discussion of the problem by Willis (1967) is particularly thorough, and we have depended on it substantially for what follows, without reproducing his full documentation. The available solutions involve deleting and/or transposing and/or revocalizing and/or suggesting different meanings for one or more words. The possible combinations seem endless. Budde (1919: 3) rearranged the sequence of words in v 1aB to obtain "Woe to those who devise iniquity upon their beds, and work evil." Wellhausen (1898: 137) deleted the second participle phrase as a gloss, and many subsequent scholars have followed him in this (list in Willis 1967: 535 n. 1). Less drastic is Duhm's deletion of "iniquity and" (1911: 84). Retaining the consonantal text and changing the vowels to make the second participle a noun, proposed by Halévy (1904) and accepted by Robinson (1954: 132), yields "planning evil and wicked deeds" (NEB, REB). A slight variation makes the noun singular (pōʿal) to match the singular number of "iniquity" in v 1aA (Sellin 1929: 317; and others). Bruno (1923: 42, 55) replaced pʿly with ṭply, "conceive," to achieve synonymous parallelism. Ehrlich (1968: V 275) argued that ʿaśîtî in Isa 37:26 means "plan," and that its synonym pʿl has this meaning in Mic 2:1aB. Willis documents this solution to Margolis and Wade and refers to Ps 58:3 as the only place (and that dubious) where ʿāśâ might refer to mental work. Peshitta's repetition of ḥšb in v 1aB seems to have arisen from a similar desire to make the two participles say the same thing. Such literalistic readings are lacking in poetic sensibility, and the results of these adjustments are insipid.

Willis points out on the one hand that ʾāwen is frequently the object of pʿl, and that other objects of this verb are nouns that refer to a range of evil deeds. On the other hand, the preferred object of the verb ḥšb is rāʿ or rāʿâ. So the common idioms "plan evil" and "do iniquity" are here switched around. Although it is theoretically conceivable that the familiar expressions were used in the original oracle and that the switch occurred in copying the text, Willis presents five reasons why this is unlikely. His fifth, and most impressive, argument is the use of a similar switch of idioms in Ezek 11:2.

| ʾēlleh hāʾănāšîm haḥōšěbîm ʾāwen | these are the men who plan iniquity |
| wěhayyōʿăṣîm ʿăṣat-rāʿ | and who advise wicked advice |

Similar modulations of standard idioms are found in Isa 59:6; Ps 21:12; and Prov 16:30.

The combination "plan" (evil) and "do" (it) is stated in reverse in Jer 18:11. In normal prose it is "plan to do evil" (ḥšb laʿăśôt rāʿâ [Neh 6:2]). Micah has broken up this phrase and made poetry out of it. The sequence of the participles and the sequence of their noun objects mark the movement from thought to deed; rāʿâ is not abstract evil, but a concrete action, a bad deed.

their beds. Retaining the Masoretic Text for the reasons given above leaves the circumstance of "doing evil upon their beds" to be explained. One would think that the bed is where the evil schemes are hatched, not where the bad deeds are done. This is clearer from Ps 36:5.

ʾāwen	yaḥšōb ʿal-miškābô	Wickedness he planned on his bed;
yityaṣṣēb ʿal-derek lōʾ-ṭôb	he stood on the road of the "Not-Good,"
rāʿ lōʾ yimʾās	"Bad" he did not reject.

The psalmist has the same ideas as Micah, but puts "on his bed" with "planned"; and "wickedness" is followed by "evil" ("Bad"), as in Micah. We note, by the way, the same poetic use of prefix verbs with past tense meaning. There is something proverbial in this repeated reference to a bed as the place where evil schemes are thought out. The use of the bed for such planning seems to be more sinister than just lying awake at night thinking up crimes to commit the next day. The night was feared in antiquity as a time when demons had more power and when evil magic could be worked by conjuring them (Fishbane 1971). Hence the need to use the bed for godly meditation (Deut 6:7; Ps 1:2). Deliberate incubation could receive revelations from night visitors—Yahweh, or his opposite. In any case, these crimes were premeditated and carefully planned and even rehearsed in bed. In Zech 7:10; 8:17 similar language is used to describe schemes against "the brother," to oppress the widow, the fatherless, the sojourner, the poor. Micah identifies specifically crimes against property (v 2).

In three respects, then, Micah has used familiar language in unfamiliar ways. The methodological flaws in most previous critical work upon the unusual features of Mic 1:1a have been: first, an expectation that the prophet will sound just like everybody else; and, second, trying to solve the problems of this half-verse by examining it in isolation from the rest of the book of Micah; and, third, the unimaginative literalism of the reading.

The splitting up of the familiar idiom *ḥšb rāʿ* over the bicolon in v 1a prepares for the idiom in v 3; and, in case we might miss it, the author has made another connection with the assonance of *ʿal-miškĕbôtām* and *ʿal-hammišpāḥâ*. And, in case we might miss *that*, he has broken up the idiom and put *ʿal-hammišpāḥâ hazzōʾt* inside *ḥšb . . . rāʿâ*, with the unusual syntax Verb + Adverb + Object. How could anyone miss it?

Once the MT of v 1a is left as it is, the puzzling collocation of "doing evil upon their beds," instead of being a problem, becomes a clue. Willis has shown that the commonest activity upon one's bed reported in the Hebrew Bible is dreaming. He concludes:

> The commonest evidence of these passages [he discussed them in detail] leads me to suggest that "upon their beds" in Mic 2,1 is an idiomatic expression equivalent to "in their dreams." I.e., the prophet does not describe nocturnal meetings of the wicked men to devise evil schemes against the innocent to be carried out the following day. Rather, he portrays the all-consuming passion for wickedness of individual evil-doers—a passion which so dominates their lives that they cannot sleep and dream without thinking about "devising iniquity" and "working evil." (1967: 538–39)

"Upon their beds" applies to both participial constructions. Moreover, the switching around of the usual objects also binds the two expressions together more closely in a kind of hendiadys—they plan and do iniquity and evil. The choice also prepares the way for v 3. Humans characteristically "do iniquity." There is no iniquity in God. God can devise "evil," something "bad" (*rāʿâ*), but he is never wicked. God even "creates evil" (Isa 45:7), the opposite of well-being (*šālôm*), a statement so theologically incorrect that most translations shy away from it. Micah has already said that "evil came down from Yahweh" (1:12). Here, as everywhere in the Hebrew Bible, God plans something bad (*rāʿâ* [2 Kgs 6:33]) and does something bad in strict equity, following the rule of equity (*jus talionis*) that the measure you give is the measure you get or you reap what you sow. The book of Micah contains several instances of this correspondence between human behavior and the divine response. Samaria gathered wealth from a prostitute's pay; that wealth will be used to pay a prostitute (1:7). They unjustly drove people from their property, so they forfeit their claim to share in the land distribution in Yahweh's congregation (2:5; the language of 2:10 may be describing their eviction). They did not heed the cry of those in distress, so Yahweh will not heed their cry of distress (3:4). Prophecy has been abused, so prophecy will be withdrawn (3:6). Jerusalem was built with violence; it will be destroyed with violence (3:12). Likewise, just as they devised evil against their victims, Yahweh is devising evil against them (2:1–3).

The similarity between a sin and its punishment is clearer in some instances than in others. Sometimes wordplay is all that is needed to make the connection. The match between "they are like a thorn hedge" and "they will suffer perplexity" (Mic 7:4) depends entirely on the assonance of *mimmĕsûkâ* and *mĕbûkātām*. Willis quotes the observation made by Beck (1898: 192) that this is *Alliteration zur Andeutung von talio*. The same could be said about the juxtaposition of *ʿal-miškĕbôtām* and *ʿal-hammišpāḥâ*. There is no logical connection between these word pairs; the resemblance lies in their sound. At the same time, each word contributes its meaning to the oracle. Amos used the expression *ʿal-kol hammišpāḥâ* to downshift Israel from the status of "people" to just another "family" among the families of the world (Amos 3:1–2). Micah's choice of the same word could be similarly derisive (see the NOTE on v 3). Whatever ties of kin might have made these people a "family," they shared the trait of such habitual evildoing that they did it in their sleep.

The need to read such a poetic text through a larger aperture than a bicolon in order to perceive the operation of the *jus talionis* is illustrated by Prov 22:22–23, where the chiastic arrangement of the quatrain provides the key to working out how the pieces fit together.

ʾal-tigzol-dal kî dal-hûʾ	Don't snatch away a poor man because he is poor;
wĕʾal-tĕdakkāʾ ʿānî baššaʿar	and don't crush a destitute man in the gate!
kî-yhwh yārîb rîbām	for Yahweh will dispute their dispute
wĕqābaʿ ʾet-qōbĕʿêhem nāpeš	and he will rob those who robbed them: [their] soul.

Verse 22 prohibits snatching the poor // afflicted by depriving them of justice "in the gate." Verse 23 gives the reason for the prohibition. Probably the chiasmus of the four colons has been missed because it is only partial. Verse 22a is parallel to v 22b in some respects (identical syntax and synonymous parallelism of the first three words—after that they part company), while v 23b is a parallel for v 22a in other respects (the verbs are close synonyms, so long as the verb in v 23b is not emended, as in BHS). The language of court procedure links v 22b and v 23a. The repetition of the verb root in each colon makes v 23 an acceptable bicolon: but it does not stand alone; the plural pronouns need nouns as referents, clearly the victims in v 22. So there is an overlay of more than one parallelistic pattern in the same unit.

The principle of talion is clearly asserted in v 23b: Yahweh will rob those who robbed. Although the root *qbˤ* is rare, its use in Mal 3:8–9 shows that it means to deprive someone of rightful property. Perhaps from squeamishness over saying that God commits robbery, or to make v 23b more synonymous with v 23a, the clear language of v 23b has been evaded, commonly by emending to *ˤqb*. This is clever, to be sure; but why do it? Part of the reason could be the incongruity between v 23a, where Yahweh acts as the champion of justice, and v 23b, where he behaves like a crook. But the legal language of v 23a matches the reference to the gate in v 22b, and God's act of robbery in v 23b matches the act of robbery in v 22a. A destitute person is crushed in the gate because he has no defender, no human advocate anyway; so Yahweh will step in and argue the case for the poor. The wrongful act in v 22a is not immediately clear; the language is terse. "Rob the poor" is not satisfactory. If the poor have nothing, how can you rob them? Here as in Mic 2:2 *gzl* means "snatch away." The available object is simply *dal*. In the context of miscarriage of justice in the gate, the crime is more likely to be illegal enslavement. If any robber seized the *dal*, Yahweh will rob them (each of his) soul. *Jus talionis*. The same rules are applied in Micah 1:1–5.

they did it. The verb is a prefix form, which in prose would normally have future time reference. The oracle can hardly be a mere prediction. The future reference of the imperfect verb might be salvaged if the action is presented as future from the time of the preceding participles, read as historic presents. Micah is not condemning things that these people might do. As the subsequent judgment speech shows, they are guilty of these crimes. In the archaic verb usage of Hebrew poetry, the prefix verb can be preterit (Hetzron 1969). Compare the last word in Mic 7:3.

it. Feminine, with no evident antecedent, since *iniquity* and *evil* are both masculine. LXX *auta* agrees with *kaka*, its free rendering of "evil." Masculine *rāˤ* and feminine *rāˤâ* (see v 3) seem to be used interchangeably in such idioms. It is masculine in the almost identical language of Gen 31:29. Feminine "it" seems to anticipate v 3. See the NOTE on "this" in Mic 1:5. Note the similar conjunction of cognate masculine and feminine nouns in v 4. Linking the masculine and feminine forms in this way, the feminine pronoun suffix in v 1bA secures a kind of merismus; Micah is talking about each and every kind of "evil."

hand. Literally "because their hand is (belongs) to El (God)" (Kogut 1987/88). If *yēš* has its normal existential use, we would not expect *l-*. The usual translation "it is in the power of their hand" (RSV) treats the infinitival construction as the subject of the sentence—"to do evil with you exists to the power of my hand" (Gen 31:29). Can *yēš* be used to predicate existence with an impersonal subject "it"? Such an idiom seems to occur here, and the interpretation that these evildoers believe that "might makes right" seems sufficient. In Gen 31:29a Laban claims superior military might and the construction is completed by the idiom "to do evil." In Prov 3:27 the similar idiom describes capacity to do good (compare "good or evil" in Gen 31:29b). The negative counterpart uses *'ên* (Deut 28:32; Neh 5:5). These idioms suggest that the unexpressed subject of *yēš* in Mic 2:1 is "to do evil."

It is suspicious that *'ēl*, whatever its etymology, is found with the meaning "strength" only in the phrase *'ēl yād* (Watson 1977). Cross (*TDOT* 1:261) explains the "frozen idiom" as the result of word misdivision from an original *l' lydy*, the first word being a derivative of the Canaanite root *l'y*, "be powerful." See also Kogut (1987/88). On *yd*, see Delcor (1967).

The obscurity of this colon evoked guesses in ancient translations. They identified *'ēl* as "God," and saw the action of the *hand* as defiant (*contra Deum*). Peshitta paraphrased "and they lift up their hands to God," a gesture associated with oath taking and prayer. They must have understood this as an accusation of falsifying a claim to property by oath, or else as a display of piety (3:11b). Perhaps the translator had in mind the association of prayer with oppression in Isa 1:10–17 (especially v 15), which, like Micah 2–3, is addressed to the rulers in Jerusalem. By adding a negative, LXX suggests that they did *not* pray. The later Greek versions rendered *'ēl* as "power." This seems to be the best solution, but the echo of "God" can also be heard; like the fisherman in Habakkuk 1, who burnt incense to his equipment, these people recognize no power higher than their own might. We need not take seriously the suggestion of Graham (1930–31: 254) that "hand" here means "phallic symbol."

Introduction to Micah 2:2

Verse 2 is a tetracolon as sophisticated in its design as any poetry in the Hebrew Bible. There are two bicolons, and each has incomplete parallelism. In each bicolon the opening verb serves for both colons. They covet both fields and houses. They defraud *geber* and *'îš*, "and" being used in spite of the fact that these parallel words are synonyms. This "and" is present in the Leningrad Codex and other prime manuscripts (unfortunately the folio with this material is lost from the Aleppo Codex) and should not be deleted as a dittograph (as in Mays and most translators and commentators). It is true that the versions (e.g., LXX) and even some Hebrew manuscripts lack this "and"; but the adjustment is obvious, whereas MT would hardly have arisen and survived from such an easy reading, if that variant had been original. There is internal support for this more difficult reading, for v 2b replicates the pattern in v 2a, even though the grammar is quaint. In v 2a each noun is followed by a verb, each of which is coordinate with the opening verb, with the same object, understood. The last words in the following colons are similarly coordinated; but they are nouns.

The pattern of "ands" in v 2bB once more imitates that in v 2aB, even though the meaning is not literal but rather "they rob a man of his home" (NEB). It is this echo of v 2a in v 2b that justifies the sequence "a man and his house and a man and his estate." It is a single crime.

The nouns describing real property are arranged chiastically—*fields* // *houses* // *house* // *estate*—showing that these are patrimonial lands. Without the plurals, it might be supposed that v 2b describes a crime against one "man"; but the sequence *bāttîm . . . bêtô* shows that the latter is distributive and individualizing. They defraud every man of his estate. These structural links between v 2a and v 2b bring the verbs together into a set of related actions. They describe illegal seizure of family estates by extortion motivated by covetousness.

The lack of the expected objects for the verbs *seized* and *stole*, which would have objects in grammatical prose, is another indication that we have here the elliptical speech of poetry. And that is not the only problem. It is not unusual in Hebrew, even in prose, for an object in one clause to do double duty in the next. On this basis the understood object of these verbs would be *fields* and *houses*, respectively. The first verb, *gzl*, means "plunder," the violent removal of property. It is mostly used of the tearing away of people from their families. In 3:2 Micah uses this verb to describe the flaying of victims (a metaphor for oppression?). Only here and in Gen 21:25 does this verb describe the snatching of a piece of immovable property ("fields," "well"). One can understand why LXX supplies the more suitable object "orphans" (contamination from Job 24:9?). The verb *nś* means "lift up and carry away." We are inclined to think that the parallelism of *fields* // *houses* // *house* // *estate* and the further references to landed property in vv 4–5 indicate that here *house* has the connotation of real estate, as the cognate often does elsewhere in the Hebrew Bible, to say nothing of similar use in other Semitic languages. For example, there is an Assyrian law in the form of a decree in Aramaic in which the phrase *bbyth wbᶜrsth*, "in his house and in his tenancy" is hendiadys—"in his rented farm" (Caquot 1971). Similarly in v 2b *bytw . . . wnḥltw* is hendiadys—"his patrimonial property"—in which the two members have been split up and spread over the poetic bicolon.

If *byt*, "house," refers to a farm as such or even to a building on the farm, the verb *nś* cannot have its literal denotation "lift up" and take away. One or the other item in the incongruous language must be figurative. "House" can mean "family," and this is precisely the metaphorical meaning of *nḥlh* in Ps 127:3; "children are the *nḥlt yhwh*." It could mean property in general—"all he possesses" (REB), viewed as God's gift. The language of physical removal is sensational when the actuality would have been the ejection of the owner from the farm, not the removal of the land from the owner. In practice both actions would be needed—expulsion of the owner and occupation of the land. As Elijah asked Ahab, "Have you murdered, and have you taken possession?" (1 Kgs 21:19). Micah does not use this available language. In his verbs, then, we have the metaphors of poetry.

Verse 2a has three verbs and two objects. By contrast v 2b has one verb and four objects. The verb *ᶜšq* refers primarily to oppression or extortion, and its object is always a person, not property. So the second object in each colon (*his house, his estate*) does not fit the verb. Once again the language is highly elliptical. As coordinated objects of *defrauded a man and his house* would be congruent if *house* meant "family." But the parallel *nḥlh* points to property, and the rest of the oracle makes it clear that the crime is the illegal seizure of patrimonial lands. The highly cryptic language requires a paraphrase: they defrauded a man by taking away his patrimonial estate. The four verbs and six nouns in v 2 are thus all interrelated in a highly complex way. This kind of artistry is characteristic of prophetic discourse. The word "powerful" (3:8) is appropriate for such a speech.

Notes on Micah 2:2

coveted . . . seized. The sequence of verbs corresponds to the participles in v 1 *planners . . . doers*. So the first *and* in v 2 does not mark continuation of action; it simply joins the verses.

The verbs in LXX—*plundering . . . oppressing*—do not match those in MT, unless the verb sequence is reversed. In LXX *diarpazein* renders both *gzlw* and *nś'w*, and the clauses are more balanced. There are no grounds for adjusting MT along the same lines. The preceding verb in Mic 2:1, *ḥšb*, "plan," is generic; one can plan good or bad. Here as in Isa 13:17, it is the object of the verb that makes the activity evil and that shows that covetousness is the motivation.

The verb *ḥmd* is the verb of the tenth commandment. In Exod 20:17 and Deut 5:21 there are two parts. Exodus uses the same verb twice, but Deuteronomy uses *tit'awweh*, "desire," as its parallel. Both verbs cover three categories of items that might be coveted—wife, real estate, livestock (including slaves). The lists differ slightly in sequence as well as detail.

Exod 20:17	*Deut 5:21*
house	
wife	wife
	house
	field
male slave	male slave
female slave	female slave
ox	ox
ass	ass
everything	everything

In the context, "house" in Exodus 20 could mean "family," with specifics ("such as") following, as if in this formulation private ownership of land as such was excluded by the belief that land belonged to God and people were clients, tenants, or stewards. Deuteronomy associates house and field as in Mic 2:2, suggesting a change in perception as the occupants of the land regarded it as their own. The tenth commandment has been singled out from the rest because it forbids desire (Rom 7:7–12); Jesus extended this detail to the seventh commandment (Matt 5:27).

It has been suggested that originally the tenth commandment was directed against seizure by fraud or violence, not just thinking about it. This interpretation was first developed by J. Herrmann (1927; see Coates 1934). In the Decalogue *ḥmd* is the only verb, no correlative action is implied. Just to covet is to break this commandment, to break the covenant. In other occurrences of this verb it is associated with action to realize the desire, notably Exod 34:24 (where there would be no problem if the enemy only desired the land while the people were busy with the festivals, but took no action), Ps 68:17 (where Elohim [God] "coveted" [*ḥmd*] the mountain [this shows that to desire something attractive is not necessarily sinful] to dwell in it, and Yahweh took up permanent residence in it), and especially Micah 2:2 (where *ḥmd* is followed by no fewer than three verbs of violent action *gzl*, *nš'*, and *'šq*). Further support for the idea that *ḥmd* implies action came from the use (twice) of *ḥmd* in the Karatepe Inscription, where it results in the replacement of the king's name by that of a usurper, i.e., dispossession, not just envy. It was Alt (1949) who pointed out the connection between this source and the Decalogue. Additional support was forthcoming in 1965 with the publication of *PRU* V. In RS 19.39 (*UT* 2001), rev:7 has *b'l yḥmdnh . yrṯy* (Baal coveted something), which, although it is obscure, links "covet" with "take possession."

In the discussion of the exact meaning of *ḥmd*, a distinction was not drawn carefully enough between denotation and connotation. In view of the parallelism of *hit'awweh* in Deut 5:21 and the interchangeability of these two verbs elsewhere in the Hebrew Bible, it seems clear that the denotation of *ḥmd* is "desire" or "craving." But it is a desire that drives the person to action, and the use of *ḥmd* in parallel with verbs of action, of violent action, shows not only that it has the connotation of such an outcome, but it also colors the verbs of action to identify them as premeditated and planned crimes. The question is then whether the use of the verb *ḥmd* all by itself in the Decalogue (which already has a general prohibition of stealing—we are not convinced that this should be restricted to kidnapping) carries the same implication of action (the real breach) or whether coveting in itself has now been identified as a covenant violation. W. L. Moran (1967) argued against Herrmann and Alt in favor of *ḥmd* as primarily an emotion. Its use alone in Exod 20:17, or paralleled by *hit'awweh* in Deut 5:21, without any development reported by verbs of action, shows that the desire itself is reprehensible, so that there is no need to deny that the Decalogue already penetrates to motive as the main consideration in its ethics. Both thought and action are combined when the crime is both premeditated and well planned, as is clearly the case in Mic 2:1–2.

Freedman (1991: 13–35) has shown that the entire Primary History (Genesis–Kings) has been edited on the basis of the Decalogue, with a blatant violation of each of the first nine commandments marking a series of crises or climaxes in the history. There is no incident that specifically involves violation of the tenth commandment. This omission or rather lack makes Micah's use of the language of that commandment all the more intriguing. In the Primary History God punishes violators of the other commandments; no one was ever punished in the Hebrew Bible for committing the covenant violation described by the verb *ḥmd*. In many cases there is no doubt that coveting provided the motivation for committing the crime, whether it was Achan who desired the banned booty and then stole it, or David who desired his neighbor's wife and then took her, or Ahab and Jezebel who coveted Naboth's property and then stole it from him through a process of judicial murder. But the fact that *ḥmd* is mentioned in connection with terrible crimes does not mean that coveting as such partakes of the criminal act. The fact that they had to use one or more additional verbs to describe what happened shows that a distinction remains between the desire and the plan and the act itself. In that distinction lies a difference between crime that human justice might be able to deal with and sin that only God can deal with. The tenth commandment prohibits a sin, not a crime. The tenth commandment stands apart from the others. The other nine prohibit various actions. The tenth means what it says—"You mustn't covet!"—and does not include action on impulse (Jackson 1975).

Micah's use of other verbs besides *ḥmd* shows that he views their activities as both a sin and a crime. There is no question that there is a close connection between the desire and the act, but they are not contained in the same word *ḥmd*. There are two parts to committing a crime: one is the plan involving desire and motivation and the other is the commission of the crime. The word *ḥmd* has only to do with the former, while other verbs have to be used for the latter.

fields . . . houses. The inverse of Deut 5:21. Compare Isa 5:8; Jer 32:15.

seized . . . stole. These verbs emphasize physical violence (Job 20:19); *ʿšq* connotes extortion or fraudulent action. The normal meanings of *nśʾ*, "lift," "carry," do not seem appropriate if "house" is a building. The property is appropriated and occupied, not destroyed or removed. If the "house" (household) is actually removed, it could refer to the dispossession and eviction of the man and his family. If the crime is seizure of territory (see the NOTE on *tribe* in v 3), then the victims are refugees or prisoners of war, forcibly removed.

man. There is a long-standing tradition that the several words in Hebrew generally translated "man" have distinct meanings or at least connotations, respected by biblical authors. Fine points of exegesis can then be struck. Donne (Sermon on Psalm 89:48 [March 28, 1619]): "*Ishe* signifies nothing but a *sound*, . . . *Adam* signifies nothing but *red earth*, . . . *Enosh* signifies nothing but a *wretched and miserable creature*. But *Gheber* . . . is the word always signifying a man accomplished in all excellencies, a man accompanied with all advantages." Similar distinctions are still maintained by Kosmala in *TDOT* 2:377–82, with *geber* featuring virility. The distinction is overdone. The word *geber* would naturally be associated with cognates that denote strength, and it usually refers to a mature male human. More than half of its occurrences are in poetry, where it often serves, as in Mic 2:2, as a (synonymous) parallel to *ʾîš*. Amos and Isaiah use three vocabulary items to refer to the victims of injustice as "poor"—*dal*,

ʿānî, ʾebyôn. None of these words are found in Micah. Hence Wolff (1990: 8) and others infer that the words for "man" in Mic 2:2 mean "citizen." Building on Alt's theory that there was long-standing hostility between the citizen-farmers of Judah and the city bureaucrats of Jerusalem (*KS* 3:373–81; cf. Beyerlin 1953: 57–59), the oppressors have been identified not as local rich owners of large estates, but as officials — magistrates (3:11), perhaps regional military governors appointed from Jerusalem. Behind this hostility lies a clash of values between the tradition that family estates had been distributed under the aegis of the old covenant league of tribes and the practices of Canaanite kings imitated by the rulers in Jerusalem (Mic 3:1, 9) and Samaria (Mic 6:16). Alt may have oversimplified the situation in mapping the ideological differences between Canaanite kingship and early Israelite tribalism onto the later differences in socioeconomic values between regional towns and the centralized bureaucracy. See the critique in Buccellati (1967). Dearman (1988: 45–48) is too sweeping is his rejection of Alt's work as relevant to Micah's indictment, drawing as he does on Jeremias's opinion that Mic 2:3–5 is Exilic (Jeremias 1971: 333–35) and Rudolph's interpretation of Mic 2:5 as referring to the eschatological future (Rudolph 1975: 55). The connection between divinely authorized occupation of land that could be identified as a person's estate and membership in the assembly of Yahweh, present in Micah, has old roots. Micah is not himself an "elder" (the word *zqn* does not occur in the book) or magistrate (Wolff), and his identification of the leaders as "heads" (3:1, 9, 11; compare the titles of officials in 7:3) is significant for recovering some sense of the struggle of power groups in his time. The data are elusive and cannot bear the interpretation of a class struggle a la Karl Marx. For a sober treatment of the problem in broad historical perspective see Reviv (1989).

   estate. Not a crime against the urban poor, who would not have a *naḥălâ*, but against the rural landowners.

Comment on Micah 2:2

Verse 2 is an explication of v 1. Verse 1 would be quite vague without v 2. The general notions *iniquity // evil* of v 1 are followed by the concrete details of v 2. Verse 1 shows that the actions in v 2 were premeditated and ruthless; v 2 shows that the motive was greed. Each verse traces the crimes from conception to execution. The crimes began with coveting (v 2aA). They planned them at night (v 1aA); they did them in the morning (v 1bA). In v 2 the more general verbs (*coveted, defrauded*) embrace the specific verbs (*seized, stole*). The similar design in the arrangement of the first six verbs in two sets of three shows that the seventh verb (*defrauded*) is climactic; it applies not just to v 2b, but to the whole enterprise. The opening verbs are generic; the follow-through is specific.

ḥšb	pʿl	ʿśh
		ʿšq
ḥmd	gzl	nśʾ

In terms of paragraph syntax, the series of verb forms *yaʿăśûhā . . . wĕḥāmĕdû . . . . wĕnāśāʾû . . . wĕgāzālû . . . wĕʿāšĕqû* would narrate or predict a string of actions in strict time succession. In the real world the events would not take place in the order in which they are reported. The artistic presentation is not logical. This is doubtless why LXX inverted the terms *plunder* and *oppress*. We are not acquainted with any commentary that faces up to the conundrum of the apparent use of *waw*-consecutive suffix verbs (which have future time reference in classical prose) in a "woe" oracle of denunciation and condemnation. The prophet's words are not a warning of misery as a consequence of things they might do, things they are planning to do. The speech is clearly an exposure of crimes that have been committed. We conclude that the suffix verbs are used here, as often in poetry, with their archaic constative aspectual reference. The prophet is exposing typical behavior on the part of these people on the basis of what they have done, what they will continue to do until and unless they are stopped. The choice of these verb forms then secured the combination of concrete specificity; the actions are typical and actual; they have done it, they are still doing it, and they will keep on doing it.

The prophet uses strong language to condemn these illegal seizures, but he does not give us any idea as to how they were done. There is, for instance, no suggestion in the text itself that the mechanism for the expropriation of these estates was foreclosure on the indebted by their creditors, the old story of rich versus poor (Gottwald 1979: 519). The rich have also been known to defraud one another.

Introduction to Micah 2:3

Compared with the elegance of v 2, v 3 is hardly poetic. It is a sentence or threat of divine judgment in conventional form, introduced by the standard messenger formula. It is remarkable that the speeches of Yahweh (vv 3 and 5), which also mark the climaxes of the oracle, are more like prose when the rest of the unit is poetic. This is the opposite of the general practice in ancient cultures, where the higher the rank of the speaker, the more elevated the style. The gods speak poetry. Against this background it is astonishing that most of the reported speech of Yahweh, especially in the Torah, is in the vernacular and in everyday prose. In three respects v 3 is more proselike than its surrounds. First, it does not exhibit the kind of parallelism on which modern students of Hebrew poetry set so much store; the nearest approach is the two negated verbs in v 3bA, and the first and last colons are linked by repeating *rāʿâ*. Second, the five clauses in v 3 are of very uneven length, and scholars have a hard time scanning them by beats. Verse 3aB has attracted suspicion because of its great length, and Renaud (1977: 67) expressed surprise at the positioning of the object in the final position. But the same syntax occurs in v 3bA. Allen, setting aside v 3aA as anacrusis, finds three bicolons (2 + 2, 3 + 2, 3 + 3) (1976: 285). It is artificial to put the caesura between *hammišpāḥâ* and *hazzōʾt*, which the Masoretes correctly tied together with conjunctive accents. Smith (1984: 23) sets

it out as we do, one colon for each clause, and scans 4 + 5 + 4, 3 + 4, in agreement with the Masoretic accents, except that each word in v 3bAα has an accent. By this measure, all but one of the colons are longer than the standard
three beats. The most remarkable of all is v 3bB in which each word (three of
them monosyllables!) is stressed, four beats in five syllables! One can almost
hear the slow, emphatic enunciation. There is a similar change of pace in the
long clauses in v 3aB and v 3bAα (fourteen, thirteen syllables). The third token
that v 3 is less poetic than its context is the use of three prose particles. These
were all deleted by Schwantes (1962: 59).

Having said all this, we must point out that v 3 is the centerpiece of the
whole oracle. It cannot be a later addition. There is no reason to suspect it just
because it is less poetic than the rest. Its place in the poem is an excellent illustration of the interweaving in the same prophetic composition of elements that
vary in their degree of attainment of standard poetic forms. There are no *textual* grounds (e.g., in versional variants) for questioning MT.

Just as v 1 began with an invocation, "Woe to those who . . . ," which could
imply direct address, "Woe to you who . . . ," and continuing with third-person
verbs, so v 3 begins with third-person (v 3aB) and switches to second-person
verbs.

Notes on Micah 2:3

Therefore. In a judgment oracle *lākēn* is the standard particle linking the sentence to the accusation. It is gratuitous to label the word as redactional (Lescow
1972: 50).

planning. We have already commented on the unique arrangement of the
participles and their objects in v 1—"planners of iniquity . . . doers of evil."
This language is echoed in v 3, giving the first participle the second object,
"planning . . . evil." The object is separated from the participle by *against this
tribe.* This is not the word sequence of prose; the pattern is found in poetry and
prophecy, particularly in Isaiah. Marti (1904 *ad loc.*) found the grammar substandard and deleted "against this family" as a corruption (cf. BHS), thus making the participial construction more like those in v 1 and overcoming what was
considered to be inordinate length in the colon. If the phrase is a gloss, it is very
inept, and the motivation for adding it is hard to imagine.

tribe. The phrase *ʿal-hammišpāḥâ* echoes *ʿal-miškĕbôtām* from v 1, and its abnormal placement between the participle and its object secures a chiastic pattern with *rāʿ ʿal-miškĕbôtām* in v 1. In spite of this structural appropriateness,
Renaud suspects the phrase *against this tribe* on four grounds: (1) on the syntactic grounds that the object should precede the adverb; (2) on stylistic grounds—
the expression is "prosaic" (Renaud 1977: 74); (3) because the addition of this
phrase wrongly extends to the whole community a condemnation that belongs
properly only to the group accused in v 1; (4) because the use of the same language in Amos 3:3 and Jer 8:3 betrays the hand of a deuteronomic redactor.
Against all this we argue that the peculiarities of vv 1–2, if left as they are, were

set up precisely to mesh with the peculiarities of v 3. Disturb one piece and the whole edifice collapses.

The noun *mišpāḥâ* is a kinship term, a social unit something less than a full tribe, more like a clan, a phratry (Andersen 1969a), larger than an extended family. The discussion in Gottwald (1979: 257–76, 315–23) does not sufficiently relate the terminology of earlier tribal organization to later political institutions to explain why Micah should use the term *mišpāḥâ* (apart from the sound-play on v 1) or what it would have meant to Micah's audience. In Amos 3:1 "the whole *mišpāḥâ*" refers to all Israel. Amos's choice is not motivated by sound play, and the use of this anachronistic word by two contemporary prophets cannot be an accident. In modern usage, the term "tribe" is colored by the superior attitude of civilized persons toward preliterate cultures as "tribal," and Micah's choice of this word has been thought to express contempt—"clique" (Haupt), "brood" (NEB), "breed" (JB), "crowd" (Allen), "gang" (Hillers). We cannot find any indications in the rest of the Hebrew Bible that this word had any but honorable associations. Renaud (1977: 73) rejects the pejorative connotation. If Micah intended it to be pejorative, his language is sarcastic. For the sound play, see the Note on v 1a.

The real problem in the choice of this word is that the talk seems to have moved away from condemnation of an element in Israelite society, which was guilty of social injustice against other members of that society, to condemnation of the nation as a whole. If the miscreants of vv 1–2 are a "tribe" within the larger entity, then the term is used metaphorically. We suggest rather that the usage is the same as in Amos 3:1–2, and we recognize here the distinctiveness of eighth-century prophecy. There can be no doubt that Micah, like Amos, is talking about the whole of Israel, seen as just one "family" among the nations. Has Micah changed the focus so that now he is talking about what will befall the whole nation as a result of the evils done by part of it? Or is it possible that the metaphor works the other way? Is the picture of one person seizing another's farm a figurative way of talking about one nation seizing the territory of another?

The term *qhl*, "community," is another traditional term used in v 5. Jacob was to be a *qhl* of *ʿammîm* (Gen 28:3; 48:4; cf Gen 35:11). It is the "*ḥēleq* [portion] of my people" that is to be forfeited as a result of this evil (v 4), a term for the covenanted land as a whole rather than the individual holdings of private citizens. All this terminology suggests that what is going on in vv 1–5 could be an intertribal land grab. Here the evidence of Hos 5:9–10 may be relevant.

> Ephraim shall be desolate in the day of rebuke; among the tribes of Israel have I made known that which shall surely be. The princes of Judah were like them that remove the boundary marker. I will pour out my wrath upon them like water.

The references to the "tribes of Israel" and "princes of Judah" go back to the older arrangements in the covenant league, as does the term *mišpāḥâ*, which was not much used under the monarchy (Andersen 1969a). Hosea condemns

Judah for removing the landmark, that is, for changing the border. The acts were reciprocal. Hosea reports a Judahite invasion of Israel; Isaiah (clearly in chapter 7) and Micah (in chapter 1) along with both Kings and Chronicles give more publicity to the retaliatory invasions of Judah from the north. Micah 1:14 says that Jerusalem(?) gave away "houses of Akzib" (these could be lands, compare "houses" in Mic 2:2) to the kings of Israel. Such seizure of the others' lands by both Israel and Judah in the frontier wars of the period would involve expulsion of the population as well—men (v 2b) and their wives and children (v 9) all being driven from their homes. All that is usually said about people losing their farms might still be true; but the background of Micah's indictment could be wars between Judah and Israel spoken of as intertribal. Micah 2 adds the detail that the action was deliberately planned (v 1) and ruthlessly carried out (v 2). Neither the northern nor the southern kingdoms are expressly identified or blamed. Perhaps both are guilty, both "peoples" summoned in 1:2. Verse 5 supplies another clue. The effect of the judgment will be that the individual addressed will not have anyone in the assembly of Yahweh to apportion the allotment. Here the language, like "tribe," evokes ancient memories. It was the individual tribes that received their territory by this means in the original distribution after the conquest. Here and now poetic justice decrees that those who did not respect these ancient and sacred arrangements will themselves be evicted, with no hope of resettlement.

If these crimes were committed by individual against individual, this could be done only with the connivance of the authorities—rulers, priests, prophets (chapter 3). If, as another reading, the evil is the seizure of traditional tribal territory, this would be in defiance of sacred boundaries set by oath within the league. This could only be done if some kind of legitimation was secured from the nation's spiritual guides (3:11).

evil. In 1:12 Micah said that "evil" had come down from Yahweh. Here Yahweh says that he is planning "evil" against this family. In chapter 1 the judgment is pronounced against Samaria and Jerusalem, which are distinguished. So here we have to ask if "this family" is only one of them (most likely Judah, because Jerusalem is prominent in chapter 3) or both together (Amos's usage).

from which. Literally "from there." The construction has been found to be anomalous on two counts. First, in the context, *there* seems to refer back to *evil.* The imagery requires a more concrete reference to a yoke on the neck. REB adds the word "yoke." NIV abandons the image. Second, it would make more sense to remove a yoke from the neck than the other way round. But compare the similar oddity of harnessing the chariot rather than the steed in Mic 1:13. J. M. P. Smith (*ICC* 54) eliminated *mšm* by deleting the first two letters as dittography from the preceding word and identifying the remaining *m* as the preposition "from" attached to the following noun—"which you will not remove from your neck." The objections to MT seem overly pedantic. NRSV, NJPS, and NJB accept MT. Either *šām* is being used as a general pronoun; or it hints at removal to a distant place from which there will be no escape. Compare the repeated "there" in 4:10 and in Hos 2:17; 10:11; 11:4.

you. The switch from third-person feminine singular (*this family*) to the second-person masculine plurals of v 3b is startling and problematical. This is one of the reasons why Marti, followed by BHS, recommends deleting "against this family" as a corruption. We have already pointed out that the three key words in v 3a ("plan," "family," "evil") echo words in v 1a, and one of these would be lost if "against this family" were deleted. We have also defended the use of "family" by comparing it with the near contemporary Amos 3:1. In Amos 3:2 reference to Israel as "the whole family" has second-person masculine plural pronouns throughout; Micah's usage has precedent. The second-person masculine plural forms continue into v 4, but v 5 has singular "thou" (m.).

your necks. The image of removing the neck suggests that "there" refers to the yoke of servitude. The implied yoke could be metaphorical; Jeremiah used a real yoke to mime political servitude (Jeremiah 27). Or Micah could be predicting actual slavery for these people. The obliqueness of the language makes it more sinister. In the light of Jer 27:8–12, there is no need to invert the image to removing the yoke from the neck, as proposed by Smith (*ICC ad loc.*)

upright. The word *rômâ* is *hapax legomenon*. For this reason, and because such a derivative of *rwm* is not found in Mishnaic Hebrew either, Ehrlich (1968: 276) reads *qômâ* instead. Cohen (1975) does not discuss this word, but his study of biblical *hapax legomena* is a caution against unneeded suspicion of a *hapax legomenon* as such. For the grammar see GKC §118q. It is usually interpreted as "proudly"; but in the context it refers to the bent attitude of one bearing a yoke. It thus reverses the liberation described in Lev 26:13.

time of evil. Amos 5:13 has an identical clause. Hence some scholars suspect it here in Micah and propose various changes. Precisely because it sounds like a stock expression, we are not surprised that more than one prophet uses it. Both prophets picked up the same cliché; it has the flavor of a proverb. Micah could have borrowed the phrase from Amos. The common phrase could be due to a common editor. The link that this phrase provides with the opening phrase in v 4 (*On that day*) secures continuity in the larger composition.

Introduction to Micah 2:4

Verse 4 consists of two parts. In v 4aAα–β Micah predicts that *on that day*, the *time of evil* of v 3bB, someone (the unidentified subject of *yiśśāʾ* in v 4aAα) *will raise* a *māšāl* consisting of a *mournful lamentation*. The rest of v 4 says that someone (the unidentified subject of *ʾāmar* in v 4aAγ) *said* the words that complete the verse. Renaud (1977: 68) found several voices.

4aAα–β	The prophet
4aAγ	The victims of judgment (2d pl.), the same as the accused of v 1
4aB	The prophet (or God)—*my people*
4bA	The people (1st sg.)
4bB	The victims of judgment (2d pl.)

If *'āmar* is set aside as anacrusis, the speech is a highly poetic quatrain.

4aAγ	[*'āmar*] *šādôd něšaddūnû*	[He said:] We have been utterly devastated,
4aB	*ḥēleq 'ammî yāmîr*	He has exchanged my people's portion.
4bA	*'êk yāmîš lî*	How he has removed (what is) mine!
4bB	*lěšôbēb śādênû yěḥallēq*	To the apostate he apportioned our fields.

The four colons have good poetic balance. The first one achieves a sound effect by repeating the root in the infinitive absolute, and the last colon has an echo in *our fields*. The last word *yěḥallēq* picks up the first word of the second colon. (Because of this similarity, Duhm [1911: 85] rejected v 4bB as a dittograph.) The verbs *yāmîr* // *yāmîš* link the middle colons, and both have singular "me."

If the verbs *he will raise* and *he said* have the same subject, then this quatrain can be identified as text of the proverb-lament. This is the usual reading. Once that decision has been made, the clash of prefix verb and suffix verb referring to the same situation can be addressed. One solution is simply to omit the second verb (NIV, REB), setting *'āmar* aside as "a scribal note" (Allen 1976: 285 n. 5). Another solution is to bring the verbs into line by adding to the second one *waw*(-consecutive), making it future (Ehrlich 1968: 276; NJPS), or *l-* (Wellhausen [1898: 138]; NEB), or reading an imperative (Rudolph 1975: 52—his translation, "I must speak," is based on revocalizing *'ōmar*). Even more tangential is a suggestion of Cazelles (1968: 151) that the root is *mrr*, the meaning "I am bitter."

We suggest that the time has come to take seriously the tense distinctions in the Hebrew verb forms of MT. The different time focus of the verbs indicates that there are two different situations, and two quite different utterances. It could be the same speaker, but on two quite different occasions. The first proverb-lament will be raised *on that day*, the coming day of doom announced by Yahweh in v 3. The second lament-complaint has already been uttered by the victim, complaining, "We have been utterly devastated," not rejoicing that "you have now been devastated." Given the same subject for both verbs, the most appropriate noun in the preceding text to be identified as the antecedent is the *man* who was defrauded in v 2. Grammatical cohesion between the two verbs can then be established once it is recognized that this poetic composition does not use the prose particle *'ăšer*. The one who will raise the taunt is (he who) *said* the words of the lament-complaint found in the latter part of v 4. The development is just like that anticipated in 7:10, and the poetic justice is the same in both situations.

The content of the second speech is quite unsuitable to be used as a proverbial lament uttered as a taunt against wrongdoers whose present misery is just punishment for their past misdeeds. There is precisely such a scenario in Habakkuk 2. Habakkuk 2:6 uses exactly the same language as Mic 2:4aA and what follows is a series of "woes" addressed *to the one being derided*. The lament in vv 4aAγ–4bB is quite different. The speaker identifies with those who have been devastated and complains on their behalf or even as one of them (using *us* and *our*). Hillers, however, thinks that "There is no insuperable difficulty involved in a lament *over an unfortunate* which includes direct speech of the unfortunate" (1984: 32 n. k).

The connections of v 4 with vv 1–3 are thus quite complex. Verse 4 picks up the earlier word *nś'* from v 2aB, and *šādôd* in v 4 could be a play on *śādôt* in v 2aA. The eschatological formula of v 4 links up with the "evil time" of v 3 and shows that it is the end of the story. Those wicked persons will be the objects of poetic justice. Having violated Yahweh's covenant allocation of fields and houses as *naḥălâ*, "patrimony" (v 2), they will be excluded from Yahweh's *qhl*, "assembly," where land is apportioned (v 5); and their allotments will be reassigned to their former owners (v 4). All five verses of the oracle are thus seen to be interconnected in many ways.

The lament-complaint in vv 4aAγ–4bB presents many textual difficulties. Koch (1969: 98) says that one of the two things that "can be asserted with certainty" concerning Hebrew metrics is the use of 3 + 2 beats rhythm (*qinah* meter) in laments. As a matter of fact, many laments in the Hebrew Bible, including the one in v 4, do not present 3 + 2 meter (Gillingham 1994: 53, 62–63). Since Budde, many scholars have seen their task as the restoration of the text of a lament so that it does have the mandated meter. We accept departures from 3 + 2 meter in laments as a permissible variation. The little lament in v 4 illustrates this. Apart from questions of meter, there are no textual grounds for changing it. Each colon in the quatrain in vv 4aAγ–4bB has three words. Each is accented in MT, so the beat rhythm is 3 + 3, 3 + 3 (R. L. Smith 1984: 23). By leaving out *he said* and by adjusting the accentuation of v 4bA (which has only four syllables compared with the nine in v 4bB!), Allen (1976: 285) arrives at 2 + 3, 2 + 3, which he thinks might be "a legitimate variation" of *qinah* meter. Alt (1955: 22) inverts the colons to obtain *qinah* meter.

The metrical puzzle is compounded by philological difficulties. Ehrlich's verdict (1968: 276): "The rest of the verse is dreadfully corrupt. Stade's attempt to establish here the original text is a distasteful [*unerquickliche*] exercise in composition that leads nowhere." Stade (1886: 122) was mainly concerned to recover the "expected" *qinah* meter (3 + 2). His result:

ḥēleq ʿammî yimmar baḥebel
wěʾên mēšîb
lěšôbênû śādênû yěḥullaq
šādôd něšaddūnû

Five of the original words survive. Most of the proposals in the apparatus of BHS derive from this 1886 study of Stade. Many of the difficulties are relieved when the chiastic arrangement of the four colons is appreciated. Although each of the four colons has three beats, they differ in length by syllable count. The word-play between the first and fourth colons (envelope construction) is associated with similar length (8 and 9 syllables). The two short inner colons (5 and 4 syllables) also have a little assonance, correctly perceived by Stade, but these correspondences do not warrant the shunting of two words from the first colon to the end of the piece. Duhm (1911) used similar methods, but arrived at substantially different results. For example, using the touchstone of parallelism, he rewrote v 4bA to obtain a statement closer in meaning to the preceding colon: *'ên môšāb lô*, "no dwelling place remains for him." This tradition has influenced the NJPS translation. Both move v 4aAγ to the last position, destroying the complex chiastic patterns of the original.

> My people's portion changes hands;
> How it slips away from me!
> Our field is allotted to a rebel.
> We are utterly ravaged.

The translation in NEB was based on different text-restoration strategies.

> We are utterly despoiled (= MT)
> the land of the LORD's people changes hands,
> How shall a man have power
> to restore our fields, now parcelled out?

Three different text-critical principles have been applied here. From G. R. Driver's theory that *yod* is sometimes an abbreviation for the Tetragrammaton (*yhwh*), *my people* becomes "the LORD's people." The word *ymšl*, "he will rule," is obtained from *ymyš ly*. The passive "parcelled out" is supported by LXX (Brockington 1973: 255). But LXX has a propensity for turning verbs without identified subjects into passives, four times in this verse alone!

In vv 4aAγ–4bB we can recognize the same kind of disjointed utterances as we met in 1:10–16, but on a smaller scale. There are several points of similarity between the two laments. "And" is not used. Both have bewildering alternation of pronouns, here "we," "I," "I," "we," in chiasmus (at least they are all first person). REB levels these pronouns to plural throughout.

Verse 4aA could refer backwards to the aspect of judgment described in v 3, while v 4aB could look forward to the aspect of judgment described in v 5. The property changes hands twice—first (v 2) when it is seized by the wicked ones of v 1, finally when it is reassigned (by God?) (v 5). Verse 4, in between, could either be the original complaint of the rightful owners linked with the denunciation in v 1 (and matching the lament for exiled children in 1:16); or the final lament of the usurpers, when these lands are seized or taken away from them. It depends in part on whether "that day" refers to the first or the second act of dispossession. While the content of the lament would be appropriate, more appropriate, for the original victims, "that day" has a futuristic tone. These lamenters call them "our fields," and this would be more correct for the original owners than for the usurpers, although that too is possible. It would, however, be ironical. The first switch in ownership was an act of human rapacity. The second was an act of God, poetic justice.

Notes on Micah 2:4

that day. The "time of evil" of divine punishment, a link with v 3. The standard phrase *bayyôm hahû'* occurs in 2:4; 4:6; 5:9. There are variants *yôm hahû'* (7:11) and *yôm hû'* (7:12). For the range of meanings, see Waltke and O'Connor (1990: 314). The phrase is often considered to be exilic or later, raising doubts about the authenticity of passages in which it occurs (Duhm 1902: 19). T. H. Robinson considered the phrase in Mic 2:4 to be anacrusis because it makes the colon so long (1964: 133). The terseness of the language shows that it required no further definition; it referred to "the day of the Lord," already established as a technical term, as the arguments in the book of Amos show. Lefevre (1957) studied the expression fully and concluded that its use in Isaiah's oracles was authentic. There it characteristically comes either first or last; so, when it comes in the middle of a piece, as here, it launches a new development.

he will raise. The verb could be impersonal, "one will raise," just as in Hab 2:6 (identical idiom), where the verb is plural. LXX and Vulgate have passive. It is possible, however, that the taunt will come from the former victim, rejoicing in divine retribution. The verb does not mean "compose" (Renaud 1977: 68), but "raise (the voice)."

proverb. As in Hab 2:6, it is possible that this signal instance of divine justice becomes a byword. The term *māšāl* has connotations of comparison, so it is possible that what is implied here is not the use of a lament in its true function, but with some second meaning, a taunt. The parallelism of *māšāl* and *něhî* makes these two words mutually self-defining—a lament functioning as a proverb. It is the preposition *'al,* "against," and the comparison with Hab 2:6 that suggest that this *māšāl* is a taunt. In content the speech in vv 4aγ–4bB is clearly a lament, and it can be fully explained as functioning as a true lament. A lament can function also as a complaint, but that would be addressed to God, appealing to his pity by expressions of misery as well as appealing to his justice. There are no vocatives or second-person pronouns in the text of the lament that might give a hint as to its intended audience.

mourn. The verb *nhh* occurs only twice, here and in Ezek 32:18. The latter is a lamentation for the downfall of Egypt, but in jubilation for her just punishment. The masculine noun *něhî* is used five times in Jeremiah (9:9, 17–19; 31:15) and once in Amos (5:16). The strange *mî* in Ezek 27:32 and *hî* in Ezek 2:10 could be worn down variant forms. This is the only occurrence of the feminine form *nihyâ* in the Hebrew Bible. As is often the case with such *hapax legomena,* emendations have been proposed. Budde (1919–20: 15) replaced it with *qînâ,* "dirge." Most commentators delete the word, attributing its presence to dittography. Those who retain it parse it as *nip'al* of *hyh,* "It has happened" (R. L. Smith 1984: 23). To improve the syntax, Duhm (1911: 84) changed the next word into a noun (*'ōmer*), thus eliminating the clash of verb tense and re-covering the first two colons (two words each) of the lament:

> Und man klagt die Klage:
> > erfüllt ist das Wort!
> > Wir sind vernichtet!

Carmignac (1955: 349) found the word *nihyâ* in the Qumran text 1QM XVII:5, with the meaning "lamentation." It is more likely that this word is another exam-ple of the participle (Yadin 1957: 355). No matter how this word is explained, the use of three words, each with the consonants *n-h*, in the same colon is re-markable and in keeping with similar assonance in other parts of this verse. De Moor suggested that the repetition of the root made the expression *nhy nhyh* elative—"the saddest lamentation" (1982: 163).

He said. A doubtful word. If it continues the discourse from v 4aAα, it does not fit the sequence (future would be followed by past). In Hab 2:6 the contin-uation verb is *wĕyō'mar*, which is followed by the words of the taunt. Some He-brew manuscripts have *wĕ-*. But is the subject of both verbs in Mic 2:4 the same? Whether there is one subject or two, there is a clash between the singu-lar *he said* and the plural *we* of the speech that follows. The first unidentified speaker here takes up the *māšāl against you*, and since the *you* are threatened with retribution in v 3, we suggest that the words carried by *he said* are a flash-back to the misery of the victims of the actions cataloged in vv 1 and 2. The land changes hands twice, the first time when seized from the rightful owners (vv 1–2), one of whom bewails their fate in the name of all in v 4aAγ–4bB (hence *we*), the second time when the usurpers are evicted (v 5). The original owners had legitimate grounds for complaint in lament; but the mocking proverb-lament (taunt) is to be made *on that day*, the future day of retribution. Then the original victims will deride their oppressors.

We. Verses 4aAγ–4bB have first-person pronouns, a mixture of singular and plural in chiastic sequence. Note the similar apposition of *-kem* (v 4aA) and *-kā* (v 5aA).

devastated. The form *nĕšaddūnû* is the only attested *nip'al* of this root; the vocalization is strange. Irregular roots often extend the stem with -ō- and one would have expected **nĕšaddōnû*. GKC §67u cannot explain how this variant could have arisen. We note that Micah's *'etmûl* (2:8) is a rare variant (it occurs again only in Isa 30:33) of the usual (*'e)tmôl*. This coincidence makes one wonder if the unexplained *'āmûr* in v 7 is a variant of *'āmôr*. The cognate in-finitive absolute before the verb is *qal*. This combination is not uncommon (Waltke and O'Connor 1990: §35.2.1d).

He. The last three verbs in v 4 have the same subject, and all are prefix (im-perfect[ive]) forms. The identity of that subject and the tense reference of the verbs are uncertain. Because the verbs follow a perfect (v 4aC) that bewails the devastation, we think that all the following verbs could take their tense from that lead item, at least the first one. Most translations recognize this, but they usually conceal the problem by translating all verbs by a bland present tense, so that it becomes a description of a general situation rather than an account of a concrete action. All four colons lament the forcible and unjust seizure of patrimonial estates, identified as *the ḥēleq* (portion) *of my people*. If this is the same action as the one denounced in vv 1–2, why the switch from the plural verbs (*they*) of vv 1–2 to the singulars (*he*) of v 4? The last statement (v 4bB) identifies the šôbēb as the one to whom "*he*" allotted (*ḥlq*) our fields. The identity and function of the person called šôbēb remains unclear; see the NOTE below. It could mean "apostate" as in Jer 31:22; 49:4, and this would introduce another motif unless the term is being used in a general way for the impious schemers of v 1. The allocation of (his) land was the prerogative of Yahweh. To conclude from this that Yahweh has actually allocated the land to them (the plotters of v 1), that is, Yahweh is the unnamed agent in v 4, would be going too far. If we think that the singular verbs in the latter part of v 4 are distributive for the plurals in vv 1–2, so that the agent of v 4 represents the evildoers of vv 1–2, then we shall have to introduce another participant again as the šôbēb. We prefer, by the rule of parsimony, to keep the number of players as small as possible. Only four are needed—Yahweh, the wrongdoers, their victims (both groups referred to in either singular or plural), with the prophet speaking it all, either in the persona of Yahweh or, when appropriate, in identification with the victims (v 4).

exchanged. See NOTE on Hos 4:7 in Andersen and Freedman (1980). This meaning for *yāmîr* is supported by Vulgate *commutata.* LXX suggests a *Vorlage ymd bḥbl.* The familiar confusion of *r* with *d* is not enough to account for this retrojected Hebrew variant, especially if the verb had the *plene* spelling of MT. LXX has brought v 4aB into line with v 5, where *ḥbl* occurs, but it has lost the chiastic pattern of the repeated root *ḥlq.* Furthermore, the assonance of *yāmîr* and *yāmîš* supports MT.

We suspect a technicality involving landownership and transfer, but we cannot pin it down exactly. Weil (1940: 147) emphasized the support given to this notion by Ruth 4:7. The language is cryptic. It bewails the loss of the inherited portion. The terms *ḥēleq* and *naḥălâ* (v 2bB) are near synonyms that in hendiadys mean "inherited portion." "My people's portion" could refer to the whole of the promised land as a national allocation from Yahweh in the covenant, now forfeited, rather than an individual allotment to just one member of the *people*. If v 4 is talking about the patrimony *naḥălâ*, whether of citizen or tribe, then it would not be appropriate for a usurper, whether another person or another nation, to refer to it as his *ḥēleq*. Nor could such a usurper call it "my people's portion." A good Israelite, the victim of the crime described in v 2, would have a double complaint. First, against the criminals themselves (v 1); second, against Yahweh for not safeguarding the title he had guaranteed under the covenant. The speech is emotional, and we suspect that it is disjointed. With such a cryptic and laconic poem, other verbs and better grammar would secure a more familiar Hebrew idiom and even a clearer statement. Schwantes (1962: 54, 62) accepts Stade's emendation to *yimmad*, "is measured," which requires the addition of *bḥbl*, "with the line" (drawn from v 5), to complete the idiom. The accumulation of such adjustments (revocalize, delete, add, transpose), which can be done in so many combinations, reduces the credibility (not the intelligibility) of the outcome, as convincing recovery of the true original text.

my people. Most occurrences of "my people" in the Hebrew Bible are Yahweh's references to Israel, a favored term. This usage is not exclusive. In Genesis, Judges, Ruth, and elsewhere, a person says "my people" to express ethnic solidarity. "My people" is comparatively frequent in Micah, occurring nine times in four clusters (not in the Book of Visions):

(1) 1:9 "He reached unto the gate of my people." The speaker most likely is Micah; it could be Yahweh. See the NOTE.

(2) 2:4 "The *ḥēleq* of my people." In the context of talk about the assignment of inalienable portions in the *qahal* of Yahweh and the forcible and illegal seizure of these lands, "the *ḥēleq* of my people" is the whole land as a covenant gift, and the expression sits well in Yahweh's speech, just as "my people" does in 2:8, 9. The main difficulty with this identification in v 4 is the first-person plural — "we have been utterly devastated . . . our fields" — with "my people" in between them. We have also tentatively concluded that Yahweh is the subject of the last three verbs, and so not the speaker. Here, then, a human, the victim, says "my people."

(3, 4) We are more confident in identifying 2:8–9 as words of Yahweh, and the two occurrences of "my people" in that speech conform to the more common biblical usage, Yahweh's reference to his covenant people.

(5) The identification of the speaker in 3:3 depends on the interpretation of "and I said" at the head of the chapter. See the NOTE. It could be the prophet, or Yahweh. (In some translations of 3:2, e.g., RSV, "My people" has been supplied for explication.)

(6) There is no doubt that Yahweh is the speaker in 3:5 and "my people" is standard usage.

(7, 8) In 6:3, 5, Yahweh clearly addresses Israel as "my people."

(9) Likewise "my people" in 6:16 is standard usage by Yahweh.

So, of the nine occurrences of "my people" in Micah, we are fairly confident that six (2:8, 9; 3:5; 6:3, 5, 16) are spoken by Yahweh, and this is possible also for 1:9 and 3:3. The balance seems against this in 2:4 because of the difficulty of understanding the rest of the speech as Yahweh's.

How . . . ! The exclamation *'êk* could be an independent ejaculation of grief, "Alas" (Hillers 1984: 31). It does not necessarily have to begin a lament, as in Lamentations; in 2 Sam 1:19 it begins the second colon, here the second bicolon. Perhaps this is why NIV and REB omitted it altogether. The particle is sometimes interrogative; so NEB. NJB reflects emendation to *'ên*, one of Stade's proposals. This reading is suggested by LXX *kai ouk*, and Peshitta has a negative particle. This emendation is still widely accepted (Mays 1976: 60).

removed. If the implied object is the real estate that is the topic throughout this oracle, this is the only place in the Hebrew Bible where the verb *m(w)š* has such an object. Nor is the preposition *l-* used with it anywhere else. For these and other reasons the reading has been doubted, and emendation to *mēšîb*, proposed by Stade (1886: 122), is commonly accepted. This part of Stade's reconstruction is not supported by LXX, whose entire rendition should be explained before just one bit of it is used. The strange use of *yāmîš* in v 4 matches the unusual idiom with *tāmîšû* in v 3. Each validates the other. In v 4 the victim complains that the oppressor has *removed* his property. As fit punishment the oppressors will not be able to remove their neck *from there*. The logic seems to be an indirect hint of *jus talionis* through assonance.

mine. The verb is transitive, but has no explicit object. *lî,* "to me," could be benefactive "for me." Or it could be the object, since poetry tends not to use the relative pronoun: [*'ăšer*] *lî,* "[what is] mine."

the apostate. The referential meaning of *šôbēb* in this context is unclear. This is the only occurrence of the masculine form of this word. The traditional understanding of the meaning as *apostate,* "turncoat" (NIV) assumes derivation from *š(w)b,* "return." The two other attestations in the Hebrew Bible are feminine forms, attributes of "daughter," referring to Israel (Jer 31:22) and Ammon (Jer 49:4), who turn back treacherously. Here the *šôbēb* is the one to whom Yahweh now apportions "our fields," assumed by many critics to be a foreign conqueror (Assyria?). If derived from *š(w)b,* "return," it could be a D form (*Polel*) participle that has lost its preformative *mem*. The ten or so verbs of this *binyān* in the Hebrew Bible are causative in meaning and are mainly used to describe Yahweh bringing people back from exile or captivity. The meaning is generally "restore" as in the famous Ps 23:3. This derivation does not fit *šôbēb*. The noun *šôbāb* (Isa 57:17; Jer 3:14, 22; perhaps Jer 50:6 [*ketib*]) refers to Israel "turning away" from Yahweh. It is hard to see how either meaning, "restorer" or "recusant," fits v 4. Why would such a recipient be called an "apostate" ("unthinkable" [Schwantes {1962: 63}])?

If *šôbēb* has the meaning of "apostate" it could refer to one of the kings of Israel, who turned back from Yahweh. So we are pointed once more to the background of intertribal war, as in 2 Chronicles 28. With this word as the only clue to the identity of the recipient of *our fields,* we are left with speculation. Scholars who conclude that *šôbēb* does not fit at all either delete it as a dittograph (Robinson 1954: 134) or resort to emendation. Connection with *šĕbî,* "captivity," has been surmised; and LXX *syntrimmon* has suggested *šeber,* parallel to *šdd*. The assonance in the colon would be improved by *šôdēd,* "plunderer" ("ravager" [NJPS, note]) as well as making an inclusion between the first and fourth colons of this quatrain. Another suggestion is to read *lĕšôbênû,* "to our captors" (Ps 137:3; 1 Kgs 8:46–50; and others). This assumes that the prophecy is talking about the Assyrian conquests, perhaps in hindsight.

The assumptions behind these procedures should be brought out into the open.

Assumption 1. The lament in vv 4aAγ–4bB is supposedly recited by the wicked "tribe" when they in their turn are removed from the lands that they took over fraudulently and by violence (vv 1–2) and which they improperly call *our fields*. We reject this assumption by taking seriously the past time reference of *he said*, which identifies the following words as the lament-complaint of the victim.

Assumption 2. The event of evicting the illegal occupants is the *evil* that Yahweh is planning against them. It will involve the imposition of a yoke on the neck that will prevent them from walking upright and from which they will not be able to extricate themselves. The language of war is not used anywhere in this oracle, but this reconstruction of the events matches the familiar pattern of conquest and capture.

Assumption 3. The lament of these now dispossessed ursurpers in vv 4aAγ–4bB, which they will use *on that day*, is quoted as a mocking *māšāl* by one of their former victims (the unidentified subject of *he will raise* in v 4aAα).

Assumption 4. The actions lamented in vv 4aAγ–4bB are (to be) carried out by Yahweh in punishment of those guilty of the acts described in vv 1–2. (We maintain, rather, that these words describe the action of a (typical) oppressor, lamented by the victim.)

Assumption 5. The outcome is that "my people's portion has changed hands . . . our fields he [Yahweh] (re-)allocated to the *šôbēb*." At the end of the chain of assumptions is the inference that the *šôbēb* must be the foreign conqueror. But "apostate" ("renegades" [NJPS]) is not an appropriate appellation for Assyria. Hence the need to find a more suitable term, such as "our captors." That kind of emendation is driven by knowledge of later history and by the theory that Micah is prophesying these developments (or that a later editor adjusted the wording of the prophecy to make it match its supposed fulfillment). If this was the editor's intention, we have to add the additional assumption that his work was spoiled by later copyists.

apportioned. If this part of v 4 is a lament-complaint over the injustices described in vv 1–2, the prefix verb form could be a poetic preterit. The Greek passive probably represents a pious attempt to distance God from the action and should not be used to support a repointing of the verb to *puˁal*, as commonly done.

Comment on Micah 2:4

The two verbs, *yiśśāˀ* and *ˀāmar*, apply to two distinct speakers and imply two different kinds of speech. Since no speakers are identified, it could be the same person on two different occasions, in different situations and in different moods. Another difference is indicated by the use of pronominal elements. The "lamentation" in v 4aA is to be spoken as a "proverb" "against *you*," against the wrongdoers who have been the concern of the oracle from the beginning. The complaint (1st sg.) in v 4aAγ–b was spoken by an individual ("my") who speaks on behalf of a larger group ("our").

The clue to understanding the second speech lies in recognizing the envelope construction secured by the chiastic arrangement of the first-person pronoun suffixes. The language is laconic and some details are not expressed. To paraphrase:

v 4aAγ   We have been utterly devastated
v 4bB   Our fields he (not identified) has apportioned (to a *šôbēb*)
v 4aB   The portion of my people he has exchanged (i.e., handed over to someone
         else in exchange for something else)
v 4bA   How he has removed (what was) mine (to turn it over to someone else)

We find no evidence in this oracle that it served as a call by the prophets to the peasants to rise up against their oppressive leaders (Pixley 1991; cf. Adas 1979).

Introduction to Micah 2:5

The assembly of Yahweh is a traditional term for the covenant league—a community of peoples (see the NOTE on 1:2). In the original occupation of the promised land the territory was parceled out tribe by tribe, by lot. Verse 5 predicts that Israel (or at least the wrongdoers of that generation) will never recover their lost status. This verse consists of one long clause. There is no development of poetic features, and the syntax is quite straightforward. Although none of the prose particles is used, there was probably no occasion for them, unless *mašlîk hebel* could have been *hammašlîk 'et-hahebel*. The verse is quite lacking in the one feature that critical scholars expected to find in Hebrew poetry, namely, parallelism. Add to this a belief that authentic Micah oracles must have been poetic, and this verse cannot pass muster. It must either be discarded as a later addition (Nowack) or heavily rewritten to recover some poetry from it. In view of the full treatment of problems of this kind by Renaud (1977: 77–79), we shall discuss only a selection of such proposals in the following NOTES.

Notes on Micah 2:5

Therefore. This conjunction is a link between v 3 and v 5. Either we have two matching judgment speeches, or one judgment in two installments, with the *māšāl* and lament of v 4 in between. The repetition of the word *Yahweh* constitutes an inclusion between v 3aA and v 5b, ending the unit. The awkwardness of having two judgment speeches in the same oracle is another reason for suspecting, even deleting v 5, the more so in view of its prose features. Graetz (*apud* Budde 1919–20: 6) eased the strain by changing *lākēn* to *'ākēn*, "indeed" ("Truly" [NJPS]), so that v 5 is resumptive and not a distinct judgment speech.

Assuming that the covenant violation condemned in vv 1–2 and lamented in v 4 is the eviction of one tribe by another from its allotted portion, the judgment describes the eviction of the guilty "family" from the promised land. The taunt in v 4 is the outcome of judgment, but where it comes in the development is not clear. If the arrangement is more or less chronological, there is a twofold response to the crimes of vv 1–2. The logical development would be that the victims would appeal to Yahweh (if that is the intent of the lament in v 4), and he would respond to their cry. But v 3 declares the divine response first, directly to the crimes of v 2. In vv 1–2 there is a double movement from plan to execution, first in the woe of v 1, then in the narrative of v 2. The planning (*ḥšb // ḥmd*) was followed by action (*pʿl // ʿśh* plus the three verbs in v 2). Verse 3 reports Yahweh's plan—an evil deed making it an evil time—but does not say what the plan is. Nor is its execution described. Verse 5 describes only the final result—*You will not have anyone working out the boundaries by lot in the assembly of Yahweh*. In between this plan (v 3, with *Therefore*) and the final result (v 5, also with *Therefore*) we assume some action, the violent eviction of the usurpers from the land violently seized. We have been unable to decide whether v 4 describes this phase of the development, but were inclined to attach it to the crimes of vv 1–2, for reasons given in the NOTES on v 4.

thou wilt not have. The First Commandment begins with the same words: *lōʾ-yihyeh lĕkā*. Since the oracle begins with a keyword from the tenth commandment, "covet," these words could be another echo from the same source. The singular pronoun *"thou"* contrasts with plural *"you"* in v 4 and is commonly emended to *lkm* to bring the pronouns into line. The subsequent loss of *mem* is explained by haplography. The singular pronoun is more difficult; a referent is not apparent. Both LXX and V confirm it.

working out the boundaries. Literally "casting (the) rope." The original *mašlîk* was Joshua. It is not clear just how this was done; whether the casting of lots was to settle the boundaries or, given the territories, to decide who gets what. In any case, Yahweh is the real *mašlîk* behind the human agent. He won't do that again.

by lot. This term is used more than a dozen times to refer to the mechanism of the original allocation of tribal territory. It is ironical that students of this verse, looking only for parallelism as an indication of poetry and, finding none, concluding that it is mere prose, have missed the artistic significance of this unique locution "casting rope by lot." The usual idiom is *hippîl gwrl* (*hšlyk gwrl* occurs in Josh 18:8, 10). Wellhausen inverted the word to obtain *gwrl bḥbl* (1898: 138). Budde (1919–20: 6) recovered the standard idioms and at the same time created a good bicolon (*zwei gute parallele Versglieder*) by emending to *mašlîk ḥebel // mappîl gôrāl*. As we saw with the participial phrases in v 1, Micah switches the words in familiar idioms. The primary reference of *ḥebel* is "rope" or "cord" used as a measuring line. By metonymy it can refer to an apportioned tract of land or a specified geographical region. When used alone with this meaning it is probably an abbreviation of *ḥebel naḥălâ* (Deut 32:9). The terms "lot" and "rope" are so closely associated that they are virtually synonymous when referring to the "lot" (= allotment) obtained by casting the *gwrl* or throwing the *ḥebel* (Josh 17:14). We retain Micah's unique expression as gathering together the associations of all these terms.

assembly. The *qāhāl* was the assembly where tribal boundaries were determined, tribal settlement decided, in the first place (cf. Deuteronomy 33 [especially vv 4–5, 21]). Another function of the *qāhāl* was to settle intertribal disputes. The archaic terminology for community leaders used in 3:1, 9 reminds one of the council of tribal chiefs. Micah seems to be harking back to an arrangement

earlier than the monarchy. It is true that the heaviest concentration of the word
qāhāl as such is in the Chronicler's history (43×), next to that P (19×), Ezekiel
(15×), and D (10×). Given the usual dating of D and P, this distribution has cast
doubt on the authenticity of the expression in Micah. Milgrom (1991) considers *qhl* to be late; but sporadic occurrence in archaic texts, such as Gen 49:6
and Num 22:4, suggests that the abundant use in the P-Ezekiel-Chronicler axis
is consciously archaizing. This word is only one of several traditional terms
used (anachronistically?) in Micah's oracle. Beyerlin (whose 1959 study of the
use of old traditions in Micah's preaching deserves more careful attention than
it has received in recent Micah research) endorses the opinion of Noth that the
language in v 5 and elsewhere in this oracle stems from the law of the ancient
amphictyonic league of tribes (Beyerlin 1959: 59). The soundness of Beyerlin's
observations is not diminished by second thoughts that scholars have had over
Noth's theory that the tribal confederation was an amphictyony (Mayes 1974).
Traditions about Israel's origins doubtless fed nostalgia, but they were not invented by nostalgia. It is reasoning in a circle to eliminate all such language
from the book of Micah on the grounds that the notions are postexilic. Micah's
choice of vocabulary was intended to evoke memories of earlier and better
days. The assembly in pre-monarchical Israel was a meeting of tribal "heads"
(Deut 33:5; cf. Mic 3:1, 9). "The profile of the functions of the early assembly,
sketchy as it is, points to tribes voluntarily in session ('ceremonial,' 'legislative,'
'executive,' or 'judicial' by turn) but retaining their respective autonomies"
(Gottwald 1979: 243). Gordis (1959 [1971a: 49–54]) brings out evidence that
the *qāhāl* was a public "people's assembly," not just a conclave of tribal leaders.
Gottwald seems to have overlooked this important article and has not done justice to the fact that it was Yahweh's *qāhāl*. The proceedings in Judges 20–21
show that the *qāhāl* was not only the institution in which tribal territories were
originally allocated; the assembly also had to preserve the integrity of tribal territory and adjudicate border disputes. To say that someone would not have a
mašlîk in the assembly of Yahweh suggests that that individual, or more likely
tribe, was expelled and became landless. This is not the same as reversing the
occupation completely, evicting the whole nation from the promised land. The
assembly is functioning; yet it sounds as if some details of the first apportionment will have to be worked out once more, but this time without the person
(*thou*) addressed in v 5. Can we identify this participant? The background that
we have just described points to an individual tribe, and this strengthens the
case, developed cautiously above, that the crime denounced in vv 1–3 could be
seizure of tribal territory.

In view of Beyerlin's discovery of cult practices behind Micah's language,
the distinctiveness of the expression *qhl yhwh*, in contrast with expressions in
which the *nomen rectum* is "Israel" or the like, should be given more weight.
This and 1 Chr 28:8 are the only places in the Hebrew Bible where the phrase
qhl yhwh is used outside the Pentateuch, where it occurs eight times (Num 16:3;
20:4; six times in Deut 23:2–9). The distinctiveness of the usage of Deut 23:2–9

points to preexilic technical term for a religious-cultic gathering where a decision is reached about the expulsion from the assembly of disqualified persons (*TWAT* 4:1212).

Expulsion from the *qhl yśr'l* is more appropriate for a tribe than an individual, since tribes made up the membership. Expulsion from the *qhl yhwh* is more appropriate for an individual. An excommunicated individual was "cut off from his people." If the case of Achan represents standard practice, his family shared his fate. But this was before the settlement on the land. The best-known case of unlawful eviction from property is that of Naboth the Jezreelite, who refused to sell Ahab "the *naḥălâ* of my fathers." It is also the classic case of a crime like those condemned in vv 1–2. There are indications that Naboth's family perished with him (2 Kgs 9:21–26). This detail is not found in the main account (1 Kings 21) (Andersen 1966); it could be a supplementary detail. In the matching sentence on Ahab there is no threat of removal of land from his family (or of his family from land). That comes out in Jehu's savagery. With or without some show of legality, the killing of Naboth's heirs was a necessary part of Jezebel's plot, and this gave Jehu grounds to carry out his plot with a scope matching Ahab's criminal behavior. Note that loss of both family and property are threatened against Amaziah by Amos, using terminology close to Micah's— *'admātĕkā baḥebel tĕḥullāq*, "thy land shall be divided by line" (Amos 7:17).

Where does the object of judgment (*thou*) in v 5 come in the hierarchy of social structure in Israel? As the largest possible unit we have the whole of Israel called *this tribe* in v 3 (if the usage is the same as that in Amos 3:1), but this word is feminine. The nation would then be only one of many to whom Yahweh allocated lands (Deut 32:9 has three of our key nouns—*ḥēleq*, *ḥebel*, *naḥălâ*). The Song of Moses focuses on the guilty nation as the offender. But the period of Micah does not know of total seizure of the territory of one nation by another. One thing is clear: The territory involved is "the *ḥēleq* of my people," i.e., the land of Israel. Yet it is Israel that is guilty, at least the leaders (we connect the "planners" of chapter 2 with the "rulers" of chapter 3). Coming down the hierarchy a bit, the emphasis of Joshua is on each tribe as a unit. There is not enough detail to show us how they worked out what each subtribal unit (the original meaning of *mišpāḥâ*) got. If Micah's analysis is on this level, we are dealing with intertribal war, or perhaps war between the northern and southern halves of Israel. This interpretation has most to be said for it. It fits in with what we know about attacks of one half on the other in the mid-eighth century. It provides a plausible background for Micah 1 and other passages, especially 2:8–10, which we believe can be understood best in the light of 2 Chronicles 28. At the same time the individualizing language, especially in vv 2 and 4, and the crimes against persons listed in vv 8–10, leave open the possibility that Micah is condemning injustices committed by powerful persons against fellow Israelites. The language of v 2 is appropriate for dispossession of one landowner by extortion, but it is equally suitable for describing the annexation of territory by a state and the forcible removal of the population. An individual or nation who grabs his neighbor's land will be evicted, not only from the property he has seized illegally, but also from his own. That is poetic justice, also divine justice, according to the Bible.

It might not be possible to resolve this dilemma. It depends on how Micah is using technical language. On the one hand there is the legal language of the civil courts (such as "a man and his estate" in v 2bB). The verbs *gzl* and *ʿšq* are used in the codes for private or civil crimes, but they could be metaphorical here for oppressive wars. Again, there is the language of larger political and social units (*the assembly of Yahweh*, in which members are tribes). We are more inclined to think that the language of the former can be used metaphorically for the latter, than that Micah is working with a theory that allocations of land in the assembly are made to individuals; yet the case of Naboth betrays great awareness of the family as the socioeconomic unit.

Comment on Micah 2:1-5

This unit has the components of a woe-oracle that functions as a message of doom.

1. Opening "Woe"—*hôy* (v 1aA)
2. Accusation (vv 1b-2)
3. Sentence (vv 3-5): in two parts, each introduced by *lākēn*

The first *lākēn*, followed by the messenger formula (v 3aA), describes the action of God. The second *lākēn* (v 5) describes the consequences. As usual with biblical justice, the punishment matches the crime. This correspondence is brought out in the repetition of key words:

Accusation	Sentence
evil [m.] (v 1)	evil [f.] (v 3)
fields (v 2)	fields (v 4)

The arguments from repeated vocabulary pull in opposite directions. The same word or phrase might be repeated by the original author for artistic reasons, or an expression used once might prompt a redactor or glossator to use it again. There are no criteria for choosing between these possibilities. Nor is it evident what style or vocabulary are "characteristic" of an author. A commonly used phrase, such as "on that day," is available to anyone, author or redactor. It identifies neither.

The same equivocation remains when the final text is neat, with a balanced structure of the kind now found in the text of vv 1-5, with the numerous interconnections that we have pointed out. Either the author got it right the first time, or else a poor (or damaged) product had to be tidied up by a later editor. When the same outcome can be imagined as reached by two quite different routes, and when all we have now is that final outcome, there is no way of deciding how it was arrived at. An untidy text, such as v 4, could be deliberately intended to convey a confused jumble of outcries; it could be a place where the author's skill failed; it could be the result of scribal carelessness; it could be due to a clumsy redactor. One or other of these explanations is preferred by this scholar or that. How to judge among the proposals? And what difference does it make? The original text is unrecoverable; the present text is unusable.

Renaud (1977: 71) has compared the structure and vocabulary of Mic 2:1–5 and Amos 5:7–17. Compare Stansell's detailed comparison of Mic 2:1–5 with Isa 5:8–10 (Stansell 1988: 121–31).

1. *hôy*   Restore *hôy* (cf. BHS)
2. Accusations of social injustice (vv 1–2)   Amos 5:7–10
3. First (part of) sentence with *lākēn* (v 3)   Amos 5:11
4. "For it is a time of evil" (v 3bB)   Amos 5:13b
5. Mourning (*nehî*) (v 4)   Amos 5:16–17
6. Second (part of) sentence with *lākēn* (v 5)   Amos 5:13

Both passages have the same kind of fluctuation between second and third persons. It seems to us just as plausible and less complicated to attribute this similarity to the influence of a common convention on both prophets, or to the continuation by Micah of prophetic rhetoric established by Amos, than to see in the common features the same kind of redactional intervention. Each piece is so distinctive and coherent on its own terms that the difference between author and redactor vanishes.

The structure of the whole unit can be understood once we recognize that the prophet is operating with a distinctively Israelite perception of what is needed to secure justice in a case like this. We think in terms of criminal justice that concentrates on the apprehension, conviction, and punishment of the criminal by the organs and instruments of the state. The Bible is equally if not more concerned with compensation and restitution, with securing the violated rights of the victim. The person who stole one sheep must return two sheep. One represents the stolen item; the other shows that what the thief did is now done to him. If it is a piece of land, the legitimate owner must be reinstated; the oppressor must be evicted, not only from the stolen property, but also from his own. The divine response to social injustice thus has two prongs, represented by the bifurcated structure of this oracle. After the opening "woe" (v 1), which identifies the *doers of evil*, their side of the story as violators of rights is described in v 2, with punishment threatened in v 3. This development is characterized by plural forms. The other prong goes over the situation again from the point of view of the victim, whose lament-complaint (vv 4aAγ–4bB) against his oppressor (the *he* identifiable only by what he is said to have done—*He has removed (what is) mine!*) results in the permanent exclusion of the culprit from any future land occupancy (v 5). The second prong is characterized by singular forms.

The general theme of vv 1–5 is clear. The oracle deals with the exposure, condemnation, and punishment of planners of iniquity and perpetrators of wickedness who deliberately and callously deprived people of their landholdings. Who they were, how it was done, and just what the punishment would be, are less clear.

Readers of this oracle have been puzzled by the way in which Micah uses standard terms but breaks familiar idioms. He does this so often that we must conclude that it was deliberate. We list a few conspicuous examples. The stock phrase pōʿălê-ʾāwen is split apart in v 1a. The idiom mšlyk gwrl is recast in v 5. The hendiadys ḥēleq wĕnaḥălâ is inverted and spread from v 2bB to v 4aB. The normal usage of the verb m(y)š is twisted.

One of the curious things about Micah's vocabulary is his use of terms that evoke memories of ancient institutions that no longer functioned in his day. On the one hand, the singular nouns in v 2b suggest that Micah is condemning crimes against individual citizens, one of whom is the "I" of v 4; and one representative of the oppressors is apparently identified by the distributive singular *thou* in v 5. On the other hand, the anachronistic terms *tribe* (v 3aB), ḥēleq ʿammî (4aB), and qhl yhwh (v 5b) place the matter on a collective basis. Is the image of *a man and his house* in v 2b a metaphor for "a tribe and its territory"? Was the evil the consolidation of small farms into *latifundia* (Bardtke 1971), or was it the frontier wars between Israel and Judah, especially those of the mid-eighth century? If so, the theme of Samaria and Jerusalem (1:1) continues, and chapters 1 and 2 go together. Chapter 1 shows that deep inroads were made in Judah, and captives dragged away (1:16). The *houses* of 1:14 and 2:2 could be the same—territories in the Shephelah ceded by Jerusalem as šillûḥîm, violently seized by Samaria. The ones who devise evil (2:1) are the kings of Israel (1:14), and the *heads of Jacob* and *rulers of the House of Israel* (3:1, 9) could be the rulers of both kingdoms, since Hos 5:10 equally condemns Judah for seizing territory. Israel had been plagued by frontier wars between the tribes from the beginning, especially since the disruption. They were particularly savage in the mid-eighth century (2 Chronicles 28). The language of 2:8 and 3:2–3 suggests war atrocities.

I.5. ATTACK ON PROPHETS (2:6–11)

TRANSLATION

MT

6a	ʾal-taṭṭīpû yaṭṭîpûn	"Don't [you (m. pl.)] preach!" they will preach.
6bA	lōʾ-yaṭṭīpû lāʾēlleh	They will not preach to these!
6bB	lōʾ yissag kĕlimmôt	He will not withdraw disgraces!
7aAα	heʾāmûr bêt-yaʿăqōb	Is it said, O House of Jacob,
7aAβ	hăqāṣar rûaḥ yhwh	Has the spirit of Yahweh been shortened?
7aB	ʾim-ʾēlleh maʿălālāyw	Are these his deeds?
7b	hălôʾ dĕbāray yêṭîbû	Did (will?) not my words achieve good
	ʾim hayyāšār hôlēk	to him who walks with the upright?

8aA	*wĕ'etmûl 'ammî*	And yesterday (against) my people
	lĕ'ôyēb yĕqômēm	he stood up as an enemy.
8aB	*mimmûl śalmâ 'eder tapšîṭûn*	You stripped off the cloak that covers the tunic
8bA	*mē'ōbĕrîm beṭaḥ*	from those who were passing through confidently,
8bB	*šûbê milḥāmâ*	those returning from war.
9a	*nĕšê 'ammî tĕgārĕšûn*	The wives of my people you expelled
	mibbêt ta'ănûgeyhā	(each) from her pleasant house,
9b	*mē'al 'ōlāleyhā*	(each) from her children
	tiqḥû hădārî lĕ'ôlām	you took away my honor forever.
10aA	*qûmû ûlĕkû*	Get up [2d m. pl.]! And go away [2d m. pl.]!
10aB	*kî lō'-zō't hammĕnûḥâ*	For the rest area is not [in] this place.
10b	*ba'ăbûr ṭom'â tĕḥabbēl*	Because of uncleanness (which) will destroy
	wĕhebel nimrāṣ	and grievous destruction.
11aAα	*lû-'îš hōlēk rûaḥ*	Let a man walking (in) spirit
11aAβ	*wāšeqer kizzēb*	and deceptively he lied:
11aB	*'aṭṭip lĕkā layyayin wĕlaššēkār*	"I will preach for thee for the wine and for the liquor"
11b	*wĕhāyâ maṭṭîp hā'ām hazzeh*	and he became (will be?) the preacher of this people.

LXX I.5. Attack on Prophets (2:6–11)

6a	Weep [pl.] not with tears;
6bA	and let them not weep over these things.
6bB	For he will not thrust aside (the) shame.
7aAα	He who says, "The House of Jacob
7aAβ	has angered the spirit of Kyrios."
7aB	Are these his practices?
7b	Are not his words good with him, and they have proceeded correctly.
8aA	And previously my people stood up as an enemy
8aB	against his peace. His skin they flayed
8bA	to take away hope,
8bB	the conflict of war.
9a	On account of this the leaders of my people will be expelled from their luxurious houses.
9b	Because of their evil practices they have been thrust aside.
	Draw near [pl.] to the eternal mountains!
10aA	Stand up [sg.] and go [sg.],
10aB	because this rest is not for thee because of uncleanness.
10b	You [pl.] have been destroyed with destruction.
11aAα	You [pl.] have been pursued, no one pursuing.
11aAβ	A spirit has established falsehood.
11aB	It has dripped to you as wine and intoxication.
11b	And it shall come to pass, from the dropping of this people.

Some Emendations of Micah 2:8aA

Masoretic Text:

| *wĕ'etmûl 'ammî lĕ'ôyēb yĕqômēm* | And-yesterday my-people as-an-enemy he-stood-up |

BH³; Procksch (1910):

wĕ'attā mûlî 'ammî lĕ'ôyēb mitqômēm	And thou against my people as an enemy dost arise

Schwantes (1962:55):

wĕ'attem mûl 'ammî lĕ'ôyĕbay qāmîm	And you against my people as my enemies arise

BH³; Bruno (1923: 51); Weiser (1963: 219); Wolff (1982: 40; 1990: 70):

wĕ'attem lō' 'ammî	And you are not my people;
lĕ'ammî lĕ'ôyēb tāqûmû	to my people as an enemy you stood up

Deissler (1964: 313):

wĕ'attem lō' 'ammî lĕ'ôyēb qāmîm	And you, not my people, as an enemy stand up

BHS; Mays (1976: 67):

wĕ'attem lĕ'ammî lĕ'ôyēb tāqûmû	But you! against my people you arise as an enemy

Wellhausen (1898: 138); Marti (1904: 275); Renaud (1977: 94):

wĕ'attem 'al 'ammî lĕ'ôyēb tāqûmû	But you! against my people as an enemy you arise

Duhm (1911: 85):

wĕ'attem 'al 'ammî lĕ'ôyēb wāqām [sic!]	But you! against my people as an enemy [?[1]]

Ehrlich (1912: 276); Allen (1976: 292):

wĕ'attem lĕ'ammî lĕ'ôyĕbîm qāmîm	And you against my people arise as enemies

Hillers (1984: 35):

wĕ'attem 'al 'ammî lĕ'ôyēb qāmîm	And you against my people as an enemy are standing up

INTRODUCTION TO MICAH 2:6–11

Confrontation Between Prophets

The main thrust of this oracle is clear. It documents Micah's confrontation with rival prophets. He accuses them of collaborating with the oppressors of the people, of hating the people (v 8a). The prophets are to blame for the ravaging of innocent men, women, and children, as if in war (or in actual war) (vv 8b–9). Some of the language suggests that these prophets legitimated the expulsion of people as "unclean" from "the resting place" (v 10).

The claims and counterclaims of rival prophets to be the official guides of the nation, authorized spokesmen of Yahweh, were one of the most extraordinary features of Israel's religion throughout the entire period when the "writing" prophets operated. The Hebrew Bible preserves many indications that in Israel prophet confronted prophet in religious controversy. Stories from Micaiah ben

---

[1] Duhm offered no translation or comment. Perhaps he understood "and he will rise up," that is, the oppressed people will retaliate.

Imlah versus Zedekiah ben Chenaanah (1 Kings 22), to Jeremiah versus Hananiah (Jeremiah 28) sometimes name the rival. Isaiah (28) and Hosea (4:5; 9:8) were opposed by other prophets, Amos (7:10–17) by a priest, Micah by prophet and priest (Mic 3:11) in alliance. The prophets proclaimed contradictory oracles and hurled contradictory messages at one another. The charge "venal" was countered by the charge "insane."

Both sides used the same techniques and the same forms of utterance. From the phenomenological point of view their behaviors were the same; from the formal point of view the composition of their oracles followed the same conventions. All were called simply *nābî'*, "prophet." There was no special term for "false prophet" (Jacob 1957). We are talking about prophets of Yahweh, not the devotees of any other god, such as "the prophets of Baal" in the entourage of Jezebel. By the time of Micaiah ben Imlah the context had already become an internal struggle within Yahwism. Both sides claimed that Yahweh had sent them. All spoke in his name. Each denounced the other in vicious, vile language. A common accusation was that the "false" prophets had not really been commissioned by Yahweh in his *sôd*, "conclave"; they had made up their messages out of their own mind. In fact, they had supplied favorable oracles of "peace" (Mic 3:5) in order to please their listeners. They purveyed spurious consolations of religion for personal gain, out of pure greed (3:5). They were drunks (2:11).

The phenomenon of rival prophets in the religion of Israel continues to be an object of intensive research. For recent discussions see Carroll (1976, 1981); Crenshaw (1971); Edelkoort (1948); Fohrer (1961); Fuerst (1982); Hossfeld and Meyer (1973); Jacob (1957); Jongeling (1971); Lindblom (1962: 210–15); Malchow (1980b); Manahan (1980); Meyer (1977); Osswald (1962); Overholt (1970); Rowley (1945); Sanders (1977); Sheppard (1988); Van Winkle (1989); De Vries (1978); Werblowsky (1956); van der Woude (1969).

Textual Problems

The general content of vv 6–11 is clear. When it comes to specific details, the passage is as obscure as any in the Hebrew Bible, perhaps the most obscure (Donat 1911). The text is incoherent to the point of unintelligibility. Yet all the individual words are familiar and their meanings are plain. It is on the level of composition that the arrangements are meaningless; or, rather, the meaning eludes us. In the NOTES we shall look at everything. Here we quote one example that gives the flavor of the whole. In v 11aA we have the string: *lû-'îš hōlēk rûaḥ wāšeqer kizzēb*, "let man walking spirit and-deception he-lied." These are some of the commonest words in the Hebrew language. What is the grammar, if any, that makes this more than a string of words?

We have three options. The first possibility is to recognize that the oracle was never intended to be a piece of rational discourse. Like Isaiah's cruel, disgusting, mockery of the gabble of the drunken prophets that he came up against (Isa 28:7–13), it is deliberate gibberish. The prophet is imitating their meaningless jabber. Micah 2:6–11 is the same kind of thing, and it should be left as it is.

The second option is to recognize in the present text the debris of a scribal calamity. The oracle was well crafted originally, but one or more scribes must have ruined the text by careless copying. We must now do our best to recover the original with the aid of the rules of Hebrew poetry and grammar as we understand them. This second option has driven research on vv 6–11 over the last century. The achievements of Ryssel (1887: 46–58), Wellhausen (1898), Graetz (1895), Duhm (1911), J. M. Powis Smith (1911), Ehrlich (1912), Budde (1919–20), Haupt (1919), Nowack (1922), Sellin (1930), Elliger (1934), Robinson (1954), and van der Woude (1969), to name only some of the more outstanding scholars who have tried their hand at the task of restoring the text to its pristine purity, are available. To illustrate the method and its results we reproduce the text reconstructed by Budde.

Budde's Restoration of Micah 2:6–11

Supposed glosses to be removed from MT are in "[. . .]." Altered words have single underlining. Words supposedly lost and now restored are in bold.

	Masoretic Text	*Budde's Restoration*
6.	ʾal-taṭṭīpû yaṭṭīpûn	ʾal-taṭṭīpû yaṭṭīpûn
	lōʾ-yaṭṭīpû lāʾēlleh	[lōʾ-yaṭṭīpû]
	lōʾ yissag kĕlimmôt	kāʾēlleh lōʾ yassig **kullānû** kĕlimmôt
7.	heʾāmûr bêt-yaʿăqōb	haʾumlāl bêt-yaʿăqōb
	hăqāṣar rûaḥ yhwh	hăqāṣar zĕrôaʿ yhwh
	ʾim-ʾēlleh maʿălālāyw	ʾim-ʾēlleh maʿălālāyw **lĕʿammô**
	hălôʾ dĕbāray yêṭîbû	hălôʾ dĕrākāyw yêṭîb[û]
	ʿim hayyāšār hôlēk	ʿim yiśrāʾēl
8.	wĕʾetmûl ʿammî lĕʾôyēb yĕqômēm	wĕʾûlām ʾattem lōʾ ʿammî
		kî lĕʿammî lĕʾôyēb tāqûmû
	mimmûl śalmâ ʾeder tapšîṭûn	bĕšālôm śalmâ mēʾōrēaḥ tapšîṭûn
	mēʿōbĕrîm beṭaḥ šûbê milḥāmâ	mēʿōbĕrîm beṭaḥ šĕbî milḥāmâ
9.	nĕšê ʿammî tĕgārēšûn	nĕšê ʿammî tĕgārēšûn
	mibbêt taʿănūgeyhā	mibbêt taʿănūgêhen
	mēʿal ʿōlāleyhā	mēʿal ʿōlālêhen
	tiqḥû hădārî lĕʿôlām	tiqḥû hădārî lĕʿôlām
10.	qûmû ûlĕkû	qûmû ûlĕkû
	kî lōʾ-zōʾt hammĕnûḥâ	kî lōʾ-zōʾt hammĕnûḥâ
	baʿăbûr ṭomʾâ tĕḥabbēl	baʿăbûr **mĕʾaṭ mĕʾûmâ**
	wĕḥebel nimrāṣ	**taḥbĕlû** ḥăbōl nimrāṣ
11.	lû-ʾîš hôlēk rûaḥ wāšeqer kizzēb	lû-**ʾānōkî** hôlēk rûaḥ wāšeqer
	ʾaṭṭip lĕkā layyayin wĕlaššēkār	kāzāb ʾaṭṭip [lĕkā] layyayin wĕlaššēkār
	wĕhāyâ maṭṭîp hāʿām hazzeh	**wĕʾehyeh** maṭṭîp hāʿām hazzeh

Only five of the colons in MT pass muster. Three words are deleted. Thirteen words are changed, some slightly, some extensively. Ten new words are introduced. About a dozen of Budde's proposals appear in the apparatus of BHS as "probable" readings. None of them has textual support. Several of Micah's unique expressions have been eliminated. The unique passives *'āmûr* (v 7aA) and *šûbê* (v 8bB) have been replaced by words with more attestation. Micah is not allowed to be different from other prophets. The expression "short of spirit" in v 7 has been deemed inappropriate for Yahweh (it means "short-tempered"); there is also a problem of gender, since *rûaḥ* is said to be usually feminine. The cliché "arm" has been substituted. The statement "You are not my people" has been imported into v 8 from Hos 1:9 (propagated by NEB, REB). The last phrase of v 7, "with the upright (he) walks" is deemed ungrammatical, and the idiom of Ps 73:1 permits "with Israel" to be restored (some suggest "with his people Israel"). (Ironically, the opposite emendation of "Israel" to "upright" in Ps 73:1 is widely favored [RSV, NAB, NEB, REB, NRSV]!)

The need for more bicolons and for more synonymous parallelism has been another driving force. The clash of number, gender, and person is such a hallmark of Micah's composition throughout the book that we should take it as a stamp of genuineness rather than the result of careless copying. This feature is in full flower in vv 6–11, and it is a prime target for textual emendation. In v 7 "his deeds" and "my words" clash; hence the change to "his words," even "his ways." In v 8 "he stood up" must be "you stood up" to match "you stripped." In v 9 "wives" is followed by the possessive pronoun "her" (twice!), so the pronouns must be changed to "their" (f.). The first-person verb "I shall preach" in v 11 has third-person forms before and after it; Budde rewrote the verse so that all three were first person.

One detail in MT that is almost universally declared to be "impossible" is the collocation of the adverb *'etmûl*, which refers to past time ("yesterday," "previously") with a prefix verb, whose salient reference is supposedly to future time. In an ingenious emendation the adverb is divided into *'tm* and *wl*, with various other adjustments. If, however, instead of permitting the supposed future reference of the verb to cancel the adverb with its past reference, the adverb is taken seriously, the adverb marks the text as a narrative of events in past time, and the verbs have to be brought into line with that. In other words, we have in vv 8–9 some more examples of the poetic use of prefix verbs with their archaic past time reference. And so we translate them.

The other scholars whose names are listed above use the same methodology as Budde, to arrive at results similar in rationale, but widely differing in detail. The diversity of these preferred solutions suggests that the quest for the historical words of Micah is hopeless. There are no controls for testing which "restoration" is most likely to be a recovery of Micah's original oracle, or even an approximation to it. Intelligibility alone cannot decide.

The Structure of Micah 2:6–11

We would like to try our hand at a third option. We shall do our best to make sense of the text as it is. This will not often be possible. Then we shall accept the limitations of our methodology. We shall refrain from using our guesses as to the meaning of the text as a guide to rewriting the text so that it validates those guesses. We shall face up to the possibility that this oracle, like so many other passages in the book of Micah, has an ineluctable unintelligibility that is partly due to our ignorance of the situation and our limited understanding of Hebrew, but that may be partly due to a studied incoherence in Micah's compositional style. We already came to such a conclusion in the case of 1:10–16. In 2:6–11 we have more of the same.

The use of the *hip'il htyp* three times in v 6 and twice in v 11 is an inclusion that provides a clue to the introverted structure of the oracle. There are five constituent units, each in a different mode. The first two and the last two form blocks of size similar to the size of the center unit.

Confrontation of prophets (v 6)	20 syllables
Questions (v 7)	32 syllables [52 syllables]
Narrative (vv 8–9)	56 syllables
Commands (v 10)	24 syllables
Confrontation of prophets (v 11)	27 syllables [51 syllables]

The distinctiveness of the narrative material at the center of the oracle and the almost exact balance in syllable length of the block before and the block after support the conclusion that the events reported in vv 8–9 are the subject of the altercation that is going on in the preceding and following material. The prominence of the verbal root *ytp* in the opening and closing bicolons shows that the situation involved a struggle between two groups (the verbs in vv 6a and 6bA are plural). Neither group is identified, except by what may be inferred from the content of the oracle. One group (the subject of the verb *yaṭṭîpûn*) preaches (or prophesies) to the other group (the subject of the verb *taṭṭipû*), telling them not to preach (or prophesy). It is of great value in understanding the peculiar use of this verb in this way to observe that the only other occurrence of the verb in the prophetic writings is in Amos 7:16. Amos quotes Amaziah as having said to him:

> *lōʾ tinnābēʾ ʿal-yiśrāʾēl // wĕlōʾ taṭṭîp ʿal-bêt yiśḥāq*
>
> You will not prophesy against Israel // and you will not preach against the house of Isaac!

The parallelism confirms that the meaning of *taṭṭîp* in a similar context of disapproval and prohibition is "prophesy." We note also the similar use of *lōʾ*, "not," for prohibition. We have every reason to suppose that Micah's situation was similar to that of Amos, especially when we add the details found in Mic 3:5–8 and the evidence of 3:11 that the priests and prophets were in collusion. Amaziah ordered Amos to leave the shrine at Bethel (Amos 7:12), using a double imperative. In Mic 2:10 there are two imperatives (both pl.) that order a rejected group to get up and go away, completing the prohibition of v 6—assuming that the two groups are the same, which is not at all clear and which might be impossible to prove.

As a further indication that vv 10–11 are a counterpoise to vv 6–7 and that all four verses are dealing with the same situation we point out that the noun "spirit" and the participle "walk(ing)" occur in v 7 and are repeated in chiasmus in v 11. This kind of structural pattern shows that we are dealing with a unified composition, and we are obliged to look for some kind of common reference for these words. Budde threw away this clue when he eliminated both these key words from v 7.

The switch of grammatical person from second to third in v 6a is generally recognized as an indication that the first two words are reported direct speech and that the second verb is the quotative verb, repeating the root instead of using the usual "say." The mix of third and first persons in v 11 can be explained in the same way. The words in v 11aB — "I will preach for thee for the wine and for the liquor" — are the reported speech of the "man of the spirit" who "walks," not "with the upright one," as in v 7, but somehow with "a deception and a lie." Verse 11b is the final comment on such a person. So we have reported speeches, albeit not very clearly identified as such, and with no identification of the speakers. The participle "said" in v 7aAα is another indication that a saying is being queried in that context. The identification of that saying is problematical; we shall address that problem in the NOTES on v 7. Here we make the preliminary observation that the oracle reports speeches made in an argument. In order to sort out that argument, to keep track of the speakers, and to distinguish the speeches from the narrative that carries them, we shall pay the closest attention to all the different pronouns that are used, trying to make sense out of them rather than changing them in order to make sense.

NOTES AND COMMENTS

Introduction to Micah 2:6

Micah built this oracle on the *hipʿil* stem of the verb root *ytp*. It occurs three times in v 6, twice in v 11. The overall structure of the oracle, embraced by this inclusion, suggests that together v 6 and v 11 constitute a single thematic unit, separated by the other material but connected with it in some way. It is hard for us to work out the logical connections between one clause and the next for lack of the usual grammatical signals, that is, conjunctions. The "and" at the beginning of v 8 marks the onset of the narrative portion. The only other clause that begins with "and" is the last one in the oracle (v 11b). The three clauses in v 6 begin with a negative particle; the four questions in v 7 begin with an interrogative particle. Without the aid of conjunctions, we do not know which of these clauses should be paired.

The three clauses in v 6 seem to be completely disjointed. The first clause (v 6a) reports that "They preached, 'Don't preach!'" The second says, "They did not (or will not) preach to these." Is v 6bA a continuation of the speech reported in v 6a, continued in the same mood, so that the verb has to be construed as jussive, in spite of the use of *lō'* rather than *'al*? So NJPS. If so, who is the "you" spoken *to* in v 6a, and the "they" spoken *about* in v 6bA? NRSV makes the second clause parallel to the speech in the first colon by taking "they" to be impersonal: "One should not preach of such things" (cf. R. L. Smith). Again, the repeated verbs (identical except for the *nun*) could have the same subject, so we have an adversative sentence: "They preach, 'Don't preach!' (but) they do not preach to these." Allen says that "[t]he subject is naturally to be taken as the same as that of the preceding verb" (1976: 292 n. 38) and paraphrases: "They should stop preaching in this vein." This makes it a comment of the author, prohibiting the prohibition. REB accepts the continuity of subject, but makes the colon a question: "But do not they hold forth about these things?"

What was the subject matter of this prophesying by one group that another group wanted to ban? The only clue is afforded by the complement *lā'ēlleh*. In v 11 the same verb has two complements with *l-*, one for the indirect object (*to thee*), one, apparently, for the subject matter ("concerning the wine and the liquor"). Which of these functions does *l-* in v 6 have? Compare Budde's suggestion (1919–20: 9) that "these" in v 6 is a cataphoric reference to "wine and liquor" in v 11, *l-* having the same function in each place. *These* is repeated in v 7, and it is best to give both occurrences the same reference, if at all possible. A matter for disagreement between the two opposing factions was whether *these* are *his ways* (clearly Yahweh's) or not. The forbidden preaching is an unacceptable or questionable identification of certain happenings (*these*) as the ways of Yahweh. In vv 1–5 there was an announcement that the people who had seized land by violence would be expelled from Yahweh's assembly, a message clearly contrary to the message of another group of prophets reported in 3:11 — "Isn't Yahweh in our midst? No evil can befall us." The "ways" of Yahweh were to keep the people safe in the land; it was blasphemy to suggest that he could ever eject them from it. There must be no more preaching along the lines of vv 1–5. *These* in vv 6 and 7 refers back to the preceding oracle. Two of the motifs in vv 1–5, removing people from their homes and treating them as war captives, reappear in vv 8–9. The collocation of women and "her house" in v 9 echoes the man and his house in v 2. Haupt (1910) recognized these similarities and reconstructed the original "elegy" consisting of 2:1, 2, 8, 9, 3, 4, and 1:8a. Needless to say, extensive emendation was required besides moving the pieces around. We see no need for that, but we recognize the validity of his insight into the affinities among the oracles in the Book of Doom.

Notes on Micah 2:6

preach. The *hip'il ytyp*, used three times in this verse and twice more in v 11, means "drip." The cognate nouns refer to drops of water (Job 36:27) or drizzle or incense gum (Exod 30:34). The use of the verb in Job 29:22 shows that words may drop like rain or dew in an altogether beneficent way (compare Deut 32:2 — same image, but not this verb, and Joel 4:18). There does not seem to be any difference between the meaning of *qal* and *hip'il*. Compare *yiṭṭĕpû hehārîm ʿāsîs*, "the mountains will drip new wine" (Joel 4:18) and *wĕhiṭṭîpû hehārîm ʿāsîs* (Amos 9:13). In all occurrences of the *hipʿil* except Amos 9:13 it is used intransitively with the meaning "prophesy." In Amos 7:16, Ezek 21:2, 7, it is in parallel with *hinnābēʾ*. While the former could be opprobrious (Amaziah's expulsion of Amos) the latter are respectable (Yahweh's command to Ezekiel). So the connotation in Micah is undetermined, and the nuance of "rant" or "dribble" in frenzy is not called for, unless by inference from the mere fact that Micah does not use the verb *nbʾ*. Ancient versions (Greek, Syriac) understood the verb to mean "shed tears."

With *qal* transitive and *hipʿil* mostly intransitive, the usual relationship between these two stem forms from a common root is inverted; *hipʿil* is usually a transitivized form. It is hard to see what the cognate object of an internal *hipʿil* would be; it may well be emphatic or intensive, but that does not help to determine its connotation. Micah is playing a tune on this word that we can no longer hear.

In an established metaphor the verb can describe the distillation of words from the lips, sweet as honey (Cant 4:11), fragrant as myrrh (Cant 5:13). This usage is morally neutral. The words thus dispensed can be beneficial (Job 29:22)—they do good (Mic 2:7b)—or deceptively seductive (Prov 5:3). In the pejorative sense the verb could describe a prophet as dribbling or driveling, like a slobbering madman with his drool running down his beard like David in the court of Achish (1 Sam 21:14).

They will not preach. The switch from second to third person in the two parts of the speech is confirmed by LXX: *mē klaiete . . . mēde dakryetōsan*, interpreting the distillation of drops as the shedding of tears. With two almost identical verb forms in close succession, one of them is often deleted as a duplicate of the other (e.g., Budde 1919–20: 8). Lindblom (1929: 59) changed both verbs to *haṭṭēp taṭṭîpû*, recasting the whole construction. It is unusual in Biblical Hebrew for a quotation formula ("he said," or the like) to come in the middle of reported direct speech. Genesis 3:3 is a rare example. Reported speech normally follows the verb. In v 6a the quotation precedes the verb and presumably continues after it. This is why v 6b is often considered to be a continuation of the one and only speech (RSV, NJPS). Mays (1976: 66) continues the speech through v 7. But some (NEB) make only the first two words the speech. The change to third person in v 6b favors this, for it reads like narrative. RSV and NRSV put two prohibitions in parallel:

Do not preach . . .

One should not preach.

The different negative particle suggests a change to indicative mood: *They will not preach.* The verb forms are not quite identical. The nunation on the first verb could be due to nothing more than its pausal position (Muraoka 1991: 137; cf. vv 8aB, 9a). If its function is grammatical, it could mark the difference between indicative mood in v 6a and jussive in v 6bA (Muraoka 1975; Hoftijzer

1985; see also Aristar 1987), notwithstanding the use of the indicative negative particle. In disagreement with previous studies that connected this suffix with Arabic energic forms, Rainey (1986: 12) showed its affinity with the Old Canaanite indicative energic. In this respect also Micah's usage is archaic and not merely an artistic flourish. If all the surrounding words are uttered by the unidentified subject of *yaṭṭîpû*, then there is a change in the direction of their attention. After directly addressing some (unidentified) group and telling them not to prophesy, these counterprophets either switch to a new audience, while still speaking *about* the same group of prophets ("They will not prophesy"); or, still speaking *to* the same prophets, they state concerning another group again: "They will not prophesy." With these three verbs, there could be three subjects (three groups of prophets), but this is rather crowding the stage.

these. The difficulties presented by this word were ingeniously solved by Sellin (1929: 320), who revocalized to *lěʾālâ*, "about a curse." After a verb of speaking the preposition *l-* would usually mark the indirect object, "to these [persons]." No referent for the demonstrative pronoun is identified. In v 11aB the same verb is followed by two complements with *l-*, one for the indirect object, one for the subject matter. There was no need on the grounds of idiom for Budde to change *l* to *k*. The same idiom occurs in v 11; the same verb is used with the same preposition, only there the nouns refer to material substances, wine and liquor. If v 6bA has the second of the complements in v 11, it means "of such things" (RSV). This was already the understanding of LXX: *epi autois*. In the immediate situation the pronoun *these* could refer to what these prophets have just been prophesying about, things they are now told not to prophesy about. The immediate listeners would know what the speaker was referring to. When such a moment is written up as literature, readers who were not there at the time would have to be told what *these* referred to. Mere literal transcription of the actual dialogue would be unsuccessful reporting. Since the editor did not supply help of this kind, he evidently assumed that the intended readers, like the original audience for the message, understood what *these* referred to.

As with our study of *this* in 1:8, English usage hides from us the fact that the Hebrew demonstratives "this" and "these" can refer backward (when we use "that," "those") as well as forward. The opposing prophets are saying that "they" (prophets with Micah's outlook) "will not" (or "should not" [RSV]) preach about the matters dealt with so far in Mic 1:2–2:5, or about the people accused in 2:1–5.

In his study of this passage van der Woude (1969) found disagreement not so much over subject matter as over ideology (*theologumena*), not the topics— current events and problems—but the analysis and commentary on the prevailing situation that splits the prophets into opposing camps. Against Micah's announcement that Yahweh is planning evil against this tribe (2:3), they assert, "He will not withdraw" (v 6bB). This is the false message of "Peace!" proclaimed by the prophets "who lead my people astray" (3:5). The repetition of "these" in v 7 suggests that *these* refers in both its occurrences to the judgments of God announced in 2:3, 5. See Strydom (1986) for a critique of van der Woude.

withdraw. The meaning of v 6bB is quite obscure. There is no subject for the verb *yissag,* "he will depart (or departed)," available in the immediate vicinity. The noun *kĕlimmôt* (f. pl.) is not eligible, unless the number and gender of one word or the other are adjusted. Emendation of the verb to *taśśîgēnû,* "reproach will not overtake us," or the like is commonly recommended (cf. Allen 1976: 292; NJPS; NJB). There does not seem to be any nearby noun that could be the subject of the verb. If this colon (v 6bB) continues the preceding speech and so is part of the object of the verb *they preach* in v 6a, then it is the counterstatement. "What you have been preaching about these things (saying that Yahweh will bring evil) is not true; on the contrary, we know that we will come to no harm because Yahweh is in our midst" (3:11), so we shall not experience *shame.* If, however, v 6bB is the object of the verb *they preach* in v 6bA, it is the message "about these things" that they must no longer preach. The first solution is better. It is possible to make sense of v 6bB as a typical false prophecy of "peace." We cannot make sense of it as part of Micah's preaching.

The verb *yissag, he will behave recreantly,* has been found unsuitable by many scholars. Because *yissag* does not seem to supply any workable meaning, emendation to *yaśśîgēnû* or the like is widely recommended. The idiom in Isa 59:9 is sometimes referred to. This assumes confusion of *śin* with *samek,* as well as other changes. This verb, root *nśg,* means "overtake," often with hostile intention. The third-person masculine singular verb does not agree with the feminine plural noun *kĕlimmôt* as the subject. Both the subject *rā',* "evil," and the object "us" can be supplied after the analogy of 3:11bB. These are extensive changes, and the neatness of the result is not a proof that it is correct.

Every step in studying *yissag* is uncertain. If the root is *swg,* then *yissag* is neither a regular *qal,* which would be *yāsôg,* nor a regular *nip'al,* which would be *yissôg.* The *hip'il* also is attested; an apparent jussive *tassēg* occurs in Mic 6:14. Reider (1954: 280) attempted to secure closer synonymous parallelism between v 6bA and v 6bB and found the needed meanings for the vocabulary of v 6bB in Arabic roots. Standard lexicons, such as BDB, find in the root *klm* only the meaning "humiliate," "humiliation." Reider proposed *kālām,* "speech," and *nsg,* "forge," both available from Arabic, to obtain "they shall not forge speeches." To achieve complete parallelism it is necessary also to make the verb plural. There is no need for such changes (see Barr 1968: 15).

Another option for resolving the clash of number and gender between the verb and the noun in v 6bB is to look for a connection of v 6bB with v 7aA, rather than within v 6. This is usually achieved only with the aid of emendation, which can be extensive. See the following NOTE.

disgraces. The understanding of the third colon in v 6 is hampered by the feminine plural noun *kĕlimmôt,* which cannot be the subject of the masculine singular verb. If "shame(s)" is the subject, the verb must be made feminine and both either singular or plural—"reproaches do not depart" (BDB 691a) or "reproaches will not come to pass" (Hillers 1984: 34). MT can be retained once it is recognized that the noun is adverbial "(causing us) shame." Perhaps the noun is instrumental. Whoever it is that speaks the words is saying that the subject of the verb *yissag* will not be deterred "by reproaches."

Prepositions and other particles are often omitted in this kind of laconic oracular poetry. In Isa 30:3 the singular *kĕlimmâ* refers to the embarrassment of those who trust in Egypt but who are let down when Egypt doesn't deliver on her promises. The analogy here would be that Yahweh will never cause such shameful feelings by deserting his people. *Kĕlimmût* (Jer 23:40) is a possible reading here. It records the outcome when human ambition is thwarted by divine judgment. To say that God would not prove renegade was one of the popular prophecies that people loved to hear. The orthodox considered it to be a fixed truth. The genuine prophets considered it to be contingent; under certain circumstances it would not hold. Yahweh behaved towards people in the way they behaved towards him, or—and this is important—he treated them the way they treated their fellow humans, so v 6bB is a proposition that God will not let us down, causing "disgraces," no matter what. It is thus a doctrine that Micah would disown. Verse 6bB can then be identified as something said by his opponents in contradiction to his prophecies of judgment and doom.

It is regrettable that the contribution of the word *klmwt* to the oracle eludes us. Hebrew words based on the root *klm* refer to shame felt, not secretly, but in sight of others, so "disgrace" is part of the notion. It does not have an active reference to the means of inducing shame. The root *b(w)š* supplies synonyms (noun and verb) that are often used in parallelism with derivatives of *klm*. Shaming a wrongdoer as an instrument of social control was characteristic of Israelite society (Bechtel 1991). Micah expects his enemies, the prophets (3:7), and Zion's enemies, the nations (7:16), to be shamed and ashamed (7:10). Perhaps v 6bB implies that their conduct at that stage was blatant, shameless.

Comment on Micah 2:6

To interpret v 6, the best working hypothesis is that one group of prophets is trying to silence another group. We could label them the "true" and the "false" prophets, but the Hebrew Bible does not supply this terminology. Prophecies, not prophets, are labeled *šeqer kizzēb*, *deception he lied* (v 11aAβ: the grammar is opaque, but the meaning of each word is clear). Each faction accused the other of that; either group could have issued the ban in v 6a. "Don't you prophesy!" The book of Amos reports that the priest Amaziah used the same language when ordering Amos out of Bethel. We can picture that dramatic situation. We have a location—the famous national shrine and royal chapel—and we have names—Amaziah versus Amos. Here we have no background, no named *dramatis personae*.

We can assume that Micah reports this incident because the ban was aimed at him. Yet the verbs are plural, prophets versus prophets. Micah is seen as one of many, sees himself as one of many, in a line, if not in a group. Van der Woude suggests that the plural includes Micah's "supporters" (1969: 247). There are no indications that the classical prophets functioned in teams. Amos, too—another loner—knew that he was in a succession. Ever since Yahweh began to raise up prophets and Nazirites they have been making the Nazirites break their vows and saying to the prophets, "You (pl.) stop prophesying!" (Amos 2:11–12).

In all the biblical accounts of confrontations between rival prophets we have only one side of the story, the side that was eventually recognized as "canonical." In the case of Amaziah versus Amos, where they hurled words at each other and quoted each other, we cannot be sure that they were careful to quote each other exactly. Amos quotes Amaziah as telling him not to "drip" (Amos 7:16). This verb does not occur in Amaziah's actual speech as reported in Amos 7:13. In other words, the root *nṭp* is not used in eighth-century contexts to refer to prophecy with approval.

Micah's situation is somewhat different from that of Amos. Amos's antagonist was a priest. Micah's enemies are other prophets (in collusion with priests, according to 3:11). When, according to Micah, they say to him and to any other prophets who follow his line, "You (pl.) stop dripping!" Micah reports their speech by using the same verb to describe what *they* are doing. They claim to speak with prophetic authority when they tell him to stop dripping, but they are the ones who are dripping when they say that.

Introduction to Micah 2:7

This verse contains four questions. The first one asks the *House of Jacob* if it is a fact that something has been said. We expect this alleged saying, the object of the first question, to be identifiable as the grammatical subject of the passive participle *ʾāmûr, is said*. Because of the difficulty of finding a subject for *is said*, and because this is the only attestation of that participle in the Hebrew Bible, v 7aAα is widely rejected as impossible as it stands, and various proposals have been made to render it meaningful. We shall look at some of these suggestions in the NOTE.

Whatever the status of the first question in v 7, the import of the following three questions is clear. These questions come in two bicolons. The first bicolon (vv 7aAβ–7aB) is a pair of correlative questions with the usual sequence of interrogative particles *h-* . . . *ʾim*. The second bicolon (v 7b) is one long question. The questions in the first bicolon concern *the spirit of Yahweh* and *his deeds*. We seem to be in the middle of a theological controversy. The questions do not expect answers. They are not requests for information. They are rhetorical. They are intended to cast doubt. They are tantamount to denial. Someone has said that the spirit of Yahweh is short (Yahweh's patience is exhausted [Hillers 1984: 34]). Someone has said that *these* are his deeds. *These* in v 7 links back through *these* in v 6 (apparently the subject matter of politically incorrect prophecy), and we have argued that *these* in both occurrences has the same referent, the preceding oracles, especially 2:1–5. The threat of impending judgment in 2:3 implies that Yahweh's patience is exhausted. The threat of permanent exclusion from the *qhl* of Yahweh (2:5) implies *deeds* of Yahweh quite out of character. Such prophecies contradict the long-held creed, central to Israel's faith, that Yahweh is slow to get angry (in fact, his *ḥesed* lasts for ever) and that the boon of occupancy of the covenanted land is permanent. The two questions in this bicolon are closely related. As a rejection of Micah's declarations, they continue the polemics of v 6. His rivals not only forbid prophets such as Micah to prophesy any more; they also refute what he has said. As Amaziah said concerning Amos, "The land is not able to bear all his words" (Amos 7:10).

The question in v 7b sounds like a rebuttal of these charges. We infer that Micah begins to deliver his own speech, his response, in v 7b. Far from being subversive to faith and injurious to national well-being, Micah insists that his words "do good." But only to the upright, or the one who walks *with the upright*. He then goes on the attack, showing that his hearers do not meet this requirement because they are guilty of terrible atrocities committed against *my people* (v 9a). At least this seems to be the general thrust of the discourse. When it comes to details, many philological problems have to be addressed. This will be done in the following NOTES.

No protagonists are identified, unless the "House of Jacob" is addressed in v 7. But who is that? See the NOTE on 1:5. The point in controversy is which faction is speaking the true word of Yahweh. It is taken for granted that the words of God are beneficial, so v 7b could suitably be spoken by Yahweh, although a prophet defending himself could say the same thing. Since Micah is here defending himself, and none of the material is identified as direct speech of Yahweh, it is quite in order to identify v 7b as Micah's *apologia*. The language used about prophets (drunks and liars) and their activity in v 11 is insulting and represents the second stage of Micah's rebuttal. In v 6 his rivals try to silence him; in v 7a they attack his theology. In v 7b he defends his words; in vv 8–9 he attacks their deeds; in v 11 he exposes the fraudulence of their prophesying.

Notes on Micah 2:7

Is it said. This verse contains several questions. Assuming the first *h-* is interrogative (on the pointing see GKC §100n), the House of Jacob is asked whether it is true that certain questions are being asked. There are three formal questions in the remainder of v 7. All three could be the object of the inquiry of the House of Jacob, at least the first two. The change to first person in v 7b convinces us that the inquiry addressed to the House of Jacob consists of the two parallel questions in vv 7aAβ–7aB. These questions to the House of Jacob are carried by the usual sequence *ha-* . . . *'im*. This has attracted suspicion to the sequence *ha-* . . . *'im* in v 7b, inviting emendation of the preposition to interrogative *'im*, thus securing another double question. We reject this proposal, not only because it requires additional emendations to shore up the change from preposition to the interrogative conjunction, but also because it is influenced by a wrong expectation that everything should be arranged in bicolons, as in BHS's display, and that there should be synonymous parallelism between the particles.

The uniqueness of the participle form attracts suspicion. Ewald (1836: 283) interpreted *h'mwr* as "an indignant exclamation" — *O dictum!* A minimal change achieves *he'ārûr*, "Is the house of Jacob cursed?" (attributed to Sellin by Hillers [1984: 35 n. e]; originated by Klostermann, according to Allen [1976: 292 — undocumented and unconfirmed; we have traced it back to Richter [1914], *via* Budde [1919–20: 7], favored by Mays); or *hămû'ār* (same consonants), same meaning (originated by Driver *JTS* 39 [1938]: 266, favored by Schwantes [1966: 62]). Van der Woude (1969: 247), taking a cue from the unique *hip'il* of Deut 26:18, reads *he'ĕmîr*, "the house of Jacob affirmed" (or perhaps with Yahweh as subject), favored by Allen. The last proposal seems improbable. Van der Woude seems to have been influenced by his belief that covenant theology and Zion theology were the stock-in-trade of the false prophets. In Deut 26:17–18 this technical use of the *hip'il* has an object that shows that it means "made covenant declarations." This meaning would deprive the verb here of its obvious object, the rest of v 7a. Hillers (1984: 35 n. e) prefers *'āmar*. LXX has *ho legōn*, as if from *h'mr*, read as *hā'ōmēr*. This would not necessarily point to a Hebrew *Vorlage h'wmr*, as inferred by Powis Smith (*ad loc.*). (In any case the vowel letter probably would not have been used in Micah's day; the spelling of word-internal *û* with *waw* begins to appear in the inscriptions only at the end of the eighth century.) LXX confirms MT. The scribe who added the vowel letter *waw* to the originally neutral *defective* spelling must have done it deliberately to secure the unique pronunciation of the passive participle. This passive of *qal* may be unique, and normally the *nip'al* is used for impersonal "it is said," but v 7aA makes sense — "Is it said (to you, or generally), O House of Jacob?"

The use of the divine or heavenly passive to refer indirectly to actions of the deity is well known in later Hebrew. Whether the usage was already in vogue in the time of Micah is not established. Early Hebrew writings betray no anxiety over using the name of God as the subject of an active verb. Whatever the motivation, Micah has many verbs that have no identifiable subjects. Since the dispute in Micah 2:6–11 is over prophecy, and who is delivering the genuine word of Yahweh, the place in the argumentation of the questions in v 7 depends on who is asking them — Micah or his rivals? Further uncertainty is introduced by the rhetorical nature of the questions. Are they intended to invoke positive or negative answers? "Is the spirit of Yahweh impatient [or *impotent*], or are these his doings?" Yes or no? By the question that begins the series, the prophet is saying that no one has posed the rhetorical question about the power of God and that those are the things that the false prophets mentioned in v 6 should be preaching about, if they were real prophets.

spirit of Yahweh. For the theology, see Dreytza (1990).

House. In 1:5; 3:1 "Jacob" // "House of Israel." In 3:9 "House of Jacob" // "House of Israel."

shortened. The colon has support from earlier tradition, including the Vulgate. But LXX has *parōrgisen*, "angered." This Greek verb translates several Hebrew verbs, most commonly *k's*, twice *kṣr*, which is closer to MT *qṣr*. Hillers is unwilling to retroject LXX to *hiqṣîp*, favored by some critics, claiming that the

Greek translation was "suggested by the context" (1984: 35 n. f), but not supplying any arguments to support this claim. Normally *nepeš*, *rûaḥ*, or *yād* is the subject of the verb *qṣr*. Here, then, "spirit" is masculine. This gender for *rûaḥ* is not as uncommon as works of reference suggest.

The collocation of derivatives of the roots *'rk*, "long," or *qṣr*, "short," with various nouns (mainly names of body organs) supplies Hebrew with various fixed expressions for describing temperaments. The most celebrated of these is the divine attribute *'erek 'appayim*, in paraphrase "it takes a long time for God to get really angry" (Exod 34:6; Num 14:18; Jon 4:2; Nah 1:3; Pss 86:15; 103:8; 145:8; Neh 9:17). The word *'erek* can refer to physical length (Ezek 17:3) as well as temporal duration. The antonym *qṣr* likewise can refer to either time or physical dimension. Man is short-lived (*qĕṣar yāmîm* [Job 14:1]; cf. Prov 10:27). With reference to body organs, *qṣr* connotes a diminution in strength, not in size. The *qiṣrê-yād* are "enfeebled" (2 Kgs 19:26 = Isa 37:27). The question *hăyad yhwh yiqṣār* means "Has Yahweh's hand become enfeebled" (Num 11:23; cf. Isa 50:2; 59:1 [where the opposite is *kōaḥ*]).

In contrast to *'erek 'appayim*, *qĕṣar 'appayim* means short- or quick-tempered (Prov 14:17), and in Prov 14:29 the expression is *qĕṣar-rûaḥ*. There is considerable overlap in reference between *nepeš* and *rûaḥ* and sometimes the phrase *qĕṣar-rûaḥ* or *qĕṣar-nepeš* refers, not to impatience (that might be expressed in an emotional outburst), but to mental exhaustion due to prolonged emotional strain (that might be manifested in torpor or apathy). Haak (1982) has shown that in Ugaritic the idiom *qṣr npš* refers either to sinful impatience requiring atonement or to innocent helplessness (as of a widow) that calls for compassion. The assumption that *qĕṣar-rûaḥ* and *qĕṣar-nepeš* always refer to impatience has not left texts in which these phrases occur open to the interpretation "weakness." Just as Esau told Jacob that he was famished to death (Gen 25:30–32), so Samson was "tired to death" by Delilah's pestering (Judg 16:16 [NRSV]). The people in Egypt didn't listen to Moses because they were worn out by heavy work (Exod 6:9). The emphasis is on psychological exhaustion and depression rather than physical weariness. Likewise in the wilderness the people were demoralized by hunger and thirst (Num 21:4). In his careful study of all such expressions Haak recognizes the two quite different possible connotations and concludes that "it is no longer possible to translate automatically 'impatience'" (1982: 167). In instances when it is not clear which connotation is intended, Haak thinks it is possible that the author was playing on both meanings. In Job 21:4 LXX took the idiom to mean anger. The current preference for "impatience" arises in part from the modern image of "impatient" Job in the dialogue in contradiction to the "patient" Job of the narrative portions of the book. But the other connotation makes better sense. Job is not quick-tempered; he is worn out by his unequal struggles with God.

Turning now to Mic 2:7, the question may be posed: Which of its two connotations does the idiom *qṣr-rûaḥ* have here? Does Yahweh's shortness of spirit mean that he has used up his patience? If the question is rhetorical and the answer is "No!" then Micah is advancing the familiar explanation that God's seeming detachment and noninvolvement is not due to indifference; it is another manifestation of his celebrated "long-suffering" (he is *'erek 'appayim*). Or is the question whether God has run out of energy? Quite apart from the notorious textual difficulties of this passage, commentators have found it difficult to link the string of questions together. The rhetorical question in v 7b is tantamount to a positive assertion: "Don't my words do good to one who walks with the upright one?" The question in v 7aB—"Are these his doings?"—implies that certain events described (in chapter 1?) are indeed deeds of God. It is not that God is inactive because he is patient; he is active, in words of prophecy and in deeds of judgment. Micah's hearers should recognize that, and they should not suppose that Yahweh has become enfeebled. The question in Mic 2:7aB is similar to the questions in Num 11:23 and Isa 59:1. His hand is not shortened; nor is his spirit. Just as in Isa 59:1, in Mic 3:8 the "power" of the Spirit of Yahweh is expressed in the message of the prophet.

When *qṣr*, "to be short," is used psychologically, with "soul," "spirit," or "hand" as the grammatical subject, it means to have insufficient resources for a task, or to have reached the limit of one's capacity. Allen (1976: 292) translates: "Has Yahweh lost his temper?" quoting Job 21:4; Eccl 7:8 in support. But, quite apart from whether those passages have that meaning, the question is whether Yahweh is more commonly reproached or mistrusted because of his slow or inadequate response to a situation than for overreaction? It is not what Yahweh has done that is the problem for the prophet, but what evildoers have apparently got away with. Yahweh's ability to keep his promises was often questioned in unbelief—"Is Yahweh's hand too short to save?" (Isa 50:2; the answer is in Isa 59:1). But Yahweh can ask such a question about himself (Num 11:23). It refers to demoralization due to exhaustion (Exod 6:9; 2 Kgs 19:26 = Isa 37:27; Num 21:4; Judg 16:16), not an energetic bad temper. In any case, the issue probably does not concern Yahweh's temperament, but the spirit of Yahweh active in prophecy (the word is used again in v 11).

Haak (1982) studied all attestations of the idioms *qṣr npš* and *qṣr rwḥ* in the Hebrew Bible and in Ugaritic. The expressions have two distinct connotations, weakness and impatience; but it is not always possible to determine which is intended. Job 21:4 refers to Job's weakness, not his impatience. Micah 2:7 probably means "Is Yahweh impotent?" with a negative answer implied (Haak 1982: 165). What is questioned is the power of his words and the validity of Micah's description of Yahweh's deeds; hence the reply in v 7b. The spirit of Yahweh is not exhausted; he has filled Micah with power to declare Israel's sin (3:8).

deeds. The noun refers almost exclusively to the evil practices of humans. It could be used here to insinuate that what Micah has been saying about God (for instance, that "evil came down from Yahweh" [1:12b]) was preposterous.

not. On the rhetorical functions of *hălô'*, see Brongers (1981) and Brown (1987).

my words. LXX "his words." The more difficult MT is confirmed by the Targum and Vulgate. Whether the speaker of v 7b is Yahweh or Micah, there has been a response to v 7a, which asked if the spirit of Yahweh has been cut short

and whether "these are *his* deeds." One can appreciate the pressure on translators and textual critics to bring "his words" into line with "his deeds." Hillers
rejects the first person because "the people are speaking" (1984: 35 n. g). But
that is not evident, and Hillers has not proved it by identifying the participants
and assigning to each their parts in the dialogue. Rather, the first-person pronoun shows that an individual (Micah more likely than Yahweh) is rebutting
the charge that his prophecies are unacceptable or subversive and must cease
forthwith. Micah is answering two rhetorical questions about the spirit of Yahweh and his deeds and defending the good effects of his own words, at least for
the upright person. This analysis excludes Hiller's translation which, by emending the first word in v 7 has the house of Jacob (whom he calls "the people") as
the ones who make the statements (questions) in v 7. It is precisely this emendation that creates the difficulty for "my words." Here it is more likely that Micah
is defending his message, which he calls "my words" rather than "the word of
Yahweh," an expression he uses only in 4:2.

   achieve good. In 1 Kgs 22:8, 18, Ahab complained about Micaiah ben Imlah:
"He does not prophesy good concerning me, but evil." Since Micah presents
his message as words from God, it is splitting hairs to try to decide whom the suffix *my* refers to. A preference for Yahweh as the referent and so the subject of the
verb changes this verb to singular — "he speaks of good" or "he makes his words
good" (Hillers's translations [1984: 35 n. h]). But "my words do good" (RV) is
quite acceptable. The idiom "do good *ʿim*" is not standard Hebrew; *l-* would be
better. Hence "*the upright* one" is not the (indirect) object of the verb. "Walking
with the upright one" is acceptable. The prepositional phrase is rarely placed
before a participle; but remember that this is poetry. The suggestion that *ʿim*
should be *ʾim* makes v 7b a double question matching the pair in v 7a. But the
good parallelism between v 7aB and v 7bA suggests something else. Together
they contain echoes of a well-known saying ("Wasn't it said, long ago, house of
Jacob?"), either Num 11:23 with slight adaptations, or something like it. The
same kinds of answers are required by these rhetorical questions.

   Is the hand (spirit) of Yahweh too short? (No!)

   Is my word to be prized by you? (Yes!)

   Cannot my words do good? (Yes!)

   walks. Mur 88 reads *hlk*, an older neutral spelling. The phrase *ʿim hayyāšār
hôlēk* is widely considered corrupt. LXX generally confirms MT, but has several
minor deviations. (1) *met' autou*, as if from *ʿimmô*; (2) an additional *w-* with the
next word would explain *kai orthoi*; (3) note the plurals *orthoi peporeuntai*. The
very early Greek text (**R**, now called 8ḤevXIIgr, published in *DJD* 8) studied
by Barthélemy has *Jenon*, agreeing with MT.

   The phrase has been emended in many different ways. The popular emendation of v 7bB to *ʿim ʿammôh yiśrāʾēl*, while highly ingenious, is far too elaborate
to be accepted, since the credibility of such a proposal rapidly diminishes with

the number of supposed changes involved. This suggestion, still made in BHS, is the end product of a great deal of work by many scholars. Nowack (in the first edition of *HKAT*) first replaced *yāšār hôlēk* with *yiśrā'ēl*. Then Marti (1904) brought in *'ammô* from v 8. Finally Budde (1919–20: 9) salvaged the article to read *'ammōh*, archaic orthography, along with the preposition, lost by haplography. That "Israel" and "upright" might be confused, or even played upon, is certainly possible; compare the celebrated emendation of Ps 73:1. MT has *ṭwb lyśr'l*, "good to Israel." Dividing the second word gives *ṭwb lyśr 'l*, "God is good to the upright" (BHS).

To be fully convincing, a textual restoration should explain how the present reading arose. In particular, why *hwlk*? If it means "with him who walks uprightly," is there any real need to change the order to **'im hôlēk yāšār* (Mays), even if the noun is adverbial? The idiom "walk with" is unobjectionable and has its most famous use in Mic 6:8. The just man walks with his God, and God walks with the just man. This reciprocity is spelled out in detail in Lev 26:21–28, using exactly the same idiom. So Mic 2:7 is reaffirming that Yahweh's covenant threats and promises will do harmful or beneficial deeds with undiminished force, depending on whether his people walk with him uprightly or not.

Finally we raise the question, suggested by the similarity of v 7b to 6:8, whether "the upright" one is Yahweh himself. Micah asks, "Do not my words [such as those in 2:1–5] bring about good for the person who walks with (Yahweh) the Upright One?"

Introduction to Micah 2:8–9

Verses 8–9 are a succinct narrative embedded in an altercation between rival factions of prophets. The conjunction *and* marks a transition to another constituent in the unit, a transition from questions to statements. Micah has just asked a rhetorical question, tantamount to an affirmative statement: "My words (which you are trying to silence) do good to anyone who walks with the Upright One." But only yesterday you were doing things to my people that I have rightly exposed and condemned, things that exclude you from further participation in the community of Yahweh (2:5). You don't know "what is good" (6:8); you are not doing justice, loving kindness, walking humbly with your God. *My words* will not *achieve good* for you. Verses 8 and 9 contain a catalog of wrongs that resemble those of 2:1–5. Instead of desisting from preaching *to these* matters, as ordered in v 6, he more openly and more directly accuses his critics. The abuses described in v 9 resemble those described in vv 1–5; the abuses described in v 9 have a background in war, perhaps the same war as was the occasion for the lament in 1:10–16. Such a report of cruel deeds can function as an accusation. The double reference to "my people" (vv 8, 9) suggests that this could be a speech of Yahweh (see the NOTE on v 4).

There are two clauses in v 8. They differ in the person of their verbs, third in v 8aA, second in v 8aB. We have already noted how Budde and other scholars level the first verb to second person. The development reported in v 8aA is not clear. The function of *l-* is ambiguous. It could mean that "my people rose up *against* an enemy." In this situation the accused had stripped the clothing from people who had been passing through trustingly as they returned from the war.

Verse 9 has two closely parallel clauses, with matching parts arranged in chiasmus.

9aA	*nĕšê ʿammî tĕgārĕšûn*	The wives of my people you expelled
9aB	*mibbêt taʿănûgeyhā*	(each) from her pleasant house,
9bA	*mēʿal ʿōlāleyhā*	(each) from her children
9bB	*tiqḥû hădārî lĕʿôlām*	you took away my honor forever.

In the usual reading of this verse, Micah accuses them of driving women from their homes and of taking away honor from their little children. A closer reading in the light of the poetic structure suggests other possibilities. First we notice that the last word, "forever," is an inclusion for "yesterday," which comes at the beginning of v 8. That arrangement marks vv 8–9 as a unit and, by the same token, detaches "forever" somewhat from the rest of v 9bB. This enhances the chiasmus between v 9aA and v 9bB (noun : verb :: verb : noun). These outer colons are an envelope construction linked, not only by the verbs (both 2d m. pl.), but also by the suffix: "*my* people" // "*my* honor." We suspect hendiadys— "my honored people." The central bicolon has four matched pairs. The pronoun suffixes (*her*) are the counterpart of *my* in the outer colons. The preposition *from* is repeated, and, since it is used with a compound preposition in v 9bA (*from upon*) we are warranted in identifying *mbyt* in this instance as another compound preposition. It is well known that Hebrew makes metaphorical use of both anatomical and architectural terms to supply directional and spatial prepositions. In *mbyt*, *byt* retains some of its connotation of "house," as in the stock phrase *mbyt wmḥwṣ*, "inside and outside." This expression is used to describe wholesale and indiscriminate slaughter "in house and in street." The collocation of *mbyt* and *mʿl* seems to be similar here and in the context of war and its atrocities describes the violent removal of women and children. This leaves the nouns *taʿănûgey-* and its parallel *ʿōlāley-*. The combination has to be read as hendiadys—"her delightful offspring," matching the phrase *bĕnê taʿănûgāyik* in Mic 1:16. One can even say that the four words in these two matching phrases are in chiasmus. The linkage that this supplies between 1:16 and 2:9 is an important clue. It suggests that the situations behind the two passages are the same or similar.

All these atrocities could be aspects of war in which property is pillaged and people are seized. Other things could be included as well, such as molesting peaceful travelers (v 8b), although these could be (repatriated?) prisoners of war or veterans.

The accusations are succinct, and there is much in these verses that is obscure to us. Since the events occurred only *yesterday*, doubtless they were all very fresh in the memory of Micah's audience, and details were not needed. As well as brevity, the verses display a certain amount of confusion not unlike the disorder found in 1:10–16, and perhaps for the same reason. The prophet is beside himself with indignation, and the recriminations tumble out in disjointed statements.

There could, however, be some order in the indictment. Traditionally in Israel there were four groups whose social position was weak and who were most vulnerable to oppression by the unscrupulous. They had a special claim on the protection of good rulers and were the particular object of the fatherly care of God himself. They were the poor, the alien, the widowed, the orphaned. We suggest that these are the victims of the crimes itemized in vv 8 and 9. War refugees could constitute a fifth group, possibly including members of the other four classes.

Notes on Micah 2:8–9

8. *yesterday.* Verse 8aA is literally "And yesterday my people as (or "to" or "for") an enemy stood up (or raised up)." Difficulties have been found in every word. Only one word (*lĕ'ōyēb*) survived in Budde's reconstruction of this colon. The past-time reference of the opening adverb *yesterday,* even when it is given its more general reference "recently," does not go with the prefix ("imperfect") verbs if they are future, or even if the prefix verbs are taken as generalizing present tense forms, as in most recent translations. The consonants of *and yesterday w'tmwl* can be rearranged to yield *w'tm wl-* (this goes back to George Adam Smith and Ehrlich). Recovery of the pronoun "you" requires that the verb be changed from third person. G. A. Smith emended the verb to the participle *qāmîm* as a suitable predicate. Changing the verb to second person brings v 8aA into line with the rest of the unit, which has second-person verbs. The *polel* form of the verb is another problem. It is normally transitive and connotes rebuilding (Isa 44:26; 58:12; 61:4). Verse 8aA has been brought into line by changing transitive *yĕqômēm* to intransitive *tāqûmû* (this goes back to Wellhausen [1898: 138]). Because "my people" is considered the victim, not the one who has turned into an enemy, or who rose up against an enemy, the last consonant of the first word has been assigned to *'ammî* as a preposition *l-*. Wellhausen made it *'al.* The status of "my people" in the situation is not obvious. In other occurrences (1:9; 2:4) the term need not be covenantal and protective, although it is that in 2:9; 3:5. In Micah, Yahweh does not call Israel "not my people" as in Hosea; but the terms "this family" (2:3), "this people" (2:11) imply reproach, if not downright renunciation. Ambivalence is to be expected; Yahweh punishes Israel as his disobedient covenant people—disobedient, but still his people. And, if the crimes are internal, whether social injustices of rich against poor, or the evil deeds of one kingdom against the other, then "my people" is both victim and enemy.

The complete liquidation of "and yesterday" in the ways reported is certainly ingenious. Too clever, perhaps. The strange form *'etmûl* occurs only here and at Isa 30:33. That meager attestation is not a sufficient reason to doubt its authenticity. See the NOTE on 2:4 for Micah's preference for *û* in several words. This opening time reference is balanced by *lĕ'ôlām* at the end of the unit. As the counterpoise of *lĕ'ôlām*, *'etmûl* could point to an indefinite past. While "yesterday" might suggest that these evil practices began only recently, the combination suggests that the consequences will stretch into the indefinite future.

stood up. The root *qwm* often has belligerent overtones. The participle *qām*, "opponent," is a synonym of *'ôyēb*. The *polel* is more problematical, since it is usually transitive, used by Second Isaiah to describe the reconstruction of Jerusalem. Or the verb could be reflexive, variant of *hitpolel*, which in its few attestations means to rise up against someone as an enemy (Job 20:27; 27:7; Pss 17:7; 59:2; and perhaps 139:21).

enemy. Like its synonym *śōnē'*, *'ôyēb* highlights a relationship to one not in covenant, or the conduct of a breaker of covenant, not animosity as such, subjectively. The idiom is incomplete. One expects "rise up *against* someone." If the words are addressed to Israel, does it mean "my people (have become) (my) enemy"? The suffix would not need to be supplied, although it would be easy to make the first letter of the next word do double duty. They became God's enemy, not by formal renunciation—their reliance on prophets with orthodox slogans and their self-deceiving piety suggest that they were religiously loyal—but by the abuses they inflicted on the disadvantaged members of society. There is no trace of such thinking in the context. The term *my people* is used protectively. The entire oracle is an attack on the prophets "who lead my people astray" (3:5). *My people* are the victims. We suggest that the preposition "against" is understood, and that the otherwise unidentified subject of the verb *he stood up* is the same as the "he" in 2:4, a representative oppressor.

stripped. The colon bristles with problems—thematic, prosodic, textual, philological. Cohesion with surrounding text is hard to find. With eleven syllables, the colon seems overweighted. As one of several accusations included in vv 8–9, it indicts a criminal act in relation to a *cloak*. The language is so cryptic that neither the perpetrators not the victims can be identified, nor what exactly was done. The verb *tapšiṭûn* has no explicit subject. The nearest connection would be with "you" of 2:4.

The *qal* of *pšṭ* (24x) is used when a person takes off all his clothes; 1 Sam 19:24 and Isa 32:11 are explicit that the person is then naked. The action of *pšṭ* is the opposite of *lbš*, "get dressed" (Lev 6:4; 16:23; Ezek 26:16; 44:19; Cant 5:3). A person might bathe between *pšṭ* and *lbš* (Lev 16:23; cf. Neh 4:17). The *hip'il* (15x) is used when someone strips the clothes from another person, alive (Joseph [Gen 37:23]) or dead (Aaron [Num 20:26, 28]), or from an adulterous woman whose punishment is exposure (Ezek 16:39; 23:26; Hos 2:5). The full *hip'il* construction has two objects; in some cases each is governed by *'et*. When there is only one object, it can be the person (Hos 2:5) or the garments (1 Sam 31:9 = 1 Chr 10:9—the removal of Saul's equipment from his dead body). In every case the result is nakedness. A similar idea is present when the *hip'il* is used to refer to skinning a slaughtered victim (Lev 1:6; Mic 3:3; 2 Chr 29:34; 35:11). Overlapping a little with the *hip'il*, the *pi'el* is used to report stripping everything, apparently, but certainly clothes, from the slain (1 Sam 31:8 = 1 Chr 10:8; 2 Sam 23:10). The salient meaning of the *qal* is "undress (oneself)," but the *hitpaᶜel* is used once with this meaning (1 Sam 18:4), and the *qal* can be used when it is the action of a thief (Hos 7:1) or of an insect pest (Nah 3:16).

Lexicons usually recognize only one root *pšṭ*. There are a dozen or so places where the *qal* is used in accounts of warfare, referring to various activities of an attacking force. Battlefield connotations are certainly present when the *piᶜel* and the *hipᶜil* refer to stripping the slain after victory, but no such picture seems to be present in the situations where the *qal* refers to activities preliminary to assault. When attacking a city (Judg 9:33, 44a, 44b; 20:37), it could mean "come out of cover"; but it is used quite generally for any kind of foray (1 Sam 23:27; 27:8, 10; 30:1, 14; Job 1:17; 1 Chr 14:9, 13; 2 Chr 25:13; 28:18), sometimes by raiding gangs more like bandits than regular armies. A common ground of meaning could be found if "pillage" is implied in these latter instances. In any case the association of *pšṭ* with warfare as well as with undressing could tie in with the connotations of war in v 8aA and the reference to *war* in v 8bB.

The difficulty with *tpšṭwn* in v 8aB is that none of the other words that occur with it there (*mmwl, ślmh, ʾdr*) occur with its root anywhere else in the Hebrew Bible. LXX read the first two words as a prepositional phrase modifying *ʾôyēb* (which it did not read as a participle)—"for enmity against his peace." The translator was evidently *au fait* with archaic orthography, for he read *ślmh* as *šĕlōmōh* (first /ō/ *defective*, terminal /ō/ archaic). He might also have felt that *war* in v 8bB requires an antonym. LXX rendered the other two words in v 8aB "they [not "you" as in MT] stripped off his skin." We have already seen above that "skin" is an attested object of *pšṭ*, and the LXX interpretation of v 8aB could have been influenced by the language of Mic 3:3 (even though the Greek vocabulary is different at each place). LXX scarcely provides a basis for recovering from *tēn doran autou* a better reading than *ʾdr*.

cloak. Here there are two words for items of clothing. The clearest word in the colon is *śalmâ*, a variant of the more usual *śimlâ*—a simple case of metathesis. There are three other Hebrew nouns that refer to a major item of clothing—*beged, mĕᶜîl, kĕtōnet*. It is hard to find any distinction among the meanings of these terms. The commonest, *beged*, seems to be generic (any garment covering the whole body), while the others could be more specific, perhaps referring to some more distinct design. Even if *kĕtōnet* is a loanword that retains its meaning of "tunic," it could nevertheless refer to an elaborate (Joseph's) or a distinctive (Tamar's) dress. Usually *kĕtōnet* seems to be the name of the inner garment, perhaps the last undergarment (Gen 37:23; Cant 5:3). The main point that is relevant to the problem of v 8aB is that all these terms seem to refer to an outer garment, of whatever design, some kind of cloak, easily removed (Gen 39:12).

When *pšṭ* has an object it is usually clothes in general—*bĕgādîm* (Lev 6:4; 16:23; Num 20:26, 28; 1 Sam 19:24; Ezek 16:39; 23:26; 26:16; 44:19; Neh 4:17; Job 22:6). The uniform use of the plural shows that *beged* is generic, referring to all and any of several garments worn by one person. This is appropriate for an action that strips a person to complete nakedness. When distinctions are made among the things removed, the outermost item removed is jewelry (*pšṭ* is never used for that action), followed by the removal of clothing (Ezek 16:39; 23:26; cf. Hos 2:5). Ezekiel 26:16 has an elaborate description of divestment: "And all the princes of the sea will come down from their thrones, and they will put aside their robes (*wĕhēsîrû ʾet-mĕʿîlêhem*), and their embroidered garments they will take off (*wĕʾet-bigdê rigmātām yipšōṭû*)." In inverse order the ceremonial investiture described in Isa 59:17 and 61:10 puts the *mĕʿîl* over the bgdym. The *mĕʿîl* is an outermost garment, the one that Jonathan removed first (1 Sam 18:4), with a *beged* underneath. Yet Ezra reverses the order (Ezra 9:3, 5).

Difficulty in identifying a person's attire in any particular case arises from the familiar usage in which the generic term becomes specific and *vice versa*. In the collocation of *ktnt* and *mĕʿîlîm* in 2 Sam 13:18 the latter seems to be generic. P prefers *beged* (94 out of 113 occurrences in the Pentateuch), and is the only source in the Pentateuch that uses *mĕʿîl* (10x—the rich outer vestment of the high priest). P never uses *śalmâ* (~ *śimlâ*), unless perhaps in Josh 22:8. Aside from that exclusion, both forms of the latter are found in every part of the Hebrew Bible, both in Exod 22:25, 26. The similar incidents in 1 Sam 15:27; 24:5 (*mĕʿîl*) and 1 Kgs 11:29–30 (*śalmâ*) suggest that these terms are alternative names for the same kind of garment. Like *beged, śalmâ* (~ *śimlâ*) can be used either generically (especially when plural) or specifically to designate a person's main (perhaps only) garment (Deut 8:4). It would be torn for grief (Gen 37:34; 44:13; Josh 7:6), so could the *mĕʿîl* (Job 1:20; 2:12). A *śimlâ* was a necessity of life, as essential as bread (Deut 10:18; Isa 3:7; 4:1). It served as a blanket (Gen 9:23; Deut 22:17). References to the *śalmâ* (~ *śimlâ*) or its equivalent in legal texts, in mourning customs, in folklore, show that this part of a person's dress has enormous social significance as a mark of status and identity. To take away a person's "cloak," especially when it was their last possession, was a devastating indignity and an ultimate crime (Job 22:6). One of the oldest and most enduring folk stories in the world, *The Poor Citizen of Nippur*, is based on the symbolism of the cloak. If taken in pledge, this garment had to be returned to its owner by nightfall so he would have something to sleep in (Exod 22:25–26; Deut 24:13). The case of the farm worker in the *Meṣad Ḥashavyahu* ostracon (*KAI* No. 200; literature in Pardee 1982: 15–20; Suder 1984: 62–63; Renz 1995, 1:315–29) is a remarkable testament to the Israelites' sensitivity to this simple, basic human value. The cloak and a person's identity were inseparable (Hallo 1997: 99 n. 9). Yahweh himself was alert to a person's right to keep his clothing (Exod 22:26). In fact, respect for this right provided a definition of what it meant to be "righteous before the LORD" (Deut 24:13). Disregard for this right is evidently the transgression condemned in Mic 2:8.

The tradition is correct that understands *šlmh* as *cloak*, even though the noun is not the object of *pšṭ* anywhere else. The problem presented by the unique collocation of these two words in Mic 2:8 is the seriousness of the offense, whether the ultimate humiliation of already destitute persons by stripping away their last possession and leaving them naked, whether the garment was taken in pledge, or whether it is just another theft (Allen 1976: 297). In view of the background presented above, especially in legal texts, this particular offense was probably chosen as an illustration of the wrongs done because of its established symbolic power. In this case *śalmâ* is probably generic, even proverbial. It might even mean the undergarment, depending on what we make of *'eder*.

that covers. This translation, or rather paraphrase, is admittedly a shot in the dark. The first word in the colon, *mimmûl*, is a problem. It rhymes with *'etmûl*, and this could be part of a deliberate pattern. To change *mimmûl* to *mē'al*, to match the same word at the beginning of v 9 and to go with the next word, changed to "peaceful," is an attractive emendation. Wellhausen, who thought of it first (1898: 138; cf. Weiser 1956: 219 and BHS), said it was "probable," but there is no textual evidence to support it, and the prior proof that *mimmûl* is impossible has not been supplied. The cryptic character of the composition is due to the sparse use of "particles" (conjunctions, prepositions) and modifiers (definite articles, pronoun suffixes), exacerbated by frequent departure from normal word order. In this clause the verb comes last, which is unusual for Hebrew, at least in prose. Taking the nearer noun, *'eder*, as the object (cf. the positions of the objects in v 9), the preceding prepositional phrase is adverbial. This suggests "You stripped the *'eder* from (on top of?) the *śalmâ*," as if the *'eder* was the overgarment, the *śalmâ* the undergarment. But then the victim would not be left naked. And we don't know what an *'eder* is (see the following NOTE). *Mimmûl* does not mean "from on top of" but "from in front of" an object usually some distance away, "over against." This preposition usually governs a word that refers to a person. It was this consideration that led Sellin (1930: 319, 321) to emend *ślmh* to *šĕlēmîm*, with the meaning it has in Gen 34:21, "peaceful." This emendation also secures parallelism with *beṭaḥ* in v 8bA, but this only implies that the peaceable ones are witnesses of the crime of stripping the *'eder*.

tunic. *'eder* (compare *hadar* in v 9) could be a loanword. It occurs only here with the apparent meaning of "cloak" (Zech 11:13 is a semantic offshoot), but this is insufficient reason for normalizing it to the more familiar *'adderet* by retrieving *t-* from the next word. Such a change is possible; even without the available *t-* to help it along, such an emendation is always conceivable. But it replaces one problem by another—how did the text get to be that way? Hebrew is rich in masculine // feminine pairs of indistinguishable meaning, and sometimes the same writer uses both. Like *beged* and *mĕ'îl*, both of the terms in v 8aB could refer to a cloak or outer garment, as distinct from a tunic, but no clear distinctions have been established among them. Hence one or other of the two has been considered redundant and omitted as a gloss on the other. Ahlström (1967), drawing on comparative evidence, tried to retain *śmlh* as the main garment with *'eder* as an accessory—"a rope or a girdle" (1967: 7), or perhaps "belt," or "buckle." The problem remains unsolved.

from. If the two following noun (participial) phrases are in apposition, *min-* governs the whole phrase; if they are parallel or coordinate, it does double duty.

passing. Safe passage of travelers could be guaranteed under treaty. A journey would not be made without advance assurances (Numbers 20–21; in Num 21:21–24 *'br* is the operational verb).

confidently. "Trust" (*beṭaḥ*) is security assured by agreement. When a way-farer is making a trip on this basis and is robbed (Hos 6:9; Judg 5:6), perfidy com-pounds the crime. The language used by Micah would be appropriate for some quite concrete outrage, and the specifics suggest something recent in memory, known to Micah's hearers and so requiring no explanation. Unfortunately we no longer have that background knowledge.

returning. The participle *'ōběrîm* supports the acceptability of *šûbê* as a par-ticiple, in spite of its uniqueness. If the second participle is passive (passive par-ticiples are often used in construct), it means those who had been returned from war, like the liberated prisoners of war in 2 Chr 28:14–15. They were sup-plied with clothes and other necessities. It would certainly have been a despica-ble crime if such a band, consisting mainly of women and children, had been robbed along the way as they were "passing through trustfully." There is no need to change *šûbê* to *šěbî* meaning "captives," the common term. Powis Smith's suggestion that it means "spoil," in parallel with the garments in v 8a, is without support. But "prisoners of war" gives a different picture. Usually they would al-ready have been stripped of their possessions, and they would hardly have been passing through peacefully. The same difficulty is present if *šwby* is retained, but read as *šûbî*, a variant of *šěbî* (Wernberg-Møller 1959: 59). A more plausible possibility is *šûb* as a variant of active *šāb*. Micah has a propensity for variants containing the vowel /u/. Compare the active meaning of *šûbâ* in Isa 30:15. The victims would then be "returning (not returned) ones." The difference is slight. The passive is intriguing because 2 Chronicles 28 reports a contemporary incident—surely without many precedents!—of captives being returned volun-tarily by their captors.

9. *wives.* In the social ethics of the Deuteronomistic tradition there were tradi-tional exhortations to public charity in behalf of four conventional and symbolic groups of disadvantaged and defenseless people—poor, homeless aliens, widows, orphans—the latter more strictly a fatherless minor with no adult male protector from among his deceased father's relatives. Economic forces and natural disas-ters, such as famine or plague, could bring about the marginalization of such persons, but war most of all would increase their number and aggravate their plight. It was the obligation of the community and more particularly the office of a king to take such unfortunates under his charge, and they would have an extra claim if their fathers had died in battle. The annals of ancient states, com-piled in the chanceries, viewed military events from the top. The glories of war are reported in epic style; the miseries of war are seldom noticed. It is otherwise in the Hebrew Bible, especially in the prophets. The horrors of war are reported; the atrocities of war are condemned. This is a prominent theme of Amos's ora-cles against all the nations in the region. The chronicles of the times catalog the eighth century B.C.E. as a time of incessant wars between Israel and Judah, among their neighbors, and with more distant imperial powers. They lined up as enemies or allies in every imaginable combination. The countryside was devas-tated (Isaiah 1; Mic 1:10–16). Whole populations were taken off into slavery

(Amos 1:6, 9). Famine and disease followed war (Amos 4:6–11). All these disasters could be interpreted in Israel as fulfillment of the curses of the covenant.

When there were casualties on the scale described in 2 Chr 28:6, however inflated the figures might be, the number of widows and orphans would be equally large. Refugees would crowd in from surrounding states (Isaiah 15–16). Micah never uses the stock vocabulary for alien, widow, and orphan. In chapter 2 he speaks more generally of men, women, and children. He does not report battles, only the aftermaths. Recent wars provide the background to chapters 1–3, and they seem to be entirely local, that is, between Israel and Judah. The crimes listed in vv 8–9 are not the immediate acts of a foreign invader, but breaches of covenant within the community of Israel. The leadership, especially the rulers in Jerusalem, with full legitimation from a conniving religious hierarchy, actually took advantage of the plight of the victims of their own civil wars, dislodging the women from their houses (v 9a), separating the children from their mothers (v 9b).

my people. The use of this term could indicate that the speaker is Yahweh, and this would give poignancy to the complaint. The speaker could be Micah; see the NOTE on v 4. Since 'am sometimes means citizenry mustered for war, its use here could be a hint that the women are war widows.

expelled. Verse 9 is part of an indictment, so the prefix ("imperfect") verbs are past tense; whether punctiliar or iterative is harder to say. The specific details suggest some particular occasion, recent according to v 8aA, which we have (provisionally) identified with the internecine strife in Israel in the reign of Ahaz. The verb *grš* describes forcible expulsion.

(each) . . . her . . . house. The almost universally recommended normalization of the singular possessive pronoun suffixes to plural "their" is not required, although it was done by all ancient translations, which, like modern ones, could not cope with the delicate nuance of the distributive singular in Hebrew. The explanation of Willi-Plein (1971: 123) is that originally the suffixes were plural *-hem* (m. for f.) and that the *mem* in the first one was lost by haplography, and then from the second by analogy. This is altogether improbable, since the singular *-hā* occurs twice. The sequence *women . . . her* means that the widows are expelled, *each* from her own house. Compare the sequence of plural and singular nouns in v 2, where the latter are similarly distributive.

pleasant. As in 1:16. The similarity of the constructions gives the obvious reading of the phrase as construct: "house of her delights," i.e., her delightful house. The question of whether the houses as such are "modest" (Mays) or luxurious does not arise. The word brings out the value of the house for the occupant. "Pleasant" is an attribute of "children" in 1:16. The repetition of this rare word in 1:16 and 2:9, found elsewhere only in Prov 19:10; Qoh 2:8; Cant 7:7, shows that there are connections in theme between chapters 1 and 2 of Micah and requires that "your darling sons" and "her beloved children" be interpreted together. "Babies," '*ôlālîm*, covers both sexes. In 1:16 the address to the bereaved mother in the singular could be taken as metaphorical for each city listed, but especially Jerusalem, as the mother of lovely children. Here, however, the plural *wives of my people* tips the balance in favor of human mothers.

from her children. Difficulty has been found in this phrase. It is thought more likely that women are taken from their homes and children are taken from their mothers, mothers being the victims in each case. Micah recognizes that children deprived of parents are victims. The expulsion of the children (not the mothers) is parallel to the exile of children from the mother in 1:16. Our analysis suggests the elimination of the literal meaning of *byt*, reading *mbyt* as a compound preposition. Only one atrocity is involved in Mic 1:16 and 2:9 — the separation of mothers and children.

my honor. The pronoun makes best sense if Yahweh is the speaker. The noun *hădārî* seems to be the object of *you took away*. The idea that the babies are deprived of *my honor* (or "their dignity" [Mays]) is rather abstract. What could *hdry* refer to? Various attempts have been made to reassign the appellative. There would be some symmetry with v 2b if *hdry* corresponds to *naḥălâ*. The women are expelled from their houses, the children from the glorious heritage that Yahweh gave them (Allen 1976: 293). But *hadar* never has this connotation in other places where it occurs; it refers to God's splendor in the cult. Although it is unthinkable that any human action can diminish (or augment) the essential and intrinsic "splendor" of God, the capture of the ark by the Philistines was seen as a departure of the glory (*kābôd*); and Ezekiel similarly saw the removal of Yahweh's presence from the Temple as loss of glory. In the present context "*my* splendor" is almost certainly Yahweh's splendor, even though we cannot work out just what is referred to under that word. Note the similar difficulty encountered in pinning down the reference of "the glory of Israel" in Mic 1:15.

One way of easing the strain of relating all this material together is to look once more at our analysis of the artistic structure of v 9. Above we discussed the symmetry and chiasmus of the two clauses, whether displayed as two or four colons.

The wives of my people you drove out	8 syllables
from inside — her lovely ones	5 syllables
from outside — her babies	5 syllables
You took away my honor — for ever.	9 syllables

We have already pointed out the structural connection between v 8aA and v 9bB. The chiasm of *'etmûl* and *'ôlām* makes an inclusion. This suggests that there might be some more long-distance connection between *my people* and *my honor*. There is a structural balance to be observed. There are two nouns with first-person singular suffix, two nouns with third-person feminine singular suffix. The latter go together. The composition is extremely intricate. The balance of *my people* and *my splendor* invites search for a closer connection for these two nouns in an envelope construction. If the two inner nouns mean "her lovely babies," the two outer ones mean "my splendid people." We can detect both grief and anger in this comment on what they have done to Yahweh's people, who are the people of his splendor in the sense that he wishes to be known as the God of Israel, to be known through the reflection of his character in their lifestyle. They are to be holy, because he is holy, splendid because he is splendid.

Introduction to Micah 2:10–11

The two verses in this concluding unit are uneven in texture. Verse 11 has three clearly bounded clauses, so the three colons can be identified with certainty. The colons in v 11 are of equal length—nine syllables. Verse 10 is less regular. The syntax of v 10a is clear; the grammar of v 10b is very difficult. We recognize four colons in v 10, with the first and fourth quite short by classical standards. The similar rhythm in the phrases *wĕḥebel nimrāṣ* and *wāšeqer kizzēb* (both obscure) is a link between v 10bB and v 11aA and could be an aid to interpretation.

In v 6a a command not to preach (2d. m. pl.) is addressed by one group of prophets to another. In the altercation that follows questions are asked and accusations are made. It has not been possible to reconstruct the dialogue with certainty. Our preferred reading identifies the speech in v 6 as an attack on prophets like Micah and vv 8–9 as the prophet's response, a reiteration of charges related to the accusations implied in the report in 2:2–3. There the oppressive acts were recounted in third person ("they"); in vv 8–9 Micah directly accuses the oppressors ("you").

Verse 10 begins with two coordinated imperative verbs (2d m. pl.). Are these commands directed (by Micah) to the same audience as vv 8–9, an act of expulsion similar to that threatened in v 5? Or do these commands represent the response of Micah's opponents, the speakers in v 6, continuing or resuming their attack, so that they not only tell the other prophets to stop preaching; they also tell them to get out, much as Amaziah told Amos to stop preaching in Bethel and to go back to Judah. Since we do not know who is speaking, or who is being addressed, and since the verbs in themselves are neutral in tone, the command to leave could be helpful advice given to the victims of the abuses described in vv 8–9.

There are difficulties in the way of reconstructing the drama as "Micah in confrontation with false prophets." We mention only two. First, the ban on preaching and its continuation with an expulsion order in v 10 (if that is the correct analysis) are addressed to a group, not just to one person (Micah), and there are no other indications that Micah was a member of a team of prophets. Second, a suitable rejoinder to the ban on prophesying in v 6 would be an attack on those prophets, such as we do find in v 11 and even more clearly in 3:5–8. The accusations in vv 8–9 are a continuation of the charges against the planners of iniquity and doers of evil of v 1, and these are not identified as prophets. It is only when we reach 3:11 that it is made clear that prophets, priests, and rulers are all in it together. In 2:6 it is the prophets, not the accused themselves, who respond to the oracle in vv 1–5 by telling the people who preach such things to stop doing it. The prophets who speak in v 6 are thus seen to be supporters of the wrongdoers of v 1, and the wrongdoers are hand-in-glove with the false prophets (3.1–12). So Micah's response has two prongs. First in vv 8–9 he rejects the ban of v 6 by going on with his message of judgment; then in v 11 he rejects the expulsion order of v 10 by attacking and discrediting these other prophets.

Verse 11 picks up the theme of v 6, using similar terms to describe prophesying. It is best interpreted as Micah's final assessment of the pseudoprophets, an inclusion for v 6. The Masoretic punctuation is preferable to the display in BHS. The syntax of the first six words in v 11 is unclear. The rendering in RSV seems to have got the general idea: "If a man should go about and utter wind and lies." All the same, it is a very free paraphrase that uses all the words in v 11aA but implies meanings for these words and grammatical relationships that are not apparent in the text and mostly do not correspond to standard usage.

Notes on Micah 2:10–11

10. *Get up.* The commands in v 10 (2d. m. pl; sg. in LXX) continue the one in v 6: "Don't preach . . . get up and get out!" When the verb in v 10b is taken as another second-person form, a continuation of direct address from v 10a, it is usually harmonized by making it plural. See the ensuing NOTE.

rest area. Or "resting place." This term is associated with *naḥălâ* (Deut 12:9), adding the idea of guaranteed security. Compare the three terms in Isa 32:18.

něwēh šālôm	safe habitation
miškěnôt mibṭāḥîm	secure dwellings
měnûḥōt ša'ănannôt	quiet resting places

Solomon climaxed his great prayer with an affirmation that Yahweh's good promise (compare v 7bA) has been perfectly fulfilled in the peace, *měnûḥâ*, enjoyed during his reign (1 Kgs 8:56). Compare the sentiments of Psalms 23:2 and 95:11. Verse 10aB could represent the cancellation of that state of affairs, similar to the eviction threatened in v 5, a counter to that eviction, this time from the other side. The word *"this"* seems to give to *měnûḥâ* a concrete meaning ("home," "haven"). The syntactic details are important. The article, which is rarely used in the poetic language employed by Micah, must be taken seriously. *The* resting place excludes the usual indefinite translations. The specificity implied by the use of the definite article could indicate possession, i.e., "your" rest (or resting place). LXX took it that way, albeit interpreting the speech as made to an individual (*soi*, "thine"), meaning Micah(?), or anticipating the *soi* in v 11. The position of the negative excludes the usual translation: "This is not a resting place." It is literally "The (your) rest is not this (or here)." It could be a warning that there are no grounds for expecting safety in this place. With such words the evildoers could be expelled from estates wrongfully occupied, developing the thought of v 5. The noun *měnûḥâ* is then the counterpart of *ḥēleq*.

It is also possible that *měnûḥâ* is connected with *beṭaḥ* in v 8b. Compare the collocation in Isa 32:18, quoted above. The latter is usually interpreted as meaning that the victims had been passing by in a peaceful manner. The reference could be to their objective, i.e., they were traversing the land in search of security (and rest). In the journey motif there are echoes of the original journey to the *měnûḥâ*, an old term for the Promised Land. The group of returnees, whoever they were and wherever they came from, included women and children, whose well-being was a matter of continual concern during the wilderness wanderings. The original trek had as its goal the land promised to the ancestors (7:20). In v 10 the prophet could be telling these people that they cannot stop on their journey; they must keep moving, because the resting place is contaminated.

uncleanness. The syntax of v 10b is problematic. There is a play on the verb and the noun with the root *ḥbl*. But this root has several meanings, or rather is several homonyms. The idea of "destruction" seems to fit in with the idea of "defilement." The first word, *baʿăbûr*, is usually a preposition, less commonly a conjunction. It is "because of uncleanness" that something has happened, or will happen. Linking v 10b with v 10a, it could mean that this place is no longer the resting place for these people, on account of *their* defilement, the anarthrous noun being definite in poetry. There are some strong words in Hosea that probably describe the conditions in Israel at this very time. He says that the land has been defiled (*ṭmʾ*) and those who did this will be hurled out (Hos 5:3; 6:10; 9:3–4). Although the word used here (*ṭomʾâ*) is sometimes identified as an infinitive, feminine in form, it is probably a uniquely attested variant of the common *ṭumʾâ*. This noun is eligible to be the subject of the following verb, that has otherwise to be changed to cope with the lack of cohesion with v 10a. Since the prepositional phrase "on account of (your) uncleanness" is an adjunct in the preceding clause (it gives the reason for the excommunication), it cannot be the direct subject of the following verb "she corrupted" (we read it as another preterit), or "will corrupt" (if you stay?). The solution once more lies in recognizing the omission of the relative pronoun in poetry: "uncleanness (that) has destroyed."

destroy. BDB recognized two roots *ḥbl*; KB and Zorrell four. The two main candidates have the meanings "pledge" or "corrupt." Each has its supporters at this place. A reference to "pledges" could be another aspect of the extortionate practices by which people had been defrauded of family estates, the property having been pledged as security for debt (so Mays 1976: 72). This requires textual changes. The interpretation assumes that the same criminals are still being addressed as in vv 8–9. The plural verb in LXX shows that they thought so too; but this evidence should be used with great circumspection, since LXX read the first two verbs in v 10a (pl. in MT) as singular. A plural verb *tḥblw* can be retrieved by reallocating *w-* from the next word (where its presence is another problem), and identifying the following *ḥebel* as cognate object, or dropping it as a dittograph (Ehrlich endorsed by Mays). A more suitable object is then found by substituting *mě'ûmâ* for *ṭom'â*. Budde (1919–20: 12), unwilling to relinquish *ṭ*, reconstructs *mě'aṭ* out of it. Result:

> For the gain of the slightest thing
> you pledge with a ruinous pledge. (Mays 1976: 72)

Only the last word of the original text survives in this reconstruction. It is better to retain the Masoretic Text, difficult though it be. The other meaning of *ḥbl*, "corrupt," is consonant with "defilement" and the attribute *nimrāṣ*. This participial form denotes sickness, and the phrase *qělālâ nimreṣet*, "a grievous curse," resembles *ḥebel nimrāṣ*, "a grievous corruption." So the two-word phrases (or clauses) are in parallel.

ṭom'â	*těḥabbel*
wěḥebel	*nimrāṣ*

Remembering that "particles" and pronouns are often omitted in this composition, and that principal clauses are often not contiguous with their subordinates, we suggest:

> Get up and go away—
> On account of (your) uncleanness (which) has corrupted (you),
> and (on account of your) corruption (which is) grievous.

If a passive is needed to improve the parallelism with the *nip'al*, then *pu'al* of *ḥbl* is attested, and **těḥubbal(û)* has been proposed.

11. **Let.** This particle (*lû*) is usually optative, "Would that . . . " When one wishes that a condition might be fulfilled, but considers fulfillment unlikely, or when a condition was not fulfilled, a more suitable translation would be: "If (only) . . . " Deuteronomy 32:29 contains an example of the latter: "If only they had been wise . . . " The particle *lû* is normally followed by a verb; but the participle, following its subject, can be used in the conditional sense: "If only my people had been listening to me" (Ps 81:14; v 12 shows that they had not done this). In 2 Sam 18:12 a similar clause seems to be simply conditional, although the condition is stated in exaggerated terms not likely to be fulfilled: "And if (or even though) I am weighing upon my palms 1000 of silver, I would not send out my hand against the king's son." This, however, is *qere*; *ketib* could be an inferior spelling of *lû* or otherwise negative *lō'*. The logic of Mic 2:11aA is not the same as any of these citations. Identifying v 11b as the apodosis with the protasis in v 11a amounts to this: "If someone comes along pretending to be 'a man of the spirit' and telling lies (but what he really means is, 'I am prepared to prophesy for wine and beer'), then he will become the 'prophet' of this people." But we have not been able to find this meaning for *lû* elsewhere. If *lû* expresses a

desire, then v 11a could contain a little dialogue. In v 11aB the bogus prophet speaks to his prospective client, making a deal. In v 11aA "this people" express a desire for a "man of the spirit." This little interchange is Micah's version of the negotiations; it is not what the parties themselves would say. This is Micah's parody, telling what is really going on—a conspiracy of mutual self-deception.

The difficulty of the MT suggests that it may be at fault. Mur 88 reads *l'*, and LXX supports the negative particle. MT could be the result of *plene* spelling of "not" followed by loss of *alef* through haplography.

a man. This noun is usually taken at face value as indefinite: "a man" (RSV), i.e., any man. This could imply that anyone could become a false prophet if he goes through the procedures; but his motivation would be personal gain (v 11aB) and his utterances would be lies (v 11aA). A more specific designation is achieved if this person is called *'îš . . . rûaḥ*, a "spirit-person." Thus *'îš . . . rûaḥ* is a discontinuous construct phrase meaning "prophet" ("a man of inspiration" [JB]).

walking. If this word has its salient meaning as a verb of motion ("walk") it lacks the usual and expected accompaniment of a locational modifier that tells us where the person walks. (In 1:8a the *hipʿil* has complements of manner, and the words after *hōlēk* are sometimes taken in this grammatical sense.) Without specifics, the verb is given a generic meaning ("go about") implying a peripatetic. Would such a description be derogatory and would such behavior be discrediting in the light of the norms and expectations of Hebrew society at that time? We know that Samuel made the rounds (1 Sam 7:15–17) but that was primarily in his capacity as an itinerant magistrate. Elijah was here, there, and everywhere (1 Kgs 18:12). But we do not hear of such wandering seers in the eighth century. The opposite of a peripatetic would be a prophet who had a permanent abode and base of operations as a member of the staff of a shrine or as a consultant with appointment and title in the bureaucracy (like Gad, David's seer). Such cult officials and experts in the royal retinue are attested in the Bible, but remarks made by the eighth-century prophets suggest that in that period such persons had become mere public servants, yes-men of the establishment. We cannot identify any institutional setting for the false prophets attacked in the books of the eighth-century prophets. In the eighth century the prophets whose messages (writings) eventually made it into the canon were evidently on the margins of power: Amos is the parade example; Micah too, so far as we can tell; but Isaiah's status as adviser to the king seems to have done a flip from hostility under Ahaz to legitimization and influence under Hezekiah, who also respected Micah, according to Jer 26:18–19. Prior to that vindication, it is more likely that the authentic prophets of the eighth century B.C.E. would seem to be self-appointed and self-supporting upstarts rather than officially licensed and salaried agents of recognized sacral and political institutions. Amos suffered conspicuously from this disadvantage and was so different from the prophets of his day that he did not want to be called a *nābî'* at all, even though he insisted that he was one, with a genuine and irresistible call and a true message from Yahweh. In the light of all this we conclude that *hōlēk* in v 11a does not describe this man as a peripatetic, in order to discredit him. The term must mean something else. We add the further point that the *binyān* for "walk around" is *hitpaʿel*.

The meaning of *hōlēk* in v 11 should be sought in the light of the occurrence of the same participle in v 7. There the one who walks is "the upright person," or perhaps one who walks "with the Upright One," the one who accepts Micah's (or Yahweh's) words and finds them beneficial. Here "walking" is a religio-ethical figure (Banks 1987: 305). The participle secures the idea of a confidence man, who resembles the crook described in Prov 6:12:

ʾādām bĕliyyaʿal	Person of wickedness,
ʾîš ʾāwen	man of iniquity,
hōlēk ʿiqqĕšût peh	walking with crooked mouth.

Here *hōlēk* is used in an ethical metaphor, to bring out the person's character, shown particularly in deceitful speech. Micah 2:11bA catches a similar aspect, the charlatan's self-advertisement, at least in the sarcastic words of his critic. The root *yšr* associated with *hōlēk* in v 7 contrasts with *šqr* and *kzb* in v 11 and sets in opposition two contrary lifestyles. Micah uses *hlk* to refer to habitual moral conduct, good or bad, several times (4:2, 2, 5, 5; 6:8, 16). To "walk" implies progress and achievement and so *hlk* sometimes functions as an auxiliary: to walk and do something is to do it on and on, more and more (Gen 8:5; cf. Gen 8:7, which uses *yš*ʾ). This is its sense in Mic 1:8. The *shophar* got louder and louder (Exod 19:19—no motion here); Samuel became taller and better (1 Sam 2:26); David got stronger and stronger, while the house of Saul got weaker and weaker (2 Sam 3:1). To have this idiom in v 11a we would have to join *hōlēk* with *šqr* and *kzb*.

spirit. As with *hōlēk* we seek help in understanding *spirit* in v 11 from its occurrence already in v 7. This link and the theme of the whole unit show that the discourse concerns the spirit of Yahweh active in prophetic utterance. The term *rûaḥ* does not connect well with *hōlēk* unless as an adverb: "walking in the spirit" (cf. Mays: "a man came in the spirit"). We think it is more likely that *rûaḥ* is a delayed modifier of *ʾîš* (the construction is a discontinuous ["broken"] construct phrase [Freedman 1972; reprint 1980: 339–41; O'Connor 1980: 371–90]), making "man . . . of spirit," i.e., a prophet. Cf. *ʾîš hārûaḥ* (Hos 9:7):

| *ʾĕwîl hannābîʾ* | the prophet is a madman, |
| *mĕšuggāʿ ʾîš hārûaḥ* | the spirit-man is crazy. |

It is an evasion of this association of *rûaḥ* with prophecy to take *rûaḥ* as no more than a reference to "wind," in the sense of something insubstantial. NASB, disregarding the Masoretic punctuation, obtains: "If a man walking after wind and falsehood [h]ad told lies *and said*, 'I will speak . . . '"

and deception a lie [he lied]. The Masoretic punctuation and colometry isolate this phrase as a poetic colon. Rhythmically it balances v 10bB. The phrase

seems to be ungrammatical. It is hard to make a clause out of it, except by paraphrase: "he lied falsely." But how does it connect with the preceding material
without emendation? The phrase "spirit and falsehood" could be hendiadys
(Rudolph 1975: *ad loc.*) ("a deceiving spirit" [Hillers 1984: 34]; "a spirit of falsehood" [NEB]). This analysis is supported by the matching "wine and beer" in
v 11aB. Note the assonance and alliteration of *šqr* and *škr*. Here "spirit" contrasts with "wine" as a source of inspiration (Durand 1982; cf. Eph 5:18). There
is also a close connection in meaning between *šqr* and *kzb*; see the following
discussion.

lied. In MT this word is a verb, "he lied." The obvious subject is "man." The
perfect (suffix) verb does not coordinate well with the participle *hōlēk*, so RSV
"go about and utter" does not have a firm foundation. RSV presumably identifies
"spirit and deception" as the object of *kizzēb*, which it translates "utter." While
we agree that *šeqer* refers to the false utterance of a pretend prophet (this usage
is quite common), we cannot find evidence to support the idea that *rûaḥ* likewise denotes utterance. And this moves it too far from the meaning of *rûaḥ* in
v 7. To contrast "the spirit of Yahweh" with "the spirit of deception," the common
term must have similar reference. "Spirit and deception" is not a simple coordination phrase ("wind and lies" [RSV]), but rather hendiadys, as noted above,
the man of the lying spirit; cf. *rûaḥ* in 1 Kgs 22:22, a very significant context (de
Vries 1978: 45). Accepting that *'îš . . . rûaḥ* (v 11aAα) is a good construction,
equivalent to *'îš hārûaḥ* in Hos 9:7, and accepting *rûaḥ wāšeqer* also, putting it
all together yields a discontinuous construct phrase in which the *nomen rectum*
is a hendiadys: "the man of the spirit of lying," i.e., a false prophet. That settled,
there remain the two verbs, likewise in discontinuous conjunction: "going . . .
he lied," meaning that he lied all the time, more and more, worse and worse.

I will preach. What follows in v 11aB is what Micah *reports* as this man's announcement, hardly what he himself would actually have said. It is too blatant
for that. If this is Micah purporting to repeat what this applicant for the job of
"people's prophet" says, then he puts in his mouth the dubious verb that began
this entire oracle, when the opponents first used this verb to insult and silence
the real prophets (v 6a), the verb that the narrator already used in v 6a. The
term clearly stung. As a con man the false prophet would be smooth and plausible; he would claim convincingly to be the real thing. But in Micah's judgment, he is only in it for the rewards, and that is something that cannot be
hidden, that people should be able to detect. Finally in v 11b Micah declares that
that is what "this people" want anyway. They are only too happy to be deceived;
they even pay the prophets to deceive them!

for thee. The verb in v 11aB has two modifiers with *l-* and this presents several possibilities: "I shall preach to (or for) you about (or for?) wine and drink."
It does not seem that liquor could be the prime topic of his proclamation, unless to legitimate the drunkenness of the national leaders (Isaiah 28, Hosea 7).
This is the interpretation in NJB: "I prophecy wine and liquor for you." The
other possibility is that the prophet expects drinks in return for his services, like
an entertainer in a tavern.

he will be. We have already considered two distinct ways of construing this clause. The commonest analysis is to take *lû* in v 11aA as a conditional conjunction, governing the whole of v 11a, which is the protasis. If a pneumatic person comes behaving as described in v 11a and speaking as reported in v 11aB, then "he would be the prophet for a people like this" (JB). The question of the time reference of the verb, however, remains open.

preacher. This participle matches *hôlēk* in v 11aA, just as *kizzēb* matches *'aṭṭîp* making chiasmus.

this people. Eissfeldt (1965: 407) recognizes vv 6–11 "as the continuation of the preceding verses." So "this people" (v 11) matches "this tribe" (v 3).

Comment on Micah 2:6–11

The whole unit is dominated by the *hip'il* of *nṭp*, which occurs three times in v 6 and twice more in v 11. In other words, this verb is used five times in the opening and closing bicolons of the unit, making a solid inclusion. The sarcastic, insulting edge of the word is clear in v 11, where the person qualified to be "the dribbler" (i.e., prophet) of this people is "a man of the spirit" who utters more and more deceptive lies and who says, "I will 'drip' for you for wine and liquor."

The false prophet is characterized in three ways, each derogatory. First as a man of spirit he perpetuates or imitates the charisma of the old pneumatic seers, who were prominent and respectable in association with Samuel, Elijah, and Elisha (Albright 1961), but who seem to have receded from view by the eighth century (Orlinsky 1965, 1974), discredited and replaced by the classical, literary prophets, who were visionaries, more individualistic, less institutionalized than the prophets of the tenth and ninth centuries. The transition is documented by the confrontation between Micaiah and Zedekiah in 1 Kings 22 (de Vries 1978). Second, they resorted to alcohol; Hosea (chapter 7), Isaiah (chapter 28), and Micah are agreed on that. Whether they used alcohol to assist inspiration is not indicated. The testimony of the canonical prophets is doubtless biased and could be just another piece of invective. To judge from 3:5, these prophets were prepared to prophesy for a consideration and to say what the people wanted them to say, which would be necessary if payments were to keep up. The most desirable message was *šālôm* — "Everything's going to be all right!" Cf. Amos 9:10.

In Mic 3:11 it is stated that prophets received money bribes, and their message, endorsed by judges and priests, was:

Is not Yahweh in our midst?
Evil will not come upon us!

The reference to "their mouth" and "their teeth" in 3:5 suggests that payment for such services was in food and drink (cf. Amos 7:12), and this could also be the significance of the reference to "wine and beer" in 2:11. "Sweeten our mouths, say Micah's enemies in prophecy, and our mouths will utter sweets for you" (Jemielity, 1992: 149). But the reference to intoxicating beverages could have another signification. Charismatics can give the impression of drunkenness (Acts 2:13–15; Eph 5:18). In Isaiah 28, however, the descriptions of vomit in connection with bouts of prophecy suggest actual drunkenness, at least in those circles. Third, Micah's use of the terms *šeqer* and *kizzēb* implies that these persons were consciously fraudulent and deliberately deceitful.

In conclusion we should mention that the strife between opposing factions of prophets in ancient Israel, of which we catch a glimpse in Micah 2, has received a lot of attention from scholars in recent years. See literature on p. 297 above. The distinction that the true prophet has a message of woe, the false prophet a message of well-being (*šālôm*) has some validity for Micah 2:6–11, but it is too simplistic to be generally useful (Rowley 1945: 35; Overholt 1970: 62). In one case there is no doubt that a prophet is false, when he recommends the worship of other gods. But the real problem lay with prophets of Yahweh, all of whom operated with the same basic theology, and manifested the same phenomenology. Even the test of who could best predict the future was not of much help, for false prophets could do this too, and often the forecasts of genuine prophets were not realized, because other factors intervened, and God changed his mind (Andersen and Freedman 1989: 638–79). The problem goes back to whether a prophet gained admission to the divine council, and was actually given a message by Yahweh himself, or only made it up out of his own head. This was no more accessible to empirical testing by ancient listeners than it is for modern readers, so the matter cannot be pursued any further in this historical and philological study.

I.6. PROMISE OF RESTORATION (2:12–13)

TRANSLATION

MT

12aAα	*'āsōp 'e'ĕsōp ya'ăqōb kullāk*	I will gather, O Jacob, all of thee,
12aAβ	*qabbēṣ 'ăqabbēṣ šĕ'ērît yiśrā'ēl*	I will assemble [the] remnant, Israel.
12aB	*yaḥad 'ăśîmennû*	A community I will make him,
	kĕṣō'n boṣrâ	like sheep in Bozrah,
12bA	*kĕ'ēder bĕtôk haddābĕrô*	like a flock inside his yard.
12bB	*tĕhîmenâ mē'ādām*	They will be in tumult (away) from man.
13aA	*'ālâ happōrēṣ lipĕnêhem*	The one who bursts through went up ahead of them.
13aBα	*pārĕṣû*	They burst through,
13aBβ	*wayya'ăbōrû ša'ar*	and they passed through the gate,
13aBγ	*wayyēṣĕ'û bô*	and they went out through it.
13bA	*wayya'ăbōr malkām lipĕnêhem*	And their king went through ahead of them,
13bB	*w-yhwh bĕrō'šām*	and Yahweh as their head.

LXX I.6. Promise of Restoration (2:12–13)

12aAα   Being assembled, Jacob will be assembled with all.
12aAβ   Receiving, I shall receive the remaining ones of Israel.
12aB   I shall put their turning aside into the same place,
12bA   as sheep in affliction, as a flock in the midst of their field.
12bB   They will leap up from men.
13aA   Through the channel in front of them they have cut through
13aBα   and have gone through a gate;
13aBβ   and they passed through it,
13aBδ   and they went out through it.
13bA   And their king went through before their face;
13bB   and Kyrios will lead them.

INTRODUCTION TO MICAH 2:12–13

Authenticity and Date

Verses 12–13 sound a note of hope quite different from the surrounding material. They promise restoration of the scattered remnant of Israel. The image of the shepherd and his flock is familiar and often used in Scripture (Isa 40:11; Ezek 34:11–16; Psalm 23). The unit fits nicely into the exilic or even postexilic circumstances of the people of Israel who had been decimated and scattered by the Assyrian and Babylonian invasions, conquests, and deportations that ended the monarchies in both kingdoms. The unit is rightly suspected of being an oracle from that later period, added to update Micah to a time when the judgments he spoke about were complete and a new future had to be faced.

A review of the history of interpretation of this unit is given by L. P. Smith (1952, especially p. 219). Micah 2:12–13 has close affinities in thought and language with portions of the Book of Visions (chapters 4–5) which, for similar reasons, are assigned to the Exile or even later. Condamin (1902) pointed out the repetition in 4:6 of key words from 2:12 — 'sp, qbṣ, śym, š'ryt, yhwh — along with the notions of Israel as a flock and Yahweh as king. Because 2:12–13 is out of place in its present position, Condamin wanted to put it between 4:7 and 4:8, where it achieves "symmetrical repetition" (1902: 385).

Opinion on the exilic origin of 2:12–13 is not unanimous. Brin (1989), quoting Kimchi, Calvin, and a minority of other more recent scholars, concludes "that there cannot be another way of interpreting our prophecy but to see in vv. 12–13 a description of judgment and punishment of Israel" (1989: 121). Brin's method is to find other places in the Hebrew Bible where the same vocabulary has a negative connotation. The verses are a threat to gather Israel "like sheep for slaughter" and to send them into exile, "because this is the punishment for their sins" (1989: 123). It is true that some of the vocabulary in vv 12–13 is ambivalent: "gather" can be used in a kindly sense (Isa 40:11); in 4:12 the purpose of gathering is malign. We have shown (Andersen and Freedman 1980: 333–38) that the verb prṣ can connote breaking either in or out.

Another theory is that, because Micah's authentic prophecies could only be messages of doom, the contradictory message of hope in vv 12–13 must be a false counter-prophecy, and vv 12–13 are a sample of the wares to be hawked by the hireling of v 11. This suggestion, first made by Ewald, has been revived by van der Woude (1969: 257). We are not convinced about this; arguments that Micah would never have said anything like vv 12–13 are *a priori*. The value of van der Woude's discussion lies in his conclusion that language like that in vv 12–13 could have been used by one of Micah's (albeit hostile) contemporaries. So why not by Micah himself?

The language of vv 12–13 can be found in sixth-century writings as well as in eighth-century prophecies. Isaiah 40:11 compares Yahweh, leading back the exiles, to a shepherd. Psalm 23 could have the same background (Freedman 1976; reprint 1980: 275–302). In Isa 52:12 Yahweh walks "in front of" them (cf. v 13b). Jer 23:12 speaks of "the remnant of my flock" (cf. v 12). Compare also Ezek 34:12. Stade (1881: 162), who called the passage "messianic," compared it with Jer 31: 8. A detailed study of all these alleged "parallels" does not yield a single phrase and very few distinct vocabulary words that might show that Mic 2:12–13 comes from the same prophetic circle, or that the editor depends on these later traditions. The same parallelism of ʾsp and qbṣ occurs in Mic 4:12. The parallelism of ʿbr and yṣʾ is attested in 1:11. There is vocabulary in common with Hos 2:2, and we have already argued for the authenticity of that passage (Andersen and Freedman 1980: 209) and for the parallelism of Yahweh and king, identified as David in Hos 3:5 (compare Mic 5:3). Here, however, Yahweh is both shepherd and king, as in 4:7.

The affinities of 2:12–13 with chapters 4–5 are not denied. The Book of Visions (chapters 4–5) is commonly dated to the Exile or later and an exilic date for 2:12–13 is then inferred from the similarity. References to Israel as "Jacob" are used throughout the book of Micah. The Jacob terminology is characteristic of Micah as well as Second Isaiah, and the phrase "remnant of Jacob" (5:6) is the counterpart of "remnant of Israel" here. Through doubt over the future of the human monarchy as a result of the disasters that had obliterated both kingdoms by the early decades of the sixth century, prophecies of restoration inclined toward theocratic government, even though the ideology of a Davidic messiah did not completely fade. The language of vv 12–13 is vague enough to fit any situation in which a scattered people are gathered together again; but there is no specific detail that fits only the Babylonian Exile. The background could equally well be the crisis of 701 B.C.E. and its aftermath, or even one of the earlier disasters in which whole populations were displaced by Israel's more immediate neighbors (Amos 1).

Whether original with Micah, or added much later by a scribe, vv 12–13 have no evident connections with the rest of chapters 1–3. They come as a unique eschatological passage among oracles of judgment aimed at both Israel and Judah, predicting the total destruction of both Samaria and Jerusalem. If that was to be the end of the story, so far as Micah was concerned, then there is no room for the sentiments of vv 12–13. But even on general grounds it is hard to believe that eighth-century prophets, making predictions like those in Mic 1:6 and 3:12 against the background of the well-known, centuries-long history of Yahweh and his people, never asked what Yahweh would do after that. Since the worst they predict (bad enough) is exile for at least a remnant and possible survival of some others in the homeland, there must always have been the chance and the hope of a revival and a renewal. The Exodus already gave a precedent and a model for such a reversal and redemption, and there is no reason to suppose that the possibility of another such cycle of events (slavery in a foreign land followed by rescue and settlement in the promised land) only occurred to people in the sixth century (Mendecki 1981). Furthermore, the curses attached to the old formulas and ceremonies of the covenant warned precisely of such an outcome, along with the hope and promise that even in that extremity repentance could secure a favorable change of policy on the part of the deity. We do not believe that these ideas came to Israelites only after they had been removed to Babylon.

The possibility that Micah saw out beyond the judgments of chapters 1–3 to some kind of recovery, as described in 2:12–13, cannot be ruled out *a priori*. This problem goes hand in hand with similar issues that arise in the Book of Visions (chapters 4–5).

The Poetry of Micah 2:12–13

This unit is highly poetic; its structure is well developed.

				syllables
12aAα	ʾāsōp	ʾeʾĕsōp	yaʿăqōb kullāk	8
12aAβ	qabbēṣ	ʾăqabbēṣ	šĕʾērît yiśrāʾēl	11
12aB	yaḥad	ʾăśîmennû	kĕṣōʾn boṣrâ	9
12bA			kĕʿēder bĕtôk haddābĕrô	8
12bB		tĕhîmenâ	mēʾādām	7
13aA	ʿālâ	happōrēṣ	lipĕnêhem	9
13aB	pārĕṣû		wayyaʿăbōrû	7
13aC		šaʿar	wayyēṣĕʾû bô	6
13bA	wayyaʿăbōr	malkām	lipĕnêhem	9
13bB		w-yhwh	bĕrōʾšām	6

Renaud reads each verse as a quatrain, with beats 4 :: 4; 4 :: 5; 4 :: 4; 3 :: 2. He comments on its "rare regularity" (1977: 107) and, in v 12, its "rigorous parallelism" (1977: 108). Renaud is comfortable with the departure of v 13b from regularity, "because the rhythm is often modified at the end of a piece" (1977: 108). The "limping" rhythm of v 12b (4 :: 5) is less acceptable, and Renaud accepts the rather drastic solution, favored by many previous commentators, of deleting v 12bB as "a marginal gloss," resulting in 4 :: 3.

Retaining all the text and recognizing ten colons in eighty syllables gives a mean of eight syllables per colon. Strange as the syntax of some of the colons as displayed above might seem, they follow the Masoretic accentuation. The intricacies of the connections are traced more readily when each verse is studied as a pentacolon, rather than as two bicolons and two tricolons. R. L. Smith (1984: 28) finds three bicolons in v 12 by reading v 12aB as a 2 : 2 bicolon; but this loses the parallelism of the two similes. These two sets of five colons are related among themselves in intricate ways, but they do not fall into bicolons with standard synonymous parallelism of the kind that we know so well from standard Hebrew poetry.

The vocabulary and syntax are representative of neither standard poetry nor standard prose. The definite article might have been used with "[the] gate." The particle *'et* is not used where it might have been (e.g., neither definite object in v 12a has it). The definite article is used only once (its use with a participle is special). The sparse use of "prose particles" puts the language in the domain of poetry. But the use of *waw*-consecutive for narration in v 13 is more like standard prose.

Scansion, whether by beats or syllable count, shows the same kinds of rhythms as the rest of the book. The colons range in length from six to eleven syllables. There is quite a lot of parallelism; the composition is figurative and rhetorical. We accept it as a good specimen of prophetic discourse in a somewhat rhapsodical vein. Several of the colons are long, some with four words; in contrast with the short colons in the preceding text, they achieve a calm, stately effect. This is especially noticeable in the use of infinitives absolute in the first bicolon of v 12. After the first three long colons, all with four words and four beats, the colons become shorter. Some have only two words and two beats. There is no need to take these as the norm in the interests of uniformity. It is artificial to construe the four-beat colons as 2 : 2.

Verse 12a is a straightforward bicolon, each colon having the same grammatical structure. A simple bicolon can be recovered from v 13 by revising the Masoretic punctuation. Here the preposition with the anaphoric pronoun does retroactive double-duty with the antecedent noun.

| 13aBβ | *wayyaʿăbōrû* | *šaʿar* | and they passed through the gate, | 5 syllables |
| 13aBγ | *wayyēṣěʾû* | *bô* | and they went out through it. | 5 syllables |

A major problem in the language of vv 12–13 is the use of the verbs. The future tense of v 12 switches to narrative past in v 13, and second-person address changes to third-person description. The provisional analysis shown above assumes that each verb achieves one clause and that each clause is likely to constitute one colon of the poem. There are three exceptions to this pattern, at least if we follow the Masoretic punctuation. MT divides v 13a into three sections by *zaqef qaton*. The identity of v 13aA as a colon is assured by both the grammar (it is a complete clause) and the exact match for v 13bA. The division of the rest of v 13a into two portions by *zaqef qaton* achieves a good balance of colon length (seven and six syllables), but here the poetic structure and the grammatical structure do not coincide. Verse 13aB has two verbs, while *gate*, which we might have thought would attach to *and they passed through*, seems to be suspended in front of the next verb *and they went out*. There are two grammatically incomplete colons, vv 12bA and 13bB, each as an echo of items in the preceding colon. Such incomplete second colons are a common feature of standard Hebrew poetry. Thus v 12b is a second simile, a very long prepositional phrase, to match or echo the brief simile at the end of v 12aC. Likewise the two-word phrase that we have made a distinct colon at the end of v 13 (v 13bB) matches and echoes the last two words in v 13bA, in synonymous parallelism, we suspect.

A different kind of problem is presented by the verb *pārĕṣû* in v 13aB. There are five verbs in this verse. They make a chain in which each has a paired relation with the next. The first two are suffixed forms, the next three *waw*-consecutive. The second verb has the same root as the participle in v 13aA, but the participle is singular while the verb is plural. Verse 13 as a whole seems to have an envelope construction, the first and last verbs being third-person masculine singular, the middle ones third-person masculine plural. If vv 13aA and 13bA can be accepted as a discontinuous bicolon wrapped around the rest of the verse, this would point to the identification of the "way-breaker" of v 13aA as Yahweh himself, who is also called "king" and "head" in v 13b. For "king" and "head" in parallel, compare Job 29:25. The repetition of "in front of them" confirms this analysis of the structure. And this detail prevents us from making a longer colon for *pārĕṣû* by reading *lpnyhm pārĕṣû* as the whole clause. Within this envelope of singular verbs are three third-person masculine plural verbs, the first two of which are the same (apart from number) as the two verbs that describe the movement of Yahweh: *prṣ* and *ʿbr*. Shepherd and sheep move in the same way. The verbs in v 13 elaborate on the nouns in v 12. There are three verbs each as the sheep imitate the action of their shepherd.

Shepherd	Flock
ʿālâ	
pōrēṣ	*pārĕṣû*
	wayyaʿăbōrû
	wayyēṣĕʾû
wayyaʿăbōr	

These correspondences among the verbs restrain us from deleting *pārĕṣû* as "a superfluous repetition" of the preceding participle (Mays 1976: 73 n. f), even though retaining it forces us either to place it in a very short colon by itself, or else to have two verbs in v 13aB. The latter is the better option. Either way the prosody is different from the common use of one colon one clause in standard Hebrew verse. The structure of verbs revealed by this analysis also renders unnecessary the attempts to make the poem more "regular" by leveling or harmonizing details that seem to be discordant. This process had already begun in the ancient versions. Syriac and Vulgate read a singular verb in place of *pārĕṣû*. BHS recommends leveling all the past-tense verb forms of v 13 to future, to harmonize with v 12.

NOTES AND COMMENTS

Notes on Micah 2:12–13

12. *I*. The speaker is Yahweh. The editor has given no indication of the change of speaker.

gather. In 1 Kgs 22:17 Micaiah prophesied that Israel would be scattered "like sheep that have no shepherd." The simile seems to have been a commonplace, and the opposite picture of gathering matches the cycle of ill and good fortune that biblical historians found throughout Yahweh's dealings with Israel.

Jacob. The emphasis is on restoration. When "Jacob" is used in chapter 3, the prime focus is on Judah, because of the explicit mention of Jerusalem. But even there Samaria is not out of the picture, so both kingdoms could be in mind here. See the NOTE on "Jacob" in 1:5.

all of thee. Compare *kullām* in 1:2. MT *kullāk* is considered to be a problem because of the third-person forms that follow. Most modern interpreters read "all of him." Support for this emendation is claimed from LXX. In view of the many other differences between MT and LXX in this verse, it is doubtful if LXX can be taken as an accurate translation of some different Hebrew original. LXX seems rather to be struggling with the problems that we still find in the Masoretic Text. The matching names *Jacob* // *Israel*, in chiastic parallelism with *kullāk* and *šĕ'ērît*, require that the latter be combined; and the second-person pronoun suffix indicates that the names are vocative. This analysis yields the paraphrase "I will gather // establish your whole remnant, O Jacob // Israel!" Compare *kol-šĕ'ērît bêt yiśrā'ēl* (Isa 46:3). Verse 12aA means that the entire scattered remnant of the people will be gathered and restored.

remnant. In the light of Hasel's work (1972, 1976), it can no longer be argued that the idea of a remnant is late and is part of the evidence that this oracle is exilic or later. The remnant could be the survivors of the destroyed northern kingdom, or of both kingdoms equally doomed so far as Micah could see at this time in his ministry. The image of a shepherd rounding up his scattered flock is not the same as mass repatriation of deported prisoners. This sequel fits just as well the follow-up of the eviction of people from their property that was denounced in vv 1–11.

community. The term *yaḥad* is literally "together." The word presents several problems, mainly grammatical. First, its position before the verb. As an adverb, *yaḥad*, more commonly *yaḥdāw*, comes later or last in a clause. And most colons in this piece begin with a verb. Even so, the three colons in v 12a have similar structure, with *yaḥad* before the verb in v 12aB matching the absolute infinitives before the verbs in the other two colons. As an adverb, *yaḥad* is a more suitable modifier of the verbs in v 12aA (*gather, assemble*), than of the verb in v 12aB, especially when the object of the verb in v 12aB is singular. How can "together" refer to a single item "him" (a feature of the text obscured by all the translations that change it to "them")? Thus Hillers "I will put them together" (1984: 38); and all translations consulted. Even though *yaḥad* on its own could describe the bringing "together" of two parts, the verb "gather" and the word "remnant" do not seem suitable for a program that simply plans the reunification of the two kingdoms, Judah and Israel. The grammatical problem, both the preverbal position of the adverb and its unsuitability for the verb "set," might be alleviated by attaching it to the previous bicolon, revising the Masoretic punctuation. Without *yaḥad* the scansion of the bicolon vv 12aB–12b is improved; but we cannot give this argument much weight, for there is no indication that the colons in vv 12–13 are meant to be of equal or regular length. Placed at the end of v 12aB, so as to modify the two preceding verbs and to bracket the two nouns "Jacob" and "Israel," *yaḥad* parallels *klk*, which contains the same strain between collective "all" and singular "thou." An objection to the relocation of *yaḥad* from the beginning of v 12aB to the end of v 12aAβ is that it makes that colon too long, and v 12aAβ is already the longest colon in the piece. Even so, *yaḥad* adds only one syllable (segholates were monosyllabic— *yaḥd*—in biblical times), and, as already said, the colons in this piece are not regular. We could make historical sense of this reading if the situation it is dealing with is not the scattering of the whole people, like sheep (as a result of war and exile), but only the division of the nation into two parts. Hosea 2:2 contains a typical example of the climactic use of *yaḥdāw* to unify two colons:

wĕniqbĕṣû	*bĕnê-yĕhûdâ*		
	ûbĕnê-yiśrā'ēl	*yaḥdāw*	

Here Judah corresponds structurally to Jacob in Mic 2:12aA, but that does not mean that "Jacob" is a name for "Judah"; we are commenting only on the structure. In our study of "Jacob" at 1:5 we found no evidence for this equation. Here, too, the same verb *qbṣ* is used and the scenario continues with the verbs *śym* and *ʿlh*. Furthermore, the reunification of the nation predicted by Hosea is achieved by the appointment of "a single leader," *rō'š*, as in Mic 2:13bB. It would be hazardous to permit Hos 2:2 to regulate the interpretation of Mic 2:12–13, but there is enough similarity to suggest that both represent ideas and ideals current in the eighth century.

In the light of Talmon's model study of this word (1989: 53–60), the possibility is now open that *yaḥad* is not always adverbial. We quote his conclusion:

This investigation was to show that the noun *yḥd*, which is a striking linguistic feature of the Qumran Scrolls, is a biblical word. The expression is found in numerous passages of the Hebrew Bible, where it is employed as a synonym for *bryt, qhl, ʿdh*, exactly in the fashion of the scrolls. The term occurs in poetic passages that are accepted as presenting early Biblical Hebrew as well as in books that are considered to be late, such as Ezra and Chronicles. (60)

Talmon did not include Mic 2:12 in his evidence, but his study permits *yaḥad* to be recognized as a noun, as the second object or object complement. The simile of the flock gathered into one pen implies a prior picture of the flock scattered (Zech 13:7). Since *ṣōʾn* is collective, all we can do with *yaḥad* in this clause is to have it refer to the reunification of the scattered flock. The simile requires a point of reference, "I will make him a something, like a flock . . ." The object "him" in v 12aB does not agree with "Jacob," which is second person in v 12aAα, nor with "remnant" in v 12aAβ, which is feminine. In fact the singular "him," which we are unwilling to change to "them," suggests that "Jacob" and "Israel" do not stand for the two parts of the divided monarchy. Each refers to the whole of Israel, and so does "him" in v 12aB. It is the regathering of a scattered flock that will make Jacob a community once more.

him. This pronoun agrees neither with "thou" (v 12aA—hence the emendation of *klk* to *klw*), nor with feminine *remnant* (v 12aAβ), nor with *them* in v 13 (hence the normalized translation "I will set them together" (RSV). In the context the most appropriate referent is "Jacob" // "Israel." There is a shift from second to third person.

Bozrah. To secure parallelism with "yard" in the next colon, the word *boṣrâ* is commonly changed to *baṣṣîrâ*, "in the fold." See Targum, Vulgate. The recovery of the preposition *b-* secures better parallelism with the following *btwk*; but the latter could govern *bṣrh* by retroactive double-duty. It is possible to make sense out of "Bozrah." Bozrah was probably one of the shearing centers, like Timnah (Genesis 38) or Karmel (1 Samuel 25). The simile could have arisen because of the reputation of Bozrah for sheep, the gathering of noisy flocks of sheep in a town could explain the parallel reference to the sheep pen.

Three towns of this name are known in the Bible. One is a city of Moab (Jer 48:24—the text is uncertain). Another is located in the Hauran, south of Damascus (1 Macc 5:26–28). The third, and the only serious candidate, is a city in Edom, an ancient seat of government (Gen 36:33). It is mentioned by other prophets (Amos 1:12; Isa 34:6; 63:1). Its presence here could be intended to evoke memories of the original divine shepherding of Israel from the land of Edom into Canaan after the Exodus. See the NOTE on *man* below.

flock. The usual expression is *ʿēder ṣōʾn*, reversed here. Compare 5:7. All four terms in these two parallel similes go together, and there is probably only one picture, in spite of the repetition of *k-*. The fine details are difficult to secure because of the obscurity (for us) of the meaning of the parallel terms *bṣrh* and *hdbrw*. Since the normal phrase *ʿēder ṣōʾn* has been reversed, perhaps *hdbrw* . . . *bṣrh* constitutes a phrase that has been broken up and inverted.

his yard. The morphology—definite article and suffix on the same noun stem—is widely rejected, although there are other examples (GKC §127i). The antecedent is not *ʿēder*, but Israel. "I shall put him in the midst of his yard— like a flock of sheep." The same kind of parallelism is used in 3:3b.

tumult. The root *hmy* (verb *hāmâ*, noun *hāmôn*) describes the noise made by a crowd (Isa 17:12). The regular imperfect would be *tehĕmeynâ* (BHS prefers *tehĕmeh*). Other roots are possible. The versions differ. Feminine plural (second or third person) seems to be indicated by the ending. If "flock" is the implied subject, the verb could be construed as singular without emendation by recognizing that the suffix *-nh* is energic, or the plural verb could be in concord with the collective meaning of "flock." Accepting the implied subject as "flock," "they (or it) will be tumultuous" (whether stampeding [NEB], or bleating [Allen 1976: 300; R. L. Smith 1984: 28], or simply noisy is another matter). In Ps 55:3 *'āhîmâ* supports the authenticity of MT here. The verb is an intensive *hip'il* and it matches *'ăśîmennû*. The clause is probably relative—"a flock (that) makes a noise."

man. The last word in v 12, literally "from man," is utterly baffling. The preposition *min* has many different meanings. If the idiom here is the same as *hmh m-* in Zech 1:17, *min* is causative. It is possible that *min-* in v 12bB is privative. Assuming that *min-* identifies cause, the commotion is due to men. RSV paraphrases "a noisy multitude of men," emphasizing the large number gathered (compare Hos 2:1). It cannot be taken as absolutely certain that *'ādām* means "man(kind)" here. Another possibility is that Adam is a place to match Bozrah. The refugees sent from Samaria to Jericho (2 Chr 28:15) might have passed by this town on their way down the Jordan Valley.

In view of the location of Bozrah in Edom, the question may be raised as to whether *'dm* in v 12bB should be read as "Edom." The parallelism of "Edom" and "Bozrah" in Isa 63:1 supports the proposal. It would make the allusion to the original Exodus certain. A difficulty in the way of accepting this emendation is the fact that the word "Edom" occurs one hundred times in the Hebrew Bible, and it is always spelled *plene*—*'dwm*. True, Zorell's lexicon cites Ezek 25:14 as *defective*. This spelling occurs in some printed editions, but, so far as we know, it is not attested in any manuscript. It could be that this unique occurrence of the *defective* spelling disguised "Edom" and prompted the reading *'ādām*. Similar difficulty with the same word, *'ādām*, in Mic 5:4b has suggested a similar emendation—to "Aram" in that case. See the NOTE there.

13. *burst through*. On the various connotations of *prṣ*, see Andersen and Freedman (1980: 333–38). An army breaks in, notably when a breach is made in a wall. Animals break out, same verb. The verb *yṣ'* with "gate" normally describes an army setting out on a campaign (compare 1:3). The definite title here suggests that Yahweh led the way, cleared the path, or broke the enclosing wall. The troops (or sheep) followed. The imagery changes from pastoral (v 12) to military (v 13). Yahweh is shepherd in v 12 and king in v 13. The roles are not incompatible. At least a king could be called a shepherd, and a shepherd could become king, prophet, or lawgiver. The two meanings of *prṣ* fit both scenes. In v 12 Yahweh speaks ("I"); in v 13 he is described ("he")—unless the "breaker" is his (messianic) agent (presented as a shepherd in 5:3). The passage through the gate could then be that of an army, not necessarily of a flock of sheep.

went up. We have from time to time mentioned the ambivalence of prefix verbs in time reference; a prefix verb may be past (archaic) or future (standard). No such ambivalence attaches to suffix verbs. Here, along with *waw*-consecutive forms, all the verbs are past tense.

their king. Unidentified. To judge from Hos 3:5, it could be David (resurrected, or a descendant), Yahweh's agent and associate as in Psalm 2. But as "king" and "head" are good parallels, only one protagonist is needed—Yahweh, shepherd, breaker, king, leader.

head. The expression *br'šm* could mean "as their head" or "at their head," leading them (*lpnyhm*). The parallelism of v 13 b is A : B : C :: B' : C'. In contrast with the heads of Jacob (3:1) *b*- could be locative—Yahweh is at their head, i.e., he leads the column of march, like a general or shepherd; but it is also a title (1 Kgs 21:12 [Andersen 1966: 57]; Job 29:25; Isa 51:1) with *bet essentiae*.

Comment on Micah 2:12–13

The transition from v 11 to v 12 is abrupt. Following Micah's diatribe, the speaker ("I") is now clearly Yahweh. This has to be inferred from the content of the speech. There are no indications of the change to a formal oracle. The change in topic and mood is equally abrupt. Micah has just exposed and ridiculed a pseudoprophet. Now Yahweh promises to gather together the scattered remnant of Israel. The oracle assumes that Israel is in need of a salvation that takes the form of bringing lost sheep back into the fold. How Israel got into that state is not a prominent feature of the preceding discourse. To be sure, in 1:16 the mother (city?) mourns her exiled children, and chapter 2 bewails the expulsion of men and women from their homes. Two pictures seem to be superimposed and mingled. One picture gives glimpses of oppressive behavior of powerful persons against property holders, and this seems to be a record of economic oppression within Israel, by other Israelites who are to be punished by exclusion from the community (2:5). The other picture shows war and its horrors, including the mistreatment of refugees. In each case people have been dispossessed and scattered, and this could be the background of the new message of hope announced in vv 12–13. Sellin (1929: 322) found the message appropriate as the aftermath of a calamity that is described by the past-tense verb forms in v 13. A group escaped through the gate of a city under the leadership of their king, and they were promised refuge; they would be gathered into safety, like sheep into a fold.

The promise of recovery and renewal in vv 12–13 expresses divine compassion for an injured nation, one that enjoys Yahweh's favor. This attitude contrasts with the mood of accusation, condemnation, rejection, and punishment found in both 2:1–11 and 3:1–12. It has seemed to many readers that these verses simply do not belong in that place. They are seen as intrusive, and many suggestions have been made to account for the presence of this unit at this location in the received text. Verses 12–13 can be accepted as a part of Micah's message, but one that should logically come after the full program of judgment has been unfolded. If Samaria is to be destroyed, as predicted in 1:6–7, and if Jerusalem is to be destroyed, as predicted in 3:12, then the reversal of fortune promised in 2:12–13 makes sense only if it is a new beginning to be made after all that. The assumption that prophecies should be written down in the temporal sequence of their fulfillment arises from *our* sense of logic and *our* rules of composition. It is not necessarily the organizing principle followed by the editor of the prophecies of Micah. There could be good artistic reasons for embedding the message of hope for a more distant future right in the middle of the prophecies of judgment. The artistic arrangement of the materials in the Book of Visions (chapters 4–5) is the mirror image of the arrangement in the Book of Doom (chapters 1–3). In chapters 4–5 the messages of disaster are embedded in oracles of cleansing (5:9–14) and re-creation (4:1–5), the last scene of the drama being in fact the first scene in the book.

Many modern scholars have operated with the simplistic assumption that Micah had only one message from Yahweh—irrevocable, terminal doom. If this were so, vv 12–13 could not be part of Micah's message at all. Hence the theory that, although it is part of the report of Micah's career, these are not his words; they are an oracle from one of the *šālôm* prophets (3:5), quoted by Micah, appropriately at this point, as a continuation of his debate with the "preacher" of v 11. This quoted "false" prophecy is implicitly refuted by the surrounding words. This idea was propounded by Ewald and can even be found in Ibn Ezra. Van der Woude (1969: 257 n. 2) supports this theory by suggesting that the last words of 2:11 might be translated "but this people prophesied, serving as a follow-up of 2:6–11 and as an introduction to the vss. 12 and 13," and pointing out that the renewal of Micah's discourse in chapter 3 is introduced by "But I said . . . " (3:1) (1969: 257). We do not think that vv 12–13 can sustain interpretation as a *shalom* prophecy, unacceptable to Micah. The *shalom* prophets' message was, "Isn't Yahweh in our midst? No harm will come to us" (3:11b). According to Amos 9:10 they said, "Calamity will not even come close, much less confront us, during our lifetime." Condamin (1902: 385) pointed out that false prophets denied altogether that any "evil" could come from Yahweh, let alone loss of nationhood and exile to a foreign country. Verses 12–13 are quite different. They make sense only as the remedy for a terrible disaster. This prophecy assumes that doom will be fulfilled; but they show that judgment would not be the end of the story of Yahweh and his people. It is only our knowledge of later developments that permits us to read "exile and return" into these words; but, even if they meant that, a promise of return from exile in Jeremiah's time was considered false only when its fulfillment was promised speedily (Jeremiah 28).

The commonest critical assessment of vv 12–13 regards these verses as a later interpolation, exilic or postexilic, intended to restore Micah's credibility when his (supposed) unqualified message of total, terminal destruction did not come true. The nation survived, albeit badly battered and widely scattered. By putting these words into the book it could now be claimed that Micah foresaw that development. There is circular reasoning here. A promise of eventual restitution as such is not to be dismissed as inauthentic unless one already knows that Micah preached nothing but doom. We have found general agreement among the eighth-century prophets that Yahweh's discipline for Israel within a continuing covenant relationship was a process of accusation leading to both plea (for recovery through repentance and reformation) and threat of disasters—the covenant curses; cf. 6:13–16—if there was no change of attitude and conduct. He continued to call them "my people" even when punishing them, and he continued to deal with them even after he had called them "not my people," according to Hosea.

Sometimes the conditional nature of an announced judgment is included in the message (Isa 1:19–20). Even when that kind of language is not used and prophecies seem to announce final judgment, subsequent developments show that the situation remains open; the messages are warnings, not final verdicts. The story of Jonah is a classic example, but it is not the only one. It is also possible for a judgment to be postponed by a prophet's intercession. And even when argument with God and exhortation of the people both fail (a not uncommon experience of prophets) and judgment becomes inevitable, that would not be the end. There would be survivors. Later on prayers for or from the remnant, appealing to the old promises or to divine compassion, might still bring about a change in God's attitude and inaugurate a new beginning. Repentance was always a possibility, either before the threatened punishment or after retribution. It was not necessary to work through and spell out the full theoretical progression of warning, chastisement, penitence, recovery so that every item in the scheme had to be in place in a coherent prophecy. The prophets were not systematic theologians. And beyond all that, such is the mystery and the power of God's grace that out of his own sheer goodness he does not need to be persuaded by prophetic mediators, or impressed by some level of human righteousness, or satisfied by justly punishing evildoers, or swayed by the broken hearts of contrite sinners. He can simply forgive and restore "because he delights in *ḥesed*" (Mic 7:18). To say that vv 12–13 cannot be an integral part of the discourse in chapters 2–3 (they are either a false prophecy or a later interpolation) is to miss the complexity of the paradoxical, ambivalent, dialectical relationship between Yahweh and Israel in the ongoing covenant (at once conditional and unconditional) as it was appreciated by the classical prophets.

INTRODUCTION TO MICAH 3

Chapter 3 consists of three units clearly marked by introductory formulas— twice a call to listen (vv 1, 9), once a messenger formula (v 5). The same people (civil rulers) are addressed in vv 1 and 9, and the accusations (vv 1–3, 9–11) are similar. Another group (prophets) is criticized in v 5. The punishment is forecast in two passages beginning "therefore" (vv 5–7; 12), and the final consequences are introduced by "then" (v 4), which logically follows v 7. In a contrasting statement (v 8), the prophet affirms his determination to declare the word of Yahweh faithfully, in contrast to the perverters of justice (v 1).

The whole message is addressed consistently to Jacob // Israel (vv 1, 8, 9). Samaria is not mentioned; the word "Judah" is not used. The oracle climaxes on Zion // Jerusalem (vv 10, 12), whose "heads, priests, prophets" (v 11) are included in a common indictment. On the significance of such "multiple class-listings," see Fishbane (1985: 34, 461).

The development of the thought is not linear. The parts are arranged in a certain symmetry, but it is not geometrical. The starting point for the action is v 8, which picks up the reference to the prophet as "man of spirit" from 2:11. The rest of the chapter is the declaration of Israel's transgression // sin. The messenger formula (v 5) carries the central indictment aimed at the prophets, "who lead my people astray" (v 5aB). Two additional indictments, twin oracles directed against the rulers (vv 1–4, 9–12), form a frame around the oracle against the prophets.

In contrast to chapters 1–2, the composition of chapter 3 is clear and coherent. The grammar and the poetry represent standard eighth-century prophetic discourse. In chapters 1–2 the colons tended to be short, and the grammatical particles were sparse. This made the text cryptic, opaque. In chapter 3 the colons are longer (average 7.9 syllables per colon), near to the standard 16-syllable bicolon of typical Hebrew verse. At the same time there are fewer omissions of particles—"and," "the," "which," prepositions, pronoun suffixes—so in this grammatical respect the language of the composition diverges from poetic usage. The use of the "prose particles," however, does not make the composition prose, that is, so long as other features, such as parallelism and meter, are taken into account as marks of poetry. And other syntactic details besides the level of use of "prose particles" have to be taken into consideration.

The bicolons in vv 1a, 2b, 3b, 8b, 9a, 10 are examples of Micah's preferred pattern—incomplete synonymous parallelism (A : B : C :: B′ : C′) with rhythmic compensation (in C′). Verses 4aB // 4bA constitute a less formal bicolon embraced by subordinate clauses of time (4aA) and reason (4bB), which have no parallels; the phrase "at that time" makes an inclusion with "then." Verse 2a is a short bicolon.

There is a tendency in this chapter to develop lists. So "heads," "priests," "prophets" are found in three successive colons of identical grammatical structure (v 11a). In vv 2–3 the terms "skin," "flesh," "bones," "meat," are used in a complex pattern of repetition. The three main terms are introduced in the first bicolon, with a participle that is the third of a series—"hating," "loving," "tearing."

skin	
flesh	bones
skin	bones

The parallelism of "skin" and "bones" is used in the fourth // fifth colons, with perfect verbs at the end. Except for the change of verb, the third colon repeats the first. Verse 3b (as emended) contains two words for flesh but deviates by using a consecutive perfect verb. It depends on the others, however, for its elliptical object "them." The pronouns are abundant—

their skin	from upon *them*
their flesh	*their* bones
———	———
their skin	from upon *them*
	their bones

The intervening colon is the only one that contains the referent of these pronouns, "my people," so there is a symmetrical arrangement of cataphoric and anaphoric pronouns. (Modern translations relieve this by supplying a noun in the first colon [RSV, NEB] or by deleting v 2b [NJB]).

Verse 12 contains the trio "Zion" // "Jerusalem" // "mountain of the house" in a tricolon, and the syntax is more sophisticated: the verbs are delayed, and the expected prepositions (*k-* in 12a, *l-* in 12bA) are missing (although *l-* in 12bB does retroactive double-duty in v 12bA, just as *tihyeh* does double-duty in v 12bB. Verse 7 begins with a simple bicolon and continues the succession of verbs into a climactic third colon (with *kullām*), followed by a reason clause (v 7b) that has no parallel.

The accusation in vv 9–10 is in two parts, switching from plural to singular. The parallelism in v 9b is lopsided, with an imperfect verb in parallel with a participle, and the second colon inflated by four "prose" particles without which *yĕšārâ yĕ'aqqēšû* would give a better balance. There is also a modicum of parallelism within v 11b.

The activities of the false prophets are described in v 5. Here two participles (in parallel) are followed by two finite verbs (in parallel). These are consecutive perfect (not imperfect, as in v 9b). The latter parallel pair (*proclaim peace* // *declare war*) are separated by a colon (v 5bC), whose need of a parallel suggests that v 5bA might serve in that capacity. This, however, is far from certain; see the discussion below.

Ideas of darkness are woven together in the four colons of v 6. "Night" and "day" are an inclusion linking the first and fourth colons. "Dark" and "black" are parallels between the second and fourth colons. Otherwise the adjacent pairs make good bicolons, switching from second to third person, which ties v 6b to v 7. The same prepositions are repeated within each of these bicolons, making for complete clarity.

It is clear that a wide range of poetic patterns has been used in a single composition; the variety is no reason for supposing that this is merely an assortment of oracles. It should be taken as one whole, an excellent specimen of eighth-century prophetic discourse.

The syntax shows a similar variation. The high incidence of the definite article is unusual for poetry. *Nota accusativi* is also used, but not consistently (only one of the several objects in vv 2–3 has it). The relative pronoun *'ăšer* is used (it is probably spurious in v 3b). There is no reason to suspect that any of these particles is secondary, the result of a later drift of poetry towards the language of prose. Micah 3 contrasts with most of Hosea in this respect. The poetic technique is similar, but Hosea 4–14 avoids the particles. In Amos they are used more freely than in Micah.

The divergence of Micah 3 from the rules of standard Hebrew grammar as found in classical narrative prose compositions, above all in the Primary History (Genesis–Kings) is seen in its inconsistent use of the verb forms in relation to clause types and paragraph development. It is generally recognized that the three main messages in this chapter are prophecies of a familiar type. There are two parts — an accusation and a sentence. The accusation describes what they have done (past) or are doing (present). We note, however, that the listing of characteristics of the accused in the form of participles is close to the use of participles in utterances of "Woe!" as in 2:1, making it appropriate and beneficial to compare the oracle of 2:1–5 with the indictments in chapter 3 (Reventlow 1996). The judgment speech announces what God will do (future) in punishment. All of the available verbal constructions are used, except for *hinnēh* plus participle for impending action (1:3; 2:3). After the audience is identified or summoned, using noun phrases (vv 1, 5a, 9a), they are further characterized by one or more participles, either definite with the article, or construct (vv 2, 5bA, 9b). The participle form does not imply that they are *now* doing such things, although that is not excluded. Such participles serve as titles acquired by a past achievement, such as "city-builder" (v 10). The identification may be continued by a coordinated relative clause beginning with *wa'ăšer* . . . (vv 3, 5bB), with verbal clauses using either perfect or imperfect verbs, with consecutive perfect as correlative of the latter. These can hardly be future. Perhaps iterative past. Conventional translation by English present tense suggests habitual action rather than a specific crime. The verdict or sentence is introduced by *'āz* (v 4) or *lākēn* (vv 6, 12) followed by imperfect verbs, or by consecutive perfect (not by both used together in this chapter).

I.7. ATTACK ON RULERS (3:1–4)

TRANSLATION

MT

1aA	*wā'ōmar*	[And] I said:
	šim'û-nā' rā'šê ya'ăqōb	Listen, you heads of Jacob,
1aB	*ûqĕṣînê bêt yiśrā'ēl*	and you rulers of the House of Israel.
1b	*hălô' lākem lāda'at 'et-hammišpāṭ*	Is it not for you to know the judgment?

2aA	*śōně'ê ṭôb*	Hating [pl.] good
2aB	*wě'ōhǎbê rā'â*	and loving [pl.] bad;
2bA	*gōzělê 'ôrām mē'ǎlêhem*	tearing [pl.] their skin from off them,
2bB	*ûšě'ērām mē'al 'aṣmôtām*	and their flesh from upon their bones;
3aAα	*wa'ǎšer 'ākělû šě'ēr 'ammî*	and who have eaten the flesh of my people,
3aAβ	*wě'ôrām mē'ǎlêhem hipšîṭû*	and have flayed their skin from off them;
3aB	*wě'et-'aṣmōtêhem piṣṣēḥû*	and their bones have broken,
3bA	*ûpārěśû ka'ǎšer bassîr*	and they chopped (them) like meat[1] in a pot,
3bB	*ûkěbāśār bětôk qallāḥat*	like flesh inside a cauldron.
4aA	*'āz yiz'ǎqû 'el-yhwh*	Then they cried out to Yahweh,
4aB	*wělō' ya'ǎneh 'ōtām*	but he did not answer them;
4bA	*wěyastēr pānāyw mēhem bā'ēt hahî'*	and he hid his face from them in that time,
4bB	*ka'ǎšer hērē'û ma'alělêhem*	as they made evil their deeds.

LXX I.7. *Attack on Rulers (3:1–4)*

1aA	And he will say,
	Hear now these things, rulers of the house of Jacob
1aB	and you who remain of the house of Israel.
1b	Is it not for you to know the judgment (*krima*)?
2aA	Hating [pl.] the good things
2aB	and loving [pl.] the bad things;
2bA	tearing [pl.] their skins from them,
2bB	and their flesh [pl.] from their bones.
3aAα	Just as they have eaten the flesh [pl.] of my people,
3aAβ	and their skins from them they have flayed;
3aB	and their bones they have broken,
3bA	and they chopped (them) like flesh into a pot (metal),
3bB	like carcasses into a cauldron (*khytra* [ceramic]).
4aA	Thus they will cry out to Kyrios,
4aB	but he will not listen to them;
4bA	and he will turn away his face from them at that time,
4bB	because they acted wickedly in their practices against them.

INTRODUCTION TO MICAH 3:1–4

This is the first of two oracles attacking the heads and rulers of Jacob-Israel. It begins with *And I said*, the only autobiographical touch in the entire book. This opening gives the impression that what follows is Micah's response to some preceding situation. This can hardly be a comment on the closing words

---

[1] MT *ka'ǎšer*, "like which," emended to *kišě'ēr*, "like flesh;" cf. LXX.

of chapter 2. We do not accept van der Woude's theory that the oracles in chapter 3 are Micah's response to a false prophecy in 2:12–13. There is nothing in chapter 3 to indicate that it was intended to contradict 2:12–13.

The Poetry of Micah 3:1–4

The invocation in v 1a is a poetic bicolon perfect in every way. The balance is good, whether measured by beats (3 : 3) or syllables (7 : 8). The parallelism is classical, a parade example of Gray's "incomplete synonymous parallelism with rhythmic compensation." These features suggest that the opening "and I said" is extrametrical; but the point is moot. Althann (1983) sometimes regards the standard oracular formulas כה אמר יהוה and נאם יהוה as part of the meter (pp. 21, 153–54) and sometimes as extrametrical (pp. 75, 206). This confusion is general in Hebrew poetry studies; such decisions seem to be purely *ad hoc*, in the interests of theory.

The oracle itself consists of two parts. The accusation in vv 1b–3 is followed by a pronouncement of doom in v 4. The indictment is composed in two five-colon units. Each has an opening colon followed by two bicolons. Verse 1b, with its second-person address, follows from the opening call to attention. It asks a question that awakens echoes of the controversial questions in 2:7. As illustration of their failure to recognize justice, Micah first characterizes the leaders as *hating good and loving evil*. These general attributes are followed by more specific charges. First a third participle is developed into a bicolon (v 2b), again straightforward incomplete synonymous parallelism. The charge is expanded further in a relative clause (v 3aAα) that carries another two well-formed bicolons (both 3 : 3 beats). The switch to third-person verbs in the five colons of v 3 does not necessarily mean that Micah is no longer addressing the rulers he called upon at the beginning of his speech (v 1). That is a grammatical option for an embedded construction.

The use of third-person forms in v 4 is not open to this explanation. The verdict is pronounced on the leaders, not to them. The difference is slight. The discontinuity is most marked in the opening adverb *then* (v 4aA). Something seems to be missing. After the evidence of their guilt in vv 2–3, punishment should be imposed in the form of some fitting disaster that will overtake them. *Then*, when trouble comes, *they will cry out to Yahweh*, and a further indication of their condemnation and rejection will be his refusal to listen to them. To find a situation for this development and a time reference for the adverb *then*, we have to go back to 2:3, where Yahweh announced that he is planning an appropriate evil *against this family*. *Then* refers to *that day* (1:4). In the NOTE, however, we shall look at this problem more closely and suggest a different solution.

The high level of formal poetry sustained in vv 1–3 does not continue in v 4. We saw the same fluctuation in 2:4a and 5. This kind of variation is characteristic of Micah's compositional style throughout. It can hardly be used to recover stages in the editorial or redactional history of the book.

NOTES AND COMMENTS

Notes on Micah 3:1–4

1. *I said.* Strictly speaking this autobiographical statement is the only piece of formal narrative in the book as history. Compare Isa 40:6; Zech 3:5 (Willis 1968; Tidwell 1975). It does not hook into any preceding narrative. The last statement that could be identified with any confidence as a personal remark by Micah was 1:8. However, 3:1 could follow from 2:11, if Micah is responding to an attempt to silence him. In this case it is even clearer that 2:12–13 is an interpolation. The argument with the pseudoprophets resumes at 3:5. What follows in vv 1–4 is clearly an oracle, spoken originally by Yahweh, now proclaimed by Micah. If he is continuing the altercation, supplying a real message from Yahweh in contrast to the fake prophecies he has just ridiculed in 2:11, then the situation is the same, and the people addressed by title now must have been part of the larger audience of chapter 2. Below we shall develop a further argument for identifying (or at least associating) the rulers of 3:1 with the plotters of 2:1.

heads. In contrast to Yahweh as "head" (2:13). For the designation of "judicial officers" as "heads" see Bartlett (1969: 2) and Reviv (1989: 15–21).

rulers. The noun *qāṣîn* is an old term for an (elected?) tribal military chief (Judg 11:6). Its elective, emergency character is seen in Isa 3:6–7. Judges 11:11 shows that *rō'š*, "head," and *qāṣîn*, "commander," when coordinated, can be hendiadys—"commander-in-chief." "Heads" is used alone in Mic 3:11, which, together with v 1b, shows that the office was judicial. In Josh 10:24 the *qĕṣînîm* are subordinate military officers. There is no reason to believe that a term like this retained its meaning unchanged for centuries. This factor and the meager evidence leave the meaning undetermined in Micah 3. In Isa 1:10 it is derogatory and, like the designation of the prophets as "diviners" (Mic 3:6), implies that they are like Philistines. Apart from historic (Josh 10:24; Judg 11:6, 11) and archaic use (Dan 11:18), the word is used only by Isaiah and Micah, and their contemporary use of the term to refer to the rulers of Jerusalem must be connected in some way. This attestation does not necessarily prove, however, that the title was then current in bureaucratic nomenclature.

These "rulers" cannot be identified. The plural suggests that they are not "kings" although kings could be included, since they must bear the ultimate responsibility for the administration of justice in Israel. In view of the scope and scale of the indictment, it is hard to believe that Micah is ignoring altogether the ultimate accountability of the king. In v 11 "heads" are on a par with priests and prophets, so we have some kind of civil magistrates. Yet Micah does not use the standard term *špṭ*. In Mic 5:1 the old-fashioned term *môšēl*, "ruler," is used rather than "king." In Isaiah and Micah *qāṣîn* does not seem to retain the military connotations it has in Joshua and Judges. Terms like this are socially mobile, moving up or down the hierarchical political scale. Whereas the *qĕṣînîm* of Josh 10:24 are subordinates, Jephthah as *qāṣîn* was supreme commander. Perhaps Micah uses the term to cover all officialdom in the civil sphere.

We can at least say that they are national and political positions, ultimately connected with the king at this time.

Here we can see the bad side of the reform of the judiciary attributed to Jehoshaphat (Freedman 1961; Whitelam 1979, especially chapter 10). According to the Chronicler:

> Jehoshaphat remained in Jerusalem a while and then went out among the people from Beer-Sheba to the hill country of Ephraim; he brought them back to the LORD God of their fathers. He appointed judges in the land in all the fortified towns of Judah, in each and every town. He charged the judges: "Consider what you are doing, for you judge not on behalf of man, but on behalf of the LORD; and He is with you when you pass judgment. Now let the dread of the LORD be upon you; act with care, for there is no injustice or favoritism or bribe taking with the LORD our God." Jehoshaphat also appointed in Jerusalem some Levites and priests and heads of the clans of Israelites for rendering judgment in matters of the LORD, and for disputes. Then they returned to Jerusalem. He charged them, "This is how you shall act: in fear of the LORD, with fidelity, and with whole heart. When a dispute comes before you from your brothers living in their towns, whether about homicide, or about ritual, or laws or rules, you must instruct them so that they do not incur guilt before the LORD and wrath be upon you and your brothers. Act so, and you will not incur guilt. See, Amariah the chief priest is over you in all cases concerning the LORD; and Zebadiah son of Ishmael is the commander (*nāgîd*) of the house of Judah in all cases concerning the king; the Levitical officials (*šōṭĕrîm*) are at your disposal; act with resolve and the LORD be with the good (*ṭôb*)." (2 Chr 19:4–11 [NJPS])

There are several features in this restructuring of the administration of justice in Judah that are worthy of attention. First, it represents a greater centralization of the judiciary. In theory the king was an ultimate court of appeal for any citizen (2 Samuel 14; 15:1–6). Jehoshaphat deputized "certain Levites, priests, and heads of families of Israel" (2 Chr 19:8) to serve as the royal court of appeals in Jerusalem. Second, we note that this new arrangement represents more than the imposition of tighter control on the previous system under which local elders could constitute a court in any town (Ruth 4); now the officers of the cult were heavily involved. Their involvement was partly an outgrowth of their ancient duty as custodians and teachers (*šōṭĕrîm*) of the codified customary laws. In this capacity Jehoshaphat had given the Levites educational duties (2 Chr 17:7–9). According to these annals, Jehoshaphat set up a national board or committee heavily weighted on the side of the cult personnel. It consisted of two priests, nine Levites, and five "princes." Third, the choice of "heads of families" as magistrates shows some acceptance of old functional structures, since the clan as the social unit served both the military and judicial organization of the tribes (Exodus 18; Deut 1:9–18 — note the use of the term "heads"). But Micah's judges are no longer heads of families or tribes; they are "heads of Jacob."

Some commentators have suspected that Micah's hostility towards these officials of his time has in it some resentment on the part of a man from the country town of Moresheth against this shift of power from the local courts to the central administration. This side of Micah's outlook has been fully studied by Wolff (1978a, 1978b, 1981). Subsequent discussion (see NOTE on 1:1) has shown that his thesis is not convincing. Under Jehoshaphat there was more management in the center and some outreach from the center to the cities of Judah; but it is going beyond the evidence (remembering too the reservations that are needed when we use Chronicles as a source of historical data) to infer that the traditional village courts had been abolished or curtailed by Micah's time. There is nothing explicit in Micah that betrays the well-known animus of "country" versus "town."

Jehoshaphat's reforms were well intentioned. His officials were commissioned with reminders that they were actually Yahweh's agents in the task (2 Chr 19:6), and they were warned against partiality and receiving bribes (2 Chr 19:7). The picture painted by Micah (which is just like the situations that the other eighth-century prophets reported) shows that Jehoshaphat's pious admonitions were not an effective safeguard against the temptations of power.

the judgment. Verse 1b probably has the same meaning as Hos 5:1—*kî lākem hammišpāṭ*, "for the judgment is yours." There it is priests and royalty together. The definite noun, and the verb "know" (Hos 4:6) suggest that Mic 3:1b is a reminder that the Israelite constitution was based on rulership under Yahweh, whose "code" was available either in traditional *tôrâ* (4:2) or in an occasional "word" declared by the prophet. Assuming that the same *mišpāṭ* is referred to in vv 1 and 8, the prophet is charging the rulers with disdain for the genuine but unpalatable word, preferring the pleasant but phony word of the pseudoprophets (2:7; 3:5). Micah's brief question leaves unexplained just what these "heads" were supposed to know and how they were to know it. The term *mišpāṭ* covers the entire process of administration of justice and can also be focused on one of the moments or parts of the action—hearing the case, coming to a decision, pronouncing a verdict, carrying out that decision. The judge had executive functions, and his responsibilities were to secure the right for the offended party by making a just decision and by seeing that it was carried out. The object of the verb *špṭ*, at least in preexilic times, was usually the innocent, not the criminal. "To know the *mišpāṭ*" meant at least acquaintance with custom and precedent, but more was involved than case law. In Israel, Yahweh was committed to *mišpāṭ*, and his "judgments" were found in traditional decisions, statutes, and *tôrâ*. Hence Hosea's elliptical statement and Micah's cryptic question, by emphasizing "knowledge," take the magistrate's task back to its foundations, the knowledge of the ways of Yahweh. This is close to Jehoshaphat's emphasis on "the fear of Yahweh" as the basis of a judge's work. We note also a balance between "to know *mišpāṭ*" and "to do *mišpāṭ*" in Mic 6:8.

The body of the accusation (vv 2–3) consists of nine colons arranged symmetrically around the middle colon (v 3aAα). Verse 2 consists of two bicolons and the rest of v 3 has two bicolons. Each of these four bicolons has synonymous parallelism, but each is different in its finer details. The series begins in v 2a with simple parallelism of two matching pairs of words—*hating good and loving bad* (A : B :: A' : B'). The next bicolon (v 2b) continues with a participle to match the two participles in v 2a. The bicolon in v 2b has incomplete synonymous parallelism (A : B : C :: B' : C'). The verb does double duty, even though this means that the coordinated *nomen rectum, their skin . . . and their flesh,* is discontinuous. Verse 2 is thus a quatrain in which the first three colons begin with a participle, while the fourth colon is incomplete. The quatrain in v 3aAβ–3bB has a similar structure, with verbs in the first three colons and the fourth incomplete. The first bicolon (v 3aAβ–3aB) matches v 2b closely; it tells once more what they did to *their skin* and *their bones.* The word *their bones* appears in two different shapes. The placement of these variant forms achieves rhyme in each bicolon: *ʿôrām // ʿaṣmôtām, mēʿălêhem // ʿaṣmôtêhem.* The choice that achieves this rhyme must have been deliberate. These four pronoun suffixes (*"their"*) all refer to *my people,* which comes symmetrically in the middle of the two bicolons with the rhyme scheme shown above. So the first two pronouns are cataphoric, the second two are anaphoric. Since pronouns refer backward, not forward in English, the arrangement in the Hebrew text has not been accepted by modern translators and commentators. Some (NIV, NJB, NRSV, REB) supply "my people" in v 2bA. Others (NJPS, Mays) move v 3aAα in front of v 2b. These changes spoil the artistic symmetry of the Hebrew poem.

The language of vv 2–3 is sensational in the extreme. Verses 2–3 describe the butchering, preparation, cooking, and consumption of a meal of human flesh. The act of slaughtering is not included; the events are not presented in natural sequence. Accepting the emendation in v 3bA, the three items "skin," "bones," "flesh," appear twice in the same sequence, making two sets of three colons. The skinning of the carcass is described twice (vv 2bA, 3aB). More logical is the sequence of removal of the flesh from the bones (v 2bB), chopping the bones (v 3aC), and chopping up the meat (v 3b) into the cooking vessels. Only one colon (v 3aA) says that these persons "ate the flesh of my people." The central colon (v 3aAα) is logically the last event in the procedure.

2. *Hating.* Love and hate are covenant terms, object "God." As in Amos 5:15 ("Love Evil and hate Good"), the close connection of "Good" with Yahweh makes it almost a name for him. Thus Amos 5:6 ("Seek Yahweh") prepares for Amos 5:14 ("Seek Good and not Evil). "Good" and "Evil" as abstractions receive their definitions, not from moral philosophy, but from the stipulations of the covenant and the character of Yahweh. Compare Isa 1:17–18. In Micah the terms "good" (1:12; 3:2; 6:8; 7:4) and "bad" (*rāʿ*— 1:12; 2:1; 3:2 [*qere*]; 7:3; *rāʿâ*— 2:3, 3; 3:2 [*ketib*]; 3:11) provide a persistent motif. The contexts and connotations of these terms show that their primary reference is to concrete events and situations. "Bad" is something planned and executed by people (2:1) or God (2:3). "Good" is defined as "doing justice" (6:8).

bad. Of the seven occurrences of this word in Micah, three are masculine, three feminine, and one uncertain. The *ketib/qere* is between feminine and masculine. The point is a fine one. Sometimes Micah prefers rare gender variants, but does not use the feminine of "good."

tearing. Compare *gzlw* in 2:2. The evildoers of 2:1 and the high national officials of chapter 3 do the same things. In both instances the victims are "my people." Micah's oracle is very much in the style of Isa 10:1–2:

hôy haḥōqĕqîm ḥiqĕqê-ʾāwen	Woe to those decreeing decrees of iniquity
ûmĕkattĕbîm ʿāmāl kittēbû	and writers (who) wrote (decrees of) wrong
lĕhaṭṭôt middîn dallîm	to deflect from judgment the poor
wĕligzōl mišpaṭ ʿăniyyê ʿammî	and to strip judgment (from) the poor of my people
lihyôt ʾalmĕnôt šĕlālām	to make widows their prey
wĕʾet-yĕtômîm yābōzzû	and orphans they despoiled

The verb *gzl* could have both a literal and a figurative meaning, with the possibility that 3:2–3 is a figurative description of the more readily identifiable actions of 2:2. Even there we could not determine whether the tearing away of a house was literal or a figure for the seizure of a country's territory. In 3:1–4 there is just one detailed picture. Is it "only hyperbole for their rapacity and cruelty" (Hillers 1984: 43)?

3. *flayed.* The same verb as in Mic 2:8. A procedure in butchering, for cult sacrifice (Lev 1:6) or otherwise. Also a common war atrocity in which the Assyrians took cold-blooded delight. It was also policy with them to boast of such deeds in order to terrify and intimidate potential rebels.

like flesh. MT has *kaʾăšer*, but LXX *hōs sarkas* requires restoration of *kišĕʾēr*, which also secures parallelism with *bāśār*, "flesh," in v 3bB. This emendation has received almost unanimous acceptance. Note, however, that MT already has *šĕʾēr* twice (2bB, 3aA), and *ʾăšer* occurs twice (vv 3a, 4b), so that confusion among four similar words occurring so close together was possible, and indeed likely. The Greek translators, with only a consonantal text, easily misread *kʾšr* in v 3bA, or a Hebrew scribe misread *kšʾr*. Allen (1973: 71) links the error with the fact that LXX seems to have a *Vorlage* with *kʾšr* for *wʾšr* in v 3. The balance is even and a decision between the two is hardly possible. We accept the emendation. See Hutton (1987).

pot. A *sîr* has been identified as a large openmouthed cauldron for stewing. Its parallel *qallāḥat* is attested only here and in 1 Sam 2:14, where it describes the pot in which sacrificial meat is being cooked for the benefit of the priests.

like . . . like. Verse 3b contains a double simile. What is being described in this grisly language? There are no similes in vv 2b–3a. These lines literally describe the preparation of meat for cooking. The imagery could be metaphorical. There are two passages in Ezekiel (11:3–8; 24:1–5) that paint a similar picture. In Ezek 11:7 the city is identified as a cooking pot. The statements could also be literally true. Atrocities like those described in chapter 2, especially if attendant on war, could be described by these horrible comparisons (Isa 9:20). But the gruesome account goes beyond mutilations with violence. Those doing it are not soldiers but rulers who should know *mišpāṭ* (v 1b). What they are doing seems to be a ritual (Ezek 16:20).

We have already noted that the "cauldron" of v 3bB is known elsewhere as a cult vessel. Is this enough to locate the activities of vv 2b–3 in a setting of religious ceremonial, of human sacrifice? Just how human sacrifices were conducted in the ancient Near East, including Israel, is not known in any detail; indeed it is vigorously debated whether such sacrifices were performed at all. The most strenuous debate against the widely held opinion that various biblical passages attest human sacrifice, even within Israel at certain times, has been waged by Weinfeld (1972, 1978; cf. Xella 1976a, 1976b). Green (1975) and Maccoby (1983) have a broad and provocative treatment of the general idea of human sacrifice in historical perspective, together with a useful review of background literature. There is no need to go into detail here; it will be discussed more fully in the NOTE on Mic 6:7. It seems to us that Weinfeld, while sounding many cautions that restrain us from making too much of this possibility (explaining the little known by the less known), did not prove that human sacrifice was never performed in that part of the world. Now, when it was carried out, how did they dispose of the body? Was there only one ritual, whole burnt offering? Or, as with other sacrifices, and as is certainly the case with ritual cannibalism conducted right up to quite recent times in various parts of the world (Fox 1989), the solemn consumption of parts of the body of the victim was an essential part of the ceremony. On cannibalism in the ancient Near East see Oeming (1989). The language of Hosea (8:13; 13:2) shows that the ultimate horror of human sacrifice was practiced in Israel at this time. They made their children "pass through the fire" (2 Kgs 17:16–17) (Weinfeld interprets this phrase otherwise), and Ahaz introduced "the sins of the house of Israel" (Mic 1:5) into Jerusalem (1:13). He too made his sons pass through the fire (2 Kgs 16:3). If the sacrifice of humans followed the ritual of animal sacrifice then the actual eating of portions of the victim's body would follow. The cooking described in Mic 3:2–3 could have no other purpose, since it says "they ate." Because the descriptions of religious actions in the ancient world that have been traditionally understood as human sacrifice (and specifically the burning of babies) are so lacking in detail that it is possible to argue that they are not human sacrifices at all, we have no information as to whether human flesh was actually consumed. At the same time we should recognize that the technical language of ritual slaughter, in fact the act itself, is not reported in 3:2–3.

If the repetition of the verb *gzl* indicates a connection between 2:2 and 3:2, then 3:2b–3 could be a figurative description of the atrocities committed in 2:2, 8–9; 3:2b–3 is an elaborate metaphor adorned with a double simile. The point of the figure is the similarity between tearing property away from an owner, stripping garments off people, and tearing off skin and stripping off flesh. There is not much correspondence between the actions described in chapter 2 and those described in 3:2b–3. The similarity could then reside in the motive and thinking of the guilty ones. Their action is clearly a calculated one (premeditated, according to 2:1–2). The most depraved motivation—hatred of good, love of evil ("Evil, be thou my good!")—is exposed in 3:2a. Cannibalism under duress and *in extremis* is one thing. To eat a human out of sheer malevolence is another. Perhaps an individual psychopath would do this. It is not likely that the entire leadership of Israel engaged in such practices together. Whatever it is they are doing, Micah chooses the most gruesome and repellent action that any human can do to another as a description of their crimes (Gal 5:15).

4. *Then.* The construction presents two grammatical problems (Mulder 1991). The first problem concerns the occasion referred to by the adverb *then*, the time when their prayers will not be (or were not) answered. Both the adverb and its parallel *in that time* (v 4bA) do not seem to have a point of reference in this unit. The second problem concerns the tense of the following verb. Normally when *'āz* is followed by a prefixed verb, the verb refers to a past situation (Rabinowitz 1984). References to a future event (let alone "a distant future" [Mays 1976: 80], namely, the eventual fall of Jerusalem, interpreted in retrospect as a fulfillment of Micah's prophecy, revised by an editor after the event!) are rare for this construction. BDB (p. 23) cites Isa 35:5, 6; 60:5; Mic 3:4, and ("rather differently") Lev 26:41 and 1 Sam 20:10. We do not include the modal use of *'āz* referring to an unfulfilled outcome in the apodosis of a hypothetical condition. Translations and commentaries seem to be unanimous that the reference in Mic 3:4 is future. Yet the accusations in vv 1–3 are not followed by a threat of judgment. If that can be assumed, then v 4 predicts the behavior of the rulers when they are punished. Punishments *are* threatened in connection with other accusations made in chapters 2–3 (2:3, 5; 3:6–7, 12). Those still future situations could be understood to be the time that the adverb *then* is referring to. If this state of affairs comes about after those punitive disasters, there is no need to make this adverb a subordinating conjunction meaning "when" (Dahood 1968: 47). As a temporal adverb pointing to the future it is balanced by "in that time," the "evil time" predicted in 2:3. It is only in 1:6–7 and 3:12 that Micah actually says what this "evil" is that is planned by Yahweh and comes down from him. Samaria and Jerusalem are targeted, more exactly their *bāmôt*. He will do evil to them because their deeds were evil (v 4bB), deeds done on the *bāmôt*. We suggest that the prophetic animus against the *bāmôt* was motivated by something more serious than concern for the claims of a centralized cultus. If these places were the scenes of human sacrifice, the placing of the term *bāmôt* in the Book of Doom (1:3, 5; 3:12) prepares for the rejection of this practice in chapter 6.

If, however, *'āz* has its normal function here, there is no need to go outside this unit to find a situation for it to refer to. In its normal use, *'āz* comes immediately after a narrative passage and reports what they did in that situation. Here, then, it goes on to report what they did when they were engaged in the activities described in vv 2–3. Are these the evil deeds carried out on the *bāmôt*? If, while carrying out those gruesome rites, they "cried out to Yahweh"—*then!*—Yahweh refused to answer them, it was because those deeds were as evil as could be. The verbs *cried out* and *answered* are used technically for intercessions in a cultic setting, associated with and reinforced by sacrifices. The notorious case of

King Mesha of Moab, who sacrificed his son on the wall in a time of peril, comes to mind (Mattingly in Dearman 1989: 229–31). In spite of the arguments of Weinfeld that this kind of thing was not done in Israel, recent studies, particularly those of Hackett (1984, 1987), make it much more likely that the incident involving Mesha (2 Kgs 3:27) was not the only one. It may not be farfetched to suggest that the prayers of v 4 were made in the context of human sacrifice as described so elaborately and with such abhorrence in vv 2–3. We bring in two other pieces of information found in the book of Micah. First, the proposal that human sacrifice should be offered to appease Yahweh is made in 6:7. Second, in that same context, there is a tie-in between the king of Moab and Balaam; and it is part of Hackett's case that the Balaam text from Deir ʿAllā (which is dated to the time of Micah) could contain further evidence of similar practices in Transjordan.

hid. Given that *ʾāz* has its normal reference to past time, all the verbs in v 4 must be preterit. This clears up the puzzle of *yastēr*, pointed as if jussive. It can be recognized as an archaic preterit spelled defectively, or rather a form whose *defective* spelling correctly indicates an originally short vowel. The two colons (vv 4aB, 4bA) are parallel:

and he did not answer them
and he hid his face from them.

This gesture of God is frequently described in the Hebrew Bible (Isa 8:17; 54:8; 64:6; etc). It is not so they cannot see God's face; he averts his gaze because his eyes are too pure to look on iniquity. Refusal to look on sin can be a token of divine forgiveness (Ps 51:11). The relationship is restored when God no longer hides his face (Ezek 39:29). If God lets his face be seen when he grants an audience to a prophet seeking an oracle, that prophet will be admitted to the divine assembly; he will "see the Lord." When this does not happen the prophet is literally "in the dark" (vv 6–7), there is no response from God (v 7bB). The consequences for prophets (v 7) and for "heads" (v 4) are similar. In the case of the general public, denial of access to the face of God implies the cessation of the festivals at which the people appeared before God, and sought his face.

deeds. This noun can be the subject (NEB) or the object (most versions) of the verb. Since *maʿalělêhem* itself means "wicked deeds," it is redundant to use a factitive verb—*hērēʿû*, "they made evil their (evil) deeds." In most of its occurrences this *hipʿil* denominative verb is intransitive (transitive in Num 16:15), the so-called absolute or elative *hipʿil* either meaning "to be as wicked as possible" (Exod 5:23; 2 Kgs 21:11; 1 Chr 21:17; Jer 7:26; Ps 74:3) or describing the total calamity brought by God (Num 11:11; Josh 24:20; Ruth 1:21; 1 Kgs 17:20). Hence the noun is referential—"They have gone to the extreme of wickedness (with) their evil practices." Compare the characterization of the rulers as "lovers of evil" in verse 2a.

The Scripture is full of encouragement to pray—at all times, but especially in time of need. There are promises that God will hear and answer those who call upon him—no conditions, no restrictions. The verbs *zā'aq,* "cry out," and *'ānâ,* "answer," are often associated in such an event. Against this expectation of open and unhindered access to God through prayer, there are warnings of times and circumstances in which prayers are futile. To be genuine, prayer must arise from an acknowledged need and with trust in the goodness of God. A willingness to walk with God (2:7) requires the renunciation of wicked deeds. Otherwise, "Their deeds (the same word as in Mic 3:4) will not permit them to return to their God" (Hos 5:4). Even when they cry to God (Hos 8:2) they won't find him, because he has withdrawn from them (Hos 5:6). Compare Isa 1:15. The language and thought of Mic 3:4 are similar to these and other like passages in Hosea and Isaiah. The people who call on Yahweh in v 4 are the "haters of good" of vv 1–3. The transition is abrupt. Why they should call on Yahweh is not explained. Although such prayer could be their reaction to punitive disasters not described in this oracle, we suggest rather that these prayers were made in the context of the barbarous ceremonies of mutilation and immolation described in vv 2–3, the extreme of wickedness according to v 4bB. What they have done (vv 1–3) is a sufficient explanation of why he has hidden his face from them and will not reply to their call. The reason for God's unresponsiveness is that their deeds are wicked (v 4bB) but even more so if they cry out to him at the very time that they are performing such deeds.

I.8. CONDEMNATION OF PROPHETS (3:5–8)

TRANSLATION

MT

5aA	*kōh 'āmar yhwh 'al-hannĕbî'îm*	Thus Yahweh has stated: Concerning the prophets
5aB	*hammat'îm 'et-'ammî*	who cause my people to go astray,
5bAα	*hannōšĕkîm bĕšinnêhem*	who bite with their teeth
5bAβ	*wĕqārĕ'û šālôm*	and cry out "Peace!"
5bB	*wa'ăšer lō'-yittēn 'al-pîhem*	and the one who does not give upon their mouth,
5bC	*wĕqiddĕšû 'ālāyw milḥāmâ*	{and} they consecrate against him war.
6aA	*lākēn laylâ lākem mēḥāzôn*	Therefore it will be night for you, from vision,
6aB	*wĕḥāšĕkâ lākem miqqĕsōm*	and it will be dark for you, from divination;
6bA	*ûbā'â haššemeš 'al-hannĕbî'îm*	and the sun will set upon the prophets,
6bB	*wĕqādar 'ălêhem hayyôm*	and the day will be dark upon them.
7aAα	*ûbōšû haḥōzîm*	And the visionaries will be ashamed,
7aAβ	*wĕḥāpĕrû haqqōsĕmîm*	and the diviners will be confounded;
7aB	*wĕ'āṭû 'al-śāpām kullām*	and they will cover themselves up to the mustache, all of them,
7b	*kî'ên ma'ănēh 'ĕlōhîm*	for God is not answering.

8aAα	*wĕʾûlām ʾānōkî mālēʾtî kōaḥ*	But, as for me, I have been filled with power
8aAβ	*ʾet-rûaḥ yhwh*	—with the Spirit of Yahweh—
8aB	*ûmišpāṭ ûgĕbûrâ*	and judgment and might;
8bA	*lĕhaggîd lĕyaʿăqōb pišʿô*	to report to Jacob his rebellion,
8bB	*ûlĕyiśrāʾēl ḥaṭṭāʾtô*	and to Israel his sin.

LXX I.8. Condemnation of Prophets (3:5–8)

5aA	Thus says Kyrios
5aB	against the prophets who cause my people to go astray,
5bAα	who bite with their teeth
5bAβ	and preach peace to it [the people].
5bB	And (if) it was not given to their mouth,
5bC	they raised up against him war.
6aA	Therefore it will be night for you, from vision,
6aB	and it will be dark for you, from divination;
6bA	and the sun will set upon the prophets,
6bB	and the day will be dark upon them.
7aAα	And those who see night-visions will be ashamed,
7aAβ	and the diviners will be ridiculed;
7aB	and all of them will rail against them,
7b	for there will be no one listening to them.
8aAα	However, I shall be filled with strength
8aAβ	with the spirit of Kyrios,
8aB	and of judgment and power;
8bA	to declare to Jacob his impieties,
8bB	and to Israel his sins.

Structure of the Text

Part I. Indictment (v 5)

5aA	*kōh ʾāmar yhwh ʿal-hannĕbîʾîm*	10
5aB	*hammatʿîm ʾet-ʿammî*	6
5bAα	*hannōšĕkîm bĕšinnêhem*	8
5bAβ	*wĕqārĕʾû šālôm*	6
5bB	*waʾăšer lōʾ-yittēn ʿal-pîhem*	9
5bC	*wĕqiddĕšû ʿālāyw milḥāmâ*	9

48 syllables

Part II. Sentence (v 6a)

6aA	*lākēn laylâ lākem mēḥazôn*	9
6aB	*wĕḥašĕkâ lākem miqqĕsōm*	9

18 syllables

Part III. Punishment (vv 6b–7)

6bA	*ûbāʾâ haššemeš ʿal-hannĕbîʾîm*	10
6bB	*wĕqādar ʿălêhem hayyôm*	8
7aAα	*ûbōšû haḥōzîm*	6
7aAβ	*wĕḥāpĕrû haqqōsĕmîm*	8
7aB	*wĕʿāṭû ʿal-śāpām kullām*	8
7b	*kî ʾên maʿănēh ʾĕlōhîm*	7

47 syllables

INTRODUCTION TO MICAH 3:5–8

The three oracles in chapter 3 consist of four verses each. The second oracle, spoken *against the prophets*, is 151 syllables in length, longer than the other two, which are about equal (135 [including the quotation formula] and 133 syllables respectively). All of these oracles have the same structure: three verses are devoted to the body of the oracle; the fourth verse is climactic and in a different style from the rest. Thus v 4 gives the outcome of the preceding situation; v 8 gives the prophet's response to the preceding situation; v 12 gives the outcome of the preceding indictment and is also the climax and finale to the whole of the Book of Doom (chapters 1–3).

The oracle *against the prophets* (vv 5–8) fits the form-critical norms for a judgment oracle. After the messenger formula (v 5aA), there is an indictment (vv 5aB–bC) followed by *lākēn*, "therefore," which introduces the sentence (v 6a) followed by the punishment (vv 6b–7). In v 8 *wĕʾûlām* marks the transition to the *apologia* of the prophet. Beginning with v 5b, the use of *zaqef qaton* is only a partial guide to the grammatical and rhetorical structure of this oracle, which requires the recognition of four colons, not three. The oracle is organized symmetrically around the formal sentence (v 6a), which addresses the prophets directly, using second-person pronouns. In the surrounding material the prophets are spoken *about* in the third-person. The symmetry of this judgment oracle is perfect. The centerpiece is a bicolon with flawless synonymous parallelism: A : B : C :: A′ : B′ : C′). This central bicolon is flanked by two blocks of material (six colons each, 48 and 47 syllables respectively). So it falls into three parts.

The central bicolon has eighteen syllables. Each bicolon immediately flanking the central one likewise has eighteen syllables. So the three bicolons in this central section are a little longer than usual for poetry (eighteen syllables each, compared with a 16-syllable bicolon average for standard poetry). The colons in the outermost blocks (two bicolons in vv 5a–5bA, two bicolons in v 7) are shorter (fourteen or fifteen syllables per bicolon).

Besides this purely quantitative balance there is more long-range parallelism between distant colons than immediate parallelism between adjacent colons.

(1) The name *yhwh* in v 5aA is matched by *ʾlhym* at the very end (v 7b). The "stereotype phrase" and double divine name has been broken up to make an inclusion for the whole.

(2) Parts I and III have *ʿal-hannĕbîʾîm* in their first colon (*ʿal* has a different meaning in each).

(3) In spite of the switch from second (Part II) to third person (Part III), the nouns "vision" and "divination" in v 6a are matched by participles for the practitioners of those techniques (*visionaries, diviners*) in v 7a.

(4) The three masculine plural nouns // participles (*the prophets, the misleaders, the biters*) in Part I match the three masculine plural nouns // participles (*the prophets, the visionaries, the diviners*) in Part III.

(5) The composition of Part III is quite straightforward. It spells out the judgment (pronounced directly *to* the prophets in v 6a) in a series of five
clauses each beginning with a consecutive perfect verb (cf. 5:9–14).
There are two bicolons (v 6b, v 7aA) with v 7aB as a climactic fifth colon
that has no formal parallel, at least not nearby. Two such clauses occur
also in Part I (vv 5bAβ, 5bC), but the construction there is much more
complicated, both in the time reference of those verbs and in their syntactic connections with the adjacent colons.

As the grammar is normally construed, "concerning (*'al*, compare 1:1) the
prophets . . . " is taken as a modifier of "said," and the following participles ("the
ones who mislead" and "the ones who bite") are in apposition with "prophets."
There is no noticeable break in the rest of v 5; the relative clause in 5bB apparently coordinates with the participle in 5bA (compare the same development
in vv 2–3). But if all these items are in apposition with "prophets," governed by
'al, then there is no formal indictment, only a long title whose characterization of
the prophets is tantamount to a charge. The oracle itself, the actual pronouncement of Yahweh, begins with v 6, and the logical conjunction *therefore* has only
an implied clause of reason—"because you led my people astray," and so on.
Hence many translations (e.g., RSV, NEB) make the actual divine pronouncement begin with v 6. This is improbable. The Masoretic use of *zaqef qaton* in
v 5aA suggests that "concerning (or against) the prophets" is part of the oracle,
and is linked by apposition to the following participle "leading astray." This could
be valid. No matter how the individual colons are identified, v 5 is a closely
knit unit. The punctuation of JB is better. It takes the four-colon unit of v 5b as
the indictment but renders it as third person. The direct address in v 6a (*lākem*,
twice) is not incompatible with the third-person description in v 5 and the
switch to third person in the remainder of the judgment speech. But second-
person address is also to be expected in v 5. To judge from vv 1 and 9, an opening
vocative, clearly second person, as *lākem* in v 1 shows, can be continued by participles. Hence we suggest that "concerning the prophets" is a parenthetical
subtitle, or at least completes the messenger formula (compare Jer 12:14; 14:1).
Thus the structure is:

Messenger Formula:	This is what Yahweh has said:
Title:	"Concerning the Prophets"
Apposition, or Beginning of Indictment:	Those who mislead my people . . .
Indictment:	Who bite . . .

If the participles are vocative ("You who lead my people astray"), then v 5b
switches to third person because the clauses are subordinate. But the indictment
could begin at once with a charge of misleading the people. The false direction
is then specifically the message of "Peace." These roundabout constructions are

only one feature of a very subtle and sophisticated composition that exploits innuendo to bring out several aspects of how these prophets lead the people astray. On the surface, the word pairs in v 5b seem to be congruent and help to define each other's meanings. They are "teeth" // "mouth" and "peace" // "war." On deeper reflection one realizes that the relationships between these pairs are skewed by ambiguity in reference. After the references to wine in 2:11, one thinks of prophets as gluttons ready to give a favorable oracle in exchange for a drink, but "upon their mouth" could mean "do what they say." The reappearance of the theme of dishonest prophets at this point does not mean that all references to this group should be found in the same place. There is no need for the proposal of Freehof (1941–42) to move 2:6 and 2:11 alongside 3:5.

The language of this unit tends to that of prose. All three "prose particles" are used. This shows that sometimes the *language* of prose can be used in a poetic *composition*.

NOTES AND COMMENTS

Notes on Micah 3:5

prophets. The charge is comprehensive, as if all prophets are under indictment, and Micah does not belong to their league. He is not called a prophet in 1:1, nor in Jer 26:18, although that verse says "he was prophesying" (*hāyâ nibbā'*, an odd construction). Micah is a "seer" (1:1), as are the prophets (v 7), even though in v 7 *hōzîm* is paralleled by the term "diviners," a profession not approved in Israel and condemned by Micah (5:11).

cause . . . to go astray. See the discussion of this root (*t'h*) at Amos 2:4 (Andersen and Freedman 1989: 304–6). This is a complaint frequently made against the false prophets. In Jer 23:13, 23, the people were led into Baʿal-worship by prophets. We have shown in our study of Amos 2:4 that apostasy in this religious sense is not the only deviation due to false prophets. It could be in mind here, if prophets as well as priests were involved in the worship on "high places" condemned in 1:5 and 3:12. But in the immediate context it would seem that the errors lie in the domain of social justice. Isaiah uses this participle ("leading astray") three times (3:12; 9:15 [elders and prophets both]; 30:28), and the victim is usually the people, easily duped by fair-seeming talk about religion or happy to be reassured that their social injustice would not forfeit the favor of God.

There are, however, other associations of this verb. The denial of justice for "my people" moves through three stages. First, the illegal confiscation of property (2:1–5), then the denial of "judgment" by the magistrates (3:1), finally the legitimation of both procedures by prophets who declare *šālôm*, "(All is) well!" While the verb sometimes means that people leave the right path, willingly to follow a false leader, it often describes the staggering gait of a person stupefied by drink. Sometimes it is the prophets themselves who are described as wandering around aimlessly under the influence: they are deceived and deceiving.

In Amos 2:4 it is false prophecies ("lies") that lead the people into errors. In some of its occurrences, the verb means to exclude people from justice.

bite. Verse 5b is generally understood as spelling out what is described briefly in v 11aC—"her prophets divine (*qsm*) for silver," ridiculing the shameless cupidity of the prophets. At the same time it deplores the gullibility of their clients. Mays's comment is characteristic: "What comes out of their mouths depends on whether anything goes in. Feed them and you hear good words; slight them and you hear of your doom (1976: 83)." Such an interpretation is supported by 2:11, which suggests that these prophets were prepared to perform in order to get rewards in the form of drinks. But we have already seen that this meaning for *l-* in that passage is far from certain. There are several reasons for doubting this traditional and popular impression. First, the language of v 5b is far from clear. The statements in v 5b are taken to mean that clients do (or don't) supply the prophets with food, and then they proclaim either peace (v 5bAβ) or war (v 5bC), as the case may be. But the terms used in v 5bAα do not describe normal eating, and v 5bB is a most unusual description of one person feeding another. The four colons of v 5b can be interpreted as two complex sentences. The participle (v 5bA) and the relative clause (v 5bB) can be interpreted as protasis, the clauses with *waw*-consecutive verbs the apodosis. In paraphrase:

> If they have something to chew with their teeth,
> then they will proclaim "Peace!"
> As for him who does not give (them)
>   (something) upon their mouth,
> they will dedicate war against him.

If v 5bAα simply means "they have something to eat," why not use the common words? The associations of *nšk* ("bite") are altogether sinister. Its primary application is to the deadly bite of a serpent (Gen 49:17; Num 21:6–9; Jer 8:17; Amos 5:19; Qoh 10:8, 11) or to wine, thought of as venom (Prov 23:32). Another meaning, which is probably a figurative extension that does not require a special root, is found in the noun *nōšek*, literally "(the) bite," which refers to an extortionate practice of usurers who secured a double dip or payment of interest in advance, enormously increasing the burden of debt. It was this crippling practice, not just money lending, that explains the banning of loans at interest in the Bible. The root probably has this secondary meaning at Hab 2:7. Its use here in Mic 3:5 does not necessarily mean that the prophets are usurers, but it does suggest that they are greedy snakes. The verb is never used to describe ordinary mastication. There is no warrant for such translations as "chew" (Mays) or "eat" (RSV; JB, etc.), in spite of the reference to teeth. The reference to "teeth" is part of the figure. The teeth of the prophets are the fangs of venomous beasts (BDB, 1042a). The comparison of the behavior of the prophets with extortionate business practices is appropriate, not only because prophets and merchants, along with priests and magistrates, were all in it together, each contributing his social function to the common enterprise, but also more directly. The prophets too were in business to make maximum profits. The image is thus congruent with vv 2a–3 (tearing the flesh of my people) and with v 11 (prophesying for money). And while the prophets gain from this religious rip-off, they still proclaim "Peace!" Such an interpretation of v 5bAα is much less strain on the grammar than making *hannōšĕkîm, the biters,* the condition and *wĕqārĕ'û* the consequence. The fault of the prophets is that they simultaneously practice wickedness and proclaim well-being. Verse 5bAβ is not an apodosis; it is simply coordinated with v 5bAα. This analysis also relaxes the obligation to make vv 5bA and 5b closely parallel in grammatical structure. Further, it enables us to recognize that both participles have the same object:

> Misleading my people,
> Biting (them) with their fangs.

They are doing two opposite things to the people at the same time. Extending the chain, we can recognize "my people" in v 5aB as the antecedent of "against him" in v 5bC. Going one step further we may now ask who are given the proclamation of "Peace!" (v 5bAβ). In view of the parallelism of "peace" and "war," we can link v 5bC with v 5bAβ (both hostile activities against the people), and contrast this hostility with the misleading proclamation of peace. Whether the people are willing to be led astray (v 5aB) or whether they are deceived, the outcome is the same: even while the prophets deceptively proclaim "Peace!" to my people, they are ripping off their skin and flesh.

Peace! The verb suggests public proclamation. The message of "Peace!" rather than an oracle of judgment was the usual means for pseudoprophets to gain popularity. Hence the counter-prophecy "No peace!" (Isa 57:21; Jer 12:12; 30:5). Both kinds of proclamation are set against each other in Jer 6:14; 8:11; 30:5; Ezek 13:10, 16.

the one who does not give. The bicolon in vv 5bB–C deals with the second kind of treatment that people receive from these prophets. If the prophets are paid (v 5bAα), they proclaim peace (v 5bAβ); if they are not paid (v 5bB), they declare war (v 5bC). There are many matches between these two bicolons. In v 5bA it is only implied that the prophets receive some kind of payment (see the Note on 2:11). The verb *yittēn,* "he will give," has no explicit object. The verb itself has many connotations. The usual translation "him who puts nothing into their mouths" requires the meaning of "into" for *ʿal* (usually "upon"). The belief that "give upon the mouth" means "give them something to eat" is encouraged by the parallelism of "teeth" and "mouth" and by the opposition of "peace" and "war." In other words, the analysis finds two contrary sets of relationships between these prophets and their hearers. It requires a fairly free and quite interpretive paraphrase to render "those who bite with their teeth" as "when they have something to eat" (RSV). The contrast implies in the first instance that they are paid something, i.e., "pay" is the connotation of *ytn* in v 5bB.

The parallelism in vocabulary between v 5bAα and v 5bB is not matched by similarity in syntax. The relative clause in v 5bB identifies the person *who does not give upon their mouth*, that is, who does not give them what they ask. This "topic" is placed in front of the main clause (v 5bC) and then "resumed" by the pronoun *him* in v 5bC. This grammatical construction, in which an item is "suspended" before a main clause, was called *casus pendens* in traditional grammar. Modern linguists prefer the terms "hanging topic" or "left location." The phenomenon in Biblical Hebrew has been fully studied by Gross (1987); see the review by Andersen (1989). Gross lists many constructions in which the suspended item is a relative clause.

upon their mouth. The idiom "give *upon* their mouth" does not mean "put something *into* their mouth." The idiom *ʿal-peh* refers to speech (tongue and lips can also be used), not to eating—Exod 23:13; compare *wattiśśāʾ bĕrîtî ʿălê-pîkā*, "and you lifted up my covenant upon your mouth" (Ps 50:16), *ûbal-ʾeśśāʾ ʾet-šĕmôtām ʿal-śĕpātāy*, "and I will not lift up their names upon my lips" (Ps 16:4). In Jer 1:9 *ʿal-pî* is used for external contact, along with the idiom *ntn b-* for putting something into the mouth. Since Mic 3:11 says that the prophets divine for silver, and v 5bA uses the language of money exaction, *nātan* could be given its contextual meaning of "pay." So v 5bB could mean "and the one who does not pay (them) (what is) upon their mouth," i.e., what they demand. At the same time the violent language of v 5bC and the association of teeth and mouth indicates that the prophet wants to convey the idea of great greed and rapacity.

consecrate. We seem to be dealing with a protection racket. The use of the term *qdš* would then be sarcastic. This declaration shows that the concepts of the "holy war" are being used. The enemy is declared "cursed" and the aim of the war is to put him under *ḥerem*, complete liquidation.

war. The language suggests that the prophets could legitimate military aggression. It must have added an even deeper bitterness to the wars between Israel and Judah, if each regarded itself as Yahweh's chosen instrument to punish the other for its sins. Of all religious wars, the worst are between the factions of the same religion. Apostates are treated worse than infidels. This doctrine is explicit in 2 Chr 28:9. But Oded the prophet adds that they went too far, forgetting their own culpability. Compare the endorsement of Jeroboam's imperialism by Jonah ben Amittai (2 Kgs 14:25), with the possibility that Amos dissented totally from such a prophetic program (Andersen and Freedman 1989: 585).

Comment on Micah 3:5

There are three parts in v 5—v 5a, vv 5bA–B, vv 5bC–D. Verse 5a is the general heading: "Thus has said Yahweh concerning (against) the prophets, the ones who lead my people astray." The proclamation is limited to the false prophets, and their crime is that they mislead the people of Yahweh. How do they do this? By proclaiming the wrong message: they proclaim peace (for a price) when in fact there will be no peace, and they proclaim war (if they are not paid) against people who deserve to be left alone (in peace as it were). So the misleading prophets are charged with double falsehood: proclaiming peace (when there is no peace) and sanctioning or sanctifying war (when there is no justification for doing so). Interlaced with these charges is the underlying condemnation of the false prophets for being motivated by vicious and violent greed. They "bite with their teeth" just like the moneylenders who insist on payment of the full interest on a loan in advance. This interest was subtracted from the amount loaned. Micah is using hyperbole or exaggerated language, but it is deliberate. The references to "peace" and "war" have as their background the traditional function of the prophet to guide and serve the nation, to proclaim either peace or well-being or to sanction war, as in 1 Kings 22. Micah has taken the standard categories and applied them to the case of an individual who comes to the prophets for help and guidance and instead gets intimidation and extortionate demands. The inquirer is then either given pablum, a deception for which he will pay dearly, or otherwise threatened with dire destruction by these greedy prophets, who do not hesitate to threaten bodily harm among other things if they do not get their fee in full and in advance.

The scenario of Micah 2 and 3 resembles the circumstances of Ahab's seizure of Naboth's estate. Just as in Mic 2:2, Naboth would not sell or exchange his property when Ahab made him a fair offer, so officials (judges) were corrupted to bring against Naboth charges of blasphemy so that he could be religiously excommunicated and executed (Andersen 1966). Hosea 7:3–7 describes a conspiracy to assassinate a king in which the cancellation of the usual immunity of "the Lord's anointed" would require endorsement of a higher divine ruling, which would usually come through one of the prophets.

If Mic 3:5 describes a purely personal retaliation of the prophets against an individual who would not pay up, then it is a rather exaggerated figure to call it "war." In v 11 Micah accuses the prophets of carrying out divinations "for silver." This is just as unethical as a priest who gives *tôrâ* "for a price" and magistrates who give a verdict "for a bribe." The terms *měḥîr* and *kesep* are neutral; they can refer to legitimate money transactions, but *šōḥad*, "bribe" shares its color with them in v 11. Now it is true that some consultants were entitled to a professional fee. We do not know how judges were compensated in Israel, but bribery is denounced often enough in antiquity to indicate that bribery was just as common then as ever. Priests were supposed to receive a subsistence from the regular oblations and not to require any supplement for occasional services that could only subvert their impartiality. There is more evidence for the payment of a consultation fee to a seer (1 Sam 9:6–10; the reference to bread shows that it could be in kind). The prophets of Baʿal who were tools of Jezebel ate at her table (1 Kgs 18:19), and Amaziah's words to Amos (Amos 7:12) hint that only in Judah could he expect to receive a handout of bread for his kind of prophecy. Elisha was absolutely firm in his refusal to receive any kind of honorarium from Naaman (2 Kgs 5:15–16), although in other circumstances he was willing to accept charitable support (2 Kgs 4:8), and Elijah even demanded it (1 Kgs 17:11). Elisha's rebuke of his servant Gehazi was exceptional. Gehazi seems to have been relying on common practice and was simply rectifying an oversight on his master's part. Under other circumstances Elisha probably accepted a fee and Gehazi collected it. Naaman was a special case. Gehazi was deceitful in hiding what he had received. Elisha's list of possible rewards—"silver, garments, olive orchards, vineyards, sheep, oxen, male slaves, female slaves"—is interesting in the light of the items mentioned by Micah.

The classical prophets of Israel were independent voices. They usually had no power base, although they could gain a following and even number kings among their adherents. They had no regular institutional support, although some could function in the cult—a very fragile connection at best. From the beginning of the monarchy David had his own seer (Gad) and court prophet (Nathan). This worked as it was supposed to, given David's kind of commitment to Yahweh, and men of integrity to hold the offices. But few would have the courage to risk their job and their life (1 Kgs 19:2; 22:27; 2 Chr 16:7–10; Jer 26:20–23; 38:15) by speaking the truth. The arrangement described in v 5b seems so transparent, so blatant, that there would be no point to it. An oracle obviously bought could have no power for any of the parties, unless they were in a psychological "conspiracy" with self-deception. This is a well-known religious phenomenon. In a skeptical age, such religious forms are maintained for the sake of the masses, as in the Roman Empire. In desperate times the prophets might command great respect from the leaders who consult them. Religious fraud and deception and gullibility are very complex social and psychological phenomena. Numerous combinations are possible. Charlatans are likely to be believed as sincere even after their racket has been exposed! Another class are sincere yet deluded, and they are the most difficult to come to terms with, in commentaries as well as in real life.

Micah 3:5 suggests that these prophets got away with their fraudulent practices because the people really believed in the power of their words and would fear their curse. In addition, the prophets would claim for themselves proprietary powers over the word of Yahweh, which they could dispense as they pleased. So it was not simply a case of collusion and bribery, but of much deeper and insidious corruption. In the phenomenology of religion it is hard, if not impossible, to draw the line between superstition and magic and genuine engagement with the spirits. There are always those who look on the priest or prophet as a kind of shaman with ability to manipulate the divine powers and with a duty to make those skills available to other persons at need. Kings especially tend to assume that prelates should be at their beck and call, and many religious professionals are happy to fit in with this expectation as timeservers and men-pleasers. It was taken for granted that it was the business of a prophet to manipulate the divine powers, and it was the right of a king to command their services. A ruler who had bought a supportive oracle ("Peace!") to legitimate a criminal regime might have a residue of conscience that could be reached by the genuine word—even Ahab could repent (1 Kgs 21:17–29). But when a rationalizing theology is provided to sanctify injustice, then the false word is sincerely believed, and religion becomes the ultimate instrument of depravity (v 11b). Formal credal orthodoxy is not an adequate test; Micah says nothing along these lines. If anything, the false prophets sounded more orthodox than he did. All systems of belief are equally vulnerable to corruption, and doctrinal correctness can blind people to their moral self-deception. This is the valid point in van der Woude's observations that Micah's rivals were in a strong position by holding to an old covenant theology augmented by a more recent political Zion mystique.

Introduction to Micah 3:6–7

Our display on p. 358 recognizes in vv 6–7 four bicolons in two pairs of comparable length (two of 18 syllables in v 6, 14 and 15 syllables in v 7). The transparent parallelism puts the poetic character of the oracle beyond doubt and supports the results of analysis based on grammar. At the same time all the colons are closely connected. The theme of light and darkness unifies the quatrain in v 6, and the list of three kinds of prophet makes a quatrain out of vv 6b and 7aA. There is a central block of six colons, each beginning in the same way with a *waw*-consecutive suffix verb (the noun *ḥoškâ* in BHS is a mistake — we follow the manuscripts and editions that read *ḥāšĕkâ*). The line forms are identical in the first bicolon in each verse, and these two bicolons both use the same root pair (*ḥzh // qsm*); there is chiasmus in v 6b.

In the book of Micah there is almost no narrative framework on which to hang the oracles. This lack leaves us guessing most of the time as to who is talking to whom. Micah is making the whole report, or the editor is presenting it as if spoken or written by the prophet. Micah says it all, so he presumably is the "I" of 1:8; 3:1, 8; 7:1, 7. Micah is the spokesman of the deity, but this is rarely made explicit by the use of the messenger formula (2:3; 3:5). For the most part it doesn't make much difference to the meaning of the oracles whether they are the direct speech of Yahweh or Micah's proclamation or version of such speech. Even the simple "And I said" of 3:1 could mean, "And I declared the word of Yahweh," because what immediately follows is a characteristic oracular speech.

In immediate dialogue we expect the participants to be identified by "I" and "thou" or "you," while the third-person verbs and pronouns refer *to* others not addressed and possibly not even present. But these simple distinctions do not always guide us safely through prophetic discourse. They are confused by some grammatical and compositional considerations. First, embedded constructions, such as relative clauses and subordinate clauses often contain third-person pronouns when the principal clauses contain first- or second-person forms. Second, in the protocol of formal and dignified speech, a social superior, supremely God, may set up a certain distance between himself and his audience by using third-person pronouns and verbs rather than first person when referring to himself. (The opposite side of this convention is the use of third-person self-reference in deferential or servile speech — "thy slave" = "I".) These somewhat unnatural circumlocutions serve the useful purpose of making the identity and role or relationship of the speaking "I" and the listening "thou" quite clear. A similar purpose is served in legal documentation, where names must be used to identify all parties. When such devices are not used, and when the narrator does not supply equivalent information by keeping track of alternating speakers ("X said to Y, ' . . . '") we are left in the dark, and can only guess at the identity of the speaker and listener from the content of the dialogue. But it is precisely because the participants in dialogue know one another, and know what is being talked about, that the explications needed by us are not present. Is the "I" of 1:8 Micah or Yahweh? Is the "thou" of 1:16 Jerusalem or a representative mother? And so on.

In Micah 3 the "I" (vv 1, 8) is Micah, but the "my" of "my people" (vv 2, 3, 5) could be Micah or Yahweh. At the beginning of a speech there may be direct address—imperative and vocative in vv 1, 9; possibly vocative in v 5; and again in concluding or climactic judgment statements (v 6—prophets; v 12—all leaders). But the indictments (vv 2–3, 5, 9b–11) are all third person, and the consequences of judgment (vv 4, 7) are spelled out obliquely. "He hid his face from *them*," says Micah (v 4b), not Yahweh, who would say, "I will hide my face from you." Why is the material presented in this way?

The transitions from one person to another in this discourse are not the seams of redactional assembly of originally disparate and unconnected scraps of oracles and editorial comment. The fabric is too closely woven for that; there are so many thematic continuities and integrating compositional devices that we are forced to recognize sustained composition. That observation, however, makes the fluctuations in person from second to third the more puzzling. The simplest hypothesis is to have as few people on stage as are needed. It does not make any difference to the meaning of the text whether that stage is an actual location in Jerusalem where Micah was able to speak directly to an assembly of heads, priests, and prophets (v 11), or whether that stage is created by an author in the imagination of readers of the book. Either way it seems strange to us that so much of the report moves from direct address *to* these persons using second-person forms to indirect talk *about* them in the third person. Does this represent any change in the direction of Micah's attention? Does it represent the author now speaking directly to his readers? Are we to suppose that Micah is talking to the same persons throughout and that switching to third person gives a touch of distance and objectivity to his speech? Or does the alternation of second- and third-person discourse mean that from time to time Micah is addressing them directly and sometimes addressing some third participant (never addressed directly, using second-person pronouns or verbs) and talking to this unidentified audience *about* the leaders?

Such a dramatic setting for chapter 3 (and indeed for the entire Book of Doom) requires then two distinct audiences. Although never identified or even addressed directly using second-person pronouns in chapter 3 (for all the second-person forms in that chapter can be referred to the accused), we do have some possible candidates in other parts of the book. First, within chapters 1–3, we have references to "my people," who are victims of their leaders' crimes. They are party to the dispute, even if they don't participate directly in it by confronting and accusing their oppressors. The situation in chapters 1–3 is thus quite different from the situation in chapter 6, where Yahweh confronts his people as such (6:2b) accusing them directly (6:3). In that covenant dispute no distinction is made between people and leaders. In chapters 2–3 the people are the victims, their leaders are the accused. There is not enough detail in chapters 1–3 to permit us to say that the speeches function in a dispute between the people of Israel and the leaders of that people. If that were so, we might consider whether the speeches about the leaders in chapters 2–3 are addressed to Yahweh by the victims.

In Micah 1:2b it is Yahweh who is the witness (*ʿēd*—see the NOTE) in that dispute, and "peoples, all of them" are summoned to hear. In 1:2 and 6:2 *šimʿû* begins an address to the adjudicators; in 3:1, 9 *šimʿû* addresses the accused. In 1:2 we were unable to decide whether *ʿammîm* (matching *hārîm* in 6:1–2) are nations other than Israel, giving an international (cosmic in chapter 6) setting to the disputation and supplying the third party (second audience) that seems to be present, but inconspicuously, in chapters 2–3; or whether in 1:2 the plural *ʿammîm* is a rare form of reference to the people(s) of Israel. The parallel in 1:2aB, the similarity to 6:2a, and the general conventions for conducting a covenant dispute incline us to believe the former, even though this panel of observers takes no detectable part in the proceedings that follow. So "my people," though referred to several times in Micah's Book of Doom, are passive and silent. It is Yahweh (or Micah his agent) who takes up the case on their behalf, functioning as advocate. It is only in 6:6–7 that we hear the voice of the people.

In chapter 6 Yahweh complains about the ungrateful way they have treated him; the Book of Doom contains no such complaints, at least not directly and explicitly. It is only indirectly implied that crimes against humanity are rebellions against the Sovereign of the Universe. In the book of Amos this point is quite explicit. In the Book of Doom, Yahweh is the defender of the defenseless and the only role we can find for the oppressed people is that of a silent and passive audience. What is said consists of charges leveled against their leaders by the prophet. We can suppose that the undoubtedly third-person passages such as 3:4, 5, 7, 10, 11 are addressed to this group.

Verse 8 stands out from all the rest in this regard. Here Micah says that he will declare to Jacob // Israel his rebellion // sin. This more personal speech is closer to chapters 1 and 6 than to the rest of chapters 2–3. Like chapters 1 and 6 it seems to be aimed at the sins of the people of Israel as a whole and in general; whereas the rest of chapters 2–3 is aimed at the specific sins of the leaders of the house of Israel. The orientation of the prophet is thus different in different parts of the book, especially in relation to the people—accused along with their leaders in chapter 6, and possibly in chapter 1, defended against their leaders in chapters 2–3.

The book thus folds together prophecies that change their focus. All (leaders and people) are involved. While the leaders are mainly responsible for the doom that now hangs over the whole nation (both Samaria and Jerusalem and the regions ruled from those cities), the people as a whole will not only share in the consequences as double victims, but even bear some responsibility for their bad leaders.

To understand the text we now have, it does not make any material difference whether this alternation of attention is actual (what Micah did when he delivered his messages orally and publicly) or notional (the way an editor wrote up and interpreted those messages). We are not now in a position to distinguish those two modes. The production and survival of the prophecies in book form mean that they were found useful and actually used for a later audience, the readership or those listening to public reading of the book. Even if originally delivered in their present form and addressed to Micah's living audience, which included representatives of both leadership and common people, when written down and used again the speeches acquire a different significance for this later audience. Yet the involvement of the later readership is not just academic. Such a prophecy has more than historical interest for them. They too are the people; they are likewise responsible. They are in similar danger of judgment; in due time such an audience will experience the book as fulfilled prophecy.

The book in its present form is not presented as fulfilled prophecy. We do not need to suppose more than two stages in the history of prophecies stemming from a prophet such as Micah. Prophecy takes its rise in an oral mode, the living utterances of Micah himself to a particular audience on a specific occasion, concrete, topical, contemporary. It comes down to us in literary mode, a finished literary composition that has attained lasting prestige in a later community that acknowledged Micah as a true prophet of Yahweh with an enduring voice and authoritative message perpetuated beyond his own time. Even if at first he was recognized as an authentic prophet of Yahweh by only a small group of faithful followers, in due time he became a prophet for the whole community of the faithful in later Judaism.

Previous studies have usually emphasized the numerous and extensive differences between the beginning and end product of this process of transformation from oracular proclamation to canonical scripture. Certainly the passage of time would place the book in a continually changing historical perspective, a process of refocusing and redefining that continues up to the present day. We do not deny any of this as part of the history of the book of Micah. The difficulties experienced by every student in recovering and reconstructing that historical development in any detail and with any certainty do not invalidate the intention of such research. The most unclear and controversial part of such investigation lies at the very beginning, in the gap between the living voice and the published book, the time taken, the changes made, the new point of view imposed upon the original material by editors and redactors, and the adjustments made to cater for ongoing use by subsequent editors and redactors. Here we are not tackling that huge question all over again. This kind of research has been fully examined by Renaud (1977). We raise the matter only in order to identify, if we can, the implied audiences of the Book of Doom, and specifically to understand why the discourse in chapter 3 fluctuates between second and third person. And, coming closer to the details, why is the judgment pronounced against the prophets in v 6a in second person, while both the accusation that precedes it in v 5 and the consequences that follow in vv 6b–7 are third person?

These alternations in the pronouns give the reader a bumpy ride everywhere in the book of Micah. The problem is prominent, the remedy is obvious and simple. Normalizing vv 5–7 to second person would make the whole pericope a uniform utterance as might have been spoken *to* the prophets originally. Normalizing vv 5–7 to third person would make a report *about* the prophets such as might have been spoken by the prophet to the people at the time or written for the community later. The perspective of vv 5–7 seems to be suspended between these two moments. We are, however, nearer to the original situation than to the later one in the very survival of at least some direct second-person address, as spoken to the original protagonists. The text has not reached the stage where a scripture-reading community have become the prime users of prophetic traditions, where they, the ongoing community, are being explicitly addressed while the prophets are seen in more remote historical perspective. Verse 6a makes sense only if the seers and diviners are actually present and condemned directly by Micah.

Verse 8 has the same immediacy. The false prophets are not yet discredited; Micah is not yet vindicated; they have yet to be humiliated and shamed. Nothing is intruded by way of later developments that settle the issue of who is right, Micah or his opponents. It is a tense moment, still alive in the text. It has about it the earnestness of a personal *apologia* by Micah himself, a bid for acceptance and credence in the face of the contrary claims and contradictory messages of the other prophets. The exposure of their policies in v 5 and the forecast of their fate in vv 6b–7 sound like warnings for the benefit of the people whom they are leading astray, some of whom might be listening in the background. Such polemics would no longer be needed once the march of events had decided between the competing claims of Micah and his rivals.

We know from Jer 26:18–19 that Micah succeeded in making at least one convert in the place where it mattered most—King Hezekiah himself. At least he was credited with having done that. That report also hints strongly at a circumstance of which the book of Micah itself contains no suggestion, unless we find it in the ominous words of v 5bD—"they consecrated war against him." Micah was personally at risk, in danger of being put to death. It is not likely that the fate of Ahijah the Shilonite (1 Kings 11), Elijah the Tishbite, Micaiah ben Imlah (1 Kings 22), and Amos of Tekoa (Amos 7:10–17) had been forgotten. The form of the oracular material in vv 5–7 thus shows a dual intention on the part of the prophet: first to denounce and condemn the false prophets in direct speech that comes to clearest expression in v 6a; second to discredit them (v 5), to warn the people against them (vv 6b–7) and to gain a hearing for his own message by affirming his own charisma (v 8).

The Poetry of Micah 3:6–7
The judgment speech in vv 6–7 comes in two parts: first direct pronouncement (second person) in v 6a, then description of the consequences (third person) in vv 6b–7. In spite of the switch from second to third person, the whole speech is an integrated composition. The first and last colons begin

with a subordinating conjunction *lākēn* (v 6aA), *kî* (v 7b), and the middle six colons all begin with consecutive perfect (future) verbs. (See the schema on page 358.) To complete this series it is necessary to follow MT and read *hāšĕkâ* rather than *hoškâ* in v 6aB. Immediate parallelism of "night" and "dark" would favor a noun (LXX *skotia*, suggesting the more familiar Hebrew *hāšĕkâ*).

"Night" (v 6aA) has "day" as its inclusion in v 6bB, suggesting that v 6 is a quatrain, in spite of the change in person. And there are other indications that vv 6–7 constitute a single compositional unit. Verse 7a contains three clauses, each beginning with a verb. Those clauses describe the reaction of the prophets to the events predicted in the three verbal clauses in vv 6aB–6b. It is not so easy to work out the subjects of the verbs in v 6. There is some parallelism in v 6b, with *the sun* as subject of the first clause, *the day* as subject of the second, placed chiastically at the end. This position for *hayyôm* also secures a chiastic inclusion with *laylâ* at the beginning of v 6.

This analysis is not compelling, however. It depends on how much weight should be given to expectations of formal parallelism in making textual judgments. The noun *hayyôm*, "the day," is a better parallel for "night" than for *the sun*. Micah continually goes against poetic conventions, particularly in the matter of fixed word pairs. Sometimes he matches a verb with a noun. This flexibility enables him to have more than one match for the same word. The fact that *hšmš* and *hywm* both have the definite article shows that they are to be taken as a pair (in chiasmus). The omission of the definite article with *lylh* and *hškh* (taken as a noun) would bring these two words together. "Night" and "day" are a conventional pair, and here they make an envelope around the quatrain. So all four words are related to each other in different combinations and in various ways, and there is nothing exclusive about any one of those relationships.

It does not follow that, because two words are related semantically and structurally, they must each be the same part of speech. This kind of leveling has often been used by text critics in making emendations, and the same process was already at work in the mind of the Greek translators. The noun *hayyôm* is often used as an adverb, and its position at the end of the unit agrees with this function. If taken as a noun, this would be the only attestation of "day" as subject of *qdr*, "to be dark." Usually it is celestial elements (sun, moon, stars, sky) that are subjects of *qal* or objects of *hipʿil* of *qdr*.

We accept v 6 as a tetracolon, in spite of the switch from second to third person; v 6a has close synonymous parallelism except for the unsolved question of the relationship between the noun "night" and the verb "it will become dark." We have seen that this tension can be resolved by reading a noun "darkness" in v 6aB; and some translations do make "night" predicative, and so quasi-verbal — "It will be night." Grammatically "night" is the subject — "Night (will be) for you," i.e., "You will have night." The parallelism within v 6b is likewise close, especially if "the day" is the subject of *qdr*. Note the repetition of the preposition *ʿal* to match the repetition of *l-* in v 6a. In addition, each half-verse has connections with the other. They are chiastic. Verses 6aA and 6bB are re-

lated by the parallelism of "night" and "day." Verses 6aB and 6bA each begins
with a third-person feminine singular verb, but only the second has an explicit
subject, "the sun." This is also a suitable, delayed subject for v 6aB, binding
the two bicolons together and explaining the verb in v 6aB. We suspect that, because readers could not wait for "day" to complete the parallelism with "night,"
the trio of verbs in v 6 (which balances the trio in v 7) was forfeited by reading
ḥoškâ as a noun rather than as a verb (already in LXX).

Notes on Micah 3:6–7

6. *night*. The first clause has no verb. "It shall be" is supplied. Taken all together,
the four colons of v 6 state quite literally that the sun will set in the daytime. This
language is frequently used in apocalyptic passages—look at Ezek 32:7–8; Joel
2:10; 4:15; Amos 5:18–20; Zeph 1:15. It is never used to describe the lack of revelation, unless it be in this one instance. The pattern in v 6 resembles that in vv
2–3, with referential pronouns flanking the nouns to which they refer.

> It will be night for you
> and it will be dark for you
> and the sun will set over the prophets
> and it will be black over them on that day.

These statements are qualified by the parallels "from vision" // "from divination." The *min-* is certainly privative (Dahood 1980: 14 n. 3). But the phrases are
not in apposition to "night"—"night . . . without vision" (RSV). After all, the
pseudoprophets could always concoct a vision, and the diviners were never
without mantic instruments. Their systems could never fail. No, these events
will take place "without vision," that is, unforeseen in their prophetic dreams
(pretended or otherwise), undetected in advance by their divinations (contrived
or otherwise). The prophets will be taken by surprise. Hence their dismay (v 7).
They had promised peace, except to those who opposed them; they expected
light. The situation is similar to that in Amos 5:18–20.

    dark. The verb is a semantic, but not a grammatical, parallel to "night." Hence
the modern preference for "darkness" supported by LXX *kai skotia*. Sperber
(1966: 658) accepts *ḥoškâ* as a noun, feminine form of *ḥōšek*. Unless we read a
noun *ḥoškâ* for *ḥāšĕkâ* at the beginning of v 6aB, the parallelism in v 6a is only
partial. Commentators who prefer the noun base their decision on a somewhat
mechanical approach to poetic parallelism. Accepting MT secures a symmetrical pattern for the eight colons of vv 6–7; but now we have to find a feminine
subject for *ḥāšĕkâ*. It cannot be "night," which is masculine. The subject is "the
sun" in the next colon. Here we have another instance of Micah's practice of
delayed declaration of a grammatical subject. Having said all that, we recognize that the claims of MT and LXX for reading *ḥāšĕkâ* or perhaps *ḥoškâ* are
nicely balanced, and we are unable to choose between them.

divination. The use of the infinitive rather than the regular noun *qesem* shows that it means "without their having divined it," not "that ye shall have no vision" (RV). The latter would imply that previously they had received visions, but that now visions will no longer be granted to them. Is it likely that Micah would make such a concession to the false prophets?

the sun will set. Other eighth-century prophets use the imagery of light and darkness as a metaphor for good and evil, but not for the speech or silence of God in revelation. In some passages the contrast between night and day corresponds to the absence or presence of Yahweh as light (not enlightenment in the intellectual sense). Micah himself uses this very image in 7:8 (cf. Isa 9:1). When Amos predicts that the Day of Yahweh will be darkness, not light (5:18), many commentators think that he was predicting a literal eclipse, and the language of Amos 8:9 supports this interpretation. The idiom used in v 6bA is the usual one for sunset, not for an eclipse of the sun at an unusual time of the day. Here it could mean metaphorically that the day of the false prophets will end. If taken more literally, it could predict some cosmic disaster (Amos 5:8), unforeseen by the false prophets, and so serving to discredit them as well as to confound them. Since v 6bA says that "the sun will set upon the prophets," this seems to be something that applies to them expressly, not to others, or not to others in the same way. Hence we conclude that it is not just a figure of speech for the end of their influence as prophets and their exercise of authority and power (their sun has set; their day is over). The main effect is upon them; v 6a is pronounced against them. They will be ashamed and abashed (v 7). The judgment is narrowly targeted on this group. But just how they will be publicly discredited is not explained. The final colon (v 7b) gives the reason for the prophets' discomfiture, dramatized by covering their mustache; it is "because there is no answer from God."

the day. This word is the obvious candidate to be the subject of *wĕqādar, and it will be dark*. *The day* is not exactly a synonym for *the sun*, but the associations are close enough. Yet the match is awkward. A better match for *day* would be *night* in v 6a, making an inclusion around the quatrain. The article with "*sun*" is appropriate for reference to a unique object. But *the day* evokes the question "Which day?" In Hebrew *hayyôm*, "the day," usually refers adverbially to present time; the article has demonstrative force—"this day," "today," or here "that day," short for *hayyôm hahû'*, "that day" (De Vries 1975: 151–277), the eschatological time when the sun and the moon will darken (Joel 2:10; 4:15).

7. *visionaries*. In eighth-century usage the terms "visionary" and "prophet" are equivalent and interchangeable. "Prophets" is used again in v 11. The participles here correspond to the nouns in v 6. The third category, *diviners*, gives its opprobrium to the other two. Note the similar list of five terms in Jer 27:9.

confounded. Or "embarrassed"; *ḥpr* is nearly always in parallel with *bwš* as here. It describes dismay when something unexpected happens.

cover. The verb describes the action of wrapping oneself completely in a robe of some kind. All the usual terms for outer garments are used—*beged* (Jer 43:12;

compare Ps 109:19), *mě'îl* (Isa 59:17), *śalmâ* (Ps 104:2). When nothing is mentioned, one of these should be understood. This mode of dress was used by a harlot (Gen 38:14), or a mourner (Ezek 24:17, 22), or a leper (Lev 13:45), the latter implying shame. In this context, the idiom "cover upon the mustache" does not mean to put some kind of covering over the upper lip as such, but to wrap oneself in a robe right up to the mustache, leaving only nose and eyes visible.

all of them. In the light of the discussion of *kullām* in 1:2, a similar adverbial meaning is possible here. They shall cover themselves *completely*, right up to the mustache. Alternatively *kullām* means that whole group—"all of them"—represented by the three classes: prophets, seers, diviners.

answering. The noun (not participle) *ma'ăneh* means "reply" not revelation. If it had been absolute, not construct, we might have read a participle—"God is not answering them"—but there is no attestation of such a *hip'il*. Verse 7b does not follow from the rest of v 7. Verse 7b matches v 4aB. Both refer specifically to the saving response of God to a call for aid, not to the granting of a vision on request.

> I will call upon Elohim
> And Yahweh will save me (Ps 55:16)

The opposite sequence is: "They call on God, but he doesn't answer" (*'ên 'ôneh* [1 Kgs 18:29]). A favorable response could be either a salvation oracle, given to the person through a prophet, or simply some action that leads to the person's safety, typically divine intervention in the course of a battle, as with a thunderstorm. Or both in combination, a promise of deliverance that is fulfilled by action.

God. The common title "Yahweh Elohim" is split to make an envelope around vv 5–7.

Comment on Micah 3:6–7

The Israelites were never able to put the detection of the false prophet on an empirical basis, except in the extreme case when he incites to apostasy (Deuteronomy 13). Although in general the prophets of weal were more suspect than the prophets of woe, there were times when the word of peace did come from God. Micah himself prophesies both judgment and salvation. In this context, however, he contrasts their false promise of well-being (v 11) with his own fearless exposure of the nation's sins (v 8). There was no unchangeable word, true for all times. In some polemics the fraudulent character of foreign prophets was tested by their ability to forecast events (Isa 41:21–29). This was the particular skill of the prognosticators or diviners. By calling his opponents "visionaries" and "diviners" (*qsm* [vv 6, 7, 11]—always an un-Israelite practice), Micah cannot be conceding that there was any validity in their practices, now to be terminated. That being so, it is not likely that the imagery of the sun going down over the prophets is metaphorical, meaning the eclipse (this is now a "dead" metaphor) of their previously successful practice. Fields (1992) has shown that the motif of "night" is used in biblical literature as a symbol of destruction: "The mere mention of evening or night in an ancient Hebrew narrative imparted to the narrative a mood of menacing and ill-omened portent" (Fields 1992: 32). Such a literary usage in Micah's prophecy obviates the need to find in the language of vv 6–7 the specifics of just how the visionaries will be discredited, references either to some meteorological happening or to some technical side of divination.

Introduction to Micah 3:8

Verse 8 seems to be a more personal statement by the prophet himself. At this point in the book it is an *apologia* for the forthrightness of the oracles in which it is embedded and which are aptly described as declaring to Jacob his rebellion and to Israel his sin. This unit contrasts Micah's endowment as a genuine prophet with the false claims of his opponents. In claiming the spirit of Yahweh, Micah lists the distinguishing marks of the true prophet—his courageous declaration of the truth about the nation's sins (v 8b), in contrast to the reassuring words of peace spoken by the pseudoprophets, and his support by supernatural power. This general claim could cover all the prophet's ministry, not just the ensuing oracle. That is, v 8 is not necessarily a preface to vv 9–12 as such; it applies to the sustained themes of chapters 1–3 as a whole.

As found elsewhere in chapter 3, the last component in an oracle is often not quite as poetic as the body. Verse 8 is just one long complex clause. The verb in v 8aAα governs a long and complex object and is followed by an elaborate infinitival construction. Verse 8b is an excellent bicolon, using Micah's preferred parallels—*rebellion // sin* (1:5; compare 1:13), *Jacob // Israel* (1:5; 2:12; 3:1, 9). Verse 8b has 8 :: 8 syllables, which is standard. But v 8a does not divide into two matching colons. It is grammatically awkward. It seems to have a list of three nouns—*power . . . and judgment and might*—interrupted by the phrase *the spirit of Yahweh*. The latter, with *nota accusativi*, seems to be the object of *I have been filled*, or "I am full"; but this leaves the other nouns (or the phrase of three coordinated nouns) unaccounted for. Perhaps they constitute a second object, or instrumental adverb.

Notes on Micah 3:8

filled. The awkward placement of the phrase "by the spirit of Yahweh" inside the coordination phrase "power . . . and judgment and might" does not mean that it is an addition, to be removed (NEB). The problem lies more on the level of formal syntax, due to the peculiarities of the verb *ml'*. The syntax of *ml'* is mercurial. An event in which agent A fills container B with substance C is usually reported using the *pi'el*. This *pi'el* is factitive of the stative *qal* (Jenni 1968: 22, 83; Lambdin 1971: 193; Waltke and O'Connor 1990: 400–4; Muraoka 1991: 155; the *pu'al* is attested only in Cant 5:14). This idiom describes the gift of the spirit (Exod 28:3) or the production of a psychological state — "you filled me (with) indignation" (Jer 5:17). In Exod 35:31 (cf. Exod 31:3) the preposition *b-* is used to mark the second object — *wayĕmallē' 'ōtô rûaḥ 'ĕlōhîm bĕḥokmâ* . . . , "and he filled him (with) the spirit of God, with wisdom . . . " When the agent A is not specified, either B or C can be the subject of *qal ml'*. "B is full (of) C" makes *ml'* a kind of stative verb, in agreement with its vocalization. The *nip'al* can be an alternative: "Joshua was full of the spirit of wisdom" (Deut 34:9). When the substance filling the container is the subject, the object B can be marked as direct using *'et*: "The cloud filled the house" (1 Kgs 8:10). Here *ml'* is transitive, in spite of the stative vocalization. B and C are interchangeable as subject and object. In Mic 3:8 *'et* shows that the spirit of Yahweh is what Micah is full of; cf. Jer 6:11. The preposition is either *nota accusativi*, or instrumental "with," not agential "by." The understood agent is Yahweh. The spirit should not be identified as the agent of the filling (so Allen). We are speaking only of the grammar. The phrase "the spirit of Yahweh" in v 8aA implies that it is Yahweh who has filled Micah with his spirit, as if *ml'ty* is functioning as passive of the *pi'el*.

Mic 3:8 is curious in that it seems to have two objects, either of which would make sense, hence the impulse to delete one of them. Either "I am filled with the spirit," or "I am filled with strength . . . and judgment and might." Does this mean that Micah is filled with both the spirit and with those other qualities? Such endowments cannot be separated. The attributes of power, judgment and might come from (or with) the spirit of Yahweh. This relationship could be secured if *rûaḥ* governs all three following nouns — the spirit of Yahweh and of judgment and of heroism. But is it acceptable to have the name Yahweh coordinated with two common nouns in this way? If it were not for the presence of the Name, the expression "spirit of judgment and might" would be acceptable (cf. Isa 11:2). In spite of its awkwardness, it is more likely that the last two nouns are in delayed coordination with *kōaḥ*.

power. A similar saying about Shoot // Branch in Isa 11:2 characterizes the spirit of Yahweh as a spirit of wisdom and other virtues, including *gĕbûrâ*. This charisma enables the Shoot to judge justly. Micah claims the same endowment. The language reminds one of the more vigorous early charismatic prophets, notably Elijah, and suggests a vehemence that could produce the kind of utterance we find in chapter 1, and arouse the kind of opposition that follows in chapter 2.

report. Compare the use of the same construction in 6:8. This suggests that the medium is the same in both cases, namely, prophetic revelation followed by public declaration.

I.9. Condemnation of Rulers (3:9–12)

TRANSLATION

MT

9aA *šimʿû-nāʾ zōʾt rāʾšê bêt yaʿăqōb*	Listen to this, you heads of the House of Jacob,
9aB *ûqĕṣînê bêt yiśrāʾēl*	and you rulers of the House of Israel:
9bA *hamătaʿăbîm mišpāṭ*	who detest what is right,
9bB *wĕʾēt kol-hayĕšārâ yĕʿaqqēšû*	and everything straight they pervert.
10a *bōneh ṣiyyôn bĕdāmîm*	He who builds Zion with blood,
10b *wîrûšālēm bĕʿawlâ*	and Jerusalem with wickedness.
11aAα *rāʾšeyhā bĕšōḥad yišpōṭû*	Her heads judged for a bribe,
11aAβ *wĕkōhăneyhā bimĕḥîr yôrû*	and her priests gave rulings for a fee,
11aB *ûnĕbîʾêhā bĕkesep yiqsōmû*	and her prophets divined for money;
11bA *wĕʿal-yhwh yiššāʿēnû lēʾmōr*	and on Yahweh they relied, saying:
11bB *hălôʾ yhwh bĕqirbēnû*	Is not Yahweh in our midst?
11bC *lōʾ-tābôʾ ʿālênû rāʿâ*	Evil will not come against us.
12aA *lākēn biglalĕkem*	Therefore, on account of you
12aB *ṣiyyôn śādeh tēḥārēš*	Zion will be plowed like a field,
12bA *wîrûšālēm ʾiyyîn tihyeh*	and Jerusalem will become rubble heaps,
12bB *wĕhar habbayit lĕbāmôt yāʿar*	and the mountain of the house *bāmôt* of the forest.

LXX I.9. *Condemnation of Rulers (3:9–12)*

9aA	Listen indeed to these things, you chiefs of the House of Jacob,
9aB	and you who remain of the House of Israel:
9bA	who abominate judgment (*krima*)
9bB	and all the straight things pervert.
10a	Those who build Zion with blood(s),
10b	and Jerusalem with wickednesses.
11aAα	Her leaders with bribes were judging,
11aAβ	and her priests for a fee were giving answers,
11aB	and her prophets for silver were divining;
11bA	and on Kyrios they were resting, saying:
11bB	Is not Kyrios among us?
11bC	Evils will not come against us.
12aA	Therefore, on account of you
12aB	Zion will be ploughed as a field,
12bA	and Jerusalem will be a fruit-shed of the field,
12bB	and the mountain of the house a grove of the thicket.

INTRODUCTION TO MICAH 3:9–12

This oracle recapitulates and completes the two units already given in chapter 3. They dealt separately with civil leaders (3:1–4) and prophets (3:5–7). Verse 11 brings these groups together, with priests added for good measure. They are one in their false reliance on Yahweh, and the pious slogan of v 11b should be assigned to them all, not just to the prophets last on the list. And all of these together are to blame for the impending devastation of Jerusalem, predicted in v 12.

This, the final oracle in the Book of Doom (chapters 1–3), has two main parts—the charge (vv 9–11) and the sentence (v 12). The judgment is pronounced in explicitly direct address (*-kem*, "you," pl.) like the opening imperative, which could cover all of v 9.

The accusation moves from a general indictment of all the leaders (v 9) to a bill of particulars that distinguishes three or four groups—an individual (the King?) (v 10) and the three main sectors of leadership—judges, priests, prophets (v 11a). Next, in a charge that probably applies to them all, they are accused of mouthing sanctimonious slogans (v 11b). Then doom is pronounced on Jerusalem (v 12).

All three oracles in chapter 3 develop in the same way. They begin to characterize the groups under accusation by listing participles. These initial characteristics are followed by more concrete reports of specific crimes, recited in narrative form using finite verbs. This pattern appears already in the bicolon in v 9b.

9bA	*hamăta'ăbîm mišpāṭ*	the (ones) detesting [part.] what is right,
9bB	*wĕ'ēt kol-hayĕšārâ*	and everything straight they pervert
	yĕ'aqqēšû	[verb].

This bicolon is followed by another participle, this time singular (*bōneh* [v 10]). The participle with the definite article in v 9b could be vocative, but the participle in v 10a, which is absolute not construct, has no definite article. The language is proverbial. This bicolon accuses a particular person of building Zion with blood. The charge continues into v 11, where the nouns are plural and the verbs switch to third person, as if the prophet, as prosecutor, is describing the crimes of the accused, addressing the judge or some other audience, perhaps the people who have been oppressed by the leaders and led astray by the prophets.

The language is mixed. In v 9b the prose particles are used as in the grammar of prose; they are sparse in the rest of the unit. The definite article in v 9bA is either vocative or equivalent to the relative pronoun; the definite article in *har habbayit* (v 12bB) is standard for the construct chain in prose and not uncommon in poetry.

The speech is not even in style and texture. There are sixteen colons, with the allocation of the quotation formula *lē'mōr* (v 11bAβ) indeterminate. Where there is parallelism, the colons are even in length (7 :: 8 syllables in v 10; 9 :: 8 in v 12b).

Verse 11 consists of two tricolons with 25 and 27 (or 24) syllables respectively. The tricolon of v 11a has neat parallelism and constant word order (verb at the end, a pattern that continues in v 11bAα). The tricolon in v 11b has quite different features; *Yahweh* common to vv 11bA, 11bB; *lō'* common to vv 11bB, 11bC; and excellent rhyme, three words ending in *-ēnû*. Verse 9 is the least well formed. The opening bicolon is close in design to 3:1a, but prose particles in v 9b show that poetic vocabulary is not being slavishly followed.

Verse 12 is a highly integrated quatrain. The authenticity of this quatrain is confirmed by its exact reproduction in Jer 26:18. Verse 12a has 13 syllables. Grammatically it is one long clause. It has five words, each a distinct clause-level constituent, and no parallelism: *lākēn biglalĕkem ṣiyyôn śadeh tēḥārēš*, "(1) Therefore, (2) on account of you (3) Zion (4) [like] a field (5) will be plowed." There is no break with a strong claim to be the position of a caesura. The position of *zaqef qaton* after the second word gives a rhythmic division into 6 (perhaps 7 or 5) :: 7 syllables. Putting the verb at the end is poetic. It sets things up for the development of the rest of the quatrain. In particular, in another context, vv 12aB–12bA would be recognized as a standard sixteen-syllable bicolon.

12aA	*lākēn biglalākem*	Therefore, on account of you,
12aB	*ṣiyyôn śādeh tēḥārēš*	Zion a field will be plowed
12bA	*wîrûšālēm 'iyyîn tihyeh*	and Jerusalem rubble heaps will be
12bB	*wĕhar habbayit lĕbāmôt yā'ar*	and the mountain of the house to high places of a forest

The Masoretic punctuation divides the verse into an introductory colon (v 12aA) that blankets all three of the following colons. These constitute a tricolon in which the noun subjects come first in each colon. All three colons are synonymous. The bicolon in vv 12aB–12bA exhibits complete synonymous parallelism (A : B : C :: A' : B' : C'). In the identical syntax of these colons the verb comes last, a very poetic touch, not uncommon in Micah but not usual in prose. Verse 12b can be read as a bicolon with incomplete parallelism. Each single matching noun in the middle bicolon has a two-noun phrase to match it in the final colon: Zion // Jerusalem // mountain of the house; field // rubble heaps // high places of a forest.

Since the three noun subjects refer to the same place, the colons are complementary. The verbs in vv 12aB and 12bA operate in v 12bB; the preposition *l-* in v 12bB operates retroactively with the nouns *field* and *heaps* in the preceding colons. Verse 12 illustrates once more a characteristic of Micah's poetry—the combination in the same unit of quite different bicolon patterns with connections among them all.

The whole unit is unusual for Micah in that every word is clear. There are no serious textual problems, except for *bnh* in v 10. See the NOTE.

NOTES AND COMMENTS

Notes on Micah 3:9–12

9. *Listen to this.* Compared with v 1, this first bicolon in the unit has two additional words. In v 1a and v 9a the second colon is identical and each has eight

syllables, the standard length. The effect of the variation is that the extra length of v 9aA matches the presence of "and I said" at the very beginning of v 1. This details suggests that *wā'ōmar* should be included in the scansion of v 1.

There is no difference in meaning between "Jacob" and "House of Jacob," and "Jacob // Israel" refers to the whole nation comprehensively, even though here the focus is on Jerusalem. The variable terminology of the parallels *(House of) Jacob // (House of) Israel* is developed throughout chapters 1–3 to become as full as possible in this final oracle. For the vocabulary, see the NOTES on v 1.

detest. Or abhor. The *pi'el* of *t'b* is used in both a factitive and a putative sense. The term *mišpāṭ* occurs in the opening address of both these matching oracles. In v 1 the *heads // chiefs* were reminded that it was their responsibility to know "the (right) judgment" (or the judgment that comes from Yahweh). Here, in the complementary statement, they repudiate the *mišpāṭ* given by God with contempt. Compare the use in other places of the comparable verb *m's* (Andersen and Freedman 1980: 353). The parallelism within v 9b points to the factitive meaning for both *pi'el* forms. Compare Hab 1:4: "the *mišpāṭ* comes out twisted." Verse 11 makes it clear that these "heads" perverted justice, that is, they made decisions (*mišpāṭ*) in the law courts that could only be considered loathsome (compare NEB—"hateful" and "hating good and loving evil" in v 2).

straight. The feminine form is comparatively rare. It is usually the attribute of *derek*. So Samuel promises to direct them "in the good and straight path" (*bĕderek haṭṭôbâ wĕhayĕšārâ*) (1 Sam 12:23). The use of the definite article in v 9bB suggests that *kol-hayĕšārâ* means "every straight path." This is confirmed by the fact that in its other occurrences the object of the verb *'iqqēš* is *derek* (Isa 59:8; Prov 10:9; compare Prov 28:6, 18.) This observation is methodologically important. It provides proof of a practice that is usually hard to demonstrate; that is, the use of compact reduced idioms. It also provides us with the clue to the use of the feminine form, agreeing with the absent but assumed *derek*. The word *derek* has its usual ethical meaning.

pervert. Literally "make crooked." The difference between the participle and its parallel imperfect verb is not great if both verbs have factitive meaning. The chiasmus shows that the two verbs have been intentionally connected to secure a kind of hendiadys: they pervert maliciously. Here we have again the question of the time reference of the prefixed verb form, especially in parallel with a participle. When the characterization of a person or group is recited as a list of participles, these are not descriptions of what they are currently doing, although they might still be behaving that way. The participles are more like titles, as in the credal recitals of the attributes of Yahweh in participial form, "Creator," etc., which culminate in a declaration that "His name is Yahweh." These are celebrations of notable achievements in the past, by which the person won the title. As such they can be expanded into a fuller report of the person's exploits, using verbal clauses. In traditional hymnic pieces, such as those in Amos and many in Psalms, the prefixed verb can be employed with its archaic reference to past events. We suggest that the same is being done here, in line with the many other occurrences of prefixed verbs with preterit meaning in the Book of

Doom. Since prefixed ("imperfect") verbs are also used in these chapters with their more familiar reference to future situations, in each case the time reference has to be settled with the aid of temporal adverbs or by purely pragmatic considerations. The choice is between past and present. Translation into English present tense is valid insofar as the parallelism is dominated by a participle: what they have done in the past defines what they are now and what they most likely keep on doing. Yet the participle "building" is more likely to refer to a specific action (giving the one who did it the lasting title of "builder") than to habitual activity.

10. *He who builds*. Literally "building." What we have said in the preceding NOTE about the time reference of the participle applies here. The participle is singular; someone is being accused of having built Jerusalem *with blood* and *with wickedness*. Most commentators and translators, beginning with the ancient versions, prefer to change the participle to plural. This is an obvious harmonization. The singular points to an individual. A king? The way Mic 3:12 is used in Jeremiah 26 suggests that his words were understood to be a criticism of the king as city-builder (Bergren 1974: 57). Compare Josh 6:26; 1 Kgs 16:34, which suggest that building a city "with blood" could refer to human foundation sacrifices—the supreme oblation in the religion of some of Israel's neighbors, the ultimate abomination in Yahwism. See the discussion on 3:2–3 and 6:7. We wonder if there is a connection between this charge and the accusations made in those verses.

Ahaz sacrificed his (two) sons, perhaps as did Hiel who rebuilt Jericho. Micah 6:7 shows that human sacrifice was a serious option at that time, although it is not clear who is making the proposal there. Ahaz also had a lot of rebuilding to do in Jerusalem. In the ancient Near East it was the exclusive prerogative of the king to be the patron of such enterprises. The importance of this tradition for Israel has been sensitively expounded by Meyers and Meyers (1987) in connection with the rebuilding of the Temple after the Exile. Ahaz's reign is the most eligible time for Micah's prophecies, as also for the early prophecies of Isaiah. The evidence of Jeremiah 26 that v 12 at least was proclaimed in the reign of Hezekiah does not necessarily mean that it was composed first at that time; it could well have been reiterated for many years, and its applicability to Jerusalem and its credibility might well have been enhanced after the part dealing with Samaria (1:5–7) had been fulfilled. In view of his reputation, we think it is unlikely that v 10 is a criticism of Hezekiah's building program.

Yet Ahaz's sacrifices if he is here the "builder of Zion" could hardly have been *foundation* sacrifices in the technical sense, unless the same ceremony was used again as part of a major rebuilding project. Ahaz's action in sacrificing his son(s) was carried out in a time of national peril under circumstances similar to those surrounding the mysterious sacrifice by Mesha of his son (cf. 2 Kgs 3:27). Such sacrifices were considered potentially very efficacious, and in and by Israel, not just by the Moabites. The Syro-Ephraimitic invasion would have been just the threat under which Ahaz would have made such a sacrifice, especially if we follow the account in 2 Chronicles 28. The report in 2 Chr 28:13 has an uncanny resemblance to 2 Kgs 3:27. The common element is the sacrifice of a royal son; this was supposed to avert the danger by bringing wrath on the enemy. The outcome in v 12 is the very opposite. Instead of saving ("building") Jerusalem "with blood," Ahaz's action (if he is the "builder" of v 10) could only lead to its complete demolition.

Zion. The usual sequence in parallelism is Zion // Jerusalem (v 12; 4:2, 8, etc.). The sequence is reversed in Mic 1:12–13. The authenticity of v 10 is supported by the fact that the pair of words Zion // Jerusalem is needed to supply the antecedent for the feminine pronouns in v 11. See Vincent (1986).

blood. Literally "bloods," which usually connotes murder rather than sacrifice. If that is the reference here, then the earlier NOTE (on *he who builds*), which speculated on a possible connection with building foundation sacrifices, will have to be modified by the stipulation that Micah viewed such an action as murder. A (dedication or foundation) sacrifice of an "innocent" victim would be regarded by the prophet as the worst kind of murder. Abraham (1975: 4), referring to 1 Kings 21; Amos 5:11; Hos 4:2; and Isa 1:15, identifies the action condemned in v 10 as "the confiscation of the property of the innocent condemned to death." This suggestion connects "building Zion" only indirectly with the shedding of innocent blood.

There is an almost identical bicolon in Hab 2:12.

12a   *hôy bōneh ʿîr bĕdāmîm*   Woe—building a city with blood,

12b   *wĕkônēn qiryâ bĕʿawlâ*   and founding a town with wickedness

In one respect this woe oracle is more general than Mic 3:10; it has two nouns ("city" // "town") where Micah has the names of a specific city ("Zion" // "Jerusalem"). In another respect Habakkuk is more specific than Micah; he has a second verb in parallel with "building." The root *knn* can refer to the founding of a city (Ps 107:36), equivalent to the root *ysd* as used in Josh 6:26 and 1 Kgs 16:34 to refer to the laying of foundations. In these several passages, then, we seem to have a traditional expression of condemnation of the use of a human for a foundation sacrifice in the construction of a city.

wickedness. Or "injustice." The noun *ʿawlâ* is a quite general term modifying "blood."

11. *Her heads.* The pronoun, used with each of the three nouns, focuses on Jerusalem, and this helps to define the reference of Jacob // Israel in this oracle, if not everywhere. Compare the list of plural nouns, similarly modified, in 1:6–7, where the suffix refers to Samaria; also "her rich ones" // "her residents" in 6:12, where the city is not identified.

judged. The root *špṭ* occurs here and in v 9b. The two colons should be interpreted together. The *heads* are magistrates. A combination of the complementary statements produces a synthesis. The bribed judges "hate good" (v 2aA) and detest justice (v 9bA).

rulings. The technical meaning of *yôrâ* is to give *tôrâ*. This service, provided to the community by priests, probably concerned mainly directions for the carrying out of various cultic procedures, including ritual purifications such as are codified in the book of Leviticus. In principle, there would be nothing wrong with accepting remuneration for such services. In parallel with v 11aA, *mĕḥîr*, "hire," does not have its innocent meaning in legitimate trade, but is a bribe (// *šōḥad*). The *tôrâ* that is sold will be made to please the buyer. Hence, picking up the other parallel with v 9bB, the priests' instruction twists the straight path. That *derek*, which we take as understood in v 9bB, is the implied object of *yôrû* in v 11aB is shown by the idiom *yôrēnû middĕrākāyw* in 4:2 (= Isa 2:3). That act of Yahweh will rectify the perversions of the priests described in 3:11.

relied. Literally "leaned," as a lame person on a stick (*miš'ān*). Yahweh is called a *miš'ān* (2 Sam 22:19 = Ps 18:19). The verb can describe both legitimate trust in and false reliance on God (Isa 10:20; 50:10). The root is used more often in Isaiah than anywhere else in the Hebrew Bible, so Micah is picking up a term current in his time. That these leaders depended heavily on Yahweh shows that they were not apostate in the formal sense of going over to other gods. Theirs is a case of false worship of the true God.

in our midst. The teaching that Yahweh is present "in the midst" of his people is good orthodox doctrine. It is prominent in both Deuteronomic and Priestly writings. Verse 11b is similar to the Zion theology with its belief in the sanctity and inviolability of Jerusalem as expressed especially in the book of Isaiah. Micah dares to contradict that belief with a threat of the actual demolition of Jerusalem. It is remarkable that Hezekiah took such unacceptable prophecy seriously.

evil. A similar slogan is found in Amos 9:10.

Calamity shall not even come close,

much less confront us, during our lifetime.

The complacent rulers in Jerusalem are confident that evil will not come to them. But Micah has already said that evil or calamity (*rā'*) has come right down from Yahweh to the gate of Jerusalem (1:12) and in 1:9 *rā'â* is the best candidate to be subject of *bā'â* just as it is of *tābô'* here. "Evil" (= "it") has come to Judah (1:9).

12. *Therefore*. This verse is quoted verbatim in Jer 26:18 (see the NOTE on 1:1). The only difference is slight. For *'yyn* Jeremiah has *'yym*, which is better Hebrew. And this could be why some Hebrew manuscripts of Micah have this reading also. The ending in Micah could be an Aramaism, current in his time (Young 1993: 60, 78). But why just this one instance? It could be a genuine dialectal variant within Hebrew, preferred because it gave a sound play on *ṣiyyôn*.

Zion. The parallelism of Zion // Jerusalem is repeated from v 10. After the first two words the rest of v 12 makes a complex tricolon. A third colon is added, which refers to the "house-mountain." This last colon is parallel to the second one; that is, v 12bA is parallel in some ways with v 12a and in others with v 12bB. The verb in v 12bA serves also in v 12bB, but the last colon supplies the preposition needed to complete the idiom in v 12bA.

plowed. If taken literally, the statement is not just a figure for demolishing the buildings.

field. A similar comparison was made with Samaria (1:6; see the NOTE). Here the point is more explicit that Jerusalem will revert to cultivation. It will be plowed.

heaps. The phrase *ʿî haśśādeh* used in Mic 1:6 is here split up, reversed, and spread over the bicolon. So the third colon in 3:12, with its reference to reforestation, resembles the second colon in 1:6, with its reference to vineyards.The apparent Aramaism of the plural form could be a dialectal feature of pre-exilic Hebrew (Young 1993: 60, 78), perhaps "northern" (Fishbane 1985: 459), with the more normal form in Jer 26:18 adjusted to later Jerusalem usage.

mountain. A catchword to hook in (domino fashion) with the next oracle, where the phrase is complete—"the mountain of the house of Yahweh." This third colon, far from being superfluous, is climactic. It is the final shocker. The Temple, the token of Yahweh's protective presence "in their midst," will be the special target of his destructive judgment. This is the final proof of divine withdrawal and rejection.

bāmôt. Or "ridges." Literally "high places." The LXX *to oros* implies singular, perhaps from a time when the Hebrew defective spelling *bmt* could be read either way. The LXX reading could be harmonizing. It secures better concord with singular *har.* The plural is a better Hebrew reading. It is in parallel with plural *rubble heaps.* More important, however, it completes a line of thought begun at 1:5, where the "high places" of Judah disturbed the symmetry of the bicolon. There Jerusalem was called "the sinful high places of Judah." It is appropriate that it revert to wooded "high places." When the Hebrew text has the same word twice, securing a structural pattern (inclusion, albeit long-distance), it is bad textual criticism to change it in both places, even though this may be supported by the fact that the versions (or even their Hebrew *Vorlagen,* for all we know) had already done it.

The difference in reference may not be great. Perhaps *bāmôt* here is a special plural referring to the most important high place of all, and now finally revealing, after the oblique reference of 1:5, that what he means by *bāmôt* is in conflict with the standard theory, say, of the Deuteronomist or Hezekiah or Josiah, namely that it is the Temple itself, the High Place *par excellence,* that is the center of corruption and the example of rebellion against God. Isaiah says practically the same thing in chapter 1, and Jeremiah and Ezekiel support the view explicitly. Micah seems to have been the first to attack the Temple in Jerusalem in so uncompromising a fashion. Not that he was an absolute first. A generation previously Amos had predicted the destruction of the temple at Bethel with similar intensity. See Vaughan (1974).

This naming of the main cult center as the prime target for Yahweh's judgment is thus a solid tradition in eighth-century prophecy. It is too simplifying to represent the prophets as moralists who "insisted that Yahweh's supreme interest was ethical, not ritualistic" (Abraham 1975: 4). Judges were condemned for corruption in the courts; priests were guilty of corrupting worship.

Comment on Micah 3:9–12

In analyzing the structure of the Book of Visions (chapters 1–3) we have pointed out several times that the placement of the oracle of judgment on Samaria (1:5–7) at the beginning of this "book" and of the oracle of judgment on Jerusalem (3:9–12) at the end is a structural feature that matches the title (1:1). The title identifies the whole book of Micah as a vision concerning "Samaria and Jerusalem." The question can now be raised as to whether what Micah says about these cities can be connected in any way with what actually happened to them during the period when Micah was prophesying. The book itself provides no such historical connections.

Micah says similar things about both cities. In particular, his language suggests total demolition and the reversion of the sites to agricultural use. In actual fact, this did not happen to either place. The point is often made that Micah's prediction about Samaria was fulfilled, even though his word against Jerusalem was not. The difference is explained in Jer 26:18 by attributing the reprieve of Jerusalem to the acceptance of Micah's message by Hezekiah. The book of Micah itself contains no inkling of these eventual outcomes. The oracles make sense if they were delivered in a time when both cities were standing and both faced the same peril for similar reasons, for the injustices condemned in chapters 1–3. They must be dated to before the onset of the final siege of Samaria by Shalmaneser V in 724 B.C.E.

To say that 1:6–7 was fulfilled in the Assyrian conquest of the northern kingdom is true in a sense. As a political entity that state came to an end. The territory of the state of Israel was split up into three or four provinces by a succession of Assyrian kings. According to the Assyrian annals, the final capture of Samaria by Sargon was quite different from what Micah describes in 1:6–7. While the Assyrians captured the city and ended Israelite rule, there was no massive destruction and the city did not need extensive rebuilding. It certainly never reverted to being plowed, as Micah predicted. Apparently Sargon repopulated the city and, indeed, increased its population (Hayes and Kuan 1991: 178).

There have been many attempts to date the lament in 1:10–16 to some actual calamity. The most favored suggestion is that it is a response to the invasion of Sennacherib in 701 B.C.E. If that is the case, then the materials have not been arranged in chronological order. We are more inclined to see in 1:10–16 a response to the wars of an earlier period, either wars between Israel and Judah or the Syro-Ephraimitic war of 734. Shaw (1994) has come to similar conclusions. The evidence is indirect. The links are so tenuous that Thompson (1982: 20) was unable to make any use of Micah in his study of the Syro-Ephraimite war. The mood and the geographical features of 1:10–16 can be compared with those of Isa 10:28–34 (note the concluding reference to a "forest"). The mood in 701 was quite different, according to the combined evidence of 2 Kings and Isaiah. On that occasion leaning on Yahweh (the term in 3:11bA), although derided by the Rabshakeh (Isa 36:15) was supported by Isaiah. If Micah had been there at the time, uttering this oracle, he and Isaiah would have been in marked disagreement.

Jeremiah (26:18) dates the final oracle in the Book of Visions (3:12) to the time of Hezekiah, quoting almost the exact words. Or, to be more precise, Jeremiah's supporters record Hezekiah's response to an oracle that had force in his reign, but that might have been standing on the record for some time. That is, such an oracle was not for the occasion of its first delivery only, but remained in force as a threat unless canceled by some appropriate change in the situation, notably repentance. The whole tenor of Hezekiah's reforms shows that the positive response to Micah's message came early in his reign, and the national posture in 701 — so very different from what Micah describes — was the result of policies pursued from the beginning of his reign. From the outset he reacted against his father's regime.

The mood in Mic 3:11b is more like that in Isa 22:7–14. In that siege of Jerusalem the mood in the capital was one of hedonistic abandonment, whether due to complacency arising from false trust, or from resignation to the inevitable ("tomorrow we die"). Unfortunately the events of Isaiah 22 remain unidentified, and some equate them with the siege of Sennacherib in 701 B.C.E. ("the only possible remaining situation" [Kaiser 1974: 139]).

The reference in Isaiah 22 to the defense works of Jerusalem — made by breaking down houses to fortify the wall — could line up with Mic 2:2 and 3:10. But the mood of confidence in v 11b contrasts with the mood of panic in Isa 7:2. Then the prophet called for resolution and high hopes, not for penitence. These differing circumstances of sieges of Jerusalem can be summarized as follows:

Source	Isaiah 7	Isaiah 22	Isaiah 36–37	Micah 1–3
Enemy	Aram-Israel	Elam-Kir	Assyria	?
King	Ahaz	?	Hezekiah	?
Mood	panic	feasting	calm trust	complacency
Prophecy	confidence	penitence	defiance	doom

All three occasions reported by Isaiah have an interest in the water supply (Isa 7:3; 22:9; cf. Hezekiah's tunnel). Micah does not confirm this factor in the circumstances of the oracle.

We conclude that there is no way of dating the oracles in chapter 3. Chapters 1–3 as a whole (if they are a whole) belong to a time when both Samaria and Jerusalem were still intact, i.e., before 724, and when Judah had been invaded, an invasion that reached Jerusalem.

COMMENT ON THE BOOK OF DOOM
(CHAPTERS 1–3)

The links between chapter 3 and chapters 1–2 show that the entire section (chapters 1–3) is a comprehensive prophecy against Samaria and Jerusalem. We have called this the Book of Doom. Micah is declaring to Jacob his rebellion and to Israel his sin (3:8b). Taken alone, the parallelism of this half-verse could be interpreted as synonymous; the equivalence of Jacob and Israel is commonplace. The rebellion of Jacob and the sin of the House of Israel were declared in 1:5 to be the reason for all the terrifying and destructive developments described and predicted in these chapters—the "evil" that the false prophets said would never happen (3:11b), the "evil" that Yahweh is planning against this family (2:3), the "evil" that has come down from Yahweh (1:12). The comments made on this "rebellion" // "sin" in 1:5 show that Jacob // Israel match Samaria // Jerusalem, and we see no reason to infer that Samaria has dropped out of the picture, just because the word "Samaria" has not been used again after 1:6. The title of the whole book (1:1) states that Micah's visions were "against" (or "concerning") Samaria and Jerusalem. In our study of the political terminology of this book we found no reason to restrict either of the names "Jacob" and "Israel" to only one of the two kingdoms. The names apply equally to either and to both, but this is because either region is identified and addressed as "Israel," "my people," disregarding the prevailing circumstance that this people happened to be divided into two kingdoms.

In chapter 3 the second oracle against the heads and rulers (vv 9–11) is more specific than the first (vv 1–4). Verse 10 names Zion // Jerusalem as the scene of their crimes, and v 12 names this city as the scene of the appropriate punishment. The heads and rulers addressed in v 1 are not located anywhere, except in Israel, and it is usually assumed that they are the same as the ones in v 9, so that the whole of chapter 3 is aimed at the Jerusalem leadership. This inference is not compelling. The echoes of chapter 1 in chapter 3 that we have already pointed out make it possible (we think likely) that 3:1–4 is an oracle against the leadership of Samaria to match the one against Jerusalem in 3:9–12. Or, since that is claiming more than can be proved, that, in view of the use of "Jacob" // "Israel" throughout the book, "heads of Jacob" covers all the leadership of Israel, north and south alike, only v 10 specifies a smaller set within that group. Even then we need to be careful; for the operative word "builder" is singular and seems to be pointing the finger at one individual who is guilty of building Jerusalem with blood.

The targets of the judgment speeches in chapter 3 are more clearly identified than those in chapter 2, but there are a number of indications that it is the same group throughout. In chapter 2 the judgment speech was delivered in two installments, each with *lākēn*, "therefore" (vv 3, 5). Similarly in chapter 3 there are two judgment speeches with *lākēn* (vv 6, 12). The social status and community functions of these miscreants are more clearly identified in chapter 3; they are "heads" and "rulers" (vv 1, 9), responsible for the administration of justice (vv 1b, 11aA). Two other groups are linked with these heads in v 11 — "priests" and "prophets." Micah 3:12 makes it clear that all these together are responsible for the impending fate of Jerusalem (which cannot be separated from the fate of Samaria predicted in 1:6–7, also introduced by *lākēn*). Part of that fate is the failure of their religion in the time of crisis. It is said of each group that Yahweh will not answer their call for help—the heads in v 4a, the seers in v7b. No technical duties of priests are discussed in chapter 3, although the word "priests" occurs only there. What is described in 1:5–7 provides the setting of their work, and in Judah this is located on the *bāmôt*; and just as 1:6–7 predicts the devastation of the cult installations of Samaria, so 3:12 predicts that the Temple mount of Jerusalem will become *bāmôt ya'ar*, "high places of a forest." The repetition of this word makes a significant inclusion and shows that cult officials are also in mind. Even though "priests" are mentioned only once, prophets also were involved in the cult, as well as the king and other government officials.

The judgment speech against the prophets in 3:5–8 is clearly a follow-up of the description of their policies and practices given in 2:6–11. The charge of corruption is repeated in 3:11aB. Not only does 3:11a link the prophets with the "heads" and priests, but also the oracle against the prophets in 3:5–8 is shown by the language of 3:8, which sets Micah's genuine prophecy against the false prophecies, to be part of the declaration of Jacob's rebellion or Israel's sin. So that verse is a ganglion with threads stretching to several other places in the text. Verse 8a is an inclusion for 3:1a and a domino link to v 9a, while all three (one in each of the parts we have identified in chapter 3) show that chapter 3 as a whole is a further exposition of the theme announced in 1:5.

Nor is there any reason to believe that those condemned in chapter 3 are any different from the ones accused in chapter 2. We have already worked out that the false prophets are the same in both chapters. The rulers who do terrible things to "my people" in 3:1–3 are facilitators of the crimes against "my people" (2:4, 9) condemned in 2:1–2, 8–9. To begin, we draw attention to the similarities between 2:1 and 3:2, where two participial phrases are used to characterize these people:

| 2:1 | *ḥšby-'wn* | *p'ly rā'* | planners of iniquity | doers of evil |
| 3:2 | *śn'y-ṭôb* | *'hby rā'* | haters of good | lovers of evil |

These epithets are followed in each case by the verb *gzl*, so Micah finds similarity in their activities. Even if the groups are not identical, there seems to be some kind of alliance. In studying chapter 2 we were unable to decide whether the seizure of a person's house was to be taken literally, reporting the oppression of the poor by rich business interests, or whether this was a figure for the violent annexation of territory of one state by another, an act of military power.

Whether merchants or soldiers, these wrongdoers act in collusion with the other main arms of the establishment—magistrates (Part I), prophets (Part II), priests (Part III).

We have a similar problem in 3:2–3, deciding whether the language is to be taken literally or whether it is a figurative description of some particularly horrifying atrocity. If figurative, it could be an additional account of the wicked deeds reported in 2:2–3, 8–9, this time highly metaphorical; or it could be describing literally murders and mutilations committed on some other occasion. Either way crimes of such enormity could be committed with impunity (for it has been left to God to step in and punish the perpetrators) only with the connivance of magistrates (3:1b, 11a). When this kind of collusion is aided by the approval of prophets and the blessings of priests (3:11), the last stages of social corruption in church and state have clearly been reached.

Having reached the end of the Book of Doom, we observe a certain consistency of mood and coherence in composition. The attack is mainly on the leadership. Leaders, and most of all judges and prophets, are accused of corruption and abuse of power. Priests are mentioned in passing in 3:11; they could hardly have been exonerated from connivance in the cult practices condemned in chapter 1. It is possible that merchants or military are in view in 2:1–5. Open criticism of those supremely responsible, the kings of the two cities named, is surprisingly lacking, although we suspect that the singular participle in 3:10 refers to Ahaz.

The Book of Doom seems to be lopsided in the attention it gives to the two capitals. Samaria does not seem to receive any attention after 1:7. Jerusalem is clearly in Micah's sights in chapter 3. The Book of Doom makes sense only if the prophecies were given before the destruction of Samaria. At that stage both capitals are on the same footing, and no one could have foreseen (Micah does not hint) that their destinies would prove to be so different. We know from Jeremiah 26 that 3:12 was still a living word in the reign of Hezekiah. After the Assyrian defeat of Samaria it would have had added urgency; but no adjustments have been made in the report in light of that development. It could be that the destruction of Samaria and the survival of Jerusalem partly confirmed, partly discredited Micah's predictions. There are indications in Isaiah that people made the inference and carried it further. In their opinion, the political survival of Judah proved that Jerusalem was different, immune. Such a response could be reflected in the slogan of 3:11b. But we know that this kind of complacency in the covenant relationship was prevalent throughout the eighth century and was not necessarily worked out first only in the last two decades, i.e., in Hezekiah's reign. Micah may have uttered his prophecies, including 3:12, first in the reign of of Jotham, certainly in the reign of Ahaz, and then repeated them in the reign of Hezekiah; and it is possible that Hezekiah was already king before the fall of Samaria. See the chronological table on p. xvii.

The prophecies about the two cities are symmetrical; the history was not symmetrical. The history has not disturbed the symmetry of the prophecy, so we are inclined to conclude that the Book of Doom was Micah's set speech and that it had already acquired its present form in the reign of Ahaz. Even though he kept on using it into the reign of Hezekiah, it did not undergo any substantial revision in the light of later developments. When eventually written down and preserved it did not reflect its great success in persuading the king into policies of repentance and reformation. If Micah was already dead before Hezekiah's reform, the preservation of his message and its protection from revision in view of its influence on the king are an indication that his words quickly attained a status that we would now call "canonical."

II. THE BOOK OF VISIONS: MICAH 4–5

◆

INTRODUCTION TO MICAH 4–5

Chapters 4 and 5 constitute a distinct block of material within the complete work. We have called this unit the Book of Visions. Its boundaries are mapped externally. The ending of the first major unit (chapters 1–3) is marked by 3:12, as discussed above. A new piece of a different genre clearly begins with chapter 6. This is generally recognized; but the unity of this section (chapters 4 and 5), its literary character, the history of its development, and its original setting are more difficult to determine.

The internal cohesion of chapters 4–5 is indicated by its overall organization. There are two focal points. The repeated use of ʿattâ, "now," suggests a focus on the present. This cannot be taken as certain, since ʿattâ does not always refer to the present instant of time; sometimes it marks a transition to a new literary component within a larger composition, e.g., at 7:10. The main transitions to new constituents are marked by the key expressions:

A			ʿattâ	(4:9–10a)
B		kîʿattâ		(4:10b)
C	wěʿattâ			(4:11–13)
A'			ʿattâ	(4:14)
B'		kîʿattâ		(5:1–3)

The reader has to establish whether the assemblage of these five units is accidental, based on no more than the use of the word "now" in all of them, but so haphazard in nature that there is no obligation to find one and the same time reference "now" in them all; or whether the glimpses they give of several situations can be integrated into a single picture of the same moment of crisis.

An assemblage of thematically related prophetic pieces can be given some literary integrity by skilful editing, even if they arose from different historical circumstances. Failure to find a common historical background can diminish appreciation of the structural features of the established text, especially if they seem to be merely redactional and superficial. Earlier critical work on chapters 4–5 concluded that they "contain seven quite unrelated poems which reveal the ideas, vocabulary, and historical background of the Exile and post-Exilic periods" (P. E. Bloomhardt in Alleman and Flack 1948: 846). "The forecasts of restoration for the Davidic kingdom and throne in Micah 4–5 are almost certainly postexilic" (D. P. Cole in Coogan, Exum, and Stager 1994: 67 n. 2). The changing circumstances of such a long period of time make it unlikely that seven short Exilic and postexilic compositions, from who knows how many authors, will hang together, no matter how skilful their editor. And it would then be inappropriate to assume connections among them that would permit the larger context to supply clues for the interpretation of individual features.

The pattern outlined above is not easily accounted for as only redactional. The repetition of *ʿattâ* is remarkable. Its positioning does not correspond to the boundaries we have recognized on other grounds, including the ancient scribal paragraph markers. For methodological considerations in the mapping of unit boundaries see Wendlund (1995). The use of conjunctions with *ʿattâ* suggests linkage of the units they initiate with other paragraphs. In normal composition the transition to a "now" paragraph is usually made by using *wĕʿattâ* to switch from indicative to precative mood (Laurentin 1964; Brongers 1965). The indicative discourse is descriptive material that analyzes the situation; the precative discourse prescribes the required course of action. The use of *wĕʿattâ* in letter writing makes it a semantically empty signal of message onset after the opening salutation (Pardee 1982: 149). In the Arad and Lachish letters, as also in *PapMur* 17 (No. 36 in Pardee's Catalogue), the form is *wʿt*, which attests a pronunciation without a terminal vowel—*waʿat(t)*. This spelling contrasts with the dominant biblical use of *wʿth*. The latter spelling records the pronunciation *wĕʿattâ*. The consistent difference between the inscriptions and the biblical text in this detail could document a distinction between the vernacular language and the language of literary Hebrew. The point is an important one since we are trying to find the milieu for the discourses in Micah 4–5. The use of *ʿattâ* could be a clue, whether of oral discourse or literary composition.

As the text now stands, the one occurrence of *wĕʿattâ* (4:11) does not fit into either pattern. It is neither epistolary nor precative. It is in the middle of the set shown above. The position of this unit (4:11–13) suggests that it is the centerpiece and that related material has been placed symmetrically around it. There are two "*ʿattâ*" pieces before 4:11–13 and two after it. The first of the pair has no conjunction; the second has *kî*. The function of this *kî* has yet to be determined. We notice first the overall structure in which these five units have symmetry around the central one. The delay of *kîʿattâ* to the last clause of the last unit is part of this symmetry. It is the middle clause (4:11) that links the whole of this body of related material (4:9–5:3) to its context.

That context does not supply the expected descriptive material to serve as the starting point for an "and now" component, if it has its standard function of marking transition from expository to precative discourse or to move from the immediate past to the imminent future. On the contrary, the surrounding material points beyond the present to the distant future. Its code word is the eschatological *wĕhāyâ*, "and it will come about." This formula marks the onset of several distinct paragraphs.

4:1aAα	wĕhāyâ	bĕ’aḥărît hayyāmîm	
4:6aA		bayyôm hahû’	nĕ’ūm-yhwh
5:4a	wĕhāyâ zeh šālôm		
5:6aA	wĕhāyâ šĕ’ērît ya‘ăqōb		
5:7aAα	wĕhāyâ šĕ’ērît ya‘ăqōb		
5:9aA	wĕhāyâ	bayyôm hahû’	

Again there are five (possibly six) pieces, and the formula is varied. The break-up of the stereotype wĕhāyâ bayyôm hahû’ (standard form in 5:9) into bayyôm hahû’ (4:6) and wĕhāyâ (5:4) achieves a most unusual chiastic pattern, and suggests that 4:6–5:4 (or 4:6–5:5) is a unit in which all the ‘attâ passages are embraced by the broken-up stereotype. Whether 5:4a is the conclusion of this unit or an integral part of 5:4–5 is a separate problem that does not change the larger picture. The five ‘attâ passages occur as a block within the five wĕhāyâ passages. The development from "and it will be" into "in that day" makes a chiastic pattern with "remnant of Jacob." The expression "in the end of the days" (4:1), different from all the others, carries the whole Book of Visions as well as opening the first oracle in the set.

Besides these structural features and the overall organization that they point to, there is another pattern that creates a second structure, superimposed on the first structure already described above. At four places the free forms of the personal pronouns are used to highlight four protagonists, and also, most likely, to set them in relationships. Two of the passages are:

| wĕ’attâ migdal-‘ēder | And thou [m.]—Tower of the Flock (4:8aA) |
| wĕ’attâ bêt-leḥem ’eprātâ | And thou [m.], Beth-lehem Ephratha (5:1aAα) |

This arrangement places the two main cities of the David tradition in juxtaposition. They come in the last unit of the first block of wĕhāyâ material and in the last unit of the central block of ‘attâ passages. Similarly "and we" (4:5b) "and they" (4:12) set in contrast the two main protagonists, Israel and the nations. The first occurs in the prime wĕhāyâ unit, the second in the prime wĕ‘attâ unit.

Additional insight into the structure of the Book of Visions is supplied by the traditional paragraph divisions, which existed in the text before the Masoretes worked out rules for preserving them. These identifications do not give as fine and detailed an analysis as the one we have already achieved on literary grounds by using all the clues provided by the repeated code words studied above. The old tradition divided the Book of Visions in to six parashiyyoth. This scheme isolates the opening (4:1–5) and closing (5:9–14) units; and it confirms the onset of new units at 4:8 and 5:1. The system identifies 5:6–8 as one parashiyyah. It does not recognize the units we have found in 4:8–14.

A salient question similar to the one we raised concerning the five ‘attâ pieces is whether these five glimpses of the future introduced by wĕhāyâ represent several aspects of the eschaton, or whether they are unrelated prophecies assembled here with nothing more in common than the use of a similar catch-phrase. Hillers (ABD 4: 809) calls it "a most superficial organizing principle."

These two sets of five pieces identified by the similar use of catchwords at their onsets account for the whole of chapters 4 and 5. The pattern in which they have all been put together, if there is one at all, is not obvious, either from the structural arrangement, or from the content of the ten portions. The five "*'attâ*" pieces come in one block that breaks the "*wĕhāyâ*" pieces into two blocks, and the three blocks are of comparable length by syllable count—324, 315, 321. The quantitative balance confirms the analysis based in the first place solely on thematic and structural features.

324 syllables	4:1–5	*wĕhāyâ bĕ' aḥărît hayyāmîm*	Yahweh supreme in Zion	A
	4:6–8	*bayyôm hahû' nĕ'ûm-yhwh*	Yahweh rules his gathered people	B
315 syllables	4:9–10a	*'attâ*	the anguish of Zion	C
	4:10b	*kî 'attâ*	redemption of Zion from Babylon	D
	4:11–13	*wĕ'attâ*	Zion defeats the nations	E
	4:14	*'attâ*	Zion (?) under threat	F
	5:1–3	*kî 'attâ*	advent of the ruler	G
321 syllables	5:4–5	*wĕhāyâ zeh šālôm*	defeat of Assyria	H
	5:6	*wĕhāyâ šĕ'ērît ya'ăqōb*	the remnant benign	I
	5:7–8	*wĕhāyâ šĕ'ērît ya'ăqōb*	the remnant malign	J
	5:9–14	*wĕhāyâ bayyôm hahû'*	Israel cleansed and avenged	K

II.1. THE END OF THE DAYS (4:1–5)

TRANSLATION

MT

1aAα	*wĕhāyâ bĕ'aḥărît hayyāmîm*	And it will come about, in the end of the days,
1aAβ	*yihyeh har bêt-yhwh*	the mountain of Yahweh's house will be established
	nākôn bĕrō'š hehārîm	as head of the mountains.
1aB	*wĕniśśā' hû' miggĕbā'ôt*	And it will be raised (higher) than the hills.
1b	*wĕnāhărû 'ālāyw 'ammîm*	And peoples will stream unto it.
2aAα	*wĕhālĕkû gôyim rabbîm*	And many nations will go (to it).
	wĕ'āmĕrû	And they will say:
2aAβ	*lĕkû wĕna'ăleh 'el-har-yhwh*	Come, and let us go up to the mountain of Yahweh,
	wĕ'el-bêt 'ĕlōhê ya'ăqōb	and to the house of the God of Jacob.
2aBα	*wĕyôrēnû middĕrākāyw*	And let him instruct us from his ways;
2aBβ	*wĕnēlĕkâ bĕ'ōrĕḥōtāyw*	and let us walk in his paths.
2bA	*kî miṣṣiyyôn tēṣē' tôrâ*	For from Zion will go forth Torah,
2bB	*ûdĕbar-yhwh mîrûšālēm*	even the word of Yahweh from Jerusalem.

3aA	*wĕšāpaṭ bên ʿammîm rabbîm*	And he will judge among many peoples,
3aB	*wĕhôkîaḥ lĕgôyīm ʿăṣūmîm* *ʿad-rāḥôq*	and he will arbitrate for powerful nations unto far off.
3bAα	*wĕkittĕtû ḥarbōtêhem lĕʾittîm*	And they will beat their swords into plowshares,
3bAβ	*waḥănîtōtêhem lĕmazmērôt*	and their spears into sickles.
3bBα	*lōʾ-yiśʾû gôy ʾel-gôy ḥereb*	They will not raise—nation against nation—a sword,
3bBβ	*wĕlōʾ-yilmĕdûn ʿôd milḥāmâ*	and they will never train for war again.
4aAα	*wĕyāšĕbû ʾîš taḥat gapnô*	And each man will sit under his own vine,
4aAβ	*wĕtaḥat tĕʾēnātô*	and under his own fig tree.
4aB	*wĕʾên maḥărîd*	And no one will terrify (them),
4b	*kî-pî yhwh ṣĕbāʾôt dibbēr*	—for the mouth of Yahweh Sebaoth has declared it.
5aA	*kî kol-hāʿammîm yēlĕkû*	For all the peoples will walk
5aB	*ʾîš bĕšēm ʾĕlōhāyw*	each in the name of its god;
5b	*waʾănaḥnû nēlēk bĕšēm-yhwh* *ʾĕlōhênû*	but we will walk in the name of Yahweh our God
	lĕʿôlām wāʿed	for ever and ever.

LXX II.1. The End of the Days (4:1–5)

1aAα	And it will be in the last of the days,
1aAβb	the mountain of Kyrios will be manifest, established on the peaks of the mountains.
1aB	And it will be exalted above the hills.
1b	And peoples will hasten to it.
2aAα	And many nations will come. And they will say:
2aAβ	Come, let us go up to the mountain of Kyrios and to the house of the God of Jacob;
2aBα	and they will show us his way [sg.],
2aBβ	and we will walk in his paths.
2bA	For from Zion will come out *nomos*,
2bB	and the word of Kyrios from Jerusalem.
3aA	And he will judge among many peoples,
3aB	and he will convict powerful nations unto far off.
3bAα	And they will beat their swords into plowshares,
3bAβ	and their spears into sickles.
3bBα	No longer will nation lift up a sword against nation;
3bBβ	and no longer will they learn to make war.
4aAα	And each will rest under his vine,
4aAβ	and each under his fig tree.
4aB	And the one who strikes terror will not be,
4b	for the mouth of Kyrios Pantokrator has declared these things.
5aA	Because all the peoples will walk,
5aB	each his own way,
5b	but we will walk in the name of Kyrios our God for ever and beyond.

INTRODUCTION TO MICAH 4:1–5

The first item in the Book of Visions is an apocalypse, a vision of the end and consummation of history. Unlike its replica in Isaiah 2, this oracle does not have its own title. R. L. Smith (1984: 36) calls it "a salvation oracle . . . with eschatological overtones." By the usual form-critical criteria for identifying a prophecy of salvation as outlined, for instance, by Koch (1967: 261–65), Micah 4:1–4(5) is lacking in the distinctive and definitive features of that genre. It is lacking in specificity, it does not arise from a situation of crisis into which the promise of deliverance comes as a welcome word, and there is no indication of its intended audience. The classical oracles of salvation are addressed to historical realities and possibilities; in this unit we float away into the dreamworld of apocalyptic vision and to the remotest boundary of conceivable time. The term "eschatological" is also inappropriate if it implies that the action takes place after "the end of the world" in another, celestial location or mode of existence beyond time. The oracle anticipates a fulfillment of God's plan for history within history, the "end" of history in the sense of completion, but not termination. The oracle is a mix of the familiar historical realities—Jacob, Zion, Yahweh, the nations (Balzer 1991; Ollenburger 1987).

Micah 4:1–5 begins with an announcement that at some unspecified time in the indeterminate future the mountain on which the Temple of Yahweh is built will be transformed so as to become the highest mountain in the world (v 1). Many (all?) nations will go on pilgrimage to this world center, to benefit from the teaching that Yahweh will provide for them there (v 2). In his role as arbitrator, Yahweh will settle international disputes, and this will result in universal disarmament and enduring peace (v 3). Each one (nation or individual) will enjoy security and prosperity (v 4). The prophecy ends with a response from the people in which they commit themselves to "walk in the name of Yahweh our God for ever and ever" (v 5).

This apocalypse is perhaps the most famous of all the visions to come from the imagination of the prophets of Israel, or revealed by the God of Israel (v 4b). It is global in scope, tranquil in mood, an impossible dream for all humankind, as hard to believe now as it must have been then. No matter where we date it in the biblical period, it is remarkable that it comes from an age of wars and tumults, of cruelty and chaos. It comes from a time of imperialist devastation, demolition, and domination of smaller nations by powers advanced in the technology of war, ruthless in conquest and control. The rest of the Book of Visions names both Assyria and Babylon in such roles.

The prophecy is intriguing in that it occurs twice in the Hebrew Bible. Isaiah 2:2–4 is almost identical to Mic 4:1–3. Tied up with the question of the literary interdependence of these two versions is the problem of the date of its original composition. See the EXCURSUS on the relationship between Isaiah 2:1–4 and Micah 4:1–5.

The Poetry of Micah 4:1–5

In order to discuss the literary organization of the piece we shall display it in twenty-eight colons. This display will point out those pairs of contiguous colons that exhibit in some measure the usual Hebrew poetic parallelism. We give also the syllable count as a convenient measure of colon length. The twenty-eight individual colons set out above are intended for discussion; they are not intended to be the last word on the stichometry of the unit.

The colons displayed above are natural grammatical units, and many of them are complete clauses. Some of the clauses are very long, too long for a single colon of standard poetry. We have shown such clauses with a caesura at a point where the Masoretic accents indicate a major break. Verse 5b is just one long clause (nineteen syllables). The Masoretic punctuation divides it into three portions. That punctuation brings out the parallelism between vv 5aA and 5b. Verse 1aAβ is a long clause (thirteen syllables), but *nākôn běrō'š hehārîm* is a distinct colon parallel to v 1aB; the poem proper begins and ends with a tricolon.

Quite apart from the fact that Isaiah 2 does not have it, Mic 4:5 is detached somewhat from vv 1–4 by the clear end to v 4. In Isaiah most prime manuscripts have an open division between v 4 and v 5; in Micah the division comes after v 5. The thematic development and structural organization show that there are five portions in the oracle (six including v 5) that might perhaps be called strophes. The poetry is most conspicuous in vv 1–3, which we have shown as four strophes of 37, 38, 38, and 38 syllables (four or five colons each). In view of this exact quantitation, we suggest that the opening colon (v 1aAα, 9 syllables) and the closing quatrain (v 4, 27 syllables) be added to give a fifth portion of 36 syllables. We do not mean that they should be moved around. The connection is provided by the larger structure. Verse 1aAα (9 syllables) and v 4b (9 syllables) make an inclusion around the body of the oracle (vv 1–4). Verse 4 does not flow on naturally from v 3. Verses 1–3 are concerned with nations; v 4 with individuals. Both are of interest and both are connected in the vision of well-being for the End-time.

Eight well-formed bicolons can be discerned in vv 1–3: the last three words of v 1aAβ with v 1aB (15 syllables), v 1aB with 2aAα (16 syllables), v 2aAβ (17 syllables), v 2aB (17 syllables), v 2b (18 syllables), v 3a (20 syllables), v 3bA (21 syllables), v 3bB (17 syllables). In terms of *parallelismus membrorum* the patterns are quite varied, although all are in keeping with standard practice. The same goes for the range in length as measured by syllables (or beats). Even the length of v 3a (20 syllables), whose last two words are often suspected because they are lacking in the recension of this oracle found in Isaiah, is not as long as the next bicolon. We must accept this whole portion as a well-composed and well-preserved poem.

The parallelism in vv 4 and 5 is less well developed; but compare the incomplete synonymous parallelism of v 4aA with that of v 2aAβ and v 3bA. Nearly all the clauses with a verb in them have that verb in clause-initial position (except when preceded by a negative or "and"). This pattern or "line form" contrasts with the many colons in Micah, especially in chapters 2–3, in which the verb comes as the last item in the colon. The exceptions are the two subordinate clauses, beginning with *kî* (v 4b and v 2b). Note the chiasmus in the latter bicolon. This sustained use of clause-initial verbs seems less than elegant. We note, too, that the use of *waw*-consecutive for future prediction is closer to the usage of standard prose than to lyrical poetry. The same features are similarly conspicuous in 5:9–14, which is the counterpoise to 4:1–5. The prose particles are not used where they might have been. The exception is the definite article. It is used three times, but only with the *nomen rectum* of a construct phrase. The latter feature is not uncommon in prophetic poetry.

These twenty-eight colons amount to 220 syllables, or 7.85 syllables per colon. This comes close to the average of fifteen or sixteen syllables in a standard bicolon. As a matter of fact only one of the well-formed bicolons present in this piece has the standard length of sixteen syllables. Several colons are nine syllables or longer. The average balances out because there are several quite short colons, at least as the Masoretes have recognized them.

There is another structure in the body of the prophecy (through v 4). It is important to recognize that v 2b is not subordinate just to the immediately preceding text; it is not part of the speech of the pilgrims, which ends with v 2aB. Verse 2b gives the reason for everything else that is said; it is the heart of the oracle. The eleven colons ahead of it amount to 75 syllables; vv 3–4a that follow have 76 syllables. This symmetry supports the analysis of v 2b as the basis of the entire development. It is not just because the mountain of Yahweh's house is so high that people will travel to it from all over the world; it is because that is where *tôrâ* is given.

Verse 2b is central in another respect as well. The final tricolon of 3:12 listed "Zion," "Jerusalem," the "Temple mountain" in successive colons. These terms are used in 4:1–5, a firm link between the Book of Doom and the Book of Visions, in our opinion (although viewed quite differently by some critics). This pattern is not fully in place until we reach v 2b, where the pair "Zion" // "Jerusalem" complete a chiastic structure that began in 3:12.

The Traditions Behind Micah 4:1–5

The ideal that this opening vision embodies is a venerable one. The whole presentation is rhapsodical. The myth of primeval paradise was one of the most enduring and widespread of the traditions of the ancient Near East, and this vision of Micah (and Isaiah) is indebted to that primal memory at several points (Clifford 1972: 156). After the opening colons about the preeminence of the Temple mountain at Jerusalem, there is a quasi-narrative sketch of future developments. The colons around the centerpiece of v 2b describe what will happen when the mountain-house of Yahweh is made highest in the world. They describe what Yahweh will do and what the nations will do.

These predictions are placed in two ranks. Verse 1 is Yahweh's achievement, at least implicitly (the verbs are passive, which makes for a quieter and more mysterious opening). Then come three verbal clauses (vv 1b, 2aA) that describe what the nations will do. Verse 3a describes what Yahweh will do (and incidentally what the *tôrâ* will do). Verse 3b forecasts what the nations will do (three verbal clauses, two with negation), with v 4 as the final picture of peace and well-being. An oracular formula (v 4b) rounds off that part of the unit. The poem continues and ends with a response from the people, who resolve to walk in the name of Yahweh their God for ever and ever.

The Structure of Micah 4:1–5

		syllables	
1aAα	*wĕhāyâ bĕ'aḥărît hayyāmîm*	9	
1aAβ	*yihyeh har bêt-yhwh*	6	
	nākôn bĕrō'š hehārîm	7	
1aB	*wĕniśśā' hû' miggĕbā'ôt*	8	37
1b	*wĕnāhărû 'ālāyw 'ammîm*	8	
2aAα	*wĕhālĕkû gôyim rabbîm*	8	
	wĕ'āmĕrû	4	
2aAβ	*lĕkû wĕna'ăleh 'el-har-yhwh*	9	
	wĕ'el-bêt 'ĕlōhê ya'ăqōb	8	38
2aBα	*wĕyôrēnû middĕrākāyw*	8	
2aBβ	*wĕnēlĕkâ bĕ'ōrĕḥōtāyw*	9	
2bA	*kî miṣṣiyyôn tēṣē' tôrâ*	8	
2bB	*ûdĕbar-yhwh mîrûšālēm*	10	38
3aA	*wĕšāpaṭ bên 'ammîm rabbîm*	8	
3aB	*wĕhôkîaḥ lĕgôyim 'ăṣûmîm 'ad-rāḥôq*	12	
3bAα	*wĕkittĕtû ḥarbōtêhem lĕ'ittîm*	11	
3bAβ	*waḥănîtōtêhem lĕmazmērôt*	10	38
3bBα	*lō'-yiś'û gôy 'el-gôy ḥereb*	8	
3bBβ	*wĕlō'-yilmĕdûn 'ôd milḥāmâ*	9	
4aAα	*wĕyāšĕbû 'îš taḥat gapnô*	8	
4aAβ	*wĕtaḥat tĕ'ēnātô*	6	27
4aB	*wĕ'ên maḥărîd*	4	(+9?)
4b	*kî-pî yhwh ṣĕbā'ôt dibbēr*	9	
5aA	*kî kol-hā'ammîm yēlĕkû*	8	
5aB	*'îš bĕšēm 'ĕlōhāyw*	6	
5b	*wa'ănaḥnû nēlēk*	6	33
	bĕšēm-yhwh 'ĕlōhênû	8	
	lĕ'ôlām wā'ed	5	

NOTES AND COMMENTS

Notes on Micah 4:1–5

1. *end.* The exact time reference intended by the stock phrase *bĕ'aḥărît hay-yāmîm*, "in the end of the days," depends on the nuance to be given to the first word and the denotation of the second. The meaning of this phrase has been discussed by Buchanan (1961), Carmignac (1969–71), Jones (1972), Kosmala (1963), van der Ploeg (1972), Rinaldi (1965), Seebass (*TWAT* 1:207–12), Staerk (1891), and Willis (1979). The first word *'aḥărît* contrasts with *rē'šît*, the two marking the onset and conclusion of a period of time. More specifically it can mean a later (the future), in contrast to an earlier (the past), phase of an epoch. The traditional "the latter days" has acquired associations with later eschatological notions of the time before the end of the world. In none of the occurrences of *bĕ'aḥărît hayyāmîm* in the Hebrew Bible do the associated statements permit the precise idea of termination (the end of time). Yet the expression is technical. It is more than a vague reference to an indeterminate future. It is more precise than "days to come" (NJB, REB). Here it marks the time of fulfillment of the Creator's intentions and purposes for the world.

Etymological arguments based on derivation from the same root as the preposition *'aḥărê*, "after," are not sufficient to establish an adverbial meaning of "afterwards." This requires reference to a situation in which something happens "after" and is the consequence of, not just the sequel to. The equivalent Akkadian expression *ana aḥrāt* or *ina aḥrāt ūmi* often refers to a permanent arrangement for all future time. It has a tone of finality. The literal meaning of the expression, "in the back of days" suggests an analysis in which the future is behind the present, following it so as to overtake it (Afanasyeva 1978).

When this phrase *bĕ'aḥărît hayyāmîm*, "in the end of the days," introduces an oracle, there is often a tone of finality, but this is the result of attaining perfection and stability, not the result of bringing history to a close. It is not the end of time, only the end of change. The emphasis is on the achievement of a destined goal. This is how Israel in the monarchy saw their own times, in the visions of Jacob (Gen 49:1) and Balaam (Num 24:14). When this ideal failed, in the later monarchy, the same expression was used to describe its recovery (Deut 4:30; 31:29; Hos 3:5; Jer 23:20; 30:24). It can even be used of God's similar dealings with other nations (Jer 48:47; 49:39; Ezek 38:16).

In Deuteronomic-prophetic usage the phrase *bĕ'aḥărît hayyāmîm* refers specifically to restoration after a calamity. The perspective is the same here. The prospect is the restoration of Israel after the appointed period of rejection to follow the destructions described in chapters 1–3. This development is not an afterthought in prophetic expectations of Israel's future. There is a common critical opinion that the expression came into use (or, if it was old, changed its connotations) in the postexilic community. Disappointment over the delay in the realization of Israel's hopes for recovery of former national identity and power caused those hopes to be projected more and more into an "eschatological" scenario. The phrase as used, for instance, in Hos 3:5 was understood by such scholars to be a much later addition to that book, adjusting the text to this later thinking. It has been much harder for scholars to explain the twin oracles of Micah 4:1-5 and Isaiah 2:1-4 as *originating* in that late milieu. This vision is not a postexilic oracle of hope added to the text to cancel the terminal judgment of oracles like those in chapters 1-3. Those punishments were corrections applied within the covenant. They were purposeful, educational, redemptive. It was expected that the lesson would be learned; the folly and futility of life lived against Yahweh would bring about a return. More than that, a regenerated Israel would give final proof to other nations that Yahweh was the only real God. Once more they would stream back to Jerusalem and live according to Torah, bringing the other nations with them.

days. The particular days are not specified. The plural *yāmîm* can refer to a unit of time, such as one year or a lifetime.

mountain. The language of the poem is drawn from a richly developed doctrine of Zion as the mountain of God (Causse 1938; Clifford 1972; Fohrer 1969: 195-241; Gordis 1971: 268-79; Kapelrud 1961; Lutz 1969; von Rad 1966; Roberts 1973; Wildberger 1957). Identification of the Temple mountain with Zion was made in 3:12, but in Micah 4 the expected parallels are delayed, making in effect a chiasmus between 3:12 and 4:1-2. The combination of *mountain* and *house* achieves a synthesis of the Sinai tradition (where the model of the Tabernacle/Temple was revealed to Moses) and the Zion tradition, where Solomon's Temple (the "house" of 3:12 and 4:1-2) was erected.

established. The use of this verb to describe building construction suggests strength and firmness. The verb describes the establishment of a throne, and this more abstract idea fits Mic 4:1. It describes the certainty of the word of God (Gen 41:32; Deut 13:15; 17:4; Hos 6:3) or a firm trust in God. With all these associations it often describes the establishment of the throne of David and of his city. Important texts are Pss 48:9; 78:67-72; 87:5. "God (or Elyon himself) established her (Zion) for ever." The name Elyon is a sign that Canaanite theology has been integrated into Israel's faith; but the roots are ancient (Gen 14:18-20). The same verb is used in Exod 15:17 for the building of the heavenly sanctuary by Yahweh with his own hands (Freedman 1981: 26; cf. Cross 1968: 23; 1973: 142-44). The noun *mēkôn* refers to the platform on which the building is erected or for the throne on which Yahweh sits as ruler of the world.

The use of the verb *kwn* in creation stories suggests, when the object is Zion, that this mountain was a special and primal creation (Clifford 1972), an idea that became fruitful in later Jewish legends. Similar notions are projected into eschatology; the cosmic mountain will be an object of special acts of creation in the End-time. So Micah, like Ezekiel after him, probably anticipated a physical transformation of the region of Jerusalem, reversing the collapse of mountains described in 1:4. On the theological aspects of the transformation, see Bruce (1990).

The periphrastic construction that uses a form of the verb *hyh*, "be," as an auxiliary with a participle is marginal to Biblical Hebrew. Some scholars consider its past-tense use to be un-Hebrew, a late intrusion under the influence of

Aramaic (Waltke and O'Connor 1990: 629). With the imperative *be!* the participle could be purely adjectival (Greenfield 1969), but there are no certain biblical examples. With the imperfect, as here, there is no agreement as to the aspect that is secured in the construction. Waltke and O'Connor (1990: 628) emphasize the "progressive" aspect. Muraoka prefers "durative" (1991: 410, 577). It is unclear whether the nuance here is "will become established" or "will stay established" (Muraoka 1991: 410). The participle *nākôn* is used periphrastically elsewhere (Exod 19:11, 15; 34:2; Josh 8:4; 2 Sam 7:16 = 1 Chr 17:14; 2 Sam 7:16 [the parallel in 1 Chr 17:24 lacks the auxiliary]; 1 Kgs 2:25). The meaning varies between "prepared" and "established." The latter is closer to the creation terminology used here.

head. Or "chief." The preposition is *bet essentiæ* (or "Bet of identity" [Waltke and O'Connor §11.2.5e; Muraoka 1991: 487]).

(higher) than. The preposition *min* is superlative. The complete idiom requires an adjective. It would mean "the highest of the mountains."

peoples. The relationships between the matched pair *ʿammîm* and *gôyim* in Biblical Hebrew poetry will be looked at in the following Excursus on the relationship between Isa 2:1–5 and Micah 4:1–5. Speiser (1960) has discussed the difference in connotation between the two terms. He concluded that while "*gôy* comes rather close to the modern definition of 'nation'," *ʿam* contains "the suggestion of blood ties and the emphasis on the individual, both of which features are peculiar to the Hebrew term" (1967: 165). When matched in poetry, as the words often are, they are correlative rather than synonymous. It is doubtful, however, whether exact technical distinctions are being sustained, requiring that *ʿammîm* be translated "ethnic groups" rather than "peoples."

stream. The verb is related to the noun that means "river," but in the Hebrew Bible it is used only to describe the movement of worshipers to a festival of their god—even Bel in Babylon (Jer 51:44). In Jer 31:12, as here, the return of scattered Israel to "the height of Zion" is celebrated with eschatological fervor, and the versions translated the verb along those lines (hence RSV). But the parallelism in both passages requires a verb of motion.

NJPS translates: "The peoples will gaze on it with joy." This draws on another root *nhr*, found in Isa 60:5; Jer 31:12; Ps 34:6 with the meaning "beam with joy."

2. *(to it).* The bicolon (vv 1b–2aAα) is spread over two verses. This obscures the fact that *ʿālāyw*, "to it," in v 1b does double duty in the next colon. The preposition *ʿal* could contribute the nuance of "around," not just "unto." The preposition also means "beside," indicating, perhaps, that, being Gentiles, the nations were not to be allowed into the Temple itself or even into the sacred precincts. They must be content to settle outside the perimeter.

let us go up. The form of the verb *naʿăleh* is ambiguous as to mood, since triconsonantal root verbs ending with the letter *hē* (such as *ʿlh*) do not receive the cohortative suffix *-â*. Its mood is determined by the preceding imperative and confirmed by the morphological cohortative *nēlĕkâ, let us walk*, in v 2aBβ. This could be the language of pilgrims; compare the "songs of ascent" in the Psalter. The ascent referred originally to the final and immediate act of entering the divine presence, which originally required the climbing of the sacred mountain, called "the hill of God // Yahweh" (Exod 4:27; 24:13), Sinai in the first place (Exod 19:23; 24:15, 18; 34:2, 4). Compare Num 10:33.

mountain of Yahweh. The rarity of the phrase *har-Yhwh* suggests that its use in Mic 4:2 is deliberate. It is part of the rhetorical structure, including a link with 3:12. Within 4:1–2 it is the result of breaking up the longer phrase *har bêt-yhwh* in v 1aA and dividing the components between the two colons in v 2a. The language was intended to stimulate definite ideas in the minds of the hearers. In the traditions, associations of Sinai were transplanted to Jerusalem—including the belief that this was the place where *tôrâ* would be given. The moral qualifications laid down in Psalm 24 for one who would be permitted to climb up Yahweh's mountain (Ps 24:3) and to seek the face of (the God of) Jacob (Ps 24:6)—the two phrases are parallel in Mic 4:2—arose from the stipulations of the covenant. The entrance ritual that provides the language of Psalm 24 is the background of the question in Mic 6:6–7, while the qualifications are summarized in Mic 6:8. It is hard to believe that the sacred mountain would be thrown open to visitors from all over the world without similar tests.

house. The phrase in "mountain of the house" in 3:12 and 4:1 is here split up and spread over two parallel colons.

instruct. The precative mood of *nēlĕkâ* extends to the parallel verbs—*naʿăleh*, which cannot receive the cohortative suffix, and *yôrēnû*. The latter is then jussive: "and let him instruct us!" This analysis is preferable to making v 2aB a consequence—"so that he may . . . " This interpretation gives the unfortunate impression that by cooperating in this way, they are helping Yahweh to do his work, confined as he is to his shrine! All the verbs express a desire, and *yôrēnû* is jussive, a prayer! The usage explains why the prefixed verb form is used here, while the normal way of continuing predictive indicative discourse (consecutive future) is found in v 3. It is anticipated that Yahweh will instruct them directly, as he did Moses at Sinai. The usual channels, which have been discredited in 3:11, are bypassed.

let us walk. Here the verb is clearly cohortative. The verb *hlk* has already been used twice, each time with a different connotation. In v 2aAα it describes the pilgrimage that the nations will make to Zion; in v 2aAβ it begins their speech. In v 2aBβ it is their ethical resolve to walk in his paths. See the following NOTE on *hlk* in v 5.

paths. The nouns *derek* and *ʾōraḥ*, both meaning "path" or "way," are conventional parallels. The prepositions with the nouns are different: *min-* "from," clashes with *b-* "in." For the parallelism, see Dahood (1970: 398). On the meaning of *b-*, see Brekelmans (1969). The inference that the prepositions must have the same meaning here is a misguided use of supposed synonymous parallelism. The preposition *min* is not partitive ("some of his ways") as suggested by Rudolph (1975: 76 n. a, 80); it identifies *his ways* as the source of the teaching—"let him teach us out of (the corpus of) his ways!" The idiom "walk in" has its metaphorical meaning and also, in the cult context, the added feature of dramatized, literal, "walking with God" in pilgrimage.

Even if we can equate the meanings of the prepositions, the two words mean-ing "way" // "path" are focused differently. In v 2aBα "teach" is literal, "ways" is figurative; in v 2aBβ the verb *hlk* is figurative (literal in v 2aAα). So the parallel-ism in v 2aB is complementary: "He will teach us to walk in his ways // paths."

For. Verse 2b is the center of the main block (vv 1–3), structurally and logi-cally. It is not necessarily part of the nations' speech. The references to Zion // Jerusalem tie v 2b back to v 1a. It is because the mountain is exalted and because Torah is given there that peoples will travel to Zion. If v 2b is included as part of the speech, it gives the reason for going up to Yahweh's mountain, not the reason for walking in his paths. The end result of it all (v 2aB, the nations fol-lowing Yahweh's instructions) is the outcome of the flanking bicolons, which contain four words referring to Jerusalem.

go forth. On the word as issuing from God's mouth, see Amos 1:2 (same par-allelism of "from Zion" // "from Jerusalem") and "going forth" in Hosea 6:3 (dis-cussed by Andersen and Freedman 1980: 423). The idiom makes it likely that here, too, *min* is locative.

Torah or "instruction." The parallelism shows that priestly *tôrâ* (compare 3:11) and prophetic word (compare Jer 18:18) are not distinguished when the one source of both speaks directly. Yet the cult setting—in the Temple, no less!—raises the question of what possible human agencies the prophet had in mind. If there are any officials on duty in that "house," their part is not worth mentioning. Micah's silence on this detail is not just due to hostility against the priests in Jerusalem, who were condemned in 3:11. It contrasts with the apologetic con-cern of the postexilic community to legitimate the greater role of priests as givers of Torah. This concern reaches the point where a priest as such (Joshua) is admitted to the divine council (Zechariah 3), a privilege previously exclusive to prophets. There Joshua is enjoined by Yahweh to "walk in my ways" (Zech 3:7).

even. This rendition of the Hebrew conjunction "and" is required because v 2bB is epexegetic. The chiasmus brings the two terms "Torah" and "the word of Yahweh" into the closest association, thus making it even clearer that they are the same, or at least equivalent.

word. Verse 3 shows that the instruction desired is a resolution of international disputes when both parties unreservedly agree to abide by Yahweh's decision.

3. *judge.* The same roots (*špṭ* and *ykḥ*) occur in parallel (twice!) in Isa 11:3–4. There it is the Davidic "branch" who is the judge. That Yahweh is "judge of all the earth" is affirmed in the patriarchal tradition (Gen 18:25), prior to the de-struction of the cities of the plain. The assertion of Yahweh's kingship in Exod 15:18 also implies more than rule just over Israel. At least his dominion extends to all the nations mentioned in the Song of the Sea, not excluding Egypt. The Exodus theme demonstrated that Yahweh was God over the whole world. The imagery of the mountain as the seat of his dominion is an important link be-tween this primal tradition of Exodus 15 and Mic 4:1. In the book of Judges, the title *haššôpēṭ* is ascribed to Yahweh, not to any human (Judg 12:27), and it is precisely as an arbitrator in international disputes that he is given this role in the book of Judges.

among. The Hebrew preposition *bên* is usually translated "between." In standard English "among" should be used when more than two entities are involved. The question, and it is a fine one, is whether the prophet has in mind that the arbitration proceedings are always between two parties although the statement extends to "many nations," but always by pairs, or whether he has in mind an adjudication that might involve several litigants all at once. English must choose a preposition for one way or the other; in Hebrew the one preposition serves for all such situations.

powerful. The adjective *'āṣûm* can be an attribute of *'am,* "people" (Exod 1:9; Num 22:6; Joel 2:2, 5 ['am = "army"]; Ps 35:18; Prov 30:26) but more frequently of *gôy* "nation" (Gen 18:18; Num 14:12; Deut 4:38; 7:1; 9:1, 14; 11:23; 26:5; Josh 23:9; Isa 60:22; Joel 1:6; Mic 4:7); once of *miqneh,* "stock" (Num 32:1), once of "kings" (Ps 135:10). Note the Deuteronomic use of *gôyim 'āṣûmîm.* The epithet *'āṣûm* is rarely without a parallel (Num 22:6) and never the lead item in parallelism. Three times it comes first in the coordinated phrase *'āṣûm wārāb* (Deut 9:14; 26:5; Isa 8:7 [plural]): *'āṣûm* is the conventional parallel for *rāb,* "numerous" (Num 32:1; Joel 2:11; Ps 35:18; plural in Isa 53:12; Amos 5:12; Mic 4:3; Zech 8:22 [which has exactly the same parallelism as Micah 4:3]; Ps 135:10; Prov 7:26). Or else *'āṣûm* is coordinated with *rāb* (Exod 1:9; Joel 2:2) or *gādôl* (Gen 18:18; Num 14:12; Dan 11:25 [army]; compare Prov 18:18; plural in Deut 4:38; 7:1; 9:1; 11:23; Josh 23:9). Zechariah 8:22 (compare Ps 135:10) has the same scenario as Micah 4:2.

> And many peoples and strong nations will come to seek Yahweh of Hosts in Jerusalem and to pray before Yahweh.

This use of the two nouns in the same sequence and the use of an adjective with each noun resembles the fuller text of the bicolon in v 3a in Micah, in contrast to the parallel in Isaiah, which has the inverse sequence and no adjective with "nations." It is likely that Zechariah depends on Micah. Isaiah's reading does not tell against *rabbîm* in Mic 4:3aA; Micah has a more complex pattern of parallelism, with a match of *rabbîm // 'āṣûmîm* secured between the colons in vv 2aAα and 3aB, in which they are attributes of "nations." This additional, long-range parallelism in Micah is more subtle than Isaiah's mere repetition of *rabbîm,* which only secures parallelism within the bicolon corresponding to vv 1b–2aAα and 3aA, whereas Micah secures parallelism between these two bicolons as well. This poetic superiority does not necessarily mean that Micah's text is prior to Isaiah's; it could be an improvement on a borrowed text. We think it more likely that Isaiah's version represents a simplification, which also involved the dropping of *'ad-rāḥôq.*

unto far off or "distant." The phrase *'ad-rāḥôq* has been suspected as not original to the composition. It is lacking in Isaiah, and it makes the colon overly long. The latter point carries little weight, however, unless one can be sure that originally all the colons in the poem were of regular if not precisely equal length. Otherwise trimming colons just because they are long is a procrustean measure. As we have already and repeatedly seen, the colons, even in this unit, range in length from two to six words, from four to twelve syllables. There is less disproportion if bicolons are taken as units. In contrast to standard Hebrew verse, where the second colon of a pair is generally equal in length to the first or shorter, prophetic poetry sometimes lengthens the second colon. In any case, this bicolon is not as long as the next one.

The presence of *ad-rāḥôq* gives Micah a perspective similar to that of Isaiah, who speaks about "all of the nations," also an addition. Micah's language is more effective. Isaiah's universalistic phrase comes at the beginning of the development (Isa 2:2b); Micah's additional phrase *unto far off* achieves a climax at the end of the scene.

If the original meaning was the settling of intertribal disputes within Israel, or between Israel and its immediate neighbors, as in Judges 12, it now embraces the most distant nations of the world. While some sort of tribal gathering may be in the background (e.g., Deut 33:2–5), that is no longer the case in Isaiah and Micah now, even without the additions. The juxtaposition of *'mym* and *gwym* would almost certainly imply more than the two kingdoms of Israel and Judah, although the vision originally included only the rest of the eight nations in the territory between Egypt and Assyria, territory to which Israel laid some claim and sovereignty over which was exercised by both David and Solomon, at least for a number of years. These would be the nations whose rebellion caused the crisis documented in Psalm 2.

swords // spears. The appearance of the "peoples" as litigants before the court of Yahweh (whether in an assembly of the Israelite league of tribes, or from all over the world) still implies hostility, settled only by the imposition of superior divine authority. The rest of the development in v 3 goes far beyond that. Enmity is set aside. Weapons are not needed. There is no longer a desire for combat. How the nations are motivated to come to Yahweh in the first place (*na'ăleh* sounds voluntary) and how this change of heart (v 2aBβ) takes place are not explained.

How realistic is the picture of the technological adaptation of weapons to tools and its reverse under opposite circumstances (Joel 4:10)? The identity of the farming implements is not certain. The *'ēt* (1 Sam 13:20–21) could be a metal point for a wooden plow or a hoe. Byington (1949: 52) argued that it would be more feasible to make a heavy hoe out of a sword rather than a plowshare. The *ḥănît*, a javelin for throwing or thrusting, was suitable for adaptation to a pruning knife, mounted perhaps on a similarly long handle to reach high branches (Isa 18:5). The emphasis on peaceful agriculture prepares the way for v 4. Note the similarly parallel emphasis on grain fields and vineyards, on plowing and pruning, in Mic 1:6 and 3:12, but in a different mood (Cannon 1930).

raise. Isaiah 2:4 has singular. The plural verb of Micah is better grammar, but the more difficult reading of Isaiah could be more original. The preceding verbs are plural. The singular subject ("nation"), singular indirect object ("nation"), and the singular object ("sword") are all distributive. The two negative statements that conclude v 3 do not have close internal parallelism—the word "sword," already used, is not followed by the expected "javelin." Instead each colon matches a preceding bicolon, chiastically. The colon in v 3bBα corresponds to the bicolon in v 3bA (disarmament). Colon v 3bBβ matches the bicolon in v 3a, since now they prefer arbitration to combat.

sword. The distributive singular object would normally be *ḥarbô*; without the suffix, prose might use the definite article. The lack of the suffix and along with this the nonuse of *nota accusativi* are poetic.

train or "learn." In view of *lĕmûdê milḥāmâ*, "trained for battle" (1 Chr 5:18), the idiom here means that they will not need to keep up their martial skills, just in case. The combined circumstances of disarmament, allocation of resources to agriculture, and discontinuation of military training, along with the security described in v 4aB, imply that there will be no threat of foreign aggression either. As the remainder of the chapter shows, this state of affairs will eventuate, not when all nations join the confederacy on the same basis as the tribes of Israel, but when they have been subjugated by victorious Zion.

If v 3b is connected logically with vv 2–3a, then the assembly (vv 1b–2aAα) for arbitration by Yahweh (v 3a) is precisely to resolve issues normally settled by armed combat. The word of Yahweh given as Torah in Zion (v 2b) must be applied precisely to this problem. The nations are willing and resolved to accept his ruling and direction (v 2aB). The outcome (v 3b) then defines or explicates what is meant by "walking in his paths." The acceptability and finality of the result come climactically in v 3bBβ; they will not go to war and they won't even prepare for it. Seen in combination, the two colons of v 3bB do not involve redundancy. Precisely because the parallelism is not formal, we should accept the combination of corresponding terms, leading to a more integrated (but dull prose) paraphrase: "They will no longer be trained to wield their swords in battle."

4. *sit* or "dwell." The language is traditional and the imagery specifically Israelite. The picture is simple, concrete, and surprisingly individualistic. The undisturbed cultivation of the vine is the preeminent sign of national and private security. There was a tradition, reflected in Gen 9:20–27, and perhaps by the Nazirites (Numbers 6) and the Rechabites (Jeremiah 35), that viewed the vine, or at least its product wine, with disfavor. Otherwise the vine was highly regarded (in one agricultural passage it is secondary to cereals [Deut 8:8]), and a man's pride in his vineyard provided a beautiful image of Yahweh's relationship to Israel (Isaiah 5).

each. The distributive use of a singular noun with a plural verb is found in vv 3b and 5a as well as here. The lack of distributive *ʾîš* in the parallel v 5a shows that there it is nations, not individual persons, who walk each in the name of its god, just as v 3 describes the fighting of nations, not persons. Yet v 4, between these two, switches attention to the individual, secure on his personal estate. It is less likely that it is a figure of speech for nations living unmolested on their territory.

To be sure, the picture is not without a national reference. Verse 4 contains a phrase that could be a direct quotation from 1 Kgs 5:5 [Eng. 4:25]—"And

Judah and Israel dwelt in safety, from Dan even to Beersheba, every man under his vine and under his fig tree, all the days of Solomon." There is nostalgia and idealization in these words. The specific national references in the source of this language are lacking in Micah's quotation, making it more general. Following on v 3, it now seems to apply to the whole world. It remembers the only period in Israel's history free from hostilities (doubtless the historian has left out those minor disturbances that must have occurred, like Tacitus's classic *sub Tiberio quies*, "under Tiberius [things were] calm" [*Annals* 5:9]). They dwelt in peace (*šālôm*) and security (*beṭaḥ*) through Solomon's entire reign, because Solomon inherited from David dominion over the whole region this side of the Euphrates. Such a thing had never happened since. But it provided the ideal for the future when Israel's former greatness would be recovered by another David (Mic 5:1), and "the one of peace" (5:4a) could be an oblique reference to Solomon.

terrify. The word is a participle, "one disturbing." This matches "in safety" (*lābeṭaḥ*) in 1 Kgs 5:5. The situation will be quite free from anxiety, particularly from fear of harm. The verb *ḥrd* describes fretting and bothering. It can include legitimate care for detail (2 Kgs 4:13) or dismay at some great catastrophe (Isa 32:11; Ezek 16:16; 32:10) or sudden alarm (Amos 3:6; Ruth 3:8). The circumstances of its use suggest agitation at danger suspected, but not clearly perceived. Sometimes it describes panic at the news of the approach of war (Isa 10:29) or after a sudden defeat (I Sam 14:15)—correspondingly at the threat of divine judgment (Isa 19:16), hardly distinguishable from impending historical disaster. Common to all these is apprehensiveness when you don't know what is going to happen, except that it will be bad. Its opposite is then a guaranteed future that excludes worry about tomorrow.

Since the sources of this "trembling," as described in the Bible, are diverse, the impression given by Mic 4:4, with its simple negation, is that all of the many possible causes of shock and agitation will be abolished in the new age. In this generalized form ("and no disturber"), the promise is a stock one, given in the old covenant guarantee (Lev 16:6; compare Jer 30:10; 46:27; Ezek 32:28; 39:26; Zeph 3:13). In Deut 28:26 and Jer 7:33 the words are given a sinister twist; the promise is turned into a curse (compare Isa 17:2; Nah 2:12).

mouth of Yahweh. The mouth of Yahweh as the source of his utterances is both personal (Yahweh himself) and specific (this oracle). To obey God is to do something *'al pî yhwh* (Exod 17:1; Lev 24:12—the phrase is characteristic of P). To ask for an oracle is to enquire at the mouth of Yahweh (Josh 9:14), to disobey an oracle is to "cross" (*'br*) the mouth of Yahweh (Num 22:18; 24:13). In contrast to the perfunctory *nĕ'ūm Yahweh* (4:6; 5:9), this rarer rubric is more majestic. It is characteristic of the book of Isaiah (1:20; 40:5; 58:14). The fuller name "Yahweh Sabaoth" is used with it only in Mic 4:4, and the lack of such a rubric for the parallel in Isaiah 2 suggests that it is original with Micah and that the title was used deliberately by him (or his editor). Isaiah would hardly have deleted it.

The name "Yahweh of hosts" has associations with earlier warfare in the period of conquest and consolidation that culminated in David's triumph. It involved the participation of heavenly troops, and its revival suits the theme of cosmic warfare in the prophets. At this point in Micah it befits the belligerent tone of the following prophecies, for a recapitulation of the *pax Solomonica* must be preceded by the wars of David.

5. *walk.* This is the only place in the Hebrew Bible where the idiom "walk in the name of (a) god" is used. The imagery of walking, though simple, is multi-layered for the pious imagination (Banks 1987). (1) Historically it evokes memories of Abraham's migration to a destination not identified at first. The promise of a land "that I will reveal to you" (Gen 12:1) is followed by "and Yahweh revealed himself" (v 7). Then he was called to "walk" to a mountain "that I will tell you" (Gen 22:2), followed by considerable play on the idea of revelation. Walking with God is thus an ancient concept, reaffirmed in Mic 6:8. The verb "walk" is also prominent in the Exodus story, with Sinai as the goal. This is already conceived in terms of pilgrimage to a cult center; and a political ingredient of paying homage (bringing tribute) to a ruler is also present.

(2) Later pilgrimages to Zion recapitulated this history, but emphases on ethical qualifications for participating in the cult also overlapped the moral teaching that covenant loyalty was walking "behind Yahweh" (Andersen and Freedman 1980: 169–70) or "in his ways."

(3) The ethical layer of meaning with its idea of a journey to God could be developed in terms of an ultimate goal for life, so that ritual marches both recapitulated historical redemption and also realized the hope of reaching the supernal mountain of God, as in Micah 4.

(4) The eschatological journey is thus rooted in history and cult and becomes explicit in the last phrase "for ever and ever."

All these layers are present in Mic 4:1–5. Going to the mountain is cultic; walking in his ways is ethical; the memories are historical; the hopes are eschatological. It is therefore inappropriate to ask what the meaning of "walk" is in this context.

The participation of the nations similarly involves an overlay of meanings, simultaneously present, or sliding from one to the other. The exegete does not have to work out which one of these several meanings is "correct." The old tribal confederation, remembered in somewhat idealized terms as the political form of Israel before the monarchy, was a group of *'ammîm*, "peoples," although Israel was usually thought of as one *'am*. Psalm 2 is a manifesto for David's empire that provided another ideal model from the past. It is an interesting political question how much the theory of David's *imperium* was worked out by regarding his vassals as adjuncts to the tribes. The great set speech of Amos 1–2 seems to be undergirded by such a political theology, since Yahweh makes equal claims or at least exercises evenhanded judgments over all the nations of the Syria-Palestine region. In any case the ideas of Psalm 2 are close to those of Micah 4–5. In particular, this model provides a basis for the mandate to conquer the nations to secure submission to Yahweh. Otherwise Mic 4:1–5 gives no hint about the reason for the nations streaming to Jerusalem.

Making the circle wider still, no limit is set; and the use of "all" in v 5 suggests the whole world. The most comprehensive tradition for that is found in the Table of Nations (Genesis 10). The fact that Nimrod is mentioned only here (5:5) and in Genesis 10 (1 Chr 1:10 derives from the latter) suggests this primal kind of universalism.

each. Verse 5 concludes the first oracle with contrasting statements about the religious preference and behavior of the "peoples" and of those who have Yahweh as their God. Verse 5 has various links with vv 1–4. Sitting and walking are two modes of life always linked in the Bible (Deut 6:7). They correspond to war and peace. Here they are linked by the distributive constructions: "they will sit *'îš* . . . ," "they will walk *'îš* . . . " In v 3b *gôy*, not *'îš*, is used as the individualizing noun; in v 5 we would have expected *'am* as the parallel (elsewhere in the oracle *'ammîm* and *gôyim* alternate). If the choice of *'îš* in v 4 marks a shift of focus from nation to individual, the choice of *'îš* rather than *'am* in v 5 leaves the focus of v 5 unclear; it is not necessarily referring to the gods of individual nations; it could refer to individuals in the nations. In any case, the distributive construction provides continuity through vv 3, 4, and 5. At the same time, the contrast between the religious orientation of the nations and of Israel seems to contradict what is said in vv 1–4. After the concluding rubric of v 4b, v 5 reads like a qualifying marginal statement. Suspicion of v 5 as an ill-fitting addition is increased when we note that the otherwise almost identical text of Isa 2:2–5 has nothing to match Mic 4:5. Each nation will continue to follow its own god.

The contradiction may be softened a little if the separation of v 5 from the rest by v 4b means that it is not referring to the same time as vv 1–4. In the end of the days all nations will eventually acknowledge the God of Jacob as the ruler of the whole world. In the meantime, even though all the nations continue to follow their own gods (the singular "its god" suggests that each nation, like Israel, has but one god, each having a different name), so far as "we" are concerned (the free form of the pronoun is emphatic), we will walk in the name of Yahweh. There is no hint as to the identity of the group that expresses this resolve.

for ever and ever. This phrase makes the last colon very long, and it has no counterpart in v 5a. Does it blanket both colons, or does it contrast the followers of Yahweh with the nations whose gods cannot guarantee the same permanent relationship? Apart from Psalms, where this expression is used twelve times, the expression *lě'ôlām wā'ed* is used only in Exod 15:18; Mic 4:5; and Dan 12:3. Compare Pss 10:16; 45:7, 18. In view of the availability of so many Hebrew expressions for the idea of eternity, this restricted occurrence is suggestive, especially so close to the idea of Yahweh as king (v 7). To say that Yahweh will reign for ever and ever (Exod 15:18) makes sense. The confession "Yahweh (is) our God for ever and ever" is implicit in the language. To say that we will walk in the name of Yahweh "for ever and ever" implies sharing in some way in his eternal life, not necessarily by the persons speaking, but by the nation to which they belong and whose continuance is connected with the fact that the God of Israel will never die. It would be anachronistic to project back into Micah's language the later developed expectations of personal immortality, living with God in heaven, that came to the fore in Jewish (and derived Christian) religious consciousness only after the end of the prophetic age. In Micah, as in the Hebrew Bible generally, the destiny of Israel and the nations is found only on this earth. It is still very political. The Zion of vv 1-2 would only later be projected into heaven. The vow of perpetual fealty that closes the unit must be seen as a resolution binding all the succeeding generations to walk with Yahweh.

Comment on Micah 4:1-5

Coming as it does after the oracle formula of v 4b, and apparently contradicting vv 1-3, verse 5 has been seen by many scholars as a later gloss, reaffirming Israel's exclusivist faith in the face of the persistent polytheism and idolatry of the nations. Whereas v 2 predicts that "many nations" will "walk" to the mountain of Yahweh, joining Jacob in common festival, here each nation "walks" its own way, each in the name of its god. It does not even set the universal dominion of the one God, Yahweh, against the regional polytheism of the Gentiles. It simply states that each nation walks in the name of its god, while "we," presumably Israel, worship Yahweh exclusively. The relationship between v 5a and v 5b, with the placement of the free subjects (kol-hā'ammîm and 'ănaḥnû) before verbs with the same root, certainly suggests contrast (Andersen 1974: 150–53; Muraoka 1983: 47–66) and warrants the translation "but we . . . "

The assumption that the compound sentence in v 5 is antithetical creates another difficulty for translation. The parallelism requires that the verbs be closely in line with each other. But it is usual to translate the first as a statement of fact ("they walk"), the second as a resolution ("we will walk"), as if the verbs differed in both tense and mood. The proper use of the cohortative for resolution in v 2 suggests that the simpler nēlēk of v 5 is indicative (unless the free pronoun makes a difference—but that construction is needed to secure the contrast).

If v 5 is seen as two statements of fact side by side—"they (will) walk in the name of their god, but we (will) walk in the name of our god"—then it is not only banal, it is something that no Israelite would say, let alone add to the sacred text. Even if it were true that Israel once had a henotheistic belief in Yahweh as their tribal god, while all the other nations similarly had theirs, it was quite another matter when the faithful from Moses onward, or at the very latest from the Exile onward, asserted the sole existence of Yahweh and the nonexistence of all other gods. Verse 5, as commonly interpreted (and appealing perhaps to contemporary pluralism), would represent a concession and a regression. It cannot be understood simply as the defiance of other religions by later diaspora Jews, as if the vision of vv 1-4 had actually been renounced! There is no indication that the Jews ever lost this hope, given as a promise to Abraham, of bringing blessing to the whole world when the nations realize that Yahweh is God. This vision was continually reaffirmed. Zechariah 8:20-23 is a shining example. In any case *kî* cannot have its usual meaning "for" here, because v 5 does not give the reason for the preceding statements in vv 1–4. Perhaps it makes a concession. Even if all the other nations continue to follow their own gods, we will keep on following Yahweh. The reiteration of the verb "walk" (three times in v 2, twice in v 5) suggests such a continuity of theme.

There are differences as well. "Walking in the name" might not be the same as "walking in the ways . . . " But walking in God's ways in v 3 is not the same as the pilgrimage; it is the consequence of learning Torah in Zion. It is important to emphasize that Israel is not distinguished from the other nations in v 2, so we cannot say that "we" in v 5a is Israel in contrast to "we" the nations in v 2. Rather is it implied that Israel, too, participates in the pilgrimage. Israel is one of the many nations. Originally Israel consisted of all the tribes. Then all David's vassals made up a larger community with Yahweh as their sovereign. In fact, "many nations" could mean "all the nations." Isaiah's addition of *kol* to v 2 is not a misinterpretation. To distinguish Israel from the rest we would have to suppose that "all the nations" in v 5a means "all the (other) nations." This is possible, but strained. If the model for the eventual Kingdom of God described in vv 1– 4 is a blend of the old tribal confederacy (Israel a company of "nations") and David's empire (the "nations" of Psalm 2, all acknowledging Yahweh and his messiah), with boundless extension, then the nations of vv 1–4 are not limited in number.

While Micah's vision of the end of the days may be idealistic and utopian, it is quite realistic compared with most apocalypses and visions reported by the prophets. That is why it has appealed to so many peoples in so many centuries, and still does. It sounds feasible. It can be imagined. It does not involve unusual miracles, unless we suppose that some kind of topographical transformation, rather than a symbolic statement is found in the elevation of Zion to the top of the mountains. The model is clearly supplied by the golden age of David and Solomon. However exaggerated the biblical stories of those reigns might be with peoples coming with tribute to the great king, they are not fantasy. If we limit the vision to the area between Assyria and Egypt (the same region as is mapped out in Amos 1–2), then there is nothing unrealistic about the vision or the picture of these nations coming to Jerusalem, as they must have previously done to pay tribute, only now they are going there to worship the great God.

EXCURSUS: THE RELATIONSHIP BETWEEN MICAH 4:1–5 AND ISAIAH 2:1–5

There are several instances in the Hebrew Bible where two passages found in different books are identical, or almost so. In some cases it is simply the same composition reproduced in two different places. The psalm of David in 2 Samuel 22 is an example. It is replicated as Psalm 18. The texts are virtually identical. But the small differences between them are considerable in number and of great interest. Some of these differences may be due to changes in either or both recensions during their independent textual transmission; but there are other differences that cannot be explained by a theory that they ultimately came from an earlier common written form. If each derived first from a distinct stream of oral transmission, one should be more willing to recognize differences of a dialectal kind, quite apart from intentional alterations that might have been made for ideological reasons.

Parts of the book of Obadiah are matched by similar passages in Jeremiah; and the question of their interrelationships and literary history is a complicated one.

Micah 4:1–4(+ 5) is essentially the same as Isaiah 2:(1)2–4(+ 5). How this came about is a mystery not yet solved—perhaps forever insoluble. Thinking of every possibility, there are seven available explanations.

1. Isaiah and Micah each composed an identical prophecy independently.
2. An earlier prophecy was taken over and used by each prophet independently.
3. Micah composed it; Isaiah borrowed it.
4. Isaiah composed it; Micah borrowed it.
5. An oracle originally part of the Micah tradition but not necessarily original with the prophet was put into his book and later introduced into the book of Isaiah in one of its many revisions.
6. An oracle originally part of the Isaiah tradition but not necessarily original with that prophet was put into his book and later borrowed into the book of Micah.
7. An independent oracle, not originally associated with either prophet, and written later than either book, perhaps much later on, found its way independently into both books.

Before discussing in detail the arguments for and against these various theories, we shall compare the two versions. It is a delicate exercise to relate the similarities and differences between these two recensions of the same composition to the literary and textual history of the two books. In comparing the text of Isa 2:1–5 with that of Mic 4:1–5, we have the benefit of two ancient manuscripts that witness to early forms or variants of the text. For Micah we have evidence of an early Greek translation in 8HevXIIgr (Tov 1990). Column 7 preserves twelve fragmentary lines containing parts of Mic 4:3–5. Where extant, 8HevXIIgr confirms the MT of Micah in every detail, including the phrase ʿad-rāḥôq in v 3aB, and all of v 4, neither of which are present in the masoretic text of Isaiah.

Among the Dead Sea Scrolls the almost complete Isaiah scroll from Cave 1 (1QIsaᵃ) is of interest. It contains a number of deviations from the traditional text. Some of these are no more than spelling peculiarities characteristic of the documents from Qumran: kwl for kl; hgwʾym for hgwym; ʾlwhy for ʾlhy; yʿqwb for yʿqb. All involve the use of waw as a vowel letter. A few are of interest for the present exercise. For textual purposes, the most significant variant is hrym in Isa 2:2aAβ, where both the MT of Isaiah and Micah have hhrym. To decide among these variants requires very fine judgment. On the one hand, since this is the only place where the definite article is used in the poetic portion of the common text, the 1QIsa[a] reading, being more poetic, could be more original. It is more likely that a small particle would be added (under pressure from prose usage) to a text from which it had previously been lacking (due to poetic usage) than that it would be removed. 1QIsa[a] gives no indications that the scribe tried to make the text more poetic. The Masoretic texts, with the additional definite article, are the result of a trend towards more prosaic language. The same parallelism of "mountains" // "hills" occurs in Nah 1:5, where the second noun has the definite article: *hārîm* // *haggĕbā'ôt*. The pressure towards leveling the parallel items by adding the definite article to the first noun is seen in the reading *hhrym* in Mur 88 (Mur XII) column xvi and in LXX *ta orē*, "the mountains."

On the other hand, the agreement of the MT Isaiah and Micah in this detail is impressive, and likely to be authentic precisely because it goes against poetic usage; that is, its inclusion must have been deliberate. The variant in 1QIsa[a] can then be explained as loss of *he'* through haplography.

Variant Readings in Isaiah 2:2–4

	MT	1QIsa[a]	
v 2	ההרים	הרים	1QIsa[a] lacks definite article
	אליו	עלוהי	different prep.; Aramaizing suffix
	כל	כול	*plene* spelling
	הגוים	הגואים	*alef* as vowel letter[1]
v 3	אל־הר־יהוה	missing	haplography in 1QIsa[a]
	אלהי	אלוהי	*plene* spelling
	יעקב	יעקוב	*plene* spelling
	וירנו	ויורינו	*plene* spelling of -ē-
	ונלכה	ונאלכה	*alef* as vowel letter
	וארחתיו	ואורחתיו	*plene* spelling
	כי	כיא	*alef* as vowel letter (?)
	וירושלם	ירוו■לים	*plene* spelling of -ē-, not a diphthong
v 4	הגוים	הגואים	*alef* as vowel letter[1]
		את	1QIsa[a] adds prose particle
	לא	ולוא	*plene* spelling, as in some manuscripts

In order to proceed, we distinguish those portions of Isa 2:1–5 and Mic 4:1–5 that are unique to each book from those portions of the text that are to all intents "the same" in both. First we shall look at the question of the place of the pericope in the larger structure of the two books.

Micah 4:1–5 comes at the beginning of the Book of Visions (chapters 4–5). It is integral to the structure of that portion of the book of Micah; indeed we

---

[1] The function of this *alef* is debated. It could be the glottal consonant, produced by palatalization of intervocalic *yod*.

have already argued that the Book of Visions is grounded in this opening vision and built on it. Besides that, it follows immediately on the Book of Doom (chapters 1–3) right after a judgment on Jerusalem (3:12) that contains a number of terms that are used in Micah 4:1–5. Isaiah 2:1–5 comes at the beginning of a collection of oracular materials that continues through chapter 4. This portion of Isaiah (chapters 2–4) and Micah 4–5 are similar in many ways. On a superficial reading, each contains diverse materials that seem to be only loosely connected, without any organizing principle. We have argued to the contrary and will do so in more detail in our final COMMENT on the Book of Visions that Micah 4–5 is a coherent literary composition. Wiklander (1985) has presented a powerful case on text-linguistic grounds for the semantic and pragmatic coherence of Isaiah 2–4 as "a persuasive discourse" (p. 245) grounded in the opening vision. Formal syntactic analysis demonstrated that Isaiah 2–4 is "a delimited text in the book of Isaiah" (p. 100). Isaiah 1 is a distinct piece that most students of Isaiah regard as a separate composition intended to serve as a general introduction to the whole book and having no immediate continuation into chapter 2.

Bearing in mind arguments presented in other places that indicate that all four eighth-century prophetic books were edited in the first place along similar lines, most likely by the same group of tradents, we are not surprised to find a lot of similarity between Isaiah 1–4 and Micah 1–5. We note four points of resemblance. First, these two "books" (Isaiah 2–4 and Micah 4–5), both concerned with Zion // Jerusalem, contain a collection of oracles held together by two eschatological visions, one at the beginning and one at the end (Mic 5:9–14 matches Isaiah 4 in this regard; it also has affinities with Isaiah 1).

Second, all these visions are suffused with mythic imagery drawn from ancient traditions of Israel, especially the Sinai theophany.

Third, each of these "books" begins with the same vision.

Fourth, far from finding a deep break between Isaiah 1 and Isaiah 2 (partly because Isaiah 2 has a fresh heading), we can interpret Isa 2:1–5 as continuing Isaiah 1 in a manner similar to the way that Mic 4:1–5 grows out of the Book of Doom. We conclude that Micah 4–5 and Isaiah 2–4 are whole compositions of the same genre. The situation in Isaiah 1 is similar to that in Micah 1–3 in many respects, and a good case can be made for giving them the same date. Isaiah 1:7–8 accurately describes the plight of Jerusalem as it is in Micah 1–3. There is flourishing religion (Isa 1:11–15; compare Mic 3:11b) coupled with social injustice (Isa 1:16; Mic 3:9). Also Isa 3:1–3 can be compared with Mic 3:11, and the common use of $q\bar{a}\hat{s}in$ is another link. Other examples: "I will hide my eyes" (Isa 1:15, same meaning as Mic 3:4b although the vocabulary is different); "blood" (Isa 1:15; Mic 3:10); contrast of evil and good (Isa 1:16–17; Mic 3:2); "the mouth of Yahweh has spoken" (Isa 1:20; Mic 4:4b); the city is a harlot (Isa 1:21; Mic 1:7); bribery (Isa 1:23; Mic 3:11). All these similarities in setting and theme mean that the oracle common to both books follows Isaiah 1 just as appropriately as it does Micah 1–3.

The usual methodology for tackling the puzzle of Isa 2:1–5 and Micah 4:1–5 as "the same" vision in two different books begins by detaching them from their present context in these integrated compositions and then comparing them with each other in isolation. The question is from what source did each book get this vision. No matter how the puzzle is solved, the impression remains that one or the other or both have "borrowed" this item, that an editor has put the vision into one or the other or both, but it does not fit either of them very well. We shall address this question in the usual way in what follows, but our conclusions, adumbrated in the present paragraph, will be different from those usually met.

Micah's Book of Visions has no title. It begins abruptly, if a distinct work; but less so if it is seen as a continuation from chapter 3. Isaiah 2:1 has a formal heading that reads like the title of a book. Here we recall the similarity of the main title of Isaiah (1:1) to the title of Micah (1:1) in presenting both books as the outcome of prophetic visions.

Comparing the contents of the two recensions more closely:

Isaiah 2	*Micah 4*
Verse 1: Title	Nothing corresponding
Verse 2 =	Verse 1
Verse 3 =	Verse 2
Verse 4 =	Verse 3
Nothing corresponding to	Verse 4
Verse 5, slight resemblance to	Verse 5

Where the texts are common (Mic 4:1–3 = Isa 2:2–4), the differences are slight. For comparison of the two texts in detail the display on pp. 425–27 uses this code:

(1) When something is present in one recension, but absent from the other, the lack is marked [. . .]. Thus Isa 2:3aAδ lacks initial "and." Isaiah 2:2aB lacks the resumptive pronoun *hû'*. Isaiah has nothing to match Mic 4:4, and nothing corresponding to the last three words of v 5. The phrase *'ad-rāḥôq* in Mic 4:3aB is lacking in the Isaiah parallel. Micah 4:1aA and Isa 2:2aA have the same words, but the participle *nākôn* has a different location in each. Both positions are awkward because the periphrastic construction is rare in standard Hebrew.

(2) When each recension has a reading at the same place, but the readings are not identical, the text of Micah will be **highlighted**, the text of Isaiah underscored. There are differences in the spelling of otherwise identical words in Mic 4:2aBα (Micah *plene*, Isaiah *defective*), Mic 4:3bAβ (the other way around). There are morphological differences in otherwise identical words (Micah has *nunation* in v 3bBβ, Isaiah has a shorter suffix form in 2:4baα. There are vocabulary differences, with alternate choices of closely similar words, such as the prepositions in Mic 4:1b = Isa 2:2c. This is a well-known

fluctuation, even in manuscripts. Micah has a greater preference for ʿal (34×) over ʾel (7×); in First Isaiah the relative frequency of ʾel is higher; so the choice here is in keeping with the general characteristics of each book.

(3) In v 5 of each recension, the language diverges considerably. Whoever borrowed from whom, he rewrote the text, adding v 4 if Micah derives from Isaiah, deleting it if it was the other way, changing vv 1–3 of Micah slightly (in either direction), changing v 5 extensively. In the latter, Micah has a resolution; Isaiah has an exhortation. Even the idiom is different. Micah walks "in the name of Yahweh;" Isaiah walks "in the light of Yahweh." Micah 7:8–9 shows that the idea of Yahweh as light does occur in the book; but "light" is also a frequent idea in Isaiah.

To sum up, of the twenty-eight colons we recognize, six (in Mic 4:4) are completely lacking from Isaiah, three (in v 5) are only partially matched; the remaining nineteen colons (in Mic 4:1–3) are essentially present in Isaiah. This common text has been punctuated by the Masoretes in the same way throughout—they even have *paseq* at the same points; but Isaiah has the "open" paragraph division marker [ס] after its v 3, whereas Micah has it after v 5. This reflects a difference of perception over the divergent continuations of the core poem.

Of the nineteen colons found in both sources, eleven are identical apart from differences in spelling or morphology noted above. The other eight differ in the use or absence of certain words; the main differences are due to the choice and disposition of the words for "peoples" and "nations."

Mic 4:1b	ʿammîm	Isa 2:2b	kol-haggôyim
Mic 4:2aAα	gôyim rabbîm	Isa 2:3aAα	ʿammîm rabbîm
Mic 4:3aA	ʿammîm rabbîm	Isa 2:3aA	haggôyim
Mic 4:3aB	lĕgôyim ʿăṣūmîm	Isa 2:4aB	lĕʿammîm rabbîm

All these matching pairs involve the same word stock. The differences are consistent, and we must assume that they were deliberate. There are three kinds of contrast. First, Isaiah uses consistently the parallelism gôyim // ʿammîm while Micah consistently uses the reverse. The conventions by which standard word pairs used as matching items in poetic parallelism had a preferred sequence ("A-word" // "B-word") were not inviolate in practice. Apart from inversion to achieve chiasmus, it would seem that variation for the sake of variety remained an option.

Second, Isaiah uses *kol* and the definite article. These are more prosaic and are secondary in all likelihood. The introduction of the phrase *kol-haggôyim* into Isa 2:2b probably went with the replacement of the series of four expressions now found in Micah (*peoples, many nations, many peoples, powerful nations*) with the different expressions now found in Isaiah. Whether these peculiarities of Isaiah are original with the author or adapter or editor or whether they are due to later scribal changes is harder to tell. Without the particles, *all* and *the*, the poetic patterns in Micah have more formal parallelism. Isaiah's language is simpler and neater, but not necessarily better or more original than the more complex pattern in Micah.

Third, Micah resembles Isaiah in the bicolon Mic 4:1b–2aAα in having a noun not modified by an attributive adjective in v 1b paralleled by a noun with the attributive adjective *rabbîm* in v 2aAα. The nouns are different, however. Isaiah 2:4a has the same pattern as in 2:2b–3aAα, except that *kol* is not used the second time around. Micah deviates from Isaiah in two ways at this matching point; first by having the adjective *rabbîm* in the lead colon, and second by using a different adjective *ʿăṣūmîm* in colon 4:3aB. The outcome of these variations in Micah is that each of his references to the nations in this poem uses a different expression, whereas Isaiah has only two expressions (unless we count the use of *kol* in Isa 2:2b as constituting a third form). Micah and Isaiah agree in that the first noun has no adjective (each has a different noun to lead the parade). The detail could be a feature of the original source. The colon in question (Mic 4:1b) has three words, eight syllables. Its bicolon has sixteen syllables, the standard ideal, and incidentally the only bicolon in the poem to meet this standard. To add the adjective, as in the other three such colons in Micah, would make ten syllables. This would not be exceptional for Micah; the addition of *kol* and the definite article to Isa 2:2b has just that effect. We do not wish to impose rigid standards mechanically and *a priori* on Micah's prosody and are unwilling to use preconceived ideas about Hebrew poetic rhythms to regulate text-critical judgments.

With all due caution, we are inclined to believe that the lack of an adjective in Mic 4:1b and Isa 2:2b is original and served poetic considerations. If this lack of an adjective in the first colon of the series is not original with the common source of both recensions, the present agreement of both recensions in this detail could be the outcome of each borrower independently dropping the original adjective. That would be a very long coincidence. Otherwise their eventual agreement could be the result of secondary contamination of Micah from Isaiah, or of Isaiah from Micah. The text shows no sign of such convergence. The arrangement in Isaiah is repetitious, whereas Micah rings the changes on nouns and adjectives. Micah uses *rabbîm* with both nouns; he uses two different adjectives with *gôyim*. Micah's introduction of a new word (*powerful*) into the second round of stock phrases (v 3a) is not unlike the introduction of *the God of Jacob* as parallel to *Yahweh* (v 2aA). In Mic 4:1aAβ *har bêt yhwh* has only *hûʾ* as its parallel (nothing in Isaiah); but in v 2aA *har bêt* is split up and spread over the bicolon and made more elaborate. Micah's arrangements are climactic in both instances. His series—*peoples, many nations, many peoples, powerful nations unto (the remote) distance*—builds up to a universalistic climax. (This accumulation of increasingly strong expressions is a further argument for the authenticity of the concluding phrase *ʿad-rāḥôq*.) By contrast, Isaiah strikes the universalistic note from the outset, using *kol*. This loses the suspense achieved by Micah's slow unfolding of his identification of the pilgrim peoples. In each recension the disposition of the four expressions for the nations achieves a symmetrical pattern that holds firm. Each has a different noun in the corresponding lines. Each arrangement seems to be the outcome of different artistic perceptions. Any subsequent trend to leveling that would bring them closer together has been resisted.

The distinctive character of each recension in this important feature makes more pungent the question of which nouns the original used. The contrast is not total. Micah has the phrase *'ammîm rabbîm* only once in the poem proper, while Isaiah has it twice; yet Micah uses it three more times in the Book of Visions (4:13; 5:6, 7). We note that Mic 4:5aA, to which nothing in Isaiah corresponds, has a similar prose construction *kol-hā'ammîm*. In each case the contrast between these prose expressions and the complete lack of such prose language in the nuclear poem in Micah's recension (Mic 4:1-3) highlights the distinctive poetic character of this portion. This suggests that Micah has preserved a version of the oracle closer to the original.

Expressions for "all the nations" in the Hebrew Bible

Portion	gôyim rabbîm	'ammîm rabbîm	kol haggôyim	kol hā'ammîm
Pentateuch	5 (Deut)	0	6 (Exod, Deut)	12 (Exod, Deut)
Former Prophets	0	0	6	7
Latter Prophets	10	18	41	8
Psalms	1	0	2	5
Other Writings	0	0	4	7
Total	16	18	59	39
Isaiah/Micah	1/2	3/4	10/0	3/1

Constructions with *kol*, "all," are used in every part of the Hebrew Bible, including the Latter Prophets. There is only one occurrence of such a phrase in Micah—"all the peoples" in Mic 4:5aA. The expression *kol haggôyim* is much preferred in the prophetic writings (41×, 10× in Isaiah). It is not used in Micah. So its occurrence in Isa 2:2b is in line with Isaiah's preference. In contrast to these widely used prose expressions (with the definite article), *'ammîm* (or *gôyim*) *rabbîm* (without the definite article, but just as definite in reference) is characteristic of prophetic (poetic) usage (28 out of 34 occurrences are in the Latter Prophets, six in Micah—a disproportionate number, and all in the Book of Visions. So here we have a hallmark of the unity of the Book of Visions and of the integral place of the opening vision (vv 1-5, or at least vv 1-3) in that larger composition. In much the same way the phrases preferred in Isa 2:1-5 are ones that occur in the rest of that book. In each case, then, this oracle has been blended with the book it is in, which could be the result of borrowing in either direction or of adaptation from a common source by the editor of each book.

Comparison of the usage of the poetic expression *'ammîm* (or *gôyîm*) *rabbîm* with the prosaic "all the nations" and "all the peoples" indicates that their meanings are essentially the same. The universal reference is clearer when *kol*, "all," is used, and Isaiah has moved in that direction. Micah's readings have a better claim to originality, and the repetition of *'ammîm* (or *rabbîm*) in Isaiah could be due to leveling.

The differences between the two recensions can now be enumerated.

A. Differences in orthography in otherwise identical words:
    1. *wywrnw* (Mic 4:2aBα) // *wyrnw* (Isa 2:3aBα);
    2. *wḥnyttyhm* (Mic 4:3bAβ) // *wḥnytwtyhm* (Isa 2:4bAβ). One each way. Otherwise the spelling in both texts conforms to standard late orthography. Note also the *defective* spelling of *'ṣmym*, a word only in Micah.

B. Differences in morphology:
    1. *ḥrbtyhm* (Mic 4:3bAα) // *ḥrbtm* (Isa 2:4bAα). Isaiah has the shorter form of the suffixed feminine plural noun. Both versions have the longer form in the following colon. On the one hand, Micah's longer form in both colons could represent a leveling and the more diverse usage in Isaiah could be more original. On the other hand, Micah's forms achieve rhyme.
    2. Micah 4:3bBβ has the more archaic verb ending *-ûn*.

C. Differences in syntax:
    1. Isaiah 2:4bBα has a singular verb, Micah 4:3bBα has plural. The equivocation does not arise because the subject, *gôy*, is collective, indifferently singular, or plural in reference. It is formally singular. But the apparent concord in Isaiah is spurious. Micah's plural is better, not because it matches the plural in the next colon (that could be due to leveling), but because the construction is distributive (hence *ḥrb* means "[his] sword"). Compare the singular distributive suffixed forms "his vine" and "his fig tree" in v 4. The implied subject is *gôyîm*.
    2. In Isa 2:2b and 2:4aA, Isaiah has the definite article *hgwym*, surely a secondary drift towards prose, in view of the general preference for the anarthrous noun in poetry and consistently in Micah.
    3. In addition, Isa 2:2b has "all *the* nations," which is more prosaic, and surely secondary. This detail was discussed above.

D. Differences in clause syntax:
    1. In the first verse Micah has pleonastic *hû'*, lacking in Isaiah. While this does not make much difference to the poetry (each colon is quite good), its consequences for grammar are far-reaching. The effect is strange; for, if *niśśā'* is considered a participle because of its parallelism with *nākôn*, the pronoun subject normally should precede it.

The use of the free form of the pronoun is in itself enough to indicate that *niśśā'* is a participle. Its presence makes it unlikely that *wĕniśśā'* is a consecutive perfect (future tense) in line with the *following* verbs. The present arrangement in Micah is artistic. The purpose of the redundant pronoun subject is structural and metrical. Its placement after the participle brings the two participles into immediate alignment. Coupled with Micah's different word patterns in v 1aA, his choices make for greater regularity in this tricolon (6, 7, 8 syllables— 4, 3, 3 words), in contrast with the uneven colons of Isaiah (8, 5, 7 syllables—5, 2, 2 words).

2. Micah has *nākôn* in the second colon in v 1aAβ, in Isaiah it precedes *yihyeh*. The apparent periphrastic *nākôn yihyeh* is problematic, no matter which version is preferred. Neither version is entirely satisfactory, neither *nākôn yihyeh* because of the unique sequence (the auxiliary should precede the participle), nor *yihyeh . . . nākôn*, because of the separation of the auxiliary verb from the participle; but compare Josh 8:4, which gives a little support to Micah. So in this detail Isaiah seems to be secondary and inferior to Micah. The loss of *hû'* from Isaiah is due to homoeoteleuton; the scribe's eye jumped from the first *alef* at the end of *niśśā'* to the *alef* at the end of *hû'*, and the pronoun was lost. Without the pronoun it is more likely that *wĕniśśā'* in Isaiah would be read as a verb with *waw*-consecutive, following on from *yihyeh*, rather than as a second participle coordinated with *nākôn*. To sum up: Micah's arrangement in v 1aA is better from a poetic point of view; it makes for a better bicolon between v 1aAβ² and v 1aB. And Micah's arrangement brings *nākôn* into parallelism with *niśśā'*, reinforcing the parallelism of *mountains // hills* (compare Isa 40:12). To that extent Micah is superior. Isaiah's two-word five-syllable colon (v 2aAβ²) is not good; in fact v 2aAβ in Isaiah constitutes one clause and reads more like prose.

3. "And" is lacking from the onset of Isa 2:3aAδ, again a movement from poetic to prose style.

E. Differences in vocabulary:

1. In Mic 4:1b *'ālāyw*, in Isa 2:2b *'ēlāyw*. This is a common confusion. These prepositions often interchange in manuscripts. Thus **P** has *'lyw* in the first hand in Micah 4:1b, with *'ayin* written over the *alef* in correction. Going the other way, 1QIsa^a has *'lywhy*. The suffix is Aramaizing, but the preposition could be authentic, with MT *'lyw* secondary, the easier reading.

2. The other vocabulary differences in the use of the nouns "peoples" and "nations" and their attendant adjectives have been discussed above.

F. Substantial difference: the presence of *'ad-rāḥôq* in Mic 4:3aB.

It is not easy to weigh these thirteen differences between the text of Mic 4:1–3 and Isa 2:2–4. Isaiah is better in 2:4aB if one thinks that the colon Mic 4:3aB is overly long (twelve syllables). Apart from this, there is no detail in which Isaiah can be judged "better" than Micah in either grammar or poetry. The differences do not prove anything about dependence in either direction. A scribe or editor can make a poor reading better or a good reading worse. A well-known text-critical stratagem would be to ask how much of one text can be best explained as the result of movement away from the other, especially if we can detect motivation. Each text seems to be slightly divergent in its own way. Differences in orthography and morphology (A and B) are neutral. Differences in vocabulary and syntax (C–E) have more significance as indices of poetic form and style. In language and poetic art, the poem fits with the rest of the book of Micah. All in all, we think that the balance lies in favor of Micah as the original, or as closer to the original if both books got it from an outside prophecy. The differences in vocabulary and syntax (C–E) can be best understood as changes made by the editor (or subsequent scribes) of Isaiah. The differences in Isaiah are not obviously motivated, except to move slightly in the direction of prose syntax (and hence away from poetic style). Some of the differences in Isaiah's text look like the outcome of scribal deterioration that could have happened well along in the copying process.

On early responses to these parallel pieces see Lohfink (1986). Alexander (1846: 96) reports the stance of numerous scholars, up to that time, on the question. While professing himself to be somewhat indifferent to the solution, he inclined to Micah as the original author. The long and continuing discussion of the puzzle of Mic 4:1–5 and Isa 2:1–5 is reviewed in detail, with full bibliography in Wilderberger (1972: 72–94), who settles for Isaiah as the source of the piece. This is the dominant opinion at the present time. In fact Renaud (1977: 160) says: "défenseurs d'une authenticité michéenne . . . ont complètement disparu de la recherche récente." See Cannawurf (1963). Here we review the options in light of the preceding analysis of the differences between the two recensions.

Option 1. Each prophecy is authentic and original for each prophet. If two authors, without collaboration, produced two identical poems, the coincidence would be remarkable, to say the least. Humanly impossible. But all things are possible with God; so perhaps the same message was given directly by God to two separate prophets on two separate occasions. A theory like this can be believed and asserted. It cannot be proved or even tested. Young (1965: 112) cites H. Bultema (*Commentaar op Jesaja* [Muskegon, 1933]) as holding this position.

Option 2. Each prophet made authentic use of an older piece, taking it over with minimal changes. This view was held by some notable scholars in the early stages of critical study of the problem. It still has its advocates. Each prophet adapted the oracle in his own way and sited it in an appropriate place among his other prophecies. Such use could have been urged on each of them if the piece were already known and recognized as traditional, if not canonical, and therefore considerably earlier than their own times. This is possible; but it would make quite a difference to the history of apocalyptic thought in Israel if a piece such as this could have been composed prior to the age of the first writing prophets.

On first reading there is hardly anything archaic in the present text—neither orthography, nor morphology, nor vocabulary, nor poetic patterns. In old poetry, for instance, *lě'ōm* was favored as a parallel of *gôy* or *'am*. Its absence here is thus surprising, especially because *lě'ōm* (the plural at least) is a favorite word in Isaiah. One might note the nonuse of the *nota accusativi* with the objects in v 3b, but this is standard poetic syntax. There is no occasion to use the relative, so its absence means nothing. The sporadic use of the definite article is a little more telling. Both recensions have *hayyāmîm, hehārîm* (Mic 4:1); Isaiah alone has *kol-haggôyim* (v 1b in Micah), which is surely secondary. The lack of the definite article with *tôrâ* "(the) Law," is more striking (compare Hab 1:4). But it need not be archaic. The parallelism shows that **tôrat yhwh* is meant.

The language cannot be said to be late either, although it has been claimed that the technical expression *bě'aḥărît hayyāmîm* is postexilic coinage; yet *all* of its occurrences are in books of preexilic provenance, and some of its settings are very old indeed—Gen 49:1; Num 24:14; Deut 4:30; 31:29; Hos 3:5; Jer 23:20; 30:24; 48:47; 49:39; Ezek 38:16. Nor are the ideas demonstrably those that arose only after the Exile, unless one assumes, as many scholars do, that eschatological notions were unknown to the classical prophets.

The task of coming to grips with this problem is made more difficult by the uniqueness of the composition from a literary point of view. It does not belong to any familiar genre, so form-criticism does not offer much help. Its global if not cosmic setting and its eschatological mood are remarkable for the eighth century, but not unique, unless one strikes all such passages out of Amos, Hosea, Micah, and Isaiah, as is frequently done.

If the piece had turned up in an early and a late prophet (say First Isaiah and Haggai), one might more readily have suspected a late insertion into the older book. But its occurrence in *two* eighth-century prophets is a powerful combination. Even if secondary in both, the fact that it was put into the collected works of old writers shows that the later editors thought it belonged there, and not, say in Haggai, even if they were not sure which of the two had the better claim. But such a solution—putting the anonymous oracle in both!—is hardly a credible action of a scribe. Even less likely is a process by which the poem, already established in the text of one or the other, would be replicated in the one that lacked it. It is hardly conceivable that any scribe would do such a thing, although we are not willing to press any argument from what we think a scribe might do. The most likely explanation is that the texts of both Isaiah and Micah came down to the scribes in their present form, and that originally both used the common passage because it had the authority of age and was already canonical enough to have a fixed form. The editor of Micah changed his source less than the editor of Isaiah did.

Option 3. Isaiah borrowed an oracle from Micah. In 1860 E. B. Pusey wrote: "It is now owned, well nigh on all hands, that the great prophecy, three verses of which Isaiah prefixed to his second chapter, was originally delivered by Micah" (1866: 289b). The direction of this alleged borrowing could be discovered if we could show (1) which prophet's work it most closely resembles; (2) that one version is an adaptation or revision of the other with the telltale marks of the borrower on the changes he made; (3) that it fits more neatly into one book rather than the other. These tests cannot be applied decisively. The specimen is too small; Isaiah and Micah are too close in background, interests, and style, to permit differentiation; the prophecies of both were probably preserved, transmitted, and edited by the same people, imposing even greater resemblance on the final outcome. The most conspicuous difference is the tendency of Isaiah's recension to be less poetic, and we think that this points to borrowing by Isaiah or by an editor of his oracles.

Option 4. Micah borrowed from Isaiah. While this is possible and widely held by scholars at the present time, for reasons already given we think that the balance of probability is the other way. Lowth (1868: 147) maintained that Isaiah was the original author. By studying vocabulary Cazelles (1980) found support for this position in the affinities between Isa 2:1–5 and other places in Isaiah, notably 11:6–9 and 32:1–4. Stade (1881: 165) argued against this explanation that the message of Mic 4:1–5 contradicts that of Mic 3:12, and since the authenticity of the latter is attested by Jer 26:18, the following vision cannot be Micah's and would not have been used by him.

Option 5. An oracle by Micah, whether circulating as an independent unit or already part of a collection, was (mistakenly, because it came to them anonymously) attributed to Isaiah by the editors of the Isaiah traditions.

Option 6. An oracle by Isaiah found its way into the Micah collection.

Option 7. If neither Isaiah nor Micah composed (options 3, 4, 5, 6) or even borrowed the passage (option 2), it must have come into both books from some other source. Because of its apocalyptic character, many scholars believe it must have been a late composition (postexilic) but anonymous. They suggest that it was independently incorporated into two earlier prophetic collections. This is perhaps the most commonly held opinion at the present time. If this is the correct explanation of the phenomenon, it implies a great deal about the status of the books at that stage and the practices of scribes. The written forms of the prophets' messages, if they were now preserved on scrolls, were nevertheless still open to revision. The books were not fixed. The position at which the piece was inserted in each book—not at the end as an appendix but in the middle of Micah and near the beginning of Isaiah—implies that the overall organization of the books remained open to editorial arrangement long after the days of the prophets themselves.

II. 1. The End of the Days (Mic 4:1–5; Isa 2:2–5)

			syllables
Mic 4:1aAα	*wĕhāyâ*	*bĕ'aḥărît hayyāmîm*	9
Isa 2:2aAα	*wĕhāyâ*	*bĕ'aḥărît hayyāmîm*	9

Mic 4:1aAβ¹	[. . .]	*yihyeh har bêt-yhwh*	6
Isa 2:2aAβ¹	*nākôn*	*yihyeh har bêt-yhwh*	8
Mic 4:1aAβ²	*nākôn*	*běrō'š hehārîm*	7
Isa 2:2aAβ²	[. . .]	*běrō'š hehārîm*	5
Mic 4:1aB	*wěniśśā' hû' miggěbā'ôt*		8
Isa 2:2aB	*wěniśśā'* [. . .] *miggěbā'ôt*		7
Mic 4:1b	*wěnāhărû ʿālāyw ʿammîm*		8
Isa 2:2b	*wěnāhărû 'ēlāyw kol-haggôyim*		10
Mic 4:2aAα	*wěhālěkû gôyim rabbîm*		8
Isa 2:3aAα	*wěhālěkû ʿammîm rabbîm*		8
Mic 4:2aAβ	*wě'āmērû*		4
Isa 2:3aAβ	*wě'āmĕrû*		4
Mic 4:2aAγ	*lěkû | wěnaʿăleh 'el-har-yhwh*		9
Isa 2:3aAγ	*lěkû | wěnaʿăleh 'el-har-yhwh*		9
Mic 4:2aAδ	*wě'el-bêt 'ělōhê yaʿăqōb*		8
Isa 2:3aAδ	[. . .]*'el-bêt 'ělōhê yaʿăqōb*		7
Mic 4:2aBα	*wěyôrēnû midděrākāyw*		8
Isa 2:3aBα	*wěyōrēnû midděrākāyw*		8
Mic 4:2aBβ	*wěnēlěkâ bě'ōrěḥōtāyw*		9
Isa 2:3aBβ	*wěnēlěkâ bě'ōrěḥōtāyw*		9
Mic 4:2bA	*kî miṣṣiyyôn tēṣē' tôrâ*		8
Isa 2:3bA	*kî miṣṣiyyôn tēṣē' tôrâ*		8
Mic 4:2bB	*ûděbar-yhwh mîrûšālēm*		10
Isa 2:3bB	*ûděbar-yhwh mîrûšālēm*		10
Mic 4:3aA	*wěšāpaṭ bên ʿammîm rabbîm*		8
Isa 2:4aA	*wěšāpaṭ bên haggôyim*		7
Mic 4:3aB	*wěhôkîᵃḥ lěgôyim ʿăṣūmîm ʿad-rāḥôq*		12
Isa 2:4aB	*wěhôkîᵃḥ lěʿammîm rabbîm* [. . . . .]*]*		8
Mic 4:3bAα	*wěkittětû ḥarbōtêhem lě'ittîm*		11
Isa 2:4bAα	*wěkittětû ḥarbōtām lě'ittîm*		10
Mic 4:3bAβ	*waḥănîtōtêhem lěmazmērôt*		10
Isa 2:4bAβ	*waḥănîtōtêhem lěmazmērôt*		10
Mic 4:3bBα	*lō'-yiś'û gôy 'el-gôy ḥereb*		8
Isa 2:4bBα	*lō' yiśśā' gôy 'el-gôy ḥereb*		7
Mic 4:3bBβ	*wělō'-yilmědûn ʿôd milḥāmâ*		9
Isa 2:4bBβ	*wělō'-yilmědû[.] ʿôd milḥāmâ* Ɔ		9
Mic 4:4aAα	*wěyāšěbû 'îš taḥat gapnô*		8
Isa 2:	[. . . . .]		

Mic 4:4aAβ	*wĕtaḥat tĕ'ēnātô*	6
Isa 2:	[. . . . .]	
Mic 4:4aB	*wĕ'ên maḥărîd*	4
Isa 2:	[. . . . .]	
Mic 4:4b	*kî-pî yhwh ṣĕbā'ôt dibbēr*	9
Isa 2:	[. . . . .]	
Mic 4:5aA	*kî kol-hā'ammîm yēlĕkû*	8
Isa 2:	[. . . . .]	
Mic 4:5aB	*'îš bĕšēm 'ĕlōhāyw*	6
Isa 2:5a	[. . . . .]	
Mic 4:5bA	**wa'ănaḥnû nēlēk**	6
Isa 2:5bA	<u>*bêt ya'ăqōb lĕkû wĕnēlēkā*</u>	9
Mic 4:5bB	*bĕšēm-yhwh 'ĕlōhênû*	8
Isa 2:5bB	*bĕ'<u>ôr</u> yhwh* [. . . . .]	4
Mic 4:5bC	*lĕ'ôlām wā'ed* ᕍ	5
Isa 2:5bC	[. . . . .]	

II.2. YAHWEH RULES THE REMNANT (4:6–8)

TRANSLATION

MT

6aA	*bayyôm hahû' nĕ'um-yhwh*	In that day—statement of Yahweh—
	'ōsĕpâ haṣṣōlē'â	I shall gather the lame,
6aB	*wĕhanniddāḥâ 'ăqabbēṣâ*	and the outcast I shall assemble,
6b	*wa'ăšer hărē'ōtî*	and those whom I have ill-treated.
7aA	*wĕśamtî 'et-haṣṣōlē'â lišĕ'ērît*	And I shall make the lame into a remnant,
7aB	*wĕhannahălā'â lĕgôy 'āṣûm*	and those who were driven off into a strong nation.
7b	*ûmālak yhwh 'ălêhem bĕhar ṣiyyôn*	And Yahweh will be king over them in Mount Zion
	mē'attâ wĕ'ad-'ôlām	from now and for ever.
8aA	*wĕ'attâ migdal-'ēder*	And thou [m.]—Tower of the Flock,
	'ōpel bat-ṣiyyôn	Ophel of Daughter-Zion.
8aB	*'ādêkā tē'teh*	To thee [m.] (she) will come . . .
8bA	*ûbā'â hammemšālâ hāri'šōnâ*	And the first rulership will come.
8bB	*mamleket lĕbat-yĕrûšālēm*	. . . the kingship to Daughter-Jerusalem.

LXX II.2. Kyrios Rules the Remnant (4:6–8)

6aA	On that day—says Kyrios—I shall gather the broken one [f.],
6aB	and the outcast [f.] I shall receive,
6b	and those whom I have rejected.

7aA   And I shall make the broken one [f.] a remnant,
7aB   and her who was rejected a strong nation.
7b   And Kyrios will be king over them in Mount Zion from now and for ever.
8aA   And thou, squalid tower of the flock, Daughter of Zion.
8aB   On thee will come
8bA   and will enter the first dominion,
8bB   the kingdom from Babylon to the Daughter of Jerusalem.

INTRODUCTION TO MICAH 4:6–8

The Constituents of Micah 4:6–8

Scholars are divided over the identity of this unit. Robinson (1954: 140), drawing attention to the similarity of the language to that in Isa 7:3; 10:20–22; and 28:5, identifies vv 6b–7 as "exilic or postexilic." Verse 6a is "an introduction supplied by the redactor" (1954: 140), while v 8 is an independent fragment that the redactor placed here because of its similarity to vv 6–7. Mays (1976: 100) draws attention to the similarity between vv 6–7 and Zeph 3:19 (between them they contain three of the four occurrences of the word "lame" in the Hebrew Bible—the fourth is in Gen 32:31). Verses 6–7 belong "to the late exilic or postexilic salvation prophecies concerned with the recovery of the scattered exiles" (1976: 100).

Hillers (1984: 56) treats 4:8 as a self-standing unit. Mays isolates v 8 from its context on the basis of the change of address (masculine in v 8, feminine in v 9). Mays draws on the work of Westermann (1964), who suggested that "salvation oracles addressed to a personified place are an adaptation of the tribe saying" (Mays 1976: 102) of the kind found in Genesis 49 and Deuteronomy 33. At the same time Mays recognized that v 8 "came into the developing book as the opening unit of the complex 4.8–5.4" (1976: 100). This is similar to a conclusion reached above in our general introduction to the structure of chapters 4–5. Our explanation of how this came about is quite different, however.

Wolfe (1935) found in vv 6–8 the work of "the eschatologists," whom he dated to 310–300 B.C.E., when "all historical setting is lost sight of" (1935: 106). Renaud (1977: 181–95) and R. L. Smith (1984: 38) treat vv 6–8 as a single unit. Renaud presents extended arguments for the redactional unity of vv 6–8, recognizing v 8 as the work of the final redactor of chapters 4–5 (1977: 149). Renaud emphasizes the affinities of v 8 with vv 6–7, especially in the continuation of its imagery.

Wolff has a more nuanced position. He recognizes vv 1–8 as a unit containing three "speech complexes" (1982: 85) that are unified by the question of the future of Jerusalem. In contrast to Robinson, who identified v 6a as redactional, Wolff finds v 7b redactional. Far from identifying v 8 as an independent fragment with its own form-critical identity (Westermann's position), Wolff (1982: 87) draws attention to the similarities between 4:8 and 5:1–3 and concludes that v 8 is entirely redactional, designed to bring together the Bethlehem promises (*Verheissungen*) of 5:1–5 with the Jerusalem promises of 4:1–7. Its opening words copied those of 5:1 in order to achieve this connection. At the same time he recognizes that 4:9–5:5 already existed as an older traditional unit (*Überlieferungsblock*) (1982: 87). Verse 8 is then a "span" or "clamp" that, because of its redactional function, is closer to vv 6–7 *thematically*, while linked with 4:9–5:5 *structurally*. In his commentary, Wolff treats the three-part unit vv 1–8 as an entity under the title "The New Jerusalem" (1982: 82–99).

Renaud emphasizes the links of v 8 with vv 6–7 a little more than Wolff does because he explains the redactor's intention in composing v 8 as the forging of a "mysterious connection between the government of the new David and the reign of God" (1977: 195). Wolff understands the redactor, by means of the similar address to the two cities at the beginning of 4:8 and 5:1, to have synthesized the Bethlehem tradition with the Zion tradition. These observations are not incompatible. They may be combined. The complete picture is one of David coming to Jerusalem from Bethlehem to rule in Zion as Yahweh's anointed (Psalm 2). That picture was not created by a postexilic redactor as a literary device to integrate fragmentary traditions that had accumulated around the original prophecies of Micah. That picture was available to the preexilic prophets of Israel, many of whom used it as background for their messages. The derivation of such ingredients from older materials is indicated by the archaisms found throughout these chapters of Micah. Verse 8, with its thematic and rhetorical linkages in both directions, is so integral to the whole presentation, that we wonder how the other pieces could have existed without it. In other words, we have in v 8 something belonging to the earliest editorial stages of the composition of the book of Micah rather than to the last redactional stages. In that capacity v 8 is an overlap piece that belongs with and completes the opening section of the restoration of Jerusalem (vv 1–8) and also inaugurates the middle section (4:8–5:8), whose two components begin in the same way with identical invocation (*wĕʾattâ*, "and thou . . . " [4:8; 5:1]) of the two cities whose destinies were joined in the past and will be joined in the future.

The recognition of these three verses as a unit depends on two considerations, one internal the other external. Externally it is marked off by the signs that v 5 ends one unit and v 9 begins the series of "now" units. The oracle formula at the beginning of v 6 certainly introduces new material; at the same time it also links to other pieces of the same kind, especially 5:9. The anaphoric *In that day* implies that the time of this development has been identified in the preceding text. Internally there are two distinct parts. The first deals with *the lame* (vv 6–7) and ends with the phrase *from now and for ever*. While this last expression usually ends a literary unit, it does not always do so (Pss 113:2; 125:2). Moreover *And thou* at the beginning of v 8 is transitional *within a speech*. Characteristically a clause that begins with "and" plus a free form of a personal pronoun makes it clear that the speech has changed its focus, here from third-person description to second-person address. There are many clauses in the Hebrew Bible that begin in this way; not one of them is the first word of a reported speech. The Masoretic tradition characteristically puts a division at such a point, as it does here. That tradition is not alone decisive for isolating literary units, for these divisions sometimes mark new paragraphs within larger literary compositions.

At the same time *And* joins these two parts together. There are other indications of internal coherence in vv 6–8 as such. The scenario has two stages—gathering the remnant of the lame and the outcasts (vv 6–7) and returning to Zion (v 8). The parallelism *Mount Zion // Daughter-Zion* is a firm domino link between v 7 and v 8. The outcome is the reinstatement of Yahweh's kingly rule, another verbal link between v 7b and v 8bB. The program is essentially the same as that in 2:12–13. These two units share the same verbs in the same parallelism ('*sp // qbṣ*); both speak about the *remnant* and about kingly rule. The image of Yahweh as shepherd is explicit in 2:12–13, implicit in 4:6–8, an image agreeable to the role of king in both contexts. Both passages together are reminiscent of Isaiah 40:1–11. On the image of Yahweh as king, see Brettler 1989.

The content of vv 6–7 follows on from vv 1–5; the designation "Mount Zion" is one link. Six of the nine occurrences of "Zion" are in chapter 4. If the term *Tower of the Flock* in v 8 is a further reference to Jerusalem, then v 8 continues the same theme. There is also a break between v 7 and v 8. The phrase "from now and for ever" in 7bB makes it sound as if the story ends there. But the end of the story is not the end of the book. There is a similar programmatic ending in v 5. Here, as often in Hebrew poems, the climactic moment is not saved up until the end; it may be placed at the beginning or in the middle. In a larger sense nothing in the entire book of Micah is more final than 4:1–5, and programmatically the return of Yahweh to Zion with the remnant must come before the world assembly of nations at that center. Quantitatively the unit divides into two equal parts—vv 6–7a (52 syllables), vv 7b–8 (52 syllables). Note also the switch from first-person speech by Yahweh in vv 6–7a to third-person speech about Yahweh in vv 7b–8. The root *mlk* then makes an inclusion for the second half, with the final outcome stated first. The repetition of "lame" is a firm link between v 6 and v 7a, and the imagery of the shepherd and his flock could explain why Jerusalem is called "Tower of the Flock" as the theme develops.

The main difference between the first unit of the Book of Visions (4:1–5) and the ones that follow it is that vv 1–5 are descriptive, while the following materials are oracular. The opening formula of v 6aA shows that. In vv 6–7 Yahweh himself speaks. In v 8 two names are mentioned: Migdal-Eder and Ophel. The words seem to be in apposition, so most likely one place with two names in Jerusalem is directly addressed, or two places that are landmarks of the same city. Along with changes in the pronouns, there are continuities in thematic development that hold the unit together. The idea of "reign" is common to v 7b and v 8, and Yahweh is the only king active. This simple picture agrees with vv 1–5, where there is no hint that Yahweh's sole sovereignty over the nations from his headquarters in Jerusalem will be administered on his behalf by a human appointee—a "messiah." As the discourse unfolds, more characters are introduced, and the action becomes more complex. In the first unit of the vision (vv 1–5), the important building in Jerusalem is "the house of the God of

Jacob" (v 2aAβ), where Torah and word of Yahweh will be issued. In v 6 Yahweh takes on the role of shepherd as well as king (v 7b) and other structures in
Jerusalem are mentioned, along with a prediction that "the first rulership" will
come to Daughter-Zion. The significance of this enigmatic remark remains
unexplained until later on. The development of the theme introduced in v 8 is
delayed. In v 9 there is an abrupt change as new participants, hostile nations
this time, are introduced, causing anguish and disaster. This scene of military
threat and defeat continues through 4:9–14 and comes to a climax with the humiliation of "the judge of Israel" in v 14.

The resumption of the constructive development promised in vv 6–7 is
signaled by the verbal link between 4:8 and 5:1, both of which begin with "And
thou [m.]," addressing a city or town, Migdal Eder in 4:8, Bethlehem in 5:1.
This formal match between 4:8 and 5:1 brings Zion and Bethlehem together,
and the root *mšl* is common to both apostrophes. Now it becomes clearer that
the plan to bring back kingly rule to Jerusalem is also intended to include a
Davidic figure. David himself is not named, but who else could it be? The associations of Bethlehem, especially the use of the old name Ephratha along
with other allusive language, could have no other intention. The knowledge
gained from reading 5:1 can then be fed back into 4:8 to clarify the obscure
expressions used there. What is in mind for the recovery of Jerusalem is collaboration between Yahweh and his human appointee, a constitutional arrangement the same as that set forth in Psalm 2. And, like Psalm 2, the plan provides
for the reestablishment of Yahweh's rule, through his Davidic messiah, over all
the surrounding nations. When first heard or read, the connections of 4:8 with
4:1–7 (as expounded in detail by Renaud [1977] and Wolff [1982]) will be to
the fore. On second reading, now that we know that 5:1 is coming up, the connections of 4:8 with the following text will also be appreciated.

The Poetry of Micah 4:6–8

The division into colons is straightforward in vv 6–7a; v 7b is less clear (two or
three colons?); v 8 is problematic since it can be analyzed in more than one way
and any way it is done yields colons of disproportionate length. The words themselves are not under any suspicion. Verse 6a contains two well-formed bicolons.

6aAβ	*'ōsĕpâ haṣṣōlē'ṣâ*	I shall gather the lame,
6aB	*wĕhanniddāḥâ 'ăqabbēṣâ*	and the outcast I shall assemble

Verse 6aAβ–6aB is a bicolon of classical merit. It has complete synonymous
parallelism with chiasmus. The length, sixteen syllables, is standard. The nouns
have the definite article, but not the object marker.

Verse 7a is a matching bicolon of standard shape (incomplete synonymous
parallelism with a ballast variant). It is long—21 syllables. We have found this
kind of variation in bicolon length throughout the book. In v 7a the nouns
have the definite article and one of them has the object marker. The two pairs

of matching nouns in v 6a and v 7a are related; the first member is the same in each pair. Between these two matching bicolons is a fifth colon (*and those whom I have ill-treated*) that adds on to the preceding bicolon, making it a tricolon, or rather making a five-colon unit.

This five-colon structure in vv 6aAβ–7a is a clue to the structure of v 8, where a similar arrangement of five colons can be recognized, even though the parallelism is less well developed.

8aAα	*wĕ'attâ migdal-'ēder*	And thou [m.]—Tower of the Flock,
8aAβ	*'ōpel bat-ṣiyyôn*	Ophel of Daughter-Zion.
8aB	*'ādêkā tē'teh*	To thee [m.] (she) will come . . .
8bA	*ûbā'â hammemšālâ hāri'šōnâ*	And will come the first rulership (f.)
8bB	*mamleket lĕbat-yĕrûšālēm*	. . . the kingship to Daughter-Jerusalem.

The parallelism of two names for the city (or of the names of two city buildings) shows that v 8aA is a bicolon, even though it has only ten syllables. Verse 8b has the same kind of parallelism as v 7a and is similarly long (nineteen syllables). The conventional pair *Zion // Jerusalem* brings the second colons of these two bicolons (8aAβ and 8bB) into a long-distance match. The fifth, middle colon (v 8aB) completes v 8aA, which is an elaborate vocative. At the same time the verb *she will come* in v 8aB sets things up for chiastic parallelism with the only verb in the final bicolon. Verse 8aB is thus a janus colon.

Verse 7b comes in between these two similarly structured five-colon units. Verse 7b is one long clause (nineteen syllables) that does not fit any standard pattern or meter or parallelism. In theme and sonority it resembles v 5b. The twelve colons that follow the opening formula (v 6aAα) thus constitute a two-layer hierarchy of concentric structures: v 7b is a bicolon in the middle of two five-colon units, and each of those has a single colon inside two bicolons. The result is a triptych in which the central panel (v 7b) contains the climactic and final statement. It is flanked by two complementary pictures of Yahweh's kingly rule, both traditional.

Along with all these highly artistic poetic structures there are no fewer than nine prose particles. These are used almost to capacity. Only one definite object has *'et* (v 7aA). The evidence of Mur 88 throws doubt on this word. It was originally lacking in the manuscript, added later between the lines. Both readings could have existed in different sources. Mur 88 was copied from one, corrected from another. In any case there is no reason for doubting that the definite articles and the relative pronoun in the present text are authentic. Their presence shows that the language of prose can sometimes be used to write excellent poetry.

NOTES AND COMMENTS

Notes on Micah 4:6–8

6. *In that day.* This phrase is repeated in 5:9 in the more complete formula "And it will happen in that day." The verb is lacking in 4:6. The verb *wĕhāyâ* occurs alone in 5:4, 6, 7, suggesting that the two incomplete parts of the usual formula should be linked across the intervening text to provide a connection between 4:6, with its talk about gathering in the flock, a remnant that is a strong nation, and 5:4–8, with its talk about the destiny of the remnant.

statement. The technical term *nĕ'ūm-yhwh* labels speech as formal utterance of the deity (Friedrich Baumgärtel 1961). The other conventional label ("Thus said Yahweh . . . ") is used in the Book of Doom (2:3; 3:5). Of the 376 occurrences of *nĕ'ūm*, 356 are in the Latter Prophets, nearly half of these in Jeremiah. The rest are spread through most of the other prophetic books. Considering its size, Micah's share is not out of line. No inference can be made about the background of the Book of Visions from the two occurrences (4:6; 5:9).

gather. The verb *'ōsĕpâ* could be no more than a variant of the expected *'e'espâ*. Prima-*alef* verbs follow one pattern or the other, but the root of "gather" is generally stable. If the loss of one *alef* was purely scribal, there was no way of vocalizing it in its normal form without the aid of a *qere*, which the scribes either did not think of or did not feel free to supply. If the loss was phonetic, then, following the usual rule, **'e'ĕs-* might have become *'es-*. But instead it has followed the analogy of verbs prima-*alef* that developed like **'a'mar* → *'ā(')mar* → *'ōmar*. It is more likely that this represents a later, sporadic switch rather than a primal systematic development parallel to the main line. The analogies that leveled the paradigms worked both ways (Blau 1979). However it happened, the result is close to *'ōsîpâ*, "I will repeat." Zephaniah 1:2–3 shows that the similarities in the sounds of the root consonants facilitated wordplay among verbs with roots *'sp*, *ysp*, and *swp*, and because all these roots are weak, confusion among the forms could easily occur. The verb *ysp*, "add," is commonly used to declare a resolution to do something more or again, or, more commonly, never to do something again — *lō' 'ōsîp 'ôd*, "I shall never do it again." This construction is followed by an infinitive in the usual idiom. Another finite verb can be used instead of the infinitive (Hos 1:6; Prov 23:35). The cohortative form is rarer, but in its one occurrence (2 Sam 12:8) it is orthographically identical with the form here. It would mean "I will gather . . . again," evoking more explicitly comparison with the first gathering at the Exodus.

The verb *'sp* is equally good as a synonymous parallel for *qbṣ* (Joel 2:16; Ezek 29:5; 39:17). The use of the same language in 2:12 with the same connotations is indisputable. Hence the proposal of some scholars to relocate 2:12–13 closer to 4:6. The verb *qbṣ* is a favorite for describing the rounding up of the scattered and injured flock. It also has associations with a military muster. If this connotation is present here, it suggests the regrouping of a defeated and scattered army. The "remnant" becomes once more a "mighty nation." This usage is exilic, referring to Israel, or postexilic, referring eschatologically to the nations. It is used by Isaiah, Jeremiah, and especially Ezekiel to predict the gathering in of the exiles. The eschatological development is illustrated by Zeph 3:8:

> to gather (*'sp*) nations,
>
> to collect (*qbṣ*) kingdoms

The picture painted by this verse resembles Mic 4:1–5, and Mic 4:7 moves to a similar eschatological conclusion. These associations, other vocabulary, and the use of the "prose particles" in poetry all point to vv 6–7 as an exilic, if not post-exilic, composition; but how ancient were the traditional materials and stock images that these later redactors might have used is less clear. Mendecki (1982, 1983) argued in detail that v 6 derives from Ezek 11:17 while Isa 49:21–23 has been taken up in v 7. The similarities are acknowledged; dependence of one passage on another is harder to prove, the direction of possible dependence even harder.

lame . . . outcast. Four terms are used to describe the objects of this collecting—*the lame*, "the chased away," "the removed," "the ill-treated." The repetition of "lame" gives a series of five references, two pairs of participles with the relative clause in the middle. The latter has no parallel, and modifies the other four. Feminine nouns are used in the same way in Zeph 3:19.

> *wĕhôšaʿtî ʾet-haṣṣōlēʿâ*
>
> *wĕhanniddāḥâ ʾăqabbēṣ*

This is the only other occurrence of *ṣōlēʿâ* in the Hebrew Bible. Zephaniah 3:19 and Mic 4:6 are variants of each other. The parallel *niddāḥâ* is not uncommon and describes the chasing away of men or animals. The third word *nahălāʾâ* is more problematical, since it is attested only here. This is no reason for replacing it by something more familiar, as is usually done. The word is related to the *hālēʾâ*, used in "be *off* with you!" (Gen 19:9; Num 17:2). It is probably an artificial *nipʿal*, imitating *niddāḥâ*, describing those who have been sent off. The feminine gender is used as a neuter, just as *ʾăbēdâ* refers to any kind of "lost" object or animal.

and. The conjunction is epexegetic: "even those whom . . . "

ill-treated. Yahweh speaks candidly about the fact that the disasters that have injured and scattered his flock were brought on by himself. Compare 1 Kgs 17:20. The root *rʿ*, "evil," runs through the book of Micah. The noun "evil, harm" occurs six times in the Book of Doom. They planned, loved (3:2), and did (2:1) "evil," yet they said, "Yahweh is in our midst; *evil* will not come upon us" (3:11). But because they had done their evil deeds (3:4), Yahweh planned evil against them (2:3), it is an evil time (2:3), evil came down from Yahweh (1:12). In contrast to this language, two other words with a homonymous root, "scream" (7:5) and "shepherd" (5:3–5; 7:14) are used. The verb and noun with this root in the next verse (4:9) have an undetermined reference. The past tense of the verb in v 6b shows that the oracle is given at a time when these terrible judgments have already been inflicted. Many modern students of the passage can think only of the Exile as a time when this could be said, so that only after that could the promised reversal be announced. We have recognized this in the INTRODUCTION above, and it is only plausible. We saw throughout the Book of Doom that Micah laments the judgments that have already fallen; the "evil" has already come down from Yahweh. In his grim pictures of suffering, some are innocent victims, some are the wicked who cried out to God in vain (3:4). And even if some of these judgments are only predicted (the one against Jerusalem in 3:12 did not come true until well after Micah's time), that does not mean that Micah could not go along with the warnings and give promises of what Yahweh would do with his people after he had punished them. The presence of such a prospect in the book of Micah does not prove that such promises could have been included only during the Exile (after the scattering had taken place) or even only after the Return (prophecy after the event). Micah was concerned for the victims of the eighth-century wars, of which he was a witness. It is arbitrary, indeed dogmatic, to assert that he had no message of hope for them. If this is the perspective of the present oracle, then the verb in v 6b will have to be translated with an English future perfect—"those whom I shall have ill-treated."

7. *And I shall make.* The verb form (consecutive perfect for future tense) is characteristic of prose. There are three such verbs in this unit, mingled with three prefixed verbs also future in reference. Verse 7 describes the second stage in the rehabilitation of the castaway people. They are not only gathered and assembled, they are made into a strong nation (7aB). "I will put" operates in both colons. To say in parallel with v 7aB that those who had been driven off will be made into a remnant seems out of place. We think of the lame outcasts as the remnant, and it requires some reading between the lines to identify them more exactly. Are they the wicked who, through a change of heart on their part or on Yahweh's part, are now pardoned? Or do they represent the "righteous" remnant who suffer along with the rest, who even suffer on behalf of the nation, in the role of the Servant of Yahweh in Isaiah? The text is too cryptic to yield answers to such questions. There is something ambivalent about the use of the term *remnant* here, and the role of "the remnant of Jacob" is similarly ambivalent in 5:6–7.

The idiom as used in Mic 4:6 is close to that in Gen 46:3: *kî lĕgôy gādôl 'ăśîmekā*. The language of Isa 54:12 shows that *l-* can mean "from" in such a construction. Yahweh will make a mighty nation "from the remnant." Compare Isa 60:22. But resort to such a marginal meaning for *l-* in order to salvage the conventional meaning of "remnant" is desperate. The difficulty with the usual interpretation is that "the lame" is not made a remnant, it is the remnant. A remnant is the very opposite of a mighty people, so how can these two items be in synonymous parallelism? The remnant is the result of decimation and the object of ingathering (2:12); but it cannot be the result of the ingathering unless the meaning of the word is reversed, unless the "mighty people," once a remnant, is still called "the Remnant," a reminder of past weakness in future strength.

Such a turn of events can transform the meaning of a word; it is retained to celebrate the transformation. Verse 7aA can then be understood as concessive: "even though only a remnant, they will be a mighty nation." These contrasting states in the history of the remnant resemble the opposite roles of the remnant among the nations described in 5:6–7, "like dew" and "like a lion." See the NOTE there.

remnant. In 2:12 the *remnant* is Israel. The same identity is doubtless implied here.

7b. This long clause, with its stately rhythm, is a match for the similar clause in v 5b. The ideas are complementary. Each is a statement about Yahweh; each ends with a similar time reference.

But we will walk in the name of Yahweh our God for ever and ever (v 5b).
And Yahweh will be king over them in Mt. Zion from now and for ever (v 7b).

Each of these statements is nineteen syllables long. Each occupies a similar position in the larger structure of the discourse.

Yahweh will be king. The role of Yahweh as universal suzerain was implied in the setup in vv 1–5. The kingship of Yahweh in the Hebrew Bible has been discussed by Herman (1988). Herman finds a royal motif in Mic 1:2–7, thus linking the opening theophany of the Book of Doom with the eschatology of the Book of Visions. See also de Fraine (1954) and Treves (1969).

over them. The preceding nouns in vv 6–7 are all singular; most of them are feminine and generic; *gôy,* "nation," is collective. The plural pronoun could hark back to all these references to Israel. But the following reference to Mount Zion gives this unit a further connection. Verses 6–7 define more fully Yahweh's role in Zion, completing the presentation that began with 4:1–5. See the following NOTE. In that larger context *them* includes all the nations that assemble at Jerusalem. Israel, the *strong nation* of v 7aB takes its place with the "strong nations" of v 3aB. Yahweh will reign *over them* all.

Mount Zion. The prospect of Yahweh's endless rule in Jerusalem returns the mind of the reader to the vision of vv 1–4. The kingly rule of Yahweh in Jerusalem is a common theme of the Psalms (e.g., Ps 99:1–2); it is found in the prophetical writings too (Isa 24:23; 52:7). This is the only place where Micah calls Jerusalem "Mount Zion." Elsewhere it is "Daughter-Zion" (1:13; 4:8, 10, 13) or simply "Zion" (3:10, 12; 4:2, 11). This terminology ties v 7 firmly into 4:1–2. The everlasting reign of Yahweh on Mount Zion augments the picture of his universal dominion in 4:1–5. Every part of v 7b has a thematic link with 4:1–5.

from now. This adverb begins the chain that continues through chapter 5 — "now" (4:9); "for now" (4:10); "and now" (4:11); "and now" (5:1); "for now" (5:3). If it refers to the present moment, the moment when the speech is made, then the installation of Yahweh as king in Zion has already taken place and will remain "from now and unto forever." In other usage, and especially in *wĕ'attâ* constructions, "and now" refers to the impending future (Brongers 1965; Laurentin 1964). Otherwise it is a semantically empty marker of transitions from the *praescriptio* to the body of a letter. In view of this usage, one must ask if the conventional English translation "now" is appropriate; sometimes "then" would be better (BDB, 774).

8. Most of the words in this verse are clear, but their connections with one another and with the surrounding passages are less so. Most of the vocabulary falls into pairs, suggesting the parallelism of poetry; but it does not scan well. No matter how the possible colons are arranged, they are uneven in length. Nevertheless, as shown in the INTRODUCTION, the verse is a five-colon unit with an introverted structure similar to that in vv 6–7a. This bespeaks some measure of integration of the components of the text, but we should not assume that all parallel items are synonymous, either as a guide to the discovery of lexical meanings or as a control on emendations.

There are two coordinated synonymous verbs in vv 8aB and 8bA: "she will come and [she] will enter." These are the only verbs in the unit and they occur right in the center. The first verb *tē'teh* is archaic and poetic. In L the initial *taw* has *dagesh*, not present in most manuscripts. Ginsburg's edition has a *rafe* sign over each of the four consonants. Knauf (1979) accounts for the peculiarity of L as a mark to alert the reader to the uncertainty of the punctuation. The construction raises various problems, but it is no solution to delete one of the verbs as "a variant reading" (Mays 1976: 102). The archaism of *tē'teh* is not an objection to its authenticity; on the contrary, in association with "primal rule" it evokes the memories of the language of old theophanies (Deut 33:2). It is true that the construction does not seem quite right, since the archaic vocabulary item *tē'teh* is followed by a *waw*-consecutive construction that is more at home in standard Hebrew. Hillers (1984: 56) finds the construction acceptable, even a "valued" feature. He translates "come and arrive" and cites a number of similar constructions from Lamentations. Micah has a propensity for such coordinated verb pairs—*ḥûlî wāgōḥî* (4:10); *qûmî wādôšî* (4:13); *teḥĕnāp wĕtahaz* (4:11). This habit makes it possible that *tē'teh ûbā'â* is another such double verb, needing only one grammatical subject consisting of the two feminine nouns in apposition in v 8b. There is only one clause, with a double verb and an elaborate subject.

The immediate availability of two feminine nouns suggests that they could be the respective subjects of the verbs. If they come in the same sequence as the verbs, the arrangement is perhaps too intricate:

tē'teh . . .   *hammemšālâ*
ûbā'â . . .   *mamleket*

It would be easier to accept just one activity of one subject if the coordination of the two verbs were matched by the coordination of the two subjects. Both nouns go with both verbs. The similar grammatical status of the two nouns would be easier to accept if the second noun had the article. Giving heed to the Masoretic punctuation, v 8bA is a good clause: *ûbā'â hammemšālâ hāri'šōnâ*, "and will come the first rule." This leaves *'ādêkā tē'teh* . . . *mamleket* as a parallel discontinuous clause wrapped around v 8bA: "unto thee will come . . . (the) kingship."

It is possible that *mamleket* lacks the article because it is a construct. Possibly the last phrase (*to Daughter-Zion*) is to be detached as the inclusion for the three names at the beginning of the verse. In any case the nonagreement of masculine "thee" with feminine "daughter" shows that the preposition *l-*, "to," cannot be the parallel to *'ad*, "unto." The preposition "to" is genitival, the arrangement is probably "Migdal-Eder . . . belonging to Daughter-Jerusalem" in an envelope around "Ophel of Daughter-Zion." There is then step parallelism.

> Unto you will come . . .
>
>> and will come the previous rulership
>>
>>> . . . kingship.

The relationship between the two nouns in v 8b is then similar to the relationship between the two names in v 8aA.

The other matching items in the verse permit the full structure to be displayed:

8aA	*wĕ'attâ*		
	migdal-'ēder . . . ❶		
	'ōpel		*bat-ṣiyyôn*
8aB	*'ādêkā*	*tē'teh* . . . ❷	
8bA		*ûbā'â*	*hammemšālâ hāri'šōnâ*
8bB		❷ . . . *mamleket*	
			❶ . . . *lĕbat-yĕrûšālēm*

The phrase *'ōpel bat-ṣiyyôn* is matched by, and surrounded by the broken phrase *migdal-'ēder* . . . ❶ ❶ . . . *lĕbat-yĕrûšālēm*. The first specific name (*migdal-'ēder*) goes with the second reference to Jerusalem (the link . . . ❶ ❶ . . .); the second specific name (Ophel) goes with the first reference to Jerusalem (Daughter-Zion). One can then see that this outer envelope construction is matched exactly by a similarly split inner construction in which the first verb goes with the second noun (the link . . . ❷ ❷ . . .), while the second verb goes with the first noun. There is a two-word phrase matched by one word in each of these patterns, with the longer expression coming first, contrary to the pattern of the familiar "ballast variant."

And thou. The new beginning is marked by the "open" Masoretic "division" at this point. The masculine singular pronoun makes a connection with the same onset in 5:1 (after a "closed" division). The use of the term *môšēl*, "ruler," in 5:1aB confirms the connection and permits the two verses to be used to interpret each other. The "first rulership" that will come (back) to Jerusalem (4:8) will be the one that came originally from Bethlehem.

Tower. Presumably all the names are related, and it is simplest to assume that they all refer to Jerusalem. There is no problem with the familiar "Daughter-Zion" // "Daughter-Jerusalem," and their parallelism links v 8a with v 8b; it is part of the introverted structure. In the syntax of v 8aA *Ophel of Daughter-Zion* is in apposition to *Tower of the Flock,* as if both had the same referential meaning. If "Tower of the Flock" is another name for the old city, or for a famous feature of it as built by David, then its significance is now lost. The hendiadys of Gen 11:4 ("city and tower" = tower-city) gives Micah's language an archaic flavor. On the relation of "tower" to "city," see Frick (1977: 47–50; 70 n. 144). The expression could have been coined by Micah to serve his poetic purpose here, providing a link with the pastoral imagery of 2:12–13 and 4:6–7. There it is the divine Shepherd, not David, who rules in Zion. Verse 8 celebrates the arrival of the human shepherd from Bethlehem into the royal city, described as a guarded fold ("tower of the flock"). Compare the fold of the "flock" in 2:12.

This tower is addressed, since "thee" is masculine, not the city Jerusalem (the noun is feminine). There must be something especially appropriate about this word, but its significance eludes us. The Song of Songs (4:4) mentions the "Tower of David." Such a tower, part of the city's defense system, as known from the time of Nehemiah, could have been associated with the people as "David's flock."

Flock. Two persons called *'ēder* are known—a Benjaminite (1 Chr 8:15) and a Levite (1 Chr 23:23; 24:30). A town in southern Judah, called *'ēder* (Josh 15:21), near the frontier with Edom has been variously identified. (Aharoni 1967: 105, 298 wanted to equate it with Arad.) A "Tower of the Flock" was the site of Jacob's encampment in the region of Hebron and Bethlehem after his return from Aram-Naharaim (Gen 35:21). If this tradition was known to Micah, it could have suggested an analogy for Jacob's latter-day return from similar exile. But a structure in or near Jerusalem would suit v 8 better. The following association with Ophel suggests that this tower was a prominent feature of the architecture of that part of the city.

Ophel. The term *'ōpel* denotes the temple mount or acropolis. It is possible, but not certain, that it denoted a similar place in Samaria (2 Kgs 5:24).

come. The root *'ty* or *'th* is archaic, poetic. One would expect the subject to be a person. The idea of an abstraction such as "kingship" coming to Jerusalem is otherwise strange for Hebrew thought (although found in Sumerian). The theme here, as in Second Isaiah, is the return of Yahweh or David (or both) and his people to Zion.

first. The adjective *hāri'šōnâ* modifies *rulership* and perhaps *kingship* as well. Its significance depends on the identity of the ruler. Verse 1 of chapter 5 emphasizes the primal origins of the one who will go out from Bethlehem. "His outgoings are *miqqedem,* from the days of *'ōlām.*" This person is called *môšēl* in 5:1, and 4:8 could describe the establishment in Jerusalem of a "rule" that originated in Bethlehem. All this evidence taken together points to the conjoint rule of Yahweh as King and David as Ruler, the arrangement celebrated in Psalm 2. David's was the first kingly rule in Zion; the terminology used here all converges on him. A minimum of history is used to develop this prophecy. David is not named. His career is not only idealized, it provides the model for the future. Just as it will endure into eternity future so it began in eternity past. The theory of the divine origin of human kingship is best known from Meso-potamia. In the king-lists, "kingship" came down from heaven and was estab-lished in a choice city as a complex of god, temple, human ruler, and *imperium*. From time to time the kingship would move to another city, as political reali-ties changed. After the major break in civilization, the Deluge, kingship came down from heaven a second time. Micah uses a similar pattern of thought. The kingship in Zion has been temporarily interrupted (v 9). But the kingship will be renewed as it was in the beginning.

This reaffirmation of the kingship of Yahweh is paralleled by a renewal of the glory of Jerusalem, which was originally *'îr haṣṣedeq qiryâ ne'ĕmānâ*, "the city of righteousness, the town of faithfulness" in Isaiah's idealization (Isa 1:26). This supposed primal status provides the standard for future restoration "as at the beginning" (*kĕbāri'šōnâ*), a suggestive coincidence in the language of Isaiah and Micah. Just as this hope in Isaiah 1 is climaxed by Isa 2:1–5, so Micah 4–5 is an exposition of the same hope in the same vein.

Comment on Micah 4:6–8

Verses 1–3 are the text of which the following verses (vv 5–8) are an exposition. The exposition proceeds in an introverted sequence; each succeeding exposi-tion develops the picture a little and then provides a hook back into the origi-nal text. Thus v 4a develops the theme of peace from v 3, and v 4b rounds it off with a hook (*kî // kî*) into v 2b. Verse 5 develops the theme of walking from v 2 and rounds it off with the phrase "for ever and ever." Verses 6–7a state the theme of assembly in another way, identifying the New Israel as a *gôy 'āṣûm* (compare v 3). Verse 7b has four hooks into the preceding text: *wmlk* matches *wšpṭ* (v 3); "over them" refers to nations (v 3); *har ṣiyyôn* echoes both words from vv 1–2; and the last phrase in v 7 picks up the last phrase of v 5. Finally v 8 focuses on Jerusalem, the dominant and opening theme.

The mountain of the house of Yahweh		(verse 1)
Gathering of peoples		(verse 2)
	Yahweh is judge	(verse 3a)
Peace		(verse 3b)
Peace		(verse 4)
Gathering of peoples		(verse 5)
and of Israel		(verse 6–7a)
	Yahweh is king	(verse 7b)
Jerusalem	David as ruler	(verse 8)

Yahweh dominates this development. He is the king in Zion in v 7. There are hints that the model for this kingdom of the End-time is the empire of David and Solomon. This notion will come out into the open in chapter 5. In chapter 4, v 4 is based on Solomon's reign; v 8 contains memories of David, who originally brought the rule to Zion. In 5:1 the ruler from Bethlehem is called *môšēl*. His is the "first rulership" that will return to Jerusalem according to v 8. Hence the two words for "rulership" in v 8 are probably not synonymous:

mamleket = the reign of Yahweh
memšālâ = the rule of David

The restoration of the original title "king" to Yahweh was accompanied by its avoidance for his human deputy. This resembles the thinking of the Exile, when the restoration of divine rule in Jerusalem was predicted, and a Davidic messiah was included in the prospectus of some of the prophets.

II.3. THE ANGUISH AND REDEMPTION OF ZION (4:9–10)

TRANSLATION

MT

9a	*'attâ lāmmâ tārî'î rēa'*	Now, why dost thou [f.] scream a scream?
9bAα	*hămelek 'ên-bāk*	Is (thy) king not in thee?
9bAβ	*'im-yô'ăṣēk 'ābād*	Has thy [f.] adviser perished?
9bBα	*kî-heḥĕzîqēk ḥîl*	For agony has gripped thee [f.]
9bBβ	*kayyôlēdâ*	—like a woman in childbirth!
10aAα	*ḥûlî wāgōḥî bat-ṣiyyôn*	Writhe [2d f. sg.] and moan [2d f. sg.], Daughter-Zion,
10aAβ	*kayyôlēdâ*	—like a woman in childbirth!
10bAα	*kî-'attâ tēṣĕ'î miqqiryâ*	For now thou [f.] wilt go out from the city,
10bAβ	*wĕšākant baśśādeh*	and thou [f.] wilt dwell in the country.
10bAγ	*ûbā't 'ad-bābel*	And thou [f.] wilt come as far as Babylon.
10bAδ	*šām tinnāṣēlî*	There thou [f.] wilt be rescued,
10bB	*šām yig'ālēk yhwh*	there Yahweh will redeem thee [f.]
10bC	*mikkap 'ōyĕbāyik*	from the grasp of thine [f.] enemies.

LXX II.3. The Anguish and Redemption of Zion (4:9–10)

9a	And now, why hast thou known bad things?
9bAα	Thou didst not have a king, didst thou?
9bAβ	Or has thy counsel failed
9bBα	because birth pangs have overcome thee—
9bBβ	like a woman in childbirth?
10aAα	Be in pain and be manly, and draw near, Daughter of Zion—
10aAβ	like a woman in childbirth!

10bAα	For now thou wilt go out of the city,
10bAβ	and thou wilt dwell in the plain.
10bAγ	And thou wilt come as far as Babylon.
10bAδ	⟨From⟩ there he will rescue thee,
10bB	⟨and from⟩ there Kyrios thy God will redeem thee
10bC	from the hand of thine enemies.

INTRODUCTION TO MICAH 4:9–10

The Theme of Micah 4:9–10

The arrangement of the lines given above shows that these verses include two units marked by the catchword "now." Each unit captures a distinct moment in the history of Zion. The first (vv 9–10a, 39 syllables) describes the torment of the city when she is bereft of her king. Verse 10b (36 syllables) predicts removal to Babylon and subsequent rescue from there. The contrast between past-tense verbs in the first unit and future verbs in the second establishes the moment of utterance as the time when Jerusalem is in her last convulsions. It is not simply a prediction of the whole sequence of events, whether written before or after the actual happening. It is not systematic enough to have been written with hindsight; it is not as close to the fulfillment as Second Isaiah.

The comparison of Zion's suffering with that of a woman in childbirth is conventional; the causes of it can be inferred only by reading between the lines. In contrast to 3:9–12, where Micah analyzed the situation and blamed the Jerusalem leadership for what would be done to the city ("on account of you" [3:12aA]), at this point Micah connects the agony of the city with the loss of her king and adviser. In 1:16 Micah used a double verb (*qorḥî wāgōzzî*, "Make thyself bald and cut off thy hair") to urge a mother (Jerusalem?) to mourn for her lost children. Here he uses a similar construction (*ḥûlî wāgōḥî bat-ṣiyyôn*, "Writhe and moan, Daughter-Zion") to urge the full experience of misery. There is no formal indication of the prophet's mood as he gives this exhortation, whether in satisfaction, because the judgment on the city is just, or in commiseration, reflecting God's compassion towards all, even towards sinners. The simile "like a woman who is giving birth," even though it is a cliché, secures the notion of extreme but endurable pain and would not normally imply blame. Moaning is part of the task of producing a child, and that part of the image contains hope for the future (John 16:21). Micah's exhortation makes the pain endurable, not by emphasizing the justice of the punishment, but by pointing to the hope of redemption (v 10b).

The Poetry of Micah 4:9–10

This is an excellent specimen of prophetic discourse. It does not fit any of the ready-made *Gattungen* of doctrinaire form criticism. There is plenty of parallelism. The individual colons vary widely in length and do not fit into the patterns of standard bicolons. This is characteristic of prophetic speech that is more emotional and agitated. The colons are shorter than usual; in fact, since parallelism and standard rhythm are not available as aids to poetic analysis, the number of colons to be displayed remains indeterminate. Verse 9bA comes closest to a standard bicolon. The parallelism of *hā-* // *ʾim* is usual; *melek* // *yôʿēṣ* is good; the suffix on the latter does retroactive double duty on the former, implying "(thy) king." This bicolon has only ten syllables. The identification of this bicolon (v 9bA) as a unit assists the recognition that vv 9a and 9bB constitute a discontinuous bicolon (envelope construction) around v 9bA. In terms of parallelism vv 9a and 9bB do not match very well. They would be closer if the fourth colon (v 9bB) were another question, making four in all. Perhaps *kî* should be interpreted as an asseverative particle rather than as a conjunction (see the NOTE).

Verse 10a picks up and expands on the last words of v 9. The verb that begins the colon has the same root as *ḥyl* and the same word ends each colon. In fact vv 9bB and 10aA match, so that v 9bB has a janus relationship with the preceding and following material. The verbal integrity of v 10a with v 9 overrides the break caused by the switch from question to command. The repetition of the root *ḥw/yl* and of the simile *like a woman in childbirth* shows that v 10a echoes v 9bB and is the climactic conclusion of this unit. Verse 10a is one clause (twelve syllables), with no place for a caesura that would yield a balanced bicolon. The Masoretes left v 10a as one prosodic unit; they did not use *zaqef qaton*. The natural breaks give a rhythm of three phrases of 5 + 3 + 4 syllables.

> *ḥûlî wāgōḥî + bat-ṣiyyôn + kayyôlēdâ*

It would have been easy enough to achieve a better balance and more formal parallelism with the same words:

> *ḥûlî . . . bat-ṣiyyôn*
> *wāgōḥî . . . kayyôlēdâ*

Compare v 13aAα and 1:16. The length of this colon (v 10aA) is due to two compositional or stylistic features, both characteristic of Micah. First the use of the double verb; second, the postponement of the vocative *Daughter-Zion*, which delays the identification of the subject of the oracle. Here, then, is another five-colon unit with intricate connections among all five colons, like the two five-colon units we found in vv 6–8. This consistent poetic practice is another reason for not identifying v 8 as merely redactional or to suggest, with Wolfe (1935), that vv 9–14 were added in mid-fourth century B.C.E., with vv 6–8 added after that at the end of the fourth century.

We arrive at the following structure for this unit:

9aA	ʿattâ	(introductory particle)	2 syllables
9aB	lāmmâ tārîʿî rēaʿ		6 syllables
9bAα	hămelek ʾên-bāk		4 syllables
9bAβ	ʾim-yôʿăṣēk ʾābād		6 syllables
9bBα	kî-heḥĕzîqēk		4 syllables
9bBβ	ḥîl kayyôlēdâ		5 syllables
10aAα	ḥûlî wāgōḥî		5 syllables
10aAβ	bat-ṣiyyôn kayyôlēdâ		7 syllables

In v 10bB the parallelism of

10bAδ	šām tinnāṣēlî
10bB	šām yigʾālēk yhwh

is good. The concluding phrase, *from the grasp of thine enemies*, is integral to the syntax of the clause in v 10bB–C. On its own, this phrase is long enough (5 syllables) to make a colon similar in length to the others in this poem. Because of the parallelism of vv 10bAδ // 10bB, v 10bC is an adverbial modifier of both of the preceding verbs. These grammatical relationships show that vv 10bAδ // 10bB // 10bC constitute a tricolon. If v 10bC is made a separate colon, it has no parallel. This consideration has no contribution to make to the assessment of the poetic quality of the poem. On the contrary, it is typical of prophetic poetry. Its function is climactic. It achieves an abrupt ending of the poem.

Verse 10bA describes the three stages of Zion's journey to Babylon. The colons are successively shorter, a pattern that can be avoided only by making the last two colons (vv 10bB–C) into one long colon. We have already given reasons for not doing that. The mean length of the six colons in v 10b is six syllables, a token of animated speech in short clauses and phrases, such as we found in 1:10–16. The clause-initial verbs in vv 10bAβ and 10bAγ identify another bicolon.

10bAβ *wěšākant baśśādeh* (6 syllables)   and thou wilt dwell in the country
10bAγ *ûbāʾt ʿad-bābel* (5 syllables)   and thou wilt come as far as Babylon

This leaves the first and last colons as an envelope around the whole. Whether the five verbs, in the sequence in which they now come in the unit, represent a sequence of events in their temporal order is less clear. The feminine *thou* addressed is the personified Jerusalem, who is told that she will go out *miqqiryâ*, "from (the) city." Since this is poetry (the choice of the noun and the lack of the definite article are tokens of that), that phrase must mean "from the city." Perhaps the prophet is telling Zion to go out from herself; but this seems a little strange. If the preposition *min-* in the first and last colons has the same meaning in each, then there is parallelism (inclusion) between v 10bAα and v 10bC. The *qiryâ* is Babylon. Once more we have delay in the disclosure of the identity of a participant, by postponement of the use of a proper noun. The parallelism of the opening and closing instances of *min-* suggests the pattern:

10bAα′	*kî-ʿattâ*		3 syllables
10bAα″	*tēṣĕʾî*	*miqqiryâ*	6 syllables
10bAβ	*wĕšākant baśśādeh*		6 syllables
10bAγ	*ûbāʾt ʿad-bābel*		5 syllables
10bAδ	*šām tinnāṣēlî*		5 syllables
10bB	*šām yigʾālēk yhwh*		6 syllables
10bC		*mikkap ʾōyĕbāyik*	5 syllables

NOTES AND COMMENTS

Notes on Micah 4:9–10

9. *a scream.* MT *rēaʿ*. The Hebrew Bible has three words with this form. The most common one, "friend," "neighbor," is not suitable here. Nor is the meaning "thought" (Ps 139:2, 17) appropriate. In Job 36:33 *rēʿô* is the subject of the verb *yaggîd*, and seems to refer to the noise that accompanies fighting. In Exod 32:17 the problematic *bĕrēʿōh* could be an archaic spelling of the same word. Gordis (1978: 423) equates the word in Mic 4:9 with these two. Here it is a cognate object of the verb.

The usual context of the verb *hērîaʿ* is a call to arms (compare Hos 5:8). The structure of v 9 (the balance of the first and last colons) shows that here the call is a cry of distress or physical pain.

king. If this king is the judge in v 14, we have an account of the humiliation and removal of a human ruler. It is important to recognize that the pronoun suffix in v 9bAβ does double duty; so *melek* means "(thy) king." There is a difference between asking "Is there no king in you?" (KJV), any king, and "Is your king not in you?" For the former the normal syntax would be **ʾēn-bāk melek*. Of course **hăʾēn-bāk melek* could be a rhetorical question meaning, "Why should you cry out? Isn't your king in you?" It depends on whether the expected answer to the next question is "No!" The mood of the poem suggests a time of great catastrophe, not a situation in which the presence of the king would be reassuring; rather a development in which the loss of the king destroys morale and causes excessive grief. In any case, it is not just the death of a king that is being mourned. He would be succeeded by the next king. This sounds more like the end of a dynasty, or at least a time when no effective ruler is present.

adviser. Assuming that the second and third questions are a bicolon and that the parallelism is synonymous, the *king* and the *adviser* are the same. If so, this is the only place in the Hebrew Bible where these two roles are combined in the same person. If two people are involved, they are the two highest civil leaders of the nation. The participle *yôʿēṣ* can be a title for the king's chief minister. It is a "messianic" title in Isa 9:6. If, as we suggest alternately, the verse consists of two bicolons in succession, the "king" and the "adviser" need not be the same.

For. The particle *kî* commonly means "because," but sometimes it has other functions. The meaning "because" would make sense here if the speaker is answering his own question. "You are to scream *because* agony has gripped you." But *like a woman in childbirth* is only a simile. Verses 9a and 9bB are a split bicolon. She is screaming *like a woman in childbirth*. Agony has gripped her because her king is not in her and her counselor has perished. Perhaps *kî* is resumptive, and *lāmmâ* brackets both colons.

gripped. Strugnell (1970: 204) has recovered *ky h[ḥz]yqkh* in a Qumran fragment, remarking that "one would like to have an explanation of the variant." The long spelling shows that they understood the suffix to be masculine. Collin (1970: 286) wondered if 4QpMic "had all these suffixes in the masculine with full spelling," continuing from the masculine suffix in *ʿādeykā* (v 8).

childbirth. Although it is a cliché, it is nevertheless interesting that this image is preferred, say, to one about a person in death throes. Even when the idea is not developed, the thought is not far away that birth pangs are necessary for new life and therefore not without hope, although fraught with danger. When used again in Mic 5:2 *yôlēdâ* has this primary meaning. Indeed it is appropriate to encourage the woman in labor to increase her painful struggles (v 10a).

10. *the city.* The series of verbs seem to describe the journey of Zion to Babylon. There is a seeming incongruity if the city in v 10bA is Jerusalem itself. How can Daughter-Zion go out from herself? When prophets address Daughter-Zion, they are talking to the people as residents of the city. Another reading of the poetic structure of v 10b is that the first noun could anticipate but not yet disclose the identification of the city as Babylon. It could be that the delay in identification of the city deliberately creates suspense by concealing vital information. The significance of going "from the city" is not clear until Yahweh is revealed as Redeemer, at the end of v 10. Compare the language of Isa 48:20.

country. Another incongruity is settling down (*škn*), not just camping, in the country and then going on to Babylon. The reverse order in time secures the right phrase. They settled in the land of Babylon, not in the city itself but beside the irrigation canals (Psalm 137). "Babel" thus modifies both "city" and "field." So the three events could tell the story backward—you will come as far as Babylon; you will dwell in that district, and (then) you will go out from the city.

rescued. Neither the means of rescue nor the return journey are described. The use of the passive delays the disclosure of the agent until the very last colon, just as Zion was not mentioned until the last colon of the preceding unit. Note also that, while *rescued* and *redeemed* are similar, the logical sequence is the reverse of their occurrence here: the ransom is paid, then the prisoner is retrieved.

redeem. Zion is the subject of the first four verbs in v 10b; Yahweh is the subject only of the last verb. The effect of delaying this identification until the very last clause is climactic.

Comment on Micah 4:9–10

The scene and the mood continually shift in this part of the poem. With the first ʿattâ "now" passage in v 9, the splendor of Zion's recovery and the glory of Yahweh's universal acclamation along with the return to the power of David (v 8) and the peace of Solomon (v 4) give way to disaster and agony. In vv 1–8 Yahweh has moved back into residence along with his reassembled people, and all the nations are streaming in to pay homage and submit to Yahweh's rule. In vv 9–10 the king and his counselor have perished, Zion is in agony, faced with removal to Babylon. In v 11 the nations have gathered against Zion in hostility.

In verse 10 several pairs of words are in the reverse of logical order. "Come" precedes "settle"; the goal of the journey (Babel) is disclosed in the last colon of the first trio; "ransom" should precede "rescue"; the identity of the Redeemer is disclosed only in the last colon of the second trio. This illogicality has evidently motivated the fad for making a break between "dwell" and "come" as in BHS, which displays each contiguous pair of colons as a bicolon, even though it means separating the two colons with šām. NIV even ends the period with "field," deletes "and," and starts a new period with "You will go." NIV ends this period with "rescued" and starts a new period with the second šām. All the colons are wrongly paired! Allen (1976: 332) does the same, as does Mays. BHS even suggests striking out the colons in vv 10bAγ–δ altogether. Is this recommended because the mention of Babel makes these colons—but only these?—an exilic addition? Not only is there no manuscript evidence for such a violent change, but one searches in vain in commentaries for serious arguments to support the result.

The major difference between our analysis and the display in BHS, which is followed by most modern translations, is the break they find after v 10bAβ. At least they are recognizing that settling in the country seems to be the end of the transition. Thus Mays (1976: 106) relaxes the tension in the first colon by making a distinction between Daughter-Zion and the city she lives in. If Jerusalem is the starting point for this move, then the "country" must be the country around Jerusalem. "The forced shift of the population from the city to open country is the prophesied disaster" (Mays 1976: 105). Removal to Babylon is then a completely different matter. In any case, the survivors of a destroyed city take temporary refuge in the countryside and then try to resettle in towns.

This problem is made more acute when, instead of accepting the overall literary structure of the text, an attempt is made to identify the "forms" of speech. Identification of the first two colons as a judgment oracle makes it harder to connect them with the last two colons as a salvation oracle. The juxtaposition does not contrast Zion the place of doom with Babel "the place of salvation" (Mays 1976: 106).

So far the three units we have identified in chapter 4 all involve travel. In vv 1–5 and vv 6–8 nations, the remnant, and kingly rule all journey to Zion. In v 10b Daughter-Zion goes out of an unidentified city, dwells in the field, and comes to Babylon. If all these movements are distinct parts of a more comprehensive series of related events, their coordination into an integrated plot is far from obvious. See the final COMMENT on the Book of Visions.

II.4. ZION DEFEATS THE NATIONS (4:11–13)

TRANSLATION

MT

11a	*wě'attâ ne'espû 'ălayik gôyīm rabbîm*	And now, many nations have mustered against thee [f.].
11bA	*hā'ōměrîm tehěnāp*	They are saying: "Let her be profaned!"
11bB	*wětahaz běṣiyyôn 'ênênû*	and: "Let our eye(s) gaze on Zion!"
12aA	*wěhēmmâ lō' yādě'û maḥšěbôt yhwh*	But they—they don't know Yahweh's schemes,
12aB	*wělō' hēbînû 'ăṣātô*	and they don't understand his plan;
12b	*kî qibběṣām ke'āmîr gōrnâ*	for he has gathered them like sheaves to the threshing floor.
13aAα	*qûmî wādôšî bat-ṣiyyôn*	Arise [2d f. sg.] and thresh [2d f. sg.] (them), Daughter-Zion!
13aAβ	*kî-qarnēk 'āśîm barzel*	For thy [f.] horn I will make iron,
13aAγ	*ûparsōtayik 'āśîm něḥûšâ*	and thy [f.] hooves I will make bronze;
13aB	*wahădiqqôt 'ammîm rabbîm*	and thou [f.] wilt pulverize many peoples,
13bA	*wěhaḥăramtî l-yhwh biṣ'ām*	and thou [f.] wilt dedicate their treasure to Yahweh,
13bB	*wěḥêlām la'ădôn kol-hā'āreṣ*	and their wealth to the Lord of the whole world.

LXX II.4. Zion Defeats the Nations (4:11–13)

11a	And now, many nations have mustered against thee,
11bA	saying: "We shall gloat,"
11bB	and: "Our eyes will look upon Zion."
12aA	But they—they did not know Kyrios' reasoning,
12aB	and they did not understand his counsel;
12b	for he has gathered them like sheaves of the threshing floor.
13aAα	Stand up [sg.] and thresh [sg.] them, Daughter of Zion!
13aAβ	For thy horns I will make iron,
13aAγ	and thy hooves I will make bronze;
13aB	and thou wilt annihilate many peoples,
13bA	and thou wilt dedicate to Kyrios the multitude of them,
13bB	and their strength to the Lord of the whole earth.

INTRODUCTION TO MICAH 4:11–13

The Situation in Micah 4:11–13

The situation described here contrasts with that in vv 1–5. There the nations are coming up to Jerusalem to seek peace; here they are coming up to wage war.

The perfect verb *have mustered* in the main statement (v 11a) suggests that the moment of crisis has been caught, and analyzed (v 12), with v 13 as the recommended response. Zion is to fight back. Extravagant promises of victory are given.

The Poetry of Micah 4:11–13

The unit consists of two parts of six colons each. The colons of the second part are of even length (7, 8, 9 syllables) and the poetic structure is easy to chart. The first part is more uneven. In 2:12aA and in 4:6a, the verbs *'sp* and *qbṣ* were used in parallel to describe the activity of Yahweh in gathering and reassembling his scattered people. In this unit the same verbs are used again, but with several differences. Here the verbs are not in contiguous colons. The root *'sp* is in the first colon (v 11a); the root *qbṣ* is in the last colon of the first half (v 12b). This makes an envelope construction for the first six-colon unit or stanza. In their other occurrences, these parallel verbs have the same grammatical function. Here the first verb is *nipʿal* (passive or middle—if passive, it is the divine passive, in line with v 12b), the second verb is *piʿel*, as in its other occurrences, and has its usual subject—Yahweh. Moreover, the final clause (v 12b) is subordinate. In their other occurrences, these verbs describe the benevolent activity of Yahweh, a kindly shepherd rounding up his flock. Here they describe the gathering of the nations in hostile array against beleaguered Zion. Within this envelope (v 11a and v 12b) marked by the parallel verb roots *'sp* and *qbṣ*, v 11b constitutes one bicolon and v 12a constitutes another. In v 11b the subject of the first verb (Zion) is not disclosed until the next clause. The bicolon in v 12a has synonymous parallelism. The extra pronoun at the beginning of the clause is antithetical—*But they*—and makes the first colon rather long. Otherwise the two colons in v 12a match closely.

The three passages in which this stock pair of synonymous verb roots has been used are clearly related; but this does not mean that they should all occur next to each other. On the contrary, we have already rejected the proposal to relocate 2:12–13 as part of 4:6–7. They are related; but they are placed at different points in the larger structure of the prophecy. In a similar manner the use of the same language (albeit with opposite reference) shows that vv 6–8 and vv 11–13 are related. They are also nearly the same length (104 and 106 syllables, respectively [vv 9–10 and 14 together have the same length, 106 syllables]). These two units with the verbal roots *'sp* and *qbṣ* are thus placed symmetrically around vv 9–10, to which both are related. As in a kaleidoscope, this section (vv 6–13, with the possible addition of v 14) gives several glimpses of Zion in contrasting states—defeated and scattered, gathered and victorious. By arranging and connecting the pieces of 4:6–14 in this way, the prophet or editor has given them their own structure, which coexists with and overlays the other structures that we have pointed out in the Book of Visions. That is, one unit can be part of more than one structure at the same time.

The bicolon in vv 13aAβ–γ (16 syllables) is impeccable. There are three pairs of matching terms, in the same sequence. The same verb is used twice.

13aAβ   *kî- qarnēk ʾāśîm   barzel*
13aAγ   *û- parsōtayik   ʾāśîm   nĕḥûšâ*

Verse 13aAα and v 13aB make a bicolon (envelope construction) around vv 13aAβ–γ, so that the consecutive perfect verb in v 13aB continues the imperatives of v 13aAα.

13aAα   *qûmî wādôśî bat-ṣiyyôn*
          . . .
13aB   *wahădiqqôt ʿammîm rabbîm*

The final bicolon (v 13b) has another shape again. The verb has no match; the other items are in chiasmus.

13bA   *wĕhaḥăramtî   l-yhwh biṣʿām*
13bB   *wĕ-   ḥēlām   laʾădôn kol-hāʾāreṣ*

In another perspective, the similar syntax of vv 13aB and 13bA shows that v 13 can be analyzed as two tricolons. Combining these two perspectives, v 13 proves to be a six-colon unit with numerous cross-linkages among the six colons. For example, the verb *thresh* (v 13aAα) requires an object, which does not turn up until v 13aB (*many peoples*). Once more we have a delayed appearance of a noun. Another notable feature of this unit is the complete absence of prose particles, even though there are many definite objects that could have taken the *nota accusativi*.

The whole unit is addressed to Zion. The two six-colon units are linked thematically and with matching phrases. The first colon (v 11a) has a distant match of *many nations* with *many peoples* (v 13aB). Verse 12b contains a simile (*like sheaves*) that supplies the basis of the figure of threshing and gathering that pervades v 13. So v 12b rounds off the first half and inaugurates the second half. Verses 11–13 can thus be read alternatively as four tricolons of approximately the same length, so two distinct superimposed structures can be discerned.

In view of all these indications that vv 11–13 are a highly integrated poetic composition, we note that the bicolon that is explicitly first-person speech (v 13aA) is flanked by portions that refer to *Yahweh* in the third-person. Such a mix of grammatical persons is scarcely tolerated in English, but is common in Hebrew, and is not in any way a mark of mixed or poor composition here. Compare the NOTE on vv 9–10 above.

Although the long opening colon (v 11a) reads like prose, the poetic character of the composition is indicated, not only by the parallelism and other structural features already described, but also by the total absence of "prose particles," except for the article with the participle (v 11bA), where it serves as a relative pronoun, and in "all *the* earth" (v 13bB), which is a fixed phrase often found in poetry. There are seven definite direct objects, but *ʾet* is never used.

This unit is one of the clearest in this part of the book. It is quite apocalyptic, even to the representation of Zion as a fabulous beast, in total contrast to the lame animals of vv 6 and 7. The fact that Yahweh is called "Lord of the whole world" indicates that the "many nations" are all the nations of the world. The fantasy of Zion conquering all these, and dedicating the spoil to Yahweh takes us back to the holy wars of Israel's earliest political formation, the prelude to the peaceful settlement that provided the inspiration for the picture in vv 1–3.

NOTES AND COMMENTS

Notes on Micah 4:11–13

11. *mustered.* The *nip'al* is ambiguous. If middle, as 1 Sam 17:1, it simply describes the preparation for war. If passive, it leaves the agent unidentified (Andersen 1971), and it is only when Yahweh is disclosed as the subject of the parallel verb at the end of v 12 that the true cause is identified. These two meanings operate simultaneously. All that the nations know is that they have assembled for war; and that is true: they are free to do that. It is also true that in the counsel of God, hidden from them, but known by the prophet (Amos 3:7), he has assembled them with a completely different aim (the divine passive).

saying. The threat, or taunt, offered by the nations is not clear in its intent. First, the delay of the subject noun "Zion" until the second clause seems abnormal. A better arrangement would be:

Let Zion be profaned
and let our eyes gaze (on her)

This presentation has a better rhythmic balance. But the delay of the noun, rather than the use of anaphora, is not unacceptable. It is a device used continually by Micah, and it has a rhetorical effect. The same pattern is used in v 13 where the phrase "many nations" is the delayed object of "thresh."

profaned. The political intentions of the various nations who invaded Israel were partly military or economic and partly religious. In the eyes of Israel an attack on their temple city would be profanity. The nations would not have used that language. The capture of the gods of other nations was standard procedure in ancient warfare, and the recapture of stolen gods was a very important objective in retaliatory measures. Desecrating the shrine of the enemy was one of the chief aims of attacking the capital city. Modern research is more aware of sociopolitical and military-economic factors underlying everything else, but the peoples of antiquity thought that they were carrying on religious warfare too, as they invoked the help of their gods against their enemies and their gods. The Bible describes Yahweh's victory over the gods of Egypt and over the Philistine gods. Even though there could be an element of parody in the biblical accounts, because the gods are reduced to mere images, in the real world the involvement of the gods was an essential element in such struggles. In a war it was not only nation against nation, but pantheon against pantheon.

In its other occurrences *ḥnp* commonly refers to the consequences of various extreme sins that put the land under a curse. Isaiah 24:5 shows that covenant violations bring on this result. It is an extreme form of cultic pollution such as idolatry (Jer 3:9) called fornication *zĕnût* (Jer 3:12). In Ps 106:38 it is child sacrifice that pollutes the land. The blood of a murdered victim for whom no reparation has been made pollutes the land (Num 35:33). This usage suggests two possibilities for interpreting v 11bA. If *teḥĕnāp* is jussive (in parallel with *taḥaz*), it declares the intention of the nations to desecrate Zion. How? By demolishing the Temple? By setting up pagan cults?

Ancient translators evidently found this verb difficult. LXX *epikharoumetha*, "we shall rejoice." This verb usually translates *śmḥ*, as it does in Mic 7:8, which is then Zion's response to this gloating. From this retrojection, Robinson (1954: 142) emended to *niśmaḥ*. Symmachus has *katakrithēsetai*, "she will be condemned," like Targum Jonathan *'ymty tḥwb*, and Syriac *ttḥyb*. Vulgate has *lapidetur*, "let her be stoned." All these interpretations show that there was general agreement about the meaning of *tḥnp*, but this could be the result of a movement of its connotation from a cultic to a legal frame of reference. Modern scholars have been dissatisfied with the reading and have made numerous proposals. Some revocalize—Haupt (1909: 218) to *hopʿal*, *tohŏnap*, "she shall be paganized"; Driver to *nipʿal*, which he translated "may she be ruthlessly treated" on the basis of an Amarna text (1938: 267—Schwantes [1962: 230] points out that this connection had already been made in the Gesenius-Buhl Lexicon). Others suggest a different root—Wellhausen: *tissāḥēp*, "let her be thrown down"; Ehrlich, declaring *teḥĕnāp* to be "misplaced" (*unpassende*) in the mouth of the enemy (1912: 282), proposed *teḥĕrab*; Sellin: *tēḥāśēp*, "let her be stripped."

There is another possibility that arises from a consideration of the poetic structure of v 11b. In standard poetry it is unusual to have the second of two parallel colons disproportionately longer than the first, as here. If we concentrate on the complete "line" (it has fifteen syllables) and do not worry about the position of the caesura, it is less appropriate to talk about a bicolon. We have another example of Micah's propensity to coordinate two verbs in immediate succession. The two verbs in sequence make a double verb, sometimes hendiadys, and they have the same subject. In the present case there are some grammatical difficulties in the way of that kind of analysis. The first verb *teḥĕnāp* (*qal*) is usually stative; hence the usual translation "Let her be profaned!" This translation gives the wrong impression that the verb is passive. The *hipʿil* is the transitivized form. It is used to describe the pollution of the land in Num 35:33 and Jer 3:2. One could revise the vocalization of the verb in v 11bA to make it transitive, with "our eye(s)" as the subject of both verbs. Even that mild emendation might not be necessary. The same *qal* form is transitive in Jer 3:9, as the use of *'ēt* makes clear. Scholars have deleted the *'ēt* or else revised the vocalization of the verb in Jer 3:9 to bring it into line with other cases. The transitive use of *qal* in Jer 3:9 makes it possible that in Mic 4:11b "our eye(s)" is the subject of both verbs. The language implies that the enemy intended to penetrate the holy precincts and pillage the sacred objects there. In the perspective of de-

vout Israelites, even for outsiders to look into the sanctuary would be profana-
tion, as we know from the response to the desecration of the Temple by the
Babylonians (as bewailed in the book of Lamentations [Lam 1:10; cf. Ps 137:7])
and later by Antiochus Epiphanes (ca. 165 B.C.E.), who erected an altar (perhaps also a statue) of Zeus Olympios (= Baal-Shamem) in the sacred area, and
by Pompey (63 B.C.E.), who went right into the Holy of Holies.

gaze. The grammatical problems of the second clause (v 11bB) are also serious. The apparent subject ("our eyes") does not agree with the (singular) verb.
This again is not insuperable. A singular verb may be used in Hebrew with a
plural subject, at least when the verb precedes. But this is more likely to occur
when the subject is plural by coordination of singular nouns, for then the verb
agrees with the first of these nouns; or when the noun is collective, the verb is
singular in form. The remedy for the grammatical discord is simple. The verb
could be emended to plural *tḥzynh*, following LXX, the singular of the present
text being due to the influence of the immediately preceding singular verb. Or
the noun could be made singular, as in some versions and some Hebrew manuscripts. Since the ancient versions have leveled the text both ways, their combined testimony confirms the antiquity, if not the authenticity of the present MT.

The expression itself is neutral. The nature of the object defines the kind of
gratification gained from gazing—beauty with enjoyment, pollution with malice
(Ps 17:4; Cant 7:1; Isa 33:17). The term is used in military annals to describe
gloating over a defeated enemy. In the Mesha Inscription (lines 4, 7) the verb root
r'h, "see," with the preposition *b-*, describes looking in triumph on a defeated
enemy. The same idiom is found in Biblical Hebrew (Ps 118:7; cf. Mic 7:10). Was
Micah's use of the Aramaic loan word *ḥzh* rather than Hebrew *r'h* intended to
give the impression that the speakers were foreigners?

12. *they.* The syntactic function of this pronoun is the same as "we" in v 5b.
It secures contrast between what they plan and what Yahweh plans.

schemes. The term is neutral. In Proverbs 12:5,

The schemes of the righteous are just;
the plans of the wicked are deceitful.

The latter indicates a well-thought-out intention to do evil. Originating in "the
heart," it is the Hebrew equivalent of "motivation," more fully *yēṣer maḥšābôt*
(Gen 6:5; 1 Chr 28:9). Human and divine intentions are opposites (Isa 55:8–9);
human schemes are only evil all the time (Gen 6:5; Ps 56:6) and detested by
Yahweh (Prov 15:26). God's schemes are for man's well-being (Jer 29:11); but
they are too numerous (Ps 40:6), too profound (Ps 92:6) for human compre-
hension. It is not simply that man's plans and God's plans push in opposite
directions. God is able to use the nefarious schemes of men to achieve, not
what they intended at all, but his own aims, and so work everything up into an
ultimately good result (Gen 50:20; Rom 8:28). The prophet's analysis of the
situation in vv 11–12 secures the biblical philosophy of evil. Evil can never be
finally successful. God does not simply counteract it or destroy it; he uses it for

just ends and transforms it into good. From Joseph (Gen 50:20) to Jesus, the victims of wrong become the God-appointed saviors.

Here the intention seems to be to lure the nations into a trap. The theory found elsewhere in the Bible that violent acts such as the invasion of Israel by Moab, Aram, Assyria, or Babylon were used by God to punish his people is muted, if not altogether absent from this unit. The point made in v 12 is similar in a general way to the response given by Isaiah to the Assyrian threat of 701 B.C.E. (Isa 36:37).

sheaves. The Temple site was originally a threshing floor (2 Samuel 24). In vv 2 and 13 the journey of all mankind to Jerusalem is a composite of politics and cult, payment of tribute for annual renewal of vassalage, and a festival of oblations (v 13b). The eschatological idea of the last battle as a harvest as well as an assize (v 2) is also present.

13. *Arise*. The double imperative matches, and contrasts with, the double imperative that begins v 10. Both commands are addressed to Daughter-Zion. The two phases in Zion's experience, anguish in v 10, recovery in v 13, are clearly related. The similarity of v 10aAα and v 13aAα contributes to the coherence between vv 9–10 and vv 11–13 and, indeed, to the thematic unity of vv 8–14 as a whole.

thresh. If war is a harvest (v 12b), threshing is its aftermath (Amos 1:3). The spoil is not the sheaves, but the grain. Atrocities committed on prisoners were worse than the cruelties of combat. Second Samuel 8 is the prototype, all to be reenacted in the End-time.

horn . . . hooves. The work animal is the ox, but this one will be fitted with terribly destructive metal attachments. The hooves were used in threshing; but the horn is more suggestive of an aggressive aurochs (Num 23:22; 24:8) or oryx, a fabulous one. The singular number of *horn* need not be pressed to identify a unicorn. At this point no human leader is mentioned for Zion as world-conqueror. Note the "ruler" and "shepherds" who are active in chapter 5.

dedicate. The verb has the archaic form of second-person feminine singular perfect. The vocabulary of the ancient "holy war" is reactivated in the language used (*ḥrm* [the "ban," i.e., total destruction], "*ʾādôn* [lord] of the whole earth").

treasure. The term *bṣ*ʿ is wealth as plunder (Judg 5:19). It not only designates legitimate spoil but also ill-gotten gain including bribes. The use of the word in this context suggests that the wealth of the nations was acquired by them by violence and fraud. In particular, the wealth of Israel, and especially the cult objects carried off from the Temple in Jerusalem, will now be retrieved. It was a frequent feature of ancient war to return captured gods to their former shrines. Thus Neriglissar (559–56 B.C.E.) brought Ammit back to Sippar from Gutium (CAH^2 III:218).

wealth. In contrast to *bṣ*ʿ, *ḥayil* represents legitimate gain, not plunder, the regular provisioning of the Temple. In the poetic combination of *bṣ*ʿ with *ḥayil* the result is merismatic, covering all the different kinds of wealth available as tribute to Yahweh.

Lord of the whole world. This title is used six times in the Bible—Josh 3:11, 13 in connection with the ark of the covenant; Ps 97:5, the eschatological kingship of Yahweh; Zech 4:14; 6:5, also eschatological. Bordreuil (1971: 25) points out that in two of these occurrences (Zech 6:5; Ps 97:1–5) the title has a cosmic-meteorological background. The language of Ps 97:5 is split between Mic 1:3 and Mic 4:13:

> The hills melted like wax at the presence of Yahweh,
> at the presence of the Lord of the whole world.

The extent of Yahweh's lordship here corresponds to the scope of the ruler's conquests in Mic 5:3 — "to the ends of the earth."

Comment on Micah 4:11–13

The mood of this unit is strangely different from that in the Book of Doom. Here Zion's sufferings are seen as undeserved. The treatment she has received from her enemies demands retribution that Zion herself will inflict upon them. As they did to her, she will do to them. The program in vv 11–13 thus fits into the larger picture of the Book of Visions.

Verses 11–13 have various verbal connections with the surrounding material: (1) *gôyim rabbîm // ʿammîm (rabbîm)* as in vv 1 and 3; (2) *Zion // Daughter-Zion*, as in vv 2, 7, 8, 10; (3) *'sp // qbṣ* as in vv 6 and 7; (4) *plan* (or "counsel"), same root as "counselor" in v 9; (5) compare what the nations *say* in v 2 with what they *say* in v 11; (6) v 13aA is just like v 10aA; in fact the overall syntax is very similar:

	Verse 10	Verse 13
Imperative	*ḥûlî*	*qûmî*
kî + imperfect	second person	first person
imperfect	—	first person
waw + perfect	*wĕšākant*	*wahădiqqôt*
waw + perfect	*ûbāʾt*	*wahahăramtî*

The things that are going on in these two units are so exactly opposite that they must go together. All roles are reversed. The opening colons, identical in form, are completely opposite in meaning. If the sequence reflects the anticipated program, Yahweh first gathers the scattered people back to Zion and then gathers the nations in order to have Zion defeat them.

Verses 11–13 sound like an oracle of salvation given at the moment of peril. The fact that the entire focus is on Zion makes it very unlikely that these messages were composed among the exiled community. The *gālût* as such was not called Zion so exclusively, and the perspective is that of the homeland. All these oracles touch historical reality at very few points. From a literary point of view they are unified around Zion, but there is no systematic chronological development from which we can reconstruct a single scenario. The structural coherence of the two chapters, of chapter 4, or even of vv 9–13 — all of which we have demonstrated—is not matched by dramatic unity. The statement that "many nations have mustered against you" could be taken as a historical fact if it sums up Jerusalem's numerous experiences in the past. The nations are "many" and "powerful." Several great nations—Egypt, Assyria, Babylon, with more to come—had invaded Israel, but only once, under David, had Israel been able to do the like to others. If v 11 is a review of the facts of the past, the opposite future of v 13 had no historical precedent.

In spite of the past tense of the first verb, this could be a practical and concrete message of Micah addressed to one of the sieges of his day only if it is exaggerated out of all reality, and then left with no shade of fulfillment. If we compare these passages with the oracles of Isaiah connected with the Syro-Ephraimite War and with Sennacherib's invasion, those oracles are quite concrete. They name names, and they keep within the bounds of historical possibility. There is some resemblance, all the same. Weiser (1961: 253) says that "the eschatological imagery of the final assault of the nations on Jerusalem and their defeat that is particularly prominent in Isaiah (Isa 17:12ff.; 10:24ff.; 29:1; 31:4f.; Ps 46:5ff.) might not be impossible in the mouth of Micah." This question of authenticity is moot. No matter what the date of their origination, these ideas and pictures are problematic. When Micah predicted the destruction of Samaria (1:6–7) and of Jerusalem (3:12), there was no hint that these judgments would be carried out by a foreign invader. The impression rather is that Yahweh will do it himself, directly, coming down from his place and trampling the "high places" (a word common to 1:2, 5; 3:12). Neither prophecy shows the benefit of hindsight, being composed or touched up to fit the actual capture of Samaria by Assyria (the city was not demolished) or the much later capture of Jerusalem by Babylonia. In this respect the cities had similar fates. With so much attention on the demolition of the Temple, there is less information about the scale of the destruction. The walls were probably broken down. Unlike in Samaria, however, there was no apparent effort to repopulate Jerusalem.

Zion is found in five quite different states in these prophecies. First, and simplest, is the helplessness of Zion and the apparent finality of the city's ruination (3:12). Another development predicts escape from the city and travel to Babylon (4:10). There is no talk of forcible eviction or forced resettlement. Is this what Micah means by the remnant being like dew (5:6)? From there Yahweh will redeem the remnant (4:10), gathering them (2:12–13) and reestablishing his rule over them in Zion (4:7–8). The walls will be rebuilt, the territory extended (7:11). A third and more complex program might be pieced together from several episodes. The nations (none are named) assemble against Zion, planning to profane her (4:11). But Zion will arise, like a mighty animal equipped for threshing, trampling them all (4:13), or like a lion, ripping them all (5:7). A fourth scenario involves only Assyria, whose invasion is repulsed so successfully that the land of Assyria itself is conquered by "seven shepherds, indeed eight princes" (5:4–5). Different again are the expectations that the nations will submit voluntarily out of fear of Yahweh (7:16–17), perhaps as a result of widespread desolation caused by Yahweh and recognized as his just judgment (7:13). They will all come streaming to Zion (7:12), as if on pilgrimage to the one legitimate worship center for the whole world (4:2), also in voluntary submission to Yahweh as adjudicator in international disputes, along with Israel. Thus universal security and well-being will be permanently established.

The one thing that these scenes have in common is their visionary character. With a bit of ingenuity, one might collage them all together. We shall attempt this in our final COMMENT on the Book of Visions. But it would require force as well as ingenuity to attach these scenes to Israel's known history. The successful defiance of foreign invaders (not named) might fit roughly Jerusalem's survival of the Syro-Ephraimitic invasion of 734 B.C.E., or perhaps Sennacherib's invasion of 701 B.C.E. But these local incidents could hardly be blown up into the global scope of Micah's vision. The ensuing counterattack into Assyria itself and even to the ends of the earth (5:3) is pure fancy.

The first and third programs sketched above, if linked, come closer to the historical facts. People were exiled to Babylon, and later many came back. The editor of Micah did not integrate these two vignettes. The historical match for Zion's ruination (3:12) would be the devastation and depopulation of the city by the Babylonians in the sixth century, but Jeremiah 26 makes it clear that that oracle was understood and believed to be genuine precisely because nothing like that had happened. Later editors left all the material untouched, even though the temptation must have been strong to bring it into connection with later developments.

The legends that grew up around the Sennacherib incident (Isaiah 36–37) stimulated extravagant expectations of similar divine help in the future. But no historical event would be described as here in Mic 4:11–13, especially if "many nations" means all the nations of the world, as it seems to do. The sole political expression of Israel is Zion, a city under siege that would turn around and conquer the whole world.

The whole of vv 11–13 is eschatological, in contrast to vv 9–10, which can be connected with history. In this respect vv 11–13 are akin to vv 1–4, and these two pieces can be put together if the subjugation of all nations to Zion is the reason why they all stream up there, bringing their wealth (v 13b). Ezekiel 38–39 can be seen as an elaboration of the theme of vv 11–13.

II.5. ZION(?) UNDER THREAT (4:14)

TRANSLATION

MT

14aA	*ʿattâ titgōdĕdî bat-gĕdûd*	Now thou [f.] shalt gather (thy) troops, O Daughter of Troops.
14aB	*māṣôr śām ʿālênû*	He put a siege against us.
14b	*baššēbeṭ yakkû ʿal-hallĕḥî ʾēt šōpēṭ yiśrāʾēl*	With the rod they struck on the jaw the judge of Israel.

LXX II.5. Zion(?) under Threat (4:14)

14aA Now the daughter will be blocked up with blockage.
14aB   Siege he has laid against us.
14b   With the rod they will strike upon the cheek the tribes of Israel.

INTRODUCTION TO MICAH 4:14

The connections of this verse with its surrounding material and the status of this verse in the whole book of Micah have been matters for extensive scholarly investigation and discussion. Renaud (1977: 198) remarks that there is hardly a text in the Bible that has led to so many divergent solutions. The most commonly advocated explanations are:

1. Verse 14 belongs somehow with the preceding material. The continuing speech takes a new direction with the opening words of 5:1 (*And thou,* ...). The break at this point was correctly perceived by the Masoretes, who placed an "open" division between 4:14 and 5:1. The present commentary prefers this reading, without, however, denying the value of observations that point in other directions.

2. Verse 14 begins a new unit. The English versions begin a new chapter with this verse, reflecting a feeling that it ties in better with what follows than with what precedes. The most influential recent advocate of this position is Willis (1968). In a study that assumed that the book of Micah reported an ongoing altercation between Micah and his adversaries and that sought to identify the various speakers, de Waard (1979: 513) identified 4:14–5:3 as Micah's "riposte" to what his opponents had said in 4:11–13. The very contrast in mood that leads some scholars to find a sharp break between 4:14 and 5:1 can be seen as a link. The disaster in which the *šōpēṭ* ("judge") of Israel is humiliated (4:14b) is met by the development in which the *môšēl* ("ruler") of Israel comes forth from Bethlehem. We acknowledge the soundness of this point, but we see it in a larger perspective. The two larger blocks of material that begin with "and thou" (4:8–14 and 5:1–8) match and balance each other in many ways. While neither of these units is entirely uniform in mood, the destructions and disasters that dominate 4:8–14 give way to the recovery and success that dominate 5:1–8.

3. Wolff is sufficiently impressed by the linkages that v 14 has with both the preceding and following text that he finds a single collection of related speeches in 4:9–5:5 (1982: 104).

4. Hillers (1984: 62) considers 4:14 to be a "fragment," and he leaves it on its own.

5. Beyerlin (1959: 17–21) has the fullest discussion of the problems of v 14 that we have come across. He reports the work of previous scholars who suggested that 4:14 was originally intended to follow 1:16. Vuilleumier

(1990: 57) summarizes the arguments for this position: (*a*) Following 1:16, 4:14 would end the list of menaced towns, with v 14aB reporting the final siege of Jerusalem. (*b*) Verse 14 (Vuilleumier claims) has the same meter as 1:8–16, namely *qinah*. We do not agree with his metrical analysis, but the point is well taken that both passages have the same desperate mood. (*c*) Verse 14 "continues the lamentation of 1:16." Vuilleumier makes the acute observation that the mourning practices mentioned separately in the two verses are found together in Lev 19:27; 21:5; and Deut 14:1. (*d*) Verse 14 contains two more examples of the highly distinctive play on the sounds of words that is such a feature of 1:10–16. Certainly *titgōdĕdî bat-gĕdûd* is the same kind of pun on what is presumably the name of a town. Possibly *baššēbeṭ* . . . *šōpēṭ yiśrā'ēl* is paronomasia rather than just assonance. (*e*) The feminine gender of the verbs in 1:16 and 4:14. (*f*) Similar indirect references to King David are found in 1:15 and 4:14. Some of these points are not very cogent. The most pertinent, in our opinion, are (*c*) and (*d*). They point strongly to common authorship; but they do not warrant relocating v 14 at the end of chapter 1. It is valid to look for a common historical background for both passages, in spite of Hillers's statement that "a search for a precise set of circumstances to match this fragment is not apt to be fruitful" (1984: 63).

This humiliating scene comes as an anticlimax after the triumph of v 13. It returns to the mood of v 9. It is possible that the "judge of Israel" in v 14 is the same as the "king" or the "counselor" of v 9 (who could be just one person). Verses 9 and 14 thus constitute an inclusion for vv 9–14 as a unit (the main body of the "now" passages). Verses 9 and 14 are the only two "now" units in which *'th* stands by itself without any qualifier. The first clause in both cases is very similar, with the verb followed by a cognate form. Verse 14 is thus part of the overall scheme of the Book of Visions, as shown in the INTRODUCTION to the Book of Visions above.

All of the constituents of chapters 4 and 5 present problems of the kind that we have just looked at in the case of v 14. Both the overall structure and the use of the same or similar words point to some kind of organization, whether original or editorial. Our interpretive strategy is then to make the most of the similarities to join everything together, rather than using the discordances and contradictions to take things apart. Thus it is simplest to assume that *bat-gĕdûd* is the last of the series of references to Zion that run through chapter 4 rather than supposing that an otherwise unidentified performer is now brought on stage (Ilan 1975). Given that equation, v 14 continues the description of Zion as belligerent. The siege of v 14aB is like the investment of v 11. The assault on the judge in v 14b could be related to the elimination of the king and counselor described in v 9.

The analysis of v 14 is made difficult by the changes in pronominal reference. The protagonists are an unidentified "Daughter Gedud" ("thou") and an unnamed judge, while the referents of *he* (subject of *put* in v 14aB), of *us* (object of that action), of *they* (subject of *struck* in v 14b) are not identified at all. These verbs could be impersonal, virtually passive. The terminology "Daughter of . . . " suggests that *bat-gĕdûd* is a city under siege, if not actually Zion (the best candidate). She is urged to respond to a threat in which her ruler (called "judge" for some reason) has suffered indignity, if not brutal injury.

With such a small piece there is not much scope for developing poetic structures. Masoretic punctuation presents four colons (mean length of 7.2 syllables). There is no parallelism. There are three clauses. Each clause has a different number and person for the verb—second-person feminine singular in v 14aA, third-person masculine singular in v 14aB, third-person masculine plural in v 14b. Verse 14b is just one long clause. It uses the prose particles (definite article and *nota accusativi*) in the normal way. The three statements have no formal connections among themselves to overcome the switches in pronouns. The verb tenses also change from colon to colon, which makes it hard to decide whether *yakkû* describes what has happened or makes a prediction.

NOTES AND COMMENTS

Notes on Micah 4:14

gather. This statement is a pun on the name of a city along the same lines as those in 1:10–15. The traditional interpretation is steered by the general impression that the verse refers to military conflict, *māṣôr* meaning "siege" and *gĕdûd* a "band" of warriors. But all these words can have other meanings. KB has four meanings for *māṣôr*, and each one is worth trying out. That it might mean "Egypt" is an intriguing possibility. Also interesting is "stress," *I māṣôr* in KB; but all their examples make sense as "siege," and an additional meaning is not required. The root *gdd* means "gather" with certainty only in *qal* (Ps 94:21). Except perhaps in Jer 5:7, the *hitpolel* means to lacerate oneself, a forbidden practice (Lev 19:27; 21:5; Deut 14:1; 1 Kgs 18:28; Jer 16:6; 41:5; 47:5). This is also Mandelkern's classification of Mic 4:14. The corresponding noun *gĕdûdâ* (Jer 48:37) has no attested masculine equivalent, unless *gĕdûd* here. The call to make incisions in herself then resembles verse 10a and would represent mourning for the judge whose sufferings are described in verse 14b. Compare JPS— "Now you gash yourself in grief." This proposal solves another problem. All the associations of *gĕdûd* are with small roving bands of brigands, which is not the way a city under siege would organize her defenders.

against us. Compare "against you" (v 11).

rod. No known historical incident suggests itself. The cultic smiting of the king in the *akītu* festival has been compared with Isa 50:6; but that was part of a ritual procedure. Interpretations of Mic 4:14 as part of such a ceremony (Kapelrud 1961: 399; Otzen 1980: 113) are not successful. There is not enough associated information.

his jaw. The article is the equivalent of the possessive pronoun.

the judge of Israel. Because of the structural signals that link v 14 closely with v 9, as discussed in the INTRODUCTION to this unit, the *judge* is probably the king. Verse 14 shows that he has been abused and humiliated, causing the "Daughter of Troops" to grieve; v 9 indicates that the king has been eliminated, causing the city to writhe in agony. There is no record of a king of Judah suffering such a fate in the time of Micah, so no identification is possible.

II.6. ADVENT OF THE RULER (5:1–3)

TRANSLATION

MT

1aAα	*wĕ'attâ bêt-leḥem 'eprātâ*	And thou [m.], Beth-lehem Ephratha,
1aAβ	*ṣā'îr lihĕyôt bĕ'alpê yĕhûdâ*	small though thou [m.] art among Judah's "thousands,"
1aB	*mimmĕkā lî yēṣē' lihĕyôt môšēl bĕyiśrā'ēl*	from thee [m.] he will go out for me to become ruler of Israel:
1b	*ûmôṣā'ōtāyw miqqedem mîmê 'ôlām*	and his origins are from antiquity, from olden days.
2aA	*lākēn yittĕnēm*	Therefore he will give them,
2aB	*'ad-'ēt yôlēdâ yālādâ*	until the time she who gives birth has given birth.
2b	*wĕyeter 'eḥāyw yĕšûbûn 'al-bĕnê yiśrā'ēl.*	And the survivors of his brothers will return to the sons of Israel.
3aA	*wĕ'āmad wĕrā'â bĕ'ōz yhwh*	And he will stand and he will shepherd them in the strength of Yahweh,
3aB	*bigĕ'ôn šēm yhwh 'ĕlōhāyw*	in the majesty of the name of Yahweh his God.
3bA	*wĕyāšābû*	And they will reside,[1]
3bB	*kî-'attâ yigdal 'ad-'apsê-'āreṣ*	because now he will be great to the ends of the earth.

LXX II.6. Advent of the Ruler (5:1–3)

1aAα	And thou Bethlehem, house of Ephratha,
1aAβ	thou art too small to be in Judah's thousands.
1aB	From thee he will go out for me to be ruler of Israel:
1b	and his goings forth (*exodoi*) are from the beginning, from the days of eternity.
2aA	Therefore he will give them,
2aB	until (the) time (when) she who gives birth has given birth.

---

[1] MT "they will sit" is problematic; emendation to "return" is generally accepted. See the NOTE.

2b   And the survivors of their brothers will return to the sons of Israel.
3aA   And he will stand ⟨and he will see⟩ and he will shepherd his flock
                in the strength of Kyrios,
3aB   and in the glory of the name of Kyrios their God they shall abide.
3b   because now he {they [MSS]} will be magnified to the ends of the earth.

INTRODUCTION TO MICAH 5:1–3

On the basis of Masoretic punctuation, we present this unit as fourteen colons. The commonly expected hallmarks of Hebrew poetry—colons with parallelism and regularity in rhythm—are not much in evidence. So far as the grammar is concerned, there are only eight finite verbs, some of which occur in subordinate clauses. Some clauses are quite long; for example, the first one (v 1a) consists of fourteen words, enough for four colons. *Zaqef qaton* is used twice; with another break after *rěbîaʿ*.

1aAα	*wěʾattâ bêt-leḥem ʾeprātâ*	8 syllables
1aAβ	*ṣāʿîr lihěyôt běʾalpê yěhûdâ*	12 [10 MT] syllables
1aBα	*mimměkā lî yēṣēʾ*	5 [6 MT] syllables
1aBβ	*lihěyôt môšēl běyiśrāʾēl*	9 [8 MT] syllables

The elaborate opening invocation (v 1aA) makes for a majestic beginning. The vocative serves as *casus pendens,* and the suffix in *from thee* is resumptive of the opening *thou;* so there is a match between v 1aAα and v 1aBα. Verse 1aB says that "a ruler in Israel" will come out from Bethlehem (v 1aB). Verses 1aAβ and 1aBβ match at several points and the statements they make are complementary. The infinitive *lihěyôt* is repeated; "Judah" is matched by "Israel," and there is a more complex relationship between "thousands" and "ruler."

Verse 1b provides more information about the origins of this mysterious personage. This bicolon has two time references in parallel. Micah often uses this pattern of a prepositional phrase as the only parallel member.

| *ûmôṣāʾōtāyw   miqqedem* | and his origins are   from antiquity, |
| *mîmê ʿôlām* | from olden days (1b) |

The individual colons in this six-colon unit range in length from five to twelve syllables; the total length (46 syllables) gives a mean length very close to the standard colon length of eight syllables.

Verse 2 contains two clauses, each of which can be construed as a bicolon. The colons are shorter than those in v 1, and there is no parallelism. Verse 3a has two features that are highly characteristic of Micah's poetry and unlike what is usual in standard poetry. There are two verbs in one colon (v 3aA). In v 3aB a prepositional phrase is an echoing match for a similar phrase in v 3aA. There are nineteen syllables in this bicolon.

wĕʿāmad wĕrāʿâ	And he will stand and he will shepherd (them)
bĕʿōz yhwh	in the strength of Yahweh,
bigĕʾôn šēm yhwh ʾĕlōhāyw	in the majesty of the name of Yahweh his God.

Only two of the seven bicolons (vv 1b and 3a) have parallelism, and it is minimal. In each case just one item, a prepositional phrase, has a match, and the matching item is the whole colon, as in v 3aA above.

The Text of Micah 5:1–3

The newly published Qumran manuscript 4QMicah (Fuller 1993; cf. Sinclair 1983) is a tiny fragment, preserving only parts of the beginnings of three lines; enough, however, to permit identification of Mic 5:1–2. Letters are fully preserved only in the middle line, but enough of the third line has been preserved to permit five letters to be restored. One letter of the first line can be restored from the tiny remains of two vertical strokes. The ten letters read or restored provide two words and parts of three others. This is not much. Even so it permits a number of inferences about the state of the text. Measurements of line length rule out support for emendations that recover a subject for the verb ("ruler," "king," "messiah") from the Targum or the New Testament; there is simply not enough room.

The most interesting feature of 4QMicah is the reading *lʾ* before *yṣʾ* where MT has *ly*.

NOTES AND COMMENTS

Notes on Micah 5:1–3

1. The LXX translation of this verse represents MT quite accurately, except for the more ample phrase "house of Ephratha." The quotation of this text in the New Testament (Matt 2:6) lacks the latter phrase. In its place it reads "land of Judah." In this respect the reading in 8HevXIIgr is noteworthy. It has *oiko* [s— —e] *fratha*, like LXX, but lacks "Bethlehem." There does not seem to be a case for recovering "house of Ephratha" from these Greek translations. The name has no other attestation. In the rendition of v 1aAβ, Matthew (or his source) has added a negative, inverting the meaning of the Hebrew original: "you are not the least among the princes of Judah." In addition, Matthew's rendition of *ʾlpy*, as *hēgemones*, "rulers," implies a reading *ʾallūpê*, which is valid in Gen 36:15; Exod 15:15; 1 Chr 1:51; Ps 54:14. Matthew has identified the word as referring to the ruler, not to Bethlehem, as a tribal entity.

Ephratha. The title *Ephratha* belongs to the early traditions. It occurs in Ps 132:6; Ruth 4:11; 1 Chr 2:24, 50 (Bethlehem occurs in v 51); 4:4. In Chronicles the name is an eponym in genealogies. The expression "Bethlehem Ephratha" is attested only in Mic 5:1 (Gorgulho 1963). The verse has an archaic flavor. Either it preserves or reworks an old Davidic tradition (Gese 1964), or it is trying to evoke nostalgia for David's time as the era of Israel's greatness by deliberate archaizing. The parallelism in Ruth 4:11 is important (see Heer [1970], Briend [1983]):

| wa'ăśēh-ḥayil bĕ'eprātâ | and make wealth in Ephratha |
| ûqĕrā'-šēm bĕbêt lāḥem | and call (thy) name in Bethlehem |

The rich suggestiveness of this bicolon has been brought out by Labuschagne (1967). Notable is the reversal in v 1aAα of the double name for David's birthplace. Psalm 132:6 associates Ephratha with David's involvement in the Ark; but that verse is obscure.

The meaning of the name and the origin of its use as a cognomen for Bethlehem are obscure. The uniqueness of the phrase in Mic 5:1 has attracted suspicion, especially because the major early witnesses do not confirm this detail. LXX retroverts to byt lḥm byt 'prth, as if Ephratha were a person's name (as in Chronicles). The quotation in Matt 2:6 has "land of Judah" in the place of Ephratha. The expression "land of Judah" occurs nowhere else in the Bible. The Gospel quotation of Mic 5:1 is clearly secondary and interpretive—hardly a quotation at all. It could have been influenced by the word "Judah" in Mic 5:1b, or by the phrase "house of Judah."

Just as the spacing of 4QMicah does not leave room for a noun subject of yṣ', so it provides room for the double name (Fuller 1993: 195). This rules out Wellhausen's adjustment: he removed "Bethlehem" as a gloss, even though what remains—"house of Ephratha"—is not attested. It rules out, as well, Hiller's deletion, on grammatical grounds, of lhywt (1984: 67).

Absalom's revolt showed that old Judaean patriotism remained strong in Hebron, with resentment, perhaps, that David had removed his capital to Jerusalem. This circumstance shows that David did not make his hometown a base for his military operations or the headquarters of his political power. So what memories is the phrase Beth-lehem Ephratha in v 1aAα meant to evoke? It would be going too far to find in Micah an anti-Jerusalem polemic, as Alt does (1955).

small. Does ṣā'îr refer to Bethlehem or to David? The verb he will go out in v 1aB has no identified subject, unless it is anticipated in the preposed noun phrase "(the) young(est) one" in v 1aAβ. The grammatical connections within v 1 are complicated by the repetition of lih[ĕ]yôt. Was Bethlehem one of the "thousands" of Judah? The term ṣā'îr refers saliently to rank or seniority in a social structure based on kinship. Does this mean that the clan that settled in this village had inferior rank in the kin structure of the tribe of Judah and that this status was conferred on the town they lived in? Bethlehem was the most junior of the "thousands" of Judah. This meaning is certain when ṣā'îr, "junior," occurs in correlation and contrast with bĕkôr, "senior" (Gen 19:31–38; 48:14; Josh 6:26; 1 Kgs 16:34), or when the pair of matching feminine abstract nouns occur together: bĕkîrâ, "seniority," ṣĕ'îrâ, "junior rank" (Gen 43:33). The terms are relative and describe the comparative rank of siblings at any stage in their lives, whether they are old or young. Genesis 25:23 is the only place where the correlative term is *rāb*, where the Babylonian background is palpable (Speiser 1964: 194). In correlation with *běkôr*, *ṣāʿîr* implies ineligibility for privileges of authority or inheritance enjoyed by the elder sibling. Even when not explicitly polarized by co-occurrence with *běkôr*, *ṣāʿîr* is still likely to retain its salient meaning of "young[est]"; or it could be used generically, not comparatively, with connotations of "young," "small," "poor," "weak." Or some other correlative could restrict its meaning to one of these connotations. Gideon (Judg 6:15) associates it with poverty (*dal*). In Job *ṣāʿîr* occurs in contrast to *yšyš*, which refers to age as such, to the elders of the community as the repositories of wisdom (Job 12:12; 15:10). It was thus an extraordinary tribute to Job when the venerable *yěšîšîm* stood up in his presence and listened to him silently (29:8) (in contrast to the proper behavior of Elihu, who listened silently to Job's three friends because they were older [*yěšîšîm*] and he was *ṣāʿîr* [Job 32:6]). There could have been no greater humiliation for Job than to be plummeted from enjoying the deference of his elders to being ridiculed by his juniors (30:1). When *ṣāʿîr* does not co-occur with a correlative term to sharpen or focus its meaning into one of these specific possibilities, we might be left with no way of knowing which of these possibilities the author intended, and a neutral translation like "least" might be appropriate, since it does not say least in what.

Yet even when the meaning intended by the author was not indicated by collocation with a conventional correlative term, such as *běkôr*, in the immediate context, the meaning might still be determined by the associations of his chosen language with tradition. The language used in Mic 5:1 is in line with a theme that turns up throughout the Hebrew Bible, the theme of the unexpected exaltation of an unlikely person to public office, the irregular, indeed illegal (Deut 21:16), supplanting of a senior brother by his junior.

There seem to be three distinct stages in the historical development of the meaning of *ṣāʿîr*. Always in Genesis, and only there, it refers to a younger *brother* (Jacob) or *sister* (Rachel—significantly his wife, in the irony of Gen 29:26); in Gen 43:33 it is Benjamin, in Gen 48:14 Ephraim. Gideon's reference to himself as the *ṣāʿîr* of his family (Judg 6:15) is not quite the same, since he is not contrasting his position with that of an elder brother. Otherwise the word *qāṭôn*, "little," is used to refer to a younger *son* (Gen 9:24; 27:15, 42; 1 Sam 16:11; 17:14) or *daughter* (1 Sam 14:49). In these contexts *gādôl*, "big," means "old[er]." If *yigdal* in v 3bB is the counterpoise, along with the references there to "strength" and "majesty," then the oracle traces the career of the "ruler" from weakness to power.

Later on, in the Former Prophets, this meaning of "youngest son" is transferred to the cadet branch, whether tribe, phratry, clan, or family, descended from a younger or youngest son. Saul protested that his tribe (Benjamin) was the "smallest" (*qṭn*) tribe of Israel, and his phratry (*mišpaḥtî*) the most "junior" (*ṣěʿîrâ*) "of all the phratries of the tribes of Benjamin" (1 Sam 9:21). In Ps 68:28 Benjamin is the *ṣāʿîr*, originally the baby brother, now the junior, but not necessarily the smallest, tribe. In the rest of the Bible these associations of *ṣāʿîr* with social status determined by the rank of one's clan in tribal structure, or one's rank in a family determined by seniority, are replaced by other determinants. In Job it refers to lower status determined by age as such. In Isa 60:22 it means "small" in size and strength, in Ps 119:141 "insignificant" (and despised). With such connotations the word can be pluralized, meaning "little ones" ("lambs of the flock"!) (Jer 14:3; 48:4; 49:20; 50:45).

The usage in Mic 5:1 seems to belong to the second of these stages. As in 1 Sam 9:20, ṣāʿîr is an attribute of a phratry. In the line of Gideon, Saul, and David, the person chosen by God is the most insignificant (junior) member of the least prestigious unit (family, clan, or tribe). As in Judg 6:15, that unit is an ʾelep, "thousand." But Mic 5:1 is different from all other contexts in that only here has the originally kin-oriented unit ʾelep become a town.

thou art. It is not easy to construe ṣāʿîr as the subject of the infinitive *lih[ĕ]yôt,* "to be." Translations paraphrase as a concessive clause ("though you are small . . . " [NIV]) or omit the verb ("least among the clans of Judah" [NJPS]). The repetition of *lih[ĕ]yôt* and the parallelism of *bĕʾalpê yĕhûdâ* and *bĕyiśrāʾēl* invite the interpretation of the two expressions along the same lines, with ṣāʿîr as the subject of *yēṣēʾ.* "The ṣāʿîr will go out from thee for me." The pattern of grammatical connections suggests that *môšēl* is the retroactive double-duty complement of the infinitive:

ṣāʿîr	lihĕyôt	↕môšēl↕	bĕʾalpê yĕhûdâ
	lihĕyôt	môšēl	bĕyiśrāʾēl

The terminology remembers that Israel under David was not a united kingdom, but a dual monarchy (David was king of Israel and Judah) like England and Scotland before 1707.

"thousands." The word ʾelep, which also means "ox," has a long history. As the name of a social unit, its meaning changes with changes in the structure of society. It is most in evidence in the old census lists, especially those in Numbers 1 and 26 (Mendenhall 1958; Gottwald 1979, *seriatim*). As the unit next below the tribe (1 Sam 10:19), it could be equivalent to the *mišpāḥâ,* at least in some contexts and periods. If ʾelep means "clan," it is doubtful that a small town like Bethlehem would be considered the "smallest" of them. On the other hand ʾelep is used in I Sam 17:18 to refer to the military unit from Bethlehem in Saul's army—a "contingent" (Mendenhall 1958; Boling 1975: 17). David was too young (qāṭān) to join it. In 11QPsᵃ 151:1 David is called qṭn // ṣʿyr (Talmon 1989: 244–72). Compare Gen 25:22. There is another possibility. In association with "shepherds" and "leaders," ʾlpy could be a *defective* spelling of ʾallûpê, "tribal chiefs of Judah." See the textual discussion of the version in Matt 2:6 above.

Judah. The word "thousands," in construct relationship with "Judah," is related also to "Israel" through the parallelism of these two names. Micah is talking about all the population units or military cadres of both Judah and Israel.

for me. Who is the speaker that this (benefactive?) pronoun refers to? Fitzmyer (1956) suggested an original *lyṣ* gave rise to *ly yṣ* by dittography, the original *l-* being "emphatic." *4QMicah* provides the unique variant *l'* before *yṣ['* and this makes Fitzmyer's solution less likely. It opens again the question of the textual status of MT *ly*. The latter yields LXX *moi*, confirmed by 8ḤevXIIgr (Tov 1990: 41 l. 33). This evidence is decisive, because the reading is as problematic in Greek as in Hebrew. At this point Matt 2:6 has *gar*, "for." This textual problem has been discussed by Willis (1967–68) and by Loretz (1977). Although line length can render unlikely restorations of *4QMicah* that require the removal or addition of longish words, Fuller has conceded that *ly* might have occurred at the end of the preceding line in *4QMicah*, with a subsequent loss of the similar *l'* (haplography) to yield MT. This is strained. If authentic, however, and if negation does not make sense, *l'* could be interpreted as the optative particle *lû*, spelled *l'*, *lw'*, or *lw* (1 Sam 14:30; Isa 48:18; 63:19).

ruler. In an old tradition only God should be *môšēl* (Judg 8:23). The term "king" could be avoided here because that title is now reserved for Yahweh (4:9). But in Gen 37:8 *mšl* and *mlk*, referring to Joseph, are synonymous. The readings "messiah" (Targum) or *hēgoumenos* (Matt 2:6) do not provide grounds for recovering a more specific title for this "ruler."

origins or "goings forth." The feminine noun means "latrine" in 2 Kgs 10:27, a doubtful reading without which Mic 5:1 is a *hapax legomenon*. The masculine form *môṣā'* has many meanings (Andersen and Freedman 1980: 423–24). It describes the place from which something goes out, e.g., the place of sunrise; and the going out can be on a journey, a military campaign, or being born. The latter connotation would make *môṣā'ôt* like *tôlĕdôt*, referring to David's ancient lineage, preserved in the old genealogies (Ruth 4). The term *môṣā'* can also describe what goes out, such as an oracle "that proceeds from the mouth of God." With this meaning v 1b would refer to the covenant guarantees that David's line would endure forever, interpreted now as ancient predictions of a Davidic messiah for the End-time (Mauchline 1970; Roberts 1973; Becker 1980; Pannell 1988). Isaiah contains such prophecies (9:1–6; cf. Crook 1954), and the expectation was still alive in the Exile (Jeremiah and Ezekiel; Luke 1:32, 69). This expectation grew out of the original covenant that promised David an enduring dynasty (2 Samuel 7). Psalm 89:35 asserts that God will not modify the *môṣā'* of his lips concerning David. In this poem the terms of reference of the original covenant are already heavily eschatologized. Psalm 2 contains another original oracle, promising David dominion "to the ends of the earth" (Ps 2:8), and Psalm 72 represents its fullest statement.

Of the two possibilities, the notion of lineage seems to be the more likely. These old prophecies about David suffered a grievous blow when that dynasty came to an end (Psalm 89, especially vv 39–46; compare Mic 4:9). The problem of Psalm 89 found a solution by projecting these old prophecies into the End-time (Hos 3:5; Isa 55:3). The stance of Proto-Zechariah is more nuanced. That prophecy contains some more delicate footwork as new political realities are accepted while old political aspirations are directed into new channels. It is noteworthy that Micah was not rewritten to bring it into line with such postexilic ideological adjustments.

olden days. In discussing the "primal rule" in 4:8 we considered whether this went back to the origins of David's dynasty or to the beginnings of time. The same possibilities exist here. A lot depends on settling the meaning of *môṣā'ôt.* But in any case the person spoken of here has some connection with the remote past. "One whose origin is from of old, from ancient times" (NJPS). A legitimate *sensus plenior* is that this Ruler will be a superhuman being, associated with God from the beginning of time. Psalm 2:7 speaks of the king as the one whom God "sired" (by adoption). Psalm 110 places the king on God's right hand. At the least the language suggests that the birth of the Messiah has been determined, or predicted in the divine council, in primal days. Micah 4–5 thus has time points in the Beginning and End as well as the Now. Even if *môṣā'ôt* means no more than an oracle expressing the divine determination, it does not require a great shift in conceptuality to move to the Son of Man figure of the later apocalypses—the *Urmensch*—and to the classical Christology of the ecumenical creeds or the heaven-created Adam of the Quran or the Metatron of the Jewish mystics. So Christians did not abuse the text when they found Jesus in it. Or to put it more cautiously in a negative way, this mysterious language relates the *môšēl* whose outgoings have been from the olden days to God (*lî*) in a special way. He will rule "for" Yahweh.

2. *Therefore.* The logical link between vv 1 and 2 is far from apparent. The connection depends on the relationship between the *ruler* and *his brothers.* Pelser (1973). See below.

he will give them. Neither subject nor object can be identified by means of anaphoric reference to nouns in the preceding text. The verb also needs an indirect object, unless the suffixed pronoun *them* is an indirect object, referring in anticipation to "his brothers" or to "the sons of Israel" in v 2b. In that case the verb would need a direct object. The only eligible preceding noun is *ruler.* God will give the ruler to the sons of Israel. In chapter 4 there are many specimens of cataphoric reference, the pronoun preceding the noun. Here the ensuing nouns are Yahweh and "his brothers." The role of the brothers depends on the meanings of the verbs *yĕšûbûn* and *yāšābû.*

If we did not know the history of David's reign, we might put up the following scenario. Because the dynasty has come to an end, the only way for the ancient oracles about David's line to be fulfilled (in answer to the prayers of Psalm 89) is to set up an interregnum. He (Yahweh) will put them (his brothers) . . . over the sons of Israel until the wonder child is born. Then he will go out from Bethlehem (v 1), rule in the name of Yahweh (v 3a), and become great to the ends of the earth (v 3b). That will bring about peace (v 4).

In vv 2–3 there is alternation of singular and plural verbs: "he will give" (v 2aA), "they will return" (v 2b), "he will stand and shepherd" (v 3a), "they will dwell" (v 3b). It sounds like a story of the ruler and his brothers, clearly David and his family (Gottlieb 1967); but what they are doing eludes us.

Is this prophecy in the same tradition as Isa 7:14 that likewise has *lākēn yittēn* and predicts the birth of Immanuel? Taken together, these two passages and similar birth oracles in Isaiah could reflect the hope that there would be an-

other David who would bring back "his brothers," the exiled or alienated north-
erners. Compare the reported efforts of Josiah. "And they will dwell" (v 3bA, as
in 4:4) reflects the ideal of the golden age of Solomon. See the NOTE there. But
this is very tenuous.

until the time. The construct noun governs the clause; compare Josh 8:29; 2
Sam 24:15.

she who gives birth. That is, the mother of the personage of v 1. The most natural
reading would be the human mother, whose identity has no special significance.
But would not the remark be then redundant? If the language is metaphorical,
the same imagery is used in Mic 4:10; the mother is Zion (Lescow 1967).

survivors. The meaning of *yeter* is quite unclear. If it means "the rest of his
countrymen" (NJPS), this implies two groups. What is the first group, so that
the others can be called "the rest"? The noun *yeter* means surplus, what is left
over, like the "remnant" (Exod 10:5; 23:11); but applied to human beings, it
probably means not "excess," but "excellent." Applied to Reuben as "firstborn"
(Gen 49:3), in the present context it could contrast with *ṣāʿîr*, "youngest." The
phrase *yeter ʾeḥāyw* then could mean "his eldest brother"—another unidentified
character! But the plural verb excludes such an interpretation.

his brothers. This could refer to his immediate or wider relatives, an echo of
the prominence of David's family in his government. A wider reference still
would be to all fellow Israelites. Compare 2 Samuel 19 where David calls the
elders of Judah "my brothers."

return. The ending is archaic. There is wordplay between the similar sounds
of the verbs *yĕšûbûn* and *yāšābû.* Doubtless they have the same subject, "his
brothers." It is tempting to bring them closer together. It is easier to read the latter
as **yāšūbû,* for it requires emendation of vowel letters to read the first as **yēšēbûn*
(cf. Ruth 4:2). "Dwell" suits the preposition *ʿal,* which has to be changed to *ʾel*
to suit "return," but can be left as it is especially if *yšb,* in its meaning "sit," here
has the connotation of "reign." The assonance of the two verbs invites recognition of connected activities: they will return and settle down.

3. *stand.* The verb *ʿāmad* can mean "he will continue," or "survive." Is this a
more suitable nuance than "stand" in the present context? Standing can be an
appropriate posture for a king, as in 2 Kgs 23:3, especially in his role as shepherd.
Compare Isa 11:10.

shepherd. This verb has no object here. In v 5a this verb describes military
action against Assyria ("And they will shepherd the land of Assyria with a
sword"). The king as shepherd is a stock image (E. Hoffmann 1987). He is be-
nign (Ps 78:70, 72) as the protector of the flock and belligerent as their protector
against enemies. He rules over Israel (v 2b) or even "to the ends of the earth"
(v 3b). Both connotations are present here, but "strength" and "majesty" are
more suited to the achievement of the soldier than the pastor.

because now. What we said above about *ʿattâ* having a future time reference
applies here—"for then." The combination *kî ʿattâ* is often assertive (Gen 22:12;
26:22; 29:32; 31:42; 43:19; Exod 9:15; Num 22:29, 33), but could be adversative
(after "No!" in 2 Sam 2:16).

he will be great. The root *gdl* has many meanings. Here a lot depends on whether "to the ends of the earth" modifies *yigdal* or whether there is a break between them and the prepositional phrase goes with something else. For instance, it could match *mimměkā* in v 1a, to make an inclusion—"He will go out from you . . . to the ends of the earth." The verbal root *gdl* can describe the ascendancy of one person or group over another (Gen 48:19). Significant in the present context is the description of Solomon as the "greatest" king in the world (1 Kgs 10:23).

the ends of the earth. David's empire (Ps 72:8—referring in this instance to Solomon's).

Comment on Micah 5:1–3

What the unit lacks in form it makes up for in atmosphere. It is not in the least prosaic. It is mysterious and majestic. It contains allusions to persons and events whose identity remains in shadow—the one who will go out from Bethlehem *to become ruler of Israel*; the one who is giving birth; the survivors of his brothers. The text is rich with sonorous phrases—"the days of old"; "the thousands of Judah"; "the ends of the earth"; and, most impressive of all, "the majesty of the name of Yahweh his God." Some of these expressions and other vocabulary are archaic—the name "Ephratha," the title *môšēl* (1aB), the image of the shepherd (3aA).

This unit presents numerous difficulties for the interpreter. The reference to Bethlehem suggests that the piece contains traditions about David's career, but, apart from the town of his birth, none of the well-known facts of his life can be identified as being alluded to with any certainty.

The verb "shepherd" to describe his rule is suitable. The statement about his greatness "to the ends of the earth" could refer to David's empire. The reference to "his brothers" could connect with the fact that many members of his large family were involved in his activities; but the statement made about them in verse 2b is quite unclear. The "one giving birth" (verse 2a) is not identifiable, unless the use of the same word in 4:9 and 10 points to Zion.

A formal connection exists between 4:8 and 5:1; both begin "And thou . . . " Note also the structural similarity in the sequences *'attā . . . 'ādeykā* and *'attā . . . mimměkā*. These two addresses could bring together the two cities of David—Zion and Bethlehem. The connection could be even closer if, as NJPS suggests, Migdal Eder is not a structure in Jerusalem, but the place near Bethlehem mentioned in Genesis 35, which could have been part of some David tradition now lost.

For interpreting the whole unit, much depends on establishing the connotation of some familiar words. Does *ṣā'îr* refer to the insignificance of Bethlehem or to the fact that David was youngest in the family (*qāṭôn* in 1 Samuel 16; cf. Ps 151)? Does *yēṣē'* (verse 2bA) refer to birth or to a military expedition? And what is the meaning of the cognate *môṣā'ôt* in the next colon? What is the meaning of "he will give them" in v 2a? Who is the speaker, referred to by *lî,* "to (or for) me," in v 1aB? Yahweh? And, in general, are the verb forms future or past tense? The answers to all these questions are interdependent, but where to begin?

The unit seems to trace the career of the "ruler" from obscurity (*ṣāʿîr* in v 1) to greatness (*yigdal* in v 3), but the steps in this career are not clear. Once again we have the problem of more referential pronouns than we can find nouns for. "Thou" is Bethlehem. "Me" is (presumably) Yahweh. "He" (subject of the singular verbs) is the "ruler," perhaps the *ṣāʿîr*. The phrase "his brothers" is the subject of the plural verbs and could be the referent of "them" (v 2aA). But other available plurals are "sons of Israel," "thousands of Judah," and "ends of the earth."

All the verbs could be future tense. Both singular and plural are used.

Verse	Verb	Tense	Meaning
1aB	*yēṣēʾ*	imperfect	he will go out
2aA	*yittĕnēm*	imperfect	he will give them
2aB	*yālādâ*	future perfect	she will have given birth
2b	*yĕšûbûn*	imperfect	they will return
3aA	*wĕ ʿāmad*	consecutive perfect	and he will stand
3aA	*wĕrāʿâ*	consecutive perfect	and he will shepherd
3bA	*wĕyāšābû*	consecutive perfect	and they will reside
3bB	*yigdal*	imperfect	he will be great

The formal character of the composition has defied the skill of the form critic. As a prophecy it does not threaten judgment or promise deliverance. The best clues are afforded by the surrounding text, but these can be used only if we can be assured that this unit is part of a larger whole. Yahweh dominates chapter 4, and no human agent is conspicuous. There are obscure references to the "king" (v 9) or the "judge" (v 14), apparently the ruler in Jerusalem. The one has been smitten (v 14) and the other has perished (v 9). Verse 8 predicted the reestablishment of "the primal rule" and the same root is found in the title of the one whose career is sketched here. This suggests that 5:1–4 describes the rise of a new David who will accomplish for Zion the great things promised in chapter 4.

In his classic study of the Israelite monarchies, Alt (*KS* 2:130; 1968: 330) emphasized the uniqueness of Micah's interest in Bethlehem as the place where the future kingship will be renewed, recapitulating its origins. By connecting Mic 5:1 with 3:9–12, Alt inferred that the original oracle excluded Jerusalem from the future destiny of the kingdom (see also *KS* 2:267 n. 2). In view of the fact that the other eighth-century prophets were interested in David, and named him, Micah's reticence in this particular is strange. Moreover, Alt's scenario, while making sense only if Mic 5:1–3 contains authentic Micah material, jars with the preeminence of Zion in the Book of Visions, and with the use of "Israel" (twice!) as the name of the future community. Even so, it is misleading to label Mic 4:1–5 as "messianic," since only Yahweh is recognized as the ruler of the future Zion in that oracle. In other words, there are tensions even within the Book of Visions, as well as between chapters 4–5 and the rest of the book.

II.7. DEFEAT OF ASSYRIA (5:4–5)

TRANSLATION

MT

4a	wĕhāyâ zeh šālôm	And he will be "The One of Peace."
4bAα	'aššûr kî-yābô' bĕ'arṣēnû	Assyria—when he invades our land
4bAβ	wĕkî yidrōk bĕ'armĕnōtênû	and when he tramples on our citadels;
4bBα	wahăqēmōnû 'ālāyw šib'â rō'îm	then we will raise up against him seven shepherds,
4bBβ	ûšĕmōnâ nĕsîkê 'ādām	even eight commanders of men.
5aA	wĕrā'û 'et-'ereṣ 'aššûr baḥereb	And they will shepherd the land of Assyria with the sword,
5aB	wĕ'et-'ereṣ nimrōd bipĕtāḥêhā	and the land of Nimrod in her entrances.
5bAα	wĕhiṣṣîl mē'aššûr	And he will save (us) from Assyria—
5bAβ	kî-yābô' bĕ'arṣēnû	when he invades our land,
5bB	wĕkî yidrōk bigĕbûlēnû	and when he tramples on our border.

LXX II.7. Defeat of Assyria (5:4–5)

4a	And this will be peace [or, she will have peace].
4bAα	Assyria—when he comes upon your land,
4bAβ	and when he comes up upon your country;
4bBα	and there shall be raised up against him seven shepherds,
4bBβ	even eight "stings" (*degmata*) of men.
5aA	And they will shepherd the Assyrian with the sword,
5aB	and the land of Nebrod in her ditch.
5bA	And he will save from the Assyrian—when he comes upon your land,
5bB	and when he comes up upon your borders.

INTRODUCTION TO MICAH 5:4–5

The Connections of Micah 5:4–5

A major problem in these verses is the function of v 4a (Luker 1987: 296). The construction wĕhāyâ, "and it [or he] will be," at the beginning of v 4a does not seem to have the same eschatological reference (or at least the formulaic function) as it has in its other occurrences in the Book of Visions. Here the verb seems to be equative, with zeh, "this," as the subject; a literal translation would be "and this will be peace." That sounds like the satisfactory conclusion of a development. So perhaps v 4a celebrates the peaceful reign of the ruler from Bethlehem "to the ends of the earth" (v 3bB), the outcome of the events sketched in vv 1–3. It could equally well anticipate the events that are traced in vv 4b–5; peace will be achieved when the Assyrian invasion has been repulsed. A third possibility is that v 4a is linked in both directions. It joins vv 1–3 to vv 4b–5 and shows that they are all part of a single story. Verses 1–5 are one *parashiyya* in the Masoretic Text.

The interpretation of v 4a depends largely on what *zeh*, *this*, refers to and on whether it refers back to something in vv 1–3 or anticipates the outcome of the events reported, predicted, in vv 4–5. Compare the similar problem of the direction of reference for "this" in 1:8 and "these" in 2:6bA. But the phrase "this peace" is very obscure. In the NOTES we shall look into the possibility that *zeh* is the archaic determinant or nominalizer—*the One of Peace*—a title. The modern tendency is to make a climax of vv 1–3, with v 4 as a new beginning. For the interpretation of this section see Cathcart (1978), Coppens (1971), Lipiński (1966), and van der Woude (1981). Perhaps it is correct to see v 4a as inaugurating a new literary unit; otherwise v 4bA begins rather abruptly. The true peace is when there is no disturbance at all (4:4a). So 5:4a could thus be a hinge between 5:1–3 and 5:4b–5 and a nexus between other passages found throughout the Book of Visions in which Israel's circumstance alternates between belligerent behavior and pacific rest.

Besides the problems in v 4a, vv 4b–5 present a number of logical differences from vv 1–3. (1) In v 3 Yahweh saves the country unaided; in vv 4b–5 victory is won by the sword. (2) In v 3b the future ruler's dominion extends to the ends of the earth; in v 6 "they" will rule the land of Assyria. (3) What is the connection between the individual ruler of vv 1–3 and the seven/eight shepherds of v 4b? (4) Before the monarchy it was Yahweh's prerogative to "raise up" a judge (cf. 4:14); in v 4b the people do it (Coppens 1971).

The Poetry of Micah 5:4–5

Apart from the problem of v 4a the rest of the unit is clearly written. It has one coherent theme. It tells a simple story of the invasion of Israel by Assyria and of a successful counterattack. The unit is composed in ten colons. Four bicolons can be identified by their simple parallelism. Two of these bicolons—the first (v 4bA) and the fourth (v 5b)—are virtually identical.

4bAα	*'aššûr kî-yābô' bĕ'arṣēnû*	Assyria—when he invades our land
4bAβ	*wĕkî yidrōk bĕ'armĕnōtênû*	and when he tramples on our citadels;
	. . .	
5bAβ	*kî-yābô' bĕ'arṣēnû*	when he invades our land,
5bB	*wĕkî yidrōk bigĕbûlēnû*	and when he tramples on our border.

These bicolons make an inclusion around the body of the unit. The first bicolon (v 4bA) is made a little long (nineteen syllables) by the suspension of *Assyria* at the beginning. The other difference between these two similar bicolons is the variation between "citadels" (v 4bAβ) and "border" (v 5bB). This variation makes a more long-range parallelism between the opening and closing bicolons.

The first and fourth bicolons describe the circumstances in which the events reported in the other two bicolons take place. Verse 4bB predicts that "we will raise up shepherds"; v 5a predicts that they will shepherd Assyria "with the sword." The term *her entrances* in v 5aB matches "our border" and "our citadels." The two outside bicolons have a verb in each colon; the two inside bicolons have just one verb each (incomplete parallelism of a familiar kind).

4bBα	*wahăqēmōnû*	*ʿālāyw*	*šibʿâ rōʿîm*
4bBβ			*ûšĕmōnâ nĕsîkê ʾādām*
5aA	*wĕrāʿû*	*ʾet-ʾereṣ ʾaššûr*	*baḥereb*
5aB	*wĕ-*	*ʾet-ʾereṣ nimrōd*	*bipĕtāḥêhā*

This leaves two unmatched colons, v 4a and v 5bA. Perhaps v 4a is not an integral part of this unit. Because of the repetition of the word "Assyria," perhaps v 5bAα (*wĕhiṣṣîl mēʾaššûr*) should be construed as part of the final bicolon. The singular verb ("and he will save") in v 5bA clashes with the preceding plurals and is commonly emended to plural (Hillers 1984: 69). But it is precisely this detail that shows that these two leftover pieces

4a	*wĕhāyâ zeh šālôm*
	. . .
5bA	*wĕhiṣṣîl mēʾaššûr*

could constitute a discontinuous bicolon, so that *the One of Peace* can be identified as the deliverer. Since each of these colons comes just before the repeated bicolon, we can analyze the entire poem as a chiastic structure of tricolon, bicolon, bicolon, tricolon, or alternatively as two pentacolons—one more illustration of Micah's liking for the pentacolon.

The colons are a little longer than standard (mean 8.5 syllables per colon). This is neither the epic nor the lyrical tradition. Each pair of colons has the same word order; there is no chiasmus within any bicolon. The repetition of *wĕkî* in vv 4aB and 5bB is redundant, but doing it twice gives the inclusion between those two bicolons a stately effect. The use of *nota accusativi* twice in v 5a shows that the language inclines towards that of prose. The use of poetic staircase parallelism seven // eight is archaizing (Bazak 1988). So is the choice of vocabulary. The verb "raise up" is a technicality for assistance through the provision of a charismatic national deliverer; but here a team, not an individual, and it is *we* who raise them up, not Yahweh, as in the old days. The terms "shepherd" and *nāsîk* (Ps 83:12) are also archaic.

Most of the parallelism in this unit is synonymous, so the "shepherds" and the "leaders of men" (v 4bB) are presumably the same, not different groups. While "border" or "territory" is a good parallel for "land," "citadels" combines with "borders" to make "border fortresses." "The land of Nimrod" is equivalent to "the land of Assyria."

The unit has verbal connections with the surrounding material. The dominant first-person plural pronouns link it to 4:14. The Assyrian threat lines up with 4:11 and 4:14 as a continuation of the catalogue of Jerusalem's sieges by "many nations." The term "shepherd" is found in 5:3. The successful conquest of Assyria explains how Israel's ruler becomes great to the ends of the earth (5:3), and it fits into 4:13 and 5:7. The association of Egypt with Assyria in Mic 7:12 and its designation there as *māṣôr* suggest a similar parallel between *māṣôr* in 4:14 and Assyria in 5:4–5 (but the meaning of *māṣôr* in 4:14 is unclear). The root *nṣl* occurs also in both 4:10 and 5:7.

NOTES AND COMMENTS

Notes on Micah 5:4–5

4. *And he will be.* This is the first of four occurrences of *wĕhāyâ* in chapter 5. This repeated expression unifies vv 4–14. At the same time v 4a goes back to 4:6, where *wĕhāyâ* was lacking. The full expression *wĕhāyâ bayyôm hahû'* is used in 5:9a. So between them 5:4a and 5:9a connect the whole of 5:4–14 to 4:6.

The question whether v 4a goes with the preceding or following material has been discussed above and in the INTRODUCTION to the Book of Visions. REB reads it as the climax to v 3 rather than a preliminary to v 4b—"Then there will be peace." Compare Hillers (1984: 64). NJB starts a new paragraph; NJPS continues without a break. So opinions about where v 4a goes are divided. The expression *wĕhāyâ* usually begins a new unit of discourse. Elsewhere in the Book of Visions this verb goes with "in that day," as commonly occurs in the Hebrew Bible. Because of this, we have speculated whether v 4a might have a long-range connection with *bayyôm hahû'* in 4:6aA, which lacks *wĕhāyâ*. It begins a series of small units, each beginning with *wĕhāyâ* that continues through vv 6 and 7, culminating in the more complete expression in v 9. The units introduced by the longer formula are more final, more eschatological—the gathering of the remnant and the cleansing of the land—while the ones with only *wĕhāyâ* are more immediate. Most of this material is concerned with war not peace, until we come to the final paragraph. Chapters 4–5, as a large entity, are embraced by units that describe peace through disarmament (4:1–5 and 5:9–14). Verse 4a could then be an axis for this arrangement, not so directly related to its immediate context in either direction.

The One. Literally "this." LXX evidently took the demonstrative as neutral, translating *hautē* (f.). From time to time scholars have toyed with the idea that in this case *zeh* is not the demonstrative "this," but the determiner "the one of," found in Arabic and in various Northwest Semitic dialects. Allegro revived the suggestion, and brought wide-ranging arguments to support the translation "Possessor of (Lord of) Peace" (1955: 311). The recovery of the Ugaritic language from the Ras Shamra tablets provided convincing arguments that the phrase *zeh sînai* in Judg 5:5 and Ps 68:9 is a divine epithet—"the One of Sinai" (Moran

1961: 61). Beyerlin (1959: 35) applied this evidence to Micah 5:4a and translated *Und er wird sein Herr des Friedens* (1959: 79). Dahood (1965b: 152; 1968: 139) has good bibliography on this question. Willis has discussed the problem on more than one occasion (1968: 543; 1969: 201 n. 53). Cathcart (1968: 512) supplies a number of parallels from the protocols of the ancient Near East and arrives at "the One of Peace." This is the best solution. It is going too far to find in the expression ideas of possession or lordship. The latter seems to have arisen through comparison with the title "Prince of Peace" in Isa 9:5. Hillers (1984: 65) recognizes "the One of Peace" as "a royal quasi-divine title." We think rather that it is a play on the name "Solomon."

It might seem incongruous to have the chief participant in the events of vv 4–5 introduced as "the One of Peace" when the following scenes are those of war. The strain is relieved once it is appreciated that the poet is not a chronicler. The outcome is stated first, then the events that lead up to it. Here, as elsewhere in Scripture, "peace" means, not the avoidance of war, but the harmony and well-being that come through victory, which is exactly what is described in the following material. What we have here in miniature is a scenario similar to the total scheme of the Book of Visions, with the grandest and most final vision of all coming first (4:1–5).

Peace. Whether human (the "ruler" from Bethlehem) or divine, such a title might seem inappropriate for a leader or deliverer who displays the military virtues of v 3a and who achieves the spectacular feat of conquering Assyria itself. We have noticed that this entire section (vv 1–5) is redolent of the age of "judges," which is precisely when Yahweh was given the accolade *yhwh šālôm* (Judg 6:24). This is the name of an altar, strictly the name of the God of the cult of that altar. Boling (1975: 134) interprets the name as "He who creates peace"—through violent destruction of the Baal cult and armed struggle against foreign invaders, the Gideon story. Psalm 83:12 shows that *nāsîk* is another rare word associated with that episode. In any case "Peace" as a name or attribute of Yahweh in the Gideon Story and possibly here in Micah 5 suggests that this story is being told like that story.

That Solomon is in mind as "the One of Peace" fits in with the similar use of the Age of Solomon to supply the idyllic picture in 4:4. Although we have tended to see in David the prototype for the "messianic" figure ("ruler," "shepherd," "judge") who will be Yahweh's human agent in all these wonderful achievements, the term "messiah" is not used and David is not named. We overlook the obvious fact that all the descendants of David who are of interest in biblical history and prophecy are descendants of Solomon, who in fame and importance for the history and religion of Israel is second only to David himself. So this new king will combine the qualities and achievements of David and Solomon.

Assyria. In Hebrew the names of countries are usually feminine. The referent is not clear. It does not refer to the nation, "Land of Assyria" (v 5a) in full, for the verbs are masculine. The feminine singular pronoun suffix in v 5aB does refer to "the land." The masculine verbs in v 4 suggest "(king of) Assyria" as the implied subject, a usage found elsewhere in the Bible. Another solution is to delete the word "land" (Hillers 1983: 138; 1984: 68).

The pronominal references point to at least four participants in this unit—Assyria ("he"; NEB takes unwarranted liberties by switching this to plural in v 6b); Israel ("we"); the shepherds (vv 4bB, 5a); and the unidentified subject of the verb "rescue." The problem of the latter is shelved, not solved, by changing the verb "he will deliver" (v 5bA) to plural (NEB), making shepherds the subject.

trample. In combination with *bw'*, "come," the verb *drk*, "tread" (cf. 1:3), describes the march of an army.

citadels. Or defense works. The opening and closing bicolons are identical, except that the second has "our border" where the first has "our citadels." Wellhausen wanted to replace "citadels" with "territory," as in v 5. LXX already read *epi tēn khōran hēmōn*. Both adjustments arise from an instinct for closer parallelism; perhaps also to remove the oddity of trampling on the citadels; the usual outcome of war is that citadels are demolished or burned. The end of the campaign seems to be reached near the beginning of the story. As Amos 1–2 shows, demolition of the "citadels" is symbolic of total destruction (Andersen and Freedman 1989: 242–44). What is more, *'armĕnôt* is a good eighth-century term, commonly used as a B word in the prophecies of the time (Amos 1–2; Hos 8:14). If the Assyrians penetrated the citadels then conquest would be complete. But "tramping" over the defenses does not necessarily imply wholesale destruction. The usual Assyrian policy was to preserve and reuse cities that they conquered and captured. This detail is lost if the piquancy of "citadels" is eliminated by reading **'admātēnû* (Hillers 1984: 68—"[it] could easily have arisen by scribal error," presumably because the two words have several consonants in common). The adjustment is slight, admittedly. The versions are divided. Syriac *bshrtn* supports MT. LXX is not helpful due to leveling with verse 5b, where LXX has *epi ta horia hēmōn* in the second colon. But the pressure toward more synonymous parallelism, which suggests "land" rather than "citadels" to modern students, could have been at work already in the Greek translator, or even in the Hebrew manuscript he used.

we will raise up. Compare the first-person pronoun in 4:14. Since the verb is used in circumstances exactly like those in the days of the judges, it is surprising that the ancient idiom ("Yahweh raised up a deliverer") is not used here. Since Wellhausen, emendation to *whqym* has enjoyed considerable favor (BHS). The verb *hqym* is the operative term for the act of raising up a deliverer, exclusively an act of God. The sequel of this act of God is "rescue," again God's act as in Mic 4:10; 5:5bA; and numerous other places. The name *yhwh* occurs twice in v 3. The question is whether the occurrence of the suffix *-nû* four times (prominent at the end of four colons, making rhyme) has contaminated v 4bBα. The consonantal spelling of *whqmnw* is ambiguous. It is possible to read the suffix as a benefactive (indirect) object—"he will raise up *for us.*" This is plausible. We should note that Wellhausen also supplied the object "us" to "deliver" in v 5bA. The supposition is that these two verbs have the same subject (Yahweh implied) and the same object "us." There is no need to emend; the one object (if correctly recovered in v 4bB) can do double duty with "deliver." These two parallel statements then act like prongs at symmetrical points that separate the four colons describing the Assyrian (two before and two after) from the four colons describing the shepherds (in the middle).

4b   Assyria   (two colons)
            And he will raise up for us against him shepherds   (four colons)
            And he will rescue (us)
5b   from Assyria   (two colons)

The proposal actually to read *whṣylnw* (Wellhausen, BHS) perceives the matter correctly, but the device of a double-duty suffix makes emendation unnecessary.

The arguments over the reading are finely balanced, the decisions not compelling either way. We surmise that the decision of NJPS to print vv 1–5 as a single paragraph, while it could be no more than the outcome of remaining neutral, might be recognizing that the *môšēl* of v 1aB is the leader throughout, "the one of Peace," and the subject of the singular verb *he will save* (v 5bA). The two opponents of Assyria are this shepherd (v 3aA) and his seven // eight associates. *They* will *shepherd* the land of Assyria; *he* will rescue "us" from Assyria.

If MT vocalization is retained, the act resembles the initiative taken by the citizens or elders to appoint a national leader in time of emergency. Compare the initiative of the elders of Gilead in the recruitment of Jephthah (Judges 11). The choice of vocabulary hints that Israel's origins are supplying the models; and certain archaisms, such as the seven // eight conventional pattern gives the poem an epic flavor. The Seven against Thebes in the Greek epic tradition may be a little removed from Near Eastern culture. We are not aware of any precedent for this kind of collegial leadership in Israel. The warrior king is accompanied by seven close companions, like the seven demons that accompany Marduk in *Enuma Elish*, the Ilu-Sibitti of the Erra poem. The latter are the immediate battle companions of the war god. The "eight" could then be this leader and his band, but these poetic numbers do not have to be taken literally. In the context it is not altogether out of the question that 7 // 8 is intended to describe David and his seven (in Samuel) brothers (but in Chronicles David is the seventh son). That is what we know from the Hebrew version of Psalm 151; language like that in Micah 5:1–5 was used in the legend of David and his brothers (Sanders 1965: 55). Similar vocabulary is underlined.

David and his brothers (Psalm 151:1)

קטן הייתי מן אחי וצעיר מבני אבי
וישימני רועה צונו ומושל בגדיותיו

> I was the smallest of my brothers,
>> and the youngest of the sons of my father;
> and he set me shepherd of his flock,
>> and ruler of his kids.

seven . . . eight. Parallelism of numbers x/x + 1 is a feature of West-Semitic literature (RSP 1:345), used sparingly elsewhere (Haran 1972). Avishur (1981: 5) reports nineteen specimens—twelve in Ugaritic, four in Aramaic, two in the Hebrew Bible (here and Qoh 11:2). In the Baal epic there are no fewer than five such matched pairs of numbers: "Like the seven cries of his mouth // yea (like) his eight shrieks" (Gordon 1949: 55, 56). In Akkadian texts number parallelism is found mainly in incantations (Watson 1984: 145). The rhetorical, form-critical, and semantic functions of such formulas have been discussed by Haran (1971), Roth (1962; 1965), and Avishur (1981). Micah also uses the sequence 1000 // 10,000 (6:7). It is not clear whether the numbers in v 4 have a precise meaning and refer to some specific group leadership pattern. In a context that has memories of David's historic role, there may be an echo of the fact that he was the eighth and youngest son of Jesse (at least in the tradition in the book of Samuel). But there is no tradition that he held the primacy in leadership shared in some way with his seven brothers.

shepherds . . . commanders. Both terms are archaic. The term *nāsîk* is an old tribal title. It is found in two connections. It belongs to the heroic age (Josh 13:21 ["officers of Sihon"]; Ps 83:12 [Midianite leaders are called *nēsîkîm*]). The term belongs to the End-time (Ezek 32:30). In Dan 11:8 the term refers to idols and is not relevant here. The parallel *nāsî'* in Ezek 32:29, followed by *nāsîk* in 32:30 does not prove that the terms are identical, but the collocation of *nĕsîkê sîḥôn* with *nĕsî'ê midyān* suggests accurate distinctions in the use of authentic political terminology. The singular is not found. The associations are with pre-monarchical Transjordan. Like the *nĕsî'îm* they are not independent rulers, but chiefs of federated tribes. If the old Israelite league had been in mind, one would have expected the number twelve. The use of the verb *nsk* in connection with the oracle appointing a messiah (presumably David) as king over Zion (Ps 2:6; cf. Prov 8:26) suggests an etymology. Its association with libation suggests a synonym of *mšḥ*, so *nāsîk* could be a synonym of "messiah."

men. There are reasons for doubting this traditional interpretation. In other occurrences the *nomen rectum* is either the name of a king (Sihon) or a country (Midian, Zaphon). In military texts, the term for warrior is *'îš*, not *'ādām*. Either the choice of this word brings out that these commanders are themselves men, or we will have to read *'ādām* = "land." Hillers solved this problem by emending to "Aram" (1983: 138; 1984: 68). The contemporary use of the term *nasīku* to refer to Aramaean chiefs supports the proposal. Even so, the weakness of the suggestion is shown up by the fact that Hillers needs five additional emendations in vv 4b–5 to secure a political-military scenario in which Israel uses Aramaean vassal states as a buffer between it and Mesopotamia.

5. *with the sword.* The unit contains three pairs of parallel terms all governed by *b-*. The idiom "shepherd . . . with the sword" requires explication. Comparison with v 3 shows that this act of the seven // eight shepherds is like that of the "ruler." If these shepherds are also rulers, then the verb shepherd means "rule." Psalm 2:9 is a close parallel—*tr'm bšbṭ brzl*. See RSV. Compare the similar use of *šbṭ* in Mic 4:14, describing, perhaps, the traditional use of the mace to brain captured enemies. A different nuance is secured if the word "sword" points to war, the response to Assyrian invasion: "And they will *conquer* the land of Assyria with the sword." The purpose of this enterprise is not so much to capture another country as to rescue their captives. Furthermore, the language of v 5b— "and he will rescue us *from* Assyria"—does not suggest merely the successful repulsion of an attack. It suggests rather that after Israel has been conquered (Assyria occupies the citadels) and prisoners have been taken back to Assyria, the shepherds will go to the land of Assyria and recover the captives from there. This is the task of a shepherd, to rescue the flock, stolen by a thief, going after him with the sword. In this perspective, the last bicolon should be seen as an inclusion of the first bicolon, a frame for the starting time of the whole story, but not as the specific time of the last moment, which is the verb *hṣyl*, "rescue."

entrances. If this comes from *ptḥ*, "doorway," it is not a good parallel to "sword." An acceptable emendation is *pĕtîḥâ*, "drawn sword." The final *he'* is the feminine suffix, not a pronoun suffix. The misreading of the latter was compounded when *yod* was added to make the noun plural. The plural *pĕtiḥôt* occurs in Ps 55:22. The adjustment is mild, involving metathesis of two letters *bpthyh* to *bptyḥh*. The Masoretes could do nothing else with the plural; but they did not make the obvious change. Compare the emendation in 3:3, which also recognizes metathesis as the origin of the error.

border. From this original denotation, the term *gĕbûl* acquired the connotation of "territory."

Comment on Micah 5:4–5

The composition is somewhat epic in tone. The moments in the story are not presented in logical or chronological sequence. The need to rescue people "from Assyria" (v 5bA) implies prior conquest with captives taken into exile (1:16). Crossing the border is mentioned last (v 5bB), trampling the citadels comes first (v 4bA). If MT is retained, we have another specimen of unfolding the story backward. First you cross the frontier, the last word in the unit; then you march through the land; finally storming the citadels crowns success by the capture of the central strongholds. The promise that Israel, or maybe with more limited scope Judah, would be able, not only to repel an Assyrian invasion, but actually to carry out a successful punitive counterattack into "the land of Nimrod" itself, seems, in view of actual historical events, to be mere wishful fancy. The language it uses conjures up memories of great moments (doubtless exaggerated) in the past, when one man could defeat a thousand, because Yahweh his God fought for him (Josh 23:10). The confidence expressed in these words is like that conveyed by Isaiah to Hezekiah, when confronted by just such an invasion (Isaiah 36–37). Hezekiah (or someone like him) could have been billed as "the One of Peace" if it was oracled that he would not only repel the Assyrian invader, as Hezekiah virtually did, but actually carry a successful counterattack right to Mesopotamia, leading resurgent Zion as described in 4:13, and so becoming great to the ends of the earth (5:3).

Gathering the details together, we can say that the Assyrians invade the Holy Land. They are successful and carry off much of the population. Those who remain in occupation are defeated by a new ruler, a Davidide raised up by the people. He then leads an army to conquer Assyria and extends his conquests to the ends of the earth. He then comes back to Zion in triumph, bringing back the scattered Israelites, and also a lot of captives. In any case all the nations of the world submit to his God and to him and bring tribute. Some parts of this scenario correspond to what happened in real history.

All these considerations make it difficult to put a date to the composition of this piece and to decide how much, if any, belongs to Micah, and how much to redaction. Compared with passages with a better claim to be authentic Micah, it lacks his tense, dense enigmatic style. Yet the poetic structure, though somewhat simple by classical standards, is so complete that editorial adjustment of an original Micah oracle by minor verbal changes is out of the question.

Nor is it possible to establish a date by historical considerations. If the reference to Assyria is realistic, it must date before the disappearance of Assyria from history; it cannot be exilic. Indeed, it must date before any major Assyrian invasion. It could reflect the confidence of Hezekiah confronted by Sennacherib. Here Micah echoes the defiance shown by Isaiah on that occasion; but Isaiah did not suggest that Hezekiah would be able to retaliate on a scale like this. Isaiah emphasizes the sole agency of Yahweh in repelling Assyria.

If Mic 5:1–5 is an eighth-century prophecy that the outcome of menacing Assyrian imperialism would be the fresh creation of David's empire, then it was not fulfilled. Israel never conquered Assyria. Such a prophecy could retain its vitality in later interpretation only by postponing it to the End-time. The End-time is the setting of chapters 4 and 5, which could have been composed as an eschatologizing reinterpretation of traditional Micah oracles, with perhaps some that were not originally Micah's at all (Micah otherwise mentions Assyria only in 7:12, which is possibly not authentic). In this later setting Assyria has now become an archetypical symbol. Assyria is named in Isa 52:4 in a context that clearly refers to Babylon. If the usage in Mic 5:4–5 is similar, it could be likewise exilic. Assyria and Egypt represented the two great world powers of the eighth century, and that is how they figure, in continual parallelism, in Hosea and Isaiah. They are also used in conjunction in prophetic eschatology (Mic 7:12).

II.8–9. THE REMNANT (5:6–8)

II.8. THE REMNANT BENIGN (5:6)

TRANSLATION

MT

6aA	*wĕhāyâ šĕ'ērît ya'ăqōb*	And the remnant of Jacob,
	bĕqereb 'ammîm rabbîm	in the midst of many peoples,
6aBα	*kĕṭal mē'ēt yhwh*	will be like dew from Yahweh,
6aBβ	*kirĕbîbîm 'ălê-'ēśeb*	like showers on the grass,
6bA	*'ăšer lō'-yĕqawweh lĕ'îš*	which does not wait for man,
6bB	*wĕlō' yĕyaḥēl libĕnê 'ādām*	and does not delay for the sons of Adam.

LXX II.8. The Remnant Benign (5:6)

6aA	And the remnant of Jacob will be ⟨among the nations⟩,
6aBα	in the midst of many peoples, like dew falling from Kyrios,
6aBβ	and like lambs on the grass;
6bA	so that no one may be gathered together
6bB	nor resist among the sons of men.

II.9. THE REMNANT MALIGN (5:7–8)

TRANSLATION

MT

7aAα	*wĕhāyâ šĕ'ērît ya'ăqōb baggôyim*	And the remnant of Jacob, in the nations
7aAβ	*bĕqereb 'ammîm rabbîm*	in the midst of many peoples,
7aBα	*kĕ'aryēh bĕbahāmôt ya'ar*	will be like a lion among beasts of the woodland,
7aBβ	*kikĕpîr bĕ'edrê-ṣō'n*	like a young lion among flocks of sheep,
7bA	*'ăšer 'im-'ābar wĕrāmas*	which went through and trampled
7bB	*wĕṭārap wĕ'ên maṣṣîl*	and mauled, and no one rescuing.
8a	*tārōm yādĕkā 'al-ṣāreykā*	Let thy [m.] hand be high over thy [m.] foes,
8b	*wĕkol-'ōyĕbeykā yikkārētû*	and let all thine [m.] enemies be cut to pieces.

LXX II.8. The Remnant Malign (5:7–8)

7aA	And the remnant of Jacob will be ⟨among the nations⟩,
7aBα	in the midst of many peoples,
7aBβ	like a lion among beasts, in the woodland;
	and like a lion-cub among flocks of sheep,

7bA   just as when he goes through, and, dividing,

7bB   seizes, and there is no one rescuing.

8a   Thy hand will be raised against those who oppress you,

8b   and all thine enemies will be annihilated.

INTRODUCTION TO MICAH 5:6–8

The Theme of the "Remnant"

These three verses develop the theme of the remnant, first introduced in 2:12. The verbs "gather" and "assemble" are used there and again in 4:6–7, and *šĕʾērît*, "remnant," occurs in those passages as the object of those verbs. The noun *šĕʾērît* occurs finally in 7:18, so it is found in each of the three "books" that make up the complete work. It is clearly an important notion in the prophecy. In 2:12 the remnant is *the remnant of Israel*; in 4:7 the noun is not qualified; in 5:6–7 the remnant is *the remnant of Jacob*; finally 7:18 has "the remnant of his inheritance." The masculine "thou" of v 8 matches *kullāk* in 2:12. If the remnant of Jacob is being addressed in all these verses (masculine for "Jacob", not feminine for "remnant"), then several problems can be solved. The three verses can be treated as a unit. Verses 6 and 7 are twin pieces; v 8 goes with them by default, since v 9 certainly begins a new section. Verse 8 could go with v 14 at longer range, and the pronoun suffix -*kā*, "thy" (m.) of v 8 continues through vv 9–13, where it refers to Jacob.

The Poetry of Micah 5:6–8

From the grammatical point of view vv 6–8 consist of just three clauses, one in each verse. Verses 6 and 7 are constructed on the same design, three bicolons each with familiar patterns of parallelism. Verse 6aAα contains the verb and the subject ("the remnant of Jacob"). Verse 6aAβ is a long locative phrase ("in the midst of many peoples"). To this point there is already enough (14 syllables) for a bicolon, but there is no parallelism. This statement is followed by a double simile (v 6aB) in a bicolon (13 syllables) with simple A : B :: A′ : B′ parallelism— "dew" and "showers" match; "from Yahweh" and "on the grass" are complementary. The clause continues with a relative clause or, rather, two clauses carried by one relative pronoun (v 6b). This use of one particle to carry two parallel co-ordinated clauses contrasts with the repetition of the subordinating conjunction with each embedded clause in vv 4b and 5b. The bicolon in v 6b has excellent complete synonymous parallelism. The only slight departure from standard practice is the longer final colon, which makes the whole bicolon eighteen syllables.

    The companion piece (v 7) begins with the same words as the first, but v 7 has one more word ("in the nations") in the first colon, making it rather long (11 syllables) and setting things up for synonymous parallelism with the next colon. The symmetry of v 6 with v 7 is disturbed in the first colon of v 7, which has *baggôyīm* extra. It is possible that originally v 6aA was the same as v 7aA, and that *bgwym* dropped out of v 6 because of haplography, owing to homoeo-archton. The scribe's eye jumped from the *bet* at the beginning of *bgwym* to the *bet* at the beginning of *bqrb*. The versions, and even an occasional Hebrew manuscript, have this word in the same position in v 6. This would be the result of leveling, if the Massoretic Text is superior. But the addition of a word by backward leveling is less likely than accidental scribal omission. Furthermore, the restoration of this missing word results in a syllable count of 48 for v 6, which is also the count for v 7. The mean colon length for each unit (8 syllables) is the standard length, and this lends additional support to the proposed emendation. Nor is there any need to drop *bgwym* from v 7, as BHS suggests. This would up-set the balance. In other words, it is more likely that *bgwym* dropped out of v 6 than that *bgwym* was added to v 7. Note, however, that the usual sequence is *ʿam // gôy*.

The double simile in v 7aB has perfect parallelism and rhythm (8 + 8 sylla-bles). So far we have had five bicolons with good parallelism. The sixth bicolon (v 7b) does not imitate its counterpart (v 6b) in having straightforward parallel-ism. Instead there are four short clauses that develop a rapidly moving narra-tive. The activity in v 7b is clearly that of the lion. Analogy in design suggests that the final relative clause in v 6 describes the activity of the dew, not Jacob or Yahweh.

	Verse 6	Both	Verse 7
		wĕhāyâ šĕʾērît yaʿăqōb	
			baggôyīm
		bĕqereb ʿammîm rabbîm	
	kĕṭal mēʾēt yhwh		*kĕʾaryēh bĕbahămôt yaʿar*
	kirĕbîbîm ʿălê-ʿēśeb		*kikĕpîr bĕʿedrê-ṣōʾn*
		ʾăšer	
	lōʾ-yĕqawweh lĕʾîš		*ʾim-ʿābar wĕrāmas*
	wĕlōʾ yĕyaḥēl libĕnê ʾādām		*wĕṭārap wĕʾên maṣṣîl*

Finally v 8 is a bicolon that addresses Jacob directly, promising military success. The contents of the two colons are parallel in only a general way. The seven bi-colons in these twin units are as close to standard poetry as anything in Micah. It is unusual for the book of Micah in consisting of nothing but well-formed bicolons.

NOTES AND COMMENTS

Notes on Micah 5:6–8

6. *remnant*. There is a grammatical anomaly in vv 6aA and 7aAα. The verb is masculine, while the following noun "remnant," which one would expect to be the subject of the verb, is feminine. There are three possible explanations for

this phenomenon. The first is that these verbs are part of a series: "And it will come to pass (that) . . . ," and it is simplest to give them the same meaning in all their occurrences, if possible. The grammar of vv 6aA and 7aAα would then be that the verb initiates a new unit and is followed by a verbless clause: "And it will come to pass (that) the remnant of Jacob (will be) in the midst of many peoples like dew." A second possible explanation is that the verb agrees with the *nomen rectum* ("Jacob") rather than the *nomen regens* ("remnant") of the construct phrase. The same thing happens in Amos 1:8, where "the remnant of the Philistines" is the subject of a plural verb. A third possibility is that "remnant of Jacob" is vocative; the subject of the verb is found in the preceding context, either the ruler from Bethlehem or "the One of Peace" (perhaps they are both the same). See the COMMENT.

in the midst of many peoples. This repeated phrase suggests more than exile of some survivors to the territory of a conquering nation, such as Assyria or Babylon. The expression *many peoples* throughout the Book of Visions seems to be almost universal in its reference. It suggests a general dispersion of prisoners and refugees into widely scattered places, not just to Mesopotamia. Large numbers had taken refuge in Egypt, and the repeated references to "islands" or "coastlands" in Second Isaiah point to other regions. This state of affairs continued under the Persians and succeeding world powers.

like dew. Psalm 72 is an idealized picture of Solomon's reign. The simile of dew is used in v 6. It expresses the concerns of a community with an agricultural subsistence economy. The just king secures the blessing of God through rain (Deut 32:2). The simile is used again in Ps 110:3, an otherwise bellicose poem. Similes of this kind are often akin to riddles. The puzzle is to work out just what is being compared to what. If it is not dew per se that the remnant is like, but rather that the situation of the remnant is like that of the grass waiting for the dew that is under divine, not human control, then the purpose of the figure is to encourage the remnant to "wait upon the Lord" (Isa 40:31). The remnant is like grass and "grass" is the antecedent. Similarly the remnant among the nations finds itself in the same situation as a flock (Micah has used this comparison for Israel more than once) being savaged by a lion. Verse 8 then promises a reversal of these helpless states, a development parallel to that which takes place in 4:11–13.

which. There are only six places in the Hebrew Bible where *'ăšer* is immediately followed by *'im* (Gen 28:15; Num 32:17; Isa 6:11 [with *'ăšer* following *'ad* in all three, and *'im* making the following suffixed verb subjunctive]; Gen 13:16; Mic 5:7; Job 9:15 [where the construction is more problematic]; Elwolde 1990). With each particle having a range of syntactic functions, which meaning of *'ăšer* and which meaning of *'im* combine here? If here and in v 7bA *'ăšer* has its normal function as the relative pronoun, it is not clear which of the preceding nouns is the antecedent. If the antecedent is immediate, v 6b tells us what dew does and v 7b tells us what the lion does. But, since the remnant of Jacob is *like* dew and *like* a lion, vv 6b and 7b tell us how the remnant behaves; the relative clause is delayed. Goshen-Gottstein's exemplary study of the problem

(1960: 143–55) deserves more attention than it seems to have received. The particle *'ăšer* sometimes serves as a subordinating conjunction. This function is commonly acknowledged; here it would mean that v 6b gives the reason why the remnant is like dew, and similarly for v 7b. How to tell when *'ăšer* is doing this is not always straightforward. Here we cautiously advance a proposal for consideration. The possibility arises here because of the puzzle of the verb forms in these clauses. In v 6b the verbs are prefixed ("imperfect"); in v 7b they are suffixed ("perfect"). The two behaviors are presented in a different time perspective. Both are stock comparisons. The usage should be sought in proverbial sayings. Because the behaviors of the two entities compared in a simile are similar (that's how a simile works!), the difference between *'ăšer* as a relative pronoun and as a subordinating conjunction may be almost indistinguishable or even have an intended ambiguity.

wait. If "dew" is the antecedent of the relative, what does it mean to say that dew does not wait for humans? The frequent poetic use of *qiwwîtî* and its usual parallel *hôḥaltî* (or *'ăyaḥēl*) expresses the human feeling of absolute dependence upon God (Gen 49:13; Isa 8:17; Ps 25:5; 30:26; 39:8; 40:2; 130:5; Job 30:26). This unique collocation of waiting for man, which is denied, could be saying that dew // rain do not depend on man in the way man depends on God. In other words, only God can send rain, a rather roundabout way of stating a truism. Three ideas are combined in the comparison of Israel's deliverer with dew: he brings refreshment, comes from God, and comes at the time of God's choosing. But these are not the only associations of "dew." Because it comes silently, uncontrollably, at night, it provides a simile for the sudden unexpected attack on an unprepared enemy (2 Sam 17:12). Has Micah deliberately chosen an ambivalent simile?

7. *like a lion*. The reading *b'r[yh* in Mur 88 is probably a scribal error. Biblical Hebrew has several different words for "lion." There are five in Job 4:10–11. The exact distinctions these words might have secured are no longer understood. The term *'aryēh* (v 7aBα) is generic; *kĕpîr* (v 7aβ) is thought to have the connotation of "young lion." Dahood (1983: 47) proposed "copper-colored lion" by connecting the word with the use of *kaparum* at Ebla for "copper." The simile is applied to Judah (Gen 49:9), to Israel (Num 23:24; 24:9), but more often to Yahweh (Hos 5:14). On the motif in ancient Near Eastern art, see Cornelius (1989).

among beasts. The parallelism between "the beasts of the forest" and "flocks of sheep" suggests, not that the lion is being compared with other wild beasts or that he is seen to ravage both wild and tame animals, but rather that the lion preys on both large and small domesticated animals. The "woodland" would then refer to the place where these animals graze (Mic 7:14—"secluded and fertile abode for flock" [BDB 420b]), not to the lion's haunts.

8. This verse resembles 4:13 in its more bellicose mood; the masculine "thou" lines up with the pronouns in 4:8 and 5:1 or otherwise refers to Jacob rather than Zion.

be high. In MT the verb is vocalized as *qal* jussive, "Let thy hand be high!" Many manuscripts have indicative *tārûm*. The jussive could be either a battle cry or a victory shout. The language of 4:13 and 5:8 shows that this is the very last scene—not of casualties in battle, but of the execution of captives after it is all over. Deuteronomy 32:40 shows that raising the hand at this stage is part of the oath of clearance made by the victorious warrior in the rituals for desacralization that round off a campaign. He affirms that he has fulfilled the vows made when he was dedicated to the campaign and is eligible for honorable discharge.

Comment on Micah 5:6–8

It is usual to interpret the twin oracles as predictions of the destiny of this remnant. "The remnant of Jacob shall be . . . like dew . . . like a lion." There are several reasons for doubting this. First, if *šĕ'ērît* is the subject, the verb should be feminine. This problem can be solved by making *wĕhāyâ* a discourse transition marker that introduces the proposition, an oracular rubric that is part of the series in this chapter. The following clause has no verb: "And (this is how) it will be: The remnant of Jacob (will be) in the midst . . . "

Second, and more serious, is the ambivalent role of the remnant, apparently benevolent in v 6, belligerent in v 7. It cannot be both in one and the same act, unless two quite different objects are in mind (friends, enemies) or unless we have a great paradox. But neither of these harmonizing explanations has support from the context. Jacob has both qualities elsewhere in these chapters, pulverizing the nations (4:13) and also bringing them into the blessings of Jacob's God (4:1–4). These two roles need not contradict each other if they are two distinct stages of the End-time, the common pattern of Armageddon before Paradise restored.

Third, the similes are conventional, but neither seems to be appropriate for the remnant. It is more likely that a king would be compared to "dew from Yahweh"; cf. Ps 72:6 (*kirĕbîbîm*). The similes are associated with the king, and the lion image with God as well. Compare "lion" and "dew" in Hosea 5–6. If the subject of these comparisons is not the remnant as such, but a participant not named here, then either Yahweh or his human deputy, the shepherd-ruler of vv 1–5, is a good candidate. "The One of Peace" (Mic 5:4a = Solomon) fits with the king of Psalm 72. "And he will be (for) the remnant like dew, like a lion." In 4:7 Yahweh is king explicitly in connection with the remnant (a role often mentioned in Second Isaiah). The boast "and none can rescue" (v 7bB) is particularly connected with assertions of Yahweh's sole power (Deut 32:39; Isa 42:22; 43:13; Hos 5:4). Yahweh does rescue his people (4:10; 5:5), and none can rescue from him. Again it does not make much difference whether these results are achieved directly by Yahweh, or by his agent.

Continuity in vv 1–8 is secured if the *môšēl* is the subject throughout, making for greater cohesion through vv 1–8. "And he will be the One of Peace . . . and he will be, O remnant of Jacob . . . like dew . . . and he will be, O remnant of Jacob . . . like a lion . . . " The difference in role, dew versus lion, is then explained by the different objects of his activity: he is like dew to the remnant he is rescuing, like a lion to all their enemies (4:10; 5:8).

II.10. ISRAEL CLEANSED AND AVENGED (5:9–14)

TRANSLATION

MT

9aA	wĕhāyâ bayyôm hahû' nĕ'ūm-yhwh	And it will happen in that day, —a statement of Yahweh—
9aB	wĕhikrattî sûseykā miqqirbekā	and I will cut off thy [m.] horses from thy [m.] midst,
9b	wĕha'ăbadtî markĕbōteykā	and I will destroy thy [m.] chariots;
10a	wĕhikrattî 'ārê 'arṣekā	and I will cut off the cities of thy [m.] land,
10b	wĕhārastî kol-mibṣāreykā	and I will demolish all thy [m.] forts;
11a	wĕhikrattî kĕšāpîm miyyādekā	and I will cut off the instruments of magic from thy [m.] hand,
11b	ûmĕ'ônĕnîm lō' yihyû-lāk	and thou [m.] wilt not have any sorcerers;
12a	wĕhikrattî pĕsîleykā ûmaṣṣēbôteykā miqqirbekā	and I will cut off thine [m.] images and thy standing stones from thy midst,
12b	wĕlō'-tištaḥăweh 'ôd lĕma'ăśēh yādeykā	and thou [m.] wilt no longer bow down to the works of thy hands.
13a	wĕnātaštî 'ăšêreykā miqqirbekā	I will extirpate thine [m.] Asherim from thy [m.] midst,
13b	wĕhišmadtî 'āreykā	and I will destroy thy [m.] cities;
14a	wĕ'āśîtî bĕ'ap ûbĕḥēmâ nāqām	and I will wreak with anger and with fury (my) vengeance
14b	'et-haggôyīm 'ăšer lō' šāmē'û	on the nations that did not obey (me).

LXX II.10. Israel Cleansed and Avenged (5:9–14)

9aA	And it will be on that day,　　—says Kyrios—
9aB	I will cut off thy horses from the midst of thee,
9b	and I will destroy thy chariots;
10a	and I will destroy the cities of thy land,
10b	and I will demolish all thy fortresses;
11a	and I will remove the sorceries from thy hands,
11b	and soothsayers will not be among (Gk. *en*) thee;
12a	and I will destroy thy carved images and thy monuments from thy midst,
12b	and thou wilt no longer worship the works of thy hands.
13a	I will cut out the groves from thy midst,
13b	and I will remove thy cities;
14a	and I will wreak with anger and with fury (my) vengeance
14b	in all the nations because they did not hearken.

INTRODUCTION TO MICAH 5:9–14

The final unit in this section predicts the completion of another task necessary for bringing in the age of purity and bliss. Israel itself must be purified. The things that have aroused Yahweh's anger will be eliminated once and for all time. The oracle is essentially an inventory of things that will be "cut off." In this context it is not clear whether the final verse (v 14) is another way of summing this up, implying that the cleanup will be universal, not just in Israel; or whether the end of the oracle (the end of the Book of Visions) returns to the theme of vengeance on "the nations that did not obey."

The Poetry of Micah 5:9–14

Verse 14 stands apart from the rest of the unit in literary form as well as in theme. It uses all three prose particles and it lacks the poetic parallelism that is so well used in the rest of this unit. Verses 9–13 consist of five bicolons that all follow the same grammatical pattern. All begin with a consecutive future verb. In four cases this is *wĕhikrattî*, "and I shall cut off"; the fifth is a variant. This pattern, one variant in a large repetitive set, is clearly a trait of eighth-century prophets (Amos 1–2; Isa 2:6–8), if not a rule. See Freedman (1986b).

It may be noted that the B noun (the matching item in the second colon of a bicolon) usually begins with *mem*. The failure of this pattern in the last bicolon (v 13b) draws attention once more to the word "cities." But the lack of parallelism there suggests that v 13 contains a summary, in chiastic order, of the two distinct lists (two sets of four items each) in vv 9–12. One list condemns trust in material strength; the other condemns trust in the illicit supernatural.

Verse 9	Verse 10	Verse 11	Verse 12	Verse 13
horses	*cities*	magic	images	Asherim
chariots	forts	sorcerers	monoliths	*cities*
			hand-made gods	

Besides the fourfold use of *wĕhikrattî* there are other verbal links from verse to verse. Four bicolons use privative *min-*; *miqqirbĕkā* occurs three times. In vv 9 and 13 this word makes an inclusion (it does double duty on each occasion). The word *miqqirbĕkā* thus links vv 9, 12, 13. "Cities" links vv 10 and 13 (if correct in the latter—we do not share the doubts of scholars who wish to emend this word). "Hand" links vv 11 and 12. These facts suggest that the composition is well preserved, and there are no other textual problems. So the oracle permits conclusions about the literary form of prophetic discourse. The abundant parallelism shows that it is poetic. None of the objects uses *'et*. But the colons tend to be long, especially if we keep v 12 in step with the others structurally and recognize just one bicolon in it. In vv 9–14 there are 127 syllables (MT 140), 9.8 syllables (MT 10.8) per colon.

The inadequacy of scanning Hebrew poetry by beats comes out clearly in the results proposed by Allen (1976: 355–56) for this unit. He recognizes eight bicolons in the present unit, i.e., 16 colons, 42 "beats" in all. We recognize only twelve colons in the oracle proper. Allen includes v 9aA and displays v 12 as four colons—overriding the parallelism by meaning and the natural speech rhythms with which these clauses (all of the same grammatical shape) would be recited. His scansion is 2 + 2 :: 3 + 2. Smith has 2 + 2 :: 2 + 2.

Allen considers that the poem is "almost completely in 3 + 2 meter" (1976: 356). But the colons to which he assigns three beats are not nearly as uniform as his figures suggest. They have 7, 9 (MT 11), 9, 10 (MT 11), 6, 10 (MT 12) syllables, or 8.5 (MT 9.3) syllables each colon on the average, while those to which he gives 2 beats are 4, 8 (9), 8 (9), 9, 7 (8), 8 (10), 5 (6), 6 (7) syllables, a little under seven (eight) each on the average. Without going into every detail, we note that Allen gives a beat to every word in v 9a (MT has three) but gives only two beats to v 11b (MT has four). The ratio 3 : 2, which Allen finds in six bicolons, suggests that the first colon is half as long again as the second. By syllables the ratio is not 1.5 but 1.2. The variation in length is less when measured by syllables. Allen's two four-beat colons (v 14) are no longer than some three-beat colons; in fact, one of his four-beat colons is as long as one of his two-beat colons. It is doubtful if v 9A should be included in any such discussion of the relative lengths of the colons in a bicolon. Leaving it out, the A colons have an average of 10 syllables each, and the B colons have an average length of 9 syllables. In other words, the lead colons are not significantly longer, on the average, than the following colons.

It is true that all the colons to which Allen assigns three beats have three orthographic words. Six of the colons to which he assigns two beats have two orthographic words. In fact four of the 3 + 2 bicolons have 3 + 2 words. But vv 10b and 11b have three and four words each; and each has nine syllables. The means by which these are estimated to have only two beats illustrates the predicament in which theories of scansion by beats have always found themselves. Small, monosyllabic words, especially if proclitic or enclitic, are not counted. In v 10b *kol* is construct and unaccented, but three beats are found in v 10a, which has the same number of syllables by giving a beat to *'ārê* (construct). Allen does not explain how he found four beats in v 14b but to do so he must have counted *'ăšer* and *lō'*, surely not *'et*. So *lō'* was counted for a beat in v 14, but not in v 11, even though the Masoretic accentuation is the same for both. We do not wish to imply that any given word, such as *lō'*, has the same degree of stress in all its occurrences. In natural speech, phrase-structure rhythms can bring about variation. All we are maintaining is that our best evidence for phrase-structure rhythms is supplied by the Masoretic accents, and these should not be overridden simply to help out a theory that the scansion of Hebrew poetry by beats must be regular.

Thematic Connections of Micah 5:9–14

Besides the structural similarities pointed out above, this piece also has thematic affinities with Mic 1:6–7 and with Isa 2:6–8. The key nouns *'ōnĕnîm, sûsîm //markĕbôt, ma'ăśēh yādāyw* occur in Isaiah's list. Isaiah makes clearer, however, that such persons and things were detested because they were foreign. This provides the link to v 14. Israel did not obey the covenant, but followed the ways of other nations.

Micah 5:9–14 balances 4:1–5. Each has a full eschatological rubric. The cleansing of the cult and the elimination of war in the latter are preliminary to the peace and security in the universalized cult of the former. And the developments in 4:6–5:8 precede both.

NOTES AND COMMENTS

Notes on Micah 5:9–14

9. *horses*. The age of Solomon provides some of the ingredients of the idealized kingdom of the future. Solomon also introduced horses and chariots. Melamed (1961: 128–31) discusses the breakup of the "stereotype phrase" *sûs wārekeb*. The elimination of this military equipment corresponds to the replacement of weapons by tools in 4:3. Both developments represent a return to the simplicity of paradise, or at least of the simpler kind of citizens' army that Israel had in the age of the Judges. In view of the other items on Micah's list and on the similar list in Isa 2:6–9, it is possible that the horses and chariots were connected with features of the cult that the prophet considered to be marked for elimination. It is reported in 2 Kgs 23:11 that Josiah "took away the horses that the kings of Judah had given to the sun, at the entrance to the house of Yahweh, . . . and he burned the chariots of the sun with fire."

10. *cities*. Does this mean all cities or just the two cities that were named as the subject matter of the book—Samaria and Jerusalem? Both were centers of social injustice (3:10) and religious corruption (1:7). The demolition of cities represents a more radical rejection of civilization. The alternative polity of Mic 4:4 is more agrarian and individualistic.

11. *magic*. The term *kešep* (Akk. *kišpu*, Ug. *ktp*) is "sorcery," while *mĕ'ōnĕnîm* are persons, "diviners" or "augurers" (Cryer 1994). They were the chief object of God's attack on the gods of Egypt (Exod 7:11). In Isa 2:6 the magicians are Philistines. The magician, male (Deut 18:10) or female (Exod 22:17), was to be executed. The extraordinary tenacity of these proscribed practices in Israel seems to have been an integral part of persistent paganizing trends, with the making of idols (v 12) as its most overt expression. All Yahweh's destructions in this oracle are directed against objects, not beliefs or practices, so here the *kĕšāpîm* are removed from the land, as if they refer to the magicians' equipment. This is the only noun of the ten that does not have the direct suffix "thy," and

it makes an excellent combination with the matching noun in the next colon. In prose they would make a construct chain. The lack of the pronoun suffix makes the fine distinction that all the people did not have instruments of magic; but they did have sorcerers (possessive *l-* in v 11b). On ancient magic, see Davies (1898) and Abusch (1990); on magic in Israel, Fishbane (1971).

13. *cities.* Even though this word is unanimously supported by the ancient versions, it has long attracted suspicion, especially in the minds of critics who expect synonymous parallelism in poetic bicolons. When the use of the same word (here "cities") for long-range inclusion (vv 10a // 13b) was not appreciated and when free emendation was in vogue, many proposals were tried (*ICC* 177; cf. *ʿăṣabbeykā* [BHS], accepted by Allen [1976: 356]). Gaster (1937: 163) claimed that *ǵr* in parallel with *psl* in an Ugaritic text, supported by an Arabic cognate, indicated the meaning of "bedaubed stone." Driver's refinement of "blood-daubed stone" (1956: 142 n. 26) supplied NEB with "blood-spattered altars," retained by REB. Dahood used a meaning of the root *ʿr*, "protect" to obtain "your gods" (1965b: 55). Jeppesen (1984b) has defended the authenticity of *thy cities* in association with Asherim in the light of the texts from Kuntillet ʿAjrud. He suggests that "Yahwism has assumed numerous forms in a variety of cities" (1984b: 464), with Yahweh associated with an Asherah in each city. Compare Koch (1988), LaRocca (1989), Lemaire (1977), and Margalit (1990). This is thus not an unnecessary repetition of "cities" from v 10. It focuses on the most conspicuous symbol of idolatry. In Mesopotamian religion certain cities attained renown because of a popular female deity, such as the Ishtar of Arbela, who had shrines in places other than her main center. Something similar in Israel lies behind the Ashimat of Samaria, and the Asherahs of the Judean cities.

14. *I will wreak.* This concluding verse rounds off earlier themes. The narrative of what Yahweh will do begins with *wěśamtî* (4:7) and ends with *wě ʿāśîtî*. A series of negated verbs begins in 4:12 and ends in 5:14: *lōʾ yādĭ0.0 ĕ ʿû . . . lōʾ hēbînû . . . lōʾ šāmĕ ʿû.* Here is another indication that Yahweh expects *the nations*, all of them (1:2), not just Israel, to *obey* him.

vengeance. The idea of "judgment" undergoes a substantial shift as the result of the Exile. Before that, the object of *špṭ* was usually the righteous, who were to be vindicated; after the Exile it was the wicked who were to be punished. In Deuteronomy *nāqām* was an act of obligation within the covenant, on behalf of the partner and only against an enemy in a secondary sense. It was not primarily punitive, but redemptive, or at least restorative.

nations. Scholars who find the reference to the *nations* out of place at this point have made various suggestions. Some would delete the whole verse as a gloss (fully reviewed by Renaud 1977: 264–66). Schwantes (1962: 142) appropriately points out that "the catchword *šmʿw* which serves as introduction to the following oracle (Cf. 6,1) also corroborates the view that v 14 is original." Others (e.g., Lippl 1937: 211) omit "the nations"; Schwantes (1962: 142) calls it "an attenuating gloss." Others again (e.g., Rudolph 1975: 105), replacing *hgwym* with a more suitable term, have accepted Bewer's proposal (1950: 68) to read *hgʾym*, "the insolent."

Comment on Micah 5:9–14

The empire of David saw the inclusion of many nations under the suzerainty of Yahweh and thus gave rise to an eschatological hope of including the whole world in a messianic kingdom. Micah 4:1–5 expresses this hope. Micah 4:6–5:8 implies wide military action by resurgent Zion to achieve a new world conquest; the nations are to be subjugated, if not exterminated. Verse 14 describes the execution of *nāqām* with the nations that did not obey (Yahweh). These could be viewed as the nations who refused to accept Yahweh's appointment of his messiah as king from Zion (Psalm 2) to the ends of the earth (Ps 72:8; Zech 9:10), or who rebelled against David their overlord. The oracle in Zech 9:9–10 has so many affinities with eighth-century prophecy, and with Micah 4–5 in particular, that one must suspect it of being a kindred piece, preserved and reused by a postexilic prophet. Or else a very good imitation.

Zechariah 9:9–10

9aAα	*gîlî mĕʾōd*	**bat-ṣiyyôn**		7 syllables
9aAβ	*hārî'î*	**bat-yĕrûšālēm**		8 syllables
9aBα	*hinnēh* **malkēk**	*yābôʾ*	*lāk*	7 syllables
9aBβ	*ṣaddîq wĕnôšaʿ*	*hûʾ*		6 syllables
9bA	*'ānî wĕrōkēb*	*'al-ḥămôr*		8 syllables
9bB		*wĕ'al-'ayir ben-'atōnôt*		7 syllables
10aAα	**wĕhikrattî**	*rekeb*	*mē'eprayim*	8 syllables
10aAβ		*wĕsûs*	*mîrûšālēm*	7 syllables
10aBα	**wĕnikrĕtâ**	*qešet*	**milḥāmâ**	8 syllables
10aBβ	*wĕdibber*	**šālôm**	**laggôyim**	8 syllables
10bA	*ûmošlô*	*miyyām*	*'ad-yām*	7 syllables
10bB		*ûminnāhār*	*'ad-'apsê-'āreṣ*	8 syllables

This composition is in strict eighth-century style. There is no use of pronoun suffixes as in Mic 5:9–14, and there are no prose particles. The twelve colons are all of a similar length. They fall into four sets of three colons each. Each tricolon has a bicolon with classical incomplete synonymous parallelism with rhythmic compensation (9aA, 9bB, 10aA, 10bB). Each of these bicolons has a third colon with less parallelism. Verse 9a is addressed to Zion; v 9b describes the king; v 10a predicts the destruction of armaments; v 10b describes the final kingdom. The patterns within vv 9 and 10 are the same; both are chiastic. The final arrangement of the four tricolons also makes a chiasmus between the two middle colons.

Zechariah 9:9–10 has at least *a dozen* key vocabulary items in common with Micah 4–5, shown in **bold italic**. None of Zechariah's expressions can be identified as a quotation or adaptation from Micah. Yet they have the same technical connotations, some quite specialized. Placing Zech 9:9–10 alongside Micah 4–5 favors the same identification of the two expected rulers. The fervor aroused by Zerubbabel after the Exile gave passing vogue to the old oracles. By the same token, Micah 4–5 could have acquired its present form under similar historical circumstances.

COMMENT ON THE BOOK OF VISIONS: CHAPTERS 4–5

The literary integrity of the Book of Visions is indicated by its thematic coherence and structural organization. The same kind of poetic craftsmanship is used throughout. The recurrence of the same vocabulary and the marking of the ten constituent units with similar introductory formulas was discussed in the INTRODUCTION to the Book of Visions. The numerous interconnections achieved by these means have been pointed out in the NOTES above.

For convenience of reference we reproduce here the structure of the Book of Visions that was worked out in the INTRODUCTION. As discussed in the NOTES and COMMENTS, the structure secured by the four colons that begin with "and" plus a free personal pronoun coexists with and is superimposed on the structure created by the two sets of units that contain "now" and "and it will be." A somewhat similar display has been worked out by Luker (1987: 293).

STRUCTURE OF MICAH 4–5

324 syllables	4:1–5	wĕhāyâ bĕ'aḥărît hayyāmîm	Yahweh supreme in Zion	A
	4:5b	wa'ănaḥnû		
	4:6–7	bayyôm hahû' nĕ'ūm-yhwh	Yahweh rules his gathered people	B
	4:8	wĕ'attâ		
315 syllables	4:9–10a	'attâ	the anguish of Zion	C
	4:10b	kî 'attâ	redemption of Zion from Babylon	D
	4:11–13	wĕ'attâ	Zion defeats the nations	E
	4:12	wĕhēmmâ		
	4:14	'attâ	Zion (?) under threat	F
	5:1	wĕ'attâ		
	5:1–3	kî 'attâ	advent of the ruler	G
321 syllables	5:4–5	wĕhāyâ zeh šālôm	defeat of Assyria	H
	5:6	wĕhāyâ šĕ'ērît ya'ăqōb	the remnant benign	I
	5:7–8	wĕhāyâ šĕ'ērît ya'ăqōb	the remnant malign	J
	5:9–14	wĕhāyâ bayyôm hahû'	Israel cleansed and avenged	K

The opening section A (4:1–5) occupies a key position in the development of the whole. In fact 4:6–5:14 could be regarded as an extended exposition of the first oracle. The first vision (4:1–5) is really *the end* of the whole story, and its position at *the beginning* of the Book of Visions suggests various possible explanations of the literary development of the unit—how it was composed and how it should now be read. If 4:1–5 (or 4:1–3 at the very least) is accepted as authentic Micah, then the rest could be understood as an accretion around this nucleus by the addition of kindred pieces composed in circles that preserved and developed Micah's prophecies. It is more probable that the greater part of chapters 4–5 comes from Micah himself, and some of it possibly contains earlier traditions (notably 4:1–3 and the nucleus of 5:1) that Micah inherited and used for his own purposes. Materials that fit into an eighth-century setting may be attributed to Micah, particularly when they have so many close affinities with Isaiah of Jerusalem; but some parts make more sense against the background of the Exile, notably 4:9 (which implies an end of David's line), 4:10 (which at least anticipates, if it does not altogether presuppose, removal to Babylon), and the promises to the remnant (4:7; 5:6, 7).

The contrast between the latter passages and the oracle about an Assyrian invasion in 5:4 requires at least two stages in the composition of the whole. If Micah (or his immediate early editor) had a major hand in the planning of this section, then the addition of the passages that must be Exilic was a revision, an adjustment in light of later developments. If the extended eschatological passages are considered to be late, then the contribution of Micah himself is correspondingly smaller. These passages are the substance of chapters 4–5, not later comments attached to identifiable Micah sayings. To the extent that chapters 4–5 are a distinct "book," we almost have a case of "all or nothing." The main act of composition must have been performed during or shortly after Micah's lifetime or else during the Exile, but early in the Exile, and certainly not after it. The prospect of release from Babylon contains no hint that Persia will be God's agent (in contrast to Second Isaiah, which casts Cyrus explicitly in this role). Nor does it betray any awareness of the state of mind of the postexilic community, especially of the doubt and perplexity caused by the failure of the glorious promises of Second Isaiah, with which Micah 4–5 shows some affinity. In fact Micah anticipates that Zion will subdue the nations.

The historical background for such hopes was provided by memories of the golden age of Israelite imperialism, the age of David and Solomon. Traditions about these two kings contribute to the Book of Visions at several points. When Micah refers to "the nations," the focus is mostly on the neighboring peoples, precisely the ones that David conquered and Solomon held in fief, and over whom especially Jeroboam II and Uzziah scored impressive victories. It was indeed Hezekiah's success in overpowering the Philistine cities that brought the Assyrians back to that area. Given the traditions associated with David and his line, and the more vigorous kings of the north, the idea of Zion conquering nations and peoples was not so farfetched. When that kind of language is used, we naturally tend to think in terms of world powers like Egypt and Assyria. Israel rarely if ever matched up to them. When the prophets talk about dominion from sea to sea and from river to river, and even "to the ends of the earth," they have in mind primarily the area with which they, and the people of Israel, were only too familiar, and where the optimum goal was to consolidate the entire region under a single king. That may not have been realizable in its totality ever (except perhaps for David), but partial conquests and possible extensions were not only conceivable but plausible.

It is beyond the capacity of criticism to reconstruct in detail the literary processes by which Micah 4–5 reached its present form. In particular we do not know what proportion of the material and what measure of the eventual structure belongs in the earliest or latest stages of composition. The general theological stance has a lot in common with First Isaiah, including the eschatological development as well as the characteristic Zion ideology. These two, in fact, are inseparable, as their fusion in 4:1–3 makes plain. The common presupposition that hopes for the future were expressed in eschatological terms only after the Exile should be relinquished, or at least gravely questioned and modified. The early date of Mic 4:1–3 (whether by Micah or Isaiah or someone before them does not matter at this point of the discussion—see the Excursus on this special problem), once conceded, makes all the other eschatological passages associated with it here equally credible as products of the eighth century. Unfortunately, except for the naming of Assyria and Babylon, there are no historical allusions, or at least none that permit any identification of known persons or events. Any of the Assyrian invasions (5:4–5—H) with Jerusalem under siege (4:14—F) (it is by no means certain that these passages should be dated together) could be in mind. But the assault on Jerusalem by "many nations" (4:11–12—E) is quite vague, perhaps deliberately so, while the conquest of Assyria is predicted in a brief poem—H, lacking in detail and corresponding to no known historical event.

Problems of this kind are found throughout the entire Book of Visions. To the form critic it presents no *Gattungen* that can be identified with certainty. In spite of the use of the oracle formula (4:4b, 9a), there is no direct address to a familiar audience, such as is found in chapters 1–3. The address to Daughter-Zion from time to time and to Bethlehem (5:1) is rhetorical apostrophe; and the identity of *migdal-ʿeder* (4:8) or *bat-gĕdûd* (4:14), the other ones addressed, remains obscure. This feature, speaking to or about cities, reminds us of Mic 1:10–16 and points to the same author. But any historical reconstruction is largely guesswork. The interpreter is thus unable to achieve the first two requirements of literary-historical exegesis: to demonstrate a conventional form and to reconstruct the historical situation.

The problems of historical reconstruction and of literary analysis go hand in hand. This has been illustrated already by the presence of both Assyria and Babylon in the text. Unless both these powers are on the stage of history at the same time, we can preserve references to historical actuality only by apportioning these parts of the text to different dates. The more we emphasize the formal literary unity of the text in terms of cohesive structural features, as sketched above, the less immediately and firmly can the Book of Visions be attached to concrete events and specific dates. This is another reason for not allowing the apparently different historical backgrounds of individual parts to dismantle the overall literary structure.

The stance of the author is one of detachment; or rather his view achieves a time perspective that sees deep into the past and far into the future, from "the days of yore" (5:1) to "the end of time" (4:1). He gives a comment on Israel's present in terms of its past and future. His language about the past is drawn from myth and legend. He recreates the atmosphere of bygone days by using archaic words rather than familiar contemporary terms. Bethlehem is "Ephrata"; Assyria is "the land of Nimrod." The human leaders are called "Ruler," "Judge," "Shepherd," *nāsîk*, but not, apparently, "King" (see NOTE on 4:9b). The glimpses of the future transcend the bounds of historical possibility. They represent a particular kind of eschatological thinking that is characteristic of the eighth-century prophets (in contrast to postexilic apocalypticists). The predictions are visionary, imaginative, evocative, poetic, and contain much more than can be squeezed into a political commentary for the occasion. They extend into the universal, the cosmic. Thus the war passages seem more like the global battles of the End-time than any episode in ancient imperialism.

This point may be illustrated by one geopolitical feature. Jacob (Judah and Israel) is on stage with Assyria and Babylon (but not Egypt!). And Zion is the center of everything. But it is Yahweh who reigns (4:7) as Lord of the whole earth (an old title) (4:13). This terminology is associated with the language of the cult and has affinities with the ideology of the postexilic theocracy. That revision of political theory was itself imbued with elements drawn from the traditions about premonarchical times, fostered by the rising prestige of the Pentateuch in the postexilic community. The theocratic and hierocratic organization of Israel embodied in the priestly materials of the Pentateuch can be interpreted as apologetic creations composed to validate a relatively recent and largely novel worldview. As such the incorporation of this priestly tradition into the latest edition of the Torah was an anachronistic projection of postexilic thought into premonarchical times, as in classical Wellhausen criticism.

Both explanations (Micah's ideology is either preexilic or postexilic) have their adherents among Old Testament scholars. Those who are convinced, as are the present writers, that P is preexilic, or at least that the traditions in it are substantially preexilic, can more readily accept the possibility that Micah 4–5 is likewise preexilic. However, if the theory of the cult community presupposed in P is largely postexilic, with Yahweh exercising the functions previously lodged in the human king, then Micah 4–5 likewise should be located in these later times. Here the theory behind 4:1–5, with its strong cult overtones, is important, and the question of its date is crucial, especially since we have argued, on purely structural grounds, that the whole of the Book of Visions is built on this oracle. The lack of a human ruler in this first vision (it is misleading to call it "messianic") contrasts with the presence of the David tradition in other parts of the Book of Visions. The model for this future kingdom seems to be the empire of David (and Solomon) and behind that the old tribal confederation.

There was continuity in the theory of divine rule, in spite of radical political changes in practice. Psalm 2 shows that David's rule was legitimated by oracles that named him as the anointed agent of Yahweh's dominion over the nations (compare Mic 5:1). This mystique, never relinquished, in spite of the trauma that followed Solomon's death, was available to serve the national and religious fervor of subsequent times. In particular, such later kings as Hezekiah and

Josiah were hopefully cast in the mold of David by Isaiah and other prophets, encouraging quite unrealistic hopes of matching the superpowers with the puny forces of Judah, or, as they viewed it, with the invincible might of Yahweh.

Isaiah 36–39 was the ultimate expression of this unbeatable combination—Yahweh, Zion, David. One can guess why Josiah was so foolhardy as to defy Pharaoh Neco at Megiddo a century later. Jeremiah knew better. The vain aspirations aroused by Zerubbabel as a possible candidate for the vacant throne of David were the last flicker of hope sparked by such beliefs. But Psalm 89 records the spiritual agony of those who had experienced some threat to the continuation of David's line, a threat that threw doubt on the durability of the promises that Yahweh had made to David (2 Sam 7:15–16). Hosea, Micah, Isaiah, Jeremiah, and Ezekiel could all think of the future in terms of David; and even Second Isaiah (see Isa 55:3). But even in *their* prophecies historical realities have been replaced by apocalyptic dreams. These kept the hope alive, as Zechariah 9 shows.

It was not until the rise of the Hasmoneans that Israel had a power base that would lure the leaders into a bid by force for political (and also religious) national sovereignty. Micah 4–5 is a major expression of this tradition. Exactly where it comes in the long development of that tradition cannot now be determined. Palpably it contains ingredients from more than one stage in the unfolding of belief in David and his line as Yahweh's king in Zion. David's original mandate and his prophetic legitimation are still in evidence. The crisis of Micah's own time was the setting for a major restatement. The whole piece shows no sign of the anguish of those who saw the end of everything in the generation after Josiah. The hope for the future is finally stated in terms of escape from Babylon, but no human king is mentioned in that connection, unless in 2:12–13, where it is more likely that the king is Yahweh (see the NOTE there).

The earlier picture of the ruler and shepherds who will subdue Assyria could hardly have been concocted after 600 B.C.E., when the downfall of Assyria was complete. Yet it was retained in the text, although it never had, and now never could have, any historical fulfillment. Conquest of Assyria was never a realistic expectation. As Isa 52:4 shows, the counterpoise of Egypt and Mesopotamia remained the political setting of Israel's plight, with Shinar (Isa 11:11; Zech 5:11), Assyria, Babylon all serving equally well as the name for the latter. So the use of "Assyria" in Mic 5:5–6 could be exilic, but only in that symbolic sense. The idea of Israel actually conquering Mesopotamia is developed even further than anything ever achieved by David, and it is stated in extravagant terms as the act of Daughter-Zion (E) and of the remnant of Jacob (J). These passages can be understood as a reaffirmation of the earlier unfulfilled program in terms of more contemporary realities. Whatever the mix of eighth-century originals and sixth-century additions or modifications, the Book of Visions bears little resemblance to subsequent history. All that later commentators could do was to spiritualize its meaning.

It is unlikely that people with realistic experiences and memories of history would be taken in by the extravagant promise of Mic 5:7–8. It sounds so much like the protreptic magic of Zedekiah ben Chenaanah (2 Kgs 22:11—the report is a parody), that one might ask if the oracle in Mic 5:7–8 is sarcastic. Noting the affinities between 5:7–8 and 2:12–13, van der Woode (1969, 1973) identified nationalistic "Zion" prophecies as "false," the message of the prophets that Micah opposed. See Sanders (1977: 25). But, if that were the case, why are they not identified more clearly as such, so that the naive reader will not take them as gospel?

III. THE BOOK OF CONTENTION
AND CONCILIATION
(MICAH 6–7)

◆

INTRODUCTION TO MICAH 6–7

We have called the third part of the book of Micah *The Book of Contention and Conciliation*. This title is generally appropriate, for the contents deal with these themes. The contention takes the form of a covenant dispute or *rîb*. The "book" begins with a double statement that Yahweh has a *rîb* with his people (6:2), and in 7:9 the prophet says in behalf of Israel that he will endure the indignation of Yahweh until the exercise is complete. This attitude shows very clearly that the condemnation of Israel takes place *within* an ongoing covenant relationship. The ambivalence of that relationship found its classical expression in the self-disclosure and self-definition that Yahweh gave to Moses at Horeb (Exodus 32–34). Side by side in a single speech are the contradictory assertions that Yahweh forgives iniquity and transgression and sin and that he will by no means clear the guilty (Exod 34:7). These opposing policies are resolved in the mystery of Yahweh's *ḥesed*, which is unlimited. The book of Micah ends with a reassertion of these ancient truths, using the traditional language (7:18). The key word *ḥesed* occurs twice here. It defines, not only the essential character of Yahweh but the required behavior of humans (6:8). God wants his people to be like himself, and he never gives up working on this project.

The themes of condemnation and forgiveness are intertwined throughout these final chapters. Their organization, however, is not straightforward; it is hard to find any overarching structure. Certainly the tones of reproach (6:3) and of accusation (6:9–12) are struck in chapter 6, followed by threats that echo the old covenant curses (6:13–16). In contrast, chapter 7 contains lamentation (7:1–6), which could express penitence, leading to confidence (7:7–12), vindication (7:13–17), and the final harmony of the covenant restored (7:18–20). The continual change of mood and the movement of thought from disputation to reconciliation thus make general sense. But the literary identity of the constituent units and their cohesion into an integral literary composition is not so easy to trace.

So far as chapter 6 is concerned, it may be divided into two parts, two distinct oracles, different in content and tone. The first (Yahweh's Covenant Dispute [6:1–8]) is an encounter between Yahweh and Israel. After the opening announcement that Yahweh is about to engage in a dispute (*rîb*), one expects charges to be laid. That does not happen immediately. In his classic study *Basic Forms of Prophetic Speech*, Westermann (1967) showed that in prophetic judgment speeches an accused person or nation could be confronted with the wrongdoing in several ways. The most direct means is a "declaratory sentence" ("You have done such-and-such"). "[T]his speech form stems from the regular judicial procedure" (Westermann 1967: 146). Less direct are questions of various kinds and pronouncements of "Woe!" In Mic 6:1–8 there is no formal indictment, so Yahweh's speech is not developed along the conventional lines of customary litigation. There is questioning, but it is startlingly different. Yahweh asks about his own conduct, not Israel's. Instead, with disarming candor, Yahweh strikes a conciliatory note from the beginning, with the astonishing suggestion that perhaps he has been at fault, inviting them to lodge their complaints against him, if they wish (v 3). The speech contains reminders of some notable moments in the past experience of Israel with Yahweh (6:4–5). The people are urged to *remember* (6:5). Israel is unable to say anything in direct answer to the question. The brief summary recitation of *the righteous acts of Yahweh* (6:5bB), the centuries-long story of Yahweh and Israel serves as a protestation of Yahweh's blamelessness; a vindication, a justification.

The second part of chapter 6 renews the call to attention (v 9b). This completes a series of six such calls, three in the Book of Doom (chapters 1–3) and three in chapters 6–7, a strong link between the first and the third parts of the whole book. The second section of chapter 6 contains a bill of charges (6:9–12) and goes on with threats of punishment (6:13–16). The penalties are assigned in the form of the curses on covenant breaches, again drawn from traditional formulations. The two parts of chapter 6 are thus complementary.

Looking further ahead, the ominous tone of condemnation and threat that dominates chapter 6 is not superseded until the evangelical note is sounded at its clearest in 7:18–20. To arrive at this restoration Israel must pass through the spiritual discipline of suffering and purgation under *the indignation of Yahweh* (7:9aA). The loss of well-being (6:14–15; 7:1) induces penitence, expressed in grief. As in 1:8–16, the revelation of impending doom is followed by lamentation (7:1–6). In these depths, the prophet, speaking personally and also in behalf of a chastened Israel, is able to wait in hope. Several things have to be set right. Broken community relationships (7:5–6) have to be mended. The desolate land (7:13) will become fertile pasture once more (7:14–15). The nations (7:16) and one particular enemy (7:8) will be confounded and subjugated (7:16–17 — this picks up a theme from chapter 5). Finally the reconciled remnant celebrates the incredible *ḥesed* of Yahweh expressed in unqualified forgiveness (7:18–20).

III.1. YAHWEH'S COVENANT DISPUTE (6:1–8)

III.1.i. YAHWEH'S INDICTMENT (6:1–5)

TRANSLATION

MT

1a	*šim'û-nā' 'ēt 'ăšer-yhwh 'ōmēr*	Listen [2d m. pl.] now to what Yahweh is saying ...
1bA	*qûm rîb 'et-hehārîm*	Stand up [2d m. sg.]! Dispute [2d m. sg.] with the mountains!
1bB	*wĕtišma'nâ haggĕbā'ôt qôlekā*	And let the hills hear thy [m.] voice!
2aA	*šim'û hārîm 'et-rîb yhwh*	Listen, mountains, to Yahweh's dispute,
2aB	*wĕhā'ētānîm mōsĕdê 'āreṣ*	and everlasting foundations of Earth!
2bA	*kî rîb l-yhwh 'im-'ammô*	For Yahweh has a dispute with his people,
2bB	*wĕ'im-yiśrā'ēl yitwakkāḥ*	and with Israel he will argue.
3aA	*'ammî meh-'āśîtî lĕkā*	My people! What have I done to thee [m.]?
3aB	*ûmâ hel'ētîkā*	And how have I wearied thee [m.]?
3b	*'ănēh bî*	Answer [2d m. sg.] me!
4aA	*kî he'ĕlitîkā mē'ereṣ miṣrayim*	For I brought thee [m.] up from the land of Egypt,
4aB	*ûmibbêt 'ăbādîm pĕdîtîkā*	and from the house of slaves I redeemed thee [m.];
4b	*wā'ešlaḥ lĕpāneykā* *'et-mōšeh 'ahărōn ûmiryām*	and I sent before thee [m.] Moses, Aaron, and Miriam.
5aAα	*'ammî zĕkor-nā'*	My people! Do remember [2d m. sg.]! ...
5aAβ	*mah-yā'aṣ bālāq melek mô'āb*	What did Balaq king of Moab scheme?
5aB	*ûmeh-'ānâ 'ōtô bil'ām ben-bĕ'ôr*	And how did Bil'am son of Be'or answer him,
5bA	*min-haššiṭṭîm 'ad-haggilgāl*	from Shittim to Gilgal?
5bB	*lĕma'an da'at ṣidqôt yhwh*	... so as to know the righteous acts of Yahweh.

LXX III.1.i. Kyrios' Indictment (6:1–5)

1a	Hear [pl.] indeed the word of Kyrios! Kyrios said ...
1bA	Stand up [sg.]! Be judged [sg.] before the mountains!
1bB	And let the hills hear thy voice!
2aA	Hear, mountains, Kyrios' dispute (*krisis*),
2aB	and (you) chasms, foundations of Earth!
2bA	For Kyrios has a dispute (*krisis*) with his people,
2bB	and with Israel he will argue.
3aA	My people! What have I done to thee?
3aB	Or how have I grieved thee?
	⟨Or how have I troubled thee?⟩
3b	Answer [sg.] me!
4aA	For I brought thee up from the land of Egypt,
4aB	and from a house of slavery I redeemed thee;
4b	and I sent before thee Moses, and Aaron, and Miriam.

5aAα	My people! Remember [sg.] indeed !
5aAβ	What did Balak king of Moab counsel against thee?
5aB	And how did Balaam son of Beor answer him,
5bA	from the reeds to Gilgal?
5bB	So that the righteousness of Kyrios might be known.

III.1.ii. ISRAEL'S RESPONSE (6:6–7)

TRANSLATION

MT

6aA	*bammâ ʾăqaddēm yhwh*	With what shall I enter Yahweh's presence?
6aB	*ʾikkap lēʾlōhê mārôm*	(With what) shall I bow down to the God of the height?
6bA	*haʾăqaddĕmennû bĕʿôlôt*	Shall I enter into his presence with burnt offerings,
6bB	*baʿăgālîm bĕnê šānâ*	with calves sons of a year?
7aA	*hăyirṣeh yhwh bĕʾalpê ʾēlîm*	Will Yahweh be pleased with thousands of rams,
7aB	*bĕribĕbôt naḥălê-šāmen*	with myriads of torrents of oil?
7bA	*haʾettēn bĕkôrî pišʿî*	Shall I give my eldest son for my transgression,
7bB	*pĕrî biṭnî ḥaṭṭaʾt napšî*	the fruit of my body for the sin of my soul?

LXX III.1.ii. Israel's Response (6:6–7)

6aA	With what shall I take hold of Kyrios?
6aB	Shall I lay hold of my God most high?
6bA	Shall I take hold of him with burnt offerings,
6bB	with calves one year old?
7aA	Will Kyrios be pleased with thousands of rams,
7aB	and myriads of fat goats?
7bA	Should I give my firstborn for ungodliness,
7bB	the fruit of my belly for the sin of my soul?

III.1.iii. YAHWEH'S REMEDY (6:8)

TRANSLATION

MT

8aA	*higgîd lĕkā ʾādām*	He told thee, O man,
8aB	*mah-ṭôb*	What is good?
8bAα	*ûmâ-yhwh dôrēš mimmĕkā*	And what is Yahweh seeking from thee?
8bAβ	*kî ʾim-ʿăśôt mišpāṭ*	Only to do justice,
8bB	*wĕʾahăbat ḥesed*	to love ḥesed,
8bC	*wĕhaṣnēaʿ leket ʿim-ʾĕlōheykā*	and to walk humbly with thy [m.] God.

LXX III.1.iii. Kyrios' Remedy (6:8)

8aA	Has it been told to you, O Man (*anthropos*),
8aB	what is good?
8bAα	Or what does Kyrios require from thee
8bAβ	but to do justice (*krima*),
8bB	to love mercy (*eleos*),
8bC	and to be ready to walk with Kyrios thy God.

INTRODUCTION TO MICAH 6:1–8

The confrontation between Yahweh and Israel is a climax in the book of Micah. It has been made famous by the popularity of its crowning verse (6:8), rightly celebrated as the supreme definition of ethical religion, "a verse often regarded as one of the great moral breakthroughs in history" (Frye 1982: 184). The "good" life, as defined here, is not "religious" at all, not if religion is thought of in terms of institutions (temple, synagogue, church) and ceremonies. The essence of what God himself expects from humans is:

> Only to do justice
> And to love goodness,
> And to walk modestly with your God. (NJPS)

"This is the greatest saying of the Old Testament" (G. A. Smith 1899, 2:425). It was the centerpiece of Robertson Smith's eloquent and enormously influential Eighth Lecture on "The Prophets of Israel" (1882).

The Constituents of Micah 6

The major components of the Book of Contention (chapters 6–7) are marked off by clear signals of the onset of each new unit. The complaint or lament (*Woe to me!*) in 7:1 marks a fresh beginning. Chapter 6 has two main portions, each marked by the call *Listen!* (vv 1, 9b). There is a very difficult question concerning v 9a, which is quite obscure, as is everything in v 9 except the word *Listen!* Verse 9a is so unintelligible that it may prove impossible to decide whether it is an afterthought to vv 1–8 (as in NJPS) or a lead-in to v 9b. The ending of v 8 is so splendid and final that any additional comment would be anticlimactic. The Masoretic Text has an open paragraph division after v 8, and the decision of NJPS to override it is puzzling.

In all its other occurrences *šimʿû* (1:2; 3:1, 9; 6:1, 2) begins a new speech without preamble except that the Book of Contention has a double beginning. By taking the first word in v 9, *qôl*, as an imperative—*Listen!*—NIV finds a similar double beginning for the second part of chapter 6. Other translations and commentaries interpret v 9a as a preliminary identification of the speaker of v 9b as Yahweh (*The voice of Yahweh* . . .). NJPS attaches v 9a to v 8, making it a kind of colophon, in which *the voice of Yahweh* makes an inclusion with *thy voice* in v 1bB, finally identifying the main speaker in vv 1–8 as Yahweh. REB preempts this by supplying "God" as the otherwise unidentified speaker of v 8. This is hardly necessary, since it is quite clear that vv 1–8 report a disputation of Yahweh *with his people* (v 2bA) in the hearing of the mountains (v 2aA). In this disputation Yahweh addresses his people (*My people!* [v 3aA]) in vv 3–5; they respond in vv 6–7; and Yahweh (or the prophet speaking in behalf of Yahweh) gives the correct answer in v 8.

Nevertheless, v 8 stands apart from the rest. It begins abruptly, without any information about the speaker. One can appreciate the need felt by the REB translators to supply this lack ("The LORD has told you mortals what is good"). In v 8 the speaker presumably addresses the person who has just made the speech in vv 6–7, calling him "Adam." The transition detaches v 8 somewhat from the preceding discourse. Perhaps v 8 is a distinct unit, centrally placed between the two parts of the disputation (vv 1–7 and 9–16).

Verses 1–8 are recognized as a unit in the traditional divisions of the Masoretic Text. The participants in the dramatic dialogue can be identified by means of vocative nouns when they are present:

Verse 1a	Unidentified "you" (m. pl.)
Verse 1b	Unidentified "thou" (m. sg.)
Verse 1bB	"Hills" (indirect precative with 3d f. pl. jussive)
Verse 2	"Mountains"
Verses 3–5	"My people," i.e., Israel (named in v 2, the only occurrence in this chapter)
Verses 6–7	No intended audience identified; presumably Yahweh is (indirectly) addressed ("Yahweh" in vv 6aA, 7aA = "thou"[?])
Verse 8	"Adam" ("man," i.e., everyman[?])

There is no identification of the speaker at any point. The prophet delivers the whole discourse, or rather the editor has written it up as a report of such a proclamation (Deissler 1959). It is a dramatic monologue, all recited by the prophet. It was actually, in Micah's utterance (or notionally, in the editor's presentation) addressed to "Israel" or to some audience or group of intended readers as representative of the whole nation. That, at least, is how the piece begins. The opening call—*Hear* (pl.) *indeed what Yahweh is saying!* (v 1a)—shows that an oracular message is about to be delivered. The verb *šimʿû* is used in this way in 1:2; 3:1, 9. The three occurrences with *-nāʾ* (3:1, 9; 6:1) constitute a series, and the pattern suggests strongly that the addressees of 6:1 are the same as those in chapter 3, namely, "the heads of the House of Jacob." These leaders were responsible, and are being held responsible, for the well-being of the whole nation.

The formal address changes to *my people* (vv 3, 5). In 2:4, 8, 9; 3:3, 5, "my people" are the victims of oppression and cruelty. In chapter 6:1–5 the people are not distinguished from the leaders. They are all held responsible for what is wrong. But in 6:9–16 wicked merchants (vv 10–12) and perhaps kings (v 16) are singled out for special blame.

In an earlier discussion we have demonstrated, or at least argued, for the integrity of chapters 4–5 as a large unit (a "book"). The thematic connections between chapter 3 and chapter 6 suggest that the Book of Visions has been placed within (and breaks apart) the discourse that began in the Book of Doom (chapters 1–3) and is resumed in chapter 6. Recognition of this connection authorizes the use of details in chapter 3 to help solve problems in chapter 6.

The Drama of Micah 6:1–8

In the presence of the people, or of their representative heads, the prophet invokes the mountains and foundations of Earth (v 2a) to listen to Yahweh's *rîb* (v 2b). The summons is conventional, a traditional acknowledgment of cosmic elements as original and continuing witnesses to the foundational covenant agreement and ongoing relationship between Yahweh and Israel (Delcor 1966). In the drama that unfolds the mountains have no active role. They fade into the background. The mythological component is minimal. The cosmic powers do not do or say anything.

Yahweh can be identified as the speaker of vv 3–5. These words are addressed to *my people*. The second-person masculine singular pronouns show that the nation as a personified entity and as a whole is being interrogated. Verses 6–7 follow immediately with no formal identification of the speaker. Someone responds on behalf of the people, but how are we to imagine this as actually being done? This is not a transcript of a trial conducted according to established procedures. Normal procedure would be to begin by laying charges against the accused; yet Yahweh does not bring accusations against them for their unsatisfactory conduct, for breaches of the covenant, as one would have expected from the way the *rîb* begins. Rather he raises questions about his own possibly unsatisfactory conduct. He invites the people to get in first with their complaints against him, if they have any.

The prophet puts into the mouth of an unidentified speaker a possible response (vv 6–7) to Yahweh's questions. Like Yahweh's opening speech, this response is out of line with what would happen in a court of law. There the accused would either confess guilt or protest innocence. Or, in this case, answering Yahweh's questions, bring a countercomplaint against him. Instead, the people bring a matching set of questions. Yahweh asked four questions and they ask four questions. The logical or organic connection of the people's response with the preceding speech by Yahweh is not direct. To discover the coherence of the dramatic recital of this imagined dialogue requires some rather devious analysis, since the roles and interactions of the two protagonists (antagonists)—Yahweh and Israel—do not conform to a standard *rîb* pattern as it has been worked out in contemporary scholarship (Nielsen 1978). Yahweh is not directly addressed in vv 6–7. In fact, the language implies that he is inaccessible.

The two parties are separated by the breach. Yahweh speaks to them, but they do not respond to him. The manner of their speech discloses their feeling of rejection, of alienation. It also implies a desire on their part to recover the lost relationship. It assumes that the relationship can be restored. In fact, the very circumstance that this dialogue is taking place at all in a mode that sounds like negotiation shows that the relationship is still operating, albeit disharmoniously. The covenant is still in place, but it requires rectification. Hence the inquiries as to the ways and means to reestablish harmony.

It is difficult to keep the intensely personal and dynamic relationship between Yahweh and Israel within a legalistic and constitutional set of constraints, worked out according to the considerations of formal justice. There is tension between the judicial background that supplies some of the concepts and vocabulary for this dispute and the literary expression of the emotional and interpersonal dimensions of the covenant in their dramatic outworking.

The Literary Genre of Micah 6:1–8

So far as the literary classification of Mic 6:1–8 is concerned, this unit presents features and problems similar to some already met in Micah's other compositions. His oracle-poems sometimes start off in one genre and then switch, or rather dissolve, into another, and then another. Thus chapter 1 begins with an invocation similar to that which begins chapter 6, switches to a theophany, proceeds to use rhetorical questions to make accusations, pronounces or threatens judgment, and goes on to lamentation.

It is greatly to the credit of the discipline of form criticism that it has recognized the various affinities of the components of such mixed compositions. It is a common vice of form criticism to categorize literary entities too rigidly (P. Watson 1963). Having recognized the dominant genre of a piece—let us say a lament—the critic proceeds to use the classification as an instrument of interpretation, assuming that the composition has its conventional function as, in the case of a lament, a sincere expression of misery or grief. But a lament can be recited perversely as an expression of scorn, taunting a defeated foe, for instance. Form and function may be skewed.

Equally unimaginative and sometimes mischievous has been the use of form criticism as a tool for text criticism. In the case of laments, the belief that they should be composed in *qinah* meter (3 : 2 beats) has provided scholars with a basis for repairing supposedly damaged texts by making them fit that meter. We saw this in the case of Mic 1:10–16.

Form criticism has not been very successful in handling compositions of mixed genre, such as are often encountered in prophetic books. The variety of genres present in chapter 1 has been explained by finding in each specimen of a distinct genre a fragment, so that the chapter as a whole is not seen as a unified composition but rather as a collection of small, possibly incomplete, oracles, loosely connected if they are connected at all. The prophetic disputation in Mic 6:1–8 is unique (Murray 1987) in biblical literature.

Our studies of the earlier portions of the book of Micah, particularly the Book of Doom (chapters 1–3), have already shown that these principles of interpretation do not work for those materials. Like other prophets, and especially like his contemporary Isaiah, Micah violates all three of these canons. He does not compose his poems line by line in uniform meter; he does not use just one distinct literary genre for each separate composition; and he does not always use a piece in accordance with the social conventions that govern the normal function of its genre.

Such sometimes puzzling practices in the original and creative use of Israel's traditional literary forms are well recognized in the case of Isaiah. The term *māšāl* ("proverb," "figure," or "parable") is sometimes used to refer to such artistic use of a composition, such as a song of grief turned into a mock dirge for threatening or perhaps taunting an enemy rather than for mourning him (Isa 14:4; Hab 2:6; the same idiom as in Mic 2:4). A "woe" oracle, normally an expression of personal misery, can be uttered, not as a lament for oneself, but as a remonstration or as a threat against evildoers in (perhaps malicious) anticipation of the sorrow that they will experience when judgment falls on them. Pieces used in this way are intended to have an effect quite opposite from the usual one.

Because Isaiah announces that he is going to sing "a love song" (*šîrat dôdî*) (Isa 5:1), it does not follow that the ensuing recital is a love song from beginning to end. Isaiah 5:1–7 is an oracle-poem that mixes ingredients from a variety of genres. The classification of "the song of the vineyard" in Isa 5:1–7 is the despair of form critics so long as they are searching for one label to attach to the whole piece. Willis (1977) lists eleven different theories as to what Isa 5:1–7 is. As a result of the sustained debate of this problem in recent years (Evans 1984, Graffy 1979, Junker 1959, Korpel 1988, Loretz 1975, Lys 1974, Schottroff 1970, Sheppard 1982, Willis 1977, Yee 1981), scholars have come slowly to the realization that successful interpretation of this piece has to cope with the blending into one poem of passages that imitate various traditional categories of composition but do not follow their canons. Isa 5:1–7 is unique. Even Yee, who classifies it as a "juridical parable," has to recognize a "major departure" from or "significant modification" (1981: 36) of the form that she has found elsewhere. In our opinion, by concentrating on the juridical affinities of the song, Yee has not been sufficiently attentive to the affinities of the piece with wisdom literature, as pointed out by Whedbee (1971: 43–51).

Similar considerations apply to the study of the form and interpretation of Mic 6:1–8. Micah's poem shares with Isaiah's the rhetorical use of interrogation. Both include a recital of the benevolent actions of Yahweh. Just as Isaiah begins by giving his poem a title that creates the expectation that it is going to be a love song and then turns it in other directions, so Micah begins by setting things up for a covenant lawsuit (*rîb*) and then fails to follow the usual procedure for such an exercise.

Mendenhall's observation (1955) that Yahweh's covenant with Israel resembled ancient suzerainty treaties had widespread and lasting influence on research into biblical accounts of confrontation between Yahweh and Israel. The formulation of covenant disputations was thought to imitate juridical procedures for dealing with breaches of various contracts (reviewed by Clark in Hayes 1974: 135–36). Following a basic statement by Gemser (1955), numerous studies (Harvey 1962, 1967; Huffmon 1959, 1966; Limburg 1969) have explored the details and worked out the standard "form" for the conduct of a *rîb* or "prophetic lawsuit" (Nielsen 1978).

The constituents of a covenant dispute conducted as a lawsuit arising from the constitutional documents of a vassal treaty have been worked out by Huffmon (1959), Harvey (1962), Wright (1962), Limburg (1969) and others. Fensham (1962), Clements (1965), Westermann (1967), and Wolff look to the analogy of process in Israel's civil courts. Psalm 50 is a specimen of the latter. A typical result of the formal, analogical approach identifies the following components:

- A summons to the custodians of the covenant to supervise the dispute (Ps 50:1–6 — Mic 6:1).
- Accusation or interrogation of the accused (Ps 50:16–20 — Mic 6:2, 3).
- A recital of Yahweh's deeds, vindicating his side of the matter (Mic 6:4–5).
- A rejection of sacrifice as a means to reconciliation (Ps 50:8–13 — Mic 6:6, 7).
- Either a verdict or an exhortation to make the right kind of reparations (Ps 50:14–15; 22–23 — Mic 6:8).

Side by side with this kind of investigation, research that goes back to Gunkel's earlier work found the background for prophetic judgment speeches in Israel's juridical procedures. The earlier preference was to locate them in the secular courts, particularly a civil process in the city gate. The presence of cultic language suggested to other scholars that temple rituals supplied the background (Hentschke 1957). Thus Würthwein (1952: 1–16) observed that the affinities of Mic 6:1–5 with the cult show that the poem derives from temple ceremonial "in einer kultischen Gerichtszene" (1952: 15). Beyerlin understood the process somewhat differently. The prophet had not adapted cultic language for prophetic purposes; rather he had taken older traditional materials, particularly those associated with the Sinai covenant, and "clothed them in cultic forms" (1959: 96). Beyerlin identified Mic 3:5–8, 9–12; 6:9–16 as well as 6:1–8 as having this character. Similarly Boecker (1964: 101–5). Ramsay (1977) concluded that Mic 6:1–8 reflects procedures in a lawsuit liturgy in the cult rather than use by the prophet of a form of litigation followed in secular courts. Some scholars even identified prophets as cultic officials. Wolff's opposite claim, that Micah was a village elder who had duties in the secular courts, is an understandable reaction against such one-sided location of the prophets in the cultus; but it goes too far in the opposite direction.

The point has now been reached where the very existence of the supposed "prophetic (or covenant) lawsuit" genre has been questioned. "Since *rîb* does not mean 'lawsuit,' but describes the ordinary experience of confronting someone with a complaint, there is no need to invoke judicial forms to interpret these passages and then try to formulate reasons why the oracles deviate from these same forms" (de Roche 1983: 571). See also Daniels (1987) and Reventlow (1996). In any case, the application of these approaches to the interpretation of Mic 6:1–8 has not been very successful. It does not fit the models at many points. Hillers (1984: 77) is obliged to recognize that the form is "incomplete and truncated."

The literary background of the constituents of Mic 6:1–8 is diverse. It seems to be a mix of genres. The opening verses (vv 1–3) announce that there is going to be a dispute (the root *ryb* is used three times). The invocation of the mountains as witnesses of the proceedings has affinities with other covenant disputation oracles, such as Isaiah 1, that have often been pointed out. Compare Mic 1:2. The language of vv 4–5 is that of the creedal recital of the mighty acts of Yahweh. It has been amply demonstrated by Begrich (1936), Beyerlin (1959), and others that the setting of vv 6–7 is cultic, either a Torah liturgy (Gunkel-Begrich 1933: 327, 408) or Temple-entrance ritual (Koch 1969: 30, 32) of which vv 6–7 are only a fragment. Lescow (1972b: 187–90) has pointed out ways in which the language actually used does not fit either of these identifications. While not denying the cultic background, he concludes from the unique features of Micah's composition that "Die Frage kann also nur eine vom Propheten selbst so formulierte prinzipielle und polemische sein" (1972b: 190). In other words, the prophet's adaptation of this material cuts across established usage in a startling way. Clements (1965: 83) recognized Isa 33:14–16 and Mic 6:6–8 as "prophetic imitations of the entrance-liturgies of Israel's sanctuaries." He was obliged to concede that "these two examples are not actual entrance-liturgies of the cult, but oracles modelled on them." Micah 6:6–8 is not itself an "oracle" in the technical sense; it is an integral part of a larger and more complex prophetic discourse that moves to its climax in v 8, where the language does become oracular. The way the drama of successful admittance to the sacred precincts is used to symbolize and ritualize acceptance by God (present in the shrine) does not permit Micah's language to be turned into a radical rejection of temple worship as such. He is not giving a "caricature" of "hypocrisy" (Craigie 1985: 46).

The final item in the unit (v 8) is different again. Although its background is harder to place, some of its vocabulary has more affinities with wisdom ethics (Fohrer 1968: 446) than with Torah regulations or covenant stipulations. In any case, in this climactic and conclusive position, v 8 does not fit the model of a prophetic lawsuit as generally recognized by form criticism. When too much is made of the diversity of the components, they are found to be so incongruent and so incompatible, that no literary unity is perceived in the oracle at all. Thus Lescow (1966: 46; 1972b: 187), struck by the difference between the juridical background of vv 1–5 and the cultic background of vv 6–7 can find no connection between them at all. Renaud (1977: 301) lists the names of other scholars who find these two portions (or even more than two) independent, at least originally.

We agree with the conclusion of Renaud that Mic 6:1–8 is an original composition of the prophet (1977: 314) who has "reused diverse literary forms in a free and flexible fashion." Where Renaud finds two elements—covenant indictment (*réquisitoire*) and sacerdotal Torah, we find as well a catechismal form of creedal recital and wisdom ethics. Knowledge of this diverse background and of these literary affinities assists interpretation, but the comparative methodology is misused when those identifications are imposed too rigidly on the whole piece.

Isaiah calls his piece a love song, but it turns out to be the very opposite. It is full of condemnation and rejection. Micah calls his piece a disputation, but the argument turns into an appeal for reconciliation. Both prophets begin by announcing a known genre, a love song in the case of Isaiah, a *rîb* in the case of Micah. Each prophet then proceeds to turn the genre upside down. Isaiah's love song becomes a judgment speech; Micah's lawsuit switches from confrontation to conciliation.

The Poetry of Micah 6:1–8

As an artistic composition, vv 1–8 are clearly poetic. Guided by the Masoretic punctuation, we find twenty-nine colons in the unit. Most of the colons are just one clause or else incomplete clauses in a parallel position (vv 2aB, 6bB, 7aB, 7bB). At some points there are longer clauses that do not scan readily (vv 4b, 8b) or that have no parallel (v 1a). There are a few prose particles, e.g., the use of *'ōtô* rather than a suffixed pronoun in v 5aB; but there are several places where the prose particles might have been used but were not. For example, *nota accusativi* is used with only one of the three objects in v 4b (the three objects are coordinated, and the one *nota accusativi* brackets them as a single group, indicating joint leadership). Suffixed nouns as objects do not have *'et*, in keeping with Micah's general practice. There are no prose particles at all in vv 6–7, in spite of many opportunities. These two quatrains are the most finished of all the poetic portions in the whole unit. In v 7b none of the noun phrases has the expected prepositions (the objects should have *'et*, the object complements should have *l-*). In contrast with the ample use of particles and prepositions elsewhere in this unit, which contributes to the solemn effect of the longer-than-average colons, their omission here in v 7b makes the speech laconic and compact, hurried and frantic, as befits the desperate mood of the speaker.

As already noted, the parallel questions make an important contribution to the structural connections between Yahweh's speech in vv 3–5 and the response in vv 6–7. There are two pairs of parallel questions in each speech.

The grouping of colons into larger units is more important than isolating them in pairs to make bicolons. Even so, there are in this unit enough bicolons of classical merit to show that Micah is as much a poet as any prophet. The bicolon in v 1b has the second colon longer (10 syllables) than the first (6 syllables), but the total length is just right (16 syllables). The two commands are parallel in thought, and *the mountains // the hills* are a standard pair. The command to speak is given obliquely in the second colon: *And let the hills hear thy voice!* The same pattern, imperative followed by jussive (*tišmaʿ!*) is used in Deut 32:1, a similar invocation.

The grammar of the nouns in v 2aB is problematical. If the whole phrase *wĕhā'ētānîm mōsĕdê 'āreṣ*, "and everlasting foundations of Earth," is a match for *hārîm*, "mountains," in v 2aA, then only one of the three items in that colon has a parallel. The length (17 syllables) is standard. The bicolon in v 2b is impeccable; the nouns are synonyms, the verb in v 2bB is placed chiastically (cf. v 4a) with a verbless predication in v 2bA.

The complex speech in vv 3–4 is a nice illustration of the mingling of some well-formed bicolons with pieces that have no matches, but which are integral to the syntax and structure of the whole. The two terse parallel questions in v 3 leave *'ammî . . . 'ănēh bî* as an envelope around them. This broken clause matches *'ammî zĕkor-nā'* in v 5aAα. The bicolon in v 4a tells the Exodus story as briefly as can be, using traditional language with the verbs placed chiastically (17 syllables). This is followed by a statement that is not poetic at all by the usual criteria (v 4b). The very uniqueness of the statement (the only mention of Miriam outside the Pentateuch) makes its authenticity indisputable. So we have a combination of two good bicolons with two small pieces and one long piece, an integral composition. Verse 5aB is a long colon (11 syllables) that matches a shorter question in v 5aAβ. Are the two prepositional phrases in v 5bA (*from Shittim to Gilgal*) a continuation of this story? This colon has no parallel, nor does v 5bB. While it is true that Shittim was the location of the Moabite troubles, Gilgal is significant as the main camp after the crossing of the river Jordan. So v 5bA charts a major part of the journey, completing the Exodus. Verse 5bA goes more appropriately with v 4a, making an inclusion. And the final colon (v 5bB) does not go at all with the preceding questions. It gives the reason for the whole exercise of remembering, "so that you might know the righteous acts of Yahweh." Verse 5bB thus closes out the whole speech.

These observations turn traditional criticism upside down. Criticism often regards such unmatched colons and isolated pieces as not belonging in the poem, as spoiling it. They can be set aside as debris of damaged bicolons, if original, or more likely as marginal glosses wrongly taken by a subsequent copyist as part of the text. That may sometimes be the case. We consider, however, that it is precisely because such colons do not have a match adjacent to them that we should study the text more carefully to see if such single colons function at a longer range. We suggest that longer-range connections help to bind everything together. A single colon at the end, or near the end, of a unit often matches something at or near the beginning, constituting an inclusion. The same device is used on an elaborate scale in v 16, where several unmatched statements are echoes of themes and motifs found earlier in the chapter.

Such compositional features are characteristic of prophetic poetry; in fact Mic 6:1–8 is an excellent specimen of the art. At no point is a correction of the text indicated for strictly poetic considerations. The least poetic component (v 8) is considered a high point in prophetic teaching and is about the only part of the unit that has not attracted text-critical improvements. The only suggestion we have come across is in Schwantes (1962: 156), who deletes *'hbt* on the grounds that this "verb is never used with *ḥsd*." But it is used here! It is specious to imply that the only passable Hebrew idioms are those attested more than once.

NOTES AND COMMENTS

Notes on Micah 6:1–8

1. *Listen.* In his dramatic role as the one who summons the disputants and witnesses to the *rîb*, the prophet is a kind of officer of the court. Whether he serves as a kind of monitor of the proceedings in the prophet's traditional capacity as mediator of the covenant is less clear. While some aspects of customary juridical procedure supply the background and even technical vocabulary (the parallel verbs in v 2b), it would be going too far to try to use an actual trial as a model for finding one's way through this text. Too many essential features are missing. There is no formal indictment; no judge is named as such; there is no pronouncement of the outcome of the *rîb* in the form of a verdict or imposition of punishment. Established juridical procedures have not driven the dramatic form, and conventional forms of speech as used "in the gate" or in the king's hall of judgment have not supplied the genres for the speeches in this unit. Knowledge of court protocol or of form-critical categories of forensic speech making should not be applied too heavily to the text in the process of interpretation. The language is allusive rather than technical.

The prophet "conducted" the *rîb* in the sense that his report is a dramatized account of such an event, like a play reading presented by one person. At least it starts that way. As we have seen, the trick is to use the ambivalence of the historical recital as a bridge to a different dramatic situation. Verse 1a is ambiguous. It could be a general call to an audience to listen to the following piece, which is identified as an oracle (*what Yahweh is saying*). The rest of v 1 through v 2 could then be Yahweh's speech, first to Israel (1b), then to the mountains (v 2). And Yahweh's speech could actually begin with v 1a. In this reading the opening call would be already part of the court proceedings. The words, from the beginning, could be the speech of Yahweh, initiating the action, calling first to the mountains (v 1a), then to his people (v 1b), and again to the mountains (v 2).

In spite of its uneven composition, it would be simpler if vv 1–5 could be interpreted as a single speech, made by Yahweh as plaintiff, addressed alternately to the panel of witnesses (vv 1a, 2a) and the defendant (vv 1b, 3–5). There is no difficulty in Yahweh referring to himself as "Yahweh" in vv 1–2, but it would be more natural in v 1a if the prophet were delivering his report and calling on all concerned. The prophet is speaking first to the people (v 1a), using a standard form of address for such proclamations (3:1, 9). So they are present. Verse 2b makes an envelope with v 1a. It gives the reason for calling the people and the mountains to attention.

When a command is given, we do not know who is being addressed unless a vocative noun is used. Sometimes the identity of the addressee can be inferred from the applicability of the content of the speech to some specific audience. The original audience did not need to be told who they were; it is only later readers who need that kind of information. That the editor did not supply such an aid suggests that he and his readers were still close to the original situation. Continuity from chapter 3 to chapter 6 suggests that the series of speeches commencing with *šimʿû* are all addressed to the same audience. But when an audience is eventually identified by the use of a noun in the vocative, *my people* (vv 3aA, 5aAα), the verbs and pronouns are singular. The first masculine plural noun in the unit is *hārîm*, *mountains* (v 2aA). When that word is supplied, we have to revise our inference that the first *šimʿû* was addressed to "the elders of Jacob" in continuation from chapter 3, or rather the point remains indeterminate.

now. The modal modifier *nāʾ* is conventionally translated "please." The command is peremptory and insistent rather than pleading.

saying. Micah does not use a standard oracle rubric or messenger formula, as if reporting, repeating, a formal pronouncement by Yahweh—something he has said—that the prophet is commissioned to proclaim. The expression is indeed unique and for that reason has attracted the scalpel of the text critic. The favored emendation is to supply *haddābār*, "the word," as antecedent of the relative clause, appealing to the variant "the word of the Lord" in LXX. This is recommended by Schwantes (1962: 145). But the continuation of LXX, "the Lord said," hardly attests *yhwh ʾāmar*, as Hillers (1984: 75) rightly points out.

Micah calls on his audience to listen to what Yahweh is going to say. So v 1a is not the title of an oracle that can be identified as vv 1b–8. One by one Micah calls on the three participants in the *rîb*—Israel, Yahweh, and the mountains. The first *šimʿû* (v 1a) is addressed to Israel; they are told to listen to Yahweh. The second *šimʿû* (v 2aA) is addressed to the mountains; they too are told to listen to Yahweh. Who, then, is addressed in v 1bA, using a singular verb—"do *thou* dispute!"? We suggest that this is the prophet calling upon Yahweh, the central figure, to engage in disputation; for, as Micah explains in v 2bA, it is Yahweh who has the *rîb* with his people. So it is not appropriate for him to begin by asking Israel to arise and engage in disputation.

Stand up! The prophet continues by calling the other participants into the action—Yahweh himself in v 1b, the cosmic guardians of the covenant in v 2. The imperatives of v 1bA are like those of a prayer. The verb *qûm* is often used as the first verb in a call for action (cf. Ps 35:1–2; Num 10:35). This is a traditional expression, continually used in prayers to Yahweh to arise and go into action as warrior or judge. The following colons make it clear that Yahweh is the one who has the *rîb* to present (v 2bA). The mountains are to listen to Yahweh's *rîb* (v 2aA), so Yahweh is the most eligible subject for the verb *rîb* in v 1bA. Another possibility is that v 1b is a command from Yahweh to the prophet, who confronts the people as Yahweh's representative and makes the speeches in this mock lawsuit on Yahweh's behalf (Huffmon 1959: 287). This suggestion makes things too complicated. The prophet does recite the whole of this dramatic poem, taking on the *personae* of the participants.

Dispute with. The idiom here is different from that in v 2, and the prepositions are different. In v 1 the noun governed by *with* (*'et*), *the mountains*, refers
to the witnesses. In v 2 the noun governed by *with* (*'im*), *his people*, refers to the
defendant in the case. Yahweh is the plaintiff, Israel the defendant. The prophet
calls on Israel to listen to what Yahweh is about to say (v 1a). He calls on the
mountains to hear the *rîb*, as if in the role of magistrate. The word *rîb* (noun and
verb) is used in the first colon of each of these three bicolons. A *rîb* is an argument, a conflict between two parties. Its connotations range from a common
brawl to formal litigation. A *rîb* consists of presentations and responses, complaints and remonstrations, with rebuttals, countercharges, explanations and ex-
cuses, overtures, negotiations, and eventually some kind of resolution, whether
reconciliation or irreparable estrangement. Such face-to-face interaction corresponds to the mutuality of covenant obligations. Each party is accountable to the
other. Yahweh has given undertakings to Israel, has made himself accountable,
and is willing to be brought to account (Schenker 1988).

the mountains. The language is that of prose. All three prose particles are used
in v 1. This befits the prophet's own speech, closer to the vernacular. The word
mountains lacks the article in the more traditional formulation in v 2aA, even
though one would have expected the vocative particle (formally identical with
the definite article) to be used with a vocative noun.

The translation, *"with the mountains,"* could be misleading. It could create a
wrong expectation that we are about to hear a dispute in which Yahweh and the
mountains have a disagreement over something. It turns out that the mountains
are to be witnesses, not disputants. There is no suitable English preposition.

hear. The precative *tšm'nh* amounts to an indirect command to Yahweh to
speak to the hills. Verse 1bB is thus transitional between v 1bA and v 2aA.

2. *Listen.* The imperative *šim'û* in v 2 is addressed to the mountains. The
scene is gradually unfolded as v 2aA repeats v 1a, adding more specific details.
What Yahweh is about to say is a *rîb*.

1a	*šim'û-nā'*	*'ēt 'ăšer-yhwh 'ōmēr*	Listen now to what Yahweh is saying . . .
. . .			
2aA	*šim'û <u>hārîm</u>*	*'et-<u>rîb</u> yhwh*	Listen, <u>mountains</u>, to Yahweh's <u>dispute</u>

We are in the domain of myth, or at least of highly imaginative dramatic poetry.
The preceding indirect command, with a jussive verb (v 1bB), is addressed to
the parallel "hills." Now the mountains are directly commanded to listen. Yet
Yahweh does not say anything directly *to* the mountains. In vv 3–5 Yahweh addresses Israel directly as "my people." Verses 1 and 2 begin with the same verb
šim'û, and it keeps things simple to suppose that each is addressed to the same
audience, namely the *mountains // hills.* The structure of v 1 supports this, for
v 1bB has the feminine verb in parallel with *šim'û*; so the masculine parallel
(*hehārîm*) of its subject (*haggěbā'ôt*) is the best candidate for subject of the

opening *šimʿû*, albeit retroactively. But why then should the identity of the audience remain undisclosed in the opening lines? Micah does this kind of thing all the time. The mountains are mentioned twice—already in v 1b (parallel "hills") and again in v 2 (parallel "foundations of Earth"). The parallelism is incomplete in each of these bicolons, and the grammatical correspondences are skewed as well. In fact, the organization of vv 1–2 is confused, or at least confusing to us; it is not obvious who the protagonists are and what their roles are— at least, not at first. A second participant is commanded to stand up and dispute in v 1b, but this litigant is not identified either. Compared with Isaiah 1, the development is not logical. The first thing to do is to secure the panel of witnesses, then to call the disputants. Israel is not expected to *Dispute with the mountains* (v 1bA), but to dispute with Yahweh (or rather to respond to Yahweh's dispute) in the presence of the tribunal consisting of the cosmic elements. The picture begins to come into focus with v 2aA, which casts two of the cosmic elements in the role of judges, or at least as observers of the proceedings.

Yet no sooner are they set up in this capacity than they recede into the background. They play no identifiable part in what follows. Verse 2b makes it clear eventually that Yahweh is disputing *with* his people. The opening call (v 1a) is thus somewhat removed from the ensuing altercation, perhaps to serve as a general heading for the whole piece, or even for the entire Book of Contention (chapters 6–7), so that it is not part of the argumentation as such. As a heading and a beginning for the whole discourse, v 1a could present the prophet as calling his audience to attention (and later the author addressing his readers). Or he could already be invoking the mountains. If so, how far do the prophet's words extend? Does his introduction to this report of a *rîb* between Yahweh and Israel go through v 2? If so, v 2b gives the reason for the prophet's sermon; it explains why he refers to Yahweh in the third person (although we cannot use this feature to determine whether Yahweh himself is present), so these words too are addressed to Micah's audience and later readers. He is functioning as a reporter and narrator, but as one outside the action that follows.

It is also possible that in this case Yahweh's speech does not begin until v 3, all of vv 1–2 being the prophet's setting of the stage. This opening speech of six lines consists of a call (by the prophet) to a litigant, unidentified at first (v 1b), and to the mountains (v 2a), followed by the naming of the litigants—Yahweh and Israel. In this way the editor has melded the two functions of prophecy: first, its immediate application to a particular situation in the career of Micah (oral mode); second, its perpetual application to Israel in all subsequent times (literary mode).

everlasting. The position of the adjective makes it unclear whether it modifies "foundations of Earth." The article is hard to explain, since it is lacking the other nouns of this bicolon. But note *hehārîm* in v 1. Perhaps the *mem* should be transposed to make a phrase "from the foundations of Earth." The phrase *môsĕdê hārîm* occurs in Deut 32:22, with the same meaning. Its associations are cosmic (Pss 8:29; 18:8; 82:5; Isa 24:18; 58:12; Jer 31:37), while *ʾētān* means "primal." Verse 2aB does not recruit *foundations* alongside *mountains* as additional members of the panel of witnesses. Rather it identifies the mountains as the primeval foundations of Earth, as in several fragments of creation stories (Ps 90:1; Job 38:4–6; Prov 8:25). See the full discussion in Andersen and Freedman 1989: 847–54.

The adjective *hā'ētānîm* is not suitable as an attribute of "the foundations of the Earth." All its associations are with perpetually flowing water (Exod 14:27; Deut 21:4; Amos 5:24; Ps 78:15). The placement of the adjective before its noun is very rare in Hebrew. For these reasons, the word has attracted suspicion. Appealing to parallelism, Wellhausen changed it to *ha'ăzînû*, "Give ear!" and this has been widely adopted (NJB, REB, and many commentators). Hillers (1984: 76) has drawn attention to the inclusion of rivers, springs, and the great deep along with heaven, earth, and mountains, in the invocation of cosmic powers in Akkadian treaty texts. He translates "streams (from) the foundations of the earth." This proposal has merit.

Putting *hā'ētānîm* at the beginning of the colon brings the four nouns "mountains," "Yahweh," "everlastings," "foundations of Earth" into a chiastic pattern. If there are two matched pairs here, then *hā'ētānîm* could perhaps be an attribute of the deity ("the Perennial" [Dahood 1983: 58]). Dahood produces evidence from Ebla; but his other examples from the Hebrew Bible involve emendation of the Masoretic Text (Dahood 1983: 64 n. 25).

with. The verb *rîb* takes either *'et* or *'im* as its idiomatic preposition. Here a distinction can be perceived. The prophet presents *to* the hills Yahweh's case *against* his people.

argue. This colon, chiastic with the preceding, has the unusual sequence of the proper noun (*Israel*) following a title (*his people*). The *hitpa'el* has reciprocal meaning and shows that there is to be altercation, not just remonstration.

3–5. Yahweh makes two speeches or a speech in two parts, each beginning with *My people!* The first reported words in v 3 sound like a response to some prior complaint on Israel's part, insinuating that Yahweh had been negligent or inconsistent. The *rîb* is not a trial but a dialogue in which Yahweh and Israel exchange statements. The opening and closing statements (vv 3, 8) are by Yahweh. The main body of the dispute is an interchange in which Yahweh expounds on his role in the founding of the nation (vv 4–5) while in vv 6–7 Israel proposes a means for making amends.

Yahweh's first speech (vv 3–5) contains fragments of the historical recital of the long epic story of Yahweh and Israel. Only two moments are reported, setting out from Egypt (v 4), getting into the land (v 5). It is hard to see what point is being made with Micah's audience by listing Moses, Aaron, and Miriam (v 4b), or by reminding them about Balaq and Balaam (v 5). Talk about those times implies that the situation in Micah's day was analogous in some way to the Exodus wanderings. In that tradition there were occasions when the people complained about the treatment they were receiving from Yahweh and expressed doubt about his capacity to look after them. They grumbled all the time in spite of the mighty deeds (*ṣidqôt yhwh* [v 5bB]). Here the recital of the gracious acts is intended to defend Yahweh from the implied charges of neglect or worse.

The charges are only implied, or they lacked specificity; for in v 3aA Yahweh asks them, "What have I done?"

What. The series of questions gives the dispute a sevenfold structure. The questions come in three pairs—*mh . . . wmh* (vv 3a, 5a, 8aB) with *bmh* in v 6aA as the added one. As in 5:9–14, the variant is in the fifth position, a pattern found in Amos also.

I wearied thee. Why does Yahweh ask the questions in this form? Are the people acting as if they had lost interest in Yahweh? Weariness is an Exodus theme, and it is applied to Yahweh several times, e.g., by Isaiah where Yahweh says he is tired of their religious antics (1:14). Perhaps the idea that Yahweh has worn them out is expressed sarcastically, since it was usually the other way around. Note similarly that in v 8 Yahweh is subject of the verb *drš*, usually a human activity towards God. Here its use could be satirical.

Answer me! The command *ʿănēh bî* could mean "Testify against me!" Yahweh is inviting them to support or defend their complaints against him. They have already found fault with him: he has done something harmful to them and he has worn them out. Now he asks them to substantiate these charges. The situation seems much like that in the book of Job, where God challenges Job to make a suitable response to various questions, based on the fact that Job has been complaining about God.

4. The recital is very abbreviated compared with some versions of Israel's national epic. The three heroes of the wilderness wanderings and two enemies are mentioned to evoke the whole story without having to tell it.

I brought thee up. Mur 88 reads *hʿlytyk, plene*. Two verbs are used in traditional formulations of the deliverance from Egypt. The verb *hôṣîʾ*, "bring out," is common and generally preferred in the Deuteronomistic tradition. The verb *haʿăleh*, "bring up," used here, is found also in Gen 50:24; Exod 17:3; 32:1, 7, 23; 33:1; Lev 11:45; Num 14:13; 16:13; 20:5; 21:5; Josh 24:17, 32; Judg 6:8, 13; 1 Sam 10:18; 2 Kgs 17:7; Hos 12:14; Amos 2:10; 3:1; 9:7; Neh 9:18; 1 Chr 17:5. It is widely used, although, not characteristic of any particular tradition; and it is not used in Psalms.

Egypt. The parallelism in v 4a is not one of simple synonymy. *The land of Egypt* followed by *the house of slaves* is a standard pattern. The second phrase is not another name for Egypt, it is a characterization of the country as a land (*byt*) whose people are slaves, captive Israelites. This political fact, as perceived by the Israelites, gave them a greater consciousness of their freedom, of the right of all Israelite citizens to freedom.

redeemed. Exodus 15 uses *gāʾal*; *pādâ* is rare.

I sent. In Hebrew prose, when the object of a verb consists of two or more proper or definite nouns, standard grammar requires the use of *nota accusativi* *ʾēt* with each noun object. In pure poetry, the object marker would not be used at all. The usage in Mic 6:4b is mixed. The particle *ʾēt* is used only once, carrying the whole phrase of three coordinated nouns. This could be no more than substandard composition, a symptom of the breakdown of classical rigor in the later stages of the language's evolution, perhaps evidence that this part of the

text is late. If, however, the choice of this remarkable construction was deliberate, the effect of using *'ēt* only once, and with one verb, is to join the three
siblings together as closely as possible, as if they were partners in a single enterprise. If *'ēt* had been used with each proper noun, this construction could be
read as implying that each person had a distinct mission.

The language used (*I sent [them] before you*) does not define their apparently
shared role in relation to Israel. Yahweh has just identified himself as their
leader (*I brought you up out of the land of Egypt*). If the three humans were
sent ahead of Israel, how do the two pictures blend? Are they commanders of
an army or shepherds leading a flock? The verb "send" is operational for the
dispatch of a messenger (Mal 4:5) to someone, thus giving Moses, Aaron, and
Miriam the role of prophets confronting the people. As a matter of fact, each of
these three is called "prophet," but in unconnected texts, never in concert.
The sequence in Mic 6:4b matches the development in Amos 2:10–11. The
Exodus was followed by the ministry of prophets, beginning with these three.

The numerous summary recitals of the "mighty acts" of Yahweh, found so
often in the Hebrew Bible, usually present a few of the highlights, easily recognized, and so carrying the full story. What makes Micah's simple statement so
remarkable, and so puzzling, is the fact that nowhere in the tradition are the
three siblings presented in a shared leadership role. Indeed, the only other place
in the Bible where they are all on stage together, they are in bitter conflict
(Numbers 12). The matter under dispute there is precisely the authority of a
genuine prophet. This issue has already dominated Micah 2–3. Here in chapter
6 it emerges again with a reminder that, from Israel's earliest beginnings, the
nation had been rebellious against the true prophets and readily seduced by
the false ones, represented here by Balaam (v 5). It is understandable that Moses
and Balaam should be selected and settled as the prototypes and enduring
models of the good and bad prophets of later times. See the following note on
Balaam for more details. But how did Aaron and Miriam come into it? There
are numerous stories of opposition to Moses. Aaron as Moses' "prophet" shared
a little of this hostility, Miriam none at all. Her status as a prophet is equivocal
and limited in scope (Exod 15:20, where she is Aaron's sister, not Moses'!). See
Trible (1989).

The portrait of Balaam remained fragmentary and contradictory in the
Hebrew Bible (Coats 1973; Dijkstra 1995; Greene 1992; Layton 1992), and the
Deir ʿAllā wall texts show that more remained in circulation about him than
found its way finally into the biblical write-up. The symmetry of the juxtaposition of Moses and Balaam as stereotypical opposites is made quite lopsided in
the traditions by the heroic stature attained by Moses and the epic scope of his
story. The classic device for confirming the credentials of a real prophet, such
as Moses, and confuting the claims of a false one, such as Balaam, would be to
have one defeat the other in open competition as Moses did with the magicians
of Egypt (Exodus 7), and as Elijah did with the prophets of Baʿal (1 Kings 18).
There are other stories along the same lines (Jeremiah 28), yet these two rivals
and opposites, Moses and Balaam, are never shown face to face.

The story about Balaam (Numbers 22–24) is in some ways the centerpiece of the book of Numbers. It serves as a watershed for the wilderness narrative and is rich with prophecies of Israel's theological status and historical destiny. Moses was excluded from all this, and one wonders why the tradents and redactors did not seize and exploit such a good opportunity to enhance the figure of Moses by giving him a decisive and defining victory in disposing of Balaam. The editors of the book of Numbers, for whatever reason, left Moses out of that part of the story. Balaam was dressed up as a curious charlatan, and at the same time, by an irony, he became an authentic prophet in spite of his contemptible mendacity and cupidity. By making Balaam such an equivocal figure, the traditions in Numbers 22–24 have done justice to the mysterious complexity of biblical prophecy. The literary treatment of Balaam showed also that the detection and exposure of a bogus prophet was not all that easy. Throughout the Hebrew Bible the same terms "prophet," "seer," "visionary" are used generically. There was no special term for "false" prophets. One is never quite sure whether Balaam is meant to be taken as a real prophet or not. So what does Micah want the people to remember? On the face of it, Balaam's reiterated assurances that he would speak only the word that God placed in his mouth (Num 22:8, 18, 35, 38; 24:13) show that he knew what real prophecy was. But that doesn't get us anywhere. Every self-advertised prophet would claim that. The remark is overused. He protests too much and the reader becomes doubtful. In the event, however, and from the point of view of the editor, there is no doubt that the words that come through are the real words of God (Num 23:5, 16) and not what Balak, the king of Moab wanted, as his indignation showed. The prophecies are genuine, but what of Balaam himself? Prophets are for hire, but the word of God is not a commodity. We seem to have here a case where the man himself does not count, and his morality is irrelevant. He is merely a passive outlet, as the phenomena reported in Num 24:4 and 16 indicate.

Israel struggled with this problem for centuries and was never able to solve it. The vital decision—how to tell a genuine prophet, actually sent from God, from a pretend prophet (whether a conscious charlatan or sincerely deluded but not in fact sent by God)—could never be made by appearances, speech forms, supportive miracles, or even the moral character of the speaker. In the end they could not handle prophecy at all and the problem was finally overcome, if that is the word, by the drastic policy of closing out the age of prophecy and refusing to consider any claimant to the office as a possible spokesperson for God. What a radical break with the past, considering the definitive role that prophets had played in the religion of Israel from Moses (or even Abraham [Gen 20:17]) down! The cessation of prophecy or at least its suspension, was taken to be a fact. But who was authorized to make such a decision? The policy was no better than a rationalization of the inability of Judaism, at least in the main line, to handle the enthusiasts. The time had come for a new kind of public leadership, scholars who interpreted the prophetic writings. Even so, such persons could often succeed better if they were considered to be inspired, and there was still some room for mystics, even if viewed with reserve. Official disapproval did not succeed in suppressing the phenomenon of prophecy. But, from the time of Ezra forward outbreaks of prophecy were more likely to contribute to the formation of sects than to the modification of established religion. Other religions supply analogies. There were various kinds of prophets in Christianity in the early days. It was this community that coined the term *pseudoprophetes*. Judaism affirmed and denied the power of prophecy by canonizing the writings of their dead prophets and denouncing the sayings of their living prophets. Institutionalized Christianity eventually did the same.

Prophets cannot be domesticated. The only safe prophet is a dead prophet. Once their sayings were fixed in writings, the scholars could keep them in their place by interpretation, manipulating the words of prophets into theologically correct doctrines. There are signs that this kind of sanitization had already begun in the redaction of sacred texts; but the problem was too tenacious and the traditions were too robust to be rendered innocuous by hermeneutical tricks. It is not uncommon for interpreters whose power rests in a right to control sacred texts, when that right is questioned, to claim a kind of ancillary status as prophets who receive authoritative interpretation by divine inspiration. The faithful still have to exercise some kind of judgment in deciding whether to allow such claims. While, on the one hand, the unique status of Moses as the unmatched prophet "whom the Lord knew face to face" (Deut 34:10) had been settled in the dispute of Numbers 12, where communication was "mouth to mouth" (Num 12:8), on the other hand the exclusiveness of Moses's privilege and power as a prophet was softened on another occasion by the recruitment of a large number of similarly charismatic colleagues, with Moses himself expressing the opinion that it would be best if prophecy could be democratized.

The simplest solution would be to have just one prophet. Micah, like Amos, is more aware of the succession of prophets. At least he does not give Moses an exclusive role, and it is not apparent what it was about Moses, Aaron, and Miriam that would help to resolve the current dispute between Yahweh and his people. There is no appeal to the writings of Moses.

Aaron. This is the only reference to Aaron in the prophetic corpus. Aaron is a character in the Hebrew Bible who does not have a story of his own. Even in the best-known incident in which he took part, the worship of the gold bull calf, his role is not central—he got involved in a story of the people. The pieces of Aaron's eventually synthesized identity are scattered and unconnected in the earliest fragmentary traditions. We know how Moses, the destined deliverer of Israel, survived the peril of Pharaoh's slaughter of the innocents; but there is no matching interest in Aaron's beginnings. He is simply there when needed. He first appears as Moses' spokesman, but often he is left out and Moses is capable of carrying on alone. In other words, there are Moses stories without Aaron, but no Aaron stories without Moses.

Aaron's relationship (brother) to Moses is not always mentioned; for instance, when Aaron accompanied Moses along with Hur to the hilltop while Joshua is fighting Amalek down below. Moses controls the outcome of the battle by manipulating the "wand of God," but he is not allowed to be a self-sufficing hero.

Moses falters through common human frailty. He needed Aaron and Hur to hold up his hands for him. The story does not explain by what qualifications Aaron and Hur were co-opted for this task. When later Moses goes up the hill with Joshua (Exod 24:14), Aaron and Hur are deputized to attend to Moses' duties as arbitrator in civil disputes during his absence. Why are not Joshua and Hur included in Micah's list? Even when installed as the main priest, Aaron is kept in his place, subservient to Moses. When he joins with Miriam in claiming status like that of Moses (Numbers 12) he is rebuffed, and even in that bid he is not affirming a unique role.

Miriam. Miriam is mentioned only twice outside the Pentateuch, here and in 1 Chr 5:29 (= Eng 6:3); the Miriam mentioned in 1 Chr 4:17 is apparently a different person, although the reference to "the daughter of Pharaoh" in v 18 may imply a mixing of traditions owing to the occurrence of the same name. The references are brief, but Micah's recognition of the three siblings as Israel's leaders in the Exodus is entirely positive. In her care for her baby brother, and in leading the celebration in Exodus 15, Miriam is a key character. Only in Numbers 12 does she become the central character of a story; her name opens and closes the chapter. It is her story. Aaron acts in collusion with her, but in a supportive way. The remarkable placement of the name of the female before the name of the male (Num 12:1) suggests that Miriam was the instigator, just as the outcome discriminates against her as the chief culprit while Aaron gets off more lightly. Too much should not be made of this detail, however. When next mentioned (Num 12:4) the names are inverted. This produces a chiastic pattern whose total effect could be to put sister and brother on an equal footing in this matter. Whether their conspiracy was a bid for power or a protest against threatened loss of status (they claim that they were already certified as agents of God's communications), the incident serves to define more clearly the supreme leadership role of Moses and to settle that point for ever. Micah's troika seems to have backed away from this resolution.

In summary, Aaron and Miriam have a mixed press in the Hebrew Bible. Aaron has a more positive image in P and in Chronicles, the late tradition. The less abundant references in earlier sources are negative and neutral (*ABD* 1:1–3). Micah alone presents the three siblings in joint leadership, and it is hard to see what point he is making.

5. In formal terms, the double question of v 3 is balanced by the double question in v 5a, both introduced by *My people*. On the use of this term in Micah compared with Isaiah, see Stansell (1988: 117–21). The intentions of the two paired questions seem different. If Israel is now tired of Yahweh, then something more contemporary might serve better than a reminder of what Balak and Balaam did. Yet nothing serves so well to define the ancient relationship between Yahweh and Israel as this one story. Balak was a king who hired a seer, a situation not unlike that reflected in Micah 3:5–7. Far from doing anything to disenchant Israel, this first encounter set the style for all subsequent "righteous deeds of Yahweh." The questions of Yahweh then serve as an oath of clearance (1 Sam 12:3), establishing his fulfillment of covenant obligations.

answer. The use of the same verb in Num 22:18, coupled with the new evidence about Balaam's role now available in the Deir ʿAllā wall inscriptions make it clearer that he was an "oracle-reciter" (Moore 1990: 99) whose trade was tied up with magic.

Shittim. Num 25:1 is the only mention of Shittim in the Pentateuch. From Shittim to Gilgal was the last long leg of the journey from Egypt to the new land. Shittim is where they were encamped when the Balaam episode took place (Num 25:1; 33:49). Shittim was their last camp of the wilderness wandering. The speeches of Deuteronomy were given there. From there the spies were sent (Josh 2:1; 3:1), and Gilgal was the first camp in the Promised Land. Ominous references to Baʿal-Peor in Hosea (compare Psalm 106) suggest a tradition that child sacrifice was part of that cult, providing a link with v 7.

the righteous acts of Yahweh. His victories in the holy wars of Israel's beginnings (Judg 5:10). This clause has no parallel; it could blanket all the preceding speech. Since Yahweh is clearly the speaker, this is as good an illustration as one could wish for of the use by a speaker of his own name rather than "I" when referring to himself. So the phrase *ṣidqôt yhwh* should not be emended to *ṣidqôtāy.* By the same token, the occurrence of "Yahweh" in v 8 does not rule out the possibility that Yahweh himself is the speaker of these words.

6–7. The speaker here is not identified. The use of the singular "I" matches the singular "thou" of vv 3–5, and we can sustain the dramatic unity and keep the action simple if all of vv 3–8 is dialogue between Yahweh and his people. The occurrence of "Yahweh" twice in vv 6–7 and the use of third-person forms could express the etiquette of indirect reference to a superior (avoiding the familiar "thou"). Yahweh can be addressed obliquely in the third person, in direct response to the questions he has asked his people in vv 3–5. If drawn from the cult, the language of vv 6–7 could correspond to that used by a would-be worshiper to a priest as a request for instruction and as part of an entrance liturgy.

The individual speaker of vv 6–7 is a representative Israelite. Burkitt found this inquiry so incredible in the mouth of any Israelite that he identified the speaker as "the earnest but ignorant settler in Palestine who knows nothing of the religion of Elijah and of Amos" (1926: 161). More recent discoveries and studies now make it quite credible that such outlandish proposals would be taken very seriously in Israel.

The inquiry uses the language of the cult. It has affinities with the "entrance liturgy" (Gunkel-Begrich 1933: 327, 408; Koch 1969: 30, 32). The four questions begin with a general one *bammâ* followed by three specific ones using *hā-.* The preposition *b-* dominates the list of proposed offerings, the typical oblations of the regular cult. Cross (1994: 99) has shown that its use is routine in votive inscriptions, with the meaning of "specification." This requires the translation "burnt offerings *consisting of* calves" rather than the accomative "with" in most translations, inferred from the parallelism. The quantities are rich, extravagant, as is fitting. They escalate to the suggestion of v 7b, horrifying to us, but not perhaps to those who made it. The prophet makes no comment about human sacrifice directly, but lists all possible offerings as inadequate for the present need.

It would seem that all such remedies, including the sacrifice of a child, were serious options for everyone, king and citizen alike, at that time. Only later, with Jeremiah and Ezekiel and the abominations of the Tophet does horror enter into it.

Each of these bicolons has one verb with two objects. "Yahweh" is repeated in v 7; but the anaphoric pronoun "him" of v 6b is not balanced by a similar object (strictly an indirect object) for "give" (him) in v 7b. The complementary parallelism shows that ʿ*ōlōt* is virtually the *nomen regens* of all the following nouns; i.e., "Will Yahweh be appeased with (holocausts of) thousands of rams?" It extends further to the proposal of human sacrifice in v 7, ʿ*ōlâ* being the usual term (2 Kgs 3:27; Jer 19:5). The Punic ostracon M 279–669 has the phrase [ʿ]*lt* *ṣmḥ*, "[ho]locaust of (his) scion," where the Punic *ṣmḥ*, "sprout," which has the same metaphorical usage in Hebrew, exactly matches "firstborn," while "the fruit of my body" in Mic 6:7 matches the use of the term "flesh" to refer to the offerer's child in Punic inscriptions.

6. *I.* The singular "I" matches the singular "thou" of the address in vv 3–5, there "my people." The response in v 6 seems to be more individual and very personal. The proposal to offer *my eldest son* could not be made by a community or on behalf of a community. Here is the voice of one concerned citizen, prepared to take the most drastic measures. Child sacrifice, as practiced in that part of the world at that time, was an option for a parent. The power and virtue of that action lay in the fact that it was one's own child who was "delivered up." Far from indicating cruelty or callousness of parent towards child, the action gained poignancy and efficacy precisely from the fact that the child was treasured; it was the person's most valuable possession. This is made clear from the language used by Phoenicians to describe their action; only a cynical reading would take the attribute in "treasured progeny"as referring to monetary value.

Recognizing that in Israel all sacrifice was not only representative, but in some sense substitutionary, then, the closer the affinity between the sacrifice and the sacrificer, the more valuable and efficacious the sacrifice. If the truly ultimate sacrifice is one's self, then the offering of the firstborn son is legally, biologically, and relationally the closest we can come to self-sacrifice. See the following NOTE on the Akeda.

Yahweh's presence. The use of third-person pronouns ("he") rather than direct address ("thou") suggests a certain distance between the speaker and Yahweh. The language could imply an actual absence of Yahweh in the perception of the speaker. To whom, in that case, would such questions be addressed? Are they purely rhetorical, as the person asks himself what he might do? Does the speaker expect the prophet to arbitrate? Directly, or indirectly, only an answer from Yahweh himself would be satisfactory. So it is possible that this oblique language is the protocol of social distance, of servility, in which an inferior avoids second-person pronouns, and even first-person forms, casting the whole into third person. Here, however, the "I" is prominent.

height. The noun *mārôm* is characteristic of Psalms and Isaiah (Ps 18:17 = 2 Sam 22:17; Pss 24:21; 33:5, 16).

burnt offerings. The reading *bʿwlwt*, doubly *plene*, has a Masora in **L** that this spelling occurs three times (גֹּמל) — Mic 6:6; Ezek 45:17; Ps 66:13 (Mm 297). The doubly *plene* spelling of the stem occurs in Ezek 43:27. In spite of the Masora, the spelling in **L** is inferior. The spelling *bʿlwt* is attested, not only in **C**, **P**, and **D**[62] but also in Mur 88. At Ezek 45:17, **D**[62] originally read *bʿlwt*; later a second *waw* was added.

7. Only in the last bicolon is the point made that these sacrifices are to deal with sin; but these terms apply to all the preceding lines. It is important to underscore the fact that the usual prepositions to mark the object ("my firstborn") and the other reference ("[for] my transgression") are not used, because this calls for recognition of the same lack in v 8 as well (see below).

thousands . . . myriads. The sequence, familiar in Canaanite literature (RSP I: 114) and in the Bible (Gevirtz 1963: 15–24), is "thousands . . . ten thousands." So far as we know, ten thousand was the largest number for which Hebrew vocabulary had a word. In sequence with "thousand," "myriad" conveyed the idea of a quantity almost unimaginable (Deut 32:30; 33:17; 1 Sam 18:7, 8; 21:12; 29:5; Pss 68:18; 91:7). Whereas number sequences with an increment of one are used in synonymous or synthetic parallelism (as pointed out in detail by Roth [1965] and Avishur [1981, 1984]), when there is an increase by a factor of ten, with reference to the same person or object, the effect is climactic. In the case of the well-known biblical example — the *contrast* of David's achievement with Saul's — the effect is antithetic (as pointed out by Gevirtz [1963: 24 n. 26]). In Micah 6:7 the movement through the list is climactic. Not that oil was superior to a ram for expiation; in fact, in the Levitical code only the blood of an animal sacrifice could make atonement. But the use of the term *nhl,* "wadi-torrent," goes beyond anything remotely feasible. Micah is using a conventional word-pair, and enough of conventional usage remains. But he uses it in his own unique and startling way, and the significance of his usage should not be restricted to that of the cliché used so widely in Ugaritic and Hebrew poetry.

torrents. Compare *palgê-šāmen* (Job 29:6).

my eldest son. The list is climactic. Proposing the holocaust of "my eldest son" // "the fruit of my belly" as more precious than thousands of rams, ten thousand streams (cosmic rivers!) of oil, shows that children were not sacrificed without great pain to natural affections, as if they were viewed as no more than another chattel to be disposed of at will. See the following NOTE on the Akeda.

8. The short clauses in this verse bring about a complete change of meter. In vv 1–5 the colons tend to be long. In vv 6–7 they are more regular, but to find three beats in all of them requires a bit of fiddling: two beats for *haʾăqaddĕmennû* (6b) one beat for two-word phrases (7aA, 7bB). To be consistent, if *pĕrî biṭnî* is given one beat because it parallels *bĕkôrî*, then *ḥaṭṭaʾt napšî* should be one beat to parallel *pišʿî* (Gordis 1971: 150 n. 0), reducing the colon to two beats. If *ḥaṭṭaʾt napšî* are given distinct beats to secure the desired three, why should not *pĕrî biṭnî* receive the same analysis? The two colons cannot be made to match by counting words or beats, but each has exactly eight syllables. Gordis (1971: 70) recognizes that v 8 departs from this pattern; but he only succeeds

in making the last bicolon 4 :: 4 by counting a beat for *'im* (1971: 67, 92). This is arbitrary, and weakens the theory of beats, since the natural stress patterns of the language, as recorded by the Masoretes, are overridden in the interests of scansion.

The words in v 8a fall into a symmetrical pattern:

higgîd				
	lĕkā			
		'ādām		
			mah-	
verb	pronoun	name	interrogative	*ṭôb*
			ûmâ-	
		yhwh		
dôrēš				
	mimmĕkā			

The parallelism suggests the same subject for *higgîd // dôrēš*. LXX makes *hgyd* passive. Cataphoric postponement of the noun subject is not unusual. The ideas are not parallel. As an act of God *drš* means to care for (Deut 11:12; Jer 30:17) or to investigate (a crime) (Gen 9:5; Deut 23:22; Ps 9:13; Ezek 34:8–14).

He told. The verb *higgîd* was used in 3:8 to describe Micah's mission, to "declare" to Jacob his sin. The same usage here indicates that Micah is talking about prophetic proclamation. The opening command to hear (v 1a) was spoken by the prophet. It was followed by a speech of Yahweh (vv 2–5) and a speech of a representative Israelite (vv 6–7). Now Micah declares the concluding word.

man. The generic *'ādām* is an unusual way to address either an individual or the people of Israel. LXX confirms the MT reading. According to *DCH* (1:127), this is the only place where "Adam" is vocative. The accompanying assertion that "Adam" is collective begs the question. The usual Hebrew term for humankind is "sons of Adam," an expression that derives from the identity of the first man. The generic usage is puzzling. The position of the vocative within the clause is also unusual. A drastic solution is to emend *'dm* to *'dny*, enhancing the parallelism to *'dny // Yhwh*, a split-up of the stock phrase. The letters *ny* are easily confused with terminal *m*. This mistake has occurred elsewhere. In 1 Sam 17:32, LXX reads "the heart of my lord." This is intrinsically better than MT "the heart of a man" (McCarter 1980: 287). See Weiss (1963: 188 n. 4) for examples and documentation.

Such a change is not necessary, however. The unusual mode of address is a striking indication that Micah is drawing on traditional formulations. The language is poetic and characteristic of wisdom ethical instruction as in Job 33:17, 23 (*lĕhaggîd lĕ'ādām yošrô*); 34:11, 15. Achtemeier (1963: 277) translates, "He has showed you, Adam, what is good." She finds in the choice of this word a reminder that the present human condition ("a life of toil and pain and guilt") derives from the first man in the biblical story. The use of the generic "Adam" gives the response a universal application. Like other great moral teachers, Micah reaffirms what has always been known and what everybody should know, in simple, but powerful terms. Achtemeier finds a similarity between the question and answer of Mic 6:6–8 and the question and answer in Mark 12:28–34. What is interesting about the latter dialogue is the way the scribe comments on Jesus' answer with a paraphrase that includes an echo of, if not an intended reference to Mic 6:6–8.

> Well, Master, thou hast said the truth: for there is one God and there is none other but he: and to love him with all the heart, and with all the understanding, and with all the soul, and with all the strength, and to love his neighbor as himself, is more than all whole burnt offerings and sacrifices (Mark 12:32–33).

What is good? There are several places in Micah where a double question is posed. There are five sets of double questions in this unit. Usually the interrogative particle comes in first position in the clause, normal for Hebrew syntax. The pattern in v 8 is different. The question follows "He told thee, man . . . ," making *mah-ṭôb* the object—"He told you what is good"—so that it is not a question at all. Translations commonly make the first an indirect question; see Zech 1:9. "In some such cases it [the interrogative] approximates in meaning to the simple rel., as Jer 7:17; 33:24; Mic 6:5, 8; Job 34:33" (BDB 552b). We think that this judgment is mistaken, arising from the exigencies of translation. It is more dramatic to leave the statements as questions.

Some translations (NJPS, REB) treat the following "interrogative" clause as a continuation of this object, but some (NRSV) see it as a real question. Taking it, like the others, as a double question, the repetition of the interrogative pronoun in v 8 discloses the introverted structure displayed above. The grammar of the first colon should then match that of the second, and the gap in one is supplied from the other:

> What good did he (Yhwh) declare to thee, O man?
> And what [good] does Yhwh seek from thee (O man)?

They are being cross-examined with a barrage of double questions on what they are supposed to know—incidents from their past, what Yahweh has done for them, what he has told them to do for him. The famous prescription that follows is not attested elsewhere in that form; but the implication is that this has always been the essential requirement. Compare Deut 10:12–13.

What is good? The parallelism requires either that two questions are asked: "What is good?" and "What does Yahweh require from you?" Or that *hgyd* has two objects, as if *mh* were a relative pronoun (NJPS; NIV makes the first an object, the second a question).

good. Micah has accused the leadership of Israel of being haters of good (3:2). Amos exhorted them to "seek good" (5:14). The question "What is good?"

even when raised by prophets (Isa 1:17; Jer 22:15–16) is a wisdom question. This has been pointed out by Brinn (1988). The language is found also in Qoh 6:11–12:

6:11	כִּי יֵשׁ־דְּבָרִים הַרְבֵּה	For when there are more words,
	מַרְבִּים הָבֶל	They make (things) more futile;
	מַה־יֹּתֵר לָאָדָם:	What more (is there) for Man?
6:12	כִּי מִי־יוֹדֵעַ מַה־טּוֹב לָאָדָם בַּחַיִּים	For who knows *what is good for Man* in life
	מִסְפַּר יְמֵי־חַיֵּי הֶבְלוֹ	(for) the number of the days of his futile life?
	וְיַעֲשֵׂם כַּצֵּל	And he spends them like a shadow,
	אֲשֶׁר מִי־יַגִּיד לָאָדָם	Because who has *declared to Man*
	מַה־יִּהְיֶה אַחֲרָיו תַּחַת הַשָּׁמֶשׁ:	what will be after him under the sun.

This is followed by a catalogue of things that are "good" for "the man," with a value system that is not at all skeptical. The word ṭôb occurs ten times in chapter 7, and in this kind of discourse means "better" or even "best." Fisch (1988: 163) suggests that Qoheleth "seems to parody" Mic 6:8. The similarity in language suggests some kind of connection. But it is more likely that the topos is an age-old question that surfaces differently in these quite different contexts. The usage in Qoheleth is important, all the same. There ṭôb has its comparative meaning — "X is better than (ṭôb min) Y." In this kind of discussion, the question is not "What is good?" Even less, the classical "What is The Good (summum bonum)?" It is concrete and practical. The poetic oracle in 1 Sam 15:22 clinches the point: "To obey is better than sacrifice." This is not splitting hairs. To say that the prescription in Mic 6:8 is "good" could imply that the other proposal in v 7 is "bad." This is the common reading, another place where reconciliation with God through sacrifice is rejected (a "thunderous rebuke" [Fishbane 1985: 182; cf. 186]). But, the comparative meaning of ṭôb implies that the suggestion in v 7 is good, but the one in v 8 is "better."

seeking. Compare diršû ṭôb, "Seek good!" (Amos 5:14).

to do . . . to love . . . to walk. There are three infinitival constructions. The compact expressions are related to one another and mutually self-defining. The ideas are not vague. The Hebrew Bible does not preach the love of abstractions. The idiom "do ḥesed" occurs; in fact it is the set idiom. To "love ḥesed" is attested only here in the Hebrew Bible. Suspecting a unique expression, Mowinckel omitted "love" and made a 3 :: 3 bicolon of the remaining two infinitival constructions (followed by and documented by Schwantes 1962: 155, 236).

The idiom "love ḥesed" is attested in the Damascus Document (XIII.18) and five times in the Rule of the Community at Qumran (II.24; V.4, 25; VIII.2; X.26). In two of these occurrences the phrase is combined with lkt. The Qumran evidence has been discussed by Hyatt (1952) and by Zimmerli (1971). It seems clear that Qumran piety was strongly influenced by the Micah passage. By the same token, it is out of the question that the word "love" "may have crept into the text" of Micah from this "*cliché* in later parlance" as suggested by Schwantes (1962: 155).

Just as in 2:1 Micah switched verbs and nouns from their stock idioms, so here, switching the idiom "do *ḥesed*" shows that both *mišpāṭ* and *ḥesed* are to be both *loved* and *done*. They are to love doing (or do lovingly) *mišpāṭ* and *ḥesed*. In Hos 2:21, *ḥesed* and *mišpāṭ* describe a faithful betrothal; the actions are inter-personal. The point being made here is that doing and loving *mišpāṭ* and *ḥesed* will atone for sins so serious that human sacrifice seems to be the only remedy. There is a tradition that God desires obedience or *ḥesed* and more than sacrifice (Hos 6:6; Holt, Else Kragelund 1987). The application of the final phrase ("with your God") to all three infinitives secures the needed synthesis even more firmly:

> to do the *mišpāṭ* (of Yahweh)
>
> to love (Yahweh) with *ḥesed*

The point may be strained. If chapter 6 is connected with chapter 3 (we have pointed out some of the evidence elsewhere), the human virtues required here involve more than piety that has only God as its interest and object. The *mišpāṭ* expected is the remedy for the injustice between humans condemned in chap-ters 2–3 (Candelaria 1983). Glueck's classic study asserted that "*ḥesed* in the pro-phetic and cognate literature [is] the reciprocal conduct of men toward one another and implicitly toward God" (1967: 63). In each connection the standards are set by Yahweh, people are accountable to Yahweh for their performance, and their conduct is expected to reflect and express the character and characteris-tic behavior of God himself. The three parts of the formula are thus mutually defining (Beck 1972).

walk humbly. The exact meaning of the third admonition cannot be estab-lished because the *hapax legomenon haṣnēaʿ* is elusive. As an infinitive absolute followed by an infinitive construct, the syntax is exceptional. The traditional meaning is "humbly," but it is possible that the meaning inclines more to "cir-cumspectly" or even "scrupulously."

Among the many discussions of this expression note Achtemeier (1963), Anderson (1951: 196—he interprets it as meaning "to live in communion with Him"), Brueggemann, Parks, and Groome (1986), Cranfield (1969—a sermon), Hemmerle (1989), Hertz (1934–35), Hyatt (1952), who discusses the Qumran evidence, Stoebe (1959), Winton Thomas (1949), who studies possible Semitic cognates, Torrance (1952), Werner (1988).

The ancient versions had difficulty with the word. Already a tendency to give the admonition a pietistic rather than a moral emphasis is discernible. In Aramaic and later Hebrew the word acquired connotations of modesty or chastity. In the Talmud the *qal* passive participle (Prov 11:2) comes to be used to refer to the person whose spiritual disposition ("modesty") qualifies him for divine blessings and privileges. Etymological inquiry has not found the key (Winton Thomas 1949). We believe that Stoebe (1959) has come closest to the meaning by recognizing its wisdom background. He translates *behutsam*, "prudently," or *bedachtsam*, "thoughtfully." This gives *haṣnēaʿ* a more intellectual slant. It justifies Hillers's translation "wisely" (1984: 75). Werner (1988) accepts Stoebe's interpretation and recognizes v 8 as a brief postexilic faith statement grounded in preexilic prophetic affirmations of Torah and of Israel's traditional creedal recital of Yahweh's saving acts. Dawes (1988), however, defends the traditional understanding of *haṣnēaʿ* as "humbly."

Comment on Micah 6:1–8

The opening formalities of vv 1b–2 create an expectation that a conventional *rîb* will follow. The disputants—Yahweh and Israel—are identified (v 2b). The mountains are commanded to listen (v 2a). It was characteristic of eighth-century prophets to create a certain expectation in the minds of listeners by starting off with the recognizable forms of a familiar genre, but then to twist the discourse away into quite unconventional development. Isaiah acted the troubador and announced that he was going to sing a love ballad (Isaiah 5), and so he did for a colon or two. But soon his song became an allegory, and then a *rîb*, and then a riddle. The composition fitted no genre, or rather it mixed ingredients that had affinities with many genres, to the despair of modern scholars who have been quite unable to classify the resultant piece. Isaiah 1 begins in a manner similar to Micah 6, as if it is going to be a covenant *rîb*. However, Yahweh takes on other roles beside that of litigant—owner of animals, father of children. Considerations of strict justice do not provide the guidelines for the debate that follows. It is not simply accusation followed by condemnation, followed by judgment. There are exhortations to reform (Isa 1:16–17), an offer of pardon (1:18–19), warnings (1:20), promises of renewal (1:25–27). Just as in Micah 6, Isaiah begins by invoking the heavens and the earth to witness the dispute to follow (Isa 1:2), and after that they disappear from view. They say nothing, do nothing.

In both of these chapters, the juridical institutions that would be the normal setting of a *rîb* have a low profile. The characteristic speeches (accusation, defense, verdict) are absent. Inversely, the genre of the speeches actually given (historical recital [Isa 1:2a = Mic 6:4], request for guidance [vv 6–7]) would be out of place in a court hearing. Comparative analysis of other passages that are considered to be documents of the covenant lawsuit, such as Isaiah 1 and Jeremiah 2, helps only in a negative way. Each of these is a sustained prophetic discourse in which various oracular materials have been worked up into a literary composition. Micah 6:1–8 represents a similar rhetorical integration of otherwise diverse ingredients, intended for proclamation or even for reading, but outside the controls of realistic simulation of courtroom procedures, or some kind of cultic re-enactment along forensic lines.

It is only in the opening verses of Micah 6 that the technical vocabulary points to such a process. The mountains are urged to hear Yahweh's *rîb* with

Israel (v 2), and v 3 sounds as if Yahweh is confronting his people in court. But there is no formal indictment. The request *'ănēh bî, Answer* [2d m. sg.] *me!* is rather an invitation to find fault with Yahweh—if they can! "Testify against me!" The recital that follows (vv 4 and 5) could be taken as a protestation of Yahweh's faithfulness, but one has to fill in a great deal to find in this a diagnosis that Israel's sins (unnamed) are the result of ingratitude. The request to remember could imply further that ingratitude rose from forgetfulness. But, unless these are only snippets from a much longer and more comprehensive recital, the events recounted are very remote from the present. The speech by Yahweh is more in his own defense than an indictment of Israel such as would be expected at this point.

In spite of the opening words, the tone of the speeches is imploring rather than accusing, encouraging rather than minatory, conciliatory ("my people!") rather than alienating. God is hurt rather than angry. If v 3 is intended to produce shame, v 5 will arouse memory and gratitude. By the time the end is reached the forbidding mood of the opening lines has been entirely replaced by a warm invitation to continue walking in covenant life.

The concluding speech is also constructive, a reaffirmation of goodwill and a reminder of past favors, with the implication that these experiences were definitive of a standing relationship. The familiar recital in v 4a is a standard way of referring to the whole complex of Exodus and wilderness wanderings. That would have been enough. But Micah adds five names. From the way in which Yahweh defends himself against implied charges, we can infer what those charges most probably were. One implied charge would be that Yahweh may have done great things in the past, but not lately—the kind of complaint that is often voiced in the Psalms. The reply is to remind the nation of its origins. Its very existence is the result of the "righteous acts of Yahweh" at the time of the Exodus. The theme of deliverance and the verbs in v 4a emphasize that Yahweh is a God of action and redemption.

The second complaint must be about leadership, or the lack of it. All the eighth-century prophets identify the failure of the leadership as the prime cause of Israel's trouble in their day, Micah as much as the others. In v 4b we have a list of the great leaders of the Exodus and wanderings, from a single family. Great leaders and great wonders are the hallmarks of Israel's past, both reflecting the concern of God for his people, his mighty deeds on their behalf, as well as the leaders whom he appointed for that purpose.

When we come to v 5, we have the reference to the conflict between the king (Balak) and the prophet (Balaam). The reminder about the confrontation between Balak and Balaam shows how a prophet of the eighth century could and would look back to the great period of Israel's beginnings for examples and analogies in dealing with contemporary problems. That episode was a historic and exemplary case of king-prophet confrontation, and although they were both foreigners, and the parallels would be skewed, this continued to be one of the prime issues throughout the entire period of Israel's monarchies. Balak wanted to bring curses down on Israel, but was thwarted by Yahweh through his (unwilling) servant Balaam, in this situation a true prophet. So the message for the current crisis is that the king, as usual with the prophets, is in the wrong, and he is being opposed by a prophet, who is in the right. Just as Balaam neutralized and reversed the king more than once in the contest of wills, so here is a prophet who is proclaiming the truth against a king who is trying to subvert the country and destroy it in the process. The king and associated leadership are behaving in ways that will bring to pass the curses of the covenant (6:14–15) instead of its blessings. As to the identity of this king, so far as Micah was concerned, there is only one candidate—Ahaz (2 Kgs 16:2–3). That Ahaz was the king who revived human sacrifice would not be lost either on the prophet or his audience. We know about the confrontation between Ahaz and Isaiah, and perhaps that is precisely what Micah has in mind here, although it is also possible, even likely, that he is thinking of himself. Chapters 2–3 show that he experienced opposition from other prophets, doubtless in the pay of the establishment. Given his messages, especially that Jerusalem would be destroyed, it is highly likely that he ran afoul of at least one king.

EXCURSUS: HUMAN SACRIFICE
IN THE HEBREW BIBLE

Religious Background

The questions asked in Mic 6:6–7 in response to a speech of condemnation made by Yahweh (vv 3–5) are a series of proposals for remedying the situation. The proposals culminate with the option to "give" that person's firstborn son. The generic ʿôlôt (v 6bA) covers all the items in the following list—calves, rams, oil—indicating that the last item—the firstborn—is to be given as a sacrificial offering. In a recent study Cross has demonstrated the use of the equivalent term in Phoenician to describe human sacrifice (1994: 97). God addressed his words to "my people" (v 3aA). The speaker who responds is not identified; presumably he is a representative of Israel. Whether he or she is a typical individual or some especially appropriate person is not indicated. In view of attested procedures, it is plausible to suppose that the king would be expected to take such an initiative.

The common use of the term "child sacrifice," while appropriate for the sacrifice of infants, even babies, as it was done in Carthage (S. Brown 1992), has a more horrifying effect because of the helplessness and innocence of the victims. The expression "innocent blood" refers generally to unwarranted homicide (Deut 19:10; 21:8, 9; 27:25; Isa 59:7; Jer 22:3; 26:15). In one clear instance the phrase applies to Canaanite child sacrifice (Ps 106:38). It is possible, then, that the sin of Manasseh, who filled Jerusalem from one side to the other with "innocent blood" (2 Kgs 21:16; cf. 2 Kgs 24:4), a sin that the LORD would not pardon, was human sacrifice on a considerable scale. But sons and daughters are not necessarily children. There is no indication of an age limit; rather that language is used because the sacrifice was made by the father, a point often over-looked. The language of Mic 6:7 is clearly that of a father.

The proposal to "give" a firstborn son needs to be understood in connection with ancient practices of ceremonial killing of humans (Derchain 1970; Green 1975; Xella 1976a; Cross 1994). It is not clear whether ritualized capital punishment, or wholesale slaughter of populations in war (*ḥerem*), or votary offering of a human should be called "sacrifice." "Sacrifice" is an interpretive term, covering not just what is done, but what the killing was believed to achieve. The word has acquired a wide metaphorical usage, but it properly denotes a formalized ritual act in which something valuable is given to a god as tribute, for appeasement, to give pleasure, or with some such aim. The proposal in Mic 6:6–7 is a means of atoning for sin. Jephthah's sacrifice (Judg 11:31) was in fulfillment of a vow. The language of Gen 22:2 is cultic, but Abraham was given no reason for the sacrifice of Isaac.

The ceremonial slaughter of animals could be followed by incineration of the whole or of selected portions; but in some procedures the flesh could be cooked and eaten as part of the liturgy. The ancient Near East does not seem to have institutionalized cannibalism as a religious activity, as it usually is in cultures that practice it (apart from emergency use of human bodies as food as the last desperate measures against starvation); but see Oeming (1989). The grisly language of Micah 3:1–3 is usually taken as metaphorical; but note the language of Ezek 16:20; Hos 13:2. Cross (1994) has shown in some detail that the term *š'r*, "flesh," refers to offspring as the donor's own flesh, emphasizing the kinship, indeed the identify of victim with offerer. The language in Micah—"the fruit of my body"—has a similar effect. This goes beyond substitution. Biblical denunciation of Canaanite religion targeted human sacrifice, especially the sacrifice of children, as its chief abomination (Deut 12:31) along with magic (Deut 18:9–14). By the end of the seventh century B.C.E., if not earlier, child sacrifice was considered abhorrent to the God of Israel ("I did not command it; it did not even enter my mind" [Jer 7:31; 19:5]). Prior to that there are indications that human sacrifice was carried out in Israel, not only by its neighbors. The clearest evidence comes from the time of Micah. Ahaz (Hezekiah's father) and Manasseh (Hezekiah's son) are named culprits. Although the dating of biblical sources is increasingly problematic, it is likely that the editorial work in the Primary History that included the two most conspicuous instances of a father sacrificing his own child (Abraham [Genesis 22], Jephthah [Judges 11]) reflected a motif that was topical in the eighth century B.C.E.

Abundant textual material (for Ugaritic practice, see DeGuglielmo 1955; Fisher 1970; Xella 1976a; for Punic, see Gianto 1987; Stager 1980; Stager and Wolff 1984) and archaeological evidence (Albright 1968: 236–44; Hennesy 1985) show that disapproving comments on human sacrifice by biblical authors were not just exaggerated polemics against Canaanite religion; the practice was widespread and long-lived among Canaanites (especially Phoenicians [Delavault and Lemaire 1976]—widely attested also by classical authors, with gruesome archaeological evidence in corroboration). Heider (1985: 404) has confirmed the position taken by the Hebrew Bible that Israel's Molek cult had Canaanite origins, and even more ancient roots, now that the evidence for the Syro-Palestinian god Maliku(m) or Milku/i has been traced back to Amorite and Eblaite (lists in Heider 1985: 409–19). Molek was a god after all. At the same time, there seems to have been a connection between the God Molek and the human king who had a special interest in this kind of sacrifice (Eissfeldt 1935; cf. Bea 1937).

The cultic rules for dedicating and redeeming the firstborn of humans and animals suggest that an animal could be substituted for a human (Exod 13:2), and this provision in Genesis 22 has been seen as an etiology for the changeover in practice in Israel (Veijola 1988; Deurloo 1994).

Biblical Evidence

Human sacrifice is reported in 2 Kgs 3:27 (king of Moab [Dearman 1989]); 16:3 [= 2 Chr 28:3] (Ahaz); 17:17; 21:6 [= 2 Chr 33:6] (Manasseh); 23:10; Jer 7:31 (a Tophet existed in the valley of the sons of Hinnom [Gehenna], where the ritual was performed); Isa 57:5; Ezek 16:20; 20:31; Hos 13:2; Amos 2:1 (reading *mōlek 'ādām, "a molek sacrifice of a human"). Cross's interpretation of 'dm as "blood" (prosthetic alef), while plausible, is hard to prove when there are so many ways of reading 'dm (DNWSI 641). His extension of the meaning to "blood relation" is a further speculation; but it gains some credibility from the use of other kinship terms in connection with mlk sacrifices. Jeremiah 19:4–5 shows that Baʿal could be the god worshiped in this way; 2 Kgs 17:31 named "Adrammalech and Anammelech"; Ps 106:37 says "demons."

The references to "Molech" (Lev 18:21; 20:1–5; etc.) gave rise to lurid speculations as to the identity and appearance of this god. Eissfeldt (1935) demonstrated that the word mulk, as used in Punic texts, indicated a supreme (royal) sacrifice of humans. (See also Bea 1937; Day 1989; Dronkert 1953.) Recently others, notably Heider (1985), Edelman (1987), and Day (1989), have argued that the Punic evidence should not be extended to Israelite practice, in spite of the common Canaanite connection. Attempts to explain these reports otherwise (Weinfeld 1972) have not been convincing (Smith 1975). Yahweh was outraged by the practice because the victims were *his children* (Deut 32:16–19; Ezek 16:21). Yet it is precisely the passion of these condemnations that makes Yahweh's command to Abraham so inexplicable to most readers (Reventlow 1968; Kilian 1970; Kreuzer 1986).

Alongside this tradition forbidding human sacrifice there is the solid teaching of the Hebrew Bible, embodied in central rituals of the cultus as set out in great detail in Leviticus, that only the shedding of the blood of an innocent or flawless victim could expiate serious sin. There is evidence of belief even in Israel that (only) human sacrifice could cope with grave emergencies and expiate extreme guilt. David agreed that the Gibeonites should "hang up [seven sons of Saul] before Yahweh at Gibeon on the mountain of Yahweh" (2 Sam 21:6) to "make expiation" (v 3). "And after that God heeded supplications for the land" (v 14). The suggestion in Micah 6:7 seems to arise from such a belief and is made in all seriousness (albeit rejected by Yahweh [Anderson 1951]).

The Rationale of Genesis 22

No reason (such as the placation of divine wrath) is given to Abraham for the command to sacrifice his son. (Later commentators came up with many suggestions, and the story was extensively rewritten to make it more intelligible, more morally acceptable; see Davies and Chilton 1978; Jacobs 1981; Milgrom 1988; Spiegel 1967.) The narrator says simply that God "tested" him. The test is made dramatic by the circumstances of Isaac's birth and his key place in the covenant (Genesis 21). The test is made poignant by the emphasis on Abraham's love for Isaac (v 2), underscored by the repetition of the terms "my father" and "my son" in the dialogue. There is no indication that children were regarded as chattels, to be disposed of without compunction. It was precisely Abraham's love for Isaac that made the test such a dreadful ordeal. The language of Mic 6:7 ("the fruit of my body") documents the same feeling. On parental attitudes toward children in antiquity, see Théodoridès, Naster, and Reis (1980) and Charlesworth (1990). The history of social attitudes toward children is not well researched. The notion that affection for children is a modern development and that until recently children were valued only as property has been refuted, at least so far as modern Europe is concerned, by Pollock (1983). There is abundant evidence for inconsolable grief over the death of children in private diaries. Similar evidence for Islam is supplied by the abundant tracts for the consolation of bereaved parents, whose roots go back to *ḥadîth* sources, with Jewish *midrashim* in the same vein (Gilʿadi 1989). The piety encouraged by these stories draws its inspiration from the legends of Eve's grief for Abel, Jacob's mourning for the (supposed) death of Joseph, David's behavior in loss (2 Sam 12:15–25; 18:33), and especially Job.

The power of these stories has been diminished in some recent writing, influenced by moral disapproval of Israel's social structures and values as "patriarchal." It has been inferred that men were inhumane toward women and children, who were valued only as property or status symbols. The genuineness of parental affection, which adds poignancy to biblical stories of bereavement, was not appreciated, and the grief of the father who surrendered a child in sacrifice, was not recognized. Tender love was ascribed to mothers, while fathers were seen as stern and callous. Texts were misread so as to provide exegetical support for these stereotypes. "God anguishes over the people's fate like a mother" (K. M. O'Connor, in Newsom and Ringe 1992: 175). "God is a mother attached to her child" (176). As if fathers were not attached to their children and did not grieve over them. In deploring his having been born, Jeremiah records that the person who brought the news to his father, made his heart rejoice. A natural reading finds this father's joy a universal human experience; it is cynical to say that he was glad because he had acquired a piece of valuable property. Both parents shared the joy. At birth the infant was placed on knees and put to breasts (Job 3:12). Since the breasts were obviously its mother's, it has been inferred that the knees were too, even though in the adduced parallels it is not the mother whose knees receive the newborn child. In Gen 30:3, it is the adopting mother whose knees receive the child from the surrogate mother. Joseph's great grandchildren were born on his knees (Gen 50:23). A particularly clear example is supplied by the Hittite story of "Appu and His Two Sons." "Appu's wife bore a son. The nurse lifted the boy and placed him on Appu's knees" (Hallo 1997: 154). There is no warrant then for the REB translation of Job 3:12: "Why was I ever laid on my mother's knees or put to suck at her breasts?" See Stade 1886b.

In the case of Abraham the repeated phrases in Gen 22:2 and 12 make the test more severe by recognizing the love that the father had for his son. But what was being tested? The story itself highlights Abraham's (apparently unquestioning) obedience (v 18) as proof that he "feared" God (v 12). This virtue remained paramount in Jewish understanding, and is the only simple moral of the miracle play (Cawley 1959). Jesus ben Sirah already interpreted the outcome: "he was found to be πιστος (*pistos*, faithful)" (44:20). An early Christian commentator identified Abraham's virtue as "faith" (Heb 11:17–19), not only as trust, but as belief in resurrection, see Dahl 1969, Veijola 1988. Jewish piety identified with Abraham's anguish when parents consented to (and even encouraged) their children's martyrdom, from the time of the Maccabees onward. This attitude came to a horrifying crescendo during the persecutions of the Middle Ages, when pious Jews, rather than fall into the hands of their (Christian!) tormenters killed their children first, and then each other, using the language of Genesis 22 and observing the sacrificial procedures (details in Spiegel 1963).

The Rationale of Judges 11

The interpretation of Judges 11 is handicapped by two limitations. First, the detachment of the narrator makes it difficult to discern the motivation of the story. We should not assume that the Bible approves of the actions of its "heroes" unless it explicitly condemns them. The stories are remarkably free from comments making value judgments. The end of the story in Judges 11 is similarly laconic: "he did with her according to his vow which he had vowed." Second, it is far from clear just how Jephthah fulfilled his vow. Embarrassed Bible students have betrayed too much eagerness to find arguments that the vow was transmuted in some way. Burney (1918: 329–31) had an excursus "Human Sacrifice among the Israelites," and in his Prolegomenon to the 1970 KTAV reprint Albright commented: "No new light has been shed by recent discovery on the meaning of the sacrifice of Jephthah's daughter, whether she was condemned to perpetual virginity, or was to be a human sacrifice. The arguments on both sides are perhaps equally weak" (Albright 1970: 22). Since then, possible evidence for human sacrifice in Jephthah's country has come from Deir ʿAllā (Hackett 1984, 1987). For a feminist reading of Judges 11, see Bal (1988) and in general Brenner and van Dijk-Hemmes (1993), and Newsom and Ringe (1992). For a critique of one-sided readings of such stories, illustrated by Fewell and Gunn (1991), see Sternberg (1992).

Common Features

Even before Christian times, in Jewish understanding of Genesis 22 the focus shifted from Abraham to Isaac as the *willing victim*, bringing his attitude close to that of Jephthah's daughter. Endless retellings of the stories gave the victims a more decisive role as models for martyrs (Davies and Chilton 1978). The New Testament contains many hints that Isaac was understood as a type of Jesus (the ram also!) (Daly 1977; Moberley 1988; Ska 1988; Lenenson 1993). The typology was already well developed in the second century A.D. by Melito of Sardis (Wilken 1976), in whose interpretation criticism of the Jews becomes very strident.

Among the midrashic elaborations, details of the story were made to yield suggestions that Abraham did in fact consummate the sacrifice, and that Isaac was miraculously restored.

Modern Critical Interpretation

Since the Enlightenment, the significance of Genesis 22, Judges 11, and Mic 6:7–8 has been trivialized by "liberal" criticism that found the very idea of sacrifice primitive and theologically unacceptable. God does not need a sacrifice in order to accept sinners. This meant that Jews were told that a God who could put Abraham through such an ordeal was unworthy; while Christians were told that their interpretation of the death of Jesus as salvific— the Lamb of God, bearing the sins of the world—was unacceptable. Judged by prevailing ethical idealism, the biblical stories were found to be crude, and their representation of Yahweh as a God who would "test" Abraham in such a cruel way, or who could be conceived as expecting Jephthah to consummate such a rash vow, was found to be morally repugnant. Such complaints were not new. Philo (*de Abrahamo*, 177–99) and Origen already replied to them. Attempts to save the stories by claiming that its intention was to teach that God did not want human sacrifice were particularly feeble; the texts do not say that at all. Abraham's merit lay precisely in his willingness to do what God told him to do. The "test" becomes vacuous, and the theological problems only break out in another place when theological requirements override the way God speaks and acts in the story *as it is actually told*. The way the story of the Akedah has been continually retold reveals endless attempts to rescue God from the complaint that he was deceptive, insincere, and far from candid. And it is only when the most troublesome components are taken seriously that the story continues to have such spiritual power for Jews, Christians, and also Muslims (who, however, replace Isaac with Ishmael in their version). The same earnestness provides the tension in the prayer of Mic 6:6–7. The situation is desperate and the proposal is serious.

It was Søren Kierkegaard who brought philosophical seriousness back to the text of Genesis 22 in *Fear and Trembling* (1843). The impact of this disturbing essay was not felt for a long time; but now it stands as posing ultimate existential questions in the most agonizing way. Biblical scholars had always been aware of specific exegetical problems, such as why the story emphasizes that father and son went off "together" (vv 6, 8), yet ends by saying simply that "Abraham returned to his young men" (v 19), suggesting that Isaac was not with him. This, and other topoi, were endlessly dealt with in comment and midrash (details in Spiegel [1967], Davies and Chilton [1978]). But Kierkegaard's three "Problems" went to the heart of the matter: (1) Is there such a thing as a teleological suspension of the Ethical? (2) Is there such a thing as an absolute duty toward God? (3) Was Abraham ethically defensible in keeping silent about his purpose before Sarah, before Eleazar, before Isaac? See Gordis (1976).

Childs (1993: 325–36) presented a study of the Akedah as the first of his experiments in doing "Exegesis in the Context of Biblical Theology." These two duties pull against each other. Exegesis gives full attention to the uniqueness of the given text, just as history requires attention to the uniqueness of the event. Theology looks for generalizations and enduring principles, with ritual reenactment or even just recital providing some kind of reactualization, aided by typological hermeneutics. Genesis 22 has supplied types, even prototypes. But much of the power of the story is lost when the Christian embellishments ("By faith, Abraham . . . offered up Isaac" [Heb 11:17]) are fed back into the plot structure of Genesis 22. Even the New Testament sees the other side ("Was not our father Abraham justified *by what he did*?" [James 2:21]). "[T]he focus of interest lies in Abraham's supreme obedience" (Sternberg 1987: 192). Abraham's reaffirmed blessing was a reward, and the enquirer in Micah 6 is told what he must do. Childs's predelection for Reformed doctrine ("Grace and reward are basically incompatible" [1993: 335]) obscures the point of the Akedah in theological sophistry.

Artistic Treatment

The iconography of the binding of Isaac has been studied by Jo Milgrom (1988). The Index of Christian Art at Princeton has 1450 entries for Genesis 22 (Spiegel 1967: xi). The theme continues to inspire Jewish writers. The poem "The Slaughter of Isaac and His Revival" by Rabbi Ephraim of Bonn (1132–1200) was the centerpiece of Spiegel's classic study. The text of the poem is to be found in Carmi (1981: 379–84). Modern poems are by Hayim Gouri and Amir Gilboa (Mintz 1966). See also Coffin (1987).

Micah 6:6–7

Against this background, the climactic offer of the firstborn son in Mic 6:7 should not be read as the end of a movement from possible offers (v 6) through impossible ones (v 7a) to the most impossible of all (v 7b), as argued by Buber and de Vaux; rather "child sacrifice is nothing other than the most valuable bid in the series" (Heider 1985: 317). The last offer was entirely possible.

There is dissonance in the text in the move from an address to Yahweh's people to the personal inquiry that follows, with its repeated "I." While the people as a whole could make a joint effort to present an impressive large-scale offering, only an individual could speak of a human as "my firstborn." This feature invalidates the argument that "Adam" in v 8 is collective. Even if there is an implication that many Israelites might be willing to do this, the personal tone is still strong. In view of past, even possibly current, practice in Israel, the person most likely to make such a proposal in Micah's day would be the king. No king is addressed anywhere in the book of Micah. But three kings are mentioned in this chapter, and we know from Jer 26:18–19 that Hezekiah took Micah's message to heart. While the alternative remedy proposed in v 8 is applicable to everybody ("Adam") it is especially appropriate for the king to do justice, love mercy, and walk humbly with his God.

III.2. MORE ACCUSATIONS AND COVENANT CURSES (6:9–16)

III.2.i. MORE ACCUSATIONS (6:9–12)

TRANSLATION

MT

9aAα	*qôl yhwh*	The voice of Yahweh!
9aAβ	*lā'îr yiqrā'*	He is calling to the city.
9aB	*wĕtûšiyyâ yir'eh šĕmekā*	And it is wisdom to fear thy [m.] name.
9bA	*šim'û maṭṭeh*	Hear [2d m. pl.], O tribe!
9bB	*ûmî yĕ'ādāh 'ôd*	And who appointed her still?
10a	*ha'iš bêt rāšā'*	Are there in the house of the wicked
	'ōṣĕrôt reša'	the treasuries of wickedness?
10b	*wĕ'êpat rāzôn zĕ'ûmâ*	And the fraudulent ephah in the detested (city[?])?
11a	*ha'ezkeh bĕmō'zĕnê reša'*	Shall I regard as pure the scales of wickedness,
11b	*ûbĕkîs 'abnê mirmâ*	and the bag of deceitful weights?
12aA	*'ăšer 'ăšîreyhā mālĕ'û ḥāmās*	—her rich men have filled (her) with violence,
12aB	*wĕyōšĕbeyhā dibbĕrû-šāqer*	and her residents have made false agreements,
12b	*ûlĕšônām rĕmiyyâ bĕpîhem*	and their tongue is deceitful in their mouth.

LXX III.2.i. More Accusations (6:9–12)

9aAα	The voice of Kyrios
9aAβ	to the city will be proclaimed.
9aB	And he will save those who fear his name.
9bA	Hear [sg.], O tribe!
9bB	And who will adorn the city?
10a	(Surely it is) not fire, and the house of the wicked
10b	heaping up unlawful riches,
	and with the pride of unrighteousness {proud unrighteousness by measure}.

11a	Shall the lawbreaker be justified by a balance,
11b	or deceitful weights in a pouch
12aA	from which their ungodly wealth they accumulated,
12aB	and her residents spoke falsehood,
12b	and their tongue was lifted up in their mouth.

III.2.ii. COVENANT CURSES (6:13–16)

TRANSLATION

MT

13a	wĕgam-ʾănî heḥălêtî hakkôtekā	And I too—I injured thee [m.] by smiting thee [m.],
13b	hašmēm ʿal-ḥaṭṭōʾtekā	I devastated (thee) for thy [m.] sins.
14aA	ʾattâ tōʾkal	Thou [m.]—thou wilt eat,
	wĕlōʾ tiśbāʿ	but thou wilt not be satisfied,
14aB	wĕyešḥăkā bĕqirbekā	and thy yšḥ in thy midst.
14bA	wĕtassēg wĕlōʾ taplîṭ	And thou [m.] wilt come to labor, but thou [m.] wilt not survive;
14bB	waʾăšer tĕpallēṭ laḥereb ʾettēn	and what thou shalt rescue I will put to the sword.
15a	ʾattâ tizraʿ wĕlōʾ tiqṣôr	Thou [m.]—thou wilt sow, but thou wilt not reap.
15bA	ʾattâ tidrōk-zayit	Thou [m.]—thou wilt tread olives,
	wĕlōʾ-tāsûk šemen	but thou wilt not be rubbed with oil,
15bB	wĕtîrôš	and must,
	wĕlōʾ tišteh-yāyin	but thou wilt not drink wine.
16aAα	wĕyištammēr ḥuqqôt ʿomrî	And he observed the statutes of Omri,
16aAβ	wĕkōl maʿăsēh bêt-ʾaḥʾāb	and all the deeds of the house of Ahab.
16aB	wattēlĕkû bĕmōʿăṣôtām	And you [m. pl.] walked in their [m.] policies.
16bAα	lĕmaʿan tittî ʾōtĕkā lĕšammâ	So that I might give thee [m.] to devastation
16bAβ	wĕyōšĕbeyhā lišĕrēqâ	and her residents to hissing;
16bB	wĕḥerpat ʿammî tiśśāʾû	and you [m. pl.] will bear the reproach of my people.

LXX III.2.ii. Covenant Curses (6:13–16)

13a	And I too—I shall begin to smite thee,
13b	I shall destroy thee in thy sins.
14aA	Thou—thou shalt eat, and thou shalt not be satisfied,
14aB	and it will grow dark in thee.
14bA	And he will depart, and thou shalt not be saved;
14bB	and as many as are saved shall be handed over to the sword.

15a   Thou—thou shalt sow, and thou shalt not reap.
15bA   Thou—thou shalt press olives,
                      and thou shalt not be anointed with oil,
15bB   and wine, and thou shalt not drink.
               And the customs of my people shall be taken away.
16aAα   And thou hast kept the statutes of Zambri,
16aAβ   and all the works of the house of Akhab.
16aB   And you [pl.] walked in their counsels,
16bAα   so that I might give thee to destruction
16bAβ   and her inhabitants to hissing;
16bB   and you will bear the reproaches of peoples.

INTRODUCTION TO MICAH 6:9–16

The Form of Micah 6:9–16

This unit consists of a bill of crimes followed by a threat of punishment. If it were not for the fact that v 8 is seen as the end of the previous unit, the *rîb*, the second half of the chapter would fit into that *Gattung* quite well. Perhaps it does. Verse 8, with its reminder that what Yahweh wants is *mišpāṭ* and *ḥesed*, is not yet a solution to the problem with Israel, but the starting point for the detailed indictment that follows. The questions in vv 10–11 continue from vv 3–5; the curses of vv 14–15 arise directly from the sanctions of the covenant.

In language and style, vv 9–16 resemble materials in chapters 1–3 that may be accepted as authentic Micah. One of the hallmarks is obscurity; obscurity to us, that is. Whether this is due to deterioration of the text as a result of long transmission, or whether it inheres in the very nature of this kind of prophecy is a point under assessment. Probably a bit of each, but the deficiency is more likely to be in our knowledge and competence than in the received text.

The Drama of Micah 6:9–16

Much of the difficulty of vv 9–16 arises from the presence of differing referential pronouns. It is worst in the opening and closing verses, both of which contain "you" (plural), not found in the others. Presumably "thy" name refers to Yahweh, but the subject of *yir'eh*, "he will fear," is unidentified. Perhaps v 9aB is an isolated saying used as part of the opening exhortation. The next verb, "Hear" (pl.) goes with "tribe" (sg.). The latter could be collective, but not if *maṭṭeh* is "scepter" (NJPS) or "rod" (NIV). It is not clear, however, why the audience is addressed in this way. The last two words of v 9 are totally obscure; the final pronoun "her" could refer to the city.

Verse 16 begins with "he," switches to "you" (pl.), then "thou" (agreeing with vv 14–15) then to "you" (plural). The isolated "thou" in v 16 comes in a *lĕmaʿan* clause, which could balance the otherwise unmatched *lĕmaʿan* clause in v 5 (v 5 has no pronouns to aid the hookup).

The intervening verses (vv 10–15) are more straightforward. They are dominated by "I" (Yahweh) and "thou" (masculine)—the individual Israelite? The addressee is not the city, to which Yahweh is apparently speaking in v 9, which would be feminine. Perhaps the alternation of singular and plural second-person pronouns is no more problematical here than in Deuteronomy, where it must simply be accepted as a characteristic of parenesis. In fact, vv 14–15, in which *'attā* is prominent, are like old curses applied individually. But the very prominence of "thou" suggests a real person. The "sins" are identified quite precisely as those of businessmen of the unnamed city. The one person most responsible for this would be the king, and evil kings are mentioned in v 16. Yet the curses are relevant to agriculturalists, not city bureaucrats.

The Poetry of Micah 6:9–16

The middle verses (10–15) display good poetic composition. Verses 10–12 are an indictment of the wicked, who have been enriched by fraudulent business practices. Verses 12aB and 12b together make a good bicolon. The common theme is false speech.

12aB	*wĕyōšĕbeyhā dibbĕrû-šāqer*	and her residents have made false agreements,
12b	*ûlĕšônām rĕmiyyâ bĕpîhem*	and their tongue is deceitful in their mouth.

Verse 12aA completes a tricolon through the parallelism of *'ăšîreyhā* and *yōšĕbeyhā*, which, by hendiadys, means "her (the city's) rich inhabitants." The relative pronoun carries the whole tricolon, which is 28 syllables long.

Verse 11 is a bicolon of standard shape (A : B :: B') and length (16 syllables).

11a	*ha'ezkeh bĕmō'zĕnê reša'*	Shall I regard as pure the scales of wickedness,
11b	*ûbĕkîs 'abnê mirmâ*	and the bag of deceitful weights?

Verse 10b with v 11 completes a tricolon dealing with dishonest weights and measures. Its three-word phrase ("the fraudulent detested ephah") resembles the one in v 11b. So vv 10b through 12b consist of two tricolons of similar design.

This leaves v 10a as an individual clause (ten syllables) with no contiguous parallel. Grammatically it continues into v 10b; the treasures of wickedness and the fraudulent ephah are in the wicked house. Verse 10a does, however, have links with the two tricolons that follow. The two kinds of fraud—dishonest measures (10b–11), deceitful words (12)—explain how the house of the wicked contains treasure stores of wickedness. The root *rš'* is used three times in vv 10–11, unifying the tetracolon.

These seven colons contain a string of words referring to various kinds of skulduggery:

10a	*rāšā'*	wicked
	reša'	wickedness
10b	*zĕ'ûmâ*	detested
11a	*reša'*	wickedness
11b	*mirmâ*	deceit
12aA	*ḥāmās*	violence
12aB	*šāqer*	falsehood
12b	*rĕmiyyâ*	deceit

These general observations provide some firm ground to stand on. But they do not help in the softer places. Verses 9 and 10a remain intractable. The expectation that similar parallelism should be found here has prompted the search for emendations. Wellhausen remains the undisputed winner of the prize for brilliance and ingenuity, and his solutions continue to hold the field, contributing largely to the suggestions still proffered by BHS and adopted silently by many translations. See the NOTES.

Verses 13–15 show similar rhetorical features. Verse 13 is a bicolon that contains complementary matching pairs in complex relationships; the second colon augments and completes the first. The same idea is expressed twice, but the two colons do not match in detail. Even the members of the one matching pair are grammatically different—the perfect verb *heḥălêtî* is matched by an infinitive absolute. The first verb has an elaborate use of the free pronoun to reinforce the subject (*gam-'ănî*), but the object is understood. Both subject and object of *hašmēm* have to be supplied—"(I) devastated (thee)."

In vv 14–15 the threefold "thou" contrasts with "I" in v 13, and carries five statements of similar construction—a curse in the figure of sorites. The four colons dealing with food constitute one set:

You will eat,	but you won't be satisfied;
You will sow,	but you won't reap.
You will tread olives,	but you won't rub (yourself with) oil;
and must,	but you won't drink wine.

Frustration is predicted for every stage in the production of three staple foods, so v 15 expounds the first colon of v 14. Mays (1976: 143) shuffles these colons together; cf. BHS footnote. The other three colons of v 14 probably constitute another set, but they are more difficult to sort out because v 14aB is unintelligible. Verse 14b contains another sorites, and it is possible that v 14aB is part of it.

Verse 16 is complicated by the changes in the pronouns. The parallelism of Omri // Ahab shows that v 16aA is a bicolon, and v 16bA has *lĕšammâ // lišrēqâ*. This leaves v 16aB // 16bB (both colons with plural "you"). A partial identification of the participants in vv 9–16 is:

maṭṭeh	"he"
"city"	"she"
"people"	"thou" (m.) as in vv 1–8
"the rich"	"they"
"Yahweh"	"I"

NOTES AND COMMENTS

Notes on Micah 6:9–16

Textual Notes on Micah 6:9

LXX attests the difficulty of the text, and back translation does not restore a better original. Instead of *tûšiyyâ*, "wisdom"(?), it reads a verb *sōsei*, "he will save" (*yôšiaʿ*)(?). Instead of *yirʾeh šĕmekā*, "he will see your name," it has *phoboumenous to onoma autou*, "those who fear his name," as if from *yĕrēʾîm* (which occurs four times in 2 Kings 17) or construct *yirʾê* (the *nomen rectum* is usually "God" or "Yahweh," but "thy name" in Ps 61:6). To recover a better Hebrew text from LXX would require almost every word of MT to be changed. LXX readings tend to be facile and harmonistic. The result is rather pious and does not fit the rest of the passage at all. It seems as if LXX is already struggling with the problems that still confront us in the Hebrew text. LXX also resolves the clash of number between "Hear" and "tribe" by reading a singular verb. LXX confirms *ûmî*, "and who," but interprets *yʿdh ʿwd* as *kosmēsei polin*, "he will beautify the city." The latter points to *ʿîr*. This is an attractive solution, since it supplies a match for *ʿîr* in v 9aA, and *ʿwd* could easily be a misreading of *ʿyr*. That would be a writing error, since the reading seems to be unintelligible.

Reading *ʿîr* for *ʿwd* solves a few problems: *ʿôd*, "still," is unsuitable at the beginning of v 10, especially before a question. The greatest problem in retaining MT lies in the meaning of *yʿdh*, "he appointed her." If *mûʿād* or *môʿēd* could be read, the latter would be a municipal assembly of some kind. The noun *môʿēd* also has connotations of business enterprise—an association of merchants. It would relieve the strain of plural *šimʿû* plus singular *maṭṭeh* if the subject is "*maṭṭeh* and her *something*." The plural *šimʿû* is fine if *maṭṭeh wmy [y]ʿdh* is a plural phrase. Wellhausen read *wmy yʿdh ʿwd* as *wmwʿd hʿyr*, "and the assembly of the city." In Josh 20:9 *mûʿādâ* is an assembly. One could read **mûʿāde(y)hā*, "those assembled (in) her" (cf. Jer 24:1). The call is addressed to *maṭṭeh* ("tribal leader") and those assembled in the city. For a similar indictment of a city, rich through dishonest commerce, see Hab 2:9, 12. On the root *yʿd* see Jeppesen (1984a), who compares Nah 1:10 and translates, "Who has made a decision about her?" He adds the comment: "God himself, of course, has made the decision about Jerusalem to punish her because of the sins enumerated in the following verses" (1984a: 574). The observation is cogent, but the identification of the city is not certain. We are inclined to agree with van der Woude (1978: 22) that the city is Samaria.

Another interpretation (NIV) makes "rod" the object of *šim'û* — "Heed the rod and the One who appointed it," presumably the ensuing punishment perceived as an ordinance of God. But *šim'û*, especially after *qôl*, must mean "listen (to words)"; and the rest is strained too far, with *mî* as relative, *y'd* as "appoint," and a feminine pronoun for a masculine noun. In the context, the best referent for "her" is the city. The verb means "appoint" a person (to a role) or a place or a time.

Grammatical Notes on Micah 6:9

The absence of a conjunction suggests that a new unit begins at this point. The Masoretic tradition recognizes an "open" division between v 8 and v 9. The sequence of words in v 9aA is unusual. On the surface, the syntax is Subject + Indirect Object + Verb: "the voice of Yahweh + to the city + he is calling (or will call)." In standard prose the preferred sequence would be to have the verb first. Less common is the placement of one item, often the subject, before the verb. Clauses of this shape have a definite function in relation to their linguistic context, usually to highlight the subject, to bring the referent either to center stage (topicalization) or into contrast with some other participant. The latter function does not seem to be operating: "the voice of Yahweh" is not placed in juxtaposition or contrast with any other participant. And it is not exactly a new theme.

It is most unusual to have two grammatical items (here subject and indirect object) before the verb. Some scholars have played with the idea that the word at the beginning of the speech, *qôl*, could be used to secure attention, a function similar to *hinnēh*, "behold," or *rĕ'ēh*, "look!" The meaning of *qôl* would be "hearken!" equivalent to *šĕma'*, "listen!" This suggestion is plausible in some situations. The voice of Yahweh was mentioned in v 1b, and the opening of v 9 can be taken as a reactivation of that theme. There Yahweh addressed the mountains; here he addressed a city.

Remembering that prose particles are likely to be omitted in prophetic discourse, it is possible that the verb comes last in v 9aAβ because it is part of a relative clause: "(It is) the voice of Yahweh (that) is calling to the city."

The tense of the verb is a distinct problem. In oracular discourse it is usual to report and repeat what Yahweh *has said* to the prophet in the council (*sôd* or *'ēdâ*) where the message originated. Hence the stock rubric, "Thus Yahweh has said" (*kōh 'āmar yhwh*). In v 1 we interpreted the (unusual) use of the participle as an indication that Yahweh is about to speak, as if his impending utterance is more personal and immediate. The construction *qôl yhwh . . . yiqrā'* can be compared to *qôl haqqôrē'* (Isa 6:4) and *qôl qôrē'* (Isa 40:3), in each case a declaration in the divine assembly (Cross 1953). As a record of what was spoken there, the verb could be preterite. Otherwise it refers to impending utterance, like the participle in v 1.

There are other indications that the two major portions of chapter 6 (vv 1–8 and vv 9–16) are linked together by their opening statements. In v 1 *šim'û-nā'* is a general call to everyone involved; there is no vocative. The statements containing *qôl* in vv 1b and 9a are each followed by *šim'û*, this time with a vocative:

"Hear, O mountains!" (v 2a); "Hear, O tribe!" (v 9b). At v 2 *šimˁû* follows "thy voice"; At v 9 *šimˁû* follows "thy name." And, just as we inferred from the parallelism of "the mountains" and "the hills" in v 1b that the whole bicolon is addressed to Yahweh, so the whole of v 9a is addressed to Yahweh and the whole is precative, as is v 1b: "Let (thy) voice, O Yahweh, call to the city!" Admittedly it is unusual to have a jussive verb last in its clause; but the methodological issue raised here is whether structural considerations can override grammatical preferences. In poetry we think that is not only possible, but probable.

voice. This word is either a noun, and subject of the verb, or else it could be an exclamation with the effect of an imperative verb: "Hearken!" (Gen 4:10).

to the city. The city is referred to by the pronoun "her" in what follows (vv 12, 16), but a city is not being addressed in vv 13–16 where "thou" is masculine. Since v 16 refers to Omri and Ahab, the city could be Samaria, and the unidentified addressee could be a king in that tradition. Again, the city could be Jerusalem, given the continuation of chapter 3 in chapter 6; and the king would be Ahaz, guilty of following Ahab's policies. For similar language see Isa 66:6.

Hark (*qôl*), tumult from the city,
(the) voice [of Yahweh] from the temple!
The voice of Yahweh paying back
retribution to his enemies.

wisdom. The noun *tûšiyyâ* is associated with prudence and knowledge in the good sense. Like its parallel terms "wisdom" (Job 11:6) and "counsel" (Isa 28:29; Prov 8:14), it is a divine gift and a human acquisition (Prov 3:21). It means the successful application of sound wisdom. No one has managed to explain it here, unless it is a sarcastic epithet for the city whose "wisdom" consists of *deceit* and *rĕmiyyâ*, a word that is placed as an inclusion for *tûšiyyâ* (they have the same ending). Recognizing that wisdom language is used in vv 8 and 9aB, NJPS has moved the latter into v 8 to provide a concluding statement: "Then will your name achieve wisdom." The Masoretic paragraph break makes this unlikely.

fear. Verse 9aB is usually taken as a pious aside—"and it is (sound) wisdom to fear thy name" (RSV). A literal translation of MT—"he will see thy name"—does not make sense. The familiar expression "the fear of Yahweh" (which is the beginning of wisdom) has associated idioms: "fear God," "fear his word," "fear (his) name" (Deut 28:58; Isa 59:19; Mal 3:20; Pss 61:6; 86:11; 102:16; Neh 1:11). LXX read this idiom *phoboumenous to onoma autou*, "those who fear his name." It has normalized MT "thy" to the supposed third person of v 9aA, whereas we suggest normalizing the other way, making the first colon vocative (see above). LXX evidently read *yrʾh* as *yirʾê* (as in Ps 61:6). No change of consonants is needed to read *yirʾâ*, "to fear." The very expression *lĕyirʾâ šĕmekā* occurs in Ps 86:11. Here the verbal noun is poised uncomfortably between its verbal and nominal function. The verbal function requires *ʾet* (as in Deut 28:58; Neh 1:11; and even in some manuscripts of Ps 86:11). The noun should be a construct; but the absolute form can be verbal without the object marker in poetry.

We suggested above that v 5bB serves as a link back to the very beginning of the unit and a stepping-stone to v 9:

And let the hills hear thy voice . . . (v 1bB)
so as to [that they may] know the righteous acts of Yahweh. (v 5bB)

The two parts of v 9 stand in a similar relationship:

Let thy voice, O Yahweh, cry to the city
(so that they may) fear thy name!

The matching items are arranged in a chiastic pattern that links the opening portions of the two large units in chapter 6.

thy voice (v 1)	acts of Yahweh (v 5)
voice of Yahweh	thy name (v 9)

Each combination has the same outcome in view for heeding the voice of Yahweh, suggesting that they are the two parts of a composite discourse whose sustained intention is to produce knowledge of Yahweh's deeds and fear of his name. The word *tûšiyyâ* fits into this setting as an indication of the desired result of heeding the voice of Yahweh. The proclamation to the city from the voice of Yahweh expresses his wisdom and is intended to instill *tûšiyyâ* into the listeners, along with (or as a facet of) the fear of his name. These thoughts are similar to those already reported in v 8 as a declaration to humans. The three items given in v 8 in answer to the question "What is good?" are augmented in v 9 by two more items, *tûšiyyâ*, practical wisdom, and the fear of God's name. The grammar of the verse remains elusive in any interpretation, and it is not clear whether the reference of *tûšiyyâ* leans to the divine or the human connotation.

fear. There does not seem to be any way of making *yiqrā'* and *yir'eh* parallel. "Thy name" would be a better object of "call." "Those who fear your name" is a pious idea (Mal 3:16), if it is the name of Yahweh. But everywhere else in this unit, Yahweh is addressing the (unidentified) "thou."

appointed. The last two words of v 9 are the despair of all students of the passage. The first two words of v 10 are likewise unintelligible, except that *ha'iš* seems to begin the first of a series of questions, leaving *'ôd* stranded. If we follow BHS and put these three unintelligible words in one colon—*ûmî yĕ'ādāh 'ôd*—we have the possibility that the third word is a cognate modifier of the verb. The meaning of the verb is not clear. The root *'dh I*, "remove" (Job 28:8; Prov 25:20), does not seem suitable. The root *'dh II*, "adorn" (Isa 61:10; Jer 4:30; 31:4; Ezek 16:11, 13; 23:40; Hos 2:15), is the source of the LXX interpretation.

Verses 10–12 contain questions apparently asked by Yahweh. The speaker in v 13 is certainly Yahweh, and *wĕgam-'ănî*, "and I too," at the commencement of that verse points to continuity in the text. All this is what the voice of Yahweh calls to the city. Recognizing vv 10–11 as a quatrain, v 10a stands apart from the other three colons. It does not present as much regularity in rhythm and parallelism in ideas as the other three colons. The temptation to bring it into line by trimming some words and replacing others has been hard for scholars to resist.

still. The position of ʿôd at the beginning of the verse seems quite unsuitable; but it does not fit the end of v 9 either. The occurrence of the same consonants ʿd in the previous word suggests a cognate, or even a *plpl* stem from that root. Otherwise emendation to "city" is favored, as in LXX.

10. *Are there*. There are no prepositions to assist unraveling the grammar. The curious *haʾiš* has been explained in three ways: as a defective spelling of *ʾîš*; as a variant of *hăyēš* (2 Sam 14:19); as a corrupt text to be emended. Popular emendations are Wellhausen's *ʾeššeh* from *nāšâ* ("Will I forget"); *ʾeśśāʾ*, "Will I forgive," (or "bear" [Duhm]); or *ʾešbît*, "Will I destroy," "extirpate," or "cause to desist" (Exod 5:5, Ezek 16:41; 34:10). Any one of these achieves parallelism with *haʾezkeh* in v 11.

Shall I give the wicked repose?
Shall I pronounce him pure?

house of the wicked. Reading *bat rešaʿ*, "*bath*-measure of wickedness," secures a nice series with "fraudulent ephah," "wicked scales," "deceitful weights." The sequence is the same as in Isa 40:12—liquid volume measure, dry volume measure, weight. This emendation was originally proposed by Duhm and "confidently" confirmed by Driver (1960: 113) on the assumption of an original abbreviation *b* for the measure; see Brockington. Hence "false measure" (NEB; REB; NJB). It is curious that *b* is attested as an abbreviation for *bn*, "son," in Ugaritic, for *byt*, "house" in Aramaic (Cowley 81: 106, 113–14), and for *bqʿ*, "half-shekel" in Hebrew (the Tell-ed-Duweir weight). There is no evidence that *b* was used for *bt, bath*. So, even if the text did once read *bršʿ*, it would not have been clear what *b* was an abbreviation for. More telling is the fact that when measuring instruments are certified to be "accurate" (*ṣedeq*), the antonym of *rešaʿ*, the code lists "scales," "weights," "ephah," "hin" (Lev 19:36), while Ezek 45:10 has "scales," "ephah," *bath*.

11. *scales of wickedness*. These are the opposite of "scales of righteousness" (Amos 8:5), so *mirmâ* in v 11b is a second epithet. Here, as in Amos, we have typical rural resentment of the notorious middlemen of urban trade.

12. *her*. The pronoun refers back to "city" in v 9. Hence NAB moved v 12 to follow v 9.

rich. It is the presence of the wicked rich inhabitants that makes the city wicked. Their victims are the righteous poor (cf. Amos 2:7).

14–15. These verses are based on the old covenant curses. The formulation is succinct, with verbs but no objects, as in vv 14aA and 15a. If each clause is taken as a colon, then these brief couplets have regular meter with two beats of four syllables in each colon. But eight syllables is standard for one colon, and this is how we have shown vv 14aA and 15a on p. 540. When an object is supplied, as in v 15bA, the unit is longer (10 syllables). Here Micah makes the verb "tread" carry two objects—olive and must. You don't normally tread olives; you tread grapes to get *tîrôš* (Amos 9:13). The technology is inexact. The choice of "must" rather than the more correct "grapes" or winepress (Isa 63:3) is subtle, telescoping the stages of the work. This gapping of an identical verb leaves v 15bB short (7 syllables), enough for one colon, hardly enough for two. If we accept vv 14aA, 15a, and 15bA as bicolons, as the lilt of the words suggests, then the correspondence of v 15bA with v 15bB requires that v 15bB be a bicolon, as shown on p. 540, even though it entails a one-word colon. With the metrical considerations balanced so evenly each way, we see no point in pressing for a choice. The alternate is to read v 15b as a bicolon of seventeen syllables. Verse 15 would then be a tricolon that deals with the three staples—grain, oil, wine. It is not clear how it fits the present context. The wicked are city merchants who trade in commodities, but do not produce them; the curses are aimed at an agrarian community.

in thy midst. What is in their midst (*yešḥăkā*, "thy" *yšḥ*) is not known. The word is *hapax legomenon*. JB omits the line. The ancient versions are a chaos—"darkness" (LXX), "humiliation" (Vulgate). In the context of food and eating, many translations go with a literal meaning for *qbr*, "stomach." To be a curse, what is in the stomach must be something bad. Hence Targum Jonathan: "sickness *mrᶜ* in thy bowels." Syriac "dysentery" is more specific, but could be no better than a guess that fits the context. If it is "hunger" (RSV), suggested by parallelism with v 14aA, "gnawing" (NJPS; cf. "gnawing hunger" [NRSV]), no etymology is known. Indigestion (NEB; REB)? Is it a substance rather than a disease? Barr (1968: 329) documents *semen virile* to Ehrlich (1912: 288). Ehrmann's derivation from *šḥḥ*, "bend," the attitude of a person defecating, seems strained (1959: 104) and does not harmonize with his enthusiasm for the scatological side of an Arabic *wasiḥa*, "be filthy" (Ehrmann 1973). The suggestion has gained some acceptance ("dung" [Holladay]; "Schmutz" [HAL]).

come to labor. This is a guess. The verb is problematical. It reads *wtsg* in L, *wtśg* in P. The latter seems to be based on *nśg*, "reach," "overtake," as in the idiom "his hand reached," i.e., he gained riches. BDB (691), with doubt, links *taśśēg* with *swg*, which has several meanings.

survive. The verb forms *hipᶜil* and *piᶜel* have the same meaning. The imagery seems to pass from childbearing to war.

16. The traditional text had a *petûḥâ* break after v 16, long before the chapter divisions were imposed. The end of the judgment speech is not well shaped internally; the contents of v 16 are rather miscellaneous, particularly in the use of pronouns, and there is no oracle formula such as *nĕʾūm yhwh* to round the unit off. It is the switch from condemnation to lamentation in 7:1 that marks the end of the judgment speech in 6:16. The lack of coherence in v 16 contrasts with the highly developed poetic designs in vv 13–15, and can be accounted for once it is realized that v 16 serves as a multiple inclusion that

gathers up themes from earlier parts of the book. A vital clue to the structure is the function of the clause *lĕma'an tittî 'ōtĕkā lĕšammâ* (v 16bA), whose lack of logical cohesion with the immediately preceding context has troubled interpreters. Here, as in v 5, the clause is not subordinate to the contiguous text, but (as the repetition of the root *šmm* makes doubly clear) links with an earlier principal clause to make an envelope. The historical reminiscences of the dynasty of Omri and Ahab are likewise retrospective.

Omri. LXX reads "my people." Allen (1973: 72) attributes the error to the proximity of "my people" in v 16bB. See Luria (1989–90).

house. The use of "house of Ahab" as parallel to "Omri" is strange in more than one way. Omri founded the dynasty, and his realm was "the house of Omri." In reputation it was "like father, like son," and both kings could be the target here. If Ahab is the exclusive, or even the main target, then "Ahab" // "son of (or house of) Omri" would be unexceptional. But Omri leads the way, so the most natural reading of the parallelism (the pattern that works in other cases) suggests that this "Ahab" was Omri's father. The name of Omri's father is not mentioned in the sources. Papponomy is certainly possible at that time, to judge from contemporary Aramaic practice. But it is difficult to imagine that Ahab would be left out of this indictment. The arrangement of the words secures more balance in the bicolon. In view of the parallel treatment of Samaria and Jerusalem in the Book of Doom (chapters 1–3), it is likely that these two kings are exemplars matching David and Solomon. In 2 Kgs 21:13 "house of Ahab" is parallel to "Samaria."

policies. The indictment of King Manasseh in 2 Kings 21 continually points out that in case after case he followed the policies of Ahab. Manasseh's sins included the worship of alien gods, the practice of magic, and passing his son through the fire; the indictment of Ahab in 2 Kgs 17:17 is more general. If this verse belong to Micah, we can speculate that already Ahaz had done the same kinds of things.

reproach. You will carry the disgrace of my people. A final threat. Is the subject "you" (pl.) the same as "my people" (objective genitive)—"You, my people, will bear your reproach"—or does it anticipate the humiliation of Israel's foes who will be taunted by (subjective genitive) "my people"? Since Micah has directed his oracles mainly against the nation's leadership, we think it is most likely that this is the group addressed in conclusion in v 16bB. The people, even though they are not as guilty as the wealthy city residents and even in spite of the fact that they are mostly the victims of oppression (chapters 2–3), suffer all the same in the punishment aimed mainly at their oppressors. The curses of the covenant do not discriminate (vv 14–15). The leaders ("you" [v 16bB]) are mainly to blame and will be punished most. The empirical factor here would be the special attention given to the privileged classes by foreign invaders, the common agents of Yahweh's punitive wrath against his people. Verse 16bB distinguishes this more accountable group from the (rest of the) people by saying that they "will bear the reproach of my people."

COMMENT ON MICAH 6

The numerous thematic linkages, vocabulary matches, and structural connections that are found in Micah 6 and that have been identified and discussed in the preceding NOTES and COMMENTS permit something to be said about the organization of the chapter as a whole. From the outset, the language of vv 1–2 indicates that the chapter is a report of a quarrel or dispute. The term *rîb* has a wide range of connotations. Its main associations are with legal disputes. From time to time disputes arose between Yahweh and his people over their failure to adhere to the stipulations of the covenant. So a quarrel such as the one we have in Micah 6 is often called a "covenant lawsuit" (Harvey 1962, 1967; Huffmon 1959). Since such quarrels were usually conducted by a prophet on behalf of Yahweh, they are sometimes designated "prophetic lawsuits" (Nielsen 1978). The cultural background of this kind of prophetic message has been sought in ancient treaty making and maintenance, in the people's courts, and in various cultic amenities and rituals. Resemblances are partial, and no certain identification has been made.

The *rîb* does not follow established juridical procedure, making use of speeches that, by form-critical criteria, can be identified as stages in some kind of court trial—summons, accusation, defense, verdict. Nor have the roles of the participants—litigants, witnesses, judges—been worked out. Whatever might have been contributed to the prophecy from such community institutions and customs in the form of dramatic roles or speech models, Micah's presentation of the dramatic confrontation of the covenant partners—Yahweh and Israel—is treated with considerable artistic freedom.

There is no formal indictment in the shape of a bill of particulars listing specific covenant violations. Breaches of covenant stipulations or of other recognized moral standards can be inferred from what some of the speeches seem to assume or imply. In v 7 a speaker acknowledges guilt of a fatal sin, but what that sin is is not disclosed. One can assume that the crimes condemned in other parts of the book, and especially in chapters 2–3, are the reasons, or some of the reasons, for the quarrel in chapter 6.

The reader is given practically no help in identifying the speakers and the intended audience of each component unit. As in the rest of the book, there is no narrative framework to tell us what is going on and to indicate who is saying what. All we have are the speeches. We are left to infer from their content and their continuity, if we can, who is speaking and who the audience is. At a few points the use of vocatives in the speeches shows who is being addressed, but there are no names: "my people" (6:3, 5—the speaker is clearly Yahweh), "man" (*'ādām*) in v 8. At other places the inferences are less certain; they have to be worked out by guessing which participant the remarks fit best.

We may assume that the prophet says all the words, whether as the original proclaimer of the message or as the putative editor of the final write-up of the discourse. As herald he declared "what Yahweh says" (v 1) to the whole people ("my people") or at least to a representative audience, "to report to Jacob his rebellion and to Israel his sin" (3:8—the same pair of words as in 6:7). As author, he kept on addressing the ongoing community throughout his book. That is one interactive situation. We are interested in what is going on *inside* the discourse. The prophet's own participation in that drama seems to be minimal. He is telling the story of Yahweh's quarrel with his people. It is possible that some of the things that the prophet says to the people are his own comments or exhortations as distinct from the quoted words of Yahweh. Perhaps v 8 is such a speech. But such a distinction is difficult to make, since the prophet in his public utterances represents Yahweh.

Tracing the prophet's mediatorial role from the other direction, it is possible that some prayers or questions addressed to Yahweh are the prophet's intercessions on behalf of the people; but once more his identification with the people makes it difficult, if not impossible (and also irrelevant), to distinguish between what he says for them and what he says as one of them.

The one and only narrative statement in the book, "And I said, . . ." (3:1), carries a series of three major speeches, each introduced by šim'û-nā', a peremptory call to attention. The vocatives that follow in 3:1 and 3:9 make it clear that the ensuing messages are addressed to the heads of the House of Jacob and administrators of the House of Israel. This comprehensive language shows that the prophecies are intended for the leadership of the whole nation, both kingdoms. The language of 6:1–8, especially the references to national origins in the Exodus, gives that speech an equally broad application.

We infer from this pattern that the third šim'û-nā' in 6:1 is calling on the same group to pay attention. Chapter 6 continues the discourse of chapter 3. The absence of a vocative after this third šim'û-nā' could imply that now everyone is required to listen, not only the leaders, but the people as well. The quarrel is with all Israel (v 2b). (This point is too fine to be capable of proof; in the NOTE we inclined to the possibility that in 6:1a Micah was invoking the mountains from the very first.)

The people are addressed explicitly in vv 3–5.

The imperative šim'û, but without the intensifying -nā', is used twice more in chapter 6, with vocatives that identify the addressees. The prophet calls on all the participants one by one. In v 1b he calls on Yahweh to arise and engage in disputation; in v 2 he calls on the mountains, right down to their primeval foundations, to listen (šim'û) to the dispute. In v 9a he calls again on Yahweh to call out to the city so as to instill the fear of his name; in v 9b he calls on the "tribe" and whoever has allocated (or adorned) (the city?) to listen (šim'û). In each instance a speech by Yahweh follows immediately, but the usual rubrics "Thus Yahweh has said," "Oracle of Yahweh," or the like, are not used.

The quarrel is with Israel, Yahweh's people, as a whole. Even so, distinctions are made within that community. Smaller groups or even individuals are dealt with, either as part of and representative of the whole nation, or else over against the rest of the people. The use of various pronouns throughout chapter 6 serves as a guide to such distinctions, and all the details of number, person, and gender in the pronoun system should be observed and exploited.

§1. "I" refers to Yahweh in the speeches he makes (vv 3–5, 10–11, 13, 16b [*tittî*, "I give"], 16bB ["my people"]).

§2. "I" is used in vv 6–7, a speech made in response to what Yahweh has just said in vv 3–5. The actual logical connection between these two successive speeches within the dramatic dialogue is a problem, discussed elsewhere. The speech in vv 6–7 could be placed in the mouth of the people as a whole, since they were addressed by the singular "thou" in vv 3–5. The person who says "I" in vv 6–7 could be an individual, a representative spokesman, since the proposal to offer "my firstborn" (v 7) could hardly be made by a community. Yet even if this language points to an individual worshiper, he would still be speaking as a representative of the nation, not as a private person, for he is responding to Yahweh's dispute with Israel, and the fatal sin for which he seeks atonement is the sin of Jacob declared by Micah in 3:8. The most likely individual to fill this role is the king, and this identification is made relatively certain when we remember that the sacrifice of the firstborn in the eighth century seems to have been a special measure taken by kings in times of great national peril.

§3. "Thou" (m.), subject of the verbs in v 1bA and referent from "thy voice" in v 1bB and "thy name" in v 9aB, is clearly Yahweh. In each case he is addressed by the prophet in the preliminaries to the main oracle. The speech made by the people or the king in vv 6–7 is an inquiry. It talks about Yahweh in the third person (*yirṣeh* in v 7aA). It is possible that the deity is being addressed obliquely rather than directly as "thou." Otherwise, to whom are the questions in vv 6–7 directed? It has been surmised, from the resemblance of the language of vv 6–7 to certain ritual exchanges that have been identified as Temple-entrance liturgies, that the questions are addressed to the appropriate cult officer who supervised admissions to the sacred precincts. The priest would give a ruling on the kind of oblation needed to deal with the particular sins of each would-be worshiper. There are no other indications that a part of such a ceremony has been incorporated into the dispute of Yahweh with Israel at this point. There is no need to bring more people onto the stage than are needed. If the questions in vv 6–7 are not addressed, albeit obliquely, to Yahweh himself, they would be directed to the prophet as his representative, as the intermediary and interpreter of God's will and wishes in the situation. They are a request for an oracle (which must come from Yahweh to be valid), rather than for a ruling from someone who knows the customary procedures. The identity of the implied addressee for vv 6–7 has a bearing on the identity of the speaker of the reply that is given in v 8.

§4. "Thou" (m.) in vv 3–5 is clearly "my people," i.e., all Israel. The language, "My people! What have I done to thee?" is quite clear on that point. Assuming coherence and consistency throughout the entire chapter, we can identify the "thou" of vv 8, 13–15, 16bA as likewise the whole people. This use of the singular pronoun to mark all Israel as an entity is particularly impressive at a time when the nation was two kingdoms. In the prophet's view, this political division had not changed the historic identity of Israel as a single people. Yahweh had only one covenant with all of them. The whole was in each part. The consistent use of "thou" to refer to all Israel shows up the use of plural "you" for addressing a group that is distinct from the (rest of the) people. It is possible that singular "thou" and plural "you" are being used interchangeably, as happens in the book of Deuteronomy, where the only distinction, if any, is an emphasis on the nation in solidarity (sg.) and the responsibility of individual citizens severally (pl.). We believe that the way the subject of the second-person masculine plural verb in v 16bB is distinguished from "my people" excludes this kind of interpretation and requires that "thou" and "you" be carefully distinguished throughout the chapter. Because the plural *šimʿû* is used in v 9b, we infer that "tribe" as used there is not equivalent to "people," but designates a portion, the leadership, oligarchy, or plutocracy.

§5. Although Yahweh is asked in v 9a to address "the city," there is no direct speech using "thou" (f.) as is the case, especially in Isaiah, when a city is personified as a woman. The feminine pronoun "she" ("her"), in vv 12 and 16bA, referring to the city, is constrained by grammatical concord with the gender of the noun.

§6. "You" (m. pl.), subject of *šimʿû-nāʾ* in v 1, refers to all the participants in general, unless the repetition of *nāʾ* is a signal that the same group as in 3:1 and 3:9 is being addressed once more; or unless this is a preliminary call to the mountains. Without a vocative noun, we are left with inferences drawn from the structure of the entire discourse, and of the whole book.

§7. "You" (m. pl.), subject of *šimʿû* in v 2, refers to the mountains. Apart from listening, they play no active role in the drama. They are not addressed again.

§8. "You" (m. pl.), subject of *šimʿû* in v 9b and of the second-person masculine plural verbs in v 16 (note the inclusion) are the "tribe," or, if our suggestion about the meaning of v 9b is correct, the tribe and whoever designated (or adorned) the city. Note the alternative identification of the city assembly in RSV, which requires an emendation but which is probably near the mark. If we are correct in recognizing the return to "you" in the last word in v 16bB as an inclusion for *šimʿû* in v 9bA, then we must reject the common text-critical resolution of the awkwardness of the singular and plural pronouns that exist side by side in v 16 by leveling them. The careful preservation of the distinction between singular and plural in the Masoretic Text of v 16bB shows that the "you" addressed in chapter 6 are a group distinct from (although they may be part of) the people as a whole (always "thou").

§9. "He." Leaving aside the obvious use of third-person masculine singular verbs to agree with the subjects "Balak" and "Balaam," we have the first verb "he observed" in v 16aAα. It has no explicit subject. The solution of this problem that emends to *wattišmōr* (leveling either to the preceding "thou" [the people] or the following "she" [the city]) is to be rejected in spite of versional support. (The adjustment of this evidence is even more heavy-handed when all the verbs are emended to yield *wtšmr . . . wtlk . . . tś*. As we have shown, the second-person masculine plural pronoun subjects of the last two verbs in v 16 make an inclusion with v 9b [perhaps also with v 1], so that the whole speech is framed by references that show that the leadership is the main target.) An eligible antecedent for this third-person masculine singular verb—its implied subject—is "the wicked [man]" (*rāšāʿ*) of v 10. This unnamed person is closely associated with the rich inhabitants of the city (v 12). His policies and practices are the same as those of Omri and Ahab, and before them Balak (v 5). These references to three notoriously wicked kings make the conclusion irresistible that these words are an attack on the king in the city, although neither the king nor the city is named.

§10. "She" in the phrases "her rich men" and "her inhabitants" (v 12) refers to "the city" of v 9. But which city? The book of Micah is about two cities, Samaria and Jerusalem (1:1). The references to Omri and Ahab in v 16 suggest Samaria; the continuity from chapter 3 suggests Jerusalem.

§11. "They" (m.) are the rich residents of the city whose behavior is described in v 12 and whose doom is announced in v 16bA. If the "you," the "tribe" addressed by *šimʿû* in v 9b, is the same as the leadership addressed by *šimʿû-nāʾ* in 3:1, 9; 6:1, the spotlight is on the "heads" and "administrators" of the whole country, and especially of Jerusalem, whereas in vv 9–16 the focus is on the city merchants whose corrupt words and deeds (v 12) have filled "the treasuries of wickedness" (v 10). When "her residents" is repeated in v 16bAβ, it occurs in an infinitival construction that is inserted inside the excellent bicolon that is made up by the two clauses with second-person masculine plural verbs.

16aB	*wattēlĕkû bĕmōʿăṣôtām*	And *you* [m. pl.] walked in *their* [m.] policies.
16bAα	*lĕmaʿan tittî ʾōtĕkā lĕšammâ*	So that *I* might give *thee* [m.] to devastation
16bAβ	*wĕyōšĕbeyhā lišĕrēqâ*	and *her* residents [*them*] to hissing;
16bB	*wĕḥerpat ʿammî tiśśāʾû.*	and *you* [m. pl.] will bear the reproach of *my* people.

Note the chiastic placement of the parallel verbs. The arrangement strongly suggests that the group addressed as "you" is being distinguished from the residents of the city ("they"). Undoubtedly all these power groups were part of the bureaucracy, a complex in which the same person might have more than one function in society. Most likely all were related by marriage or collusion (3:11).

Micah does not attack the religious establishment in chapter 6 unless the reminder about Balaam is an indirect attack on similar latter-day sorcerers and v 12b refers to false prophecies. The treasuries of wickedness (v 10) could be in either the Temple or the king's palace, where accumulated wealth was stored on behalf of the nation but in fact as the capital of the oligarchy/plutocracy. We conclude that, just as "he" (the king) is one of "them" (the rich residents of the city), so "they" are part of the larger "you" (the whole leadership). And "you" are part of the people ("thou"). The leadership can be distinguished from the people, but it cannot be separated from it. All share a common fate. The curses of the covenant come on the whole people ("thou") (vv 14–15), but the leaders are chiefly to blame and will receive a worse punishment: "You will bear the reproach of my people" (v 16bB).

§12 "They," the pronoun suffix on "their counsels" (v 16aB), refers to Omri and Ahab. There could be a more distant reference to Balak and Balaam because of the repetition of the root yᶜ$ṣ$ and the insinuation that Israel's kings were like Balak.

§13 "They" (f.), subject of the verb "let them hear" in v 1bB, are the hills, whose role is passive.

The preceding inventory of pronouns that identify and distinguish all the participants in the drama of the "dispute" of Yahweh with his people enables us to sort out the otherwise bewildering profusion of pronouns in the last verse of the chapter.

§1 "I" = Yahweh in *tittî*, "I give," and in *ᶜammî*, "my people."

§4 "Thou" = the people in *'ōtĕkā* (v 16bAα).

§8 "You" = the leadership, subject of "you walked" (v 16aB) and "you will bear" (16bB).

§9 "He" = the king(?); he kept Omri's statutes (v 16aAα).

§10 "She" = the city in "her inhabitants," identified in v 12 as the city's wealthy residents.

§11 "They" = the city's wealthy residents.

§12 "They" = Omri and Ahab, referred to by "their" in "their policies" (v 16aB).

Here we can remark once more that the evidence of the pronouns, so problematic at first glance, is vital for disentangling the complex web of relationships and interactions among all of these participants, especially in the dispute between Yahweh and the various sections of the community. Note that we were not able to identify the prophet as a member of the cast. We reject outright the well-established and now hardly questioned strategy of simplifying this problem by leveling the pronouns. This mischief already began in the ancient versions, and their variants are available to support the usual emendations. Those variants are only evidence of the problem, not pointers to its solution.

The main distinction secured by the careful and consistent use of the pronouns is that between the singular "thou" (the people) and the plural "you" (the leaders). The plural "you" with this reference is not used at all in the first half of the chapter (vv 1–8). The verb "Listen!" in v 2 is addressed to the mountains, and *šimʿû-nāʾ* in v 1 we take to be general, but it would make little difference to the main point if v 1a continues the address to the leaders from chapter 3. In any case, in the first part (vv 1–8) Yahweh addresses only the people in general and as a whole, the "thou" of vv 3–5.

In the second part (vv 9–16), Yahweh addresses both the people—"thou" of vv 13–15 and v 16bA—and the leaders—"you" of vv 9 and 16. Although they are separated from each other, these two addresses to the people (vv 3–5 and vv 13–15) make up a single speech. The introductory *wĕgam-ʾănî* (v 13a) is a firm link back to vv 3–5. The similarity of the verbs *helʾētîkā . . . heʿĕlitîkā . . . heheĕlētî* is another indicator that the two speeches are connected. Verses 3–5 recall what Yahweh did to them in the past; vv 13–15 predict what he will do to them in the future, what, in fact, he has already begun to do. The last word of the people's speech in v 7—"my fatal sin"—reappears in the first bicolon of Yahweh's renewed address to the people in v 13:

| v 3 | *helʾētîkā* | → | v 13a | *heheĕlētî* |
| v 7bB | *hattaʾt* | → | v 13b | *hattōʾtekā* |

The two *lĕmaʿan* constructions (vv 5bB, 16bA) have comparable functions in the two speeches. Each is separated by intervening text from the statements whose purpose it explains. "I brought you out of the land of Egypt, . . . so that you might know the righteous deeds of Yahweh." The righteous deeds or victories of Yahweh are the achievements of the Exodus and conquest of which an abbreviated selection is recited in v 4. "I have begun to smite you (v 13), . . . so that I might give you to desolation." The curses of the covenant enumerated in vv 14–15 (again an abbreviated selection) are only the first stages of punishment that could be devastating if it went on long enough. The cognates *hašmēm* and *šammâ* make an inclusion for v 13 at v 16bA.

There is a marked difference in tone between the two parts of chapter 6. The whole speech to the leadership in vv 9–16 is more severe and so is the speech to the people (vv 13–15) included within it. This speech approaches the classical judgment oracle in both form and content. In vv 3–5, by contrast, the note is affirmative and conciliatory. It is quite surprising to begin a covenant dispute in this way. The double address to "my people" is accepting, even affectionate. There is no condemnation, no accusation, not even reproach. Yahweh is hurt rather than angry. There is an ominous undercurrent to the words, all the same. The call to remember (v 5aA) suggests that they have forgotten, a serious lapse. The question "(In) what have I wearied thee?" (v 3aB) implies that the people felt, and perhaps had even said, that he *had* wearied them. Yahweh is on the defensive. He seems to be replying to criticism. There was provision in the covenant for the people to call on Yahweh to keep his part of the agreement; if the people called him to account by lodging complaints, it showed that they believed that the covenant was still in place but it wasn't working very well.

One of the benefits of the covenant on which the people counted was a promise to deliver them in time of trouble. That's how the whole thing started in the first place. Micah's predecessor, Amos, had recorded such an outlook in the minds of people (actually the leadership) a generation previously. He considered their expectation presumptuous and preposterous in view of their own track record. Coming from the oppressed people, the complaint that Yahweh had exhausted them (worn out their patience by his inactivity) could be an appeal for action in defending them against oppressors within Israel (cf. the atrocities reported in chapters 2–3). A stock expression in such prayers for deliverance (often in the Psalms) was ʿănēnî, "Answer me!" It could be ironic that Yahweh calls on *them* to answer *him* (v 3b), as if he is praying to them. He is giving them an opportunity to speak.

Even though the tone of vv 3–5 is conciliatory, even neutral, there is friction in the relationship. The people are dissatisfied and Yahweh is defending himself. In showing them that they have no reason to feel that he has wearied them, it is interesting that Yahweh does not point out any recent achievement or acts of beneficence that might have been experienced by the present generation, to silence their complaints. Rather, he goes right back to the beginnings of their experience together, recollecting and rehearsing only the earliest stages, from Egypt, to Shittim, to Gilgal. That should be enough. That is all they needed to value Yahweh forever.

Beneath these familiar and conventional reminders of Yahweh's unblemished record there lurk hints of a darker side to the story. From the beginning, and especially at Shittim, their own conduct was nothing to remember. The Balak/Balaam episode, in particular, was long kept in mind as an object lesson. On the one side, Shittim was the scene of the second great apostasy (Numbers 25 — the first was the Mt. Horeb incident), as a result of which Israel forfeited its claim on Yahweh as covenant partner. On the other side, Yahweh did not exercise his option to renounce them and abandon the whole enterprise. He didn't keep his side of the arrangement either.

The moral of the Balak story was that Yahweh wouldn't listen to Balaam (Josh 24:10). He turned the curse into a blessing (Neh 13:2). So the reminders are both bitter and sweet. They set the record straight, but they leave the situation indeterminate. As a legacy of these rough beginnings, the threat of doom was not canceled; it was suspended. Israel was on probation, and they had better remember it. The reminders given in vv 3–5 are a vindication of Yahweh's restraint. He has been violating his own pledged word all along by not punishing them promptly.

The recital also reminds them that the terms of the covenant have been radically different since Horeb and Shittim. They are on a bond of good behavior under a suspended sentence. Any good treatment they received from Yahweh from then on was a bonus, a gift of grace, not a reward for satisfactory conduct. Now all that covenant obedience can do is avert, or rather continue to postpone, the dissolution of the covenant. They had long since lost their right to covenant standing, but Yahweh kept on conferring it on them anyway. They were still his people, in spite of everything.

These are the implied terms on which the covenant is now being reviewed. It is not an assize. In one sense the judgment has already been passed; in another the day of final reckoning has not yet come (Exod 32:34b). This reading of the situation helps to explain why the *rîb* in Micah 6 is not conducted along strict juridical lines. The quarrel has not yet reached the court.

The positive element in the contemporary relationship between Yahweh and his people is expressed also from their side. The transition from Yahweh's speech in vv 3–5 to the people's speech in vv 6–7 is abrupt. It is usual for interpreters to fill in the missing development by supposing that the conventional elements of accusation and condemnation are to be understood at this point. This is a lot to supply. What is clear at least is that the people reply with concern and contrition. They show themselves eager to please Yahweh, willing to do anything to set things right. They propose the most extreme measures, even to the point of the ultimate sacrifice, that of the firstborn son. The speech of the people shows that they are not apostate. It is Yahweh, named twice, whom they wish to appease. Shocking as the proposal of a human sacrifice seems to us, it is the ultimate in seriousness. Micah has not set it up in order to denounce or refute it. He bypasses it.

In v 6 the aim of the sacrifices was to gain access to Yahweh and to bow down to the God of Heaven. In v 7 the aim is to deal with "my rebellion" // "my fatal sin." It is because of the seriousness of the obstacle that the people wonder if the regular sacrifices, even in enormous quantities, will be enough to propitiate Yahweh for this terrible sin, whatever it was. They were supposed to know what Yahweh required of them as "good." There is a whole book in the Pentateuch devoted to this subject of sacrifices for sins of various kinds. But nowhere in the Hebrew Bible is there any ritual remedy for extreme sins. When seeking pardon for the fatal sin of rebellion, however, the audience here, or some spokesman, asks questions as if they do not really know how to proceed. But that same fact of asking the questions of vv 6–7 expresses also faith that there ought to be a way of regaining the divine favor, however extreme their fault.

The precedent might be found in the outcome of the apostasy of the golden calf, which wasn't remedied by sacrifice, but instead by Yahweh's self-affirmation that he "bears iniquity, transgression, and sin," language that reappears at the end of Micah.

There were grounds for this hope in the national creed, of which the recital in vv 3–5 has just reminded them. The apostasies in the wilderness threatened to sabotage the covenant before it had fairly started. That bitter breach at the very beginning left a legacy of guilt and insecurity. The same incident also revealed Yahweh's deepest character as the "kind and sensitive God," "forgiving iniquity, rebellion, and sin" (Exod 34:7). That assurance was made without conditions. There was no proviso that forgiveness would result only after appeasement or satisfaction through sacrifice. Against this background, the questions in vv 6–7, especially the final one, however well intentioned, would seem to be on the wrong track.

The prophet answers the question indirectly by taking the discussion onto new ground, or rather to what has always been the basis of a right relationship with God. The answer given in v 8 is couched in terms different from the preceding questions. Verse 8 answers the question, "What is good?" defined further as "What is Yahweh seeking from you?" Following vv 6–7, v 8 is not just an answer to the general question, "What is good?" It is the answer to the question of how to overcome the barrier of rebellion against God as a fatal sin. The answer is brief, but comprehensive. It has become the classic definition of true religion, in line with 1 Sam 15:22; Hos 6:6; Isa 1:16; Amos 5:14–15, 24. The requirement is ethical; it is also intensely religious, not in terms of formalized ceremonial, but in the simplest language. What Yahweh wants from people is that they should walk with him. Scholars have been so preoccupied with trying to find out the meaning of the word *haṣnēaʿ* that they have missed the simple part that is as clear as day. "Walk with your God," whether humbly or circumspectly or wisely or however is not the main point. Walk with your God by doing justice and loving mercy! These terms derive their definitions from Yahweh, the exemplary doer of *ḥesed* and lover of justice. In sum, then, vv 3–8 are full of encouragement and hope, in spite of the fact that they start off as a quarrel.

This positive mood is quite lacking in vv 9–16. This speech is more disputatious, more like what we would expect in a *rîb*. There is still a note of reluctance and hesitation on Yahweh's part. In v 13 he says he has only begun to smite them for their sins. The frustrations described in vv 14–15 are conventional, the curses of the covenant. They are the kind of experiences that could serve as disciplines and correctives within a covenant relationship that was still intact and functioning. The people suffer them all in solidarity.

It is otherwise with the "wicked man" (v 10aB), the wealthy residents of the city (v 12), who are accused of deceptive talk and fraudulent business practices. These two are closely associated in vv 10–12. The statement that *he* observed the statutes of Omri (v 16aA) permits a provisional identification of this chief culprit with some king of Micah's time. The accusation is not spelled out in detail, but the names of Omri and Ahab are enough to give an idea of the kind of behavior of which he (and they) are guilty. The crimes described in 2:1–2 sound like the "deed of the house of Ahab": in seizing Naboth's vineyard (1 Kings 21).

The study of the pronouns and related evidence in this chapter permitted us to recognize four levels in the social pyramid. At the bottom the people ("thou"); above them the leadership ("you"); within that group the wealthy residents of the city ("they"); and in their number one conspicuously wicked person ("he") whom we surmise to have been the king. All but the last of these receive attention in v 16, which wraps everything up. The people are made a desolation, and "her residents" a hissing (v 16Aβ). The leaders are the ones who have to bear the reproach of "my people."

III.3. Lamentation (7:1–6)

TRANSLATION

MT

1aAα	'alĕlay lî	Woe to me!
1aAβ	kî hāyîtî kĕ'ospê-qayiṣ	For I have become like summer's gatherings,
1aB	kĕ'ōlĕlōt bāṣîr	like vineyard gleanings.
1bA	'ên-'eškôl le'ĕkôl	There is no bunch of grapes to eat,
1bB	bikkûrâ 'iwwĕtâ napšî	no ripe fig (that) my soul desires.
2aA	'ābad ḥāsîd min-hā'āreṣ	The devout man has perished from the earth,
2aB	wĕyāšār bā'ādām 'āyin	and there is no one upright among humankind.
2bA	kullām lĕdāmîm ye'ĕrōbû	All of them lie in wait for blood;
2bB	'îš 'et-'āḥîhû yāṣûdû ḥērem	each one hunts his brother with a net.
3aA	'al-hāra' kappayim lĕhêṭîb	Their hands are upon evil, to do it well.
3aBα	haśśar šō'ēl	The administrator asks
3aBβ	wĕhaššōpēṭ baššillûm	—and the judge—for a payoff;
3bA	wĕhaggādôl dōbēr hawwat napšô hû'	—and the great—he demands whatever he likes.
3bB	wayĕ'abbĕtûhā	And they wove it together.
4aA	ṭôbām kĕḥēdeq	Their good is like briers;
4aB	yāšār mimmĕsûkâ	[their] upright one more than thorns.
4bAα	yôm mĕṣappeykā	The day of thy [m.] watchmen,
4bAβ	pĕquddātĕkā bā'â	thy [m.] punishment has come.
4bB	'attâ tihyeh mĕbûkātām	Now their [m.] confusion will come.
5aA	'al-ta'ămînû bĕrēa'	Don't trust [2d m. pl.] (your) friend!
5aB	'al-tibṭĕḥû bĕ'allûp	Don't rely [2d m. pl.] on (your) close friend!
5bA	miššōkebet ḥêqekā	From her who lies in thy [m.] bosom
5bB	šĕmōr pithê-pîkā	guard the doors of thy [m.] mouth.
6aA	kî-bēn mĕnabbēl 'āb	For (the) son thinks (his) father is a fool;
6aB	bat qāmâ bĕ'immāh	(the) daughter stands against her mother;
6aC	kallâ baḥămōtāh	(the) daughter-in-law against her mother-in-law;
6b	'ōyĕbê 'îš 'anšê bêtô	the enemies of a man are the men of his house.

LXX III.3. Lamentation (7:1–6)

1aAα	Woe for me!
1aAβ	For I have become like one gathering stubble in harvest,
1aB	like small grapes in vintage.
1bA	There is no cluster, to eat the firstfruits.
1bB	Alas, my soul!

2aA   For the godly has perished from the earth,
2aB   and one who sets things right among men does not exist.
2bA   All of them for blood go to law;
2bB   each one his neighbor oppresses with oppression.
3aA   They prepare their hands for evil.
3aBα   The ruler requests,
3aBβ   and the judge spoke peaceful words;
3b   it is the desire of his soul.
4aA   ⟨And⟩ I shall take away their good things like a moth that consumes
4aB   that consumes and acting by rule
4bAα   in the day of visitation.
4bAβ   ⟨Woe, woe!⟩ thy reckonings have come.
4bB   Now will be their lamentations.
5aA   Don't trust [pl.] in friends!
5aB   And don't hope [pl.] in leaders!
5bA   From thy conjugal partner
5bB   be on guard, not to impart anything to her!
6aA   For son dishonors father,
6aB   daughter stands up against her mother;
6aC   daughter-in-law against her mother-in-law;
6b   all the enemies of a man (*aner*) those in his house.

INTRODUCTION TO MICAH 7:1–6

The Themes of Micah 7

This chapter rounds off the whole book with an assemblage of themes that have already been declared. Here they are brought to an eschatological climax. Their expression at the end reaches the highest pitch, and both the judgment and mercy of God are affirmed in the fullest terms.

The chapter begins with a lament (vv 1–6), as if the curses of 6:14–15 have come about. The corruption in society (6:10–13) has reached the ultimate stage in the breakdown of integrity at the highest levels of government (3:11) down to the intimate relations of family life (7:2–6). In spite of this, or perhaps because of it, the faithful look to God in hope that the ordeal will end (7:7 — the vocabulary of 5:6b). Then all the present circumstances will be reversed. Zion, once fallen and despised (4:11), will see the downfall of her enemy (7:10); she will rise again, rebuild, and expand (7:10–12). God's ancient promises (7:20) will be fulfilled. All will be forgiven and forgotten (7:18–19), a thing that chapter 6 said was impossible. Israel will be revered by all the nations, and so will Israel's God (4:1–5), who will shepherd them (7:14–15; compare 4:6–8) as in the days of old. Verse 13 interrupts this movement from grief to glory with a general statement about the universal devastation that must precede the final joy. The chapter is thoroughly eschatological but not in the least apocalyptic; it is prophetic, but not oracular; it is liturgical but not cultic.

It is eschatological in the sense of bringing the divine plan to a finality after which no further developments can be conceived. But it is not apocalyptic, because it does not use arcane visions or symbols, but rather openly realistic language. It is prophetic, in the sense that it uses the vocabulary and forms of prophetic discourse, as found elsewhere in Micah and in the classical prophets; but the normal rubrics are not used, and only one verse (18) can be identified as a speech of God. It is liturgical in that it uses the conventional forms of prayer (lamentation [1–4], trust [7], contrition [8–9], supplication [14], expectation [8, 10, 16–17, 19–20], praise [19–20]), but not cultic, for it is not manifestly the text for a religious ceremony.

It is literature. But it is raw and immediate, as if coming straight from a prophet; not reflective and analytical, as if from a scholar.

Its perspective is not unlike that of Second Isaiah, but its background is not so demonstrably exilic. The destiny of Israel is set against Assyria and Egypt, as in Hosea, not against Babylon. Since hope is set on the recovery of Transjordan (v 14), the situation could be as early as the eighth century. The defiance in v 10 could be that expressed against Assyria by Jerusalem in the reign of Hezekiah.

The total effect is harmonious, but the individual pieces are disparate. Quite apart from the diversity of form (in the technical form-critical sense) already pointed out, and the range of mood, the variety of referential pronouns makes the participants and their connections hard to identify.

Verses 1–6 are marked as a unit by "I" in the opening and closing colons. By the same token, perhaps v 7 should be included, especially as it picks up the root *ṣph* from v 4. The speaker could be the prophet himself, or the nation. There is no real difference here if the prophet is speaking on behalf of the nation. But his posture is somewhat distanced from the people since there are descriptions of the evils rampant in society (third person) in vv 2–3 and 6.

At one point the prophet seems to be addressing, exhorting the nation. Verses 4–5 contain second-person address, with plural verbs in v 5a. Verse 4 also contains some third-person passages. There is some symmetry in the arrangement, but it is not a complete introversion, and the matching parts do not balance quantitatively.

The alternation between singular and plural can be explained, for the most part, as the distributive construction. Thus, in v 6, "son," "daughter," "daughter-in-law" are "the members of a man's household." The construction is evident in v 2b (singular subject with plural verb). Exactly as in v 6, v 3 has a series of three singular nouns—*haśśar, haśśōpēṭ, haggādôl* (but the nouns in v 6 do not have the article), all comprehended in a plural verb. The switch to singular at the end of v 5 is connected with the focus on the individual and his wife.

The connections of v 4 are harder to work out. In any case, the overall introversion is clear.

First person (v 1)
      Third person (vv 2–3)
            Second person (v 5)
      Third person (v 6)
First person (v 7)

The last colon of v 2 (brother against brother) links with v 6, but a more prominent pattern is the division into public (vv 2–3) and private (vv 5–6) relationships.

The Poetic Form of Micah 7:1–6

In terms of poetic composition, the result is not very elegant. The article is not used consistently. The colons are of irregular length, some very long indeed. The occasional bicolons, with reasonable parallelism (1a, 1b, 2a, 2b, 5a, 7a) are interspersed with single colons or with bicolons of rough shape.

Using the Masoretic cantillations as a guide to the prosody, we display 27 colons on p. 561. (It could be done in other ways; the scansion of v 3 is problematic.) The mean length is 7.1 syllables per colon, shorter than standard. As pointed out in the opening discussion of Micah's poetry, shorter colons go with the agitation of more emotional discourse, as here. At the same time the range of colon length is wide, from four to eleven syllables. When there is parallelism, the colons are more even, and the bicolon length is consistent.

There is one bicolon in the unit that realizes complete parallelism without chiasmus (v 5a). The bicolon in v 2a (15 syllables) has complete parallelism with chiasmus.

2aA ʾābad ḥāsîd min-hāʾāreṣ   has-perished devout-man from the earth,

2aB wĕ- yāšār bāʾādām ʾayin   and   upright among-mankind is not

The bicolon in v 1aAβ–1aB (15 syllables) has incomplete parallelism, two similes as in 5:6, 7. The bicolon in v 2b has complementary matching items. The verbs are complementary—they lie in wait to snare someone. The first subject, *All of them,* is matched by the distributive *each.* The adverbials are complementary; a paraphrase is prosaic: "to catch him (in) a net to murder him." The bicolon in v 1b is even more complex. The two items of fruit match, but the other items have to be integrated to yield "that my soul desires to eat." The two similes in v 1a make the single idea of the gatherings and gleanings of a vineyard at the end of the season. Three typical officials are listed in v 3aB–bA, making a 22-syllable bicolon. The two participles, *ask, demand,* are parallel, each following one of the nouns:

the administrator asks

. . .

the great one demands

The middle noun, *the judge,* is followed by the object of both participles, the term "for a bribe." Furthermore, the adjective *haggādôl,* "the great one," does not necessarily list a third functionary. Just as the phrase *hakkōhēn haggādôl* means "the high (or chief) priest," so this adjective goes with both the preceding titles. It is the chief prince and the head judge who are guilty of graft. This complex unit is preceded by a statement that does not seem to be grammatical (v 3aA) and followed by a one-word colon (v 3bB) that does not seem to have any match. We suggest that these two colons constitute an envelope construction around the other two colons, and that v 3bB supplies the verb needed in v 3aA.

More interesting than the bicolon patterns is the way the successive bicolons are linked in a chain. The first four colons develop a figure of speech based on the harvest. The four colons in vv 1b–2a are linked by the inclusion of *'yn;* at the end of v 2aB *'yn* is chiastic, not only to the verb at the beginning of v 2aA, but also to the same word at the beginning of 1bB. This connection explains the simile. Micah himself is not "like summer's gatherings." He is looking for an honest person, and his failure to find even one is as grievous as a failure of the fruit yield would be. The word *All of them* at the beginning of v 2bA is expounded twice. First in the distributive parallel in v 2bB, then in the list in v 3.

Verse 3bA contains a long-range link with v 1bB, contrasting a good and bad desire of the soul. Verse 4a uses "good" in contrast to "evil" (v 3aA) and returns to the imagery of v 1 by using another congruent simile. The lamenter looked for a devout, honest person, as for good fruit; but the leading members of the community were "like briers and thorns," repeating the word *yāšār* (vv 2aB, 4aB) in bitter sarcasm.

The structure of vv 5–6 is very complex and the colons are even shorter (mean 6.4 syllables). The poetic colons are related to one another in a variety of ways. As usual with Micah, he does not use the same pattern routinely in any one composition. So v 5a has complete synonymous parallelism. In v 6aB–C the verb *qāmâ* does double duty; the other words match in pairs. Around this bicolon, which deals with the female members of a family, there are two colons that deal with males (vv 6aA, 6b). Since *son* and *daughter* are parallel, v 6a can be read as a tricolon. There are two climaxes. After the bicolon in v 5a, v 5b is one long clause (11 syllables) that intensifies the point. It has to be construed as a bicolon for reasons of rhythm. The last colon rounds everything off. In some ways it completes the series that began in v 5a, moving from friend and acquaintance to family members.

In vv 2–4 Micah deplored and bewailed the fact that not one honest person could be found in public life; in vv 5–6 he finds a complete breakdown of trust in family life. Little wonder that he concludes that the day of reckoning has come (v 4b).

NOTES AND COMMENTS

Notes on Micah 7:1–6

1. This verse, all in first person, is a distinct unit, the introduction to what follows. It has the form of a poem of grief. Neither Robinson (1954: 149), nor Allen (1976: 383), nor Smith (1984: 54) can find a single 3 :: 2 bicolon in it. The

poet compares his misery with that when the vintage has failed and the long-awaited fruit cannot be found.

Woe. Not the usual *'ôy* or *hôy*, but *'alĕlay.* The only other occurrence of this word is in Job 10:15. The consonant *l-* is prominent in conventional Hebrew expressions of grief. The opening *'alĕlay* is matched by *'ôlĕlōt* in the first colon, in the second by *'eškôl* followed by *le'ĕkôl.*

I have become. The poet could be expressing the distress of the land in the time of drought. But the figure is really connected with what follows. Like Jeremiah, who combed the streets of Jerusalem looking for just one honest person (Jer 5:1), Micah is bewailing the fact that there are no good people left (v 2). Even at the end of harvest there is always a hope of gleanings. For the poor it would be a great relief, their only food, to find a little leftover fruit, and it would be starvation for them if there were none. The mourner himself is not "like" the gleanings: he is a person who finds nothing.

like. The double use of *k-,* "like," shows that two similes have been combined in one picture. The two comparisons are formally congruous, "gatherings of summer [fruit]" // "gleanings of the vintage." The indirectness of the comparison has troubled some commentators, and already LXX read a participle—*synagōn,* "a gatherer." Reading of the first word as abstract "gathering(s)" has been blamed on the influence of "gleanings" in the next colon; but, by the same token, recovering the participle in the first colon puts the noun "gleanings" out of balance. So changes have to be made in v 1aB to bring it into line with the now emended v 1aA. Several ways of doing this are cataloged by Schwantes (1962: 175). None of this is necessary once it is perceived that Micah is using an image that is more like a condensed Homeric simile than a simple one-step comparison. Cf. Isa 24:13.

gatherings. The singular *'ōsep* occurs in Isa 32:10; 33:4. Micah 7:1 is the only occurrence of the plural. The variant *'āsîp* (Exod 23:16; 34:22) has the same meaning, "harvest" (of summer fruits, at the end of the agricultural year). In the Gezer Calendar *'sp* is the task of the first (double) month, *qṣ* is the task of the last (single) month of the agricultural year. Micah's combination of terms could be merismus; the season yielded nothing, from beginning to end.

vineyard. Or "vintage." In Isa 32:10 *bāṣîr* // *'ōsep,* the inverse of here. Jeremiah 48:32 has *qyṣ* // *bṣyr* in the same sequence as Micah. Vintage came between threshing and sowing.

gleanings. The word is always plural. It refers to the second going-over of field, vineyard, or olive grove. The gleanings (*'ôlĕlôt* [Judg 8:2]) were the last pickings of inferior quality (Isa 24:13).

ripe fig. The vine and fig are staples (Brueggemann 1981), and their association is conventional (4:4). Micah does not name either fruit. Because of its etymology *bikkûrâ* is generally assumed to be the first-ripe fruit of the season, "before the summer," when a person plucks it eagerly and devours it speedily (Isa 28:4). It represents something utterly delectable and desirable. The masculine plural *bikkûrîm* refers generally to the first yield of a new crop of grain or fruit. This was reserved for God, to be offered at the feast of Pentecost, *yôm hab-bikkûrîm* (Num 28:26). Grain yielded *leḥem habbikkûrîm* (Lev 23:20). The word *bikkûrâ* (f. sg.) contrasts with this masculine plural form. The singular does not occur often enough for us to be sure that it refers specifically or exclusively to a fig. There are, however, two reasons for thinking that it does. First, there is no place where the word is associated with any other identifiable fruit except a fig. Second, the expression *tĕ'ēnê bakkūrôt* (Jer 24:2 — vocalization slightly different) refers to the very best figs (*tĕ'ēnîm ṭōbôt mĕ'ōd*). The *bikkûrâ* in Hos 9:10 is a fig, the most precious firstfruit of all, that of its first bearing season (*bĕrē'šî-tāh* [Andersen and Freedman 1980: 540]). Whatever the taste, this first-picked fig evidently had enormous emotional and symbolic value as welcome proof that the tree would bear and as further proof, year by year — and the earlier the better (Isa 28:4) — that it would be a good season. In Hos 9:10, as in Mic 7:1, grapes are mentioned first. Nouns for a grape or bunch of grapes are masculine, "fig" is feminine. The proverbial excellence of the *bikkûrâ* was due to the fact that it satisfied the craving due to long abstinence (Isa 28:4). But one would not be expecting to find a first-ripe fig at the end of summer. Because of its associations, *bikkûrîm* could mean simply "choice" or "tasty," grapes as well as figs, and this notion could extend to *bikkûrâ* as well. Knowledge of the exact fruit specified by Micah is unimportant for the point he is making.

To remove the anomaly of the soul craving a first-ripe fig at the time of gleaning, the last two words, instead of being parsed as a relative clause without the relative pronoun, could be intended as an inclusion for the first two:

1aAα	*'alĕlay lî*	Woe to me!
	. . .	
1bB	*'iwwĕtâ napšî*	my soul desires [in vain]

The arrangement of the four colons is chiastic: *bikkûrâ* goes with "summer's gatherings," with the two middle colons referring to grapes.

The threats of 6:15 mention specifically the failure of the olive and the grape crops. Micah 7:1 laments over just such a disaster. The verse has two parts, each a distinct unit with its own pattern of poetic parallelism. The two parts are unified by the references to the summer harvest of fruits — grape and fig — from its onset to gleaning. The time sequence seems to be inverted, since the gleanings (the last thing to be done) are mentioned in v 1a while the first-ripe fig (the first thing to be expected) is mentioned in v 1b. There was no fruit at any stage: there was nothing at the end (v 1a) and there wasn't even anything at the beginning (v 1b). The poet is bewailing a season-long famine.

One could strain the text and take vv 1a and 1b in their given sequence. The poet could be bewailing the famine after the end of summer and gleanings (v 1a) when there is not yet any cluster (of grapes) or first-ripe (fig) (v 1b) to mark the onset of the next harvest season. In spite of the unusual time sequence, the first reading is to be preferred. The poet compares his case to a situation in which the harvest yields no fruit at all, from beginning (v 1b) to end (v 1a), not a period of waiting for the next round. His perspective from the end of the season, when the observation is made, is that there was nothing then and, looking back, there was nothing at the beginning either.

Verse 1b on its own could be taken literally. There was no cluster (of grapes) (nor) first-ripe (fig) that my soul (appetite) desired to eat. The poet *is* the hungry person who finds nothing. The use of the preposition *k-*, "like," twice in v 1a shows that it employs a double simile, but it requires some paraphrase to bring out the idea. The poet is not like the harvest or the barren land; he is the disappointed farmer, like Yahweh in Isaiah 5. Some of the parables of Jesus work in the same way. They begin with "The kingdom of Heaven (God) is like a householder" (say); but it is a story or situation involving a householder and the comparison comes out at a different point.

The word *'ên*, "there is not" (v 1bA) is repeated in v 2aB, and its long-range chiastic placement there suggests a linkage between v 1 and v 2. In v 2 the speaker deplores the disappearance of the faithful and upright from the land. Verse 1 is a figurative description of this state of affairs. If the analogy holds, we have to find out why the land has become barren of good people.

2. *devout . . . upright.* Verse 2 gives the solution to the riddle in v 1. The use of *'yn* as inclusion for v 1b–2a brackets the list:

1b	*'ên-*	*'eškôl*	. . .	*bikkûrâ*	
2a		*ḥāsîd*	. . .	*yāšār*	*'āyin*

The parallelism of *min-hā'āreṣ // bā'ādām* makes it possible that the latter means "land." But the combination could mean "land and people." The nonuse of the article with the nouns *ḥāsîd* and *yāšār* contrasts with the use of the article with the nouns *administrator* and *judge* in v 3; these are generic, those specific. The nouns *ḥāsîd* and *yāšār* go together, defining the perfect man, as *tām wĕyāšār* do in Job 1:1.

All of them. "Them" does not refer back to the nouns in v 2a. As in Hos 7:7 it anticipates an upcoming list. They are all lying in wait for blood; each catches his brother in a net.

brother. That the crime is committed against a "brother" suggests that this is a power struggle among equals, not just the oppression of the weak by the strong. Or the prophet could be reminding the rich and powerful that even the poorest Israelite, their victim, is their brother.

with a net. Psalm 10 uses similar imagery of the chase (compare Hab 1:15). They regard one another as animals to be hunted. In this well-integrated bicolon, the comprehensive subject (*kullām*) and the distributive subject (v 2bB) both go with both verbs, and so do the other items "for blood" and "with a net." The two verbs are complementary, they are all lying in wait to catch one another; everybody is hunting everybody. Compare v 6b.

3. This verse contains an elaborate introversion:

		Syllables
3aA	ʿal-hāraʿ	3
	kappayim lĕhêṭîb	5
3aBα	haśśar šōʾēl	4
3aBβ	wĕhaśśōpēṭ baśśillûm	7
3bA	wĕhaggādôl dōbēr	6
	hawwat napšô hûʾ	5
3bB	wayĕʿabbĕtûhā	6

The structure of the inner section displays three definitive substantives "prince," "judge," "great one." These are the subjects of two parallel verbs "asking," "speaking," with one adjunct (baśśillûm, "for a payoff") common to both participles. None of the colons exhibited above is a complete clause, and they are too short for the usual kind of poetry.

Almost every word in this verse has been altered by modern text critics in one way or another in attempts to make the text more intelligible, to make the grammar more normal, to make the poetry more regular. The verdict of Hillers is an honest facing of the problem: "The MT is corrupt beyond convincing restoration, and where the versions are more intelligible they seem to have wrested a meaning from the same Hebrew text rather than to have had a better one" (1984: 84). Schwantes's extended discussion can be consulted (1962: 180–85), but the textual situation seems to be hopeless.

Omitting the definite article from haśśōpēṭ turns it into a participle coordinated with šōʾēl. This change makes a straightforward clause—"The prince asks and *judges* for a bribe"—a rather pedestrian result that loses some of the parallelism in the received text.

When two words in succession have the same root, it is always possible that one will be lost by haplography. The emendations behind the NEB translation of v 3aB assume that this happened twice. It is too optimistic to grade these conjectural emendations as "probable." They have been abandoned in REB.

Putting all the parts of v 3 together as complementary, we can overcome, to some extent, the impression that the seven constituents displayed above are *disjecta membra*. The relationships among these constituents are semantic, grammatical, and poetic. Our task is to find out the semantic references that permit one piece to be linked to another, to discover the grammatical relationships among them, and to work out the poetic structures that the composition realizes. Assuming that the composition is coherent—intended to be the way it is and preserved by the copy makers—our problem is to determine the clues that resolve the enigmatic result.

There could be play on the opposite meaning of "evil" and "good," but one is a noun, the other an infinitive, so they do not match on the level of grammar. The word hāraʿ could belong to the series of definite substantives that lines up in a pattern that could be chiastic, the outer adjectives being attributes of the inner nouns—the evil administrator, the great judge.

3aA	*hāraʿ*		the evil	
3aBα		*haśśar*		the administrator
3aBβ		*haššōpēṭ*		the judge
3bA	*haggādôl*		the great	

One can apply both adjectives to both nouns. The title *haggādôl*, as in *hakkōhēn haggādôl*, could mean the "chief." Micah is talking about two individuals, the head administrator and the chief magistrate, and both are evil. The three nouns are related to the plural verb distributively, and *napšô hûʾ* is also distributive, qualifying them all. If it were not for the plural verbs and pronoun suffixes, one could consider that all four definite nouns might refer to just one person. Melamed (1961: 131) pointed out that *śar* and *šōpēṭ* can be used in hendiadys (Exod 2:14), so their occurrence in parallelism as in Mic 7:3 could be a breakup of that "stereotype phrase."

If this structure of four definite nouns provides a framework for the rest of the words used, the problem is to find matching grammatical and poetic functions. The word *hāraʿ*, "the evil one," could be balanced by words with the root *ṭwb*, "good," either *hêṭîb* in the same colon or *ṭôbām* in v 4. Both of the latter seem to be used sarcastically. The nouns *kappayim*, "palms (of the hand)" and *napšô*, "his soul (or throat)," body parts, could be correlative, and their symmetrical placement invites the search for corresponding grammatical and poetic relationships.

A lot depends on discovering the reference and grammatical function of *hûʾ* at the end of v 3bA. First, it could be reinforcement of the preceding suffix— "his soul, (even) his," usually *napšô gam-hûʾ*. Or it could be resumptive of *haggādôl* as subject *casus pendens*—"And, as for the great man, he speaks the desire of his soul." The objection to this suggestion is that the normal syntax of such a clause is to have the subject, including a resumptive pronoun, precede the participle predicate (analysis in Gross 1987: 121). The place in the syntax and poetry of the last word, a complete clause (v 3bB), assuming that it does belong with the rest, is another component of the problem.

And they wove it together. Both subject ("they") and object ("her") require referents if there is cohesion. Presumably "they" are all the persons listed above. Their activity of "weaving" is conspiring together to subvert justice. The image of weaving could be a continuation of catching people in a net, the whole an elaborate metaphor for organized crime. But *ḥēdeq* is masculine, so the suffix *-hā* cannot refer to that word. The nearest candidate to be antecedent of *-hā* is the noun *hawwat*. Its meaning "desire" is associated with *nepeš* (Prov 10:3). It also means "destruction" or violence. It is associated with perverse speech in Ps 5:19; 38:13 (*dibbĕrû hawwôt ûmirmôt kol-hayyôm yehgû*, "they spoke destruction and treachery all the day they meditated"); 52:4 (*hawwôt taḥšōb lĕšônekā* . . .

ʿōśēh rĕmiyyâ, "treachery you planned [with] your tongue . . . you doer of deception"); 55:12 (hawwôt bĕqirbāh . . . ûrĕmiyyâ, "destruction is in her midst . . . and
deception"); and Prov 17:4. The meaning "desire" has been influenced by ʾiw-
wĕtâ napšî in v 1, and the methodological problem is to work out whether the
poet is repeating the root with the same meaning or playing on two meanings
or giving it both meanings at once. And with either meaning hawwat is a suitable object for "weave." The result of all this is a glimpse of the network of corruption among the rich leaders of the community, so that the good and upright
become their victims.

upon evil. The first phrase ʿal-hārāʿ is the hardest piece of all to fit into the rest
of the verse. If ʿal means "on account of," v 3 could give the reason why good
persons have disappeared or another reason for the mourning in v 1. Or, in view
of Hos 9:7, ʿal-hārāʿ could be an interrupted beginning of a clause continued
in v 4b—the day of your punishment has come "on account of the evil."

to do well. This verb usually has a positive meaning. Here sarcastic? To do
themselves a bit of good? The idea might match šlm, with the idea of well-
being. Guided by the above analysis, the symmetry of hawwat napšô going with
dōbēr suggests that lĕhêṭîb goes with šōʾēl. If one tries to imagine what people
like this would do, it is more likely that the wicked would ask the prince and
judge for favorable treatment. If the judges take the initiative in asking for a
bribe, things are really bad.

payoff. "Repayment," perhaps "retribution," not clearly "bribe," for which there
is available vocabulary (compare Hos 9:7).

wove. The verb is *hapax legomenon.* If it continues the plural verbs of v 2b
it could describe catching and tying them up. This leaves the object *her*
unexplained.

4. The interweaving of the pronouns in this verse has already been noted.
The suffixes are chiastic—-ām, -kā, -kā, -ām. Hosea 9:7 contains similar vocabulary—yĕmê happĕquddâ // yĕmê haššillûm—as well as ṣōpeh, "watchman."

good. The parallelism shows that ṭôb matches yāšār, with the following *mem*
as a suffix, and v 2 shows that humans are in mind. Double-duty *k-* makes two
similes. But if "from" is retained, there is intensification—"like briers . . . more
than thorns." For a similar sequence of *k-* . . . *min-,* see 2 Sam 23:4.

briers. Proverbs 15:19. The noun mĕsûkâ is *hapax legomenon,* traditionally a
thorn hedge. Note the assonance with mĕbûkâ. How can the good and honest be
like the brier, fit for burning? In whose opinion? In a judgment speech the
wicked are like fuel for the flames. Has v 3 inverted the meaning of yāšār from
v 2? The ones sarcastically called the yāšār of the community (in fact wicked)
will be like thorns when the day of visitation comes (linking v 4aA with what follows). But v 4aA is unmatched and could complete the development of vv 2–3.

day. If this noun is construct (compare Hos 9:7), "day" (m.) would be subject
of "came" (f.) but not in agreement. Perhaps the verb is in concord with the
nomen rectum. But if yôm is parallel to ʿattâ, along with parallelism of perfect
bāʾâ, "she came," with imperfect tihyeh, "she will (be)come," and chiasmus, then
there is a general match.

4bA   *yôm . . . pĕquddātĕkā bā'â* The day . . . of thy punishment has come.

4bB   *'attâ tihyeh mĕbûkātām*   Now their confusion will come about.

BHS wants to level -*kā* to -*ām*, a typical result of reading Hebrew poetry through a narrow window that shows only two colons at a time.

watchmen. The word *mĕṣappeykā* makes the first colon very long. One can understand why BH[3] wanted to delete it. Not BHS, however. The *pi'el* is not as common as *qal*, but it occurs again in v 7 and should by all means be retained. Hosea 9:7 shows that *ṣôpeh*, "watchman," is a prophet. Possibly *yôm* is construct to two nouns—the day of your punishment, predicted by the prophets. To whom is v 4b spoken? By the prophet to the people (singular collective), a judgment? By the Lord to the lamenter, an assurance? Like its parallel *šlm*, *pqd* can have the idea of visitation for vindication of the oppressed as well as for retribution on the oppressor. Hence the pronouns: *Your* redemption has come (to the lamenter); now *their* confusion will take place (against the wicked).

has come. The feminine verb agrees with the gender of the *nomen rectum*, not with the implied subject ("day"). The same grammar is found in Amos 1:8 and Mic 5:6 (see the NOTE there).

5-6. Here the parallelism is more like that of standard poetry. "And" is not used. The singulars are related to the plurals as distributive. The plurals are second person in the first bicolon, third in the last colon. The bicolons are matched—13, 11, 11, 15 syllables. The plurals are more general, but already in v 5a the singular nouns point to the distributive, the subject *'îš* being omitted. In v 6b the singular noun finally has this function.

Don't rely. LXX has "and" before the second negative particle. Mur 88 reads *w'l*.

fool. The *pi'el* is possibly deliberative ("thinks that his father is a fool"), but action could be implied ("treats his father as a fool").

stands. In v 6, *qāmâ* does double duty. More fascinating is the use of pronoun suffixes in v 6aB, but not with "father" in v 6aA. The feminine "her" does retroactive double duty for the missing "his."

The statements cover all the relationships that prevail in a person's house. The minimum size of a family that realizes all the possible relationships is five: (1) A father-husband who is head of the household, directly related to his wife (v 5b) and his son (v 6aA); (2) a wife-mother, wife of the head of the family and so related to him (v 5b) and in charge of the women of the next generation (daughter [v 6aBα] and daughter-in-law [v 6aBβ]); (3) son—if only one, he must be married, for there is a daughter-in-law—and that son could be in mind in v 5b as well as v 6aA (but v 6aA could apply to an unmarried son also); (4) daughter (responsible to her mother [v 6aBα]); (5) son's wife (v 6aBβ), related more directly to her mother-in-law than to her husband. If the network of relationships shown by reading vv 5b-6 at face value charts at least the main lines of responsibility and authority, then the household is divided into two sections—males and females—so that the matriarch exercises her own authority over the younger women, including her son's wife. A similar division is reflected in Psalm 123:2; and this arrangement gives significance to the relationship between Naomi and Ruth.

The number of persons involved was recognized as five by Jesus (Luke 12:52). He saw the household divided "three against two and two against three." There could be two splits—two males against three females, or two parents against the next generation. That both are meant is indicated by the fact that v 5b records mistrust between spouses. But it could be that Luke reports a double split because his more detailed version has the hostility going in both directions, not just from the younger towards the older generation, as in Mic 7:6 and Matt 10:35. So Luke 12:53:

father against son	and son against father,
mother against daughter	and daughter against the mother,
mother-in-law against her daughter-in-law	and daughter-in-law against the mother-in-law

Not recognized are the relationships between son-in-law and his parents-in-law because the bride's parents belong to a different household. The position of Moses in Jethro's house was thus anomalous; and so was Jacob's with Laban, hence his desire to set up his own household (Gen 30:3). The move described in Gen 2:24 does not match what actually happened, for a husband remained with his parents: unless this practice, too, is not Israelite, reflecting a matriarchal society in which a bridegroom moves in with his wife's family. Lot had no daughters-in-law in his household (Gen 19:12); his married sons had gone to live in their wives' households. In either case Gen 2:24 highlights a breach of the authority structure of the extended family in which all males are under the *pater familias* and all females, including sons' wives, are under the matriarch. This is why there is no mention of a relationship of daughter to father or of son to mother. This list thus reflects the authority structure as well as the living arrangements. The daughter in the household would be either unmarried or widowed (Genesis 38; Ruth 1). The males and females constitute distinct units. The man is over his wife and son; the wife is over her daughter *and* her daughter-in-law. Not all relationships are covered in both directions. There is no talk of parents abusing their responsibilities to children, and v 5b is not balanced by a similar warning to a wife! See Grelot (1986).

The state of affairs described in v 6 is a commonplace in ancient literature. In the Erra Epic the breakdown of the fabric of society is described by saying:

A son will not ask after the health of his father, nor the father of his son.

A mother will happily plot harm for her daughter. (Dalley 1991: 297)

Such ills are often part of longer lists of plagues seen as curses for faulty human behavior and marks of divine disfavor. The Cuthean Legend of Naram Sin (lines 138–41) says:

City will be hostile to city, house to house,
father [to son, brother] to brother,
man to man, friend to companion;
they will not speak the truth with one another.

The diviners had techniques for counteracting such social ills. Tablet II, lines 20–28 of the Akkadian *Šurpu* incantations list estrangements of son from father, father from son, and so on (Reiner 1958: 13):

20. who estranged son [from] [father],

21. who estranged father [from] son,

22. who estranged daughter [from] mother,

23. who estranged mother [from] daughter,

24. who estranged daughter-in-law [from] mother-in-law,

25. who estranged mother-in-law [from] daughter-in-law,

26. who estranged brother [from] brother,

27. who estranged friend [from] friend,

28. who estranged companion [from] companion.

Micah's list is shorter, but has interesting similarities. In Micah the intergenerational conflict is from young to old; in the *šurpu* spell it goes in both directions, as well as with peers. The focus is on the family; there is no son-in-law in either series.

Similar language was used in Egypt. The Instruction of Amenemhet gives this advice:

Trust not a brother, know not a friend,
Make no intimates, it is worthless. (Hallo 1997: 67)

The *Admonitions of Ipuwer* similarly:

A man looks upon his son as his enemy. (Hallo 1997: 94)

III.4. SONG OF CONFIDENCE (7:7–12)

TRANSLATION

MT

7aA	wa'ănî bayhwh 'ăṣappeh	And, as for me, I will watch for Yahweh,
7aB	'ôḥîlâ lē'lōhê yišʿî	I will wait for the God of my salvation;
7b	yišmāʿēnî 'ĕlōhāy	(until) my God hears me.

8aA	'al-tiśmĕḥî 'ōyabtî lî	Don't rejoice [2d f. sg.] at me, my enemy [f.]!
8aB	kî nāpaltî qāmtî	Although I fell down, I got up again.
8b	kî-'ēšēb baḥōšek	When I shall sit in darkness,
	yhwh 'ôr lî	Yahweh will be light for me.
9aA	za'ap yhwh 'eśśā'	The indignation of Yahweh I will bear,
9aB	kî ḥāṭā'tî lô	for I have sinned against him;
9bAα	'ad 'ăšer yārîb rîbî	until he concludes his case against me
9bAβ	wĕ'āśâ mišpāṭî	and carries out his sentence against me.
9bBα	yôṣî'ēnî lā'ôr	He will bring me out to the light,
9bBβ	'er'eh bĕṣidqātô	I will see his justice.
10aAα	wĕtēre' 'ōyabtî	And let my enemy [f.] see,
10aAβ	ûtĕkassehā bûšâ	and let shame cover her!
10aB	hā'ōmĕrâ 'ēlay	who says [f.] to me:
	'ayyô yhwh 'ĕlōhāyik	Where is he—Yahweh, thy [f.] God?
10bA	'ênay tir'ennâ bāh	My eyes will look upon her,
10bB	'attâ tihyeh lĕmirmās	Now she will become a trampling place,
	kĕṭîṭ ḥûṣôt	like mud of the streets.
11a	yôm libĕnôt gĕdērāyik	The day for rebuilding thy [f.] fences,
11b	yôm hahû' yirḥaq-ḥōq	that day, he will expand (thy) boundary.
12aA	yôm hû' wĕ'ādeykā yābô'	That day—and he will come to thee [m.]
12aB	lĕminnî 'aššûr wĕ'ārê māṣôr	from Assyria and the cities of Egypt
12bA	ûlĕminnî māṣôr wĕ'ad-nāhār	and from Egypt, and as far as the River,
12bBα	wĕyām miyyām	and (to the) sea from (the) sea,
12bBβ	wĕhar hāhār	and (to the) mountain (from) the mountain.

LXX III.4. Song of Confidence (7:7–12)

7aA	But I—I will look to Kyrios,
7aB	I will wait for God my savior;
7b	my God will hear me.
8aA	Don't rejoice [sg.] over me, my enemy [f.]!
8aB	because I have fallen. And I shall arise.
8b	For, though I should sit in darkness, Kyrios will be light for me.
9aA	The indignation of Kyrios I will bear,
9aB	for I have sinned against him;
9bAα	until he executes justice for me
9bAβ	and carries out my sentence (*krima*).
9bBα	And he will bring me out into the light,
9bBβ	I shall see his righteousness.
10aAα	And my enemy [f.] shall see,
10aAβ	and she shall be covered with shame,
10aB	who says [f.] to me: Where is Kyrios thy God?
10bA	My eyes will look upon her;
10bB	now she will become a thing to be trampled,
	like mud of the paths.
11a	The day of plastering brick—
11b	that day will be thy destruction,
	and that day will get rid of thy customs.
12aA	And thy cities will be leveled and into division of Assyrians.

12aB	and the strong cities into division
12bA	from Tyre as far as the River,
12bBα	a day of water and tumult {and from sea to sea,
12bBβ	and from mountain to the mountain}.

INTRODUCTION TO MICAH 7:7–12

The Themes of Micah 7:7–12

This unit is an expression of confidence in future vindication by Yahweh, in spite of the present desolation. Two processes are at work. The speaker is bearing the wrath (za'ap) of Yahweh and the scorn of an enemy. Verse 7 declares an attitude to Yahweh; v 8 addresses the enemy. Because of this change in the direction of the poet's thought, the connection of v 7 with vv 8–12 is not certain. Neither the speaker nor the enemy is identified, but both are female — most likely the reference is to two countries or two cities (the capitals of kingdoms). The speaker could be Zion, challenging one of her numerous assailants. The unit itself contains no identification. The enemy could be any of the many invaders of Judah who attacked Jerusalem. We should not assume too hastily that the enemy is Babylon, for there are other candidates. Solving this problem does not matter for the present exercise, except insofar as we are trying to date the language. There are no historical allusions. The only clue is the theology. It reflects attitudes appropriate for Israel after the destruction of Jerusalem in the sixth century, attitudes that find full expression in Lamentations, and especially in Second Isaiah. It has been inferred from these affinities that the unit Mic 7:7–12, along with many other portions of the book, belongs in the same period, the Exile or even later.

Modern study of this passage has been dominated by a famous paper by Gunkel (1923). His work represented a reaction against the conclusions of some earlier scholars, notably Haupt, Marti and Nowack, who dated this appendage to the book of Micah to the Maccabean age. Gunkel identified vv 7–20 as a cultic composition from the time of Third Isaiah put together out of a lament (vv 7–10), an oracle (vv 11–13), a lament (vv 14–17), a hymn (vv 18–20). Eissfeldt (1962) identified vv 8–20 as "a psalm from North Israel" to be related to the disasters that brought about the fall of the northern kingdom. In other words, he found an eighth-century date believable. The majority opinion still seems to side with Gunkel (Dus 1965). Even scholars such as Lippl (1937) who assign most of the book to Micah consider that vv 8–20 are the only portion of the book that was not authentic Micah, being a later editorial or scribal addition.

The allocation of v 7 is a distinct problem. Scholars seem to be evenly divided as to whether it sounds a note of hope at the end of the lament in vv 1–6 or whether the change of mood marks the onset of a fresh composition. The use of the personal pronoun ("and I . . . ") at the beginning of v 7 marks a contrast; but, insofar as it contrasts with the preceding material (if not the immediately preceding material in vv 5–6 with its admonitions, at least with the mood of lamentation in vv 1–3) it takes the "confession" forward into a new phase of hope. This tone continues into v 8. At this point the Masoretic tradition has a "closed" paragraph break; but the language of v 8 is sustained ("my enemy" in vv 8 and 10 must be the same). So in this instance we do not fully accept the traditional divisions. Similar indeterminacy prevails in the case of v 13 (after which the Masoretes preserved a "closed" break). It does not fit very well with either v 12 or v 14.

The sentiments of Micah 7, and especially of vv 7–12 are close to those of the book of Lamentations. The Lamentations were written right after the fall of Jerusalem, early in the sixth century B.C.E., in the heat of the moment, but their theology is the already matured expression of insights that are found in the writings of the prophets of the two preceding centuries. One could say that the piety of the book of Lamentations, which became so influential and enduring in the religious mentality of the people of Israel from that point onwards, was nurtured by the teachings of the prophets more than any other source. The acceptance of the prophetic interpretation of Israel's history by the survivors of the Babylonian conquest ensured, not only that the nation would survive by reaffirming its indelible identity as the people of Yahweh, but also that the prophetic writings that took the same position would survive with the nation. The religious stamina of the exiles did not create pieces like Mic 7:7–20; it was itself created by prophecies of that kind. The hope for the resurrection of Zion, expressed in Second Isaiah, was not invented in the middle of the sixth century. It was nurtured by all the previous prophecies, and Mic 7:7–20 could be one such prophecy.

The Song of Confidence in vv 7–12 is close in thought to Mic 4:14 in which fallen Zion will stand up (compare 7:8) and trample her enemies (compare v 10b). They had feasted their eyes on her (4:11), with humiliating taunts (*hā'ōmĕrîm* in 4:11, *hā'ōmĕrâ* in 7:10). Now she will do the same to them. All this suggests that 7:8–12 is another poem for Zion.

Verse 7 balances v 1 and contrasts with it. This is why some translations (NJPS, NJB, NRSV) and commentators (Rudolph 1975: 126; Allen 1976: 383; Wolff 1982: 174; Vuilleumier 1990: 82; and others) make vv 1–7 the unit. For many of these scholars v 7 is the absolute end of the real book of Micah, vv 8–20 being a much later scribal addition. Others (REB) make a break between v 6 and v 7. In this case, as in most others, the use of *and* plus a free personal pronoun at the onset of a clause achieves at once both continuity (through the conjunction) and contrast (through the pronoun). So the question is whether that construction sets only v 7 into that relationship with vv 1–6, or whether v 7 inaugurates a song of confidence that continues through v 12 and which, as a whole, contrasts with the mood of sadness in the lament of vv 1–6. The confidence that "my God will hear me" (v 7b) is the basis for the defiance of the enemy and the constructive developments that are expressed in vv 8–12. We incline to the latter view; but the point is finely balanced.

In v 7 the prophet expresses hope that the cause of the grief will be removed. A situation so desperate, when all social safeguards, public (vv 2–4a) and private (vv 5–6), have broken down, can only be remedied by drastic intervention by God. The prophet does not indicate just how he expects God to solve the problem. Verse 7b is then the center of the double poem, the pivot between grief and hope and the logical conclusion of the overall development, the end of despair, the recovery of confidence.

In 7:8 *kî nāpaltî qāmtî* is literally "When I fell down, I stood up." Yet this is scarcely possible in the context. The whole of vv 8–12 constitutes a coherent unit in theme and structure, but the verb forms are mixed. The focus is clearly on the future, and translations from LXX onwards have brought everything into line with that perception. There is no problem in v 9Aβ with *wĕ'ăśâ*, which is a consecutive construction following the imperfect *yārîb* in v 9bA. However, v 8 presents several difficulties; the four clauses match, but only partly:

8aB	*kî nāpaltî*	Although I fell down,
	qāmtî	I got up again.
8b	*kî-'ēšēb baḥōšek*	When I shall sit in darkness,
	yhwh 'ôr lî	Yahweh will be light for me.

The scenario of vv 8–12 is familiar in prophetic writings, especially in Isaiah, who uses the same imagery. The moments in the dramatic development can be identified. Zion has suffered a disaster described as "I fell down." This is stronger than "I stumbled" or tripped up; it commonly describes death in battle. As a result, the speaker is dwelling in darkness. The situation is that of a prisoner in a dungeon, which is most probably a figure of speech for the plight of a dead person in the netherworld. The enemy is rejoicing over her defeat (v8aA), gloating over her with the taunt: "where is he—Yahweh, thy God?" (v 10aB).

The speaker does not accept the theory that her defeat was due to the inactivity, absence, or even nonexistence of her God. On the contrary, as 4:11–13 has already explained, the enemy doesn't understand what is going on. The speaker knows that it is the wrath of Yahweh that has brought her into this situation (v9aA), because she had sinned against him (v 9aB), and she accepts that. Paradoxically, although confessedly guilty in relation to God, Zion is the innocent victim of the enemy's attack, and she is confident that Yahweh himself will take up her case and vindicate her, and that openly on the stage of history. That decision involves not only a favorable verdict, but *doing* justice (v 9bA); and doing justice means both the liberation of Zion from her prison ("He will bring me out to the light" [v 9bB]) and defeat of the enemy (v 9–10bB) by Zion herself, if we may add 4:13 to the picture. Then the roles will be reversed, as poetic justice requires; then it will be Zion's turn to gloat over her fallen enemy (v 10bA).

It is necessary to go into these details and to show that the situation in 7:8–12 is specific and concrete, in order to avoid the error of reducing the verbs in v 8 to the bland present tense of a general rule:

When I fall, I arise;
When I sit in darkness,
the Lord is a light for me.

The analysis requires that *kî* be concessive—"although" or "even though," excluding both "when" (KJV, RSV, etc.) and "because" (LXX). Instances of concessive *kî* are discussed by Aejmelaeus (1986: 199 n. 19). The context here requires that the protasis in each instance be future tense: "I shall arise," and "Yahweh will be light for me," even though the suffixed "I fell down" is problematical. If v 9bB is a restatement of v 8bB, both affirm the expectation of rescue from the dark prison; and this excludes the spiritualizing interpretation of v 8b as the present experience of the presence of Yahweh as a light for the prisoner:

Though I live in darkness,   Yahweh is my light (NJB).

The grammatical problem is now manifest. Verse 8aB records the past punctiliar event—"I fell down"; v 8b reports the resultant situation with no specific time reference, except that the state is ongoing—"sit in darkness." In that situation the speaker predicts the future, using imperfect verbs in vv 9–10—eight of them—with one *waw*-consecutive *wĕʿāśâ* (v 9bAβ). This detail makes the clauses in v 8 stick out. Everyone agrees that *qāmtî* means "I shall stand up," but how can that be? LXX has *kai anastēsomai*, as if from *wĕqāmtî*. It is possible that this retrojected reading stood in LXX's *Vorlage*, indeed likely, since the Greek would be all right, even better, without "and." But this improvement in the syntax of the Hebrew text, in line with standard grammar, is not necessarily the better, more original Hebrew text. It still needs to survive additional tests. The difficulty of MT is a point in its favor; for who would have deleted "and"? The lack of "and" with *qmty* matches its absence from its parallel v 8bB. The suffix verb *qmty* with future meaning resembles *ʿbr* in 5:7. See the NOTE there. The understanding of *qmty* as future tense must go hand in hand with v 8bB as future. There, too, LXX has future (*phōtiei*), as if it read *ʾwr* as a verb, another perfect with future tense. The verb *ʾôr* is attested in Gen 44:3 and 1 Sam 29:10, the latter future, "and it will be light for you." If *ʾôr* has the same meaning in v 8bB, as a parallel with v 8aB requires, then we cannot say that an original *wʾwr* (like 1 Sam 29:10) has lost "and," as could be said for *qmty*. So we have two perfect verbs with future meaning in this passage.

The faith that lives with such buoyant hope when everything has been lost is rooted in two convictions. All events are under the management of the sovereign lord Yahweh; and his purposes (*maḥšĕbôt yhwh* [4:12]) are altogether just. When Israel affirmed the rightness of the punishment sustained under God's anger (v 9), they could be confident that they would be vindicated when that anger was expended. The historical enemy was no more than God's agent for achieving his justice. But the enemy had no idea of that. Zion and her enemy perceive the same event in completely opposite ways. For the enemies, the absence of Yahweh (v 10aB) gives license for wickedness. For Zion, the injustice inflicted by the enemy is the justice of God (v 9b). This ambivalent analysis of historical experience is worked out as hope for the future. With Yahweh, the downfall of Zion must work through darkness into light; with the enemy, the defeat of Zion must be compensated for by victory over the enemy with gloating to match and repay the attitude of that enemy to Zion. In this ambivalence, Zion is acquiescent toward Yahweh (v 9), defiant toward the enemy (v 8). Although carrying out the just sentence of God on Zion (v 9)—albeit unknowingly (4:12)—the enemy is guilty of cruelty and blasphemy (4:11; 7:10) and for this must be punished. This is also the theology of First Isaiah.

The continuation of the Song of Confidence is in the manner of a taunt song. This portion (vv 8–10) is an excellent specimen of prophetic composition. It is not standard poetry, although there is plenty of parallelism; nor is it standard prose, although there is prose syntax (*'ad 'ăšer* in v 9bA) and v 10aB is prose. There are several good bicolons in verses 9bA (*rîb // mišpāṭ*), 10aA and 10bB, but the whole piece was not organized in this way as a string of bicolons. Verse 8b parallels v 8Ab by expanding the single verbs in v 8aB to longer phrases.

> I have fallen down . . . I sit in darkness;
> I will stand up . . . Yahweh will shine for me.

There are other pairs of colons that are related thematically, but they are not contiguous. Thus v 8aA has no formal parallel, but the vocative *'ōyabtî* is taken up again in v 10aB—"You who say . . . "—quoting the taunt with which the enemy exults over Zion. Verse 9bB is usually taken as one grammatical period, even though there is no "and" to join the two clauses.

> He will let me out into the light;
> I will enjoy my vindication by Him (NJPS).

Instead, one should recognize here the midpoint of the unit. "He will bring me out to the light" ends the first section; "I will see him in his vindication" begins the last section. Instead of complaining because the two colons in v 9bB do not make good poetry, we should observe that they hook into good parallels further away.

> Yahweh [will be] light for me (8bB)
>
> . . .
>
> He will bring me out to the light (9bB)

Note the chiasmus of "me" and "light." The fact that there is no "and" with *yôṣî'ēnî* shows that this clause does not continue the paragraph governed by *'ad 'ăšer*.

> 9bBβ *'er'eh bĕṣidqātô* I will see in his justice
> . . .
> 10bA *'ênay tir'ênnâ bāh* My eyes will look upon her

Each of these colons serves a dual purpose. Each is followed by a bicolon that describes the coincident state of the enemy. After "I will see" (v 9bBβ) v 10 follows with "And let my enemy see . . . " After "My eyes will look upon her" (v 10bA), v 10bB adds "Now she will become like a trampling place, . . . "

The object in view in vv 9bB and 10aA is Yahweh in his vindication; seen by both, one colon for Zion, two colons for the enemy. The repetition of *'ōyabtî* (vv 8aA, 10aAα) from the first colon of this unit marks the onset of the second main section. At the midpoint all three participants are on stage:

Yahweh	*yôṣî'ēnî lā'ôr*	He will bring me out to the light (v 9bBα)
Zion	*'er'eh bĕṣidqātô*	I will see his justice (v 9bBβ)
Enemy	*'ênay tir'ennâ bāh*	My eyes will look upon her (v 10bA)

All roles are now reversed. Yahweh brings light instead of darkness; Zion stands in righteousness instead of sin; the enemy is ashamed instead of exultant. The object in view in v 10b is the enemy in her defeat, one colon for Zion, two colons for the enemy.

The effect of this arrangement is that the final outcome is anticipated early in the presentation (v 8), but the development turns back to an early point to bring out the great contrast when Zion's condition is completely reversed. Thus vv 9a–9bA expand "sit in darkness" under the wrath of God, and this moves on into light. Verse 10bB returns to the very first colon (the enemy's original taunt), inverted because it is now the enemy's turn to fall into the mud.

Zion's predicament is thus stated three times, in vv 8, 9, 10, and the remedy is stated three times. This is much more effective then simply telling the story once, logically and chronologically.

NOTES AND COMMENTS

Notes on Micah 7:7–12

8. *rejoice*. The verb for a victory ode and for votary thanksgiving (Sirhan bottle). See NOTES on Hosea 9:1 in Andersen and Freedman (1980: 522).

enemy. The noun is feminine singular. It is unnecessary for Allen to change this word to plural throughout; cf. REB. Mays (1976: 159) says that this is the only passage in the Hebrew Bible in which the "enemy" of traditional laments is female. He interprets it as a confrontation of Jerusalem and Edom; and brings Isaiah 34, Obadiah, and Psalm 137 as evidence. NJPS suggests Damascus. The Targum glossed the word with "Rome." If Mic 1:1 may be used as a clue, v 8 could be Jerusalem regarding Samaria as the enemy. But the taunt of v 10bA seems to come from a non-Israelite. The language of Mic 7:8–10 is not specific enough to support such identifications. The speaker is certainly Zion, so prominent elsewhere in the prophecy, and her plight is similar to that in 4:11, but at a later stage (the enemy rejoices over the fallen city). The sequel here is quite different from the outcome in 4:12–13. There the Lord's plan was to lure the nations to Zion whom they imagine to be defenseless. But Zion is able to counterattack successfully. While Zion's defiance of Sennacherib (Isaiah 37) is similar in some ways, the city then saw Yahweh's role differently: "I will turn you back on the road by which you came." In both cases (Isaiah 37, Micah 4), Zion survives and triumphs; at least there is no intervening period of total humiliation. In Mic 7:8–10, by way of contrast, Zion goes into darkness. This is interpreted along the lines that became classic during the Exile. The fall of Jerusalem was really an act of God, indignant with his people because of their sin (v 9a). Against this background, the completion of Yahweh's case against Zion comes when she has received from the Lord's hand "double for her sins" (Isa 40:1). Only when this penalty has been inflicted and accepted will Zion regain a position in which Yahweh will once more be her champion and advocate in her just case (rîbî, mišpāṭî—[his] disputation, judgment [for] me) against the nations. (In the translation above, the suffix is taken to be objective—"his case against me"; in the note below we discuss the reading as benefactive—"his judgment for me.") The formal ambiguity in this language thus matches the ambivalent status of Zion as both guilty towards Yahweh, but an innocent victim of the Babylonians (or whoever the "enemy" is). When that enemy is dealt with, Yahweh's vindication (his victorious act) will not be so much a punishment of this enemy as a rescuing of the victim. Yahweh was declared by the enemy to be incompetent because Zion was left helpless. It is precisely because of this misreading of the situation that Yahweh's vindication required a demonstration of his ability to take care of Zion by rescuing her. This rescue is described as bringing Zion from darkness to light, the language of resurrection from Sheol. Then the roles will be reversed. The enemy will be trodden down (presumably by Zion; compare 4:13), and Zion will gloat over her.

although. Concessive kî (Vriezen 1958).

fell down. The verb is used to describe war casualties. This language and the imagery of darkness show that this piece is presented as a song from Sheol.

got up. This action, and bringing out to the light, describes resurrection from the dead (Hos 6:2, with associated light imagery). It was an ancient belief of Israel that Yahweh could perform this miracle (Deut 32:3; 1 Sam 2:6). It could be used as a figure of speech for the revival of a dead city only because the idea of personal resurrection already existed. This belief included the notion of waiting in Sheol in hope until Yahweh brings out the dead, after his wrath has subsided. The use of similar verbs in Job (13:15; 14:13; 19:20–26) gives grounds for including Mic 7:7 as the preface of this piece rather than the conclusion of the preceding one.

The verbs have aspect rather than tense: nāpaltî (past punctual), qāmtî (future punctual), 'ēšēb (durative). This leaves 'ôr to complete the series. It is usual to interpret 'ôr lî as "my light." Why not 'ôrî? To complete the pattern, 'ôr can be read as a verb (future punctual) "will shine." This verb is used to describe the rising of the sun (BDB 21a), and this fits in with the imagery of the current passage.

9. *his case.* Literally "my *rîb.*" The parallel expressions *yārîb rîbî // wĕʿāśâ mišpāṭî* are formally ambiguous, depending on whether the pronoun suffixes are subjective-genitive or accusative-dative. If the speaker considered herself to be in the right, then the case (*rîbî*) and its verdict (*mišpāṭî*) would be set in motion by a plea for justice and the combination would mean "my righteous cause." As in Ps 17:2, *mišpāṭî* would mean "my vindication." Such an interpretation does not jibe with the admission of guilt that the speaker has just made in the preceding bicolon (v 9a). The verdict against a sinner is condemnation, with infliction of divine indignation as the penalty. The situation in v 9a is the experience of the procedures in v 9bA. The Greek translators read it this way, rendering the parallel terms by *dikē // krima,* "penalty" // "sentence."

It is possible that the author wished to preserve the formal ambiguity of these suffixed nouns as a means of presenting the ambivalent status of Zion as both guilty (towards God) and innocent (victim of aggression). Two quarrels are encapsulated in the ambiguity. First is the Lord's case against Zion, leading to the punishment described in v 9a, reflected in the misery lamented in vv 1–7. In the context, the term *rîbî* would mean "(his) case (against) me." Verse 9bA then describes the endurance of the Lord's fury until the case is finished, finished when the sentence is served. The second quarrel is Zion's suit against the enemy. Zion expects the Lord to take up this dispute (*rîbî*) on her behalf, and will wait in hope

> Until he champions my cause,
> And upholds my claim. (NJPS)

The term *rîbî* then means "(his) case (for) me" against the enemy of v 10.

carries out. The sequence *yārîb . . . wĕʿāśâ* is used in standard Hebrew to predict a series of completed future actions: "until he will have conducted his dispute on my behalf and secured justice for me." The use of imperfect *yôṣîʾēnî* after this, with no "and," shows that v 9bB is a different development, picking up from v 8bB, as the repetition of the word *light* shows.

I will see. An object is needed. The link with v 8bB suggests that Zion will see Yahweh once more as its "light." NJPS paraphrases: "I will enjoy vindication by Him." Doubtless *ṣidqātô* does mean "his act of vindicating (me)," just as *rîbî* means "(his) disputation on my behalf." But the animus directed against Zion in 4:11 and 7:10 requires that Zion look with triumph on her defeated foe. Verse 9bB is then continued in v 10bA:

9bBβ	*ʾerʾeh bĕṣidqātô*	I will see his justice	A
10aAα	*wĕtērēʾ ʾōyabtî*	And let my enemy [f.] see,	B
10aAβ	*ûtĕkassehā bûśâ*	and let shame cover her!	B′
10aB	*hāʾōmĕrâ ʾēlay*	who says [f.] to me:	
	ʾayyô yhwh ʾĕlōhāyik	Where is he—Yahweh, your God?	
10bA	*ʿênay tirʾênnâ bāh*	My eyes will look upon her	A′

The object *bāh*, *her*, in the last colon is also the object of "I will see" in v 9bBβ.

10. *my enemy*. As in v 8aA, the feminine singular implies confrontation between two cities.

let . . . see. Jussive: "Let her see." But the position of "my eyes" before "will look" in v 10bA suggests indicative mood. The complex development of this theme of seeing has already been traced in the Notes above. One motif is enabling sight by providing light. Another is the gaze of elation. The unspecified object of "I will see" in v 9bBβ could be either Yahweh or the defeated foe. For structural reasons we suggested "her." But the omission of the object in v 9bBβ could be intended to leave the seeing general. These readings need not be mutually exclusive; it is the whole situation that is viewed. Similarly *tēreʾ* in v 10aA has no object. The enemy sees the new situation. Yahweh has vindicated Zion. We are not told how he does this, or what he does to the enemy to cause "shame." This theme of shame is renewed in v 16.

cover. The spelling suggests jussive, or else that the object is understood. The precative mood of the verbs in this unit seems to have been overlooked by translators. The mood could be extended to v 9: "Let him bring me out to the light!" Hebrew can use simple coordination of clauses as an alternative surface realization of subordination (Andersen 1974: 190); but the translation of the first *wě-* in v 10 as "when" (REB, NAB, NJB, NJSV] is arbitrary. "Then" (NRSV) preserves the continuity. Even if v 10aA is read as conditional (Wolff 1982: 188), the quasi-relative clause in v 10aB clamps the two colons in v 10aA together, with v 10bA as the consequence clause. This is better than reading v 10aB as *casus pendens* for v 10bA (REB).

who says. The participle construction is in apposition with "my enemy" in v 10aA, rather than *casus pendens* to the following object *bāh*. Perhaps it might be vocative, continuing v 8aA. The present tense favors that, but the rest of v 10 has switched from second to third person. In any case this taunting question is part of the enemy's glee referred to in v 8aA. The situation resembles that in Mic 4:11, but seems to be more specific and historical. The gathering of all the nations of the earth to attack Jerusalem seems to be an End-time scenario (Zech 12:3; 14:2).

Where is he? One can only be amused at the pedantic mentality that wants to correct *ʾayyô* to *ʾayyēh* (BHS). Look at the same construction in 2 Kgs 19:13; Isa 19:12; compare Jer 37:19. It is a stock taunt, similar to the categorical *ʾēn ʾĕlōhîm*, a charge of incompetence rather than nonexistence.

will look. The unique spelling with double *n* could be a mixture of *tirʾeynâ* and *tirʾennâ*.

now. The literal meaning is not suitable, especially with the imperfect. Hence "Lo" (NJPS), "This time" (NJB), omitted in REV. Some English speakers use "presently" and "momentarily" in a way that is substandard for purists.

for a moment	momentarily
in a moment, soon, shortly	momentarily *or* presently
currently, now	presently

In v 10bB *ʿattâ* with a future tense verb means "soon," "shortly," "immediately."

mud. The trampling could represent the conventional abuse of a defeated enemy.

11–12. The connections are harder to trace in this part of the unit. NJPS makes vv 8–13 a unit, following the traditional paragraph divisions at the end, but not at the beginning. One can see why. The feminine suffix in v 11 continues from vv 5–10, where a city was the speaker. It is simplest to assume that v 11 is a response to that speaker. But the pronoun in v 12 is masculine (BHS wants to level to feminine); and, if the referent is Yahweh, then the theme of journey from all corners of the world continues through v 17. Verse 13 interrupts this with a prophecy about devastating the land, an event that, at this stage, would seem to have been left behind long ago, and must be understood as a reprise. Hence we take v 13 to be the onset of the next unit, but without confidence.

After the well-made colons in chapter 7 so far, vv 11–12 come as a bit of a shock. They (vv 7–10) were not without difficulties, but these (vv 11–12) are terrible. Like 1:10–16, this is either very raw, but authentic stuff, or it is corrupt beyond repair. As with the earlier specimen, one can only presume that it was perpetuated with all its difficulties because it was presented to the scribes in this form with a prestige that forbade alteration. As with 1:10–16, there is not much poetry in the formal sense. It would be a capital error to assume that it must have been more regular originally and to use the rules of poetry to restore the pristine work. The difficulties are reflected in LXX, which is very different from MT. If LXX is clearer, it does not follow that it is better.

rebuilding. Allocation of vv 11–12 to the middle of the fifth century B.C.E. because the language reminds us of Nehemiah's project to erect a fortification wall around Jerusalem (Wolff 1990: 5) makes too much of meager evidence. This was not the only time that the wall of Jerusalem needed repairs. The use of *gdr* rather then *ḥômâ* in line with the following parallel and the expansion of the vision to a cosmic scale makes the prophecy too eschatological to match Nehemiah's task.

day. The variations are intriguing:

11a	*yôm libĕnôt gĕdērāyik*	day for rebuilding thy fences,
11b	*yôm hahû' yirḥaq-ḥōq*	that day, he will expand (thy) [m.] boundary.
12aA	*yôm hû' wĕʿādeykā yābô'*	That day, and he will come to thee [m.]

The standard *hayyôm hahû'* and substandard *hayyôm hû'* are not used. The discrepancy is so conspicuous that the temptation to level them to the textbook norm *hayyôm hahû'* would be hard for a scribe to resist unless the text had acquired a status that restrained such changes. Since everyone (author first, scribe later) knew how to do it right, this extraordinary text should be given a chance to vindicate itself. However, "restoring" *hayyôm hahû'*, or leveling the first two expressions to *yôm hû'* does not solve the more serious problem, which is the relationship of these expressions to the other words present. "And he will come to thee . . . " seems to be a fresh start. This leaves the pattern:

11a	yôm	the day
	libĕnôt gĕdērāyik	for rebuilding thy fences
11b	yôm hahû'	that day
	yirḥaq-ḥōq	he will expand (thy) boundary
12aA	yôm hû'	that day
	wĕ'ādeykā yābô'	and to thee he will come

boundary. If *ḥōq* means "boundary," chosen here for the sake of assonance, then the suffix *-ayik*, "thy," does double duty, and expanding thy frontier is parallel to rebuilding thy walls. It is even possible that *gdr*, rather than *qîr* or *ḥômâ*, was used to indicate the fence around a property rather than a city wall. We suggest that the grammar consists of verbless clauses, predicate before subject. The first *yôm* is construct, governing the infinitive (cf. Hag 1:2). The second and third *yôm* lack the article under the influence of the first *yôm*, but all are definite. Mur 88 reads *bywm* in v 11b, doubtless under the influence of the more familiar construction.

The theme of the wide extension of Israel's territory is not new. It is a restatement of the hope of recovering the ancient glory of David's kingdom. No agent is identified—Yahweh or the messianic hero—the same problem as in chapters 4–5. The term *ḥōq*, "bound," is used in creation traditions for the bounds set by God. Its use here gives a mythological taste to the messianic kingdom. The bounds emerge from the promise to Abraham, realized in David's kingdom, projected on to an apocalyptic screen. It is not cosmic enough to be eschatological, yet not specific enough to be historical.

The idiom *rḥq ḥq* is found here only. Another explanation reads *rḥqḥq* as a partially reduplicated root—"That is a far-off day" (NJPS). Cf. *hr hhr* (v 12bBβ).

12. The map of the empire seems overelaborate. It is a distinct tradition, with a less common name for Egypt. If the River is the Euphrates, then the north-south distance is stated twice. This arrangement matches what are apparently two statements about sea and mountain in v 12bB; but the use of *min-* there is reversed. We would expect some statement for east to west. Defining the territory exactly requires that the seas and mountains be identified. A consistent use of *min-* as correlate of *'ad* can be recognized if we note that the prepositions are placed chiastically and are omitted from some of the nouns.

12aB	lĕminnî 'aššûr wĕ'ārê māṣôr	*from* Assyria and [*unto*] the cities of Egypt
12bA	ûlĕminnî māṣôr wĕ'ad-nāhār	and *from* Egypt, and <u>unto</u> (the) River,
12bBα	wĕyām miyyām	and [*unto*] sea *from* sea,
12bBβ	wĕhar hāhār	and [*unto*] mountain [*from*] the mountain.

Compare Ps 72:8 where the prepositions are used normally (Ps 72:9 is like Mic 7:17).

will come. If the singular verb *yābô'* describes this migration, one can understand why LXX made it plural. Compare the similar idiom in 4:8. If the subject of the singular verb is the messianic hero, the following words describe the scope of his kingdom (5:3b).

cities. Emendation to *w'd(y)* is attractive.

Egypt. It is not certain that *māṣôr* is Egypt (Calderone 1961), although that country is the usual match for Assyria. But then it is usually called *miṣrayim*, which occurs in v 15. In 4:14 *māṣôr* is "siege" (but the interpretation is not certain). LXX reads "Tyre"; hence NAB, NJB. But the alternate name could reflect a different tradition of geographical terminology. The vocabulary is archaic, perhaps affected. Note the peculiarity of *lĕminnî* instead of the usual *min*, and *nāhār* instead of the usual *hannāhār*.

sea. On the use of *yām*, "sea," as a cardinal point see Sirat (1971).

mountain . . . the mountain. This unique expression possibly means "the remotest mountain" (de Moor 1982: 163).

III.5. VINDICATION (7:13–17)

TRANSLATION

MT

13aA	*wĕhāyĕtâ hā'āreṣ lišĕmāmâ*	And the land will become desolate,
13aB	*'al-yōšĕbeyhā*	on account of her inhabitants,
13b	*mippĕrî ma'alĕlêhem*	from the fruit of their [m. pl.] evil deeds.
14aAα	*rĕ'ēh 'ammĕkā bĕšibṭekā*	Shepherd thy [m.] people with thy [m.] staff,
14aAβ	*ṣō'n nahălātekā*	the flock of thine [m.] inheritance;
14aBα	*šōkĕnî lĕbādād ya'ar*	dwelling alone (in) woodland,
14aBβ	*bĕtôk karmel*	in the midst of Carmel.
14bA	*yir'û bāšān wĕgil'ād*	Let them graze (in) Bashan and Gilead
14bB	*kîmê 'ôlām*	as in the ancient days,
15a	*kîmê ṣē'tĕkā mē'ereṣ miṣrāyim*	as in the days when thou camest out from the land of Egypt.
15b	*'ar'ennû niplā'ôt*	I showed him marvels.
16aA	*yir'û gôyīm*	Let the nations see (them),
16aB	*wĕyēbōšû mikkōl gĕbûrātām*	and let them be ashamed of all their might.
16bA	*yāśîmû yād 'al-peh*	Let them put hand over mouth;
16bB	*'oznêhem teḥĕrašnâ*	let their ears become deaf.
17aA	*yĕlaḥăkû 'āpār kannāḥāš*	Let them lick up dust like the snake,
17aBα	*kĕzōḥălê 'ereṣ*	like those who slither on the ground;
17aBβ	*yirgĕzû mimmisgĕrōtêhem*	let them come trembling out of their dens.
17bA	*'el-yhwh 'ĕlōhênû yiphādû*	El Yahweh, our God, let them fear (thee),
17bB	*wĕyîrĕ'û mimmekkā*	and let them be afraid of thee [m.]!

LXX III.5. Vindication (7:13-17)

13aA   And the earth will become desolate,
13aB   together with her inhabitants,
13b   because of the fruit of their practices.
14aAα   Shepherd thy people with thy staff,
14aAβ   the sheep of thine inheritance;
14aBα   those who dwell by themselves in the thicket
14aBβ   in the midst of Carmel.
14bA   They will graze in the (land of) Bashan and in the (land of) Gilead
14bB   as in the days of old,
15a   ⟨and⟩ as according to the days when thou didst go forth from the land of Egypt,
15b   You will see amazing things.
16a   The nations will see it and will be ashamed
16bA   of all their might. They will put hands over their mouth;
16bB   their ears will become deaf.
17aA   They will lick dust like snakes,
17aBα   crawling on the earth;
17aBβ   they will be confused in their confinement.
17bA   At Kyrios our God they will be out of their minds,
17bB   and they will be afraid of thee.

INTRODUCTION TO MICAH 7:13-17

The Themes of Micah 7:13-17

Verse 13 is transitional. The Masoretic paragraph division sĕtûmâ embodies an analysis that attaches it to vv 9-12. Verse 13 is an interlude. It predicts a phase of destruction that does not seem to fit either the triumphal tone of vv 11-12 or the reconstructive tone of vv 14-17.

Verses 14-17 begin as a prayer to Yahweh to resume his ancient role as shepherd of his people (Psalm 23; Isa 40:11; Mic 4:6-7), "as in the olden days" (v 15). The prayer is replete with memories of old traditions, secured by traditional vocabulary: šibṭekâ, "thy rod" (Ps 23:4), ʿam // ṣōʾn, "people" // "flock" (Ps 100:3); naḥălâ, "inheritance" (very common); niplāʾôt, "marvels" (frequent in psalms of historical recital; cf. Forshey 1975).

Because of "our" in v 17, the whole is spoken by Israel, and "thou" in the first and last colons shows that the whole is addressed to Yahweh. Verse 15b is exceptional. "I showed him" sounds like part of an account given by Yahweh. The problem created by this dissonance can be solved by concocting a different text altogether—harʾēnû, proposed by BHS, or some other remedy (see the NOTE). Verse 15a also contains a curious detail if addressed to Yahweh: "thou camest out from the land of Egypt." Usually it is Israel who went out (qal); Yahweh brought them out (hipʿil). But see Judg 5:4; Ps 68:8.

Verse 14 begins and ends with "shepherd" (root rʿh) and describes Yahweh and Israel. Verses 16-17 begin and end with yrʾw (the verb has a different meaning in each occurrence) and describe Yahweh and the nations. Assonance of *rʿh* and *rʾh* thus provides a chain through vv 14–17. In verse 16 the imperfect verbs in clause-initial position, without "and" (compare Habakkuk 3), are archaic epic preterit; but the time references in verse 15 and the matching imperative in v 14aAα suggest that the verb *yirʿû* (v 14bA) is jussive, "Let them graze!"

The Poetry of Micah 7:13–17

On the basis of the Masoretic accentuation we find seventeen colons in this unit. The Masoretes did not supply *zaqef qaton* in v 13a. The whole of v 13 is just one long clause (21 syllables); there is no natural place to put a caesura. The poetry in vv 14–17 is better developed. Colons range in length from four to twelve syllables. The text in vv 14–15a contains three statements. The first and third begin with a precative verb, each with the same root—imperative in v 14aAα, jussive in v 14bA. The statement in the middle (v 14aB) begins with a participle of archaic form, either an ancient title for Yahweh, used vocatively, or a description of the flock dwelling in the woodland. Each of these statements has a similar grammatical shape. Each begins with a verbal element, and at least one item in the first colon has a match in the next colon. Thus v 14aA has *thy people // the flock of thine inheritance*; v 14aB has *woodland // in the midst of* (which does retroactive double duty) *Carmel*; vv 14b–15a have *as in the ancient days // as in the days when thou camest out from the land of Egypt*.

First statement:

14aAα	*rēʿēh ʿammĕkā bĕšibṭekā*	Shepherd thy [m.] people with thy [m.] staff,
14aAβ	*ṣōʾn naḥălātekā*	the flock of thine [m.] inheritance;

Second statement:

14aBα	*šōkĕnî lĕbādād yaʿar*	dwelling alone (in) woodland,
14aBβ	*bĕtôk karmel*	in the midst of Carmel.

Third statement:

14bA	*yirʿû bāšān wĕgilʿād*	Let them graze (in) Bashan and Gilead
14bB	*kîmê ʿôlām*	as in the ancient days,
15a	*kîmê ṣēʾtĕkā mēʾereṣ miṣrāyim*	as in the days when thou camest out from the land of Egypt.

If each of these units is given the same rank, each a bicolon, the third statement (vv 14b–15a—21 syllables) is about as long as the first two together (v 14a—22 syllables). It would seem that the greater length of the third statement was intended to achieve this balance. Leaving out v 15a, the three statements in v 14 have virtually the same length (11, 11, 12 syllables), but then the third (v 14b) has no parallelism like that in the other two. Verse 15a supplies parallelism of greater precision (Clines) for v 14bB. Leaving the imbalance between these two matching items highlights the concluding effect of v 15a, which gives the time setting for the entire recital. The poetic structure does not fit the verse structure inherited by the Masoretes and their system of binary divisions did not permit them to handle the three metrically similar statements in v 14 in the same way. They were able to divide v 14a with *zaqef qaton* and to use *rĕbîaʿ* in v 14aA, but the disjunctive accents in vv 14aB and 14b have less power. If they had been followed, the result would be as shown above, a seven-colon unit. The three bicolons are rhythmically similar, but the third (v 14b) has no parallelism like that in the first two, which have incomplete synonymous parallelism of a familiar kind. This kind of parallelism does obtain between v 14b and v 15a. The result is a unit (however we wish to display the colons) of great complexity, with connections among all the components. As the piece unfolds, new items of information are added. There is only one picture, a shepherd with his flock. The grammar of each successive statement contains a series of adverbial adjuncts that supply the details.

14aA   Verb: *Shepherd*   Object: *thy people*   Instrument: *with thy staff*
14b   Verb: *Let them graze* Place: *Bashan*   Time: *as in days of old*

The object in v 14aA is doubled. The location in v 14bA is given a mythic setting in v 14aB—Bashan and Gilead are compared to the fabulous woodland of Carmel. The time reference in v 14b is expanded in v 15a. With all this rich detail and repetition, one hardly notices the most remarkable feature of all: after the imperative verb that begins the piece (v 14aA) the focus shifts to the activity of the flock (in spite of its singular number, most interpreters have concluded that *šōkĕnî* in v 14aB refers to the flock). The first verb has no explicit subject; the shepherd is not identified, except by implication. Only in the last colon (v 15a) does the reference to coming out of Egypt make that identity clear, and even then the name of Yahweh is not used. It is supplied only at the very end of the unit, in v 17.

Just as vv 14–15a, dealing with Israel the flock, are embraced by the repeated verb *rʿh*, so vv 16–17, dealing with the nations, are embraced by the repetition of *yrʾw* (vv 16aA, 17bB). The parallelism and the use of *metheg* show that the latter means *fear*. The nine colons in this second main part of the unit consist of four bicolons and an extra colon or rather three bicolons (16a, 16b, 17a) and a tricolon (v 17b). Other arrangements are possible. There are actually seven clauses describing what the nations will do. After the first colon (v 16aA), which has no formal parallel, there is a tricolon describing the disgrace of the nations (vv 16aB–16b). The bicolon in v 16b has parallelism with chiasmus. Verse 16b expounds the colon in v 16aB. The bicolon in v 17aA–17aBα has incomplete parallelism, and is followed by a single colon (v 17aBβ). The six colons in vv 16aB–17aB thus have an introverted structure: colon (v 16aB), bicolon (v 16b), bicolon (17aA–17aBα), colon (17aBβ). The first and last colons constitute an envelope around the rest, as the parallelism of *their might // their dens* shows. At the same time v 17aBβ has v 17bA as its chiastic parallel, so that vv 17abβ–17b makes another tricolon. Finally we note that the outermost colons (v 16aA and v 17bB) constitute an envelope around the other seven colons.

This leaves v 15b. This is the only part of the entire poem that can be identified as a statement of the deity. It is exactly in the middle: the preceding seven colons have 64 syllables; the following nine colons have 65 syllables.

In vv 14–17 there were twelve opportunities to use a prose particle. Not one was used. The language is clearly that of poetry. A remarkable feature of vv 14–17 is the high incidence of prefixed verb forms, ten in all. The only other verb is the opening imperative: "Shepherd!" The mood of the initiating verb determines the salient reading of the entire ensuing paragraph unless there are indications to the contrary. The verb in v 14bA is certainly jussive. (The verb in v 15b is a distinct problem. In any case it is the only one that is first person, so it stands apart from the other series.) Quite aside from the continuing force of the opening imperative, the clause-initial position of a prefixed verb is itself an indication of precative mood, and there is no reason why all eight prefixed verbs in vv 16–17 should not be taken as jussive. All have the same subject, "(the) nations" of v 16aA (virtually with "their eyes" in the variant gender of v 16bB). It is also remarkable that only two of the eleven verbal clauses in vv 14–17 begin with "and," considering the ubiquity of this conjunction in typical Hebrew. The two clauses introduced by "and" (vv 16aB, 17bB) have important functions in the total structure of the extended imprecation against the nations in vv 16–17. The first (v 16aA) and the last (v 17bB) clause make an inclusion with the help of the assonance of the verbs.

16aA   *yir'û gôyīm*   Let (the) nations see (them),

       . . .

17bB   *wĕyirĕ'û mimmekkā* and let them be afraid of thee.

In effect, these two clauses make a discontinuous bicolon (envelope construction) with the "and" joining the two colons. The other "and," at the beginning of v 16aB, introduces the body of this prayer against the nations (vv 16aB–17bA). The verbal clauses come in two sets of three, with the verb in the third clause of each set at the end of its clause (vv 16bB, 17bA). The first set (in v 16) expresses a wish that the nations be confounded; the second set (in v 17) hopes for their servile submission to Yahweh. It is all highly structured, but the thematic, syntactic, and prosodic structures do not coincide. The whole of vv 14–17 is thus a sustained prayer expressing an interest in all three participants in the End-time drama—Yahweh, that he might shepherd his flock (v 14a); Israel, that they might graze as in the olden days (vv 14b–15); the nations, to be subdued (vv 16–17).

NOTES AND COMMENTS

Notes on Micah 7:13-17

13. Some of this language has been used in 6:16. The use of three prepositional phrases makes the construction rather ponderous. The thematic connection of v 13 with the surrounding material is not evident. Clause-initial *wĕhāyĕtâ* usually marks the introduction of a new paragraph, and the salient reading would be future tense: "and it will be." Some of the strain could be relieved if the conjunction "and" in *wĕhāyĕtâ* were taken, not as *waw*-consecutive, but as coordinating, with the verb as past tense. Assuming that *the land* is Israel, the verse would then describe once more the desolation due to the anger of Yahweh (v 9), "their evil deeds" having the same reference here and in Mic 3:4. But with so many other passages in Micah having a global reference, and in a context that describes the vindication of Yahweh and his people in full view of the whole world, it is more likely that v 13 is speaking about the devastations of the earth in universal judgment on its wicked inhabitants. It prepares for the submission of the nations described in vv 16-17.

14. *dwelling.* The archaic participle could be a title of Yahweh (Ps 68:17, associated with Bashan; Deut 33:16; Ps 74:2, several words in common with Mic 7:14-17) or Israel, preferred by most translators. The plural verb *yirʿû* suggests that the singular participle is a title of God. The language of Num 23:9, especially its use of *lĕbādād* suggests Israel. Either way, the expression emphasizes the uniqueness of Israel, and of Israel's God.

Bashan and Gilead. These names remind us first of a particular phase of the Exodus, but they have many other associations. They represent disputed territory whose recapture was often symbolic of recovery of ancient rights. Note the symbolic use of "Gilead" in Jer 22:6. In the present context the following reference to the Exodus fits in with the memories of that event already present in chapter 6.

15. *thou camest out.* The tradition usually says that Israel went out of Egypt (Ps 114:1). Verse 15 could be a remark addressed to Israel in the middle of its prayer. The identification of the subject of *camest out* as Yahweh is indicated by the unity of the prayer (Yahweh is *thou*), but this result is complicated by the first-person verb in v 15b.

land. LXX lacks "land," and some scholars recommend its removal from the Hebrew text. Wolff (1982: 189) says that this would improve the *qinah* meter. But "the land of Egypt" is the common expression, and prior decisions about what the meter should be cannot be used to make text-critical judgments without falling into circular reasoning.

I showed him. We recognize the prefix verb as an archaic preterit. If v 15 is a snippet of a historical recital, with Yahweh the speaker, then the Hebrew text can stand, but a change of speakers between the otherwise parallel constructions with "as in the days" is harsh. The Masoretic Text is confirmed by the reading *deiksō autois* (or *autous*), "I shall show them," in several Greek manuscripts, and by the Targum, Peshitta, and Vulgate. LXX "you shall see" does not provide a plausible retrojection; it seems to be interpretive. MT is widely rejected, however, and various suggestions have been made to change the verb so that v 15 becomes part of the prayer. Wellhausen's emendation to *har'ēnû*, "cause us to see!" is the most widely accepted (NJB, NRSV, REB). Allen (1976: 392 n. 43) retains the consonants and repoints to *'ar'ēnû*, "show us!" This would be an Aramaizing *Ap'el*, which is going rather far afield. (Allen attributes the suggestion to Ewald—not confirmed.) With so many memories of Israel's early days in this unit, it is simplest to retain a historical reference. Yahweh says, "When you came out from Egypt, I showed him marvels." The very next verse goes on to anticipate, to pray, that now the nations "will see" similar wonders, with similar results. These words, in the middle of the prayer, could be a quotation (by the person praying) of a recognizable saying of Yahweh. The words are quoted as grounds for the request that Yahweh would do the same thing again for his people in a time of similar need.

marvels. The Lord showed wonders to Pharaoh (Exod 3:20), who does not otherwise figure in these colons. He is evidently the one referred to by the object *him* of the verb in the preceding colon: *I showed him.* The term *marvels* is common in the Psalms, but otherwise it is found in the basic tradition only in Exod 34:10.

16. *nations.* The response described here is very similar to that in Exodus 15 and Habakkuk 3.

see. The second last word in v 17 is spelled the same—*yr'w*, but MT *metheg* distinguishes *yr'w* as *defective* spelling of *yyr'w*. This spelling occurs in Mur 88. The verbs could have the same pronunciation but different meanings, the second being rather the biconsonantal by-form based on the alloroot *r'*, "fear" (Andersen 1970). "The sea feared and fled" (Ps 114:3—*rā'â* preserves the ancient masculine ending).

ashamed. There is a similarity in the behavior of the disgraced prophets, who cover themselves completely, except for the mustache (3:7), and Zion's enemies, who put their hands on their mouths and crawl in the dust.

might. If the pronoun suffix refers to the nations, their military might is disgraced. The noun is usually a reference to an act of God. "From all their might" then means "because of all (your) might to them." The suffix is datival. Otherwise the *min-* must be privative—"deprived of all their might."

mouth. The silence of Exodus 15.

17. *the snake.* The image derives from Gen 3:14. Barré (1982) found a similar collocation of ideas—humiliation and eating dust—in the Amarna letter EA 100.

El Yahweh. The same expectation is found in Hos 3:5. Because the preposition *'el,* "unto," does not fit the idiom of the verb "fear," we speculate that it might be part of the compound divine name *El Yahweh.* Note *El* in 7:18.

(thee). Yahweh, if v 17bB is an inclusion from v 14 as we argued above. This is the most natural reading, since the whole of vv 14–17 is a prayer. It is not easy to account for the idiom *from thee,* rather than identifying Yahweh as the object of "fear." Israel is involved also. Zion has her own account to settle with the

enemy. She will see (vv 9bB, 10bB) when Yahweh's righteous action brings shame (v 10aA) to the foe; and the nations will see (v 16aA) and be ashamed (the root of the noun in v 10aA is repeated in the verb in v 16aB). The thematic connection between vv 7–12 and vv 13–17 is seen also in the match between the taunt "Where is Yahweh, thy God?" (v 10aB) and the submission of the nations to "Yahweh, our God" in v 17bA. The nations will fear Yahweh on account of Israel, because of the wonders Yahweh did on Israel's behalf. Part of the political outcome is respect for Israel by the nations.

III.6. THE COVENANT MENDED (7:18–20)

TRANSLATION

MT

18aA	mî-'ēl kāmôkā nōśē' 'āwōn	Who is a god like thee, forgiving iniquity,
18aB	wĕ'ōbēr 'al-peša'	and passing by treachery
	lišĕ'ērît naḥălātô	for the remnant of his heritage;
18bA	lō'-heḥĕzîq lā'ad 'appô	(the one who) did not sustain his anger for ever,
18bB	kî-ḥāpēṣ ḥesed hû'	because he delights in ḥesed . . .
19aA	yāšûb yĕraḥămēnû	He will once more have compassion on us;
19aB	yikbōš 'ăwōnōtênû	he will trample on our iniquities.
19b	wĕtašlîk bimĕṣūślôt yām	And thou shalt hurl into the depths of the sea
	kol-ḥaṭṭō'wtām	all their sins
20aA	tittēn 'ĕmet lĕya'ăqōb	Thou shalt give truth to Jacob,
20aB	ḥesed lĕ'abrāhām	ḥesed to Abraham.
20bA	'ăšer-nišba'tā la'ăbōtênû	. . . which thou didst swear to our fathers
20bB	mîmê qedem	from the days of old.

LXX III.6. The Covenant Mended (7:18–20)

18aA	Who is a god like thee, taking away iniquities,
18aB	and passing over the ungodlinesses
	of the remnant of his inheritance?
18bA	And he has not sustained his anger for a testimony,
18bB	because he is desirous of mercy (eleos).
19aA	He will turn again and will pity us;
19aB	he will sink our iniquities,
19b	and they shall be cast into the depths of the sea—all our sins.
20aA	Thou wilt {He will} give truth to Jacob,
20aB	mercy (eleos) to Abraham,
20bA	as thou didst swear to our fathers
20bB	according to the former days.

INTRODUCTION TO MICAH 7:18–20

The Themes of Micah 7:18–20

The prophecy ends on an altogether positive note. This is an acclamation of God that concentrates on his faithfulness in keeping his promises, and especially his eagerness to forgive rather than punish. This thematic unity is disturbed by changes of dialogue posture as shown by the variety of pronouns used. The unit opens and closes with direct address to God ("thou"), but the middle section is third person narrative. The switch to third person for the rest of v 18 after the opening address does not indicate a loss of cohesion; it can be explained if the clauses are relative.

The opening question, *Who is a god like thee?* is immediately answered by setting forth the incomparability of Yahweh (Lang 1981). This is done by listing his attributes as a series of characteristic activities. This kind of composition was a popular form of hymnic recital with a credal effect. The participial titles of Yahweh frequently celebrate his power in creation or his mighty acts in history. Gunkel and Begrich (1933: 44) call them "hymnic participles." Here the titles go back to the revelation of the name of Yahweh to Moses (Exod 34:7). The definite article is often used with the participles in compositions of this kind, and then it is clearly equivalent to the relative pronoun—"the one who forgives iniquity." Their absence here is another sign that the unit contains archaizing poetry. Relative clauses switch to third person even when the antecedent is not third person, and this grammar continues through v 18b, even though the verbs are now perfect. Even the final subordinate clause is brought under this rule.

In v 19a imperfect verbs (third person) are used with a first-person object, but v 19b has a second-person verb with a third-person object. Verse 20 continues with a second-person description, and the second person kept up even in the relative clause along with first person in the indirect object.

18a   Who is a god like *thee,* . . . for the remnant of *his* heritage;

18b   *he* did not sustain *his* anger . . . because *he* delights in *ḥesed* . . .

19aA   *he* will return . . . *he* will have compassion on *us*

19aB   *he* will trample on *our* iniquities

19b   *thou* shalt hurl . . . all *their* sins

20aA   *thou* shalt give truth to Jacob

20bA   which *thou* didst swear to *our* fathers

It is altogether too easy to smooth out these fluctuations in the pronouns by leveling the third-person pronouns to either second person (when the referent is God) or first person. This is what NIV has done, without giving the reader the slightest intimation that they have changed the text in five places to achieve this result. The variations in the pronouns are a guide to the overall structure of the unit. After the opening question, addressed to Yahweh in the second person (v 18a—20 syllables), there is a description in the third person of Yahweh's compassion and willingness to forgive (vv 18b–19a—26 syllables), followed by a further address to God in the second person (vv 19b–20—38 syllables). The references to the objects of Yahweh's forgiveness, the Israel of the prophet's day, alternate in a different pattern: third (v 18), first (19a), third (19b), first (20b). It is strange that the changes in the pronouns ("he" to "thou" in the case of Yahweh; "our iniquities" to "their sins" in the case of Israel) occur in the middle of a verse that is otherwise unified by the theme of forgiveness.

The incomparability of Yahweh is thus asserted in two parts—his attributes (v 18) and his achievements (vv 19b–20). In the middle v 19a is a prophecy that he will do the same thing again.

The changes in the pronouns are matched by changes in the verb forms. These variations raise the question of the time reference intended in the choice of verb forms. A spread of time is in view. The opening question is found in ancient odes celebrating Yahweh's achievements. Notable among past achievements is Yahweh's faithfulness to the ancestors. The promises made to Abraham and Jacob were fulfilled in the Exodus and in the gift of the promised land. In all this variegated use of the traditions, mainly patriarchal and Exodus, some are transparent and formal, some secondary and associative. Fishbane (1985: 430) found in this passage a "taxemic form" of haggadic interpretation of ancient traditional formulations.

The Poetry of Micah 7:18–20

To arrive at the ten colons displayed on p. 594 we have followed the Masoretic accents except in the case of v 18a. There MT has *zaqef qaton* with *pešaʿ*. We suggest that considerations of poetic parallelism should override that decision, with the caesura after *ʿāwōn* so that the two matching participle constructions come in parallel colons. Another possibility is to read v 18 as a quatrain (2 : 2 :: 2 : 2 beats):

18aA   *mî-ʾēl kāmôkā*
         nōśēʾ ʿāwōn
18aB   *weʿōbēr ʿal-pešaʿ*
       lišěʾērît naḥălātô

The two colons in the middle have good parallelism. This leaves the outer colons as an envelope and brings the last phrase into closer attachment to the opening question. The next bicolon (v 18b) is a complex sentence (12 syllables). The middle bicolon (v 19a) is remarkable for having three verbs. The first could be auxiliary. The bicolon is unified by the repetition of *-nû*, "our," and by the third-person verbs in parallel. In v 18a the parallel words for sin are ʿāwōn and pešaʿ. The first derives from the tradition, and is matched by the plural form in v 19aB. Micah himself elsewhere prefers the pair pšʿ // ḥ ṭʾt (1:5; 3:8; 6:7). In spite of the parallelism of the plural nouns *iniquities* (v 19aB) and *sins* (v 19b), the verbs in v 19 change from third to second and the pronoun suffixes change from first to third. The final section (19b–20) is another envelope construction with two long colons embracing a bicolon that is an impeccable specimen of standard incomplete parallelism:

> 20aA   *tittēn   ʾĕmet lĕyaʿăqōb*   Thou shalt give truth   to Jacob,
>
> 20aB   *ḥesed lĕʾabrāhām*   *ḥesed*   to Abraham.

One could display v 19b (13 syllables) and v 20b (14 syllables) as bicolons to match v 20a (12 syllables), but the stately effect of these long flowing clauses would still be the same. The last colon (v 20bB) is a relative clause modifying the broken-up stereotype phrase "truth and kindness" (usually in the inverse sequence), with *our fathers* in parallel with "Jacob and Abraham" (also inverted). The book thus ends with an affirmation of the reliability of God's sworn promises, especially the promise of compassion upon our sins.

NOTES AND COMMENTS

Notes on Micah 7:18–20

18. It is surprising that Yahweh is nowhere named in this concluding hymn. The original question was "Who is like thee among the gods, O Yahweh?" (Exod 15:11). This question, in its original formulation and in its literal reading could imply that there are other gods, but none is like Yahweh in forgiving sins. The adherents of other ancient religions did not have any fixed doctrines that their gods would never forgive sins. They also hoped and believed that the gods might be compassionate. Worshipers always hoped that there would be some way of moving the gods to pity. In the West-Semitic religious tradition the same kind of language was used as we find in the central affirmations of Yahwism. The god Hadad in the Tel Fekherye bilingual inscription was *rḥmn*, "compassionate" (line 5).

The question is asked in two forms: by Yahweh—"Who is like me?" (Isa 44:7; Jer 49:19; 50:44), or by Israel—"Who is like thee?" (Exod 15:11; Ps 35:10; 71:19; 77:14; 89:9; 113:5; Job 36:22). The only possible answer is "None!" (Labuschagne 1966).

The original question in Exodus 15 highlighted Yahweh's incomparable power in quelling Pharaoh at the Sea of Reeds. The most memorable act of pardoning sin occurred at Sinai/Horeb. The phrase "carrying (away) iniquity" is the only item that Mic 7:18 has in common with the great revelation given then, so what we have here is only an indirect allusion. Even so, in view of the widespread evidence for this classic credo throughout the Hebrew Bible (Andersen 1986: 44–52), there is enough common vocabulary between Exodus 34 and Mic 7:18–20 to support the inference that Micah had that tradition in mind and expected his listeners to recognize it. In its own way Micah's affirmation is even stronger than the original, especially in the reason given in v 18bB and the extraordinary image used in v 19b.

remnant. This latter phrase is not necessarily extraneous in its present setting. BH3 thinks it is an addition. Left as it is, this diction secures a linkage with the reference to the remnant in chapter 5. The use of *naḥălâ* in verse 14 is also important for filling out the picture.

sustain. This use of the root *ḥzq* is unique. Literally "he did not strengthen his anger," i.e., he did not keep it up. Rather he allowed it to subside. Here *ḥesed*, rather than, say, "compassion" is the opposite of *'ap*. But the usual correlate *rḥm*, "pity," is used in v 19.

he delights in ḥesed. For a recent survey of the extensive literature on this word, see Andersen (1986) and Romerowski (1990).

19a. This is the one perfectly formed bicolon in the piece. The lines are exactly equal in length, and have rhyme provided by the pronoun suffixes (the usual source of rhyme in Hebrew poetry).

once more. The verb *yāšûb* is an auxiliary like *hôsîp*, "add," i.e., do again. It is not followed by an infinitive because both the following verbs are coordinated, and *yāšûb* governs them both. Compare 1:6.

trample. See R. P. Gordon (1978).

19b. Whether recital of a past event or promise of a future one, the highly figurative language of hurling sin into the sea provides a unique metaphor. It is as dramatic as the ceremony of the scapegoat that symbolically carried the sins of Israel off into the wilderness. That ritual leaves the impression that sins were believed to be effectively disposed of by this means. We know of no matching concretized dramatization of the idea that God can get rid of sins by throwing them into the sea. The following NOTE opens up the possibility that the destruction of Pharaoh provided the picture, just as Exodus 15 provided some of the language in this unit.

thou. It is too drastic to level all the third-person forms that come between v 18aA and v 19b to second person (REB [wholly]; NJB [partly]).

depths of the sea. The *mĕṣūlôt yām* (Ps 68:23) are quasi-mythological deeps, like Sheol (Ps 88:7). The "deep" was feared, personified like a monster (Ps 69:16). Water is both purifying and destructive. The Flood is the prototypical instance, and its dual imagery—saving life and causing death—continues to turn up in the Bible. The dramatic action of hurling something undesirable or harmful into deep water is part of ancient magical rituals. A Hittite example: "May the pure water cleanse the evil tongue, impurity, bloodshed, sin, curse . . . Just as the wind blows away the chaff and carries it into the sea, let it likewise blow away the bloodshed and impurity of this house, and let it carry it into the sea. Let it go into the sacred mountains. Let it go into the deep wells" (Hallo 1997: 170a). For Mesopotamia, see Abusch (1990). The parallelism of Exod 15:4–5 is

yārâ bayyām . . . yārĕdû bimṣôlōt

The idiomatic use of the same verb in Jon 2:4 shows that the act of God against a sinner could be described in these terms, in Jonah's case, literally: "And thou didst hurl me into the deep." The currency of the idiom is shown also by Neh 9:11: "And their pursuers thou didst hurl into the deeps like a stone." This is clearly dependent on Exodus 15; it has been adapted to standard prose. In these traditions it is the sinner (or an enemy) who is hurled into the sea. Analogy with sins is evident in Isa 38:17—"You have hurled all my sins behind your back."

their sins. The nearest available referent (cataphoric) is "our fathers." Otherwise it goes back to "the remnant of his heritage" in v 18. The strain caused by the third-person pronoun "their" could be relieved by recognizing the suffix -*m* as enclitic (Dahood *CBQ* 20 [1958]: 45). It is usually corrected to "*our* sins," which has considerable support in the versions and even in a few manuscripts. Hence REB; see Brockington. Yet this correction is obvious, and all this evidence can be set aside as secondary. An orthographic explanation suggested by Weiss (1963: 192) is that -*nw* could have been misread as -*m*.

20. *give.* The verb *ntn*, give, is operational for this act, and *tittēn* (v 20aA) can be taken either as indicative (continuing from v 19b) or jussive.

ḥesed. The use of this word in vv 18bB and 20aB is a long-range link between the opening and closing sections of the unit. The usual sequence is "mercy and truth," hendiadys for "reliable mercy," the second noun defining the first (Zimmerli *TDNT* 9:383). Here it is inverted (cf. Hos 4:1; Ps 89:24). The names Abraham and Jacob are also inverted, perhaps to make it clear that the real ancestors are in mind, not just Israel the nation of the prophet's times. Since Yahweh has already given his truth and mercy to the ancestors, the use of *tittēn* is problematic. Whether the verb is past or future, it is not evident what the "truth" and "mercy" is that the Lord gave // will give to these two men. In any case a complex hendiadys is involved; and both blessings are given to both patriarchs. "Mercy and truth" are not normally the objects of "give"; they are used as adverbs to show *how* God keeps his promises. The preposition *b*- is understood. We may fill out the laconic speech: "(In) (his) mercy and truth he will give (us) [the remnant] (the inheritance) that he swore to our fathers, Abraham and Jacob."

which. The nearest antecedent for the relative pronoun in v 20b is "heritage" in v 18. The usual antecedent of that kind of clause in the Deuteronomic tradition is "the land of Canaan." The related verbs "give" // "swear" are used in all the sources for promises made to patriarchs. The description of the land in v 12 arises from both the patriarchal map and the empire of David.

days of old. Micah uses several phrases to refer to the beginnings from which all present developments were determined—*miqqedem* (5:1); *mîmê ʿôlām* (5:1); *kîmê ʿôlām* (7:14); *mîmê qedem* (7:20).

COMMENT ON MICAH 7

The most common analysis divides the book into two sections (chapters 1–3 and chapters 4–7). The last four chapters are generally divided into 4–5 and 6–7, and we have followed this scheme. Schneider (1979: 25) disagrees and argues that "each summons to hear, 1:2; 3:1; 6:1, begins a new section." We can concur, so far as 6:1 is concerned; but arguments for the unity of chapters 1–3 prevent us from isolating chapter 3. We have recognized some continuity between chapter 3 and chapter 4. The repeated calls to hear can be viewed rather as unifying signals that span the Book of Visions (chapters 4–5). At the same time we can recognize that chapter 7 serves as a review and summary of the whole prophecy. There are four main portions. Chapter 7 begins with a lamentation (7:1–6), an echo of the lamentations in chapter 1. The third portion 7:13–17 also recapitulates several themes previously used, notably the humiliation and later triumph of Zion as described in chapter 5. These two portions strike negative notes. But they are interwoven with two other passages in which countervailing faith and confidence are affirmed—7:7–12 (a song of confidence) and 7:18–20 (reaffirmation of the ancient covenant).

The contrastive use of the construction wa'ănî, "but, as for me . . ." at the beginning of v 7 marks a major transition from the mood of grief and depression expressed in the opening unit (vv 1–6) to the exultant hope that comes to fuller and fuller expression in the remainder of the book. The confidence affirmed in v 7 rises to a great climax in the final acclamation of God's inexhaustible compassion and unfailing love (vv 18–20).

The whole of chapter 7 can be understood as a prayer. The abundant use of "I" makes it intensely personal. This is the voice of the prophet. He speaks for himself. At the same time, in his capacity as a prophet, he acts in solidarity with the people and speaks for them. In this intercessory role, the prophet presents the community of God under several aspects, each of which is found in a distinct block of material. These major units can be identified through their consistent use of a dominant image. In vv 9–12 the *personae* are two enemies confronting one another with taunts and threats. The pronoun suffixes indicate that they are females. The reference to "thy [f.] walls" (v 11a) discloses that the speaker is a personified city. In the context of the whole book this can only be Jerusalem // Zion, even though neither name is used in this chapter. No clues are given about the identity of the enemy or about the historical circumstances. We accept the author's reticence on this point, and recognize that this anonymity permits sense to be made of the text in more than one setting.

The prayer in vv 14–17 casts God in the role of shepherd, with the people as "the flock of [his] inheritance." This language supplies another link to the final unit (vv 18–20), where the people are "the remnant of his heritage" (v 18aB). This diction then serves as an echo of the oracles about the remnant in chapter 5.

Keeping the number of participants as small as is necessary to account for all the references, the dramatis personae, besides Yahweh (the only one named), are the main speaker ("I" in vv 1–10, perhaps the same as the "we" [in vv 17 and 19]) and the enemy, identified as "the nations" in vv 16–17), represented by the female antagonist in v 10.

As spokesman for the people, the prophet assumes two stances towards God. One stance is a frank acknowledgment of guilt ("I have sinned against him" [v 9]), along with the recognition that the miserable situation lamented in vv 1–6 is part of bearing the indignation of the Lord (v 9). At the same time the prophet is confident that God will hear him (v 7b). He can watch expectantly and wait hopefully (v 7a) because he is assured that God will not retain his anger forever. The sins will be completely disposed of (v 19).

The other stance towards God arises from the expectation that God will devastate the earth on account of the evil deeds of its inhabitants (v 13). This judgment will satisfy Zion for the shame she experienced when the enemy jeered, "Where is he— Yahweh, thy God?" (v 10aB). The restoration of the flock to safe pasture (v 14) will be a replay of the Exodus story (v 15), when the nations will be once again discredited and forced to recognize "Yahweh, our God" (v 17bA).

The eschatological themes that conclude the book of Micah are developed in three distinct cycles. The transition from misery to hope is clearly marked by "and I" at the beginning of v 7, and the first-person speech continues through v 10. The outcome of Zion's vindication will be the arrival of the nations from all points of the compass, a movement presented again in v 17, a movement already prophesied in Mic 4:1–3. The whole story thus ends, not only with the recovery of the relationship promised to the ancestors (v 20), but also with the expansion of Israel (v 11) and with the settlement of old disputes and the universal recognition of Yahweh as God. Micah 4:3; 7:12; and 7:17 all strike a similar note of finality.

In the middle of this material there is a small unit (v 13) whose opening verb predicts the devastation of the world. This development cannot follow the submission of the nations described in v 12. It sounds more like a mighty act of God that will make the nations ashamed of all their might (v 16). In other words, v 13 is the starting point for the vindication of Yahweh and the rehabilitation of his people that are sketched in vv 14–17. Verse 13 thus makes a better beginning for vv 13–17 than an end for vv 7–13.

As the eschatological vision goes through each of its three cycles (vv 7–12, vv 13–17, vv 18–20), there is some backtracking and overlap as the anticipated events unfold. The scope expands with each round. At first we see the two enemy cities in confrontation (vv 7–12); then the whole world becomes the stage (vv 13–17); and finally the plan of God for all creation is seen in its full development "from the days of old."

INDEX OF AUTHORS

◆

INDEX OF SUBJECTS

◆

INDEX OF BIBLICAL AND OTHER ANCIENT REFERENCES

◆

INDEX OF LANGUAGES

◆